THE CRB COMMODITY YEARBOOK 1998

BRIDGE Commodity Research Bureau

John Wiley & Sons, Inc.
New York • Chichester • Weinheim • Brisbane • Singapore • Toronto

Published by John Wiley & Sons, Inc.

ISBN 0-471-24705-7

Printed in the United States of America
10 9 8 7 6 5 4 3 2 1

Bridge Commodity Research Bureau
30 South Wacker Drive, Suite 1810
Chicago IL 60606
312-454-1801
800-621-5271
http://www.crbindex.com
Email: crbinfo@bridge.com

TABLE OF CONTENTS

ACKNOWLEDGMENTS

The editors wish to thank the following for source material:

American Bureau of Metal Statistics
American Gas Association
American Iron and Steel Institute
American Metal Market
American Paper and Pulp Association
American Petroleum Institute
Atomic Industrial Forum Inc.
Chicago Board of Trade
Chicago Mercantile Exchange
Citrus Associates of the N.Y. Cotton Exchange
Coffee, Sugar & Cocoa Exchange
Commodity Exchange, N.Y.
Commodity Futures Trading Commission
The Conference Board
Edison Electric Institute
F.W. Dodge Corp.
Federal Power Commission
Federal Reserve Board
Florida Department of Citrus
Futures Industry Association
General Services Administration
Gill & Duffus Ltd.
Gold Fields Mineral Services Ltd.
Handy & Harman
International Cotton Advisory Committee
International Monetary Market (Chicago)
International Rubber Study Group
Johnson Matthey Ltd.
The Journal of Commerce
Kansas City Board of Trade
Leather Industries of America Inc.
London Metal Exchange
MidAmerica Commodity Exchange
Minneapolis Grain Exchange
National Coffee Association of U.S.A., Inc.
New York Cotton Exchange
New York Futures Exchange
New York Mercantile Exchange
Newsprint Service Bureau
Nuclear Exchange Corp.
Nuclear Regulatory Commission
Oil World
Organization for Economic Co-operation and Development (OECD)
Portland Cement Association
Random Lengths
Rubber Manufacturers Association
The Silver Institute
Society of the Plastics Industry Inc.
Textile Economics Bureau Inc.
Textile Organon
U.N. Conference on Trade and Development
U.N. Food and Agriculture Organization
U.S. Bureau of Mines
U.S. Department of Agriculture
U.S. Department of Commerce
U.S. Department of Energy
U.S. Department of the Interior
U.S. Department of Labor
U.S. Department of the Treasury
The Wall Street Journal
Winnipeg Commodity Exchange
Wool Services Co.
Zinc Institute

THE COMMODITY PRICE TREND

In 1997, the Bridge Commodity Research Bureau's Futures Price Index declined for the second consecutive year and closed at the lowest level since 1993. The December 31, 1997 closing value of 229.14 was 10.47 lower, or 4.37 percent below the December 31, 1996 closing level of 239.61.

For the year, only one of the six sub-indices advanced. The 25.17 percent rise in the imported group was countered by declines of 22.21 and 20.87 percent in the industrial and energy groups, respectively.

Energy

The energy index fell 20.87 percent for the year led by declines in excess of 31 percent in both crude oil and heating oil. Natural gas prices fell by 17 percent from the year earlier level.

Crude oil traded in a broad range in 1997, beginning the year near $26.00 per barrel; falling to $18.50 by June; recovering to $23.00 in the fall; and dropping to $17.60 by the end of the year.

The status of Iraqi oil exports, as mandated by the United Nations oil for food program, bounced the market around for ten months, but the year-long decline accelerated in November when OPEC ministers agreed to raise their official crude oil production ceiling from 25.0 to 27.5 million barrels per day.

Grains

The grains index dropped only 0.27 percent in 1997, stemming the sharp decline the index experienced in 1996. Wheat prices were the weakest of the index components, dropping 14.5 percent on the year. A 2.9 percent decline in soybean prices was balanced by a 2.6 percent rise in corn prices.

Record foreign wheat production and rising world surpluses combined to depress the wheat market.

Industrials

The industrial index experienced the deepest losses of any of the CRB indices in 1997 as it fell 22.2 percent from the ending 1996 value. Copper prices declined 22 percent and cotton fell by nearly 11 percent.

The decline in the index began at the end of July when the world was awakened to the emerging financial crisis in the Pacific Rim countries. Simultaneously, the copper market turned lower and remained in a severe downtrend for the rest of the year based on expectations that Asian demand, the primary bullish factor through 1996 and early 1997, would evaporate.

Livestock

The 11.85 percent decline in the livestock index was solely attributable to a 27 percent drop in lean hog prices. Live cattle, the other livestock index component, experienced a market price rise of just over 2.2 percent for the year.

1997 was a disasterous year for hog producers. They began the year expanding herd sizes because of lower feed costs and expectations of increased demand from Japan due to the abolishment of the Japanese 24 percent pork import tax. Unfortunately, Japanese demand never materialized and domestic demand declined as well, resulting in a buildup of stocks held in cold storage and reduced hog slaughter numbers.

Precious Metals

The precious metals sub-index fell 1.28 percent for the year. A 21 percent decline in the price of gold was countered by a 25 percent rise in the price of silver. Platinum prices for the year were flat.

Both rumored and actual selling from European central banks eroded gold values while silver mysteriously bucked the trend and moved higher. In late January of 1998, the mystery was solved when Warren Buffet announced he had purchased 130 million ounces of silver in the last half of 1997 on behalf of Berkshire Hathaway, his investment unit.

Softs

The softs index rose 25.17 percent in 1997 as all four components registered gains. Coffee rose 41 percent, cocoa rose 19 percent, sugar rose 11 percent, and orange juice was up 8 percent for the year.

Coffee futures rallied strongly in 1997 due to tight Arabica supplies and small crops in Columbia and Brazil. Cocoa prices moved higher all year as El Nino related weather problems combined with increased consumption to drive prices. Sugar prices rose on declining world stocks and Russian crop concerns.

On July 1, 1997, the Bridge CRB Sub-Indices were modified to match the CRB Futures Price Index components and real-time calculation was initiated.

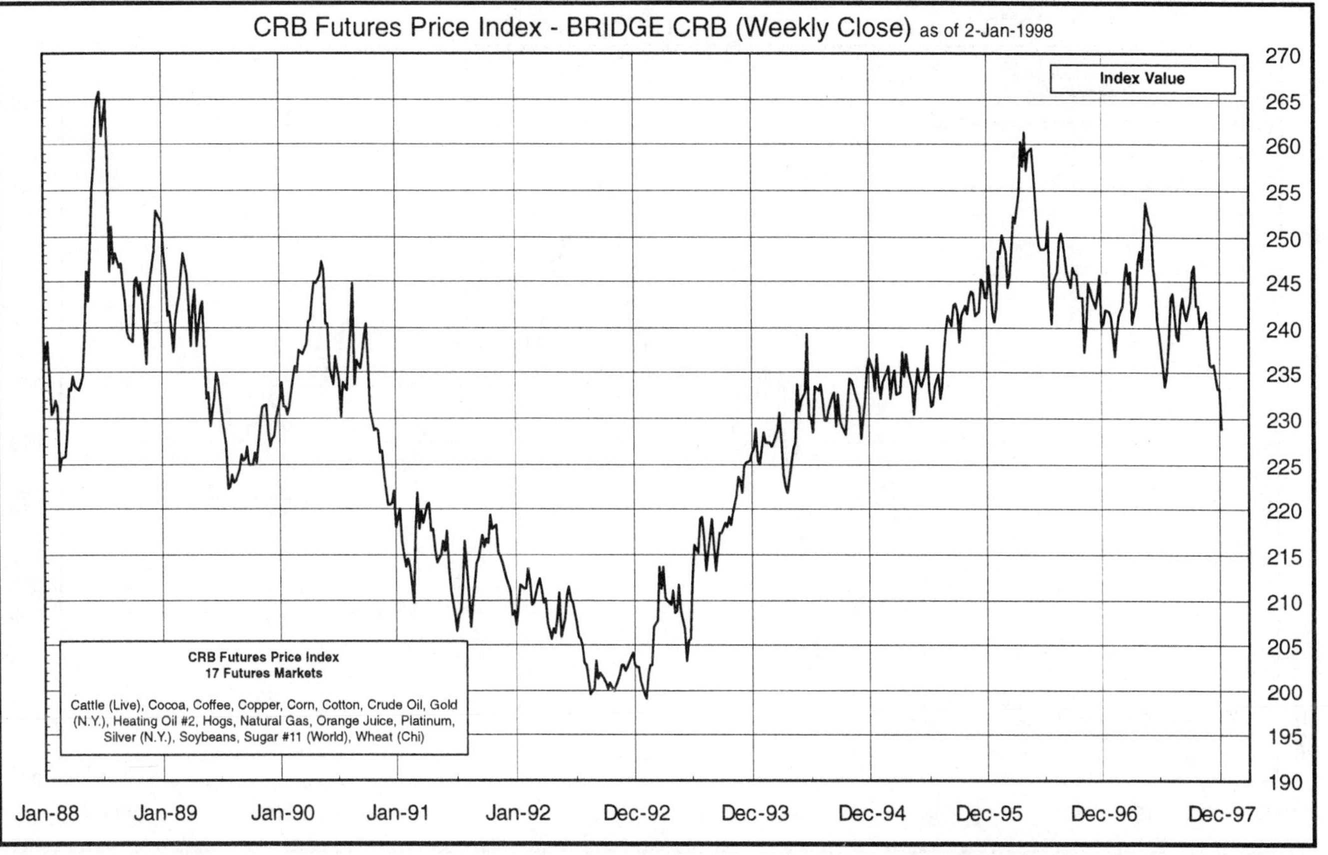

Monthly CRB Futures Price Index High, Low and Close 1967 = 100

Year		Jan.	Feb.	Mar.	Apr.	May	June	July	Aug.	Sept.	Oct.	Nov.	Dec.	Range
1988	High	239.3	232.9	233.5	236.0	248.4	270.5	265.8	251.0	248.6	246.5	247.0	252.8	270.5
	Low	230.4	224.3	224.5	232.7	232.5	249.8	242.0	243.7	237.1	237.6	236.0	244.1	224.3
	Close	230.4	225.7	233.0	234.4	248.4	265.1	246.2	246.2	238.8	243.9	244.9	251.8	------
1989	High	251.6	243.3	248.1	244.6	242.8	235.4	237.0	225.5	226.8	228.1	231.7	229.9	251.6
	Low	241.1	236.6	241.7	237.7	229.4	227.9	221.2	221.5	222.9	223.0	226.0	225.6	221.2
	Close	242.4	243.2	242.1	238.0	229.4	234.4	221.2	225.5	226.8	225.7	228.8	229.9	------
1990	High	235.1	236.3	239.0	245.8	247.8	241.2	240.0	244.7	239.8	242.0	231.1	223.8	247.8
	Low	228.8	229.9	234.2	238.4	241.5	233.8	230.3	233.1	234.9	228.6	223.2	220.1	220.1
	Close	229.9	234.6	238.2	245.8	241.5	236.9	235.0	233.7	239.2	229.8	223.3	222.6	------
1991	High	222.8	215.6	221.8	222.2	217.0	217.7	214.1	216.5	217.6	219.8	218.6	213.9	222.8
	Low	214.1	209.7	217.3	216.2	214.1	208.4	205.9	204.7	211.9	216.2	213.3	207.2	204.7
	Close	214.1	215.6	218.5	216.2	215.4	208.4	214.1	211.8	215.6	218.2	213.3	208.1	------
1992	High	212.2	215.3	212.9	210.3	211.7	212.9	209.1	204.9	203.5	202.9	203.6	204.3	215.3
	Low	206.9	207.2	208.6	204.5	204.9	208.0	203.0	198.2	199.3	199.1	199.2	201.2	198.2
	Close	211.2	209.6	209.8	204.8	208.0	209.3	203.1	201.0	200.4	199.9	203.1	202.8	------
1993	High	203.2	204.9	214.3	213.9	211.8	210.0	219.7	223.5	217.8	220.6	223.8	226.8	226.8
	Low	199.3	198.4	203.4	207.8	207.4	202.6	207.2	212.1	211.9	216.6	217.4	218.4	198.4
	Close	199.5	202.9	212.5	210.9	208.7	207.1	219.3	217.2	216.1	218.4	218.0	226.3	------
1994	High	229.8	229.2	231.0	227.8	239.2	239.7	234.7	235.4	234.4	235.2	234.7	237.2	239.7
	Low	226.2	225.7	227.4	227.8	225.2	235.9	230.4	228.0	228.6	227.0	228.8	227.0	225.2
	Close	225.6	227.6	227.7	225.0	235.5	230.4	233.7	231.9	229.9	233.3	229.2	236.6	------
1995	High	238.0	236.2	236.9	237.7	237.1	238.0	235.9	240.3	245.8	242.7	244.5	246.5	246.5
	Low	232.6	231.0	231.1	233.2	229.6	232.2	229.3	231.7	239.4	238.3	240.9	240.9	229.3
	Close	232.8	234.3	232.9	235.3	232.7	233.4	233.2	240.0	241.7	242.2	241.8	243.2	------
1996	High	247.6	251.2	253.5	263.8	261.2	252.9	251.9	252.0	250.4	249.6	247.1	246.9	263.8
	Low	238.6	245.6	242.7	250.2	251.8	246.6	240.1	242.8	243.1	237.8	236.0	238.1	236.0
	Close	247.5	248.8	251.4	256.1	254.1	248.7	242.0	249.5	245.6	237.8	243.4	239.6	------
1997	High	244.3	243.9	248.0	249.0	254.8	250.0	243.4	245.3	244.5	247.6	243.5	238.4	254.8
	Low	238.9	236.1	241.6	237.6	245.5	238.5	232.0	236.7	240.0	238.3	235.3	228.8	228.8
	Close	239.0	242.4	245.2	248.3	251.0	239.4	242.8	242.0	243.1	240.0	235.9	229.1	------

Source: BRIDGE - Commodity Research Bureau

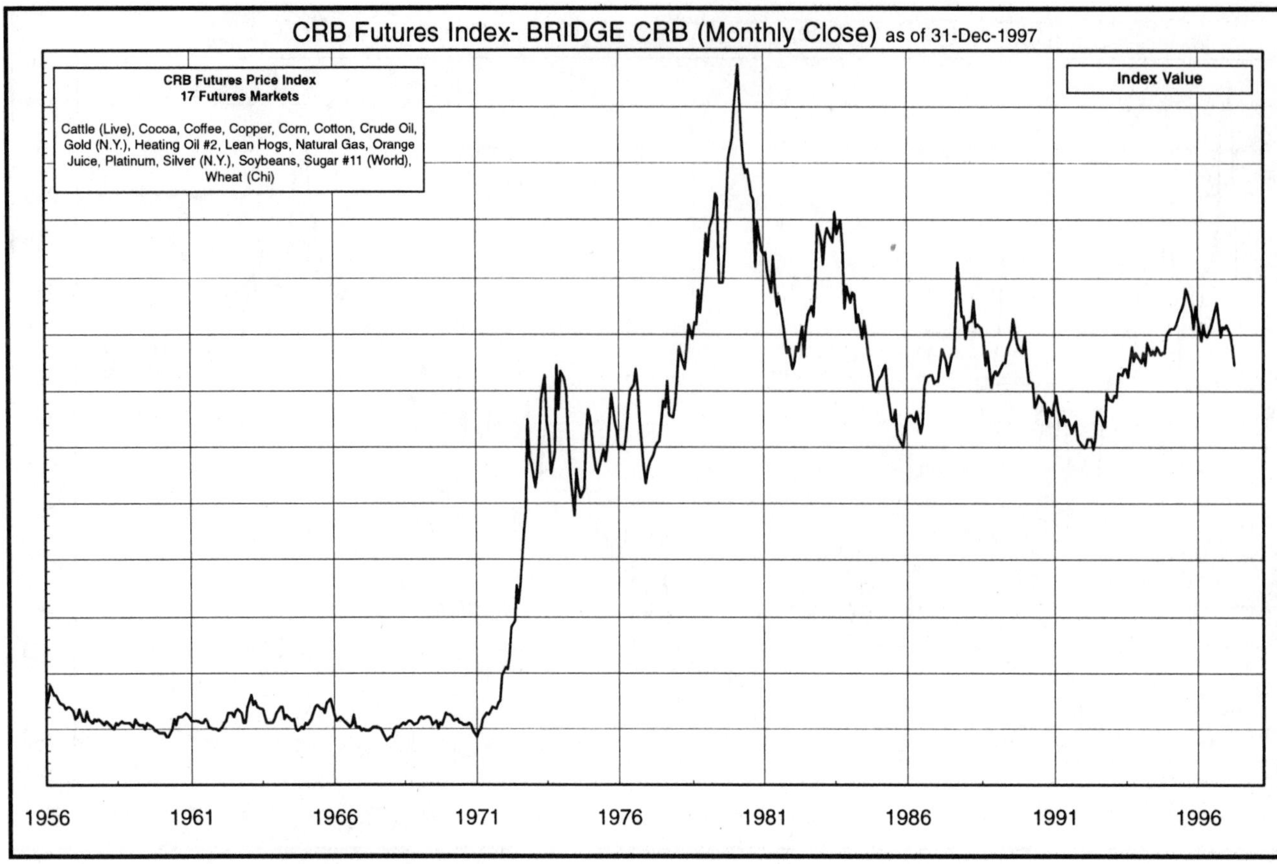

CRB Futures Index- BRIDGE CRB (Monthly Close) as of 31-Dec-1997

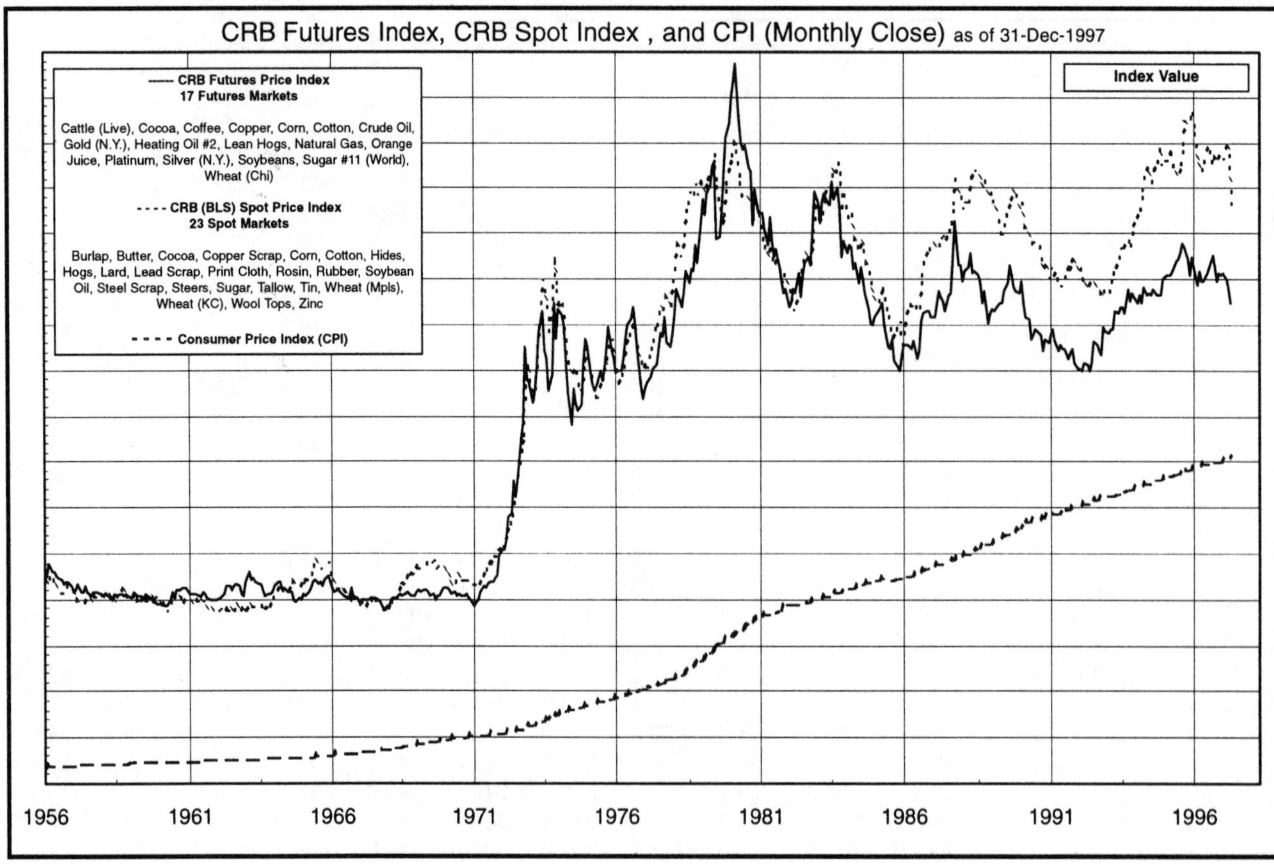

CRB Futures Index, CRB Spot Index , and CPI (Monthly Close) as of 31-Dec-1997

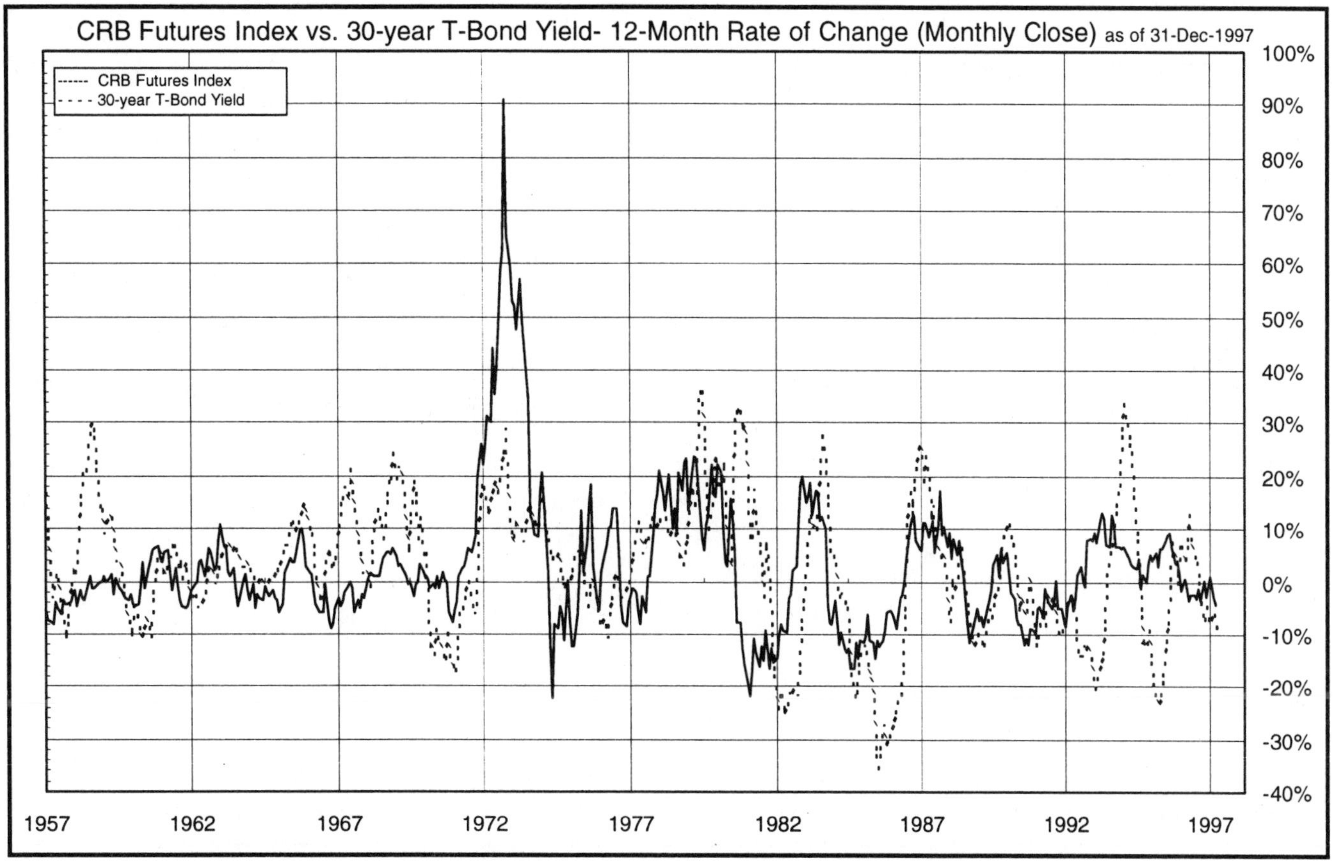

CRB Futures Index vs. 30-year T-Bond Yield- 12-Month Rate of Change (Monthly Close) as of 31-Dec-1997

------ CRB Futures Index
- - - - 30-year T-Bond Yield

100%
90%
80%
70%
60%
50%
40%
30%
20%
10%
0%
-10%
-20%
-30%
-40%

1957 1962 1967 1972 1977 1982 1987 1992 1997

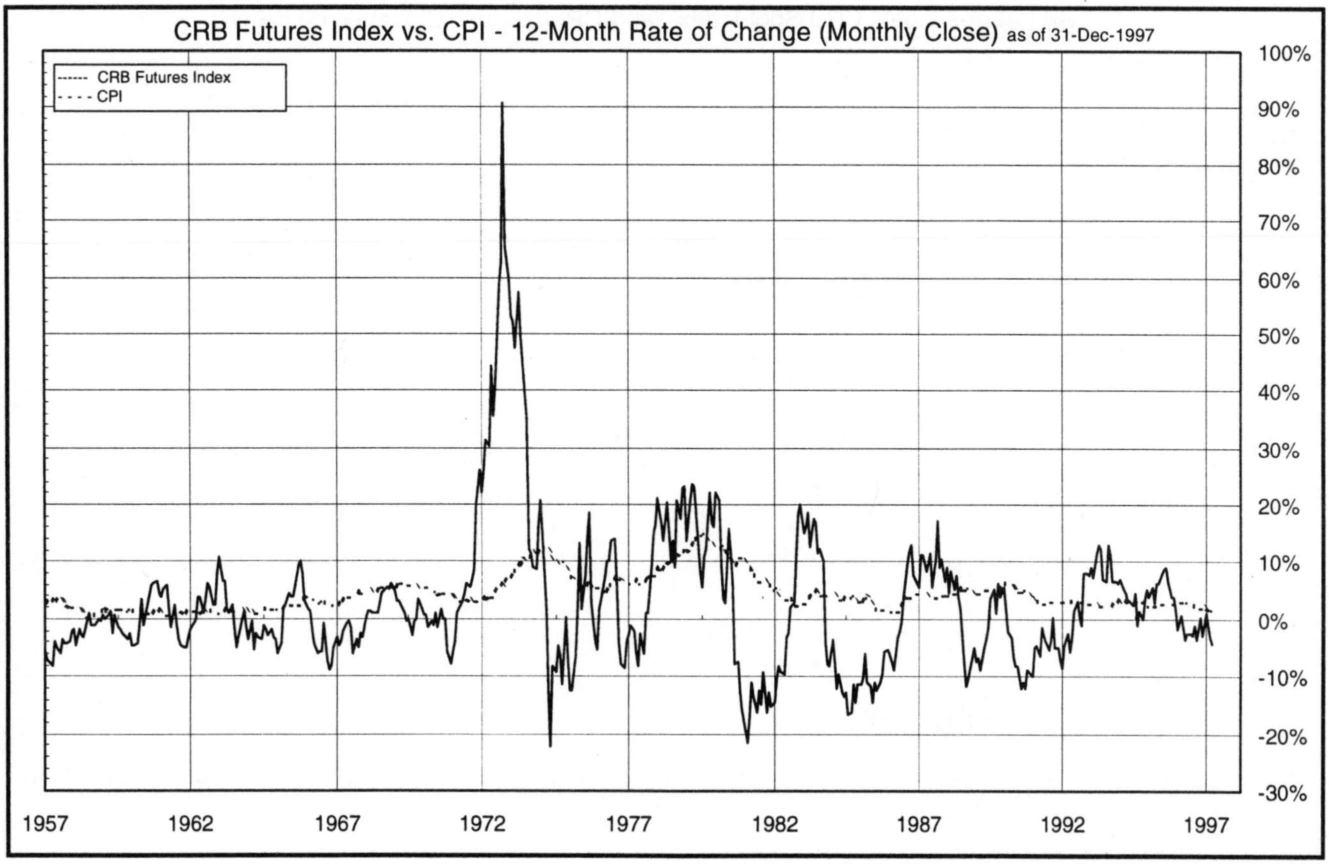

CRB Futures Index vs. CPI - 12-Month Rate of Change (Monthly Close) as of 31-Dec-1997

------ CRB Futures Index
- - - - CPI

100%
90%
80%
70%
60%
50%
40%
30%
20%
10%
0%
-10%
-20%
-30%

1957 1962 1967 1972 1977 1982 1987 1992 1997

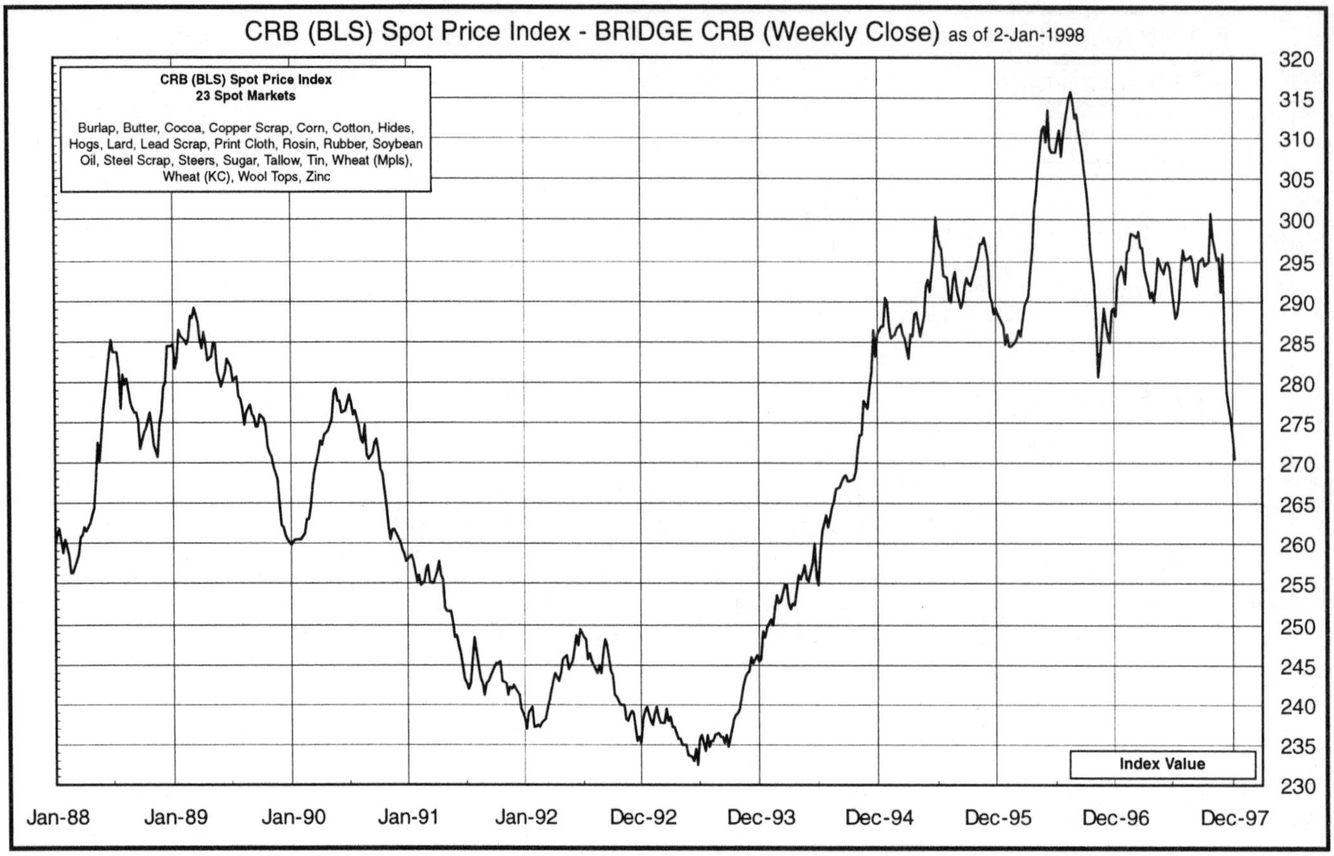

CRB (BLS) Spot Price Index - BRIDGE CRB (Weekly Close) as of 2-Jan-1998

CRB (BLS) Spot Price Index
23 Spot Markets

Burlap, Butter, Cocoa, Copper Scrap, Corn, Cotton, Hides, Hogs, Lard, Lead Scrap, Print Cloth, Rosin, Rubber, Soybean Oil, Steel Scrap, Steers, Sugar, Tallow, Tin, Wheat (Mpls), Wheat (KC), Wool Tops, Zinc

Index Value

320 315 310 305 300 295 290 285 280 275 270 265 260 255 250 245 240 235 230

Jan-88 Jan-89 Jan-90 Jan-91 Jan-92 Dec-92 Dec-93 Dec-94 Dec-95 Dec-96 Dec-97

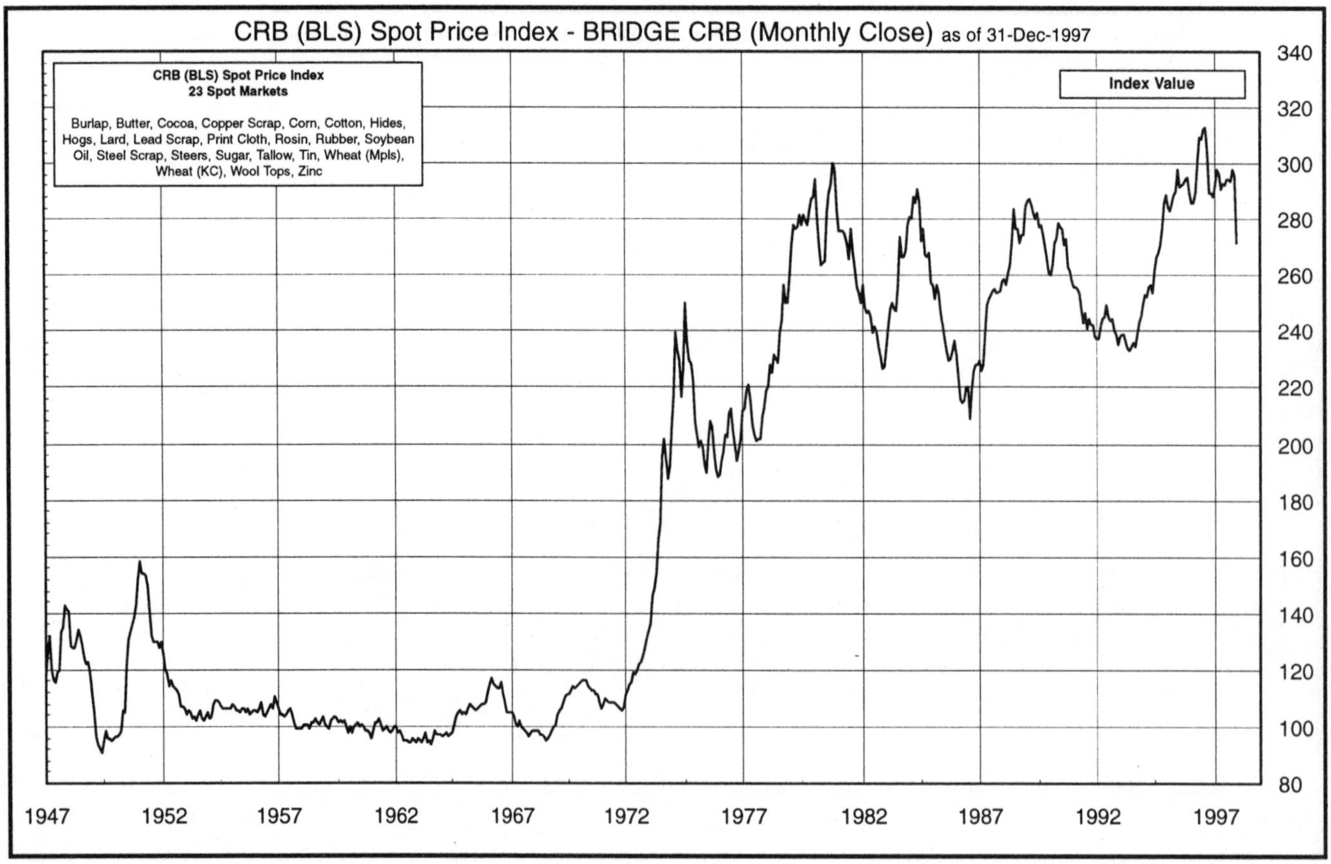

CRB (BLS) Spot Price Index - BRIDGE CRB (Monthly Close) as of 31-Dec-1997

CRB (BLS) Spot Price Index
23 Spot Markets

Burlap, Butter, Cocoa, Copper Scrap, Corn, Cotton, Hides, Hogs, Lard, Lead Scrap, Print Cloth, Rosin, Rubber, Soybean Oil, Steel Scrap, Steers, Sugar, Tallow, Tin, Wheat (Mpls), Wheat (KC), Wool Tops, Zinc

Index Value

340 320 300 280 260 240 220 200 180 160 140 120 100 80

1947 1952 1957 1962 1967 1972 1977 1982 1987 1992 1997

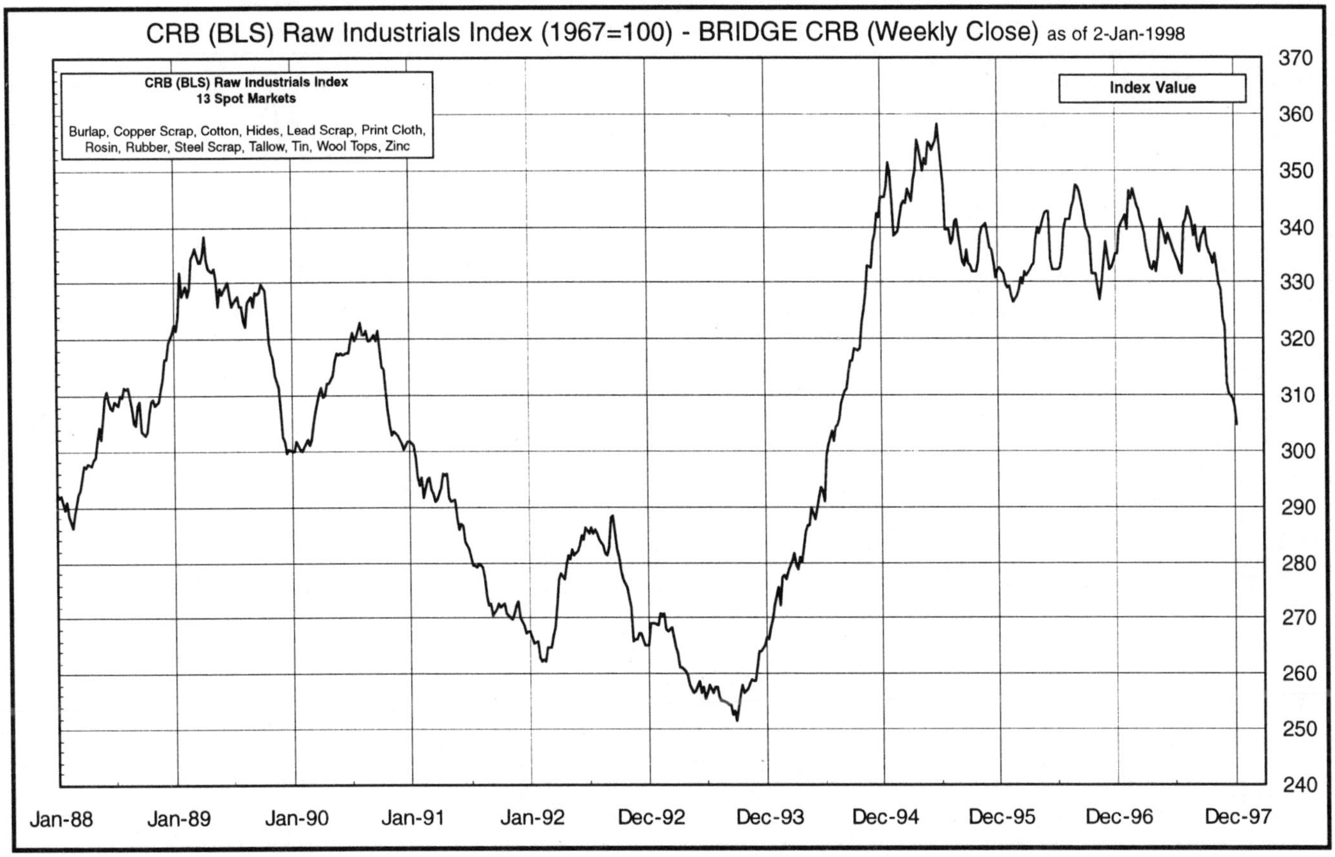

CRB (BLS) Raw Industrials Index (1967=100) - BRIDGE CRB (Weekly Close) as of 2-Jan-1998

CRB (BLS) Raw Industrials Index (1967=100) - BRIDGE CRB (Monthly Close) as of 31-Dec-1998

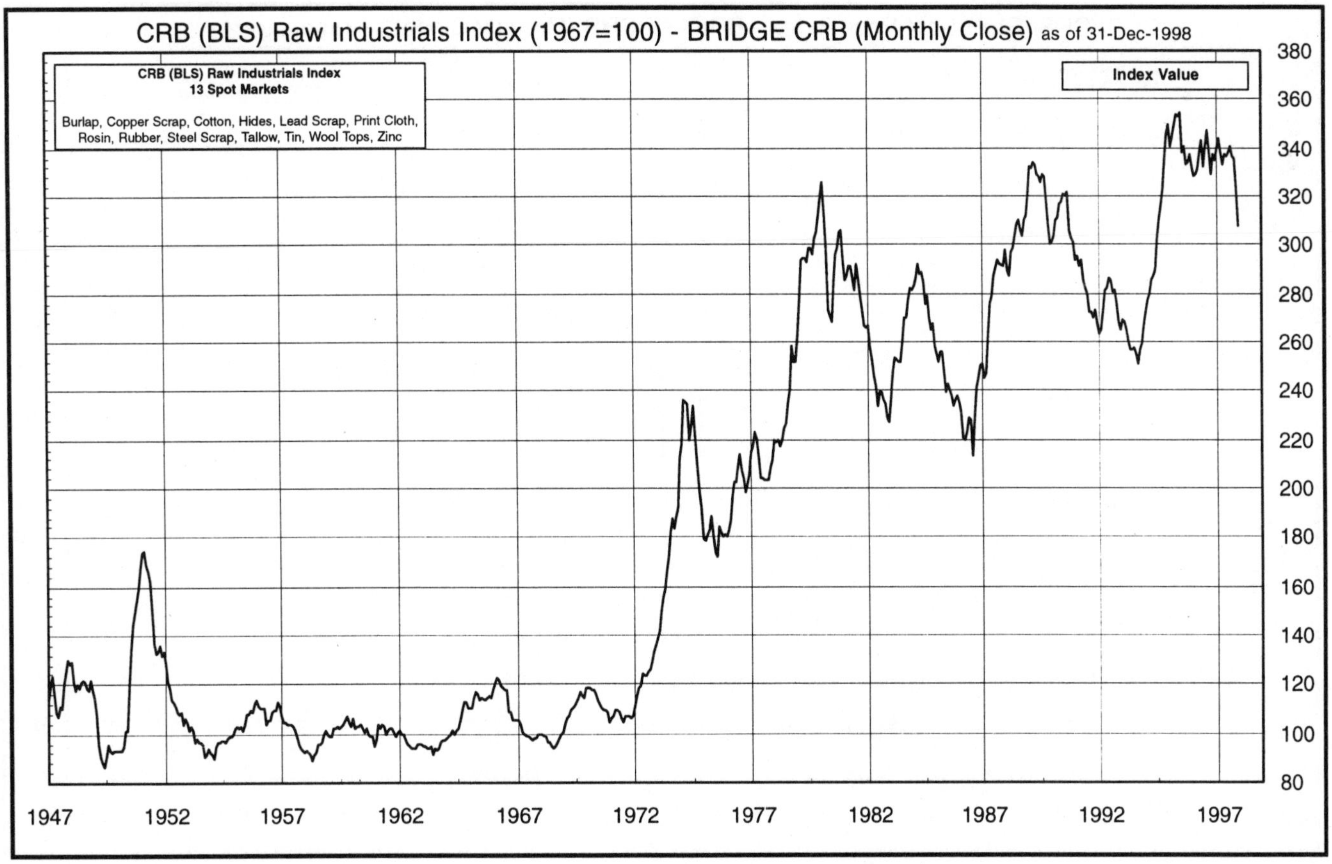

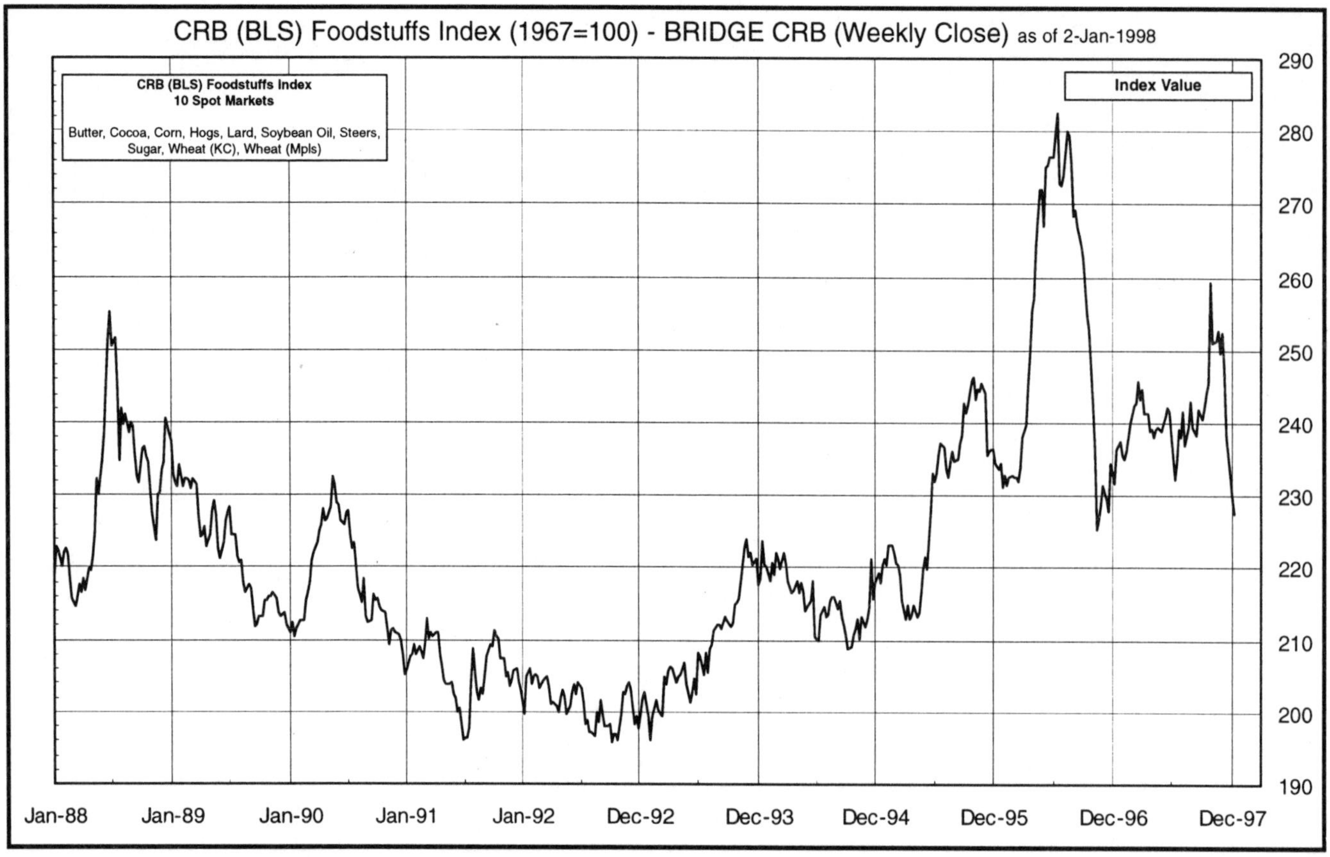

CRB (BLS) Foodstuffs Index (1967=100) - BRIDGE CRB (Weekly Close) as of 2-Jan-1998

CRB (BLS) Foodstuffs Index
10 Spot Markets

Butter, Cocoa, Corn, Hogs, Lard, Soybean Oil, Steers, Sugar, Wheat (KC), Wheat (Mpls)

Index Value

290
280
270
260
250
240
230
220
210
200
190

Jan-88 Jan-89 Jan-90 Jan-91 Jan-92 Dec-92 Dec-93 Dec-94 Dec-95 Dec-96 Dec-97

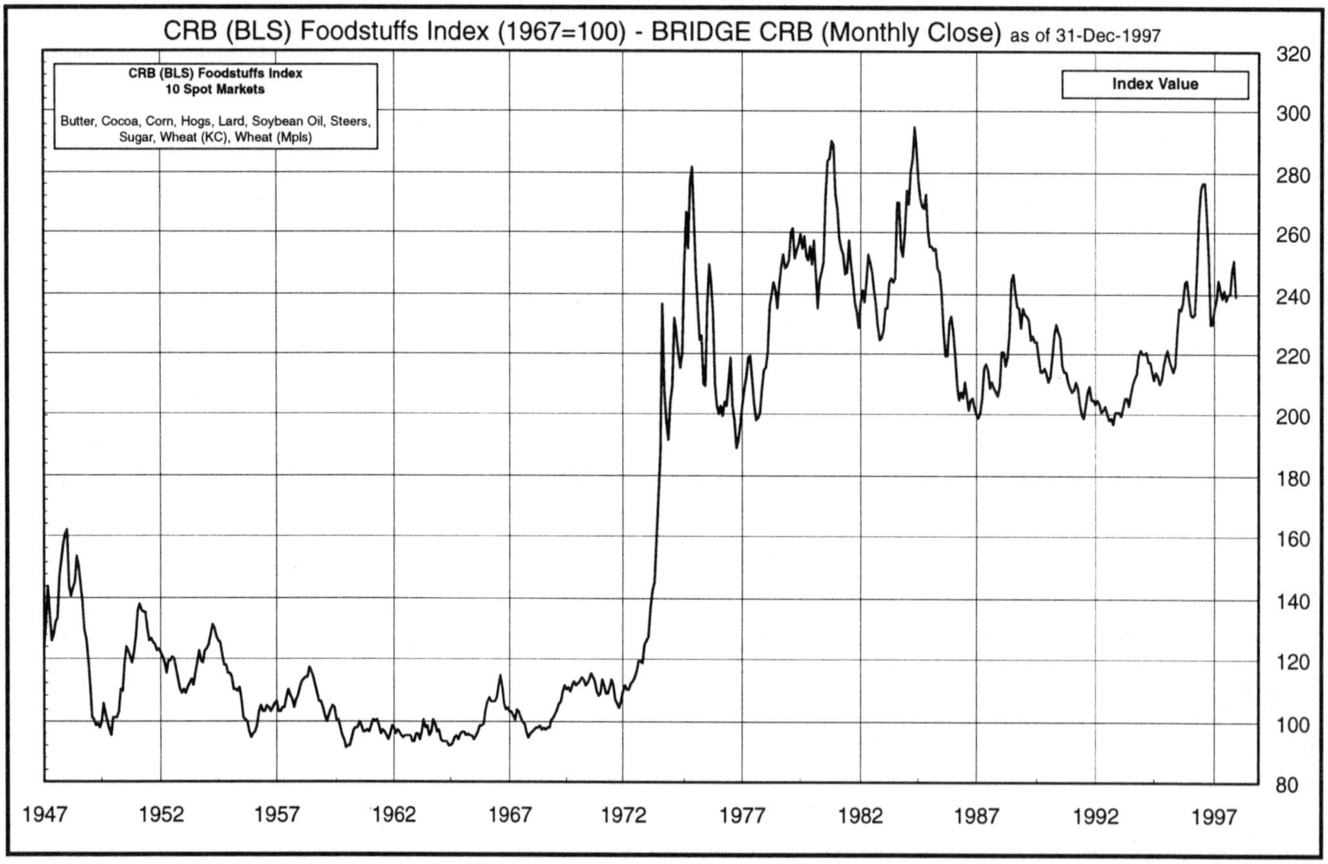

CRB (BLS) Foodstuffs Index (1967=100) - BRIDGE CRB (Monthly Close) as of 31-Dec-1997

CRB (BLS) Foodstuffs Index
10 Spot Markets

Butter, Cocoa, Corn, Hogs, Lard, Soybean Oil, Steers, Sugar, Wheat (KC), Wheat (Mpls)

Index Value

320
300
280
260
240
220
200
180
160
140
120
100
80

1947 1952 1957 1962 1967 1972 1977 1982 1987 1992 1997

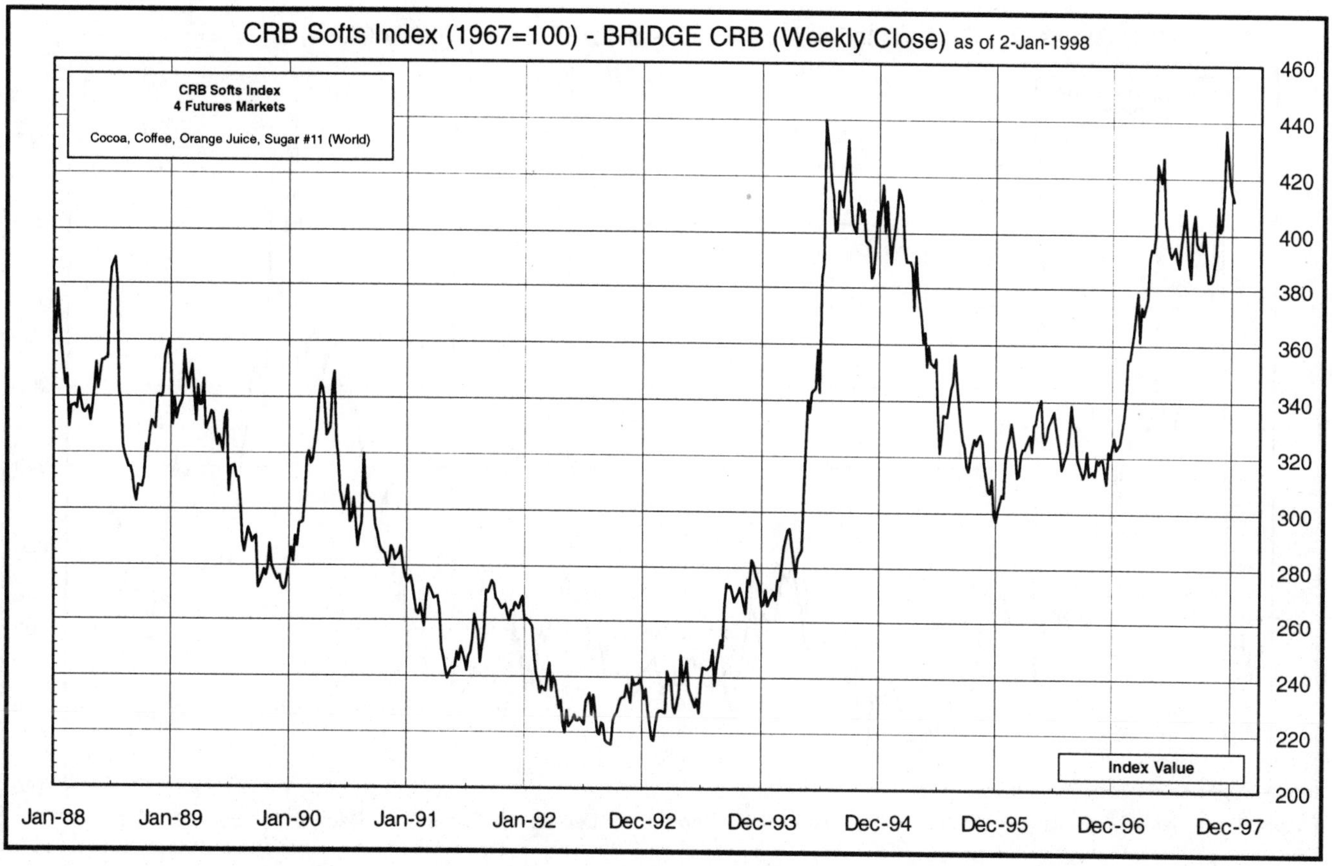

CRB Softs Index (1967=100) - BRIDGE CRB (Weekly Close) as of 2-Jan-1998

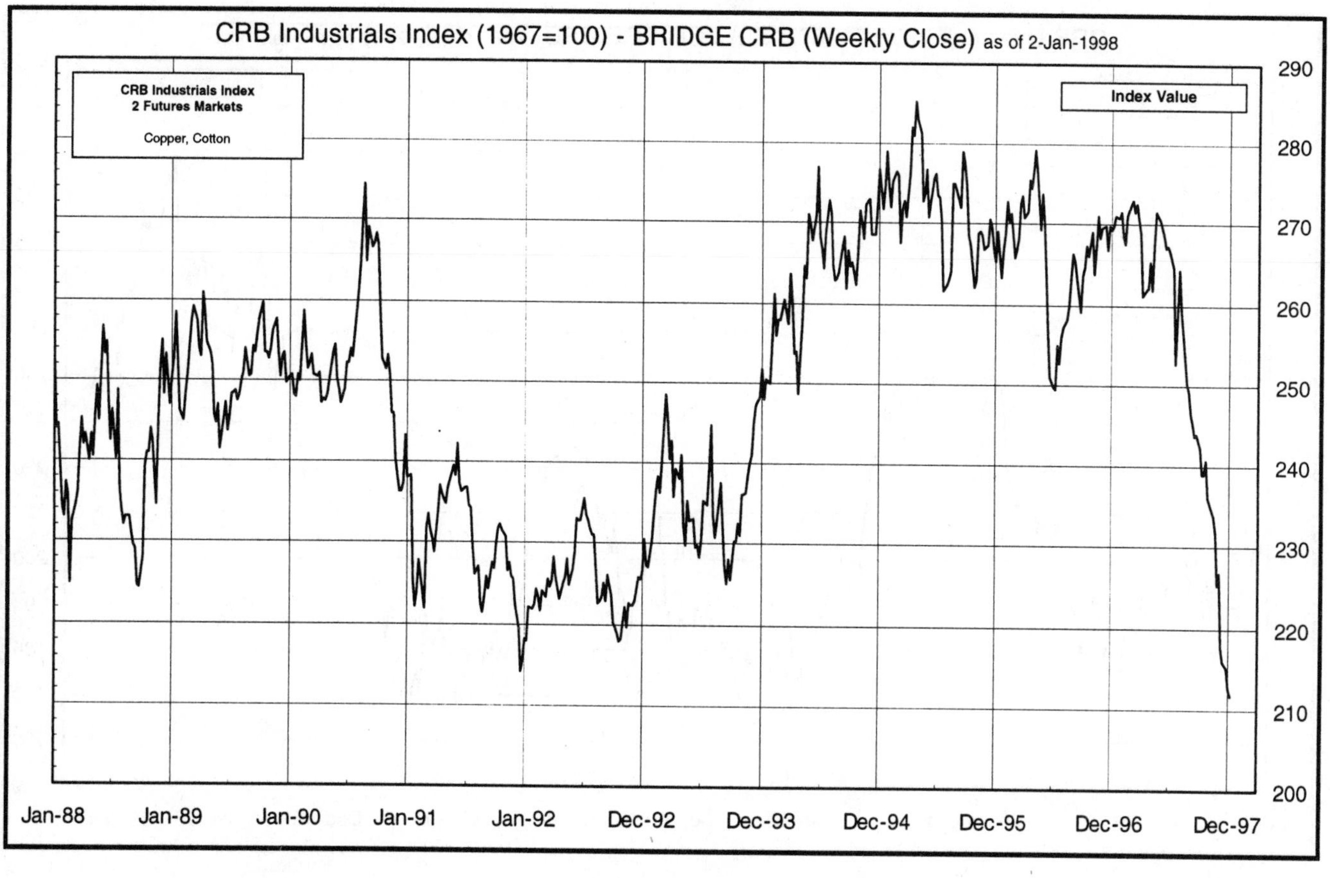

CRB Industrials Index (1967=100) - BRIDGE CRB (Weekly Close) as of 2-Jan-1998

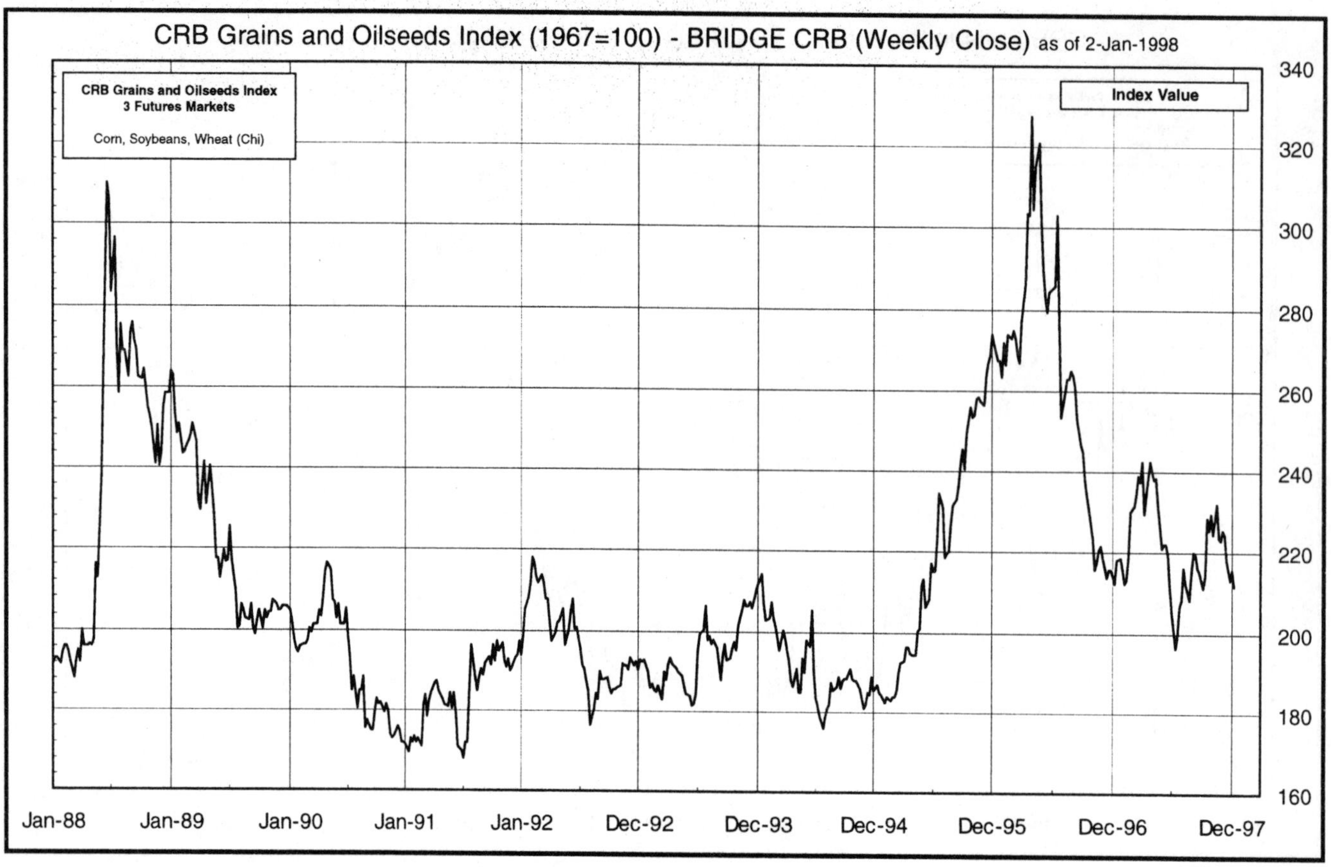

CRB Grains and Oilseeds Index (1967=100) - BRIDGE CRB (Weekly Close) as of 2-Jan-1998
CRB Grains and Oilseeds Index
3 Futures Markets
Corn, Soybeans, Wheat (Chi)
Index Value
340
320
300
280
260
240
220
200
180
160
Jan-88
Jan-89
Jan-90
Jan-91
Jan-92
Dec-92
Dec-93
Dec-94
Dec-95
Dec-96
Dec-97

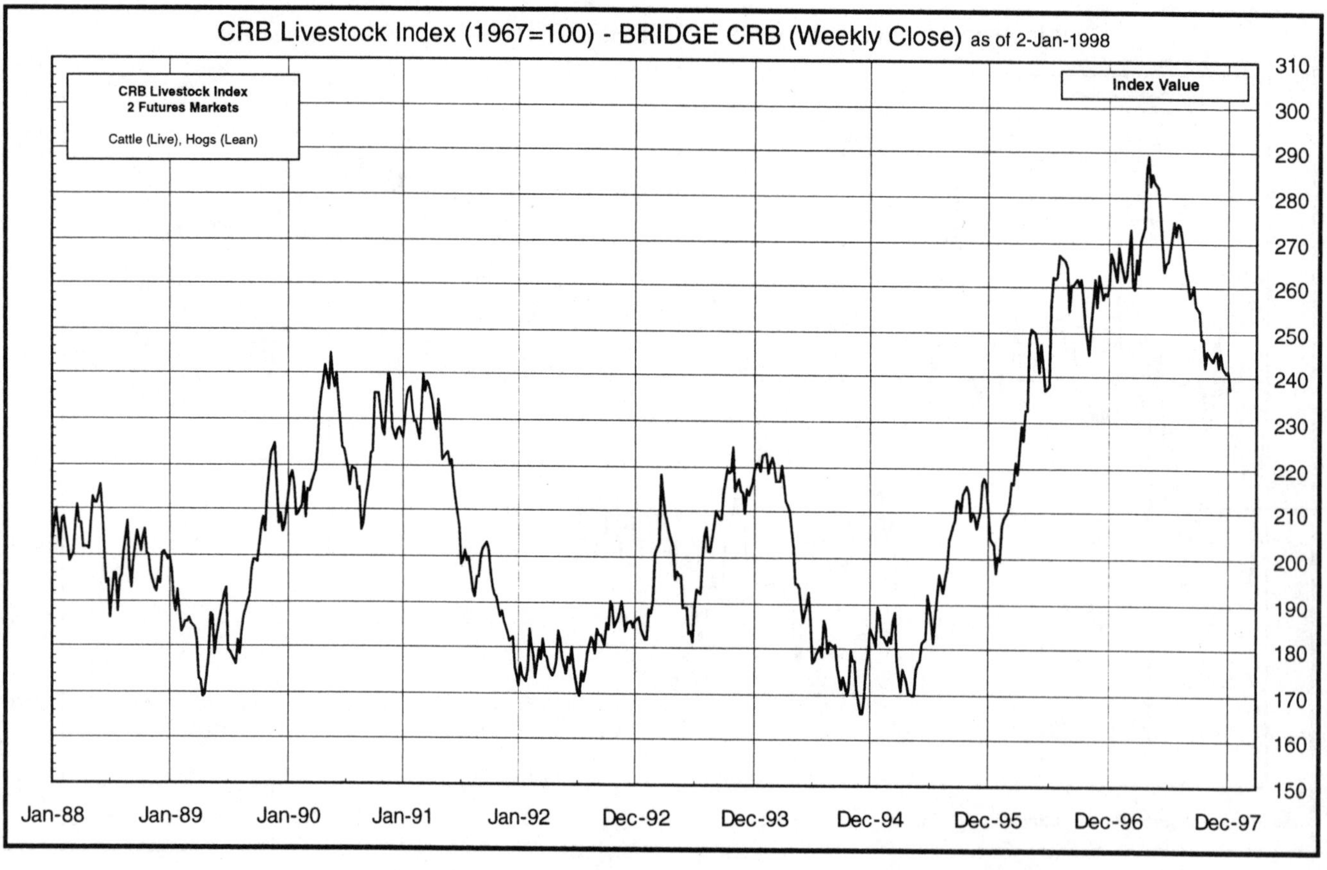

CRB Livestock Index (1967=100) - BRIDGE CRB (Weekly Close) as of 2-Jan-1998
CRB Livestock Index
2 Futures Markets
Cattle (Live), Hogs (Lean)
Index Value
310
300
290
280
270
260
250
240
230
220
210
200
190
180
170
160
150
Jan-88
Jan-89
Jan-90
Jan-91
Jan-92
Dec-92
Dec-93
Dec-94
Dec-95
Dec-96
Dec-97

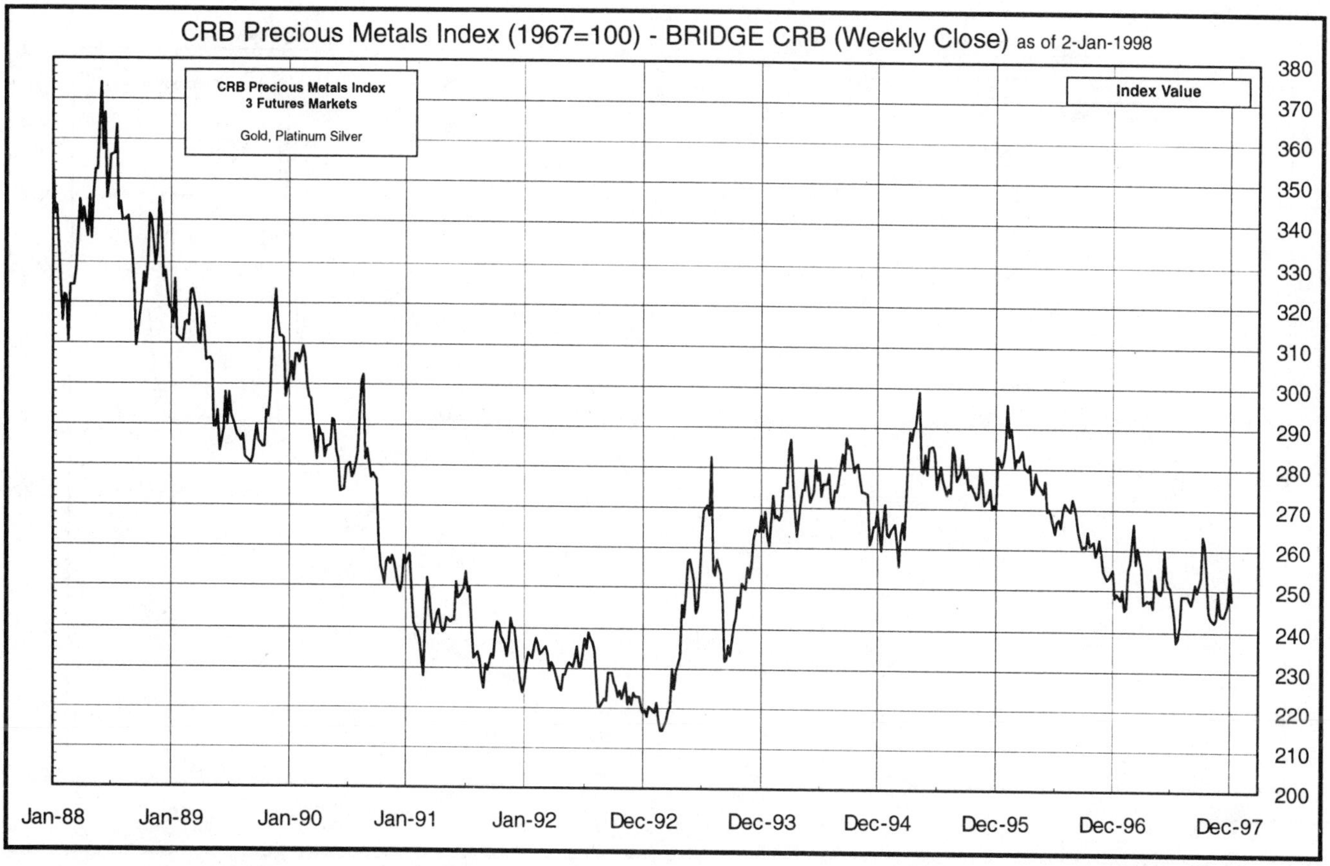
CRB Precious Metals Index (1967=100) - BRIDGE CRB (Weekly Close) as of 2-Jan-1998
CRB Precious Metals Index
3 Futures Markets
Gold, Platinum Silver
Index Value
380
370
360
350
340
330
320
310
300
290
280
270
260
250
240
230
220
210
200
Jan-88
Jan-89
Jan-90
Jan-91
Jan-92
Dec-92
Dec-93
Dec-94
Dec-95
Dec-96
Dec-97

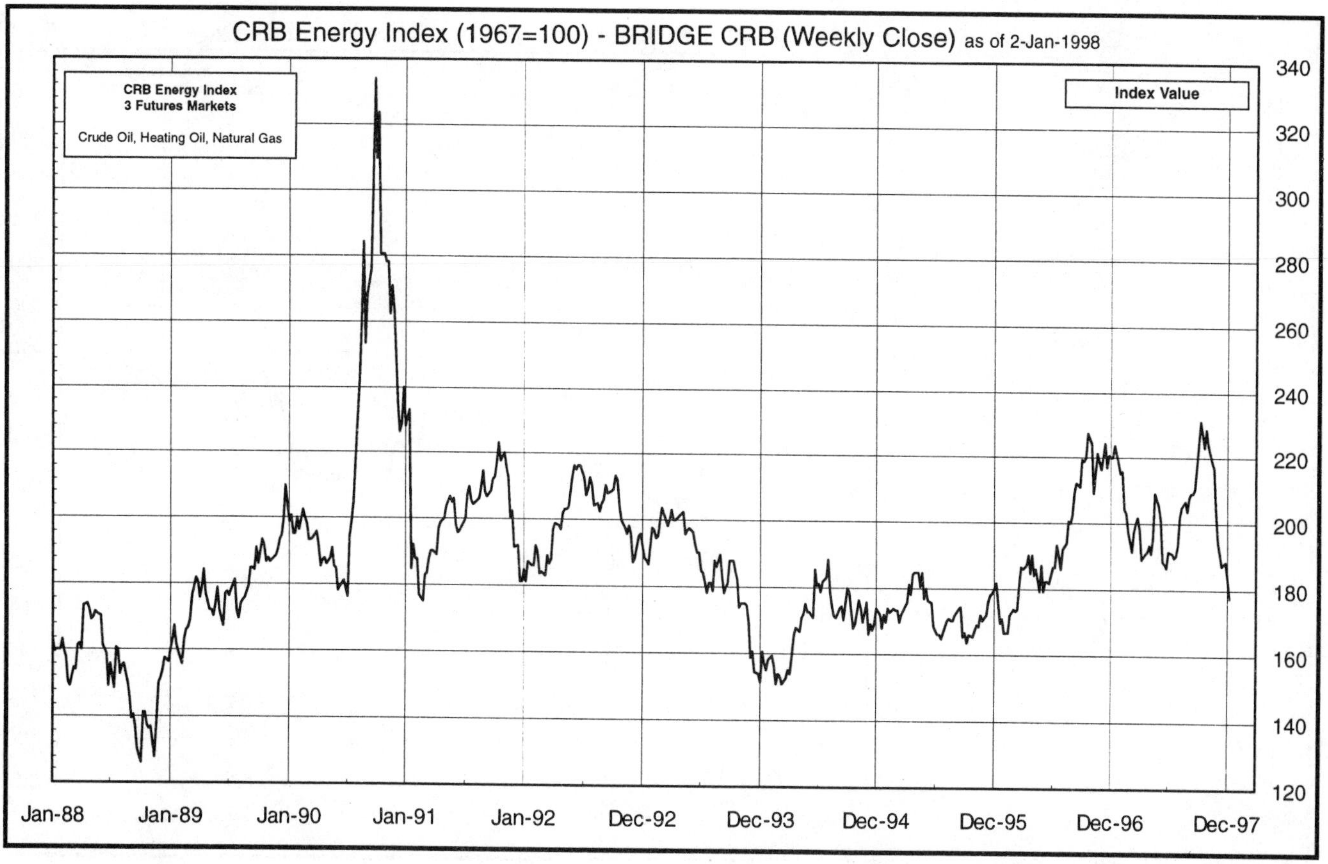
CRB Energy Index (1967=100) - BRIDGE CRB (Weekly Close) as of 2-Jan-1998
CRB Energy Index
3 Futures Markets
Crude Oil, Heating Oil, Natural Gas
Index Value
340
320
300
280
260
240
220
200
180
160
140
120
Jan-88
Jan-89
Jan-90
Jan-91
Jan-92
Dec-92
Dec-93
Dec-94
Dec-95
Dec-96
Dec-97

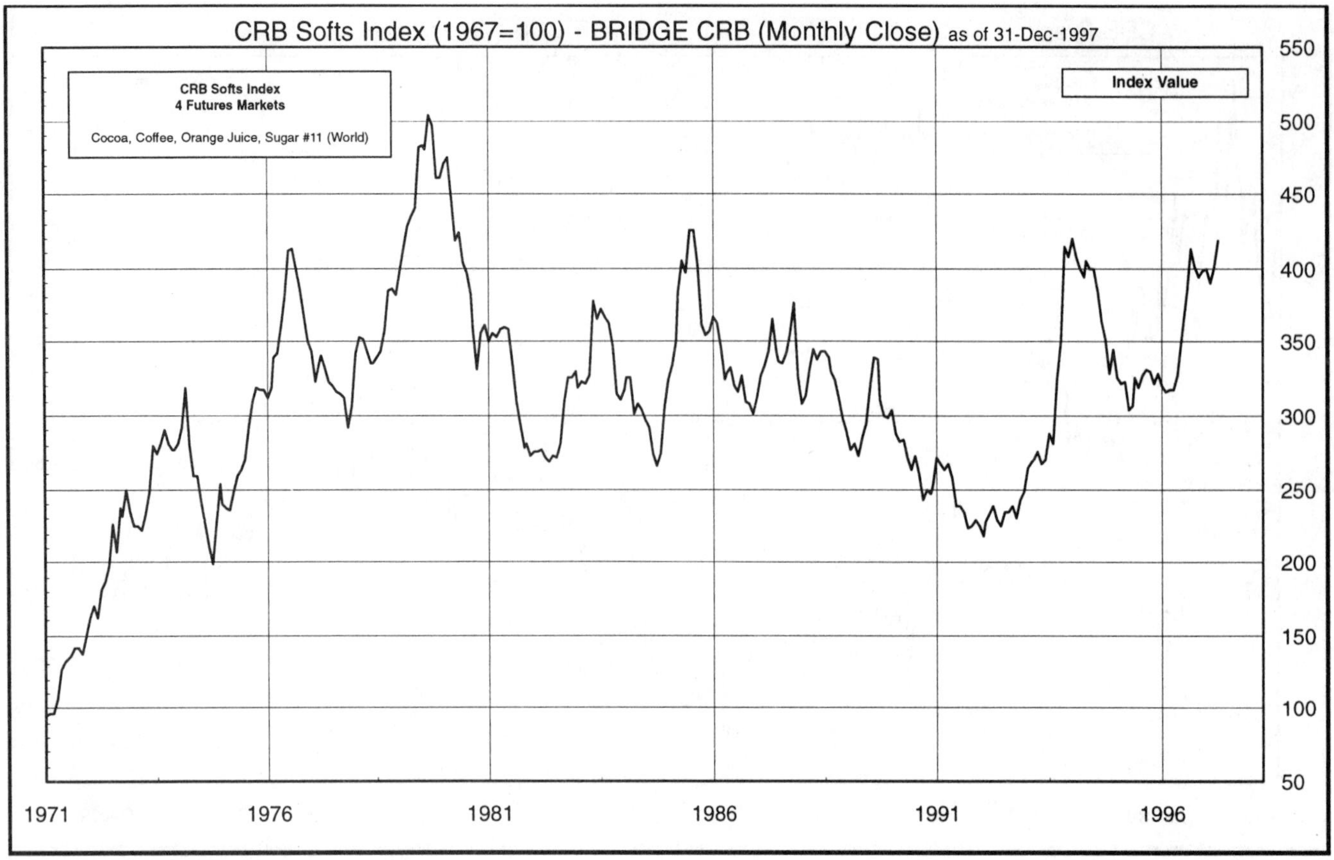

CRB Softs Index (1967=100) - BRIDGE CRB (Monthly Close) as of 31-Dec-1997

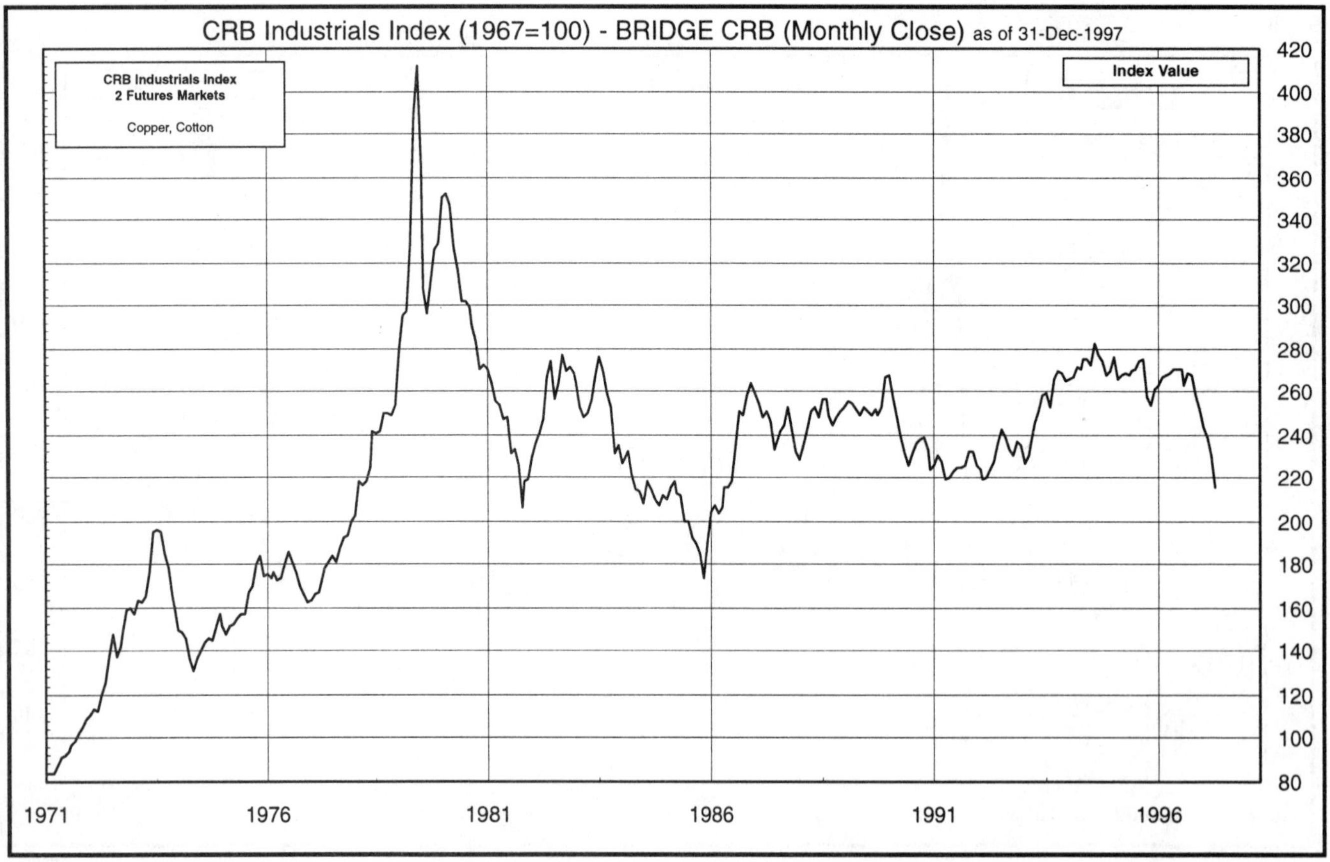

CRB Industrials Index (1967=100) - BRIDGE CRB (Monthly Close) as of 31-Dec-1997

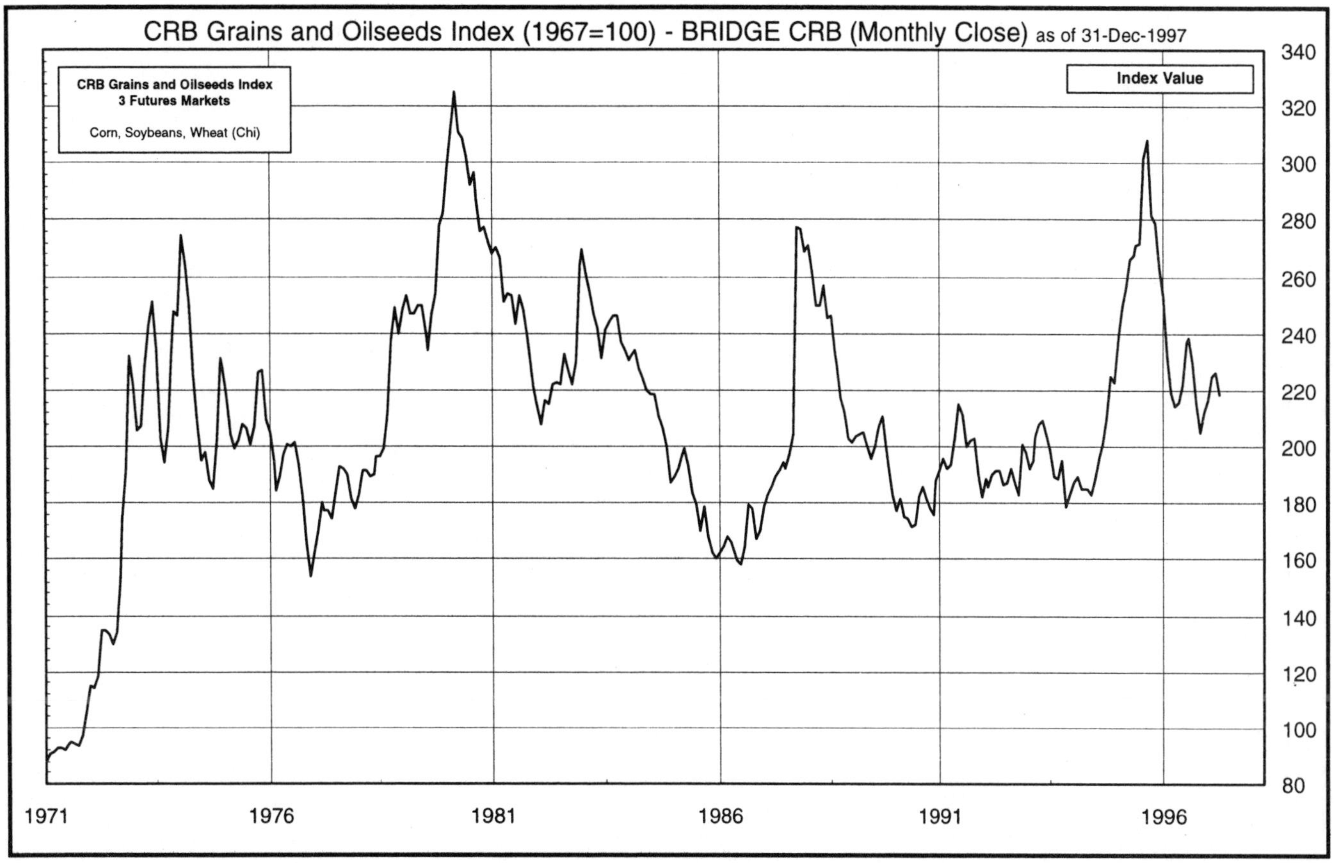

CRB Grains and Oilseeds Index (1967=100) - BRIDGE CRB (Monthly Close) as of 31-Dec-1997

CRB Grains and Oilseeds Index
3 Futures Markets

Corn, Soybeans, Wheat (Chi)

Index Value

340
320
300
280
260
240
220
200
180
160
140
120
100
80

1971 1976 1981 1986 1991 1996

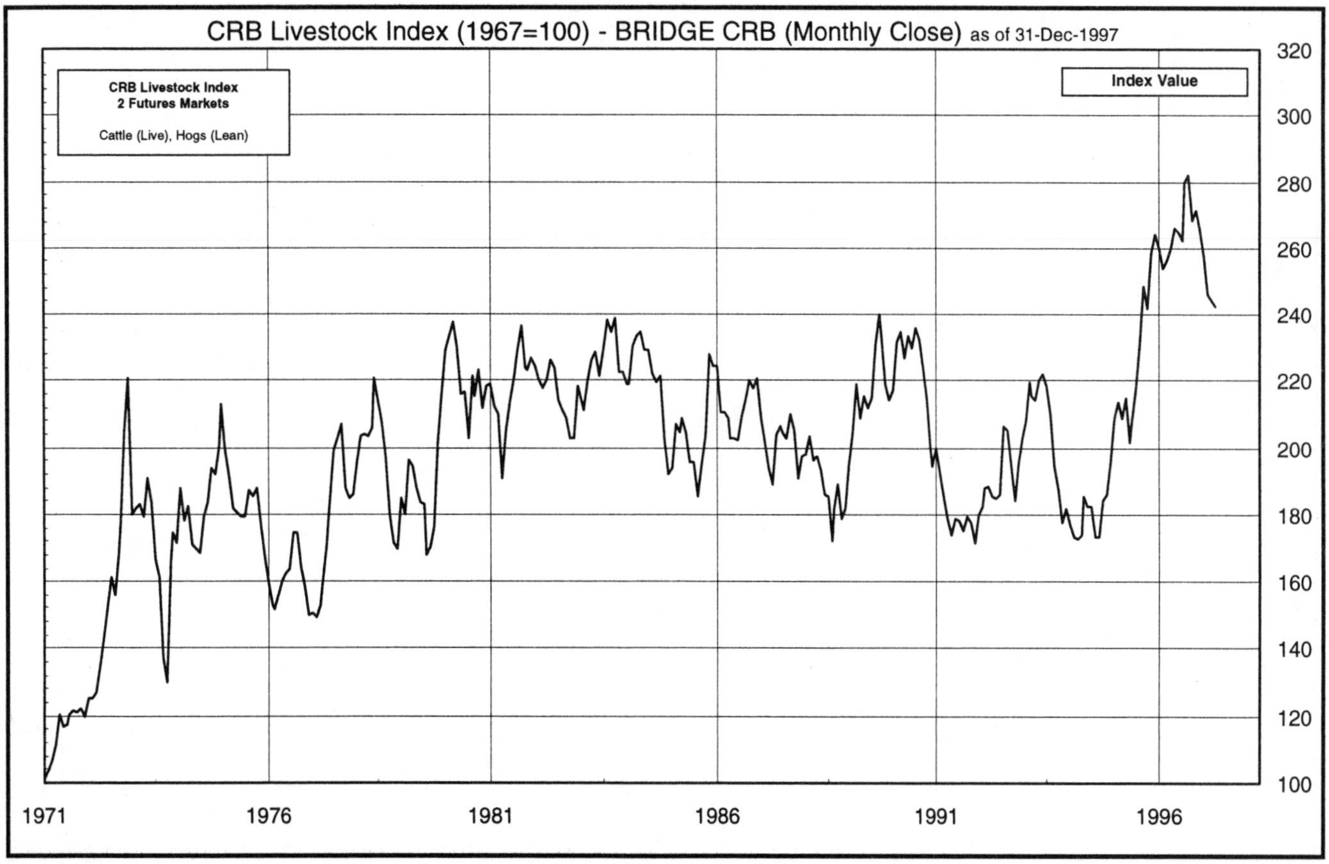

CRB Livestock Index (1967=100) - BRIDGE CRB (Monthly Close) as of 31-Dec-1997

CRB Livestock Index
2 Futures Markets

Cattle (Live), Hogs (Lean)

Index Value

320
300
280
260
240
220
200
180
160
140
120
100

1971 1976 1981 1986 1991 1996

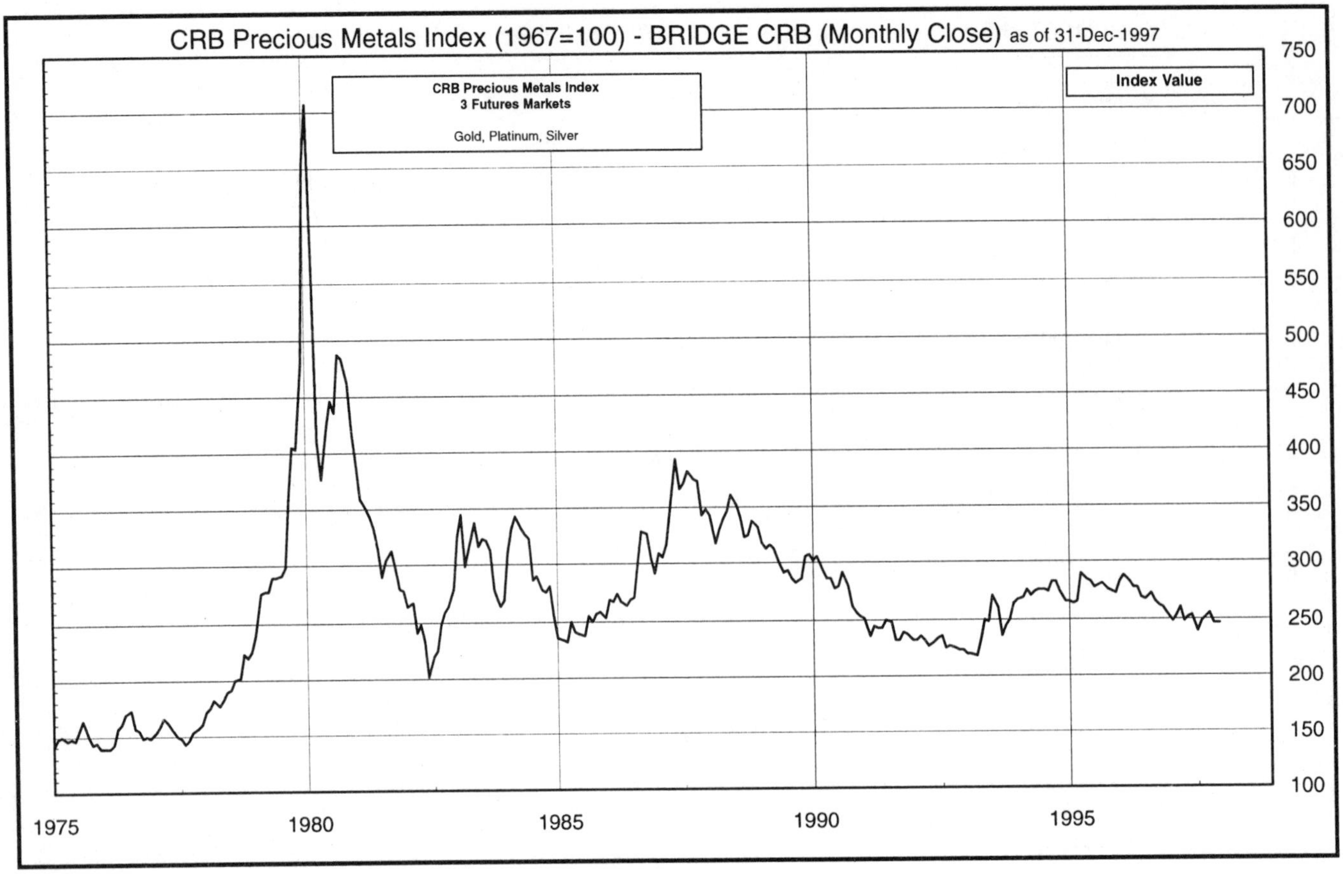
CRB Precious Metals Index (1967=100) - BRIDGE CRB (Monthly Close) as of 31-Dec-1997
CRB Precious Metals Index
3 Futures Markets
Gold, Platinum, Silver
Index Value
750
700
650
600
550
500
450
400
350
300
250
200
150
100
1975
1980
1985
1990
1995

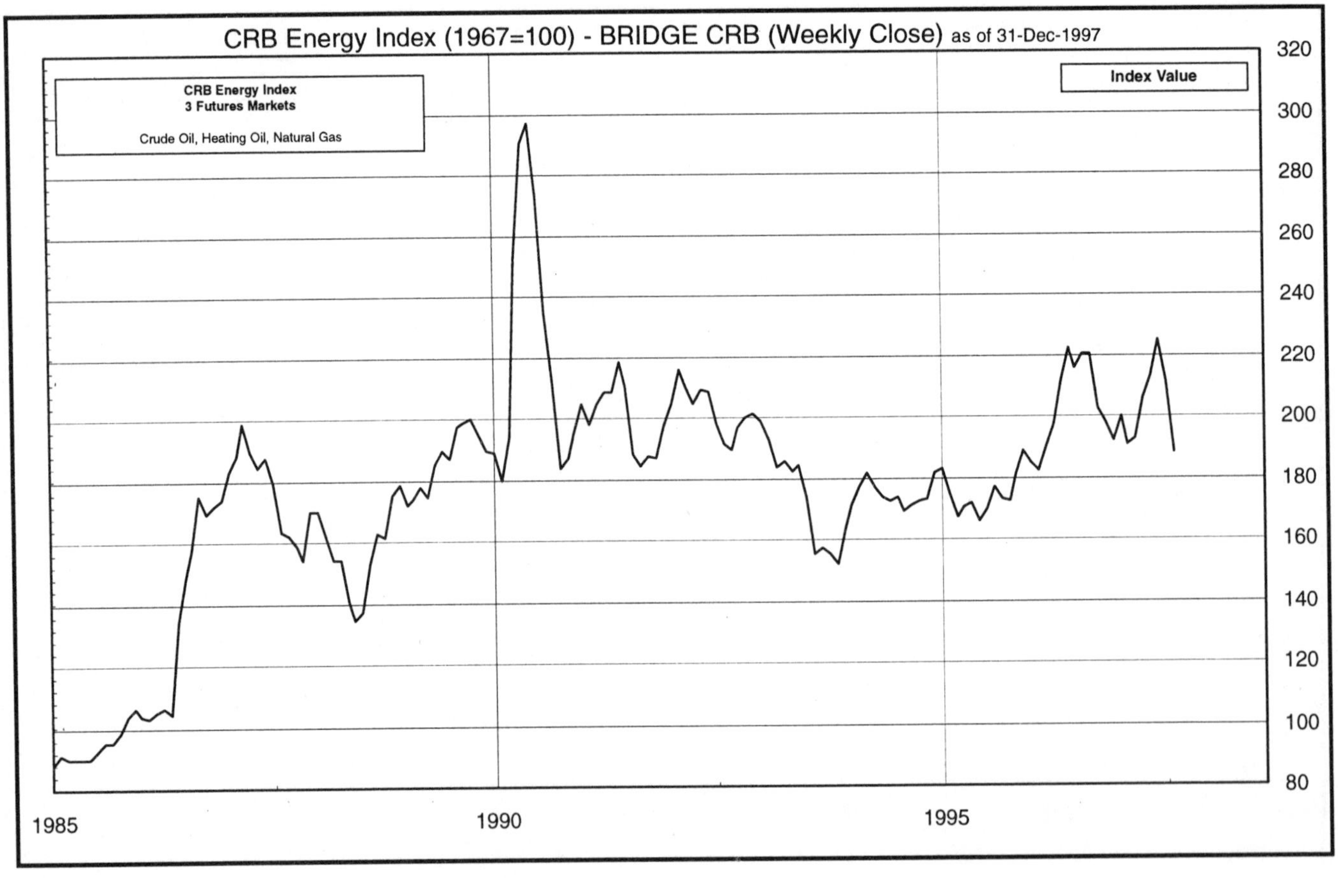
CRB Energy Index (1967=100) - BRIDGE CRB (Weekly Close) as of 31-Dec-1997
CRB Energy Index
3 Futures Markets
Crude Oil, Heating Oil, Natural Gas
Index Value
320
300
280
260
240
220
200
180
160
140
120
100
80
1985
1990
1995

CRB Futures Index (1967=100) and Goldman Sachs Commodity Index (GSCI™/SM) - (Weekly Close) as of 31-Dec-1997

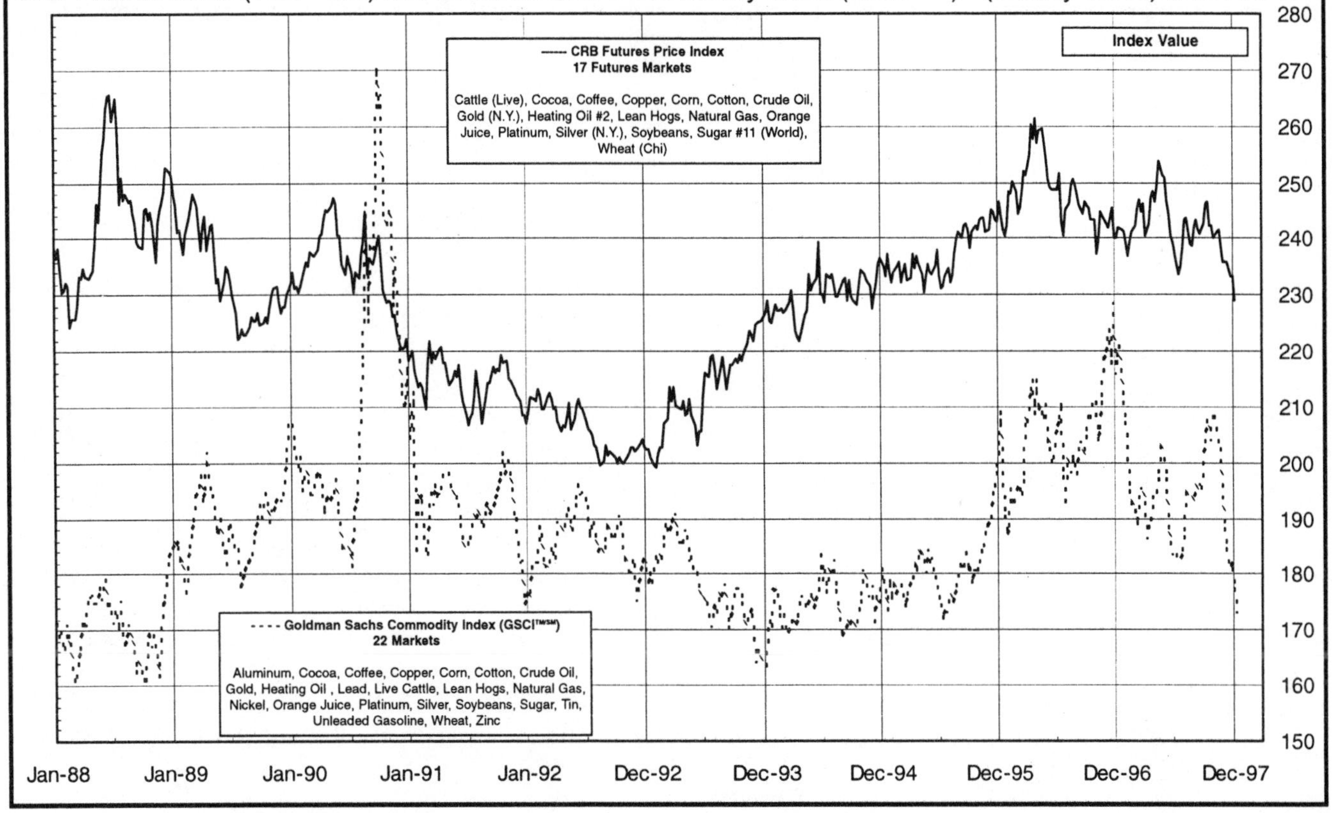

Index Value

—— CRB Futures Price Index
17 Futures Markets

Cattle (Live), Cocoa, Coffee, Copper, Corn, Cotton, Crude Oil, Gold (N.Y.), Heating Oil #2, Lean Hogs, Natural Gas, Orange Juice, Platinum, Silver (N.Y.), Soybeans, Sugar #11 (World), Wheat (Chi)

- - - - Goldman Sachs Commodity Index (GSCI™/SM)
22 Markets

Aluminum, Cocoa, Coffee, Copper, Corn, Cotton, Crude Oil, Gold, Heating Oil , Lead, Live Cattle, Lean Hogs, Natural Gas, Nickel, Orange Juice, Platinum, Silver, Soybeans, Sugar, Tin, Unleaded Gasoline, Wheat, Zinc

280, 270, 260, 250, 240, 230, 220, 210, 200, 190, 180, 170, 160, 150

Jan-88, Jan-89, Jan-90, Jan-91, Jan-92, Dec-92, Dec-93, Dec-94, Dec-95, Dec-96, Dec-97

CRB Futures Index and CRB (BLS) Spot Price Index (1967=100)- BRIDGE CRB (Weekly Close) as of 27-Feb-1998

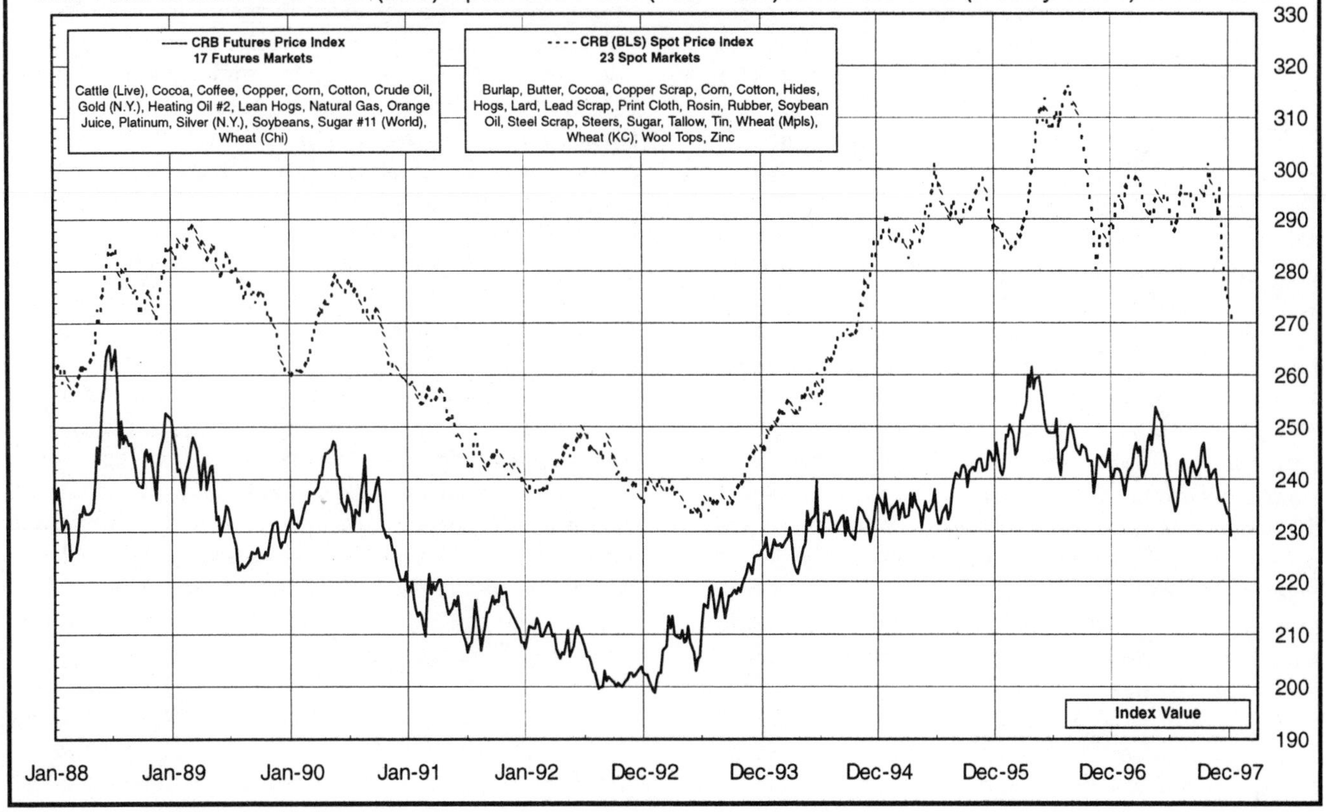

—— CRB Futures Price Index
17 Futures Markets

Cattle (Live), Cocoa, Coffee, Copper, Corn, Cotton, Crude Oil, Gold (N.Y.), Heating Oil #2, Lean Hogs, Natural Gas, Orange Juice, Platinum, Silver (N.Y.), Soybeans, Sugar #11 (World), Wheat (Chi)

- - - - CRB (BLS) Spot Price Index
23 Spot Markets

Burlap, Butter, Cocoa, Copper Scrap, Corn, Cotton, Hides, Hogs, Lard, Lead Scrap, Print Cloth, Rosin, Rubber, Soybean Oil, Steel Scrap, Steers, Sugar, Tallow, Tin, Wheat (Mpls), Wheat (KC), Wool Tops, Zinc

Index Value

330, 320, 310, 300, 290, 280, 270, 260, 250, 240, 230, 220, 210, 200, 190

Jan-88, Jan-89, Jan-90, Jan-91, Jan-92, Dec-92, Dec-93, Dec-94, Dec-95, Dec-96, Dec-97

El Niño – Not Just a Media Child

By John Dee

INTRODUCTION

Decades (maybe even longer) before the rest of the world paid any attention to the sea surface temperatures in the Tropical Pacific, fisherman in the coastal sections of Peru and Equador noticed a seasonal warming of the sea in their region. Because this seasonal warming occurred near the time of the celebration of the birth of Jesus Christ, the local fisherman called the occurrence El Niño, or "The Boy Child." Occasionally, this seasonal warming occurred to a greater magnitude and lasted longer than it did on average. About 30-40 years ago, Atmospheric Scientists and Oceanographers began to notice this abnormal warming and its effects on the region. Within the past 20-30 years, a link has been made between the abnormal fluctuation in sea surface temperatures in the Tropical Pacific and regional and world weather anomalies. Recently, the term El Niño has become known to refer to the abnormal warming of the sea surface in the Tropical Pacific and the effects on the atmosphere that it causes. Working in conjunction with the sea surface temperature fluctuation (El Niño) is a fluctuation in the normal air pressure measured at specific locations in the same general area. This fluctuation in sea level pressure has been given the term "Southern Oscillation," and the combination of **E**l **N**iño and the **S**outhern **O**scillation has been given the acronym ENSO.

It is the purpose of this report to try and clear up any misunderstanding about El Niño and the Southern Oscillation (to be referred to in the future as ENSO) and to also try and draw conclusions between ENSO and world supply and demand of Agricultural and Industrial Commodities. There are several points which will be made through the course of this report, and at this time, I would like to make my first point. While it may appear as though the scientific community fully understands the causes and effects of an ENSO event, quite the reverse is true. I do not mean to criticize those involved in the study of this phenomenon. There have been great advances in knowledge made by them over the past several decades. Yet, the study of ENSO is quite young and scientists are still learning more about what makes this event occur. At this point, scientists are not fully sure of the mechanisms causing the development of an El Niño, or what makes it go away. Any forecasting tools used to date on ENSO use statistical methods rather than mechanical or physical formulas. At times, these statistical models perform quite well, while at other times, they fail quite miserably. It is believed that the El Niño and SO are related and work off of each other to some extent, but to what extent and what exactly causes them to have these fluctuations, they do not know. Thus it is important to keep in mind that the study of ENSO is still in its infantile stages and little is truly known about what causes it to occur and what causes it to go away. Progress is being made towards better understanding this phenomenon and hopefully in the not-so-distant future, a much better understanding will be available for use in predicting worldwide weather anomalies.

While little is known about what the mechanisms are which cause the ENSO to occur, quite a bit is known about what goes on in the ocean and atmosphere of the Tropical Pacific during an event. During the warm phase of an ENSO, the sea surface temperatures in the central and eastern Pacific Ocean in the vicinity of the Equator become warmer than average *(figure 1)*. In addition, the sea level pressures in the eastern Pacific become lower than average, while those in the western Pacific become higher than normal. During a cold episode (commonly called La Niña) the reverse happens. Sea surface temperatures in the same general area of the central and eastern Pacific Ocean become cooler than average, the sea level pressures in the eastern Pacific become higher than normal, and those in the western Pacific become lower than average. During a warm episode, the warmer than average water and lower than average pressures at sea level combine to bring enhanced cloud development and also enhanced rainfall. Regions of coastal Peru, which are usually a desert and see less than 1-4" of rainfall occur all year, sometimes see rainfall amounts of 1-2" occur during a single event!

Another product of the enhanced cloud cover in the eastern tropical Pacific is hurricane development in areas where these storms are usually quite rare.

Figure 1

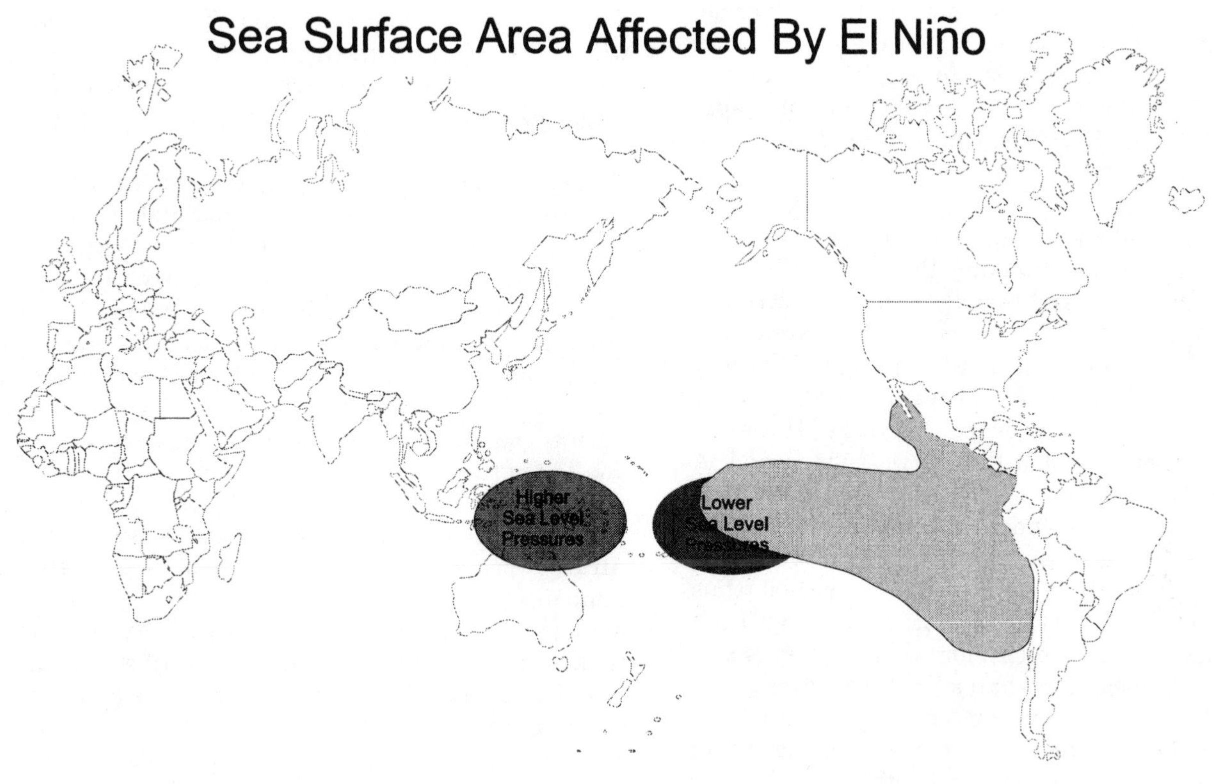

WARM EPISODE (El Niña) Years
1902, 1909, 1911, 1914, 1918, 1923, 1925, 1930, 1932, 1939, 1941, 1951, 1953, 1957, 1965, 1969, 1972, 1976, 1982, 1986, 1991, 1994, 1997
COLD EPISODE (La Niña) YEARS
1904, 1909, 1910, 1915, 1917, 1924, 1928, 1938, 1950, 1955, 1956, 1964, 1970, 1971, 1973, 1975, 1988, 1995

Table 1

Western Samoa and the region around Fiji normally do not see much in the way of tropical storm development. However, during a warm episode, this region can experience tropical activity to the magnitude of strong hurricanes. In the western Pacific, just the opposite occurs. The cooler than average sea surfaces and higher than average surface pressures lead to a decrease in cloud development and a decrease in rainfall, hence the droughts in Indonesia and in northern Australia. More on how the ENSO effects weather around the world will be discussed later.

Another point which I would like to make is that it seems to be common thinking that every ENSO is relatively the same and that there is little variance in strength, size or life between one event and another. In reality, each El Niño is different. Typically, the development of warm episodes occur on the average of once every 3-7 years. However, sometimes they repeat within a two year period. A typical warm ENSO event will also begin to form sometime during the June-October period, reach its maximum strength during the December-March period and dissipate in the March-June period, thus lasting close to a year. However, there have been some which have lasted for more than two years and others which lasted less than a year. The strength of an ENSO will also vary from one event to another. Some ENSO's produce sea surface anomalies of eight degrees C or greater, while others reach their maximum intensity at 2-3 degrees C above average *(figure 2)*.

Impacts On Regional and World Weather Patterns

The development of an El Niño or La Niña can and does impact on the weather not just in the vicinity of the tropical Pacific, but also around the world from South Africa to Newfoundland *(figures 3,4,5,6)*. I will first start out with the impact this phenomenon has on the weather patterns in the region of the tropical Pacific.

As touched on earlier, during a warm episode, the cooler sea surface temperatures and higher sea-level pressures in the western Pacific lead to a suppression of tropical cloud development and also a decrease in tropical rainfall in Indonesia and sections of southeast Asia. Locations such as Indonesia, Australia, Malaysia and India see a significant threat of below average precipitation during the duration of the warm episode *(figures 3&4)*. Another location in the general area of the tropics which experiences below average precipitation during a warm episode is southeast Africa. Specifically the countries of South Africa, Zimbabwe Mozambique and the island of Madagascar *(figure 3)*. These areas see the drier than average weather occur during different times of the year. The dry weather in Indonesia typically occurs throughout the duration of the warm episode. The dryness in northern Australia also typically occurs throughout the duration of the ENSO, and can also expand into the southern and eastern regions of this country. The drier than average weather in southeast Africa is most notable during the southern hemisphere's summer from December to March.

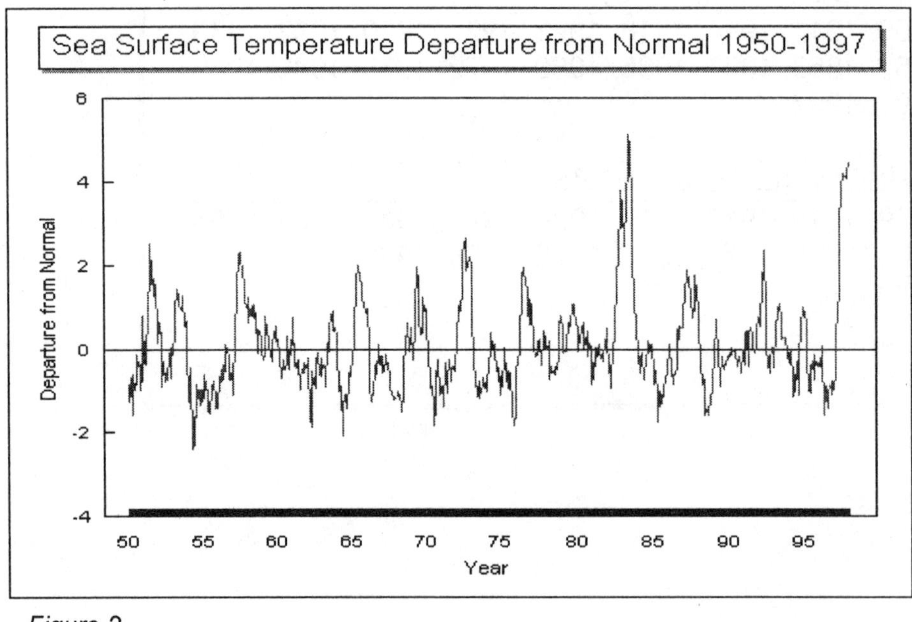

Figure 2

The Southwest Asian Monsoon, of which the Indian Monsoon is a part, is also adversely affected by an El Niño *(figure 4)*. The suppression of tropical cloud development over Indonesia also can extend west into the Indian sub-continent and the critical monsoon rains can be lessened in this region. One of the worst Indian Monsoon events in modern times happened during the El Niño year of 1987. Rainfall in the 1987 monsoon was a fraction of what normally occurs and crop production nationwide suffered. Production areas of Thailand, Cambodia, Vietnam and the Philippines also see less than normal rainfall occur while an El Niño is present.

There are other areas affected by an El Niño. Above average precipitation in northeast Argentina and southern Brazil occurs during their summer months *(figure 4)*. An increase in the sea surface temperatures leads to greater than average available moisture and energy which provides the rainfall for these areas. Further north, warmer than average weather occurs in northeast Brazil during their winter months and a decrease in precipitation amounts occurs in the Amazon Basin throughout much of the year *(figure 3)*.

While North America is quite a distance from the region where the ENSO is occurring, it does not escape the unusual weather which an ENSO can create. The warmer waters create a situation similar to that which occurs in the southern hemisphere, with more moisture and an increase in upper air energy (the jet stream) occurring. This increase in moisture and upper air energy is most prevalent during the winter months and occurs most noticeably in the southern third of the Nation. During the winter months while an ENSO is occurring, the sub-tropical jet stream (the jet which divides the tropical weather in the south from the cooler weather of the mid-latitudes) becomes stronger than usual. This enhanced jet leads to more and stronger storms across the southern U.S. One area which can be affected by the stronger than average sub-tropical jet is southern and central California. The storms which usually move into this region from the Pacific during the winter months are enhanced by a feed of tropical moisture and the energy it holds. Significant economic impacts occur as a result of coastal and river flooding brought on by these stronger than usual winter storms. Snowpack is also increased in the Sierra Nevada. This snowpack feeds much of the state of California with water throughout the year. The 1994 ENSO has been credited with ending the six year drought in California and returning the reservoirs to near capacity. The stronger than average sub-tropical jet can also strengthen the weather systems which move along the Gulf of Mexico Coast. Thus the Gulf Coast States tend to be wetter than average during the winter months while a warm ENSO is occurring.

The strengthening of the sub-tropical jet drains energy from the polar jet decreasing its efficiency at drawing cold air from the Polar Regions southward. The polar jet is what Americans associate with the term *jet stream* and is actually the stream of air separating the mild air of the mid-latitudes with the cold air from the Polar Regions. Thus the Canadian Prairies, Canadian Rockies, and the northern sections of the U.S. Plains and Midwest see warmer than average temperatures occur during the winter months. It is also important to note that there has been no correlation made to the occurrence of an ENSO and drought in the Midwestern U.S. This does not mean that while an ENSO is occurring a drought in the Midwest is impossible. However, the finger cannot be pointed at El Niño.

One last impact an ENSO has on the U.S. is a drop in tropical storm and hurricane development in the Atlantic Basin. Residents and governments along the Gulf Coast and Atlantic Coast can usually breathe a sigh of relief at the development of a warm episode, as the chances of a hurricane affecting this region are diminished. However, it must be stressed that the presence of a warm episode does not eliminate the threat of a hurricane. One example of this anomaly is Hurricane Andrew of 1992.

It is also important to point out that with the exception of southern Africa, the entire continent of Africa, all of Europe and all of the former Soviet Union are also not effected by an ENSO.

The effects that a cold episode or La Niña have on the weather patterns around the world is nearly opposite to that which occurs during an El Niño *(figures 5 & 6)*. Areas which tend to be drier than average during an El Niño tend to be wetter than average during a La Niña, and those areas which are cooler than average during an El Niño are warmer during a La Niña and vice-versa.

It is also very important to note that the occurrence of these weather anomalies is not a guarantee while an ENSO is occurring. As mentioned, each ENSO is different in its characteristics and thus has a different effect on the weather around the world.

Figure 3

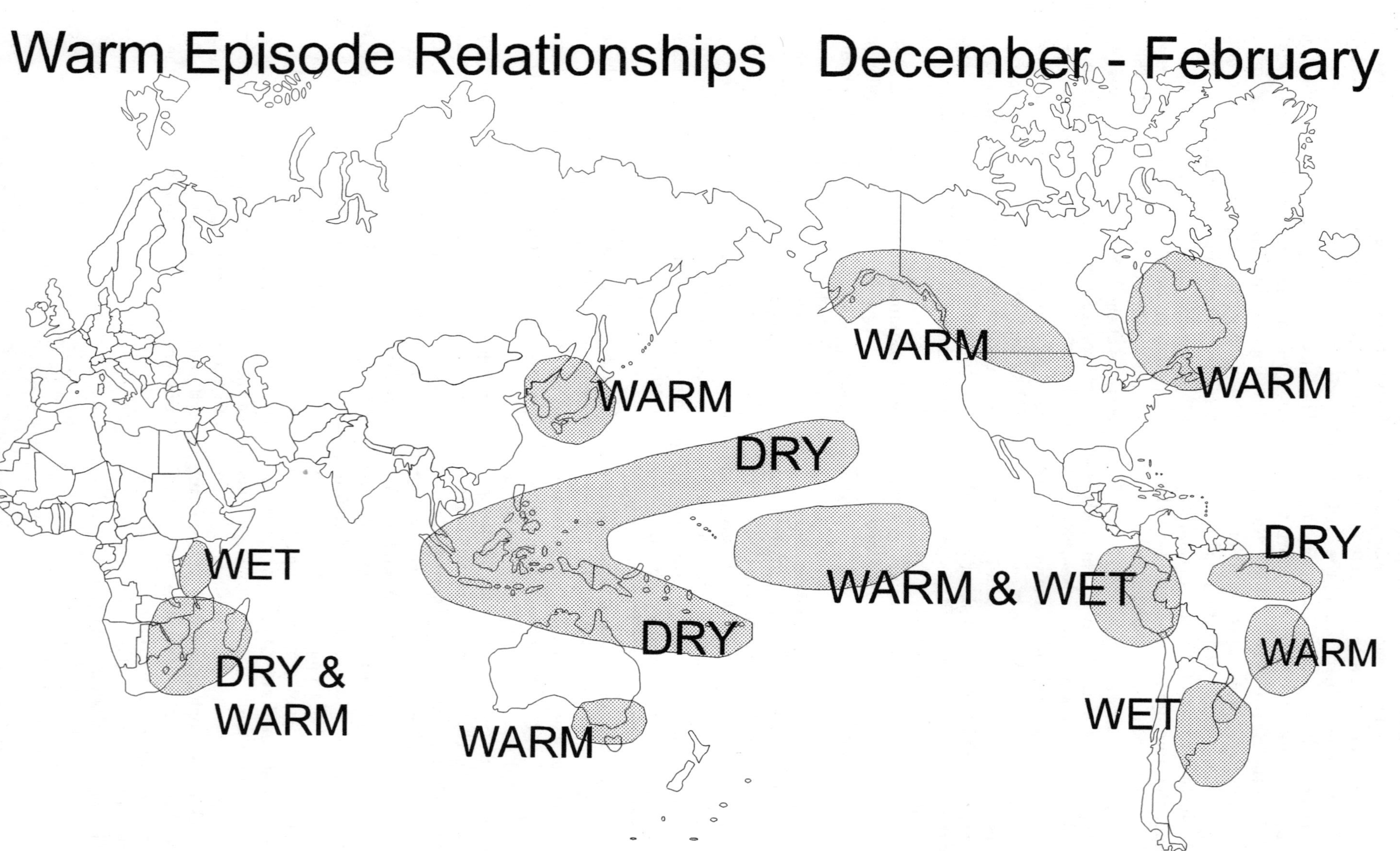

Warm Episode Relationships December - February
WARM
WARM
WARM
DRY
WET
DRY
WARM & WET
DRY
DRY &
WARM
WARM
WARM
WET

Figure 4

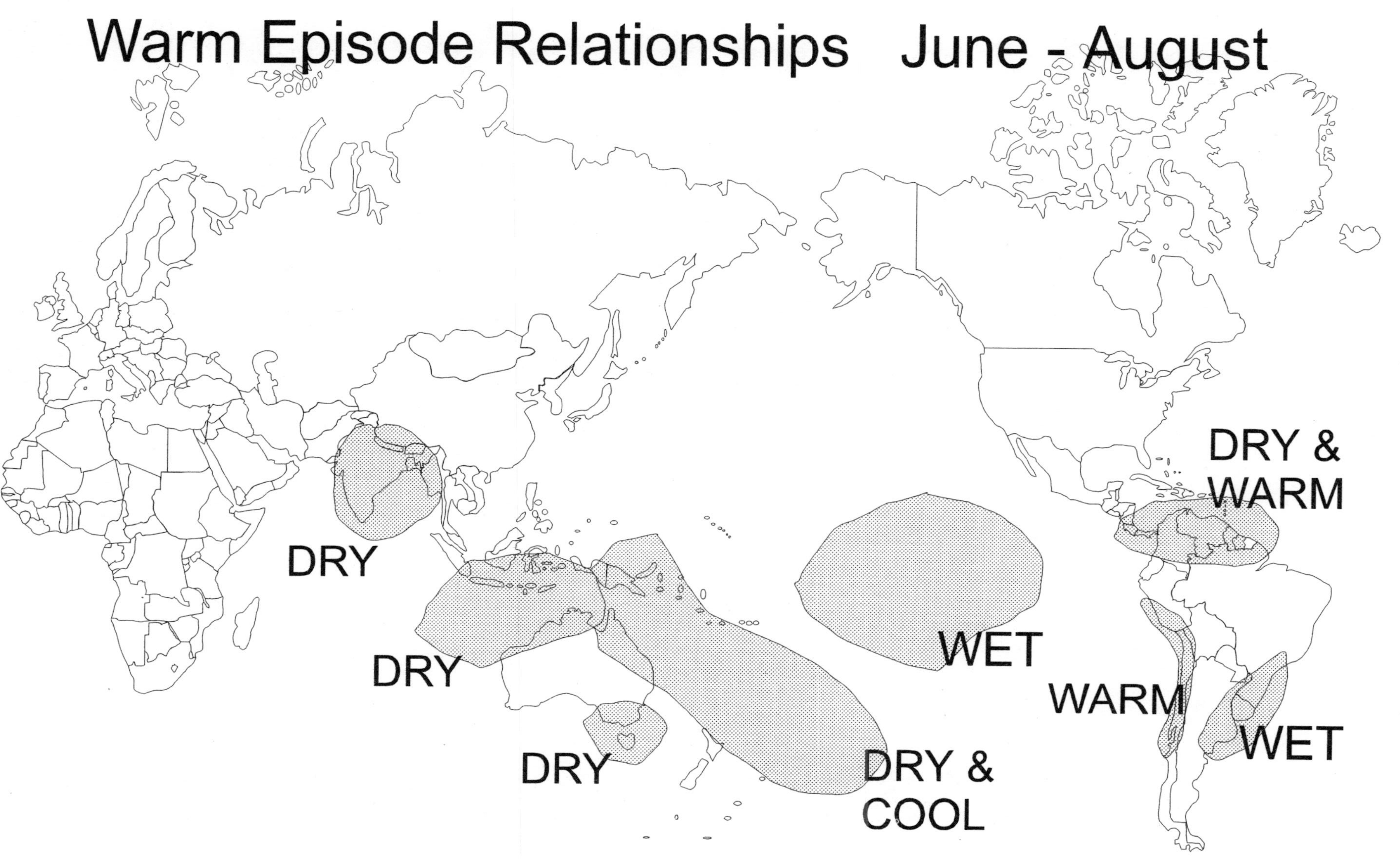
Warm Episode Relationships June - August
DRY & WARM
DRY
DRY
DRY
WET
WARM
WET
DRY & COOL

Figure 5

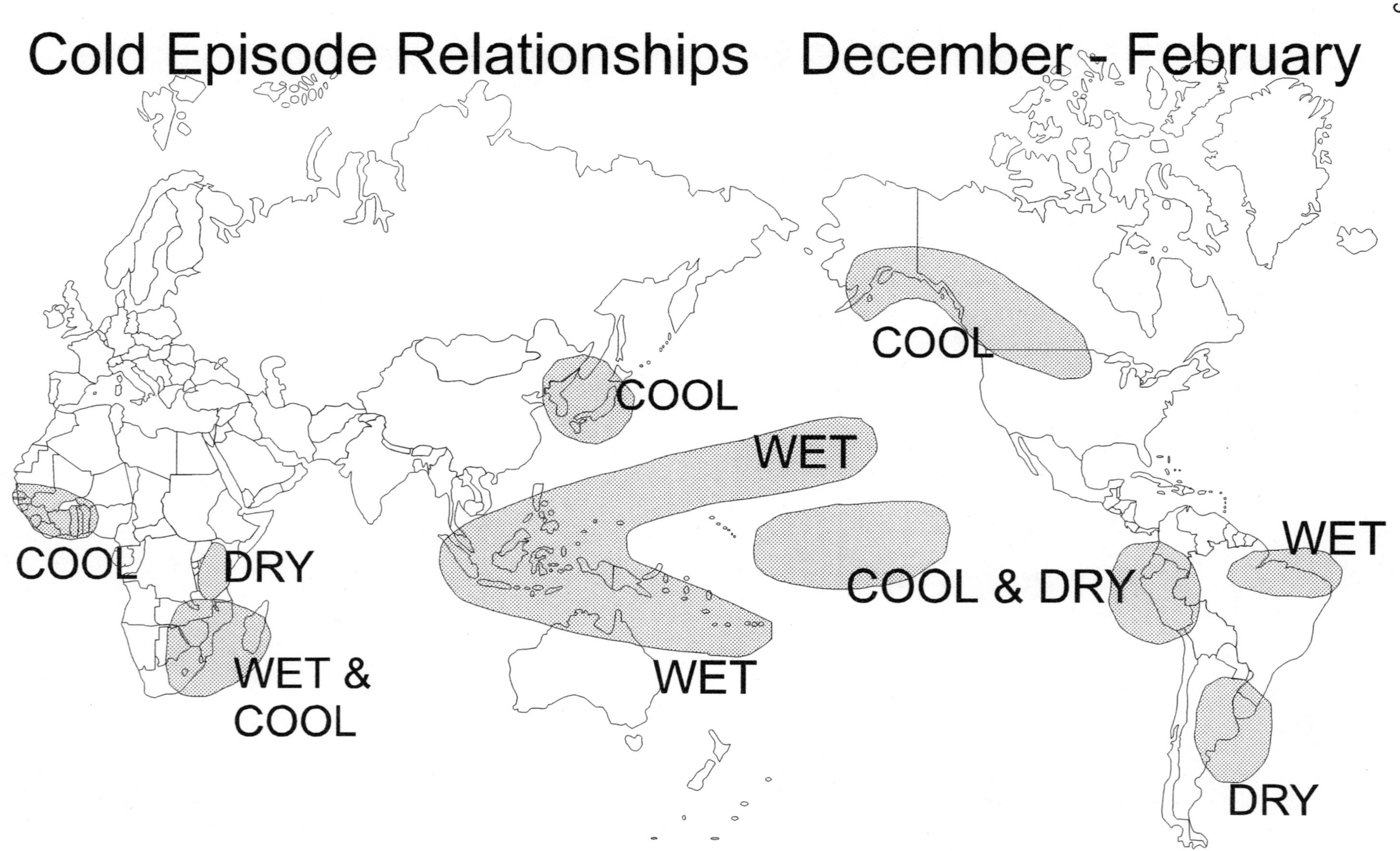

Cold Episode Relationships December - February
COOL
COOL
WET
WET
COOL & DRY
WET
DRY
COOL
DRY
WET & COOL

Figure 6

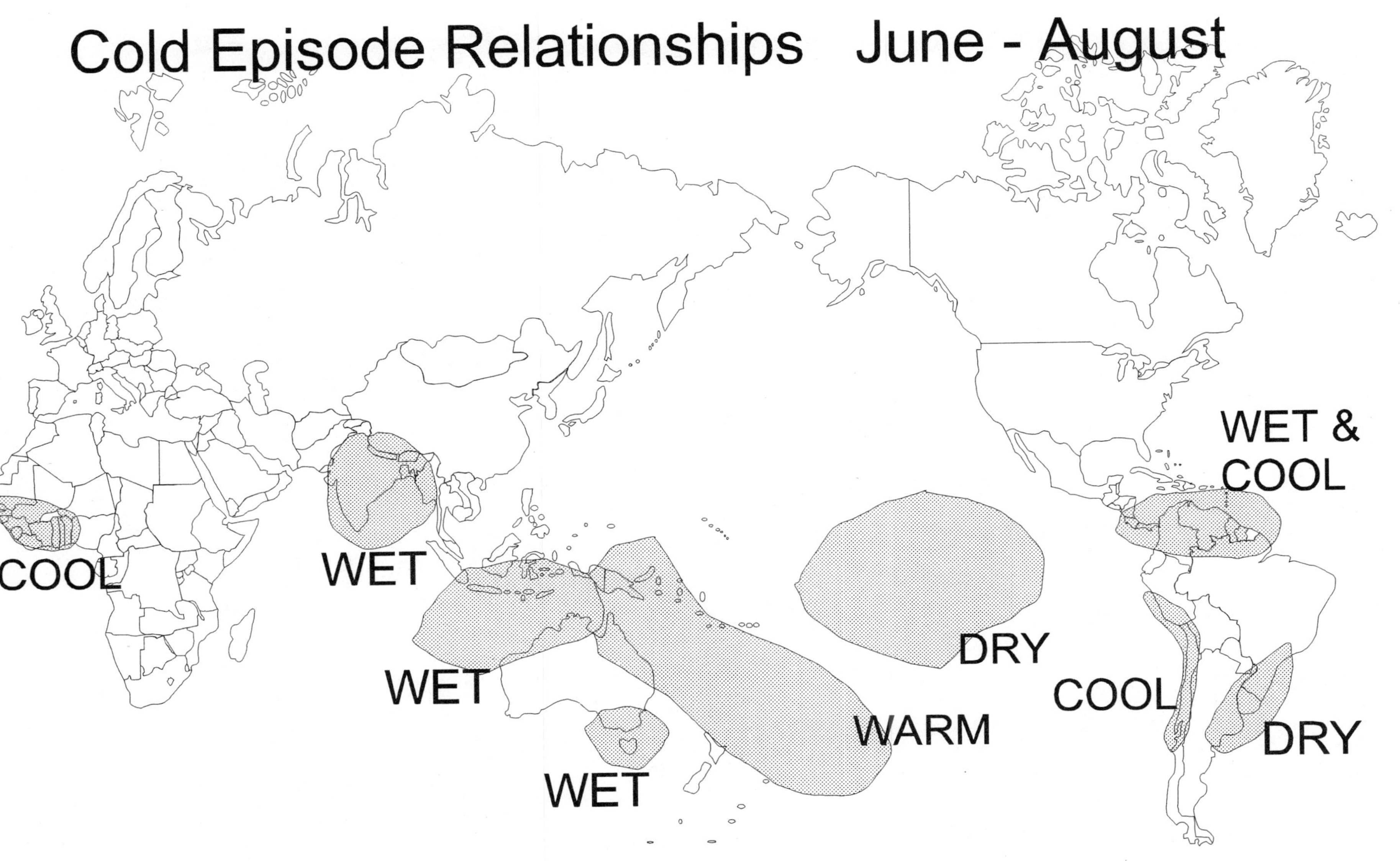

Cold Episode Relationships June - August
COOL
WET
WET
WET
WARM
DRY
WET & COOL
COOL
DRY

Take the recent ENSO episode for example. While sea surface temperatures were in El Niño-like levels of 3-5 degrees C higher, and sea level pressures were also in El Niño-like levels, the Indian Monsoon did not experience much of a deviation from average with close to average rainfall occurring. South Africa has also seen fairly frequent and plentiful rainfall to date (Feb. 1, 1998). The anomalies which did verify with this episode were the wet weather in Argentina and Brazil, wet weather in both the west coastal and the Gulf Coastal regions of the U.S., warm weather in the Canadian and U.S. Plains and dry weather in Indonesia.

Effects of El Niño on World Agricultural Production

Now that you have a better idea what an ENSO is and which areas are affected by it, let's turn our attention to which crops around the world stand the greatest chance for declines or improvements in their yields due to the presence of an El Niño or La Niña.

As is the case with the impacts that an El Niño has on the weather, the greatest impacts on crop production can also be found closest to the tropical Pacific. Most notably is the drop in production of tropical crops of coffee, cocoa, sugar, rice, and also the tropical oils of coconut and palm oil. The drier than average weather which can develop during an El Niño in Indonesia, Malaysia and the Philippines can, and has, cut production of these crops. The drier than average weather in this area generally occurs during the duration of the El Niño, and thus all stages of development of these crops can experience drier than average weather. The most critical phases of development for Coffee and Cocoa are the reproductive stages of flowering and fruiting. It is during this stage that the harvested portions of the plant are produced. The flowering and fruiting of the crops differ from region to region, but the growth cycles of the different crops of Coffee and Cocoa are the same and are tied into the wet and dry seasons. Planting and flowering is done during the beginning of the wet season and harvesting occurs at the end of the wet season. Because of the dependance that the coffee and cocoa crops have on the pronounced wet season developing, a delayed or erratic wet season can have serious effects on the production of these crops.

The wet season for the coffee and cocoa crops in South America occurs from November through March. The far northern coffee and cocoa producing regions of Brazil can experience dry weather during their critical stages and yields can be effected.

On the other side of the Pacific, Indonesian coffee and cocoa production can be inhibited by a lack of rainfall throughout their growth. Coffee production on the island of Madagascar can also be negatively affected by dry weather during its flowering and fruiting stages.

Tropical oils are another crop which can, and have been, negatively affected by the dry weather associated with El Niño. Once again, it is Indonesia, Malaysia and the Philippines which are most under the gun for a drop in production due to dryness created by El Niño. However, tropical oil production, as well as soybean oil production in India can, and has been, affected by dryness due to El Niño. In the 1987 Indian monsoon year, oil production in India was cut by 10-15%. The drop in Indian Vegetable Oil production was compounded by significant drops in tropical oil production in areas of Indonesia and Malaysia, as well as dry weather in the soybean growing regions of the U.S. This created a decrease in world oil supplies and prices for all oils rose dramatically in 1988.

Another crop affected by a warm ENSO episode is rice. The years of 1987-88 and 1992-93 saw significant drops in rice production across Indonesia and India. The main reason for the drop in production in India was the failure of normal monsoon rains to occur across much of the Indian sub-continent. The monsoon rains are extremely important to the production of crops across India. For most of the year, India sees little rainfall and the region is basically a desert. In an average year, most of India receives between 70-95% of its annual rainfall during the wet season. Beginning in June and continuing through September, the winds shift their direction and come off of the oceans. This reversal of windflow pumps in the warm and humid air off of the oceans and disturbances in the weather lead to waves of showers and thunderstorms occurring across India during these months. The timely arrival of the monsoon is critical as farmers there wait for the first rains to arrive before planting the crops. Additional rainfall is needed throughout the season as little in the way of irrigation occurs in India and the soils accumulate no additional water during the winter months. The only crops which see a significant amount of irrigation are the wheat fields in northern and northwest India. Here, farmers actually wait for the retreat of the monsoon before they plant their wheat

Impact of El Niño on World Crop Production

Stage of ENSO	Regional Impact	Time of Maximum Effects	Crops Affected
Warm	India - Dry	June - Sept	Sugar - Decrease in Production Possible
Warm	Indonesia - Dry	Duration of Episode	Sugar - Decrease in Production Possible
Warm	Australia - Dry & Cool	June - August	Sugar - Decrease in Production Possible
Warm	Brazil(Amazon) - Dry	Dec - Feb	Cocoa - Decrease in Production Possible
Warm	Brazil(NE Coast) - Warm	Dec - Feb	Cocoa – Minor Impact
Warm	Indonesia - Dry	Duration of Episode	Cocoa - Decrease in Production Possible
Warm	Madagascar - Dry & Warm	June - August	Coffee - Decrease in Production Possible
Warm	Indonesia - Dry	Duration of Episode	Coffee - Decrease in Production Possible
Warm	Indonesia - Dry	Duration of Episode	Rice - Decrease in Production Possible
Warm	India - Dry	Duration of Episode	Autumn Rice - Decrease in Production Possible
Warm	India - Dry	June - Sept	Winter Rice - Decrease in Production Possible
Warm	Indonesia - Dry	Duration of Episode	Coconut Oil - Decrease in Production Possible
Warm	Indonesia - Dry	Duration of Episode	Oil Palm - Decrease in Production Possible
Warm	Malaysia - Dry	Duration of Episode	Oil Palm - Decrease in Production Possible
Warm	India - Dry	June - August	Rapeseed - Decrease in Production Possible
Warm	India - Dry	June - August	Peanut - Decrease in Production Possible
Warm	Indonesia - Dry	Duration of Episode	Peanut - Decrease in Production Possible
Warm	India - Dry	June - August	Cottonseed - Decrease in Production Possible
Warm	Australia - Dry	Duration of Episode	Cottonseed - Decrease in Production Possible
Warm	Brazil & N. Argentina - Wet	Dec - Feb	Soybeans - Increase in Production Possible
Warm	South Africa - Dry	Dec - Feb	Corn - Decrease in Production Possible
Warm	Zimbabwe - Dry	Dec - Feb	Corn - Decrease in Production Possible
Warm	Mozambique - Dry	Dec - Feb	Corn - Decrease in Production Possible
Warm	Eastern Australia - Dry	June - August	Wheat - Decrease in Production Possible
Warm	Brazil & N. Argentina - Wet	Dec - Feb	Wheat - Minor Impact

Impact of La Niña on World Crop Production

Stage of ENSO	Regional Impact	Time of Maximum Effects	Crops Affected
Cold	India - Wet	June - Sept	Sugar - Moderate Increase in Production Possible
Cold	Indonesia - Wet	Duration of Episode	Sugar - Moderate Increase in Production Possible
Cold	Australia - Wet & Warm	June - August	Sugar - Moderate Increase in Production Possible
Cold	Brazil(Amazon) - Wet	Dec - Feb	Cocoa - Minor Impact
Cold	Brazil(NE Coast) - Cool	Dec - Feb	Cocoa - Decrease in Production Possible
Cold	Indonesia - Wet	Duration of Episode	Cocoa - Minor Impact
Cold	Madagascar - Wet & Cool	June - August	Coffee - Minor Impact
Cold	Indonesia - Wet	Duration of Episode	Coffee - Minor Impact
Cold	Indonesia - Wet	Duration of Episode	Rice - Minor Impact
Cold	India - Wet	Duration of Episode	Autumn Rice - Moderate Increase in Production Possible
Cold	India - Wet	June - Sept	Winter Rice - Moderate Increase in Production Possible
Cold	Indonesia - Wet	Duration of Episode	Coconut Oil - Moderate Increase in Production Possible
Cold	Indonesia - Wet	Duration of Episode	Oil Palm - Moderate Increase in Production Possible
Cold	Malaysia - Wet	Duration of Episode	Oil Palm - Moderate Increase in Production Possible
Cold	India - Wet	June - August	Rapeseed - Increase in Production Possible
Cold	India - Wet	June - August	Peanut - Increase in Production Possible
Cold	Indonesia - Wet	Duration of Episode	Peanut - Minor Impact
Cold	India - Wet	June - August	Cottonseed - Increase in Production Possible
Cold	Australia - Wet	Duration of Episode	Cottonseed - Moderate Increase in Production Possible
Cold	Brazil & N. Argentina - Dry	Dec - Feb	Soybeans - Decrease in Production Possible
Cold	South Africa - Wet & Cool	Dec - Feb	Corn - Increase in Production Possible
Cold	Zimbabwe - Wet & Cool	Dec - Feb	Corn - Increase in Production Possible
Cold	Mozambique - Wet & Cool	Dec - Feb	Corn - Increase in Production Possible
Cold	Eastern Australia - Wet	June - August	Wheat - Minor Impact
Cold	Brazil & N. Argentina - Dry	Dec - Feb	Wheat - Moderate Decrease in Production Possible

fields in September and October, and then irrigate them throughout the dry season.

Another area which sees a strong impact due to El Niño is the corn production areas of South Africa, Zimbabwe and Mozambique. This is another area of the world which sees pronounced dry and wet seasons. While the wet and dry seasons here are not as pronounced as they are in India, local crops are also planted in tune with the annual arrival of the wet season and harvested as the dry season arrives. This dependence on the annual wet season was demonstrated quite well in the 1992-1993 production year. It was during that year that an El Niño-induced drought developed in South Africa, Zimbabwe, and Mozambique, the corn production in some of these areas was cut 50%.

One area which sees favorable growing conditions due to El Niño is northeast Argentina and southern Brazil. Above average rainfall occurs in this region during the months of December through February. These are the critical reproductive and vegetative months for corn and soybeans and the increase in rain during this period can have yield increasing effects for both crops.

The only effects of an ENSO episode in North America on the supply or demand of commodities is a drop in demand for Natural Gas across the north central U.S. during the winter months. As mentioned, a warm anomaly develops in the Canadian Plains, the northern Plains, and northern Midwest in the winter time. This warm anomaly causes the arctic air to remain in the arctic and as a result, demand for Natural Gas for heating is reduced. Just the opposite can occur when a La Niña or absence of an El Niño is occurring. The cold air is allowed to come down and is often colder and longer lasting than average. This creates abnormally high demands for Natural Gas. The winter of 1996-97 was one such year.

There is one other area which sees a significant impact due to La Niña and that is the production regions of northeast Argentina and southern Brazil. During a La Niña, drier than average conditions develop and the production of corn and soybeans can be negatively affected. All of the other anomalies, when reversed during a La Niña, do not show a significant impact on the crops produced. In most cases, the impact to the weather is an increase in rainfall. This increase in rainfall does not benefit the crops in these regions dramatically because the region sees ample rainfall in an average year anyway. If anything, a modest increase in crop production occurs in places like Indonesia, India, and South Africa.

CONCLUSIONS

In conclusion, it is safe to say that an ENSO event does have a significant impact on the weather in different areas of the world and these weather impacts can also have a direct impact on crop production in that region. Over the course of the past decade or two, certain governments around the world have made changes in their policies involving the production and consumption/distribution of their crops due to the status of the ENSO.

It is also important to note that while ENSO's have been observed by humans for hundreds of years, it has only been within the last several decades that a concerted effort has been made to study and understand what causes an ENSO and its full impact on the weather worldwide. Much has been learned so far, but there is still much, much more to learn, including what causes the sea surface to warm or cool and possibly new impacts on the weather in different areas of the world.

It is important to keep in mind that each ENSO is different and will have different effects on the weather patterns worldwide. Not all El Niños bring super storms to southern California or drought to Australia. Even if the anomalies associated with an El Niño or La Niña do develop, they can still develop to varying degrees. Sometimes the anomaly is severe enough to cause a reduction or increase in crop production and sometimes it is not.

In the future, it is likely that much more will be known about the El Niño - Southern Oscillation mechanism, including what causes it to occur. Forecasting this event more accurately will also likely result, and it is my opinion that as advances in the knowledge of ENSO are made, so will advances in long-range (seasonal) forecasts. Who knows, maybe some day meteorologists will be able to forecast the weather for next summer or winter as accurately as they forecast this afternoons weather!

John Dee received a Bachelor of Science degree from Purdue University in Agricultural Meteorology. He has worked for the National Weather Service in Washington DC at the Climate Prediction Center (formerly the Climate Analysis Center) as well as for the U.S. Department of Agriculture. Since 1991, Mr. Dee has owned and operated Global Weather Monitoring, a private weather forecasting firm located in Chicago. Currently, The Iowa Grain Company in Chicago has an exclusive contract with Global Weather Monitoring to supply all of their weather forecasts. Mr. Dee also provides consultation for other companies in the world, including Agri-business, industrial and the media. To obtain his forecasts for the commodity markets, use the world wide web and go to: www.johndee.com or www.iowagrain.com/weather.

UNDERSTANDING OPTIONS

by Michele Ruston Gowda and Mark Taborsky

INTRODUCTION – UNRAVELING THE MYSTERY OF OPTIONS

The thousands of different exchange-traded options contracts now available to investors—whether on individual securities, stock indices or futures contracts—can seem intimidating, even to an experienced hand. There is virtually no limit to the ways options can be used, and their growing popularity as investment vehicles reflects the flexibility they offer large and small investors alike.

The purpose of this article is to provide investors with a brief explanation of how options work, show how they are used, and to help determine which options strategies, if any, can be used for a particular investment objective. This booklet can provide no more than an introduction to this complex product, and it assumes familiarity with the underlying financial instruments the options are based on. Used appropriately, options can help the investor limit risk, lock in profits, and sleep at night. They can be used to increase leverage and enhance potential profits while limiting financial risk. Or they can be used by speculators who are willing to assume unlimited risk. Like any tool, options must be used carefully with a full understanding of the underlying risk involved. An investment that is appropriate for one investor could be completely unacceptable for another. In other words, the investor himself must determine which tool to use, which market to use it in, and whether its use is appropriate.

Fortunately for us, the many different kinds of options share a common vocabulary and a common set of responses to similar changes in their underlying investments. For some, the vocabulary surrounding options trading may seem difficult at first but there is nothing secret or mysterious about it. This booklet will help explore what many of the commonly used terms mean and how they relate to options trading. For quick reference, a glossary is included at the end of this article.

I. OPTION BASICS

An option is any contract where one party pays another party for the opportunity, but not the obligation, to enter into a financial transaction at a specified price by or on a stated date in the future. Options contracts can be negotiated by the individual parties, by a broker in the over-the-counter market, or they can be bought and sold on regulated exchanges. Today, attesting to the popularity and benefits provided by options trading, there are literally thousands of standardized options contracts available on individual stocks, on commodity and financial futures, and on indexes which can be bought and sold around the world.

An option is a contract between two parties that is legally binding only on the seller of the option. An option grants the purchaser of the option the right—but not the obligation—to enter into a financial transaction at a specified price. For the buyer, honoring the contract is literally optional; it is his choice whether to consummate the deal. The buyer has paid the seller of the option for the right to back out of the deal. The seller of the option, whether it is the right to buy or the right to sell the underlying instrument, must honor the contract if the purchaser decides to go through with the deal by exercising his option. The option buyer gladly pays for the right to change his mind. The seller grants that right for the premium he receives.

CALLS AND PUTS

There are two basic types of options: calls and puts. The following descriptions represent the most basic and simplest option strategies, however you will later see that these calls and puts can be used in a variety of combinations to create much more sophisticated ways of hedging or speculating on different aspects of different markets.

A Call

A person who buys a call pays a premium for the "right" to ***buy*** the underlying instrument at a specific price (strike price) within a certain period of time (before exercise date or expiration). Conversely, the seller (writer) of a call receives the premium but has to deliver the underlying instrument if the owner of the call exercises his right. Generally, the call *purchaser* believes the price of the underlying instrument will rise and the call *writer* believes the underlying instrument will not increase in price sufficiently to offset the premium he has received for writing the call.

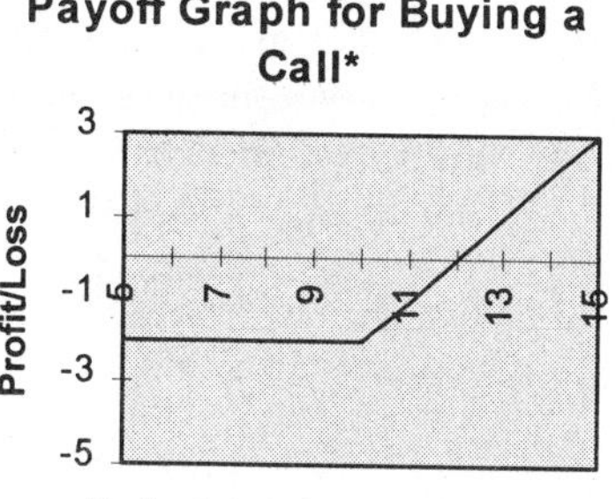

*Assumes strike price of $10 and $2 in premium

Buying a call represents the simplest bullish strategy. A person long a call will earn unlimited profits as the price of the underlying instrument rises, but has limited downside. No matter how far the price of the underlying instrument falls, the loss is limited to the option premium. When prices drop, the option is left to expire without being exercised.

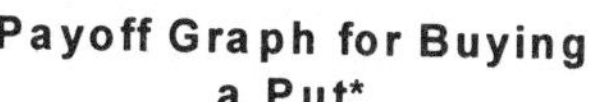

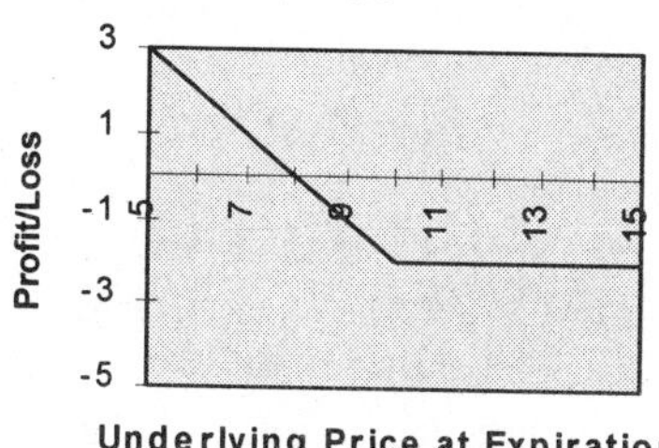

*Assumes strike price of $10 and $2 in premium

A put purchaser will earn profits when the price of the underlying instrument falls, but limits risk to the premium paid if the price of the underlying instrument rises. Buying puts provides an alternative bearish strategy to selling equity stock short. Whereas investors can only sell short on an "uptick" in the equity price, there are no such restrictions for buying puts.

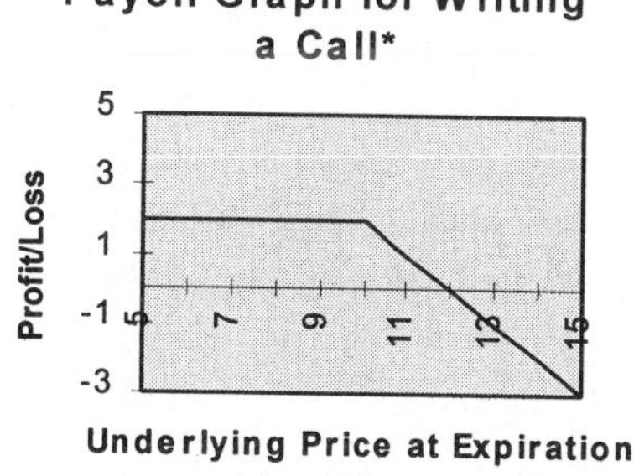

*Assumes strike price of $10 and $2 in premium

The person who sells a call is paid for assuming the risk that the price of the underlying instrument will rise. The call writer will make money as long as the price of the underlying instrument stays constant or falls. The call writer has almost unlimited risk on the upside, given that he will have to sell stock at the strike price, even if the market price is much higher. Writing calls works in declining and sideways markets and requires adequate capital to purchase the stock—or buy back the call—in a rising market.

A Put

A person who buys a put pays a premium for the "right" to ***sell*** the underlying instrument at a specific price within a certain period of time. The seller of a put receives the premium but is required to buy the underlying instrument at the strike price if the owner of the put exercises his right. Generally, the call purchaser and the put writer believe that the price of the underlying instrument will rise.

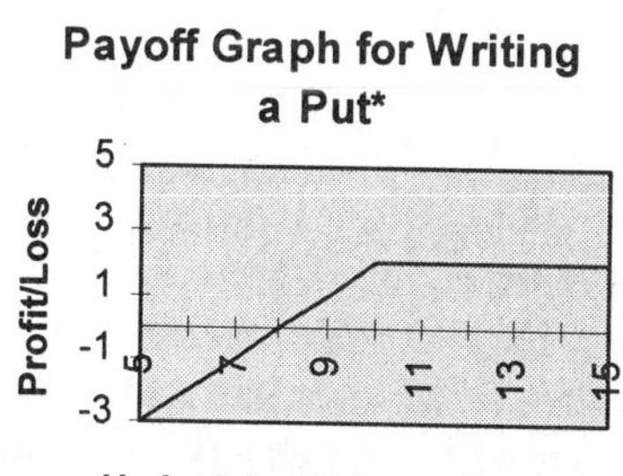

*Assumes strike price of $10 and $2 in premium

Selling or writing puts is another bull strategy. Put writers earn a premium for assuming the risk that the price of the underlying instrument will fall. The put writer will make money at expiration as long as the price of the underlying instrument falls by less than the option premium. The put writer has almost unlimited risk on the downside (stock can't fall below zero), given that he will have to buy at the strike price and sell at the market price. Writing puts works in rising and sideways markets and requires adequate capital to buy the stock—or buy back the put—in a falling market.

UNLISTED OPTIONS

As mentioned, you don't need an option to be listed on an exchange to be involved in an options transaction. In fact, before formal exchanges were created, most options contracts had to be negotiated by the individual parties wanting to set up the agreement.

However, as the following example demonstrates, there can be several disadvantages to using these unlisted options.

Let's take a look at an example of an option on a piece of real estate. Suppose a farmer had a piece of land for sale near a highway cloverleaf that would be a perfect site for shopping mall. The land is currently zoned as a farmland and is worth $5,000 an acre in that area. A developer believes that the land value will increase dramatically if the zoning is changed to allow the development of the shopping mall. Because of the uncertainty with respect to zoning, the developer offers the farmer $75,000 for an option to purchase the land at $10,000 an acre at any point during the next nine months. The farmer sells the option and receives the $75,000 premium (amount paid for the option), which is his to keep regardless of what happens. If the developer, armed with the option to buy the land, can obtain financing and approval of the zoning board, the option will be exercised, and the farmer's land will become a very valuable home to a shopping mall.

But suppose the zoning board, citing the traffic created by the new mall, decides not to approve the zoning change. The developer's option now allows him to buy the land at twice its market value. Obviously, he will not exercise his option. The developer has lost his $75,000, but this is far less than he would have lost if the land had been purchased outright before going to the zoning board. Meanwhile, the farmer has earned $75,000 for holding the land off the market for the nine-month life of the option. He has been compensated for his risk of not selling sooner.

Risk of Default:

So far, so good. The option provided a value to both the buyer and the seller. But what if the farmer discovers that his land is worth $40,000 an acre as a mall and refuses to honor the option agreement after the developer gets the zoning change? The developer has the legal right to exercise the option, but he may have to sue the farmer and pay high legal costs in order to enforce that right.

Inability to Offset a Contract:

The farmer may offer to buy out the option by paying the developer $40,000 an acre, but the developer does not have to let the farmer out of the deal at any price, including the fair market value. The transaction cannot be reversed without the consent of both parties.

Poor Liquidity:

One of the most basic problems with unlisted options is the fact that you need to go out and find another party to fulfill the other side of the contract. The farmer may have wanted to sell an option, but in order to do so, he had to seek out a developer who was interested in his land and interested in this type of arrangement. Furthermore, even if he found a willing party to fulfill the other side of the contract, the other party may not have been willing to pay him as much in option premium as someone else.

Customization:

With these disadvantages it may seem strange why anyone would use unlisted options. However, one of the greatest benefits of unlisted options is the ability to customize a contract. With an unlisted option, the parties can set up a contract for any instrument, any strike price, any premium and any expiration date. Given the unique aspects of the land in question, the farmer and the developer did not have the luxury of setting up their contract on a formal exchange.

It is worth mentioning the existence of the over-the-counter (OTC) options markets. For certain customized options trades, a broker may be able to fulfill the opposite side of the contract for a particular customer, generally a large institutional client. The broker may be willing to take the opposite position with its own proprietary account or may be able to match one side of an option trade with that of another customer. Because the broker needs to be able to determine a fair market price for the transaction, over-the-counter options are generally done only for actively traded instruments, however a plethora of exotic options (e.g., look-back options, compound options, barrier options, etc.) have been developed in recent years in response to customer interest in refining their investments or hedges.

LISTED OPTIONS

In order to offset the problems with unlisted and OTC options, options exchanges were created to standardize and centralize the purchase and sale of a wide variety of options contracts. Formal exchanges bring together buyers and sellers in a regulated marketplace and add to the liquidity of these securities. The exchanges' clearinghouses guarantee the integrity of each and every trade executed on their trading floors and thus eliminate the risk of counterparty default.

One of the best ways to learn about options is to simply look at how they are listed in the daily newspapers. The vast array of options available for trading are too numerous to list here, but the Wall Street Journal lists almost all actively traded options daily. However the broad categories of options are worth mentioning. The types of listed options include the following:

Equity Options:

The first represents an equity option on International Business Machines (IBM). As with all equity options, the contract is listed for a round lot of 100 shares of the underlying IBM stock. Standard equity options are for expirations within a one year period while LEAPS (Long Term Options) represent equity options with an initial expiration date greater than two years.

While this list of contracts for IBM may seem long, it represents only the most actively traded contracts. The internet, Barron's or a broker can provide investors with a more complete listing. As with any investment decision, it is important to have full information.

The first column in the table next page shows the closing price for the underlying stock from the previous day's trading. The second column reflects the different strike prices. The third column identifies the expiration date. The remaining columns reflect

IBM			Call	Call	Put	Put
Close	Strike	Exp.	Vol.	Last	Vol.	Last
158 1/8	100	Jan	410	59 1/2	434	1/16
158 1/8	110	Jan	329	49 3/8	338	3/16
158 1/8	120	Jan	994	40 1/8	928	5/16
158 1/8	125	Jan	36	34 1/4	1005	1/4
158 1/8	130	Dec	72	27 1/2	---	---
158 1/8	130	Jan	399	30	636	3/8
158 1/8	130	Apr	13	31	86	2 1/4
158 1/8	135	Jan	318	24 1/2	910	9/16
158 1/8	140	Dec	319	17 7/8	4	1/16
158 1/8	140	Jan	427	19 1/2	505	15/16
158 1/8	140	Apr	4	23 3/8	106	4
158 1/8	145	Dec	314	13 1/8	1176	1/16
158 1/8	145	Jan	587	15 1/8	427	1 1/2
158 1/8	150	Dec	746	7 7/8	747	1/16
158 1/8	150	Jan	152	11 3/4	1452	2 9/16
158 1/8	155	Dec	3090	3 1/2	3904	3/8
158 1/8	155	Jan	1141	7 3/4	1253	4 1/4
158 1/8	155	Apr	114	14 1/4	154	8 5/8
158 1/8	155	Jul	109	17 7/8	---	---
158 1/8	160	Dec	6938	1/2	2038	2 3/8
158 1/8	160	Jan	1598	4 7/8	321	6 3/8
158 1/8	160	Apr	78	11	6	11
158 1/8	165	Dec	1654	1/16	144	7 3/4
158 1/8	165	Jan	1473	3 1/8	39	9 1/2
158 1/8	170	Jan	746	2	1	13
158 1/8	170	Apr	156	7	---	---
158 1/8	175	Jan	657	1	---	---
158 1/8	175	Apr	109	5 3/8	3	20 1/4

Source: Wall Street Journal, December 20, 1996

the daily volume and the last price quoted for the option call and the option put, respectively. You will notice that trading activity is almost always concentrated in the two or three strike prices closest to the stock's current price.

While over-the-counter options can be written at any strike price the parties agree on and for any length of time, it is necessary for the exchanges to standardize its strike prices and expiration dates to avoid confusion and to maximize the liquidity of individual contracts. If a stock is selling for less than $10 a share, no new options will be listed on it as existing ones expire. For stocks selling for up to $25 a share, strike prices are listed every $2.50, then at every $5 from $25 to $200, then at every $10 for stocks selling for more than $200. If a stock has traded under $8 for six months, the exchange delists its options. Existing puts and calls are traded until they expire, but no new months or strike prices are added. Once listed, a strike price remains eligible for trading until the end of its contract month's trading period. For a volatile stock in a prolonged bull or bear market, this could result in a plethora of possible puts and calls eligible for trading.

Suppose a company splits its stock. An option also would be split so that it continued to represent the same level of risk and reward. If a $30 stock is split 2-for-1, each $30 put and call would be split, giving the holder two $15 calls or puts and leaving the writer short two calls or puts for each one originally written. In more complicated deals, such as corporate restructuring, the size of the new pieces may not work out so neatly, but the exchanges will balance the pieces as closely as possible. Fractional shares of stock would be settled in cash if needed, but the adjustments themselves will not create any profits or losses to the options traders.

Index Options:

Index options are contracts to buy or sell a market index at a given level. An investor's exposure to the index is calculated with the use of a multiplier. The multiplier is fixed by the exchange when the option is first listed. Index options can be for a particular market or for a particular industry and can be on the cash market or on the futures market. Generally, the multiplier is 100 for options on underlying cash securities and 500 for options on futures contracts (again, check with your broker to ensure a complete understanding of the terms and conditions). Unlike a stock option or an option on a commodity futures contract, an index option has no single item to deliver. In order to keep things simple, deliveries in index options have to be made in cash. For example, the writer of a call on an index which is exercised must pay the holder cash equal to the difference between the closing level of the index on the exercise date and the exercise price of the option, multiplied by the index's multiplier. In the example below, if the Utility Index closed at 255.42 and the Jan. 255 call holder decided to exercise (versus closing the position by selling the call), he would earn $42 = (255.42 - 255) x $100.

Utility Index (UTY)

Expiration	Strike	Volume	Last	Net Change	Open Interest
Feb	250c	20	9-3/8	---	---
Mar	250p	3	4-1/2	-1-1/8	106
Jan	255c	10	3-1/2	+11/16	238
Jan	260c	30	1-3/8	+3/8	223
Feb	260c	2	3-5/8	-1/8	20
Jan	265c	20	1/4	---	194
Call Volume:	0	Open Interest: 1,713			
Put Volume:	16	Open Interest: 7,499			

Source: Wall Street Journal, January 9, 1997

In this listing, the newspaper also provides information on the amount of open interest. This simply refers to the number of contracts outstanding as of the previous day's trading. In this example, there are significantly more put contracts in play than call contracts. Contrarian traders believe that the put-call ratio is a good contra-indicator, with a high put/call ratio indicating bullishness. This is explained by the fact that with a high put/call ratio many people have already bought puts to protect their long stock positions and the market has already had this bearishness priced into the market.

Options on Futures:

Investors can also buy and sell options on underlying futures contracts. All options on futures contracts are quoted in the same terms as that of the underlying future contract. In general, the newspaper will indicate the contract size for the underlying instrument. Looking at the example below; the options on the Japanese Yen future is listed at 12,500,000 yen. An investor wanting to buy a February 87.00 put would have to pay $1,362.50 for the contract (12,500,000 yen x $.0109/100 cents per yen).

Notice that the newspaper provides a settlement price for the option. Although the option may not have traded all day, the prices provided here are listed daily

Japanese Yen(CME) 12,500,000 yen, cents per 100 yen	Calls-Settle			Puts-Settle		
Strike	Jan	Feb	Mar	Jan	Feb	Mar
8600	---	---	1.77	0.00	0.65	0.99
8650	0.29	---	1.49	0.00	0.85	1.20
8700	0.00	0.88	1.23	0.21	1.09	1.45
8750	0.00	0.68	1.03	0.71	1.39	1.73
8800	0.00	0.53	0.86	1.21	1.74	2.06
8850	0.00	0.41	0.72	1.71	2.12	2.41
Est. vol 4,738 Th 2,929 calls 2,010 puts Op Int Thur 45,209 calls 43,946 puts						

Source: Wall Street Journal, January 6, 1997

based on their time to expiration, the current volatility of the underlying futures contract and the price of the underlying future itself. More discussion on the use of pricing models is included in Chapter 2.

On U.S. exchanges, options on futures expire the month before the futures contract ceases trading. This allows those who have taken delivery to get out of the futures position in an orderly fashion, without the need to engage in a transaction in the actual market.

American vs. European Options:
It is important to note that when an option is listed, it can either be an "American" option or a "European option". American in this context only refers to the right to exercise the contract at will, at any point up to the expiration date. It has nothing to do with the exchange the option is traded on. A European option, on the other hand, can only be exercised on the date of its expiration. Obviously, the European option offers much less flexibility. Today, most individual stock options are American and most index options are European, but it is still advisable to check with your broker to confirm all aspects of the option before entering into the contract.

II. OPTION PRICING

Now that we have a basic understanding of what it means to buy or sell calls and puts, and we have seen how option prices are quoted in the newspapers, there is clearly a need to understand how the price of the option premium is derived. The investor needs to know whether he is paying a fair price for the option he is buying, or conversely, whether he is being fairly compensated for the risk he is assuming by selling an option.

While the option premium is derived by market forces, there are a number of financial models used to determine the theoretical value of an option, such as the Black-Scholes formula for calls on common stocks and Black's modification of his model for options on commodity futures. These formulas are beyond the scope of this discussion, however it is worth discussing the basic concepts underlying these formulas, namely, the fact that the price paid for an option is based on a combination of its intrinsic value and its time value.

Option Premium = Intrinsic Value + Time Value

INTRINSIC VALUE

Intrinsic value is what the option is worth if exercised immediately. Let's look at an example from December 20, 1996 for the Netscape options listed below. Since the current underlying stock is valued at 54 5/8 (spot price), any call with a strike price less than this spot price has intrinsic value. For example, the January 50 call is said to be "in the money" because if the call purchaser decides to exercise the option, he can purchase stock at $50 versus the $54 5/8 that he would have to pay in the regular market. The option has an intrinsic value of $54 5/8 - $50 = $4 5/8. A January 50 put, however, has no intrinsic value and is said to be "out of the money" because there is no value to exercising the option. There is no reason why the put purchaser would exercise the right to sell the Netscape stock at $50 when he could sell it on the regular market for $54 5/8. A put option only has intrinsic value when the strike price is more than the spot price. When the spot price is equal to the strike price, an option is said to be "at the money" and the intrinsic value will always be zero.

Netscape			Call		Put	
Close	Strike	Exp.	Vol.	Last	Vol.	Last
54 5/8	45	Jan	61	10 1/2	40	1
54 5/8	50	Dec	83	4 1/4	240	1/16
54 5/8	50	Jan	8	6 1/2	65	2 3/16
54 5/8	55	Dec	274	5/8	206	1
54 5/8	55	Jan	149	4	71	3 7/8
54 5/8	60	Dec	185	1/16	40	5 3/8
54 5/8	60	Jan	120	2 1/4	24	7 ½
54 5/8	75	Jan	10	1/4	205	20 7/8

Source: Wall Street Journal, December 19, 1996

TIME VALUE

Look again at the Netscape option prices. You will notice that the price of the January 50 call is listed at 6 1/2 even though its intrinsic value is only 4 5/8. Also, the January 55 call which has no intrinsic value is still listed as having a price of 4. Time value accounts for these differences. It is possible that the price of Netscape can fluctuate before expiration so that either the 50 call will become more profitable or the 55 call will move into the money. The option's remaining life gives it time value—time in which to become intrinsically valuable.

The time value portion of the premium will be determined by the number of days to the option's expiration, the expected volatility of the underlying instrument, and the carrying costs associated with holding the option to expiration.

Time Decay:

Obviously the more time remaining before expiration, the greater the time value. However, investors should be aware of a phenomenon called time decay. An option's time value decreases slowly in value when there is a lot of time remaining until expiration, but loses value at an increasing rate as the time to expiration gets closer. This is because the time value of an option decreases exponentially as the time remaining on an option nears expiration. Generally an option with less than 45 days until expiration begins to show signs of rapidly decreasing time value. Because of this effect, it is generally more profitable for a trader to close out a long option position before it expires. As soon as an option reaches its expiration, it will have lost all of its time value.

For this reason, options traders need to have a much more accurate picture of the timing of a market shift in order to make a profitable trade. While many traders have made the correct decision as to where the market is heading, they often need to determine within weeks, and sometimes days, as to when that shift will take place. Sudden consolidations can wipe out profits quickly. Traders who try to buy options with long expirations to get around this problem have to pay much more in option premium and thus don't experience the same leverage as with a shorter dated option.

Volatility:

The more volatile the price of the underlying stock, the greater the time value. High volatility increases the chance that the underlying stock will move sufficiently, either up or down, to become profitable within the remaining time period.

There is a need to be cautious when discussing volatility. Volatility is the only unknown variable in theoretical option pricing equations and for this reason often reflects the market forces. An investor can look at the historical volatility of the underlying instrument and find that the implied volatility incorporated in the theoretical pricing model is much higher. The investor is paying more for the option than the historical volatility would dictate because there is greater demand than supply.

Determining whether this option is too expensive is a matter of opinion on whether too much or too little volatility has been priced into the option. If history says that a future's recent implied volatility is 15% and the current option price implies a volatility of 20%, the option may be expensive. It may also reflect that future volatility will be higher than historical volatility. For an options trader, he must determine how long this high volatility period will last. If it will last beyond his time horizon for the trade, the relatively high premium paid for the option is inconsequential to the trading strategy. The high premium will be recouped upon selling the option.

On the other hand, many traders use options to trade around big market announcements where there is a great deal of uncertainty surrounding the outcome. The implied volatility and thus the price paid for the option premium can be very high preceding the market announcement and drop dramatically once the outcome is known. The change in the price of the option due to the underlying price move can be less than the fall in the price of the option as a result of lower volatility. In other words, an investor can still lose money with an option, even if a market announcement has favored the investor's position for the underlying instrument.

PRICE MOVEMENT (DELTA)

By definition, the option premium has to be exactly equal to the sum of the time value and the intrinsic value. A deep out-of-the-money option is 100% time value and a deep in-the-money option will be almost completely composed of intrinsic value. It is equally important to understand how the price of the option moves as the price of the underlying instrument moves from being out-of-the money to being in-the-money. This rate of change is called the option's "delta."

The price of a deep out-of-the money option tends to move much more slowly than the underlying instrument. This is because it is highly unlikely that the option will be exercised. For example, if the underlying stock increases in value by $2, and the option is still very unlikely to be exercised, its price may only increase by $.50. This rate of change in the option price relative to the rate of change of the underlying instrument is its delta and in this case, the delta is said to be .25. A point move in the underlying instrument corresponds to a quarter point move in the option price.

What is interesting about options is that as the price of the underlying instrument moves closer to the option's strike price, the delta increases because the likelihood of the option being exercised increases. An at-the-money option with a reasonable amount of time remaining until expiration will have a delta of approximately .50. This makes sense since there is approximately a 50/50 chance that the option will be exercised. Once the option becomes deep in-the-money, a $1 move in the underlying instrument will likely correspond to a $1 move in the option price. The option's delta is now one and moves point for point with the underlying instrument. The chance of the option being exercised is virtually 100%.

This change in delta means that options automatically adjust the amount of leverage as the underlying instrument moves in or out of the investor's favor. The delta decreases as the underlying instrument moves against the trader and increases as the underlying price moves in the investor's favor.

Deep-out-of-the-money options make the smallest absolute changes in value, but they can provide the biggest bang for the buck in return on risk capital because of their lower premiums. Since they have the least chance of winding up in the money, they also have the greatest probability of a 100% loss on that investment.

PUT-CALL PARITY

According to option pricing theory, puts and calls with the same strike price and same expiration should sell at the same value relative to the underlying price (at times there may be a small discrepancy since the downside risk associated with writing a put is limited by zero but the upside liability is unlimited when writing a call).

$$\text{Call Price} - \text{Put Price} = \text{Current Price} - \text{Strike Price}/(1+ \text{carrying costs})^{\text{time remaining}}$$

We can see why this relationship holds true by comparing two strategies. In the first strategy we pay P_P for a put on a stock and we pay P_S to buy the underlying stock. In the second strategy we pay P_C for a call on the same stock (with the same strike price and the same expiration) and we put an amount of money into the bank equal to the present value of the strike price at expiration. If the stock price is higher than the strike price upon expiration in the first strategy the put is worthless and the investor ends up owning a share of stock. In the second strategy, the call is exercised and the bank balance is used to purchase the stock. Both strategies end up with the same outcome. If the stock price ended up lower than the strike price at expiration, both strategies still arrive at the same outcome. In the first strategy, the investor exercises the put and ends up with cash equal to the strike price. In the second strategy, the call is worthless and the investor ends up with a bank balance equal to the exercise price.

For example, on January 28, 1997, Dell Computer stock traded at $66, the February 65 call sold for 4-1/8 and the put sold for 3-1/8. Since there is very little time remaining on the options, the carrying costs are negligible and the put-call relationship holds true ($4-1/8 - $3-1/8 = $66 - $65). Whenever this relationship does not hold true, an arbitrage opportunity exists. This will be discussed in greater detail in Chapter 3. Let's assume in the above example that the put sold for 3-3/8 while everything else stayed the same. A trader could take advantage of this violation of put-call parity by buying the relatively cheap side of the equation and selling the more expensive side of the equation.

III. EXECUTING A TRADE

BUYING AN OPTION

Assume an investor has decided to buy 10 Wal-Mart March 25 calls. The underlying stock is currently selling at 23-3/8 and the call has last been listed in the newspaper as having last traded at $11/16. She tells her broker to execute the trade.

The broker calls his firm's booth on the floor of the Chicago Board of Options Exchange (CBOE), with the order to buy 10 Wal-Mart March 25 calls at $11/16 or better. The firm's floor broker is handed the order and attempts to fill it immediately through open outcry in the ring where the Wal-Mart options are traded.

Some floor brokers work for other commission houses, but others hold the unique title of market maker. A market maker is a floor trader who, after passing tests and being registered by the SEC, is obligated to trade with the public—namely, the floor brokers holding the public's orders. Market makers are not in the business of holding long-term positions, but of providing market liquidity and earning the spread between the bid and the asked price. Unlike their specialist counterparts who trade common and preferred stock, they are not obligated to see that the customer's limit orders are filled in an orderly manner. That is done by exchange employees called order book officials (OBO's).

Our floor broker bids 11/16 and gets offers at to sell at 3/4. Since he has a limit order, he cannot execute the order. The OBO nearest the broker goes to him and verifies the order. The OBO has offers to sell in the market at 3/4 and previous bids at 5/8. The 11/16 now becomes the highest bid "on his book" and is entered into the exchange's quote system, which displays the market as 11/16 bid, 3/4 asked. A few minutes later, another broker comes to the pit with 5 Wal-Mart March 25 calls to sell at the market. He offers them at 3/4, the current offering price, and finds no takers. Next, he checks with the OBO and finds our investor's bid of 11/16 for 10. Having a market order, he sells 5 at 11/16. Later, a market maker who had been offering at 3/4 drops his price to 11/16 and sells the remaining 5 lots to our investor. The OBO then informs our floor broker that the order has been filled, and oral and written confirmations of the fill are sent to the customer by her broker.

Once the initial trade was consummated, it was recorded on the clearing association's books. Our investor was listed as long 10 options in effect owed to her by the clearing house. Each seller was listed as short 5 options, which were owed to the clearing house. Most likely, the market maker would have covered his short position before going home that evening by buying from another seller.

It is now two weeks later, and Wal-Mart is trading at $22-5/8 and the March 25 call has last been traded at $9/16. Our investor has decided that she has made the wrong decision and wants to sell her call option (to offset her position) before it loses any more value. She calls her broker and tells him to sell a March 25 call "at the market". This starts the same process over again except that the broker will not have to wait to find a particular price. He will simply sell the option at whatever price is bid. Her broker is able to fulfill the sell order at 5/8 and our investor has lost $62.50 (1/16 x 10 x 100) plus commission costs in the transaction. Unlike the situation with unlisted options, the broker does not have to find the same parties who sold him the options in order to close the position.

SELLING AN OPTION

While there are many similarities in how buy and sell orders are executed, there is one major difference. Writing options requires margin. Because option writing has virtually unlimited liability, clearing houses require traders to submit cash or securities, to insure that investors can meet the financial obligations associated with their trading activity. The clearing house needs assurance that the option writer will be able to meet the obligation to buy or sell the underlying stock if the contract is exercised. The margin requirement for every contract is set by the clearing house and additional margin calls can be made by the clearinghouse as the option position moves against the trader or as volatility increases. Although investors receive premium for assuming the risk associated with writing a call, they should also consider the cash flow implications of margin to determine whether a trade is desirable. Margin requirements can alter the trade's return profile.

Let's assume that an investor wants to sell a call and he owns the underlying stock. He tells his broker to sell 10 Wal-Mart March 25 calls at the market. For margin, the option writer puts 1000 shares (10 x 100 shares) of Wal-Mart stock in safekeeping at the commission house and he immediately receives the premium generated from selling the calls. Why does he get to keep the cash immediately? His Wal-Mart shares are in the hands of his commission house, which is ultimately responsible for seeing that he fulfills his obligation if exercised. No matter what happens to Wal-Mart—even a takeover at $100 a share—the covered writer has no additional liability beyond the provision of those shares.

While it may be obvious, note that an options position can only be offset by reselling or repurchasing the same option. The purchase of a put cannot be offset by purchasing a call. The investor must resell the put in order to eliminate his position in the market.

PLACING ORDERS

When placing an order with a broker, it is important to convey exactly how and at what price you wish the order to be fulfilled. Different exchanges allow different types of order fulfillment, so be sure to check with your broker on the best way to place your trade.

Market Orders:
Orders to place a trade at whatever level the market is currently trading. These orders are given first priority for fulfillment.

Stop Orders:
Orders become activated only when the market price trades at or better than the stop price. A buy stop order is placed above the market price and is transformed into a market order once the market trades at or above the stop price. A sell stop order is placed below the market price and is traded once the market trades at or below the stop price.

Limit Orders:
Limit orders are the lowest in priority and are filled after market and stop orders have been filled. Unlike stop orders they do not become market orders once the limit price has been reached. These orders can only be fulfilled when they trade at or better than the limit price. A buy limit order is placed below the current market price and will be filled only at or below the limit price. A sell limit order is placed above the market price and is filled only if the market price rises to or above the limit price.

Time Limit Orders:
Investors can place an order which must be filled within a particular time frame or else it becomes void. All orders are assumed to be good for a day unless the investor states otherwise.

EXERCISING AN OPTION

Although we have mentioned that it is almost always better to offset an option in order to retain the time value, it is worthwhile discussing how options can be exercised. An exercised index option is settled at that evening's settlement price. Suppose a speculator exercises an index call in an extremely volatile market, and the call was in the money when the order to exercise was given at 1:30. However, it was out of the money when the index closed for the day. The unfortunate exerciser then must pay the seller the difference between the strike price and the settlement price. If an October 965 S&P 500 call were exercised when the index was at 963 and it were to expire that day at 968, the exerciser would not get paid. He must pay the call writer the difference between the strike price and the settlement price.

IV. OVERVIEW OF GENERAL OPTIONS STRATEGIES

Now that we have a basic understanding of what options are and how they are traded, these next chapters will help describe some of ways options can be used to accomplish various investment objectives. It is important to note that these represent only the most basic strategies and that there are a myriad of creative uses for options; unfortunately it would be impossible for us to describe all of these in full detail.

SPECULATING

An investor is very bullish on Motorola (MOT) which is currently trading at $65. It's the middle of December and he suddenly has $6000 cash available to invest. Let's assume he wants exposure to 100 shares of Motorola. First, he could buy 104 shares outright at a total cost of $5750 plus commissions (which for simplicity's sake we will ignore in all our examples). Second, he could buy 50 shares on margin, paying $2875 and borrowing $2875 at the broker loan rate plus 2%. Third, he could buy one January 60 call at 1-7/16 for $143.75 (1-7/16 x 100 x 1). Assume that the investor, being highly bullish on Motorola, buys the option.

Motorola			Call		Put	
Close	Strike	Exp.	Vol.	Last	Vol.	Last
57 1/2	55	Jan	941	4	484	1-1/4
57 1/2	60	Dec	452	1/8	75	2-1/2
57 1/2	60	Jan	2192	1-7/16	128	3-5/8
57 1/2	60	Apr	724	3-5/8	87	5-3/8
57 1/2	65	Jan	214	7/16	---	---

Source: Wall Street Journal, December 19, 1996

Motorola			Call		Put	
Close	Strike	Exp.	Vol.	Last	Vol.	Last
61-3/4	55	Jan	638	7-1/4	219	3/8
61-3/4	60	Dec	---	---	---	---
61-3/4	60	Jan	2356	3-3/8	853	1-1/2
61-3/4	60	Apr	255	5-7/8	460	3-1/8
61-3/4	65	Jan	2996	1-1/8	114	4-1/8

Source: Wall Street Journal, December 30, 1996

Now it is December 30, 1996, and because this trade was done with hindsight, MOT is selling at 61-3/4. The investor now has the right to buy stock worth $6,175 ($61-3/4 a share x 100 shares) for only $6,000 ($60 a share x 100 shares), an intrinsic value of $175. But the options are trading at 3-3/8, a value of $337.50 ($3-3/8 x 100). The difference is the remaining time value, and it is enough that our trader decides to sell the calls now instead of exercising them or waiting for an additional price appreciation on the stock. Now let's compare the profit earned by using options versus the two other alternatives:

Strategy	**Buy Stock** Buy 100 shares for cash	**Buy Stock on Margin** Buy 100 shares at 50% margin	**Buy Options** Buy a Jan 60 call at 1-7/16
Cost	$5,750	$2875	$143.75
Risk	$5,750	$5750*	$143.75
Profit	$425	$425*	$193.75 (3-3/8-1-7/16)x100
Return	7.4%	14.8%	134.8%

**does not include the interest on the broker loan which increases the funds at risk and reduces the profit.*

Buying 100 shares at 57-1/2 and selling them at 61-3/4 gives a return of over 7% in less than two weeks, certainly nothing to sneeze at. Buying on 50% margin (ignoring the interest expense which does decrease the return slightly) doubles the return. Of course, when the investor buys on margin, he is risking total capital of $5,750, but this provides leverage for aggressive investors. However, the real leverage champion is the option trade. With only $143 of capital at risk, the investor earned a far greater return on his capital than in the other scenarios.

The investor, had he invested all of his money in options, could have generated over $8,000 in profits. However, our investor did not have the advantage of hindsight. Leverage can cut both ways and while it was almost impossible that Motorola's shares would lose 100% of its value in under two weeks, the option buyer clearly faced that possibility. Whereas stock is assumed to have an eternal life (until it is retired and bought back by the corporation), all options which expire out of the money automatically become worthless.

HEDGING

Suppose an investor owns a great deal of Phillip Morris stock. She is bullish on the company but is concerned that rising interest rates, fears of inflation and an increase in the overall volatility of the stock market may cause her to bail out. She doesn't want to sell the stock unless she absolutely has to. One of the ways she can protect her position is to purchase the right to sell her stock in the future by buying a put. In this way, options can provide a form of insurance. Purchasing an option locks in a worst-case price. Whether that produces a profit or loss is not relevant to the true hedger. She is asking herself "Can I live with the price I am guaranteed?"

However, as you will see, there is a dilemma in determining what level of protection to buy; similar to deciding how much collision deductible to take on an insurance policy. Investors have to pay more now to guarantee paying less later.

Phillip Morris			**Call**		**Put**	
Close	**Strike**	**Exp.**	**Vol.**	**Last**	**Vol.**	**Last**
114	100	Jun	5	16-7/8	660	2-3/4
114	105	Jan	93	9-7/8	25	1/2
114	110	Jan	162	5-1/2	130	1-5/16
114	115	Jan	203	2-1/2	70	3-5/8
114	115	Feb	100	4-5/8	---	---
114	115	Jun	92	8	71	7-3/4

Source: Wall Street Journal, December 30, 1996

Let's assume our investor wants the highest level of insurance over the near term and will hold the option until expiration (no time value). She decides to buy the 115 January put. By doing this, she guarantees a price of $111-3/8 price for the underlying stock. She has paid net $2-5/8 for this guarantee. She paid $3-5/8 in option premium for the right to sell her stock for $115, a dollar more than it is currently worth ($111-3/8 is equal to $115 less $3-5/8 in premium or $114 less $2-5/8).

What happens when the price of the underlying stock changes? Let's assume the price of Phillip Morris rises to $115. As the price of the underlying Phillip Morris stock rises, the put loses its intrinsic value. However, the gain in the price of the underlying Phillip Morris stock has compensated for this loss. As the price of Phillip Morris rises above $115, the option will not be exercised but the investor continues to benefit from the price appreciation of the underlying stock. If the price of the underlying stock drops below $114, she can still sell her stock for $115, increasing the intrinsic value of the option which will offset decreases in the price of the underlying stock. Regardless of what happens to Phillip Morris, she can sleep soundly, knowing that the lion's share of her profits remains lock in.

Now let's assume our investor decided to pay a lower premium and bought the January 110 put for $1-5/16. She has paid less for the option but she will only be protecting the profits associated with a $108-11/16 price level ($110 less the $1-5/16 premium). She will make more if the price of the stock stays constant or increases since she paid less for the option, but if prices fall, she will only benefit if they fall to below $110, the point at which the option will have value if exercised.

It is worth mentioning that hedging decisions will be somewhat more complicated if the trader does not expect to hold the option until expiration. Since time value can change the value of the option dramatically, the trader needs to consider the delta of the option. If the delta is .5, then the trader will need two options to offset a 1 point move in the underlying security. Note that because the delta can move quickly, this is a hedge strategy which must be closely monitored.

The table below may seem a bit obvious, but even experienced traders have been known to put on the wrong hedging positions.

Position to be Protected	Call Strategy	Put Strategy	Futures Strategy*
Own Inventory of a Commodity	Write Call	Buy Put	Short Futures (Lock in selling prices today)
Will Need to Buy Commodity in the Future	Buy Call	Write Put	Long Futures (Lock in buying prices today)

**See Chapter VI Strategies for Options on Futures*

COVERED OPTION WRITING

Many investors who are confident of their ability to pick a stock have considerable trouble determining when to take profits or cut losses. Options can help provide the discipline needed to trade effectively. Say a trader believes a particular stock has the potential to rise as high as $100. Some traders will sell covered calls, (out-of-the-money calls with a strike of $100) against their stock holdings, hoping that they will be forced to take profits at that level. If the price of the underlying stock doesn't reach $100, the trader will have earned the additional income from the option premium received. If the stock does reach $100 or higher, the trader can sell his existing position in the stock to offset his option obligation. Selling the out-of-the-money call has forced the trader to sell his holdings in the stock once it reached his predetermined level. Whenever a trader writes a call against an existing stock position it is called a covered call.

Traders can also use covered calls to help generate additional income when they have already made the decision to sell a particular stock holding, say to rebalance their portfolio. With this strategy, they sell a call which they believe will be exercised upon expiration. They will be forced to honor the option contract and sell their stock as they had originally intended to do, but they would have received the additional premium for writing the call.

Note that when an investor writes calls or puts without having a position in the underlying instrument, he or she is said to be writing "naked" options. There is unlimited risk in this type of investing since the investor has to honor the contract regardless of market conditions.

STRADDLES AND STRANGLES (TRADING VOLATILITY)

Investors can also use options to speculate on changes in the volatility of the underlying instrument by using an option straddle strategy. With a short straddle, the investor sells a call and a put at the same strike price with the same expiration and hopes to benefit from a relatively flat (low volatility) market. The investor receives the premium from selling the call and the premium from selling the put. If the market price remains relatively close to the original strike price, the investor will earn more in premium than he or she will have to pay out to fulfill either the put or the call contract.

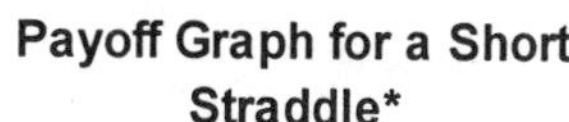

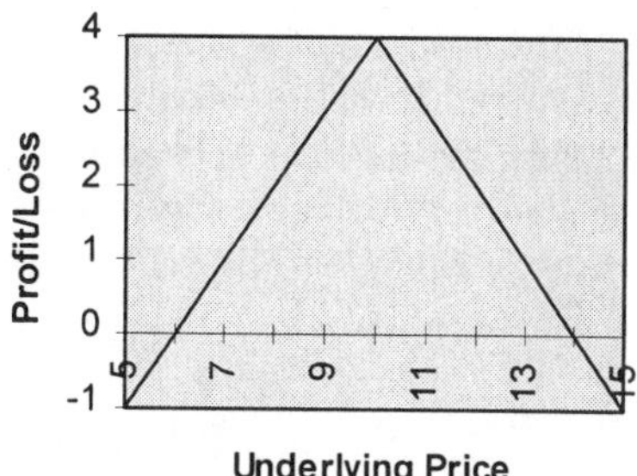

*Assumes strike price of 10 and $2 in premium

For example, assume that an investor believes that implied volatility for a certain stock's call and put options is high relative to historical volatility. The investor will receive $2 for selling the call and $2 for selling the put. The stock is currently trading at $10. If the stock does not move more than $4 ($2 + $2) above or below the strike price of 10, the investor will retain more premium than will be paid out to honor whichever contract is exercised upon expiration. Ideally, the stock will continue to trade at $10 and the investor will keep both premiums with neither contract being exercised. The investor still faces unlimited upside or downside risk. Say an unexpected earnings report is announced and the stock suddenly starts trading at $20. Since the short straddler wrote both a put and a call, he will have to honor the call contract and sell stock to the purchaser for $10 which will he will have to provide at a cost of $20. The straddle writer will lose $6 ($4 - $20 + $10). In a whipsaw market, being short a put and a call at the same strike price can be extremely painful. Traders have been known to close out the losing position only to find the other option going against them shortly thereafter.

With a long straddle, the investor buys a call and a put at the same strike price with the same expiration and benefits from a highly volatile market. The investor's risk is limited to the total amount paid for both options and will earn a profit when a price change in either direction is sufficient to offset or exceed the amount paid out. But even the buyers of volatility must be willing to act quickly, taking profits and cutting losses from time decay when the volatility fails to materialize.

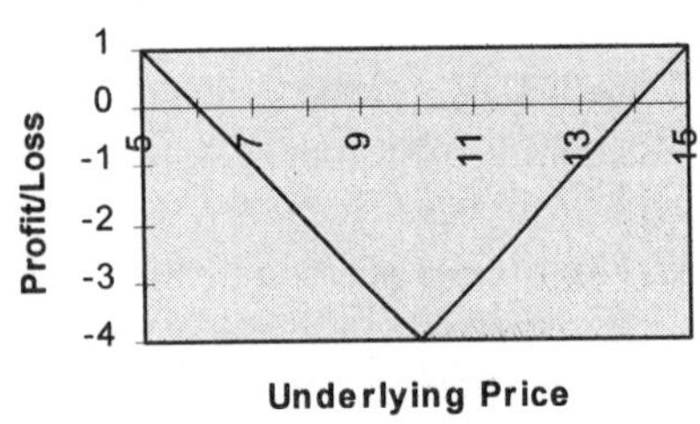

*Assumes strike price of 10 and $2 in premium

There are other ways to trade volatility. A strangle is similar to a straddle but uses different out-of-the-money strike prices to take advantage of decaying time value. Let's assume a speculator believes PepsiCo, which is currently trading at 29-1/4, will continue to trade within a range bounded by $28 on the downside and $30 on the upside over the next few weeks. She sells the $27-1/2 put for $1-3/8 and the $30 call for $2-1/8 and receives a net credit of $350. Recall, that all of the premium is time value since there is no intrinsic value with these out-of-the-money options. If PepsiCo continues to trade within this range, she will keep all of the premium. However, if PepsiCo rallies above $30 or sells off to below $27-1/2, the speculator would find out why selling volatility by writing a put and a call is called a "strangle." As the profitability diagram illustrates, the potential liability on a strangle can be unbearable, and it is not a strategy for the inactive or the timid investor.

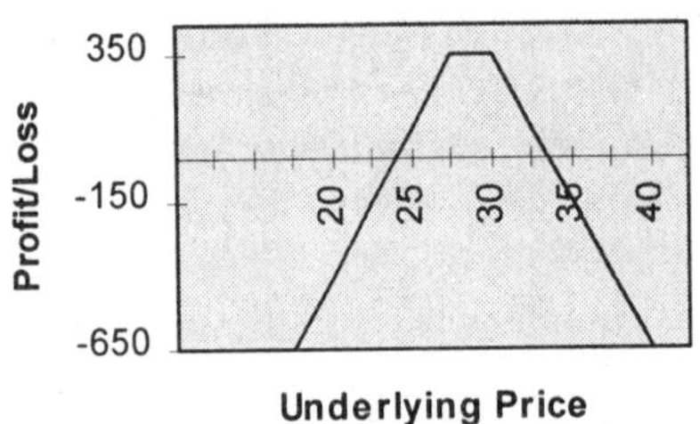

*Source: Wall Street Journal, Jan 7, 1997

OPTION SPREADS

As discussed earlier, options with different parameters (i.e., strike prices, expiration, etc.) will react differently to changes in the same underlying instrument. As such, speculators can take positions which will take advantage of a larger movement in one option over another. This difference in the change between the two options prices is known as the spread. Investors can utilize many different spread strategies.

Vertical (Price) Spread:

A vertical price spread involves the simultaneous purchase and sale of calls (or puts) with different strike prices but with the same expiration date. One of the attractions of this type of investment is that the maximum profit and the maximum loss can be ascertained in advance. For example, in a *bull call spread* an investor buys a call with a low strike price and sells a call with a higher strike price. The investor limits his profits but also subsidizes the amount paid to purchase the call by selling another call. As the price of the underlying instrument rises, the call option gains intrinsic value, but at the higher strike price, the profits from the purchased call are offset by the written call.

For example, a bullish investor could buy the January 760 S&P 500 call for 8-1/4 and sell the January 775 for 2-1/4. The total cost to establish the spread is $1500 (($8.25 - $2.25) x 250), ignoring commissions. If the January S&P index expires at $775 or above, the profit is $2,250. (($775 - $760) x $250 - $1500). If the S&P index expires at 760, the investor will lose the entire price paid for establishing the trade. The spread breaks even when the index expires at a level of $766.

Similarly, there are bull put spreads where the investor buys a put at a lower strike price and sells a put with a higher strike price to profit when the underlying price moves upward. With bear call and put spreads the investor buys an option at the higher strike price and sells the same type of option at the lower strike price. With bear spreads, investors make money when the underlying instrument falls in price.

Payoff Graph for a Bull Call Spread*

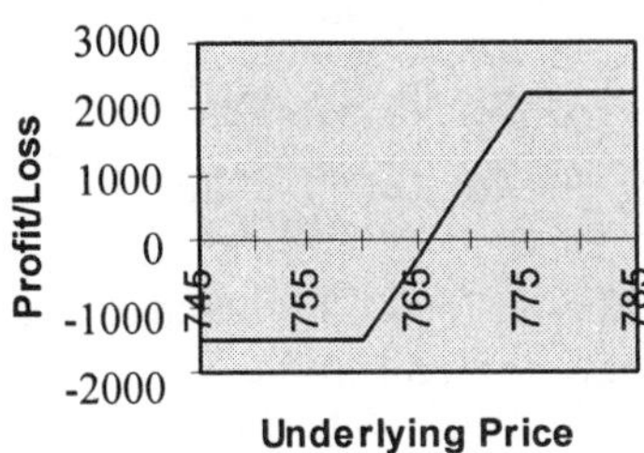

Source: Wall Street Journal, January 13, 1997

Horizontal (Calendar) Spread:

A horizontal spread, often called a calendar spread, involves buying options with the same strike price but with different expiration dates. Calendar spreads are used to take advantage of differences in time values during periods of relatively flat prices. Remember that options lose time value exponentially as the time to expiration draws closer, so that a call with a near term expiration will lose value significantly faster than an option with a later expiration. Assume an investor believes that a particular stock will stay relatively calm over the next few months. He sells the March 73 call for $250 and buys the May 73 call for $550 for a maximum net loss of $300 (the written call is covered by the bought call). If the March call expires at or out of the money, the May call will still have remaining time value. If the remaining time value is greater than the net $300 paid for the calls, the investor can sell the remaining option and make a profit. Note that a diagonal spread involves buying and selling calls with both different strike prices and different expiration dates.

Ratio Spreads:

Another popular form of options trading is a ratio spread strategy which takes advantage of delta changes. A close-to-the-money option will have a delta equal to approximately double or triple the delta of a farther out-of-the-money option, but the prices of the respective options may not match that ratio. Suppose we are interested in Compaq and the February 77 call is selling for $1.50 when the price of the underlying stock is at 76. Assume it has a delta of .5 as predicted by the pricing model. Now assume that the February 80 call has a delta of .20 and is selling for $.90. If we are modestly bullish on Compaq, we could buy the 77 call for $150 and sell two 80 calls for $180, receiving a net credit of $30. Since we are long only one call, there will be a margin requirement on the extra short call, but it will not be too high because the 80 strike is out of the money. If the underlying Compaq stock is at $77 or less when the February options expire, the ratio spread earns the net credit of $30.

But suppose Compaq immediately rallies $2 to $78. The delta on the 77 call is .5, so theoretically it will rise in value by $1 ($2 price move x .5 delta) from $1.50 to $2.50. The 80 calls will move only $.40 each ($2 price move x .20 delta) from $.90 to $1.30. We now unwind the spread, selling the 77 call for $250 and buying back the 105 calls for a total of $260. We have a profit of $10, consisting of a gain of $100 on the long call and a loss of $80 on the short calls.

This type of trade requires low transaction costs along with continual monitoring of the deltas which are constantly changing as the price of the underlying instrument changes. If the rally raised the delta on the 77 call to .70 and on the 80 calls to .40, the 77 call gains only $70 and the two 80 calls gain a total of $80. At some point in a rising market, incremental losses on the short legs will become larger than incremental gains on the long side, and there will be a call for additional margin on the short side.

Another popular ratio trading strategy, particularly in options on common stocks, is combining a position in the underlying instrument with the options. For example, a holder of 200 shares of Hershey on October 5, 1987 (pre-market crash), could have purchased a February 35 call for 3 and sold three February 40 calls for 1-5/8, receiving a net credit of $187.50 (ignoring transaction costs). For margin purposes, the trader is fully covered. If all the options expire worthless, there is a small profit on the options position. However, the downside protection provided by the premium income is considerably less than would have been the case if the trader had decided just to write two covered calls.

ARBITRAGE

Recall that in options pricing theory, puts and calls with the same strike price and same expiration should sell at the same value relative to the underlying price.

Call Price - Put Price =
Current Price - Strike Price/(1+ carrying costs)$^{\text{time remaining}}$

Whenever this relationship does not hold true, an arbitrage opportunity exists; that is, a trader can generate returns without assuming any risk. At the end of January, Dell Computer stock traded at $66, the February 65 call sold for 4-1/8 and the put sold for 3-1/8, all of which upheld put-call parity. If we now assume that the put sold for $4 while everything else stayed the same, we can demonstrate how a trader could take advantage of this mispricing by buying the relatively cheap side of the equation (left side) and selling the more expensive side of the equation (right side). On the left side of the equation the trader would have bought the call for 4-1/8 and sold the put for 4 for a net investment of 1/8. On the right side of the equation, the trader would have agreed to sell the underlying stock for $66. Upon expiration, if the price of the underlying stock rose to 67, the trader would have a call option with a value of $2, the put would expire worthless and the underlying stock position could be offset for a loss of $1. The investor earns a return of $7/8 ($1 - 1/8 investment).

If the price of the underlying stock had dropped to $64, the call would expire worthless, the put would be exercised for a loss of $1, but the sale of the underlying stock would have earned $2. Again, the trader earned a return of $7/8 ($1 - 1/8 investment). If the stock had not changed in price, the call would have been worth $1, the put would go unexercised and the sale of the underlying stock would have no implications. Again, the trader has earned a return of $7/8. As you can see, regardless of whether the price of the underlying stock goes up or down, the investor is guaranteed a return of $7/8.

It is important to note that these arbitrage opportunities generally involve very small discrepancies and don't arise very often. As such, taking advantage of arbitrage opportunities requires very low transaction costs and constant monitoring of the markets.

V. STRATEGIES FOR INDEX OPTIONS

Buying a put as insurance for a profitable stock position is often an attractive strategy, but what if your portfolio contains dozens of common stocks, many of which do not have listed options? Or suppose you are one of those people who feels very confident about the overall direction of the stock market but extremely unsure about which individual securities to buy or sell?

One solution to both of the above problems is to use options on financial indices. Often, the most cost-efficient way to hedge a portfolio is to hedge the entire basket of stocks at once. Likewise, the speculator who wants a leveraged investment in a particular market or sector can benefit from using a market or industry index option.

SELECTING THE APPROPRIATE INDEX

In order to hedge a particular portfolio effectively, it is critical that an investor select an index which accurately reflects his or her own stock holdings. This means looking for an index which incorporates the same types of stocks with similar weightings as those in an individual portfolio. There should be a very high correlation between the index and the individual portfolio, that is, moves in the index should correspond to similar moves in the portfolio. For example, there are significant differences between the Major Market Index (MMI) and the S&P 500. The MMI is price-weighted, which means the index portfolio includes an equal number of each of its stocks, regardless of the price of each stock. On the other hand, the Institutional Index, is value-weighted which means that each stock in the portfolio represents an equal dollar value. IBM, which is included in both indexes, could make up a different proportion of each of these indices. It is important to note that value-weighted indices are rebalanced every three months, so even if there is a good match to your portfolio in March, it could turn out to be a very poor fit by December if your portfolio no longer closely matches the weights of the index.

USING INDEX OPTIONS FOR INSTITUTIONAL TRADING

For the institutional investor, one strategy for dealing with a large infusion of cash is to write puts on a particular index. Because it can take weeks for some institutional accounts to fully implement a buy program without disrupting market prices in individual stocks, the put sales provide premium income to help lock in a potential price level until the funds are fully invested. In a declining market, however, the benefit of actually buying the stocks at lower prices is offset by the losses on the puts, which would be bought back as soon as stock positions are added.

To avoid the day-to-day cash flow involved with margin calls, an institution might prefer to buy calls at the onset of a stock buying program or to buy puts at the start of divestiture, rather than writing the options suggested at the start of this chapter. Profits on calls in a rising market will offset the higher prices for the stocks, and profits on puts will help cut losses from selling into a declining market. Losses on the options will be offset by better prices paid for the stocks in a buying program and better prices received in a selling program. Often there are several ways to hedge. Sometimes one appropriate method will be as good as another, but things are not always that simple.

Alternatively, the institutional investor could buy calls on the appropriate index or indices, expecting gains on the calls to compensate for any rally in the stocks actually purchased. In a declining market, the losses on the calls would be compensated for by the lower prices paid for the securities as the hedge position is unwound.

VI. STRATEGIES FOR OPTIONS ON FUTURES

So far all our discussion has been based on options for a particular underlying instrument. However, another category of options has become particularly popular, namely options on futures contracts. In fact, in many instances investors can find more activity surrounding options on futures contracts than on options for the same underlying instrument. This is because options on futures often provide more flexibility to investors. Options on futures provide investors with the opportunity to avoid quantity risk when hedging, to create artificial futures contracts (where none are available), or to transform the risk profile of a futures position into that of a synthetic option.

FUTURES BASICS

It is worthwhile to briefly review the basics surrounding futures contracts. Futures contracts were developed primarily because of a need for financial insurance. Futures contracts allow individuals or companies to lock in future prices, whether it be to sell or to buy. The key difference between an option and a future is that the holder of a futures contract has no choice whether or not to exercise; the investor is obligated to fulfill the terms of the contract. The futures contact can still be offset at any point up until its expiration. It is also important to note that there is no premium involved with a futures contract since both sides of the contract are assuming price risk. However, all futures contracts require margin to ensure fulfillment of the contract and this cash flow requirement should be incorporated into any return calculations.

With futures, a traditional hedger might be a farmer who has a field of grain and who wants to sell his crop in advance of his harvest in order to ensure a reasonable price for his crop. The farmer sells a futures contract (sells a standard quantity and quality of grain to a buyer for a future delivery date). If the price of grain drops, the farmer does not have to worry since he has already arranged the terms of sale. However, if the price of grain rises, he has lost his opportunity to sell at a higher price. Although he has guaranteed a reasonable price for his crop, he is still assuming the risk that the price will rise and that he cannot reap the benefits.

On the other hand, a bread manufacturer who is also interested in hedging might have bought the opposite side of the same futures contract. The bread manufacturer wants to insure his profit margins by locking in a reasonable price for his required inputs. He is hedging the risk that prices could rise before he is required to take delivery. With a futures contract he has guaranteed a price for his inputs, yet he is still assuming the risk that prices will decrease within the time period of his contract.

Of course, futures can also be used to speculate. Speculators underwrite the risk of holding an inventory or contracting to sell an unharvested crop in the future in exchange for the potential to profit from favorable price movements.

The difference between the price of the futures contract and of the underlying instrument is called "basis." In a normal market, the price of a futures contract is higher than the current market or "spot" price of the underlying instrument because there are costs incurred by those who are holding the inventory until the date of expiration. These "carrying costs" can include storage, insurance and interest. The price differential will decrease (basis increases or becomes more positive) as the date to expiration nears and prices adjust to reflect the lower carrying costs. In order to prevent arbitrage, the futures price must converge toward the spot price by the date of expiration. In cases of unusual demand or a current shortage of a particular instrument, the spot price can be higher than the futures price. In this case, there is said to be an inverted market. Futures hedgers and speculators alike are subject to basis risk, or the change in price differential between the spot and the futures price over time. *Remember:*

Basis = Cash or "Spot" Price - Futures Price

Options on futures are simply contracts which provide the right but not the obligation to buy or sell a futures contract. There is still a premium paid to the call or put writer for fulfilling the opposite side of the contract if the buyer decides to exercise. Options on futures generally expire one month prior to the expiration date of the future so that the future can be settled on a cash basis. Very few investors want actual delivery of a futures contract, e.g. 3000 bushels of corn, delivered to their door. Check with your broker to get more detail on the actual expiration dates of the option and its underlying future.

Now that we have a basic understanding of options on futures, we need to know what benefits they offer over using a straightforward future or using an option on the direct underlying instrument?

HEDGING QUANTITY RISK

With a futures contract the quantity to be delivered of a given commodity is set in advance. When a hedger knows the exact amount of a commodity he wants to hedge, a futures contract often provides the best way of avoiding price risk. However, a hedger often doesn't know the exact amount of the commodity he will be producing in the future. Since the hedger is obliged to fulfill the futures contract, he may be forced to go out into the market to provide the required commodity. This inability to match quantities exposes the hedger to unwanted risk. However, by using an option on a futures contract, a hedger can minimize quantity risk.

Let's look at an example. It is spring of 1997, and the U.S. long-term weather forecast is for a hot, dry summer in the corn belt. A farmer normally yields 35 bushels per acre on 150 acres planted to corn. He usually hedges the average harvest of 5,250 bushels by selling one November futures contract, which calls for delivery of 5,000 bushels. He is concerned that his yield this year may be hurt by the weather but he also does not want to give up the chance for price appreciation if his crops are okay but supply is hampered elsewhere. Sure enough, shortly after he gets his seeds planted, a drought leads to supply constraints and November corn climbs to over $3/bushel. Since he breaks even at $2.70, he knows he should hedge, but it is almost as dry and just as hot where he is and he doesn't want to short corn he may not have to sell in November.

One choice would be to write a November $3.00 call for which he earns $.05 in premium. At this price, he could lock in a profit of $.35 a bushel if the call is exercised ($3.00 - $2.70 + $.05) and he has a sufficient corn crop to meet the obligations of the contract. However, he still couldn't afford to buy corn on the market to compensate for a crop shortage on his farm because the premium he received does not provide much downside protection (this example does not consider basis risk for reasons of simplification).

However, let's assume he decides to buy a November $3.00 put selling for $.10 cents. If prices fall and he exercises the option, his profit is locked in at $.20 ($3.00 - $.10 - $2.70) a bushel. If corn continues to rise in price above $3.00, he will not exercise the option and will sell whatever crop he has at the higher price. If mid-summer rains save the crop yields and in mid-August November corn futures sell for under $2.50, the intrinsic value of the put would insure a healthy profit because the farmer can sell the puts. Even if the farmer's crop was one of the few seriously affected by the weather, he has still locked in profits. The put has worked just like term insurance.

CREATING NEW FUTURES CONTRACTS

Options can also be used to create futures contracts where none exist. Since equity holders are rarely looking to hedge on individual stocks, there is no futures market for individual stocks. However, a particular investor may believe that a certain stock will increase in price but is uncertain about the timing of the price move. Since the investor doesn't want to pay for the time value associated with buying a long expiration call, he may prefer assuming a futures position. By buying a call and writing a put, a speculator can artificially create a long futures position.

Assume Phillip Morris is trading at 120. The March 120 call is selling for $5 and the put is selling for $6. The investor buys the call and sells the put earning $1 (ignoring commissions) and provides the required margin for writing the put option. Our new long October futures contract has a strike of $119. The $1 earning on the options opening transactions is our basis risk. If the price of Phillip Morris does not change, the options will expire at the money, and the convergence will eat the basis, just as in any storable commodity. If Phillip Morris price goes up, so will the profits once the price of the stock is over 120, but there is also unlimited downside price risk. If Phillip Morris fell to $100, the synthetic futures contract would lose $1,900 ($120 - $100 + $1) * 100.

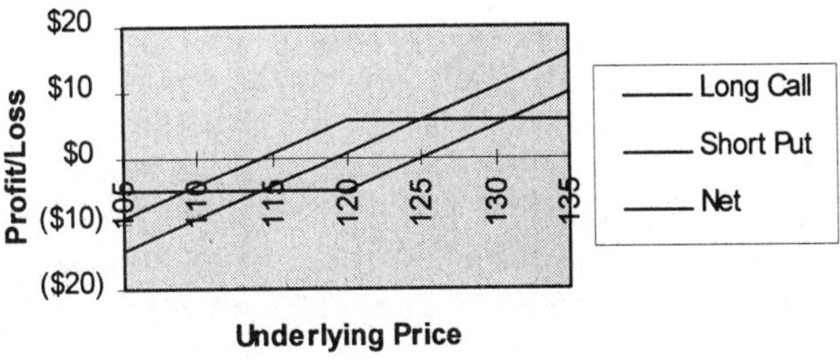

*Source: Wall Street Journal, January 23, 1997

ARBITRAGE WITH SYNTHETIC CALLS AND PUTS

As we have seen above, there is a formula for making a synthetic future. This same formula can be manipulated to create other synthetic options as well.

Future	=	Call	-	Put
-Future	=	-Call	+	Put
Put	=	Future	-	Call
-Put	=	-Future	+	Call
Call	=	Future	+	Put
-Call	=	-Future	-	Put

Note: negative sign indicates short position, positive sign indicates long position.

Also note that in order to have an equivalent futures position, investors also need to consider the delta of the option being used. If you are long 8 calls and short 8 puts with a delta of .50, then that position has an equivalent futures position of 8 futures contracts ((8+8) x .50).

With synthetic options and futures, investors can also exploit arbitrage opportunities; that is, taking advantage of discrepancies in the price of various options or futures without assuming any risk. For example, an arbitrageur might buy the synthetic option when its price is lower than the listed options price and sell the offsetting listed option to maintain a neutral position. However, these arbitrage opportunities are also rare and short-lived. In order to participate in these opportunities, traders need to be watching the markets continuously and have very low transaction costs.

Equivalent Futures Position =
Delta of the Option x Quantity of Options

SPLIT-SYNTHETIC FUTURES

Assume December gold is trading at exactly 330, and we are bearish. We can short December directly, or we can write the 330 call and buy the 330 put. But suppose we would like a little cushion around our basically bearish position. We can buy the December 320 put for, say $1.50, and we can sell the October 340 call for $1.60, getting the extra 10 cents for the call's unlimited upside risk. If we ignore commissions, as long as the price stays between 320 and 340, both options expire worthless, and the trade makes $10 ($.10 X 100 oz). If the price drops below 320, the put adds value to the $10 earned on the initial transaction. If the futures price goes over 340.10, the position at expiration loses money. However, suppose gold begins to move lower soon after the options are opened, say to 325. The put would gain value and the call would lose. Because the put was closer to being at the money, it probably would rise in price about twice as fast as the call lost value, and the entire position could be unwound quickly. If gold moved higher, the position could be liquidated at a loss before the put became worthless.

VII. RISKS ASSOCIATED WITH OPTIONS TRADING

While we have focused on the various strategies and benefits of options trading, it is imperative that we reiterate some of the risks associated with trading these instruments. When options are used by knowledgeable, skilled and experienced traders they can be very effective in protecting positions or generating returns. To the uninitiated trader, options can present their own surprises. It is worth mentioning some of the most common pitfalls.

TIME DECAY

Options are unique in the fact that their value is subject to time decay. For this reason, options traders need to have a much more accurate picture of the timing of a market shift in order to make a profitable trade. While many traders have made the correct decision as to where the market is heading, they often need to determine within weeks, and sometimes days, as to when that shift will take place. Sudden consolidations can wipe out profits quickly. Traders who try to buy options with long expirations to get around this problem have to pay up on the option premium and thus don't experience the same leverage as a shorter dated option.

LIQUIDITY

In general, options are less liquid than futures and as a result often have wider bid/offer spreads. When an option has a wide bid/offer spread, the trader has less opportunity to take advantage of small shifts in the market. By confining trading to the most liquid contracts at the largest exchanges, traders can somewhat overcome this problem, however this issue still limits the opportunities available to trade markets with lower volatility.

One of the other factors to be aware of is the fact that markets can suddenly become completely illiquid. On October 19, 1987, the stock markets crashed and investors were all clamoring to sell their positions at the same time. The market infrastructure simply couldn't handle the volume of activity and investors had to wait days and even weeks to change their positions. By this point, many investments were completely worthless. While trading automation has drastically reduced the risk of this type of incident, there can be many unforeseen reasons why you may not be able to offset an options position in a timely manner. Trading limits on a given day can also dramatically affect your ability to accurately price or offset your position.

CHANGES IN VOLATILITY

Many people are skeptical about the opportunity to generate profits with options when option premiums are high. This skepticism is not always warranted. Futures options are mathematically valued rights to purchase underlying futures. Their "richness" or "cheapness" are all a matter of opinion on whether too much or too little volatility has been priced into the option. If history says that a future's recent implied volatility is 15% and the current option price implies a volatility of 20%, the option may be expensive. It may also reflect that future volatility will be higher than historical volatility. For an options trader, he must determine how long this high volatility period will last. If it will last beyond his time horizon for the trade, the relatively high premium paid for the option is inconsequential to the trading strategy. The high premium will be recouped upon selling the option. For example, someone who bought an option on the Japanese Yen in June of '95 might have been concerned about paying a relatively high premium (relative to historical volatility), but in fact would have benefited from even higher volatility over the following month.

On the other hand, many traders use options to trade around big market announcements where there is a great deal of uncertainty surrounding the outcome. The implied volatility and thus the price paid for the option premium can be very high preceding the market announcement and drop dramatically once the outcome is known. The change in the price of the option due to the underlying price move can be less than the fall in the price of the option as a result of lower volatility. For example, buying and holding a Japanese Yen option in February of '94 could have been hazardous, regardless of whether the directional move was correct or not.

OVERNIGHT TRADING

Many of the instruments underlying listed options can trade overnight when the options markets are closed. Stocks can trade on Instinet and many futures contracts trade on evening sessions leaving options traders to wait until the following morning to take any action. Because options prices are mathematically tied to the underlying price, much of the value of an option can be lost in overnight trading. For this reason option traders can wake up to significant surprises. Traders have to be aware of this fact and may want to confine their option positions to instruments which only trade during day sessions.

BASIS RISK

Investors who wish to invest in futures options have to be aware of basis risk. For example, in a calendar spread using straight forward options, both options contracts are based on the exact same underlying instrument, e.g. 100 shares of Dell. However, if an investor conducts a calendar spread using futures options, e.g. buys the May call for corn and sells the March call for corn, these are related but different entities. While the underlying commodities are the same, the delivery dates are not the same and as such the investor must be aware of the relationship between the two contracts to determine whether he or she feels comfortable incurring the basis risk. Even though the calendar spread might work, all profits can be wiped out by an unexpected change in the basis.

WRITING OPTIONS

Although we have discussed the risks associated with writing naked options, the risks are worth reiterating. There is unlimited downside risk when writing a put or a call contract. Even the greatest investors can be caught off guard by unexpected market events which can make their investments worthless. When writing options, the results can be far more destructive. While the old saying "buyer beware" is generally true, in options trading "seller beware" is far more appropriate.

* * *

This discussion is intended to provide the novice with an understanding of the risks as well as the rewards of options trading. The strategies discussed in this booklet are not exhaustive nor are they appropriate in all markets. The examples have been simplified to insure clarity. They do not include commissions nor the impact of tying up cash in margin deposits. All these factors and any other issues and concerns should be discussed in detail with your broker before entering any options trades. Options trading generally requires far more attention than other investments, but once their use has been mastered they can provide both convenience and value to the investor.

GLOSSARY OF TERMS

The following list of terms may be helpful to new options traders. While most have been discussed and explained within this book, others are simply terms which a new options trader may come across. This list is not complete nor is it intended to state or to suggest the correct legal significance or meaning of any word or term. Investors should consult a broker to clarify any unfamiliar terms or expressions.

actuals: Commodities on hand, ready for shipment, storage and manufacture.

arbitrage: Simultaneous purchase and sale of two different contracts (or a combination of cash and futures to take advantage of perceived mispricing.) In a pure arbitrage, mispricing is locked in and a risk-free profit made through trades.

at-the-market: An order to buy or sell at the best price possible at the time an order reaches the trading pit.

at-the-money: In options, when the strike price equals the price of the underlying financial instrument.

basis: The difference between the price of a futures contract and the underlying commodity's spot (or cash) price.

basis grade: Specified grade, or grades named in the exchange's futures contract. Other grades deliverable are subject to price differentials from the basis or "contract" grade.

bear: A market trending downward; or a person who expects prices to go lower.

bid: An offer to buy, subject to immediate acceptance made on the floor of an exchange for a definite number of financial instruments at a specified price.

bull: A market trending upward; or a person who expects price to go higher.

buy on close: To buy at the end of the trading session at a price within the closing range.

buy on opening: To buy at the start of the trading session at a price within opening range.

call: An option that gives the buyer the right to a long position in the underlying instrument at a specific price; the call writer (seller) may be assigned a short position in the underlying item if the buyer exercises the call.

cash commodity: The actual physical product on which a futures contract is based. This product can include agricultural commodities, financial instruments or the cash equivalents of index futures.

cash delivery: (See delivery)

cash market: Markets where trades take place for spot (immediate or near immediate) delivery as opposed to future delivery.

CFTC: Commodity Futures Trading Commission.

CTA: Commodity Trading Advisor.

close: The period at the end of the trading session officially designated by the exchange during which all transactions are considered made "at the close."

closing price or range: The price or price range recorded during the period designated as the official close.

commission house: A concern that buys and sells actual commodities or futures contracts for the accounts of customers.

cover: The cancellation of a short position in any financial instrument or cash commodity by the purchase of an equal quantity of the same item (see liquidating).

covered writing: The sale of a call against a long position in the underlying financial instrument or cash commodity.

cross hedge: When one cash commodity or financial instrument is hedged by using futures or options based on another.

day orders: Orders at a limited price which are understood to be good for the day, unless expressly designated as an open order or "good till-canceled" order.

delivery: The tender and receipt of the actual financial instrument or commodity, or in the case of agricultural commodities, warehouse receipts covering such a commodity, in settlement of a futures or options contract. Some contracts settle in cash

(cash delivery) in which case open positions are marked to market on the last day of the contract based on the cash market close.

delivery month: Specified month in which delivery may be made under the terms of a futures contract.

delivery notice: A notice of a clearing member's intention to deliver a stated quantity of a commodity in settlement of a short futures position.

delta: The change in the price of an option relative to the change in price of the underlying instrument.

differentials: The premiums paid for the grades better than the basis grade and the discounts allowed for grades lower than the basis grades. These differentials are fixed by the contract terms on most exchanges.

financial futures: Futures contracts based on interest-rate instruments (T-bonds, T-bills, etc.), foreign currencies, and indices.

fundamental analysis: An approach to market forecasting that emphasizes the analysis of factors affecting supply and demand (opposite of technical analysis).

futures contract: A commitment to deliver or receive a standardized quantity and quality of a commodity (or financial instrument) on a specified future delivery date at a specified price.

futures commission merchant (FCM): a broker who is permitted to accept orders to buy and sell futures contracts for customers.

futures funds: Usually limited partnerships for investors who participate in the futures market by buying shares in a fund managed by professional traders or commodity trading advisors.

hedge: A sale of futures or options to offset the ownership or purchase of the underlying cash commodity in order to protect it against adverse price moves; or conversely, a purchase of futures or options to offset the sale of the underlying cash commodity, again for protection against adverse price moves.

in-the-money: In call options, when the strike price is below the price of the underlying instrument. In put options, when the strike price is above the price of the underlying instrument. In-the-money option premiums always include intrinsic value.

index futures: Futures contracts based on indices such as the S&P 500 or Value Line Index. These are cash settlement contracts.

intrinsic value: For in-the-money call and put options, the difference between the strike price and the underlying instrument's price.

limit: The maximum daily price change above or below the previous close in a specific futures market. Trading limits may be changed during periods of unusually high market activity.

limit order: An order given to a broker by a customer which has some restrictions upon its execution, such as price or time.

liquidation: A transaction made in reducing or closing out a long or short position, but usually used to mean a reduction or closing out of a long position.

local: Independent trader who trades his own money on the floor of an exchange. Some locals act as brokers as well, but are subject to certain rules that protect customer orders.

long: (1) The buying side of an open futures or options contract. (2) A trader whose net position in the futures or options market shows an excess of open purchases over open sales.

margin: Cash or equivalent posted as a guarantee of fulfillment of a futures or options contract (not a down payment).

margin call: Demand for additional funds or equivalent because of adverse price movements or some other contingency.

mark-to-market: The practice of crediting or debiting a trader's account based on the daily closing prices of the futures or options contracts he is long or short.

market order: An order for immediate execution at the best available price.

naked position: The sale of an option, futures, or cash commodity not covered by a position in the underlying instrument or item.

nearby: The futures contract closest to expiration.

net position: The difference between the open contracts long and the open contracts short held in any one commodity or option by any individual or group.

offer: A quotation indicating willingness to sell at a given price (opposite of bid).

on opening: A term used to specify execution of an order during the opening.

open contracts: Contracts which have been bought or sold without the transaction having been completed by subsequent sales, repurchase, or actual delivery or receipt of commodity, or by expiration of the option.

open interest: The number of "open contracts." It refers to unliquidated purchases or sales, not their combined total.

open order: An order which is good until canceled.

opening, the: The period at the beginning of the trading session officially designated by the exchange during which all trades are considered made "at the opening."

options: See puts and calls.

opening prices (or range): The price or price range recorded during the period designated by the exchange as the official opening.

out-of-the-money: Calls with strike prices above the price of the underlying financial instruments, and puts with strike prices below the price of the underlying items. They contain no intrinsic value.

pit: A platform on the trading floor of an exchange, consisting of steps upon which traders and brokers stand while trading (if circular, called a "ring").

point: The minimum unit in which changes in futures prices may be expressed (minimum price fluctuation may be in multiples of points).

position: An interest in the market in the form of open commitments.

premium: (1) The amount by which a given futures contract's price or commodity's quality exceeds that of another contract or commodity (opposite of discount). (2) In options, the price of a call or put, which the buyer pays to the option writer (seller).

price limit: The maximum fluctuation in price of a futures contract permitted during one trading session, as fixed by the rules of a contract market.

purchase and sale statement: A statement sent by the FCM to a customer when his futures position has been reduced or closed out (also called "P and S").

put: In options, the buyer of a put has the right to acquire a short position in the underlying futures contract at the strike price until the option expires; the seller (writer) of the put obligates himself to take a long position in the futures at the strike price if the buyer exercises his put.

range: The difference between the high and low price of the futures contract during a given period.

ratio hedging: Hedging a cash position with futures or options on a less or more than one-for-one basis.

reaction: The downward tendency of a commodity after an advance.

round-turn commission: The cost to the customer for executing a futures contract, which is charged only when the position is liquidated.

scalping: For floor traders, the practice of trading in and out of contracts throughout the trading day in hopes of making a series of small profits.

settlement price: The official daily closing price of a futures contract, set by the exchange for the purpose of settling margin accounts.

short: (1) The selling of an open futures or options contract. (2) A trade whose net position in the futures market shows an excess of open sales over open purchases (see "long").

speculator: A trader who takes an outright long or short position in the market (opposite of "hedger"). Some speculators also trade spreads.

spot commodity: See cash commodity.

spot price: The price at which the spot or cash commodity is selling on the cash or spot market.

spread: A simultaneous purchase of one contract and sale of another. Spreads can be transacted between contracts with the same underlying commodity but different months; the same month but different commodities; or the same month and commodity but traded on different exchanges.

straddle: The simultaneous purchase (or sale) of both a put and a call in the same option month and strike price.

strangle: The sale of both a put and a call in the same option month, usually as a strategy assuming that the volatility of the market is stabilizing or falling.

strike price: In options, the price at which a position will be established if the buyer exercises his option. Also called strike or exercise price.

synthetic: A futures or options position created artificially by combining other options or options and futures.

technical analysis (charting): The use of charts and other devices to analyze price change patterns and changes in volume and open interest to predict futures market trends (opposite of fundamental analysis).

time value: In options, the value of the premium is based on the amount of time left before the contract expires and the volatility of the underlying futures contract. Time value is that portion of the premium in excess of intrinsic value. Time value diminishes as the expiration of the option draws near and/or if the underlying futures becomes less volatile.

volume of trading (or sales): A simple addition of successive futures transactions (a transaction consists of a purchase and matching sale).

writer: The seller of an option, who collects the premium payment from the buyer.

Volume U.S.

U.S. FUTURES VOLUME HIGHLIGHTS

1997 in Comparison with 1996

1997 Rank	Top 50 Contracts Traded in 1996	1997 Contracts	1997 %	1996 Contracts	1996 %	1996 Rank
1	T-Bonds, CBT	99,827,659	22.50%	84,725,128	21.32%	2
2	Eurodollar, CME	99,770,237	22.49%	88,883,119	22.37%	1
3	Crude Oil, NYMEX	24,771,375	5.58%	23,487,821	5.91%	3
4	T-Notes (10 Year), CBT	23,961,819	5.40%	21,939,725	5.52%	4
5	S&P 500 Index, CME	21,294,584	4.80%	19,899,999	5.01%	5
6	Corn, CBT	16,984,951	3.83%	19,620,188	4.94%	6
7	Soybeans, CBT	14,539,766	3.28%	14,236,295	3.58%	7
8	T-Notes (5 Year), CBT	13,488,725	3.04%	11,463,640	2.88%	8
9	Natural Gas, NYMEX	11,923,628	2.69%	8,813,867	2.22%	10
10	Gold (100 oz.), COMEX Div. of NYMEX	9,541,904	2.15%	8,902,179	2.24%	9
11	#2 Heating Oil, NYMEX	8,370,964	1.89%	8,341,877	2.10%	11
12	Unleaded Regular Gas, NYMEX	7,475,145	1.68%	6,312,339	1.59%	12
13	Deutsche Mark, CME	7,044,783	1.59%	5,979,464	1.50%	13
14	Soybean Meal, CBT	6,424,945	1.45%	5,955,977	1.50%	14
15	Japanese Yen, CME	6,034,565	1.36%	5,101,819	1.28%	16
16	Soybean Oil, CBT	5,284,994	1.19%	4,980,277	1.25%	19
17	Sugar #11, CSC	5,284,971	1.19%	4,751,852	1.20%	18
18	Wheat, CBT	5,058,645	1.14%	8,385,967	1.36%	15
19	Silver (5,000 oz), COMEX Div. of NYMEX	4,893,520	1.10%	4,870,808	1.23%	17
20	Swiss Franc, CME	4,222,268	0.95%	3,929,225	0.99%	20
21	Live Cattle, CME	3,919,642	0.88%	3,926,192	0.99%	21
22	Cotton, NYCE	2,837,280	0.64%	2,373,855	0.60%	23
23	British Pound, CME	2,664,401	0.60%	2,961,782	0.75%	22
24	Canadian Dollar, CME	2,542,102	0.57%	1,932,729	0.49%	27
25	High Grade Copper, COMEX Div. of NYMEX	2,356,170	0.53%	2,311,919	0.58%	24
26	Coffee "C", CSC	2,294,181	0.52%	2,039,576	0.51%	26
27	Cocoa, CSC	2,274,509	0.51%	2,121,576	0.53%	25
28	Lean Hogs, CME	2,100,909	0.47%			
29	Wheat, KCBT	1,937,140	0.44%	1,830,276	0.46%	28
30	Mexican Peso, CME	1,707,706	0.38%	850,040	0.21%	35
31	T-Bonds, MIDAM	1,513,925	0.34%	1,281,967	0.32%	30
32	One Month LIBOR, CME	1,504,230	0.34%	1,190,652	0.30%	31
33	Euroyen, CME	1,119,827	0.25%	503,104	0.13%	44
34	Orange Juice (Frozen Conc.), NYCE	1,029,861	0.23%	654,937	0.16%	39
35	Soybeans, MIDAM	1,026,830	0.23%	976,134	0.25%	33
36	Wheat, MGE	1,024,523	0.23%	996,780	0.25%	32
37	T-Notes (2 Year), CBT	1,018,545	0.23%	643,845	0.16%	40
38	Municipal Bond Index, CBT	983,877	0.22%	883,901	0.22%	34
39	NYSE Composite Index, NYCE	916,716	0.21%	791,325	0.20%	37
40	30 Day Federal Funds, CBT	910,747	0.21%	608,308	0.15%	42
41	E Mini S&P, CME	885,825	0.20%			
42	Feeder Cattle, CME	837,165	0.19%	772,222	0.19%	38
43	NASDAQ 100, CME	807,604	0.18%	380,963	0.10%	50
44	Goldman Sachs Commodity Index, CME	773,088	0.17%	446,186	0.11%	49
45	Dow Jones Industrial Index, CBOT	755,476	0.17%			42
46	Platinum, NYMEX	698,597	0.16%	802,468	0.20%	36
47	Australian Dollar, CME	595,573	0.13%	461,084	0.12%	48
48	Pork Bellies, CME	595,319	0.13%	612,649	0.15%	41
49	U.S. Dollar Index, NYCE	485,481	0.11%	509,067	0.13%	43
50	Corn, MIDAM	432,461	0.10%	462,318	0.12%	47
	Top 50 Contracts	438,748,885		390,907,421 *		
	Contracts Below the Top 50	4,904,872	1.11%	6,494,732	1.63%	
	TOTAL	**443,653,757**	**100.00%**	**397,402,153**	**100.00%**	

* For 1996 Top 50 contracts totaled 393,695,915 including 3 contracts that are not among 1997's Top 50.

U.S. FUTURES VOLUME HIGHLIGHTS

1997 in Comparison with 1996

1997 RANK	EXCHANGE	1997 CONTRACTS	1997 %	1996 CONTRACTS	1996 %	1996 RANK
1	Chicago Board of Trade (CBT)	190,056,287	42.84%	171,134,185	43.06%	1
2	Chicago Mercantile Exchange (CME)	159,975,955	36.06%	141,600,469	35.63%	2
3	New York Mercantile Exchange (NYMEX) *	70,634,699	15.92%	64,223,291	16.16%	3
4	Coffee, Sugar & Cocoa Exchange (CSCE)	10,022,427	2.26%	9,102,029	2.29%	4
5	New York Cotton Exchange (NYCE) **	6,201,235	1.40%	4,967,176	1.25%	5
6	MidAmerica Commodity Exchange	3,500,791	0.79%	3,229,710	0.81%	6
7	Kansas City Board of Trade (KCBT)	2,192,694	0.49%	2,084,493	0.52%	7
8	Minneapolis Grain Exchange (MGE)	1,040,594	0.23%	1,012,598	0.25%	8
9	Philadelphia Board of Trade (PBOT)	29,075	0.01%	48,202	0.01%	9
	TOTAL	**443,653,757**	**100.00%**	**397,402,153**	**100.00%**	

* Includes Comex Division.
** Includes the New York Futures Exchange.

U.S. FUTURES VOLUME 1993 - 1997

CHICAGO BOARD OF TRADE (CBT)

FUTURE	CONTRACT UNIT	1997	1996	1995	1994	1993
Wheat	5,000 bu	5,058,645	5,385,967	4,955,067	3,620,631	3,019,629
Corn	5,000 bu	16,984,951	19,620,188	15,105,147	11,529,884	11,462,618
Oats	5,000 bu	397,332	501,858	475,538	492,504	455,335
Soybeans	5,000 bu	14,539,766	14,236,295	10,611,534	10,749,109	11,649,333
Soybean Oil	60,000 lbs	5,284,994	4,980,277	4,611,336	5,063,188	4,612,229
Soybean Meal	100 tons	6,424,945	5,955,977	5,601,242	4,593,814	4,718,095
Rice	200,000 lbs	171,973	119,900	121,914	16,693	
Crop Yield	Crop yield est. X 10	1,472	1,343	3,123		
Diammonium Phosphate	100 tons	144	3,935	6,755	15,588	45,314
Anhydrous Ammonia	100 tons	19	351	1,060	2,811	9,831
Edible Oil Index	100 tons			21	298	
Barge Freight Index	%BF x $5/ton					6
Structural Panel Index	100,000 sq. ft.			885	7,033	
Eastern Catastrophe Insurance	Loss/EP x $25,000					4,600
Midwest Catastrophe Insurance	Loss/EP x $25,000					74
National Catastrophe Insurance	Loss/EP x $25,000				4	4,782
Silver	5,000 oz	61	110	8,617	10,278	1,022
Silver	1,000 oz	30,771	41,575	76,667	88,663	89,141
Gold	100 oz	138	335	647	984	778
Gold	Kilo	13,620	17,687	20,245	22,712	22,220
T-Bonds	$100,000	99,827,659	84,725,128	86,375,916	99,959,881	79,428,444
T-Notes (6 1/2-10 Year)	$100,000	23,961,819	21,939,725	22,445,356	24,077,828	16,601,258
T-Notes (5 Year)	$100,000	13,488,725	11,463,640	12,637,054	12,462,838	8,123,939
T-Notes (2 Year)	$200,000	1,018,545	643,845	744,866	939,043	532,203
30-Day Federal Funds	$5,000,000	910,474	608,308	643,717	416,200	182,319
German Bund	250000	200,588				
Municipal Bond Index	$1,000 x Index	983,877	883,901	1,169,470	1,600,533	1,120,510
Treasury Note Inflation Indices	$100,000	22				
Canadian Government Bonds	$100,000 CAD				27,163	
Dow Jones Industrial Index	$10 x Index	755,476				
Brady Bond Index	$1,000 x Index		69			
Yield Curve Spread	$25,000 x 100YC	271	3,771			
US Dollar Index	$1,250 x Index					733
MMI Maxi	$500 x Index					155,338
Wilshire Small Cap Index	$500 x Index					1,626
Total		**190,056,287**	**171,134,185**	**165,616,177**	**175,697,680**	**142,241,377**

Volume U.S.

CHICAGO MERCANTILE EXCHANGE (CME)

FUTURE	CONTRACT UNIT	1997	1996	1995	1994	199
Live Hogs	40,000 lbs		1,784,564	1,669,680	1,554,022	1,401,75
Lean Hogs	40,000 lbs	2,100,909	311,347	984		
Pork Bellies, Frozen	40,000 lbs	595,319	612,649	561,913	633,646	698,79
Boneless Beef	200,000 lbs 90% lean	4,245				
Boneless Beef Trimmings	200,000 lbs 50% lean	4,876				
Butter	40,000 lbs	2,805	273			
Cheddar Cheese	40,000 lbs	533				
Fluid MIlk	50,000 lbs	4,188	2,336			
Live Cattle	40,000 lbs	3,919,642	3,926,192	3,257,105	3,580,896	3,306,95
Feeder Cattle	44,000 lbs	837,165	772,222	511,895	446,639	419,88
Lumber	160,000 bd ft		26,293	179,538	172,963	178,18
Orient Strand Board Lumber	100,000 bd ft	1,115	235			
Random Lumber	80,000 bd ft	260,318	277,781	3,148		
T-Bills (90-day)	$1,000,000	199,084	251,353	620,223	1,020,491	1,017,35
T-Bills (1 Year)	$500,000				586	
Eurodollar (3-month)	$1,000,000	99,770,237	88,883,119	95,730,019	104,823,245	64,411,39
Euroyen	$1,000,000,000 xy	1,119,827	503,104			
Euromark (3-month)	$1,000,000				566	26,05
Federal Funds Rate	$3,000,000	2,790	47,495	52,412		
One Month LIBOR	$3,000,000	1,504,230	1,190,652	1,707,062	1,911,184	1,128,32
Argentine FRB Bond	$1,000 X Bond	1,553	9,610			
Brazilian C Bond	$500 x Bond	2,995	10,198			
Brazilian EL Bond	$500 x Bond		253			
Mexican PAR Bond	$500 x Bond	366	1,926			
Mexican CETES	2,000,000	8,598				
Mexican TIIE	6,000,000	1,897				
BP/DM Crossrate	125,000 GBP	127				
JY/DM Crossrate	250,000 DEM	180				
DM/JY Cross (New)	125,000 x dm/jy X			106		17
British Pound	62,500	2,664,401	2,961,782	2,610,510	3,562,865	3,701,42
Brazilian Real	100,000	49,092	87,323	20,364		
Canadian Dollar	100,000	2,542,102	1,932,729	1,756,569	1,740,205	1,410,81
Deutschemark	125,000	7,044,783	5,979,464	7,186,476	10,956,479	12,866,45
Japanese Yen	12,500,000	6,034,565	5,101,819	5,630,053	6,612,993	6,023,13
Mexican Peso	500,000	1,707,706	850,040	133,791		
Swiss Franc	125,000	4,222,268	3,929,225	4,399,932	5,217,236	5,604,84
Australian Dollar	100,000	595,573	461,084	346,823	355,183	198,95
French Franc	250,000	112,520	67,835	48,621	49,005	19,34
New Zealand Dollar	100,000	3,506				
South African Rand	500,000	6,287				
Deutschemark Forward	$250,000			38,582	46,979	
Japanes Yen Forward	$250,000			16,898		
British Pound Rolling Spot	250,000 sterling					1,72
Japanese Yen Rolling Spot	$250,000			15,310		
Deutschemark Rolling Spot	$250,000			44,013	126,994	28,93
Nikkei 225	$5 x Index	417,541	502,072	609,720	548,233	356,52
Mexican IPC Index	$25 x Index	88	4,481			
E-Mini S&P	$50 x S&P Index	885,825				
S&P 500 Index	$500 x 500 Index	21,294,584	19,899,999	18,852,149	18,708,599	13,204,41
S&P 500 Barra Growth Index	$500 x 500 Index	6,196	3,400	1,240		
S&P 500 Barra Value Index	$500 x 500 Index	11,203	7,531	1,478		
S&P MidCap 400 Index	$500 x 400 Index	262,017	289,989	253,741	285,962	218,53
FT-SE 100	50 x FTSE Index					9
Major Market	$500 x Index	732	4,592	58,048	150,308	49,28
NASDAQ 100 Index	$500 x Index	807,604	380,963			
Dow Jones Taiwan Stock Index	$250 x Index	8,558				
Russell 2000	$500 x Index	182,717	78,353	43,857	36,239	19,47
Goldman Sachs Commodity Index	$250 x GSCI	773,088	446,186	270,504	154,511	122,28
Total		**159,975,955**	**141,600,469**	**146,662,764**	**162,696,029**	**116,415,11**

COFFEE, SUGAR & COCOA EXCHANGE (CSCE)

FUTURE	CONTRACT UNIT	1997	1996	1995	1994	1993
Coffee "C"	37,500 lbs	2,294,181	2,039,576	2,003,014	2,658,073	2,489,223
Sugar #11	112,000 lbs	5,284,971	4,751,852	4,711,082	4,719,218	4,285,945
Sugar #14	112,000 lbs	158,431	182,393	119,508	150,472	133,898
White Sugar	50 metric tons	10	333			
Cocoa	10 metric tons	2,274,509	2,121,576	2,090,098	2,417,006	2,128,384
Brazil-Diff Coffee	37,500 lbs					11
Cheddar Cheese	40,000 lbs	289	980	977	1,366	669
Non Fat Dry Milk	44,000 lbs	559	282	90	905	1,276
Butter	10,000 lbs.	1,482	93			
BFP Milk		7,084				
Milk	50,000 lbs	911	4,944	436		
Total		**10,022,427**	**9,102,029**	**8,925,205**	**9,947,040**	**9,039,406**

KANSAS CITY BOARD OF TRADE (KCBT)

FUTURE	CONTRACT UNIT	1997	1996	1995	1994	1993
Wheat	5,000 bu	1,937,140	1,830,276	1,560,538	1,502,348	1,348,500
Western Natural Gas	10,000 MMBtu	86,723	89,706	77,595		
Value Line Index	$500 x Index	14,047	28,663	35,185	50,259	45,806
Mini Value Line	$100 x Index	154,784	135,848	74,346	51,901	40,662
Total		**2,192,694**	**2,084,493**	**1,747,664**	**1,604,508**	**1,434,968**

MIDAMERICA COMMODITY EXCHANGE (MidAm)

FUTURE	CONTRACT UNIT	1997	1996	1995	1994	1993
Wheat	1,000 bu	130,968	151,755	137,573	102,145	101,353
Corn	1,000 bu	432,461	462,318	305,347	232,855	276,502
Oats	1,000 bu	4,916	8,449	5,846	5,208	4,555
Soybeans	1,000 bu	1,026,830	976,134	868,577	797,803	966,244
Soybean Meal New	20 tons	23,773	11,638	4,060	3,757	3,800
Soybean Oil	30,000 lbs	37,962	14,248	6,658		
Live Cattle	20,000 lbs	16,316	20,983	18,811	15,895	16,314
Lean Hogs	20,000 lbs	1,312				
Live Hogs	20,000 lbs	4,152	21,118	24,059	19,614	17,841
Rice, Rough New	200,000 lbs				68,379	65,970
New York Silver	1,000 oz	8,928	8,398	13,320	17,170	10,986
New York Gold	33.2 oz	15,161	15,876	18,964	24,926	19,803
Platinum	25 oz	4,248	6,949	3,055	2,841	1,750
T-Bonds	$50,000	1,513,925	1,281,967	1,341,877	1,385,904	1,125,645
T-Bills	$500,000	461	753	754	826	1,129
T-Notes (10 Year)	$50,000	49,700	41,849	38,494	35,303	11,615
T-Notes (5 Year)	$50,000	479	383	37	4	39
Eurodollars	$500,000	5,997	8,893	23,550	8,987	7,229
U.S. Dollar Index	$1,250 x USDI					7
Australian Dollar	50,000	585	266	221		
British Pound	12,500	28,094	21,424	23,620	66,162	67,208
Swiss Franc	62,500	47,504	48,027	50,201	64,501	73,532
Deutschemark	62,500	84,344	79,093	95,775	113,166	123,573
Japanese Yen	6,250,000	48,585	42,085	55,213	67,641	62,874
Canadian Dollar	50,000	14,090	7,104	11,970	9,522	8,505
Total		**3,500,791**	**3,229,710**	**3,047,982**	**3,042,609**	**2,966,474**

MINNEAPOLIS GRAIN EXCHANGE (MGE)

FUTURE	CONTRACT UNIT	1997	1996	1995	1994	1993
Wheat	5,000 bu	1,024,523	996,780	914,882	737,089	822,898
White Wheat	5,000 bu	14,284	14,602	20,411	27,446	10,895
Oats	5,000 bu					4,025
Barley	180,000 lbs.	452	631			
White Shrimp	5,000 lbs	737	56	336	854	1,437
Black Tiger Shrimp	5,000 lbs	598	529	387	119	
Total		**1,040,594**	**1,012,598**	**936,016**	**765,508**	**839,255**

Volume U.S.

NEW YORK COTTON EXCHANGE (NYCE)*

FUTURE	CONTRACT UNIT	1997	1996	1995	1994	1993
Cotton #2	50,000 lbs	2,837,280	2,373,855	2,525,434	2,289,998	1,603,027
Potato	85,000 lbs.	540	744			
Cotlook World Cotton	50,000 lbs X CWC				79	3,363
Orange Juice Frozen Concentrate	15,000 lbs	1,029,861	654,937	688,932	653,824	640,131
European Currency Unit	$100,000					
Mark Pound	125,000 GBP	86,166	87,757	32,804	12,351	
Mark Peseta	250,000 DEM	754				
Mark Paris	500,000 DEM	158,740	77,263	36,649	10,295	
Mark Yen	125,000 DEM	172,612	167,093	66,405	30,566	
Mark Lira	250,000 DEM	137,077	74,997	31,604	3,572	
Mark Swiss Franc	125,000 DEM	121,303	37,566	1,209		
Mark Krona	125,000 DEM	63,685	8,378			
Pound Swiss	125,000 GBP	5,699				
Pound Yen	125,000 GBP	9,629				
U.S. Dollar/Mark	$125,000	33,917	32,441	29,441	30,385	
U.S. Dollar/Canadian	$200,000	830				
U.S. Dollar/Swiss Franc	$200,000	4,282	4,098	1,586	10	
U.S. Dollar/Japanese Yen	$200,000	9,060	9,037	4,943	2	
U.S. Dollar/British Pound	125,000 GBP	6,375	2,290	3,021	2	
U.S. Dollar/Rand	$100,000	4,683				
U.S. Dollar/Australian	$200,000 AUD	5,393				
U.S. Dollar/New Zealand	$200,000 NZD	9,499				
U.S. Dollar/Rupiah	$500,000,000 RUD	2				
U.S. Dollar/Ringgit	$500,000 RIN	228				
U.S. Dollar/Baht	$5,000,000 BAH	2				
U.S. Dollar Index	$1,000 x Index	485,481	509,067	456,859	558,439	599,112
Emerging Markets Debt Index	$1,000 x Index	261	341	732		
T-Note (5 Year)	$100,000	18,040	45,064	44,959	69,858	50,200
T-Note (2 Year)	$200,000	1,790	1,147	11,072	3,233	734
NYSE Composite Index	$500 x Index	916,716	791,325	685,922	729,231	848,522
NYSE Utility Index	$500 x Index				11	10
PSE Tech 100	$500 x Index	9,848	8,663			
Commodity Research Bureau Index	$500 x Index	71,482	81,113	81,413	109,986	91,908
Total*		**6,201,235**	**4,967,176**	**4,702,985**	**4,501,842**	**3,837,007**

NEW YORK MERCANTILE EXCHANGE (NYMEX)**

COMEX DIVISION

FUTURE	CONTRACT UNIT	1997	1996	1995	1994	1993
High Grade Copper	25,000 lbs	2,356,170	2,311,919	2,519,414	2,737,967	2,064,629
Silver	5,000 oz	4,893,520	4,870,808	5,183,236	5,994,345	4,855,924
Gold	100 oz	9,541,904	8,902,179	7,781,596	8,503,366	8,916,195
Platinum	50 oz					342
Paladium	100 oz					2
Eurotop 100 Index	$100 x Price	47,427	38,925	49,328	62,231	56,497
Total		**16,839,021**	**16,123,831**	**15,533,574**	**17,297,909**	**15,893,589**

NYMEX DIVISION

FUTURE	CONTRACT UNIT	1997	1996	1995	1994	1993
Palladium	100 oz	238,716	205,610	166,713	143,773	113,681
Platinum	50 oz	698,597	802,468	846,693	895,805	651,222
No. 2 Heating Oil, NY	1,000 bbl	8,370,964	8,341,877	8,266,783	8,986,835	8,625,061
Unleaded Gasoline, NY	1,000 bbl	7,475,145	6,312,339	7,071,787	7,470,836	7,407,809
Natural Gas	10,000 MMBTU	11,923,628	8,813,867	8,086,718	6,357,560	4,671,533
Gulf Coast Unleaded Gas	42,000 gal			252	300	510
Alberta Natural Gas	10,000 MMBTU	110	2,876			
Palo Verde Electricity	736 Mwh	155,977	17,548			
California Oregon Border Electricity	737 Mwh	120,896	52,340			
Permian Basin Natural Gas	10,000 MMBTU	15	8,811			
Propane	42,000 gal	40,255	53,903	49,532	45,100	44,923
Crude Oil	1,000 bbl	24,771,375	23,487,821	23,613,994	26,812,262	24,868,602
Total		**53,795,678**	**48,099,460**	**48,102,472**	**50,712,471**	**46,383,341**
Total**		**70,634,699**	**64,223,291**	**63,636,046**	**68,010,380**	**62,276,930**

PHILADELPHIA BOARD OF TRADE (PBOT)

FUTURE	CONTRACT UNIT	1997	1996	1995	1994	1993
Australian Dollar	100,000	1,270	2,532	1,716	265	142
British Pound	62,500	2,543	1,761	4,147	2,485	1,493
Canadian Dollar	100,000	80	91	208	639	
ECU	125,000	158	616		1,768	
Deutschemark	125,000	12,510	23,904	17,121	21,661	11,469
Swiss Franc	125,000	3,913	4,723	3,915	3,038	614
French Franc	500,000	3,489	3,704	4,162	7,167	8,814
Japanese Yen	12,500,000	5,112	10,871	7,372	5,323	2,564
Total		**29,075**	**48,202**	**38,641**	**42,346**	**25,096**

		1997	1996	1995	1994	1993
TOTAL FUTURES		**443,653,757**	**397,402,153**	**395,313,480**	**426,307,942**	**339,075,626**
PERCENT CHANGE		**11.64%**	**0.53%**	**-7.27%**	**25.73%**	**14.83%**

* The New York Cotton Exchange volume now includes the New York Futures Exchange.

** In August 1994, the Commodity Exchange and the New York Mercantile Exchange merged and is now listed as one exchange.

OPTIONS TRADED ON U.S. FUTURES EXCHANGES VOLUME HIGHLIGHTS

1997 in Comparison with 1996

1997 RANK	EXCHANGE	1997 CONTRACTS	1997 %	1996 CONTRACTS	1996 %	1996 RANK
1	Chicago Board of Trade (CBT)	52,642,632	47.40%	51,304,320	50.31%	1
2	Chicago Mercantile Exchange (CME)	40,738,473	36.68%	35,421,726	34.74%	2
3	New York Mercantile Exchange (NYMEX) *	13,216,647	11.90%	11,576,001	11.35%	3
4	Coffee, Sugar & Cocoa Exchange (CSCE)	3,043,615	2.74%	2,287,750	2.24%	4
5	New York Cotton Exchange (NYCE) **	1,232,052	1.11%	1,261,109	1.24%	5
6	Kansas City Board of Trade (KCBT)	103,879	0.09%	68,479	0.07%	6
7	Minneapolis Grain Exchange (MGE)	47,710	0.04%	26,891	0.03%	7
8	MidAmerica Commodity Exchange (MidAm)	34,337	0.30%	27,531	0.03%	8
	TOTAL	**111,059,345**	**100.00%**	**101,973,807**	**100.00%**	

* Includes Comex Division.

** Includes the New York Futures Exchange.

OPTIONS VOLUME ON U.S. FUTURES EXCHANGES 1993 - 1997

CHICAGO BOARD OF TRADE (CBT)

OPTION	CONTRACT UNIT	1997	1996	1995	1994	1993
Corn	5000 bu	4,963,603	6,602,010	3,783,446	2,144,461	2,031,284
Soybeans	5000 bu	5,339,936	5,135,124	3,149,635	2,710,656	2,927,072
Oats	5000 bu	21,654	45,037	35,250	20,495	17,373
Wheat	5000 bu	1,698,969	1,886,909	1,243,567	827,930	713,670
Soybean Oil	60,000 lbs	381,193	285,274	232,635	287,905	181,938
Soybean Meal	100 tons	716,079	593,165	304,835	263,734	306,523
Rice	200,000 lbs	37,769	14,658	14,336	1,750	
Diammonium Phosphate	100 tons		50			
Crop Yield	Crop yield est. X 10	165	1,061	3,519		
Silver	1,000 oz	68	515	1,476	5,952	12,423
Eastern Catastrophe Insurance	Loss/EP x $25,000		66	3,274	7,742	2,482
Midwest Catastrophe Insurance	Loss/EP x $25,000			50	44	
National Catastrophe Insurance	Loss/EP x $25,000				1,590	4,102
Westerm Insurance-Annual	Loss/EP x $25,000				44	
PCS Castastrophe Insurance		15,706	14,688	1,064		
T-Bonds	$100,000	30,805,885	25,930,661	25,639,950	28,142,549	23,435,164
T-Notes (10 Year)	$100,000	6,032,088	7,907,650	6,887,102	6,437,215	4,844,272
T-Notes (5 Year)	$100,000	2,105,792	2,723,525	3,619,462	2,675,097	1,976,924

Volume U.S.

CHICAGO BOARD OF TRADE (CBT) (continued)

OPTION	CONTRACT UNIT	1997	1996	1995	1994	1993
T-Notes (2 Year)	$200,000	4,268	2,806	13,189	12,862	8,235
German Bund	250000	15,620				
Muni Bonds	$1,000 x Index	210,990	43,219	13,018	24,772	68,816
Brady Bond Index	$1,000 x Index		440			
Yield Curve Spread	$25,000 x 100 YCS	360	3,284			
Canadian Government Bonds	$100,000 C$				1,385	
Flexible U.S. T-Bonds		118,895	94,453	59,804	174,295	
Flexible T-Notes (10 Year)		15,910	12,735	36,425	46,606	
Flexible T-Notes (5 Year)		1,350	6,990	14,730	19,060	
Flexible T-Notes (2 Year)		200		100	250	
Dow Jones Industrial Index	$10 x Index	156,132				
Major Market Index	$500 x Index					1,368
Wilshire Small Cap Index	$500 x Index					52
Total		**52,642,632**	**51,304,320**	**45,056,867**	**43,806,394**	**36,531,698**

CHICAGO MERCANTILE EXCHANGE (CME)

OPTION	CONTRACT UNIT	1997	1996	1995	1994	1993
Live Hogs	40,000 lbs		169,214	137,435	109,448	79,046
Lean Hogs	40,000 lbs	210,429	35,831			
Live Cattle	40,000 lbs	540,804	539,523	463,455	519,813	500,664
Fluid Milk	40,000 lbs		307			
Boneless Beef	20,000 lbs 90% lean	997				
Boneless Beef Trimmings	20,000 lbs 50% lean	1,054				
Butter	50,000 lbs	479	92			
Cheddar Cheese	40,000 lbs	54				
Fluid Milk	50,000 lbs	4,078				
Pork Bellies, Frozen	40,000 lbs	29,324	52,040	21,156	24,173	32,698
Feeder Cattle	44,000 lbs	161,100	174,518	109,096	95,845	79,264
Lumber	160,000 bd ft		1,753	14,433	17,603	25,934
Orient Strand Board	100,000 bd ft	489	86			
Random Lumber	80,000 bd ft	19,826	26,922	491		
One Month LIBOR	$3,000,000	28,809	16,031	54,219	79,172	90,604
Brazilian C Bond	$500 x Index		30			
Mexican PAR Bond	$500 x Index		130			
Mexican TIIE	6,000,000	110				
Euromark (3-month)	$1,000,000					8,923
Eurodollar (3-month)	$1,000,000	29,595,246	22,234,888	22,363,853	28,145,929	17,008,764
Euroyen	100,000,000 JPY	41,577				
T-Bill (90-day)	$1,000,000		80	3,594	5,269	14,485
DM/JY Cross (New)	125,000 x dm/jy X					82
British Pound	62,500	986,950	2,886,041	1,668,624	920,109	528,239
Brazilian Real	100,000	114,464	74,106	3,700		
Deutschemark	125,000	1,411,110	1,822,649	2,642,904	4,793,639	5,916,463
Mexican Peso	500,000	186,594	13,466	1,114		
Swiss Franc	125,000	591,509	753,418	630,016	767,583	627,923
Japanese Yen	12,500,000	1,661,417	1,734,186	2,141,043	2,946,432	2,261,977
Canadian Dollar	100,000	253,075	197,741	259,857	185,652	176,930
New Zealand Dollar	100000	32				
Australian Dollar	100,000	25,465	5,785	9,892	7,800	3,482
French Franc	250,000	1,884	2,149	4,935	1,064	5,562
British Pound Rolling Spot	250,000 sterling					286
Deutschemark Rolling Spot	250,000 U.S.					420
Nikkei 225	$5 x Index	7,834	5,722	8,986	7,982	9,684
Mexican IPC Index	$25 x Index		75			
S&P 500 Index	$500 x Index	4,734,950	4,636,236	4,568,232	3,820,893	2,916,047
E-Mini S&P	$50 x S&P Index	8,661				
S&P 500 Barra Value Index	$500 x Index	1,791	4,765	30		
S&P 500 Barra Growth Index	$500 x Index	962	2,960			
S&P MidCap 400 Index	$500 x Index	3,272	2,201	5,435	3,622	5,129
FT-SE 100	$50 x FTSE Index					2
Major Market	$500 x Index	20	729	289	804	251
NASDAQ 100 Index	$500 x Index	108,922	23,992			
Dow Jones Taiwan Index	$250 x Index	146				
Russell 2000	$500 x Index	2,849	2,089	1,532	2,793	1,428
Goldman Sachs Commodity Index	$250 x GSCI	2,190	1,971	28,028	33,949	37,590
Total		**40,738,473**	**35,421,726**	**35,142,349**	**42,489,574**	**30,331,877**

COFFEE, SUGAR & COCOA EXCHANGE (CSCE)

OPTION	CONTRACT UNIT	1997	1996	1995	1994	1993
Sugar	112,000 lbs	1,369,465	1,094,879	1,203,779	1,166,748	916,170
Flexible Sugar		155				
Coffee	37,500 lbs	1,272,767	856,710	867,303	1,208,925	1,022,017
Cocoa	10 metric tons	399,408	335,173	319,513	341,131	326,760
Cheddar Cheese	40,000 lbs		4	76	150	174
Non Fat Dry Milk	44,000 lbs		21		58	296
BFP Milk		1,364				
Butter	10,000 lbs	77				
Milk	50,000 lbs	379	963	103		
Total		**3,043,615**	**2,287,750**	**2,390,774**	**2,717,012**	**2,265,417**

NEW YORK MERCANTILE EXCHANGE (NYMEX)*

COMEX DIVISION

OPTION	CONTRACT UNIT	1997	1996	1995	1994	1993
Gold	100 oz	2,064,883	2,079,663	2,006,695	1,589,065	1,717,015
5 Day Gold	100 oz		150	688	911	418
Silver	5,000 oz	842,923	949,239	1,146,513	1,316,650	1,094,702
5 Day Silver	5,000 oz		96	221	368	1,262
High Grade Copper	25,000 lbs	133,603	150,339	134,212	184,125	146,060
5 Day Copper	25,000 lbs			34	41	534
Eurotop 100 Index	$100 x Price					533
Total		**3,041,409**	**3,179,487**	**3,288,363**	**3,091,160**	**2,960,524**

NYMEX DIVISION

OPTION	CONTRACT UNIT	1997	1996	1995	1994	1993
Heating Oil	42,000 gal	1,147,034	1,108,935	703,388	699,325	803,216
Crude Oil	1,000 bbl	5,790,333	5,271,456	3,975,611	5,675,072	7,156,518
Unleaded Gasoline	1,000 bbl	1,033,778	655,965	766,557	573,502	660,886
Natural Gas	10,000 MMBTU	2,079,607	1,234,691	921,520	493,491	345,814
Alberta Natural Gas	10,000 MMBTU		15			
Gas-Crude Oil Spread	1,000 bbl	41,867	31,743	64,285	13,932	
Heating Oil-Crude Oil Spread	1,000 bbl	18,657	45,920	72,969	13,965	
Palo Verde Electricity	736 Mwh	19,328	3,964			
California Oregon Border Electricity	737 Mwh	13,495	7,650			
Platinum	50 oz	31,139	36,175	43,601	90,556	62,661
Total		**10,175,238**	**8,396,514**	**6,547,931**	**7,559,843**	**9,029,095**
Total*		**13,216,647**	**11,576,001**	**9,836,294**	**10,651,003**	**11,989,619**

KANSAS CITY BOARD OF TRADE (KCBT)

OPTION	CONTRACT UNIT	1997	1996	1995	1994	1993
Wheat	5,000 bu	99,092	65,190	75,849	89,960	87,214
Western Natural Gas	10,000 MMBtu	240	1,850	2,546		
Mini Value Line	$100 x Index	4,547	1,439	3,014	3,404	1,797
Total		**103,879**	**68,479**	**81,409**	**93,364**	**89,011**

MIDAMERICA COMMODITY EXCHANGE (MidAm)

OPTION	CONTRACT UNIT	1997	1996	1995	1994	1993
Soybeans	1,000 bu	19,594	13,689	11,908	13,498	19,062
Soybean Oil	30,000 lbs	3		5		
Soft Red Winter Wheat	5,000 bu	4,491	3,422	2,425	3,536	2,652
Corn	1,000 bu	8,904	9,753	7,296	5,765	6,274
Rough Rice	200,000 lbs				5,588	6,013
T-Bonds	$50,000	1,282	530	721	3,149	1,966
Gold	33.2 oz	63	137	772	417	39
Total		**34,337**	**27,531**	**23,127**	**31,953**	**36,006**

Volume U.S.

MINNEAPOLIS GRAIN EXCHANGE (MGE)

OPTION	CONTRACT UNIT	1997	1996	1995	1994	1993
American Spring Wheat	5,000 bu	40,383	21,126	26,893	26,441	27,822
European Spring Wheat	5,000 bu	88	44	184	284	48
Oats	5,000 bu					177
White Wheat	5,000 bu	6,320	5,175	5,333	13,556	9,009
Barley	180,000 lbs.		8			
White Shrimp	5,000 lbs	180	7	118	102	465
Black Tiger Shrimp	5,000 lbs	739	531	138	28	
Total		**47,710**	**26,891**	**32,666**	**40,411**	**37,521**

NEW YORK COTTON EXCHANGE (NYCE)**

OPTION	CONTRACT UNIT	1997	1996	1995	1994	1993
Cotton	50,000 lbs	648,154	816,550	1,416,054	816,031	372,074
Cotlook World Cotton	50,000 lbs X CWC					206
Orange Juice Frozen Concentrate	15,000 lbs	457,143	316,469	171,209	159,365	101,214
Potato	85,000 lbs.	14	26			
U.S. Dollar Index	$500 x Index	22,539	50,461	23,987	42,268	67,603
Mark Pound	$125,000 BP	3,484	9,247	116		
Mark Paris	$500,000 DM	105	1,473	570		
Mark Yen	$125,000 DM	458	2,010	160		
Mark Swiss Franc	$125,000 DM	675	7,313	33		
Mark Lira	$250,000 DM	1,637	367	354		
Dollar Mark	$125,000 DM	912	266			
U.S. Dollar / British Pound	$125,000 BP	32	22			
U.S. Dollar / Japanese Yen	$12,500,000 JY	1,225	1,209			
NYSE Composite Index	$500 x Index	81,038	48,714	26,457	26,636	29,571
PSE Tech 100	$500 x Index	8,801	2,211			
Commodity Research Bureau Index	$500 x Index	5,835	4,771	6,384	7,495	6,818
Total**		**1,232,052**	**1,261,109**	**1,645,324**	**1,051,795**	**577,486**

	1997	1996	1995	1994	1993
TOTAL OPTIONS	**111,059,345**	**101,973,807**	**94,208,810**	**100,881,506**	**81,858,635**
PERCENT CHANGE	**8.91%**	**8.24%**	**-6.61%**	**23.24%**	**18.22%**

* In August 1994, the Commodity Exchange and the New York Mercantile Exchange merged and is now listed as one exchange.

** The New York Cotton Exchange volume now includes the New York Futures Exchange volume.

Volume Worldwide

Agricultural Futures Markets (AFM), Netherlands

	1997	1996	1995	1994	1993
Live Hogs	57,069	49,986	30,877	41,382	46,117
Piglets	2,610	2,529	1,047	3,417	3,358
Wheat		536			
Potatoes	76,646	75,046	165,313	229,071	154,832
Total	**136,325**	**128,097**	**197,237**	**273,870**	**204,307**

Austrian Futures & Options Exchange (OTOB), Austria

	1997	1996	1995	1994	1993
Austrian Government Bond	107,421	151,633	176,527	124,070	43,410
ATX Index	566,459	412,047	498,234	348,291	174,095
CeCe (5 Eastern European Indices)	464,480				
Austrian Government Bond Options	5,412	6,835			
ATX Index Options	572,644	960,513	1,748,567	1,252,782	672,985
ATX LEOs (Long-term Equity Options)	4,693	43,990	71,555	9,077	
CeCe (5 Eastern European Indices) Options	43,424				
All Options on Individual Equities	1,346,990	1,266,960			
Total	**3,111,523**	**2,841,978**	**2,494,883**	**1,734,220**	**890,490**

Belgian Futures and Options Exchange (BELFOX), Belgium

	1997	1996	1995	1994	1993
Belgian Government Bonds	200,413	390,013	507,254	687,987	584,970
Belgian Medium Term Government Bond (BMB)	7,887				
BIBOR 3 Months	230,714	157,909	175,082	150,238	190,936
Bel 20 Index	551,044	326,542	187,686	154,574	12,281
Belgian Government Bonds Options	302	1,509	4,504	51,989	
Bel 20 Index Options	954,238	1,170,948	862,492	561,012	345,510
USO (Dollar/Belgian Franc)	119,251	128,548	108,471	29,546	
Gold Index Options	61,269	82,442	81,897		
All Options on Individual Equities	402,547	378,034			
Total	**2,527,665**	**2,635,945**	**1,927,386**	**1,635,346**	**1,133,697**

Bolsa Brasileira de Futuros (BBF), Brazil

(Merged with BM&F)	1997	1996	1995	1994	1993
R$/US$ Exchange Rate	5,225	41,130	22,948		
U.S. Denominated Arabica Coffee	570	7,308	6,733		
Stock Price Future Return Index	335,908	189,773			
Long Term Interest Rate		15,985	20,422		
Average Interest Rate on Interbank Deposits	7,140	58,325	78,662	999,617	
R$ (Brazilian Real)/US$ Exchange Rate Options	178,000	1,819,120	89,700		
U.S. Denominated Arabica Coffee Options		14,628	591,752		
Average Interest Rate on Interbank Deposits Options	502,820	48,213,690	127,924,464	2,049,380	
Total	**1,029,663**	**50,047,438**	**128,734,681**	**3,048,997**	

Budapest Commodity Exchange (BCE), Hungary

	1997	1996	1995	1994	1993
Milling Wheat	108,431	65,454	18,065		
Corn	77,992	44,253	16,954		
Euro Wheat	2,263				
Feed Wheat	13,693	6,179	1,790		
Feed Barley	10,330	5,982	767		
Black Seed	4,448	2,580	2,933		
BL-55 Flour		10	39		
Europe I Live Hogs	249	191	150		
Europe II Live Hogs	101	322	358		
Deutsche Mark	2,731,592	751,130	697,200		
U.S. Dollar	1,097,502	871,174	357,610		
Japanese Yen	852,629	916,857	269,826		
European Currency Unit	134,048	1,303,920	31,435		
British Pound	201,974	304,872			
Swiss Franc	849,185	419,885			
Czech Crown	2				
Italian Lira	83,692	710,455			
3 Month BUBOR	405,726	22,333			
1 Month BUBOR		135			
3 Month Hungarian Interbank Deposit Rate		1,661	2,016		
Total		**5,427,393**	**1,399,143**		

Volume Worldwide

Beijing Commodity Exchange (BCE), China

	1997	1996	1995	1994	199
Peanuts		18,875	1,957		
Greenbean	9,275,688	81,081,235	141,662,184		
Total	**9,275,688**	**81,100,110**	**141,664,141**		

Bolsa de Mercadorias & Futuros (BM&F), Brazil

	1997	1996	1995	1994	199
Arabica Coffee	114,521	116,071	76,206	79,220	87,75
Live Cattle	109,261	117,395	39,174	5,687	7,43
Sugar Crystal	8,330	6,212	4,301		
Cotton	13,689	2,339			
Corn	18,907	3,696			
Soybean Futures	16,082	20,274	3,750	11	37
Gold Futures	195,310	219,567	607,288	132,240	11,72
Gold Spot	173,752	278,476			
Bovespa Stock Index Futures	14,914,692	15,122,751	15,304,666	10,583,594	10,374,8
Interest Rate	36,466,961	49,541,598	35,152,630	28,474,764	18,996,1
Interest Rate Swap	11,660,972	6,313,852	3,592,277	6,002,555	1,860,8
Interest Rate x Exchange Rate Swap	3,504,600	2,069,329	1,500,685	3,666,097	17,47
Interest Rate x Reference Rate Swap	139,929	161,159	127,796	119,229	
Interest Rate x Inflation Index Swap (formerly Inflation)	10,324	6,486	7,601		
Interest Rate x Gold Swap	1,500				
Interest Rate x Ibovespa Swap		1			
ID x U.S. Dollar Spread Futures	52,587	99,631			
C-Bond	296,758	608,798			
El-Bond	4,060	1,850			
U.S. Dollar	40,387,111	45,132,135	74,241,367	39,231,744	7,608,6
Exchange Rate Swap	71,713	58,885	174,177	170,662	
Reference Rtae x Price Index swap		1,022			
Reference Rate x Exchange Rate Swap	1,922	328	813		
Interest Rate x FGV-100 Swap	5				
Price Index x Exchange Rate	773	564			
Robusta Coffee					[illegible]
Interest Rate x Gold Price Variation Swap (Not Guaranteed) Futures				737	
Inflation Rate Future				75,513	258,3
Interest Rate x Basic Financial Rate Swap			2		
Interest Rate Options Exercise				120	
Central Bank Bills				10	
Gold Options on Actuals	141,880	363,089	1,882,502	6,772,894	9,406,1
Gold Options Exercise	81,542	150,144	1,124,792	2,246,674	1,401,3
U.S. $ Denominated Arabica Coffee Options	3,210	14,767	2,810,322	3,290,667	1,504,7
U.S. $ Denominated Arabica Coffee Options Exercise	1,256	29,249	1,375,756	1,359,128	268,1
Live Cattle Options	392	5,882	34,240	88,428	
Live Cattle Options Exercise		1,500	38,504		
Bovespa Stock Options	359,846	201,757	74,469	11,875	
Bovespa Stock Options Exercise	31,971	15,722	1,765		
Interest Rate Options	375,435	761,541	42,200	320	
Interest Rate Options Exercise	57,390	30,550			
Interbank Deposit Rate Index Options	348,990				
Fexible Bovespa Stock Index Options	618,424	167,918			
U.S. Dollar Options on Actuals	7,211,258	5,180,578	3,338,020	588,911	359,4
U.S. Dollar Options Exercise	974,381	142,710	403,456	80,703	50,1
Flexible Currency Options	3,809,659	7,662,050	6,097,019		
Total	**122,179,393**	**134,609,876**	**148,055,778**	**102,981,783**	**52,213,6**

Budapest Stock Exchange (BSE), Hungary

	1997	1996	1995	1994	199
3 Month Hungarian T-Bills	3,409	30,933	6,333		
1 Year Hungarian T-Bills	8,126				
1 Month BUBOR	101	4,585			
3 Month BUBOR	3,679	161			
Budapest Stock Index (BUX) Futures	1,208,388	136,920	3,207		
DEM/HUF	183,470	25,429	1,407		
USD/HUF	55,116	20,439	940		
ECU/HUF	2,339	24,299	494		
Total	**1,464,628**	**242,766**	**12,381**		

Deutsche Terminborse (DTB), Germany

	1997	1996	1995	1994	1993
DAX	6,623,287	5,452,505	4,788,661	5,140,803	3,976,882
MDAX	180,668	47,865			
BUND	31,337,633	16,496,809	12,525,264	14,160,460	7,624,604
Medium Term Notional Bond (BOBL)	24,299,906	18,269,169	7,351,783	5,647,859	4,533,543
1 Month Euromark	166,936	85,519			
3 Month Euromark	964,096				
SCHATZ	4,805,755				
FIBOR		2,414	99,809	428,516	
BUXL			4,584	89,150	
DAX Options	31,521,286	26,042,463	24,299,078	23,499,552	21,419,890
BUND Options	702,882	205,520	194,036	261,110	251,859
Medium Term Notional Bond (BOBL) Options	1,640,211	663,502	123,019	46,145	54,373
Options on DAX Futures	3,415	24,544	21,073	49,642	62,976
US$/DM Options	250,783				
All Options on Individual Equities	9,667,248	10,024,170			
Total	**112,164,106**	**77,314,480**	**49,407,307**	**49,323,237**	**37,924,127**

Amsterdam Exchanges (AEX), Netherlands

(formerly European Options Exchange (EOE)	1997	1996	1995	1994	1993
AEX Stock Index (FTI)	2,554,776	2,426,699	1,004,005	1,031,333	811,882
Dutch Top 5 Index (FT5)	58,891	70,873	63,751	61,957	58,483
Eurotop 100 Index	249	31	233	435	1,102
Old U.S. Dollar/Guilder (OFUS)	16,604	7,955	14,663	13,395	22,000
US Dollar / Guilder (FUS)	323				
US Dollar / Euro (FDE)	2,987				
Guilder Bond (FTO)	6,052	21,368	8,051	14,132	70,388
Gold Options	59,871	89,779	45,283	133,412	284,040
Silver Options	4,320	7,799	5,704	5,100	
US Dollar/Guilder (FUS) Options	408,820	539,799	552,452	482,961	672,632
US Dollar / Euro (FDE) Options	270,088				
Dutch Government Bond Options	286,808	474,525	406,500	449,511	436,199
AEX Stock Index Options	8,232,719	6,039,984	3,681,781	2,851,170	2,694,680
Eurotop 100 Options	12,127	5,090	5,204	853	2,647
Dutch Top 5 Index Options	414,956	861,025	561,611	393,584	411,757
Major Market Index Options				1,563	6,227
All Options on Individual Equities	36,340,078	18,754,623			
Total	**48,669,669**	**29,299,550**	**6,349,238**	**5,439,406**	**5,472,037**

Finnish Options Market Exchange (FOM), Finland

	1997	1996	1995	1994	1993
Finnish Government Bond	374,214	291,658	125,298		
STOBOR-FRA Interest Rate		4,600			
FRA Interest Rate	1,827,730	1,167,155	4,375		
FRX Currency	8,940				
STOX Stock Future	640,268	275,172			
FOX Index	246,907	203,138	181,428		
FRX Currency Options	31,125	1,800	9,669		
FOX Index Options	684,704	404,161	521,008		
All Options on Individual Equities	1,699,591	1,143,787			
Total	**5,513,479**	**3,491,471**	**841,778**		

FUTOP Clearing Centre, Denmark

	1997	1996	1995	1994	1993
Danish Government Bonds 9% 2000		16,351	14,520		1,250
Danish Government Bonds 8% 2001	40,534	27,126			
Danish Government Bonds 8% 2003	422				
Danish Government Bonds 8% 2006	114,618	194,430	7,679		
Danish Government Bonds 7% 2004	18,962	4,789	159,778	74,220	
Danish Government Bonds 7% 2007	49,768				
6% 2026 Mortgage Bonds	44,395	58,590	54,885	172,239	28,618
7% 2029 Mortgage Bonds	390				
3 Month CIBOR	23,995	6,843	14,260	32,718	34,727
KFX Stock Index	252,571	303,856	263,537	429,466	339,024
Danish Government Bonds 9% 1995					480
Danish Government Bonds 9% 1998			8,395	103,103	185,953
Danish Government Bonds 8% 2003				343,101	391,969
9% 2022 Mortgage Bonds					1,408
All Futures on Individual Equities	39,633	6,625			

Volume Worldwide

FUTOP Clearing Centre, Denmark (continued)

	1997	1996	1995	1994	1993
Danish Government Bonds 8% 2006 Options	22,375	40,923	1,204		
Danish Government Bonds 7% 2004 Options		794	77,767	24,045	
Danish Government Bonds 7% 2007 Options	7,859				
Danish Government Bonds 9% 2000 Options					170
Danish Government Bonds 8% 2003 Options				76,548	85,580
KFX Stock Index Options	31,638	42,586	51,053	79,952	87,246
All Options on Individual Equities	34,306	44,810			
Total	**681,466**	**747,723**	**653,078**	**1,335,392**	**1,156,425**

International Petroleum Exchange (IPE), United Kingdom

	1997	1996	1995	1994	1993
Crude Oil	10,301,918	10,675,389	9,773,146	10,082,761	8,852,549
Gasoil	4,031,608	4,361,062	4,491,463	3,779,064	3,608,637
Natural Gas (NBP)	81,445				
Unleaded Gasoline			3,030	3,977	32,062
Crude Oil Options	250,176	374,233	571,308	531,742	1,059,222
Gasoil Options	68,195	110,226	116,424	136,859	217,508
Unleaded Gasoline Options					
Total	**14,733,342**	**15,520,910**	**14,955,371**	**14,534,403**	**13,769,978**

Italian Derivatives Market of the Italian Stock Exchange, Italy

	1997	1996	1995	1994	1993
MIB 30 Index	4,463,034	2,675,238	1,140,636		
MIB 30 Index Options	1,159,059	476,138	12,464		
All Options on Individual Equities	2,444,424				
Total	**8,066,517**	**3,151,376**	**1,153,100**		

Korea Stock Exchange (KSE), Korea

	1997	1996	1995	1994	1993
KOPSI 200	3,252,060	715,621			
KOPSI 200 Options	4,528,424				
Total	**7,780,484**	**715,621**			

Kuala Lumpur Commodity Exchange (KLCE), Malaysia

	1997	1996	1995	1994	1993
Crude Palm Oil	935,595	498,118	524,665	567,902	355,743
Crude Palm Kernel Oil (15 tonne)					4,474
Crude Palm Kernel Oil (25 tonne)				230	2,741
Total	**935,595**	**498,118**	**524,665**	**568,132**	**362,958**

Kuala Lumpur Options & Financial Futures Exchange, Malaysia

	1997	1996	1995	1994	1993
KLSE Composite Index	382,974	71,278			
Total	**382,974**	**71,278**			

London Metal Exchange (LME), United Kingdom

	1997	1996	1995	1994	1993
High Grade Primary Aluminum	22,484,144	14,552,878	14,060,243	14,604,218	10,083,34
Aluminum Alloy	389,558	292,429	210,787	148,685	111,45
Copper - Grade A	15,099,842	18,484,367	17,530,263	17,236,317	14,855,43
Standard Lead	2,352,731	2,202,864	1,758,742	1,942,234	1,020,57
Primary Nickel	4,627,929	3,104,514	3,319,697	3,404,942	2,118,71
Special High Grade Zinc	7,390,436	4,852,942	5,241,931	5,303,060	4,167,83
Tin	1,119,776	1,121,836	1,275,718	1,192,735	613,95
High Grade Primary Aluminum Options	1,659,879	1,030,703	1,241,596	1,231,794	900,26
Aluminum Alloy Options	535	242	96		
Copper - Grade A Options	1,732,509	1,623,575	2,212,821	2,155,587	1,156,35
Standard Lead Options	34,531	30,992	22,262	45,769	17,29
Primary Nickel Options	60,645	54,646	83,637	142,107	70,60
Special High Grade Zinc Options	285,453	126,094	177,005	253,782	163,47
Tin Options	13,005	8,925	15,532	26,487	10,63
Primary Aluminum TAPOS	47,447				
Copper TAPOS	74,080				
Total	**57,372,500**	**47,487,007**	**47,150,330**	**47,687,717**	**35,289,93**

London International Financial Futures Exchange (LIFFE), United Kingdom

(LCE merged with LIFFE in 1996)	1997	1996	1995	1994	1993
3 Month Short Sterling	20,370,846	15,793,775	15,314,576	16,603,152	12,135,981
3 Month Euromark	43,326,030	36,231,178	25,737,379	29,312,222	21,318,942
1 Month Euromark	113,408	48,644			
3 Month Eurolira	14,894,163	6,936,873	4,005,125	3,456,437	1,479,012
3 Month Euroswiss	4,746,234	3,299,058	1,749,774	1,698,736	1,846,376
3 Month ECU	534,457	602,518	693,526	622,457	720,788
3 Month Euroyen	162,686	242,413			
Long Gilt	19,651,565	15,408,010	13,796,555	19,048,097	11,808,998
German Government Bund	44,984,029	39,801,928	32,231,210	37,335,437	20,440,442
Medium Term German Government Bond (BOBL)	731,865				
Italian Government Bond	15,260,072	12,603,754	9,612,899	11,823,741	6,344,233
Japanese Government Bond	813,241	816,059	845,329	610,925	421,454
U.S. T-Bond	58,180				4,660
Financial Time Index (FT-SE 100)	3,698,368	3,627,044	3,373,259	4,227,490	3,119,971
Financial Time Index (FT-SE Mid 250 Index)	68,280	34,068	35,068	40,674	
Barley	15,325	17,892	18,088	8,072	13,479
BIFFEX (Baltic Freight Index)	45,059	60,577	74,696	47,805	43,105
Cocoa	1,857,065	1,688,921	1,653,790	1,600,746	1,908,136
U.S. Dollar Coffee	1,544,193	1,182,528	1,062,744	1,269,477	908,963
Potatoes in Bulk	22,933	21,330	27,268	36,672	23,073
Wheat	128,411	115,869	101,025	84,212	62,546
White Sugar	686,302	579,463	575,734	480,973	329,414
3 Month Eurodollar			2,720	91,738	244,728
Spanish Government Bond					28,318
German BOBL				73,043	1,049,640
3 Month Short Sterling Options	2,662,716	2,213,494	3,348,945	4,057,878	2,666,711
3 Month Euromark Options	4,225,874	4,888,942	3,427,376	2,943,936	2,906,476
3 Month Euroswiss Options	31,390	45,568	33,781	19,245	32,163
3 Month Eurolira Options	2,402,371	953,558	100,129		
Long Gilt Options	1,799,660	1,361,344	1,756,533	2,357,348	2,059,142
German Government Bond Options	10,082,217	8,462,806	6,988,655	8,574,137	4,416,480
Medium Term German Gov't Bond (BOBL) Options	196,128				
Italian Government Bond Options	2,544,870	2,456,177	1,130,762	1,030,672	602,096
U.S. T-Bond Options	6,868				2,626
Financial Times Index Options (FT-SE 100)	7,188,349	6,738,955	4,434,086	4,786,656	3,439,460
Financial Times FLEX Index Options (FT-SE 100)	32,985	65,701	60,699		
Barley Options	206	22	103	64	110
BIFFEX (Baltic Freight Index) Options	149	728	447	94	10
Cocoa Options	27,838	57,094	48,196	87,215	107,102
U.S. Dollar Coffee Options	184,975	129,844	169,130	204,945	282,263
Potatoes Options	5	35			
Wheat Options	9,326	8,758	12,907	6,866	1,769
White Sugar Options	21,062	13,268	23,016	8,196	
3 Month Eurodollar Options			2	12,400	20,015
Hi Pro Soy					7,020
Lamb					110
Raw Sugar			34,219	30,959	14,898
Pigs					2,291
Sugar (FOB)				1,104	
Hi Pro Soy Options					1
Pigs Options					25
All Options on Individual Equities	4,295,877	4,298,010			
Total	**209,425,578**	**170,805,206**	**128,678,388**	**148,726,421**	**97,108,712**

Volume Worldwide

Marche a Terme International de France (MATIF), France

	1997	1996	1995	1994	1993
CAC 40 Index	6,461,308	5,853,172	6,549,953	7,464,449	5,908,739
ECU Bond	357,094	579,493	657,152	618,715	873,002
Notional Bond	33,752,483	35,321,843	33,610,221	50,153,150	36,804,824
5-Year Bond	2,100,683				
German Notional Bond (BOBL)	2,692				
Long-Term Yield Spread	5				
3 Month Pibor	14,417,310	14,133,278	15,488,076	13,176,354	11,863,798
Potatoes	1,944	11,663	29,619	33,302	11,029
Sugar	144,849	193,024	305,598	297,940	262,940
Sugar 100	7,086				
Wheat	13,673	7,236			
Rapeseed	74,387	60,148	51,135	7,026	
French Treasury Bond					29,213
French Medium Term				63	99,260
Coffee				170	490
Notional Bond Options	8,376,474	8,894,196	9,517,932	18,024,502	11,572,671
3 Month Pibor Options	2,788,126	3,107,113	4,615,434	3,361,277	4,830,198
5-Year Bond Options	70,416				
German Notional Bond (BOBL) Options	27,147				
U.S. Dollar/French Franc Options	3,429	32,364	67,286	75,436	
U.S. Dollar/Deutschemark Options	4,871	31,637	116,127	225,497	
Sterling/Deutschemark Options	2	3,244	35,734		
Deutschemark/Italian Lira Options	3,395	12,652	11,249		
Deutschemark/French Franc Options	600	46,751	34,491		
Sugar Options	730	5,424	505		
ECU Bond Options				790	7,79[illegible]
Total	**68,608,704**	**68,293,238**	**71,090,512**	**93,438,671**	**72,263,96[illegible]**

MEFF RENTA FIJA (RF), Spain

	1997	1996	1995	1994	1993
90 Day MIBOR Plus	2,462,893	1,275,222	302,681		
360 Day MIBOR Plus	80,555	61,702	15,403		
German Diff	17,446	123,311			
French Diff		5,229			
Italian Diff	55	8,269			
3 Year Notional Bond	4,930	212,933	456	12,112	15,58[illegible]
5 Year Notional Bond	9,731				
10 Year Notional Bond	21,046,078	18,535,566	13,035,805	13,191,835	4,537,76[illegible]
90 Day MIBOR		7	3,153,112	3,730,008	2,319,13[illegible]
360 Day MIBOR			177,964	446,160	44,13[illegible]
Spanish Peseta/U.S. Dollar					2[illegible]
Spanish Peseta/Deutschemark					3,17[illegible]
3 Year Notional Bond Options	50	11,440			
10 Year Notional Bond Options	2,563,370	3,372,235	1,888,547	2,047,754	1,087,97[illegible]
90 Day MIBOR Plus Options	400,311	249,806	58,297		
90 Day MIBOR Options		75,288	450,310	307,460	139,55[illegible]
Total	**26,585,419**	**23,931,008**	**19,082,575**	**19,735,329**	**8,147,33[illegible]**

MEFF RENTA VARIABLE (RV), Spain

	1997	1996	1995	1994	1993
IBEX 35 Plus	6,053,283				
IBEX 35		2,924,367	28,096,670	2,702,089	1,085,60[illegible]
IBEX 35 Plus Options	1,411,101				
IBEX 35 Options		863,961	8,179,560	754,155	356,34[illegible]
All Options on Individual Equities	1,485,074	951,271			
Total	**8,949,458**	**4,739,599**	**3,627,630**	**3,456,244**	**1,441,95[illegible]**

Mercato Italiano Futures (MIF), Italy

	1997	1996	1995	1994	1993
10 Year BTP	2,851,585	2,240,085	2,636,161	3,702,802	2,776,992
5 Year BTP	28,585	68,697	166,002	667,115	1,637,256
RIBOR	135,414				
10 Year BTP Options	140,597	130,307	113,665		
Total	**3,156,181**	**2,439,089**	**2,915,828**	**4,369,917**	**4,414,248**

Marche des Options Negociables de Paris (MONEP), France

	1997	1996	1995	1994	1993
CAC 40 Index (Short Term) Options	6,250,090	2,465,497	2,425,363	2,755,289	2,451,512
CAC 40 Index (Long Term) Options	3,285,383	2,126,001	3,013,926	2,996,181	1,760,763
All Options on Individual Equities	5,565,057	3,980,856			
Total	**15,100,530**	**8,572,354**	**5,439,289**	**5,751,470**	**4,212,275**

Montreal Exchange (ME), Canada

	1997	1996	1995	1994	1993
3 Month Bankers Acceptance	4,139,777	2,415,563	2,326,709	1,918,976	724,158
1 Month Bankers Acceptance		314	7,225	12,172	24,552
10 Year Canadian Government Bond	1,272,970	1,072,111	1,026,854	1,496,543	895,047
5 Year Canadian Government Bond	50,944	35,649	63,842		
5 Year Canadian Government Bond Options	933	703	2,191	6,363	9,489
3 Month Bankers Acceptance Options	155,308	75,224	51,855	29,464	
10 Year Canadian Government Bond Options	23,175	30,159	40,147	51,305	61,455
All Options on Individual Equities	1,016,945	660,962			
Total	**6,660,052**	**4,290,685**	**3,518,823**	**3,514,823**	**1,714,701**

New Zealand Futures Exchange (NZFOE), New Zealand

	1997	1996	1995	1994	1993
3 Year Government Stock	46,363	15,046	26,912	101,229	74,128
10 Year Government Stock	17,965	8,565	8,456	42,541	20,996
90 Day Bank Bill	1,019,686	655,270	478,806	608,460	463,141
Trade Weighted Index	40				
NZSE-10 Captial Share Price Index	3,037	5,686	2,971		
New Zealand Electricity	4,596				
5 Year Government Stock					50,836
U.S. Dollar			19	21	9
NZSE-40 Captial Share Price Index			3,936	7,397	3,633
3 Year Government Stock Options		30		80	1,000
90 Day Bank Bill Options	1,811	8,845	16,321	6,870	8,193
NZSE-10 Captial Share Price Index Options	7	23	24		
5 Year Government Stock Options					1,652
10 Year Government Stock Options			200	4,200	120
NZSE-40 Captial Share Price Index Options			2,194	1,985	596
All Options on Individual Equities	117,669	144,207			
Total	**1,211,174**	**837,672**	**539,839**	**772,783**	**624,304**

Oslo Stock Exchange (OSE), Norway

	1997	1996	1995	1994	1993
OBr10	58,518	55,376	52,001	165,443	28,245
OBr5	33,422	50,673	49,187	43,745	
Forwards	1,630				
OBX	135,284	36,366	18,615	4,151	16,650
OBX Options	926,646	512,460	481,865	422,430	385,540
OBX Long Options			12,100	1,370	
All Options on Individual Equities	1,086,171	815,396			
Total	**2,241,671**	**1,470,271**	**613,768**	**637,139**	**430,435**

Swiss Options and Financial Futures Exchange (SOFFEX), Switzerland

	1997	1996	1995	1994	1993
Swiss Market Index	1,810,698	1,720,053	1,457,108	1,694,260	914,021
Swiss Government Bond (CONF)	638,638	913,466	955,895	949,657	270,653
Medium Term Swiss Government Bond (COMI)	20,055	42,007			
3 Month Euro Swiss Franc					353
5 Year Swiss Franc					28,548
Swiss Market Index Options	8,632,768	8,018,333	6,027,308	6,678,779	5,595,388
Swiss Government Bond Options	5,289	26,446	35,695	49,749	
All Options on Individual Equities	22,087,258	28,802,225			
Total	**33,194,706**	**39,522,530**	**8,476,006**	**9,372,445**	**6,808,963**

Volume Worldwide

Singapore International Monetary Exchange (SIMEX), Singapore

	1997	1996	1995	1994	1993
Eurodollar	7,400,058	8,184,887	8,394,933	8,687,969	5,535,806
Deutschemark			66	8,727	16,368
Japanese Yen			106	16,825	21,009
British Pound			8	1,741	3,912
Deferred Spot US$/JY	61,468	86,833	58,922	68,605	13,182
Deferred Spot US$/DM	49,264	70,651	109,181	131,210	26,298
Nikkei 225 Index	4,844,495	4,887,912	6,456,984	5,801,098	5,162,199
Nikkei 300 Index	129,695	156,482	174,234		
MSCI Taiwan Index	677,295				
Gold		133		26	436
High Sulfur Fuel Oil	1,766	42	19,421	171,896	300,201
Brent Crude	33,067	63,535	73,445		
Euroyen	9,624,680	8,162,548	6,549,295	6,820,673	3,532,998
Euromark			1,800	231,068	23,127
Japanese Government Bond	132,104	138,471	297,426	443,564	29,253
MSCI Hong Kong Index				317	80,245
Gasoil					23,288
Eurodollar Options	7,825	3,319	5,247	13,545	6,525
Euroyen Options	481,138	208,363	128,944	126,280	57,395
Japanese Government Bond Options	11,658	18,709	35,071	39,808	
Nikkei 225 Index Options	628,222	58,660	1,943,096	1,496,922	897,545
Nikkei 300 Index Options			3,160		
MSCI Taiwan Index Options	7,550				
Total	**24,090,285**	**22,568,545**	**24,251,339**	**24,060,274**	**15,729,787**

South African Futures Exchange (SAFEX), Africa

	1997	1996	1995	1994	1993
All Share Index	2,599,489	1,943,973	1,816,846	2,185,672	1,670,540
Industrial Index	1,960,260	1,493,987	1,030,714	920,786	422,203
Financial Index	3,710	10,080	4,290		
Gold Index	491,351	603,205	656,696	933,591	895,772
Krugerrand		4,152	5,901	5,664	
3 Month Bank Bill	106	1,360	5,154	3,901	2,135
R 150	8,489	37,982	30,472	1,750	
R 153	5,924	101			
E168 (Long Bond)			530	8,495	6,903
All Share Index Options	4,873,560	3,759,424	2,932,564	2,804,855	1,236,263
Industrial Index Options	1,282,555	913,342	481,053	377,593	148,101
Financial Index Options	3,533	11,168			
Gold Index Options	248,765	1,015,065	195,720	132,230	102,136
Krugerrand Options			203	3,300	
R 150 Options	10,467	26,682	29,683		
R 153 Options	20,085	2,060			
3 Month Bank Bill Options			820		
E168 (Long Bond) Options			60	100	920
Total	**11,508,294**	**9,822,581**	**7,218,914**	**7,377,937**	**4,484,973**

OM Stockholm (OMS), Sweden

	1997	1996	1995	1994	1993
Interest Rate	12,704,397	15,642,920	10,949,860	14,123,881	11,272,285
Interest Rate Index	46	3,434			
OMSX Index		130			
OMX Index	2,163,560	1,625,391	1,593,408	1,706,984	627,706
Financial Times Index (FT-SE Mid 250)				9,565	
All Futures on Individual Equities	288,841	272,514			
Interest Rate Options	5,846	32,825	42,783	86,410	
OMSX Index Options		274			
OMX Index Options	3,545,967	5,399,227	6,067,268	5,812,435	4,073,852
Financial Times Index (FT-SE Mid 250) Options				2,140	
All Options on Individual Equities	19,485,816	12,920,145			
Total	**38,194,473**	**35,896,860**	**18,653,319**	**21,741,415**	**15,973,843**

Sydney Futures Exchange (SFE), Australia

	1997	1996	1995	1994	1993
ll Ordinaries Share Price Index	3,204,266	2,675,754	2,476,331	2,552,546	980,866
) Day Bank Bills	5,918,447	4,977,945	6,172,512	9,369,008	6,415,394
Year Treasury Bonds	10,378,357	9,209,228	8,820,651	9,709,791	6,939,811
) Year Treasury Bonds	5,819,677	5,315,845	5,740,870	6,814,733	4,781,905
SW Electricity	1,191				
IC Electricity	1,129				
/ool (Cash Set)			1,221	4,833	3,271
/heat	7,937	6,482			
reasy Wool	10,127	7,554	4,799		
ifty Leaders Share Price Index				1	1
ll Futures on Individual Equities	29,157	54,463			
ll Ordinaries Share Price Index Options	896,340	896,880	652,607	833,667	466,896
0 Day Bank Bills Options	984,363	911,005	712,834	943,749	663,317
Year Treasury Bond Options	418,081	457,808	426,836	507,252	514,539
vernight 3 Year Treasury Bond Options	43,540	42,461	7,443	2,078	320
0 Year Treasury Bonds Options	545,359	845,571	580,091	800,263	712,686
vernight 10 Year Treasury Bond Options	149,817	128,426	24,419	18,656	2,082
/heat Options	1,740	788			
reasy Wool Options	11	41			
Total	**28,409,539**	**25,530,251**	**25,620,614**	**31,556,584**	**21,481,096**

Toronto Futures Exchange (TFE), Canada

	1997	1996	1995	1994	1993
SE 35 Index	317,408	155,652	110,011	104,209	69,058
SE 100 Index	19,317	8,135	2,963	10,819	
SE 35 Options	431,623	254,199	337,764	247,482	221,232
SE 100 Index Options	51	845	7,824	13,200	
ilver Options			656	8,300	4,583
Total	**768,399**	**418,831**	**459,218**	**384,010**	**294,877**

Winnipeg Commodity Exchange (WCE), Canada

	1997	1996	1995	1994	1993
Vheat	197,619	206,120	155,699	191,696	210,074
)ats	3,205	3,496	32,761	52,550	59,244
;anadian Barley			18,523	31,600	4,150
₹ye			104	1,022	7,829
laxseed	140,756	99,889	132,525	105,338	104,110
;anola (Rapeseed)	1,387,675	1,345,952	1,075,683	1,167,447	972,354
eed Peas	14,247	17,979	7,802		
Vestern Barley	284,614	334,809	172,733	115,376	40,248
hunder Bay Barley				5,378	63,643
Vheat Options	250	355	734	3,145	5,274
laxseed Options	66	466	1,567	1,692	4,907
;anadian Barley Options			435		80
Vestern Barley Options	959	3,166	274	1,716	10
;anola Options	31,810	61,233	71,197	82,565	44,121
Total	**2,061,201**	**2,073,465**	**1,670,037**	**1,759,525**	**1,615,044**

Hong Kong Futures Exchange (HKFE), Hong Kong

	1997	1996	1995	1994	1993
lang Seng Index	6,446,696	4,656,084	4,546,613	4,192,574	2,415,739
Red-Chip Index	143,078				
)eutschemark Rolling Forex	121,173	76,075	12,633		
lapanes Yen Rolling Forex	109,578	106,888	8,688		
3ritish Pound Rolling Forex	20,475	12,392			
3 Month HIBOR	87,819				
3old				490	972
All Futures on Individual Equities	4,453				
lang Seng Index Options		1,093,871	645,538	606,674	282,283
Red-Chip Index Options	1,234				
Total	**8,081,880**	**5,945,310**	**5,213,472**	**4,799,738**	**2,698,994**

Volume Worldwide

Kanmon Commodity Exchange (KCE), Japan

	1997	1996	1995	1994	1993
Red Beans	95,982	118,438	237,745	492,294	579,751
Imported Soybeans	1,382,063	496,376	130,520	213,271	486,850
Refined Sugar	1,421	1,438	1,449	1,432	1,437
Corn	5,069,142	4,346,586	2,890,258	1,709,248	1,077,057
Total	**6,548,608**	**4,962,838**	**3,259,972**	**2,416,245**	**2,145,095**

Kansai Agricultural Commodities Exchange (KANEX), Japan

	1997	1996	1995	1994	1993
Red Beans	483,330	877,474	1,723,230	2,931,256	3,092,743
Imported Soybeans	4,022,023	2,656,174	1,695,414	1,298,180	2,113,812
Refined Sugar	2,842	2,876	2,886	2,864	2,874
Raw Sugar	643,742	577,641	730,582	664,683	1,063,480
Raw Silk (formerly at Kobe Raw Silk Exchange)	327,009	458,243	591,922	695,172	687,723
Raw Sugar Options	47,189	71,145	79,365	63,789	26,793
Total	**5,526,135**	**4,643,553**	**4,823,399**	**5,655,944**	**6,987,425**

KOBE Rubber Exchange (KRE), Japan

	1997	1996	1995	1994	1993
Total		**2,606,706**	**3,984,347**	**2,933,883**	**1,275,051**

Maebashi Dried Cocoon Exchange (MDCE), Japan

	1997	1996	1995	1994	1993
Dried Cocoon	565,423	864,703	443,411	475,978	1,782,394
Total	**565,423**	**864,703**	**443,411**	**475,978**	**1,782,394**

Chubu Commodity Exchange (CCE), Japan

(formerly NGSE, NTE, and TDCE)	1997	1996	1995	1994	1993
Red Beans	241,008	287,220	502,369	919,371	1,217,337
Sweet Potato Starch	48	48	48	48	48
Imported Soybeans	1,010,201	620,703	307,451	177,513	287,612
Refined Sugar	1,421	1,438	1,449	1,789	2,874
Dried Cocoon	684,141	1,202,536	488,709	488,558	1,066,374
Cotton Yarn (40S)	126,684	296,455	755,844	1,100,388	822,683
Staple Fiber Yarn (Dull)	9,948	10,001	9,967	13,114	18,279
Wool Yarn	35,315	27,277	53,811	87,240	79,114
Total	**2,108,766**	**2,445,678**	**2,119,648**	**2,788,021**	**3,494,321**

Osaka Securities Exchange(OSE), Japan

	1997	1996	1995	1994	1993
Nikkei 225 Index	7,484,182	7,043,977	7,220,900	6,208,754	8,461,458
Nikkei 300 Index	1,526,538	1,872,983	2,318,652	4,184,480	
Nikkei 225 Index Options	4,910,359	3,924,543	5,174,571	4,273,641	6,090,375
Nikkei 300 Index Options	7,798	44,254	122,084	269,067	
All Options on Individual Equities	222,094				
Total	**14,150,971**	**12,885,757**	**14,836,207**	**14,935,942**	**14,551,833**

Osaka Mercantile Exchange (OME), Japan

(formerly KRE and OTE)	1997	1996	1995	1994	1993
Staple Fiber Yarn (Bright)	687	3,109	4,128	3,507	2,928
Staple Fiber Yarn (Dull)	4,952	2,928	2,940	2,910	2,928
Wool Yarn	22,589	18,624	64,073	266,974	524,699
Cotton Yarn (20S)	1,245,452	1,109,607	2,151,580	2,000,530	648,345
Cotton Yarn (40S)	147,444	254,828	659,110	833,307	574,724
Rubber (RSS3)	1,200,850	2,232,827	3,810,938	2,933,883	1,275,051
Rubber Index	382,913	373,879	173,409		
Aluminum	160,060				
Total	**3,164,947**	**3,995,802**	**6,866,178**	**6,041,111**	**3,028,675**

Tokyo Commodity Exchange (TOCOM), Japan

	1997	1996	1995	1994	1993
Gold	8,871,965	9,510,941	10,945,134	12,481,095	8,764,441
Silver	792,844	752,995	1,440,297	1,042,185	661,452
Platinum	10,839,577	6,895,464	5,975,872	4,551,406	4,984,480
Palladium	3,817,892	434,163	629,034	774,284	2,275,843
Aluminum	567,175				
Rubber	4,758,390	9,085,709	14,287,783	9,021,881	2,973,241
Cotton Yarn	524,717	874,052	1,838,448	2,573,963	1,865,469
Woolen Yarn	5,789	6,830	8,859	36,499	32,869
Total	**30,178,349**	**27,560,154**	**35,125,427**	**30,481,313**	**21,557,795**

Tokyo Grain Exchange (TGE), Japan

	1997	1996	1995	1994	1993
American Soybeans	9,966,257	7,120,741	2,699,926	2,559,288	3,750,291
Red Beans	2,542,760	2,847,511	3,384,267	5,122,015	6,353,667
Corn	13,840,721	16,034,716	6,899,593	3,053,244	1,263,357
Refined Sugar	2,842	2,876	2,898	2,864	2,874
Raw Sugar	1,279,550	1,045,438	1,291,441	1,220,931	2,218,688
American Soybean Options	263,990	275,269	206,993	96,505	60,420
Corn Options	44,220				
Raw Sugar Options	186,698	182,724	158,044	67,636	38,450
Total	**28,127,038**	**27,509,275**	**14,643,162**	**12,122,483**	**13,687,747**

Tokyo International Financial Futures Exchange (TIFFE), Japan

	1997	1996	1995	1994	1993
3 Month Euroyen	25,523,583	29,334,830	36,329,959	37,425,846	23,386,958
1 Year Euroyen		23,200	25,300	25,100	4,434
U.S. Dollar /Japanese Yen	63,755	44,194	5,037	13,770	48,241
Euroyen Options	535,895	567,793	361,920	570,237	686,514
Total	**26,123,233**	**29,970,017**	**36,722,216**	**38,034,953**	**24,126,147**

Tokyo Stock Exchange (TSE), Japan

	1997	1996	1995	1994	1993
5 Year Government Yen Bond	118,447	220,955			
10 Year Government Yen Bond	11,873,549	12,450,925	14,010,374	12,999,698	15,162,159
20 Year Government Yen Bond	2,167	2,242	2,734	3,194	3,106
TOPIX Stock Index	3,035,724	2,857,272	2,745,614	2,623,067	2,156,960
30 Year U.S. T-Bond	30,650	31,030	102,340	115,750	112,600
TOPIX Options	9,356	13,444	16,742	20,078	37,831
10 Year Government Yen Bond Options	2,002,357	1,975,274	2,017,031	1,691,834	1,506,836
Total	**17,072,250**	**17,551,142**	**16,877,804**	**15,761,787**	**17,472,656**

Yokohama Raw Silk Exchange, Japan

	1997	1996	1995	1994	1993
Raw Silk	658,176	1,083,386	1,256,094	998,686	1,512,132
Total	**658,176**	**1,083,386**	**1,256,094**	**998,686**	**1,512,132**

	1997	1996	1995	1994	1993
TOTAL FUTURES	**756,538,888**	**703,482,637**	**783,168,145**	**637,865,283**	**428,375,632**
PERCENT CHANGE	**7.54%**	**-1.68%**	**0.35%**	**48.67%**	**37.99%**
TOTAL OPTIONS	**268,531,426**	**271,860,316**	**265,921,807**	**141,969,616**	**109,987,845**
PERCENT CHANGE	**-1.22%**	**-26.70%**	**87.30%**	**27.21%**	**18.18%**
TOTAL	**1,025,070,314**	**975,342,953**	**1,049,089,952**	**779,834,899**	**538,363,477**
PERCENT CHANGE	**5.10%**	**-8.03%**	**16.18%**	**44.29%**	**33.46%**

Conversion Factors

Commonly Used Agricultural Weights and Measurements

Bushel Weights:
wheat and soybeans = 60 lbs.
corn, sorghum and rye = 56 lbs.
barley grain = 48 lbs.
barley malt = 34 lbs.
oats = 32 lbs.

Bushels to tonnes:
wheat and soybeans = bushels X 0.027216
barley grain = bushels X 0.021772
corn, sorghum and rye = bushels X 0.0254
oats = bushels X 0.014515

1 tonne (metric ton) equals:
2204.622 lbs.
1,000 kilograms
22.046 hundredweight
10 quintals

1 tonne (metric ton) equals:
36.7437 bushels of wheat or soybeans
39.3679 bushels of corn, sorghum or rye
45.9296 bushels of barley grain
68.8944 bushels of oats
4.5929 cotton bales (the statistical bale used by the USDA and ICAC contains a net weight of 480 pounds of lint)

Area Measurements:
1 acre = 43,560 square feet = 0.040694 hectare
1 hectare = 2.4710 acres = 10,000 square meters
640 acres = 1 square mile = 259 hectares

Yields:
wheat: bushels per acre X 0.6725 = quintals per hectare
rye, corn: bushels per acre X 0.6277 = quintals per hectare
barley grain: bushels per acre X 0.538 = quintals per hectare
oats: bushels per acre X 0.3587 = quintals per hectare

Commonly Used Weights

The troy, avoirdupois and apothecaries' grains are identical in U.S. and British weight systems, equal to 0.0648 gram in the metric system. One avoirdupois ounce equals 437.5 grains. The troy and apothecaries' ounces equal 480 grains, and their pounds contain 12 ounces.

Troy weights and conversions:
24 grains = 1 pennyweight
20 pennyweights = 1 ounce
12 ounces = 1 pound
1 troy ounce = 31.103 grams
1 troy ounce = 0.0311033 kilogram
1 troy pound = 0.37224 kilogram
1 kilogram = 32.1507 troy ounces
1 tonne = 32,151 troy ounces

Avoirdupois weights and conversions:
27 11/32 grains = 1 dram
16 drams = 1 ounce
16 ounces = 1 lb.
1 lb. = 7,000 grains
14 lbs. = 1 stone (British)
100 lbs. = 1 hundredweight (U.S.)
112 lbs. = 8 stone = 1 hundredweight (British)
2,000 lbs. = 1 short ton (U.S. ton)
2,240 lbs. = 1 long ton (British ton)
160 stone = 1 long ton
20 hundredweight = 1 ton
1 lb. = 0.4536 kilogram
1 hundredweight (cwt.) = 45.359 kilograms
1 short ton = 907.18 kilograms
1 long ton = 1,016.05 kilograms

Metric weights and conversions:
1,000 grams = 1 kilogram
100 kilograms = 1 quintal
1 tonne = 1,000 kilograms = 10 quintals
1 kilogram = 2.204622 lbs.
1 quintal = 220.462 lbs.
1 tonne = 2204.6 lbs.
1 tonne = 1.102 short tons
1 tonne = 0.9842 long ton

U.S. dry volumes and conversions:
1 pint = 33.6 cubic inches = 0.5506 liter
2 pints = 1 quart = 1.1012 liters
8 quarts = 1 peck = 8.8098 liters
4 pecks = 1 bushel = 35.2391 liters
1 cubic foot = 28.3169 liters

U.S. liquid volumes and conversions:
1 ounce = 1.8047 cubic inches = 29.6 milliliters
1 cup = 8 ounces = 0.24 liter = 237 milliliters
1 pint = 16 ounces = 0.48 liter = 473 milliliters
1 quart = 2 pints = 0.946 liter = 946 milliliters
1 gallon = 4 quarts = 231 cubic inches = 3.785 liters
1 milliliter = 0.033815 fluid ounce
1 liter = 1.0567 quarts = 1,000 milliliters
1 liter = 33.815 fluid ounces
1 imperial gallon = 277.42 cubic inches = 1.2 U.S. gallons = 4.546 liters

ENERGY CONVERSION FACTORS

U.S. Crude OIl (average gravity)
1 U.S. barrel = 42 U.S. gallons
1 short ton = 6.65 barrels
1 tonne = 7.33 barrels

Barrels per tonne for various origins

Abu Dhabi	7.624
Algeria	7.661
Angola	7.206
Australia	7.775
Bahrain	7.335
Brunei	7.334
Canada	7.428
Dubai	7.295
Ecuador	7.58
Gabon	7.245
Indonesia	7.348
Iran	7.37
Iraq	7.453
Kuwait	7.261
Libya	7.615
Mexico	7.104
Neutral Zone	6.825
Nigeria	7.41
Norway	7.444
Oman	7.39
Qatar	7.573
Romania	7.453
Saudi Arabia	7.338
Trinidad	6.989
Tunisia	7.709
United Arab Emirates	7.522
United Kingdom	7.279
United States	7.418
Former Soviet Union	7.35
Venezuela	7.005
Zaire	7.206

Barrels per tonne of refined products:

aviation gasoline	8.9
motor gasoline	8.5
kerosene	7.75
jet fuel	8
distillate, including diesel	7.46

(continued above)

residual feul oil	6.45
lubricating oil	7
grease	6.3
white spirits	8.5
paraffin oil	7.14
paraffin wax	7.87
petrolatum	7.87
asphalt and road oil	6.06
petroleum coke	5.5
bitumen	6.06
LPG	11.6

Approximate heat content of refined products:
(Million Btu per barrel, 1 British thermal unit is the amount of heat required to raise the temperature of 1 pound of water 1 degree F.)

Petroleum Product	**Heat Content**
asphalt	6.636
aviation gasoline	5.048
butane	4.326
distillate fuel oil	5.825
ethane	3.082
isobutane	3.974
jet fuel, kerosene	5.67
jet fuel, naptha	5.355
kerosene	5.67
lubricants	6.065
motor gasoline	5.253
natural gasoline	4.62
pentanes plus	4.62

Petrochemical feedstocks:

naptha less than 401*F	5.248
other oils equal to or greater than 401*F	5.825
still gas	6
petroleum coke	6.024
plant condensate	5.418
propane	3.836
residual fuel oil	6.287
special napthas	5.248
unfinished oils	5.825
unfractionated steam	5.418
waxes	5.537

Source: U.S. Department of Energy

Natural Gas Conversions

Although there are approximately 1,031 Btu in a cubic foot of gas, for most applications, the following conversions are sufficient:

Cubic Feet					**MMBtu**
1,000	(one thousand cubic feet)	=	1 Mcf	=	1
1,000,000	(one million cubic feet)	=	1 MMcf	=	1,000
10,000,000	(ten million cubic feet)	=	10 MMcf	=	10,000
1,000,000,000	(one billion cubic feet)	=	1 Bcf	=	1,000,000
1,000,000,000,000	(one trillion cubic feet)	=	1 Tcf	=	1,000,000,000

Aluminum

The U.S. Geological Survey reported that U.S. primary aluminum production increased slightly in 1996 to 3.6 million metric tonnes. Thirteen companies operated 22 primary aluminum reduction plants and one plant remained closed. Aluminum recovered from purchased scrap increased to 3.3 million tonnes. Of the total, 52 percent came from new manufacturing scrap while the remainder was from old scrap of discarded aluminum products. Aluminum from beverage cans accounted for about one-half of the reported old scrap consumption in 1996. The largest domestic markets for aluminum products were transportation and the container and packaging industries. Other uses were the building and construction industry and electrical and consumer durables.

World inventory levels of aluminum at the end of 1996 were mixed. Inventories at the London Metal Exchange (LME) were higher while world producer stocks were lower. U.S. inventories were slightly lower. Primary aluminum was produced in 44 countries in 1996. World production was estimated at 20.7 million tonnes, up four percent from the 1995 total. The U.S. was by far the largest producer with 1996 output of 3.58 million tonnes, up six percent from 1995. The next largest producer was Russia with 1996 output of 2.8 million tonnes, up almost three percent from 1995. The third largest producer of primary aluminum was Canada with output of 2.28 million tonnes, up five percent. Other large producers are China, Australia and Brazil.

U.S. primary aluminum production in July 1997 was 305,000 tonnes, up from 296,000 tonnes in June 1997. In the January-July 1997 period, primary aluminum production was 2.09 million tonnes which was slightly higher than the comparable period in 1996. U.S. secondary recovery of new aluminum in July 1997 was 168,000 tonnes compared to 161,000 tonnes in June 1997. In the first seven months of 1997, secondary recovery of aluminum was 1.13 million tonnes, up from 1.03 million tonnes a year before. Secondary recovery of old aluminum in July 1997 was 141,000 tonnes, up from 135,000 tonnes in June 1997. For the January-July 1997 period, secondary recovery of old aluminum was 971,000 tonnes, up close to ten percent from the same period of 1996.

U.S. imports for consumption of crude aluminum metals and alloys in June 1997 were 167,000 tonnes. That was down 16 percent from June 1997. In the first six months of 1997, imports of crude aluminum metals and alloys were 1.06 million tonnes. Imports for consumption of aluminum plates, sheets, bars and other materials in June 1997 were 47,000 tonnes, down from 49,000 tonnes the month before. In the first six months of 1997, imports of plates, sheets, bars and other aluminum materials were 271,000 tonnes. Total new supplies of aluminum, including primary production, secondary recovery and imports for consumption in June 1997 were 806,000 tonnes, down five percent from the previous month.

U.S. stocks of aluminum, including scrap, at the end of June 1997 were 1.79 million tonnes. That was up slightly from stocks at the end of May 1997. At the end of 1996, U.S. aluminum stocks were 1.83 million tonnes. U.S. exports of aluminum in June 1997 were 131,000 tonnes. Exports of crude metals and alloys were 34,900 tonnes. Exports of aluminum plates, sheets, bars and other materials were 69,300 tonnes. Scrap exports in June 1997 were 27,200 tonnes.

Futures Markets

Aluminum futures and options are listed on the London Metals Exchange (LME).

World Production of Primary Aluminum In Thousands of Metric Tons

Year	Australia	Brazil	Canada	China	France	Germany	Norway	Russia[3]	Spain	United Kingdom	United States	Venezuela	World Total
1988	1,150	874	1,534	710	328	753	864	2,400	323	300	3,944	437	17,548
1989	1,244	890	1,555	750	335	796	863	3,300	352	297	4,030	540	19,010
1990	1,230	931	1,570	850	326	740	845	3,523	353	294	4,050	590	19,300
1991	1,228	1,140	1,822	963	286	690	833	3,251	355	294	4,121	601	19,700
1992	1,236	1,193	1,972	1,100	418	603	838	2,700	359	244	4,042	561	19,500
1993	1,381	1,172	2,308	1,220	426	552	887	2,820	356	239	3,695	568	19,800
1994	1,317	1,185	2,255	1,450	384	505	858	2,670	338	231	3,299	585	19,200
1995[1]	1,297	1,188	2,172	1,870	365	575	847	2,722	362	238	3,375	630	19,900
1996[2]	1,372	1,190	2,282	1,780	365	577	874	2,800	362	240	3,577	600	20,700

[1] Preliminary. [2] Estimate. [3] Formerly part of the U.S.S.R.; data not reported separately until 1992. *Source: U.S. Geological Survey (USGS)*

Production of Primary Aluminum (Domestic and Foreign Ores) in the U.S. In Thousands of Metric Tons

Year	Jan.	Feb.	Mar.	Apr.	May	June	July	Aug.	Sept.	Oct.	Nov.	Dec.	Total
1988	320	304	330	324	336	323	334	333	327	339	332	344	3,944
1989	346	312	347	334	347	335	346	341	323	328	328	343	4,030
1990	345	311	345	331	342	330	340	341	332	347	337	347	4,048
1991	349	317	352	340	353	343	354	350	336	347	337	343	4,121
1992	344	320	343	330	342	330	339	340	330	343	335	347	4,043
1993	335	292	323	313	325	315	316	302	291	303	287	294	3,696
1994	292	261	286	269	277	268	275	274	267	277	270	280	3,296
1995	281	253	280	272	285	277	288	286	280	289	285	299	3,375
1996	301	283	303	293	303	293	301	302	292	304	295	305	3,577
1997[1]	305	277	307	295	304	296	305	304	294	307	295	305	2,996

[1] Preliminary. *Source: U.S. Geological Survey (USGS)*

ALUMINUM

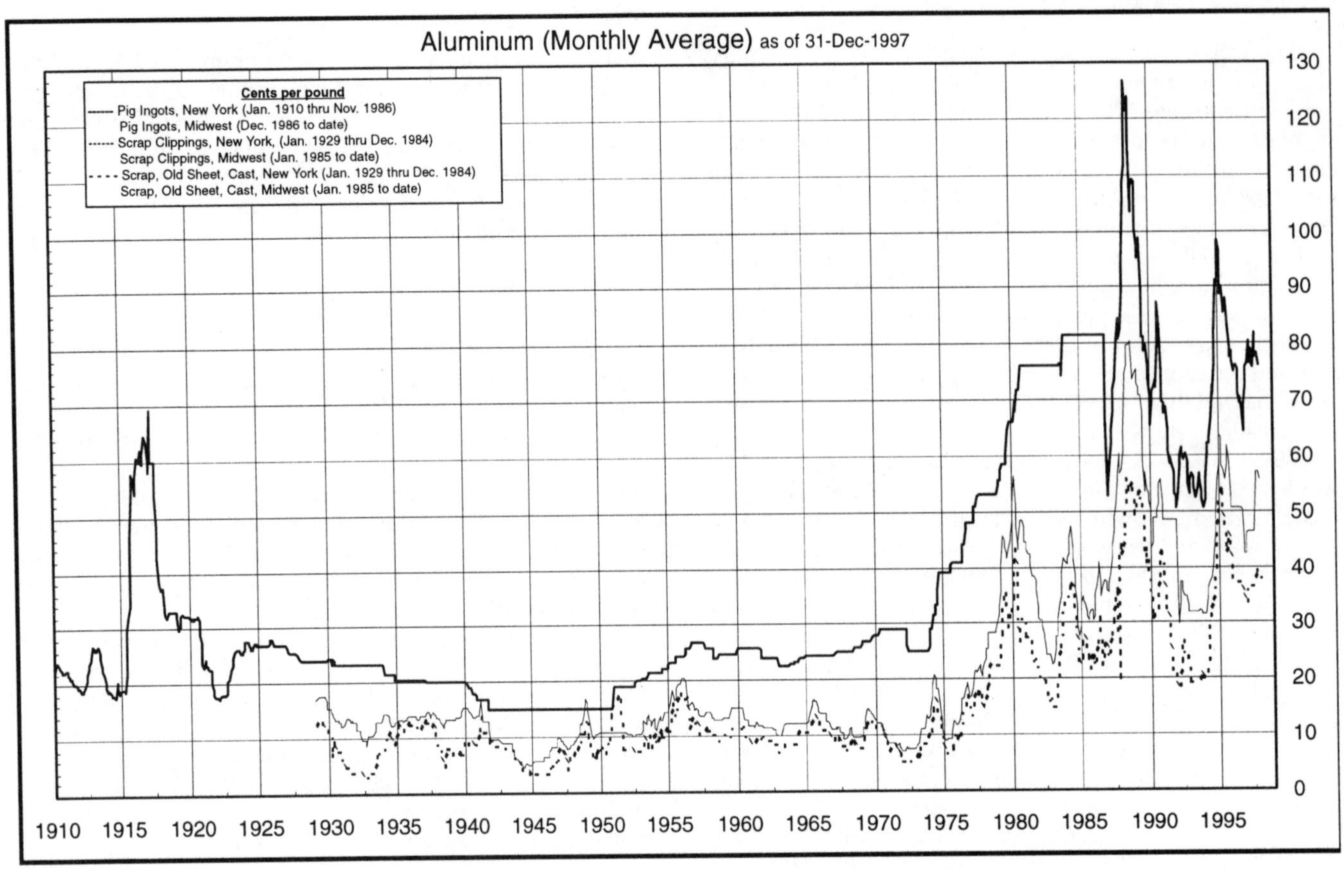

Salient Statistics of Aluminum in the United States   In Thousands of Metric Tons

								Net Shipments[5] by Producers								
								Wrought Products				Castings				
Year	Net Import Reliance as a % of Apparent Consumption	Production Primary	Production Secondary	Primary Shipments[2]	Recovery from Scrap Old	Recovery from Scrap New	Apparent Consumption	Plate Sheet, Foil	Rolled Structural Shapes[3]	Extruded Shapes[4]	All	Permanent Mold	Die	Sand	All	Total All Net Shipments
1987	23	3,343	1,986	6,813	852	1,134	5,469	3,740	346	1,351	5,549	181	685	113	1,012	6,562
1988	7	3,944	2,122	6,851	1,045	1,077	5,373	3,787	343	1,341	5,589	201	700	115	1,055	6,621
1989	E	4,030	2,054	6,751	1,011	1,043	4,957	3,900	339	1,280	5,633	210	740	110	1,096	6,728
1990	E	4,048	2,390	6,590	1,360	1,030	5,260	3,799	301	1,211	5,425	208	620	103	968	6,393
1991	E	4,121	2,290	6,400	1,320	969	5,040	3,787	311	1,096	5,300	168	575	97	864	6,156
1992	1	4,042	2,760	6,810	1,610	1,140	5,730	4,097	303	1,186	5,691	198	595	99	804	6,609
1993	19	3,695	2,940	7,300	1,630	1,310	6,600	4,030	297	1,300	5,770	225	645	103	994	6,770
1994	30	3,299	3,090	8,160	1,500	1,580	6,880	4,810	296	1,420	6,690	247	551	208	1,050	7,740
1995	23	3,375	3,190	8,260	1,510	1,680	6,320	4,900	526	1,540	7,130	442	627	207	1,440	8,580
1996[1]	21	3,577	3,290	8,260	1,570	1,710	6,620	4,370	352	1,550	6,430	NA	NA	NA	NA	NA

[1] Preliminary. [2] To domestic industry. [3] Also rod, bar & wire. [4] Also rod, bar, tube blooms & tubing. [5] Consists of total shipments less shipments to other mills for further fabrication. NA = Not available. E = Net exporter. *Source: U.S. Geological Survey (USGS)*

Supply and Distribution of Aluminum in the United States   In Thousands of Metric Tons

Year	Apparent Consumption	Production Primary	Production From Old Scrap	Imports	Exports	Inventories December 31 Private	Inventories December 31 Government[3]	Year	Apparent Consumption	Production Primary	Production From Old Scrap	Imports	Exports	Inventories December 31 Private	Inventories December 31 Government[3]
1985	5,174	3,500	850	1,420	908	2,343	2	1991	5,040	4,121	1,320	1,490	1,762	1,780	2
1986	5,143	3,037	784	1,967	753	2,235	2	1992	5,730	4,042	1,610	1,725	1,453	1,880	57
1987	5,469	3,343	852	1,850	917	2,000	2	1993	6,600	3,695	1,630	2,540	1,210	1,980	57
1988	5,373	3,944	1,045	1,620	1,247	1,883	2	1994	6,880	3,299	1,500	3,380	1,370	2,070	57
1989	4,957	4,030	1,011	1,470	1,615	1,822	2	1995[1]	6,320	3,375	1,510	2,970	1,610	2,000	57
1990	5,260	4,048	1,360	1,514	1,659	1,820	2	1996[2]	6,620	3,577	1,570	2,810	1,500	1,830	57

[1] Preliminary. [2] Estimate. *Source: U.S. Geological Survey (USGS)*

Aluminum Products Distribution of End-Use Shipments in the United States In Thousands of Metric Tons

Year	Building & Construction	Consumer Durables	Containers & Packaging	Electrical	Exports	Machinery & Equipment	Trans-portation	Other	Total
1987	1,441	576	2,052	620	569	401	1,500	223	7,382
1988	1,316	588	2,036	671	787	435	1,536	269	7,638
1989	1,294	544	2,112	663	1,060	436	1,448	264	7,821
1990	1,208	509	2,157	594	1,131	452	1,388	261	7,700
1991	1,052	472	2,210	579	1,357	426	1,414	241	7,752
1992	1,144	523	2,259	587	1,236	448	1,591	256	8,045
1993	1,240	563	2,180	609	1,090	477	1,970	259	8,390
1994	1,400	647	2,270	682	1,200	572	2,310	276	9,360
1995	1,220	621	2,310	657	1,310	570	2,610	279	9,570
1996[1]	1,310	633	2,180	665	1,290	567	2,630	281	9,550

[1] Preliminary. *Source: U.S. Geological Survey (USGS)*

World Consumption of Primary Aluminum In Thousands of Metric Tons

Year	Brazil	Canada	China	France	Ger-many	India	Italy	Japan	Rep. of Korea	Russia	United Kingdom	United States	World Total
1987	430.3	423.1	727.0	615.6	1,185.7	326.0	548.0	1,696.8	207.9	2,830.0	383.6	4,546.2	18,137.5
1988	324.2	437.1	658.0	660.6	1,232.6	327.0	581.0	2,123.2	268.0	2,900.0	427.4	4,601.9	18,877.9
1989	420.1	450.2	920.0	685.5	1,289.1	420.0	607.0	2,211.6	287.6	2,700.0	454.7	4,381.4	19,281.1
1990	341.2	387.2	861.0	720.9	1,295.4	433.3	652.0	2,415.2	368.9	2,790.0	453.7	4,330.4	19,275.4
1991	354.2	408.2	938.0	734.2	1,360.9	430.2	670.0	2,431.6	383.5	2,409.0	412.4	4,137.2	18,778.2
1992	377.1	420.4	1,253.8	722.8	1,457.1	414.3	660.0	2,271.6	397.0	1,352.0	483.3	4,616.9	18,475.4
1993	378.9	486.6	1,318.0	665.0	1,300.0	475.3	554.0	2,138.3	524.8	767.0	475.0	4,877.1	18,278.7
1994	413.8	532.8	1,484.0	735.0	1,501.5	415.0	660.0	2,345.8	603.9	585.9	500.0	5,407.1	19,723.9
1995	500.2	532.4	1,859.9	747.0	1,715.6	469.1	668.1	2,443.4	692.6	590.0	500.0	5,054.8	20,114.7
1996[1]	499.6	598.6	2,033.1	706.0	1,323.2	576.4	585.0	2,492.0	703.0	-----	600.0	5,400.0	20,320.2

[1] Preliminary. *Source: American Metal Market (AMM)*

Salient Statistics of Recycling Aluminum in the United States

Year	Percent Recycled	New Scrap[1]	Old Scrap[2]	Recycled Metal[3]	Apparent Supply	New Scrap	Old Scrap	Recycled Metal	Apparent Supply
		In Thousands of Metric Tons				Value in Millions of Dollars			
1987	30	1,134	852	1,986	6,603	1,807	1,358	3,165	10,524
1988	33	1,077	1,045	2,122	6,450	2,614	2,536	5,150	15,654
1989	34	1,043	1,011	2,054	6,000	2,020	1,958	3,978	11,620
1990	38	1,034	1,359	2,393	6,298	1,688	2,218	3,906	10,280
1991	38	969	1,320	2,290	6,010	1,270	1,730	3,000	7,880
1992	40	1,140	1,610	2,760	6,870	1,450	2,040	3,500	8,710
1993	37	1,310	1,630	2,940	7,920	1,540	1,920	3,460	9,300
1994	36	1,580	1,500	3,090	8,460	2,480	2,360	4,840	13,300
1995	40	1,680	1,510	3,190	8,010	3,190	2,850	6,040	15,200
1996	39	1,710	1,570	3,290	8,340	2,690	2,470	5,160	13,100

[1] Scrap that results from the manufacturing process. [2] Scrap that results from consumer products. [3] Metal recovered from new plus old scrap.
Source: U.S. Geological Survey (USGS)

Producer Prices for Aluminum Used Beverage Can Scrap In Cents Per Pound

Year	Jan.	Feb.	Mar.	Apr.	May	June	July	Aug.	Sept.	Oct.	Nov.	Dec.	Average
1987	37.15	39.93	42.59	44.50	47.40	50.55	52.73	54.50	54.36	57.14	55.50	59.45	49.65
1988	65.80	70.50	72.93	72.50	72.50	72.50	72.50	71.63	66.21	63.92	61.50	64.93	68.95
1989	72.64	73.76	73.15	69.50	71.55	66.59	57.92	55.50	54.68	55.50	54.30	51.50	63.05
1990	48.50	45.50	47.55	50.50	50.77	50.50	49.71	51.13	57.53	52.15	48.00	44.67	49.71
1991	49.00	49.11	48.67	42.09	37.86	37.00	39.79	37.50	37.50	35.76	35.18	34.50	40.33
1992	35.38	38.32	40.73	43.91	44.40	41.50	41.50	41.69	39.93	38.07	38.00	38.68	40.18
1993	41.00	41.00	38.04	36.63	35.00	35.00	37.52	37.59	36.50	34.19	33.60	34.78	36.74
1994	38.45	43.08	42.50	46.60	45.50	48.98	56.40	56.00	56.00	62.64	70.40	71.00	53.13
1995	74.85	72.24	65.00	65.00	65.00	65.00	65.00	67.98	64.80	58.45	57.00	58.50	64.91
1996	57.73	56.00	56.24	58.90	59.00	49.70	47.50	49.25	50.20	48.50	49.03	53.50	52.96

Source: American Metal Market (AMM)

ALUMINUM

Average Price of Cast Aluminum Scrap (Crank Cases) in Chicago   In Cents Per Pound

Year	Jan.	Feb.	Mar.	Apr.	May	June	July	Aug.	Sept.	Oct.	Nov.	Dec.	Average
1990	34.68	30.50	30.77	32.50	32.50	32.50	35.93	37.50	41.97	42.50	40.58	39.00	35.91
1991	33.50	32.00	32.00	30.64	28.45	22.40	21.50	21.50	21.13	19.00	18.11	18.00	24.85
1992	18.71	23.00	26.91	27.00	24.45	24.00	24.00	24.00	21.21	19.50	19.50	19.50	22.65
1993	19.50	19.50	19.50	19.50	19.50	19.50	20.79	21.00	20.62	20.00	20.00	20.00	19.95
1994	20.00	25.79	28.33	32.50	32.50	33.18	35.90	36.50	41.07	44.45	50.50	53.50	36.19
1995	53.53	54.08	49.02	48.50	44.41	42.50	43.76	45.80	45.05	39.27	37.50	37.50	45.08
1996	37.50	37.50	37.50	37.50	37.50	37.50	37.50	36.50	35.40	33.80	33.50	33.50	36.27
1997	36.09	36.50	36.50	36.50	36.50	36.50	36.50	39.36	38.60	38.50	38.50	38.07	37.34

Source: American Metal Market (AMM)

Aluminum Products (Ingot and Mill Products) Shipments[1] in the United States   In Million Pounds

Year	Jan.	Feb.	Mar.	Apr.	May	June	July	Aug.	Sept.	Oct.	Nov.	Dec.	Total
1990	1,234	1,154	1,313	1,224	1,355	1,318	1,257	1,272	1,224	1,247	1,098	1,120	14,761
1991	1,177	1,087	1,261	1,244	1,313	1,287	1,387	1,389	1,276	1,371	1,265	1,241	15,298
1992	1,324	1,280	1,376	1,298	1,277	1,339	1,330	1,333	1,361	1,453	1,333	1,360	16,081
1993	1,251	1,291	1,486	1,408	1,377	1,440	1,296	1,410	1,382	1,306	1,364	1,284	16,294
1994	1,584	1,620	2,007	1,679	1,895	1,758	1,679	1,934	1,744	1,760	1,868	1,811	20,295
1995	1,632	1,472	1,704	1,594	1,605	1,576	1,368	1,493	1,533	1,571	1,469	1,404	18,422
1996	1,420	1,457	1,555	1,642	1,735	1,564	1,516	1,661	1,510	1,639	1,473	1,451	18,623
1997[2]	1,199	1,175	1,293	1,320	1,326	1,319	1,267	1,301	1,320	1,299	1,158		13,976

[1] Mills products & pig & ingot (net shipments). [2] Preliminary. *Source: Bureau of the Census, U.S. Department of Commerce*

Aluminum Inventories of Ingot, Mill Products and Scrap in the U.S., on First of Month   In Million Pounds

Year	Jan.	Feb.	Mar.	Apr.	May	June	July	Aug.	Sept.	Oct.	Nov.	Dec.
1990	4,016	4,019	4,035	3,914	3,974	3,808	3,916	4,070	3,980	4,040	4,119	4,013
1991	4,013	4,068	4,169	4,256	4,212	4,135	4,044	3,990	4,028	4,008	3,992	3,923
1992	3,913	4,321	4,346	4,375	4,411	4,486	4,482	4,333	4,376	4,418	4,336	4,263
1993	4,093	4,124	4,179	4,250	4,274	4,327	4,398	4,417	4,387	4,360	4,294	3,020
1994	4,372	4,646	4,758	4,778	4,784	4,790	4,725	4,659	4,637	4,605	4,540	4,551
1995	4,572	4,710	4,845	4,691	4,743	4,745	4,639	4,691	4,594	4,403	4,366	4,346
1996	4,403	4,382	4,481	4,433	4,451	4,327	4,358	4,318	4,216	4,174	4,061	4,030
1997[1]	4,040	4,033	3,993	3,990	3,966	3,989	4,045	4,026	4,029	4,032	4,105	

[1] Preliminary. *Source: Bureau of the Census, U.S. Department of Commerce*

Aluminum Exports of Crude Metal and Alloys from the United States   In Cents Per Pound

Year	Jan.	Feb.	Mar.	Apr.	May	June	July	Aug.	Sept.	Oct.	Nov.	Dec.	Total
1990	79.0	65.1	55.3	61.4	41.4	48.6	41.5	39.0	53.6	59.6	62.2	76.0	679.8
1991	61.1	54.8	46.7	82.8	56.4	71.3	69.0	80.1	54.6	68.0	80.7	67.3	792.8
1992	50.8	43.8	49.7	38.6	33.6	39.8	50.0	50.3	40.4	82.1	50.5	73.5	603.1
1993	54.8	38.6	41.7	26.3	38.6	30.7	33.9	24.5	27.9	31.7	24.1	27.6	400.4
1994	22.1	18.3	28.3	17.9	37.5	30.5	30.6	38.3	40.3	24.8	26.1	24.1	338.9
1995	26.1	32.7	25.4	31.1	31.4	20.7	26.6	39.2	38.9	33.0	30.4	33.6	369.1
1996	23.1	27.9	31.2	34.3	46.2	54.3	36.3	33.7	30.2	40.3	33.2	26.2	416.9
1997[1]	31.0	25.5	22.5	33.0	24.1	34.9	23.9	33.2	34.4				262.5

[1] Preliminary. *Source: U.S. Geological Survey (USGS)*

Aluminum General Imports of Crude Metal and Alloys into the United States   In Cents Per Pound

Year	Jan.	Feb.	Mar.	Apr.	May	June	July	Aug.	Sept.	Oct.	Nov.	Dec.	Total
1990	84.4	73.4	85.4	85.1	90.4	94.0	102.6	82.1	76.4	66.8	58.7	60.6	959.6
1991	79.5	79.4	84.3	88.2	85.1	75.9	97.3	89.0	86.6	90.4	81.0	88.0	1,024.7
1992	100.7	93.1	97.1	94.6	96.3	87.8	82.4	103.4	94.3	108.4	100.5	96.8	1,155.4
1993	120.8	123.9	165.8	172.0	152.1	152.6	125.1	162.7	173.5	149.4	182.9	155.6	1,836.4
1994	200.2	157.8	282.0	206.9	251.9	179.3	202.8	198.3	160.0	183.4	240.1	222.2	2,484.9
1995	214.0	168.0	204.0	195.0	184.0	172.0	136.0	134.0	117.0	137.0	139.0	133.0	1,933.0
1996	158.0	150.0	148.0	188.0	176.0	169.0	139.0	149.0	136.0	170.0	147.0	180.0	1,910.0
1997[1]	145.0	147.0	209.0	196.0	198.0	167.0	157.0	152.0	150.0				1,521.0

[1] Preliminary. *Source: U.S. Geological Survey (USGS)*

Antimony

Antimony is primarily a byproduct of mining, smelting and refining of other metals, primarily lead and silver-copper ores. It finds use in flame retardants, fabrics, plastics and ammunition. Reductions in the use of antimonial lead are an indication that demand for antimony is shifting from metal products to plastics and pigments. Most antimony is found in Idaho, Nevada, Alaska and Montana.

According to the U.S. Geological Survey, domestic primary smelter production of antimony increased in 1996, but consumption of primary antimony declined slightly. The estimated distribution of primary antimony uses in the U.S. was: flame retardants, 62 percent; transportation including batteries, 15 percent; chemicals, 10 percent; ceramics and glass, 8 percent; and other uses, 5 percent.

A small amount of antimony is recovered as a byproduct of the smelting of domestic lead and silver-copper ores, but almost all primary antimony metal and oxide produced domestically originated from imports. Primary antimony metal and oxide were produced by six companies operating six plants using domestic and foreign feed material. Two plants were in Texas, one each in Idaho, Montana, Nebraska and New Jersey.

U.S. production of primary smelter antimony trioxide in the second quarter of 1997 was 6,210 metric tonnes, antimony content. That was up very slightly from the first quarter's production total. For all of 1996, primary smelter production of antimony trioxide was 25,700 tonnes. Secondary lead smelting produced 562 tonnes of antimony in the second quarter of 1997, about the same as the first quarter. For all of 1996, secondary antimony production was 7,900 tonnes.

U.S. imports for consumption of antimony ore and concentrate in the first half of 1997 were 503 tonnes, antimony content. For all of 1996 they were 1,000 tonnes. U.S. imports of antimony metal for consumption in the January-June 1997 period were 7,460 tonnes while for all of 1996 they were 18,300 tonnes. Antimony oxide imports for consumption were 9,300 tonnes, antimony content, in first half 1997, and 18,300 tonnes for all of 1996. U.S. consumption of primary antimony in the second quarter of 1997 was 3,160 tonnes, down from 3,240 tonnes in the first quarter. For all of 1996, U.S. consumption of primary antimony was 13,100 tonnes, antimony content.

World Mine Production of Antimony (Content of Ore) In Metric Tons

Year	Australia	Bolivia	Canada	China[2]	Guatemala	Kyrgyzstan[4]	Mexico[5]	Peru[6]	Russia[4]	South Africa	Thailand	Turkey	World Total
1993	1,700	5,556	673	60,000	600	2,500	1,469	240	8,000	4,111	620	111	87,800
1994	1,700	7,050	750	91,000	600	2,000	267	460	6,000	4,534	500	75	117,000
1995[1]	900	6,426	574	125,000	610	1,500	-----	460	6,000	5,537	230	100	154,000
1996[2]	1,300	6,600	1,405	98,000	610	1,200	-----	460	6,000	4,800	250	100	126,000

[1] Preliminary. [2] Estimate. [3] Formerly part of Czechoslovakia, data not reported separately until 1993. [4] Formerly part of the USSR; data not reported separately until 1992. [5] Includes antimony content of miscellaneous smelter products. [6] Recoverable W=Withheld proprietary data. *Source: U.S. Geological Survey*

Salient Statistics of Antimony in the United States In Metric Tons

Year	Avg. Price ¢ per lb. CIF U.S. Ports	Production[3]: Primary[2] Mine	Production[3]: Primary[2] Smelter	Production[3]: Secondary (Alloys)[2]	Imports for Consumption: Ore Gross Weight	Imports for Consumption: Ore Antimony Content	Imports for Consumption: Oxide (Gross Weight)	Exports (Oxide)	Industry Stocks, December 31[3]: Metallic	Oxide	Sulfide	Residues & Slag	Total[4]
1993	76.9	266	22,000	9,620	1,720	543	19,322	3,896	2,790	3,320	20	W	9,080
1994	177.7	215	25,500	12,200	7,680	5,640	21,300	6,500	2,770	5,000	W	W	10,900
1995[1]	227.8	262	23,500	10,500	6,140	4,260	18,600	6,950	2,450	4,450	W	W	10,600
1996[2]	146.6	242	25,700	7,900	1,610	1,000	18,300	3,990	3,480	4,330	W	W	11,200

[1] Preliminary. [2] Estimate. [3] Antimony content. [4] Including primary antimony residues & slag. W = Withheld proprietary data
Source: U.S. Geological Survey (USGS)

Industrial Consumption of Primary Antimony in the United States In Metric Tons (Antimony Content)

Year	Metal Products: Ammunition	Antimonial Lead	Sheet & Pipe	Bearing Metal & Bearings	Solder	Total All Metal Products	Flame Retardents: Plastics	Flame Retardents: Total	Non-Metal Products: Ceramics & Glass	Pigments	Plastics	Total	Grand Total
1993	W	1,110	W	44	242	2,810	5,440	7,250	848	489	786	2,310	12,400
1994	W	1,990	W	36	183	3,740	6,690	8,570	980	369	1,030	2,490	14,800
1995	W	2,230	W	53	192	3,760	6,690	7,800	1,080	492	1,090	2,770	14,300
1996[1]	W	1,760	W	44	255	3,110	6,830	7,770	1,030	450	1,080	2,690	13,600

[1] Preliminary. [2] Estimated coverage based on 77% of the industry. W=Withheld proprietary data. *Source: U.S. Geological Survey (USGS)*

Average Price of Antimony[1] in the United States In Cents Per Pound

Year	Jan.	Feb.	Mar.	Apr.	May	June	July	Aug.	Sept.	Oct.	Nov.	Dec.	Average
1994	73.00	73.00	78.04	87.50	111.07	153.75	182.50	235.00	250.00	260.00	288.00	293.00	173.74
1995	293.00	293.00	284.00	284.00	201.00	142.00	188.00	240.00	244.00	213.00	170.00	170.00	226.83
1996	153.00	152.50	152.50	150.12	142.50	142.50	132.50	127.50	127.50	127.50	127.50	127.50	138.59

[1] Prices are for antimony metal (99.65%) merchants, minimum 18-ton containers, c.i.f. U.S. Ports. *Source: American Metal Market (AMM)*

Apples

The USDA forecasts U.S. apple production in the 1997-98 (July-June) marketing year at 4.7 million metric tonnes, slightly above a year ago. There were improved production prospects in the eastern and central states which offset prospects in the western states.

Apple production in the western states in the 1997-98 season is forecast to be 3 million tonnes which is 6 percent less than a year ago. Most of the decline is in Washington state, the largest apple producer. The Washington crop was forecast to decline 5 percent to 2.4 million tonnes. Washington produces about half the U.S. apple crop.

Production of apples in 1997-98 in the central states is forecast at 635,030 tonnes which is 32 percent above the 1996-97 crop. Michigan, the major producing state in the central region, is forecast to produce 454,000 tonnes or some 38 percent more than in 1996-97. Apple production in the eastern states is forecast by USDA at 1.1 million tonnes, 6 percent above a year ago. New York, the second largest U.S. producing state was forecast to have a crop up 9 percent from last season at 508,000 tonnes. There was favorable weather late in the season. U.S. apple exports in 1997-98 were forecast to decline by 9 percent to 610,000 tonnes.

World Production of Apples[3], Fresh (Dessert & Cooking) In Thousands of Metric Tons

Year	Argentina	Canada	France	Germany	Hungary	Italy	Japan	Netherlands	South Africa	Spain	Turkey	United States	World Total
1987	925	506	1,985	1,077	1,064	2,273	998	340	526	971	1,680	4,873	20,922
1988-9	1,030	501	1,935	2,467	1,131	2,443	1,042	383	534	845	1,950	4,140	22,662
1989-90	1,050	538	1,818	1,727	959	2,162	1,045	417	557	747	1,850	4,519	21,654
1990-1	950	540	1,895	2,222	945	2,102	1,053	431	542	635	1,900	4,398	21,224
1991-2	1,043	513	1,236	1,165	859	1,869	760	223	605	517	1,900	4,413	18,250
1992-3	947	564	2,398	3,228	666	2,394	1,039	640	633	1,095	2,100	4,798	35,443
1993-4	1,006	488	2,079	1,719	819	2,145	1,011	670	638	891	2,080	4,847	36,505
1994-5	1,146	554	2,166	2,080	610	2,153	989	590	577	739	2,095	5,217	37,712
1995-6[1]	1,147	591	2,089	1,373	353	1,889	963	595	703	843	2,100	4,801	38,773
1996-7[2]	1,276	560	2,049	1,776	475	2,100	936	490	675	875	2,100	4,733	42,265

[1] Preliminary. [2] Estimate. [3] Commercial crop. [4] Formerly part of Yugoslavia; data not reported separately until 1992. NA = Not available.
Source: Foreign Agricultural Service, U.S. Department of Agriculture (FAS-USDA)

Salient Statistics of Apples[2] in the United States

Year	Production: Total	Production: Utilized	Growers Prices: Fresh ¢ Lb.	Growers Prices: Processing $ Ton	Utilization of Quantities Sold: Fresh	Processed[5]: Canned	Processed[5]: Dried	Processed[5]: Frozen	Processed[5]: Juice & Cider	Processed[5]: Other[3]	Avg. Farm Price ¢ Per Lb.	Farm Value Million $	Foreign Trade[4]: Domestic Exports Fresh	Foreign Trade[4]: Domestic Exports Dried[5]	Foreign Trade[4]: Imports Fresh & Dried[5]	Fresh Per Capita Consumption Lbs.
	Millions of Pounds												Metric Tons			
1987	10,742	10,451	12.7	79.3	5,610	1,306	284	249	2,929	74	8.6	903.1	296.2	7.7	132.7	20.8
1988	9,120	9,070	17.4	123.0	5,230	1,399	285	266	1,824	67	12.7	1,147.8	254.5	12.0	133.0	19.9
1989	9,917	9,871	13.9	107.0	5,822	1,320	282	322	2,068	57	10.4	1,024.6	357.4	23.7	119.7	21.2
1990	9,657	9,618	20.9	144.0	5,515	1,378	270	304	2,077	74	15.1	1,447.7	371.3	55.5	122.0	19.6
1991	9,707	9,637	25.1	171.0	5,447	1,311	299	286	2,194	100	17.9	1,727.0	530.1	44.2	143.9	18.2
1992	10,569	10,463	19.5	130.0	5,767	1,498	324	247	2,472	155	13.6	1,428.0	487.8	22.1	139.3	19.2
1993	10,685	10,574	18.4	107.0	6,124	1,335	366	282	2,382	85	12.9	1,363.9	662.9	19.2	130.9	19.2
1994	11,501	11,331	18.6	114.0	6,366	1,406	415	304	2,707	133	12.9	1,467.1	663.1	25.1	115.8	19.6
1995	10,585	10,390	24.0	159.0	5,843	1,292	334	305	2,538	78	17.0	1,765.6	611.3	-----	154.4	18.9
1996[1]	10,355	10,304	20.9	176.0	6,304	1,215	310	241	2,169	65	16.2	1,670.4	590.7	-----	182.3	19.3

[1] Preliminary. [2] Commercial crop. [3] Mostly crushed for vinegar, jam, etc. [4] Year beginning July. [5] Fresh weight basis. *Source: Economic Research Service, U.S. Department of Agriculture (ERS-USDA)*

Average Price of Apples Received by Growers (for Fresh Use) in the United States In Cents Per Pound

Year	Jan.	Feb.	Mar.	Apr.	May	June	July	Aug.	Sept.	Oct.	Nov.	Dec.	Average
1988	11.1	12.9	12.5	11.0	10.9	10.4	22.8	27.7	23.7	18.5	17.5	17.4	16.4
1989	18.1	17.9	16.5	14.4	13.5	10.8	11.5	15.9	16.7	14.3	13.3	12.1	14.6
1990	12.2	12.4	12.3	12.0	12.6	13.7	20.3	22.3	22.2	19.3	19.6	20.9	16.7
1991	20.1	20.5	20.3	20.2	22.5	23.2	24.6	23.2	26.4	23.8	25.1	25.7	23.0
1992	24.6	24.8	24.3	24.1	25.0	25.2	28.6	33.3	27.1	21.2	19.4	19.9	24.8
1993	18.3	16.7	14.5	14.3	14.9	16.1	17.8	24.4	24.1	21.1	19.3	18.6	18.3
1994	18.7	17.8	16.6	15.5	14.3	13.5	19.4	29.0	20.8	19.2	16.4	19.2	18.4
1995	19.5	18.3	18.2	16.6	15.4	15.6	17.5	24.5	26.0	25.1	23.5	24.0	20.4
1996	25.4	24.2	25.1	22.6	21.9	21.9	23.3	25.2	30.2	24.6	23.2	22.6	24.2
1997[1]	22.5	20.3	17.6	15.5	14.3	14.6	14.1	19.0	24.7	25.3	22.9	23.7	19.5

[1] Preliminary. *Source: Economic Research Service, U.S. Department of Agriculture (ERS-USDA)*

Arsenic

According to the U.S. Geological Survey, the United States was the world's largest consumer of arsenic in 1996. The U.S. accounts for about two-thirds of world demand. U.S. demand for arsenic metals and compounds has remained relatively stable for the last four years, averaging about 2,000 metric tonnes of contained arsenic per year. All domestic arsenic requirements are met by imports. On a contained metal basis, arsenic trioxide accounted for 99 percent of imports in 1996. China is the world's leading producer of both arsenic trioxide as well as arsenic metal.

The largest market for arsenic in the U.S. is in the production of arsenical wood preservatives. Demand for arsenic is closely tied to the home construction market. Wooden decks use arsenical preservatives. Because arsenic is a toxic substance, there are questions about how much it will be used in the future in the construction industry. There appears to be a greater acceptance of alternative preservatives which could affect the use of arsenic in the coming years.

Where arsenic does appear to have a future is in the rapidly growing semiconductor industry. It is here that high-purity arsenic, which is 99.9999 percent pure or greater, is finding increased use. In the production of integrated circuits, gallium arsenide is being used as it has unique properties. One of the more important ones is the ability to operate at higher speeds or frequencies. This is becoming of critical importance in the communications industry where there are increasing demands to move more information at higher speeds. Integrated circuits made with gallium arsenide have better signal reception. Additionally, gallium arsenide integrated circuits have lower power consumption.

While gallium arsenide has a number of advantages, there are also disadvantages. These include higher costs than silicon due in part to less availability of arsenide. Additionally, arsenide is a deadly element leading to environmental and safety concerns.

U.S. imports of arsenic metal in 1996 were 252 tonnes, arsenic content. That was down significantly from 557 tonnes in 1995. In 1996, China supplied 212 tonnes with Japan and Germany supplying smaller amounts of arsenic metal. Imports of arsenic compounds in 1996 were 21,200 tonnes, arsenic content, which was down 4 percent from 1995. The total U.S. supply of arsenic in 1996 was 21,400 tonnes.

Of the total supply of 21,400 tonnes, demand for wood preservatives used 19,200 tonnes or 90 percent of the total. Agricultural chemicals used 950 tonnes while glass production used 700 tonnes. Use in nonferrous alloys and electronics consumed 250 tonnes. Other uses took 300 tonnes, arsenic content, in 1996.

U.S. imports for consumption of arsenic trioxide in 1996 were 28,000 tonnes, down from 29,000 tonnes in 1995. The major supplier was China with 11,000 tonnes followed by Chile with 8,790 tonnes. Other major suppliers of arsenic trioxide are Mexico and France. The U.S. imported one metric ton of arsenic acid in 1996.

World production of arsenic trioxide in 1996 was estimated at 42,100 tonnes, down 13 percent from 1995. In 1996, the major producer of arsenic trioxide was China with 15,000 tonnes, down from 21,000 tonnes in 1995. The next largest producer was Chile with 9,000 tonnes, up sharply from 6,400 tonnes in 1995. Mexico produced 4,300 tonnes in 1996 followed by France with output of 3,000 tonnes.

World Production of White Arsenic (Arsenic Trioxide) In Metric Tons

Year	Belgium	Bolivia	Canada[4]	Chile	China	France	Germany	Mexico	Namibia[3]	Peru	Phillippines	Russia[5]	World Total
1989	3,500	338	1,825	5,000	7,000	10,000	360	5,551	2,399	563	4,652	8,100	61,026
1990	3,000	300	485	5,830	9,000	6,480	360	4,810	1,640	500	5,090	7,800	53,400
1991	2,500	463	236	6,820	10,000	2,000	300	4,920	1,800	661	5,000	7,000	46,000
1992	2,000	633	250	6,020	15,000	2,000	300	4,293	2,456	644	5,000	2,500	45,800
1993	2,000	663	250	6,200	14,000	3,000	300	4,447	2,290	391	2,000	2,000	41,700
1994	2,000	341	250	6,300	18,000	6,000	300	4,400	3,047	286	2,000	1,500	47,600
1995[1]	2,000	362	250	6,400	21,000	5,000	250	4,500	1,661	285	2,000	1,500	48,200
1996[2]	2,000	370	250	9,000	15,000	3,000	250	4,300	1,100	285	2,000	1,500	42,100

[1] Preliminary. [2] Estimate. [3] Output of Tsumeb Corp. Ltd. only. [4] Includes low-grade dusts that were exported to the U.S. for further refining. [5] Formerly part of the U.S.S.R.; reported seperately until 1992. *Source: U.S. Geological Survey (USGS)*

Salient Statistics of Arsenic in the United States In Metric Tons (Arsenic Content)

	Supply				Distribution		Estimated Demand Pattern						Average Price			
	Imports												Trioxide	Metal		
Year	Metal	Compounds	Industry Stocks Jan. 1	Total	Apparent Demand	Industry Stocks Dec. 31	Agricultural Chemicals	Glass	Wood Preservatives	Non-Ferrous Alloys & Electric	Other	Total	Mexican (¢ Per Pound)	Chinese (¢ Per Pound)	Imports Trioxide[3]	Exports
1989	928	21,498	100	22,526	22,300	100	4,900	900	15,600	700	200	22,300	27	47	28,348	126
1990	796	19,900	100	20,796	20,500	100	4,200	800	14,400	800	300	20,500	23	180	26,256	149
1991	1,010	20,700	100	21,810	21,600	----	5,000	900	14,300	1,000	400	21,600	25	68	27,142	233
1992	740	23,300	----	24,040	23,900	----	3,900	900	17,900	800	400	23,900	29	56	30,671	94
1993	767	20,900	----	21,667	21,300	----	3,000	900	16,200	800	400	21,300	33	44	27,500	364
1994	1,330	20,300	----	21,630	21,500	----	1,200	700	18,000	1,300	300	21,500	32	40	26,800	79
1995[1]	557	22,100	----	22,657	22,300	----	1,000	700	19,600	600	400	22,300	33	66	29,000	430
1996[2]	252	21,200	----	21,452	21,400	----	950	700	19,200	250	300	21,400	33	40	28,000	36

[1] Preliminary. [2] Estimate. [3] For Consumption. *Source: U.S. Geological Survey (USGS)*

Barley

World barley production declined steadily from the mid-1980's into the mid-1990's, but the slide has since slowed. Production in 1997/98 of 154.9 million metric tonnes compares with 153.1 in 1996/97 and average production in the early 1990's of 165 million tonnes. Collectively, the E.U. is the largest producing area with 52.5 million tonnes in 1997/98, unchanged from 1996/97. Russia, once the world's largest producer, had seen a steady drop in production from 27 million tonnes in 1992/93 to 15.9 million in 1996/97, but due to a higher average yield output jumped to an estimated 21 million tonnes in 1997/98 which if realized would reinstate Russia as the top producer. Canada is a close second with 13.5 million tonnes in 1997/98 vs. 15.6 million in 1996/97, the decline reflecting a drop in average yield. In the U.S., barley is the third largest produced feed grain but only accounts for 5 percent of total world production.

The slippage in world barley use may have also bottomed; the total of 153.2 million tonnes in 1997/98 compares with 149.7 million in 1996/97 and more than 165 million early in the 1990's. The 1997/98 supply/demand forecasts are expected to increase ending world carryover to 24.9 million tonnes vs. 23.3 a year earlier. World stocks formerly averaged over 30 million tonnes consistently.

The U.S. barley crop year begins June 1. Production peaked in the 1980's as producers found returns more favorable to wheat and sunflower crops. Barley production in 1997/98 of 374 million bushels compares with 395.7 million in 1996/97 and record low 359.6 million in 1995/96. In 1997/98, average yield per acre of 58.3 bushels was marginally under 1996/97, but the harvested acreage of 6.4 million acres was down 5percent. North Dakota is the largest producer followed by four other states whose combined production accounted for 75 percent of the 1997/98 crop.

U.S. disappearance in 1997/98 of 427 million bushels compares with 422 million in 1996/97. Feed and residual use were estimated at 185 million bushels vs. 219 million in 1996/97. Industrial use, mostly for beer and alcohol, is forecast as unchanged at 172 million bushels. Exports may rise to 70 million vs. 31 million in 1996/97, the lowest total so far of the 1990's. Imports are up marginally, estimated at 40 million bushels, most of which is malting quality barley from Canada. Carryover stocks on May 31, 1998 of 97 million bushels compare with the year earlier 110 million.

World barley trade was forecast at 16.3 million metric tonnes in 1997/98, unchanged from 1996/97. The European Union exports almost a third of the total with Canada and Australia much of the balance. Importing countries are numerous, but Saudi Arabia is foremost with 6 million tonnes in 1997/98, followed by China with 2.2 million.

U.S. farmer's barley prices were forecast to average $2.25-$2.65 per bushel in 1997/98 vs. $2.74 in 1996/97.

Futures Markets

Barley futures and options are traded on the Winnipeg Commodity Exchange (WCE) and the London Commodity Exchange (LCE). Futures are traded on the Budapest Commodity Exchange.

World Barley Supply and Demand In Thousands of Metric Tons

	Exports						Imports			Utilization				Ending Stocks		
Crop Year	Australia	Canada	EC-12	Total Non-U.S.	U.S.	Total Exports	Saudi Arabia	Unaccounted	Total Imports	Production	Russia[3]	U.S.	Total Utilization	Canada	U.S.	Total Stocks
1988-9	1,364	3,419	8,349	14,137	1,718	15,855	4,714	-12	15,855	162,722	44,245	7,540	162,536	2,800	4,276	30,674
1989-90	2,447	3,773	7,905	15,905	1,798	17,703	4,146	467	17,703	164,761	22,433	8,030	167,440	2,056	3,501	28,789
1990-1	2,683	4,460	7,053	17,016	1,507	18,523	4,342	742	18,523	178,056	29,156	8,283	174,898	2,646	2,948	32,317
1991-2	1,951	3,379	9,459	16,929	2,090	19,019	6,873	77	19,019	169,136	25,635	8,735	165,833	2,615	2,800	32,471
1992-3	2,600	2,859	5,816	15,084	1,611	16,695	3,917	807	16,695	165,767	28,368	7,916	166,065	3,271	3,292	31,923
1993-4	4,232	3,789	6,793	16,986	1,553	18,539	4,497	415	18,539	169,962	27,041	9,053	169,633	3,376	3,023	32,252
1994-5	1,356	2,556	5,061	13,314	1,355	14,669	3,002	213	14,669	161,469	24,711	8,726	167,531	1,820	2,451	27,287
1995-6	3,375	2,603	2,480	10,664	1,181	11,845	2,966	87	11,845	142,747	18,002	7,640	150,160	1,749	2,168	19,874
1996-7[1]	4,020	3,440	5,800	15,130	1,213	16,343	5,750	81	16,343	153,689	16,251	8,531	149,997	3,362	2,383	23,566
1997-8[2]	2,700	3,200	6,000	15,280	1,350	16,630	6,000	414	16,630	156,451	18,150	7,228	153,978	2,672	2,110	26,039

[1] Preliminary. [2] Estimate. [3] Formerly part of the U.S.S.R.; data not reported separately until 1989-90. NA = Not available.
Source: Foreign Agricultural Service, U.S. Department of Agriculture (FAS-USDA)

World Production of Barley In Thousands of Metric Tons

Year	Australia	Canada	China	Denmark	France	Germany	India	Kazakhstan[3]	Spain	Turkey	United Kingdom	United States	World Total
1988-9	3,306	10,212	6,041	5,419	9,800	9,587	1,577	44,500	12,070	6,000	8,775	6,314	167,302
1989-90	4,044	11,666	6,180	4,982	9,840	9,716	1,721	48,500	9,100	4,900	8,025	8,784	169,680
1990-1	4,184	13,441	3,930	4,990	10,150	13,990	1,490	8,500	9,410	6,600	7,900	9,192	178,056
1991-2	4,606	11,617	3,928	5,041	10,789	14,494	1,640	3,085	9,140	6,800	7,700	10,110	169,136
1992-3	5,460	11,032	4,000	2,974	10,580	12,196	1,700	8,511	6,105	6,500	7,350	9,908	165,767
1993-4	6,956	12,972	4,200	3,369	8,981	11,000	1,510	7,149	9,520	7,300	6,040	8,666	169,962
1994-5	2,913	11,690	4,411	3,450	7,650	10,900	1,310	5,100	7,600	6,500	5,950	8,162	161,469
1995-6	5,823	13,035	4,089	3,860	7,740	11,890	1,730	2,178	5,200	6,900	6,830	7,829	142,747
1996-7[1]	6,632	15,562	4,000	4,190	9,540	12,070	1,650	2,700	9,600	7,200	7,780	8,616	153,689
1997-8[2]	5,500	13,650	4,000	4,200	10,200	13,400	1,700	2,600	8,500	7,200	7,800	8,153	156,451

[1] Preliminary. [2] Estimate. [3] Formerly part of the U.S.S.R.; data not reported separately until 1990-91. *Source: Foreign Agricultural Service, U.S. Department of Agriculture (FAS-USDA)*

Barley Acreage and Prices in the United States

Year Beginning-June 1	Acreage -- 1,000 Acres -- Planted	Harvested for Grain	Yield Per Harvested Acre -- Bushels --	Received by Farmers[3]	Seasonal Prices: Duluth or Better Feed (No. 2)	Malting (No. 3)	Portland No. 2 Western	Government Price Support Operations: National Average Loan Rate	Target Price	Put Under Support (Mil. Bu.)	% of Production
				Dollars per Bushel							
1989-90	3,125	8,313	48.6	2.42	2.20	3.28	2.61	1.34	2.43	24.0	5.9
1990-1	8,221	7,529	56.1	2.14	2.13	2.42	2.65	1.28	2.36	33.8	8.0
1991-2	8,941	8,413	55.2	2.10	2.17	2.38	2.66	1.32	2.36	38.0	8.2
1992-3	7,762	7,285	62.5	2.04	2.11	2.37	2.57	1.40	2.36	42.9	9.4
1993-4	7,786	6,753	58.9	1.99	2.05	2.48	2.40	1.40	2.36	37.7	9.5
1994-5	7,159	6,667	56.2	2.03	2.02	2.75	2.51	1.54	2.36	28.2	7.5
1995-6[1]	6,689	6,279	57.3	2.89	2.67	3.69	3.51	1.54	2.36	14.9	4.1
1996-7[2]	7,174	6,787	58.5	2.74	2.32	3.18	NA	1.55	NA	NA	NA

[1] Preliminary. [2] Estimate. [3] Excludes support payments. *Source: Economic Research Service, U.S. Department of Agriculture (ERS-USDA)*

Salient Statistics of Barley in the United States In Millions of Bushels

Year Beginning-June 1	Supply: Beginning Stocks	Production	Imports	Total Supply	Disappearance: Domestic Use: Food & Alcohol Beverages	Seed	Feed & Residual	Total	Exports	Total Disappearance	Ending Stocks: Gov't Owned	Privately Owned[3]	Total Stocks
1990-1	160.8	422.2	13.5	596.5	161.1	14.6	204.8	380.5	80.6	461.1	8.4	127.0	135.4
1991-2	135.4	464.3	24.5	624.2	163.3	12.9	224.9	401.1	94.5	495.6	6.5	122.1	128.6
1992-3	128.6	455.1	11.4	595.1	158.4	13.1	192.1	363.6	80.3	443.9	5.4	145.8	151.2
1993-4	151.2	398.0	71.5	620.7	162.9	11.8	241.1	415.8	66.1	481.8	5.2	133.7	138.9
1994-5	138.9	374.9	65.9	579.6	163.8	11.2	225.8	400.8	66.2	467.0	5.0	107.6	112.6
1995-6	112.6	359.6	40.7	512.9	160.1	11.8	179.0	350.9	62.4	413.3	5.0	94.6	99.6
1996-7[1]	100.0	396.0	37.0	532.0	160.0	11.8	220.0	391.8	31.0	423.0	0	100.4	100.4
1997-8[2]	109.0	374.0	35.0	519.0	----	----	160.0	235.0	90.0	422.0	----	----	97.0

[1] Preliminary. [2] Estimate. [3] Uncommitted inventory. [4] Includes quantity under loan & farmer-owned reserves. *Source: Economic Research Service, U.S. Department of Agriculture (ERS-USDA)*

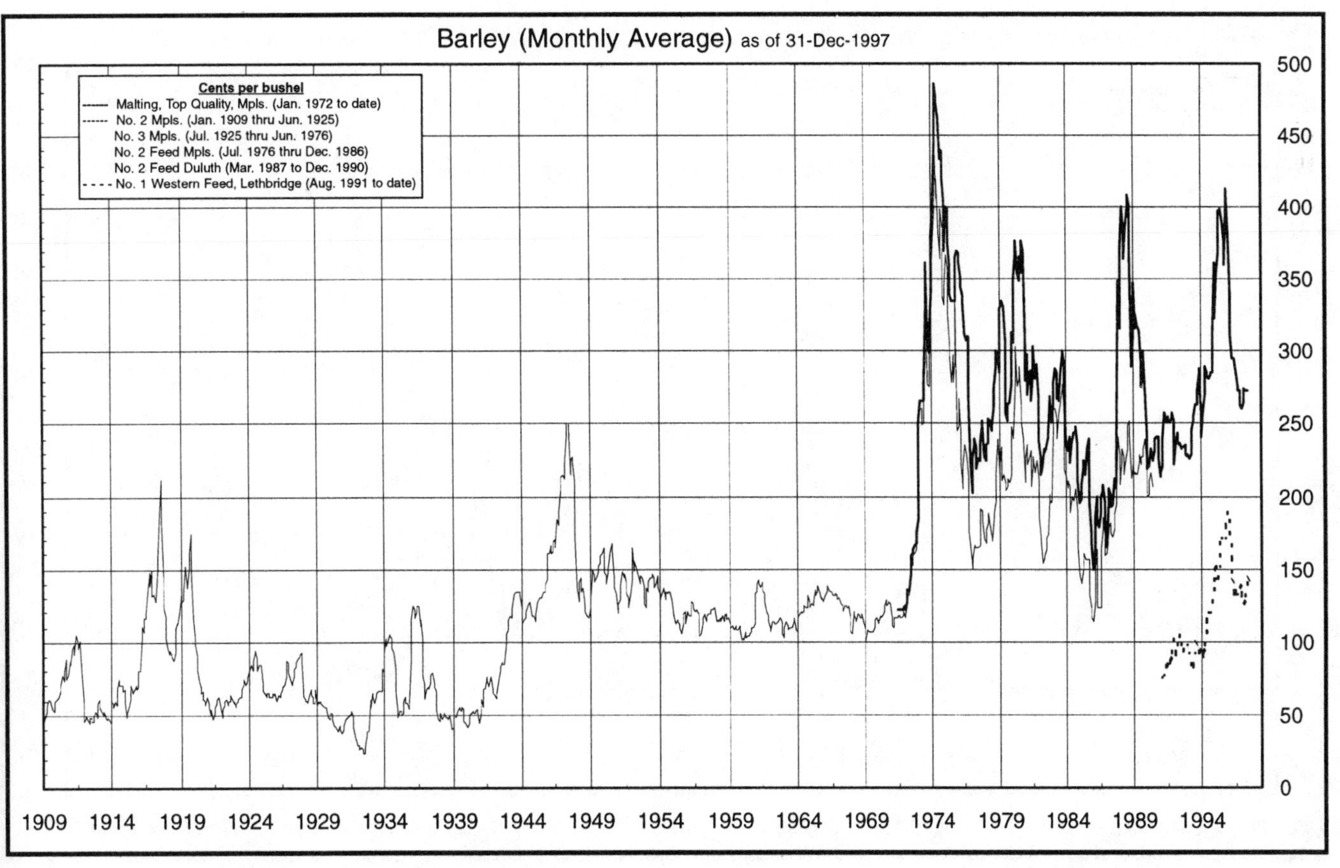

BARLEY

Average Price of No. 2 (or Better) Feed Barley, in Duluth   In Cents Per Bushel

Year	June	July	Aug.	Sept.	Oct.	Nov.	Dec.	Jan.	Feb.	Mar.	Apr.	May	Average
1990-1	239	217	199	201	211	216	207	209	215	214	212	213	213
1991-2	202	189	192	208	218	223	218	220	228	230	235	238	217
1992-3	230	215	203	212	211	208	206	206	208	210	212	205	211
1993-4	199	196	189	189	201	216	214	215	216	207	208	211	205
1994-5	205	202	199	204	195	204	200	202	206	202	197	211	202
1995-6	222	225	209	206	258	298	292	294	300	286	299	320	267
1996-7	322	279	260	234	210	190	196	195	201	222	233	245	232
1997-8[1]	231	204	210	229	205	198							213

[1] Preliminary. NQ = No quote. *Source: Economic Research Service, U.S. Department of Agriculture (ERS-USDA)*

Average Prices Received by Farmers for All Barley in the United States   In Cents Per Bushel

Year	June	July	Aug.	Sept.	Oct.	Nov.	Dec.	Jan.	February	Mar.	Apr.	May	Average
1990-1	229	216	213	213	204	216	213	214	213	215	210	205	213
1991-2	190	173	206	206	210	220	224	221	215	212	214	222	209
1992-3	209	226	216	184	192	205	195	207	200	200	209	197	203
1993-4	195	190	202	187	182	201	202	215	207	201	202	206	199
1994-5	191	192	207	193	193	209	199	205	213	213	215	221	204
1995-6	225	241	262	257	288	309	315	315	328	324	324	345	294
1996-7	355	318	299	278	269	265	267	252	244	236	227	231	270
1997-8[1]	225	227	237	239	245	258	243	239					239

[1] Preliminary. *Source: National Agricultural Statistics Service, U.S. Department of Agriculture (NASS-USDA)*

Average Open Interest of Western Feed Barley Futures in Winnipeg   In Contracts -- 20 Tonnes

Year	Jan.	Feb.	Mar.	Apr.	May	June	July	Aug.	Sept.	Oct.	Nov.	Dec.
1992	940	662	1,060	1,572	2,025	2,692	3,168	2,605	2,994	2,746	1,519	1,685
1993	1,471	1,000	1,369	2,318	2,818	3,500	2,287	2,016	2,580	3,643	4,743	5,946
1994	7,600	8,164	7,650	8,212	8,153	9,019	8,511	8,558	9,633	12,340	10,802	9,457
1995	8,900	9,295	9,965	8,657	7,279	8,731	9,297	9,770	10,704	12,043	10,324	12,089
1996	13,803	12,979	15,746	18,022	19,045	18,502	15,504	14,190	16,647	20,143	21,233	24,590
1997	22,718	19,290	15,080	14,620	14,385	12,291	10,023	13,641	12,909	13,147	14,473	13,576

Source: Winnipeg Commodity Exchange (WCE)

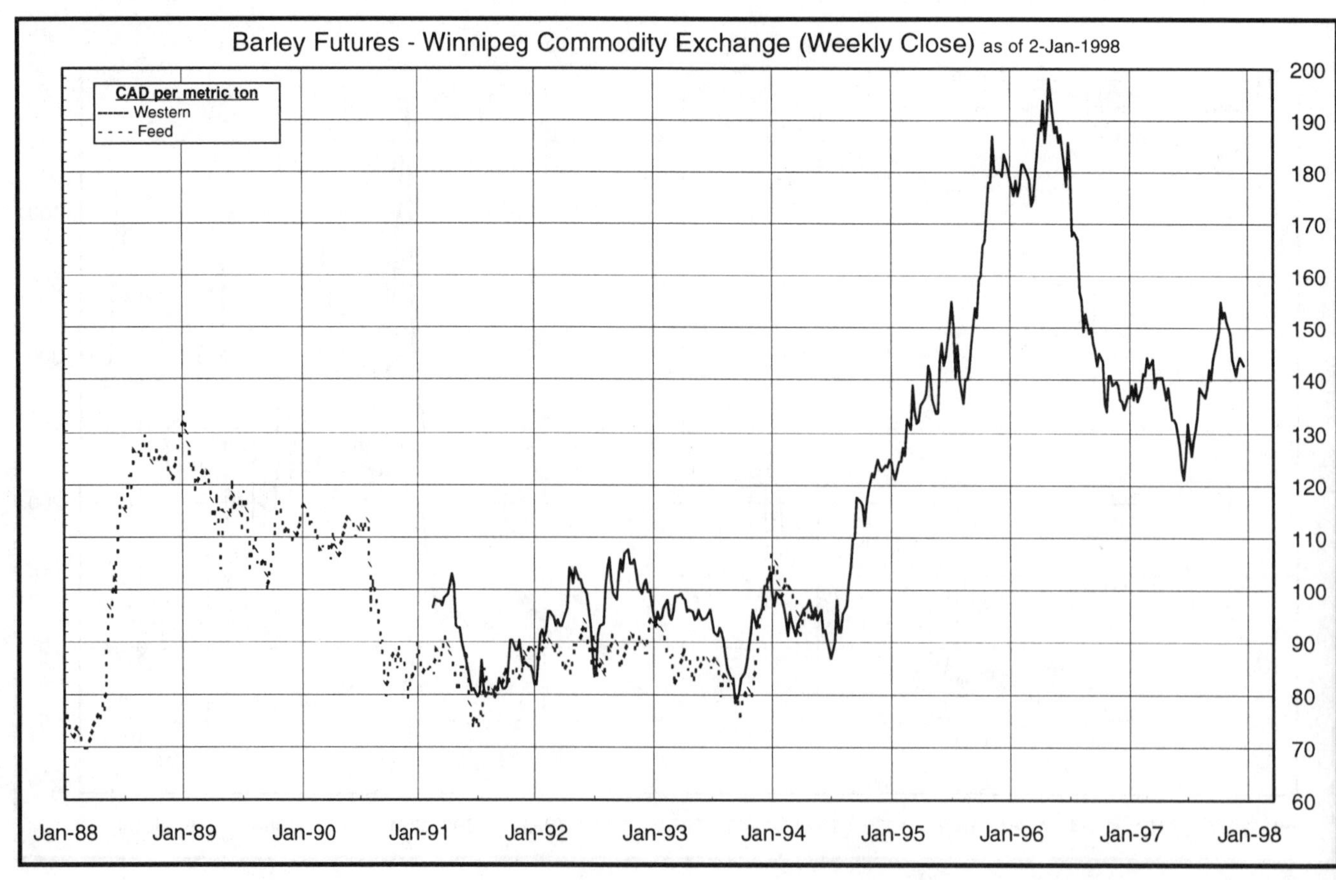

Bauxite

Bauxite is a naturally occurring, heterogeneous material composed primarily of one or more aluminum hydroxide materials, plus various mixtures of silica, iron dioxide, titania, alumina silicates and other impurities in trace amounts.

Bauxite is the only raw material used in the production of alumina on a commercial scale in the U.S. Bauxites are typically classified according to their intended commercial applications: abrasive, cement, chemical, metallurgical, refractory. Of all bauxite mined, about 85 percent is converted to alumina for the production of aluminum metal. An additional 10 percent goes into nonmetal uses as various forms of specialty alumina and the remaining 5 percent goes to nonmetallurgical bauxite applications.

In 1996, 25 countries reported bauxite mine production. Total world production amounted to 114 million metric tonnes, a 6 percent increase from 1995. About 70 percent of total 1996 production was mined in Australia, Brazil, Guinea and Jamaica. Total known world reserves of bauxite are considered sufficient to meet world primary aluminum metal demand well into the 21st century.

U.S. production of alumina (calcined equivalent), derived almost exclusively from imported metallurgical-grade bauxite, increased 4 percent in 1996 compared to 1995. Most of the alumina shipped by U.S. refineries went to domestic smelters for aluminum metal production.

U.S. bauxite production is less than 1 percent of the U.S. requirement for bauxite. As such, bauxite production figures cannot be published as it would reveal company proprietary information. U.S. imports of crude and dried bauxite in the January-May 1997 period were 4.24 million tonnes. Of the total, Guinea supplied 1.67 million tonnes and Jamaica supplied 1.6 million tonnes. Other large suppliers were Brazil and Guyana. For all of 1996, U.S. imports of bauxite were 10.2 million tonnes. The U.S. also exported small amounts of bauxite, primarily to Canada. Total exports in the first five months of 1997 were 24,400 tonnes, and for all of 1996 they were 92,500 tonnes.

U.S. imports of calcined bauxite in the first five months of 1997 were 146,200 tonnes with refractory calcined bauxite making up 94,700 tonnes. The primary suppliers were China and Guyana. For all of 1996, U.S. imports of calcined bauxite were 352,000 tonnes supplied primarily by China and Guyana. The U.S. exported small amounts of calcined bauxite to Canada, Japan and Mexico.

World Production of Bauxite In Thousands of Metric Tons

Year	Australia	Brazil	China	Greece	Guinea	Guyana[2]	Hungary	India	Jamaica[3]	Russia[3/4]	Sierra Leone	Suriname	World Total
1985	31,839	5,846	2,800	2,435	13,956	2,206	2,815	2,341	6,239	6,400	1,185	3,738	89,747
1986	32,384	6,446	2,900	2,231	14,835	2,600	3,022	2,322	6,964	6,275	1,242	3,731	92,534
1987	34,102	6,567	3,200	2,467	16,282	2,785	3,101	2,816	7,660	5,700	1,391	2,581	96,517
1988	36,192	8,083	2,300	2,433	15,624	1,339	2,593	3,961	7,305	5,500	1,403	3,434	103,105
1989	38,584	8,665	2,388	2,550	15,792	1,321	2,644	4,471	9,601	5,500	1,548	3,530	103,722
1990	41,391	9,678	2,400	2,496	15,772	1,424	2,559	4,852	10,921	5,500	1,430	3,283	113,000
1991	40,510	10,365	2,600	2,133	15,466	2,204	2,037	4,735	11,552	5,000	1,288	3,198	111,000
1992	39,746	9,366	2,700	2,078	13,800	2,376	1,721	4,898	11,302	4,578	1,250	3,250	105,000
1993	41,320	9,669	3,500	2,205	14,100	2,130	1,561	5,277	11,391	4,260	1,165	3,412	109,000
1994	41,733	8,673	3,700	2,196	14,400	2,100	830	4,809	11,564	3,000	735	3,772	107,000
1995[1]	42,655	8,761	5,000	1,916	14,400	2,100	1,100	4,800	10,857	3,100	280	3,300	109,000
1996[2]	43,062	10,000	6,500	2,241	14,400	2,093	1,044	5,162	11,829	3,100	280	3,695	114,008

[1] Preliminary. [2] Estimate. [3] Dry Bauxite equivalent of ore processed. [4] Formerly part of the U.S.S.R.; data not reported separetely until 1992.
Source: U.S. Geological Survey (USGS)

Salient Statistics of Bauxite in the United States In Thousands of Metric Tons

Year	Net Import Reliance as a % of Apparent Consumption	Average Price FOB Mine $ per Ton	Consumption by Industry: Total	Alumina	Abrasive	Chemical	Refractory	Dry Equivalent: Imports[3] (for Consumption)	Exports[3]	Consumption	Stocks, December 31: Producers & Consumers	Government	Total
1985	96	13-20	8,206	7,219	305	219	408	7,158	69	8,206	3,643	18,357	22,000
1986	96	13-17	6,901	5,980	259	231	372	6,456	85	6,901	3,319	18,472	21,791
1987	96	13-17	9,548	8,601	224	243	422	9,156	231	9,548	3,019	18,472	21,491
1988	97	13-17	10,074	8,970	274	236	524	9,944	71	10,074	3,021	18,474	21,495
1989	96	15-20	11,810	10,782	275	223	407	10,893	44	11,810	2,891	18,474	21,365
1990	98	15-20	12,042	11,064	276	212	387	12,144	74	12,042	2,318	18,477	20,795
1991	100	15-18	12,204	11,383	204	218	328	11,871	51	12,204	2,620	18,477	21,097
1992	100	15-18	11,873	11,066	223	190	334	10,939	63	11,873	2,319	17,805	20,124
1993	100	15-24	11,917	11,002	203	225	429	11,621	90	12,200	1,590	16,938	18,500
1994	99	15-24	11,200	10,400	197	192	350	10,700	129	11,200	1,560	17,200	18,800
1995[1]	99	15-18	10,900	10,100	133	201	394	10,100	108	10,900	1,730	16,300	18,100
1996[2]	100	15-18	10,900	10,300	118	21	386	10,200	132	10,900	2,060	15,700	17,800

[1] Preliminary. [2] Estimate. [3] Including concentrates. W = Withheld proprietary data. *Source: U.S. Geological Survey (USGS)*

Bismuth

Bismuth finds a wide variety of uses ranging from pharmaceutical compounds to glass ceramics to chemicals and pigments. Bismuth is used for treating stomach ulcers and is found in household pharmaceuticals. In recent years, bismuth has been of interest as a non-toxic substitute for lead in many chemical and metallurgical applications. Bismuth is being tested as an additive to brass for plumbing fixtures, and there has been research into using it to replace lead in shotgun pellets. Because of the limited supply of bismuth, neither of these applications are likely to find extensive usage. Bismuth is also being substituted for lead in ceramic glazes for china. Bismuth has the same durability as lead without being hazardous.

The U.S. Geological Survey reported that the Omaha, Nebraska lead refinery of ASARCO Incorporated has been scheduled to be closed in February 1998. Lead refinery operations were stopped in June 1996, and bismuth recovery operations were to continue until the deadline but were shut down in June 1997 according to ASARCO. The Omaha plant was the last domestic source of primary bismuth.

U.S. consumption of bismuth in the second quarter of 1997 was 367,000 kilograms, down slightly from the first quarter consumption of 387,000 kilograms. Bismuth consumption for all of 1996 was 1.52 million kilograms. By use, bismuth consumption in the first half of 1997 fell into four categories. Consumption for chemicals, including industrial and laboratory chemicals as well as cosmetics and pharmaceuticals was 397,000 kilograms, and for all of 1996 it was 855,000 kilograms. Use of bismuth in bismuth alloys in the first half of 1997 was 222,000 kilograms while for all of 1996 use in alloys was 401,000 kilograms. Use in metallurgical additives in the January-June 1997 period was 122,000 kilograms while for all of 1996 it was 231,000 kilograms. Use of bismuth in other products in the first half of 1997 was 12,000 kilograms. For all of 1996, bismuth use in other categories was 35,000 kilograms.

U.S. imports for consumption of bismuth metal in the first five months of 1997 were 132,000 kilograms. Imports of bismuth metal for all of 1996 were 1.49 million kilograms. In 1996, Belgium supplied 39 percent of the total. Mexico supplied another 30 percent while the United Kingdom supplied 13 percent and China provided 10 percent.

U.S. exports of bismuth metal, alloys, and waste and scrap in the January-May 1997 period were 83,100 kilograms. In the first quarter of 1997, exports were 38,300 kilograms. For all of 1996, exports were 151,000 kilograms. Of the total, Belgium was the primary market taking 43 percent while Canada took 39 percent. Other markets were Guatemala, France and Switzerland.

World Production of Bismuth In Metric Tons

	Mine Output, Metal Content						Refined Metal						
Year	Canada	China	Japan	Mexico	Peru	Total	Belgium	China	Kazakhastan[3]	Japan	Mexico	Peru	Total
1987	165	260	165	1,065	412	2,886	865	600	85	546	561	387	4,078
1988	181	750	160	958	363	3,220	795	750	85	524	622	341	3,669
1989	205	850	150	883	687	3,750	800	850	85	502	597	646	3,970
1990	87	1,060	133	733	555	3,440	1,000	1,060	80	442	549	521	4,190
1991	65	1,040	138	651	610	3,230	800	1,260	70	461	500	377	3,820
1992	224	820	159	807	550	2,740	800	1,060	45	530	550	419	3,670
1993	144	740	149	908	1,000	3,220	950	1,050	170	497	650	937	4,360
1994	129	610	152	900	1,000	3,060	900	850	170	505	650	871	4,070
1995[1]	187	740	177	995	1,000	3,490	800	800	165	591	924	870	4,260
1996[2]	185	700	169	1,000	1,000	3,440	800	800	160	563	925	870	4,230

[1] Preliminary. [2] Estimate. [3] Formerly part of the U.S.S.R.; data not reported separately until 1992. *Source: U.S. Geological Survey (USGS)*

Salient Statistics of Bismuth in the United States In Metric Tons

	Bismuth Consumed, By Uses							Imports of Metallic Bismuth from				
Year	Metallurgical Additives	Other Alloys & Uses	Fusible Alloys	Chemicals[3]	Total Consumption	Consumer Stocks Dec. 31	Exports of Metal & Alloys	Belgium	Mexico	Peru	Total	Dealer Price $ Per Pound
1987	494	22	334	748	1,597	294	38	435.0	391.3	440.4	1,581	3.65
1988	493	27	332	679	1,531	433	147	340.2	448.5	188.9	1,641	5.78
1989	396	25	272	659	1,352	440	122	835.7	390.8	271.4	1,880	5.76
1990	424	24	249	577	1,274	331	122	668.1	404.8	262.7	1,612	3.56
1991	341	26	271	789	1,427	247	75	345.1	535.0	169.8	1,411	3.00
1992	381	33	278	758	1,450	272	90	467.4	550.5	75.7	1,621	2.66
1993	232	59	256	750	1,300	323	70	275.1	479.1	117.2	1,330	2.50
1994	306	26	276	841	1,450	402	160	512.0	665.0	114.9	1,660	3.25
1995[1]	257	27	544	1,320	2,150	390	261	636.0	444.0	10.9	1,450	3.85
1996[2]	231	35	401	855	1,520	122	151	584.0	453.0	19.5	1,600	3.60

[1] Preliminary. [2] Estimate. [3] Includes pharmaceuticals. *Source: U.S. Geological Survey (USGS)*

Broilers

Federally inspected U.S. broiler production is expected to reach 29.2 billion pounds in 1998, up from a record high 27 billion pounds in 1997. In the early 1990's, production averaged about 20 billion pounds. Production of ready-to-cook (RTC) broiler meat in the second half of 1997 of 13.8 billion pounds compares with 13.2 billion a year earlier and forecasts of 14.5 billion in the first half of 1998. Hot summer weather in 1997 may have contributed to lower egg sets, but the broiler hatchery supply as of August 1 was still 9 percent larger than a year ago. Net returns for broiler processors in 1997 were expected to be 3 cents per pound higher than the 5 cents realized in 1996. Wholesale whole broiler prices in early 1997 were higher than a year earlier, but turned lower later in the year. Lower feed costs more than offset the lower broiler prices and allowed the increase in net returns. The 12-City average wholesale price averaged near 60 cents per pound in 1997 vs. the 1996 average of 61.24 cents with little change expected in 1998. Retail prices in mid-1997 averaged around 85 cents a pound vs. about 82 cents a year earlier. U.S. per capita broiler consumption in 1997 at a record high 73.1 pounds, retail weight, compares with the previous year's record of 70.8 pounds. An even sharper gain is forecast for 1998 with consumption expected to reach 77.5 pounds, suggesting that publicity directed towards the need for proper cooking of poultry meat, especially at fast-food outlets, will not dampen consumption.

A key factor for the steady gains in U.S. broiler production is strong foreign demand, reflecting a combination of attractive prices of U.S. broilers, notably leg quarters, and the rapid development of foreign markets. Exports in the first half of 1997 of 2.2 billion pounds compares with 2.1 billion the year before. Russia was the major importer with over 1 billion pounds vs. 854 million pounds in 1996. However, exports to Asia in late 1997 were clouded by currency and financial uncertainties in the region.

Broiler Supply and Prices in the United States

Year & Quarters	Federally Inspected Slaughter: Number (Millions)	Average Weight (Pounds)	Liveweight Pounds (Mil. Lbs.)	Certified RTC Weight (Mil. Lbs.)	Total Production RTC[3] (Mil. Lbs.)	Per Capita Consumption RTC Basis (Pounds)	Prices: Farm (Cents per Pound)	Georgia Dock[4] (Cents per Pound)
1992	6,425	4.51	28,998	21,052	20,904	75.7	31.85	50.21
1993	6,681	4.56	30,474	22,178	22,015	77.7	34.40	53.65
1994	7,270	4.64	33,595	23,846	23,666	79.4	35.06	54.40
1995	7,371	4.66	34,348	25,021	24,827	79.2	34.68	54.73
1996[1]	7,546	4.78	36,034	26,336	26,125	81.4	38.67	61.09
1997[2]	7,668	4.81	36,891	26,974	27,287	83.7	37.38	59.96
I	1,858	4.86	9,026	6,527	6,628	20.3	39.17	61.59
II	1,965	4.81	9,463	6,843	6,948	21.7	36.97	60.01
III	1,956	4.72	9,233	6,866	6,861	21.3	39.57	61.74
IV	1,888	4.86	9,169	6,738	6,850	20.4	33.80	56.50

[1] Preliminary. [2] Estimate. [3] Total production equals federally inspected slaughter plus other slaughter minus cut-up and futher processing condemnation. [4] Ready-to-cook-basis. *Source: Economic Research Service, U.S. Department of Agriculture (ERS-USDA)*

Salient Statistics of Broilers in the United States

Year	Commercial Production: Number (Millions)	Commercial Production: Liveweight (Mil. Lbs.)	Average Liveweight Per Bird (Pounds)	Average Price (¢/Pound)	Value of Production (Mil. $)	Total Chickens[3] Supply and Distribution — Production: Federally Inspected (In Millions of Pounds)	Production: Other Chickens	Production: Total	Storage Stocks January 1	Exports	Broiler Feed Ratio in Pounds	Consumption: Total (Mil. Lbs.)	Consumption: Per Capita[4] (in Lbs.)
1991	6,137	27,203	4.43	30.8	8,383	19,728	32	19,760	242	1,261	4.9	18,271	63.55
1992	6,402	28,829	4.51	31.8	9,174	21,052	36	21,088	300	1,489	5.1	19,347	66.57
1993	6,694	30,618	4.56	34.0	10,417	22,178	36	22,015	368	1,966	5.3	20,059	68.50
1994	7,018	32,529	4.64	35.0	11,372	23,846	38	23,666	358	2,876	5.2	20,690	69.50
1995	7,326	34,222	4.66	34.4	11,762	25,021	39	24,827	458	3,894	5.2	20,832	68.80
1996[1]	7,598	36,486	4.74	38.1	13,906	26,336	38	26,124	560	4,420	4.5	21,626	70.80
1997[2]						27,281	39	27,055	641	4,655	5.1	22,421	72.70

[1] Preliminary. [2] Estimate. [3] Ready-to-cook. [4] Retail weight basis. *Source: Economic Research Service, U.S. Department of Agriculture (ERS-USDA)*

Average Wholesale Broiler[1] Prices RTC (Ready-to-Cook) In Cents Per Pound

Year	Jan.	Feb.	Mar.	Apr.	May	June	July	Aug.	Sept.	Oct.	Nov.	Dec.	Average
1991	51.72	50.63	51.41	51.96	52.03	52.66	54.25	54.61	53.61	51.61	50.30	49.54	52.03
1992	50.14	50.28	50.24	49.45	55.06	52.38	56.04	56.13	51.29	53.67	54.98	51.17	52.57
1993	52.14	53.01	54.02	54.66	57.86	55.04	55.36	57.77	57.59	55.72	55.82	53.17	55.18
1994	52.67	55.22	57.56	57.80	61.39	60.71	57.36	54.65	55.80	54.02	50.50	50.87	55.71
1995	51.14	51.73	52.32	51.51	52.94	55.88	58.76	61.74	61.48	58.79	61.08	58.87	56.35
1996	59.00	55.31	54.31	56.01	61.71	65.52	64.58	64.07	64.01	62.64	64.37	63.50	61.25
1997[2]	61.99	59.53	58.41	59.77	58.53	59.05	63.04	63.25	59.86	55.39	54.62	52.25	58.81

[1] 12-city composite wholesale price. [1] Preliminary. *Source: Economic Research Service, U.S. Department of Agriculture (ERS-USDA)*

Butter

U.S. butter production during 1997 stabilized following a five-year slide in output, reflecting a soft market for cheese which in turn increased the supplies of milk available for butter production. The U.S. produced 535,000 metric tonnes in 1997, up 2,000 from 1996, but 84,000 tonnes below the 1992 record high. U.S. consumption also increased marginally to 525,000 tonnes, up 7,000 from 1996 but 45,000 tonnes below 1994. Since the late 1980's the annual new supply has outpaced domestic demand; the differential has narrowed in recent years and is not likely to repeat the 1992 excess of 94,000 tonnes. There is a definite production seasonality: January is the highest producing month and August the lowest. U.S. butter stocks, once mostly government owned, dropped sharply during the 1990's; from a high at year-end 1991 of 249,000 tonnes, to only 8,000 at year-end 1997. Annual U.S. per capita butter use in 1996 of 4.3 pounds was the lowest since 1982.

Butter production is derived directly from milk production. Butter manufacture is the third largest use of milk production, the first being milk as a fluid and then its conversion into cheese. California is the largest producing state with a third of total U.S. production, followed by Wisconsin.

World butter production in 1997 of 5.3 million metric tonnes compares with 5.2 million in 1996 and a 1992-96 average of 5.3 million tonnes. A combined Russia and the Ukraine were once the world's largest producers with 1,065,000 tonnes in 1992, but their year-to-year-totals have since dropped sharply with only 540,000 tonnes in 1997. The U.S. generally produces about 10 percent of the world total. Statistically India is the largest producer with a record 1.45 million tonnes in 1997 vs. 1.4 million in 1996, but their product is mostly Ghee, a butter-like substance which is consumed almost entirely in India.

World consumption mirrors production: India is first, Russia and the Ukraine second. Germany's annual use during 1995-1997 of about 570,000 tonnes topped the U.S.

Global foreign trade in butter is small. U.S. imports are insignificant, 4,000 tonnes in 1997, slightly above average; but exports show sharp variance, totaling 145,000 tonnes in 1993 and only 12,000 tonnes in 1997. New Zealand is the largest exporter with 310,000 tonnes in 1997, 43 percent of the world total. Russia was the largest importer in 1997 with 245,000 tonnes, 57 percent of total world imports. World stocks have been trending lower, 469,000 tonnes at year-end 1997 vs. ending stocks in excess of 800,000 in the early 1990's. The key to increased world demand and higher prices rests largely on Russia, but whether they will be available to increase imports is questionable although underlying buying interest is strong.

World market prices of butterfat in 1997 maintained a well balanced market with stable to firm prices. The reasons were twofold: E.U. exportable supplies were low and stocks of non-government butter were relatively tight. Butter prices, basis North Europe FOB, fell from $2,300 per ton at the start of 1996 to $1,650 by year-end, recovering during 1997 to more than $1,800 by mid summer. U.S. prices of wholesale Grade A butter slipped during the first half of 1997 bottoming at 86.1 cents per pound in May before rebounding to $1.02 by September. The year earlier monthly average was $1.455 per pound. Domestic prices were forecast to hold firm or rise during late 1997 and into early 1998.

Supply and Distribution of Butter in the United States In Millions of Pounds

	Supply				Distribution							93 Score AA Wholesale Price	
					Domestic Disapearrance			Department of Agriculture					
Year	Production	Cold Storage Stocks[3] Jan. 1[6]	Imports	Total Supply	Total	Per Capita (Pounds)	Exports	Jan 1. Stocks[5]	Dec. 31 Stocks[5]	Removed by USDA Programs	Total Use	California ($ per Pound)	Chicago ($ per Pound)
1987	1,104	193	4.769	1,361	1,198	4.7	16	220	96	187.3	1,215	1.6748	1.4172
1988	1,208	143	5.328	1,359	1,131	4.5	15	96	173	312.6	1,147	1.6097	1.3412
1989	1,295	215	4.621	1,515	1,127	4.4	112	173	223	413.4	1,243	1.5660	1.2951
1990	1,302	256	4.798	1,582	1,039	4.4	126	223	373	400.3	1,167	1.3050	1.0346
1991	1,336	416	4.740	1,759	1,181	4.4	26	373	511	442.8	1,208	1.2856	1.0182
1992	1,365	539	4.153	1,919	1,323	4.4	142	511	430	439.5	1,466	1.1386	.8427
1993	1,315	448	4.374	1,774	1,327	4.7	204	430	229	288.8	1,532	1.0612	.7693
1994	1,296	235	3.340	1,543	1,362	4.8	101	229	67	204.3	1,464	.9581	.7068
1995[1]	1,261	79	1.536	1,340	1,326	4.5	141	67	----	78.5	----	----	.8188
1996[2]	1,174	19	2.205	1,175	1,142	4.3	42	----	----	0.0	----	----	----

[1] Preliminary. [2] Estimates. [3] Includes butter equivalent. [4] Includes USDA shipments to territories. [5] Includes butteroil. [6] Includes stocks held by USDA.
Source: Economic Research Service, U.S. Department of Agriculture (ERS-USDA)

Commercial Disappearance of Creamery Butter in the United States In Millions of Pounds

Year	First Quarter	Second Quarter	Third Quarter	Fourth Quarter	Total	Year	First Quarter	Second Quarter	Third Quarter	Fourth Quarter	Total
1986	198.6	220.1	234.4	269.8	922.9	1992	214.6	216.6	236.8	276.2	944.3
1987	222.7	222.1	218.4	239.3	902.5	1993	224.6	231.5	271.9	312.7	1,040.6
1988	194.5	221.6	219.7	274.0	909.8	1994	261.7	254.9	285.0	298.3	1,097.3
1989	188.3	145.6	228.8	291.3	854.1	1995	335.7	269.0	261.2	304.9	1,170.8
1990	197.5	218.1	218.1	281.8	915.2	1996	325.6	301.8	237.5	294.1	1,159.0
1991	186.8	184.0	255.6	276.5	903.5	1997[1]	322.7	280.9	259.4		863.0

[1] Preliminary. *Source: Economic Research Service, U.S. Department of Agriculture (ERS-USDA)*

World (Total) Butter[3] Production In Thousands of Metric Tons

Year	Australia	Canada	France	Germany[4]	India	Ireland	Netherland	New Zealand	Poland	Russia[5]	Ukraine[5]	U.K.	United States
1987	104	95	569	553	750	150	234	248	293	----	1,742	174	501
1988	98	105	521	585	850	139	214	276	293	----	1,724	140	547
1989	96	99	525	711	880	156	213	246	325	820	441	130	588
1990	111	100	514	640	970	159	209	276	300	833	444	138	591
1991	111	97	496	555	1,020	146	196	269	220	729	376	132	606
1992	116	86	454	474	1,060	142	191	268	180	762	303	127	619
1993	131	83	444	480	1,110	135	184	276	180	732	312	152	596
1994	147	88	444	461	1,200	136	159	297	160	488	254	154	588
1995	138	93	453	486	1,300	150	132	280	163	419	219	130	573
1996	153	93	462	480	1,400	150	127	309	160	290	163	130	533
1997[1]	163	92	450	442	1,470	146	136	320	176	250	120	129	522

[1] Preliminary. [2] Forecast. [3] Factory (including creameries and dairies) and farm. [4] Includes the former East Germany after 1988. [5] Formerly part of the U.S.S.R.; data not reported seperately until 1989. *Source: Foreign Agricultural Service, U.S. Department of Agriculture (FAS-USDA)*

Production of Creamery Butter in Factories in the United States In Millions of Pounds

Year	Jan.	Feb.	Mar.	Apr.	May	June	July	Aug.	Sept.	Oct.	Nov.	Dec.	Total
1987	111.9	97.4	105.4	102.6	98.2	81.5	75.2	66.4	77.9	91.2	87.9	108.5	1,104.1
1988	126.1	119.7	115.5	113.8	108.0	90.8	76.3	74.1	83.3	92.3	95.6	112.0	1,207.5
1989	129.0	124.7	135.7	124.7	122.5	95.3	72.2	80.1	81.6	95.1	94.4	107.4	1,262.7
1990	134.0	127.3	136.2	125.6	118.6	96.7	84.6	84.2	83.4	106.7	110.1	112.2	1,319.6
1991	142.1	126.3	131.6	133.7	126.0	98.3	88.9	85.0	84.7	105.2	108.5	130.1	1,360.4
1992	156.0	132.0	129.9	119.7	118.2	103.0	97.8	86.7	96.6	101.6	98.3	119.8	1,365.2
1993	147.3	127.2	131.6	121.8	116.4	102.3	86.2	80.7	86.3	97.8	97.3	120.3	1,315.2
1994	135.3	118.4	118.0	119.4	118.2	99.2	84.2	88.2	91.2	101.8	100.7	121.4	1,295.9
1995	135.6	121.7	127.3	120.6	119.4	98.4	85.0	76.0	80.2	93.5	90.5	112.4	1,260.7
1996[1]	132.4	114.7	111.9	109.3	100.9	72.7	75.2	73.2	80.7	96.6	95.3	111.3	1,174.5
1997[2]	124.0	108.3	104.1	117.5	103.1	81.8	81.9	70.3	79.7	83.2	88.2	111.2	1,041.8

[1] Preliminary. [2] Estimate. *Source: Economic Research Service, U.S. Department of Agriculture (ERS-USDA)*

Cold Storage Holdings of Creamery Butter on First of Month in the United States In Millions of Pounds

Year	Jan.	Feb.	Mar.	Apr.	May	June	July	Aug.	Sept.	Oct.	Nov.	Dec.
1987	193.0	206.6	231.6	254.0	247.9	251.1	237.9	211.2	187.3	176.2	165.6	158.5
1988	143.2	157.3	198.9	221.1	240.4	280.5	293.4	295.8	294.4	253.4	237.3	226.2
1989	214.7	246.6	314.4	341.9	377.2	438.3	464.1	461.3	439.7	407.9	370.6	294.1
1990	256.2	269.7	293.8	335.4	358.8	399.6	420.0	420.8	427.9	412.3	413.6	407.6
1991	416.1	470.8	524.8	555.9	620.5	646.7	662.7	659.8	629.4	597.2	567.1	539.4
1992	539.4	565.4	624.8	645.3	678.7	712.6	747.0	755.8	705.7	608.1	541.7	487.6
1993	447.7	489.1	492.5	515.6	552.7	559.0	569.0	516.4	473.3	395.4	341.1	276.3
1994	234.7	251.0	243.2	253.5	265.7	281.4	275.1	245.9	206.6	163.4	124.6	84.5
1995	79.5	89.9	88.3	74.8	79.1	81.3	79.2	68.3	50.2	32.8	23.6	15.7
1996	18.6	25.5	33.7	48.7	39.8	34.0	29.7	31.7	27.3	21.4	20.5	17.6
1997[1]	13.7	21.2	24.3	26.7	43.9	63.9	59.5	62.8	48.7	43.9	26.6	15.4

[1] Preliminary. *Source: Agricultural Statistics Board, U.S.Department of Agriculture (ASB-USDA)*

Wholesale Price of 92 Score Creamery (Grade A) Butter in Chicago In Cents Per Pound

Year	Jan.	Feb.	March	April	May	June	July	Aug.	Sept.	Oct.	Nov.	Dec.	Average
1987	137.3	136.8	137.8	138.8	138.4	144.6	149.0	148.1	145.3	136.8	135.6	134.0	140.2
1988	131.9	131.0	131.0	131.0	131.0	133.5	135.9	135.6	134.3	132.0	131.3	131.3	132.5
1989	131.0	131.0	131.0	131.0	131.0	131.0	130.3	132.8	125.1	120.5	120.5	120.0	127.9
1990	110.9	108.3	108.3	106.9	99.0	98.4	100.3	98.9	98.9	98.9	98.9	98.0	102.1
1991	97.3	97.3	97.3	97.3	97.3	98.6	98.9	98.9	100.7	106.3	104.6	98.4	99.3
1992	94.9	86.3	86.3	86.3	83.8	76.6	76.6	76.6	81.7	82.2	80.7	78.6	82.5
1993	75.3	75.3	75.3	75.3	75.3	76.2	73.5	74.6	74.3	74.2	73.6	69.7	74.4
1994	64.0	64.0	65.5	65.5	64.5	65.1	66.9	71.5	71.5	71.5	71.5	67.0	67.4
1995	64.0	65.5	66.5	66.5	66.5	69.9	74.5	79.5	80.9	95.4	103.5	74.4	75.6
1996	75.4	66.4	65.5	69.0	87.8	129.3	145.3	145.5	145.5	128.6	74.1	71.9	100.4
1997	81.9	98.4	106.3	95.6	86.1	105.5	102.7	102.7	101.6	135.3	148.8	120.1	107.1

Source: Economic Research Service, U.S. Department of Agriculture (ERS-USDA)

Cadmium

Cadmium is a rare chemical element that is the by-product of the smelting and refining of zinc ores. It is used primarily for the plating of iron and steel to protect them from corrosion. Due to the cost of waste disposal and assorted problems with its toxicity, the use of cadmium in electroplating has decreased. Due to environmental concerns, the outlook for increased cadmium use is not very positive. Cadmium is highly toxic and its disposal represents a problem for users.

For 1995, two companies in the U.S. recovered cadmium as a by-product of the smelting and refining of zinc concentrates. A third company recovers cadmium from other nonferrous sources, such as lead smelter baghouse dust, but these operations were halted in 1993. The estimated consumption pattern for cadmium includes batteries 65 per cent; pigments 14 per cent; coatings and platings 9 per cent; stabilizers for engineering plastics and similar synthetic products 9 per cent; nonferrous alloys 2 per cent; and other including electrooptics 1 per cent.

Cadmium recycling has proved to be feasible only for nickel-cadmium batteries, some alloys, and dust from electric arc furnaces operated by the steel industry. The exact amounts of cadmium that are recycled are not known. In 1994, the U.S. steel industry generated more than 500,000 tonnes of electric furnace dust, typically containing .003 per cent to .07 per cent cadmium. Seventeen states were reported to be setting up collection networks for recycling nickel-cadmium batteries. The U.S. imports cadmium metal from a number of countries. These include Canada, Mexico, Belgium, and Germany among others.

U.S. refinery production of cadmium in 1995 was estimated at 1,300 tonnes, up 29 per cent from 1994. Imports of cadmium metal for consumption in 1995 were 1,040 tonnes, down 6 per cent from the previous year. U.S. exports of cadmium metal, alloys, and scrap in 1995 were 1,050 tonnes, down 28 per cent from the previous year. Shipments of cadmium from the government stockpile in 1995 were 450 tonnes, up from 209 tonnes the previous year and 185 tonnes in 1993. As of September 30, 1995, the government stockpile of cadmium showed 2,020 tonnes of uncommitted inventory, 243 tonnes of committed inventory, and 2,020 tonnes authorized for disposal. U.S. apparent consumption of cadmium in 1995 was estimated at 1,600 tonnes, up 57 per cent from 1994. Stocks at year end 1995 that were held by producers and distributors were 540 tonnes, up from 439 tonnes the previous year.

World production of cadmium in 1995 was estimated at 18,900 tonnes, up over 4 per cent from the previous year. The major producer of cadmium was Japan with 2,800 tonnes, followed by Canada with 2,300 tonnes, and Belgium with 1,600 tonnes. Other important producers include Germany, Australia, and Mexico. Estimated world resources of cadmium were about 6 million tonnes based on zinc resources containing about .3 per cent cadmium.

World Refinery Production of Cadmium In Metric Tons

Year	Australia	Belgium	Canada	China	Finland	Germany	Italy	Japan	Kazakhstan[4]	Mexico	United Kingdom	United States[3]	World Total
1987	944	1,308	1,481	680	690	1,125	320	2,450	3,000	935	498	1,515	19,066
1988	855	1,836	1,694	750	703	1,186	686	2,614	3,000	1,117	399	1,885	21,869
1989	696	1,764	1,620	800	612	1,234	776	2,694	3,000	976	395	1,550	20,873
1990	638	1,960	1,470	1,100	569	990	691	2,450	2,800	882	438	1,680	20,200
1991	1,076	1,807	1,829	1,200	593	1,048	658	2,889	2,500	688	449	1,680	20,900
1992	1,001	1,550	1,963	1,150	590	961	742	2,986	1,000	602	383	1,620	19,600
1993	951	1,573	1,944	1,160	785	1,056	517	2,832	1,000	797	458	1,090	19,000
1994	910	1,556	2,173	1,280	548	1,145	475	2,629	995	646	469	1,010	18,500
1995[1]	838	1,710	2,349	1,200	539	1,150	308	2,652	1,209	689	549	1,270	18,900
1996[2]	682	1,580	2,540	1,300	648	1,150	296	2,343	1,200	675	541	1,530	18,900

[1] Preliminary. [2] Estimate. [3] Primary and secondary metal. [4] Formerly part of the U.S.S.R.; data not reported separately until 1992.
Source: U.S. Geological Survey (USGS)

Salient Statistics of Cadmium in the United States In Metric Tons of Contained Cadmium

Year	Net Import Reliance as a % of Apparent Consumption	Production (Metal)	Producer Shipments	Cadmium Sulfide Production	Production Other Compounds	Imports of Cadmium Metal[3]	Exports[4]	Apparent Consumption	Industry Stocks Dec. 31[5]	N.Y. Dealer Price $ per Pound[6]
1987	61	1,515	1,916	540	1,497	2,701	241	4,178	720	1.60
1988	59	1,885	2,074	345	1,451	2,482	613	3,620	854	6.91
1989	62	1,550	2,015	267	1,451	2,787	369	4,096	726	6.28
1990	55	1,680	1,860	228	1,144	1,740	385	2,800	653	3.38
1991	58	1,680	1,740	263	1,089	2,040	448	3,080	835	2.01
1992	55	1,620	2,080	270	1,073	1,960	213	3,330	868	.91
1993	64	1,090	1,320	303	731	1,420	38	2,940	579	.45
1994	3	1,010	1,290	170	898	1,110	1,450	1,040	423	1.13
1995[1]	E	1,270	1,280	105	936	848	1,050	1,160	542	1.84
1996[2]	33	1,530	1,310	119	720	843	201	2,250	750	1.24

[1] Preliminary. [2] Estimate. [3] For Consumption. [4] Cadmium Metal, alloys, dross, flue dust. [5] Metallic, Compounds, Distributors (including in compounds from 1985). [6] Sticks and Balls in 1 to 5 short ton lots. E = Net exporter. *Source: U.S. Geological Survey (USGS)*

Canola (Rapeseed)

World canola (or rapeseed, the terms are interchangeable) production during the 1990's has increased about 30 percent. Among major vegetable oilseeds canola is now vying for second place with cottonseed in crop size, although only about 20 percent that of soybeans. In 1997/98 a near record 33.2 million metric tons were produced vs. 30.6 million in 1996/97 and the record high 34.6 million in 1995/96. On a protein meal basis rapeseed is the world's second largest, production of which totaled 18 million tons in 1997/98 vs. 17.4 million in 1996/97; but for oil, rapeseed ranks third (after soybean and palm) with production of 10.9 million tons in 1997/98 vs. 10.5 million in 1996/97. Total rapeseed 1997/98 world supplies are estimated at 34.3 million tons vs. 32.2 million in 1996/97. The world 1997/98 (July/June) crush of 29.7 million tons compares with the previous year's 28.5 million tons and the 1995/96 record of 30.6 million.

China accounts for nearly a third of total world production--a record high 9.4 million tons in 1997/98 vs. the previous year's 9.2 million. Canada and India produced more than six million tons each in 1997/98. Collectively, the European Union is the second largest producing area with 8.1 million tons in 1997/98 vs. 7.1 million in 1996/7. E.U. rapeseed production, with Germany the largest producer, is double that of the region's second largest oilseed crop--sunflowerseed. In terms of protein meal consumption, E.U. 1997/98 rapeseed usage of 5.1 million tons is one-fourth that of soybean meal (23.1 million). E.U. rapeseed oil usage, however, about equals soybean oil use: 1.97 million tons in 1997/98 vs. 2.0 million, respectively. Foreign trade in canola is second only to soybeans. World exports totaled 5.4 million tons in 1997/98, unchanged from 1996/97.

U.S. production of canola seed is small. About 893 million pounds were produced in 1997/98 (June/May) vs. 479 million in 1996/97, the increase reflecting a near doubling in planted acreage to 733,000 acres from 366,000 in 1996/97. The acreage and crop size were well above normal but to suggest a major uptrend was taking hold would be premature. Average yield, however, is erratic: 1,249 pounds per acre in 1997/98 vs. 1,384 pounds in 1996/97 and 1,278 in 1995/96. The crop is grown mostly in the Northern Plain states. U.S. production fails to cover disappearance, estimated at 1.3 billion pounds in 1997/98 vs. 1.1 billion in 1996/97. Canola seed imports, mostly from Canada, bridge the domestic supply/demand imbalance. Imports of 441 million pounds in 1997/98 compare with 570 million in 1996/97 and the record high 773 million in 1993/94. The U.S. also exports canola seed, 276 million pounds in 1997/98 vs. 173 million in 1996/97. The U.S. crush in 1997/98 was forecast to be a record 1,024 million pounds, up from 866 the year prior. 1997/98 production of canola oil (October/September) of 350 million pounds compares with 341 million in 1996/97, while canola oil imports, mostly from Canada, of 1.2 billion million pounds compares with 1.1 billion in 1996/97. A decade earlier, oil production totaled 50 million pounds and imports 400 million pounds. Domestic oil demand was forecast at a record high 1.3 billion pounds in 1997/98.

Contributing to the sharp gains in U.S. canola production since the mid-1980's include (1) government enticements to increase canola acreage; (2) development of low-erucic canola varieties that can be grown in the U.S.; and (3) the wider acceptance of canola oil in cooking due to its lower content of saturated fats. Canola oil is said to be 94 percent saturated fat free, the lowest of any leading oil. Demand for canola meal has also grown impressively as a livestock feed. Domestic usage of meal in 1997/98 of a record high 1.3 million short tons compares with 1.2 million in 1996/97.

The average price received by farmers for canola seed in 1997/98 was forecast to range between $10-12.00 per cwt. against $13.40 in 1996/97. Canola oil's price was forecast at $.235-.265 per pound vs. $.258 in 1996/97. Canola meal's price of $135-160 per short ton compares with $209 in 1996/97.

Futures Market

Canola futures and options are traded on the Winnipeg Commodity Exchange (WCE) and quoted in Canadian dollars per ton. Rapeseed futures are traded on the Marche a Terme International de France (MATIF).

World Production of Canola (Rapeseed) In Thousands of Metric Tons

Year	Australia	Canada	China	Czechoslovakia	France	Germany	India	Pakistan	Poland	Sweden	United Kingdom	former U.S.S.R.	World Total
1984-5	32	3,412	4,205	300	1,305	1,017	3,073	234	911	327	925	55	16,935
1985-6	87	3,498	5,607	285	1,340	1,184	2,681	250	1,073	320	895	74	18,699
1986-7	77	3,787	5,881	306	1,071	1,472	2,605	217	1,298	321	940	144	19,550
1987-8	66	3,847	6,605	337	2,645	1,723	3,455	204	1,192	250	1,353	296	23,435
1988-9	58	4,218	5,044	380	2,303	1,642	4,377	249	1,199	250	1,040	420	22,646
1989-90	78	3,209	5,436	387	1,748	1,908	4,125	233	1,586	370	976	424	22,096
1990-1	98	3,266	6,958	380	1,926	2,155	5,152	228	1,206	367	1,258	506	25,321
1991-2	170	4,224	7,436	446	2,270	3,030	5,863	219	1,043	252	1,308	409	28,489
1992-3	179	3,872	7,653	430	1,810	2,617	4,872	207	758	247	1,159	388	25,588
1993-4	294	5,480	6,939	466	1,550	2,848	5,390	215	594	313	1,256	325	27,039
1994-5	309	7,228	7,492	452	1,800	2,896	5,884	312	756	214	1,254	363	30,626
1995-6[1]	584	6,436	9,777	662	2,782	3,103	6,070	385	1,377	216	1,235	415	34,911
1996-7[2]	641	5,062	9,201	521	2,912	2,150	6,220	460	449	120	1,410	440	31,257
1997-8[3]	769	6,198	9,300	575	3,400	2,843	6,100	----	584	130	1,509	400	34,253

[1] Preliminary. [2] Estimate. [3] Forecast. *Source: The Oil World*

CANOLA

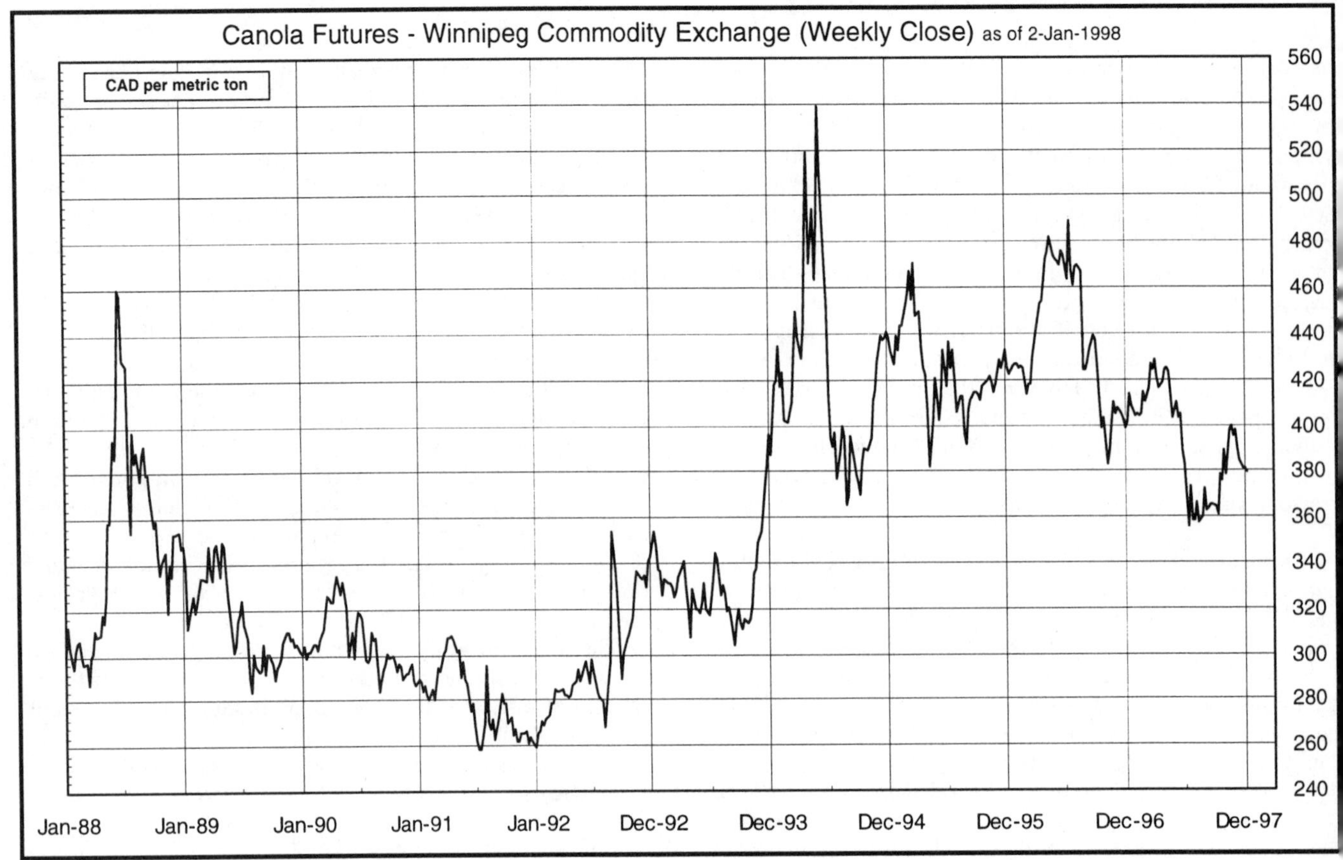

Volume of Trading of Canola Futures in Winnipeg   In Contracts

Year	Jan.	Feb.	Mar.	Apr.	May	June	July	Aug.	Sept.	Oct.	Nov.	Dec.	Total
1987	105,790	144,081	101,293	119,194	143,831	97,003	87,229	71,845	93,376	121,599	102,507	127,547	1,315,295
1988	137,387	131,618	92,012	104,171	170,733	132,602	72,880	61,506	66,555	81,043	57,266	60,999	1,168,772
1989	53,322	62,513	53,926	53,143	80,411	62,378	52,661	51,673	50,701	76,917	76,173	50,947	724,765
1990	52,473	66,423	52,720	55,158	82,685	53,085	51,270	61,642	56,933	57,302	49,450	58,994	698,135
1991	67,489	59,380	64,193	67,572	68,849	59,270	90,575	65,541	76,966	75,457	53,660	66,421	815,373
1992	57,429	54,546	57,174	38,674	87,638	75,018	50,157	72,971	79,034	93,692	99,577	73,805	839,715
1993	73,411	74,362	63,737	73,358	61,996	70,117	94,286	77,325	56,377	73,953	107,485	112,377	938,784
1994	119,691	103,517	85,125	100,923	111,962	79,307	83,903	95,712	54,893	87,350	101,727	96,797	1,120,907
1995	75,068	87,113	86,340	67,937	95,447	85,126	94,576	70,904	94,794	126,210	84,991	107,177	1,075,683
1996	99,542	95,034	76,704	128,169	148,189	103,892	135,652	87,896	108,490	161,894	90,105	110,453	1,346,020
1997	121,433	133,056	131,473	148,647	117,219	116,117	80,867	72,602	93,967	150,065	97,984	124,245	1,387,675

Source: Winnipeg Commodity Exchange (WCE)

Average Open Interest of Canola Futures in Winnipeg   In 20 Metric Ton Units

Year	Jan.	Feb.	Mar.	Apr.	May	June	July	Aug.	Sept.	Oct.	Nov.	Dec.
1987	25,143	32,141	34,152	31,564	30,761	28,903	26,599	24,083	25,075	25,893	23,049	26,576
1988	28,875	33,387	31,798	34,056	34,587	31,318	30,224	29,509	26,289	29,510	28,974	29,221
1989	22,435	20,889	18,591	22,690	24,587	21,025	22,280	22,027	16,153	21,556	20,981	21,749
1990	18,431	20,340	17,599	19,825	24,718	22,546	23,073	24,353	24,872	25,688	18,706	22,057
1991	22,000	22,829	24,815	26,637	30,072	28,240	28,288	27,547	27,558	29,079	23,880	20,117
1992	15,943	17,556	20,559	21,410	23,727	28,885	26,013	25,674	28,049	32,724	35,693	37,375
1993	34,098	37,658	36,715	38,210	38,231	29,743	39,763	43,844	50,616	55,107	54,998	54,475
1994	50,335	55,280	54,899	58,012	60,567	55,434	54,733	57,044	57,049	54,375	55,045	49,475
1995	47,579	43,662	36,530	32,580	38,361	42,961	43,607	42,828	51,067	57,638	46,640	45,444
1996	42,646	43,808	45,126	47,989	54,228	52,176	49,387	40,619	42,242	52,273	53,121	54,323
1997	48,681	48,281	50,815	50,025	49,212	43,941	35,496	30,039	25,255	36,674	38,702	42,510

Source: Winnipeg Commodity Exchange (WCE)

World Supply and Distribution of Canola and Products In Thousands of Metric Tons

Crop Year	Canola					Canola Meal					Canola Oil				
	Production	Exports	Imports	Crush	Ending Stocks	Production	Exports	Imports	Consumption	Ending Stocks	Production	Exports	Imports	Consumption	Ending Stocks
1988-9	22,646	4,417	4,610	20,252	3,760	12,160	2,709	2,675	12,213	81	7,671	1,939	1,807	7,775	687
1989-90	22,096	2,831	2,891	21,075	3,240	12,709	1,681	1,773	12,721	160	7,944	1,624	1,730	8,000	743
1990-1	25,321	2,433	2,474	23,318	3,130	14,083	1,950	1,877	14,056	114	8,786	1,577	1,550	8,697	781
1991-2	28,489	2,674	2,645	25,111	3,700	15,203	2,527	2,507	15,169	128	9,469	1,529	1,633	9,518	836
1992-3	25,588	3,058	3,003	23,634	780	14,304	2,705	2,626	14,206	147	8,990	1,129	1,134	9,120	742
1993-4	27,039	4,150	4,087	25,270	790	15,151	2,623	2,736	15,287	124	9,726	1,590	1,527	9,532	849
1994-5	30,626	4,506	4,579	27,511	1,040	16,519	2,630	2,558	16,405	167	10,648	2,038	2,052	10,276	1,236
1995-6[1]	34,911	4,302	4,291	30,356	1,120	18,282	3,023	3,021	18,254	192	11,729	1,887	1,930	11,665	1,334
1996-7[2]	31,257	3,898	3,865	29,840	1,120	17,906	2,890	2,967	17,953	222	11,492	1,661	1,554	11,560	1,160
1997-8[3]	34,253	3,938	3,960	31,220		18,739	2,815	2,798	18,750	194	12,032	1,846	1,921	12,187	1,080

[1] Preliminary. [2] Estimate. [3] Forecast. *Source: The Oil World*

Salient Statistics of Canola and Canola Oil in the United States In Millions of Pounds

Crop Year Beginning June 1	Canola Supply				Canola Disappearance			Canola Oil Supply				Canola Oil Disappearance		
	Stocks June 1	Production	Imports	Total	Crush	Exports	Total[3]	Stocks June 1	Production	Imports	Total	Domestic	Exports	Total
1988-9	2	39	37	78	71	4	75	29	54	430	513	486	8	494
1989-90	3	95	231	329	298	10	308	20	130	391	541	510	6	516
1990-1	21	97	141	259	195	32	227	24	18	583	625	577	7	584
1991-2	32	191	2	225	109	97	212	41	32	815	888	801	15	816
1992-3	13	144	27	184	59	104	174	71	49	861	981	898	16	914
1993-4	10	252	773	1,036	850	78	941	67	406	902	1,375	1,228	76	1,304
1994-5	95	447	630	1,173	899	227	1,139	137	299	938	1,374	1,165	153	1,318
1995-6	34	548	558	1,140	899	138	1,052	54	355	1,086	1,496	1,270	147	1,417
1996-7[1]	88	479	570	1,137	866	173	1,057	79	341	1,075	1,495	1,136	293	1,429
1997-8[2]	80	914	441	1,435	1,057	260	1,338	66	362	1,126	1,554	1,290	187	1,477

[1] Preliminary. [2] Estimate. [3] Forecast. *Source: Economic Research Service, U.S. Department of Agriculture (ERS-USDA)*

Wholesale Price of Canola Oil, Refined (Denatured), in Tanks in New York In Cents Per Pound

Year	Jan.	Feb.	Mar.	Apr.	May	June	July	Aug.	Sept.	Oct.	Nov.	Dec.	Average
1988	63.56	63.50	63.50	63.50	63.50	63.50	63.50	63.50	63.50	64.63	66.25	70.00	64.37
1989	70.00	70.00	80.25	80.25	80.25	80.75	80.25	80.25	80.25	80.25	80.25	80.25	78.58
1990	81.75	82.25	82.23	82.25	82.25	82.25	82.25	82.25	79.25	77.25	77.25	81.00	81.02
1991	82.25	82.25	82.25	82.25	82.25	82.25	82.25	82.25	82.25	82.25	82.25	82.25	82.25
1992	82.25	82.25	82.25	82.25	82.25	82.25	82.25	82.25	67.25	62.25	62.25	62.25	76.00
1993	62.25	62.25	62.25	62.25	55.88	53.75	53.25	53.00	53.00	52.00	52.50	50.00	56.03
1994	53.75	53.75	53.75	53.75	53.75	53.75	53.75	53.75	53.75	53.75	53.75	53.75	53.75
1995	53.75	53.75	53.75	53.75	53.15	50.75	50.75	50.75	50.75	50.75	50.75	50.75	51.95
1996	50.75	50.75	50.75	50.75	50.75	50.75	50.75	50.75	50.75	60.56	90.00	90.00	58.11
1997[1]	90.00	90.00	90.00	90.00	90.00	90.00	90.00	90.00	90.00				90.00

[1] Preliminary. *Source: Economic Research Service, U.S. Department of Agriculture (ERS-USDA)*

Average Price of Canola in Vancouver In Canadian Dollars Per Tonne

Year	Jan.	Feb.	Mar.	Apr.	May	June	July	Aug.	Sept.	Oct.	Nov.	Dec.	Average
1987	242.61	227.73	219.03	221.67	243.97	256.27	247.85	235.66	243.24	257.22	267.19	281.15	245.30
1988	302.56	303.16	294.22	305.27	336.31	413.98	395.28	381.19	379.83	349.68	333.96	344.35	344.98
1989	329.54	321.64	333.29	331.44	335.18	306.10	300.49	289.44	297.10	293.79	303.10	302.54	311.97
1990	300.01	301.45	311.00	318.78	322.24	303.89	300.83	299.43	292.74	295.23	290.08	290.01	302.14
1991	285.01	280.36	291.50	298.57	293.83	277.25	258.12	269.40	275.00	270.30	262.90	261.60	276.99
1992	264.15	273.35	282.70	276.85	288.08	292.35	272.20	282.26	320.62	302.10	327.22	331.57	292.79
1993	344.22	329.26	328.67	325.06	318.85	319.23	331.29	322.85	311.29	311.66	331.44	366.37	328.35
1994	408.60	413.10	422.23	454.90	481.44	484.95	388.63	382.54	381.70	379.99	401.38	432.35	419.32
1995	431.85	440.41	456.13	425.40	404.27	414.31	426.49	405.94	405.89	413.29	416.03	423.77	421.98
1996	424.07	422.60	417.55	443.94	473.04	469.28	470.38	453.86	453.53	444.01	432.30	439.79	445.36
1997	441.96	441.68	457.95	448.09	446.00	428.47	395.58	400.68	390.38	398.81	419.12	410.21	423.24

Source: Winnipeg Commodity Exchange (WCE)

Cassava

Cassava, or tapioca root, is used primarily as an animal feed and as a foodstuff in tropical countries. For some time, cassava has been looked upon as a possible solution to world hunger problems. Technology advances have held forth the promise of increasing yields substantially. New strains of cassava root are being developed in Africa and they could eventually be used in the fight against hunger.

The major producers of cassava are scattered around the world. For 1994, the Food and Agricultural Organization of the United Nations reported that world production of cassava was 152.4 million tonnes. This was down about 1 per cent from the previous year. For the five year period of 1990-1994, world cassava production averaged 152.7 million tonnes per year. Cassava production has been fairly steady in recent years. Among the major producers of cassava are Brazil, Nigeria, Zaire and Thailand. Other major producers include Indonesia, Tanzania, Ghana and China. In 1994, Brazil was the largest producer of cassava. Production was estimated at just over 24 million tonnes or almost 16 per cent of the world total. Over the most recent five year period, average cassava production was 23.3 million tonnes. The next largest producer is Nigeria with 1994 output at 21 million tonnes or almost 14 per cent of the world total. Average production over the last five years was 20.5 million tonnes. Production of cassava in Zaire was estimated at 19.6 million tonnes, down 6 per cent from the previous year. Production over the last five years averaged 19.5 million tonnes.

Thailand is both a major producer and exporter of tapioca root. For 1994, Thailand produced 19.1 million tonnes or almost 13 per cent of the world total. About 25 per cent of Thailand's production is exported making Thailand by far the world's largest exporter of cassava.

World exports of tapioca root in 1995 were estimated at 3.7 million tonnes, down 36 per cent from the previous year. One strong trend has been that world exports of cassava have been declining. In 1990, world cassava exports were 9.1 million tonnes. This appears to be the result of the exporting countries consuming their own production. Thailand is the world's largest exporter of cassava with over 90 per cent of the market. Indonesia exports smaller amounts of cassava.

World imports of cassava in 1995 were estimated at 3.7 million tonnes, down 26 per cent from the previous year. World imports of cassava have been on the decline. By far the world's largest importer is the 12 nation European Community. Imports in 1995 were 3.3 million tonnes or 90 per cent of the world total. China is a smaller importer of cassava. In part, the decline in imports of cassava may be due to the fact that other animal feeds are being substituted for tapioca root.

World Cassava Production — In Thousands of Metric Tons

Year	Brazil	China	Ghana	India	Indonesia	Mozambique	Nigeria	Paraguay	Tanzania	Thailand	Uganda	Zaire	World Total
1991	24,538	3,310	3,600	5,416	15,954	3,690	20,000	2,585	7,460	20,356	3,229	19,500	153,562
1992	21,919	3,357	4,000	5,469	16,516	3,239	21,320	2,591	7,112	20,356	2,896	20,210	153,058
1993	21,837	3,403	4,500	5,413	16,799	3,511	29,900	2,656	6,833	20,203	3,139	20,835	163,002
1994	24,464	3,501	6,025	5,784	15,729	3,352	31,005	2,518	7,209	19,091	2,080	18,051	163,514
1995	25,316	3,501	6,899	6,000	15,438	3,597	31,404	3,000	5,969	18,164	2,625	17,500	164,163
1996[1]	24,587	3,501	6,899	6,000	15,438	4,733	31,500	2,770	5,912	16,000	2,650	18,000	162,942

[1] Estimate. *Source: Food and Agricultural Organization of the United Nations (FAO-UN)*

Prices of Tapioca, Hard Pellets, F.O.B. Rotterdam — U.S. Dollars Per Metric Ton

Year	Jan.	Feb.	Mar.	Apr.	May	June	July	Aug.	Sept.	Oct.	Nov.	Dec.	Average
1992	197	184	179	177	179	181	184	192	195	187	172	170	183
1993	160	150	140	149	145	133	130	131	136	127	120	125	137
1994	122	123	128	133	138	141	147	154	158	161	161	161	144
1995	164	170	180	178	174	176	183	176	178	184	182	178	177
1996	167	160	155	158	163	154	149	154	146	139	140	133	152
1997	133	118	112	108	114	110	100	97	100	102	102	100	108

Source: The Oil World

World Trade in Tapioca — In Thousands of Metric Tons

	Exports					Imports						
Year	China	Indonesia	Thailand	Viet Nam	Total World Exports	China	EC-12[2]	Japan	Rep. of Korea	United States	Former U.S.S.R.	Total World Imports
1991	410	859	6,187	3	7,571	175	5,692	162	444	127	----	7,353
1992	316	873	8,045	32	9,422	230	6,128	181	876	217	22	8,951
1993	269	936	6,707	29	8,089	149	6,449	151	658	60	8	8,417
1994	77	686	4,703	28	5,642	92	5,441	94	132	18	----	6,076
1995	10	481	3,297	1	3,865	362	2,924	16	140	----	----	3,580
1996	11	410	3,607	1	4,080	69	3,370	22	550	----	----	4,220
1997[1]	8	168	3,062	27	3,300	126	2,641	11	282	----	----	3,345

[1] Estimate. [2] Excluding trade between the EEC members. *Source: The Oil World*

Castor Beans

World production of castorseed beans in the 1996-97 season was estimated by the USDA at 1.17 million metric tonnes, down six percent from the previous season. Over the last five seasons, global production of castorseed beans has averaged 1.18 million tonnes. India is the largest producer of castor beans with 1996-97 production estimated at 850,000 metric tonnes, down nine percent from the previous year. India produces nearly three-quarters of the world's castor beans. China is the next largest producer of castor beans with 1996-97 production estimated at 200,000 tonnes, 11 percent more than in 1995-96. The next largest producer of castor beans is Brazil. The 1996-97 crop was 35,000 tonnes. Other producers include Paraguay, the Philippines, Pakistan and Ecuador.

Castor beans are used to produce castor oil. India is the largest producer of castor oil and the largest exporter. The U.S. is a major importer and user of castor oil.

The USDA reported that in June 1997, U.S. imports of castor oil were 6,880 tonnes. That was up sharply from June 1996 when imports were 36 tonnes. In October-June 1996-97, U.S. imports of castor oil were 24,661 tonnes, down 33 percent from the comparable period in 1995-96. The USDA reported that the value of castor oil imports in October-June 1996-97 was $18 million. This was 35 percent under the value of castor oil imports in the October-June 1995-96 period.

World Production of Castorseed Beans In Thousands of Metric Tons

Crop Year	Brazil	China	Ecuador	India	Mexico	Paraguay	Pakistan	Philip-pines	Sudan	Tanzania	Thailand	Former U.S.S.R.	World Total
1991-2	133	310	5	575	1	33	13	7	6	3	13	32	1,163
1992-3	102	291	12	617	1	20	6	7	8	3	24	20	1,140
1993-4	45	280	13	700	1	15	7	7	6	3	22	4	1,135
1994-5	53	230	7	850	1	10	5	7	4	3	15	8	1,226
1995-6[1]	33	165	5	930	1	9	3	7	2	3	16	3	1,209
1996-7[2]	48	220	4	770	1	8	3	7	1	2	15	3	1,116
1997-8[3]	110	220	4	800	----	9	3	7	----	----	15	3	1,210

[1] Preliminary. [2] Estimate. [3] Forecast. *Sources: Foreign Agricultural Service, U.S. Department of Agriculture (FAS-USDA); The Oil World*

Castor Oil Consumption[2] in the United States In Thousands of Pounds

Crop Year	Oct.	Nov.	Dec.	Jan.	Feb.	Mar.	Apr.	May	June	July	Aug.	Sept.	Total
1991-2	----------	12,073	----------	3,877	2,914	3,766	2,806	3,516	3,606	3,203	3,708	3,019	42,488
1992-3	4,712	3,250	3,100	3,287	4,271	3,924	4,098	3,965	4,496	4,902	5,073	4,400	49,478
1993-4	5,046	5,649	5,092	5,510	4,982	5,766	4,548	6,335	5,258	4,603	4,929	4,543	62,261
1994-5	5,032	4,204	5,092	6,001	5,179	4,911	4,722	3,740	5,067	4,891	6,452	4,834	60,125
1995-6	5,228	5,463	6,232	5,794	6,979	5,545	3,369	5,864	5,469	5,439	4,332	3,818	63,532
1996-7[1]	3,921	4,460	4,555	3,738	4,679	4,256	4,476	4,006	3,851	3,855	3,763	5,050	50,610
1997-8[1]	3,276	4,353	4,514										12,143

[1] Preliminary. [2] In inedible products (Resins, Plastics, etc.). *Source: Bureau of the Census, U.S. Department of Commerce*

Castor Oil Stocks in the United States, on First of Month In Thousands of Pounds

Crop Year	Oct.	Nov.	Dec.	Jan.	Feb.	Mar.	Apr.	May	June	July	Aug.	Sept.
1991-2	----------	22,921	----------	20,382	23,499	17,293	21,511	19,429	13,036	20,383	16,066	11,346
1992-3	7,158	5,383	5,364	4,124	10,076	13,154	19,345	14,983	17,094	24,652	20,616	25,070
1993-4	22,981	21,275	23,482	21,132	29,871	9,946	18,394	25,249	22,550	21,795	27,911	20,950
1994-5	21,066	23,484	23,357	21,132	29,245	20,986	10,387	5,492	22,765	33,557	37,542	42,516
1995-6	27,143	35,329	43,189	51,713	45,746	37,210	29,718	36,829	55,687	43,954	37,802	25,535
1996-7[1]	23,831	38,785	41,016	31,755	23,630	15,157	7,200	24,164	14,166	27,754	17,426	20,656
1997-8[1]	25,098	24,188	25,425	18,661								

[1] Preliminary. NA = Not available. *Source: Bureau of the Census, U.S. Department of Commerce*

Average Wholesale Prices of Castor Oil No. 1, Brazilian Tanks in New York In Cents Per Pound

Year	Jan.	Feb.	Mar.	Apr.	May	June	July	Aug.	Sept.	Oct.	Nov.	Dec.	Average
1991	39.30	36.00	36.75	37.00	37.00	36.50	35.50	35.00	35.00	35.40	35.00	37.50	36.33
1992	37.50	37.50	37.50	36.00	34.50	34.50	34.50	34.50	34.50	34.00	34.00	34.00	35.21
1993	34.00	32.00	32.00	32.00	37.00	37.00	37.00	37.00	38.50	41.50	44.00	44.00	37.17
1994	44.00	41.75	41.00	41.00	46.00	45.00	45.00	45.00	45.00	45.00	45.00	45.00	44.06
1995	45.00	45.00	45.00	45.00	45.00	45.00	45.00	45.00	45.00	45.00	45.00	45.00	45.00
1996	43.50	41.50	41.50	41.50	41.50	41.50	41.50	41.50	41.50	41.50	41.50	41.50	41.67
1997	44.20	44.00	42.88	42.50	42.50	35.00	36.50	36.50	37.00				40.12

Source: Foreign Agricultural Service, U.S.Department of Agriculture (FAS-USDA)

Cattle and Calves

The world cattle inventory has held relatively steady for several years; the January 1, 1998 total of 1,029 million head was marginally lower than a year earlier and compares with the 1990's low of 1,025 million in 1993. However, some large changes have occurred in selected areas, notably the decline in cattle numbers in the former U.S.S.R. and the increase in China. The early 1998 cattle inventory in Russia and the Ukraine was estimated at 53 million head vs: 58 million in 1997 and nearly 90 million in 1990. China's January 1, 1998 inventory of a record 147 million head compares with 140 million a year earlier and an annual average of 102 million early in the 1990's; if the uptrend is maintained China's cattle inventory should total 160 million head by the year 2000. India, who holds 25 percent of the world's total cattle inventory, 275 million head, has shown little cattle number change in recent years.

The U.S. cattle inventory may have peaked in the 1980's at around 110 million head, then sliding to 96 million by early 1990. A moderate cyclical expansion then took hold that carried the nation's inventory to about 100 million head by early 1998. However, the mid 1997 inventory of 108.8 million head was the lowest midyear total since 1992. First half commercial cattle slaughter was down about 2percent, largely reflecting reduced beef cow and steer slaughter, but total cow slaughter was down nearly 8percent and beef slaughter was off 12percent. As of late 1997 there was little sign that any major cyclical expansion in cattle numbers would take hold until 1999, if then. The three largest cattle inventory states are Texas, Kansas and Nebraska.

The world beef market during 1997 was considerably more placid than in 1996 when European consumption and trade was disrupted by the "mad cow" disease outbreak. Although the beef safety fears largely eased in 1997, little recovery in world beef usage was expected due largely to a continued contraction in the Russian republics, from 4.1 billion tonnes in 1997 to 3.8 billion in 1998. Asian beef consumption, however, continues to expand; nearly doubling from the early 1990's to over 8 billion tonnes in 1998, with China setting the pace.

U.S. cattle slaughter in 1997 (through October) of 30.7 million head compares with 30.8 million in the like 1996 period. Fed cattle slaughter in 1998 is expected to follow a fairly normal seasonal pattern and peak in the second and third quarters. However, slaughter is likely to decline three-four percent due to lower placements on feed during the second half of 1997. Cow slaughter may drop about 12 percent. Average dressed slaughter weights are expected to increase to 705-710 pounds due to the reduced cow slaughter. U.S. beef production in 1998 is forecast at 24.8 billion pounds vs. 25.3 billion in 1997 and 25.4 billion in 1996. On a worldwide basis, U.S. cattle slaughter generally accounts for about 15-20 percent of world slaughter, but accounts for about 25 percent of world beef production. U.S. per capita beef consumption, however, has shown little growth in recent years as consumers opt for less red meat in their diet. Per capita use in 1997 of 67.2 pounds (retail weight) compares with 67.7 pounds in 1996 and a 1998 estimate of 65.7 pounds.

U.S. beef (and veal) exports in 1997 of 1.92 billion pounds compare with 1.88 billion in 1996 and forecasts of 2.1 billion in 1998. The gain in 1998 was based on increased demand from Japan and Korea, but a downward revision is likely due to the financial difficulties in both nations. Typically, Japan has been the largest market for U.S. beef, but Mexico has been the most rapidly growing market recently. U.S. beef imports in 1997 of 2.5 billion pounds compare with 2.1 billion in 1996 and 2.7 billion estimated for 1998. Australia, New Zealand and Canada are the largest foreign beef suppliers to the U.S. while live cattle is imported from Canada and Mexico.

Fed cattle prices are expected to remain strong for some time, after rising about $2/cwt. to $67/cwt. in 1997. On the retail level, choice beef prices in late 1997 were expected to reach the upper $2.80's per pound, the highest since 1994.

Futures Markets

Live cattle futures and options are traded on the Chicago Mercantile Exchange (CME), the Bolsa de Mercadorias & Futuros (BM&F), and the MidAmerica Commodity Exchange (MidAm). Feeder cattle futures are traded on the CME and the BM&F, and feeder cattle options are traded on the CME.

World Cattle and Buffalo Numbers as of January 1 In Thousands of Head

Year	Argentina	Australia	Brazil	China	Colombia	France	Germany	India	Mexico	Russia[3]	Ukraine[3]	United States	World Total (Mil Head)
1987	51,683	23,540	128,000	91,670	18,819	22,171	21,109	274,822	33,603	----	122,103	102,118	1,073
1988	56,482	23,469	130,000	94,650	18,400	21,053	20,608	268,720	35,378	----	115,824	99,622	1,070
1989	56,482	23,938	130,500	97,948	17,627	21,340	20,369	268,470	34,999	59,300	25,621	98,065	1,037
1990	56,482	24,673	140,400	100,752	16,835	21,394	20,287	270,070	31,747	58,800	25,195	95,816	1,035
1991	56,982	25,026	142,900	102,884	16,225	21,446	19,488	272,300	29,847	57,000	24,623	96,393	1,036
1992	55,229	25,857	141,800	104,592	16,008	20,970	17,134	271,200	30,232	54,677	23,728	97,556	1,032
1993	55,577	25,182	143,700	107,840	16,391	20,383	16,207	271,255	30,649	52,226	22,457	99,176	1,032
1994	54,875	25,758	144,900	113,157	16,614	20,112	15,897	272,655	30,702	48,914	21,607	100,988	1,036
1995	54,207	25,736	149,315	123,317	16,725	20,524	15,962	274,155	30,191	43,296	19,580	102,755	1,033
1996	53,569	26,500	149,228	132,058	16,768	20,662	15,890	276,105	28,140	39,700	17,526	103,487	1,038
1997[1]	51,696	26,300	146,110	140,010	16,856	20,563	15,770	277,045	26,900	36,400	15,295	101,209	1,032
1998[2]	50,277	26,300	144,500	147,000	16,941	20,300	15,650	278,565	25,630	34,000	13,500	99,118	1,029

[1] Preliminary. [2] Forecast. [3] Formerly part of the U.S.S.R.; country data not shown seperately prior to 1989. *Source: Foreign Agricultural Service, U.S. Department of Agriculture (FAS-USDA)*

Cattle Supply and Distribution in the United States In Thousands of Head

Year	Cattle & Calves on Farms January 1	Imports	Calves Born	Total Supply	Livestock Slaughter - Cattle and Calves: Commercial: Federally Inspected	Other[3]	All Commercial	Farm	Total Slaughter	Deaths on Farms	Exports	Total Disap-pearance
1986	105,378	1,407	41,182	147,967	39,108	1,588	40,696	350	41,046	4,992	108	46,146
1987	102,118	1,200	40,152	143,470	37,148	1,314	38,462	330	38,792	4,800	131	43,723
1988	99,622	1,332	39,318	141,247	36,459	1,126	37,585	295	37,889	4,573	321	42,774
1989	96,740	1,459	38,817	139,626	35,110	980	36,089	240	36,329	4,361	169	40,859
1990	95,816	2,135	38,613	139,546	34,133	800	35,032	245	35,277	4,327	120	39,724
1991	96,393	1,939	38,583	139,861	33,285	841	34,126	242	34,368	4,247	311	38,927
1992	97,556	2,255	38,933	141,104	33,428	817	34,245	244	34,489	4,366	322	39,177
1993	99,176	2,499	39,448	142,750	33,752	767	34,519	227	34,746	4,630	153	39,529
1994	100,988	2,083	40,059	143,799	34,719	745	35,465	227	35,700	4,268	231	40,190
1995	102,755	2,694	40,211	145,660	36,128	785	36,913	387	37,300	4,400	88	41,800
1996[1]	103,487	1,965	39,776	145,229	35,718	863	36,583	----	38,600	4,600	174	43,300
1997[2]	101,500	1,958	38,718	142,176	35,567	784	36,350	----	38,100	4,800	280	43,100

[1] Preliminary. [2] Estimate. [3] Wholesale and retail. *Source: Economic Research Service, U.S. Department of Agriculture (ERS-USDA)*

Beef Supply and Utilization in the United States

Year/Quarter	Beginning Stocks	Production: Commercial	Production: Total	Imports	Total Supply	Exports	Ending Stocks	Total Disap-pearance	Per Capita Disappearance: Carcass Weight	Per Capita Disappearance: Retail Weight
	Million Pounds								Pounds	
1994	529	24,278	24,386	2,368	27,283	1,611	548	25,124	96.4	67.0
I	529	5,745	5,783	682	6,994	359	562	6,073	23.4	16.4
II	562	6,042	6,058	603	7,223	391	506	6,326	24.3	17.0
III	506	6,377	6,393	587	7,486	416	543	6,527	25.0	17.5
IV	543	6,114	6,152	499	7,194	445	548	6,201	23.7	16.6
1995	548	25,115	25,222	2,104	27,874	1,821	519	25,534	97.0	67.4
I	548	5,888	5,925	572	7,045	368	514	6,163	23.5	16.3
II	514	6,325	6,341	540	7,395	452	471	6,472	24.6	17.1
III	471	6,625	6,641	539	7,651	499	464	6,688	25.4	17.6
IV	464	6,277	6,315	453	7,232	502	519	6,211	23.5	16.4
1996	519	25,419	25,525	2,073	28,117	1,877	377	25,863	97.4	67.7
I	519	6,302	6,340	508	7,367	452	461	6,454	24.4	17.0
II	461	6,642	6,658	526	7,645	544	406	6,695	25.2	17.5
III	406	6,390	6,406	555	7,367	436	414	6,517	24.5	17.0
IV	414	6,084	6,121	484	7,019	445	377	6,197	23.2	16.2
1997[1]	377	25,301	25,407	2,467	29,493	1,918	400	25,933	96.7	67.2
I	377	6,112	6,149	536	7,062	455	387	6,220	23.3	16.2
II	387	6,419	6,435	716	7,538	513	425	6,600	24.7	17.1
III	425	6,620	6,636	680	7,741	500	430	6,811	25.4	17.6
IV	430	6,150	6,187	535	7,152	450	400	6,302	23.4	16.3
1998[2]	400	24,825	24,931	2,680	29,061	2,095	325	25,566	94.5	65.7
I	400	6,050	6,087	680	7,167	475	375	6,317	23.4	16.3
II	375	6,200	6,216	725	7,316	540	325	6,451	23.9	16.6

[1] Preliminary. [2] Forecast. *Source: Economic Research Service, U.S. Department of Agriculture (ERS-USDA)*

United States Cattle on Feed in 13 States In Thousands of Head

Year/Quarter	Number on Feed[3]	Placed on Feed	Marketings	Other Disappearance	Year/Quarter	Number on Feed[3]	Placed on Feed	Marketings	Other Disappearance
1994	11,196	23,449	22,979	1,060	1996[1]	10,346	23,210	22,085	913
I	11,196	5,372	5,559	275	I	10,346	5,210	5,531	213
II	10,734	4,675	5,951	334	II	9,812	4,226	5,937	261
III	9,124	6,315	5,996	191	III	7,840	6,664	5,481	182
IV	9,252	7,087	5,473	260	IV	8,841	7,050	5,076	257
1995	9,117	22,576	21,111	732	1997[2]	10,558	24,271	22,774	930
I	9,117	5,455	4,956	197	I	10,558	5,605	5,563	239
II	9,409	4,982	5,493	199	II	10,391	4,856	6,014	275
III	8,699	5,904	5,685	152	III	8,958	7,135	5,975	155
IV	8,766	6,235	4,977	184	IV	9,963	6,675	5,222	261

[1] Preliminary. [2] Estimate. [3] Beginning of Period. *Source: Economic Research Service, U.S.Department of Agriculture (ERS-USDA)*

CATTLE AND CALVES

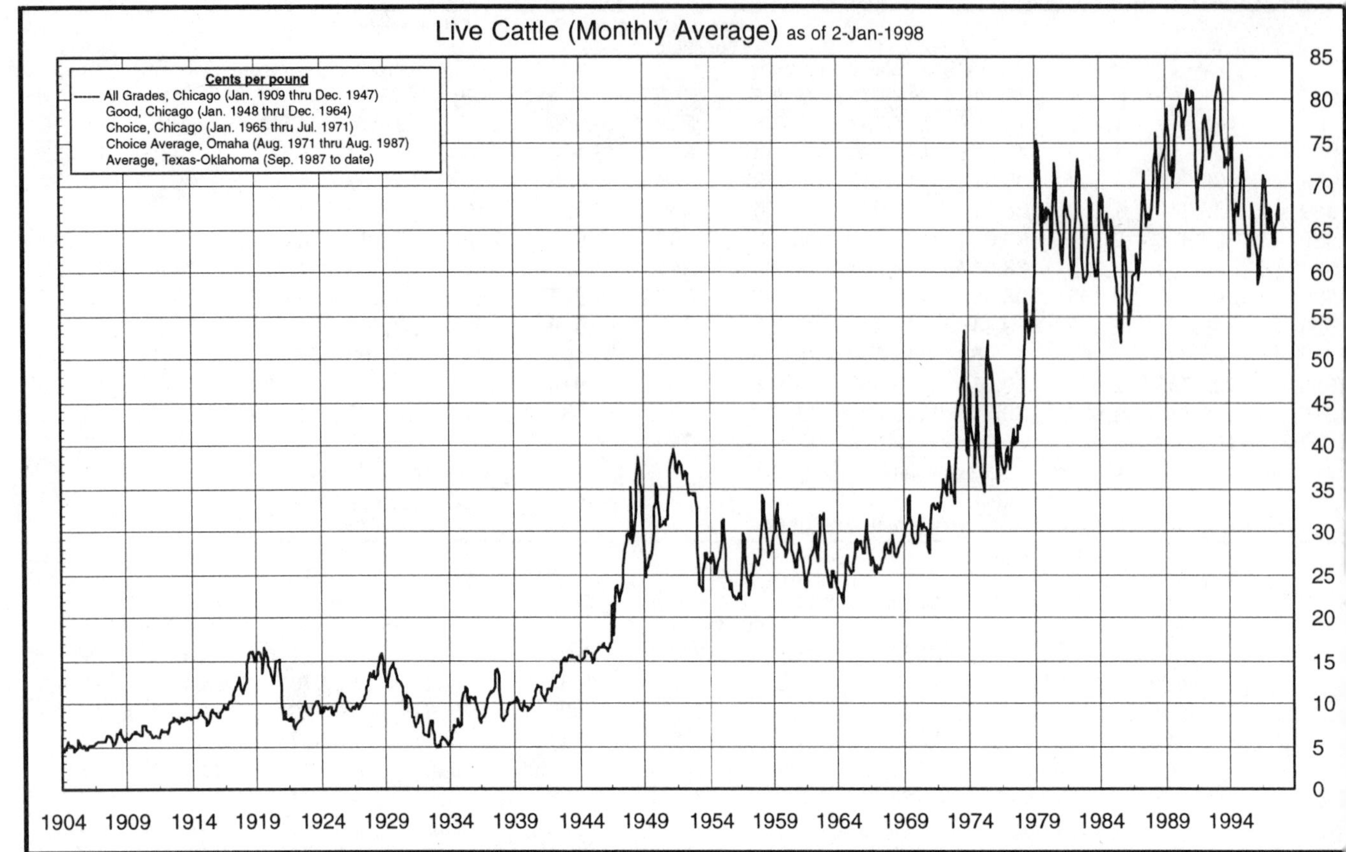

United States Cattle on Feed in 7 States, on First of Month In Thousands of Head

Year	Jan.	Feb.	Mar.	Apr.	May	June	July	Aug.	Sept.	Oct.	Nov	Dec
1987	7,953	7,614	7,473	7,527	7,548	7,875	7,488	6,983	7,098	7,830	8,659	8,752
1988	8,411	8,204	7,912	8,056	7,829	8,134	7,736	7,140	6,944	7,404	8,194	8,255
1989	8,045	7,970	7,931	8,252	8,087	7,795	7,235	6,763	6,631	6,958	7,911	8,331
1990	8,378	8,526	8,319	8,483	8,181	7,867	7,310	6,998	6,975	7,635	8,669	9,039
1991	8,992	8,963	8,874	8,941	8,590	8,570	7,877	7,388	7,064	7,216	8,013	8,477
1992	8,397	8,223	8,195	8,058	7,868	7,876	7,377	7,050	7,018	7,565	8,704	8,984
1993	9,163	9,140	8,851	8,781	8,409	8,393	7,973	7,703	7,794	8,224	8,219	8,418
1994	8,256	8,139	7,981	7,960	7,772	7,511	6,910	6,841	6,949	7,295	7,988	8,198
1995	8,031	8,119	8,227	8,328	8,233	8,182	7,734	7,391	7,189	7,722	8,420	8,685
1996	8,667	8,304	8,152	8,286	7,758	7,253	6,578	6,337	6,612	7,486	8,534	9,003
1997[1]	8,943	8,813	8,769	8,904	8,484	8,231	7,679	7,536	7,850	8,558	9,390	9,718

[1] Preliminary. *Source: Economic Research Service, U.S. Department of Agriculture (ERS-USDA)*

United States Cattle Placed on Feedlots in 7 States In Thousands of Head

Year	Jan.	Feb.	Mar.	Apr.	May	June	July	Aug.	Sept.	Oct.	Nov.	Dec.	Total
1987	1,581	1,442	1,719	1,701	1,984	1,432	1,289	1,915	2,474	2,614	1,676	1,390	21,217
1988	1,663	1,379	1,848	1,521	2,175	1,387	1,251	1,660	2,209	2,450	1,690	1,421	20,654
1989	1,706	1,610	1,975	1,539	1,624	1,293	1,291	1,638	1,953	2,652	2,001	1,537	20,819
1990	1,881	1,383	1,862	1,362	1,597	1,325	1,530	1,745	2,199	2,726	1,987	1,433	21,030
1991	1,721	1,455	1,703	1,427	1,772	1,102	1,327	1,459	1,826	2,539	1,917	1,456	19,704
1992	1,565	1,502	1,516	1,425	1,724	1,319	1,432	1,641	2,189	2,688	1,813	1,694	20,508
1993	1,641	1,262	1,626	1,326	1,801	1,430	1,513	1,865	2,148	2,494	1,610	1,215	19,931
1994	1,416	1,256	1,518	1,310	1,359	1,113	1,520	1,761	1,915	2,244	1,642	1,345	18,863
1995	1,631	1,532	1,681	1,403	1,673	1,356	1,404	1,653	2,173	2,278	1,804	1,446	20,353
1996	1,312	1,441	1,666	1,150	1,242	1,068	1,483	1,965	2,267	2,536	1,953	1,423	19,506
1997[1]	1,663	1,552	1,694	1,296	1,612	1,224	1,751	2,111	2,278	2,454	1,826	1,304	20,765

[1] Preliminary. *Source: Economic Research Service, U.S. Department of Agriculture (ERS-USDA)*

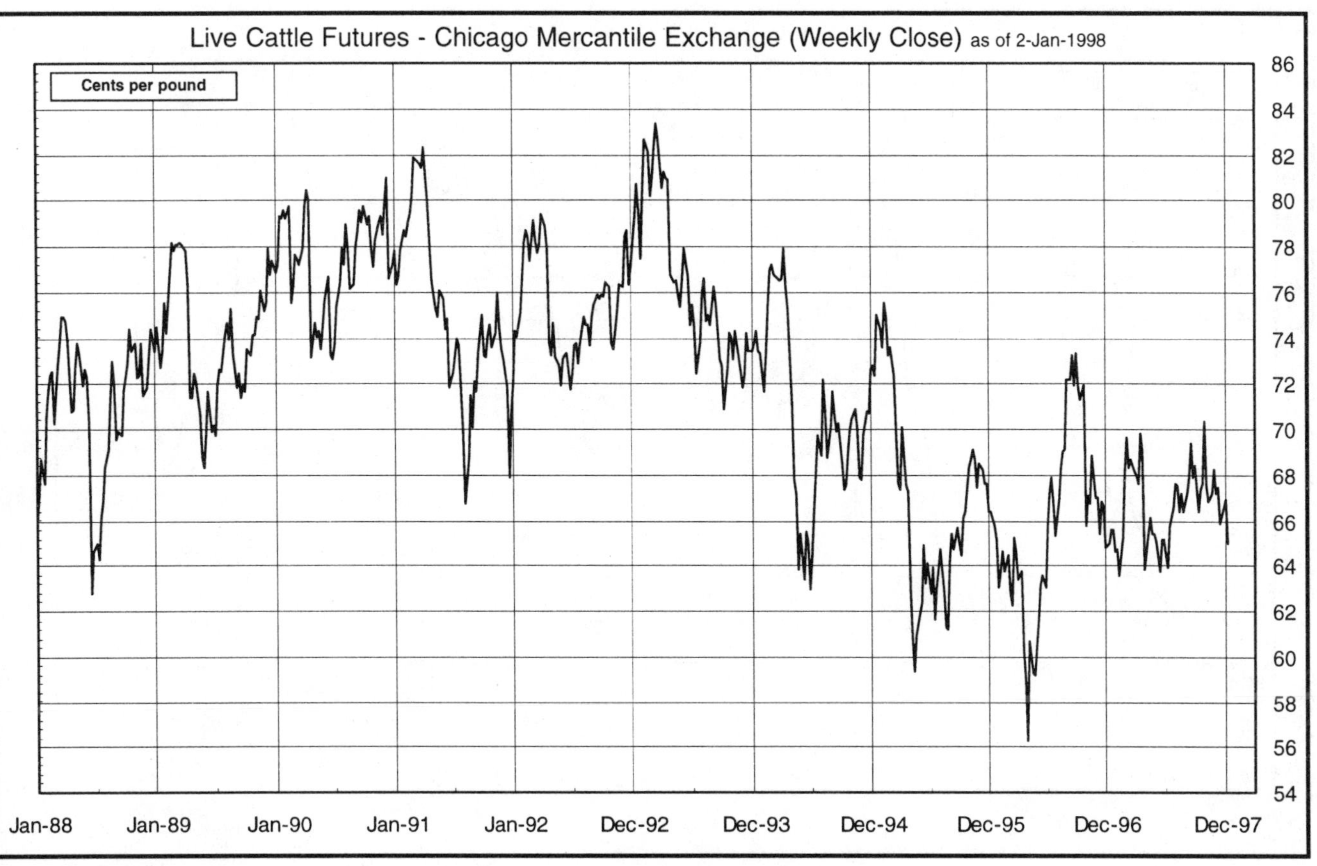

United States Cattle Marketings in 7 States In Thousands of Head

Year	Jan.	Feb.	Mar.	Apr.	May	June	July	Aug.	Sept.	Oct.	Nov.	Dec.	Total
1987	1,793	1,478	1,571	1,541	1,514	1,732	1,723	1,732	1,671	1,700	1,478	1,612	19,545
1988	1,764	1,545	1,593	1,609	1,724	1,717	1,785	1,790	1,682	1,576	1,517	1,516	19,818
1989	1,677	1,534	1,579	1,580	1,752	1,791	1,700	1,694	1,579	1,628	1,490	1,403	19,407
1990	1,619	1,495	1,578	1,539	1,761	1,809	1,765	1,686	1,460	1,605	1,522	1,359	19,198
1991	1,632	1,431	1,499	1,650	1,651	1,681	1,724	1,716	1,598	1,665	1,376	1,443	19,066
1992	1,640	1,410	1,536	1,490	1,594	1,702	1,674	1,592	1,581	1,473	1,442	1,414	18,548
1993	1,534	1,441	1,585	1,572	1,681	1,743	1,702	1,692	1,652	1,546	1,322	1,305	18,775
1994	1,481	1,357	1,467	1,430	1,542	1,632	1,550	1,602	1,525	1,504	1,370	1,432	18,317
1995	1,484	1,372	1,513	1,437	1,667	1,754	1,698	1,815	1,594	1,529	1,478	1,412	19,038
1996	1,626	1,541	1,476	1,613	1,747	1,696	1,678	1,653	1,342	1,431	1,418	1,415	18,636
1997[1]	1,728	1,554	1,497	1,648	1,785	1,732	1,852	1,755	1,528	1,545	1,429	1,499	19,552

[1] Preliminary. *Source: Economic Research Service, U.S. Department of Agriculture (ERS-USDA)*

Quarterly Trade of Live Cattle in the United States In Head

	Imports					Exports				
Year	First Quarter	Second Quarter	Third Quarter	Fourth Quarter	Annual	First Quarter	Second Quarter	Third Quarter	Fourth Quarter	Annual
1987	433,872	334,037	75,635	356,940	1,200,484	27,096	25,861	33,194	44,547	130,698
1988	731,806	216,269	131,503	252,628	1,332,206	22,563	28,008	157,642	113,236	321,449
1989	515,682	287,158	132,072	524,503	1,459,415	72,822	37,867	24,117	34,334	169,140
1990	566,516	577,328	301,668	689,488	2,135,000	33,929	28,384	23,335	34,266	119,914
1991	599,398	551,390	225,710	562,556	1,939,054	49,497	62,134	103,866	95,465	310,962
1992	599,255	505,568	389,417	801,025	2,255,265	97,683	100,282	74,827	48,998	321,790
1993	672,447	635,341	469,439	721,819	2,499,046	50,733	33,286	22,049	47,348	153,416
1994	569,466	540,845	386,596	585,597	2,082,504	51,803	43,115	62,729	73,144	230,791
1995	868,694	804,686	488,515	624,350	2,786,245	26,597	18,441	19,794	29,716	94,548
1996	605,648	467,059	391,633	501,108	1,965,448	33,906	42,796	42,757	54,848	174,307
1997[1]	494,637	500,052	423,838	213,401	1,631,928	63,217	58,153	81,095	31,053	233,518

[1] Preliminary. *Source: Economic Research Service, U.S. Department of Agriculture (ERS-USDA)*

CATTLE AND CALVES

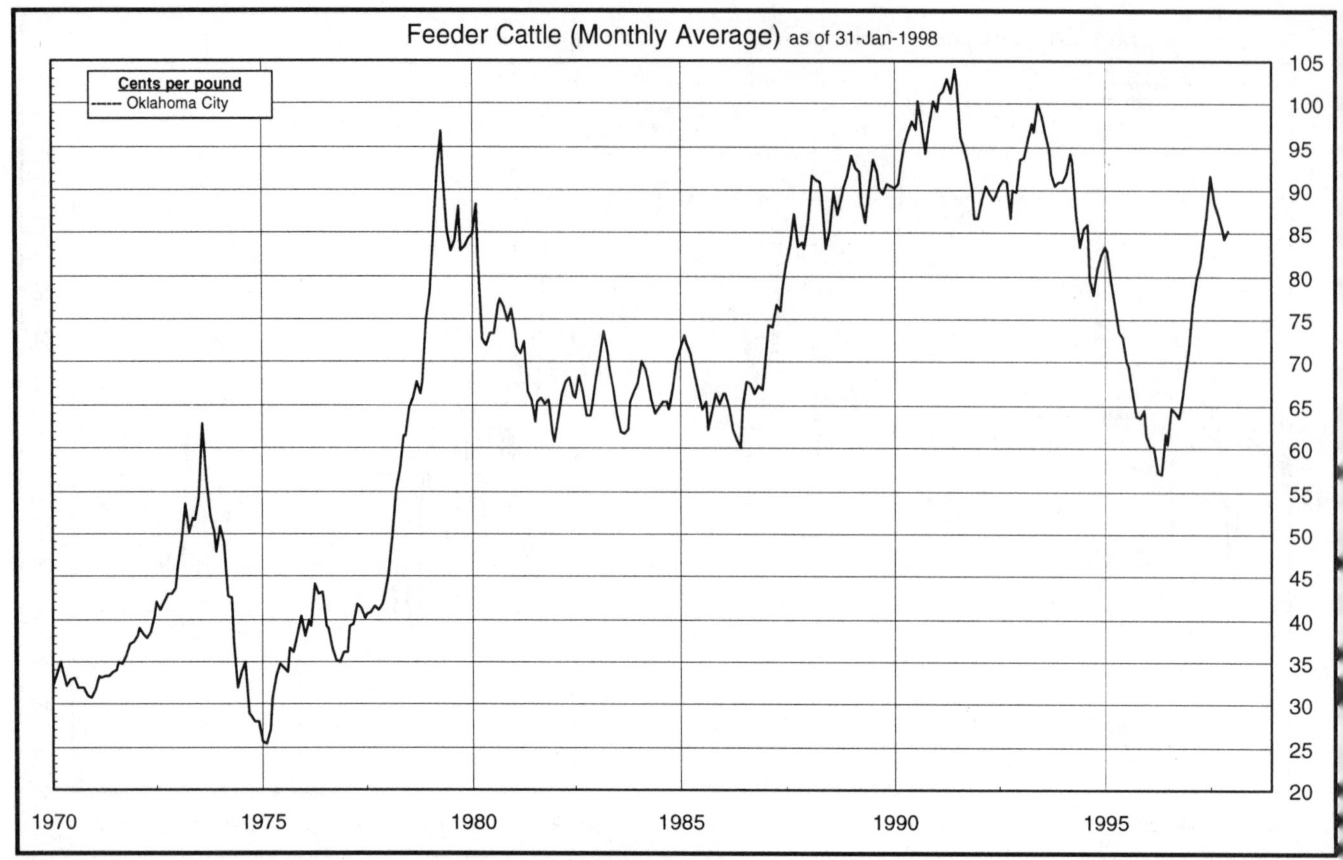

Average Wholesale Price of Slaughter Steers in Texas, Choice 2-4 (1100-1300 Lbs.) In Dollars Per 100 Lbs.

Year	Jan.	Feb.	Mar.	Apr.	May	June	July	Aug.	Sept.	Oct.	Nov.	Dec.	Average
1991	79.42	79.56	80.90	80.73	78.22	74.29	72.44	67.38	69.19	71.16	72.16	70.68	74.68
1992	73.88	77.21	78.18	77.83	75.98	73.55	73.02	74.26	75.04	75.97	75.29	78.35	75.71
1993	80.05	80.91	82.66	81.78	80.84	77.31	74.32	75.09	73.46	72.13	73.23	72.42	77.02
1994	72.88	73.03	75.41	75.48	68.12	63.60	66.58	68.04	66.79	66.51	69.43	69.35	69.60
1995	73.60	73.79	70.64	67.54	64.27	63.08	61.81	61.95	63.80	64.89	67.94	66.14	66.62
1996	64.63	63.00	61.77	59.85	59.78	61.37	64.07	67.15	71.12	70.95	70.70	66.25	65.05
1997	65.07	65.35	67.44	67.66	67.36	63.53	63.80	65.19	66.04	66.93	67.66	65.91	66.00

Source: Economic Research Service, U.S.Department of Agriculture (ERS-USDA)

Average Price of Steers (Feeder) in Oklahoma City In Dollars Per 100 Pounds

Year	Jan.	Feb.	Mar.	Apr.	May	June	July	Aug.	Sept.	Oct.	Nov.	Dec.	Average
1991	99.22	101.01	101.50	103.00	101.22	104.05	102.32	96.09	94.62	92.90	89.93	86.69	97.71
1992	86.63	88.90	90.43	89.48	88.96	89.27	90.43	91.30	90.87	86.65	90.12	89.83	89.41
1993	93.59	93.80	95.82	97.65	96.85	100.09	98.58	96.48	94.78	91.82	90.57	91.04	95.09
1994	90.90	91.88	94.34	93.18	87.21	83.45	85.48	85.97	79.77	77.88	80.99	82.58	86.14
1995	83.41	83.05	79.50	76.62	73.69	72.89	70.09	69.62	66.71	68.60	63.45	64.44	72.67
1996	61.38	60.16	60.03	57.20	57.06	61.66	60.56	64.79	64.33	63.45	66.33	68.26	62.10
1997	71.52	76.77	79.66	81.60	85.43	87.04	91.67	88.69	87.23	85.66	84.37	85.25	83.74

Source: Wall Street Journal

Federally Inspected Slaughter of Cattle in the United States In Thousands of Head

Year	Jan.	Feb.	Mar.	Apr.	May	June	July	Aug.	Sept.	Oct.	Nov.	Dec.	Total
1991	2,809	2,408	2,444	2,674	2,786	2,650	2,784	2,843	2,634	2,855	2,508	2,491	31,887
1992	2,856	2,377	2,599	2,525	2,688	2,863	2,802	2,721	2,748	2,793	2,490	2,632	32,094
1993	2,601	2,411	2,712	2,623	2,720	2,957	2,811	2,883	2,810	2,729	2,632	2,706	32,593
1994	2,679	2,501	2,799	2,656	2,780	2,984	2,770	3,001	2,885	2,878	2,744	2,806	33,483
1995	2,802	2,524	2,890	2,591	3,064	3,187	2,878	3,160	3,019	2,982	2,897	2,741	34,735
1996	3,046	2,855	2,834	3,039	3,257	3,078	3,080	3,148	2,693	3,074	2,801	2,800	35,721
1997[1]	3,169	2,726	2,795	2,998	3,125	3,003	3,127	3,050	2,909	3,156	2,698	2,811	35,567

[1] Preliminary. *Source: Agricultural Statistics Board, U.S. Department of Agriculture (ASB-USDA)*

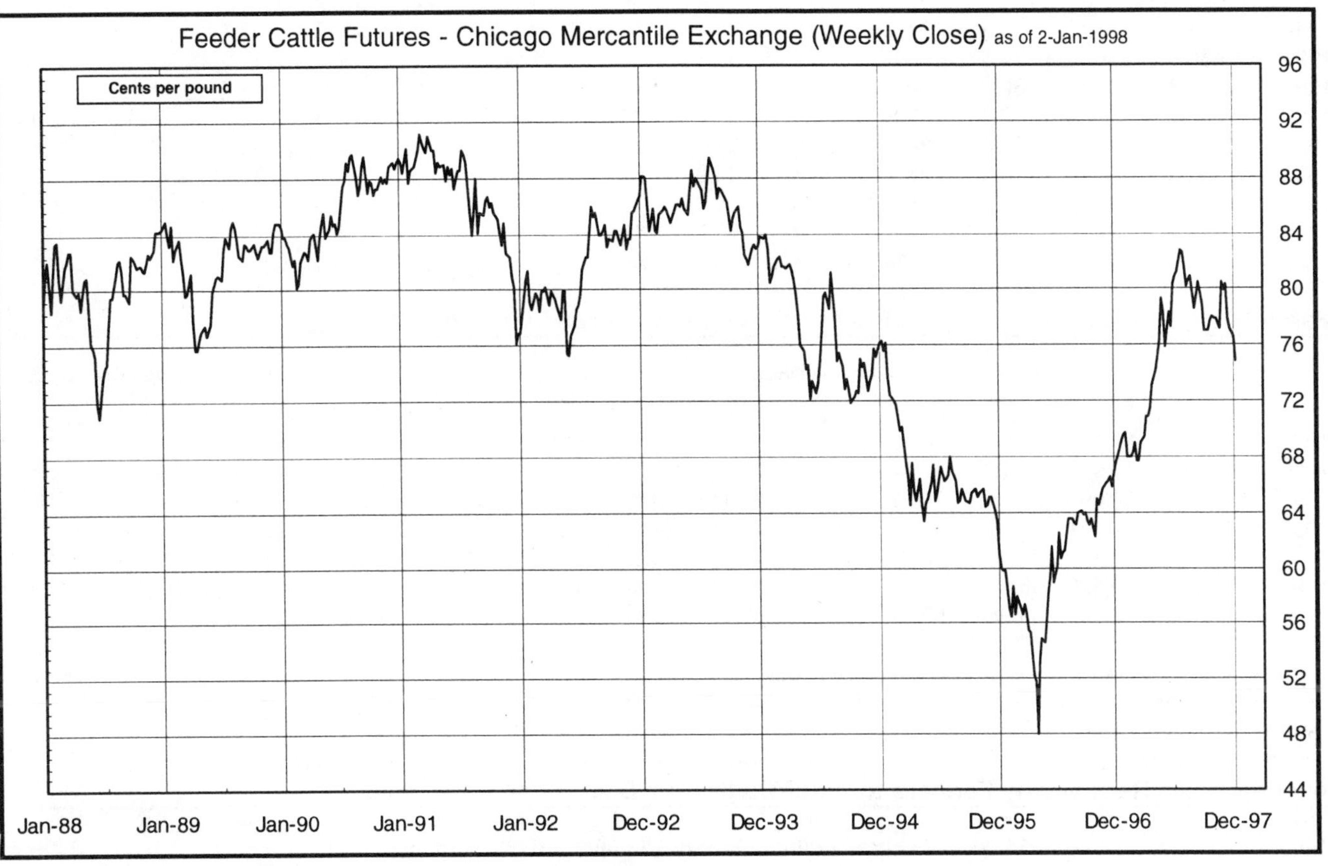

Average Open Interest of Live Cattle Futures in Chicago In Contracts

Year	Jan.	Feb.	Mar.	Apr.	May	June	July	Aug.	Sept.	Oct.	Nov.	Dec.
1987	62,770	83,958	91,018	89,818	98,350	86,144	81,399	81,315	90,915	80,156	75,379	74,839
1988	77,436	92,363	105,307	97,582	91,480	85,257	82,080	81,025	80,935	80,356	82,790	76,683
1989	80,464	84,909	93,240	82,267	81,588	69,981	78,045	76,582	73,530	65,807	73,962	71,508
1990	95,515	108,149	104,647	95,709	86,875	76,130	70,462	68,375	69,611	67,122	70,576	69,647
1991	74,392	79,695	84,574	83,322	78,284	70,107	67,868	68,359	74,483	70,395	75,788	74,687
1992	79,638	97,500	97,222	90,823	83,112	68,135	67,828	62,656	61,783	60,761	63,945	67,125
1993	78,481	79,256	88,113	78,144	72,183	68,287	66,617	66,560	70,275	70,559	73,571	76,042
1994	87,923	87,578	83,949	70,287	72,851	75,470	76,663	72,988	73,391	67,924	74,152	68,600
1995	80,306	78,793	76,821	64,763	61,460	56,783	58,077	55,511	58,319	62,222	69,495	69,065
1996	72,870	83,064	91,348	97,315	97,911	96,320	96,547	93,557	92,804	88,467	88,062	87,305
1997	97,014	103,437	108,157	98,354	99,640	96,279	99,042	98,590	94,137	93,579	100,368	102,741

Source: Chicago Mercantile Exchange (CME)

Volume of Trading of Live Cattle Futures in Chicago In Thousands of Contracts

Year	Jan.	Feb.	Mar.	Apr.	May	June	July	Aug.	Sept.	Oct.	Nov.	Dec.	Total
1987	376.6	426.7	474.2	456.6	523.7	357.8	394.8	412.7	485.8	580.4	363.1	377.0	5,229.3
1988	425.1	455.6	543.9	468.0	467.8	571.3	463.4	511.8	415.0	417.5	383.9	353.9	5,477.2
1989	452.9	357.7	409.0	404.2	382.9	370.3	327.9	331.9	376.9	345.4	266.2	240.2	4,265.7
1990	400.5	350.0	354.1	327.6	372.2	263.9	298.5	327.7	273.3	320.3	268.4	240.8	3,797.4
1991	344.2	252.1	288.9	300.4	247.2	254.8	311.2	406.1	321.2	386.3	327.7	352.8	3,792.9
1992	375.6	322.5	353.8	319.1	275.9	263.9	268.9	231.0	196.0	227.9	203.8	246.7	3,319.6
1993	328.8	294.2	363.4	263.5	199.7	255.4	269.3	226.0	269.5	297.6	248.4	291.1	3,307.0
1994	280.8	291.8	262.4	264.2	372.9	363.9	318.2	317.1	270.0	308.9	275.9	254.6	3,580.9
1995	289.7	259.2	391.7	287.2	285.7	290.2	245.3	266.8	233.4	220.1	246.7	241.1	3,257.1
1996	312.0	275.4	333.2	457.5	385.9	303.1	319.8	299.5	278.1	339.4	312.6	309.7	3,926.2
1997	361.6	352.2	312.1	331.9	285.9	303.4	387.5	324.9	316.8	374.6	238.0	330.6	3,919.6

Source: Chicago Mercantile Exchange (CME)

CATTLE AND CALVES

Beef Steer-Corn Price Ratio[1] in the United States

Year	Jan.	Feb.	Mar.	Apr.	May	June	July	Aug.	Sept.	Oct.	Nov.	Dec.	Average
1990	34.1	33.8	32.9	31.5	29.9	29.4	29.2	31.5	34.0	36.6	37.6	36.6	33.1
1991	36.0	35.0	34.5	33.9	33.4	33.2	32.9	30.6	30.7	32.2	31.6	30.7	32.9
1992	30.3	31.0	30.7	30.8	30.2	29.8	31.7	34.7	35.0	37.3	38.2	38.7	33.2
1993	38.8	39.8	38.8	37.8	37.8	37.1	33.8	33.4	33.7	31.8	29.8	27.0	35.0
1994	27.1	26.3	27.5	28.5	26.8	24.0	28.4	31.6	30.2	32.1	34.4	31.9	29.1
1995	32.6	32.4	30.5	28.4	26.3	25.2	23.5	23.5	23.0	22.3	22.7	21.1	26.0
1996	20.3	18.1	17.2	15.1	13.9	14.2	14.0	15.0	19.1	23.6	25.8	24.9	18.4
1997[2]	24.2	24.6	24.3	24.3	25.4	25.4	26.9	26.6	26.6	26.5	27.1	26.5	25.7

[1] Bushels of corn equal in value to 100 pounds of steers and heifers. [2] Preliminary. *Source: Economic Research Service, U.S. Department of Agriculture.*

Farm Value, Income and Wholesale Prices of Cattle and Calves in the United States

Year	January 1 Per Head Dollars	January 1 Total Million $	Gross Income From C. & C.[2] Million $	At Omaha[3] Steers[3] Choice	At Omaha Steers Select	At Omaha Heifers Select	At Omaha Heifers Choice	Feeder Heifers at Oklahoma City[5]	Cows, Boning Utility Sioux Falls[6]	Cows, Commercial Sioux Falls	Wholesale Prices, Central U.S. Choice, 700-850 lb.	Wholesale Prices, Central U.S. Select, 700-850 lb.	Wholesale Prices, Central U.S. Cow[6], Canner[7]
				Dollars per 100 Pounds									
1990	616	58,990	39,192	77.40	75.24	73.94	76.82	85.31	53.60	57.13	123.11	116.49	99.96
1991	655	63,090	38,697	74.03	72.46	71.44	73.86	86.04	50.66	56.08	117.24	112.73	99.42
1992	630	61,451	37,272	75.17	73.65	72.88	74.95	78.41	44.84	51.22	116.02	111.66	93.85
1993	649	64,436	39,362	76.23	74.09	73.77	76.01	82.79	47.52	56.47	117.71	113.53	95.43
1994	659	66,490	36,395	67.60	66.33	66.14	67.93	74.55	42.51	48.28	106.73	102.08	84.39
1995	615	63,157	33,983	65.64	63.94	63.69	65.46	64.43	35.58	39.03	106.09	98.45	68.67
1996[1]	503	52,010	NA	74.50	61.83	61.22	64.18	57.21	30.45	33.70	102.01	95.70	58.16

[1] Preliminary. [2] Excludes interfarm sales and Government payments. Cash receipts from farm marketings and value of farm consumption. [3] 1,000 to 1,100 pound weight range. [4] 1,000 to 1,200 pound weight range. [5] 700 to 750 pound weight range. Prior to 1992, 600 to 700 pound weight range. [6] All weights. [7] & cutter. NA=Not available. *Source: Economic Research Service, U.S. Department of Agriculture (ERS-USDA)*

Average Price Received by Farmers for Beef Cattle In Dollars Per 100 Pounds

Year	Jan.	Feb.	Mar.	Apr.	May	June	July	Aug.	Sept.	Oct.	Nov.	Dec.	Average
1990	73.70	74.60	74.20	74.60	74.60	74.20	73.60	76.00	75.00	75.50	75.30	77.10	74.87
1991	76.60	77.00	78.50	78.20	75.90	73.60	71.60	68.80	68.70	70.40	67.90	67.40	72.88
1992	68.90	72.50	72.80	72.60	71.90	70.20	70.60	71.80	71.80	71.80	70.20	70.80	71.33
1993	75.10	75.80	77.20	77.30	77.10	74.50	72.50	72.70	71.40	69.10	69.30	68.50	73.38
1994	69.90	70.10	72.30	72.00	67.20	62.70	62.90	65.90	63.50	62.90	64.40	64.40	66.52
1995	67.50	68.70	66.90	63.80	60.80	60.90	59.50	59.40	59.10	58.80	60.70	60.60	62.23
1996	59.10	57.90	56.80	54.90	54.70	56.40	59.10	61.30	63.80	63.30	63.40	61.00	59.31
1997[1]	61.40	74.90	64.80	64.80	65.10	62.30	62.80	63.90	63.60	63.30	63.30	62.90	64.43

[1] Preliminary. *Source: Crop Reporting Board, U.S. Department of Agriculture (CRB-USDA)*

Average Price Received by Farmers for Calves In Dollars Per 100 Pounds

Year	Jan.	Feb.	Mar.	Apr.	May	June	July	Aug.	Sept.	Oct.	Nov.	Dec.	Average
1990	90.80	95.80	98.80	100.00	101.00	98.10	95.90	98.90	95.40	92.80	93.80	96.80	96.51
1991	98.00	104.00	106.00	109.00	107.00	106.00	103.00	98.30	96.20	93.90	90.20	87.60	99.93
1992	88.30	92.80	94.10	92.00	89.60	88.50	90.10	90.40	87.40	86.00	86.50	87.00	89.39
1993	94.70	96.00	98.60	99.60	99.20	99.10	96.90	95.10	93.50	93.90	91.60	92.80	95.92
1994	93.90	94.90	97.60	95.80	89.40	84.80	83.80	84.40	80.00	78.20	81.00	81.90	87.14
1995	85.00	86.90	84.40	81.80	77.00	76.90	72.00	70.90	68.50	66.20	64.00	63.30	74.74
1996	61.80	60.20	59.40	55.10	54.40	55.10	56.80	59.30	61.00	60.10	61.20	61.80	58.85
1997[1]	68.10	74.90	80.00	82.20	84.30	85.40	86.90	88.00	86.90	84.30	82.90	83.30	82.27

[1] Preliminary. *Source: Crop Reporting Board, U.S. Department of Agriculture (CRB-USDA)*

Federally Inspected Slaughter of Calves and Vealers in the United States In Thousands of Head

Year	Jan.	Feb.	Mar.	Apr.	May	June	July	Aug.	Sept.	Oct.	Nov.	Dec.	Total
1990	175	145	165	128	137	131	139	147	132	158	149	136	1,743
1991	150	120	119	105	102	90	108	108	115	127	125	131	1,408
1992	128	111	120	108	103	105	106	107	107	111	109	121	1,328
1993	101	97	116	96	82	91	90	95	94	94	101	103	1,159
1994	99	94	112	92	90	98	93	106	106	112	114	121	1,237
1995	121	104	118	96	114	115	111	121	119	124	125	125	1,393
1996	140	140	141	128	133	131	156	153	146	159	139	149	1,715
1997[1]	143	122	128	126	114	115	131	123	133	137	121	142	1,534

[1] Preliminary. *Source: Crop Reporting Board, U.S. Department of Agriculture (CRB-USDA)*

Cement

The use of cement in the United States corresponds to areas where construction activity is the greatest. According to the U.S. Geological Survey, portland cement shipments in the U.S. and Puerto Rico were 9.01 million metric tonnes in June 1997. This was 6 percent more than shipments a year earlier in the same month. Cumulative shipments of portland cement for the January-June 1997 period were 42.6 million tonnes, a 5 percent increase from the same period of 1996. The leading portland-cement-producing states are California, Texas, Pennsylvania, Michigan and Missouri. Together they shipped 36 percent of the June total. The leading consuming states for portland cement are California, Texas, Florida, Ohio and Illinois. They received 33 percent of the June total. For all of 1996, portland cement production was 89.5 million tonnes.

Masonry cement shipments in June 1997 were 315,636 tonnes. That was 1 percent less than in June 1996. For all of 1996, masonry cement shipments were 3.47 million tonnes. Over the January-June 1997 period, cumulative shipments of masonry cement were 1.7 million tonnes which represented a 5 percent increase over the same period in 1996. The leading masonry-cement-producing states are Alabama, Florida, Indiana, Michigan and Pennsylvania. The leading consuming states are Florida, Georgia, North Carolina, Ohio and Texas.

Over the first half of 1997, the major destination for finished portland cement was Florida with 3.2 million tonnes. The second leading destination was Southern California with 2.8 million tonnes. The third largest user was southern Texas with 2.2 million tonnes followed by northern Texas at 2.1 million tonnes.

For the January-June 1997 period, the major destination for prepared masonry cement was Florida with 269,116 tonnes. The next largest destination was North Carolina at 148,462 tonnes. Georgia was next largest at 119,551 tonnes.

U.S. imports of hydraulic cement and clinker in the January-May 1997 period were 6.1 million tonnes. The major supplier of hydraulic cement and clinker was Canada followed by Venezuela, Spain, Greece and Mexico. U.S. imports of white cement in the first five months of 1997 were 208,955 tonnes with the major suppliers being Canada, Denmark, Mexico and Spain.

World Production of Hydraulic Cement In Thousands of Metric Tons

Year	Brazil	China	France	Germany	India	Italy	Japan	Rep. of Korea	Russia[3]	Spain	Turkey	United States	World Total
1990	25,800	210,000	26,400	37,700	49,000	40,000	84,400	33,600	151,371	28,100	24,500	71,400	1,160,000
1991	27,490	252,610	26,507	34,396	51,000	40,806	89,564	34,999	140,000	25,119	26,091	68,465	1,181,793
1992	23,903	308,220	21,165	37,529	50,000	41,347	88,253	44,444	61,700	24,615	28,607	70,883	1,239,683
1993	24,843	367,880	20,464	36,649	53,812	34,771	88,046	47,313	49,900	22,878	31,241	75,117	1,301,527
1994	25,229	421,180	21,296	40,380	60,000	33,192	91,624	50,730	37,200	25,150	29,493	79,353	1,380,052
1995[1]	25,500	445,610	21,000	40,000	70,000	35,000	90,474	55,130	36,400	25,000	33,153	78,320	1,421,342
1996[2]	30,000	450,000	20,000	40,000	70,000	35,000	90,000	56,500	36,000	25,000	35,000	84,000	1,460,000

[1] Preliminary. [2] Estimate. [3] Formerly part of the U.S.S.R.; data not reported separately until 1992. *Source: U.S. Geological Survey (USGS)*

Salient Statistics of Cement in the United States

Year	Net Import Reliance as a % of Apparent Consumption	Production: Portland	Production: Others[3]	Production: Total	Capacity Used at (Portland Mills) %	Shipments From Mills: Total Mil. Tons	Shipments From Mills: Value[4] Mil. $	Average Value (F.O.B. Mill) $ per ton	Stocks at Mills Dec. 31	Exports[5]	Apparent Consumption	Imports for Consumption[5] by Country: Canada	Japan	Mexico	Spain	Total
		Thousand Tons							Million Tons			Thousands of Short Tons				
1990	14	67,044	2,911	69,954	76.3	78,199	4,280	54.73	5,637	503	81,305	3,216	2,101	2,307	1,309	13,273
1991	10	64,165	3,028	67,193	72.2	68,999	3,832	55.54	6,009	633	72,413	3,127	331	1,044	699	8,701
1992	6	66,841	2,744	69,585	76.0	69,203	3,779	54.61	5,272	746	74,124	2,997	278	825	446	6,166
1993	7	70,845	2,962	73,807	79.1	74,079	4,175	56.36	4,788	625	79,198	3,629	43	783	597	7,060
1994	10	74,335	3,613	77,948	82.3	80,490	4,981	61.88	4,805	633	86,370	4,268	14	640	1,342	11,303
1995[1]	11	73,303	3,603	76,906	81.2	77,650	5,471	68.46	5,813	759	86,612	4,886	[6]	850	1,501	13,848
1996[2]	12			78,600				70.00	5,000	750	89,400					

[1] Preliminary. [2] Estimate. [3] Masonry, natural & pozzolan (slag-line). [4] Value received F.O.B. mill, excluding cost of containers. [5] Hydraulic & clinker cement. [6] Less than $^1/_2$ unit. NA = Not available. *Source: U.S. Geological Survey (USGS)*

Shipments of Finished Portland Cement from Mills in the United States In Thousands of Metric Tons

Year	Jan.	Feb.	Mar.	Apr.	May	June	July	Aug.	Sept.	Oct.	Nov.	Dec.	Total
1992	3,739.2	3,814.2	4,781.0	6,011.0	6,455.1	7,017.0	6,956.4	6,942.4	7,015.2	7,516.3	5,018.3	4,370.6	69,698.3
1993	3,370.8	3,664.1	4,882.0	5,784.1	6,617.4	7,329.2	7,199.8	7,557.4	7,237.4	7,414.5	6,269.0	5,033.3	72,359.1
1994	3,406.1	3,790.2	5,884.3	6,227.3	7,320.8	7,689.9	6,877.4	7,938.1	7,461.9	7,237.8	6,203.5	5,093.2	75,130.4
1995	3,685.2	3,959.7	5,556.6	5,668.6	6,720.6	7,336.8	6,748.1	7,660.9	7,177.0	7,736.3	6,238.3	4,667.7	73,155.6
1996	3,913.3	4,312.7	5,234.1	6,801.6	7,621.3	7,395.1	7,749.4	8,193.4	7,178.3	8,276.7	6,011.4	4,763.3	77,550.0
1997[1]	4,097.9	4,498.5	5,728.9	6,972.7	7,434.7	7,679.7	8,065.2	7,846.5	8,119.8	8,625.1			69,068.8

[1] Preliminary. *Source: U.S. Geological Survey (USGS)*

Cheese

World cheese production in 1997 totaled a record 12.1 million metric tonnes vs. 11.9 million in 1996, with U.S. production accounting for 3.33 million and 3.27 million tonnes, respectively. France produces half the U.S. total to rank in second place globally. World consumption of 11.7 million tonnes in 1997 compares with 11.5 million in 1996, with the U.S. totals 3.45 million and 3.36 million. France and Italy consume 2.3 million tonnes annually. Worldwide, the supply and demand for cheese has set new highs in each year of the 1990's. Most of the world's cheese is consumed where produced. However, record per capita cheese consumption in the U.S. of 13 kilograms pales relative to Europe where use tops 20 kg. in some countries, notably France.

World foreign trade of cheese is biased towards exports; one million metric tonnes in 1997 vs. 959,000 in 1996; imports in both years hovered around 700,000 tonnes. 1997's largest single exporter was New Zealand with 225,000 tonnes while collectively the European Union exported about half the world total. U.S. exports are small, averaging 32,000 tonnes during 1995-97. The U.S., however, runs a close second to Japan as the largest importer: 155,000 tonnes to the U.S. in 1997 vs. Japan's 170,000 tonnes. 1997 ending world stocks of 1.89 million tonnes compare with 1.96 million a year earlier.

Cheese is a $10 billion-a-year industry in the U.S. and American cheese, mostly cheddar, accounts for the largest individual variety of U.S. production and consumption. However, since the late 1980's, other varieties--mostly Italian--have had a combined production that exceeds American cheese. Per capita consumption of American has slipped in recent years to 12 pounds while other cheese use has climbed to over 10 pounds. Mozzarella makes up the bulk of Italian cheese use.

For most dairy products statistical data is a product of the fat or skim solids content. Not so for cheese. Making cheese exhausts virtually all the value of the skim component of raw milk, even though most of the solids-not-fat are left in the liquid whey. To account for this, the factors used for cheese reflect the total skim solids needed to produce a pound, not just the casein and minerals in the cheese.

Wholesale American cheese prices (40-pound blocks, Wisconsin) averaged $1.25 per pound in mid-1997, 40 cents lower than in 1996.

Futures Markets

Cheddar Cheese futures and options are traded on the Coffee, Sugar & Cocoa Exchange, Inc. (CSCE).

World Production of Cheese In Millions of Metric Tons

Year	Argentina	Australia	Brazil	Canada	Denmark	France	Germany	Italy	Netherlands	New Zealand	United Kingdom	United States	World Total
1988	265	176	200	252	258	1,378	849	737	559	128	299	2,527	10,489
1989	260	190	220	247	275	1,485	885	760	568	128	280	2,546	10,743
1990	270	175	245	255	293	1,471	749	811	593	122	316	2,749	10,873
1991	290	178	290	262	285	1,500	777	885	610	125	303	2,747	10,366
1992	310	197	296	262	290	1,489	783	890	634	142	324	2,943	10,931
1993	350	211	310	271	321	1,509	821	885	637	145	331	2,961	11,172
1994	385	234	330	282	286	1,541	855	913	648	192	326	3,054	11,194
1995	370	241	360	277	311	1,579	875	942	680	197	354	3,138	11,349
1996	390	268	385	289	298	1,594	947	950	688	230	364	3,274	11,686
1997[1]	405	261	405	300	287	1,600	980	945	702	240	365	3,345	11,819
1998[2]	420	275	425	290	285	1,605	1,000	945	714	260	368	3,425	12,036

[1] Preliminary. [2] Estimate. [3] Formerly part of the U.S.S.R.; data not reported seperately prior to 1989. *Source: Foreign Agricultural Service, U.S. Department of Agriculture (FAS-USDA)*

Supply and Distribution of All Cheese in the United States In Millions of Pounds

	Supply					Cheese	Distribution						
	Production		January 1			40-Lb. Blocks Wisconsin Assembly Points		Gov't	American Cheese Removed by USDA Programs		Domestic Disapparence		
Year	Whole Milk[2]	All Cheese[3]	Commercial Stocks	Imports[4]	Total Supply	¢ per lb.	Exports & Shipments[5]	Dec. 31 Stocks		Total Disappearance	American Cheese Donated	Total	Per Capita
1986	2,798	5,209	945	295	6,449	127.30	97	420.1	468.4	5,660	560	5,602	23.11
1987	2,717	5,344	789	265	6,399	123.19	88	81.2	282.0	5,939	607	5,861	24.09
1988	2,757	5,572	460	253	6,284	123.80	76	36.7	238.1	5,886	257	5,801	23.70
1989	2,674	5,615	361	279	6,289	138.79	74	6.6	37.4	5,959	67	5,901	23.81
1990	2,894	6,059	323	302	6,689	136.69	75	8.2	21.5	6,231	21	6,168	24.64
1991	2,769	6,055	450	301	6,810	124.41	72	23.1	76.9	6,393	60	6,337	25.01
1992	2,937	6,488	393	285	7,191	131.91	78	16.5	14.4	6,720	0	6,661	26.01
1993	2,957	6,528	454	321	7,303	131.52	87	2.2	8.3	6,853	0	6,766	26.24
1994	2,974	6,735	464	345	7,544	131.45	55	.9	6.9	7,086	0	6,994	26.82
1995	3,129	6,940	436	337	7,714	132.77	65	NA	6.1	7,275	0	7,198	27.20
1996[1]	3,291	7,218	449	335	8,002	149.14	NA	NA	5.0	7,473	0	NA	27.70

[1] Preliminary. [2] Whole milk American cheddar. [3] All types of cheese except cottage, pot and baker's cheese. [4] Imports for consumption. [5] Commercial.
NA = Not available. *Source: Economic Research Service, U.S. Department of Agriculture (ERS-USDA)*

Production of Cheese in the United States In Millions of Pounds

	American			Swiss,				Cream &				Total	Cottage Cheese		
Year	Whole Milk	Part Skim	Total	Including Block	Munster	Brick	Limburger	Neufchatel Cheese	Italian Varieties	Blue Mond	All Other Varieties	of All Cheese[2]	Lowfat	Curd[3]	Creamed[4]
1986	2,798	2.1	2,800	227.3	88.5	20.4	1.1	321.5	1,632.9	34.2	82.1	5,209	265.5	600.1	704.8
1987	2,717	.9	2,718	227.2	92.6	28.9	1.1	342.2	1,799.8	35.9	99.1	5,344	270.5	573.8	674.8
1988	2,757	1.1	2,758	250.1	83.3	24.8	1.0	375.9	1,937.1	37.8	104.3	5,572	290.9	556.7	647.1
1989	2,674	.8	2,675	231.2	91.1	17.5	.9	401.0	2,042.9	34.6	121.2	5,615	300.9	526.9	572.3
1990	2,894	.8	2,895	261.1	100.2	17.3	.8	430.8	2,207.0	36.4	110.7	6,059	301.8	493.5	530.6
1991	2,769	.8	2,770	234.5	106.4	15.3	.7	446.7	2,328.6	34.3	118.5	6,055	321.1	490.9	497.9
1992	2,937	1.2	2,938	237.3	116.4	15.5	1.0	516.7	2,508.6	33.3	121.9	6,488	329.5	502.4	457.3
1993	2,957	3.7	2,961	231.4	117.5	12.5	.9	539.9	2,494.5	33.3	137.2	6,528	317.0	471.4	430.5
1994	2,974	24.7	2,999	221.2	113.6	12.2	.8	573.4	2,625.7	36.5	152.1	6,735	321.1	463.3	410.0
1995	3,131	24.0	3,155	221.7	109.1	10.4	.9	543.8	2,674.4	36.6	164.6	6,917	325.9	458.9	384.9
1996[1]	3,281	NA	3,281	219.0	106.8	10.6	.7	574.7	2,812.4	38.3	106.7	7,218	329.9	448.3	360.4

[1] Preliminary. [2] Excludes full-skim cheddar and cottage cheese. [3] Includes cottage, pot, and baker's cheese with a butterfat content of less than 4%. [4] Includes cheese with a butterfat content of 4 to 19%. *Source: Economic Research Service, U.S. Department of Agriculture (ERS-USDA)*

Wholesale Price of Cheese, 40-lb. Blocks, Wisconsin Assembly Points In Cents Per Pound

Year	Jan.	Feb.	Mar.	Apr.	May	June	July	Aug.	Sept.	Oct.	Nov.	Dec.	Average
1987	127.8	122.5	122.3	122.4	122.0	122.0	123.2	125.5	126.6	121.9	121.3	120.8	123.2
1988	118.4	116.1	115.6	115.1	115.0	116.2	118.3	127.6	134.6	136.4	136.3	136.0	123.8
1989	129.1	117.6	117.9	120.4	123.9	130.8	140.6	143.3	155.8	160.3	163.6	162.2	138.8
1990	152.3	131.6	130.7	140.5	145.8	149.5	151.0	150.3	142.6	114.9	112.0	112.7	136.2
1991	111.4	111.5	111.5	111.7	115.0	121.4	128.4	136.1	139.7	140.2	135.8	130.2	124.4
1992	125.4	119.0	119.8	131.9	140.0	141.3	141.8	142.0	136.9	132.4	129.4	123.2	131.9
1993	119.3	118.6	124.3	140.8	141.8	133.7	126.3	124.8	137.4	138.9	138.7	133.7	131.5
1994	132.2	134.2	140.0	143.3	125.7	120.2	129.1	132.2	135.6	135.4	127.9	121.3	131.5
1995	124.5	130.4	131.1	122.8	122.1	126.9	126.7	132.2	141.3	145.0	145.8	144.6	132.8
1996	139.3	139.3	140.9	145.1	151.8	151.5	158.2	167.6	145.5	162.3	133.9	126.0	146.8
1997[1]	127.9	132.3	134.0	125.6	116.5	117.9	123.3	137.6	141.4	142.4	143.8	146.1	132.4

[1] Preliminary. *Source: Economic Research Service, U.S. Department of Agriculture (ERS-USDA)*

Production[2] of Cheese in the United States In Millions of Pounds

Year	Jan.	Feb.	Mar.	Apr.	May	June	July	Aug.	Sept.	Oct.	Nov.	Dec.	Total
1987	422.0	398.6	457.4	462.1	477.8	465.6	453.8	426.0	430.7	448.6	431.8	469.7	5,344
1988	439.5	436.2	491.6	475.3	488.2	476.7	454.9	442.0	451.9	470.0	458.9	486.5	5,572
1989	456.6	419.5	488.4	472.6	494.9	485.5	464.6	460.4	448.5	464.0	453.0	489.5	5,614
1990	483.7	471.9	531.7	521.1	542.8	522.8	502.2	495.0	472.6	505.9	495.5	522.1	6,061
1991	501.7	458.0	530.1	515.4	532.3	509.0	499.5	498.2	485.0	521.0	502.3	533.7	6,061
1992	514.1	497.1	542.7	534.7	550.9	549.8	541.8	534.6	528.3	558.2	547.5	571.6	6,488
1993	517.3	492.5	563.2	561.4	576.9	563.2	537.9	525.8	531.1	560.0	540.1	558.9	6,528
1994	538.3	505.8	591.8	554.3	590.4	558.7	550.7	562.4	565.5	574.5	559.3	578.3	6,730
1995	559.3	523.3	596.0	559.6	595.3	579.2	556.5	550.8	571.3	588.6	584.7	618.4	6,883
1996	590.0	576.0	625.4	606.0	636.5	595.8	582.2	589.5	584.5	612.2	595.5	623.9	7,218
1997[1]	596.1	574.6	638.1	601.7	640.5	627.5	615.3	601.0	605.7	619.6	602.2	629.2	7,351

[1] Preliminary. [2] Excludes cottage cheese *Source: National Agricultural Statistics Service, U.S. Department of Agriculture (NASS-USDA)*

Cold Storage Holdings of All Varieties of Cheese in the U.S., on First of Month In Millions of Pounds

Year	Jan.	Feb.	Mar.	Apr.	May	June	July	Aug.	Sept.	Oct.	Nov.	Dec.
1987	693.6	683.9	652.4	646.5	645.1	666.8	659.0	642.5	606.6	580.8	538.0	495.9
1988	457.1	455.1	448.3	443.8	451.9	460.1	480.9	496.1	460.8	421.3	400.7	366.7
1989	388.1	395.3	404.4	396.6	412.1	431.9	429.6	430.4	419.8	370.2	331.4	330.6
1990	328.0	358.4	374.9	395.8	413.4	441.6	465.0	484.6	475.7	459.9	445.4	437.3
1991	457.8	483.9	475.1	492.4	510.3	512.1	521.5	511.5	494.1	477.9	429.3	409.0
1992	415.4	440.9	445.9	449.0	449.7	455.9	465.2	496.2	487.3	449.7	441.1	462.0
1993	462.0	476.1	454.4	460.0	453.6	480.5	541.2	533.3	517.7	500.1	471.9	462.4
1994	465.2	495.2	473.6	473.3	487.9	513.4	521.4	506.3	474.7	453.0	448.3	434.2
1995	436.9	449.7	448.7	458.8	466.1	465.8	473.6	482.4	458.1	428.5	418.7	393.6
1996	412.1	441.3	466.4	490.9	525.5	541.8	542.8	536.6	506.9	495.8	494.6	480.2
1997[1]	487.0	498.8	493.3	517.0	557.2	584.0	603.8	605.0	582.3	531.2	489.7	476.1

[1] Preliminary. [2] Quantities are given in "net weight." *Source: National Agricultural Statistics Service, U.S.Department of Agriculture (NASS-USDA)*

Chromium

Chromite is the ore mineral of chromium. It is used in making stainless steel and other alloys for which resistance to oxidation and corrosion is important. Chromium has uses as a tanning agent and for plating. The mineral chromite is used in refractory linings for steel-making furnaces. Chromium is an essential trade element for human health. Some chromium compounds are acutely toxic, chronically toxic or carcinogenic. The U.S. has no chromite ore reserves and limited reserve base.

World chromite resources, mining capacity and ferrochromium production capacity are concentrated in the Eastern Hemisphere. Global chromite ore reserves are more than adequate to meet anticipated world demand. Since the U.S. mines no chromite ore, imports are essential. Recycling is the only domestic supply source of chromium.

South Africa is the leading producer of ferrochromium and its exports to the U.S. are used in the defense industry. Other large chromite producers are the former Soviet republic of Kazakhstan and Albania. Cuba and Brazil in the Western Hemisphere produce smaller amounts.

U.S. production of chromium ferroalloys and metal in the January-July 1997 period were 36,600 metric tonnes, gross weight, and 25,000 tonnes, chromium content. Total 1996 production was 36,800 tonnes, gross weight. U.S. production of stainless steel in 1996 was 1.92 million tonnes.

In terms of the components of the U.S. supply, stainless steel scrap receipts in 1996 were 579,000 tonnes. For January-June 1997, they were 404,000 tonnes. Chromite ore imports for the first seven months of 1997 were 163,000 tonnes while for all of 1996 they were 250,000 tonnes. Imports of chromium ferroalloys, including high-, medium, and low-carbon ferrochromium silicon were 198,000 tonnes in the first half of 1997. For 1996 they were 469,000 tonnes. Chromium metal imports, including waste and scrap, were 5,190 tonnes in January-June 1997 and 8,730 tonnes for all of 1996.

U.S. consumption of chromite ore over the first seven months of 1997 was 197,000 tonnes while for all of 1996 it was 282,000 tonnes. Consumption of chromium ferroalloys and metal were 213,000 tonnes in January-July 1997 and 333,000 tonnes for all of 1996.

The U.S. exports smaller amounts of chromium. For all of 1996, chromite ore exports were 69,400 tonnes. Chromium ferroalloy exports in 1996 were 15,800 tonnes and chromium metal exports were 1,330 tonnes. Exports of stainless steel scrap were 303 tonnes.

At the end of July 1997, industry stocks of chromite ore were 160,000 tonnes. Of this total, chemical and metallurgical chromite ore was 151,000 tonnes while refractory chromite ore was 8,420 tonnes. Stocks of chromium ferroalloys and metal were 24,320 tonnes at the end of July 1997, with producer stocks 3,520 tonnes and consumer stocks 20,800 tonnes. Government stocks of chromite ore at the end of July 1997 were 1.14 million tonnes. Stocks of chromium ferroalloys were 1.02 million tonnes while stocks of chromium metals were 7,720 tonnes.

World Mine Production of Chromium In Thousands of Metric Tons (Gross Weight)

Year	Albania	Brazil	Cuba	Finland	India	Iran	Kazakhstan[3]	Madagascar	Philippines	South Africa	Turkey	Zimbabwe	World Total
1987	1,075	338	52	543	624	92	3,570	107	188	3,789	762	570	11,919
1988	1,109	410	52	700	821	60	3,700	64	129	4,245	851	561	12,896
1989	900	476	51	513	1,003	73	3,800	63	217	4,951	1,077	627	14,006
1990	950	263	50	504	1,050	77	3,800	151	183	4,620	836	573	13,200
1991	587	340	50	473	940	90	3,800	149	191	5,100	940	564	13,300
1992	322	449	50	499	1,158	130	3,500	161	81	3,363	531	522	11,000
1993	282	308	50	511	1,070	115	2,900	144	62	2,838	767	252	9,560
1994	223	360	50	573	909	129	2,020	90	76	3,599	1,270	517	10,100
1995[1]	246	448	50	598	1,536	129	2,871	103	111	5,085	2,080	707	14,300
1996[2]	236	450	50	582	1,363	129	1,190	137	78	5,018	2,000	697	12,200

[1] Estimate. [2] Preliminary. [3] Formerly part of the U.S.S.R.; data not reported seperately until 1992. *Source: U.S. Geological Survey (USGS)*

Salient Statistics of Chromium in the United States In Thousands of Metric Tons (Gross Weight)

Year	% Net Import Reliance of Apparent Consumption	Production of Ferrochromium	Exports	Imports for Consumption	Reexports	Consumption by Primary Consumer Groups: Total	Consumption: Metallurgical & Chemical	Consumption: Refractory	Consumer Stocks, Dec. 31: Metallurgical & Chemical	Consumer Stocks: Refractory	Consumer Stocks: Total Stocks	$ per Metric Ton: South Africa[3]	$ per Metric Ton: Turkish[4]
1987	75	107	1	490	5	506	459	48	309	23	332	46	115
1988	78	120	4	615	1	551	495	56	366	23	390	56	180
1989	78	147	40	525	2	561	517	44	368	24	392	65	185
1990	80	109	6	347	4	405	361	44	333	21	355	55	135
1991	75	68	9	310	----	375	339	36	310	11	321	50	130
1992	86	61	7	324	----	362	335	27	308	13	321	60	110
1993	81	63	10	329	2	337	314	23	259	16	275	60	110
1994	75	67	47	273	----	322	302	20	250	17	266	60	110
1995[1]	80	73	18	416	----	W	W	W	194	11	205	80	230
1996[2]	79	37	69	362	----	W	W	W	165	8	173	80	230

[1] Preliminary. [2] Estimate. [3] Cr_2O_3, 44% (Transvaal). *Source: U.S. Geological Survey (USGS)*

Coal

U.S. coal production in the first quarter of 1997 was 274 million short tons. This was up 6 percent from the first quarter of 1996. For all of 1996, U.S. coal production was 1.06 billion tons. Coal production in the first quarter of 1997 was a record due to increased demand for coal by the electric utility sector.

Regional coal production in the first quarter of 1997 increased 8 percent in Appalachia and 7 percent in the West. Coal production in the Interior Region fell 2 percent. Coal production east of the Mississippi River increased 7 percent while west of the Mississippi it increased 5 percent. Most of the increased coal production was in West Virginia and Colorado.

Coal consumption in the first quarter of 1997 was 246 million tons, a record. In the first quarter of 1996, coal consumption was 243 million tons. U.S. coal consumption in 1996 was 983 million tons. In first quarter 1997, electric utility plants used 218 million tons of coal. Coke plants used 7.6 million tons while other industrial plants used 18.3 million tons. Residential and commercial use was 1.7 million tons.

U.S. coal exports in the first quarter of 1997 were 20 million tons. Metallurgical coal exports in the first quarter of 1997 were 12 million tons. Steam coal exports were 8 million tons in first quarter 1997. There were increased exports to Canada and the United Kingdom. U.S. coke exports were 63,000 tons. U.S. coal imports in first quarter 1997 were 1.3 million tons, down 22 percent from a year ago.

World Production[3] of Coal (Monthly Average) In Thousands of Metric Tons

Year	Australia	Canada	China	Czech Rep.[4]	Germany	India	Indonesia	Kazakhstan[5]	Poland	Russia[5]	Ukraine[5]	United Kingdom	United States
1989	12,317	3,233	87,833	2,089	6,454	16,569	380	----	14,830	48,083	----	8,190	67,608
1990	13,236	3,139	90,000	1,842	6,363	16,819	611	----	12,306	39,300	----	7,442	71,137
1991	13,720	3,326	88,212	1,623	6,063	18,905	1,143	----	11,698	33,769	----	8,028	68,755
1992	14,594	2,693	91,278	NA	6,013	19,490	1,760	10,546	10,960	16,123	----	7,273	75,413
1993	14,711	2,943	96,177	1,574	5,347	20,503	2,299	9,323	10,873	16,200	9,545	5,683	71,473
1994	14,721	3,664	100,508	1,530	4,802	20,974	2,603	8,696	11,136	14,622	7,650	3,976	78,102
1995	15,921	3,215	107,624	2,958	4,905	22,131	3,460	6,933	11,347	13,866	6,717	4,282	86,081
1996[1]	NA	3,190	116,117	NA	4,428	23,782	3,945	6,638	11,796	13,756	5,852	4,109	88,574
1997[2]	NA	NA	112,221	NA	4,348	26,870	3,299	6,293	11,643	13,971	5,509	NA	NA

[1] Preliminary. [2] Estimate. [3] All grades of anthracite and bituminous coal, but excludes recovered slurries, lignite and brown coal. [4] Formerly part of Czechoslovakia; data not reported separately until 1993. [5] Formerly part of the U.S.S.R.; data not reported separately until 1992. NA = Not available.
Source: United Nations (UN)

Production of Bituminous & Lignite Coal in the United States In Thousands of Short Tons

Year	Alabama	Colorado	Illinois	Indiana	Kentucky	Montana	Ohio	Pennsylvania	Texas	Virgina	West Virgina	Wyoming	Total U.S.
1988	26,518	15,913	58,594	31,271	157,852	38,881	34,043	67,091	52,281	45,886	145,005	164,014	950,265
1989	27,992	17,123	59,267	33,641	167,389	37,742	33,689	67,248	53,854	43,006	153,580	171,558	980,729
1990	29,030	18,910	60,393	35,907	128,396	37,616	35,252	67,008	55,755	46,917	169,205	184,249	1,029,076
1991	27,269	17,834	60,258	31,468	158,980	38,237	30,569	61,936	53,825	41,954	167,352	193,854	995,984
1992	25,796	19,226	59,857	30,466	161,068	38,889	30,403	65,498	55,071	43,024	162,164	190,172	997,545
1993	24,768	21,886	41,098	29,295	156,299	35,917	28,816	55,394	54,567	39,317	130,525	210,129	945,424
1994	23,266	25,304	52,797	30,927	161,642	41,640	29,897	62,237	52,346	37,129	161,776	237,092	1,033,504
1995	24,640	25,710	48,180	26,007	153,739	39,451	26,118	61,576	52,684	34,099	162,997	263,822	1,032,974
1996[1]	24,637	24,886	46,656	29,670	152,425	37,891	28,572	67,942	55,164	35,590	170,433	278,440	1,063,856
1997[2]	25,039	27,769	42,785	34,878	155,148	41,268	30,793	72,077	54,484	37,044	168,340	289,001	1,094,837

[1] Preliminary. [2] Estimate. *Source: Energy Information Administration, U.S. Department of Energy (EIA-DOE)*

Production[2] of Bituminous Coal in the United States In Thousands of Short Tons

Year	Jan.	Feb.	Mar.	Apr.	May.	June	July	Aug.	Sept.	Oct.	Nov.	Dec.	Total
1988	75,325	76,757	83,943	75,324	73,981	76,443	69,176	88,175	83,196	80,799	82,925	80,260	946,304
1989	81,969	75,040	88,981	77,233	82,486	78,544	66,269	90,824	84,618	87,657	85,043	72,554	971,218
1990	90,304	81,796	91,357	83,350	86,615	84,720	79,585	91,558	83,107	93,418	86,772	75,676	1,028,258
1991	85,810	82,592	85,012	79,324	79,917	76,896	79,745	88,851	81,533	90,307	81,730	79,383	991,100
1992	87,979	82,102	85,835	82,364	80,197	79,968	80,768	84,401	83,555	86,265	80,240	83,021	996,695
1993	80,508	76,341	84,782	79,329	73,759	80,949	70,771	76,209	79,705	80,628	79,404	79,905	942,290
1994	76,578	81,569	95,969	87,534	82,105	86,223	77,421	93,881	88,346	85,085	86,317	87,856	1,028,884
1995	88,351	83,893	93,020	80,092	83,291	84,210	79,511	88,035	89,052	90,573	86,779	81,292	1,032,974
1996	83,013	83,671	90,392	88,158	88,562	83,824	88,331	94,664	87,388	94,195	86,400	86,493	1,059,104
1997[1]	92,425	88,394	92,757	86,226	92,882	84,942	90,230	89,878	92,783	96,173	84,959	97,057	1,089,494

[1] Preliminary. [2] Includes small amounts of lignite. *Source: Energy Information Administration, U.S. Department of Energy (EIA-DOE)*

COAL

Production[2] of Pennsylvania Anthracite Coal In Thousands of Short Tons

Year	Jan.	Feb.	Mar.	Apr.	May	June	July	Aug.	Sept.	Oct.	Nov.	Dec.	Total
1988	215	268	279	265	296	282	246	360	315	377	302	253	3,458
1989	281	282	337	273	280	256	197	311	299	373	339	291	3,519
1990	237	221	259	297	329	327	225	280	323	354	310	183	3,345
1991	248	243	259	230	224	235	253	313	285	346	299	238	3,173
1992	247	257	279	296	274	287	305	337	311	322	321	306	3,542
1993	272	266	290	175	305	358	222	277	351	603	315	271	3,705
1994	318	335	415	380	375	379	346	457	412	453	452	395	4,717
1995	304	304	372	332	335	353	307	396	428	445	388	347	4,682
1996	302	349	367	371	361	335	367	418	385	557	505	434	4,751
1997[1]	351	366	492	498	467	519	513	561	551	621	532	575	5,342

[1] Preliminary. [2] Represents production in Pennsylvania only.. *Source: Energy Information Administration, U.S. Department of Energy (EIA-DOE)*

Salient Statistics of Coal in the United States In Thousands of Short Tons

				Exports						Losses &
Year	Production	Imports	Consumption	Brazil	Canada	Europe	Asia	Total	Total Ending Stocks[2]	Unaccounted For[3]
1988	950,265	2,134	883,642	5,252	19,232	45,137	23,075	95,023	188,831	-1,316
1989	980,729	2,851	889,699	5,681	16,777	51,604	22,734	100,815	178,087	6,811
1990	1,029,076	2,699	895,480	5,847	15,511	58,382	22,725	105,804	201,629	3,949
1991	995,984	3,390	887,621	7,052	11,178	65,520	21,788	108,969	200,682	3,731
1992	997,545	3,803	892,421	6,370	15,140	57,255	20,540	102,516	197,685	9,407
1993	945,424	7,309	925,944	5,197	8,889	37,575	19,500	74,519	145,742	4,213
1994	1,033,504	7,584	930,201	5,482	9,193	35,825	17,957	71,359	169,358	15,912
1995	1,032,974	7,201	940,638	6,351	9,427	48,620	19,095	88,547	169,083	7,786
1996	1,063,856	7,126	982,805	6,540	12,029	47,193	17,980	90,473	154,089	14,585
1997[1]	1,094,838	6,989	999,619	7,509	10,038	43,752	14,356	84,499	143,805	10,768

[1] Preliminary. [2] Producer & distributor and consumer stocks, excludes stocks held by retail dealers for consumption by the residential and commercial secor. [3] Equals production plus imports minus the change in producer & distributor and consumer stocks minus consumption minus exports.
Source: Energy Information Administration, U.S. Department of Energy (EIA-DOE)

Consumption and Stocks of Coal in the United States In Thousands of Short Tons

	Consumption								Stocks, Dec. 31[3]			
	Electric Utilities				Industrial				Consumer			
Year	Anthracite	Bituminous	Lignite	Total	Coke Plants	Other Industrial[2]	Residential and Commercial	Total	Electric Utilities	Coke Plants	Other Industrials	Producers and Distributors
1988	1,063	681,048	76,260	758,372	41,888	76,252	7,130	883,642	146,507	3,137	8,768	30,418
1989	1,049	688,504	77,335	766,888	40,508	76,134	6,167	889,699	135,860	2,864	7,363	29,000
1990	1,031	694,317	78,201	773,549	38,877	76,330	6,724	895,480	156,166	3,329	8,716	33,418
1991	994	691,275	79,999	772,268	33,854	75,405	6,094	887,621	157,876	2,773	7,061	32,971
1992	986	698,626	80,248	779,860	32,366	74,042	6,153	892,421	154,130	2,597	6,965	33,993
1993	951	732,736	79,821	813,508	31,323	74,892	6,221	925,944	111,341	2,401	6,716	25,284
1994	1,123	737,102	79,045	817,270	31,740	75,179	6,013	930,201	126,897	2,657	6,585	33,219
1995	978	749,951	78,078	829,007	33,011	72,796	5,824	940,638	126,304	2,632	5,702	34,444
1996	1,009	795,252	78,421	874,681	31,706	70,594	5,824	982,805	114,669	2,667	5,688	31,065
1997[1]	1,030	815,674	76,830	893,533	30,073	69,979	6,036	999,619	103,589	1,970	5,246	33,000

[1] Preliminary. [2] Including transportation. [3] Excludes stocks held at retail dealers for consumption by the residential and commercial sector.
Source: *Energy Information Administration, U.S. Department of Energy (EIA-DOE)*

Average Prices of Coal in the United States In Dollars Per Short Ton

	End-Use Sector				Exports				End-Use Sector				Exports		
Year	Electric Utilities	Coke Plants	Other Indust-rial[3]	Imports[4]	Steam	Metal-lurgical	Total Average[4]	Year	Electric Utilities	Coke Plants	Other Indust-rial[3]	Imports[4]	Steam	Metal-lurgical	Total Average[4]
1988	30.64	47.70	33.43	29.96	38.59	44.17	42.23	1993	28.58	47.44	32.23	29.89	36.03	44.11	41.41
1989	30.15	47.50	33.03	34.14	37.64	45.19	42.52	1994	28.03	46.56	32.55	30.21	34.34	42.77	39.93
1990	30.45	47.73	33.59	34.45	36.81	46.51	42.63	1995	27.01	47.34	32.42	34.13	34.51	44.30	40.27
1991	30.02	48.88	33.54	33.12	36.91	46.15	42.39	1996	26.45	47.33	32.32	33.45	34.09	45.49	40.76
1992	29.36	47.92	32.78	33.46	35.73	45.41	41.34	1997[1]	26.52	48.14	32.50	34.56	33.09	46.09	41.26

[1] Preliminary. [2] Estimate. [3] Manufacturing plants only. [4] Based on the free alongside ship (F.A.S) value. NA = Not available.
Source: Energy Information Administration, U.S. Department of Energy (EIA-DOE)

Trends in Bituminous Coal, Lignite and Pennsylvania Anthracite in the U.S. In Thousands of Short Tons

	Bituminous Coal and Lignite							Pennsylvania Anthracite					All Mines
	Production				Labor Productivity								
Year	Underground	Surface	Total	Miners[1] Employed	Underground - Short Tons	Surface Per Miner	Average Per Hour	Underground	Surface	Total	Miners[1] Employed	Labor Product. Short Tons Miner/Hr.	Labor Product. Short Tons Miner/Hr.
1980	336,925	486,719	823,644	224,938	1.21	3.27	1.94	583	5,473	6,056	3,631	1.11	1.93
1981	315,875	502,477	818,352	226,250	1.29	3.50	2.11	621	4,802	5,423	3,052	.92	2.10
1982	338,572	494,951	833,523	214,400	1.37	3.48	2.14	579	4,009	4,588	2,717	.59	2.11
1983	299,882	478,111	778,003	173,543	1.62	3.87	2.52	487	3,602	4,089	2,099	1.01	2.50
1984	351,474	540,285	891,759	175,746	1.72	4.10	2.65	576	3,586	4,162	2,102	1.02	2.64
1985	350,073	528,856	878,930	167,009	1.79	4.32	2.76	727	3,982	4,708	2,272	1.05	2.74
1986	359,800	526,223	886,023	152,668	2.00	4.69	3.04	638	3,654	4,292	1,977	1.03	3.01
1987	372,238	542,963	915,202	141,065	2.21	5.06	3.32	636	2,925	3,560	1,602	1.13	3.30
1988	381,546	565,164	946,710	133,913	2.38	5.41	3.58	610	2,945	3,555	1,453	1.21	3.55
1989	393,322	584,058	977,381	130,103	2.46	5.70	3.73	513	2,835	3,348	1,394	1.12	3.70
1990	424,119	601,449	1,025,570	129,619	2.54	6.07	3.86	427	3,080	3,506	1,687	1.03	3.83
1991	406,901	585,638	992,539	119,441	2.70	6.51	4.12	324	3,121	3,445	1,161	1.39	4.09
1992	406,815	587,248	994,062	108,979	2.95	6.73	4.41	424	3,058	3,483	1,217	1.33	4.36
1993	350,637	590,482	941,119	100,099	3.24	7.84	4.74	416	3,889	4,306	1,124	1.85	4.70

[1] Excludes miners employed at mines producing less than 10,000 tons. *Source: Energy Information Adminstration, U.S. Department of Energy (EIA-DOE)*

Average Mine Prices of Coal in the United States In Dollars Per Short Ton

	Average Mine Price by Method			Average Mine Prices by Rank						All Coal
Year	Underground	Surface	Total	Lignite	Subbituminous	Bituminous	Anthracite[1]	Bituminous & Lignite FOB Mines[2]	Anthracite FOB Mines[2]	CIF[3] Electric Utility Plants
1980	33.50	18.78	24.65	W	11.08	29.17	42.51	24.52	42.51	28.76
1981	35.78	20.60	26.40	W	12.18	31.51	44.28	26.29	44.28	32.32
1982	35.78	21.46	27.25	W	13.37	32.15	49.85	27.14	49.85	34.91
1983	34.47	20.68	25.98	W	13.03	31.11	59.29	25.85	52.29	34.99
1984	33.36	20.59	25.61	10.45	12.41	30.63	48.22	25.51	48.22	35.12
1985	32.91	20.13	25.20	10.68	12.57	30.78	45.80	25.10	45.80	34.53
1986	30.33	19.34	23.79	10.64	12.26	28.84	44.12	23.70	44.12	33.30
1987	29.63	18.58	23.07	10.85	11.32	28.19	43.65	23.00	43.65	31.83
1988	28.97	17.43	22.07	10.06	10.45	27.66	44.16	22.00	44.16	30.64
1989	28.44	17.38	21.82	9.91	10.16	27.40	42.93	21.76	42.93	30.15
1990	28.58	16.98	21.76	10.13	9.70	27.43	39.40	21.71	39.40	30.45
1991	28.56	16.60	21.49	10.89	9.68	27.49	36.34	21.45	36.34	30.02
1992	27.83	16.34	21.03	10.81	9.68	26.78	34.24	20.98	34.24	29.36
1993	26.92	15.67	19.85	11.11	9.33	26.15	32.94	20.56	37.80	28.64

[1] Produced in Pennsylvania. [2] FOB = free on board. [3] CIF = cost, insurance and freight. W = Withheld data. *Source: Energy Information Administration, U.S. Department of Energy (EIA-DOE)*

Cobalt

Cobalt is a strategic metal used in many diverse industrial and military applications. Cobalt is found widely in the ores of iron and copper. The largest use of cobalt is in superalloys, which are used to make parts for gas turbine aircraft engines. Cobalt has numerous additional applications. Cobalt is used to make magnets; corrosion and wear-resistant alloys; cemented carbides and diamond tools; high-speed steels; catalysts for the petroleum and chemical industries; drying agents for paints, varnishes, and inks; ground coats for porcelain enamels; pigments; steel-belted radial tires; battery electrodes; and magnetic recording media.

The U.S. is the world's largest consumer of cobalt. With no mine or refinery production, the U.S. relies on imports to meet its primary cobalt needs. The U.S. government maintains significant quantities of cobalt metal in the National Defense Stockpile for military, industrial and civilian use in the event of a national emergency.

According to the U.S. Geological Survey, the supply of cobalt in expected to increase in the next few years. U.S. government sales of cobalt from the National Defense Stockpile are expected to continue at the rate set each year under the annual materials plan until the amount authorized for disposal has been sold. Current producers are expected to expand their output. Increased cobalt production will come from newly mined ore and from the refining of intermediate materials such as tailings and slags.

World cobalt demand is also expected to increase. Cobalt consumption by the superalloy industry should increase with the growth in the production of commercial aircraft and land-based gas turbines for power generation. The use of cobalt in rechargeable batteries is also expected to show significant growth. The increase in supply is expected to exceed the increase in use and that is expect to result in a oversupply of cobalt and lower prices.

U.S. reported consumption of cobalt materials in July 1997 was 574 tonnes, contained cobalt. Cobalt metal consumption was 273 tonnes. Consumption of cobalt oxide and other cobalt chemical compounds was 128 tonnes while consumption of cobalt scrap was 172 tonnes. In the January-July 1997 period, U.S. consumption of cobalt materials was 4,120 tonnes. In the comparable period of 1996, consumption was 3,740 tonnes while for all of 1996 it was 7,010 tonnes.

U.S. reported stocks of cobalt materials, contained cobalt, held by industry at the end of July 1997 were 714 tonnes. U.S. government reported stocks of cobalt metal at the end of July 1997 were 17,800 tonnes. At the end of 1996, industry stocks of cobalt materials were 762 tonnes while U.S. government stocks of cobalt metal were 18,700 tonnes.

U.S. imports for consumption of cobalt in the first half of 1997 were 4.35 million kilograms, cobalt content. For all of 1996, they were 6.71 million kilograms.

World Mine Production of Cobalt In Metric Tons (Cobalt Content)

Year	Australia	Botswana	Canada	Cuba	Finland (Refinery)	France (Refinery)	Japan (Refinery)	New Caledonia	Norway (Refinery)	Russia[3]	Zaire	Zambia	World Total
1987	1,261	181	2,490	1,566	1,234	136	124	750	1,576	2,800	23,200	7,365	41,245
1988	1,200	291	2,398	1,783	1,132	176	109	800	1,951	2,850	26,000	7,090	43,819
1989	1,100	215	6,167	1,825	1,295	165	99	800	1,946	5,700	18,400	7,255	42,873
1990	1,200	205	5,470	1,460	1,300	150	199	800	1,830	5,500	19,000	7,000	42,300
1991	1,400	208	5,274	1,100	1,503	123	185	800	1,983	5,800	9,900	6,994	33,300
1992	1,600	208	5,102	1,150	2,100	150	105	800	2,293	4,000	5,700	6,910	27,800
1993	1,800	205	5,108	1,060	2,200	150	190	800	2,414	3,500	2,459	4,840	21,900
1994	2,200	225	4,265	972	3,000	600	480	800	2,900	3,000	826	3,600	17,800
1995[1]	2,200	270	5,339	1,561	4,000	600	480	800	2,900	3,500	1,647	5,908	23,800
1996[2]	2,300	410	5,803	1,968	4,700	600	480	800	3,700	3,300	2,000	7,900	27,000

[1] Preliminary. [2] Estimate. [3] Formerly part of the U.S.S.R.; data not reported seperately until 1992. *Source: U.S. Geological Survey (USGS)*

Salient Statistics of Cobalt in the United States In Metric Tons (Cobalt Content)

					Consumption by End Uses											
Year	Net Import Reliance as a % of Apparent Consumption	Cobalt Secondary Production	Processors and Consumer Stocks Dec. 31	Imports for Consumption	Ground Coat Frit	Stainless & Heat Resisting	Catalysts	Super-Alloys	Tool Steel	Magnetic Alloys	Pigments	Drier in Paints, etc.[3]	Cutting & Wear-Resistant Material	Welding Materials	Total Apparent Uses	Price $ Per Pound[4]
1987	87	1,025	2,043	8,832	360	26	497	2,873	174	666	258	799	654	W	7,986	6.56
1988	87	1,018	1,766	7,051	332	26	617	2,865	180	878	378	892	522	206	7,824	7.09
1989	83	1,184	1,456	5,793	366	74	819	2,860	219	870	319	718	538	136	7,172	7.64
1990	84	1,225	1,853	6,530	357	41	W	3,345	123	710	W	751	541	180	7,512	10.09
1991	80	1,578	1,622	6,920	W	51	W	3,066	W	713	W	781	525	135	7,240	16.92
1992	76	1,613	840	5,760	257	26	949	2,697	47	670	197	745	522	128	6,471	22.93
1993	79	1,566	819	5,950	W	41	935	2,530	59	569	193	732	569	171	7,310	13.79
1994	81	1,570	914	6,780	W	41	871	2,810	84	698	198	809	723	312	8,470	24.66
1995[1]	82	1,540	818	6,440	196	38	732	2,940	146	757	172	770	748	287	8,640	29.21
1996[2]	83	1,670	762	6,710	159	38	652	3,230	95	728	191	733	722	284	8,810	25.50

[1] Preliminary. [2] Estimate. [3] Or related usage. [4] Annual spot for cathodes. W = Witheld proprietary data. *Source: U.S. Geological Survey (USGS)*

Cocoa

Cocoa is a tropical crop found mostly in a zone that extends approximately 15 degrees north and 15 degrees south of the equator. Cocoa trees can grow to a height of 30-35 feet producing fruits which are called pods. A mature cocoa pod is six to ten inches long and can contain 20 to 50 seeds or beans. In the course of a year, the cocoa tree will produce thousands of flowers but only a very small number will produce a mature pod. Flowers and pods are present on the tree throughout the year but at times they will have a greater concentration. After successful pollination, the pod reaches maturity in five to six months and is then harvested. After a cocoa tree is planted, it becomes productive in four or five years and reaches peak productivity by the tenth or eleventh year. Cocoa trees can remain productive for 50 years.

The main growing region for cocoa is West Africa where about 60 percent of the world's cocoa production originates. The four major producers in West Africa are the Ivory Coast, Ghana, Nigeria and Cameroon. Southeastern Asia is another important production region with Indonesia, Malaysia and Papua New Guinea the primary producers. In South America, Brazil and Ecuador are the largest producers. Cocoa production is very difficult to estimate and forecasts are often subject to major revisions.

The USDA estimated world cocoa production for the 1997-98 (October-September) season at 2.76 million metric tonnes. That represents a 2 percent increase from the previous season.

The Ivory Coast crop was forecast to be 1.18 million tonnes, a four percent increase from the previous year but some three percent less than the 1995-96 record crop of 1.22 million tonnes. It was an interesting season in that the weather was very dry between July and September with good rains during October and November. There were also adequate rains in the important May-June period which were enough to keep the crop from having any serious problems.

The Ghana cocoa crop is forecast to be 350,000 tonnes, up eight percent from the previous season but still 13 percent less than the 1995-96 crop. There is a biennial cycle in cocoa production that is common among tree crops with large crops followed a year later by smaller crops which are in turn followed by larger crops.

Brazil's 1997-98 cocoa production is forecast at 152,000 tonnes which is up five percent from the 1996-97 crop of 145,000 tonnes. That crop was the smallest ever. Brazilian cocoa production has been adversely affected by a number of factors including poor weather as well as disease. After a period of dry weather, there were beneficial rains that may increase the size of the crop despite the continuing problems with disease. Due to declining production Brazil has started to import small amounts of cocoa, primarily from Indonesia.

Despite a severe drought, the USDA has forecast Indonesia's 1997-98 cocoa crop at 325,000 tonnes, up one percent from the 1996-97 crop of 322,000 tonnes. The number of bearing trees is increasing and growers have improved maintenance. Despite this, the drought has been severe and it looks possible the crop could in fact be smaller. Indonesia has been rapidly increasing its production capacity in cocoa and is now a major exporter of cocoa beans.

Malaysia's 1997-98 cocoa crop is forecast at 115,000 tonnes, down four percent from a year ago. Malaysian cocoa production has been on the decline since the 1989-90 record crop of 240,000 tonnes. In Malaysia, cocoa is being replaced by other crops like palm oil.

Papua New Guinea has had a severe drought related to El Nino and cocoa production in 1997-98 is expected to decline over 20 percent from the year before.

World consumption of cocoa continues to trend higher. The 1997-98 world cocoa grind is estimated at 2.88 million tonnes, almost three percent more than the year before. Cocoa consumption has been increasing as countries with low per capita rates of use begin to use more cocoa. World stocks of cocoa are expected to decline in 1997-98 as they did in 1996-97.

Futures Markets

Cocoa futures and options are traded on the Coffee, Sugar and Cocoa Exchange (CSCE) in New York, and in London on the LIFFE. Futures are traded on the Kuala Lumpur Commodity Exchange (KLCE).

World Supply and Demand of Cocoa In Thousands of Metric Tons

Crop Year Beginning October	Stock Oct. 1	Net World Production[4]	Total Availability	Seasonal Grindings	Closing Stocks	Stock Change	Crop Year Beginning October	Stock Oct. 1	Net World Crop[4]	Total Availability	Seasonal Grindings	Closing Stocks	Stock Change
1982-3	749	1,533	2,282	1,635	647	-102	1990-1	1,300	2,501	3,796	2,343	1,457	158
1983-4	647	1,524	2,170	1,726	444	-202	1991-2	1,457	2,270	3,685	2,297	1,394	-27
1984-5	444	1,920	2,364	1,862	502	58	1992-3	1,394	2,385	3,716	2,427	1,277	-42
1985-6	502	1,942	2,444	1,877	567	65	1993-4	1,277	2,488	3,706	2,483	1,224	5
1986-7	567	1,993	2,535	1,896	639	97	1994-5	1,224	2,380	3,571	2,544	1,027	-164
1987-8	639	2,191	2,811	1,998	808	193	1995-6[1]	1,027	2,906	3,875	2,694	1,187	212
1988-9	808	2,445	3,245	2,125	1,124	320	1996-7[2]	1,187	2,686	3,747	2,795	985	-109
1989-90	1,124	2,395	3,518	2,222	1,300	173	1997-8[3]	NA	2,731	NA	2,875	NA	-144

[1] Preliminary. [2] Estimate. [3] Forecast. [4] Obtained by adjusting the Gross World Crop for one percent loss in weight. *Source: E D & F Man Cocoa, Ltd.*

COCOA

World Production of Cocoa Beans In Thousands of Metric Tons

Crop Year Beginning October	Brazil	Cameroon	Colombia	Dominican Republic	Ecuador	Ghana	Indonesia	Ivory Coast	Malaysia	Mexico	Nigeria	Papua New Guinea	World Total
1987-8	400	133	53.8	50.0	76.0	188	70.0	674	227	47.5	145	35.0	2,214.2
1988-9	334	124	56.3	44.3	82.0	300	98.0	849	225	41.0	160	48.0	2,471.3
1989-90	356	122	58.0	57.0	102.0	295	135.0	710	240	38.5	155	41.0	2,419.1
1990-1	375	100	60.0	42.3	104.0	293	165.0	804	235	38.9	160	34.0	2,525.5
1991-2	301	107	60.5	48.8	82.4	243	200.0	747	217	41.5	110	41.0	2,301.0
1992-3	330	100	60.0	50.8	76.0	312	240.0	700	225	43.5	140	39.0	2,415.5
1993-4	281	105	60.0	58.7	80.0	312	280.0	850	204	34.0	130	31.0	2,519.2
1994-5	228	108	60.0	56.8	82.0	315	257.0	873	134	38.5	130	29.0	2,403.7
1995-6[1]	221	130	60.0	58.0	95.0	403	305.0	1,219	127	40.5	140	35.0	2,934.8
1996-7[2]	145	120	60.0	54.5	105.0	324	322.0	1,131	120	41.0	155	36.0	2,713.5
1997-8[3]	152	120	60.0	57.0	85.0	350	325.0	1,180	115	42.0	145	28.0	2,759.3

[1] Preliminary. [2] Estimate. [3] Forecast. *Source: Foreign Agricultural Service, U.S. Department of Agriculture (FAS-USDA)*

World Consumption of Cocoa[1] In Thousands of Metric Tons

Crop Year Beginning October	Belgium	Brazil	Cote d'Ivoire	France	Germany	Italy	Malaysia	Netherlands	Singapore	United Kingdom	United States	Former USSR	World Total
1986-7	34	233	89	35	205	43	36	190	33	94	228	164	1,896
1987-8	35	241	102	40	245	46	40	215	40	100	241	132	1,998
1988-9	41	210	110	44	265	46	47	234	46	112	237	201	2,121
1989-90	47	239	111	59	287	51	72	241	52	120	270	106	2,217
1990-1	45	275	115	70	295	56	77	268	51	145	272	83	2,339
1991-2	46	216	108	67	306	62	87	294	50	153	307	25	2,291
1992-3	47	218	100	80	331	58	99	309	46	169	326	95	2,439
1993-4	50	224	110	95	319	65	103	331	51	170	317	90	2,483
1994-5[2]	53	194	108	108	318	69	101	350	51	154	331	80	2,544
1995-6[3]	54	205	135	111	289	69	96	385	54	191	345	80	2,688
1996-7[4]	55	205	165	111	268	70	93	400	55	180	365	85	2,762

[1] Figures represent the "grindings" of cocoa beans in each country. [2] Preliminary. [3] Estimate. [4] Forecast. *Source: Foreign Agricultural Service, U.S. Department of Agriculture (FAS-USDA)*

Raw Cocoa Grindings in Selected Countries In Metric Tons

Year	Total	First Quarter	Second Quarter	Third Quarter	Fourth Quarter	Total	First Quarter	Second Quarter	Third Quarter	Fourth Quarter
	Germany[2]					Netherlands				
1987	208,684	55,190	49,224	46,424	57,846	195,627	49,141	47,399	42,772	56,315
1988	232,794	60,039	53,990	53,008	65,757	216,499	56,074	51,712	50,539	58,174
1989	245,997	61,960	59,211	56,994	67,832	233,529	61,071	56,392	55,129	60,937
1990	281,855	69,125	64,613	70,994	77,123	247,590	62,243	58,817	58,702	67,828
1991	290,703	73,172	72,396	70,934	73,661	274,741	64,299	71,643	63,973	74,826
1992	319,251	78,661	73,797	80,111	86,682	293,157	77,954	71,537	69,871	73,795
1993	298,681	74,119	69,805	74,010	80,747	320,060	78,338	75,548	81,183	84,991
1994	296,219	80,242	68,033	67,706	80,238	334,384	83,963	78,055	84,249	88,117
1995	258,817	69,441	56,478	61,523	71,375	355,492	91,314	85,248	85,311	93,619
1996	251,070	69,520	59,471	65,824	56,255	388,412	100,866	90,724	99,549	97,273
1997[1]	245,352	61,379	57,402	65,233		405,716	102,338	100,132	101,817	
	United Kingdom					United States[3]				
1987	95,396	24,469	22,941	22,405	25,581	180,811	39,665	45,930	49,864	45,352
1988	100,507	26,309	24,997	22,407	26,794	186,885	45,197	47,327	48,376	45,985
1989	114,669	28,506	30,113	26,873	29,177	192,837	43,802	49,185	47,071	52,779
1990	124,791	32,116	29,322	29,419	33,934	216,740	51,559	51,683	58,278	55,220
1991	148,191	32,902	36,016	41,863	37,410	255,781	51,191	64,365	66,544	73,681
1992	159,284	39,831	37,903	37,120	44,430	313,921	70,335	74,515	84,109	84,962
1993	171,343	44,575	41,975	37,496	47,297	321,905	78,968	77,720	84,593	80,624
1994	163,170	44,131	39,063	39,591	40,385	322,629	71,398	78,805	86,247	86,179
1995	159,877	43,410	35,348	34,431	46,688	338,401	78,835	78,886	87,360	93,320
1996	189,037	50,500	44,535	48,855	45,147	351,042	79,044	82,713	93,933	95,352
1997[1]	170,588	44,059	42,702	41,180		398,189	95,435	97,223	105,984	

[1] Preliminary. [2] Beginning October 1990, includes former East Germany. [3] Data incomplete January 1984-March 1991, excludes one major processor. *Source: Foreign Agricultural Service, U.S. Department of Agriculture (FAS-USDA)*

Imports of Cocoa Butter in Selected Countries In Metric Tons

Year	Australia	Austria	Belgium	Canada	France	Germany	Italy	Japan	Netherlands	Sweden	Switzerland	United Kingdom	United States
1985	8,538	3,682	15,416	5,535	19,908	33,378	3,056	8,632	24,595	4,920	11,175	31,372	70,146
1986	8,204	4,387	13,795	5,377	19,397	25,513	3,246	8,474	14,925	4,866	11,369	32,669	70,264
1987	8,370	3,879	14,312	5,833	23,704	27,436	3,509	9,330	16,152	5,272	11,932	29,689	79,773
1988	9,405	4,315	12,869	7,371	24,562	33,590	4,731	12,497	20,431	5,596	12,821	34,329	78,285
1989	10,291	4,599	17,748	8,224	26,597	41,765	5,932	15,280	22,924	5,735	16,276	35,045	64,353
1990	10,025	6,047	22,125	8,830	28,539	49,999	6,187	15,686	34,529	5,855	16,306	34,604	92,165
1991	11,218	5,171	24,795	8,682	28,628	54,452	7,813	15,245	29,729	6,299	16,544	26,876	90,004
1992	10,697	5,249	31,836	10,706	28,560	44,906	8,431	15,835	29,999	5,885	17,422	26,300	99,509
1993	13,129	5,417	28,989	10,225	30,611	37,269	9,851	16,422	51,559	6,390	16,711	25,941	85,400
1994	13,030	5,410	34,061	11,551	36,698	59,170	9,173	15,937	43,192	7,079	17,242	35,453	54,550
1995[1]	2,600	54	26,185	11,146	40,245	69,928	12,027	12,898	38,300	7,078	17,835	30,654	57,210

[1] Preliminary. [2] Formerly part of the U.S.S.R.; data not reported separately until 1992. NA = Not available. *Source: Food and Agricultural*

Imports of Cocoa Liquor and Cocoa Powder in Selected Countries In Metric Tons

	Cocoa Liquior						Cocoa Powder						
Year	France	Germany	Netherlands	Japan	United Kingdom	United States	Belgium	France	Germany	Italy	Japan	Netherlands	United States
1985	24,031	3,570	14,822	2,792	3,400	53,042	4,586	8,269	16,624	8,313	3,841	4,669	81,775
1986	28,426	2,006	10,915	3,346	4,091	50,705	4,844	8,984	15,654	9,059	4,844	4,669	89,454
1987	31,171	391	8,805	3,402	1,870	38,105	5,229	8,967	16,989	9,330	5,517	3,624	103,455
1988	31,157	793	9,014	3,445	3,022	34,454	5,572	9,750	16,455	9,498	6,470	3,432	91,337
1989	29,257	1,040	9,315	3,451	2,524	27,556	6,138	10,920	18,470	10,233	6,033	5,862	53,736
1990	35,146	1,860	9,875	3,123	1,713	25,047	6,235	12,244	21,294	11,418	6,284	6,446	58,280
1991	40,251	3,242	7,443	2,057	1,918	25,320	6,665	12,215	25,315	12,189	6,557	6,239	55,636
1992	45,056	2,540	7,130	2,246	3,611	24,255	6,700	14,896	27,745	14,469	6,067	9,412	56,089
1993	41,999	1,694	15,543	2,468	1,490	31,641	6,600	16,773	25,732	13,221	5,771	5,626	66,533
1994	42,392	2,682	14,913	2,312	4,443	26,846	8,748	19,215	28,806	12,884	6,461	10,078	67,207
1995[1]	46,570	5,083	6,822	1,832	5,030	19,192	NA	17,081	32,247	15,265	6,310	10,048	66,075

[1] Preliminary. NA = Not available. *Source: E D & F Man Cococa, Ltd.*

Imports of Cocoa and Products in the United States In Thousands of Metric Tons

Year	Jan.	Feb.	Mar.	Apr.	May	June	July	Aug.	Sept.	Oct.	Nov.	Dec.	Total
1987	27	28	23	31	21	10	11	14	6	23	24	45	263
1988	27	31	27	19	15	21	15	20	9	9	14	31	237
1989	44	24	30	29	25	18	18	23	14	20	10	10	266
1990[2]	72	53	70	110	83	60	NA	61	41	NA	72	49	716
1991	70	53	51	74	62	66	65	59	53	NA	NA	73	761
1992	83	66	62	55	50	60	52	60	67	67	64	69	755
1993	67	57	56	61	58	61	77	58	59	71	71	98	801
1994	67	68	56	61	49	51	49	58	58	61	45	48	672
1995	68	54	44	48	47	48	48	51	53	49	54	48	672
1996	90	87	90	80	55	49	62	53	53	60	60	89	828
1997[1]	82	47	77	71	64	54	59	47	54	61	56		733

[1] Preliminary. [2] Prior to 1990, data for cocoa bean imports only. NA = Not available. *Source: Foreign Agricultural Service, U.S. Department of Agriculture (FAS-USDA)*

Visible Stocks of Cocoa in Port of Hampton Road Warehouses[1], at End of Month In Thousands of Bags

Year	Jan.	Feb.	Mar.	Apr.	May	June	July	Aug.	Sept.	Oct.	Nov.	Dec.
1988	140.8	274.8	347.3	434.9	480.8	474.3	511.2	464.1	486.4	465.8	442.1	419.6
1989	528.4	653.3	777.7	775.0	875.0	741.6	655.8	583.2	509.1	594.2	567.0	552.3
1990	403.6	445.9	583.2	674.3	807.4	1,064.7	917.2	67.2	1,046.5	19.0	996.5	958.2
1991	946.5	953.3	910.1	946.0	906.1	1,036.6	1,174.5	1,291.2	1,386.2	1,429.0	1,426.0	1,502.9
1992	1,588.3	1,892.1	2,233.1	2,236.2	2,236.9	2,204.8	2,150.8	2,087.4	1,982.4	2,018.6	2,043.9	2,188.5
1993	2,209.9	2,497.3	2,443.9	2,676.8	2,771.8	2,689.7	2,920.0	2,708.6	2,740.1	2,418.7	2,328.3	2,356.9
1994	2,329.6	2,441.1	2,443.9	2,522.9	2,533.1	2,460.2	2,445.4	2,335.0	2,308.4	2,360.2	2,306.9	2,253.7
1995	2,152.7	2,098.6	2,195.7	2,212.3	2,120.2	2,016.0	1,919.8	1,786.6	1,713.1	1,598.2	1,463.9	1,470.3
1996	1,439.8	1,492.8	1,458.0	1,549.6	1,561.7	1,493.9	1,412.3	1,315.4	1,239.6	1,338.9	1,108.1	1,116.2
1997	1,128.3	1,132.1	1,133.0	1,094.0	1,010.5	970.2	872.4	840.1	727.3	763.9	695.7	704.8

[1] Licensed and unlicensed warehouses approved by the CSCE. *Source: Coffee, Sugar & Cocoa Exchange, Inc. (CSCE)*

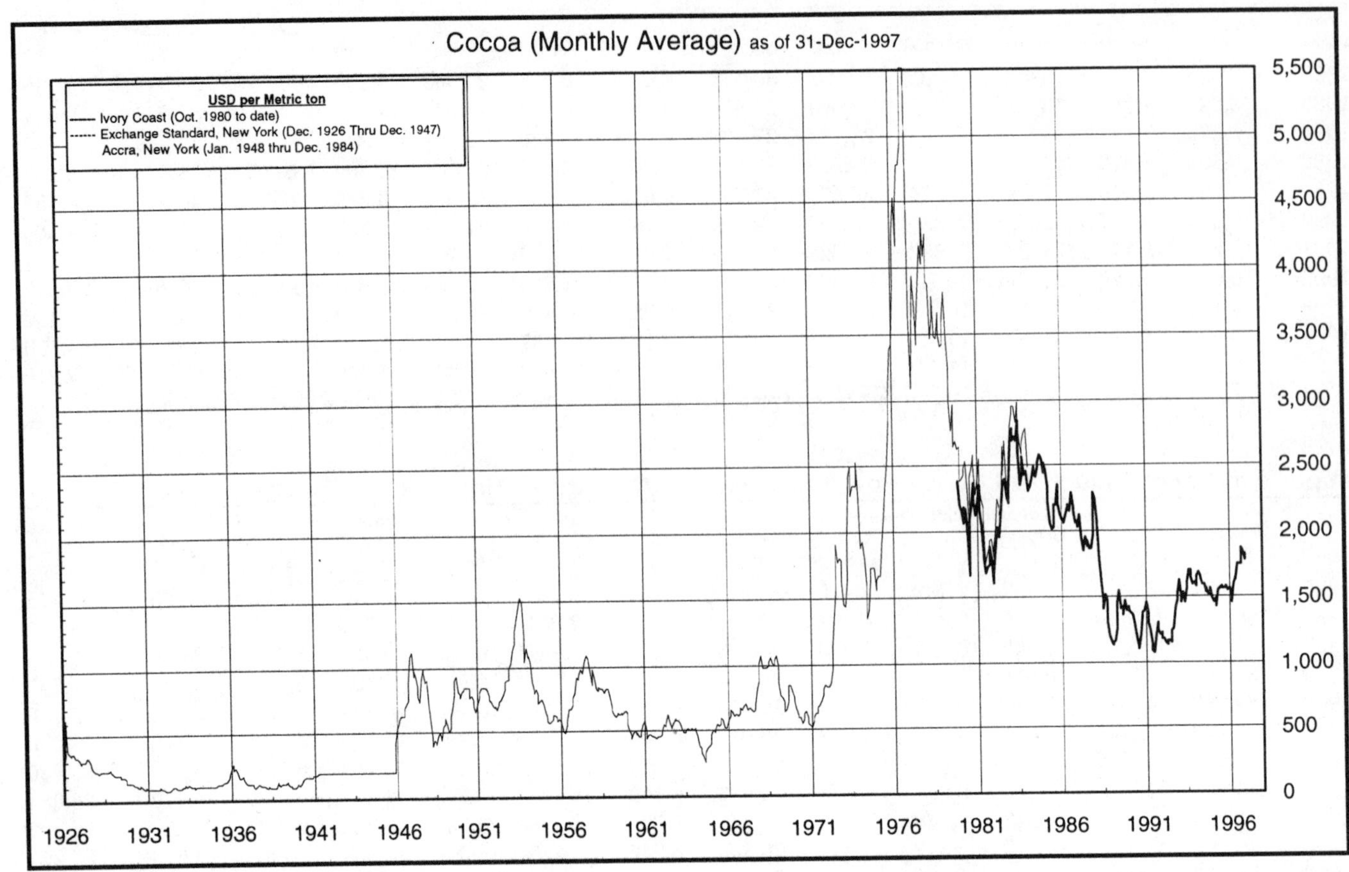

Visible Stocks of Cocoa in Philadelphia (Delaware River) Warehouses[1], at End of Month In Thousands of Bags

Year	Jan.	Feb.	Mar.	Apr.	May	June	July	Aug.	Sept.	Oct.	Nov.	Dec.
1987	209.8	210.8	228.9	224.1	243.6	276.2	291.4	259.7	236.6	177.9	189.6	206.3
1988	164.6	149.2	154.9	211.1	227.3	232.0	238.1	193.3	185.5	157.6	123.4	112.0
1989	86.0	67.5	88.7	96.2	114.0	112.5	100.3	100.0	54.6	46.1	51.9	53.5
1990	35.1	61.1	87.5	107.9	120.5	204.4	297.1	231.2	185.9	193.0	195.3	215.1
1991	216.2	226.9	249.3	254.9	309.2	376.8	382.8	376.8	375.5	355.1	280.5	282.7
1992	344.6	345.5	412.1	547.6	576.7	632.0	637.7	654.0	616.4	606.0	565.8	612.4
1993	562.2	589.8	603.9	606.0	653.1	678.0	665.7	648.9	600.6	611.5	685.2	781.8
1994	831.5	937.7	1,004.2	1,010.9	1,055.4	1,095.2	1,076.0	1,029.8	968.5	857.1	843.9	818.9
1995	807.5	1,034.3	1,038.9	1,020.2	963.7	924.3	860.7	759.2	852.2	727.0	666.0	735.6
1996	960.2	1,005.2	1,205.6	1,658.8	1,871.3	1,851.7	1,969.1	1,816.2	1,851.1	1,705.1	1,671.7	1,696.5
1997	1,753.0	1,634.4	1,579.6	1,641.0	1,578.7	1,625.9	1,696.2	1,637.6	1,530.9	1,491.8	1,414.2	1,394.0

[1] Licensed and unlicensed warehouses approved by the CSCE. *Source: Coffee, Sugar & Cocoa Exchange, Inc. (CSCE)*

Visible Stocks of Cocoa in New York Warehouses[1], at End of Month In Thousands of Bags

Year	Jan.	Feb.	Mar.	Apr.	May	June	July	Aug.	Sept.	Oct.	Nov.	Dec.
1987	51.9	43.5	40.0	39.4	55.2	46.1	58.7	43.5	49.4	44.8	107.7	149.1
1988	138.7	115.4	100.1	96.8	102.8	135.4	140.8	146.8	114.3	105.8	73.7	59.8
1989	65.0	81.9	47.3	82.2	214.8	245.3	274.2	215.6	181.3	247.7	313.6	293.5
1990	288.4	267.5	311.9	335.3	294.8	359.2	431.3	409.0	442.2	406.3	413.4	397.2
1991	355.6	219.6	295.9	294.1	250.4	292.6	313.3	317.1	271.5	253.9	292.9	282.4
1992	321.2	303.7	278.7	302.6	273.4	287.8	329.7	301.5	280.5	252.3	212.7	183.3
1993	150.9	144.1	122.0	125.0	119.8	119.8	119.8	119.8	119.8	118.6	132.4	187.7
1994	271.0	275.0	280.8	296.6	358.6	394.1	447.5	447.5	467.3	427.3	407.2	556.1
1995	560.5	634.5	559.2	539.4	510.4	561.1	579.3	595.4	459.9	598.7	679.7	598.7
1996	667.6	646.1	632.7	627.2	656.1	633.5	1,191.7	1,154.2	1,121.4	973.2	950.1	919.0
1997	984.7	981.3	945.0	1,250.0	1,574.4	1,524.7	1,512.8	1,348.0	1,217.3	1,073.7	1,020.0	980.4

[1] Licensed and unlicensed warehouses approved by the CSCE. *Source: Coffee, Sugar & Cocoa Exchange, Inc. (CSCE)*

Spot Cocoa Prices[1] for Selected Origins of Cocoa Beans and Products in the U.S. Dollars Per Metric Ton

Crop Year Beginning October	Cocoa Beans: Brazil	Cote d'Ivoire	Dominican Republic	Ecuador	Malaysia	Chocolate Liquor: Brazil	Chocolate Liquor: Ecuador	Cocoa Butter: African	Cocoa Butter: Other	Cocoa Cake 10-12% Fat
1987-8	1,807	1,952	1,664	1,700	NA	2,280	2,216	4,001	3,919	916
1988-9	1,669	1,773	1,442	1,466	1,364	2,136	1,912	3,543	3,515	945
1989-90	1,259	1,307	1,142	1,250	1,162	1,775	1,640	3,176	3,151	666
1990-1	1,222	1,289	1,091	1,168	1,131	1,704	1,646	3,232	3,199	394
1991-2	1,234	1,262	1,051	1,136	1,111	1,656	1,540	2,763	2,815	393
1992-3	1,109	1,199	969	1,123	1,020	1,571	1,513	2,517	2,572	539
1993-4	1,378	1,560	1,277	1,393	1,326	2,076	2,028	3,348	3,393	649
1994-5	1,547	1,596	1,347	1,436	1,434	2,202	2,105	3,730	3,737	560
1995-6	1,539	1,522	1,387	1,390	1,449	2,167	2,023	3,780	3,795	519
1996-7	1,641	1,631	1,498	1,511	1,539	2,305	2,163	4,022	4,021	553

[1] All prices are nominal and are net ex-dock or ex-warehouse, U.S. eastern seaboard north of Hatteras, for merchandise physically available in interstate commerce, in truckload and regular commercial quantities. NA = Not available. *Source: Foreign Agricultural Service, U.S. Department of Agriculture*

Average Open Interest of Cocoa Futures in New York In Contracts

Year	Jan.	Feb.	Mar.	Apr.	May	June	July	Aug.	Sept.	Oct.	Nov.	Dec.
1988	27,704	28,713	32,178	33,589	35,239	36,444	37,772	38,841	38,762	38,222	37,834	36,697
1989	36,747	35,492	32,917	36,597	41,341	45,016	47,222	45,700	42,731	46,366	48,062	49,553
1990	52,094	52,599	55,796	51,299	51,076	50,385	49,603	49,083	47,332	50,084	44,944	41,955
1991	42,446	38,205	40,198	45,250	47,764	49,111	53,153	53,886	53,974	54,854	53,390	53,412
1992	54,464	54,797	52,110	49,904	48,076	47,690	49,924	50,532	51,706	56,101	57,426	60,521
1993	64,886	68,307	69,464	68,533	71,802	71,792	87,011	83,057	88,000	94,844	96,507	91,573
1994	89,174	87,349	91,715	82,500	82,970	72,288	72,249	69,614	73,436	74,163	72,232	75,995
1995	78,873	80,786	82,299	78,435	80,547	75,496	74,975	65,794	68,547	72,758	76,680	79,844
1996	90,478	93,533	98,049	95,390	96,346	88,232	80,873	77,134	77,942	79,572	77,139	78,592
1997	86,960	90,589	96,771	96,956	94,651	97,385	101,815	101,138	106,487	108,263	99,544	97,009

Source: Coffee, Sugar & Cocoa Exchange, Inc. (CSCE)

Volume of Trading of Cocoa Futures in New York In Contracts

Year	Jan.	Feb.	Mar.	Apr.	May	June	July	Aug.	Sept.	Oct.	Nov.	Dec.	Total
1988	84,590	83,826	92,644	85,144	111,277	121,184	128,859	106,031	87,684	137,635	142,016	87,160	1,268,050
1989	138,883	122,374	116,082	132,208	135,783	129,943	98,922	137,879	73,741	95,531	101,152	59,352	1,341,850
1990	121,610	128,357	166,277	191,007	194,759	181,377	126,596	143,323	75,757	120,689	116,175	69,990	1,635,917
1991	94,609	92,450	104,973	99,176	76,435	104,327	96,840	146,379	104,136	135,677	106,888	72,629	1,234,519
1992	122,576	119,375	94,131	116,804	66,185	135,373	104,660	145,815	113,589	109,888	137,815	95,024	1,397,235
1993	145,378	139,932	111,751	149,771	82,961	189,474	225,901	215,044	240,371	217,697	229,752	183,352	2,128,384
1994	178,303	190,804	205,623	188,004	267,188	251,300	193,883	241,340	142,589	183,975	210,635	164,917	2,417,006
1995	197,032	183,784	191,328	208,707	169,061	199,211	140,789	205,169	120,433	149,810	211,171	113,603	2,090,098
1996	177,720	226,701	213,189	242,988	164,749	183,544	159,070	164,719	107,634	167,227	185,226	128,809	2,121,576
1997	180,669	172,510	219,896	235,020	130,041	251,471	186,280	200,707	168,981	204,394	180,805	143,735	2,274,509

Source: Coffee, Sugar & Cocoa Exchange, Inc. (CSCE)

Coconut Oil and Copra

World copra production is small at only about 2 percent of total world oilseed production and crop size has shown relatively little increase during the past decade. Copra, dried coconut meat, is crushed or processed to yield coconut oil and copra meal. Coconut oil, an important ingredient in cosmetics and soap, is also used as a food ingredient. As an edible oil, however, foodstock use is shrinking, particularly in the U.S., as the oil has a very high level of 92 percent saturated fat. U.S. coconut oil imports are mostly processed into inedible products.

Coconut oil use in U.S. food products has dropped about one-third from the mid-1980's to an average of about 225,000 tonnes in the mid-1990's. Its use in inedible products, soap being the most prominent, has also fallen.

Most of the world copra crop is processed into oil. 1997/98 copra production of 5.5 million metric tonnes was about unchanged from 1996/97. From that total 3.92 million tonnes of coconut oil were obtained vs. 3.5 million in 1996/97. Copra meal output at 1.86 million tonnes was approximately the same as in the previous year. Percentagewise, coconut oil accounts for less than 3 percent of the world's vegetable and marine oils. The Philippines and Indonesia account for about two-thirds of world copra output. Copra production is not only dependent on the weather, but also appears to have a biological cycle that historically has triggered relatively sharp fluctuations in output.

Foreign trade in copra products is small: coconut oil exports in 1997/98 totaled less than one million tonnes; copra meal exports were placed at 1.1 million tonnes, about unchanged from 1996/97. World carryover stocks of both coconut oil and copra are also small. Coconut oil is estimated at 280,000 tonnes at the end of 1997/98, and copra stocks are estimated at 6,000 tonnes.

U.S. imports of coconut oil in 1996/97 (October/June) totaled 384,599 metric tonnes vs. 344,313 in the like year earlier period, with a value of $285 million vs. $239 million, respectively. Manufacturers are not adverse to switching to palm oil should coconut oil's premium to palm oil widen too far.

U.S. coconut oil prices in mid-1997 were below those of the previous year, but the 12-month average ending in August of $795 per metric ton was unchanged from the year earlier period. World copra prices, basis Rotterdam, in 1996/97 averaged $457 per ton vs. $487 during 1995/96; the Rotterdam coconut oil price of $700 per metric ton compares with $746, respectively.

World Production of Copra In Thousands of Metric Tons

Year	India	Indonesia	Ivory Coast	Malaysia	Mexico	Mozambique	New Guinea	Philippines	Sri Lanka	Thailand	Vanuatu	Vietnam	World Total
1988	487	1,021	52	97	203	70	134	1,710	130	62	24	139	4,444
1989	470	1,381	70	96	202	70	117	2,345	128	59	45	188	5,488
1990	450	1,392	75	76	175	72	91	1,950	61	62	28	192	4,933
1991	440	1,110	79	82	175	72	110	1,845	70	65	27	220	4,612
1992	440	1,110	65	82	200	72	117	1,845	70	65	24	220	4,624
1993	445	1,100	60	65	173	73	120	1,950	60	68	26	200	4,648
1994	455	1,270	65	60	170	74	101	1,930	60	69	27	200	4,801
1995	610	1,080	72	66	160	74	125	2,500	113	103	30	208	5,446
1996[1]	630	1,155	75	60	155	75	178	1,725	88	90	28	210	4,779
1997[2]	580	1,320	75	60	150	76	188	2,080	100	100	28	215	5,285
1998[3]	620	1,120	75	55	150	76	150	1,850	95	90	NA	210	4,826

[1] Preliminary. [2] Estimate. [3] Forecast. *Source: The Oil World*

World Supply and Distribution of Coconut Oil In Thousands of Metric Tons

	Production							Consumption						Ending Stocks		
Year	India	Indonesia	Malaysia	Philippines	Total	Exports	Imports	European Union	India	Indonesia	Philippines	United States	Total	Philippines	United States	Total
1987-8		721	38	1,141	2,851	1,451	1,490	535	246	479	304	416	2,891	122	151	589
1988-9	285	669	40	957	2,685	1,219	1,287	473	282	517	297	396	2,911	100	68	432
1989-90	284	782	34	1,314	3,217	1,506	1,490	535	284	576	278	386	3,061	115	128	571
1990-1	272	843	34	1,283	3,192	1,450	1,490	664	279	682	279	402	3,332	51	127	473
1991-2	267	701	33	1,110	2,852	1,343	1,321	513	278	380	257	409	2,883	115	85	420
1992-3	267	681	29	1,294	3,004	1,655	1,270	516	279	430	249	491	2,960	38	114	379
1993-4	272	746	24	1,051	2,804	1,354	1,443	547	275	379	266	483	2,950	50	74	322
1994-5	363	666	36	1,664	3,478	1,772	1,748	664	367	520	269	491	3,334	109	74	440
1995-6[1]	380	675	35	1,172	2,998	1,380	1,418	606	383	436	295	427	3,120	87	38	352
1996-7[2]	351	806	33	1,218	3,171	1,711	1,685	699	354	291	291	503	3,119	66	68	377
1997-8[3]	352	706	31	1,304	3,124	1,643	1,652	660	357	311	302	492	3,143	67	72	368

[1] Preliminary. [2] Estimate. [3] Forecast. *Source: The Oil World*

Supply and Distribution of Coconut Oil in the United States In Millions of Pounds

Year	Rotterdam Copra Tonne $ U.S.	Rotterdam Coconut Oil, CIF $ U.S.	Imports For Consumption	Stocks Oct. 1	Total Supply	Exports	Disappearance Total Domestic	Disappearance Edible Products	Disappearance Inedible Products	Production of Coconut Oil (Refined) Total	Oct. - Dec.	Jan. - March	April - June	July - Sept.
1986-7	285	413	1,087	308	1,395	49	1,076	319	720	685.5	151.8	197.9	180.4	155.4
1987-8	385	547	1,074	271	1,344	77	935	233	700	786.1	181.7	194.2	214.9	195.3
1988-9	371	545	778	332	1,110	55	904	211	713	712.7	199.3	165.1	182.0	166.3
1989-90	251	371	1,038	152	1,190	44	866	161	705	703.1	195.4	163.8	187.3	156.6
1990-1	247	364	946	279	1,225	51	897	169	742	754.6	196.8	150.8	141.8	265.2
1991-2	397	605	838	277	1,115	22	906	164	699	733.9	145.3	158.8	159.3	270.5
1992-3	292	446	1,162	187	1,349	15	1,082	202	692	650.5	156.0	158.8	166.6	169.1
1993-4	388	564	999	251	1,250	20	1,067	234	716	536.2	155.6	129.0	131.8	119.8
1994-5	432	656	1,100	163	1,263	18	1,082	247	694	546.8	137.5	142.7	144.3	122.3
1995-6	487	746	873	163	1,036	11	840	221	453	445.0	127.5	118.4	132.8	66.4
1996-7[1]	452	693	1,014	185	1,199	20	959	120	471	324.2	77.0	61.5	101.5	84.2

[1] Preliminary. NA = Not available. *Source: Bureau of the Census, U.S. Department of Commerce*

Consumption of Coconut Oil in End Products (Edible and Inedible) in the U.S. In Millions of Pounds

Year	Jan.	Feb.	Mar.	Apr.	May	June	July	Aug.	Sept.	Oct.	Nov.	Dec.	Total
1987	63.7	58.0	76.2	74.1	72.8	81.4	73.8	79.1	82.5	89.6	70.0	72.8	894.0
1988	76.1	71.2	59.1	59.6	66.8	65.8	55.1	53.8	48.7	65.2	57.8	57.9	737.1
1989	52.6	51.6	64.3	55.0	65.9	58.0	60.5	51.3	48.7	55.1	49.7	39.6	652.3
1990	45.4	44.9	44.3	44.6	43.2	39.4	39.8	39.5	39.2	49.7	41.0	43.9	514.9
1991		137.6			150.6			134.4			122.1		544.7
1992	72.5	70.6	76.5	70.7	78.7	74.8	65.2	70.6	77.4	75.8	76.2	66.4	875.4
1993	74.4	75.9	81.3	77.6	72.1	71.0	73.6	78.2	72.6	85.9	90.9	84.6	938.1
1994	74.4	77.4	77.5	80.4	86.6	88.8	76.0	88.4	65.1	74.6	85.1	95.0	969.3
1995	78.2	79.5	86.5	81.0	79.7	82.0	76.5	71.4	61.6	62.1	59.8	59.9	878.0
1996	47.0	54.3	60.1	60.2	68.6	54.6	55.1	47.9	44.9	49.6	50.3	47.9	640.7
1997[1]	44.1	44.8	52.8	46.1	41.9	49.4	49.9	48.3	66.9	53.4	43.9	47.7	589.1

[1]Preliminary. *Source: Bureau of the Census, U.S. Department of Commerce*

Stocks of Coconut Oil (Crude and Refined) in the United States, on First of Month In Millions of Pounds

Year	Jan.	Feb.	Mar.	Apr.	May	June	July	Aug	Sept	Oct.	Nov.	Dec.
1987	323.3	323.6	355.7	318.1	336.9	271.2	203.6	243.9	240.8	270.2	288.5	370.9
1988	367.7	358.8	370.7	371.1	356.0	353.6	336.6	290.2	287.5	335.0	332.7	307.0
1989	275.7	278.9	247.4	205.3	167.7	134.7	189.9	177.5	149.8	150.8	218.6	238.5
1990	297.3	304.4	307.0	348.0	305.6	306.6	292.2	264.3	315.4	281.1	309.3	304.6
1991	NA	NA	359.0	NA	NA	364.3	NA	NA	279.3	NA	NA	298.0
1992	NA	266.3	274.2	239.7	211.2	173.7	178.3	141.1	187.1	187.7	225.1	278.8
1993	355.7	406.7	418.9	348.7	338.3	305.2	257.2	233.8	321.4	250.8	335.0	299.1
1994	291.7	316.5	284.5	251.5	237.6	199.9	151.4	163.7	156.0	164.1	166.2	152.9
1995	155.6	173.6	168.1	163.7	148.5	183.5	163.8	136.9	124.1	162.9	199.7	187.7
1996	164.7	229.1	200.4	217.7	173.6	175.9	171.5	116.7	113.8	84.0	78.6	65.0
1997[1]	125.9	147.4	141.1	204.5	174.5	161.3	143.8	143.4	154.3	149.6	162.1	194.2

[1] Preliminary. NA = Not avaliable. *Source: Bureau of the Census, U.S. Department of Commerce*

Average Price of Coconut Oil (Crude) Tank Cars in New York In Cents Per Pound

Year	Jan.	Feb.	Mar.	Apr.	May	June	July	Aug.	Sept.	Oct.	Nov.	Dec.	Average
1987	21.40	20.88	19.30	20.38	21.44	24.25	25.75	25.13	24.40	24.69	24.50	27.15	23.27
1988	28.81	26.06	25.45	25.25	26.50	30.45	31.88	28.30	27.38	27.44	28.06	27.81	27.78
1989	26.75	27.63	27.90	28.94	29.90	29.56	28.94	27.75	28.63	27.25	26.35	24.75	27.86
1990	24.31	23.69	22.10	21.63	21.15	20.31	19.16	18.58	18.26	18.18	20.45	20.13	20.66
1991	20.22	20.31	20.50	19.38	19.69	21.69	26.19	25.63	25.63	28.50	31.50	32.38	24.30
1992	39.33	36.00	34.57	34.63	33.56	32.13	29.63	27.31	27.88	26.95	27.00	25.50	31.21
1993	24.94	24.37	23.65	23.13	24.13	24.95	25.35	25.61	24.44	23.88	26.69	34.25	25.45
1994	30.30	29.69	27.31	28.19	29.45	30.25	29.56	30.35	30.63	30.60	34.19	33.69	30.35
1995	32.50	32.00	31.13	31.00	30.50	35.00	37.90	35.63	35.00	36.00	37.88	33.69	34.02
1996	35.80	36.63	36.75	38.75	39.50	42.25	41.80	42.80	47.20	48.00	49.50	50.00	42.42
1997[1]	44.20	44.00	42.88	42.50	42.50	35.00	36.50	36.50	37.00	34.76	34.26	32.95	38.59

[1] Preliminary. NA = Not available. *Source: Economic Research Service, U.S. Department of Agriculture*

Coffee

Coffee prices were extremely volatile in 1997. In the second quarter of 1997, prices staged a spectacular rally only to see a steep price decline in the third quarter. That was followed by another rally and setback and then a third rally occurred in late 1997. The initial rally was caused by very tight supplies of arabica coffee along with ideas that production in Colombia could be less than had been expected. That proved to be the case as Colombia's 1996-97 (October-September) coffee crop was the smallest in several years. World stocks of coffee, particularly arabica coffee, had been drawn down due to the very small Brazilian crop in 1995-96. That crop was damaged by two frosts in the June-July 1994 period. As the 1996-97 season drew to a close, coffee stocks were again tight and prices rallied in response.

As the 1997-98 coffee year got underway in October, the market was contending with the combination of still tight stocks of arabica coffee along with poor weather in a number of major coffee producing countries. El Nino related conditions brought some very dry weather to parts of Colombia and Brazil as well as Central America. Hurricanes were spawned in the Pacific and they damaged the coffee crops in Mexico and Guatemala. El Nino related droughts struck Southeast Asia and damaged the Indonesian robusta crop.

For the 1997-98 season, it appeared that world production of coffee would be similar to the 1996-97 season. The USDA forecast world production at 102.6 million bags, just about the same level as in 1996-97. Many of the differences in various estimates of world coffee production are related to difficulties in estimating the huge Brazilian coffee crop. The sheer size of the crop and its geographical expanse make it problematic to obtain an accurate estimate of production. The 1996-97 (April-March) crop in Brazil was estimated at 28 million bags. Coffee, like other tree crops, exhibits biennial production cycles. Large crops tend to be followed by smaller crops which in turn are followed by larger crops. The large 1996-97 Brazilian crop was in turn followed by a somewhat smaller crop in 1997-98. That crop was estimated at between 24 and 26 million bags. Recent stocks data from Brazilian farm cooperatives indicates that the crop could in fact have been closer to 24 million bags or less.

The Brazilian harvest was about over by September 1997 and at that time the other major producing countries began the harvest of their 1997-98 crops. The major producers of arabica coffee besides Brazil are Colombia, Mexico and the Central American countries, Ethiopia, Kenya and India. Colombia is the second largest producer of coffee. The Colombian 1996-97 (October-September) crop was damaged by heavy rains and came in at 10.8 million bags, 17 percent less than the previous season. The 1997-98 crop is forecast at 12 million bags though that is subject to change. Colombia has been experiencing very dry weather for several months, an El Nino effect. There remain questions as to whether the crop will in fact reach 12 million bags. Colombia has also been plagued by insect infestation and social unrest. In 1997, there were a number of labor stoppages by truckers and port workers, all of which slowed the movement of coffee to export locations.

Mexico was forecast to produce 5.5 million bags of coffee in 1997-98, four percent more than in the previous season. The weather in Mexico has been extreme. The coffee growing regions were struck by two hurricanes which appeared to cause some damage in the producing states of Oaxaca and Chiapas. In addition to hurricanes, there was a cold wave in late 1997 that adversely impacted production in the central producing states. As a result of these events, coffee production could turn out to be closer to five million bags.

In Central America, the major coffee producers are Guatemala, Honduras, El Salvador, Costa Rica and Nicaragua. These countries also experienced some dry weather followed by beneficial rains. Guatemala appeared to lose some of its crop as a result of storms. Overall, the 1997-98 coffee crop in Central America is projected to be 12.6 million bags, two percent more than the year before.

World robusta coffee production in 1997-98 should be about the same or slightly lower than in the previous season. Among the major producers of robusta coffee are Brazil, Uganda, the Ivory Coast, Indonesia and Vietnam. The most interesting development in the robusta market has been in Indonesia where there has been a severe El Nino related drought. There have been a wide range of estimates of the coffee crop with some pointing to a decline of 20 percent followed by another decline in 1998-99. It was also interesting to see that robusta production in Vietnam was not impacted by the weather and the 1997-98 crop of 5.8 million bags will just about offset the losses in Indonesia.

A key fundamental factor in the coffee market in 1998 will be the size of the 1998-99 Brazilian crop. Harvest of that crop begins in late April. With the 1997-98 crop being smaller, the biennial production cycle would call for a larger crop in 1998-99. Weather for this new crop in early 1998 has been good if not excellent. Some of the initial estimates put the crop at between 30 and 40 million bags. In the 1987-88 season, Brazil produced a coffee crop that was over 40 million bags.

World consumption of coffee in 1997-98 is expected to be close to the level of production. Consumption could reach 106 million bags. Coffee consumption has recovered from the low levels seen in the 1994-95 and 1995-96 seasons. The substantial price increases that followed the Brazilian frosts of 1994 resulted in a sharp increase in retail prices for coffee. That led to lower coffee consumption. Coffee roasters since then have been trying to keep prices steady. While coffee continues to face competition from other beverages, consumption has been on the rise especially in the countries that produce coffee.

Futures Markets

Coffee futures are traded on the Bolsa de Mercadorias & Futuros (BM&F), the Manila International Futures Exchange Inc. (MIFE), the Singapore Commodity Exchange Ltd., the London International Financial Futures and Options Exchange (LIFFE), and the Coffee, Sugar and Cocoa Exchange Inc. (CSCE) in New York. Options are traded on the BM&F, the LIFFE and the CSCE.

World Supply and Distribution of Coffee In Thousands of 60 Kilogram Bags (132.276 Lbs. Per Bag)

Crop Year	Beginning Stocks	Production	Imports	Supply	Total Exports	Bean Exports	Rst/Grn Exports	Soluble Exports	Domestic Use	Ending Stocks
1988-9	48,174	94,165	415	142,754	71,371	68,108	162	3,101	21,280	50,193
1989-90	50,193	96,958	258	147,409	83,402	80,034	129	3,239	21,065	43,012
1990-1	43,012	100,181	352	143,545	76,319	73,434	83	2,802	22,489	44,997
1991-2	44,997	103,731	349	149,077	81,387	78,341	53	2,993	22,198	45,492
1992-3	45,492	92,888	770	139,150	77,772	73,615	113	4,044	21,650	39,728
1993-4	39,728	93,303	1,002	134,033	77,332	72,610	108	4,614	23,340	33,361
1994-5	34,575	98,126	1,145	133,846	69,337	65,130	228	3,979	23,013	41,496
1995-6[1]	41,496	89,743	1,156	132,395	75,082	70,141	229	4,712	24,337	32,976
1996-7[2]	32,976	102,665	1,173	136,814	83,810	79,689	172	3,949	24,711	28,293
1997-8[3]	28,293	102,619	1,003	131,915	84,611	80,258	164	4,189	25,921	21,383

[1] Preliminary. [2] Estimate. [3] Forecast. *Source: Foreign Agricutural Service, U.S. Department of Agriculture (FAS-USDA)*

World Production of Green Coffee In Thousands of 60 Kilogram Bags (132.276 Lbs. Per Bag)

Crop Year	Brazil	Cameroon	Colombia	Costa Rica	El Salvador	Ethiopia	Guatemala	India	Indonesia	Ivory Coast	Mexico	Uganda	World Total
1988-9	25,000	1,760	10,700	2,758	1,492	3,400	3,022	3,590	6,750	3,989	5,500	3,300	94,363
1989-90	26,000	1,440	13,300	2,453	2,787	3,400	3,472	2,150	7,100	4,734	5,100	2,500	97,286
1990-1	31,000	1,450	14,500	2,565	2,603	3,500	3,282	2,970	7,480	3,300	4,550	2,700	100,417
1991-2	28,500	1,920	17,980	2,530	2,357	3,000	3,549	3,200	7,100	3,967	4,620	2,900	103,731
1992-3	24,000	837	14,950	2,620	2,894	3,500	3,584	2,700	7,350	2,500	4,180	2,800	92,888
1993-4	28,500	1,250	11,400	2,475	2,361	3,700	3,078	3,465	7,400	2,700	4,200	2,700	93,303
1994-5	28,000	1,000	13,000	2,492	2,314	3,800	3,500	3,060	6,400	3,733	4,030	3,100	98,126
1995-6[1]	16,800	1,000	12,939	2,595	2,325	3,800	3,827	3,717	5,800	2,900	5,400	4,200	89,743
1996-7[2]	28,000	1,000	10,779	2,376	2,498	3,800	4,275	3,417	7,900	4,667	5,300	4,350	102,665
1997-8[3]	26,000	1,000	12,000	2,455	2,378	3,800	4,280	4,000	7,100	4,200	5,500	4,000	102,619

[1] Preliminary. [2] Estimate. [3] Forecast. *Source: Foreign Agricultural Service, U.S. Department of Agriculture (FAS-USDA)*

World Exportable[4] Production of Green Coffee In Thousands of 60 Kilogram Bags (132.276 Lbs. Per Bag)

Crop Year	Brazil	Cameroon	Colombia	Costa Rica	El Salvador	Ethiopia	Guatemala	Indonesia	Ivory Coast	Kenya	Mexico	Uganda	World Total
1988-9	15,500	1,725	8,891	2,508	1,332	1,767	2,717	5,478	3,957	1,787	3,880	3,250	71,891
1989-90	17,000	1,405	11,538	2,198	2,607	2,239	3,162	5,820	4,700	1,665	3,650	2,450	75,944
1990-1	21,500	1,420	12,885	2,305	2,423	1,800	2,972	6,185	3,264	1,433	3,150	2,650	78,271
1991-2	19,500	1,895	16,580	2,270	2,173	1,400	3,239	5,550	3,929	1,483	3,170	2,845	81,729
1992-3	15,500	812	13,647	2,365	2,677	2,000	3,274	5,570	2,461	1,195	2,880	2,745	71,631
1993-4	19,100	1,225	9,700	2,225	2,131	2,200	2,777	5,535	2,661	1,208	3,000	2,640	70,315
1994-5	18,300	975	11,564	2,252	2,079	2,300	3,220	4,440	3,687	1,562	3,030	3,040	75,649
1995-6[1]	6,300	975	11,439	2,360	2,055	2,300	3,527	3,750	2,852	1,788	4,340	4,140	66,095
1996-7[2]	17,000	970	9,279	2,126	2,268	2,300	3,990	5,820	4,616	1,115	4,330	4,280	78,578
1997-8[3]	14,000	970	10,500	2,205	2,144	2,300	3,970	5,000	4,145	1,479	4,579	3,930	77,239

[1] Preliminary. [2] Estimate. [3] Forecast. [4] Marketing year begins in October in some countries and April or July in others. Exportable production represents total harvested production minus estimated domestic consumption. *Source: Foreign Agricultural Service, U.S. Department of Agriculture (FAS-USDA)*

Green Coffee Imports in the United States In Thousands of 60 Kilogram Bags[2]

Year	Brazil	Colombia	Costa Rica	Domin. Republic	Ecuador	El Salvador	Ethiopia	Guatemata	Indonesia	Mexico	Peru	Venezuela	Grand Total
1988	4,213	2,235	233	366	811	829	218	609	731	1,719	436	72	15,348
1989	4,155	2,413	393	402	1,137	790	432	1,404	635	3,937	673	87	19,377
1990	3,633	2,771	403	445	876	843	234	1,871	830	3,305	473	222	19,566
1991	5,335	3,048	603	343	785	868	31	1,489	536	2,993	610	108	18,849
1992	4,253	4,852	662	254	753	1,344	23	1,812	581	3,042	526	104	21,673
1993	3,376	2,957	437	213	671	1,274	192	1,815	542	2,947	158	444	18,023
1994	2,850	2,372	325	207	969	376	215	1,403	558	2,516	249	295	14,913
1995	2,302	2,485	388	266	745	284	109	1,637	513	2,887	621	89	15,886
1996	1,852	2,966	482	255	665	401	137	1,748	1,246	3,734	441	445	17,947
1997[1]	2,587	3,273	585	147	486	515	323	1,896	1,454	2,912	649	125	19,415

[1] Preliminary. [2] 132.276 pounds per bag. *Source: Bureau of the Census, U.S. Department of Commerce*

COFFEE

Monthly Green Coffee Imports in the United States   In Thousands of 60 Kilogram Bags[2]

Year	Jan.	Feb.	Mar.	Apr.	May	June	July	Aug.	Sept.	Oct.	Nov.	Dec.	Total
1988	1,175	1,683	1,427	1,179	1,141	832	1,543	1,621	1,238	1,272	1,195	1,040	15,348
1989	1,646	1,323	1,368	1,398	1,296	1,199	1,634	1,974	1,951	2,180	1,748	1,660	19,337
1990	1,950	1,989	2,358	1,783	1,658	1,548	1,451	1,261	1,229	1,611	1,140	1,591	19,566
1991	2,106	1,946	1,590	1,748	1,556	984	1,056	1,335	1,424	1,368	1,616	2,122	18,849
1992	2,262	1,944	2,125	1,698	1,534	1,795	1,806	1,692	1,644	1,615	1,508	2,050	21,673
1993	1,782	1,663	2,012	1,481	1,631	1,253	1,442	1,344	1,374	1,464	1,018	1,561	18,023
1994	1,538	1,152	1,409	1,077	1,082	1,151	1,195	1,560	1,266	1,127	1,103	1,213	14,872
1995	1,469	1,253	1,702	1,221	1,190	1,240	1,117	1,094	1,220	1,326	1,492	1,563	15,886
1996	1,824	1,657	1,753	1,395	1,444	1,236	1,329	1,341	1,364	1,279	1,485	1,828	17,936
1997[1]	1,582	1,837	1,966	1,792	1,738	1,583	1,783	1,391	1,147	1,215	1,184	1,629	18,848

[1] Preliminary. [2] 132.276 pounds per bag. *Source: Bureau of the Census, U.S. Department of Commerce*

Average Price of Brazilian[1] Coffee in New York   In Cents Per Pound

Year	Jan.	Feb.	Mar.	Apr.	May	June	July	Aug.	Sept.	Oct.	Nov.	Dec.	Average
1988	117.35	130.40	126.21	123.30	121.02	122.81	120.01	111.89	118.79	115.65	118.53	136.10	121.84
1989	145.29	128.72	128.06	131.45	128.94	115.02	78.75	67.32	67.75	60.32	65.53	67.93	98.76
1990	70.36	77.59	86.17	87.45	86.31	82.94	78.94	90.25	92.20	85.78	77.46	80.17	82.97
1991	75.59	79.39	83.83	81.58	75.56	72.44	69.24	68.15	75.08	65.91	66.03	62.14	72.91
1992	62.03	58.05	59.60	54.94	51.11	49.08	48.53	46.40	49.43	59.64	64.64	74.39	56.49
1993	67.13	66.34	62.60	54.92	57.26	55.70	65.76	73.25	75.58	71.65	74.20	74.51	66.58
1994	71.42	80.14	84.72	87.14	118.37	136.43	211.81	192.38	212.73	191.21	172.83	159.73	143.24
1995	162.81	161.07	171.48	166.54	161.72	145.22	139.68	149.54	130.26	127.23	125.33	110.46	145.95
1996	127.54	144.05	140.99	132.92	134.76	125.44	106.93	108.28	103.10	105.77	103.76	103.71	119.77
1997	127.28	160.21	179.75	183.73	209.62	184.21	158.52	158.25	167.77	152.12	149.07		166.41

[1] And other Arabicas. NA = Not available. *Source: Foreign Agricultural Service, U.S. Department of Agriculture (FAS-USDA)*

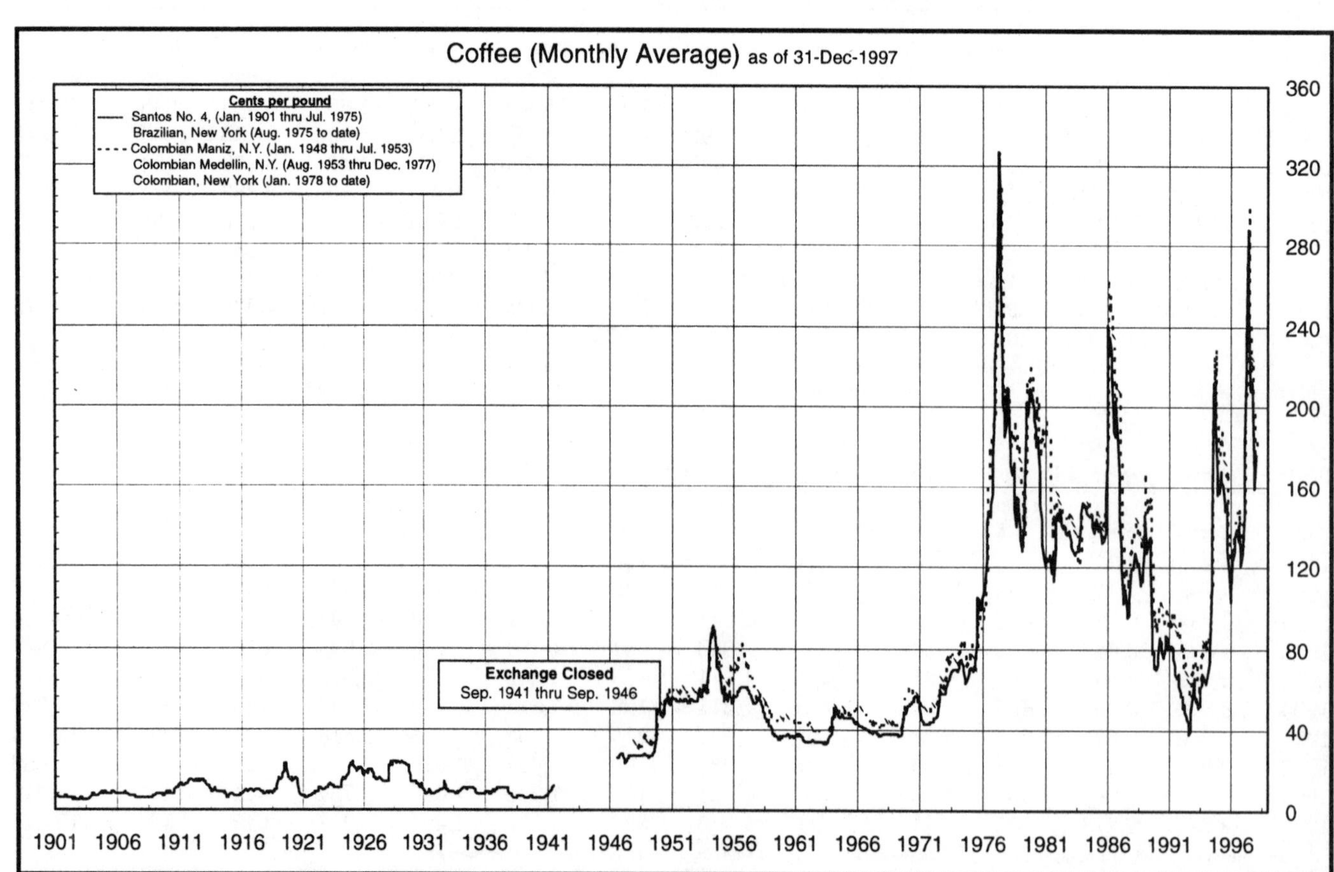

Average Monthly Retail[1] Price of Coffee in the United States In Cents Per Pound

Year	Jan.	Feb.	Mar.	Apr.	May	June	July	Aug.	Sep.	Oct.	Nov.	Dec.	Average
1990	291.7	296.5	289.1	288.5	293.8	297.7	305.4	302.7	302.5	303.0	294.5	294.1	296.6
1991	294.5	297.1	289.4	292.4	287.9	286.6	280.5	272.4	269.2	270.6	267.3	262.5	280.9
1992	266.8	268.8	263.1	261.2	266.0	262.5	265.2	261.3	253.7	249.2	239.1	236.4	257.8
1993	235.2	245.2	246.2	247.7	251.4	253.3	254.8	250.0	249.3	241.5	243.3	248.0	247.2
1994	253.0	252.9	251.5	251.6	253.5	259.8	334.1	448.0	445.8	445.0	448.2	438.2	340.1
1995	439.8	423.4	410.8	408.4	406.7	405.9	402.7	405.1	399.6	386.5	381.4	375.2	401.8
1996	357.7	359.0	355.0	352.7	344.4	343.8	338.0	339.0	333.3	334.4	328.3	330.7	343.0
1997	330.0	331.6	351.2	389.4	410.9	442.8	462.8	466.9	461.7	439.2	430.3		410.6

[1] Roasted in 13.1 to 20 ounce cans. *Source: Foreign Agricultural Service, U.S. Department of Agriculture*

Average Price of Colombian Mild Arabicas[1] in the United States In Cents Per Pound

Year	Jan.	Feb.	Mar.	Apr.	May	June	July	Aug.	Sep.	Oct.	Nov.	Dec.	Average
1990	82.07	91.55	103.24	101.79	99.14	96.01	92.45	103.30	102.21	97.20	92.38	97.06	96.53
1991	91.55	94.23	99.36	97.27	91.51	90.18	88.02	88.09	91.95	82.88	82.43	79.70	89.76
1992	78.40	71.75	73.67	69.55	64.93	64.10	62.50	56.49	56.18	64.77	71.72	81.52	67.97
1993	71.61	72.45	67.07	59.77	67.35	68.13	76.40	84.18	86.58	83.02	85.56	87.33	75.79
1994	85.85	93.04	93.23	97.53	133.90	151.85	222.75	210.57	231.52	206.07	186.96	173.94	157.27
1995	177.23	175.07	185.75	180.30	177.18	170.87	157.22	163.21	141.49	132.08	129.09	110.47	158.33
1996	119.08	134.94	160.60	134.31	142.56	133.25	135.39	137.68	123.30	127.77	129.41	126.41	133.73
1997	146.18	188.62	212.96	199.22	318.50	227.15	190.57	193.46	196.29	169.40	161.38		200.34

[1] ICO monthly and composite indicator prices on the New York Market, 1979 ICA Agreement Basis. *Source: Foreign Agricultural Service, U.S. Department of Agriculture*

Average Price of Other Mild Arabicas[1] in the United States In Cents Per Pound

Year	Jan.	Feb.	Mar.	Apr.	May	June	July	Aug.	Sep.	Oct.	Nov.	Dec.	Average
1990	75.83	84.01	93.96	93.73	92.02	88.26	86.48	94.42	94.92	91.41	84.84	89.89	89.15
1991	86.32	89.57	93.72	91.73	87.50	85.50	82.73	81.63	87.45	79.87	78.46	75.11	84.97
1992	72.99	67.88	69.96	65.23	60.14	58.38	57.68	52.42	52.73	61.40	67.36	77.46	63.64
1993	68.66	67.46	62.77	56.88	61.48	61.61	71.46	76.56	79.87	75.05	77.07	80.00	69.91
1994	77.21	82.69	85.57	89.23	121.97	142.57	217.67	198.07	220.10	199.06	180.76	167.47	148.53
1995	171.74	168.71	178.22	172.81	168.63	151.56	143.83	151.41	131.87	125.38	123.23	103.99	149.28
1996	109.38	122.71	119.05	122.01	128.56	124.46	120.47	122.49	114.05	120.62	119.90	115.01	119.89
1997	131.83	167.20	193.82	204.43	264.50	212.55	186.52	185.17	184.38	161.45	154.15		186.00

[1] ICO monthly and composite indicator prices on the New York Market, 1979 ICA Agreement Basis. *Source: Foreign Agricultural Service, U.S. Department of Agriculture*

Average Price of Robustas 1976[1] in the United States In Cents Per Pound

Year	Jan.	Feb.	Mar.	Apr.	May	June	July	Aug.	Sep.	Oct.	Nov.	Dec.	Average
1990	50.52	51.30	57.68	57.39	55.03	52.38	51.47	55.10	57.09	58.05	56.79	57.04	54.99
1991	53.92	52.46	52.13	52.38	48.22	47.10	46.49	46.57	48.11	47.31	51.47	51.45	49.80
1992	49.44	43.22	43.08	42.32	38.79	38.07	39.60	39.92	42.39	45.50	49.08	52.09	43.63
1993	48.13	48.25	46.86	45.51	46.91	47.65	50.39	59.29	63.44	60.05	62.53	62.90	53.49
1994	60.91	62.25	66.46	72.64	96.05	113.31	164.65	162.68	182.95	170.09	154.19	130.48	119.72
1995	132.26	135.22	146.83	145.47	141.89	129.53	120.89	131.28	116.41	114.15	112.79	94.72	126.79
1996	91.99	98.99	91.99	91.45	92.10	86.46	78.14	80.16	74.83	72.97	70.51	63.08	82.72
1997	67.66	76.65	81.31	78.48	95.74	91.94	82.52	76.92	77.43	76.90	78.20		80.34

[1] ICO monthly and composite indicator prices on the New York Market, 1979 ICA Agreement Basis. *Source: Foreign Agricultural Service, U.S. Department of Agriculture*

Average Price of Composite 1979[1] in the United States In Cents Per Pound

Year	Jan.	Feb.	Mar.	Apr.	May	June	July	Aug.	Sep.	Oct.	Nov.	Dec.	Average
1990	62.75	67.01	75.25	75.34	73.30	69.91	68.36	74.10	75.55	73.89	70.10	72.83	71.53
1991	69.39	70.55	72.47	71.45	67.47	65.58	64.31	63.38	66.86	62.83	64.30	63.07	66.81
1992	61.12	55.51	56.48	53.64	49.27	48.13	48.70	45.89	47.11	52.88	57.49	64.00	53.35
1993	58.14	57.32	54.76	51.38	54.18	54.54	60.61	67.69	71.64	67.78	70.03	71.53	61.63
1994	69.17	72.37	76.11	81.19	108.42	127.91	191.44	181.53	202.39	185.64	168.12	149.14	134.45
1995	152.08	152.24	162.73	159.59	155.96	141.66	132.71	141.70	124.75	120.02	117.99	99.57	138.42
1996	100.33	110.50	105.89	107.09	110.24	105.79	99.97	102.73	96.52	98.56	97.14	90.04	102.07
1997	100.03	121.89	137.47	142.20	180.44	155.38	135.04	132.63	132.51	121.09	118.16		134.26

[1] ICO monthly and composite indicator prices on the New York Market, 1979 ICA Agreement Basis. *Source: Foreign Agricultural Service, U.S. Department of Agriculture*

COFFEE

Average Open Interest of Coffee 'C' Futures in New York In Contracts

Year	Jan.	Feb.	Mar.	Apr.	May	June	July	Aug.	Sept.	Oct.	Nov.	Dec.
1987	15,317	16,034	17,415	20,445	22,455	21,160	22,536	23,943	25,857	26,418	22,757	21,064
1988	22,581	26,100	24,591	21,413	22,228	23,346	21,570	24,525	22,460	21,961	19,424	20,356
1989	24,544	23,684	23,246	25,870	23,663	24,716	27,184	31,410	32,404	35,019	32,687	32,096
1990	37,352	43,516	46,187	43,978	41,756	40,464	39,856	41,428	39,278	39,523	43,750	41,365
1991	42,320	41,326	39,948	39,410	41,726	43,717	42,037	40,661	42,126	43,940	41,819	40,628
1992	47,042	51,183	48,961	51,979	59,275	58,304	59,096	58,401	56,446	59,808	57,527	58,257
1993	59,193	54,249	53,618	55,578	51,797	50,918	53,871	48,541	47,649	49,809	46,901	48,812
1994	54,796	50,230	53,713	57,226	58,574	54,589	43,056	35,052	35,800	34,258	31,046	31,134
1995	34,455	35,391	36,925	34,387	34,615	34,462	30,156	27,448	27,800	28,408	24,505	26,412
1996	28,430	28,224	28,127	28,793	28,394	25,096	26,188	25,799	23,929	26,202	27,599	27,201
1997	38,516	42,888	39,092	32,644	30,324	22,552	21,497	19,818	22,788	25,109	23,636	28,577

Source: Coffee, Sugar & Cocoa Exchange, Inc. (CSCE)

Volume of Trading of Coffee 'C' Futures in New York In Contracts

Year	Jan.	Feb.	Mar.	Apr.	May	June	July	Aug.	Sept.	Oct.	Nov.	Dec.	Total
1987	69,564	81,427	78,671	104,350	71,189	86,564	77,621	106,182	77,207	85,315	72,846	53,650	964,586
1988	67,955	119,075	85,154	80,772	73,379	125,684	91,569	118,956	88,460	83,713	85,366	129,627	1,149,710
1989	141,903	106,019	102,594	129,018	95,902	134,848	100,700	122,207	97,744	104,100	111,434	82,484	1,328,953
1990	130,223	174,115	211,105	144,641	128,121	147,605	127,767	172,947	119,088	113,569	175,067	119,802	1,774,050
1991	138,642	174,688	188,842	153,436	103,344	135,887	107,058	170,113	180,017	148,640	159,099	112,882	1,772,648
1992	153,332	199,420	174,662	188,232	156,944	164,586	177,493	182,741	163,214	108,707	211,678	199,374	2,152,383
1993	290,120	214,771	183,354	209,607	176,559	197,761	193,002	233,479	202,363	187,763	217,947	182,486	2,489,223
1994	188,508	219,455	208,113	284,734	380,119	304,542	210,479	196,685	159,574	177,424	184,172	142,713	2,658,073
1995	169,250	191,352	213,326	156,191	163,248	186,550	162,562	161,076	165,337	152,959	157,240	123,923	2,003,014
1996	203,369	186,526	152,797	197,442	137,454	158,929	171,800	196,991	136,054	196,696	135,305	166,213	2,039,576
1997	242,719	280,014	267,369	223,330	219,214	186,227	135,664	136,807	142,610	151,171	145,610	163,446	2,294,181

Source: Coffee, Sugar & Cocoa Exchange, Inc. (CSCE)

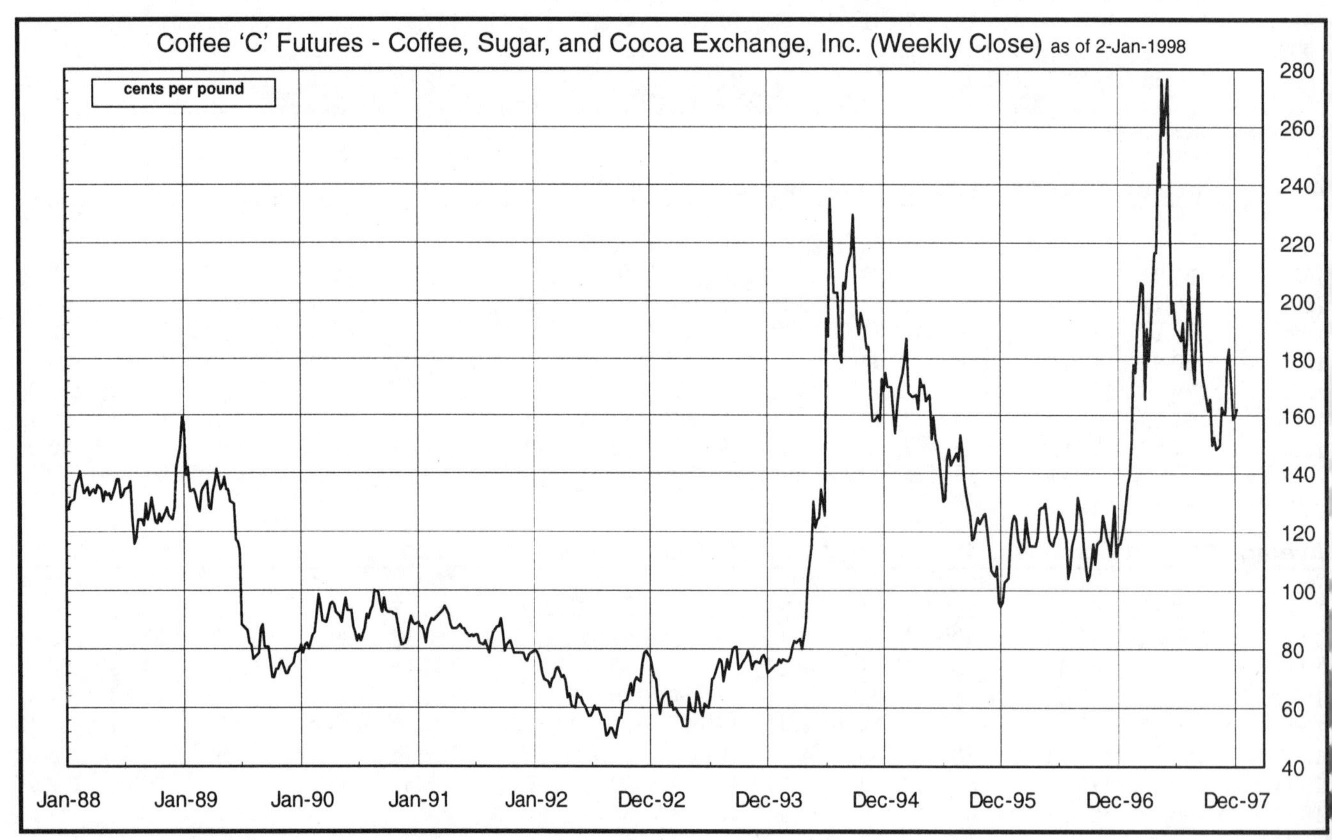

Coke

U.S. coke production in the January-March 1997 quarter was 5.55 million short tons vs. 5.75 million tons in the comparable quarter of 1996. For all of 1996, U.S. coke production was 23.1 million tons. U.S. imports of coke in the first quarter of 1997 were 271,000 tons which was well below the 418,000 tons in first quarter 1996. For all of 1996, U.S. coke imports were 1.11 million tons.

U.S. producer and distributor stocks of coke at the end of March 1997 were 1.37 million tons. That was up 19 percent from the end of first quarter 1996. U.S. consumption of coke in the first quarter of 1997 was 5.72 million tons which represented an 8 percent decline from the comparable quarter of 1996. For calendar year 1996, U.S. consumption of coke was 23 million tons. The United States also exports coke. In the January-March 1997 period, exports were 63,000 tons. That was well below the comparable quarter of 1996 when exports were 128,000 tons. For calendar year 1996, exports were 1.12 million tons.

Salient Statistics of Coke in the United States   In Thousands of Short Tons

	Production at Coke Plants							Exports			
Year	Merchant Coke Plants	Furance Coke Plants	Total Coke	Breeze	Imports	Consumption[2]	Total	Canada	Mexico	Producer & Distributor Ending Stocks	Avg. Price of Coal Receipts at Coke Plants
1991	3,251	20,795	24,046	1,734	1,099	24,216	740	239	98	2,107	48.95
1992	3,248	20,162	23,410	1,721	1,739	24,731	642	310	76	1,883	47.92
1993	3,209	19,973	23,182	3,424	1,534	24,303	835	417	92	1,461	47.44
1994	3,244	19,443	22,686	1,392	1,612	24,163	660	371	94	986	46.56
1995	3,239	20,509	23,749	1,463	1,816	24,500	750	579	60	1,302	47.34
1996[1]	3,105	19,971	23,076	1,402	1,111	23,043	1,121	491	143	1,323	47.33

[1] Preliminary. [2] Equal to production plus imports minus the change in producer and distributor stocks minus exports.
Source: Energy Information Administration, U.S. Department of Energy (EIA-DOE)

Production of Petroleum Coke in the United States   In Thousands of Barrels[2]

Year	Jan.	Feb.	Mar.	Apr.	May	June	July	Aug.	Sept.	Oct.	Nov.	Dec.	Total
1991	17,590	15,280	16,380	16,515	17,635	17,020	17,685	17,875	17,050	17,505	3,505	19,040	207,465
1992	18,550	16,330	17,825	17,615	18,460	18,685	19,330	18,280	17,845	17,665	3,540	19,385	217,995
1993	18,551	17,289	19,226	18,200	18,587	18,715	20,196	19,319	18,547	18,695	18,954	19,737	226,016
1994	19,170	16,873	18,695	18,454	19,748	19,325	20,008	19,473	17,868	18,753	18,995	19,697	227,059
1995	19,079	17,117	18,556	18,519	19,774	19,949	19,527	19,722	19,184	19,292	19,349	19,887	229,955
1996	19,536	18,706	21,015	20,663	20,426	19,927	19,836	20,328	20,124	20,558	20,447	21,389	242,955
1997[1]	19,798	17,594	20,603	21,274	22,210	21,052	21,619	22,229	21,630	21,782			251,749

[1] Preliminary. [2] Prior to 1993, data converted from thousands of short tons (5 barrels = 1 short ton). *Source: Energy Information Administration, U.S. Department of Energy (EIA-DOE)*

Coal Receipts and Carbonization at Coke Plants in the United States   In Thousands of Short Tons

	Coal Receipts at Coke Plants							Coal Carbonized at Coke Plants						
	By State					By Plant Type		By State					By Plant Type	
Year	Alabama	Indiana	Ohio	Pennsylvania	Total	Merchant Coke Plants	Furance Coke Plants	Alabama	Indiana	Ohio	Pennsylvania	Total	Merchant Coke Plants	Furance Coke Plants
1991	3,114	8,141	3,595	8,912	33,090	4,399	28,692	3,166	8,234	3,698	8,812	33,854	4,482	29,371
1992	3,334	6,894	3,717	9,761	32,027	4,295	27,732	3,297	7,153	3,755	9,868	32,366	4,316	28,050
1993	3,184	6,515	2,853	10,424	31,104	4,184	26,921	3,206	6,591	2,892	10,333	31,323	4,267	27,056
1994	3,242	5,023	3,064	10,776	31,719	4,205	27,514	3,253	4,841	3,092	10,849	31,740	4,218	27,522
1995	3,183	5,731	2,758	10,959	33,036	4,189	28,848	3,257	5,883	2,777	10,858	33,011	4,248	28,763
1996[1]	3,213	5,884	1,770	10,562	31,672	4,135	27,537	3,247	5,823	1,842	10,689	31,706	4,135	27,570

[1] Preliminary. *Source: Energy Information Administration, U.S. Department of Energy (EIA-DOE)*

Coke Distribution and Stocks in the United States   In Thousands of Short Tons

	Distribution							Coke Plant Stocks, Dec. 31			
	By Plant Type		By Consumer Category						By Plant Type		
Year	Merchant Coke Plants	Furance Coke Plants	Blast Furance	Foundries	Other Industrial Plants	Total Coke	Breeze	Total Coke	Merchant Coke Plants	Furance Coke Plants	Breeze
1991	3,246	24,267	25,669	1,213	630	27,513	2,057	2,107	252	1,856	259
1992	3,253	26,718	28,075	1,290	606	29,971	2,255	1,883	267	1,616	215
1993	3,226	27,009	28,295	1,373	567	30,235	3,563	1,461	272	1,189	486
1994	3,400	25,949	27,248	1,480	621	29,349	1,735	986	122	864	105
1995	3,284	25,103	26,346	1,401	639	28,386	1,638	1,302	112	1,189	136
1996[1]	NA	NA	NA	NA	NA	NA	NA	1,323	160	1,163	161

[1] Preliminary. *Source: Energy Information Administration, U.S. Department of Energy (EIA-DOE)*

Copper

Copper metal and copper alloys have considerable commercial importance due to their electrical, mechanical and physical properties. Copper for commercial purposes is obtained by the reduction of copper compounds in ores, followed by electrolytic refining. Copper finds widespread use in alloys such as brass, which is composed of copper and zinc.

The world's largest producer of copper is Chile with about a quarter of the world's output, followed by the U.S., Canada, Australia, Peru and Zambia. In the U.S., the principal mining states are Arizona, New Mexico, Utah, Michigan and Montana.

Copper prices have been volatile due to a tight balance between world copper production and consumption. World stocks of copper are at low levels but there has been a lot of expectation that world production will start to increase. The International Copper Study Group reported that in the first five months of 1997 there was a close balance between supply and demand for refined copper. Total global inventories, or those held by producers, consumers, merchants and exchanges, at the end of June 1997 were only 700,000 tonnes. At the current rate of consumption, that was less than a three week supply.

U.S. mine production of copper in June 1997 was 162,000 metric tonnes, up from 161,000 tonnes in May 1997. In the first half of 1997, mine production of copper was 945,000 tonnes while for all of 1996 it was 1.91 million tonnes. Of the 1996 total 1.24 million tonnes, or 65 percent, was mined in Arizona with the remainder in other states such as Montana and Utah. U.S. smelter production of copper in June 1997 was 112,000 tonnes, up sharply from 90,100 tonnes in May 1997. For January-June 1997, smelter production of copper was 662,000 tonnes while for all of 1996 it was 1.3 million tonnes. Of the copper produced at smelters, about 82 percent was from domestic and foreign ores and 18 percent was from scrap.

U.S. production of copper in refineries in June 1997 was 148,000 tonnes, down from 162,000 tonnes in May 1997. For the first half of 1997, refinery production of copper was 979,000 tonnes. For 1996 it was 2.01 million tonnes. In the first half of 1997, domestic production of electrolytically refined copper was 643,000 tonnes. Electrowon production of refined copper from scrap in first half 1997 was 201,000 tonnes. Of the total, electrolytically refined production was 128,000 tonnes while fire refined production was 72,900 tonnes.

U.S. reported consumption of refined copper in June 1997 was 217,000 tonnes compared to 219,000 tonnes in May 1997. In the first half of 1997, consumption was 1.38 million tonnes and for all of 1996 it was 1.64 million tonnes. Consumption of purchased copper-base scrap in June 1997 was 151,000 tonnes and in first half 1997 it was 887,000 tonnes. For all of 1996, copper-base scrap consumption was 1.64 million tonnes. U.S. refined copper stocks at the end of June 1997 were 163,000 tonnes.

Futures Markets

Copper futures and options are traded on the London Metals Exchange (LME) and the New York Mercantile Exchange, COMEX division. Copper futures are traded on the Beijing Commodity Exchange (BCE).

World Mine Production of Copper (Content of Ore) In Thousands of Metric Tons

Year	Australia	Canada[3]	Chile	China	Indonesia	Mexico	Peru	Poland	Russia[4]	South Africa	United States[3]	Zambia	World Total[2]
1987	232.7	802.2	1,418.1	250	102.1	252.7	417.6	438.0	630	188.1	1,244	463.2	8,24
1988	238.3	776.5	1,451.0	282	121.5	284.9	337.5	437.0	1,000	168.5	1,420	456.6	8,72
1989	296.0	723.1	1,609.3	276	144.0	264.2	387.9	384.0	1,000	181.9	1,507	466.3	9,05
1990	330.0	793.7	1,588.4	285	164.1	293.9	339.3	330.0	950	178.7	1,588	421.0	8,95
1991	320.0	811.1	1,814.3	304	211.7	292.1	357.2	320.0	900	184.6	1,531	390.6	9,09
1992	378.0	768.6	1,932.7	334	280.8	279.0	345.6	331.9	699	176.1	1,760	429.5	9,47
1993	402.0	732.6	2,055.4	345	298.6	301.1	348.3	383.6	584	166.3	1,800	396.2	9,45
1994	415.6	617.3	2,219.9	396	322.2	305.5	343.6	378.0	573	160.1	1,820	373.2	9,50
1995[1]	419.9	728.7	2,488.6	445	443.6	343.2	443.1	383.6	525	161.6	1,850	323.7	10,10
1996[2]	525.0	688.8	3,115.8	439	507.5	340.7	572.4	422.0	520	152.6	1,920	334.0	11,00

[1] Preliminary. [2] Estimate. [3] Recoverable. [4] Formerly part of the U.S.S.R.; data not reported separately until 1992. *Source: U.S. Geological Survey*

Commodity Exchange, Inc. Warehouse Stocks of Copper, on First of Month In Thousands of Short Tons

Year	Jan.	Feb.	Mar.	Apr.	May	June	July	Aug.	Sept.	Oct.	Nov.	Dec
1988	18.5	16.9	16.8	11.8	10.2	19.0	16.9	24.6	22.3	13.6	9.5	5.
1989	13.4	14.9	17.3	29.7	21.2	25.2	23.0	20.4	15.2	11.4	10.4	9.
1990	16.3	7.2	4.1	4.5	6.0	14.7	18.1	11.5	8.9	6.7	8.3	9.
1991	20.2	14.7	16.4	30.2	30.9	25.0	25.1	35.9	33.6	24.4	26.8	29.
1992	33.7	34.8	29.5	28.2	30.3	32.4	31.8	36.0	40.4	51.7	70.1	73.
1993	105.9	124.0	114.8	107.6	110.8	108.3	105.5	113.8	100.1	94.1	96.6	80.
1994	74.0	56.7	49.8	37.2	31.6	30.4	36.0	37.4	28.5	17.9	20.3	21.
1995	26.7	18.7	17.7	9.0	11.5	7.0	13.1	16.7	16.5	11.2	6.0	5.
1996	23.7	12.1	12.4	13.9	20.7	13.2	7.6	17.7	22.1	21.7	30.8	36.
1997	29.3	18.4	24.8	43.3	48.9	42.6	44.7	30.0	46.5	61.5	68.0	82.

Source: New York Mercantile Exchange, COMEX division

Salient Statistics of Copper in the United States   In Thousands of Metric Tons

Year	New Copper Produced: From Domestic Ores: Mines	New Copper Produced: From Domestic Ores: Smelters	New Copper Produced: From Domestic Ores: Refineries	New Copper Produced: From Foreign Ores[3]	New Copper Produced: Total New	Secondary Recovered[4]	Imports[3]: Unmanufactured	Imports[3]: Refined	Exports: Ore, Concentrate[6]	Exports: Refined[7]	Stocks, Dec. 31: COMEX	Stocks, Dec. 31: Primary Producers (Refined)	Stocks, Dec. 31: Blister & Material in Solution	Apparent Consumption: Refined Copper (Reported)	Apparent Consumption: Primary & Old Copper[8]
1987	1,244	972	1,127	W	1,127	498	568	469	125	9	17	113	150	2,127	2,197
1988	1,417	1,043	1,282	124	1,406	518	513	332	211	58	12	97	121	2,210	2,214
1989	1,498	1,120	1,352	125	1,477	548	515	300	267	130	15	107	132	2,203	2,185
1990	1,588	1,158	1,502	75	1,577	537	512	262	258	211	18	101	119	2,150	2,168
1991	1,631	1,123	1,501	77	1,577	518	512	289	253	263	31	132	135	2,048	2,105
1992	1,765	1,180	1,615	96	1,711	555	593	289	266	177	96	205	166	2,178	2,311
1993	1,800	1,270	1,210	89	1,790	543	637	343	227	217	67	153	146	2,364	2,510
1994	1,850	1,310	1,280	64	1,840	500	763	470	261	157	24	119	171	2,680	2,680
1995[1]	1,850	1,250	1,300	91	1,930	442	825	429	239	217	22	163	174	2,530	2,540
1996[2]	1,920	1,300	1,290	147	2,010	428	924	543	195	169	27	170	173	2,620	2,830

[1] Preliminary. [2] Estimate. [3] Also from matte, etc., refinery reports. [4] From scrap only. [5] For consumption. [6] Blister (copper content). [7] Ingots, bars, etc. [8] Old scrap only. *Source: U.S. Geological Survey (USGS)*

Consumption of Refined Copper[3] in the United States   In Thousands of Metric Tons

Year	By-Products: Cathodes	By-Products: Wire Bars	By-Products: Ingot & Ingot Bars	By-Products: Cakes & Slabs	By-Products: Billets	By-Products: Other[4]	By Class of Consumer: Wire Rod Mills	By Class of Consumer: Brass Mills	By Class of Consumer: Chemical Plants	By Class of Consumer: Ingot Makers	By Class of Consumer: Foundries	By Class of Consumer: Miscellaneous[5]	Total Consumption
1987	1,852.9	13.8	74.0	71.9	92.7	20.3	1,593.9	488.6	1.1	1.4	14.2	26.4	2,125.7
1988	1,967.4	14.0	54.2	63.0	99.0	12.7	1,667.2	493.2	1.0	2.6	14.5	31.9	2,210.4
1989	1,981.6	6.1	34.4	64.9	104.9	11.2	1,698.4	461.0	.9	1.3	14.9	26.5	2,203.1
1990	1,922.4	6.6	50.5	57.9	W	113.0	1,653.5	445.2	1.1	4.5	14.6	31.6	2,150.4
1991	1,854.9	W	24.7	33.3	W	135.4	1,591.8	458.5	.9	3.4	12.7	25.3	2,048.3
1992	1,974.9	W	20.0	43.7	W	139.6	1,675.0	458.5	.9	3.0	15.0	25.8	2,178.2
1993	2,130.0	W	37.7	55.5	W	136.0	1,819.1	503.0	.9	2.2	10.2	27.6	2,360.0
1994	2,410.0	W	37.3	73.2	W	164.0	2,060.0	568.0	1.1	4.5	11.1	30.4	2,680.0
1995[1]	2,250.0	W	31.3	75.9	W	181.0	1,950.0	533.0	W	W	W	55.9	2,530.0
1996[2]	2,340.0	W	27.0	80.8	W	170.0	1,980.0	588.0	W	W	W	49.4	2,620.0

[1] Preliminary. [2] Estimate. [3] Primary & secondary. [4] 1991 to date include Wire Bars and Billets. [5] 1995 to date include Chemical Plants, Ingot Makers, and Foundries. *Source: U.S. Geological Survey (USGS)*

London Metals Exchange Warehouse Stocks of Copper, at End of Month   In Thousands of Metric Tons

Year	Jan.	Feb.	Mar.	Apr.	May	June	July	Aug.	Sept.	Oct.	Nov.	Dec.
1988	59.6	74.4	69.4	54.8	86.8	109.1	145.8	148.4	122.4	86.2	78.3	79.9
1989	96.6	104.2	117.4	138.7	125.2	99.2	96.1	100.8	126.7	117.8	142.2	131.2
1990	121.5	106.8	71.9	67.0	92.8	67.7	126.8	161.1	227.1	221.1	199.9	220.6
1991	189.0	202.8	213.9	237.9	275.0	264.9	266.5	307.1	308.4	291.7	308.3	332.3
1992	308.6	302.7	296.4	279.7	265.4	259.1	246.8	275.2	299.7	317.8	327.0	315.8
1993	313.5	333.1	365.8	403.5	429.1	446.9	464.3	521.7	600.7	612.3	590.9	599.5
1994	597.6	554.5	504.3	446.4	379.0	350.9	338.9	367.8	359.3	333.1	318.4	301.8
1995	309.9	280.9	239.9	204.9	197.9	166.5	151.5	163.1	178.2	193.6	222.2	364.8
1996	355.1	348.4	322.3	303.9	309.7	263.0	227.6	275.5	240.7	122.1	96.1	119.6
1997[1]	194.2	216.2	177.2	145.8	133.0	128.3	234.9	278.7	332.8			

[1] Preliminary. *Source: American Bureau of Metal Statistics (ABMS)*

Copper Refined from Scrap in the United States   In Thousands of Metric Tons

Year	Jan.	Feb.	Mar.	Apr.	May	June	July	Aug.	Sept.	Oct.	Nov.	Dec.	Total
1988	34.2	35.2	42.9	38.1	38.0	38.4	30.4	37.9	42.3	37.0	37.5	40.2	453.3
1989	37.4	40.8	47.0	40.1	40.8	41.1	36.6	41.4	40.6	41.3	35.9	37.1	479.9
1990	37.3	35.2	37.1	38.5	39.3	38.1	34.6	39.2	29.9	34.3	31.9	32.0	440.8
1991	35.4	32.8	40.5	39.6	38.2	35.7	32.6	33.0	28.5	37.3	32.1	32.6	417.7
1992	27.8	34.1	39.8	34.8	36.7	39.4	27.8	35.4	39.8	40.0	34.3	35.8	433.2
1993	38.1	45.9	38.9	37.8	36.4	41.1	35.0	37.6	37.4	43.0	35.4	32.2	459.8
1994	33.3	28.3	37.9	30.7	37.1	28.7	26.9	33.0	38.7	27.0	34.3	37.3	391.7
1995	30.9	30.6	36.0	32.7	33.7	28.2	18.7	25.1	25.4	25.0	26.2	24.4	319.0
1996	25.0	23.7	25.5	22.5	26.8	30.9	24.4	25.0	26.8	30.6	25.9	26.3	333.0
1997[1]	35.9	30.0	36.4	32.6	35.4	30.8	26.4	28.4	31.6				383.3

[1] Preliminary. *Source: U.S. Geological Survey (USGS)*

COPPER

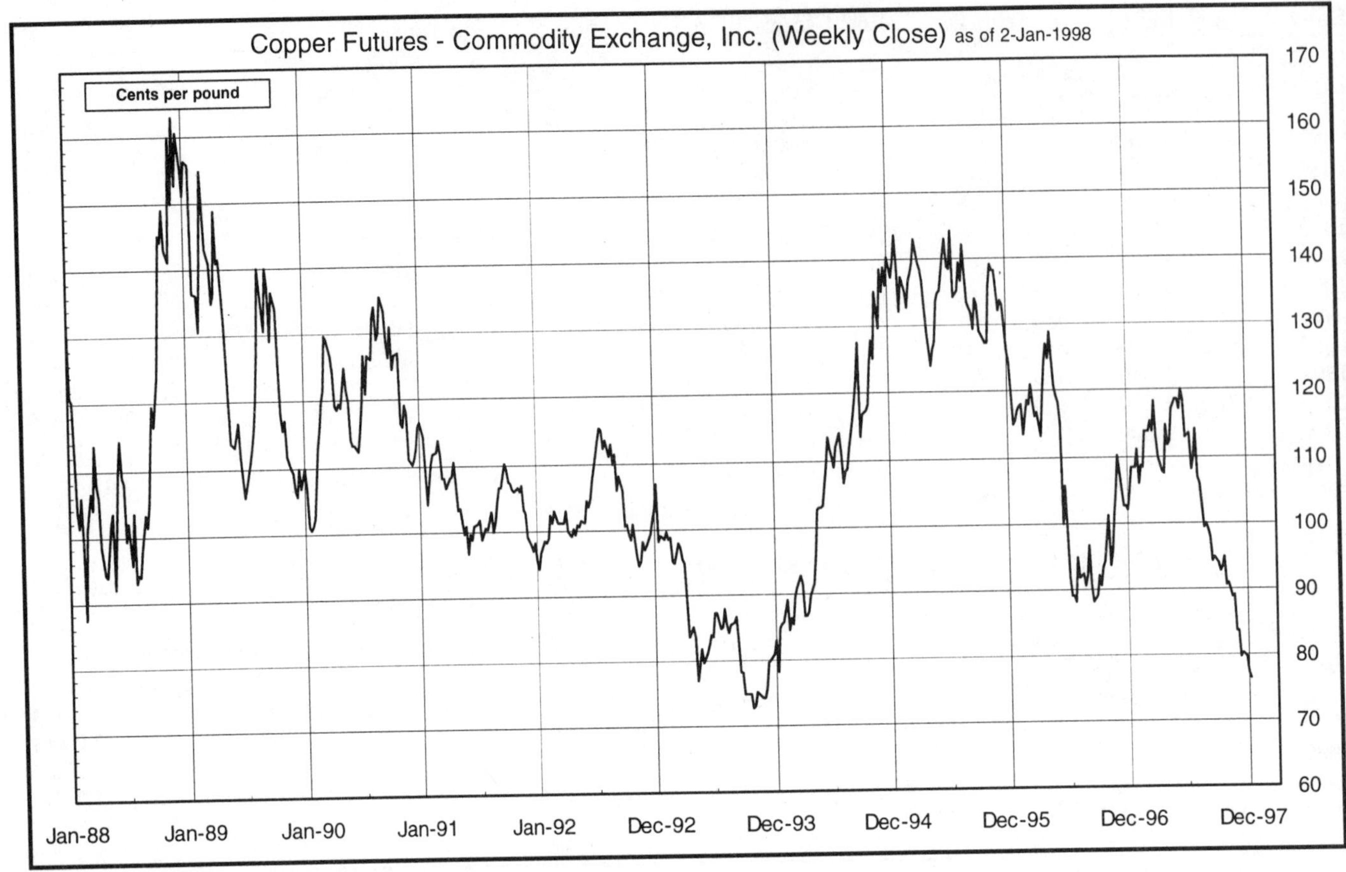

Average Open Interest of Copper Futures[1] in New York In Contracts

Year	Jan.	Feb.	Mar.	Apr.	May	June	July	Aug.	Sept.	Oct.	Nov.	Dec.
1988	43,177	41,220	35,505	34,787	31,410	35,949	31,750	29,563	35,094	35,998	37,039	33,510
1989	33,819	34,199	35,058	36,021	30,901	28,527	26,534	28,420	28,849	27,287	31,240	32,343
1990	31,466	33,908	34,654	34,405	31,552	30,113	32,780	31,515	32,578	36,145	35,088	30,128
1991	34,927	35,978	35,026	34,096	44,153	39,879	33,100	33,333	40,347	42,028	41,618	44,283
1992	47,109	47,929	48,700	45,114	39,986	48,129	47,065	38,397	37,041	41,658	44,927	45,541
1993	47,433	48,707	48,220	51,217	52,762	56,856	54,861	54,571	54,929	57,406	63,632	69,311
1994	65,518	65,446	66,177	59,346	63,825	60,383	51,616	46,855	56,344	59,060	59,158	51,078
1995	52,632	50,770	47,267	47,793	50,089	48,200	40,968	37,744	33,709	36,476	38,475	35,996
1996	47,771	45,706	42,732	46,771	47,284	52,558	56,564	56,549	55,408	58,124	61,031	55,807
1997	54,468	56,022	58,205	50,574	56,740	56,774	47,767	44,632	49,612	54,912	67,026	67,502

[1] Data for May 1988 thru December 1989 include Old copper and High Grade copper contracts. *Source: New York Mercantile Exchange, COMEX Division*

Volume of Trading of Copper Futures[1] in New York In Contracts

Year	Jan.	Feb.	Mar.	Apr.	May	June	July	Aug.	Sept.	Oct.	Nov.	Dec.	Total
1988	210,209	222,625	194,722	151,177	130,289	179,991	120,108	143,103	142,041	186,479	258,834	173,805	2,113,383
1989	216,528	201,132	219,910	201,997	193,956	174,055	132,793	173,273	151,097	176,822	154,241	93,243	2,089,047
1990	152,156	148,766	179,445	181,726	164,489	163,372	141,602	154,383	156,924	161,814	133,718	114,790	1,853,185
1991	159,621	131,044	108,191	150,390	148,777	139,207	110,025	149,702	132,354	125,757	153,910	135,132	1,643,310
1992	145,245	168,015	105,003	157,473	77,722	182,091	138,225	177,581	137,423	121,392	146,062	117,931	1,674,163
1993	152,387	148,388	132,705	212,086	160,751	181,427	165,727	169,428	222,099	133,364	203,729	182,538	2,064,629
1994	197,959	233,016	231,239	207,963	247,143	297,393	188,644	242,393	219,788	208,957	290,585	178,887	2,737,967
1995	242,760	267,883	232,229	242,302	195,554	274,587	167,836	213,110	169,689	181,945	185,141	146,378	2,519,414
1996	184,431	173,689	157,553	210,836	200,469	255,172	150,445	174,351	166,537	250,420	227,800	160,216	2,311,919
1997	193,543	221,504	190,000	218,607	164,728	238,918	191,609	198,156	197,746	202,615	203,376	135,368	2,356,170

[1] Data for May 1988 thru December 1989 include Old copper and High Grade copper contracts. *Source: New York Mercantile Exchange, COMEX Division*

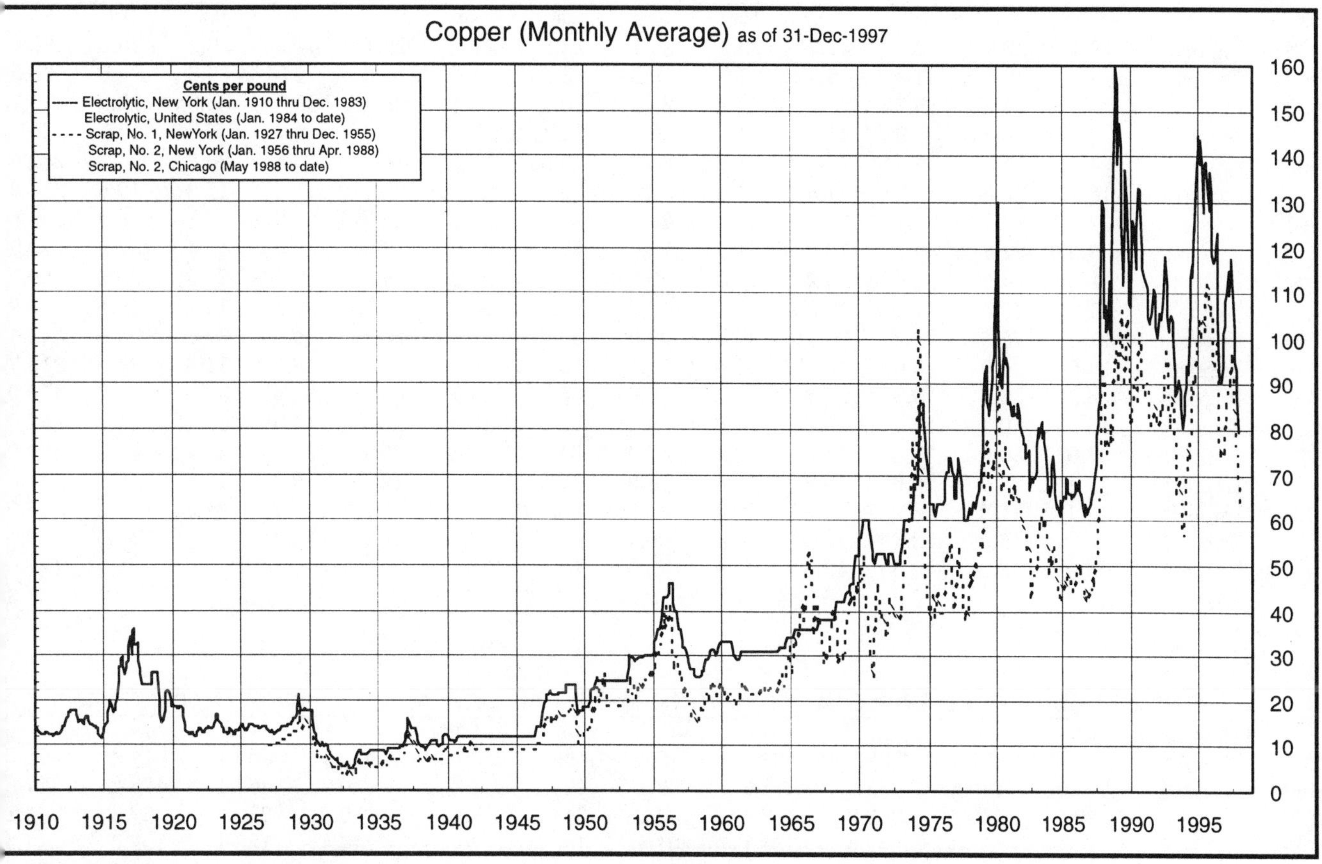

Producers' Price of Electrolytic (Wirebar) Copper, Delivered to U.S. Destinations In Cents Per Pound

Year	Jan.	Feb.	Mar.	Apr.	May	June	July	Aug.	Sept.	Oct.	Nov.	Dec.	Average
1988	135.63	110.58	111.99	107.51	106.91	116.46	107.90	103.62	118.04	126.38	159.08	167.80	122.66
1989	164.21	146.17	154.89	150.26	132.72	121.45	119.27	133.75	143.60	137.61	123.59	115.64	136.93
1990	116.36	119.35	136.22	134.38	132.32	124.93	133.91	142.53	142.45	138.41	127.76	124.39	131.08
1991	122.59	122.73	121.24	120.35	133.11	111.72	111.90	113.48	118.92	118.90	117.26	110.33	118.54
1992	108.16	112.52	113.56	112.35	112.56	116.74	125.66	124.30	119.39	112.09	108.23	111.13	114.72
1993	112.57	110.26	107.80	99.03	92.35	94.98	93.41	97.06	92.36	81.69	86.07	91.08	96.56
1994	95.65	99.13	101.76	99.87	112.30	120.58	123.68	121.38	132.53	130.91	141.92	148.86	119.05
1995	152.02	146.00	151.14	146.03	139.80	149.51	150.00	149.77	144.14	140.00	148.48	143.78	146.72
1996	130.09	128.75	130.20	131.29	135.33	116.33	102.68	104.14	102.51	105.46	112.78	114.78	117.86
1997	120.29	122.22	126.80	121.70	127.25	129.57	121.94	114.11	107.14	105.08	99.53	95.65	115.94

Source: American Metal Market (AMM)

Dealers' Buying Price of No. 2 Heavy Copper Scrap In the Chicago[1] In Cents Per Pound

Year	Jan.	Feb.	Mar.	Apr.	May	June	July	Aug.	Sept.	Oct.	Nov.	Dec.	Average
1988[1]	77.10	68.00	63.50	63.12	70.07	70.59	69.80	69.54	72.36	78.93	83.66	85.50	72.68
1989	89.83	87.13	95.33	95.95	91.14	80.27	74.45	75.54	86.50	90.32	86.00	80.25	86.06
1990	78.27	71.00	78.73	88.00	88.00	84.38	84.00	85.50	91.84	89.50	86.48	83.00	84.06
1991	83.00	79.50	82.21	82.50	78.66	72.40	71.00	71.00	72.05	75.39	75.08	74.50	76.44
1992	73.21	73.37	75.23	75.16	74.00	74.27	77.18	78.38	75.38	70.27	69.00	67.18	73.55
1993	67.95	67.00	67.00	62.95	55.12	53.59	56.33	54.18	52.67	49.10	47.00	48.00	56.74
1994	50.80	56.11	59.61	62.00	64.86	72.32	76.40	74.30	75.69	76.45	78.10	82.95	69.13
1995	89.48	90.79	89.39	91.75	85.91	88.73	92.32	92.65	92.70	90.64	92.00	92.00	90.70
1996	87.17	82.90	83.24	83.29	82.95	71.48	61.43	62.00	62.00	63.00	64.84	66.00	72.53
1997	68.73	71.63	77.50	79.18	77.33	78.19	72.64	70.24	65.67	63.74	61.31	58.43	70.38

[1] Data prior to May 1988 are for the New York. *Source: American Metal Market (AMM)*

COPPER

Foreign Trade of Refined Copper in the United States   In Thousands of Metric Tons

Year		Jan.	Feb.	Mar.	Apr.	May	June	July	Aug.	Sept.	Oct.	Nov.	Dec.	Total
1988	Imports	49.4	38.0	39.0	33.7	25.9	25.1	22.3	27.7	25.7	44.2	39.2	20.2	390.4
	Exports	4.9	2.0	3.8	5.7	7.7	9.5	3.5	4.4	14.3	2.3	4.0	4.5	66.5
1989	Imports	32.7	24.8	18.7	20.9	24.1	25.9	20.9	24.4	28.1	30.5	32.3	16.9	300.1
	Exports	6.2	4.8	5.9	13.5	4.3	6.6	21.4	15.8	23.4	13.7	6.3	12.1	130.2
1990	Imports	24.7	15.8	26.5	25.3	31.3	24.0	20.6	18.0	21.4	18.4	20.8	16.7	263.6
	Exports	18.1	20.8	12.2	7.6	15.6	12.2	23.9	20.1	22.4	21.5	17.2	19.8	211.3
1991	Imports	22.7	27.1	21.7	30.9	17.5	23.6	23.7	17.4	22.9	36.3	26.8	18.0	288.6
	Exports	33.6	21.4	37.4	16.8	31.5	23.9	20.6	20.9	17.9	13.4	15.4	17.9	270.7
1992	Imports	22.6	24.5	31.9	25.2	25.3	26.1	24.7	25.3	24.0	19.6	20.3	20.8	289.1
	Exports	21.7	18.4	10.8	12.3	11.7	12.0	9.3	13.0	13.6	24.1	14.1	16.1	176.9
1993	Imports	21.8	25.6	28.2	35.9	29.5	26.9	30.6	28.3	22.5	31.6	32.2	30.5	343.4
	Exports	14.0	24.9	23.6	16.3	15.4	13.1	10.7	10.1	19.5	19.5	14.9	14.5	216.7
1994	Imports	28.7	33.6	49.8	36.8	36.1	46.8	35.6	34.4	34.7	62.4	35.9	36.2	470.0
	Exports	13.0	10.2	10.7	6.8	14.8	9.1	15.6	10.9	15.4	15.9	13.1	21.1	157.0
1995	Imports	34.9	30.0	37.1	36.9	36.5	37.9	31.5	31.8	28.7	38.7	44.4	40.3	429.0
	Exports	11.1	24.0	25.6	18.2	23.4	38.9	16.3	16.6	12.1	9.0	12.5	9.5	217.0
1996	Imports	43.1	41.2	48.2	49.6	56.8	44.6	53.8	64.8	62.3	46.1	61.8	47.2	543.0
	Exports	13.7	16.5	12.7	12.3	10.8	10.7	15.7	17.7	14.5	16.4	12.8	16.0	170.0
1997[1]	Imports	55.4	48.0	43.6	43.6	61.0	42.0	53.1	73.3					420.0
	Exports	11.1	9.8	6.5	6.5	71.9	8.2	6.9	7.5					128.3

[1] Preliminary. *Source: U.S. Geological Survey (USGS)*

Stocks of Refined Copper in the United States   In Thousands of Short Tons (Recoverable Copper Content)

Year	Jan. 1	Feb. 1	Mar. 1	Apr. 1	May 1	June 1	July 1	Aug. 1	Sept. 1	Oct. 1	Nov. 1	Dec. 1
1983	484.5	489.6	501.6	508.9	524.1	519.4	498.7	509.0	522.7	509.1	514.2	505.2
1984	475.3	497.8	499.6	483.3	478.3	463.4	483.2	493.4	490.7	467.1	475.2	457.3
1985	469.7	452.9	380.9	368.2	358.4	363.2	344.1	331.4	310.9	275.7	257.3	264.1
1986	270.7	271.0	261.6	242.0	231.1	201.4	188.0	209.6	214.4	188.1	189.0	211.3
1987	238.4	211.5	206.8	170.1	175.7	161.6	136.4	141.0	140.4	151.3	121.1	86.7
1988	81.4	79.8	81.6	89.0	83.1	75.7	42.0	48.8	52.5	42.9	40.6	39.8
1989	56.3	67.5	56.3	60.6	54.3	54.4	49.1	61.8	66.1	42.3	48.1	48.2
1990	72.7	42.4	38.6	45.2	55.9	60.2	67.5	67.2	67.6	27.4	27.9	45.4
1991	72.3	72.8	53.2	68.6	63.2	52.8	52.4	71.4	64.4	48.5	48.3	63.1
1992	75.3	76.3	67.2	69.7	75.9	65.0	62.2	71.2	87.1	99.5	110.3	107.1
1993	135.4	152.7	144.3	132.3	146.0	153.6	137.1	151.0	128.4	117.2	124.6	107.1
1994	103.0	87.7	83.6	72.8	70.7	70.4	73.3	81.1	74.6	66.5	52.7	53.6
1995[2]	55.8	39.6	37.0	22.6	33.1	30.8	27.0	50.0	60.6	71.1	69.4	73.4
1996	120.0	131.4	125.5	123.1	126.3	107.9	102.8	106.2	104.7	68.0	76.0	77.5
1997[1]	88.2	98.8	104.4	116.0	117.9	121.7	122.9	148.8	177.9			

[1] Preliminary. [2] New reporting method beginning January 1995. *Source: American Bureau of Metal Statistics (ABMS)*

Stocks of Refined Copper in the United States   In Thousands of Short Tons (Recoverable Copper Content)

Year	Jan. 1	Feb. 1	Mar. 1	Apr. 1	May 1	June 1	July 1	Aug. 1	Sept. 1	Oct. 1	Nov. 1	Dec. 1
1983	699.9	760.8	766.4	759.1	795.5	780.0	722.2	683.0	757.4	767.2	765.2	810.4
1984	832.8	817.5	730.0	653.0	618.5	519.3	551.9	526.5	516.0	493.9	483.9	430.0
1985	425.0	420.7	385.7	361.9	364.6	380.4	368.8	464.0	546.7	558.4	533.6	486.6
1986	502.8	501.5	451.8	435.7	422.6	418.7	396.8	430.4	455.1	455.4	458.5	464.8
1987	473.7	467.5	410.5	397.5	387.4	348.5	337.8	336.8	341.1	314.7	254.9	269.6
1988	260.9	292.1	301.1	290.2	277.4	317.9	329.9	374.7	348.7	310.9	282.8	272.2
1989	337.5	325.7	341.0	350.3	406.5	385.7	374.2	389.8	335.8	368.7	348.1	358.3
1990	362.3	382.0	335.6	320.0	332.6	356.3	291.8	370.9	417.9	484.6	483.0	447.6
1991	439.5	464.2	447.1	501.1	559.5	595.4	593.1	605.4	664.7	653.5	644.9	676.9
1992	640.4	718.1	704.2	715.7	714.9	723.2	726.4	737.9	816.5	822.5	873.8	896.1
1993	757.1	765.9	789.6	817.2	885.1	912.2	910.4	943.8	1,040.3	1,124.3	1,133.9	1,106.1
1994	1,075.0	1,095.5	1,046.8	984.9	913.7	859.5	843.7	839.7	874.6	870.7	835.1	818.4
1995[2]	611.6	655.8	622.2	577.9	537.0	525.6	494.9	464.7	465.7	467.7	481.4	503.5
1996	560.2	566.0	552.5	517.5	498.7	563.9	507.9	476.6	544.4	499.5	391.8	362.0
1997[1]	405.4	469.5	476.3	445.7	413.5	402.4	408.3	489.6	550.8			

[1] Preliminary. [2] New reporting method beginning January 1995. *Source: American Bureau of Metal Statistics (ABMS)*

Production of Refined Copper in the United States In Thousands of Short Tons (Recoverable Copper Content)

Year	Jan.	Feb.	Mar.	Apr.	May	June	July	Aug.	Sept.	Oct.	Nov.	Dec.	Total
1987	118.0	110.5	105.4	127.7	118.5	95.5	107.7	106.4	121.8	131.3	123.3	127.7	1,394
1988	124.5	127.2	145.6	122.5	133.7	116.7	112.7	146.0	133.8	121.1	137.7	131.8	1,553
1989	129.5	128.1	137.2	118.3	132.2	142.6	121.3	150.8	116.5	137.0	127.4	130.7	1,572
1990	136.0	122.0	150.4	140.1	147.5	136.1	125.5	132.5	130.1	141.6	141.0	125.5	1,628
1991	129.0	127.7	134.9	119.7	137.1	124.8	136.8	142.7	135.6	153.1	141.0	149.7	1,632
1992	139.9	135.6	150.6	142.8	123.0	138.5	140.3	150.1	146.9	155.3	156.8	153.7	1,734
1993	153.9	153.8	173.2	166.0	160.3	177.0	151.4	153.7	160.2	157.3	157.2	166.2	1,930
1994	160.9	150.0	167.8	157.2	165.5	160.4	148.9	165.6	162.1	157.3	153.3	159.8	1,909
1995[2]	202.7	185.5	204.8	194.6	210.0	198.3	193.8	208.8	199.0	206.5	211.3	208.1	2,423
1996	210.8	197.6	209.7	212.4	213.5	193.4	206.1	199.5	198.8	223.1	199.3	212.0	2,476
1997[1]	220.7	200.7	216.7	216.3	205.9	196.5	222.1	213.5	226.2				2,558

[1] Preliminary. [2] New Reporting method beginning January 1995. *Source: American Bureau of Metal Statistics (ABMS)*

Production of Refined Copper Outside the United States In Thousands of Short Tons (Recoverable Copper Content)

Year	Jan.	Feb.	Mar.	Apr.	May	June	July	Aug.	Sept.	Oct.	Nov.	Dec.	Total
1987	385.8	375.4	410.6	412.2	399.9	403.6	393.3	370.6	391.2	402.7	402.5	407.5	4,755
1988	397.7	387.8	434.2	370.6	389.4	391.5	366.6	386.9	365.9	412.8	417.0	414.9	4,735
1989	387.8	372.7	411.9	404.3	430.1	388.7	409.5	413.5	421.7	436.1	434.0	402.7	4,913
1990	423.7	396.7	424.6	412.8	414.1	395.6	372.6	407.1	404.6	422.6	417.4	411.0	4,902
1991	416.5	381.1	427.7	405.5	425.3	404.5	375.1	378.7	411.4	411.8	409.2	424.5	4,871
1992	441.2	412.6	447.0	418.0	438.7	449.5	418.5	425.8	418.7	438.9	431.3	426.1	5,166
1993	429.2	405.6	475.1	426.2	440.9	447.5	421.6	449.4	448.0	425.9	447.2	436.5	5,253
1994	432.5	390.8	432.7	400.6	432.9	421.1	387.8	413.8	421.5	416.3	437.4	428.8	5,016
1995[2]	817.5	797.6	868.4	858.2	859.4	844.8	849.7	825.7	819.8	865.2	833.8	872.2	10,112
1996	903.2	869.3	929.3	922.2	916.3	918.3	908.3	931.1	938.2	972.9	935.8	992.4	11,137
1997[1]	962.5	936.0	981.1	1,007.9	1,032.8	1,021.5	1,024.0	1,008.2	990.0				11,952

[1] Preliminary. [2] New Reporting method beginning January 1995. *Source: American Bureau of Metal Statistics (ABMS)*

Deliveries of Refined Copper to Fabricators in the United States In Thousands of Short Tons[3]

Year	Jan.	Feb.	Mar.	Apr.	May	June	July	Aug.	Sept.	Oct.	Nov.	Dec.	Total
1987	160.2	138.7	166.9	152.3	165.6	152.3	131.6	127.2	121.8	188.3	192.7	168.2	1,885
1988	152.0	151.5	162.5	149.6	150.1	161.2	116.5	164.7	133.8	148.2	159.1	139.0	1,824
1989	127.8	147.7	148.4	141.1	153.2	168.4	131.4	173.2	116.5	156.8	149.2	121.9	1,781
1990	167.4	132.8	163.3	156.6	153.3	144.5	129.5	132.5	130.1	140.9	130.7	108.6	1,733
1991	128.4	153.3	125.3	126.7	152.7	115.0	125.4	152.8	135.6	167.7	130.4	132.9	1,684
1992	144.9	159.0	165.9	155.5	149.4	161.4	145.8	144.1	146.9	150.4	166.2	130.0	1,813
1993	142.9	165.3	201.6	170.4	162.5	209.6	144.8	191.4	178.9	164.3	194.8	182.7	2,109
1994	193.3	168.6	204.6	178.3	187.8	171.9	154.3	194.6	188.2	188.7	167.5	175.1	2,173
1995[2]	233.8	209.2	239.1	200.9	230.0	210.5	187.1	208.8	202.9	224.7	222.4	175.5	2,545
1996	221.6	227.2	240.0	242.2	270.7	222.1	233.8	246.8	277.5	239.7	240.6	231.9	2,882
1997[1]	246.3	234.5	240.6	247.4	254.9	228.1	241.1	257.4	242.1				2,923

[1] Preliminary. [2] New reporting method beginning January 1995. [3] Recoverable copper content. *Source: American Bureau of Metal Statistics (ABMS)*

Deliveries of Refined Copper to Fabricators Outside the United States In Thousands of Short Tons[3]

Year	Jan.	Feb.	Mar.	Apr.	May	June	July	Aug.	Sept.	Oct.	Nov.	Dec.	Total
1987	386.0	413.0	413.9	406.8	426.7	401.8	384.1	359.4	416.4	468.8	377.1	396.8	4,851
1988	359.6	375.2	448.7	385.1	366.8	403.2	340.9	405.9	401.8	437.4	455.6	356.6	4,737
1989	426.0	369.9	411.8	360.9	459.0	398.0	386.8	464.2	393.2	456.9	423.0	399.1	4,949
1990	419.9	466.3	436.7	392.9	408.3	466.7	303.7	373.5	370.8	448.9	469.1	420.7	4,972
1991	405.0	404.4	391.5	361.2	406.3	433.5	368.5	323.4	420.7	499.1	391.4	483.4	4,807
1992	453.7	408.9	441.8	416.4	413.4	432.4	410.4	364.7	432.6	403.5	406.1	461.3	5,045
1993	427.9	392.9	452.3	361.7	422.2	442.6	384.4	347.9	387.5	414.8	463.4	458.5	4,956
1994	399.8	429.5	481.2	466.5	468.9	428.1	387.9	369.2	423.5	448.9	457.1	436.0	5,197
1995[2]	758.5	810.1	892.8	882.2	853.0	867.3	863.7	814.1	803.4	835.1	796.6	726.2	9,903
1996	875.2	859.4	934.3	907.2	816.7	950.7	908.3	817.4	911.5	1,056.0	922.7	918.3	10,878
1997[1]	862.2	889.7	977.9	1,007.1	991.1	982.7	897.8	874.0	912.8				11,194

[1] Preliminary. [2] New reporting method beginning January 1995. [3] Recoverable copper content. *Source: American Bureau of Metal Statistics (ABMS)*

Corn

The U.S. 1997/98 (September/August) corn crop of 9.36 billion bushels, the third highest on record, compares with 9.29 billion in 1996/97. The record high 10.1 billion bushel crop was realized in 1994/95. The 1997 crop proved larger than initially expected as a larger harvested acreage offset a lower average yield; acreage of 74 million acres was up from 73.1 million in 1996 while average yield of 125.8 bushels per acre compares with 127.1, respectively.

In the key producing midwestern states crop conditions in early fall were very favorable for the maturing crop, although initial harvest results were variable due to mixed growing conditions at critical times during the summer. The large crop and moderate dip in 1997/98 exports placed the carryover forecast as of August 31, 1998 at a larger than expected 928 million bushels vs. 884 million a year earlier. In the late 1980's carryover averaged almost 4 billion bushels with much of it Government's owned. The stock-to-use ratio in 1997/98 was forecast at 8.3 percent vs. 10 percent in 1996/97, and the 1995/96 season's very low 5 percent.

Despite the large U.S. 1997/98 crop, futures values held steady during the second half of calendar year 1997, pivoting about $2.70 per bushel, basis the nearest Chicago futures contract. Indeed, for the entire year futures held within a tight 70 cent range and at yearend were within a few cents of late 1996 values. The price action was in sharp contrast to 1996 when futures soared during the first half of the year from $3.50 per bushel to $5.50. and then quickly lost almost $3.00 closing the year near $2.70. In 1997/98 the average price received by farmers was forecast to range between $2.55-$2.95 per bushel vs. the 1996/97 average of $2.70, and the 1994/95 record high of $3.24.

Corn is the leading U.S. feed grain with usage in 1997/98 expected to top the combined total disappearance of sorghum, barley and oats by about 8 billion bushels. Domestic feed and residual use in 1997/98 of a record 5.6 billion bushels compares with 5.4 billion in 1996/97. Food, seed, and industrial use (FSI) were estimated at a record 1.8 billion bushels vs. 1.7 billion in 1996/97. FSI demand once again shows sign of quickening following some hesitation in 1995/96. High Fructose corn syrup (HFCS) production of 525 million bushels compares with 506 million in 1996/97 and 482 million in 1995/96. Corn's use in the manufacture of fuel alcohol was put at 475 million bushels vs. 427 million the year before and a large 533 million in 1994/95.

The U.S. exports about 75 percent of the world's total corn trade (67 million tonnes in 1997/98 vs. 65.4 million in 1996/97); Argentina is a distant second with about 12 percent. Importers are numerous, but the leaders are generally in Asia, paced by Japan (15.5 million tonnes), South Korea (8.7 million) and Taiwan (5 million). China's imports have dropped sharply since 1994/95, from 4.32 million tonnes to about 300,000 in 1997/98, but China has not yet built its corn production enough to meet the feed demand of its increasing poultry inventory. U.S. exports in 1997/98 of 1.75 billion bushels compare with 2.22 billion in 1996/97. U.S. corn imports are minimal, on average about 13 million bushels.

The near record world corn production in 1997/98 of 570 million tonnes was lower than initially expected and compares with the record 590 million in 1996/97, of which the U.S. share was about 40 percent. China, since 1987/88 the second largest producer, produced 105 million tonnes in 1997/98 vs. a record 127 million tonnes in 1996/97, with the slippage reflecting a moderate drop in acreage and sharper decline in average yield to 4.47 tonnes per hectare from 5.2 tonnes the year before. Other large producing countries are Brazil, Mexico, Argentina and France. Global use in 1997/98 of a record 591 million tonnes compares with the previous high of 572 million in 1996/97. China's use of 122 million tonnes compares with 115 million in 1996/97. Brazil's consumption in recent years has averaged about 36 million tonnes, Mexico about 24 million and Japan around 16 million. The U.S. is the largest world consumer with almost a third of the total, 188 million tonnes in 1997/98. World corn stocks are forecast to decrease in 1997/98 by at least 20 million tonnes, ending the season with 64 million tonnes vs. initial forecasts of 71 million.

U.S. #2 yellow corn prices vary with the location. Typically, Gulf port prices are about 30¢ per bushel higher than prices in Central Illinois while quotes at St. Louis run about 10¢-12¢ higher than Illinois prices. Typically the seasonal price pattern hits bottom around harvest and then begins to rise to reflecting the costs of carrying the crop in storage. In late 1997, #2 yellow corn in Central Illinois was trading around $2.75 per bushel, up about 30 cents from the September low with the increase partially reflecting spillover from a robust soybean market and hopes that China's import needs would prove stronger than expected.

Futures Markets

Corn futures are traded on the Beijing Commodity Exchange (BCE), the Budapest Commodity Exchange, the Tokyo Grain Exchange (TGE), the Chicago Board of Trade (CBOT), and the Mid-American Commodity Exchange (MidAm). Corn options are traded on the CBOT and the MidAm.

The CBOT also trades Iowa Corn Yield Insurance futures and options. A contract for U.S. corn yield insurance futures and options also exists although volume is very low at this time.

World Production of Corn or Maize In Thousands of Metric Tons

Crop Year	Argentina	Brazil	Canada	China	France	India	Italy	Mexico	Romania	South Africa	United States	Yugo-slavia	World Total
1988-9	5,000	26,050	5,369	77,350	14,578	8,229	6,318	10,100	10,000	12,384	125,194	7,697	401,962
1989-90	5,200	22,300	6,571	78,928	13,400	9,409	6,359	9,750	6,760	8,900	191,156	9,415	460,484
1990-1	7,600	24,330	7,067	96,820	9,500	8,962	5,864	14,100	6,800	8,300	201,534	6,724	477,855
1991-2	10,600	30,800	7,413	98,770	12,930	8,060	6,240	14,689	10,500	3,125	189,868	11,500	487,307
1992-3	10,200	29,200	4,883	95,380	14,870	9,992	7,410	18,631	6,829	9,990	240,719	6,650	538,552
1993-4	10,000	32,934	6,501	102,700	14,840	9,600	8,030	19,141	8,000	13,275	160,954	5,912	475,471
1994-5	11,360	37,440	7,043	99,280	12,640	9,120	7,480	17,005	8,500	4,845	256,621	7,500	561,839
1995-6[1]	11,100	32,480	7,271	112,000	12,390	9,440	8,450	17,780	9,923	10,200	187,305	7,700	515,491
1996-7[2]	15,000	36,160	7,380	127,470	14,430	10,100	9,550	19,500	9,610	9,012	236,064	7,600	592,479
1997-8[3]	15,000	33,000	7,180	105,000	16,500	10,000	9,500	18,500	12,000	8,000	237,897	9,500	576,044

[1] Preliminary. [2] Estimate. [3] Forecast. *Source: Foreign Agricultural Service, U.S. Department of Agriculture (FAS-USDA)*

World Supply and Demand of Course Grains In Millions of Metric Tons/Hectares

Crop Year Beginning Oct. 1	Area Harvested	Yield	Pro-duction	World Trade	Total Con-sumption	Ending Stocks	Stocks as % of Consump-tion[3]
1988-9	323.1	2.23	720.8	98.0	786.2	146.6	18.7
1989-90	320.8	2.47	791.1	104.5	815.4	122.3	15.0
1990-1	315.1	2.62	826.5	89.5	814.3	134.5	16.5
1991-2	320.4	2.52	808.4	96.0	808.4	134.5	16.6
1992-3	322.0	2.70	869.1	91.7	840.8	162.7	19.4
1993-4	315.7	2.53	798.0	85.6	837.5	123.2	14.7
1994-5	323.4	2.70	873.7	97.1	861.3	136.2	15.8
1995-6	313.4	2.56	801.8	87.9	842.6	95.4	11.3
1996-7[1]	323.0	2.81	907.6	92.4	883.6	119.4	13.5
1997-8[2]	318.4	2.80	890.0	91.1	906.2	103.1	11.4

[1] Preliminary. [2] Estimate. [3] Represents the ratio of marketing year ending stocks to total consumption. *Source: Foreign Agricultural Service, U.S. Department of Agriculture (FAS-USDA)*

Acreage and Supply of Corn in the United States In Millions of Bushels

Crop Year Beginning Sept. 1[3]	Planted	Harvested: For Grain	Harvested: For Silage	Yield Per Harvested Acre Bushels	Carry-over, Sept. 1: On Farms[3]	Carry-over, Sept. 1: Off Farms[3]	Supply: Beginning Stocks	Supply: Pro-duction	Supply: Imports	Supply: Total Supply
	In Thousands of Acres									
1988-9	67,717	58,250	8,294	84.6	2,002.8	2,256.3	4,259	4,929	3	9,191
1989-90	72,322	64,783	6,606	116.3	967.5	962.9	1,930	7,525	2	9,458
1990-1	74,166	66,952	6,124	118.5	754.8	589.7	1,344	7,934	3	9,282
1991-2	75,957	68,822	6,101	108.6	691.2	830.0	1,521	7,475	20	9,016
1992-3	79,311	72,077	6,069	131.5	605.0	494.8	1,100	9,477	7	10,584
1993-4	73,235	62,921	6,831	100.7	1,070.7	1,042.0	2,113	6,336	21	8,470
1994-5	79,175	72,887	5,601	138.6	395.4	454.7	850	10,103	10	10,962
1995-6	71,245	64,995	5,295	113.5	740.9	816.9	1,558	7,374	16	8,948
1996-7[1]	79,507	73,147	5,415	127.1	196.6	229.3	426	9,293	13	9,733
1997-8[2]	80,227	73,720	5,758	127.0	475.0	408.2	883	9,366	10	10,259

[1] Preliminary. [2] Estimate. [3] Data prior to 1986-87 are as of October 1. NA = Not available. *Source: Economic Research Service, U.S. Department of Agriculture (ERS-USDA)*

Production of Corn (for Grain) in the United States In Millions of Bushels

Year	Illinois	Indiana	Iowa	Kansas	Mich-igan	Minn-esota	Missouri	Nebraska	Ohio	South Dakota	Texas	Wis-consin	Total
1988	700.8	415.0	898.8	143.8	112.0	347.8	153.5	818.4	255.0	132.0	129.6	130.7	4,921.2
1989	1,322.3	691.6	1,445.5	155.0	222.6	700.0	219.8	847.0	342.2	190.8	148.4	310.8	7,525.5
1990	1,320.8	703.1	1,562.4	188.5	238.1	762.6	205.8	934.4	417.5	234.0	130.5	354.0	7,934.0
1991	1,177.0	510.6	1,427.4	206.3	253.0	720.0	213.4	999.6	326.4	240.5	165.0	380.8	7,475.5
1992	1,646.5	877.6	1,903.7	259.5	241.5	741.0	324.0	1,066.5	507.7	277.2	202.5	306.8	9,476.7
1993	1,300.0	712.8	880.0	216.0	225.5	322.0	166.5	785.2	360.8	160.7	212.8	216.2	6,336.5
1994	1,786.2	858.2	1,930.4	304.6	260.9	915.9	273.7	1,153.7	486.5	367.2	238.7	437.1	10,102.7
1995	1,130.0	598.9	1,402.2	244.3	249.6	731.9	149.9	854.7	375.1	193.6	216.6	347.7	7,373.9
1996	1,468.8	670.4	1,718.1	357.2	216.2	868.8	355.1	1,186.9	305.3	370.0	201.6	333.0	9,293.4
1997[1]	1,425.5	719.6	1,656.0	386.1	263.3	857.9	332.9	1,151.7	462.3	333.2	248.4	402.6	9,365.6

[1] Preliminary. *Source: National Agricultural Statistics Service, U.S. Department of Agriculture (NASS-USDA)*

CORN

Supply and Disappearance of Corn in the United States In Millions of Bushels

Crop Year Beginning Sept. 1	Supply				Disappearance: Domestic Use							Ending Stocks		
	Beginning Stocks	Pro-duction	Imports	Total Supply	Food, Alcohol & Industrial	Seed	Feed & Residual	Total	Exports	Total Disap-pearance	Gov't Owned[3]	Privately Owned[4]	Total
1993-4	2,113	6,337	20.8	8,470	1,591	20.1	4,700	6,311	1,328	7,620	45	805	850
Sept.-Nov.	2,113	6,337	5.2	8,455	380	0	1,703	2,083	435	2,518	53	5,884	5,937
Dec.-Feb.	5,937	------	8.0	5,945	376	0	1,243	1,619	330	1,949	50	3,946	3,996
Mar.-May	3,996	------	6.3	4,002	418	19.5	955	1,372	270	1,642	48	2,312	2,360
June-Aug.	2,360	------	1.4	2,361	418	.6	800	1,218	293	1,511	45	805	850
1994-5	850	10,103	9.6	10,962	1,686	18.2	5,523	7,227	2,178	9,405	42	1,516	1,558
Sept.-Nov.	850	10,103	2.1	10,955	409	0	2,016	2,425	449	2,875	55	8,026	8,080
Dec.-Feb.	8,081	------	3.7	8,084	409	0	1,493	1,902	590	2,493	50	5,542	5,592
Mar.-May	5,592	------	3.0	5,595	434	14.7	1,163	1,612	568	2,180	50	3,365	3,415
June-Aug.	3,415	------	.8	3,416	434	3.5	850	1,288	570	1,858	42	1,516	1,558
1995-6[1]	1,558	7,374	16.0	8,948	1,612	20.2	4,682	6,314	2,228	8,522	42	575	426
Sept.-Nov.	1,558	7,374	4.0	8,935	413	0	1,756	2,169	660	2,830			6,106
Dec.-Feb.	6,106	------	5.0	6,111	401		1,348	1,749	562	2,311			3,800
Mar.-May	3,800	------	5.0	3,805	429		1,048	1,477	610	2,180			1,718
June-Aug.	1,718	------	3.0	1,721	370		530	900	396	1,295			426
1996-7[2]	426	9,293	13.0	9,733	1,691		5,362	7,053	1,795	8,849			884
Sept.-Nov.	426	9,293	3.0	9,723	386		1,946	2,332	487	2,819			6,904
Dec.-Feb.	6,904	------	2.0	6,906	398		1,490	1,888	525	2,412			4,494
Mar.-May	4,494	------	4.0	4,498	463		1,108	1,571	431	2,001			2,497
June-Aug.	2,497	------	4.0	2,500	444		819	1,263	353	1,616			883
1997-8[2]	883	9,366	10.0	10,259	1,815		5,850	7,665	1,750	9,415			844
Sept.-Nov.	883	9,366	3.0	10,252	436		2,201	2,637	385	3,022			7,230

[1] Preliminary. [2] Estimate. [3] Uncommitted inventory. [4] Includes quantity under loan and farmer-owned reserves. *Source: Economic Research Service, U.S. Department of Agriculture (ERS-USDA)*

Corn Production Estimates and Cash Prices in the United States

Crop Year	Corn for Grain Production Estimates (In Thousands of Bushels)					Dollar Per Bushel						Value of Pro-duction (Million Dollars)
	Aug. 1	Sept. 1	Oct. 1	Nov. 1	Final	St. Louis No. 2 Yellow	Omaha No. 2 Yellow	Gulf Ports No. 2 Yellow	Kansas City No. 2 White	Chicago No. 2 Yellow	Average Farm Price[2]	
1989-90	7,348,155	7,321,005	7,448,875	7,589,715	7,525,493	2.58	2.41	2.79	3.10	2.54	2.36	17,897
1990-1	7,850,164	8,118,117	8,021,697	7,934,892	7,934,028	2.49	2.28	2.67	2.98	2.41	2.28	18,192
1991-2	7,474,480	7,295,071	7,479,421	7,485,901	7,475,480	2.53	2.36	2.74	3.06	2.52	2.37	17,864
1992-3	8,762,060	7,873,436	8,592,821	9,328,850	9,476,698	2.25	2.10	2.46	2.49	2.22	2.07	19,723
1993-4	7,423,142	7,229,427	6,961,902	6,503,237	6,336,470	2.67	2.56	2.85	2.78	2.68	2.50	16,032
1994-5	9,214,420	9,257,170	9,602,340	10,010,310	10,102,735	2.51	2.33	2.78	2.91	2.43	2.26	22,992
1995-6	8,121,520	7,832,140	7,541,400	7,373,700	7,373,876	4.06	3.87	4.30	4.14	3.97	3.24	24,118
1996-7[1]	8,694,628	8,803,928	9,012,148	9,265,288	9,293,435						2.71	24,853
1997-8[1]	9,275,870	9,267,655	9,311,705	9,359,485	9,365,574						2.45-2.75	

[1] Preliminary. [2] Season-average price based on monthly weighted by monthly marketings. *Source: Economic Research Service, U.S. Department of Agriculture (ERS-USDA)*

Distribution of Corn in the United States In Millions of Bushels

Year Crop Beginning Sept. 1	Food, Seed and Industrial Use								Livestock Feed[4]	Exports (Including Grain Equiv. of Products)	Domestic Disap-pearance	Total Utilization
	HFCS	Glucose & Dextrose	Starch	Alcohol: Fuel	Alcohol: Beve-rage[3]	Seed	Cereal & Other Products	Total				
1989-90	368	193	230	321	109	19	115	1,355	4,389	2,368	5,745	8,120
1990-1	379	200	232	349	80	19	114	1,373	4,663	1,725	6,036	7,761
1991-2	392	210	237	398	81	20	116	1,454	4,878	1,584	6,332	7,916
1992-3	414	214	238	426	83	19	117	1,493	5,296	1,663	6,808	8,471
1993-4	444	223	223	458	106	20	118	1,571	4,704	1,328	6,292	7,620
1994-5	465	231	226	533	100	18	132	1,686	5,523	2,177	7,228	9,405
1995-6	482	237	219	396	125	20	133	1,592	4,696	2,228	6,294	8,522
1996-7[1]	504	246	229	429	130	20	135	1,672	5,325	1,825	6,995	8,820
1997-8[2]	540	250	235	500	133		136	1,794	5,600	2,050	7,360	9,410

[1] Preliminary. [2] Estimate. [3] Also includes nonfuel industrial alcohol. [4] Feed and waste (residual, mostly feed). *Source: Economic Research Service, U.S. Department of Agriculture (ERS-USDA)*

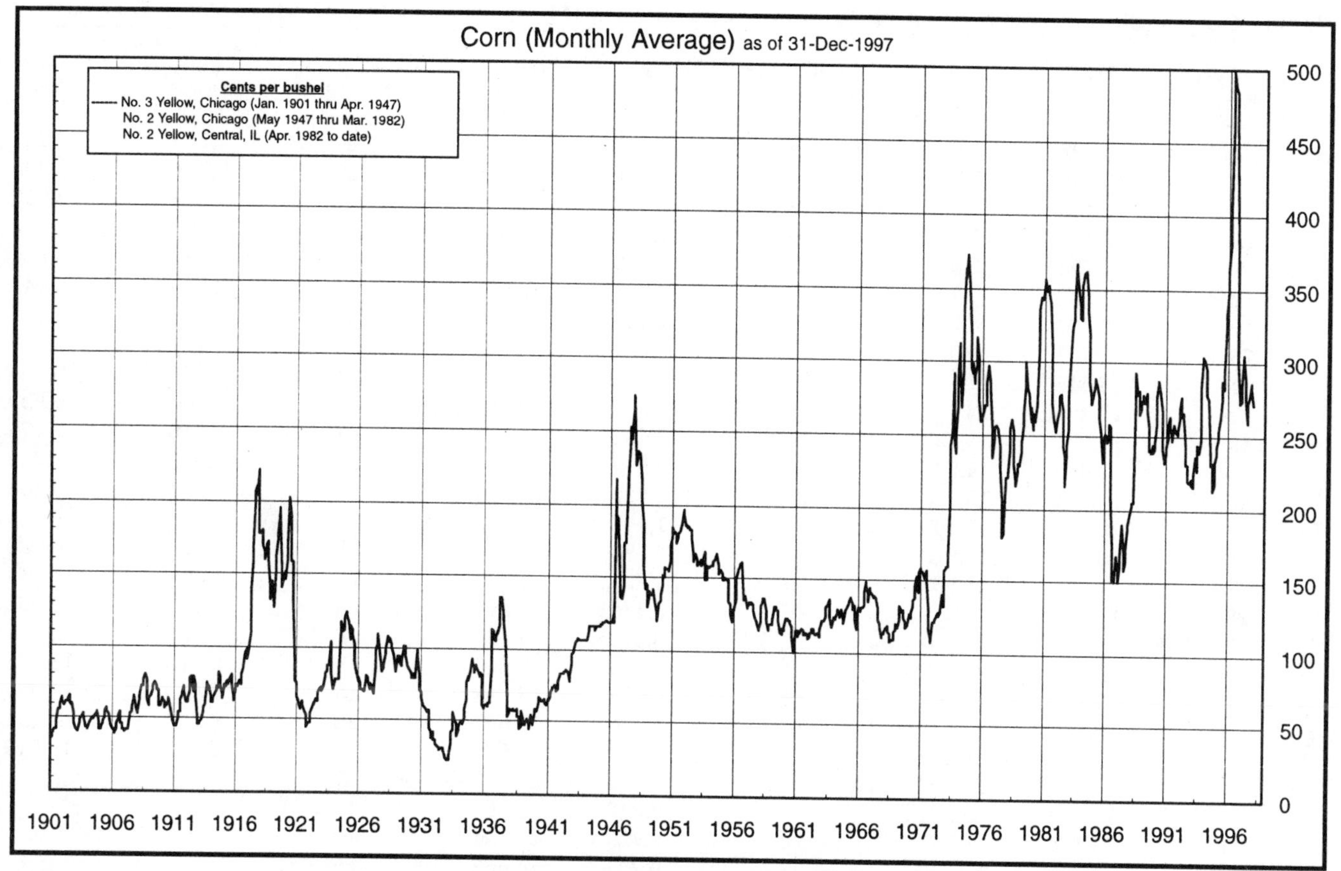

Average Cash Price of Corn, No. 2 Yellow in Central Illinois In Dollars Per Bushel

Crop Year	Sept.	Oct.	Nov.	Dec.	Jan.	Feb.	Mar.	Apr.	May	June	July	Aug.	Average
1988-9	2.68	2.70	2.54	2.56	2.62	2.60	2.64	2.58	2.64	2.53	2.44	2.30	2.57
1989-90	2.35	2.25	2.29	2.29	2.29	2.34	2.44	2.64	2.73	2.70	2.68	2.54	2.46
1990-1	2.25	2.18	2.20	2.27	2.31	2.36	2.45	2.50	2.41	2.34	2.34	2.45	2.34
1991-2	2.39	2.41	2.41	2.42	2.49	2.58	2.64	2.50	2.51	2.51	2.31	2.17	2.45
1992-3	2.13	1.97	1.99	2.05	2.07	2.05	2.16	2.23	2.20	2.09	2.25	2.27	2.12
1993-4	2.22	2.27	2.63	2.81	2.89	2.83	2.76	2.61	2.58	2.61	2.19	2.13	2.54
1994-5	2.08	1.92	2.03	2.16	2.22	2.27	2.36	2.41	2.50	2.65	2.79	2.68	2.34
1995-6	2.83	3.12	3.22	3.36	3.53	3.71	3.92	4.47	4.86	4.74	4.70	4.48	3.91
1996-7	3.39	2.81	2.63	2.62	2.62	2.71	2.90	2.87	2.74	2.59	2.44	2.60	2.74
1997-8[1]	2.61	2.66	2.70										2.66

[1] Preliminary. *Source: Economic Research Service, U.S. Department of Agriculture (ERS-USDA)*

Average Cash Price of Corn, No. 2 Yellow at Gulf Ports[2] In Dollars Per Bushel

Crop Year	Sept.	Oct.	Nov.	Dec.	Jan.	Feb.	Mar.	Apr.	May	June	July	Aug.	Average
1988-9	3.08	3.07	2.89	2.99	3.01	2.99	3.02	2.93	2.99	2.87	2.73	2.57	2.93
1989-90	2.60	2.40	2.75	2.75	2.69	2.70	2.72	3.01	3.08	3.05	2.92	2.79	2.79
1990-1	2.59	2.55	2.54	2.60	2.68	2.70	2.77	2.80	2.69	2.65	2.67	2.79	2.67
1991-2	2.76	2.76	2.72	2.71	2.70	2.89	2.96	2.77	2.77	2.80	2.61	2.48	2.74
1992-3	2.50	2.40	2.42	2.39	2.39	2.40	2.48	2.55	2.50	2.36	2.59	2.55	2.46
1993-4	2.57	2.68	2.94	3.08	3.22	3.14	3.05	2.88	2.81	2.85	2.51	2.44	2.85
1994-5	2.48	2.44	2.43	2.61	2.72	2.72	2.79	2.79	2.84	3.04	3.23	3.21	2.78
1995-6	3.32	3.57	3.63	3.76	4.00	4.18	4.34	4.80	5.17	4.99	5.07	4.73	4.30
1996-7	3.69	3.27	2.97	2.97	3.02	3.08	3.25	3.17	3.01	2.86	2.69	2.86	3.07
1997-8[1]	2.88	3.05	2.98										2.97

[1] Preliminary. [2] Barge delivered to Louisiana Gulf. *Source: Economic Research Service, U.S. Department of Agriculture (ERS-USDA)*

CORN

Weekly Outstanding Export Sales and Cumulative Exports of U.S. Corn In Thousands of Metric Tons

Marketing Year 1995/96 Week Ending	1995/96 Out-standing Sales	1995/96 Cumu-lative Exports	Marketing Year 1996/97 Week Ending	1996/97 Out-standing Sales	1996/97 Cumu-lative Exports	Marketing Year 1997/98 Week Ending	1997/98 Out-standing Sales	1997/98 Cumu-lative Exports
Sept. 7, 1995	16,892	985	Sept. 5, 1996	14,289	169	Sept. 4, 1997	7,730	207
14	16,576	2,354	12	14,671	557	11	7,761	793
21	16,456	3,898	19	14,851	1,163	18	7,750	2,097
28	16,176	5,244	26	14,714	1,860	25	7,693	2,914
Oct. 5	15,798	6,510	Oct. 3	14,778	2,590	Oct. 2	7,487	3,602
12	15,721	7,720	10	15,080	3,145	9	7,279	4,445
19	16,208	8,956	17	14,555	3,890	16	7,126	5,118
26	16,757	9,979	24	14,487	4,727	23	7,121	5,593
Nov. 2	3,548	17,182	31	14,298	5,776	30	7,299	6,207
9	17,351	12,478	Nov. 7	14,082	6,789	Nov. 6	7,606	6,829
16	17,785	13,428	14	13,921	8,117	13	7,810	7,776
23	17,387	14,508	21	13,279	9,340	20	7,673	8,329
30	16,881	15,973	28	12,222	10,626	27	7,565	9,138
Dec. 7	16,754	17,103	Dec. 5	11,447	11,908	Dec. 4	7,459	9,919
14	16,717	17,910	12	10,573	13,481	11	6,921	10,830
21	17,474	18,962	19	10,708	14,340	18	6,701	11,617
28	17,362	20,299	26	10,175	15,319	25	6,634	12,031
Jan. 4, 1996	17,975	21,154	Jan. 2, 1997	9,344	16,367	Jan. 1, 1998	6,481	12,764
11	18,538	22,389	9	9,371	17,249	8	6,318	13,280
18	19,142	23,649	16	9,297	18,568	15	6,469	14,007
25	18,811	24,973	23	9,490	19,661	22	6,276	14,771
Feb. 1	18,541	26,252	30	9,434	20,574	29	6,531	15,519
8	18,370	27,398	Feb. 6	9,236	21,656	Feb. 5		
15	18,713	28,201	13	9,342	22,365	12		
22	18,119	29,367	20	8,729	23,471	19		
29	18,264	30,667	27	9,224	24,482	26		
Mar. 7	18,289	31,784	Mar. 6	9,274	25,422	Mar. 5		
14	17,669	33,217	13	9,152	26,412	12		
21	17,202	34,391	20	8,684	27,432	19		
28	16,664	35,621	27	8,145	28,252	26		
Apr. 4	16,732	36,628	Apr. 3	8,054	29,273	Apr. 2		
11	16,204	37,678	10	7,873	30,119	9		
18	15,411	39,216	17	7,706	30,777	16		
25	15,283	40,284	24	7,731	31,491	23		
May 2	14,778	41,642	May 1	7,320	32,495	30		
9	14,795	42,579	8	7,418	32,872	May 7		
16	14,054	43,695	15	7,394	33,511	14		
23	12,941	44,681	22	7,438	34,469	21		
30	11,980	45,715	29	7,379	35,118	28		
June 6	11,287	46,776	June 5	7,301	35,811	June 4		
13	10,466	47,440	12	7,151	36,477	11		
20	9,724	48,060	19	6,845	37,139	18		
27	8,694	49,010	26	6,809	37,729	25		
July 4	7,661	50,075	July 3	6,647	38,353	July 2		
11	6,678	50,897	10	6,270	38,974	9		
18	6,005	51,506	17	5,863	39,551	16		
25	5,419	52,163	24	5,077	40,325	23		
Aug. 1	4,608	52,976	31	4,388	41,018	30		
8	3,411	53,780	Aug. 7	3,713	41,667	Aug. 6		
15	2,320	54,532	14	3,074	42,287	13		
22	1,883	54,970	21	2,003	43,432	20		
29	1,163	55,623	28	6,297	0	27		

Source: Foreign Agricultural Service, U.S. Department of Agriculture (FAS-USDA)

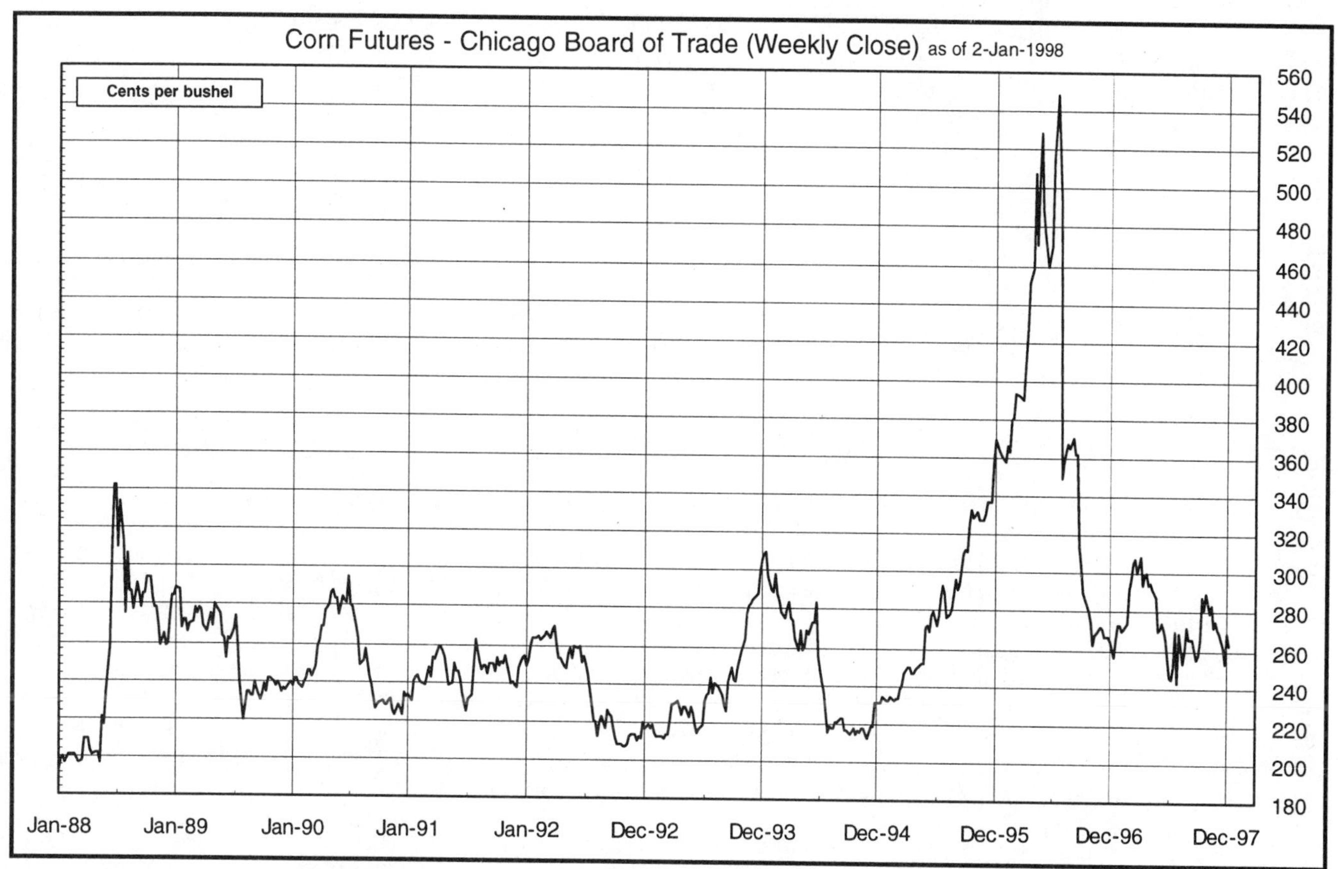

U.S. Exports[1] of Corn (Including Seed), by Country of Destination In Thousands of Metric Tons

Year Beginning Oct.	Algeria	Canada	Egypt	Israel	Japan	Mexico	Rep. of Korea	Russia[3]	Saudi Arabia	Spain	Taiwan	Vene-zuela	Total
1987-8	1,113	158	1,078	415	14,816	2,900	4,411	5,585	545	1,836	4,169	0	43,955
1988-9	973	896	1,014	304	13,016	3,113	4,591	15,573	616	1,280	3,625	0	50,676
1989-90	1,146	637	1,135	250	13,885	4,585	5,680	16,371	707	1,712	5,009	593	59,854
1990-1	1,328	302	1,756	299	13,639	1,901	1,982	9,077	725	1,434	5,086	321	44,497
1991-2	827	314	1,058	369	13,481	1,041	1,508	6,533	602	1,273	4,998	552	40,693
1992-3	1,224	1,189	1,543	539	14,235	396	1,021	3,380	787	1,075	5,450	777	41,766
1993-4	1,182	640	1,437	268	12,032	1,678	631	2,337	851	1,116	4,955	751	33,057
1994-5	846	1,135	2,608	671	16,107	3,166	8,921	9	864	2,497	6,210	886	58,645
1995-6	507	735	1,854	625	14,900	6,268	7,333	58	844	1,156	5,600	479	52,681
1996-7[2]	862	879	2,364	NA	15,425	3,141	5,404	NA	1,025	NA	5,609	NA	46,579

[1] Excludes exports of corn by-products. [2] Preliminary. [3] Formerly part of the U.S.S.R.; data not reported separately until 1992.
Source: Economic Research Service, U.S. Department of Agriculture (ERS-USDA)

Stocks of Corn (Shelled and Ear) in the United States In Millions of Bushels

	On Farms				Off Farms				Total Stocks			
Year	Mar. 1	June 1	Sept. 1	Dec. 1	Mar. 1	June 1	Sept. 1	Dec. 1	Mar. 1	June 1	Sept. 1	Dec. 1
1988	4,421.0	3,241.0	2,002.8	4,280.2	3,214.6	2,594.5	2,256.3	2,791.4	7,635.6	5,835.5	4,259.1	7,071.6
1989	3,021.0	2,022.0	967.5	4,698.8	2,182.9	1,397.3	962.9	2,383.3	5,203.9	3,419.3	1,930.4	7,082.1
1990	2,910.5	1,623.5	754.8	4,874.0	1,901.9	1,219.7	589.7	2,066.3	4,812.4	2,843.2	1,344.5	6,940.3
1991	3,064.5	1,755.0	691.2	4,294.5	1,724.5	1,237.0	830.0	2,246.6	4,789.0	2,992.0	1,521.2	6,541.1
1992	2,610.2	1,517.5	605.5	5,736.9	1,950.8	1,221.1	494.8	2,169.5	4,561.0	2,738.6	1,100.3	7,906.4
1993	3,630.0	2,216.5	1,070.7	3,803.0	2,048.2	1,492.9	1,042.3	2,133.5	5,678.2	3,709.4	2,113.0	5,936.5
1994	2,210.0	1,203.0	395.4	5,417.5	1,785.5	1,156.9	454.7	2,663.0	3,995.7	2,359.9	850.1	8,080.5
1995	3,502.0	2,072.0	740.9	3,960.0	2,089.7	1,342.9	816.9	2,145.8	5,591.7	3,414.9	1,557.8	6,105.8
1996	2,000.2	780.1	196.6	4,800.0	1,799.3	937.8	229.3	2,103.7	3,799.5	1,717.9	425.9	6,903.7
1997[1]	2,870.0	1,501.0	475.0	4,822.0	1,624.1	995.6	408.2	2,407.8	4,494.1	2,496.6	883.2	7,229.8

[1] Preliminary. NA = Not available. *Source: National Agricultural Statistics Service, U.S. Department of Agriculture (NASS-USDA)*

CORN

Volume of Trading of Corn Futures in Chicago   In Thousands of Contracts

Year	Jan.	Feb.	Mar.	Apr	May	June	July	Aug.	Sept.	Oct.	Nov.	Dec.	Total
1988	608	667	642	696	847	1,580	1,364	1,070	871	932	1,119	710	11,106
1989	834	677	764	828	786	897	865	687	565	940	870	559	9,271
1990	650	798	925	1,148	1,429	1,353	1,102	908	606	788	1,136	580	11,423
1991	847	697	933	1,041	845	1,013	1,254	1,097	692	884	908	632	10,853
1992	901	1,003	952	869	938	1,015	866	795	689	688	996	644	10,357
1993	518	636	774	895	688	1,047	1,396	1,014	896	1,036	1,574	988	10,539
1994	1,251	1,036	1,046	1,109	1,079	1,455	748	602	615	703	1,025	861	11,530
1995	787	832	974	988	1,214	1,760	1,294	1,319	1,220	1,613	1,743	1,356	15,105
1996	1,992	1,820	1,608	2,655	2,085	1,545	1,591	1,145	1,183	1,436	1,515	1,046	19,620
1997	1,161	1,483	1,693	1,780	1,292	1,347	1,528	1,318	1,060	1,700	1,434	1,188	16,985

Source: Chicago Board of Trade (CBT)   *Note: The CBT changed the volume figures from Bushels to Contract in January 1998.*

Average Open Interest of Corn Futures in Chicago   In Contracts

Year	Jan.	Feb.	Mar.	Apr.	May	June	July	Aug.	Sept.	Oct.	Nov.	Dec.
1988	145,703	151,802	157,448	162,651	165,394	214,463	245,871	234,992	232,953	247,369	242,342	222,420
1989	216,220	198,812	192,640	183,544	163,888	156,782	143,806	145,405	141,379	171,513	194,251	167,944
1990	178,094	202,845	229,946	252,155	250,020	242,462	212,749	207,951	206,603	211,222	230,333	203,881
1991	210,006	219,236	229,010	229,404	204,828	202,100	198,527	219,700	215,527	242,466	257,065	228,347
1992	254,195	294,957	285,429	260,527	230,359	232,189	211,221	219,796	208,613	239,888	262,345	244,803
1993	256,113	260,986	248,638	250,000	229,016	232,590	265,672	264,938	243,892	275,792	332,445	327,226
1994	346,077	336,342	327,539	305,722	262,621	246,308	215,081	208,990	212,983	243,678	262,849	250,646
1995	292,090	311,372	336,433	355,443	368,381	427,744	413,839	418,450	439,170	473,698	490,970	487,977
1996	500,837	508,496	469,697	453,707	403,118	350,066	304,265	298,894	302,170	326,373	332,809	306,256
1997	305,779	347,392	382,261	351,852	290,649	274,760	267,531	281,194	307,415	378,453	379,045	331,386

Source: Chicago Board of Trade (CBT)   *Note: The CBT changed the open interest figures from Bushels to Contract in January 1998.*

Corn Price Support Data in the United States

Crop Year Beginning Sept. 1	National Average Loan Rate[3]	Target Price	Placed Under Loan	% of Production	Acquired by CCC	Owned by CCC Aug. 31	CCC Inventory As of Dec. 31: CCC Owned	CCC Inventory As of Dec. 31: Under CCC Loan	Quantity Pledged	Face Amount
	$ Per Bushel		Millions of Bushels						Ths. Bu	Ths. $
1988-9	1.77	2.93	756	15.3	151	363	679	982	755,895	1,313,581
1989-90	1.65	2.84	920	12.2	361	233	676	1,110	920,068	1,487,026
1990-1	1.57	2.75	1,071	13.5	285	371	214	1,071	1,071,040	1,616,948
1991-2	1.62	2.75	1,006	13.5	291	113	265	678	26,636	45,609
1992-3	1.72	2.75	1,646	17.4	0	56	125	1,021	15,245	28,947
1993-4	1.72	2.75	618	9.7	0	45	54	812	13,697	26,052
1994-5	1.89	2.75	2,002	19.8	NA	NA	44	1,598	26,318	53,474
1995-6[1]	1.89	2.75	970	9.2	NA	NA	42	579	NA	NA
1996-7[2]	1.89	NA	561	NA	NA	NA	30	756	NA	NA
1997-8[2]	1.89	NA	NA	NA	NA	NA	2	81	NA	NA

[1] Preliminary. [2] Estimate. [3] Finley or announced loan rate. *Source: National Agricultural Statistics Service, U.S. Department of Agriculture (NASS)*

Average Price Received by Farmers for Corn in the United States   In Dollars Per Bushel

Crop Year	Sept.	Oct.	Nov.	Dec.	Jan.	Feb.	Mar.	Apr.	May	June	July	Aug.	Average
1988-9	2.60	2.58	2.51	2.53	2.60	2.59	2.60	2.56	2.58	2.52	2.47	2.27	2.54
1989-90	2.29	2.22	2.24	2.27	2.31	2.32	2.37	2.51	2.62	2.63	2.62	2.51	2.36
1990-1	2.32	2.19	2.16	2.22	2.27	2.32	2.39	2.42	2.38	2.31	2.27	2.33	2.28
1991-2	2.33	2.31	2.29	2.33	2.40	2.46	2.49	2.48	2.49	2.47	2.33	2.15	2.37
1992-3	2.16	2.05	1.98	1.97	2.03	2.00	2.10	2.16	2.14	2.09	2.22	2.25	2.07
1993-4	2.21	2.28	2.45	2.67	2.70	2.79	2.74	2.65	2.60	2.61	2.29	2.16	2.50
1994-5	2.19	2.06	1.99	2.13	2.19	2.23	2.30	2.36	2.41	2.51	2.63	2.63	2.26
1995-6	2.69	2.79	2.87	3.07	3.09	3.37	3.51	3.85	4.14	4.22	4.43	4.80	3.15
1996-7	3.55	2.89	2.66	2.63	2.69	2.65	2.79	2.80	2.69	2.56	2.43	2.50	2.74
1997-8[1]	2.52	2.54	2.51	2.52	2.57								2.53

[1] Preliminary. *Source: Economic Research Service, U.S. Department of Agriculture (ERS-USDA)*

Corn Oil

The steady year to year uptrend in U.S. corn oil produc-ion carried to a record high 2.3 billion pounds in 1997/98 s. the previous record of 2.2 billion in 1996/97. Production n the late 1980's averaged about 1.4 billion. Seasonally, nonthly production tends to peak around March and touch-es a low in either November or July. Seasonal consumption patterns are clouded, but on a total basis the gain in domes-tic usage pales against exports.

Total 1997/98 disappearance of 2.3 billion pounds was marginally higher than in 1996/97, and equaled the record high set in 1995/96. Domestic usage of 1.27 billion pounds compares with 1.25 billion in 1996/97 and the record high 1.3 billion in 1995/96. Corn oil is cholesterol free which has enhanced its appeal among health conscious consumers.

1997/98 corn oil exports totaled 1 billion pounds, the same as in 1996/97. The European Union is a major importer of U.S. corn oil, led by Italy, Spain and Greece. Saudi Arabia and Turkey are the largest individual importing nations. South Korea is Asia's largest buyer. U.S. imports are insignificant. Carryover stocks show considerable variation: from a low of 4.4 million pounds at the end of 1989/90 to a high of 24.1 million five years later. Estimated ending 1997/98 stocks are 117,000,000 pounds.

Crude corn oil prices, basis wet/dry-milled Central Illinois, averaged 24.63 cents a pound in calendar 1997 (vs a marketing year avg. of 24.05 cents). Prices a year earlier were 24.52 cents (and 25.24). Calendar year prices in the 1990's have ranged from 21.77 (1993) to 28.39 (1991).

Supply and Distribution of Corn Oil in the United States In Millions of Pounds

Crop Year Beginning Oct. 1	Supply: Stocks Oct. 1	Supply: Production	Supply: Imports	Supply: Total Supply	Disappearance: Baking and Frying Fats	Disappearance: Salad and Cooking Oil	Disappearance: Margarine	Disappearance: Total Edible Products	Disappearance: Domestic Disappearance	Disappearance: Exports	Disappearance: Total Disappearance
1991-2	138	1,821	5.0	1,965	411	565	185	1,085	1,202	566	1,768
1992-3	196	1,878	7.0	2,081	241	547	W	945	1,220	712	1,931
1993-4	150	1,906	7.0	2,062	86	413	W	649	1,228	717	1,944
1994-5	118	2,227	10.0	2,356	100	446	W	636	1,250	865	2,115
1995-6	241	2,139	11.0	2,391	82	434	79	595	1,298	977	2,275
1996-7[1]	116	2,231	14.0	2,361	73	386	68	527	1,244	988	2,232
1997-8[2]	129	2,276	15.0	2,420					1,268	1,000	2,268

[1] Preliminary. [2] Estimate. W = Withheld proprietary data. *Source: Economic Research Service, U.S. Department of Agiculture (ERS-USDA)*

Production[2] of Crude Corn Oil in the United States In Millions of Pounds

Year	Oct.	Nov.	Dec.	Jan.	Feb.	Mar.	Apr.	May	June	July	Aug.	Sept.	Total
1991-2		436.7		138.1	137.5	164.5	153.3	150.2	160.0	165.0	162.4	153.6	1,821
1992-3	168.1	151.8	151.6	135.5	139.0	165.6	153.5	161.6	164.5	163.0	158.5	165.1	1,878
1993-4	160.8	153.4	162.5	140.6	138.6	166.9	155.3	164.2	171.8	164.8	162.3	165.1	1,906
1994-5	175.5	165.3	180.9	163.2	161.8	232.7	188.4	191.2	193.6	193.5	180.3	188.5	2,215
1995-6	179.5	173.8	184.5	180.6	160.4	192.9	192.1	175.9	178.4	147.1	162.2	171.2	2,099
1996-7	183.8	182.3	208.2	172.5	170.9	209.9	188.3	182.5	184.3	174.0	180.6	182.2	2,220
1997-8[1]	199.2	207.5	202.0										2,435

[1] Preliminary. [2] Not seasonally adjusted. *Source: Bureau of the Census, U.S. Department of Commerce*

Consumption of Corn Oil, in Refining, in the United States In Millions of Pounds

Year	Oct.	Nov.	Dec.	Jan.	Feb.	Mar.	Apr.	May	June	July	Aug.	Sept.	Total
1991-2		287.2		138.1	137.5	164.5	153.3	150.2	160.0	165.0	162.4	153.6	1,672
1992-3	168.1	151.8	151.6	81.2	93.6	110.5	102.4	85.8	99.9	88.0	90.9	96.4	1,320
1993-4	106.7	101.7	114.3	71.8	76.5	92.6	79.4	91.5	91.7	90.6	106.4	109.1	1,132
1994-5	103.5	107.2	116.9	100.7	92.3	109.9	97.3	95.6	108.9	97.2	78.2	95.5	1,203
1995-6	82.9	97.9	102.0	78.6	91.6	100.0	84.8	90.0	90.5	74.5	66.5	90.2	1,049
1996-7	82.0	83.0	84.7	69.7	71.0	79.5	71.4	76.1	80.4	86.9	90.8	58.5	934
1997-8[1]	87.5	83.8	100.6										1,088

[1] Preliminary. *Source: Bureau of the Census, U.S. Department of Commerce*

Average Corn Oil Price, Wet Mill in Chicago In Cents Per Pound

Year	Oct.	Nov.	Dec.	Jan.	Feb.	Mar.	Apr.	May	June	July	Aug.	Sept.	Average
1991-2	27.75	27.25	28.75	29.00	28.45	27.19	26.75	26.04	24.75	22.48	20.40	21.00	25.82
1992-3	20.43	20.60	20.75	20.75	20.87	20.79	20.80	20.75	20.60	20.67	21.50	22.23	20.90
1993-4	22.25	23.06	26.93	28.00	29.89	30.30	29.63	29.48	29.43	27.20	25.02	24.87	27.17
1994-5	24.73	24.75	24.75	28.01	27.26	28.17	27.30	26.42	26.61	27.38	26.35	25.93	26.47
1995-6	26.05	25.54	24.99	24.52	24.30	24.34	25.60	27.98	25.66	25.46	24.33	24.14	25.24
1996-7	22.67	21.96	22.27	23.39	23.97	24.38	24.60	24.66	24.82	25.34	25.36	25.15	24.05
1997-8[1]	25.20	26.25	26.28	24.95									25.67

[1] Preliminary. *Source: Economic Research Service, U.S. Department of Agriculture (ERS-USDA)*

Cotton

U.S. cotton production in the 1997-98 (August-July) season was forecast by the USDA at 18.82 million bales. This was some 120,000 bales less than in the previous season. The record crop of 1994-95 was 19.66 million bales. Texas was once again the largest producing state with a cotton crop of 5.36 million bales, some 22 percent more than in 1996-97. It was an interesting season in Texas as the crop did not get off to a good start but then the weather improved in the middle and late stages of the crop's growth cycle. Texas harvested 5.33 million acres of cotton and the yield was 482 pounds per acre. The yield was down six percent from the year before.

California cotton production in 1997-98 was forecast to be 2.62 million bales, down five percent from the previous year. Acreage harvested was 1.15 million acres while the yield was 1,188 pounds per acre. The yield was up four percent from the year before. Mississippi's cotton crop was estimated at 1.8 million bales, down four percent from the 1996-97 season. Some 960,000 acres were harvested. The yield in Mississippi was 900 pounds per acre, up ten percent from 1996-97. Georgia's cotton crop was 1.98 million bales, down five percent from the previous year. Georgia harvested 1.44 million acres and the yield was 662 pounds per acre, down 11 percent from the year before.

The U.S. upland cotton crop was 18.29 million bales, down one percent from the previous season. The pima or long staple cotton crop was 533,000 bales, one percent more than the previous season. California is the largest producer of pima cotton with 1997-98 production estimated at 420,000 bales, 12 percent more than in 1996-97. U.S. acreage planted to cotton in 1997-98 was 13.91 million while harvested acreage was 13.45 million acres. The abandonment rate, or amount of cotton acreage planted but not harvested, was three percent, well below the previous season's 12 percent rate. The national average yield was 672 pounds per acre, down five percent from 1996-97. The record yield was set in the 1994-95 season at 708 pounds.

U.S. cotton stocks at the beginning of the 1997-98 season were 3.97 million bales, a substantial increase from 1996-97 when they were 2.61 million bales. U.S. imports of cotton had been very high in the previous two seasons. In 1995-96 they were 410,000 bales while in 1996-97 they were 400,000 bales. The high level of imports was due in part to high prices for domestic cotton which forced some textile mills to import cotton. With lower prices expected in 1997-98, U.S. cotton imports are forecast to be 20,000 bales. The U.S. total supply of cotton in 1997-98 is forecast at 22.81 million bales, up four percent from the previous season. That would be the largest supply since the 1994-95 season.

Domestic use of cotton in the U.S. is forecast at 11.4 million bales, up two percent from 1996-97. This would be the highest rate of domestic cotton use in many years. How much cotton is consumed by U.S. textile mills is dependent on a number of factors including the direction and strength of the U.S. economy as well as consumer tastes. In years of economic weakness or recession, textile mills use of cotton declines. In the 1982-83 season, when there was economic weakness, mill use of cotton was only 5.5 million bales. In the 1973-74 season, when there was recession, mill use was 7.5 million bales. While the rate of growth of the U.S. economy is expected to slow in 1998, the trend of growth will remain higher. In November 1997, the Census Bureau reported that the seasonally adjusted daily rate of cotton consumption was nearly 43,000 bales. That implied that the annual rate of cotton use was nearly 11.6 million bales.

U.S. exports of cotton in the 1997-98 season were forecast to be 7.1 million bales, three percent more than in 1996-97. If there is a major area of concern in the cotton market, it is in the export sector. In late 1997 and early 1998, cotton prices were trending lower as a result of concerns about prospects for U.S. exports. In particular, there was severe financial turmoil in Asia resulting in a significant devaluation of those currencies versus the dollar. Countries like South Korea, Japan, Indonesia, Malaysia and Thailand all saw their currencies decline in value relative to the dollar. All of these countries are importers of U.S. cotton fiber. As of early 1998, there was no strong evidence that U.S. cotton exports were being impaired as a result of this.

One other complication was that China, traditionally a major importer of U.S. cotton, had imposed some restrictions on cotton imports. In part, China was trying to reduce its already large domestic inventory of cotton. While China was likely to import less U.S. cotton, other countries like Mexico were buying more cotton. Going into 1998, the outlook for exports was mixed. It still appeared very possible that exports would exceed the year ago level by three percent. U.S. use of cotton in 1997-98 was forecast at 18.5 million bales. Ending stocks were projected to be 4.3 million bales or eight percent more than at the end of the 1996-97 season.

World production of cotton in 1997-98 was forecast at 90.11 million bales, one percent more than in the previous season. World domestic use of cotton was estimated at 89.63 million bales, one percent more than in 1996-97. For the 1997-98 season, China's cotton crop was forecast to be 18.5 million bales, down four percent from the previous season. China was expected to import 2.2 million bales which would be down almost 40 percent from the prior season. China is projected to have ending stocks of 14.3 million bales.

India's cotton production in 1997-98 was forecast to be 12.8 million bales, seven percent less than in the previous season. Pakistan's 1997-98 cotton crop was projected to be 7.5 million bales, up three percent from the previous season. Production in Central Asian countries was forecast to increase in 1997-98. Uzbekistan's crop was estimated to be 5.4 million bales, up 14 percent from the previous year. Uzbekistan was expected to export 4.4 million bales of cotton. Turkmenistan's cotton crop was projected to be 900,000 bales, 50 percent higher than the year before. Exports were projected to be 650,000 bales.

Futures Markets

Cotton futures and options are traded on the New York Cotton Exchange (NYCE). Cotton futures are traded on the Bolsa de Mercadorias & Futuros (BM&F). Cotton Yarn futures are traded on the Nagoya Textile Exchange, the Osaka Textile Exchange, and the Tokyo Commodity Exchange (TOCOM).

Supply and Distribution of All Cotton in the United States In Thousands of 480-Pound Bales

Crop Year Beginning Aug. 1	Area: Planted	Area: Harvested	Yield Lbs./acre	Supply: Beginning Stocks[3]	Supply: Production[4]	Supply: Imports	Supply: Total	Disappearance: Mill Use	Disappearance: Exports	Disappearance: Total	Unaccounted	Ending Stocks	Farm Price[5]	"A" Index Price[6]	of Production Million $
	--- 1,000 acres ---												-- Cents Per Lb. --		
1988-9	12,515	11,948	619	5,771	15,412	5	21,187	7,785	6,148	13,930	-165	7,092	56.6	66.42	4,190.5
1989-90	10,587	9,538	614	7,092	12,196	2	19,290	8,759	7,694	16,453	163	3,000	66.2	82.34	3,877.9
1990-1	12,348	11,732	634	3,000	15,505	4	18,509	8,657	7,793	16,450	285	2,344	67.1	82.87	5,075.8
1991-2	14,052	12,960	652	2,344	17,614	13	19,971	9,613	6,646	16,259	-8	3,704	58.1	62.90	4,913.2
1992-3	13,240	11,143	699	3,704	16,219	1	19,923	10,250	5,201	15,451	190	4,662	54.9	56.87	4,273.9
1993-4	13,438	12,783	606	4,662	16,134	6	20,802	10,418	6,862	17,280	8	3,530	58.4	70.75	4,520.9
1994-5	13,720	13,322	708	3,530	19,662	20	23,212	11,198	9,402	20,600	38	2,650	72.0	92.66	6,796.7
1995-6	16,931	16,007	537	2,650	17,900	408	20,958	10,604	7,675	18,322	-27	2,609	76.5	85.61	6,574.6
1996-7[1]	14,634	12,868	707	2,609	18,942	403	21,954	11,126	6,865	17,991	8	3,971	70.4	78.66	6,524.4
1997-8[2]	13,905	13,437	673	3,971	18,848	25	22,844	11,400	7,000	18,400	-44	4,400			

[1] Preliminary. [2] Estimate. [3] Excludes preseason ginnings (adjusted to 480-lb. bale net weight basis). [4] Includes preseason ginnings. [5] Marketing year average price. [6] Average of 5 cheapest types of SLM 1 3/32" staple length cotton offered on the European market. *Source: Economic Research Service, U.S. Department of Agriculture (ERS-USDA)*

World Production of All Cotton In Thousands of 480-Lb. Bales

Crop Year Beginning Aug. 1	Argentina	Brazil	China	Egypt	India	Iran	Mexico	Pakistan	Sudan	Turkey	United States	Uzbekistan[3]	World Total
1988-9	896	3,376	19,100	1,405	8,276	551	1,416	6,547	700	2,985	12,196	12,621	84,774
1989-90	1,272	3,030	17,400	1,324	10,599	524	769	6,687	584	2,835	12,196	7,605	79,780
1990-1	1,355	3,215	20,700	1,378	9,135	553	813	7,522	380	3,007	15,505	7,317	86,980
1991-2	1,148	3,445	26,100	1,338	9,291	543	831	10,000	386	2,578	17,614	6,628	95,992
1992-3	666	2,113	20,700	1,620	10,775	465	138	7,073	276	2,635	16,218	5,851	82,709
1993-4	1,075	1,860	17,200	1,882	9,487	310	110	6,282	250	2,666	16,134	6,067	76,049
1994-5	1,608	2,526	19,900	1,225	10,814	542	458	6,250	400	2,886	19,662	5,778	85,610
1995-6	1,930	1,791	21,900	1,088	12,649	800	860	8,200	490	3,911	17,900	5,740	92,174
1996-7[1]	1,493	1,300	19,300	1,568	13,781	700	1,077	7,300	460	3,600	18,942	4,750	89,247
1997-8[2]	2,100	1,750	19,500	1,450	12,800	NA	900	7,000	400	3,300	18,977	5,400	90,878

[1] Preliminary. [2] Estimate. [3] Formerly part of the U.S.S.R.; data not reported separately until 1989. *Source: Foreign Agricultural Service, U.S. Department of Agriculture (FAS-USDA)*

World Supply and Demand of Cotton In Thousands of 480-Lb. Bales

Crop Year Beginning Aug. 1	Beginning Stocks: United States	Beginning Stocks: Uzbekistan[3]	Beginning Stocks: China	Beginning Stocks: World Total	Production: United States	Production: Uzbekistan[3]	Production: China	Production: World Total	Consumption: United States	Consumption: Russia[3]	Consumption: China	Consumption: World Total	Exports: United States	Exports: Uzbekistan[3]	Exports: China	Exports: World Total
1988-9	5,771	1,302	7,559	32,850	15,412	12,704	19,056	84,423	7,782	9,200	20,533	85,352	6,148	3,656	1,636	25,869
1989-90	7,092	473	5,971	31,423	12,196	7,605	17,400	79,741	8,759	5,831	20,000	86,579	7,694	6,810	865	31,275
1990-1	3,000	460	4,379	25,771	15,505	7,317	20,700	86,968	8,657	5,469	20,000	85,677	7,793	5,393	928	29,656
1991-2	2,344	1,555	5,956	27,073	17,614	6,628	26,100	95,659	9,613	4,539	20,500	86,045	6,646	5,200	602	28,196
1992-3	3,704	2,295	12,284	37,403	16,218	5,851	20,700	82,445	10,250	2,200	21,500	85,765	5,201	5,500	684	25,583
1993-4	4,662	1,845	10,442	35,121	16,134	6,067	17,200	76,697	10,418	2,200	21,300	85,353	6,862	5,800	749	26,731
1994-5	3,530	737	6,101	26,507	19,662	5,778	19,900	85,534	11,198	1,263	20,200	84,688	9,402	5,006	183	28,476
1995-6	2,650	956	9,678	28,977	17,900	5,740	21,900	92,174	10,647	1,150	19,500	85,444	7,675	4,500	21	27,359
1996-7[1]	2,609	1,304	13,202	33,813	18,942	4,750	19,300	89,247	11,126	950	21,000	88,482	6,865	4,550	10	26,533
1997-8[2]	3,971	709	15,105	36,403	18,977	5,400	19,500	90,878	11,400	1,050	21,500	89,175	7,300	4,200	10	26,432

[1] Preliminary. [2] Estimate. [3] Formerly part of the U.S.S.R.; data not reported separately until 1989. *Source: Foreign Agricultural Service, U.S. Department of Agriculture (FAS-USDA)*

World Consumption of All Cotton in Specified Countries In Thousands of 480-Lb. Bales

Crop Year Beginning Aug. 1	Brazil	China	Egypt	France	Germany	India	Italy	Japan	Mexico	Pakistan	United States	Uzbekistan[3]	World Total
1988-9	3,766	20,500	1,300	640	910	8,139	1,424	3,408	650	3,904	7,782	9,100	85,565
1989-90	3,445	20,000	1,352	600	1,435	8,667	1,450	3,229	725	4,801	8,759	9,200	86,579
1990-1	3,215	20,000	1,457	530	955	9,018	1,470	3,027	712	5,648	8,657	8,700	85,677
1991-2	3,215	19,000	1,465	484	830	8,674	1,447	2,783	772	6,482	9,613	860	86,136
1992-3	3,445	21,500	1,640	470	680	9,761	1,400	2,301	740	6,634	10,250	950	85,770
1993-4	3,675	20,900	1,530	500	750	9,950	1,375	2,060	825	6,500	10,418	925	85,325
1994-5	4,000	20,200	1,350	500	660	10,334	1,525	1,800	800	6,750	11,198	750	84,574
1995-6	3,904	19,500	1,010	450	610	12,282	1,470	1,529	1,000	7,000	10,647	875	85,444
1996-7[1]	3,900	21,000	900	440	600	13,000	1,560	1,400	1,550	7,000	11,126	800	88,482
1997-8[2]	3,400	21,500	1,000	450	615	13,200	1,560	1,250	2,050	6,800	11,400	850	89,175

[1] Preliminary. [2] Estimate. [3] Formerly part of the U.S.S.R.; data not reported separately until 1991. *Source: Foreign Agricultural Service, U.S. Department of Agriculture (FAS-USDA)*

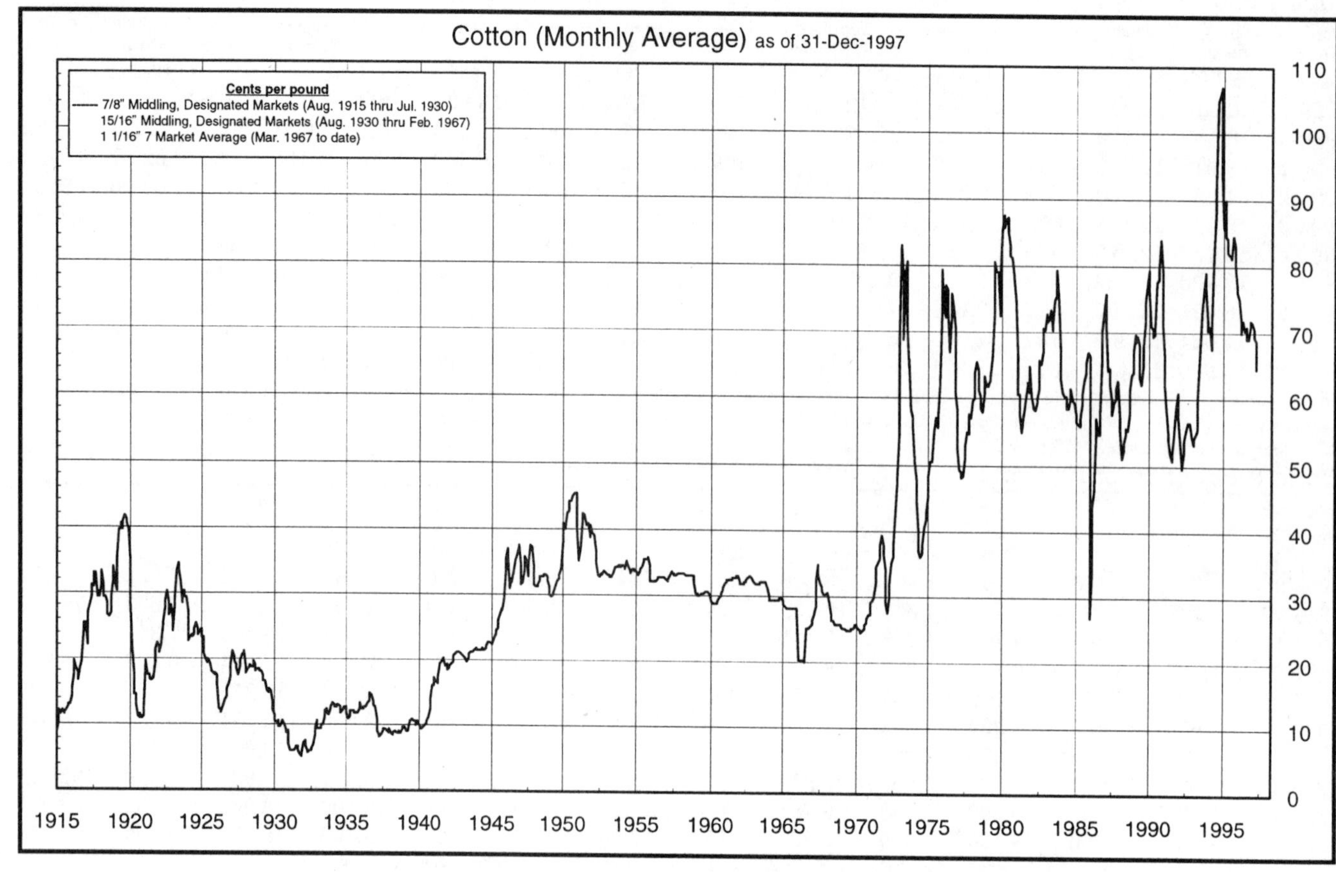

Average Spot Cotton Prices[2], C.I.F. Northern Europe In U.S. Cents Per Pound

Crop Year Beginning Aug. 1	Argentina "C"[3] 1 1/16"	Australia M 1 3/32"	Cotlook Index A	Cotlook Index B	Egypt Giza[4] 81	Greece M 1 3/32"	Mexico[5] M 1 3/32"	Pakistan Sind/ Punjab[6]	Tanzania AR'[7] Type 3	Turkey Izmir[8] 1 3/32"	U.S. Calif. ACALA SJV[9]	U.S. Memphis Terr.[10] M 1 3/32"	U.S. Orleans/ Texas[11] M 1 1/32"
1980-1	82.06	------	94.20	84.20	137.66	100.41	95.48	85.11	103.78	97.43	101.85	99.99	89.14
1981-2	63.55	------	73.80	64.40	115.73	81.06	75.36	65.56	87.92	77.65	79.79	75.87	66.76
1982-3	62.63	------	76.65	66.60	110.07	85.25	76.37	65.58	87.19	83.28	84.94	77.95	68.11
1983-4	83.32	90.83	87.65	80.40	134.07	94.42	87.54	75.51	95.23	92.64	94.90	87.23	78.41
1984-5	60.95	60.33	69.15	59.55	134.01	76.14	70.10	56.20	77.29	75.92	76.20	73.88	65.95
1985-6	49.42	50.05	49.00	40.95	111.40	50.98	53.16	37.92	55.81	57.06	59.43	65.01	52.26
1986-7	68.97	66.59	62.05	55.05	112.59	63.53	64.64	55.11	67.41	64.63	74.27	61.96	56.38
1987-8	64.13	76.14	72.30	67.50	145.11	83.85	73.75	65.88	87.96	86.43	81.17	74.24	72.07
1988-9	64.11	72.14	66.35	61.30	176.85	63.07	61.54	56.98	69.09	68.98	77.13	69.00	63.92
1989-90	77.05	84.16	82.40	77.40	189.54	83.76	82.50	76.75	86.68	90.49	88.59	83.90	78.93
1990-1	77.06	85.58	82.90	77.80	177.43	84.24	84.46	77.19	89.62	81.32	92.84	88.13	80.35
1991-2	55.08	65.97	63.05	58.50	128.10	65.90	68.19	58.14	68.90	74.66	74.47	66.35	63.41
1992-3	64.31	64.01	57.70	53.70	99.24	56.92	------	52.66	62.24	------	68.37	63.08	58.89
1993-4	80.20	72.81	70.60	67.30	88.35	58.81	------	54.42	69.83	59.80	77.55	72.80	69.78
1994-5	101.88	81.05	92.75	92.40	93.70	88.64	82.65	73.75	------	------	106.40	98.67	95.70
1995-6	82.98	93.75	85.61	81.06	------	84.95	94.94	81.86	96.20	90.38	103.49	94.71	90.37
1996-7[1]	79.71	83.24	78.59	74.80	------	75.85	79.60	73.37	79.22	------	89.55	82.81	79.77

[1] Preliminary. [2] Generally for prompt shipment. [3] 1 1/32" prior to January 20, 1984; 1 1/16" since. [4] Giza 67 until December 1983; Giza 69/75/81 until November 1990; Giza 81 since. [5] S. Brazil Type 5, 1 1/16" until 1987/88; Brazilian Type 5/6, 1 1/16" since. [6] Sind SG until June 1984; Sind/Punjab SG until January 1985; Afzal 1" until January 1986; Afzal 1 1/32" since. [7] No. 1/2 until February 1986; AR' Mwanza No. 3 until January 1992; AR' Type 3 since. [8] Izmir ST 1 White 1 1/16" RG prior to 1981/82; 1 1/32" from 1981/82 until January 1987; Izmir/Antalya ST 1 White 1 3/32" RG since. [9] SM 1 1/8". [10] SM 1 1/16" prior to 1981-82; Middling 1 3/32 inches since. [11] Middling 1" prior to 1988/89; Middling 1 1/32" since. NA = Not available. *Source: International Cotton Advisory Committee (ICAC)*

Average Price of Strict Low Middling 11/16", Cotton[2] at Designated U.S. Markets ¢ Per Pound (Net Weight)

Year	Aug.	Sept.	Oct.	Nov.	Dec.	Jan.	Feb.	Mar.	Apr.	May	June	July	Average
1987-8	75.89	71.41	64.30	64.66	62.26	59.69	57.83	59.64	60.07	61.55	62.86	57.40	63.13
1988-9	55.20	51.25	52.20	53.40	54.80	55.67	55.37	57.59	61.43	63.70	64.06	67.39	57.67
1989-90	69.88	68.46	69.40	68.33	63.56	62.21	64.95	68.06	71.31	74.61	77.06	79.53	69.78
1990-1	76.27	71.01	70.54	69.48	69.92	70.50	77.69	77.92	79.94	83.94	79.05	71.33	74.80
1991-2	66.44	62.39	58.28	54.70	53.89	51.54	50.76	52.01	54.97	55.45	58.82	60.93	56.68
1992-3	57.56	53.49	49.47	49.98	51.85	53.72	55.38	56.45	56.17	56.37	54.38	54.35	54.10
1993-4	53.04	54.01	54.58	55.61	60.29	66.53	72.69	72.74	76.12	79.30	76.85	71.71	66.12
1994-5	70.32	71.10	67.58	72.00	81.92	88.11	91.89	104.20	104.94	105.38	106.96	93.26	88.14
1995-6	85.90	90.00	84.65	84.16	82.18	81.81	81.56	81.13	84.69	83.22	80.23	76.84	83.03
1996-7	76.15	75.24	72.21	70.12	71.98	70.53	70.53	71.12	69.09	69.30	71.03	71.83	71.59
1997-8[1]	71.61	70.75	69.46	68.90	64.57	62.75							68.01

[1] Preliminary. [2] Color 41, leaf 4, staple 34, mike 35-36 and 43-49, strength 23.5-26.4. *Source: Agricultural Marketing Service, U.S Department of Agriculture (AMS-USDA)*

Average Spot Cotton, 13/32", Price (SLM) at Designated U.S. Markets In Cents Per Pound (Net Weight)

Year	Aug.	Sept.	Oct.	Nov.	Dec.	Jan.	Feb.	Mar.	Apr.	May	June	July	Average
1987-8	78.02	73.59	66.12	66.19	64.12	61.79	60.36	62.35	63.00	64.43	65.90	60.71	65.55
1988-9	58.64	54.52	54.26	54.91	56.55	57.81	57.80	59.75	63.49	66.07	66.53	69.90	60.02
1989-90	72.45	71.24	71.55	70.23	65.61	63.83	66.39	69.55	72.85	76.32	78.73	81.34	71.67
1990-1	78.06	72.87	72.19	70.97	71.61	72.14	79.38	79.86	81.99	85.94	81.02	73.28	76.61
1991-2	68.24	64.18	59.74	55.57	54.62	52.39	51.84	53.11	56.30	56.90	60.26	62.35	57.96
1992-3	59.08	54.99	50.96	51.41	53.37	55.24	56.86	58.30	58.03	58.23	56.24	56.22	55.74
1993-4	54.89	55.90	56.46	57.34	61.76	67.97	73.99	74.15	77.55	80.42	78.01	72.97	67.62
1994-5	71.46	72.42	68.82	73.38	83.41	89.92	94.25	106.66	107.50	107.93	109.52	96.31	90.13
1995-6	88.31	92.71	87.06	86.43	84.25	84.32	84.04	83.65	87.25	85.90	82.71	78.86	85.46
1996-7	77.97	76.92	73.90	71.74	75.75	72.53	72.86	73.60	71.23	71.38	73.25	74.04	73.76
1997-8[1]	73.69	72.64	71.13	70.35	66.30	64.55							69.78

[1] Preliminary. *Source: Economic Research Service, U.S. Department of Agriculture (ERS-USDA)*

Average Spot Prices of U.S. Cotton,[1] Base Quality--(SLM) at Designated Markets In Cents Per Pound

Crop Year Beginning Aug. 1	Dallas (East Tex.-Okl.)	Fresno (San Joaquin Valley)	Greenville (South-east)	Green-wood (South Delta)	Lubbock (West Texas)	Memphis (North Delta)	Phoenix Desert (South-west)	Average
1987-8	61.14	66.02	63.37	62.41	61.09	62.54	65.69	63.13
1988-9	55.88	63.30	57.26	56.67	55.77	56.71	59.67	57.90
1989-90	67.11	73.47	70.64	69.50	67.06	69.51	71.19	69.78
1990-1	71.40	78.30	75.90	75.53	71.09	75.49	75.90	74.80
1991-2	55.63	57.50	57.70	56.21	55.79	56.18	57.77	56.68
1992-3	53.78	52.84	56.73	55.03	53.53	55.03	51.61	54.10
1993-4[2]	66.22	65.04	67.46	67.04	65.92	67.04	64.16	66.12
1994-5	86.96	93.73	87.17	87.25	86.66	87.25	87.96	88.14
1996-7	70.29	74.47	72.06	71.84	69.98	72.11	69.88	71.59
1997-8[3]	66.92	69.80	68.95	68.05	66.82	68.05	67.47	68.01

[1] Prices are for mixed lots, net weight, uncompressed in warehouse. [2] 1993/94 prices are for mixed lots, net weight, compressed, F.O.B. car/truck. *Source: Agricultural Marketing Service, U.S. Department of Agriculture (AMS-USDA)*

Average Price[1] Received by Farmers for Upland Cotton in the United States In Cents Per Pound

Year	Aug.	Sept.	Oct.	Nov.	Dec.	Jan.	Feb.	Mar	Apr.	May	June	July	Average
1987-8	63.8	65.4	65.1	65.6	64.6	61.7	57.0	57.9	59.9	58.3	62.0	59.5	63.7
1988-9	53.9	51.9	55.1	57.5	55.3	54.7	52.8	55.6	58.7	58.3	57.2	59.5	55.6
1989-90	60.4	63.8	65.8	65.6	61.9	60.2	61.0	63.9	65.8	66.2	64.0	63.9	63.6
1990-1	64.6	65.1	67.7	68.4	67.1	64.9	67.9	68.9	69.5	70.1	67.5	66.3	67.1
1991-2	66.3	64.9	62.9	61.2	55.7	51.7	49.8	50.3	53.1	53.2	58.0	56.3	56.8
1992-3	52.7	52.8	53.9	52.7	54.3	53.0	53.8	56.3	55.1	54.4	53.6	53.7	53.7
1993-4	52.4	51.4	52.4	53.3	56.5	62.7	65.7	66.6	67.5	69.0	63.3	58.7	58.1
1994-5	66.8	65.9	66.2	68.5	73.3	78.7	80.2	82.6	77.6	76.2	86.5	80.1	72.0
1995-6	72.2	74.8	74.2	75.0	75.7	76.4	75.7	76.8	78.9	76.7	76.9	73.6	75.4
1996-7	71.9	71.6	71.5	69.7	69.3	67.9	68.1	69.3	67.6	68.3	67.1	67.5	69.3
1997-8[2]	67.1	69.4	69.6	67.6	63.8	62.6							66.7

[1] Weighted average by sales. [2] Preliminary. *Source: Agricultural Marketing Service, U.S. Department of Agriculture (AMS-USDA)*

COTTON

Purchases Reported by Exchanges in Designated U.S. Spot Markets[1] In Running Bales

Year Beginning Aug. 1	Aug.	Sept.	Oct.	Nov.	Dec.	Jan.	Feb.	Mar.	Apr.	May	June	July	Market Total
1987-8	152,935	252,669	650,349	718,829	1,065,457	622,727	571,851	463,739	266,545	572,702	336,191	117,645	5,791,639
1988-9	288,187	166,692	230,724	163,642	323,025	383,699	811,630	388,169	307,937	282,564	261,958	282,288	3,890,515
1989-90	119,516	49,237	89,853	214,910	258,849	388,519	333,417	206,528	157,187	86,966	42,299	46,312	1,993,593
1990-1	36,735	53,948	154,499	376,790	600,752	516,421	180,949	66,869	138,503	101,180	45,731	40,551	2,312,928
1991-2	50,469	55,637	179,671	347,393	776,233	1,043,190	1,063,959	699,026	302,102	110,764	134,500	105,795	4,868,739
1992-3	81,778	233,424	325,600	853,846	1,049,780	1,321,861	317,451	330,381	224,874	208,962	189,401	231,390	5,368,748
1993-4	143,237	173,896	321,119	1,071,518	1,213,655	500,246	602,766	318,008	234,331	318,244	83,083	40,699	5,020,802
1994-5	92,401	98,251	426,371	1,075,829	1,491,429	608,701	233,159	149,762	49,192	44,228	43,821	13,244	4,326,388
1995-6	60,442	38,855	73,857	209,279	381,943	765,502	153,758	241,197	225,797	73,459	59,042	31,324	2,314,455
1996-7	62,884	73,925	148,337	477,331	613,430	696,494	412,095	242,606	72,234	130,163	201,557	93,205	3,224,261
1997-8	48,504	106,503	323,400	367,010	617,470	655,432							2,118,319

[1] Commencing March 28, 1983, spot transactions are for eight markets; and commencing September 1, 1988, spot transactions are for seven markets.
Source: Agricultural Marketing Service, U.S. Department of Agriculture (AMS-USDA)

Production of Cotton (Upland and American-Pima) in the United States In Thousands of 480-Pound Bales

Year	Upland: Alabama	Arizona	Arkansas	California	Georgia	Louisiana	Mississippi	Missouri	North Carolina	South Carolina	Tennessee	Texas	Total American-Pima
1981	422	1,556	604	3,535	159	742	1,565	168	95	164	315	5,663	79.6
1982	460	1,095	534	3,073	235	870	1,760	204	102	155	339	2,700	98.7
1983	183	725	323	1,971	112	532	900	73	43	53	151	2,380	94.7
1984	447	1,097	612	2,913	281	1,056	1,650	187	120	170	337	3,680	130.4
1985	545	928	703	3,114	370	742	1,655	204	117	180	419	3,910	155.1
1986	330	675	602	2,245	185	673	1,190	196	109	87	396	2,535	205.9
1987	397	849	901	2,989	338	977	1,745	330	98	106	634	4,635	284.6
1988	380	865	1,044	2,824	370	948	1,825	306	133	140	584	5,215	334.2
1989	383	649	851	2,661	342	868	1,555	269	141	154	476	2,870	691.7
1990	375	811	1,081	2,734	405	1,177	1,850	314	263	145	495	4,965	358.5
1991	553	898	1,576	2,548	722	1,414	2,275	429	640	344	701	4,710	398.4
1992	621	725	1,681	2,817	744	1,299	2,131	541	468	226	834	3,265	508.3
1993	469	790	1,094	2,918	733	1,105	1,550	376	429	204	545	5,095	369.3
1994	726	862	1,772	2,902	1,537	1,512	2,132	615	829	393	885	4,968	337.7
1995	492	793	1,468	2,312	1,941	1,375	1,841	513	798	376	724	4,460	367.6
1996[1]	789	778	1,636	2,390	2,079	1,286	1,876	591	1,002	455	675	4,345	528.5
1997[2]	550	820	1,730	2,200	1,900	985	1,810	580	930	400	656	5,300	537.0

[1] Preliminary. *Source: Agricultural Statistics Board, U.S. Department of Agriculture (ASB-USDA)*

Cotton Production and Yield Estimates

Year	Forecast of Production (1,000 Bales of 480 Lbs.[1]): Aug.1	Sept.1	Oct. 1	Nov. 1	Dec. 1	Jan. 1	Actual Crop	Forecasts of Yields (Lbs. Per Harvested Acre): Aug.1	Sept.1	Oct. 1	Nov. 1	Dec. 1	Jan. 1	Actual Yield
1983	7,810	7,776	7,550	7,497	7,725	------	7,771	503	501	487	504	506	------	508
1984	12,569	13,276	13,272	13,271	13,292	------	12,982	583	615	620	613	610	------	600
1985	13,780	13,655	13,638	13,875	13,810	13,534	13,432	638	632	633	644	644	630	630
1986	10,676	10,506	10,006	9,875	9,792	9,785	9,731	573	565	539	546	539	553	552
1987	12,907	12,846	13,336	13,936	14,281	14,724	14,760	615	616	640	671	695	703	706
1988	14,934	14,709	14,714	14,837	15,197	15,446	15,411	616	605	605	612	627	623	619
1989	11,834	12,279	11,991	12,102	12,083	12,233	12,196	618	603	607	608	619	619	614
1990	14,864	14,722	14,540	14,905	15,399	15,617	15,499	622	616	609	622	640	640	634
1991	17,648	17,868	17,614	13,429	14,052	17,542	17,614	630	638	620	635	630	656	652
1992	16,533	16,943	15,885	16,204	16,259	16,260	16,219	696	685	694	698	696	700	699
1993	18,545	17,867	17,014	16,297	16,284	16,176	16,134	668	645	614	594	597	607	606
1994	19,195	19,025	19,303	19,453	19,573	19,728	19,662	690	690	690	695	699	710	708
1995	21,811	20,266	18,771	18,838	18,236	17,971	17,900	663	615	574	567	551	540	537
1996	18,577	17,900	18,189	18,594	18,738	18,951	18,942	686	661	673	698	704	709	707
1997	17,783	18,418	18,410	18,848	18,819	18,977	18,977	637	658	665	673	672	686	686

[1] Net weight bales. *Source: Agricultural Statistics Board, U.S. Department of Agriculture (ASB-USDA)*

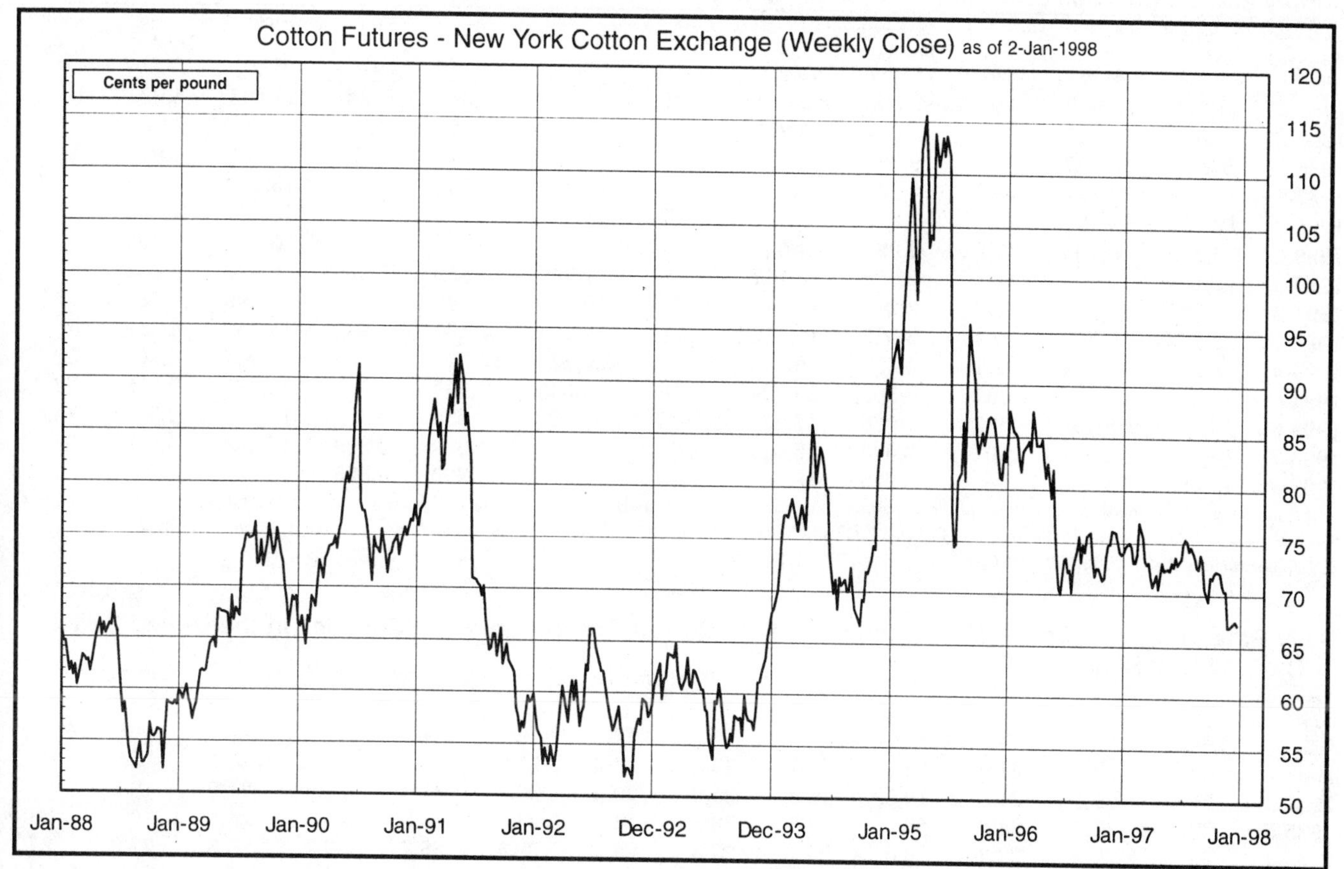

Average Open Interest of No. 2 Cotton Futures in New York In Contracts

Year	Jan.	Feb.	Mar.	Apr.	May	June	July	Aug.	Sept.	Oct.	Nov.	Dec.
1988	35,240	35,974	30,507	29,933	29,753	31,804	28,307	34,637	38,453	37,162	33,210	30,682
1989	31,415	30,978	36,725	36,657	40,761	38,693	40,059	45,894	49,629	49,072	48,136	42,349
1990	40,237	36,291	36,073	37,829	37,908	38,556	36,083	34,042	35,250	40,431	43,997	40,241
1991	43,003	46,793	44,001	43,957	50,086	46,637	40,924	39,616	38,252	39,772	39,295	36,066
1992	38,097	40,095	38,592	36,228	37,839	36,861	35,891	42,241	46,168	46,577	40,425	38,487
1993	41,946	38,657	38,576	33,641	33,012	34,057	32,118	33,872	37,393	36,479	38,567	45,975
1994	54,424	55,558	53,724	54,670	52,830	51,001	52,357	50,597	50,955	51,561	53,563	59,065
1995	71,353	75,100	79,090	71,488	71,714	68,159	65,656	69,653	69,528	65,768	38,475	35,996
1996	58,001	60,231	57,542	61,795	64,555	62,342	61,921	60,182	58,168	58,415	57,397	47,652
1997	59,909	65,392	72,130	76,779	73,464	70,296	73,893	79,309	87,134	92,430	89,150	87,120

Source: New York Cotton Exchange (NYCE)

Volume of Trading of No. 2 Cotton Futures in New York In Contracts

Year	Jan.	Feb.	Mar.	Apr.	May	June	July	Aug.	Sept.	Oct.	Nov.	Dec.	Total
1988	114,672	119,832	97,533	118,614	127,880	149,303	89,907	100,447	108,285	135,221	124,221	84,334	1,370,249
1989	124,764	135,963	113,028	118,573	135,044	167,442	91,381	151,034	165,255	143,713	178,889	124,034	1,649,120
1990	135,260	116,806	126,820	121,203	139,489	135,040	132,329	129,081	103,936	142,670	150,958	98,895	1,534,611
1991	133,415	179,656	148,918	156,978	174,690	122,242	116,458	115,175	107,742	125,558	150,545	82,867	1,614,244
1992	134,531	134,184	149,711	167,778	173,128	153,194	105,534	142,323	144,844	129,680	161,194	105,157	1,701,258
1993	171,180	135,400	136,965	135,300	105,920	128,985	130,886	122,280	110,989	107,571	178,350	139,344	1,603,027
1994	210,011	207,421	210,363	252,614	179,591	208,945	161,688	128,879	140,574	179,604	205,936	203,021	2,289,998
1995	223,073	290,600	286,098	219,187	214,052	185,276	183,171	199,050	191,534	196,676	195,601	141,116	2,525,434
1996	215,882	196,225	147,393	251,786	236,684	264,047	131,183	177,430	166,629	229,305	229,281	128,010	2,373,855
1997	201,610	253,475	302,609	258,851	175,227	314,406	234,718	202,008	212,966	216,771	266,800	197,839	2,837,280

Source: New York Cotton Exchange (NYCE)

Supply and Distribution of Upland Cotton in the United States In Thousands of 480-Pound Bales

Crop Year Beginning Aug. 1	Area: Planted (1,000 Acres)	Area: Harvested (1,000 Acres)	Yield Lbs./Acre	Supply: Beginning Stocks[3]	Supply: Production[4]	Supply: Imports	Supply: Total	Disappearance: Mill Use	Disappearance: Exports	Disappearance: Total	Ending Stocks	Farm Price[5] Cents/Lb.
1984-5	11,065	10,300	599	2,693	12,851	21	15,566	5,490	6,125	11,615	4,024	58.7
1985-6	10,601	10,145	628	4,024	13,277	33	17,334	6,352	1,855	8,207	9,289	56.8
1986-7	9,933	8,357	547	9,289	9,525	3	18,817	7,385	6,570	13,955	4,942	51.5
1987-8	10,259	9,894	702	4,942	14,475	2	19,419	7,565	6,345	13,910	5,718	63.7
1988-9	12,325	11,759	615	5,718	15,077	5	20,800	7,711	5,883	13,594	7,026	55.6
1989-90	10,210	9,166	602	7,026	11,504	2	18,532	8,686	7,242	15,928	2,798	63.6
1990-1	12,117	11,505	632	2,798	15,147	4	17,949	8,592	7,378	15,970	2,262	67.1
1991-2	13,802	12,716	650	2,262	17,216	13	19,491	9,548	6,348	15,896	3,583	56.8
1992-3	12,977	10,863	694	3,583	15,710	1	19,294	10,190	4,869	15,059	4,456	53.7
1993-4	13,248	12,594	601	4,456	15,764	6	20,226	10,346	6,555	16,901	3,303	58.1
1994-5	13,552	13,156	705	3,303	19,324	18	22,645	11,109	8,978	20,087	2,588	72.0
1995-6	16,717	15,796	533	2,588	17,532	400	20,520	10,538	7,375	17,913	2,543	75.4
1996-7[1]	14,376	12,612	701	2,543	18,413	403	21,359	11,020	6,399	17,419	3,920	69.3
1997-8[2]	13,655	13,188	666	3,920	18,300	25	22,245	11,290	6,575	17,865	4,326	

[1] Preliminary. [2] Estimate. [3] Excludes preseason ginnings (adjusted to 480-lb. bale net weight basis). [4] Includes preseason ginnings. [5] Marketing year average price. [6] Average of 5 cheapest types of SLM 1 3/32" staple length cotton offered on the European market. *Source: Economic Research Service, U.S. Department of Agriculture (ERS-USDA)*

Daily Rate of Upland Cotton Mill Consumption[2] on Cotton-System Spinning Spindles in the United States In Thousands of Running Bales

Crop Year Beginning Aug. 1	Aug.	Sept.	Oct.	Nov.	Dec.	Jan.	Feb.	Mar.	Apr.	May.	June	July	Average
1983-4	22.6	22.4	22.9	22.3	18.7	23.5	22.4	21.9	21.5	22.1	20.1	17.7	21.6
1984-5	21.4	20.4	21.4	19.5	16.9	20.0	20.9	20.8	21.0	21.9	21.0	18.5	20.3
1985-6	22.9	22.5	24.6	23.9	19.5	23.8	24.9	24.6	24.8	25.2	24.4	20.9	23.4
1986-7	26.7	26.2	27.3	26.5	23.1	27.3	28.1	29.4	28.7	29.3	28.3	27.0	27.3
1987-8	30.3	30.1	31.0	30.3	24.4	28.4	29.5	29.5	27.8	27.6	26.5	21.7	28.1
1988-9	28.8	27.7	27.6	26.1	22.9	28.3	29.2	30.0	31.2	32.2	31.9	27.9	28.6
1989-90	32.9	32.8	33.0	30.6	25.9	29.9	31.4	31.5	30.9	31.8	32.8	27.8	30.9
1990-1	33.8	41.4	33.2	30.2	29.7	---	32.3	---	---	34.0	---	---	33.5
1991-2	33.6	---	---	33.1	---	34.6	36.3	35.7	35.6	37.3	35.2	33.9	35.0
1992-3	38.5	37.8	39.7	37.6	31.5	39.1	39.5	38.8	38.7	39.4	37.8	34.5	37.8
1993-4	39.8	38.4	39.4	36.4	31.4	36.9	37.9	39.0	39.3	39.5	40.4	40.3	38.2
1994-5	41.0	41.4	41.1	41.8	41.7	42.6	42.1	42.4	41.1	40.2	39.2	37.2	41.0
1995-6	38.8	39.4	37.6	38.1	37.9	37.5	38.1	39.5	39.4	39.6	40.6	39.8	38.9
1996-7	40.5	40.7	40.5	41.5	41.1	41.2	40.4	39.4	41.0	41.0	40.9	42.5	40.9
1997-8[1]	40.8	42.4	42.0	42.5	43.9								42.3

[1] Preliminary. [2] Not seasonally adjusted. *Source: Bureau of the Census, U.S. Department of Commerce*

Consumption of American and Foreign Cotton in the United States In Thousands of Running Bales

Year	Aug.	Sept.	Oct.	Nov.	Dec.	Jan.	Feb.	Mar.	Apr.	May	June	July	Total
1983-4	453	560	459	446	468	469	448	548	430	442	503	354	5,628
1984-5	428	509	428	390	423	399	418	519	419	439	525	369	5,268
1985-6	458	562	493	477	486	595	499	492	620	503	489	522	6,198
1986-7	534	523	683	529	576	546	562	734	573	586	708	540	7,096
1987-8	606	753	621	606	610	568	590	738	556	551	662	433	7,294
1988-9	577	693	552	523	572	568	584	751	623	645	798	559	7,444
1989-90	689	860	690	642	685	630	658	826	650	667	826	559	8,383
1990-1	680	835	671	610	601	---	2,068	---	---	2,212	---	---	8,367
1991-2	2,215	---	---	2,199	---	870	730	898	718	752	885	682	9,949
1992-3	776	950	799	756	792	788	796	976	778	792	951	694	9,846
1993-4	801	965	792	731	790	743	785	999	806	830	1,032	744	10,019
1994-5	870	1,070	873	838	897	858	878	1,097	847	842	999	681	10,750
1995-6[1]	829	1,020	798	761	801	744	787	1,029	810	824	1,040	731	10,174
1996-7	847	1,028	829	816	858	810	819	1,014	834	840	1,044	781	10,519
1997-8[1]	868	1,100	872	855	954								11,157

[1] Preliminary. *Source: Bureau of the Census, U.S. Department of Commerce*

Exports of All Cotton[2] from the United States In Thousands of Running Bales

Year	Aug.	Sept.	Oct.	Nov.	Dec.	Jan.	Feb.	Mar.	Apr.	May	June	July	Total
1983-4	369	329	308	438	566	821	737	783	839	494	429	370	6,483
1984-5	454	249	340	472	712	755	705	692	556	435	359	299	6,028
1985-6	166	218	180	198	236	189	202	206	125	69	68	19	1,876
1986-7[2]	374	496	489	525	664	591	518	750	500	465	554	439	6,365
1987-8	355	304	316	612	536	698	879	649	565	537	486	359	6,296
1988-9	248	173	292	352	524	756	514	597	575	795	515	649	5,990
1989-90	431	384	507	469	516	909	840	882	818	495	510	550	7,311
1990-1	480	355	433	591	639	1,112	950	804	960	488	404	273	7,489
1991-2	219	126	239	396	674	961	725	791	787	535	430	466	6,349
1992-3	252	263	277	342	528	501	502	533	639	401	317	395	4,950
1993-4	287	248	345	405	571	738	512	743	761	854	770	626	6,860
1994-5	531	333	341	710	1,098	1,115	1,383	1,392	1,104	684	410	300	9,402
1995-6	315	245	452	733	1,230	1,262	1,295	777	576	343	263	183	7,675
1996-7	257	171	277	573	899	666	728	848	711	631	604	501	6,866
1997-8[1]	458	299	400										4,628

[1] Preliminary. [2] Data prior to 1986-7 are for American Cotton only. *Source: Foreign Agricultural Service, U.S. Department of Agriculture (FAS-USDA)*

U.S. Exports of American Cotton to Countries of Destination In Thousands of 480-Pound Bales

Crop Year Beginning Aug. 1	Canada	China	Hong Kong	Indo-nesia	Italy	Japan	Rep. of Korea	Mexico	Philip-pines	Taiwan	Thai-land	United Kingdom	Total
1983-4	227	12	283	320	252	1,709	1,269	------	59	495	244	67	6,785
1984-5	195	6	125	258	301	1,464	1,257	------	58	513	139	72	6,211
1985-6	98	------	1	105	91	520	513	------	8	46	17	35	1,958
1986-7	70	------	52	324	263	1,723	1,330	------	153	907	239	56	6,685
1987-8	153	------	88	287	406	1,569	1,450	------	135	424	248	69	6,582
1988-9	148	793	108	307	239	1,381	1,302	------	50	254	172	37	6,147
1989-90	197	670	244	499	431	1,594	1,365	117	134	320	375	74	7,694
1990-1	191	1,233	306	561	425	1,437	1,168	202	132	358	317	36	7,793
1991-2	181	792	335	739	240	1,107	1,024	213	181	380	368	60	6,646
1992-3	154	1	100	429	144	839	1,031	557	117	279	150	65	5,201
1993-4	165	1,183	314	653	96	790	976	653	168	356	277	65	6,862
1994-5	253	2,257	347	925	83	1,061	951	558	173	352	441	89	9,402
1995-6[1]	294	1,847	223	794	115	940	769	618	144	255	331	85	7,675
1996-7[2]	253	1,756	129	594	46	630	568	733	84	255	197	66	6,865

[1] Preliminary. [2] Estimate. *Source: Foreign Agricultural Service, U.S. Department of Agriculture (FAS-USDA)*

Cotton[1] Government Loan Program in the United States

Crop Year Beginning Aug. 1	Support Price	Target Price	Put Under Support	% of Pro-duction	Acquired	Owned July 31	Crop Year Beginning Aug. 1	Support Price	Target Price	Put Under Support	% of Pro-duction	Acquired	Owned July 31
	--- ¢ per Pound ---		Ths Bales		----- Ths. Bales -----			--- ¢ per Pound ---		Ths Bales		---- Ths. Bales ----	
1985-6	57.30	81.0	7,287	54.9	161	792	1991-2	50.77	72.9	6,312	36.6	8	[3]
1986-7	55.00	81.0	6,170	64.8	12	24	1991-2	50.77	72.9	6,312	36.6	8	[3]
1987-8	52.25	79.4	5,362	37.0	131	3	1993-4	52.35	72.9	7,721	49.0	3	14
1988-9	51.80	75.9	11,231	74.5	66	35	1994-5	50.00	72.9	4,716	24.4	[3]	[3]
1989-90	50.00	73.4	3,732	32.4	2	27	1995-6[2]	51.92	72.9	3,478	19.8	0	0
1990-1	50.27	72.9	3,205	21.1	1	4	1996-7[2]	51.92	-----	-----	-----	-----	-----

[1] Upland. [2] Preliminary. [3] Less than 500 bales. NA = Not available. *Source: Economic Research Service, U.S. Department of Agriculture (ERS)*

Production Cotton Cloth[1] in the United States In Millions of Square Yards

Year	First Quarter	Second Quarter	Third Quarter	Fourth Quarter	Total Year	Year	First Quarter	Second Quarter	Third Quarter	Fourth Quarter	Total Year
1986	1,037	1,103	1,095	1,129	4,364	1992	1,154	1,172	1,130	1,144	4,600
1987	1,158	1,217	1,219	1,178	4,772	1993	1,150	1,144	1,071	1,039	4,403
1988	1,252	1,255	1,072	1,052	5,632	1994	1,073	1,125	1,131	1,143	4,473
1989	1,157	1,192	1,134	1,106	4,589	1995	1,169	1,137	1,090	1,093	4,488
1990	1,202	1,127	1,087	1,048	4,463	1996	1,067	1,109	1,072	1,076	4,323
1991	1,081	1,148	1,082	1,093	4,404	1997[2]	1,133	1,164	1,132		4,573

[1] Cotton broadwoven goods over 12 inches in width. [2] Preliminary. *Source: Bureau of the Census, U.S. Department of Commerce*

COTTON

Cotton Ginnings[1] in the United States To: In Thousands of Running Bales

Crop Year	Aug. 1	Aug. 15	Sept. 1	Sept. 15	Oct. 1	Oct. 15	Nov. 1	Nov. 15	Dec. 1	Dec. 15	Jan. 1	Jan. 15	Feb. 1	Total Crop
1985-6	70	NA	681	1,073	2,431	4,342	6,246	8,216	10,052	11,372	12,365	12,776	12,948	13,063
1986-7	145	NA	624	1,022	2,407	3,618	5,292	6,369	7,491	8,263	8,588	9,093	9,270	9,294
1987-8	1	NA	429	1,242	3,196	5,359	7,531	9,135	11,082	12,588	13,276	13,733	14,177	14,493
1988-9	136	NA	804	1,147	2,279	4,116	6,922	9,535	11,845	13,257	14,248	14,686	14,904	14,939
1989-90	90	NA	382	523	981	2,772	5,948	8,388	10,353	11,246	11,548	11,681	11,771	11,913
1990-1	120	NA	583	1,090	2,616	4,739	7,955	10,207	12,428	13,863	14,516	14,809	14,963	15,082
1991-2	NA	NA	699	983	2,467	4,955	8,351	10,752	13,260	15,067	15,888	16,402	16,765	17,146
1992-3	14	NA	446	740	1,664	4,046	7,584	10,296	12,597	14,083	14,944	15,311	15,527	15,786
1993-4	9	NA	435	748	1,846	4,471	7,975	10,952	13,244	14,695	15,321	15,517	15,590	15,675
1994-5	113	NA	680	943	2,324	5,002	8,878	12,479	15,587	17,465	18,438	18,842	19,028	19,127
1995-6	17	433	898	2,455	4,795	8,430	11,262	14,199	16,102	17,011	17,292	17,416	17,469	
1996-7	48	342	637	2,146	4,780	8,876	11,943	14,659	16,664	17,685	18,110	18,321	18,436	
1997-8[2]	2	366	683	1,295	3,829	8,115	11,603	14,746	16,796	17,761	18,062	18,346		

[1] Excluding linters. [2] Preliminary. NA = Not available. *Source: National Agricultural Statistics Service, U.S. Department of Agriculture (NASS-USDA)*

Fiber Prices in the United States In Cents Per Pound

Year		Cotton[1] Actual	Cotton[1] Raw[5] Equivalent	Rayon[2] Actual	Rayon[2] Raw[5] Equivalent	Polyester[3] Actual	Polyester[3] Raw[5] Equivalent	Price Ratios[4] in Percent Cotton/Rayon	Price Ratios[4] in Percent Cotton/Polyester
1985		65.83	73.15	78.83	82.12	66.33	69.10	.89	1.06
1986		60.99	67.77	75.75	78.91	62.33	64.93	.86	1.04
1987		72.71	80.79	81.00	84.38	65.75	68.49	.96	1.18
1988		64.89	72.10	90.67	94.44	73.83	76.91	.77	.94
1989		71.99	79.99	109.75	114.32	85.67	89.24	.70	.90
1990		79.29	88.10	119.92	124.91	82.58	86.02	.71	1.03
1991		79.05	87.83	122.00	127.08	73.50	76.56	.69	1.15
1992		61.92	68.80	114.08	118.84	73.50	76.56	.58	.90
1993		62.43	69.37	111.42	116.06	72.50	75.52	.60	.92
1994		78.69	87.43	103.00	107.29	74.92	78.04	.82	1.12
1995		100.76	111.95	118.67	123.61	88.83	92.53	.91	1.21
1996		86.24	95.83	118.00	122.92	81.10	84.48	.78	1.14
1997	Jan.	77.97	86.63	115.00	119.79	70.00	72.92	.72	1.19
	Feb.	77.68	86.31	115.00	119.79	70.00	72.92	.72	1.18
	Mar.	77.95	86.61	115.00	119.79	70.00	72.92	.72	1.19
	Apr.	75.18	83.53	115.00	119.79	68.00	70.83	.70	1.18
	May	75.54	83.93	115.00	119.79	68.00	70.83	.70	1.18
	June	77.09	85.66	115.00	119.79	68.00	70.83	.70	1.19
	July	78.47	87.19	115.00	119.79	68.00	70.83	.73	1.23
	Aug.	77.59	86.21	115.00	119.79	68.00	70.83	.72	1.22
	Sept.	76.56	85.07	115.00	119.79	71.00	73.96	.71	1.15
	Oct.	74.96	83.29	115.00	119.79	71.00	73.96	.70	1.13
	Nov.	74.97	83.30	115.00	119.79	71.00	73.96	.70	1.13

[1] SLM-1 1/16" at group B Mill points, net weight. [2] 1.5 and 3.0 denier, regular rayon staples. [3] Reported average market price for 1.5 denier polyester staple for cotton blending. [4] Raw fiber equivalent. [5] Actual prices converted to estimated raw fiber equivalent as follows: cotton, divided by 0.90, rayon and polyester, divided by 0.96. *Source: Economic Research Service, U.S. Department of Agriculture (ERS-USDA)*

Average Producer Price Index of Gray Cotton Broadwovens Index 1982=100

Year	Jan.	Feb.	Mar.	Apr.	May	June	July	Aug.	Sept.	Oct.	Nov.	Dec.	Average
1987	101.8	101.8	101.9	102.5	103.0	103.3	106.0	103.9	107.1	109.5	110.6	111.5	105.2
1988	112.7	114.3	114.5	115.9	116.2	116.1	115.9	115.6	114.8	111.9	112.5	112.3	114.4
1989	112.4	111.3	110.9	110.9	110.5	110.1	109.4	109.8	109.8	110.8	110.9	113.5	110.9
1990	113.7	113.8	113.8	114.0	114.1	109.9	115.1	115.1	112.3	112.5	116.1	116.4	113.8
1991	113.3	113.6	114.1	114.5	114.9	115.2	115.3	115.3	115.3	115.4	115.7	115.6	114.9
1992	116.9	116.8	116.7	116.7	116.8	117.5	117.3	117.3	117.2	116.9	117.1	117.2	117.0
1993	117.0	116.8	115.9	116.3	115.7	115.7	115.2	115.2	112.5	114.1	114.1	114.9	115.3
1994	109.9	110.8	115.4	115.7	114.9	114.9	115.0	117.5	117.6	118.9	117.2	118.0	115.5
1995	117.8	120.2	120.7	121.6	123.4	123.6	124.1	125.4	125.3	123.7	123.7	123.8	122.8
1996	123.6	123.7	122.0	122.0	121.1	120.7	120.7	119.9	119.7	120.4	120.0	120.4	121.2
1997[1]	120.3	120.8	120.7	120.8	121.2	120.6	121.4	121.6	121.5	121.3	122.1	121.5	121.1

[1] Preliminary. *Source: Bureau of Labor Statistics (0337-01), U.S. Department of Commerce (BLS)*

Cottonseed and Products

Cottonseed production is directly related to the amount of cotton produced. In the 1997-98 (Aug.-Sept.) marketing year, the U.S. planted 13.91 million acres to cotton and harvested 13.44 million, 570,000 acres more than in 1996-97. The season got off to a poor start in the Delta states where it was cold and wet. Problems with seed germination led a number of producers in northern Alabama, Mississippi and Tennessee to plow up planted cotton acreage. Overall, the season turned out well as weather was generally favorable. Production was estimated by the USDA at 18.85 million bales with a national average yield of 673 pounds per acre.

The USDA reported that cottonseed stocks on August 1, 1997 were 523,000 short tons. Cottonseed production was estimated at 7.06 million tons, down about one percent from a year earlier. The total supply of cottonseed was estimated at 7.58 million tons, down slightly from the previous year. The cottonseed crush was estimated at 3.85 million tons. Cottonseed exports were forecast to be 100,000 tons, down almost 14 percent from the year before. Use of cottonseed for other purposes, such as feeding livestock, was estimated at 3.18 million tons, about the same as the previous year. Total use of cottonseed in 1997-98 was estimated at 7.13 million tons. Ending stocks on July 31, 1998 were projected to be 450,000 tons.

U.S. cottonseed oil stocks on October 1, 1997 were 74 million pounds. Cottonseed oil production in 1997-98 was forecast by USDA to be 1.23 billion pounds, unchanged from 1996-97. U.S. domestic use of cottonseed oil was estimated at 1.03 billion pounds and exports were estimated at 200 million pounds. Projected stocks on September 30, 1998 were 80 million pounds.

Cottonseed meal production in 1997-98 was forecast to be 1.74 million tons. U.S. domestic use was projected to be 1.64 million tons with exports of 105,000 tons. Projected stocks of cottonseed meal on September 30, 1998 were 51,000 tons.

World Production of Cottonseed In Thousands of Metric Tons

Crop Year	Argentina	Australia	Brazil	China	Egypt	Greece	India	Mexico	Pakistan	Turkey	United States	Former U.S.S.R.	World Total
1989-90	495	493	1,255	7,008	498	440	4,610	255	2,911	987	4,243	4,600	31,242
1990-1	538	686	1,352	8,340	504	365	3,980	294	3,275	977	5,415	4,550	33,919
1991-2	435	724	1,313	10,499	491	355	4,090	307	4,352	878	6,283	4,283	37,691
1992-3	275	528	800	8,340	571	410	4,740	52	3,080	905	5,652	3,557	32,196
1993-4	390	466	920	6,655	655	460	4,120	31	2,740	892	5,754	3,600	29,688
1994-5	631	474	980	7,727	411	574	4,709	187	2,959	930	6,898	3,360	33,105
1995-6	760	595	690	8,487	384	725	5,339	344	3,604	1,263	6,213	3,150	35,254
1996-7[1]	590	859	580	7,481	560	540	5,900	375	3,230	1,200	6,480	2,600	34,301
1997-8[2]	800	903	700	7,000	570	590	5,600	265	3,600	1,150	6,404	3,050	34,696

[1] Preliminary. [2] Estimate. *Source: Oil World*

Salient Statistics of Cottonseed in the United States

Crop Year Beginning Aug. 1	Supply: Stocks	Supply: Production	Supply: Total Supply	Disappearance: Crush	Disappearance: Exports	Disappearance: Other	Disappearance: Total Disappearance	Farm Price $/Ton	Value of Production Mil. $	Products Produced: Oil Millions Lbs.	Products Produced: Meal Thousand Sh. Tons
	In Thousands of Short Tons										
1989-90	665	4,677	5,342	2,974	46	1,957	4,977	105	492.7	1,039	1,327
1990-1	366	5,969	6,337	3,369	53	2,264	5,686	121	722.3	1,154	1,691
1991-2	651	6,926	7,579	3,981	161	2,977	7,119	71	492.3	1,279	1,765
1992-3	460	6,230	6,690	3,629	192	2,504	6,325	98	608.4	1,137	1,533
1993-4	365	6,343	6,708	3,470	157	2,649	6,276	113	714.4	1,119	1,563
1994-5	432	7,604	8,036	3,947	232	3,306	7,485	101	771.3	1,312	1,830
1995-6	551	6,849	7,399	3,882	114	2,886	6,882	106	730.4	1,229	1,748
1996-7[1]	517	7,144	7,661	3,860	116	3,162	7,138	126	892.9	1,216	1,752
1997-8[2]	523	7,278	7,801	3,850	125	3,226	7,251	106-120	NA	1,250	1,755

[1] Preliminary. [2] Estimate. *Source: Economic Research Service, U.S. Department of Agriculture (ERS-USDA)*

Average Wholesale Price of Cottonseed Meal (41% Solvent) at Memphis In Dollars Per Short Ton

Year	Jan.	Feb.	Mar.	Apr.	May	June	July	Aug.	Sept.	Oct.	Nov.	Dec.	Average
1989	200.50	191.25	196.25	184.40	161.50	163.30	157.50	172.00	190.00	181.25	180.00	180.00	179.83
1990	160.00	150.00	146.25	150.00	155.00	147.50	161.50	169.50	178.75	163.00	147.50	141.25	155.85
1991	125.00	118.10	125.00	122.50	118.10	117.20	127.50	130.90	133.10	131.00	144.40	162.00	129.57
1992	156.25	140.10	124.25	121.25	127.50	132.50	133.75	146.90	163.00	154.40	157.50	174.50	144.33
1993	164.40	149.40	153.50	149.00	143.10	153.00	170.30	178.50	193.75	173.10	181.00	180.00	165.75
1994	170.30	173.10	174.00	166.25	157.75	154.10	152.50	144.50	145.00	134.40	120.50	114.20	150.55
1995	106.75	97.50	100.30	98.10	92.75	108.75	116.90	116.50	137.60	153.25	165.00	185.80	123.27
1996	208.80	202.80	195.60	220.00	191.25	192.20	201.56	193.10	193.10	183.25	196.60	224.50	200.23
1997[1]	207.20	183.75	189.10	189.10	193.75	190.30	170.75	176.25	192.00	189.10	189.10	190.50	188.41

[1] Preliminary. *Source: Economic Research Service, U.S. Department of Agriculture (ERS-USDA)*

COTTONSEED AND PRODUCTS

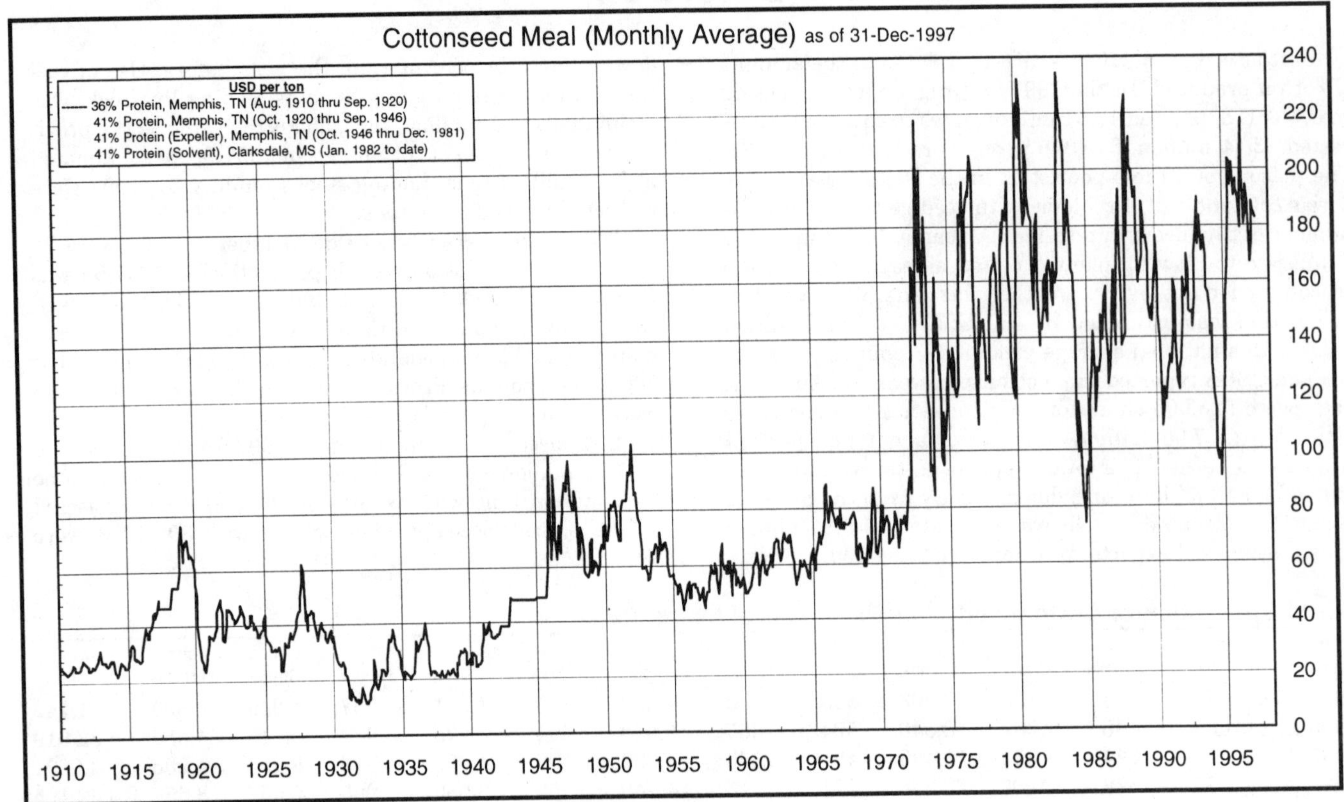

Supply & Distribution of Cottonseed Oil in the United States In Millions of Pounds

Crop Year Beginning Oct. 1	Supply: Stocks	Supply: Production	Supply: Imports	Supply: Total Supply	Disappearance: Domestic	Disappearance: Exports	Disappearance: Total	Per Capita Consump. of Salad & Ck. Oils -- In Lbs.--	Utilization Food Uses: Shortening	Utilization Food Uses: Salad & Cooking Oils	Utilization Food Uses: Total	Prices: U.S.[3] (Crude) $/Tonne	Prices: Rott[4] (Cif) $/Tonne
1991-2	137	1,279	18	1,434	1,075	281	1,356	25	247	375	685	443	545
1992-3	78	1,137	38	1,253	995	177	1,172	26	238	353	640	551	688
1993-4	81	1,119	26	1,226	873	248	1,121	25	217	289	558	684	750
1994-5	106	1,312	0	1,417	1,006	329	1,335	26	217	262	532	683	671
1995-6	82	1,229	.3	1,311	996	221	1,217	27	218	235	497	575	613
1996-7[1]	94	1,216	.3	1,310	1,012	232	1,244	27	271	265	556	564	590
1997-8[2]	66	1,250	.3	1,317	1,015	220	1,235					619	663

[1] Preliminary. [2] Estimate. [3] F.O.B.; Greenwood, MS. (Tank Cars). [4] Rotterdam;U.S. PBSY *Source: Economic Research Service, U.S. Department of Agriculture (ERS-USDA)*

United States Consumption of Crude Cottonseed Oil in Refining In Millions of Pounds

Year	Oct.	Nov.	Dec.	Jan.	Feb	Mar.	Apr.	May	June	July	Aug.	Sept.	Total
1991-2		265.0		104.6	108.9	101.3	88.7	76.0	84.2	84.6	72.7	48.6	1,034.6
1992-3	75.7	93.3	95.5	107.3	85.1	77.5	92.8	79.3	74.7	65.1	68.6	57.6	972.5
1993-4	82.7	113.0	103.8	110.8	96.7	111.5	69.6	74.8	73.2	74.6	88.4	64.2	1,063.3
1994-5	81.9	97.2	109.8	107.7	87.1	96.2	87.2	72.8	73.4	76.0	83.3	71.6	1,044.4
1995-6	76.1	91.8	89.7	94.5	87.2	92.2	83.4	77.3	55.5	56.2	64.3	54.4	922.5
1996-7	67.2	85.1	85.1	88.7	83.3	80.8	77.4	79.2	58.4	55.3	59.0	39.2	858.7
1997-8[1]	73.1	73.1	77.2										893.9

[1] Preliminary. *Source: Bureau of the Census, U.S. Department of Commerce*

United States Exports of Cottonseed Oil (Crude and Refined) In Thousands of Pounds

Year	Jan.	Feb.	Mar.	Apr.	May	June	July	Aug.	Sept.	Oct.	Nov.	Dec	Total
1991		55,378			67,155			52,469			38,291		213,293
1992	68,977	69,631	19,704	19,753	13,071	13,443	16,027	7,947	13,090	8,101	4,625	17,308	271,677
1993	23,904	14,238	6,294	27,370	25,849	17,685	5,066	7,065	19,246	7,079	15,103	14,075	182,974
1994	32,011	11,093	21,156	26,595	34,921	11,583	24,303	24,644	25,265	17,487	33,385	36,613	299,056
1995	18,808	43,454	48,471	34,500	28,775	22,692	18,490	11,973	NA	9,896	30,268	13,223	280,550
1996	26,407	8,103	38,597	24,628	16,052	14,135	7,827	21,197	10,903	12,526	10,345	20,918	211,638
1997[1]	25,722	26,835	22,647	22,230	30,319	9,535	25,207						278,563

[1] Preliminary. NA = Not available. *Source: Economic Research Service, U.S. Department of Agriculture (ERS-USDA)*

Cottonseed Crushed (Consumption) in the United States   In Thousands of Short Tons

Year	Aug.	Sept.	Oct.	Nov.	Dec.	Jan.	Feb.	Mar.	Apr.	May	June	July	Total
1989-90	218.8	150.6	273.4	338.3	335.1	346.6	285.1	254.8	245.5	201.5	194.9	129.3	2,974
1990-1	157.3	176.1	274.9	339.4	320.8		973.0			864.5		------	3,106
1991-2	813.6			1,145.2		420.6	378.3	381.3	297.8	245.4	292.1	270.2	4,245
1992-3	245.7	162.9	323.2	353.3	372.1	413.3	334.6	324.1	323.8	296.4	242.7	237.2	3,629
1993-4	182.9	162.6	300.4	391.4	375.0	391.0	335.2	358.6	265.7	257.7	239.4	210.2	3,470
1994-5	192.1	195.5	343.9	386.2	397.5	404.6	360.5	391.0	345.4	304.0	316.5	310.0	3,947
1995-6	264.4	245.5	337.1	386.7	362.4	402.3	373.5	381.4	349.6	325.2	223.7	209.2	3,861
1996-7	229.2	225.0	331.7	355.1	352.6	381.0	362.8	362.2	334.4	351.3	280.8	294.0	3,860
1997-8[1]	244.4	178.6	329.7	374.5	379.3								3,616

[1] Preliminary. *Source: Economic Research Service, U.S. Department of Agriculture (ERS-USDA)*

Production of Cottonseed Cake and Meal in the United States   In Thousands of Short Tons

Year	Aug.	Sept.	Oct.	Nov.	Dec.	Jan.	Feb.	Mar.	Apr.	May	June	July	Total
1988-9	100.7	80.1	135.4	170.0	172.5	183.2	151.6	175.3	152.7	157.6	126.7	106.1	1,712
1990-1	68.7	77.4	128.2	160.1	148.8		456.2			409.1		-------	1,449
1991-2	388.6			533.9		192.6	170.5	173.5	138.2	111.7	129.9	127.8	1,967
1992-3	111.2	76.0	143.7	150.2	160.5	176.2	146.6	136.4	140.9	126.1	103.0	101.0	1,572
1993-4	76.7	71.5	130.1	172.2	166.6	161.8	151.8	164.0	119.6	116.1	106.9	93.4	1,531
1994-5	90.6	89.4	154.2	171.5	176.9	184.1	162.2	174.3	154.2	137.4	143.9	137.2	1,776
1995-6	120.1	113.6	159.9	178.2	161.0	183.8	169.8	168.3	158.7	147.1	102.4	102.7	1,766
1996-7	100.9	99.1	146.1	161.5	158.2	174.5	164.6	162.1	152.2	160.7	128.6	123.2	1,732
1997-8[1]	128.2	92.1	147.8	168.7	177.3								1,714

[1] Preliminary. *Source: Bureau of the Census, U.S. Department of Commerce*

U.S. Production of Crude Cottonseed Oil[2]   In Millions of Pounds

Year	Aug.	Sept.	Oct.	Nov.	Dec.	Jan.	Feb.	Mar.	Apr.	May	June	July	Total
1989-90	81.9	56.8	97.6	115.3	117.4	118.4	98.2	89.4	88.8	74.7	75.4	48.0	1,062
1990-1	58.7	57.6	86.2	104.0	102.3		309.9			283.0		------	1,002
1991-2	263.7			398.9		137.4	127.2	121.5	97.5	79.3	91.8	91.3	1,409
1992-3	77.8	56.8	99.5	110.2	117.6	134.7	107.2	104.9	101.7	96.1	77.7	76.5	1,161
1993-4	59.1	51.7	93.5	122.2	117.5	124.7	99.9	119.6	85.3	85.2	78.4	69.8	1,107
1994-5	61.7	61.0	109.8	122.6	125.6	133.4	115.6	125.2	110.4	97.7	102.4	96.6	1,262
1995-6	87.8	84.3	105.2	121.6	111.6	130.9	121.4	125.6	110.4	101.9	73.3	76.7	1,251
1996-7	70.3	69.4	98.9	114.8	115.9	123.9	114.8	114.7	103.7	109.8	86.9	85.9	1,209
1997-8[1]	80.6	66.0	97.8	120.3	122.2								1,169

[1] Preliminary. [2] Not seasonally adjusted. *Source: Bureau of the Census, U.S. Department of Commerce*

United States Production of Refined Cottonseed Oil   In Millions of Pounds

Year	Aug.	Sept.	Oct.	Nov.	Dec.	Jan.	Feb.	Mar.	Apr.	May	June	July	Total
1989-90	86.6	69.1	79.8	111.8	111.6	122.3	94.4	109.7	80.4	74.8	65.0	50.8	1,056
1990-1	57.8	53.7	75.4	96.0	90.0		253.9			256.3		-------	883
1991-2	209.3			205.0		103.2	105.6	97.9	85.6	73.4	82.1	81.1	1,043
1992-3	69.3	46.3	72.6	90.2	91.9	103.1	82.0	74.5	88.8	75.6	70.8	62.4	928
1993-4	65.1	54.6	79.4	109.1	100.6	107.2	93.4	107.8	66.9	71.6	70.0	72.2	998
1994-5	86.3	62.9	80.0	94.4	106.2	104.2	94.4	92.6	84.2	70.1	70.7	72.6	1,019
1995-6	80.5	69.0	74.0	89.5	86.9	91.7	84.6	89.8	81.7	75.0	53.8	54.5	931
1996-7	62.4	53.0	64.9	82.8	82.2	85.9	80.7	78.1	75.2	76.9	56.4	53.6	852
1997-8[1]	57.4	38.1	48.3	71.0	74.8								695

[1] Preliminary. *Source: Bureau of the Census, U.S. Department of Commerce*

U.S. Stocks of Cottonseed Oil (Crude & Refined) at End of Month   In Millions of Pounds

Year	Aug.	Sept.	Oct.	Nov.	Dec.	Jan.	Feb.	Mar.	Apr.	May	June	July
1989-90	191.4	147.3	138.3	163.2	189.6	186.8	180.9	174.8	168.8	156.1	135.6	111.8
1990-1	75.9	80.4	83.0	93.5	102.7		145.8			124.3		-------
1991-2	136.3			163.3		193.1	183.6	180.3	171.5	154.0	139.9	119.8
1992-3	94.3	81.0	93.1	101.7	123.2	148.4	152.6	167.1	157.0	159.2	144.8	143.8
1993-4	85.8	54.6	79.4	109.1	100.6	107.2	93.4	107.8	66.9	71.6	70.0	72.1
1994-5	112.4	105.6	103.5	117.0	114.7	122.2	150.5	129.9	120.8	95.7	96.9	92.2
1995-6	87.8	82.1	82.6	89.3	94.8	118.2	147.2	151.2	155.6	143.3	128.1	125.4
1996-7	101.2	94.1	97.5	102.5	106.0	120.9	133.7	137.5	131.7	116.1	103.4	85.9
1997-8[1]	78.0	66.4	68.6	86.4	104.6							

[1] Preliminary. *Source: Bureau of the Census, U.S. Department of Commerce*

COTTONSEED AND PRODUCTS

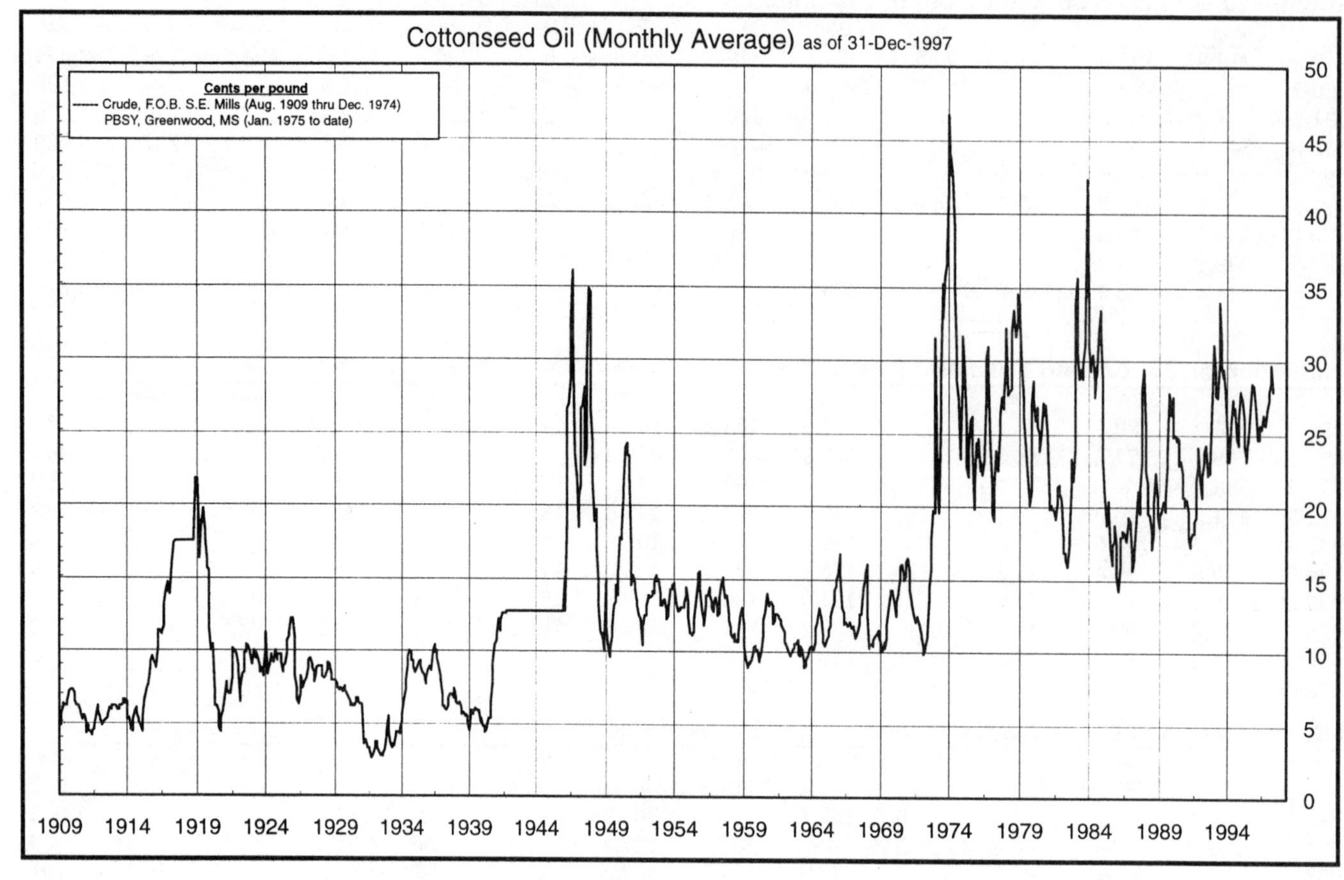

Average Price of Crude Cottonseed Oil, PBSY, Greenwood, MS[1] (Tank Cars) In Cents Per Pound

Year	Jan.	Feb.	Mar.	Apr.	May	June	July	Aug.	Sept.	Oct.	Nov.	Dec.	Average
1988	21.31	20.19	19.60	21.00	22.88	26.65	30.25	15.00	23.00	21.44	19.70	19.94	21.75
1989	19.19	17.56	20.25	21.06	21.80	20.25	19.63	18.60	19.75	19.95	20.81	20.50	19.95
1990	19.95	20.19	22.88	22.83	26.90	26.94	26.00	24.60	24.88	24.80	24.19	24.75	24.08
1991	23.75	22.88	23.00	22.13	20.67	20.31	20.50	21.00	19.88	17.98	17.41	18.07	20.63
1992	18.50	18.13	19.25	19.38	21.38	22.58	24.45	21.86	21.04	22.17	22.96	23.91	21.30
1993	24.09	22.03	22.24	22.55	22.70	26.76	30.74	30.45	28.98	24.79	26.69	30.39	26.03
1994	33.16	29.96	29.60	29.06	29.66	27.55	24.20	23.71	24.51	23.64	24.85	25.50	27.12
1995	28.70	29.95	27.14	27.61	27.51	30.04	30.63	30.26	28.61	27.61	26.27	26.10	26.36
1996	24.45	24.35	24.25	26.77	28.46	27.94	28.25	27.81	26.13	24.55	24.28	24.29	25.96
1997	25.21	25.44	26.18	25.10	25.19	25.01	26.53	27.11	28.03	28.47	29.11	26.78	26.51

[1] Data prior to 1995 are F.O.B. Valley Points, Southeastern mills. *Source: Economic Research Service, U.S Department of Agriculture (ERS-USDA)*

United States Exports of Cottonseed Oil to Important Countries In Thousands of Metric Tons

Year	Canada	Dominican Republic	Egypt	Guat-emala	Japan	Mexico	Nether-lands	Salvador	South Korea	Turkey	Venez-uela	Total
1987	3.2	5.0	1.9	2.4	15.7	3.1	2.9	15.6	7.8	-----	47.3	109.9
1988	4.8	3.1	29.6	.5	21.5	8.2	2.7	26.3	7.7	13.5	46.2	167.8
1989	6.6	5.1	39.4	6.0	34.3	3.2	3.4	30.5	21.0	2.0	53.7	209.4
1990	6.8	6.0	14.7	.4	36.7	1.4	2.9	21.0	36.0	-----	9.2	136.3
1991	7.8	2.1	14.7	-----	24.1	4.8	3.4	13.0	13.0	5.5	4.2	97.0
1992	11.3	1.0	8.2	3.2	15.3	8.5	17.4	26.5	10.9	7.0	3.7	123.3
1993	10.9	-----	-----	.5	17.6	5.8	.2	30.8	6.6	.5	1.5	83.1
1994	10.8	-----	7.5	12.3	29.8	10.3	1.9	26.1	16.9	-----	4.5	135.7
1995	12.0	-----	10.3	1.9	17.9	5.7	1.5	37.8	19.2	-----	2.8	133.7
1996[1]	23.2	-----	-----	1.7	15.8	3.3	-----	20.6	7.2	2.0	-----	100.0

[1] Prelminary. *Source: The Oil World*

CRB Futures Index

The Commodity Research Bureau Futures Price Index was first calculated by Commodity Research Bureau, Inc. in 1957 and made its innaugural appearance in the 1958 CRB Commodity Year Book.

The Index was originally comprised of two cash markets and 26 futures markets which were traded on exchanges in the U.S. and Canada. It included barley and flaxseed from the Winnipeg exchange; cocoa, coffee "B", copper, cotton, cottonseed oil, grease wool, hides, lead, potatoes, rubber, sugar #4, sugar #6, wool tops and zinc from New York exchanges; and corn, oats, wheat, rye, soybeans, soybean oil, soybean meal, lard, onions, and eggs from Chicago exchanges. In addition to those 26, the Index also included the spot New Orleans cotton and Minneapolis wheat markets.

Like the Bureau of Labor Statistics spot index, the CRB Futures Price Index is calculated to produce an unweighted geometric mean of the individual commodity price relatives. In other words, a ratio of the current price to the base year average price. Currently, 1967 is the base year the Index is calculated against (1967 = 100).

The formula considers all future delivery contracts which expire on or before the end of the sixth calendar month from the current date, up to a maximum of five delivery months per commodity. However, a minimum of two delivery months must be used to calculate the current price, even if the second contract is outside of the six month window. Contracts are excluded from the calculation when in their delivery period.

The 1997 closing Index value of 229.14 was 4.37 percent lower than 1996's close of 239.61 and marked the second consecutive yearly lower close. Among the six CRB Index sub-indices, only the Imported index was up for the year.

Futures Markets

Futures and options on the CRB Futures Index are traded on the New York Futures Exchange (NYFE).

CRB Futures Price Index Component Commodities by Group

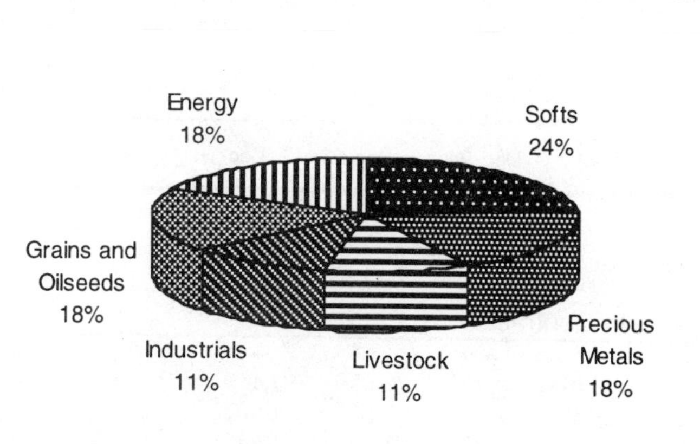

Groups:	*Components:*
Energy -	Crude Oil, Heating Oil, Natural Gas
Grains and Oilseeds-	Corn, Soybeans, Wheat
Industrials -	Copper, Cotton
Livestock -	Live Cattle, Live Hogs
Precious Metals -	Gold, Platinum. Silver
Softs -	Cocoa, Coffee, Orange Juice, Sugar

The CRB Futures Price Index is computed using a three-step process:

1) Each of the Index's 17 component commodities is arithmetically averaged using the prices for all of the designated contract months which expire on or before the end of the sixth calendar month from the current date, except that: a) no contract shall be included in the calculation while in delivery; b) there shall be a minimum of two contract months for each component commodity (adding contracts beyond the six month window, if necessary); c) there shall be a maximum of five contract months for each commodity (dropping the most deferred contracts to remain at five, if necessary). The result is that the Index extends six to seven months into the future depending on where one is in the current month. For example, live cattle's average price on October 30, 1995 would be computed as follows:

$$\text{Cattle Average} = \frac{\text{Dec. '96 + Feb. '97}}{2}$$

2) These 17 component averages are then geometrically averaged by multiplying all of the numbers together and taking the 17th root.

$$\text{Geometric Average} = \sqrt[17]{\text{Crude Avg. x Heating Avg. x ...Sugar Avg.}}$$

3) The resulting average is divided by 30.7766, the 1967 base-year average for these 17 commodities. That result is then multiplied by an adjustment factor of .8486. This adjustment factor is necessitated by the nine revisions to the Index since its inception in 1957. Finally, that result is multiplied by 100 in order to convert the Index into percentage terms:

$$\text{CRB Futures Index} = \frac{\text{Current Geometric Average}}{\text{1967 Geometric Avg. (30.7766)}} \text{ x .8486 x 100}$$

CRB FUTURES INDEX

Average Open Interest of CRB Futures Index in New York In Contracts

Year	Jan.	Feb.	Mar.	Apr.	May	June	July	Aug.	Sept.	Oct.	Nov.	Dec.
1988	2,597	2,607	2,682	2,819	3,592	3,934	2,846	2,795	2,659	2,419	2,529	2,556
1989	2,679	3,008	2,491	2,274	2,117	2,104	1,891	1,992	1,861	1,907	2,215	2,209
1990	1,889	1,229	1,476	1,858	1,499	1,459	1,289	1,286	1,181	1,247	1,505	1,530
1991	1,443	1,593	1,524	1,620	1,511	1,524	1,168	1,071	1,045	1,172	1,357	1,383
1992	1,435	1,472	1,185	1,347	1,311	1,087	951	1,179	1,075	1,226	1,283	1,406
1993	1,969	1,984	1,842	2,201	2,564	2,947	2,616	2,409	2,128	2,383	2,432	2,351
1994	2,607	3,146	2,680	2,691	2,339	2,698	3,838	5,146	4,562	4,942	4,535	2,800
1995	2,144	2,164	2,147	2,370	2,016	2,144	2,053	2,070	2,062	1,942	2,003	1,640
1996	1,934	1,826	1,753	2,355	1,881	1,890	1,562	1,345	1,596	1,853	1,861	1,866
1997	1,944	2,128	2,090	2,245	2,192	1,817	1,957	1,741	1,656	1,843	1,789	1,752

Source: New York Futures Exchange (NYFE)

Volume of Trading of CRB Futures Index in New York In Contracts

Year	Jan.	Feb.	Mar.	Apr.	May	June	July	Aug.	Sept.	Oct.	Nov.	Dec.	Total
1988	9,557	10,726	13,841	9,480	20,299	43,591	31,043	22,020	15,615	9,044	9,691	11,044	205,951
1989	8,805	10,045	12,035	11,437	13,145	13,824	11,917	9,846	7,918	7,412	9,613	8,551	124,548
1990	6,505	5,829	7,042	6,670	7,191	6,687	6,477	6,415	4,096	4,744	4,409	3,842	69,907
1991	5,835	5,391	6,715	6,432	3,671	5,557	4,853	5,876	4,414	3,766	4,132	4,543	61,185
1992	4,895	6,031	4,136	5,697	5,496	4,487	4,162	4,617	3,874	3,183	5,277	4,400	56,255
1993	3,620	5,720	8,050	7,340	8,680	10,722	12,418	8,590	6,192	4,350	8,535	6,954	91,908
1994	6,956	7,473	10,085	10,274	11,298	14,652	10,560	8,967	7,445	6,575	10,186	5,515	109,986
1995	6,151	5,545	5,763	7,955	7,877	7,573	6,875	10,094	7,376	5,030	5,865	5,309	81,413
1996	7,490	6,041	6,428	10,784	9,526	5,543	7,476	5,816	6,311	6,527	5,990	3,181	81,113
1997	6,645	4,942	5,245	8,600	8,156	7,776	6,248	7,685	4,537	4,588	3,468	3,592	71,482

Source: New York Futures Exchange (NYFE)

Currencies

Trading in the world's currencies during 1997 was estimated to total $1.5 trillion per day. During the first half of 1997, the world's major currencies tended to trade in relatively narrow ranges against the U.S. dollar; but the stability unraveled in the fourth quarter when a number of Asian countries seemed to be edging towards a financial abyss, triggering in its wake an international flight to the apparent safety of the dollar.

The Asian debacle began in Thailand and quickly spread throughout Asia, but by yearend it was the collapse of the South Korean won that attracted the most attention while heightening concern about the Japanese yen and the Hong Kong dollar. The Hong Kong dollar has survived previous financial crises largely because it is pegged at a fixed exchange rate to the U.S. dollar; in effect the U S. dollar could be legally declared legal tender in Hong Kong. A major uncertainty as 1998 unfolds is whether the Chinese government will be willing to defend the H.K.'s peg value or tie it more directly to China's yuan. In mid-1997 the J-yen was trading around 115 yen to the U.S. dollar, by yearend the parity was close to 130, only slightly below the five and a half year high of 130.78 reach in mid-December, but still a gain for the year of 12.5 percent. Even a late 1997 shift in Japan's fiscal policy, focusing on a broad based tax cut and corporate restructuring, failed to arrest traders' fears. However, Japan's central bank appears determined to prevent the yen from weakening during 1998 by intervening "on a scale that will surprise the market." Indeed, for the first time in five years, Japan's central bank sold U.S. dollars in late 1997, but the impact proved short lived as traders were looking for more than intervention in the FOREX market to reverse Japan's six-year economic slump.

The U.S. dollar closed 1997 almost 17 percent higher against the D-mark, at 1.77 D-M, down from an eight year high of 1.8815 in early August, reflecting traders preference towards America's strong economic growth and worries about the stability of Europe's planned common currency. The U.K. has already indicated it is not likely to participate in at least the first round of the European union. A basic tenet of the single-currency plan is that the various governments must bring down budget deficits to three percent of their gross domestic product; while the U.K. is thought capable of reaching that objective, it may be out of France's reach, if not also Germany's. In an effort to bolster the-mark's value, Germany's Bundesbank in early October surprised other European nations and raised a key interest rate, the first such increase in five years, although the move had only a short-term bullish effect on the mark.

The dollar closed 1997 up 2.7 percent against the British pound. In the fourth quarter, against both the Swiss and French francs, the dollar strengthened to its highest level since late summer. The Canadian dollar traded in a narrow range for much of 1997, pivoting around $0.72 U.S dollars. However, in the fourth quarter it fell to an 11-year low following the collapse of two Japanese firms which heightened fears they would need to sell their Canadian dollar holdings to raise badly needed cash. The C-dollar's weakness prompted the Bank of England and Canada's central bank to intervene in the FOREX market in an effort to temper the selling, but the C-dollar still closed the year under $0.70.

The FINEX U.S. Dollar Index strengthened during the first quarter of 1997, retaining much of the gain into midsummer when another rally carried it to its high for the year. Then a two-month dip was soundly reversed when the Asian domino effect changed everything, carrying the dollar back to its high by yearend.

The dollar is likely to remain strong into 1998 even though the U.S. economy's strong growth rate is apt to slow. The uncertainty for the dollar is likely to focus on Asia. Should the Asian crisis prove to have deep roots, the dollar's perceived safety will likely offset any negative U.S. economic data that may develop during 1998.

Futures Markets

The Chicago Mercantile Exchange International Monetary Market (IMM) trades futures and options on the Deutsche mark, Japanese yen, Mexican peso, Australian dollar, British pound, Canadian dollar, French franc, Swiss franc, Brazilian real, South African rand and the New Zealand dollar. Additional currency futures are likely to begin trading there in 1998. Chicago's MidAmerica Commodity Exchange (MidAm) trades smaller futures contracts on many of the IMM currencies. The FINEX division of the New York Cotton Exchange (NYCE) trades futures and options on a composite Dollar Index and also offers crossrate futures contracts: D-mark/J-yen, D-mark/French franc and D-mark/B-pound. Currency futures and options are also traded on the Philadelphia Board of Trade (PBOT).

CRB Currency Index 1977 = 100

Year	Jan.	Feb.	Mar.	Apr.	May	June	July	Aug.	Sep.	Oct.	Nov.	Dec.	Average
1987	117.32	119.22	120.88	124.17	125.74	123.36	121.20	121.22	124.24	125.14	131.66	136.41	124.21
1988	135.47	133.03	135.76	137.40	136.26	133.02	128.23	126.15	126.26	129.90	134.12	134.61	132.52
1989	130.38	129.50	127.85	126.75	121.86	119.28	123.21	121.77	120.01	122.28	122.64	125.11	124.22
1990	126.68	127.50	124.71	125.11	127.77	127.85	131.67	136.42	137.52	141.69	143.64	140.48	132.59
1991	140.91	142.85	134.41	130.85	130.02	126.44	126.33	128.27	130.86	131.57	134.66	136.78	132.83
1992	136.15	133.37	129.33	129.78	132.13	135.42	139.83	142.26	140.65	136.30	129.70	129.91	134.57
1993	127.91	126.74	127.99	132.20	132.73	131.17	129.44	130.64	132.87	131.38	129.31	129.14	130.13
1994	128.54	129.57	130.89	130.57	132.23	134.18	137.60	137.51	139.78	141.94	140.29	137.85	135.08
1995	139.31	140.54	147.85	152.52	150.20	150.85	150.58	145.41	143.89	146.33	145.21	143.83	146.38
1996	141.69	141.01	141.12	139.61	138.11	138.37	139.53	140.52	139.51	138.74	139.92	137.47	139.63
1997	134.61	130.36	129.56	128.71	130.83	131.75	130.14	126.84	128.02	129.07	129.58	126.93	129.70

Closing value. *Source: BRIDGE CRB*

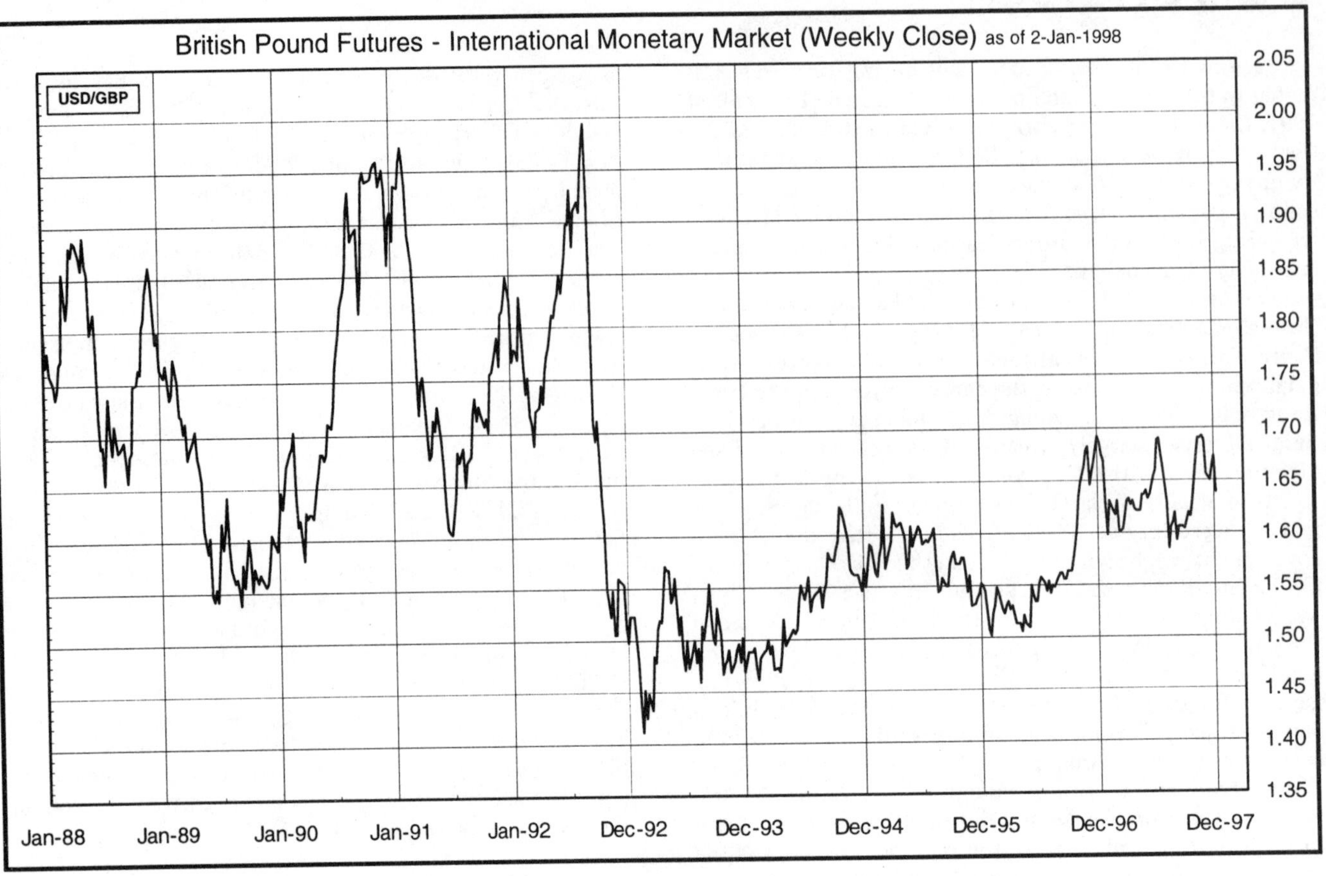

British Pound Futures - International Monetary Market (Weekly Close) as of 2-Jan-1998

USD/GBP

2.05
2.00
1.95
1.90
1.85
1.80
1.75
1.70
1.65
1.60
1.55
1.50
1.45
1.40
1.35

Jan-88 Jan-89 Jan-90 Jan-91 Jan-92 Dec-92 Dec-93 Dec-94 Dec-95 Dec-96 Dec-97

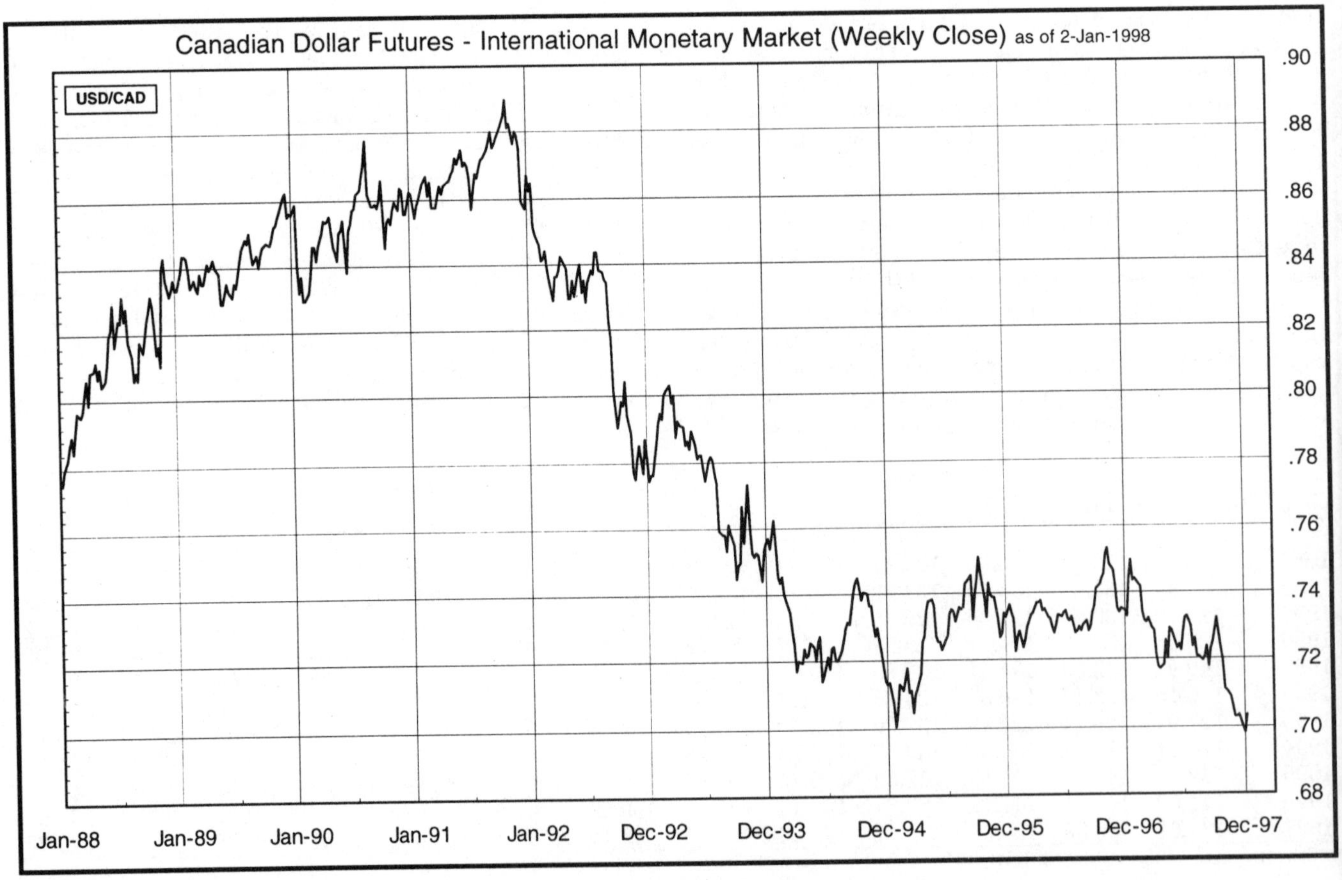

Canadian Dollar Futures - International Monetary Market (Weekly Close) as of 2-Jan-1998

USD/CAD

.90
.88
.86
.84
.82
.80
.78
.76
.74
.72
.70
.68

Jan-88 Jan-89 Jan-90 Jan-91 Jan-92 Dec-92 Dec-93 Dec-94 Dec-95 Dec-96 Dec-97

Deutsche Mark Futures - International Monetary Market (Weekly Close) as of 2-Jan-1998

Japanese Yen Futures - International Monetary Market (Weekly Close) as of 2-Jan-1998

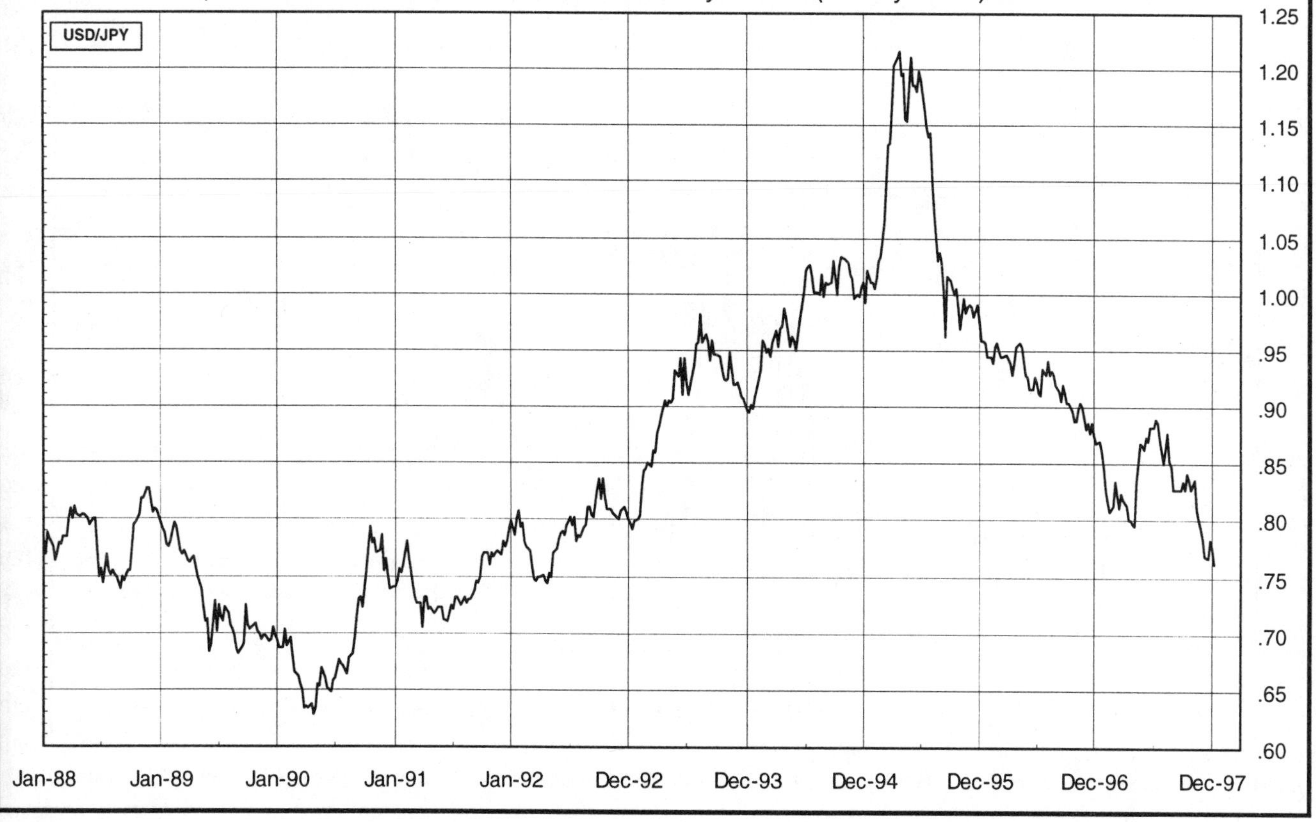

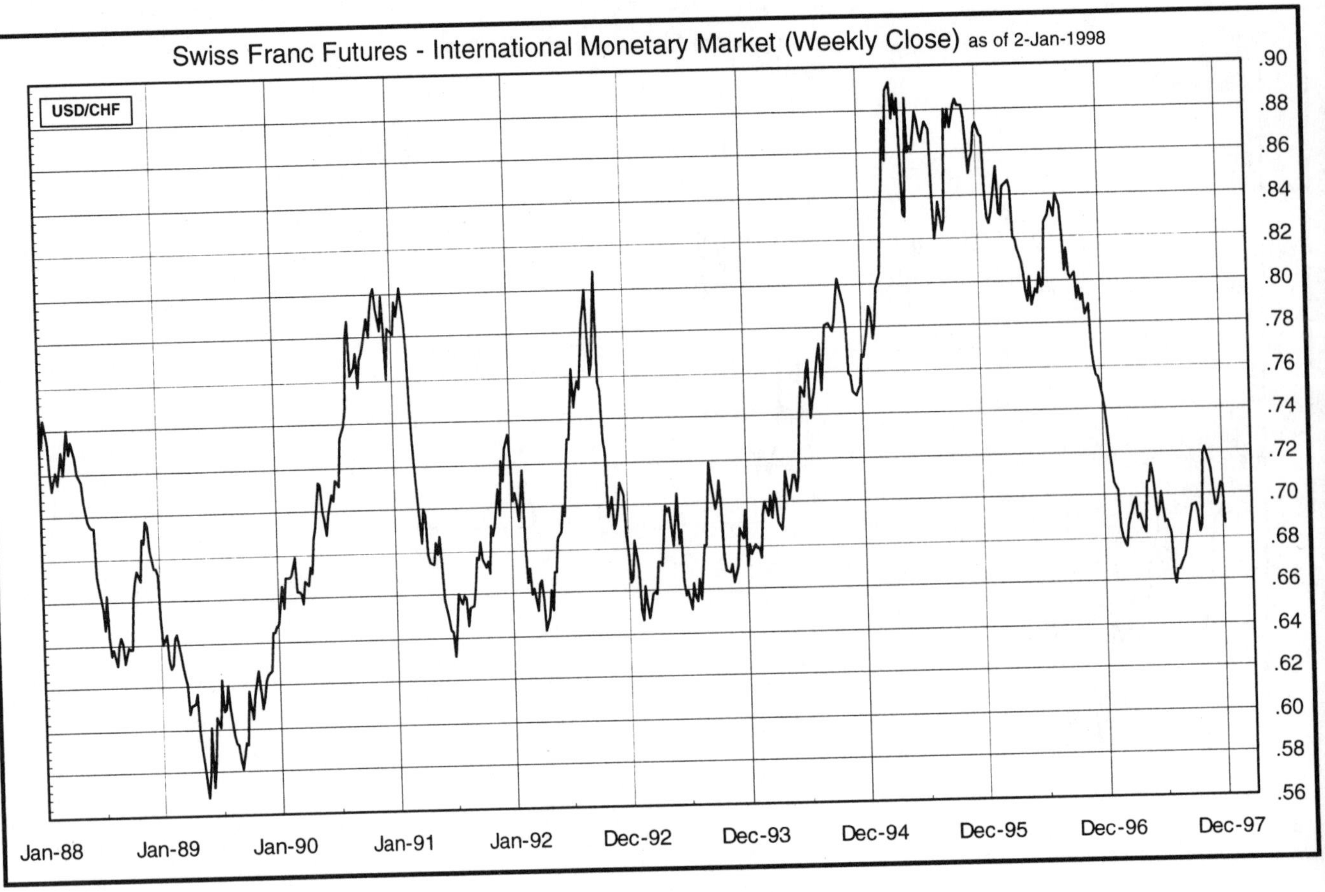

Swiss Franc Futures - International Monetary Market (Weekly Close) as of 2-Jan-1998

USD/CHF

.90
.88
.86
.84
.82
.80
.78
.76
.74
.72
.70
.68
.66
.64
.62
.60
.58
.56

Jan-88 Jan-89 Jan-90 Jan-91 Jan-92 Dec-92 Dec-93 Dec-94 Dec-95 Dec-96 Dec-97

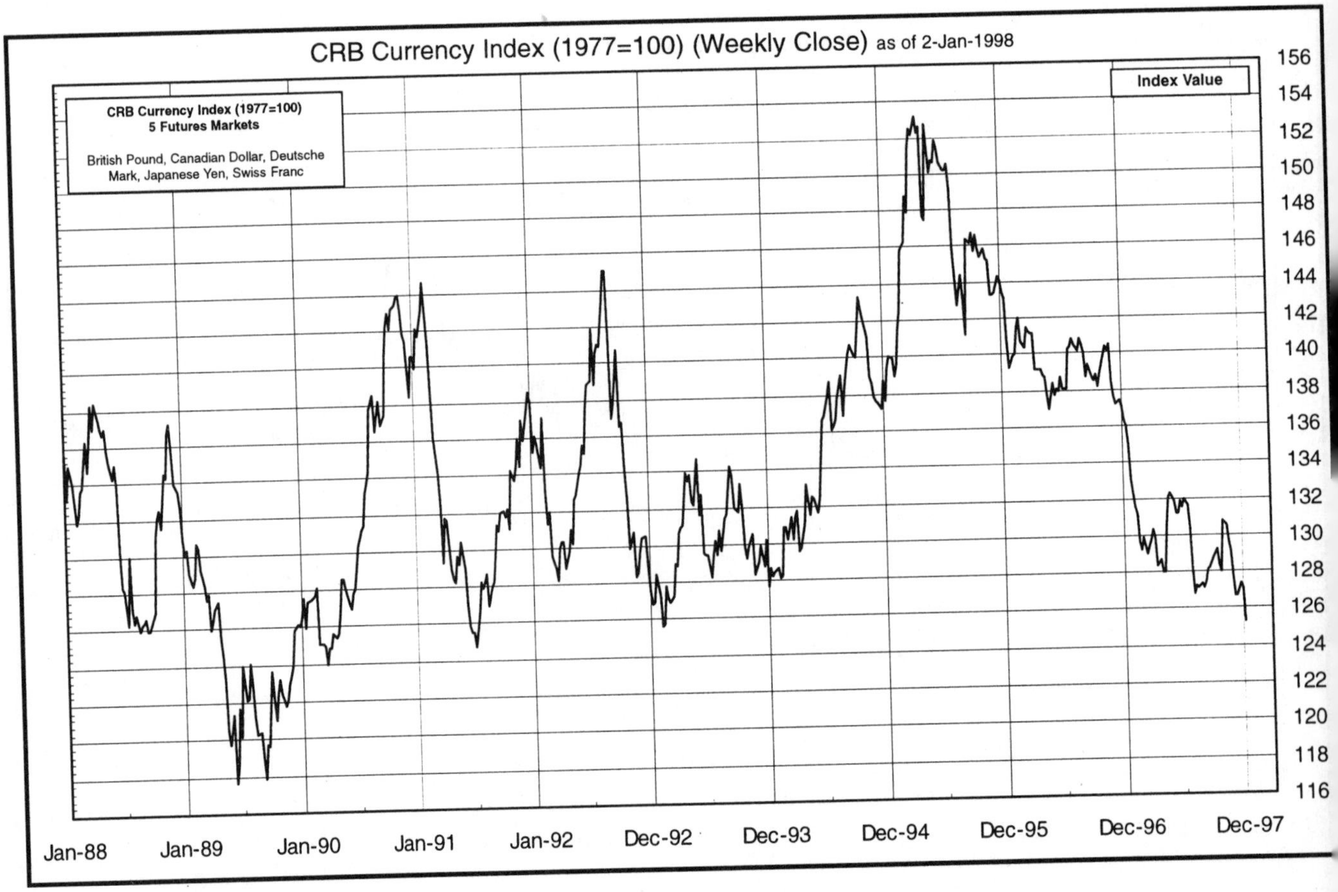

CRB Currency Index (1977=100) (Weekly Close) as of 2-Jan-1998

Index Value

CRB Currency Index (1977=100)
5 Futures Markets

British Pound, Canadian Dollar, Deutsche Mark, Japanese Yen, Swiss Franc

156
154
152
150
148
146
144
142
140
138
136
134
132
130
128
126
124
122
120
118
116

Jan-88 Jan-89 Jan-90 Jan-91 Jan-92 Dec-92 Dec-93 Dec-94 Dec-95 Dec-96 Dec-97

Canadian Dollars per U.S. Dollar

Year	January	February	March	April	May	June	July	August	September	October	November	December	Average
1989	1.1916	1.1893	1.1949	1.1883	1.1932	1.1982	1.1891	1.1758	1.1824	1.1749	1.1695	1.1610	1.1840
1990	1.1718	1.1967	1.1800	1.1640	1.1749	1.1728	1.1571	1.1453	1.1578	1.1600	1.1637	1.1604	1.1670
1991	1.1563	1.1545	1.1572	1.1535	1.1497	1.1438	1.1493	1.1451	1.1372	1.1281	1.1310	1.1474	1.1461
1992	1.1569	1.1827	1.1923	1.1871	1.1990	1.1955	1.1916	1.1906	1.2208	1.2440	1.2683	1.2711	1.2083
1993	1.2774	1.2595	1.2467	1.2616	1.2686	1.2788	1.2817	1.3078	1.3210	1.3253	1.3166	1.3307	1.2896
1994	1.3175	1.3419	1.3645	1.3821	1.3805	1.3831	1.3818	1.3777	1.3536	1.3495	1.3649	1.3896	1.3656
1995	1.4120	1.3995	1.4065	1.3749	1.3607	1.3772	1.3609	1.3550	1.3495	1.3449	1.3525	1.3685	1.3718
1996	1.3664	1.3753	1.3651	1.3591	1.3690	1.3649	1.3687	1.3717	1.3691	1.3501	1.3382	1.3621	1.3633
1997	1.3484	1.3555	1.3727	1.3947	1.3793	1.3844	1.3769	1.3894	1.3865	1.3863	1.4127	1.4272	1.3845

Average. *Source: BRIDGE*

German (Deutsche) Marks per U.S. Dollar

Year	January	February	March	April	May	June	July	August	September	October	November	December	Average
1989	1.8365	1.8500	1.8689	1.8699	1.9494	1.9770	1.8920	1.9303	1.9506	1.8666	1.8288	1.7364	1.8797
1990	1.6936	1.6764	1.7056	1.6857	1.6646	1.6828	1.6373	1.5711	1.5703	1.5235	1.4850	1.4969	1.6161
1991	1.5092	1.4812	1.6132	1.7013	1.7178	1.7833	1.7886	1.7440	1.6951	1.6913	1.6222	1.5597	1.6589
1992	1.5802	1.6193	1.6594	1.6486	1.6209	1.5713	1.4892	1.4459	1.4486	1.4860	1.5866	1.5826	1.5616
1993	1.6144	1.6427	1.6459	1.5939	1.6050	1.6541	1.7137	1.6927	1.6198	1.6396	1.6997	1.7106	1.6527
1994	1.7422	1.7340	1.6907	1.6969	1.6557	1.6269	1.5705	1.5637	1.5488	1.5188	1.5410	1.5705	1.6216
1995	1.5312	1.4996	1.4044	1.3792	1.4085	1.3988	1.3874	1.4457	1.4599	1.4133	1.4178	1.4397	1.4321
1996	1.4627	1.4644	1.4763	1.5053	1.5329	1.5274	1.5026	1.4819	1.5068	1.5277	1.5124	1.5517	1.5043
1997	1.6056	1.6749	1.6940	1.7120	1.7029	1.7269	1.7932	1.8398	1.7867	1.7556	1.7317	1.7787	1.7335

Average. *Source: BRIDGE*

Japanese Yen per U.S. Dollar

Year	January	February	March	April	May	June	July	August	September	October	November	December	Average
1989	127.41	127.65	130.58	132.09	138.10	143.74	140.41	141.57	145.04	142.25	143.55	143.67	138.01
1990	145.13	145.70	153.35	158.52	153.77	153.74	149.00	147.47	138.76	129.56	129.18	133.88	144.84
1991	133.67	130.58	137.48	137.05	138.12	139.66	137.97	136.87	134.41	130.78	129.74	127.93	134.52
1992	125.24	127.65	132.79	133.51	130.61	126.72	125.69	126.10	222.58	121.23	123.80	123.94	134.99
1993	124.94	120.77	116.99	112.22	110.10	107.29	107.57	103.74	105.41	107.00	107.78	109.89	111.14
1994	111.33	106.22	105.00	103.36	103.76	102.37	98.65	99.88	98.78	98.36	98.08	100.08	102.16
1995	99.67	98.14	90.40	83.59	84.96	84.55	87.22	94.72	100.49	100.76	101.93	101.84	94.02
1996	105.66	105.57	105.90	107.23	106.42	108.91	109.21	107.84	109.87	112.40	112.35	114.01	108.78
1997	117.93	122.90	122.72	125.66	118.93	114.25	115.30	117.90	120.85	121.06	125.35	129.62	121.04

Average. *Source: BRIDGE*

Swiss Francs per U.S. Dollar

Year	January	February	March	April	May	June	July	August	September	October	November	December	Average
1989	1.5624	1.5735	1.6112	1.6472	1.7290	1.7060	1.6294	1.6631	1.6866	1.6317	1.6182	1.5671	1.6355
1990	1.5179	1.4885	1.5128	1.4851	1.4202	1.4253	1.3909	1.3086	1.3061	1.2814	1.2563	1.2802	1.3894
1991	1.2712	1.2690	1.3891	1.4382	1.4557	1.5304	1.5507	1.5204	1.4819	1.4797	1.4357	1.3825	1.4337
1992	1.4045	1.4567	1.5072	1.5179	1.4895	1.4234	1.3322	1.2948	1.2763	1.3193	1.4276	1.4231	1.4060
1993	1.4775	1.5197	1.5199	1.4572	1.4471	1.4767	1.5138	1.4947	1.4158	1.4421	1.4966	1.4629	1.4770
1994	1.4707	1.4558	1.4295	1.4363	1.4120	1.3723	1.3256	1.3176	1.2895	1.2636	1.2974	1.3275	1.3665
1995	1.2865	1.2694	1.1691	1.1362	1.1678	1.1564	1.1542	1.1958	1.1868	1.1444	1.1440	1.1624	1.1811
1996	1.1810	1.1942	1.1945	1.2194	1.2546	1.2574	1.2324	1.2022	1.2333	1.2583	1.2757	1.3296	1.2361
1997	1.3925	1.4543	1.4622	1.4614	1.4298	1.4419	1.4810	1.5123	1.4702	1.4507	1.4057	1.4393	1.4501

Average. *Source: BRIDGE*

British Pounds per U.S. Dollar

Year	January	February	March	April	May	June	July	August	September	October	November	December	Average
1989	1.7740	1.7534	1.7132	1.7006	1.6281	1.5541	1.6257	1.5925	1.5720	1.5864	1.5727	1.5974	1.6392
1990	1.6513	1.6960	1.6246	1.6376	1.6775	1.7112	1.8101	1.9008	1.8803	1.9481	1.9635	1.9208	1.7852
1991	1.9347	1.9641	1.8214	1.7514	1.7259	1.6491	1.6482	1.6839	1.7253	1.7214	1.7780	1.8311	1.7695
1992	1.8083	1.7776	1.7251	1.7562	1.8101	1.8555	1.9193	1.9445	1.8510	1.6547	1.5269	1.5497	1.7649
1993	1.5330	1.4383	1.4621	1.5465	1.5492	1.5090	1.4973	1.4928	1.5251	1.5027	1.4808	1.4904	1.5023
1994	1.4933	1.4787	1.4921	1.4832	1.5038	1.5261	1.5446	1.5421	1.5647	1.6073	1.5864	1.5582	1.5317
1995	1.5742	1.5727	1.6004	1.6087	1.5886	1.5960	1.5955	1.5668	1.5595	1.5782	1.5612	1.5411	1.5786
1996	1.5289	1.5376	1.5278	1.5159	1.5154	1.5417	1.5538	1.5501	1.5595	1.5863	1.6629	1.6660	1.5622
1997	1.6590	1.6258	1.6095	1.6285	1.6325	1.6457	1.6717	1.6044	1.6020	1.6331	1.6887	1.6606	1.6385

Average. *Source: BRIDGE*

CURRENCIES

Average Open Interest of Canadian Dollar Futures in Chicago In Contracts

Year	January	February	March	April	May	June	July	August	September	October	November	December
1989	24,221	27,726	23,102	21,146	24,900	24,807	20,007	31,041	27,206	25,903	29,645	29,116
1990	26,426	29,204	23,848	24,048	33,823	30,809	39,843	42,092	34,998	29,434	31,250	25,272
1991	29,072	28,214	25,550	24,894	29,310	33,136	25,113	25,310	30,909	28,805	27,453	22,311
1992	19,724	24,020	24,118	21,354	24,020	22,860	24,773	27,665	28,221	27,827	28,025	24,923
1993	20,410	24,376	25,877	23,639	27,438	29,784	29,385	45,397	40,639	43,476	32,469	28,879
1994	28,277	38,157	48,411	42,730	44,363	42,845	35,370	39,582	49,312	40,706	42,353	59,763
1995	55,863	44,677	33,706	45,394	47,832	36,677	44,930	42,629	49,526	43,032	40,047	40,592
1996	31,028	37,674	38,551	41,411	46,470	37,141	37,522	42,063	44,014	68,674	82,817	72,586
1997	55,949	56,600	72,803	82,732	73,747	57,243	43,937	59,112	56,387	59,265	75,027	74,221

Source: International Monetary Market (IMM), division of the Chicago Mercantile Exchange (CME)

Average Open Interest of Deutsche Mark Futures in Chicago In Contracts

Year	January	February	March	April	May	June	July	August	September	October	November	December
1989	51,439	65,251	52,869	52,693	70,062	72,766	62,365	66,520	65,666	70,976	91,393	93,491
1990	63,745	73,216	72,357	63,058	70,475	65,113	64,765	72,684	58,241	61,839	76,650	67,322
1991	51,211	73,463	72,824	71,737	79,162	80,318	68,046	73,860	70,525	59,236	85,248	77,632
1992	60,390	69,246	76,614	74,945	85,123	74,761	79,297	93,027	82,287	87,679	126,380	132,676
1993	134,432	140,184	126,046	118,747	131,816	159,334	165,356	147,140	108,958	103,720	135,960	145,414
1994	146,742	144,594	118,301	99,177	125,321	108,586	94,767	106,647	108,742	88,784	101,376	101,548
1995	79,425	92,975	79,700	61,954	71,050	60,698	46,832	63,789	63,820	53,300	59,123	70,267
1996	74,553	79,549	70,804	75,370	86,672	71,984	65,130	73,623	74,561	71,361	70,936	72,887
1997	79,970	97,156	94,187	81,216	83,567	84,285	116,221	115,947	88,075	68,767	76,424	84,700

Source: International Monetary Market (IMM), division of the Chicago Mercantile Exchange (CME)

Average Open Interest of Japanese Yen Futures in Chicago In Contracts

Year	January	February	March	April	May	June	July	August	September	October	November	December
1989	39,467	48,400	53,654	52,013	67,213	73,355	48,261	30,235	71,230	50,594	60,283	57,748
1990	60,012	67,723	82,783	71,709	79,850	62,252	62,760	65,050	77,686	74,890	77,115	65,365
1991	43,552	64,694	57,115	49,060	52,964	55,727	53,045	56,496	66,174	74,353	74,585	64,219
1992	63,856	67,714	71,702	63,938	63,079	64,596	56,465	58,353	53,462	44,488	45,941	46,887
1993	50,066	70,195	81,979	76,696	82,028	81,103	72,186	80,780	73,002	83,097	84,812	95,817
1994	101,792	94,470	73,286	57,281	65,835	70,759	73,734	72,798	63,419	63,091	80,053	92,834
1995	86,569	86,852	77,649	63,379	67,644	56,285	48,680	63,463	73,830	67,336	73,335	70,268
1996	80,645	78,915	71,643	76,655	73,832	85,398	77,941	73,535	86,723	76,620	72,130	67,301
1997	73,391	82,542	78,466	81,117	85,984	73,322	62,488	82,369	96,468	90,080	130,606	121,001

Source: International Monetary Market (IMM), division of the Chicago Mercantile Exchange (CME)

Average Open Interest of Swiss Franc Futures in Chicago In Contracts

Year	January	February	March	April	May	June	July	August	September	October	November	December
1989	27,442	31,287	34,749	34,074	42,256	36,445	35,625	41,613	38,429	31,432	39,757	47,927
1990	36,339	42,435	34,953	32,853	45,464	42,862	39,769	48,544	40,269	37,216	44,166	37,220
1991	31,489	36,483	49,061	40,026	38,601	43,476	36,031	35,881	29,833	24,949	32,342	32,439
1992	24,653	33,640	42,825	36,230	38,269	36,668	30,159	33,707	33,167	34,767	45,428	44,901
1993	52,713	49,472	48,002	43,514	47,832	42,343	40,703	44,329	60,446	49,320	58,406	49,670
1994	41,914	46,280	44,134	37,450	42,071	49,162	45,223	43,746	44,495	39,587	51,539	55,424
1995	39,726	44,364	39,358	30,270	30,586	26,766	23,121	30,267	34,228	34,889	38,033	44,741
1996	42,280	42,902	36,924	39,233	46,810	44,848	38,300	40,298	43,695	47,613	53,581	59,405
1997	51,652	54,114	51,121	45,725	48,651	42,530	55,279	58,098	49,296	43,585	51,822	48,560

Source: International Monetary Market (IMM), division of the Chicago Mercantile Exchange (CME)

Average Open Interest of British Pound Futures in Chicago In Contracts

Year	January	February	March	April	May	June	July	August	September	October	November	December
1989	22,870	24,705	27,436	21,170	25,871	26,512	22,899	22,559	27,661	21,971	24,850	26,124
1990	23,272	30,729	26,219	23,909	33,355	35,528	37,898	41,820	33,458	32,213	39,623	32,790
1991	23,686	34,680	33,558	29,900	30,697	33,792	26,443	21,578	28,215	22,882	31,792	26,443
1992	21,578	28,215	22,882	31,595	36,426	35,529	27,160	28,041	30,137	30,330	33,121	27,935
1993	26,614	41,752	40,238	38,544	39,654	34,953	26,056	32,446	33,560	29,733	37,246	33,606
1994	39,223	43,878	35,554	44,725	46,577	41,801	37,633	34,988	40,751	42,648	49,684	65,834
1995	47,740	44,935	36,805	23,161	26,571	28,402	22,662	34,932	38,900	34,485	43,634	49,804
1996	40,315	50,106	52,349	54,954	52,573	61,461	55,080	50,862	53,868	51,934	62,128	47,652
1997	40,479	38,370	43,742	37,701	40,956	48,890	60,592	50,829	41,801	35,752	56,825	44,667

Source: International Monetary Market (IMM), division of the Chicago Mercantile Exchange (CME)

United States Merchandise Trade Balance[1] In Millions of Dollars

Year	January	February	March	April	May	June	July	August	September	October	November	December	Total
1988	-9,874	-11,179	-7,656	-8,233	-7,915	-11,738	-10,211	-11,006	-9,237	-10,251	-10,824	-10,402	-126,959
1989	-8,639	-8,622	-6,954	-7,191	-9,463	-8,724	-10,582	-11,034	-8,971	-11,780	-10,754	-6,687	-115,245
1990	-9,640	-6,150	-6,369	-6,527	-7,308	-6,476	-10,759	-10,509	-9,157	-12,805	-10,529	-6,211	-109,030
1991	-7,079	-4,201	-1,889	-3,411	-4,158	-3,948	-7,894	-7,450	-7,111	-8,735	-4,942	-5,908	-74,068
1992	-5,470	-2,178	-3,527	-5,772	-5,409	-6,718	-9,893	-10,218	-9,693	-9,706	-8,644	-7,276	-96,106
1993	-6,113	-5,905	-8,886	-8,428	-6,542	-11,749	-12,609	-11,949	-12,516	-12,638	-11,521	-9,115	-132,575
1994	-11,999	-13,573	-11,477	-13,405	-14,079	-14,009	-15,831	-14,232	-14,566	-14,926	-15,292	-13,272	-166,123
1995	-15,746	-14,221	-14,487	-16,051	-16,010	-15,862	-15,887	-13,415	-13,243	-13,108	-12,324	-12,600	-173,560
1996	-15,623	-12,911	-14,574	-15,897	-16,826	-14,839	-17,757	-16,759	-17,976	-15,320	-15,176	-17,695	-191,170
1997[2]	-18,149	-16,761	-14,877	-15,528	-16,363	-15,244	-16,849	-16,559	-18,538	-17,082			-199,140

[1] Not seasonally adjusted. [2] Preliminary. *Source: Bureau of Economic Analysis, U.S. Department of Commerce (BEA)*

Index of Real Trade-Weighted Dollar Exchange Rates for Total Agricultural[2] 1985 = 100

Year		Jan.	Feb.	Mar.	Apr.	May	June	July	Aug.	Sept.	Oct.	Nov.	Dec.
1990	U.S. Markets	78.3	78.1	79.3	79.4	78.5	78.9	79.2	79.1	78.5	76.6	74.7	75.3
	U.S. Competitors	80.1	81.2	79.6	79.2	77.8	77.5	76.4	76.1	76.3	75.0	75.3	73.5
1991	U.S. Markets	75.8	75.0	78.4	79.4	79.7	80.8	80.5	79.8	78.4	78.3	77.1	76.3
	U.S. Competitors	75.3	75.1	76.4	77.0	77.3	77.8	77.8	76.9	75.8	77.0	76.4	76.2
1992	U.S. Markets	75.5	76.4	80.9	78.2	76.5	76.0	74.7	74.2	74.2	75.2	77.6	77.3
	U.S. Competitors	76.2	76.8	81.1	76.6	77.4	76.6	75.6	75.1	77.2	75.7	77.7	77.4
1993	U.S. Markets	78.2	78.4	78.3	77.0	77.3	76.0	77.1	76.8	76.0	76.6	77.4	77.9
	U.S. Competitors	78.3	78.6	79.1	78.4	78.9	77.7	78.5	78.7	78.0	78.3	78.6	78.1
1994	U.S. Markets	77.0	77.0	97.1	97.4	97.0	96.9	95.3	95.2	94.3	93.8	94.2	96.7
	U.S. Competitors	78.3	78.3	107.3	107.6	105.7	104.5	101.5	101.2	100.1	98.4	99.1	100.5
1995	U.S. Markets	99.2	98.6	96.7	92.5	92.0	92.0	92.2	94.8	96.6	96.7	98.3	98.0
	U.S. Competitors	98.9	98.0	95.3	93.9	94.5	93.8	92.7	94.5	95.6	94.4	94.4	94.8
1996	U.S. Markets	99.4	99.2	99.4	99.4	99.4	100.1	100.4	99.4	100.1	101.1	100.8	101.5
	U.S. Competitors	96.0	96.0	96.3	97.0	97.9	97.5	96.7	96.2	96.8	97.4	96.5	97.8
1997[1]	U.S. Markets	103.0	105.3	106.2	106.4	104.3	103.4	104.3	105.7	105.8	106.0	108.8	
	U.S. Competitors	99.8	102.8	103.8	104.4	103.9	104.9	106.7	109.5	109.1	108.5	107.9	

[1] Preliminary. [2] Real indexes adjust nominal exchange rates for differences in rates of inflation to avoid the distortion caused by high-inflation countries. A higher value means the dollar has appreciated. Federal Reserve Board Index of trade-weighted value of the U.S. Dollar against ten major currencies. Weights are based on relative importance in world financial markets. *Source: Economic Research Service, U.S. Department of Agriculture (ERS-USDA)*

United States Balance on Current Account[1] In Millions of Dollars

Year	1st Quarter	2nd Quarter	3rd Quarter	4th Quarter	Annual
1988	-29,145	-30,998	-34,670	-33,623	-128,245
1989	-22,132	-25,670	-31,115	-26,659	-104,231
1990	-17,433	-20,023	-31,333	-25,869	-91,892
1991	14,997	2,611	-17,526	-9,600	-5,657
1992	-6,112	-13,796	-15,976	-20,499	-56,383
1993	-16,121	-22,303	-24,713	-27,638	-90,771
1994	-26,153	-32,000	-36,362	-39,020	-133,538
1995	-34,709	-35,704	-33,132	-25,554	-129,095
1996	-32,884	-35,585	-42,833	-36,874	-148,184
1997[2]	-39,972	-37,852	-42,156		-159,973

[1] Not seasonally adjusted. [2] Preliminary. *Source: Bureau of Economic Analysis, U.S. Department of Commerce (BEA)*

Merchandise Trade and Account Balances In Billions of Dollars

	Merchandise Trade Balance					Current Account Balance				
Year	Canada	Germany	Japan	Switzerland	U.K.	Canada	Germany	Japan	Switzerland	U.K.
1989	6.5	75.0	80.0	-4.4	-40.4	-21.6	56.6	63.1	7.0	-36.6
1990	9.5	69.2	69.4	-3.5	-33.4	-19.7	48.7	44.7	8.6	-33.3
1991	6.1	19.0	96.1	-2.5	-18.1	-22.2	-18.1	68.2	10.6	-14.0
1992	7.5	27.9	124.5	2.4	-23.0	-20.8	-19.4	112.4	15.1	-17.8
1993	9.9	41.2	139.3	4.9	-20.2	-21.7	-14.3	131.9	19.4	-15.5
1994	14.1	50.9	144.1	5.2	-17.0	-14.7	-20.6	130.5	18.4	-2.5
1995	24.6	65.0	131.2	5.1	-18.3	-5.4	-23.6	110.4	21.5	-5.8
1996	30.1	71.3	83.6	4.9	-19.7	2.8	-13.1	65.8	20.3	-.7
1997[1]	19.4	78.0	98.9	4.5	-20.6	-6.0	-5.5	91.8	16.8	3.9
1998[2]	19.5	93.7	112.9	6.0	-33.5	-5.7	10.0	104.8	18.5	-13.9

[1] Estimate. [2] Projection. *Source: Organization for Economic Cooperation and Development (OECD)*

CURRENCIES

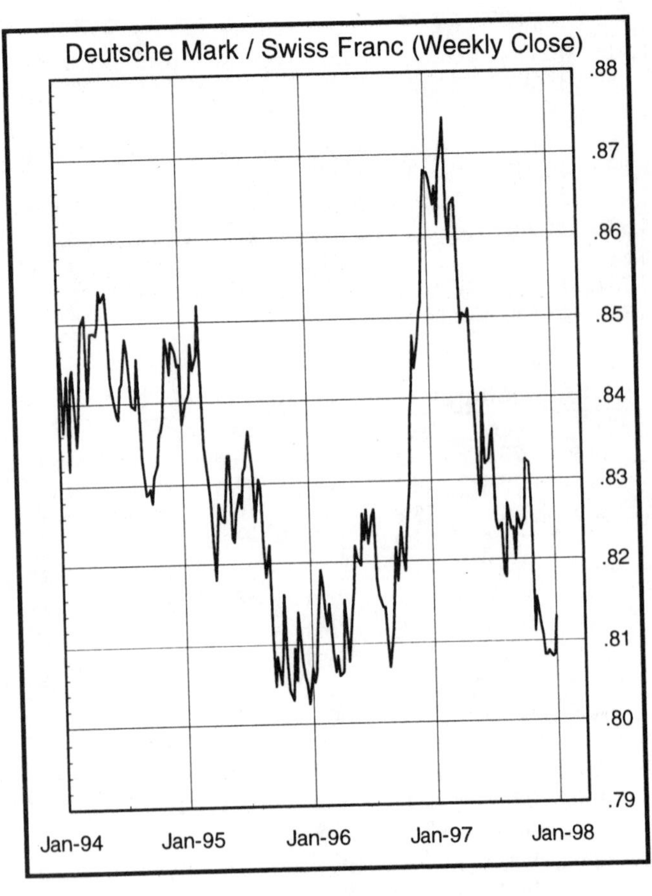

Deutsche Mark / Swiss Franc (Weekly Close)
.88
.87
.86
.85
.84
.83
.82
.81
.80
.79
Jan-94
Jan-95
Jan-96
Jan-97
Jan-98

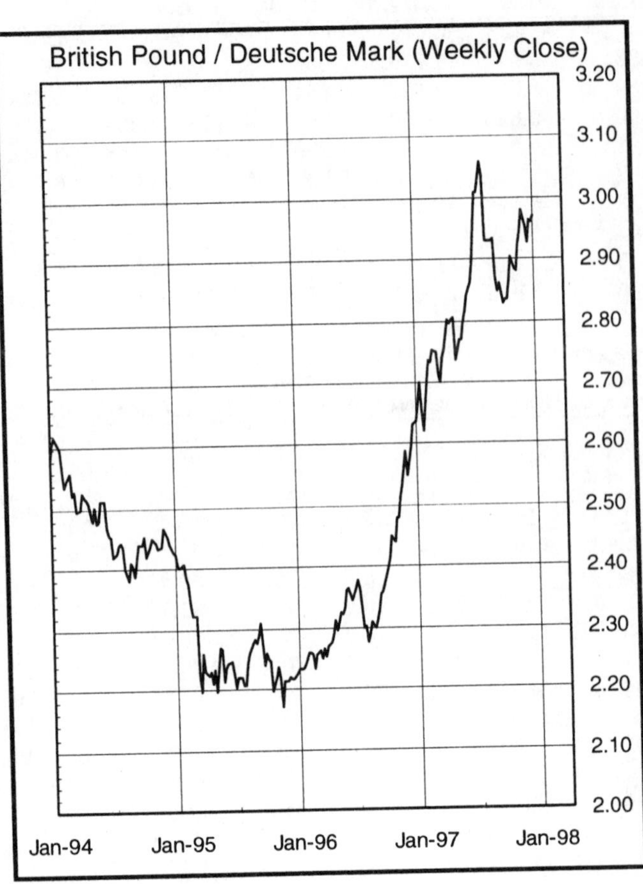

British Pound / Deutsche Mark (Weekly Close)
3.20
3.10
3.00
2.90
2.80
2.70
2.60
2.50
2.40
2.30
2.20
2.10
2.00
Jan-94
Jan-95
Jan-96
Jan-97
Jan-98

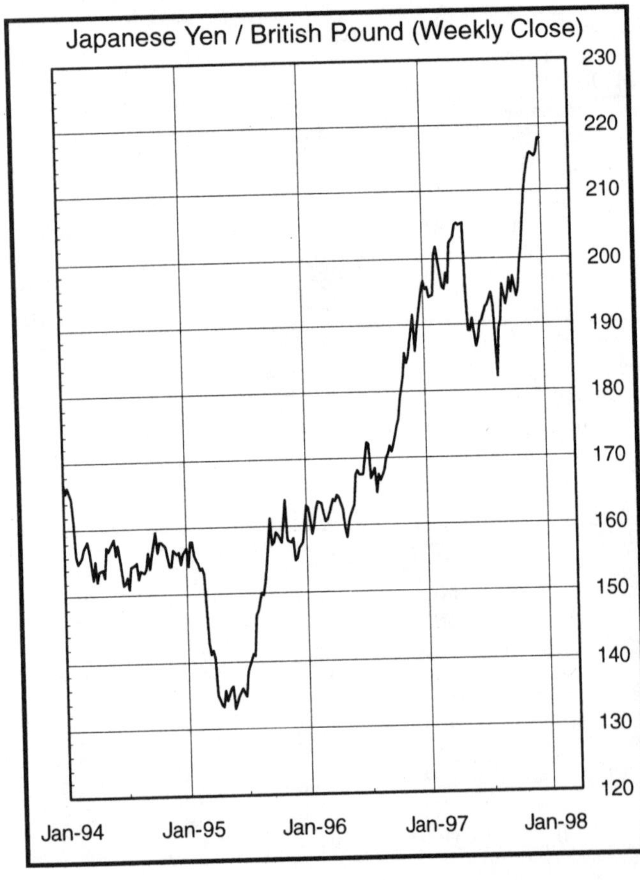

Japanese Yen / British Pound (Weekly Close)
230
220
210
200
190
180
170
160
150
140
130
120
Jan-94
Jan-95
Jan-96
Jan-97
Jan-98

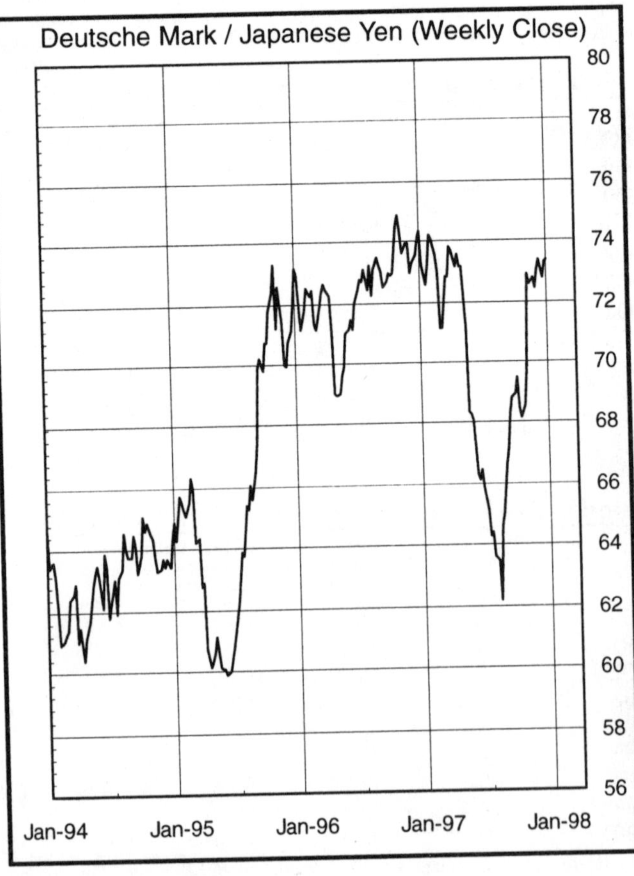

Deutsche Mark / Japanese Yen (Weekly Close)
80
78
76
74
72
70
68
66
64
62
60
58
56
Jan-94
Jan-95
Jan-96
Jan-97
Jan-98

Diamonds

Diamonds have unique properties that give them their value in industrial and research applications. Diamonds are the hardest substance known and as such find multiple uses in cutting, drilling, grinding and polishing. Industrial-grade diamonds are used primarily as abrasives. Diamonds have excellent optical properties as well as superior electrical and thermal characteristics. As such, they find use in special lenses, heat sinks in electrical circuits, wire drawing as well as other technologies.

The U.S. is one of the world's leading producers of synthetic industrial diamonds. In 1996, the U.S. accounted for output of 114 million carats. More than 20 million carats of industrial diamonds were estimated to have been recycled in the U.S. in 1996. Four U.S. companies recovered and sold industrial diamonds as their principal product in 1996. The U.S. Geological Survey reported that a new diamond mine under development near Fort Collins, Colorado, may prove to be the first significant domestic source of natural industrial diamonds in the United States. A diamond processing plant at the mine began operating in May 1996. About 65% of the recovered diamonds were gem quality.

World Production of Natural Gem Diamonds In Thousands of Carats

Year	Angola	Australia	Botswana	Brazil	Central African Republic	China	Ghana	Namibia	Russia[3]	Sierra Leone	South Africa	Zaire	World Total
1991	899	17,978	11,550	600	296	200	560	1,170	10,000	160	3,800	3,000	51,090
1992	1,100	18,078	11,160	653	307	200	570	1,520	9,000	180	4,600	8,934	57,300
1993	130	18,844	10,310	1,000	370	230	106	1,120	8,000	90	4,600	2,006	47,600
1994	270	19,485	10,550	300	400	230	118	1,312	8,500	155	5,050	4,000	51,400
1995[1]	2,700	18,312	11,502	700	400	230	126	1,382	9,000	113	5,070	4,000	54,800
1996[2]	3,600	18,897	11,000	700	350	230	125	1,300	9,250	162	5,360	3,000	55,400

[1] Preliminary. [2] Estimate. [3] Formerly part of the U.S.S.R.; data not reported separately until 1992. *Source: U.S. Geological Survey (USGS)*

World Production of Natural Industrial Diamonds In Thousands of Carats

Year	Angola	Australia	Botswana	Brazil	Central African Republic	China	Ghana	Russia[3]	Sierra Leone	South Africa	Venezuela	Zaire	World Total
1991	62	17,978	4,950	900	82	800	140	10,000	83	4,600	112	14,814	54,737
1992	80	22,095	4,790	665	107	800	140	9,000	116	5,600	176	4,567	48,500
1993	15	23,032	4,420	600	125	850	484	8,000	68	5,700	155	13,620	57,400
1994	30	23,815	5,000	600	131	850	473	8,500	100	5,800	214	13,000	58,900
1995[1]	300	22,381	5,300	600	130	900	505	9,000	101	5,880	64	13,000	58,600
1996[2]	400	23,096	5,000	600	120	900	505	9,250	108	6,000	60	15,000	61,600

[1] Preliminary. [2] Estimate. [3] Formerly part of the U.S.S.R.; data not reported separately until 1992. *Source: U.S. Geological Survey (USGS)*

World Production of Synthetic Diamonds In Thousands of Carats

Year	Belarus[3]	China	Czech Republic[4]	France	Greece	Ireland	Japan	Russia[3]	South Africa	Sweden	Ukraine[3]	United States	World Total
1991	------	15,000	10,000	4,000	1,000	60,000	30,000	120,000	60,000	25,000	------	90,000	423,000
1992	30,000	15,000	10,000	3,500	750	60,000	30,000	80,000	60,000	25,000	10,000	90,000	422,000
1993	30,000	15,500	5,000	3,500	1,000	65,000	32,000	80,000	60,000	25,000	10,000	103,000	440,000
1994	25,000	15,500	5,000	3,500	1,000	65,000	32,000	80,000	60,000	25,000	8,000	104,000	434,000
1995[1]	25,000	15,500	5,000	3,000	1,000	60,000	32,000	80,000	60,000	25,000	8,000	115,000	440,000
1996[2]	25,000	15,500	5,000	3,000	750	60,000	32,000	80,000	60,000	25,000	8,000	114,000	439,000

[1] Preliminary. [2] Estimate. [3] Formerly part of the U.S.S.R.; data not reported separately until 1992. [4] Formerly part of Czechoslovakia; data not reported separately until 1993. W = Withheld proprietary data. *Source: U.S. Geological Survey (USGS)*

Salient Statistics of Industrial Diamonds in the United States In Millions of Carats

	Bort, Grit & Powder & Dust — Natural and Synthetic								Stones (Natural)						
	--- Production ---														
Year	Manufactured Diamond	Secondary	Imports for Consumption	Exports & Reexports	In Manufactured Products	Gov't Sales	Apparent Consumption	Price Value of Imports $ Per Carat	Secondary Production	Imports for Consumption	Exports & Reexports	Gov't Sales	Apparent Consumption	Price Value of Imports $ Per Carat	Net Import Reliance % of Consumption
1991	90.0	3.5	70.0	78.8	.6	5.0	89.1	.83	.3	7.6	2.9	-----	5.0	6.68	94
1992	95.0	3.4	97.3	83.6	.6	10.4	121.9	.70	.1	9.8	5.6	-----	4.3	4.56	98
1993	105.0	15.9	133.0	107.0	.6	-----	146.0	.61	.1	5.2	3.4	1.3	1.9	6.85	95
1994	104.0	16.0	174.0	153.0	.4	2.0	141.0	.51	.1	2.8	4.4	3.1	NA	9.41	NA
1995[1]	115.0	26.1	188.0	101.0	NA	.2	228.0	.43	.3	4.1	5.2	.3	NA	6.62	NA
1996[2]	110.0	48.0	212.0	107.0	NA	1.0	263.0	.45	.3	3.2	3.8	.6	NA	6.97	NA

[1] Preliminary. [2] Estimate. NA = Not avaliable. W = Withheld proprietary data. *Source: U.S. Geological Survey (USGS)*

Eggs

U.S. shell (table) egg and egg product exports fell during 1997 from a year earlier to 235 million dozen from 253 million, of which shell egg exports accounted for 100 million vs. 114 million, respectively. Forecasts for 1998 place exports at a record 255 million dozen with shell eggs accounting for 115 million. Japan is one of the largest importer of U.S. eggs, but total shipments in the first half of 1997 fell to 26 million dozen from 32 million a year earlier. Canada, Mexico and Hong Kong are also large importers, but only Canadian demand increased during 1997 while Hong Kong imports dropped sharply. As of late 1997 it was uncertain what effect the Asian currency turmoil might have on U.S. egg exports to the region. The European Union, paced by the Netherlands, imports U.S. eggs but the demand within the union has relatively large variance and is also subject to currency fluctuations.

China is the world's largest producer and consumer of eggs. China's production has more than doubled since the early 1990's with nearly a record 400 billion (33.3 billion dozen) produced in 1997, about half of the world's total. The U.S. is the world's second largest egg producer with 1997 production estimated at 78 billion (6.5 billion dozen). However, a major difference persists between the two nations in respect to usage. Much of China's production is directly consumed as fresh brown eggs whereas in the U.S. about a third of production is processed and white eggs are favored for table use. U.S. per capita table egg consumption in 1997 was forecast at 171 vs. 175 in 1996 and estimated at 169 in 1998. U.S. consumer preference has shifted to egg products relative to table eggs although per capita use is skewed towards tablestock. Per capita egg usage is much higher abroad than in the U.S. Japan's white egg use, in excess of 260, is the world's highest.

Foreign trade in eggs is small. The net totals favor exports. The E.C. generally accounts for about a third of world exports while Asia, paced by Japan and Hong Kong, import about 75% of the total. Japan's import breakdown includes hatched, table, dried and preserved eggs as well as egg albumen and yolks.

There are definitive seasonal swings in U.S. egg production and table consumption. The table egg flocks typically reach a low in mid-summer and then increase throughout the year with monthly production peaking in the winter. Table egg consumption tends to be highest when consumers have more time for leisurely meals, generally in the summer. Wholesale prices lack a clear seasonality, but on balance are highest during the winter months. U.S. total egg production in 1997 of 6.44 billion dozen compares with 6.36 billion in 1996 and forecasts of 6.58 billion in 1998.

The New York wholesale market egg price in 1996 averaged 88.18 cents per dozen, the 1997 average was estimated to have fallen to $.77-$.83, reflecting some slack in domestic demand and lower exports. Prices are forecast to fall again in 1998 to a range of $.72-$.78 per dozen.

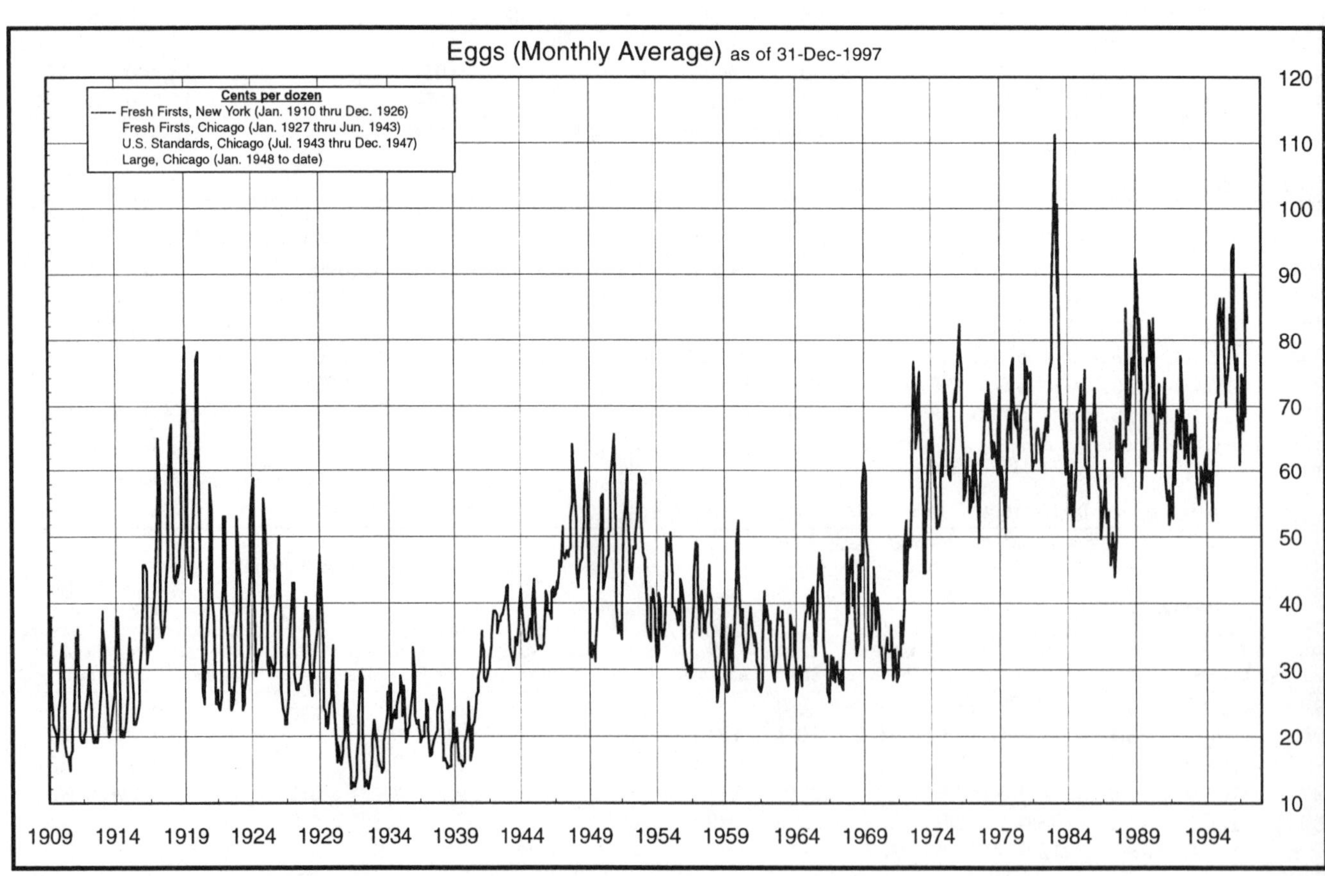

Vorld Production of Eggs In Millions of Eggs

ear	Brazil	China	France	Germany	Italy	Japan	Mexico	Russia[4]	Spain	Ukraine[4]	United Kingdom	United States	World Total[4]
989	12,174	140,900	15,050	17,794	11,223	40,356	17,950	49,042	10,140	17,393	10,547	67,178	534,736
990	13,454	158,920	14,629	16,800	11,454	40,318	18,040	47,470	10,659	16,287	10,658	67,987	526,296
991	13,655	184,400	15,300	15,525	11,568	41,638	19,840	46,900	10,184	15,188	12,485	69,612	529,075
992	14,190	230,980	15,375	15,165	11,454	42,911	19,650	42,900	8,675	13,445	10,699	70,860	541,859
993	12,700	235,960	15,355	13,678	11,502	43,252	21,471	40,300	8,454	11,766	10,645	72,072	593,734
994	13,460	281,010	16,370	13,960	11,599	43,047	25,896	37,400	9,670	10,145	10,620	74,136	644,545
995	16,065	301,860	16,911	13,838	12,017	42,167	25,760	33,720	9,983	9,500	10,644	74,592	668,567
996	15,932	317,560	16,500	13,940	11,923	42,891	26,045	31,500	8,952	8,760	10,668	76,296	687,053
997[1]	16,890	328,000	16,350	13,900	12,050	43,200	26,500	32,000	9,600	8,320	10,700	77,256	702,963
998[2]	17,735	360,000	16,450	13,900	12,000	43,000	26,100	32,500	9,900	7,800	10,600	78,960	738,576

[1] Preliminary. [2] Estimate. [3] Forecast. [4] Formerly part of the U.S.S.R.; data not reported separately until 1987. [4] Selected countries.
ource: Foreign Agricultural Service, U.S. Department of Agriculture (FAS-USDA)

Salient Statistics of Eggs in the United States

ear	Hens & Pullets: On Farm Dec. 1[3] (Thousands)	Hens & Pullets: Average Number During Year (Thousands)	Rate of Lay Per Layer During Year[4] (Number)	Eggs: Total Produced (Millions)	Eggs: Price in ¢ Per Dozen	Value of Production[5] Million $	Total Egg Production (Million Dozen)	Imports[6] (Million Dozen)	Exports[6] (Million Dozen)	Used for Hatching (Million Dozen)	Consumption: Total (Million Dozen)	Consumption: Per Capita Eggs[6] (Number)
.988	275,447	278,587	251	69,878	52.8	2,073	5,784	5.3	141.8	606.0	5,060	247.8
.989	271,064	270,415	250	67,503	68.9	3,877	5,598	25.2	91.6	641.8	4,917	238.6
.990	271,963	270,946	251	68,134	70.8	4,021	5,666	9.1	100.8	678.5	4,916	236.0
.991	279,325	275,451	252	69,465	67.6	3,915	5,779	2.3	154.5	708.6	4,938	234.6
.992	282,034	278,824	254	70,749	57.6	3,397	5,885	4.3	157.0	732.0	5,020	235.9
.993	290,626	284,770	253	71,936	63.4	3,800	5,960	4.7	158.9	769.6	5,082	236.2
1994	298,509	291,018	254	73,911	61.4	3,780	6,177	3.7	187.6	803.0	5,186	238.7
1995	298,753	293,854	253	74,591	62.4	3,880	6,216	4.1	208.9	847.2	5,167	235.7
1996[1]	303,754	297,958	256	76,281	75.0	4,757	6,359	5.4	253.1	864.7	5,249	237.1
1997[2]	311,084	303,166	255	77,401			6,555	4.0	258.0	900.0	5,398	241.7

[1] Preliminary. [2] Estimate. [3] All layers of laying age. [4] Number of eggs produced during the year divided by the average number of all layers of laying age on hand during the year. [5] Value of sales plus value of eggs consumed in households of producers. [6] Shell-egg equivalent of eggs and egg products.
Source: National Agricultural Statistics Service, U.S. Department of Agriculture (NASS-USDA)

Average Wholesale Price of Shell Eggs (Large) Delivered, Chicago In Cents Per Dozen

Year	Jan.	Feb.	Mar.	Apr.	May	June	July	Aug.	Sept.	Oct.	Nov.	Dec.	Average
1988	48.10	45.90	50.57	45.15	44.10	49.82	66.85	62.39	68.48	60.10	59.24	63.29	55.33
1989	64.57	63.79	84.68	69.10	67.27	69.55	69.30	77.09	74.70	76.90	86.48	92.25	74.64
1990	86.50	72.63	83.14	72.35	57.41	63.90	61.19	70.91	72.37	77.09	77.00	83.00	73.12
1991	80.19	69.00	83.10	64.59	59.93	63.35	73.07	71.30	68.80	67.96	68.50	74.12	70.33
1992	59.16	55.68	55.73	57.17	52.00	56.05	52.82	57.86	64.83	58.14	69.30	68.05	58.90
1993	65.65	63.61	77.50	71.07	61.90	67.64	62.79	67.59	60.64	64.21	65.55	65.55	66.14
1994	62.07	64.89	68.28	58.34	55.12	55.05	58.75	60.63	59.21	55.93	61.50	62.88	60.22
1995	58.55	58.24	60.22	59.87	52.50	56.84	68.10	65.93	71.10	71.34	83.93	86.35	66.08
1996	85.25	80.00	86.12	78.88	69.77	73.00	74.73	80.59	83.80	79.13	93.68	94.60	81.63
1997	79.77	75.18	77.25	68.55	64.40	61.02	74.66	66.07	74.26	68.39	89.87	82.68	73.51

[1] Preliminary. *Source: National Agricultural Statistics Service, U.S. Department of Agriculture (NASS-USDA)*

Total Egg Production in the United States In Cents Per Dozen

Year	Jan.	Feb.	Mar.	Apr.	May	June	July	Aug.	Sept.	Oct.	Nov.	Dec.	Total
1988	6,047	5,667	6,050	5,767	5,839	5,575	5,740	5,762	5,589	5,838	5,697	5,839	69,410
1989	5,758	5,182	5,782	5,569	5,696	5,498	5,648	5,613	5,450	5,658	5,543	5,781	67,178
1990	5,708	5,172	5,838	5,655	5,769	5,533	5,703	5,718	5,533	5,783	5,696	5,879	67,987
1991	5,865	5,316	5,935	5,666	5,796	5,643	5,840	5,855	5,675	5,915	5,811	6,035	69,352
1992	5,951	5,558	6,042	5,832	5,918	5,693	5,908	5,919	5,753	6,019	5,913	6,112	70,618
1993	6,030	5,432	6,067	5,861	6,009	5,816	5,992	6,015	5,876	6,144	6,085	6,296	71,623
1994	6,186	5,598	6,320	6,073	6,189	5,992	6,205	6,272	6,125	6,377	6,265	6,516	74,121
1995	6,369	5,714	6,448	6,177	6,251	6,010	6,145	6,146	5,990	6,260	6,232	6,523	74,265
1996[1]	6,398	5,954	6,495	6,243	6,340	6,169	6,440	6,447	6,235	6,495	6,409	6,698	76,323
1997[2]	6,574	5,904	6,620	6,351	6,507	6,276	6,443	6,483	6,350	6,646	6,549	6,812	77,515

[1] Preliminary. [2] Estimate. *Source: National Agricultural Statistics Service, U.S. Department of Agriculture (NASS-USDA)*

EGGS

Shell Eggs: Per Capita Disappearance in the United States In Number of Eggs

Year	First Quarter	Second Quarter	Third Quarter	Fourth Quarter	Total	Total Consumption (Million Dozen)	Year	First Quarter	Second Quarter	Third Quarter	Fourth Quarter	Total	Total Consumption (Million Dozen)
1986	55.2	52.7	52.6	55.2	215.8	4,327	1992	45.1	44.1	44.4	46.7	180.3	3,838
1987	53.6	52.2	52.2	53.7	211.6	4,282	1993	46.1	44.0	43.8	46.0	179.7	3,825
1988	53.2	49.3	49.4	50.7	202.6	4,138	1994	45.0	43.0	43.9	46.0	177.9	3,864
1989	49.2	47.2	47.5	49.0	192.2	3,978	1995	44.0	43.1	42.7	45.0	174.9	3,834
1990	47.0	46.3	46.0	47.7	186.8	3,891	1996[1]	44.5	42.1	43.4	45.0	175.0	3,873
1991	46.7	43.8	45.1	47.0	182.6	3,844	1997[2]	44.0	42.1	42.3	44.3	172.7	3,856

[1] Preliminary. [2] Estimate. *Source: Economic Research Service, U.S. Department of Agriculture (ERS-USDA)*

Egg-Feed Ratio[1] in the United States

Year	Jan.	Feb.	Mar.	Apr.	May	June	July	Aug.	Sept.	Oct.	Nov.	Dec.	Average
1988	8.2	7.5	8.0	6.9	6.0	5.5	6.9	7.1	8.3	7.7	8.0	8.2	7.3
1989	8.3	8.2	11.1	9.0	8.4	8.8	9.2	11.6	11.8	12.1	13.6	14.3	10.5
1990	14.3	11.5	13.0	11.0	8.5	9.0	7.9	9.9	10.9	12.1	12.4	12.3	11.1
1991	13.2	11.1	12.6	10.0	8.6	8.8	10.4	9.8	9.4	9.7	9.9	11.2	10.4
1992	8.4	7.8	7.4	7.6	6.7	7.0	7.3	8.1	9.6	9.3	11.2	11.1	8.5
1993	10.5	10.3	11.7	10.6	9.2	9.8	8.2	8.9	8.1	8.8	8.8	8.3	9.4
1994	7.9	8.0	8.6	7.9	7.2	7.1	7.9	9.0	9.2	9.0	10.3	10.2	8.5
1995	9.7	9.6	9.2	9.2	7.8	7.8	8.0	8.7	9.2	8.9	10.4	10.6	9.1
1996	10.1	8.9	9.3	8.1	6.6	6.7	6.3	6.9	8.1	9.3	11.3	12.5	8.7
1997[2]	10.0	9.9	8.6	7.4	7.2	6.6	8.2	7.8	9.3	8.7	11.4	11.0	8.8

[1] Pounds of laying feed equivalent in value to one dozen eggs. [2] Preliminary. *Source: Economic Research Service, U.S. Department of Agriculture (ERS)*

Total Eggs -- Supply and Distribution in the United States In Millions of Dozen

	Supply				Utilization			Consumption	
Year & Quarters	Beginning Stocks	Production	Imports[4]	Total Supply	Exports[4]	Eggs Used for Hatching	Ending Stocks	Total	Per Capita (Number)
1992 I	13.0	1,464	.8	1,477	40.5	180.0	15.8	1,241	58.5
II	15.8	1,454	1.0	1,471	36.1	186.9	17.0	1,231	57.9
III	17.0	1,464	1.3	1,482	34.5	180.6	15.8	1,251	58.7
IV	15.8	1,501	1.2	1,518	45.9	178.9	13.5	1,280	59.8
1993 I	13.5	1,461	.9	1,475	37.1	187.3	11.9	1,237	57.7
II	11.9	1,474	1.5	1,487	34.5	196.6	11.7	1,244	57.9
III	11.7	1,490	1.4	1,503	42.0	192.4	11.4	1,258	58.4
IV	11.4	1,535	.9	1,548	45.3	191.4	10.7	1,300	60.2
1994 I	10.7	1,509	1.0	1,520	40.2	195.3	12.1	1,273	58.8
II	12.1	1,521	1.1	1,535	45.5	205.3	11.9	1,272	58.6
III	11.9	1,550	1.0	1,563	49.3	202.8	13.8	1,297	59.6
IV	13.8	1,597	.6	1,611	52.6	199.6	14.9	1,344	61.6
1995 I	14.9	1,549	1.1	1,565	45.5	207.1	14.9	1,297	59.4
II	14.9	1,545	1.2	1,561	50.1	214.1	17.9	1,279	58.4
III	17.9	1,533	1.0	1,552	47.0	213.0	13.0	1,279	58.3
IV	13.0	1,589	.8	1,602	66.4	212.9	11.2	1,312	59.6
1996[1] I	11.2	1,571	1.5	1,583	59.3	217.4	9.8	1,297	58.8
II	9.8	1,563	1.6	1,574	65.6	217.2	9.6	1,282	58.0
III	9.6	1,594	1.2	1,604	66.0	215.8	11.9	1,311	59.1
IV	11.9	1,632	1.0	1,645	62.2	214.3	8.5	1,360	61.2
1997[2] I	8.5	1,587	1.9	1,597	61.7	220.3	6.5	1,309	58.8
II	6.5	1,591	1.5	1,599	50.3	225.8	6.5	1,317	59.0
III	6.5	1,603	1.5	1,611	51.0	224.1	8.2	1,328	59.4
IV	8.2	1,655	1.0	1,664	57.0	225.0	10.0	1,372	61.2
1998[3] I	10.0	1,605	1.0	1,616	62.0	230.0	10.0	1,314	58.5
II	10.0	1,615	1.0	1,626	63.0	240.0	10.0	1,313	58.3
III	10.0	1,670	1.0	1,681	65.0	235.0	10.0	1,371	60.8

[1] Preliminary. [2] Estimate. [3] Forecast. [4] Shell-egg equivalent of eggs and egg products. *Source: Economic Research Service, U.S. Department of Agriculture (ERS-USDA)*

Hens and Pullets of Laying Age (Layers) in the United States, on First of Month In Thousands

Year	Jan.	Feb.	Mar.	Apr.	May	June	July	Aug.	Sept.	Oct.	Nov.	Dec.
1988	286,470	285,670	283,225	279,221	277,449	272,482	270,282	271,220	273,136	275,191	276,415	275,447
1989	272,243	272,780	271,590	269,278	267,269	267,239	267,088	266,253	267,656	267,919	270,006	271,064
1990	271,164	272,826	271,921	272,813	270,664	269,040	265,647	266,767	267,004	268,835	270,274	271,963
1991	273,917	275,533	274,446	272,541	272,150	272,944	272,779	272,998	274,277	276,187	278,433	279,325
1992	280,697	279,274	279,117	279,009	276,757	275,645	275,179	275,091	274,010	279,233	280,183	282,034
1993	281,639	282,933	282,005	282,480	281,468	280,795	280,517	282,201	282,341	284,771	285,298	290,626
1994	290,413	289,625	290,416	290,979	289,125	288,398	287,454	288,484	292,116	294,576	295,719	298,509
1995	300,331	298,202	297,689	296,290	294,697	290,806	289,018	286,519	289,595	290,889	294,486	298,293
1996	299,261	298,320	298,348	298,029	295,123	293,740	294,044	296,612	296,911	298,433	299,910	303,754
1997[1]	304,040	302,486	303,406	303,035	302,250	300,171	298,641	298,417	299,578	305,864	306,583	311,084

[1] Preliminary. *Source: National Agricultural Statistics Service, U.S. Department of Agriculture (NASS-USDA)*

Eggs Laid Per Hundred Layers in the United States In Number of Eggs

Year	Jan.	Feb.	Mar.	Apr.	May	June	July	Aug.	Sept.	Oct.	Nov.	Dec.	Average
1988	2,154	2,027	2,189	2,103	2,150	2,081	2,150	2,150	2,073	2,152	2,105	2,179	2,126
1989	2,154	1,937	2,178	2,111	2,165	2,089	2,148	2,135	2,071	2,142	2,098	2,181	2,117
1990	2,149	1,940	2,185	2,120	2,171	2,105	2,179	2,181	2,104	2,189	2,140	2,208	2,139
1991	2,186	1,977	2,217	2,124	2,168	2,108	2,186	2,190	2,106	2,175	2,124	2,208	2,147
1992	2,176	2,036	2,216	2,148	2,186	2,110	2,196	2,204	2,125	2,200	2,140	2,226	2,164
1993	2,192	1,970	2,209	2,132	2,182	2,112	2,175	2,183	2,124	2,209	2,167	2,237	2,158
1994	2,199	1,987	2,246	2,160	2,204	2,142	2,222	2,230	2,152	2,227	2,180	2,176	2,177
1995	2,130	1,919	2,173	2,092	2,137	2,075	2,137	2,135	2,065	2,140	2,108	2,183	2,108
1996	2,141	1,996	2,178	2,105	2,153	2,099	2,180	2,172	2,094	2,171	2,124	2,199	2,134
1997[1]	2,161	1,943	2,176	2,093	2,156	2,092	2,155	2,164	2,097	2,172	2,121	2,193	2,127

[1] Preliminary. *Source: National Agricultural Statistics Service, U.S. Department of Agriculture (NASS-USDA)*

Egg-Type Chicks Hatched by Commercial Hatcheries in the United States In Thousands

Year	Jan.	Feb.	Mar.	Apr.	May	June	July	Aug.	Sept.	Oct.	Nov.	Dec.	Total
1988	29,274	28,433	35,615	34,749	35,984	33,049	24,876	27,838	30,918	31,007	27,181	27,311	366,235
1989	26,602	27,271	32,597	36,135	38,376	34,708	29,828	32,217	32,862	33,456	29,666	29,284	383,002
1990	32,004	32,107	36,509	36,915	37,895	34,471	31,582	32,949	31,219	32,926	29,809	31,046	398,432
1991	34,487	34,837	37,041	39,775	38,404	36,227	33,696	33,656	34,007	34,307	30,400	32,717	419,554
1992	32,496	31,950	36,490	35,755	38,513	34,568	32,265	28,349	28,760	32,843	27,718	31,612	391,319
1993	34,885	34,009	38,264	37,163	36,742	35,587	33,980	31,455	31,775	31,634	30,074	30,448	405,986
1994	33,236	31,086	33,489	35,657	35,322	31,985	29,613	31,295	31,587	32,066	26,075	30,166	381,577
1995	32,374	32,743	36,019	35,078	37,540	34,996	29,572	31,442	33,586	33,383	29,129	30,639	396,501
1996	31,523	34,627	37,474	35,628	38,607	34,076	33,331	32,393	32,070	33,065	31,437	33,017	407,248
1997[1]	33,331	35,318	37,648	38,746	38,891	36,955	33,954	32,903	35,794	35,175	27,803	35,604	422,122

[1] Preliminary. *Source: National Agricultural Statistics Service, U.S. Department of Agriculture (NASS-USDA)*

Cold Storage Holdings of Frozen Eggs in the United States, on First of Month In Millions of Pounds[1]

Year	Jan.	Feb.	Mar.	Apr.	May	June	July	Aug.	Sept.	Oct.	Nov.	Dec.
1988	17.3	18.3	18.3	14.1	17.3	20.3	25.3	22.9	24.5	22.2	20.0	17.9
1989	19.6	19.7	19.0	14.8	15.3	16.2	15.1	16.5	15.0	14.4	14.9	13.4
1990	13.6	14.2	15.2	16.8	19.7	16.8	18.1	17.1	17.1	16.6	16.8	17.2
1991	14.7	14.8	14.0	14.1	13.0	13.5	14.2	18.1	16.3	16.5	17.0	15.1
1992	16.0	20.0	19.2	19.7	18.8	18.9	21.1	19.5	20.2	20.0	21.7	18.7
1993	17.2	16.7	16.9	15.1	14.3	15.5	15.1	17.6	18.1	14.4	14.0	13.5
1994	13.7	14.8	15.8	15.6	16.3	15.2	15.4	19.0	19.7	17.8	20.0	19.1
1995	19.5	19.5	18.3	18.5	17.3	18.1	22.9	20.6	18.0	16.2	14.4	12.5
1996	13.8	15.6	16.2	12.4	11.5	11.4	11.7	13.5	15.0	14.9	12.6	10.4
1997[2]	10.2	11.0	11.5	8.5	8.5	8.4	8.6	9.2	11.1	10.9	10.9	10.3

[1] Converted on basis 39.5 pounds frozen eggs equal 1 case [2] Preliminary. *Source: National Agricultural Statistics Service, U.S. Department of Agriculture*

Electric Power

U.S. net generation of electric power in the January-July 1997 period was 1.8 trillion kilowatthours. That was virtually unchanged from the comparable period of 1996 and up from the same period in 1995 when it was 1.72 trillion kilowatthours. For all of 1996, U.S. electric power generation by electric utilities was 3.08 trillion kilowatthours.

In July 1997, U.S. generation of electric power was 904 billion kilowatthours. That was some 14 percent above the June 1996 total. Cooling demands in the summer and heating demands in the winter lead to increased electric power generation in those seasons. Of the July 1997 total electric power output, some 167 billion kilowatthours were provided by coal-powered electric utilities. Another 9.2 billion kilowatthours came from petroleum-powered electric utilities. Gas-powered electric utilities generated 40.1 billion kilowatthours while nuclear-powered electric utilities provided 57.4 billion kilowatthours. Hydroelectric based utilities generated 30.1 billion kilowatthours in July 1997. Geothermal-powered utilities provided 512 million kilowatthours while other alternative powered utilities such as biomass, wind, photovoltaic and solar thermal generated 169 million kilowatthours.

Electric utility stocks of coal in July 1997 were 110 million short tons which was down from 121 million tons in June 1997. In July 1996, electric utility coal stocks were 120 million tons. Utilities in Pennsylvania had the most coal on hand in July 1997 with 8.2 million tons, followed by Texas with 7.6 million tons.

Electric utility stocks of petroleum in July 1997 were 45.7 million barrels. That was down from 46.9 million barrels in June 1997. In July 1996, electric utility petroleum stocks were 46 million barrels. In July 1997, Florida had the largest petroleum stocks at 6.8 million barrels followed by California utilities at 5.8 million barrels.

U.S. electric utility retail sales of electricity in July 1997 were 294 billion kilowatthours. That was up from 259 billion kilowatthours in June 1997. In the January-July 1997 period retail sales of electricity were 1.78 trillion kilowatthours. For the comparable period of 1996 retail sales were 1.79 trillion kilowatthours.

In July 1997, U.S. electric utility retail sales of electricity to residential customers totaled 108.9 billion kilowatthours. Retail sales to the commercial sector were 87.6 billion kilowatthours. Sales to the industrial sector were 88.5 billion kilowatthours. Sales to others, which includes public and street lighting, sales to railroads and railways, and interdepartmental sales were 8.9 billion kilowatthours. For all of 1996, retail sales of electricity to the residential sector were 1.08 trillion kilowatthours. Sales to the commercial sector were 892 billion kilowatthours, while sales to the industrial sector were 1.01 trillion kilowatthours. Sales to other sectors were 100 billion kilowatthours.

World Electricity Production (Monthly Average) In Millions of Kilowatt Hours

Year	Australia	Canada	China	Germany	India	Italy	Japan	Rep. of Korea	Russia[3]	South Africa	Ukraine[3]	United Kingdom	United States
1987	11,027	41,361	41,442	34,873	16,824	16,748	58,248	6,166	138,744	12,550	------	25,161	226,561
1988	11,592	42,164	49,460	35,228	18,427	16,931	62,811	7,122	142,090	13,062	------	25,761	239,875
1989	12,316	41,628	49,549	36,716	20,428	17,570	66,563	7,873	143,500	13,527	------	25,153	246,659
1990	12,923	40,169	51,500	37,433	22,025	18,074	71,439	8,972	139,455	13,782	------	26,581	250,979
1991	13,071	42,326	55,918	44,949	23,893	18,503	74,007	9,885	136,156	14,026	------	26,900	254,818
1992	13,313	41,803	61,562	44,761	25,081	18,854	74,611	10,914	84,038	14,008	21,044	27,240	256,209
1993	13,646	42,591	67,723	37,722	26,961	18,566	75,559	12,036	79,716	14,572	19,159	26,834	262,158
1994	13,929	44,502	75,312	37,786	29,250	19,292	80,361	13,754	75,740	15,650	17,425	27,637	272,354
1995	14,450	44,868	81,979	38,207	31,675	20,093	82,497	15,388	72,291	15,752	16,167	27,635	278,776
1996[1]	14,119	45,747	88,275	45,586	32,808	21,227	73,058	17,124	71,811	16,679	15,086	30,356	257,872
1997[2]	14,027	45,898	90,209	47,167	33,899	22,329	72,931	18,576	63,720	17,528	17,100	29,312	285,455

[1] Preliminary. [2] Estimate. [3] Formerly part of the U.S.S.R.; data not reported separately until 1992. *Source: United Nations*

Installed Capacity, Capability & Peak Load of the U.S. Electric Utility Industry In Millions of Kilowatt Hours

	Installed Generating Capacity at Dec. 31															
		Type of Prime Mover				Type of Ownership										
Year	Total Electric Utility Industry	Hydro	Gas Turbine & Steam	Nuclear Power	Internal Combustion	Investor Owned	Cooperative	Sub-total Gov't.	Municipal Utilities	Federal	Power Districts, State Projects	Capability at Winter Peak Load	Non-Coincident Winter Peak Load	Capacity Margin Non-Coincident Peak Load (%)	Total Electric Utility Industry Generation	Annual Peak Load Factor (%)
1987	718.1	85.9	524.3	101.6	6.2	552.8	26.4	138.9	39.4	64.7	34.9	663.0	448.3	23.4	2,572.1	60.8
1988	723.9	86.9	526.6	103.4	7.0	557.8	26.4	139.7	40.4	64.8	34.5	676.9	466.5	20.0	2,704.3	59.5
1989	730.9	87.5	529.1	106.7	7.5	562.1	26.4	142.4	40.7	67.2	34.5	685.2	496.4	22.3	2,784.3	62.2
1990	735.1	87.2	531.1	108.0	8.7	568.8	26.3	139.9	40.1	65.4	34.4	696.8	484.0	20.4	2,808.2	60.4
1991	740.0	88.7	534.1	108.4	8.8	573.0	26.5	140.5	40.4	65.6	34.5	703.2	485.4	20.2	2,825.0	60.9
1992	741.7	89.7	534.5	107.9	9.6	572.9	26.0	142.7	41.6	66.1	35.0	707.8	493.0	21.1	2,797.2	61.1
1993	744.7	90.2	536.9	107.8	9.8	575.2	26.1	143.4	41.8	66.1	35.5	712.0	521.7	17.1	2,882.5	61.0
1994	746.0	90.3	537.9	107.9	9.9	574.8	26.4	144.7	42.0	66.3	36.4	715.1	518.3	16.7	2,910.7	61.2
1995[1]	750.5	91.1	541.6	107.9	9.9	578.7	27.1	144.8	42.2	65.9	36.6	727.7	544.7	13.2	2,994.5	59.8
1996[2]	754.9	90.9	544.8	109.2	10.0	581.1	26.9	146.9	42.7	67.2	36.9	740.5	545.1	14.9	3,073.1	61.0

[1] Preliminary. *Source: Edison Electric Institute (EEI)*

Available Electricity and Energy Sales in the United States In Billions of Kilowatt Hours

	Net Generation									Sales to Ultimate Customers							
	Electric Utility Industry																
Year	Total[2]	Hydro	Natural Gas	Coal	Fuel Oil	Nuclear	Other Sources[3]	Total	Total Million $	Total	Residential	Inter-Departmental	Commercial	Industrial	Street & Highway Lighting	Other Public Auth.	Railways & Railroads
1983	2,310	332.1	274.1	1,259	144.5	293.7	6.5	2,368	129,589	2,160	750	5.4	545.6	783	13.9	57.3	4.3
1984	2,416	321.2	297.4	1,342	119.8	327.6	8.6	2,488	143,093	2,281	782	5.8	578.1	835	14.2	59.9	4.5
1985	2,470	281.1	291.9	1,402	100.2	383.7	10.7	2,568	149,162	2,306	792	5.3	605.9	820	14.6	62.2	4.7
1986	2,487	290.8	248.5	1,386	136.6	414.0	11.5	2,599	152,467	2,355	820	5.2	629.0	819	15.0	61.9	4.7
1987	2,572	249.7	272.6	1,464	118.5	455.3	12.3	2,719	155,700	2,435	846	4.5	658.4	843	14.4	63.0	4.9
1988	2,704	222.9	252.8	1,541	148.9	527.0	12.0	2,879	162,388	2,554	886	4.2	697.8	881	14.6	64.6	5.1
1989	2,784	265.1	266.6	1,554	158.3	529.4	11.3	2,985	169,627	2,621	898	4.3	715.9	912	14.6	69.3	5.3
1990	2,808	279.9	264.1	1,560	117.0	576.9	10.7	3,041	176,468	2,684	915	4.2	738.9	931	15.2	72.8	5.3
1991	1,825	275.5	264.2	1,551	111.5	612.6	10.1	3,100	185,118	2,764	948	2.6	753.3	934	15.6	76.1	5.3
1992	2,797	239.6	263.9	1,576	88.9	618.8	10.2	3,107	187,283	2,735	929	2.6	755.7	949	15.8	77.2	5.2
1993	2,883	265.1	258.9	1,639	99.5	610.3	9.6	3,210	197,992	2,860	994	2.7	803.1	957	18.1	69.7	5.4
1994	2,911	243.7	291.1	1,635	91.0	640.4	8.9	3,283	202,597	2,936	1,008	3.0	833.5	990	18.5	70.6	5.8
1995	2,995	293.7	307.3	1,653	60.8	673.4	6.4	3,395	207,652	3,017	1,042	2.1	863.5	1,006	17.9	69.9	5.5
1996[1]	3,073	324.5	262.3	1,737	67.0	674.7	7.2	3,473	212,390	3,103	1,082	2.5	887.1	1,028	18.0	70.3	5.3

[1] Preliminary. [2] Includes internal combustion. [3] Includes electricity produced from geothermal, wood, waste, wind, solar, etc.
Source: Edison Electric Insititute (EEI)

Electric Power Production by Electric Utilities in the United States In Millions of Kilowatt Hours

Year	Jan.	Feb.	Mar.	Apr.	May	June	July	Aug.	Sept.	Oct.	Nov.	Dec.	Total
1983	195,579	172,479	182,488	170,372	174,392	191,048	220,165	229,957	195,604	182,931	183,949	212,319	2,310,285
1984	216,632	189,564	200,107	181,084	192,217	209,648	221,245	229,296	195,198	190,936	190,380	199,996	2,416,304
1985	227,856	198,242	194,970	184,877	196,790	205,363	226,722	226,050	202,499	194,789	192,427	219,255	2,469,841
1986	217,470	192,336	196,834	186,074	197,315	215,015	242,672	225,166	206,692	197,754	196,432	213,551	2,487,310
1987	222,749	194,034	201,849	189,496	206,074	225,589	247,915	247,645	213,008	203,009	200,258	220,500	2,572,127
1988	237,897	216,937	214,013	196,000	208,371	232,747	257,461	267,693	220,179	210,608	209,593	232,752	2,704,250
1989	232,747	219,826	226,742	208,042	220,124	235,689	257,050	258,687	227,150	219,910	219,300	259,038	2,784,304
1990	237,289	212,880	226,034	211,070	222,908	249,175	266,375	268,527	237,017	224,694	213,748	237,434	2,808,151
1991	248,455	210,821	221,400	209,004	234,373	248,427	271,976	268,115	233,885	223,430	221,377	233,760	2,825,023
1992	243,970	217,761	224,665	210,837	220,355	236,842	266,148	255,203	234,760	221,289	221,263	244,126	2,797,219
1993	245,782	224,617	234,801	211,374	222,396	249,633	282,292	279,132	236,603	223,629	225,855	246,412	2,882,525
1994	261,697	225,011	231,544	214,817	227,703	263,859	278,149	274,645	237,663	227,972	224,745	242,906	2,910,712
1995	253,077	228,127	233,675	217,381	236,381	256,083	292,827	304,709	245,574	234,409	234,117	258,170	2,994,529
1996	268,713	245,388	247,989	226,423	251,570	268,644	289,329	290,458	250,672	240,674	241,077	258,138	3,079,074
1997[1]	274,177	234,315	244,569	231,045	243,206	266,565	304,344	294,386	266,690	253,430			3,135,272

[1] Preliminary. *Source: Energy Information Administration, U.S. Department of Energy*

Use of Fuels for Electric Generation in the United States

	Consumption of Fuel									
Year	Coal (Thousand Short Tons)	Fuel Oil (Thousand Barrels)[2]	Gas (Million Cubic Feet)	Total Fuel in Coal Equivalent[3] (Thousand Short Tons)	Net Generation by Fuels[4] (Million Kw. Hr.)	Pounds of Coal Per Kw. Hr. (Pounds)	Cost of Fossil-Fuel at Elec. Util. ¢ Mil. BTU	Average Cost of Fuel Per Kw. Hr. (¢)	Heat Rate BTU Per Kw. Hr.	Cost Per Million BTU Consumed (¢)
1983	625,211	245,497	2,910,767	867,621	1,678,021	.993	220.6	2.40	10,547	227.1
1984	664,399	204,479	3,111,342	909,156	1,758,882	.990	219.1	2.41	10,385	232.0
1985	693,841	173,414	3,044,083	926,793	1,794,276	.990	209.4	2.27	10,429	217.7
1986	685,056	230,482	2,602,370	907,720	1,770,925	.989	175.0	1.92	10,423	184.5
1987	717,894	199,378	2,844,051	944,420	1,854,895	.981	170.6	1.84	10,354	177.7
1988	758,372	248,096	2,635,613	984,969	1,942,353	.984	164.3	1.76	10,328	170.7
1989	766,888	267,451	2,787,012	1,004,964	1,978,577	.987	167.5	1.79	10,312	174.0
1990	773,549	196,054	2,787,332	988,300	1,940,712	.997	168.9	1.80	10,366	174.1
1991	772,268	184,886	2,789,014	987,469	1,926,801	.996	160.3	1.75	10,322	169.6
1992	779,860	147,335	2,765,608	983,484	1,928,683	.990	159.0	1.72	10,340	166.6
1993	813,508	162,454	2,682,440	1,017,086	1,997,605	.993	159.5	1.72	10,351	166.6
1994	817,270	151,004	2,987,146	1,033,575	2,017,646	.999	152.6	1.59	10,425	152.6
1995	829,007	102,150	3,196,507	1,039,174	2,021,064	1.003	145.3	1.48	10,173	145.2
1996[1]	874,616	112,565	2,732,496	1,063,755	2,066,666	1.007	151.9	1.55	10,176	151.9

[1] Preliminary. [2] 42-gallon barrels. [3] Coal equivalents are calculated on the basis of Btu instead of generation data. [4] Excludes wood & waste fuels.
Source: Edison Electric Institute (EEI)

Fertilizer

The three primary fertilizer chemicals used in the United States are nitrogen, phosphorus and potassium. These chemicals provide the basic nutrients to plants. The basic nitrogen fertilizer is ammonia, which is comprised of natural gas and nitrogen. Ammonia can be applied in liquid form below the surface of the soil or converted into solid nitrogenous fertilizers. Crop plants cultivated for both human consumption and as animal feed require nitrogen for proper nutrition and maturation. Certain plants such as soybeans are able to convert atmospheric nitrogen into a usable form through a process called fixation.

All commercial fertilizers contain their nitrogen in the ammonium and/or nitrate form or in a form that is converted to these forms once the fertilizer is applied to the soil. According to the U.S. Geological Survey, in 1996 there were 25 ammonia producers with 41 plant locations in the U.S. Many companies in the fertilizer industry were expanding their operations to include production of all three major plant nutrients.

U.S. production of synthetic anhydrous ammonia in 1996 was 14.6 million metric tonnes, contained nitrogen. That was 12 percent higher than in 1995. U.S. exports of ammonia in 1996 were 435,000 tonnes, up 36 percent from 1995. Imports for consumption of synthetic anhydrous ammonia in 1996 were 2.46 million tonnes, down six percent from the previous year. U.S. apparent consumption of ammonia in 1996 was 16.6 million tonnes, up eight percent from the year before. Producer stocks of ammonia on December 31, 1996 were 953,000 tonnes, about the same as the year before. World production of anhydrous ammonia in 1996 was 97.5 million tonnes, up one percent from 1995. World trade in anhydrous ammonia was 11 million tonnes in 1996.

Potash denotes a variety of mined and manufactured salts, all containing the element potassium in water soluble form. As a fertilizer, potassium in water-soluble form activates plant enzymes, aids photosynthesis in the leaves, and increases disease resistance. U.S. production of potash in 1996 was 2.89 million tonnes, down five percent from 1995. Exports of potash in 1996 were 1.1 million tonnes, up 17 percent from the previous year. Imports for consumption in 1996 were 8.14 million tonnes, up two percent from 1995. U.S. apparent consumption of potash in 1996 was 10 million tonnes, up one percent from 1995.

Phosphorus is an essential element for plant and animal nutrition. Phosphate rock minerals are the only significant global resources of phosphorus. The U.S. is the world's leading producer and consumer of phosphate rock, used to manufacture phosphate fertilizers. U.S. marketable phosphate rock production in July 1997 fell four percent from the previous month. Production in 1996 was 46.5 million tonnes. Domestic use of phosphate rock in July 1997 was 3.3 million tonnes.

World Production of Ammonia In Thousands of Metric Tons of Contained Nitrogen

Year	Canada	China	France	Germany	India	Indonesia	Japan	Mexico	Netherlands	Poland	Russia[3]	United States	Total
1989	3,339	17,000	1,476	2,932	6,661	2,526	1,539	2,100	2,901	2,360	19,400	12,280	99,331
1990	3,054	17,500	1,586	2,690	7,010	2,789	1,531	2,164	3,188	1,962	18,200	12,680	97,160
1991	3,016	18,000	1,604	2,123	7,132	2,706	1,553	2,221	3,033	1,531	17,100	12,803	93,800
1992	3,104	18,000	1,848	2,113	7,452	2,688	1,602	2,203	2,588	1,490	8,786	13,400	93,600
1993	3,410	19,000	1,871	2,100	7,176	2,888	1,471	1,758	2,472	1,163	8,138	12,600	91,700
1994	3,470	20,100	1,480	2,170	7,334	2,800	1,483	2,030	2,500	1,230	7,500	13,400	92,200
1995[1]	3,773	22,600	1,470	1,470	7,713	2,850	1,584	1,992	2,500	1,415	7,500	13,000	96,100
1996[2]	3,800	23,000	1,500	1,200	7,800	2,870	1,560	2,150	2,500	1,400	7,000	14,600	97,500

[1] Preliminary. [2] Estimate. [3] Formerly part of the U.S.S.R.; data not reported separately until 1992. *Source: U.S. Geological Survey (USGS)*

Salient Statistics of Nitrogen[3] (Ammonia) in the United States In Thousands of Metric Tons

	Net Import Reliance as a % of Apparent	-- Production[3] (Fixed) --					--- Nitrogen[5] Compounds ---		- Stocks, Dec. 31 -			--------- Average Price ($ Per Tonne) ---------			
										Fixed Nitrogen	Ammonia	---------- Urea ----------		Ammonium Nitrate:	Ammonia F.O.B.
Year	Consumption	Fertilizer	Non-fertilizer	Total	Imports[4] (Fixed)	Exports	Produced	Consumption	Ammonia	Compounds	Consumption (Apparent)	F.O.B. Gulf[6] Coast	F.O.B. Corn Belt	F.O.B. Corn Belt	Gulf Coast
1989	17	11,131	1,148	12,280	2,861	346	9,634	9,687	849	787	14,871	139-145	110-120	105-115	104
1990	15	11,573	1,107	12,680	2,673	482	9,851	9,902	797	1,451	14,923	155-156	155-165	120-125	106
1991	14	11,559	1,244	12,803	2,742	580	9,770	9,815	936	1,607	14,826	142-143	146-160	108-130	117
1992	14	12,000	1,349	13,400	2,690	354	10,404	10,448	1,059	1,789	15,600	142-146	149-160	138-149	106
1993	17	11,300	1,320	12,620	2,657	378	10,000	10,100	852	1,600	15,100	139-141	141-165	138-149	121
1994	19	11,600	1,750	13,350	3,450	215	10,000	11,700	956	1,650	16,500	219-226	204-215	165-176	211
1995[1]	15	11,600	1,410	13,010	2,630	319	10,400	10,700	959	1,580	15,300	217-222	220-235	162-170	191
1996[2]	18	12,600	1,930	14,530	2,460	435	10,300	11,100	953	1,510	16,600	188-190	197-210	160-170	225

[1] Preliminary. [2] Estimate. [3] Anhydrous ammonia, synthetic. [4] For consumption. [5] Major downstream nitrogen compounds. [6] Granular.
Source: U.S. Geological Survey (USGS)

World Production of Phosphate Rock, Basic Slag & Guano   In Thousands of Metric Tons (Gross Weight)

Year	Brazil	China	Egypt	Israel	Jordan	Morocco	Russia[3]	Senegal	Syria	Togo	Tunisia	United States	World Total
1987	4,777	15,000	1,175	3,798	6,800	21,300	34,100	1,874	1,986	2,644	6,390	40,954	151,962
1988	4,672	17,000	1,154	3,479	6,611	25,015	37,000	2,326	2,186	3,464	6,103	45,389	166,436
1989	3,655	20,000	1,355	3,922	6,900	18,067	37,500	2,273	2,256	3,355	6,610	49,817	167,342
1990	2,968	21,550	1,151	3,516	6,082	21,396	36,800	2,147	1,633	2,314	6,258	46,343	162,783
1991	3,280	22,000	1,652	3,370	4,433	17,900	28,400	1,741	1,359	2,965	6,352	48,096	150,731
1992	2,850	21,400	2,000	3,595	4,296	19,145	11,500	2,284	1,266	2,083	6,400	46,965	139,000
1993	3,419	21,200	1,585	3,680	4,129	18,193	9,400	1,667	931	1,794	5,500	35,494	119,000
1994	3,937	24,100	1,500	3,961	4,217	19,764	8,000	1,587	1,203	2,149	5,699	41,100	128,000
1995[1]	3,590	19,300	1,500	4,063	4,984	20,200	8,800	1,500	1,551	2,560	7,241	43,500	130,000
1996[2]	3,600	21,000	1,500	3,800	5,350	20,800	8,500	1,600	2,000	2,600	7,100	45,400	133,000

[1] Preliminary. [2] Estimate. [3] Formerly part of the U.S.S.R.; data not reported separately until 1992. *Source: U.S. Geological Survey (USGS)*

Salient Statistics of Phosphate Rock in the United States   In Thousands of Metric Tons

Year	Mine Production	Marketable Production	Value Million $	Imports for Consumption	Exports	Apparent Consumption	Stocks, Dec. 31 (Producer)	Price - $ Avg. Per Metric Ton (F.O.B. Mine)	Avg. Price of Florida & North Carolina - $ Tonne - F.O.B. Mine (-60% to +74%) - Domestic	Export	Average
1987	148,426	40,954	793	464	8,454	35,683	10,884	19.37	18.93	22.87	19.77
1988	162,299	45,389	888	676	8,092	41,025	9,323	19.56	18.29	25.24	19.56
1989	170,268	49,817	1,084	705	7,842	42,143	11,027	21.76	20.65	28.67	21.76
1990	151,277	46,343	1,075	451	6,238	43,967	8,912	23.20	22.44	30.43	23.55
1991	154,485	48,096	1,109	552	5,082	40,177	10,168	23.06	22.67	31.69	23.69
1992	154,936	46,965	1,058	1,530	3,723	42,920	12,612	22.53	22.47	31.69	23.32
1993	107,000	35,500	759	534	3,200	38,300	9,220	21.38	21.26	28.51	21.89
1994	157,000	41,100	869	620	2,800	42,900	5,980	21.14	21.79	25.60	22.08
1995[1]	165,000	43,500	947	1,080	2,990	42,000	5,710	21.75	21.29	28.35	21.75
1996[2]	172,000	44,200	1,020	1,790	2,200	42,100	6,880	23.10	22.50	34.23	23.10

[1] Preliminary. [2] Estimate. *Source: U.S. Geological Survey (USGS)*

World Production of Marketable Potash   In Thousands of Metric Tons (K_2O Equivalent)

Year	Belarus[3]	Brazil	Canada	China	France	Germany	Israel	Jordan	Russia[3]	Spain	United Kingdom	United States	World Total
1987	------	62	7,668	40	1,539	5,709	1,253	734	10,888	741	429	1,262	30,526
1988	------	54	8,154	22	1,502	5,800	1,244	785	11,301	855	460	1,521	31,820
1989	------	97	7,333	42	1,195	5,388	1,273	792	10,200	741	462	1,595	29,276
1990	------	66	6,989	29	1,292	4,960	1,311	841	9,000	686	488	1,713	27,493
1991	------	101	7,406	32	1,129	3,855	1,320	818	8,560	585	495	1,749	26,136
1992	3,311	85	7,270	21	1,141	3,460	1,300	794	3,470	594	529	1,705	23,900
1993	1,947	173	3,836	25	890	2,861	1,309	822	2,628	661	555	1,510	20,400
1994	3,021	242	8,037	74	870	3,286	1,259	930	2,498	684	580	1,400	23,100
1995[1]	3,211	370	8,855	80	799	3,280	1,320	1,070	2,800	650	582	1,480	24,700
1996[2]	3,200	375	8,170	110	800	3,200	1,320	1,200	2,800	600	580	1,390	23,900

[1] Preliminary. [2] Estimate. [3] Formerly part of the U.S.S.R.; data not reported separately until 1992. *Source: U.S. Geological Survey (USGS)*

Salient Statistics of Potash in the United States   In Thousands of Metric Tons (K_2O Equivalent)

Year	Net Import as % of Consumption	Production	Sales by Producers	Value Million $	Imports for Consumption	Exports	Apparent Consumption	Producer Stocks, Dec. 31	$ Per Ton: Avg. Value Per Ton of Product - $	$ Per Ton: Avg. Value of K2O Equiv.	Avg. Price[3] $ Per Tonne
1987	71	1,262	1,485	197.7	4,073	470	5,088	155	67.98	131.73	93.00
1988	73	1,521	1,427	240.3	4,217	380	5,264	248	85.75	168.37	132.00
1989	66	1,595	1,536	271.5	3,410	446	4,500	307	90.28	176.74	137.00
1990	68	1,713	1,716	303.3	4,164	470	5,410	303	89.46	176.80	130.00
1991	67	1,749	1,709	304.5	4,158	624	5,243	343	91.52	178.20	131.00
1992	67	1,705	1,766	334.4	4,248	663	5,351	283	96.45	189.36	134.00
1993	72	1,510	1,480	286.0	4,360	415	5,430	305	94.36	192.72	130.74
1994	76	1,400	1,470	284.0	4,800	464	5,810	234	95.93	193.50	125.34
1995[1]	75	1,480	1,400	284.0	4,820	409	5,820	312	98.58	202.43	137.99
1996[2]	76	1,390	1,430	299.0	4,940	481	5,890	265	101.08	208.86	134.07

[1] Preliminary. [2] Estimate. [3] Unit of K_2O, standard 60% muriate F.O.B. mine. *Source: U.S. Geological Survey (USGS)*

Fish

The USDA reported that farmer sales of catfish to processors are forecast to reach 520 million pounds in 1997, ten percent higher than in 1996. This would mark the first time that production was over half a billion pounds. In the first eight months of 1997, catfish deliveries to processing plants were 355 million pounds, 12 percent more than in the comparable period of 1996. This was the third year of higher sales. The early outlook for 1998 is that production growth will likely slow due to smaller fish inventories.

At the beginning of July, growers in the four major producing states (Mississippi, Alabama, Arkansas and Louisiana) reported holding larger inventories of broodfish than in 1996. At the same time, growers reported that inventories of stocker and fingerling fish were lower than the previous year. Broodfish numbers were only slightly higher than in 1996 with increases in Mississippi and Arkansas offsetting declines in Louisiana. The USDA notes that as the catfish industry expands, more specialized firms are likely to enter the industry. Current growers, who have their own broodfish and hatchery operations, are likely to purchase stockers or fingerlings from these firms.

After increasing almost 15,000 acres between July 1995 and July 1996, the total pond acreage in the four major producing states in the first half of 1997 was up one percent from the previous year. With farm prices in 1997 lower, any additions to pond acreage are likely to be small. In July 1997, growers in the four major states reported that there were 4,500 acres of ponds under construction and 5,600 acres under renovation. Expected higher prices in 1998 and low feed costs should mean pond acreage will expand further.

During the first half of 1997, the U.S. imported 76 million pounds of Atlantic salmon, up 12 percent from the first half of 1996. For all of 1997, Atlantic salmon imports are expected to be 155-165 million pounds. The major suppliers of salmon to the U.S. are Canada and Chile. Chile is the dominant supplier of filleted salmon products to the U.S. but Canada has increased its share of the market. In the first half of 1997, U.S. imports of salmon totaled 40.5 million pounds while imports from Chile were 29.9 million pounds.

In the 1990's, U.S. per capita seafood consumption remained between 14.8 and 15.2 pounds of edible meat per year. Growth in seafood consumption has come from an increasing population. The industry showing the most long-term growth has been the catfish industry.

Fishery Products -- Supply in the United States In Millions of Pounds[2]

					Domestic Catch					Imports				
		-For Human Food-		For Industrial		% of Grand	-For Human Food-		For Industrial		% of Grand	-For Human Food-		For Industrial
Year	Grand Total	Finfish	Shellfish[3]	Use[4]	Total	Total	Finfish	Shellfish[3]	Use[4]	Total	Total	Finfish	Shellfish[3]	Use[4]
1986	14,368	7,087	2,533	4,748	6,031	42.0	2,240	1,153	2,638	8,337	58.0	4,847	1,380	2,110
1987	15,744	7,919	2,642	5,183	6,896	43.8	2,769	1,177	2,950	8,848	56.2	5,150	1,465	2,233
1988	14,628	7,786	2,719	4,123	7,192	49.2	3,306	1,282	2,604	7,436	50.8	4,480	1,437	1,519
1989	15,485	9,735	2,533	3,217	8,463	54.7	4,897	1,307	2,259	7,022	45.3	4,838	1,226	958
1990	16,349	10,120	2,542	3,687	9,404	57.5	5,747	1,294	2,363	6,945	42.5	4,373	1,248	1,324
1991	16,364	10,186	2,834	3,344	9,484	58.0	5,564	1,467	2,453	6,879	42.0	4,622	1,367	890
1992	16,106	10,297	2,945	2,864	9,637	59.8	6,182	1,436	2,019	6,469	40.2	4,115	1,509	845
1993	20,334	10,796	3,025	6,513	10,467	51.5	6,770	1,444	2,253	9,867	48.5	4,026	1,581	4,260
1994	19,309	10,719	2,995	5,595	10,461	54.2	6,612	1,324	2,525	8,848	45.8	4,107	1,671	3,070
1995[1]	16,600	10,809	2,891	2,900	9,904	59.7	6,531	1,252	2,121	6,696	40.3	4,278	1,639	779

[1] Preliminary. [2] Live weight, except percent. [3] For univalue and bivalues mollusks (conchs, clams, oysters, scallops, etc.) the weight of meats, excluding the shell is reported. [4] Fish meal and sea herring. *Source: Fisheries Statistics Division, U.S. Department of Commerce*

Fisheries -- Landings of Principal Species in the United States In Millions of Pounds

	Fish									Shellfish					
													Oysters	Scallops	
Year	Cod, Atlantic	Flounder	Halibut	Herring, Sea	Men-haden	Pollock	Salmon, Pacific	Tuna	Whiting	Clams (Meats)	Crabs	Lobsters (American)	(Meats)	(Meats)	Shrimp
1987	59	200	76	207	2,712	598	562	100	35	134	386	46	40	41	363
1988	76	229	82	222	2,086	1,290	606	111	36	132	456	49	32	43	331
1989	78	202	75	209	1,989	2,385	786	89	39	138	458	53	30	41	352
1990	96	255	70	221	1,962	3,129	733	62	44	139	499	61	29	42	346
1991	93	405	66	230	1,977	2,873	783	36	37	134	650	63	32	40	320
1992	62	646	67	282	1,644	2,952	716	57	36	142	624	56	36	34	338
1993	51	599	63	216	1,983	3,258	888	55	36	148	604	57	34	19	293
1994	39	427	58	214	2,324	3,133	901	72	36	131	447	66	38	25	283
1995[1]	30	423	45	265	1,847	2,853	1,137	14	34	134	364	66	40	20	307

[1] Preliminary. NA = Not available. *Source: Fisheries Statistics Division, U.S. Department of Commerce*

U.S. Fisheries: Quantity & Value of Domestic Catch & Consumption & World Fish Oil Production

	Disposition					For Human Food	For Industrial Products	Ex-vessel Value[3]	Average Price	Fish Per Capita Consumption	World[2] Fish Oil Production
	Fresh & Frozen	Canned	Cured	For Meal, Oil, Etc.	Total						
Year	Millions Pounds							Million $	¢ Lb.	Lbs.	1,000 Tonnes
1989	5,585	798	128	1,952	8,463	6,204	2,259	3,238	38.3	15.6	1,393
1990	6,501	751	126	2,026	9,404	7,041	2,363	3,522	37.4	15.0	1,386
1991	6,541	674	119	2,150	9,484	7,031	2,453	3,308	34.9	14.8	1,105
1992	7,288	543	110	1,696	9,637	7,618	2,019	3,678	38.2	14.7	1,187
1993	7,744	649	115	1,959	10,467	8,214	2,253	3,471	33.2	14.9	1,184
1994	7,475	622	95	2,269	10,461	7,936	2,525	3,807	36.8		1,470
1995[1]	7,215	769	90	1,830	9,904	7,783	2,121	3,770	38.2		1,302

[1] Preliminary. [2] Crop year on a marketing year basis. [3] At the Dock Prices. *Source: Fisheries Statistics Division, U.S. Department of Commerce*

Imports of Seafood Products into the United States In Thousands of Pounds

	Fresh			Frozen								
Year	Atlantic Salmon	Pacific Salmon	Shrimp	Trout	Atlantic Salmon	Pacific Salmon	Shrimp	Oysters[2]	Mussels[3]	Clams[4]	Canned Salmon	Prepared Shrimp[5]
1992	48,843	40,075	8,347	6,197	5,302	10,199	558,580	16,800	7,657	6,192	2,671	36,782
1993	62,860	33,920	11,649	4,741	7,714	11,659	556,213	17,293	9,658	5,818	2,053	44,765
1994	68,254	31,952	NA	3,878	7,851	11,210	580,010	15,415	11,032	8,265	3,190	47,912
1995	95,739	33,371	NA	4,076	9,982	8,849	539,630	14,866	15,483	5,930	3,582	57,577
1996	116,606	43,962	NA	4,552	10,752	8,514	507,823	14,222	21,241	6,596	4,182	74,648
1997[1]	150,135	38,999	NA	5,403	14,956	25,662	572,111	14,531	26,903	5,703	3,675	76,213

[1] Preliminary. [2] Oysters fresh or prepared. [3] Mussels fresh or prepared. [4] Clams, fresh or prepared. [5] Shrimp, canned, breaded or prepare.
NA = Not available. *Source: Bureau of the Census, U.S. Department of Commerce*

Exports of Seafood Products into the United States In Thousands of Pounds

	Fresh			Frozen								
Year	Atlantic Salmon	Pacific Salmon	Shrimp	Trout	Atlantic Salmon	Pacific Salmon	Shrimp	Oysters[2]	Mussels[3]	Clams[4]	Canned Salmon	Prepared Shrimp[5]
1992	1,396	20,655	3,558	1,201	406	240,072	18,082	1,105	2,317	4,999	85,369	11,134
1993	4,018	24,275	2,776	955	373	257,751	16,524	1,454	2,291	4,217	84,520	11,539
1994	1,184	22,483	NA	1,958	384	260,469	13,622	2,634	1,935	3,785	90,393	15,778
1995	6,823	26,142	NA	1,545	231	266,706	14,795	2,531	1,896	3,968	95,611	14,837
1996	7,280	42,999	NA	1,867	322	223,346	11,180	2,097	1,603	5,126	94,842	17,665
1997[1]	7,504	25,529	NA	1,709	322	152,516	11,967	2,890	1,157	4,916	81,407	14,826

[1] Preliminary. [2] Oysters fresh or prepared. [3] Mussels fresh or prepared. [4] Clams, fresh or prepared. [5] Shrimp, canned, breaded or prepare.
NA = Not available. *Source: Bureau of theCensus, U.S. Department of Commerce*

World Production of Fish Meal In Thousands of Metric Tons

Year	Chile	Spain	Denmark	EU-12	FSU-12	Iceland	Japan	Norway	Peru	South Africa	Thailand	United States	World Total
1989-90	1,124.6	129.6	256.4	502.8	705.0	140.9	1,000.8	166.8	1,180.4	103.8	265.5	299.5	6,352.0
1990-1	1,144.2	123.9	302.6	556.2	643.9	87.6	841.8	220.8	1,308.5	87.9	292.8	310.4	6,303.6
1991-2	1,322.1	122.1	351.7	602.5	465.1	158.9	509.6	239.9	1,095.6	150.3	313.4	312.2	5,948.5
1992-3	1,091.2	101.6	300.1	531.2	355.0	197.7	395.0	250.8	1,767.3	128.3	349.3	352.5	6,202.4
1993-4	1,526.1	91.0	352.7	569.5	295.0	190.5	343.0	216.8	2,254.4	75.4	372.8	447.8	7,085.7
1994-5	1,549.7	83.0	363.4	571.2	280.0	173.8	239.0	225.0	2,052.6	56.2	383.5	338.3	6,657.2
1995-6[1]	1,392.9	84.0	322.9	530.9	260.0	271.0	197.0	233.8	1,702.7	61.0	380.0	329.1	6,284.0
1996-7[2]	1,200.0	84.0	340.0	549.0	260.0	253.0	190.0	235.0	2,000.0	60.0	385.0	345.0	6,447.0

[1] Preliminary. [2] Estimate. [3] Forecast. *Source: The Oil World*

World Production of Fish Oil In Thousands of Metric Tons

Year	Canada	Chile	China	Denmark	Iceland	Japan	Norway	Peru	South Africa	FSU-12	United States	World Total	Fish Oil CIF[4]
1989-90	9.5	204.9	11.6	73.2	66.2	445.7	49.2	209.2	12.7	124.9	127.3	1,438.2	238
1990-1	10.7	201.0	12.4	107.2	39.4	331.7	97.6	215.1	12.1	132.0	127.8	1,383.0	307
1991-2	11.0	155.9	8.7	114.5	63.0	186.1	92.9	102.1	16.1	104.2	84.4	1,042.1	361
1992-3	11.8	165.3	9.4	90.3	86.0	102.0	112.3	250.9	17.0	71.6	119.0	1,140.6	375
1993-4	9.9	280.0	11.0	112.0	96.5	90.9	122.7	426.5	8.5	52.7	141.2	1,457.5	332
1994-5	10.1	323.1	12.0	118.3	84.0	63.0	94.1	380.2	3.8	48.5	109.6	1,356.9	405
1995-6[1]	10.3	280.2	12.4	120.0	121.0	47.0	93.7	411.0	8.0	43.0	110.4	1,369.0	461
1996-7[2]	11.0	173.0	12.0	118.0	136.0	51.0	73.0	411.0	7.0	41.0	110.0	1,253.0	502

[1] Preliminary. [2] Estimate. [3] Forecast. [4] Any origin, N.W. Europe, $ per tonne. *Source: The Oil World*

Monthly Production of Catfish--Round Weight Processed--in the U.S. In Thousands of Pounds (Live Weight)

Year	Jan.	Feb.	Mar.	Apr.	May	June	July	Aug.	Sept.	Oct.	Nov.	Dec.	Total
1988	26,018	27,786	28,179	20,805	20,351	22,839	23,687	26,941	24,611	26,221	25,037	22,634	295,109
1989	26,948	28,559	29,458	27,310	28,892	27,598	27,827	28,371	30,366	31,670	29,096	25,805	341,900
1990	33,066	31,884	33,120	30,980	31,542	28,967	29,540	31,108	27,566	29,211	27,913	25,538	360,435
1991	32,206	33,036	35,951	31,205	31,322	31,588	32,720	32,912	33,244	35,400	31,114	30,172	390,870
1992	36,200	39,228	45,048	41,177	39,111	36,813	36,128	37,958	37,857	39,212	35,073	33,562	457,367
1993	40,327	40,277	43,521	39,920	37,030	35,496	37,086	37,706	37,072	39,472	36,557	34,549	459,013
1994	36,714	35,035	40,446	34,494	34,163	34,595	35,901	39,813	38,716	39,072	36,054	34,266	439,269
1995	38,807	38,515	42,200	36,588	37,030	36,047	35,800	38,827	37,634	39,456	34,119	31,863	446,886
1996	38,475	38,004	46,376	38,557	39,583	36,810	39,025	40,463	38,807	42,070	37,210	36,874	472,254
1997[1]	42,409	45,067	48,431	45,721	43,409	42,282	43,376	44,154	43,472	46,275	40,137	40,216	524,949

[1] Preliminary. *Source: Economic Research Service, U.S. Department of Agriculture (ERS-USDA)*

Average Price Paid to Producers for Farm-Raised Catfish in the U.S. In Cents Per Pound (Live Weight)

Year	Jan.	Feb.	Mar.	Apr.	May	June	July	Aug.	Sept.	Oct.	Nov.	Dec.	Average
1988	68	72	75	75	75	78	80	80	79	79	78	78	76.4
1989	78	78	77	76	76	75	71	68	65	64	64	68	71.7
1990	72	74	78	78	78	78	76	76	76	76	75	72	75.8
1991	69	69	69	69	66	65	63	60	59	58	57	53	63.1
1992	53	56	60	63	63	61	59	58	59	61	62	63	59.8
1993	63	67	70	71	72	72	72	73	73	73	73	73	71.0
1994	74	77	79	80	80	80	80	80	80	77	77	77	78.4
1995	78	79	79	79	79	79	79	79	78	78	78	78	78.6
1996	77	78	78	78	79	79	79	78	77	76	75	73	77.3
1997[1]	73	73	73	73	73	72	71	70	69	69	69	69	71.2

[1] Preliminary. *Source: Economic Research Service, U.S. Department of Agriculture (ERS-USDA)*

Sales and Prices of Fresh Catfish in the United States

Year	Jan.	Feb.	Mar.	Apr.	May	June	July	Aug.	Sept.	Oct.	Nov.	Dec.	Total/Avg.
						In Thousands of Pounds							
SALES--Whole													
1994	3,664	3,677	3,752	3,192	3,176	2,892	3,036	3,173	3,179	3,197	2,888	2,862	38,688
1995	3,221	3,373	3,856	3,086	2,997	2,903	2,951	3,184	3,108	3,166	2,962	2,847	37,654
1996	3,673	3,593	4,168	3,508	3,230	2,868	3,001	3,107	3,215	3,324	2,763	2,925	39,375
1997[1]	3,402	3,632	4,133	3,770	3,456	3,447	3,481	3,284	3,370	3,598	3,002	3,051	41,626
Fillets[2]													
1994	3,101	3,204	3,550	3,061	3,103	3,015	3,046	3,383	3,183	3,212	2,784	2,665	37,307
1995	3,054	3,281	3,646	3,369	3,350	3,246	3,115	3,348	3,162	3,295	2,897	2,845	38,608
1996	3,439	3,866	4,366	3,883	3,824	3,374	3,556	3,615	3,645	3,758	3,254	3,222	43,802
1997[1]	3,627	4,272	4,531	4,084	4,126	3,894	4,033	4,135	4,009	4,464	3,623	3,543	48,341
Other[3]													
1994	967	926	1,019	912	1,079	907	914	959	965	965	821	790	11,224
1995	998	1,115	1,437	1,328	1,234	1,172	934	1,035	1,067	1,166	1,049	938	13,473
1996	1,097	1,263	1,438	1,154	1,124	937	1,045	1,128	1,081	1,228	1,063	982	13,540
1997[1]	1,287	1,497	1,562	1,530	1,430	1,307	1,385	1,332	1,358	1,498	1,212	1,147	16,545
						In Dollars Per Pound							
PRICE--Whole													
1994	1.54	1.62	1.71	1.73	1.73	1.74	1.76	1.76	1.72	1.72	1.70	1.66	1.70
1995	1.69	1.69	1.68	1.69	1.69	1.71	1.70	1.69	1.68	1.67	1.63	1.65	1.68
1996	1.63	1.64	1.68	1.68	1.73	1.77	1.73	1.71	1.67	1.65	1.64	1.60	1.68
1997[1]	1.59	1.60	1.58	1.56	1.56	1.52	1.51	1.53	1.54	1.52	1.54	1.50	1.55
Fillets[2]													
1994	2.69	2.73	2.86	2.91	2.91	2.92	2.93	2.94	2.93	2.93	2.91	2.91	2.88
1995	2.89	2.90	2.92	2.93	2.90	2.90	2.91	2.90	2.91	2.92	2.90	2.89	2.91
1996	2.88	2.85	2.86	2.87	2.88	2.92	2.91	2.88	2.85	2.83	2.84	2.81	2.87
1997[1]	2.80	2.79	2.80	2.78	2.78	2.77	2.75	2.74	2.73	2.69	2.67	2.71	2.75
Other[3]													
1994	1.92	1.82	1.90	1.93	2.02	2.02	1.95	1.95	1.92	1.89	1.91	1.87	1.93
1995	1.82	1.80	1.93	1.99	1.99	1.97	1.81	1.86	1.84	1.84	1.87	1.81	1.88
1996	1.77	1.75	1.77	1.84	1.87	1.90	1.86	1.81	1.77	1.74	1.75	1.73	1.80
1997[1]	1.72	1.67	1.68	1.64	1.68	1.68	1.70	1.69	1.65	1.60	1.66	1.64	1.67

[1] Preliminary. [2] Includes regular, shank and strip fillets; excludes breaded products. [3] Includes steaks, nuggets and all other products not reported.
Source: Economic Research Service, U.S. Department of Agriculture (ERS-USDA)

Flaxseed and Linseed Oil

In the U.S. the area planted to flaxseed has been in a downtrend for several years. Although planted acreage in 1997/98 rose to 152,000 vs. the record low 1996/97 acreage of 96,000, during the 1980's planted acreage often exceeded 500,000 acres. Flaxseed (from which linseed oil is derived) is now officially considered a minor U.S. oilseed with production in recent years under three million bushels, well below the total amount imported.

Flaxseed production in 1997/98 (June/May) of 2.6 million bushels compares with 1.6 million in 1996/97 and the high for the 1990's of 6.2 million bushels in 1991/92. Since the mid-1970's U.S. flaxseed production has dropped nearly 80 percent. The U.S crop is produced mostly in the Northern Plains states, primarily North Dakota. Imports of flaxseed, mostly from Canada, the world's largest producer with about a third of production, were forecast at 7.8 million bushels in 1997/98 vs. a record 8.4 million bushels in 1996/97. Imports in the 1990's have averaged almost seven million bushels, twice the 1980's yearly rate. The U.S. has been a net importer of flaxseed since 1978. Total 1997/98 supplies of 10.8 million bushels compares with 11.2 million in 1996/97. Disappearance in 1997/98 was forecast at 10.2 million bushels vs. 10.8 million in 1996/97. Most of the crop is crushed, 9.75 million bushels in 1997/98 vs. ten million in 1996/97. U.S. exports of flaxseed are insignificant.

U.S. domestic demand for linseed oil in 1997/98 of 155 million pounds is unchanged from the previous two seasons and compares with annual averages of 200 million pounds in the mid-1980's. Exports were put at 45 million pounds vs. a record high 66 million in 1996/97. 1997/98 production of 195 million pounds compares with 200 million in 1996/97. Linseed oil is used as a drying agent in paint, but its domestic usage has fallen due to the acceptance of water based latex paints. Annual disappearance in the 1990's has averaged about 180 million pounds, at least 25 million under the like 1980 period. Carryover stocks as of May 31, 1998 are estimated at 35 million pounds, unchanged from a year earlier. Linseed meal production in 1997/98 of 180,000 short tons compares with 185,000 in 1996/97. Meal disappearance of 181,000 tons compares with 186,000 the prior year. About 40 percent of the production was exported in both years.

The average price received by U.S. farmers for flaxseed in 1997/98 was expected to average between $4.45-$5.95 per bushel vs. the 1996/97 average of $6.21. Linseed oil prices in 1997/98 were forecast between $.35-.38 per pound vs. $.36 in 1996/97, basis Minneapolis. Linseed meal prices, basis 34% protein Minneapolis, in 1997/98 were forecast between $115-S145 per ton vs. $159.25 in 1996/97.

Futures Markets

Flaxseed futures are traded on the Winnipeg Commodity Exchange (WCE). Prices are quoted in Canadian dollars per metric ton.

World Production of Flaxseed In Thousands of Metric Tons

Crop Year	Argentina	Australia	Bangladesh	Canada	China	Egypt	France	Hungary	India	Romania	United States	Former USSR	World Total
1987-8	535	8	43	701	400	29	21	20	393	38	189	228	2,755
1988-9	446	3	43	328	490	28	32	11	361	38	41	220	2,215
1989-90	526	2	47	498	400	21	31	11	326	49	31	227	2,352
1990-1	458	4	48	889	535	28	34	10	339	53	97	197	2,923
1991-2	341	5	55	635	410	24	26	13	292	23	158	140	2,458
1992-3	177	5	49	334	430	21	29	10	268	18	84	130	1,969
1993-4	112	8	49	627	410	22	27	11	330	28	88	120	2,177
1994-5	152	6	48	960	511	23	44	11	325	27	74	110	2,533
1995-6[1]	149	15	49	1,105	420	23	27	12	308	26	56	113	2,532
1996-7[2]	68	7	50	851	480	23	15	12	319	24	41	100	2,249

[1] Preliminary. [2] Estimate. [3] Forecast. *Source: The Oil World*

Supply and Distribution of Flaxseed in the United States In Thousands of Bushels

Crop Year Beginning June	Planted	Harvested	Yield Per Acre Bushels	Supply: Beginning Stocks	Production	Imports	Total Supply	Distribution: Seed	Crush	Exports	Residual	Total Distribution
	---- 1,000 Acres ----											
1988-9	275	226	7.1	2,325	1,615	6,730	10,670	158	8,500	764	-59	9,363
1989-90	195	163	7.5	1,307	1,215	7,260	9,782	211	8,250	1,054	23	9,538
1990-1	260	253	15.1	244	3,812	6,715	10,771	288	8,800	549	163	9,800
1991-2	356	342	18.1	971	6,200	4,371	11,542	139	9,050	541	256	9,986
1992-3	171	165	19.9	1,556	3,288	6,035	10,879	167	8,600	230	337	9,334
1993-4	206	191	18.2	1,545	3,480	5,118	10,143	144	8,650	126	69	8,989
1994-5	178	171	17.1	1,155	2,922	6,005	10,082	134	8,550	72	156	8,912
1995-6[1]	165	147	15.0	1,170	2,211	7,248	10,681	91	9,000	119	202	9,399
1996-7[2]	96	92	17.4	1,230	1,601	8,390	11,222	123	10,000	144	502	10,769
1997-8[3]	152	146	17.5	453	2,555	7,800	10,808	142	9,750	135	181	10,769

[1] Preliminary. [2] Estimate. [3] Forecast. NA = not avaliable. *Source: Economic Research Service, U.S. Department of Agriculture (ERS-USDA)*

FLAXSEED AND LINSEED OIL

Production of Flaxseed in the United States, by States   In Thousands of Bushels

Crop Year	Minne-sota	North Dakota	South Dakota	Other States	Total	Crop Year	Minne-sota	North Dakota	South Dakota	Other States	Total
1988	110	1,295	210	------	1,615	1993	170	2,886	323	101	3,480
1989	95	980	140	------	1,215	1994	126	2,450	304	42	2,922
1990	238	3,118	456	------	3,812	1995	171	1,725	260	55	2,211
1991	640	4,860	578	122	6,200	1996	60	1,386	126	30	1,602
1992	220	2,730	322	16	3,288	1997[1]	84	1,760	252	75	2,171

[1] Preliminary. *Source: National Agricultural Statistics Service, U.S. Department of Agriculture (NASS-USDA)*

Factory Shipments of Paints, Varnish and Lacquer in the United States   In Millions of Dollars

Year	First Quarter	Second Quarter	Third Quarter	Fourth Quarter	Total	Year	First Quarter	Second Quarter	Third Quarter	Fourth Quarter	Total
1988	2,531.8	3,071.1	2,870.1	2,479.3	10,783	1993	2,894.1	3,600.5	3,448.9	2,993.7	12,937
1989	2,614.4	3,149.9	3,100.0	2,665.7	11,239	1994	3,039.8	3,783.0	3,736.2	3,240.8	13,800
1990	2,754.7	3,188.6	3,080.1	2,632.6	11,762	1995	3,330.3	3,838.0	3,814.5	3,423.4	14,406
1991	2,498.4	3,158.7	3,123.0	2,611.2	11,707	1996	3,420.8	4,144.7	3,938.5	3,413.5	14,918
1992	2,852.3	3,464.1	3,308.7	2,816.4	12,442	1997[1]	3,416.2	3,907.5	3,814.1	3,229.3	14,367

[1] Preliminary. *Source: The Oil World*

Consumption of Linseed Oil in Inedible Products in the United States   In Millions of Pounds

Year	July	Aug.	Sept.	Oct.	Nov.	Dec.	Jan.	Feb.	Mar.	Apr.	May	June	Total
1990-1	9.5	10.2	6.8	8.3	6.3	4.7		19.4			24.2		89.4
1991-2		29.0			23.2		15.5	15.5	13.0	15.0	15.3	11.4	133.4
1992-3	16.3	14.8	11.5	11.2	6.9	8.0	8.3	8.5	11.8	10.5	12.6	13.0	133.4
1993-4	14.9	8.1	11.2	9.0	7.2	10.7	10.2	7.5	9.9	8.5	11.5	11.7	120.4
1994-5	10.7	10.8	12.3	12.2	9.0	10.0	12.6	8.2	11.4	8.1	10.0	9.7	124.9
1995-6	8.8	10.0	9.4	10.6	7.4	6.9	8.8	8.5	7.2	8.1	10.1	9.5	105.3
1996-7	9.0	10.8	7.8	6.0	6.7	6.1	6.7	7.1	6.3	8.3	8.9	8.5	92.3
1997-8[1]	8.9	7.7	8.6	6.7	7.5	6.4							91.6

[1] Preliminary. *Source: Bureau of the Census, U.S. Department of Commerce*

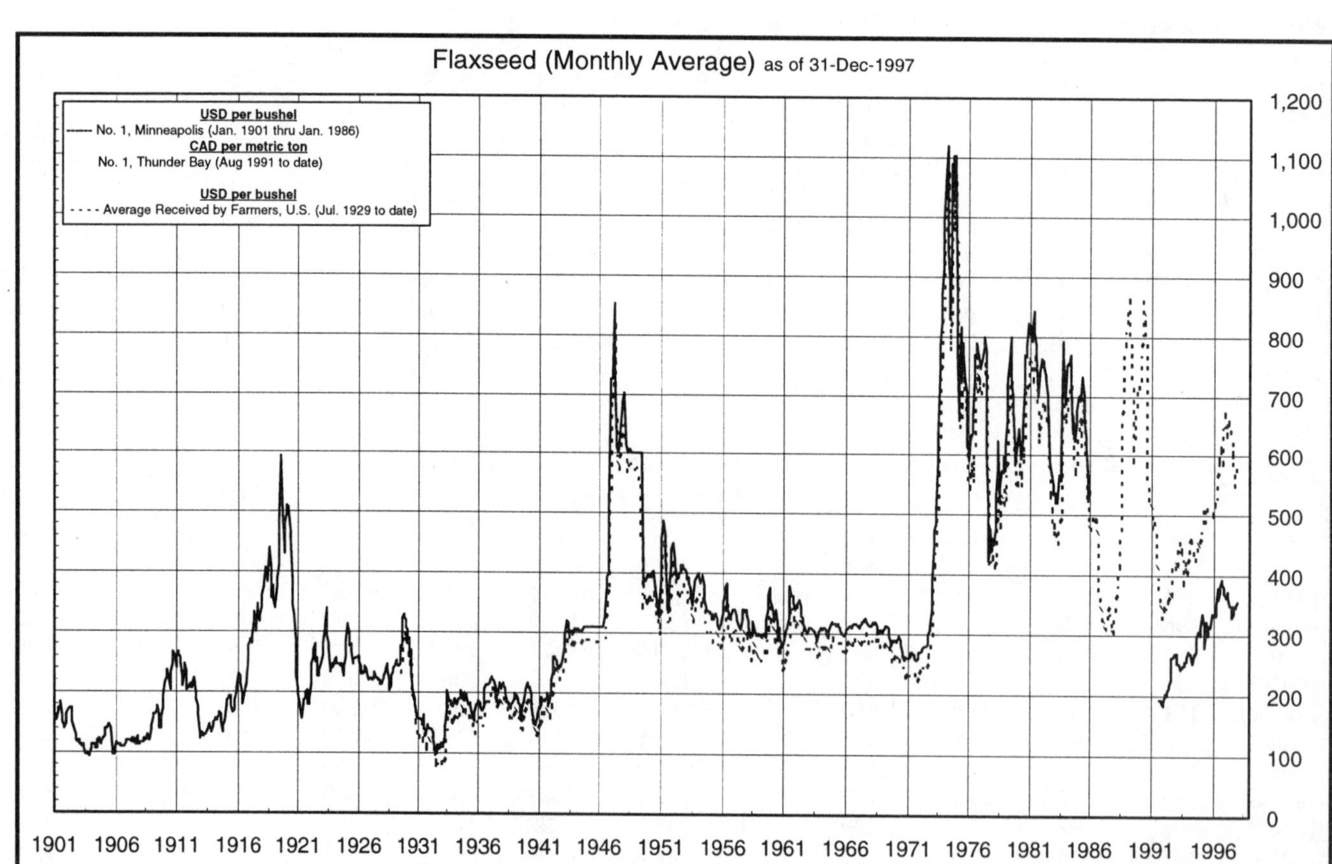

Supply and Distribution of Linseed Oil in the United States In Millions of Pounds

Crop Year Beginning June	Supply: Stocks June 1	Supply: Production	Supply: Total	Disappearance: Exports	Disappearance: Domestic	Disappearance: Total Disappearance	Average Price at Minneapolis Cents/Lb.
1987-8	51	217	268	8	219	227	24.7
1988-9	41	170	211	12	151	163	39.5
1989-90	48	165	213	12	164	176	40.2
1990-1	37	176	213	6	167	173	38.0
1991-2	40	182	222	12	170	182	32.0
1992-3	40	172	212	8	150	158	31.5
1993-4	54	174	228	7	162	165	31.8
1994-5	63	171	237	24	168	192	33.7
1995-6	45	180	228	23	155	178	36.5
1996-7[1]	50	200	256	66	155	221	36.0
1997-8[2]	35	195	235	45	155	200	34.5-38.5

[1] Preliminary. [2] Forecast. *Source: Economic Research Service, U.S. Department of Agriculture (ERS-USDA)*

World Production and Price of Linseed Oil In Thousands of Metric Tons

Year	Argentina	Bangladesh	Belgium	China	Egypt	Germany	India	Japan	United Kingdom	United States	Former U.S.S.R.	World Total	Rotterdam Ex-Tank $ Tonne
1988-9	137.7	10.8	9.6	127.5	11.8	41.6	103.4	33.2	12.2	76.0	10.5	658.3	716
1989-90	158.8	11.6	12.9	104.1	11.7	44.9	92.9	31.4	11.4	76.1	11.5	646.6	756
1990-1	141.5	12.0	12.2	126.9	12.3	57.5	94.2	34.7	16.8	84.0	10.1	685.8	502
1991-2	114.0	13.5	14.7	111.0	11.3	56.1	83.8	31.9	27.0	87.9	9.1	638.4	377
1992-3	62.3	12.6	25.5	114.0	8.1	56.8	78.0	28.4	27.2	80.0	9.6	571.5	450
1993-4	32.2	12.7	28.8	121.8	8.7	77.2	90.7	30.7	35.2	78.7	9.9	617.9	476
1994-5	46.8	13.0	35.2	127.8	9.3	104.0	91.4	29.2	41.4	81.7	10.2	700.3	657
1995-6	47.8	13.0	44.3	117.3	9.9	72.0	88.0	30.0	28.9	80.0	11.6	659.0	579
1996-7[1]	17.0	13.0	37.1	114.0	10.0	75.9	89.0	31.0	32.1	99.0	11.0	644.0	560
1997-8[2]	29.0	NA	NA	120.0	10.0	NA	85.0	31.0	NA	98.0	11.0	670.0	NA

[1] Preliminary. [2] Forecast. *Source: The Oil World*

Average Price Received by Farmers for Flaxseed in the United States In Dollars Per Bushel

Year	July	Aug.	Sept.	Oct.	Nov.	Dec.	Jan.	Feb.	Mar.	Apr.	May	June	Average
1988-9	6.29	7.19	7.67	7.85	8.09	8.34	8.34	8.70	8.09	7.78	7.54	6.79	7.72
1989-90	5.90	6.49	7.07	7.09	7.15	7.14	7.24	7.69	8.03	8.60	8.23	8.31	7.41
1990-1	7.56	5.86	5.36	5.15	5.16	5.15	5.12	4.82	4.90	4.66	4.33	3.98	5.17
1991-2	3.92	3.69	3.55	3.39	3.31	3.46	3.39	3.43	3.51	3.53	3.61	3.66	3.54
1992-3	3.70	3.68	4.12	4.09	4.08	4.24	4.11	4.46	4.52	4.40	4.42	4.45	4.19
1993-4	4.29	3.79	4.24	4.09	4.05	4.18	4.38	4.61	4.64	4.60	4.43	4.25	4.30
1994-5	4.28	4.52	4.54	4.49	4.51	4.71	4.76	4.94	5.13	5.10	4.91	5.03	4.74
1995-6	5.11	5.21	5.11	5.11	5.17	5.03	5.26	5.21	5.28	5.31	6.13	5.90	5.32
1996-7	6.19	6.15	5.89	6.49	6.38	6.77	6.43	6.30	6.66	6.49	6.50	6.03	6.36
1997-8[1]	6.07	5.53	5.72	5.81	5.71	5.72	5.54						5.73

[1] Preliminary. *Source: National Agricultural Statistics Service, U.S. Department of Agriculture (NASS-USDA)*

Stocks of Linseed Oil (Crude & Refined) at Factories & Warehouses in the U.S. In Millions of Pounds

Year	July 1	Aug. 1	Sept. 1	Oct. 1	Nov. 1	Dec. 1	Jan. 1	Feb. 1	Mar. 1	Apr. 1	May 1	June 1
1987-8	52.2	45.9	40.2	52.1	54.3	50.4	50.8	56.0	39.0	35.5	35.6	40.8
1988-9	35.6	36.0	44.8	24.4	33.5	36.6	46.8	54.6	47.6	49.1	54.6	47.5
1989-90	48.4	43.8	23.2	21.5	23.9	30.3	29.9	39.5	36.7	39.1	38.3	36.8
1990-1	28.2	21.9	17.2	41.8	41.4	47.5	-----------	61.7	-----------	-----------	75.4	-----------
1991-2	-----------	60.6	-----------	-----------	64.2	-----------	73.1	51.2	62.3	45.6	45.7	41.4
1992-3	34.6	35.5	29.7	41.3	49.1	47.7	39.9	44.2	45.1	49.1	42.8	43.1
1993-4	45.2	39.0	42.1	47.0	27.9	19.3	22.5	38.0	42.0	49.4	52.0	62.6
1994-5	60.3	56.5	49.4	60.6	48.1	39.3	38.6	38.9	31.0	35.7	37.9	44.8
1995-6	39.5	44.6	37.4	46.0	48.0	44.5	45.3	58.9	64.0	62.0	60.6	47.2
1996-7	51.3	50.9	59.0	46.1	38.8	41.8	49.2	48.1	53.9	50.5	44.5	45.6
1997-8[1]	39.9	35.2	40.3	33.3	38.6	40.3	46.0					

[1] Preliminary. *Source: Bureau of the Census, U.S. Department of Commerce*

FLAXSEED AND LINSEED OIL

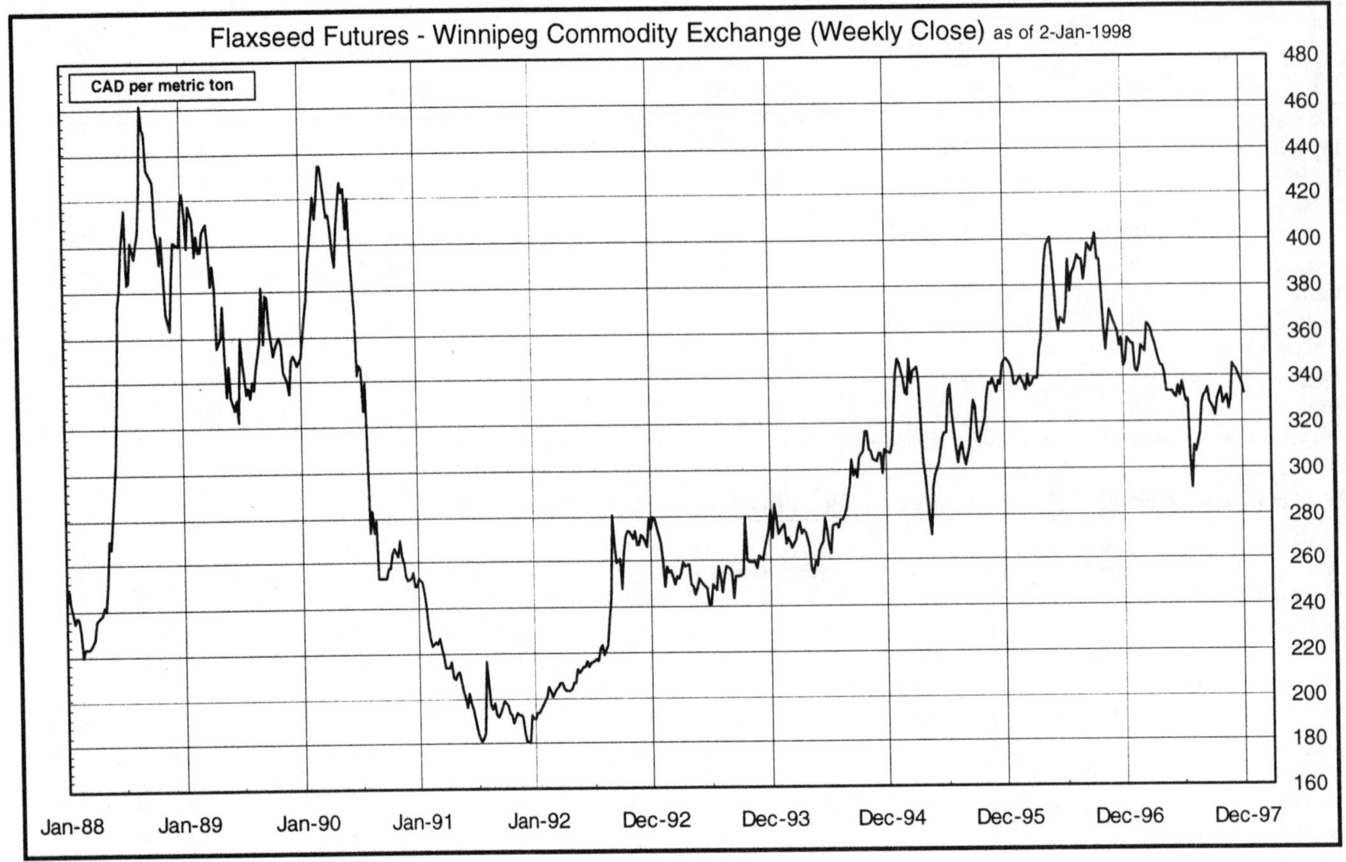

Wholesale Price of Raw Linseed Oil at Minneapolis in Tank Cars In Cents Per Pound

Year	July	Aug.	Sept.	Oct.	Nov.	Dec.	Jan.	Feb.	Mar.	Apr.	May	June	Average
1987-8	25.00	25.00	25.00	22.75	24.25	25.00	25.00	25.00	25.00	24.75	24.75	28.20	24.98
1988-9	35.00	37.00	41.50	42.00	42.00	41.50	41.00	41.00	41.40	42.00	42.00	39.75	40.51
1989-90	39.00	39.00	39.50	40.00	40.00	40.00	40.00	40.00	41.60	42.00	42.00	43.00	40.51
1990-1	44.00	40.40	39.75	36.80	36.00	36.00	36.00	36.00	36.00	36.00	36.50	36.00	37.45
1991-2	36.00	36.00	36.00	30.00	30.00	30.00	30.00	30.00	30.00	30.00	30.00	30.00	31.50
1992-3	30.00	30.00	32.00	32.00	32.00	32.00	32.00	32.00	32.00	32.00	32.00	28.50	31.38
1993-4	32.00	32.00	32.00	32.00	32.00	32.00	32.00	32.00	32.00	32.00	32.00	32.00	32.00
1994-5	30.31	32.00	32.00	33.50	35.00	35.00	35.00	35.00	35.00	35.00	35.00	35.00	33.98
1995-6	35.00	35.50	37.00	37.00	37.00	37.00	37.00	37.00	37.00	37.00	37.00	37.00	36.71
1996-7	37.00	37.20	37.50	37.00	33.75	32.12	36.00	36.00	36.00	36.00	36.00	36.00	35.88
1997-8[1]	36.00	36.00	36.00										36.00

[1] Preliminary. *Source: Economic Research Service, U.S. Department of Agriculture (ERS-USDA)*

Average Open Interest of Flaxseed Futures in Winnipeg In Contracts

Year	Jan.	Feb.	Mar.	Apr.	May	June	July	Aug.	Sept.	Oct.	Nov.	Dec.
1988	5,838	6,341	5,583	6,189	6,089	7,219	5,964	7,018	7,791	8,777	10,662	7,621
1989	7,864	7,875	5,422	6,038	6,479	8,297	8,609	9,234	8,191	5,120	4,613	3,349
1990	3,812	5,165	5,701	5,790	4,839	4,985	4,950	4,908	4,651	4,477	5,079	4,502
1991	4,033	4,140	4,175	4,861	4,137	4,642	5,317	6,106	6,173	5,733	5,669	5,333
1992	5,620	6,772	7,864	7,984	7,786	7,321	6,299	6,553	5,623	4,860	6,734	5,979
1993	7,810	8,052	6,203	5,672	5,505	5,321	4,246	5,777	5,923	3,568	3,763	3,922
1994	6,118	6,201	5,946	5,519	4,683	3,945	4,301	4,654	4,997	3,077	4,888	5,251
1995	6,242	8,731	7,505	7,121	8,107	7,212	6,436	5,557	6,230	5,245	5,937	4,414
1996	6,059	6,056	4,402	5,192	6,970	4,435	3,102	2,989	3,257	3,438	4,326	5,119
1997	5,420	5,356	5,591	5,151	4,923	4,075	3,891	4,031	7,131	8,284	7,255	7,955

Source: Winnipeg Commodity Exchange (WCE)

Fruits

The USDA indicated that grower prices for many citrus and noncitrus fruits were likely to remain below the year ago level for the remainder of 1997 and into 1998. Larger grape and pear crops are expected in important Western producing states while the U.S. apple crop is expected to be larger as well. A record orange crop is forecast for Florida and the grapefruit crop will also be large. During the first seven months of 1997, the grower price index for fruit and nuts averaged eight percent below a year ago. Part of the decline was due to a record Florida orange crop and a large grapefruit crop.

U.S. apple production in the 1997-98 (July-June) season was forecast to be 4.7 million tonnes, slightly above a year ago. A smaller crop in Washington, the largest producing state, will be offset by larger crops in New York and Michigan. Washington produces about half of the U.S. apple crop but this year's harvest is expected to be down five percent. New York, the second largest apple-producing state, was expected to have a crop some nine percent above the 1996-97 output.

U.S. grape production was forecast to increase 20 percent from last season. It was expected to surpass the previous record of 1982. California, by far the largest producer of grapes, was expecting a 1997 crop of 12 billion pounds, 20 percent higher than in 1996. Wine grape production was forecast at 5.4 billion pounds, up 21 percent from 1996. California table grape production was estimated at 1.4 billion pounds, up almost 19 percent from 1996. Raisin grape production was estimated at 5.2 billion pounds, also 19 percent above the 1996 level. U.S. production of grapes in 1997 was forecast at 13.3 billion pounds.

The 1997 U.S. pear crop is forecast to be 2.04 billion pounds, up 24 percent from 1996. California is the second largest producer of pears with the 1997 crop forecast at 660 million pounds, up four percent from 1996. Bartlett pear production was forecast at 600 million pounds, up almost five percent. Washington is the largest producer of pears with 1997 production estimated at 820 million pounds, almost 37 percent above 1996.

U.S. peach production is forecast to increase almost 28 percent in 1997 to 2.64 billion pounds. California is the major producer of peaches with production in 1997 of 1.86 billion pounds. California clingstone peach production was estimated at 1.1 billion pounds, up less than one percent from 1996, while freestone peach production was up 20 percent. Georgia and South Carolina recovered from the crop failure of 1996 with Georgia production forecast at 160 million pounds and South Carolina at 150 million pounds.

Commercial strawberry production in the six major producing states of California, Florida, Oregon, Washington, Michigan and New Jersey was forecast to decline four percent in 1997 compared to a year ago.

Commercial Production for Selected Fruits in the United States In Thousands of Short Tons

Year	Apples	Cherries[2]	Cranberries	Grapes	Grapefruit	Lemons	Nectarines	Oranges	Peaches	Pears	Pineapples	Prunes & Plums	Strawberries	Tangelos	Tangerines	Total All Fruits
1992	5,284	373	208	6,052	2,224	766	236	8,909	1,336	923	550	829	668	117	260	29,482
1993	5,342	339	196	6,023	2,791	942	205	10,992	1,330	948	370	588	724	137	247	31,750
1994	5,750	359	234	5,874	2,661	984	242	10,329	1,257	1,046	365	879	825	150	318	31,872
1995	5,293	363	210	5,922	2,912	897	176	11,432	1,151	948	345	744	804	142	287	32,155
1996	5,196	290	234	5,554	2,718	992	247	11,427	1,058	821	347	952	814	110	349	31,831
1997[1]	5,113	367	275	6,836	2,888	859	264	12,827	1,326	1,044	324	884	817	177	418	34,954

[1] Preliminary. [2] Sweet and tart. *Source: Economic Research Service, U.S. Department of Agriculture (ERS-USDA)*

Utilized Production of Selected Fruits in the United States In Thousands of Short Tons

Year	Utilized Production (In Thousands of Short Tons): Citrus[1]	Noncitrus[2]	Total	Value of Production (In Thousands of Dollars): Citrus[1]	Noncitrus[2]	Total
1991	11,285	15,740	27,025	2,414,933	6,021,210	8,436,143
1992	12,452	17,124	29,576	2,401,351	6,036,615	8,437,966
1993	15,274	16,563	31,837	2,151,173	6,135,411	8,286,584
1994	14,561	17,341	31,903	2,268,330	6,269,879	8,542,929
1995	15,799	16,353	32,178	2,328,915	6,816,378	9,145,293
1996[3]	15,714	16,054	31,768	2,515,419	7,120,584	9,636,003

[1] Year harvest was completed. [2] Includes bushberries (beginning 1992), cranberries and strawberries. [3] Preliminary. *Source: Economic Research Service, U.S. Department of Agriculture (ERS-USDA)*

Average Retail Prices for Selected Fruits in the United States In Dollars Per Pound

Year	Red Delicious Apples	Bananas	Anjou Pears	Thompson Seedless Grapes	Lemons	Grapefruit	Oranges: Navel	Oranges: Valencias
1992	.890	.458	.837	1.288	1.007	.607	.574	.559
1993	.834	.439	.846	1.465	1.084	.529	.557	.654
1994	.803	.462	.802	1.642	1.090	.513	.545	.587
1995	.835	.490	.774	1.551	1.136	.548	.625	.648
1996	.930	.490	.916	1.685	1.114	.574	.707	.703
1997[1]	.913	.508	1.009	1.745	1.100	.502	.555	NA

[1] Estimate. *Source: Economic Research Service, U.S. Department of Agriculture (ERS-USDA)*

FRUITS

Utilization of Fruit Production, and Value in the U.S. In Thousands of Short Tons (Fresh Equivalent)

Year	Utilized Pro-duction	Fresh	Processed: Canned	Dried	Juice	Frozen	Wine	Other	Value of Utilized Production $1,000
1988	15,911	5,909	2,374	2,546	1,415	459	2,983	224	5,102,962
1989	16,345	6,104	2,266	2,857	1,580	479	2,869	190	5,279,382
1990	15,640	6,093	2,244	2,440	1,448	506	2,717	192	5,525,279
1991	15,740	6,215	2,119	2,417	1,583	501	2,739	167	6,021,210
1992	17,124	6,522	2,386	2,369	1,743	584	3,256	264	6,036,615
1993	16,563	6,400	2,042	2,339	1,743	627	3,029	181	6,135,411
1994	17,341	6,711	2,092	2,816	1,881	669	2,711	227	6,269,879
1995	16,356	6,292	1,754	2,400	1,852	652	2,992	205	6,817,748
1996[1]	16,117	6,325	1,873	2,275	1,577	610	3,043	180	7,255,293

[1] Preliminary. *Source: Economic Research Service, U.S. Department of Agriculture (ERS-USDA)*

Average Price Indexes for Fruits in the United States

Year	Index of all Fruit and Nut Prices Received by Growers (1990-92 = 100)	Producer Price Index (1982 = 100): Fresh Fruit	Dried Fruit	Canned Fruits and Juices	Frozen Fruits and Juices	Consumer Price Index (1982-84 = 100): Fresh Fruit	Processed Fruit
1988	96	112.8	98.9	120.3	130.0	143.0	121.9
1989	99	110.4	103.1	122.6	124.5	152.4	125.9
1990	97	116.1	107.0	126.9	138.9	170.9	136.6
1991	112	129.4	111.5	128.6	115.1	193.9	131.8
1992	99	83.2	114.3	134.6	125.7	184.2	137.7
1993	91	84.3	117.6	126.1	110.9	188.8	132.3
1994	89	82.2	120.9	126.0	111.9	201.2	133.1
1995	99	85.8	121.0	129.4	115.8	219.0	137.2
1996	118	100.8	124.2	137.5	123.9	234.4	145.2
1997[1]		98.8	125.2	137.6	117.2	235.5	149.5

[1] Estimate. *Source: Economic Research Service, U.S. Department of Agriculture (ERS-USDA)*

Fresh Fruit: Per Capita Consumption[1] in the United States In Pounds

Year	Citrus Fruit: Oranges	Tangerines & Tangelos	Lemons	Grapefruit	Total	Noncitrus Fruit: Apples	Apricots	Avocados	Bananas	Cherries	Cran-berries
1988	13.90	1.77	2.47	6.69	25.39	19.84	.15	1.58	24.29	.53	.11
1989	12.17	1.71	2.39	6.60	23.56	21.22	.10	1.54	24.71	.62	.20
1990	12.38	1.31	2.60	4.43	21.37	19.60	.16	1.07	24.36	.39	.24
1991	8.46	1.38	2.60	5.87	19.07	18.18	.13	1.41	25.11	.40	.26
1992	12.91	1.94	2.54	5.95	24.36	19.24	.15	1.43	27.25	.53	.24
1993	14.24	1.87	2.65	6.23	25.95	19.16	.13	2.17	26.79	.43	.19
1994	13.06	2.11	2.68	6.12	24.95	19.57	.15	1.34	28.05	.53	.08
1995	11.97	2.01	2.87	6.06	24.11	18.94	.10	1.37	27.41	.29	.08
1996[2]	12.77	2.19	2.90	5.83	24.85	19.34	.09	1.60	28.01	.41	.09

[1] All data on calendar-year basis except for citrus fruits; apples, August; grapes and pears, July; grapefruit, September; lemons, August of prior year; all other citrus, November. [2] Preliminary. *Source: Economic Research Service, U.S. Department of Agriculture (ERS-USDA)*

Fresh Fruit: Per Capita Consumption[1] in the United States In Pounds

Year	Noncitrus - Continued: Grapes	Kiwifruit	Mangos	Nectarines & Peaches	Pears	Pine-apples	Papaya	Plums & Prunes	Straw-berries	Total Noncitrus	Total Fruit
1988	7.70	.25	.38	6.75	3.22	1.81	.16	1.72	3.33	71.82	97.21
1989	7.94	.33	.51	5.86	3.20	2.04	.14	1.41	3.25	73.07	96.63
1990	7.92	.49	.54	5.54	3.22	2.05	.18	1.55	3.24	70.55	91.92
1991	7.26	.44	.85	6.43	3.15	1.92	.17	1.42	3.58	70.73	89.80
1992	7.19	.33	.68	6.02	3.14	2.00	.24	1.78	3.61	73.84	98.20
1993	7.04	.53	.90	5.95	3.38	2.05	.28	1.28	3.64	73.92	99.87
1994	7.32	.57	.98	5.49	3.48	2.04	.30	1.62	4.09	75.62	100.57
1995	7.52	.56	1.13	5.44	3.40	1.93	.37	.94	4.15	73.62	97.73
1996[2]	6.94	.55	1.36	4.29	3.10	1.92	.55	1.41	4.39	74.05	98.90

[1] All data on calendar-year basis except for citrus fruits; apples, August; grapes and pears, July; grapefruit, September; lemons, August of prior year; all other citrus, November. [2] Preliminary. *Source: Economic Research Service, U.S. Department of Agriculture (ERS-USDA)*

Gas

The U.S. Energy Information Agency reported that gross withdrawals of natural gas in July 1997 were 2.05 trillion cubic feet, up three percent from the previous month and two percent more than a year ago. For all of 1996, gross withdrawals were 24.3 trillion cubic feet. Natural gas repressuring in July 1997 was 311 billion cubic feet, up three percent from June 1997 and eight percent above the same month in 1996. For all of 1996, natural gas repressuring amounted to 3.71 trillion cubic feet.

Nonhydrocarbon gases removed in July 1997 were 43 billion cubic feet, some five percent above the previous month. It was also nearly 39 percent more than the same month a year ago. Vented and flared natural gas in July 1997 amounted to 21 billion cubic feet, the same as the previous month, but five percent less than the same month in 1996.

Marketed production (wet) of natural gas in September 1997 was 1.62 trillion cubic feet, some three percent less than the previous month but the same amount as a year earlier. For the January-September 1997 period, marketed production (wet) of natural gas was 14.8 trillion cubic feet, about the same as in the comparable period of 1996. For all of 1996, marketed wet production was 19.95 trillion cubic feet.

Extraction loss in September 1997 was 75 billion cubic feet, the same as the previous month and the same as a year earlier. In the January-September 1997 period, extraction loss totaled 689 billion cubic feet, just slightly lower than the 693 billion cubic feet in the same period of 1996. For all of 1996, natural gas extraction loss was 930 billion cubic feet. Extraction loss annually amounts to between four and five percent of marketed production.

Natural dry gas production in the U.S. in September 1997 was 1.55 trillion cubic feet. That was three percent less than in August 1997 but almost the same as a year ago. In the January-September 1997 period, dry gas production was 14.1 trillion cubic feet, down less than one percent from the comparable period in 1996, but two percent more than the same period in 1995. For all of 1996, dry gas production was 19 trillion cubic feet. U.S. dry gas production has been trending higher.

End-use natural gas consumption was estimated to be 1.43 trillion cubic feet in September 1997, down almost three percent from the previous month. For the January-September 1997 period, end-use consumption in 1997 was about one percent lower than in 1996. Industrial consumption over the first nine months of 1997 increased relative to 1996 while residential and commercial use declined. Total natural gas consumption in September 1997 was 1.43 trillion cubic feet.

Futures Markets

Natural gas futures and options are traded on the New York Mercantile Exchange (NYMEX) and the Kansas City Board of Trade (KCBT). Futures are traded on the International Petroleum Exchange (IPE).

World Production of Natural Gas (Monthly Average Marketed Production[3]) In Terajoule[4]

Year	Australia	Canada	China	Germany	Indonesia	India	Italy	Mexico	Netherlands	Romania	Russia[5]	United Kingdom	United States
1988	50,286	313,592	46,331	45,312	120,227	28,441	47,009	79,163	173,213	102,977	2,184,357	134,778	1,550,343
1989	51,406	331,923	48,816	44,734	128,193	33,715	49,618	75,131	210,184	92,312	2,245,667	143,708	1,569,198
1990	66,445	342,826	49,380	44,162	195,448	36,795	54,389	79,594	211,717	79,931	2,311,092	158,628	1,614,310
1991	62,194	362,029	49,955	52,460	158,214	43,284	53,037	79,009	239,349	68,977	2,286,626	176,344	1,609,083
1992	67,696	397,229	50,052	51,911	165,761	43,297	57,117	95,688	240,043	67,900	1,743,167	176,661	1,614,941
1993	72,848	437,922	52,297	47,904	171,828	44,475	60,792	93,646	244,205	68,891	1,708,083	196,792	1,667,401
1994	87,356	438,335	55,230	50,535	190,775	47,219	64,142	97,285	207,317	65,057	1,525,232	203,875	1,700,081
1995	78,460	607,608	55,872	55,451	203,633	53,422	64,467	100,488	209,229	60,258	1,936,092	213,987	1,683,692
1996[1]	95,082	625,469	63,792	60,310	291,490	59,452	63,864	160,347	236,803	58,843	1,915,492	360,395	1,727,420
1997[2]	82,143	624,904	76,355	56,568	297,371	60,324	62,852	168,111	297,018	48,139	1,792,141	256,558	NA

[1] Preliminary. [2] Estimate. [3] Compares all gas collected & utilized as fuel or as a chemical industry raw material, including gas used in oilfields as a fuel by producers. [4] Terajoule = 10 to the 12th power Joule = approximately 10 to the 9th power BTU. [5] Formerly part of the U.S.S.R., data not reported separately until 1992. NA = not avaliable. *Source: United Nations*

Marketed Production of Natural Gas in the United States, by States In Million of Cubic Feet

Year	Alaska	California	Colorado	Kansas	Louisiana	Michigan	Mississippi	New Mexico	Oklahoma	Texas	Wyoming	Total
1987	359,837	424,621	164,557	457,050	5,122,509	146,996	139,727	823,773	2,004,797	6,126,315	497,980	17,348,537
1988	378,638	399,663	191,544	592,845	5,180,267	146,145	124,053	791,819	2,167,050	6,286,029	509,058	17,918,465
1989	393,729	362,860	216,737	601,196	5,078,125	155,988	102,645	854,615	2,237,037	6,241,425	665,699	18,095,147
1990	402,907	362,748	242,997	573,603	5,241,989	172,151	94,616	965,104	2,258,471	6,343,146	735,728	18,593,792
1991	437,822	378,384	285,961	628,459	5,034,361	195,749	108,031	1,038,284	2,153,852	6,280,654	776,528	18,532,439
1992	443,597	365,632	323,041	658,007	4,914,300	194,815	91,697	1,268,863	2,017,356	6,145,862	842,576	18,711,808
1993	430,350	315,851	400,985	686,347	4,991,138	204,635	80,695	1,409,429	2,049,942	6,249,624	634,957	18,981,915
1994	555,402	309,427	453,207	712,730	5,169,705	222,657	63,448	1,557,689	1,934,864	6,353,844	696,018	19,709,525
1995	469,550	279,555	523,084	721,436	5,108,366	238,203	95,533	1,625,837	1,811,734	6,330,048	673,775	19,506,474
1996[1]	480,828	286,494	572,071	712,796	5,240,747	245,740	103,263	1,554,087	1,734,887	6,449,022	666,036	19,750,793

[1] Preliminary. *Source: Energy Information Administration, U.S. Department of Energy (EIA-DOE)*

GAS

World Production of Natural Gas Plant Liquids — Thousand Barrels Per Day

Year		Algeria	Canada	Mexico	Saudi Arabia	Former USSR	United States	Persian Gulf[2]	OAPEC[3]	OPEC[4]	World
1989	Average	130	410	384	503	425	1,546	851	1,041	1,188	4,502
1990	Average	130	426	428	620	425	1,559	930	1,107	1,281	4,632
1991	Average	140	431	457	680	420	1,659	931	1,113	1,299	4,827
1992	Average	140	460	454	713	390	1,697	1,003	1,185	1,364	4,973
1993	Average	145	506	459	704	380	1,736	1,040	1,238	1,435	5,169
1994	Average	140	539	461	698	340	1,727	1,081	1,272	1,475	5,297
1995	Average	145	581	447	701	180	1,762	1,106	1,301	1,506	5,474
1996	Average	145	599	423	697	248	1,830	1,082	1,274	1,452	5,625
1997[1]	Average	145	628	384	721	248	1,855	1,106	1,298	1,476	5,665

[1] Preliminary. [2] Bahrain, Iran, Iraq, Kuwait, Qatar, Saudi Arabia and the United Arab Emirates. [3] Organization of Arab Petroleum Exporting Countries. [4] Organization of Petroleum Exporting Countries. *Source: Energy Information Administration, U.S. Department of Energy (EIA-DOE)*

Recoverable Reserves and Deliveries of Natural Gas in the United States — In Billions of Cubic Feet

Year	Gross Withdrawals Natural Gas	Recoverable Reserves of Natural Gas Dec. 31[2]	Deliveries: Residential	Deliveries: Commercial	Deliveries: Electric Utility Plants[3]	Deliveries: Industrial	Deliveries: Total Deliveries	Consumption: Lease & Plant Fuel	Consumption: Used as Pipline Fuel	Heating Value BTU per Cubic Foot
1988	20,999	168,024	4,630	2,670	2,636	6,383	16,320	1,096	614	1,029
1989	21,074	167,116	4,781	2,718	2,787	6,816	17,102	1,070	629	1,031
1990	21,523	169,346	4,391	2,623	2,786	7,018	16,819	1,236	660	1,031
1991	21,750	167,062	4,556	2,729	2,789	7,231	17,305	1,129	601	1,030
1992	22,132	165,015	4,690	2,803	2,766	7,527	17,786	1,171	588	1,030
1993	22,726	162,415	4,956	2,863	2,682	7,981	18,483	1,172	624	1,027
1994	23,581	163,837	4,848	2,895	2,987	8,167	18,899	1,124	685	1,028
1995	23,744	165,146	4,850	3,031	3,197	8,580	19,660	1,220	700	1,027
1996[1]	24,052	N/A	5,241	3,158	2,732	8,870	20,006	1,250	711	1,027

[1] Preliminary. [2] Estimated proved recoverable reserves of dry natural gas. [3] Figures include gas other than natural (impossible to segregate); therefore, shown separately from other consumption. *Source: Energy Information Administration, U.S. Department of Energy (EIA-DOE)*

Gas Utility Sales in the United States by Types and Class of Service — In Trillions of BTU's

Year	Total Utility Sales	Number of Customers (Millions)	Class by Service: Residential	Class by Service: Commercial	Class by Service: Industrial	Class by Service: Electric Generation	Class by Service: Other	Revenue -- Million $ From Sales to Customers: Total	Revenue: Residential	Revenue: Commercial	Revenue: Industrial	Revenue: Electric Generation	Revenue: Other
1988	10,705	52.4	4,695	2,306	2,208	1,336	160	46,162	24,828	10,681	6,713	3,400	538
1989	10,551	53.4	4,798	2,322	1,963	1,280	188	47,493	26,172	11,074	9,217	449	582
1990	9,842	54.3	4,468	2,192	1,890	1,120	171	45,153	25,000	10,604	6,034	2,962	553
1991	9,601	55.2	4,546	2,198	1,743	888	226	44,647	25,729	10,669	5,326	2,250	674
1992	9,907	56.1	4,694	2,209	1,959	813	231	46,178	26,702	10,865	5,837	2,077	698
1993	10,151	57.0	5,054	2,397	2,009	524	168	50,137	29,787	12,076	6,162	1,480	632
1994	9,248	57.9	4,845	2,253	1,690	420	159	49,852	30,552	12,276	5,529	1,170	597
1995[1]	9,221	58.7	4,803	2,281	1,591	328	218	46,436	28,742	11,573	4,816	836	549
1996[2]	9,532	59.8	5,198	2,395	1,519	271	148	51,115	32,021	12,726	4,257	783	545

[1] Preliminary. [2] Estimate. NA = Not available. *Source: American Gas Association (AGA)*

Salient Statistics of Gas in the United States

Supply, Disposition: In Billions of Cubic Feet. Average Price Delivered to Consumers: $ Per Thousand Cubic Feet.

Year	Supply: Marketed Production	Supply: Extraction Loss	Supply: Dry Production	Supply: Storage Withdrawals	Supply: Imports (Consumed)	Supply: Total Supply	Disposition: Consumption	Disposition: Exports	Disposition: Added to Storage	Disposition: Total Disposition	Wellhead Price	Imports	Exports	Residential	Commercial	Industrial	Electric Utilities
1988	17,918	816	17,103	2,270	1,294	20,315	18,030	74	2,211	20,315	1.69	1.84	2.74	5.47	4.63	2.95	2.33
1989	18,095	785	17,311	2,854	1,382	21,435	18,801	107	2,528	21,435	1.69	1.82	2.51	5.64	4.74	2.96	2.43
1990	18,594	784	17,810	1,986	1,532	21,302	18,716	86	2,499	21,300	1.71	1.94	3.10	5.80	4.83	2.93	2.38
1991	18,532	835	17,698	2,752	1,773	21,836	19,035	129	2,672	21,836	1.64	1.82	2.59	5.82	4.81	2.69	2.18
1992	18,712	872	17,840	2,772	2,138	22,360	19,544	216	2,599	22,360	1.74	1.85	2.25	5.89	4.88	2.84	2.36
1993	18,982	886	18,095	2,799	2,350	23,254	20,279	140	2,835	23,254	2.04	2.03	2.59	6.16	5.22	3.07	2.61
1994	19,710	889	18,821	2,508	2,624	23,782	20,708	162	2,796	23,581	1.85	1.87	2.50	6.41	5.44	3.05	2.28
1995[1]	19,506	908	18,599	2,974	2,841	24,260	21,581	154	2,566	23,744	1.55	1.49	2.39	6.06	5.05	2.71	2.02
1996[2]	19,751	958	18,793	2,883	2,868	20,589	21,967	152	2,872	24,281	2.17	1.97	2.98	6.34	5.40	3.42	2.69

[1] Preliminary. [2] Estimate. *Source: Energy Information Administration, U.S. Department of Energy (EIA-DOE)*

verage Open Interest of Natural Gas Futures in New York In Contracts

ar	Jan.	Feb.	Mar.	Apr.	May	June	July	Aug.	Sept.	Oct.	Nov.	Dec.
990	-----	-----	-----	1,320	2,699	4,268	6,130	8,760	11,077	12,998	13,813	10,814
991	10,523	13,825	13,125	13,225	16,782	18,502	19,235	21,460	23,853	24,003	21,692	19,065
992	24,718	28,661	29,851	33,626	41,456	49,642	49,829	57,346	68,306	77,034	80,349	74,569
993	69,499	77,053	91,132	116,366	136,074	132,667	124,038	126,443	129,940	130,619	124,627	129,963
994	127,254	128,336	118,480	119,908	120,894	120,956	111,044	135,652	156,238	145,766	139,471	139,054
995	148,448	151,882	157,097	150,101	148,797	144,402	143,942	140,297	135,226	133,969	140,301	166,227
996	155,024	150,521	149,809	159,132	147,616	156,959	151,913	135,191	138,657	144,944	147,854	151,498
997	156,231	162,567	171,467	181,745	206,685	197,637	199,296	213,640	235,509	242,184	231,556	210,259

Source: New York Mercantile Exchange (NYMEX)

olume of Trading of Natural Gas Futures in New York In Thousands of Contracts

ear	Jan.	Feb.	Mar.	Apr.	May	June	July	Aug.	Sept.	Oct.	Nov.	Dec.	Total
990	-----	-----	-----	4.1	6.4	10.5	14.3	17.3	15.2	25.3	15.9	22.3	131.4
991	29.2	14.9	22.8	20.3	28.7	51.2	37.0	33.1	42.3	46.6	49.0	50.2	425.3
992	89.0	45.4	77.9	98.9	137.5	116.4	156.0	192.2	268.7	300.0	213.5	227.6	1,923.2
993	194.3	274.4	318.8	443.0	471.5	365.9	335.6	353.3	459.6	417.1	449.7	613.9	4,697.1
994	667.6	470.9	373.5	344.7	411.1	465.8	438.8	724.2	578.7	594.2	621.9	721.8	6,413.2
995	733.0	557.8	676.1	524.5	621.3	622.5	641.8	745.6	548.3	664.4	763.0	988.5	8,086.7
996	887.2	655.7	694.6	620.0	590.7	681.3	829.0	628.8	679.1	924.4	802.8	820.4	8,813.9
997	922.8	693.6	664.7	836.3	945.4	803.7	812.9	1,313.8	1,377.1	1,394.0	1,104.8	1,054.6	11,923.6

Source: New York Mercantile Exchange (NYMEX)

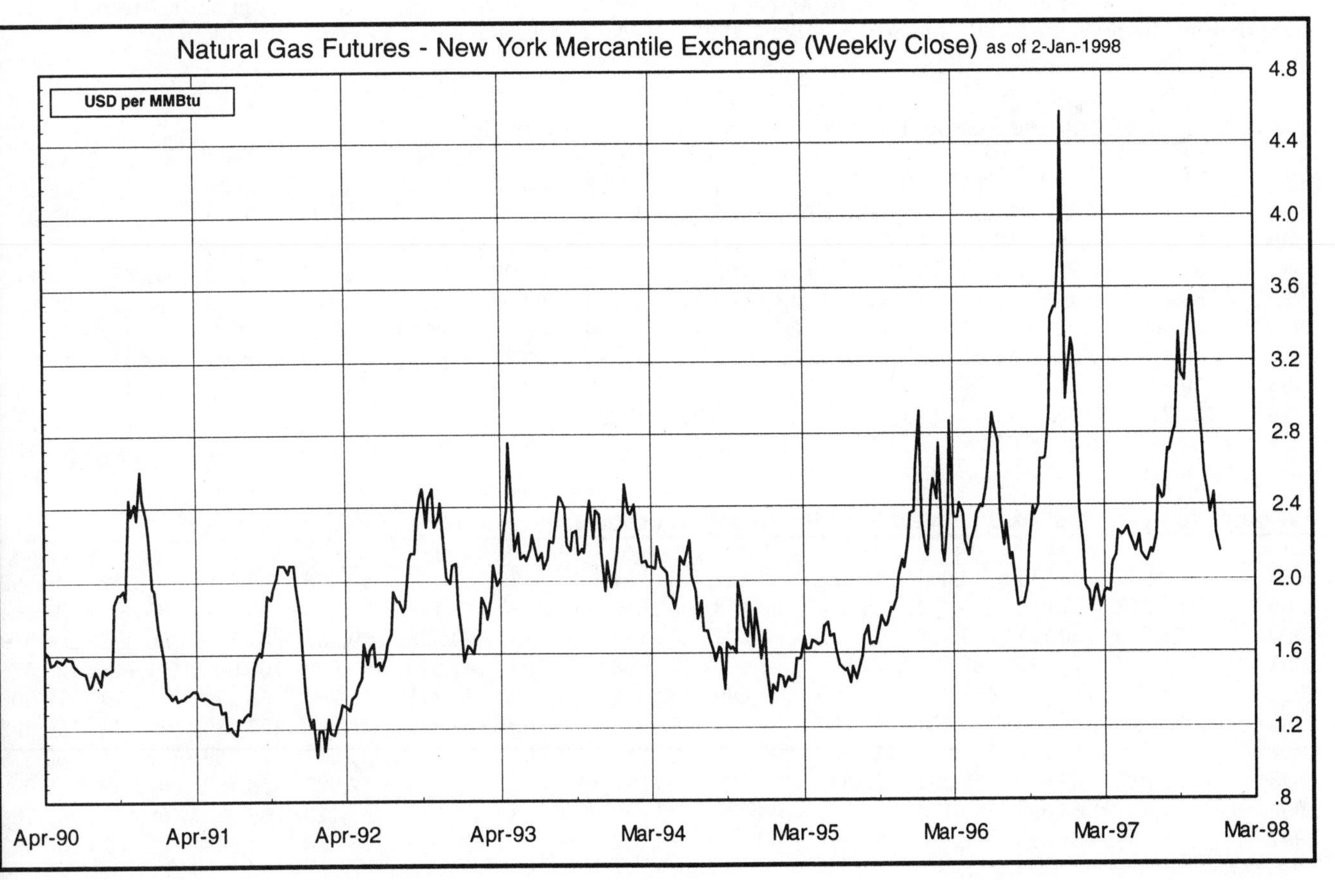

Gasoline

After moving sharply higher in the September-October 1997 period, unleaded gasoline prices fell back in the fourth quarter of 1997. Two reasons for the decline were low seasonal demand and higher levels of gasoline production. U.S. gasoline demand held up fairly well in the fourth quarter but was more than offset by increased production. Production of unleaded gasoline has been higher than use, resulting in a buildup of gasoline stocks. U.S. gasoline stocks in the fourth quarter of 1997 were running about four percent above a year ago. Gasoline stocks, while larger than they were, are not considered to be a burden at these levels.

It was expected that in the first quarter of 1998 a number of refineries would be undergoing maintenance resulting in a January-February 1998 decline in the U.S. production of gasoline. Ahead of this, refiners were producing more gasoline in expectation of a drawdown in stocks in the first quarter and possibly the second quarter as well. The peak driving season in the U.S. extends from the second quarter through the third quarter.

U.S. production of finished motor gasoline in August 1997 averaged 8.04 million barrels per day. That was one percent above the output in July 1997 and three percent more than in August 1996. Over the first eight months of 1997, finished motor gasoline production averaged 7.75 million barrels per day which was almost two percent more than in the comparable period of 1996. For all of 1996, gasoline production averaged 7.65 million barrels per day.

U.S. imports of finished gasoline in August 1997 averaged 284,000 barrels per day which was nearly ten per cent more than in the previous month. Imports in August 1997 were 18 percent less than in August 1996. In the January-August 1997 period, U.S. gasoline imports averaged 324,000 barrels per day which was 11 percent less than in the same period of 1996. For all of 1996, gasoline imports averaged 336,000 barrels per day. That represented an increase of 27 percent from 1995. U.S. exports of finished gasoline in August 1997 were 89,000 barrels per day. For the January-August 1997 period, gasoline exports averaged 110,000 barrels per day, some seven percent more than in the comparable period of 1996. For all of 1996, U.S. gasoline exports averaged 104,000 barrels per day.

Total product supplied in August 1997 averaged 8.32 million barrels per day, down two percent from the previous month. In the first eight months of 1997, product supplied averaged 8.01 million barrels per day, up one percent from the comparable period in 1996. For all of 1996, product supplied in the U.S. averaged 7.89 million barrels per day.

Total U.S. stocks of motor gasoline (including blending components) at the end of August 1997 were estimated at 186 million barrels. That was down from 190 million barrels at the end of July 1997. Stocks at the end of 1996 were 195 million barrels. Stocks of finished motor gasoline at the end of August 1997 were 147 million barrels, down from 151 million barrels at the end of July 1997. At the end of 1996, finished motor gasoline stocks were 157 million barrels.

Futures Market

Unleaded gasoline futures and options are traded on the New York Mercantile Exchange (NYMEX).

Average Price of Unleaded Gasoline in New York In Cents Per Gallon

Year	Jan.	Feb.	Mar.	Apr.	May	June	July	Aug.	Sept.	Oct.	Nov.	Dec.	Average
1988	45.14	45.79	45.25	50.89	52.20	51.70	55.12	48.18	46.40	51.15	52.39	47.22	49.29
1989	50.24	48.47	54.91	69.98	67.97	63.75	56.34	52.81	59.29	55.76	50.80	53.94	57.02
1990	64.20	59.59	56.15	61.86	64.24	64.55	65.25	89.61	99.85	95.68	88.10	68.07	73.10
1991	68.88	65.82	74.25	72.07	70.28	63.59	65.23	69.90	62.17	64.41	65.10	55.55	66.44
1992	53.04	55.14	54.10	59.75	63.48	64.51	59.94	62.06	61.63	60.81	58.22	53.24	58.83
1993	52.96	52.54	54.33	59.35	59.37	54.78	51.80	53.13	48.61	50.22	44.30	37.68	51.59
1994	42.40	43.75	44.04	48.98	50.62	52.84	54.52	55.61	46.53	51.14	52.32	46.87	49.14
1995	50.99	51.43	50.74	61.01	64.76	59.47	51.45	53.45	56.10	48.89	51.15	53.44	54.41
1996	50.70	53.26	58.56	69.17	65.10	58.03	61.65	61.17	62.43	65.52	69.23	68.58	61.95
1997	67.64	62.49	61.28	58.59	62.08	55.17	58.58	70.42	62.17	58.35	55.60	51.75	60.34

Source: New York Mercantile Exchange (NYMEX)

Average Open Interest of Unleaded Regular Gasoline Futures in New York In Contracts

Year	Jan.	Feb.	Mar.	Apr.	May	June	July	Aug.	Sept.	Oct.	Nov.	Dec.
1988	39,887	43,055	44,006	46,094	46,517	50,754	57,897	51,064	49,636	49,649	49,877	50,893
1989	55,838	57,011	59,012	69,547	68,478	61,519	56,913	52,158	51,910	55,312	65,392	71,464
1990	77,580	80,425	75,368	71,132	62,121	72,105	68,826	59,528	60,558	61,253	56,332	56,569
1991	54,807	75,337	81,393	74,801	71,900	73,633	74,503	87,073	90,680	100,606	111,745	125,578
1992	124,896	117,155	108,388	89,775	79,680	80,394	81,110	76,741	71,264	68,059	71,110	77,508
1993	80,610	93,630	100,657	96,607	88,311	94,926	104,260	103,371	100,921	107,339	126,649	150,359
1994	135,366	120,204	118,977	122,092	96,525	89,854	86,401	76,213	67,881	70,258	71,245	63,679
1995	61,015	67,631	65,201	76,323	76,269	69,676	64,379	58,426	62,089	58,782	57,902	70,098
1996	64,561	64,990	70,100	71,895	66,172	52,882	55,394	55,618	57,119	59,993	58,416	62,760
1997	68,188	84,693	92,520	97,619	90,407	78,492	83,082	103,538	103,250	94,602	92,852	103,497

Source: New York Mercantile Exchange (NYMEX)

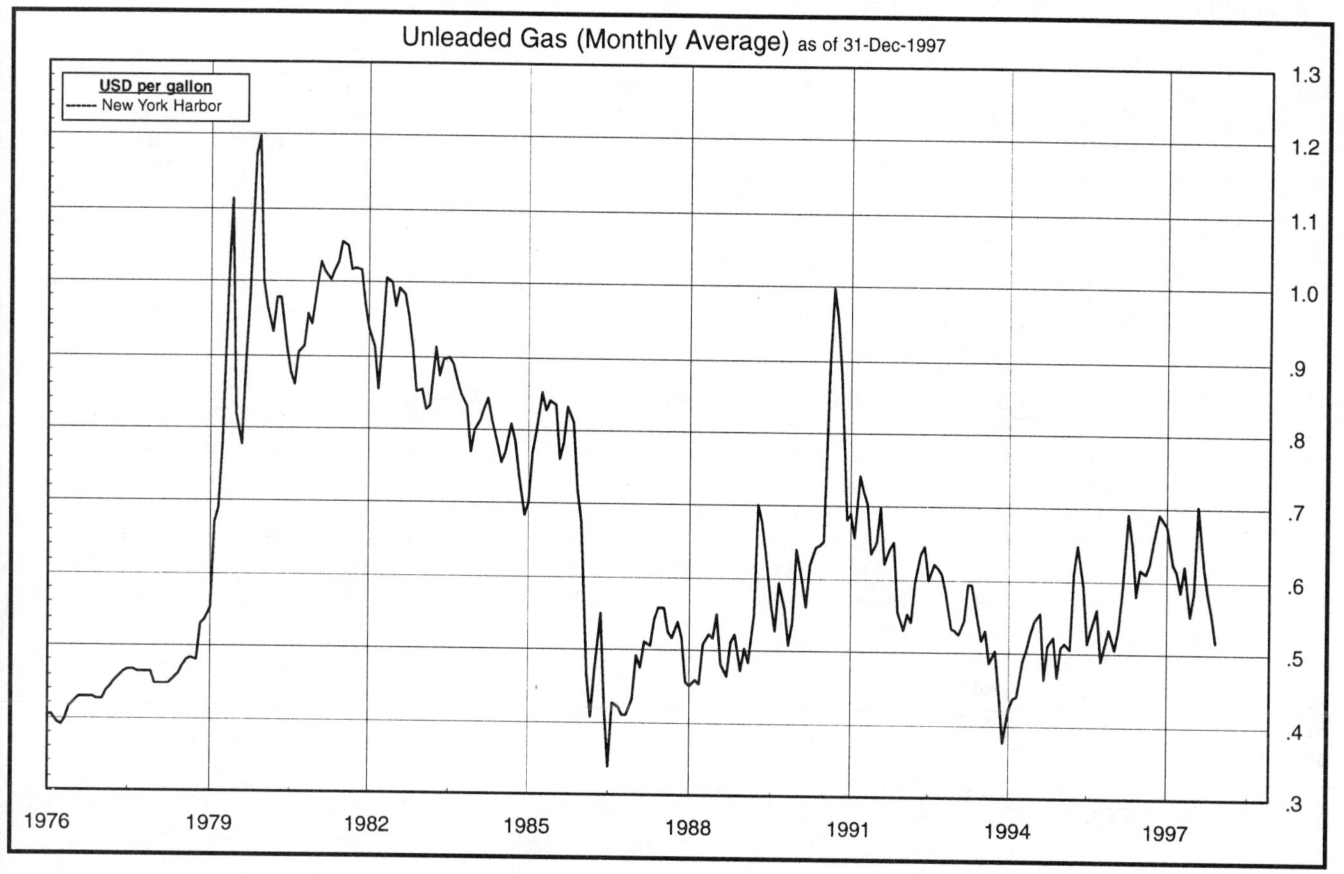

Volume of Trading of Unleaded Regular Gasoline Futures in New York In Contracts

Year	Jan.	Feb.	Mar.	Apr.	May	June	July	Aug.	Sept.	Oct.	Nov.	Dec.	Total
1988	196,616	191,231	245,019	217,139	257,507	330,009	401,196	254,010	294,512	355,982	308,438	240,366	3,292,025
1989	354,167	258,669	373,936	510,964	407,445	443,205	356,939	310,546	412,753	375,489	328,277	352,168	4,484,558
1990	540,633	349,439	461,438	481,665	527,637	472,377	456,342	549,702	373,102	386,472	314,051	248,137	5,160,995
1991	366,772	351,188	525,432	541,073	482,943	446,350	396,429	562,085	386,421	477,111	537,834	529,940	5,603,578
1992	565,922	558,476	604,678	668,490	580,088	620,114	600,897	545,520	469,844	563,856	435,847	461,025	6,674,757
1993	531,780	558,770	584,899	539,785	571,860	611,951	594,740	721,852	642,959	629,733	674,814	729,717	7,392,860
1994	634,027	526,505	615,594	677,891	636,990	673,034	601,980	748,415	569,384	684,670	582,359	519,987	7,470,836
1995	592,329	506,640	736,704	663,743	780,568	680,792	565,655	556,589	573,551	473,014	480,507	461,695	7,071,787
1996	543,818	449,537	570,341	676,193	623,347	467,953	533,793	463,830	469,036	527,553	487,624	499,314	6,312,339
1997	590,066	563,180	605,121	623,169	618,312	555,543	721,386	795,404	664,906	613,557	509,893	614,608	7,475,145

Source: New York Mercantile Exchange (NYMEX)

Production of Finished Motor Gasoline in the United States Thousand Barrels Per Day

Year	Jan.	Feb.	Mar.	Apr.	May	June	July	Aug.	Sept.	Oct.	Nov.	Dec.	Average
1988	6,730	6,736	6,715	6,907	6,851	6,983	7,159	7,209	6,948	6,858	7,060	7,303	6,956
1989	6,937	6,650	6,612	6,811	6,894	7,275	7,360	7,155	7,069	6,845	7,046	6,884	6,963
1990	6,879	6,989	6,613	6,775	6,610	7,101	7,238	7,326	7,274	6,880	6,940	6,887	6,959
1991	6,629	6,573	6,643	6,742	7,063	7,351	7,274	7,247	7,030	6,749	7,018	7,354	6,975
1992	7,013	6,726	6,683	6,954	7,092	7,198	7,195	6,817	7,071	7,198	7,323	7,411	7,058
1993	7,228	7,144	6,904	7,126	7,446	7,442	7,337	7,335	7,573	7,394	7,652	7,725	7,360
1994	7,097	6,790	6,760	7,195	7,348	7,455	7,380	7,432	7,385	7,151	7,849	7,867	7,312
1995	7,303	7,243	7,168	7,529	7,678	7,843	7,747	7,642	7,785	7,544	7,739	7,821	7,588
1996	7,333	7,303	7,242	7,475	7,724	7,820	7,811	7,696	7,585	7,496	7,835	7,784	7,593
1997[1]	7,308	7,315	7,322	7,822	8,056	8,180	7,947	8,048	8,147	8,039	7,984	8,208	7,867

[1] Preliminary. *Source: Energy Information Adminstration, U.S. Department of Energy (EIA-DOE)*

GASOLINE

Disposition of Finished Motor Gasoline, Total Product Supplied in the U.S. Thousand Barrels Per Day

Year	Jan.	Feb.	Mar.	Apr.	May	June	July	Aug.	Sept.	Oct.	Nov.	Dec.	Average
1988	6,693	7,039	7,323	7,430	7,303	7,817	7,482	7,556	7,404	7,271	7,379	7,344	7,336
1989	6,745	7,119	7,421	7,157	7,381	7,780	7,296	7,717	7,240	7,302	7,353	7,410	7,328
1990	6,643	7,179	7,338	7,121	7,358	7,519	7,496	7,796	6,914	7,226	7,241	6,978	7,235
1991	6,645	6,838	7,017	7,137	7,437	7,456	7,561	7,528	7,083	7,281	7,008	7,224	7,188
1992	6,869	6,963	7,137	7,238	7,328	7,460	7,639	7,380	7,344	7,338	7,102	7,396	7,268
1993	6,639	7,112	7,389	7,435	7,585	7,700	7,785	7,864	7,607	7,382	7,533	7,661	7,476
1994	6,980	7,275	7,395	7,564	7,644	7,922	7,884	7,975	7,615	7,548	7,464	7,924	7,601
1995	7,163	7,481	7,788	7,651	7,894	8,220	7,888	8,187	7,786	7,781	7,866	7,742	7,789
1996	7,254	7,552	7,729	7,869	7,998	8,089	8,135	8,216	7,641	8,038	7,875	7,775	7,849
1997[1]	7,312	7,651	7,808	8,067	8,128	8,260	8,471	8,195	8,004	8,166	7,955	8,093	8,012

[1] Preliminary. *Source: Energy Information Adminstration, U.S. Department of Energy (EIA-DOE)*

Stocks of Finished Gasoline[2] on Hand in the United States In Millions of Barrrels

Year	Jan.	Feb.	Mar.	Apr.	May	June	July	Aug.	Sept.	Oct.	Nov.	Dec.
1988	203.1	205.1	196.4	192.1	190.8	176.7	181.2	185.4	184.6	182.3	185.8	192.0
1989	207.8	205.7	191.1	190.6	185.8	180.1	192.1	183.8	187.5	184.8	187.1	179.1
1990	197.6	203.3	187.9	186.3	180.3	177.7	182.0	175.4	190.5	181.9	178.7	182.4
1991	189.1	182.7	174.4	171.9	173.7	178.5	173.5	172.8	179.1	168.3	173.3	183.3
1992	192.8	191.4	182.9	185.0	187.4	189.5	182.0	168.2	170.0	168.7	178.2	179.1
1993	197.8	201.9	189.0	184.0	186.8	184.2	176.8	166.7	171.2	175.6	182.6	187.1
1994	194.1	186.2	175.6	176.4	179.0	176.9	172.9	167.6	169.2	161.7	176.6	175.9
1995	182.7	180.0	167.8	167.1	167.1	163.5	166.0	154.6	158.9	155.6	155.6	161.3
1996	168.7	168.4	158.3	159.8	161.8	163.8	163.7	154.9	161.3	149.1	150.7	157.0
1997[1]	164.9	161.3	153.8	152.0	157.8	163.9	150.6	149.6	158.1	158.0	161.1	166.0

[1] Preliminary. [2] Includes oxygenated and other finished. *Source: Energy Information Administration, U.S. Department of Energy (EIA-DOE)*

Refiner Sales Prices of Finished Motor Gasoline to End Users (Excluding Taxes)[1] In Cents Per Gallon

Year	Jan.	Feb.	Mar.	Apr.	May	June	July	Aug.	Sept.	Oct.	Nov.	Dec.	Average
1988	64.9	63.3	62.5	66.0	68.4	68.1	69.9	71.8	70.0	68.0	67.6	66.1	67.3
1989	65.6	66.1	68.4	81.7	85.5	84.5	82.0	76.6	74.9	74.7	72.7	72.1	75.6
1990	78.8	76.5	75.1	77.9	80.2	81.5	80.8	92.4	101.2	108.7	107.2	98.4	88.3
1991	88.8	79.5	74.0	77.0	82.0	81.9	78.9	81.1	80.2	77.9	79.1	76.0	79.7
1992	71.2	70.2	71.0	74.6	80.3	84.0	83.5	82.3	82.3	81.3	81.4	78.5	78.4
1993	76.9	76.1	75.7	77.8	80.1	79.8	77.6	76.2	74.9	75.3	72.5	68.0	75.9
1994	66.8	67.6	67.3	69.5	71.1	74.1	77.0	81.5	79.6	76.9	77.5	75.1	73.8
1995	74.5	73.3	73.1	77.3	83.4	83.9	80.0	76.9	75.8	73.6	71.8	73.0	76.5
1996	74.6	74.8	79.8	88.1	92.7	90.3	87.5	84.9	84.4	84.4	86.7	85.9	84.7
1997[2]	86.6	86.1	84.3	83.9	84.5	83.3	81.5	86.8	87.2	84.4			84.9

[1] Excludes aviation. [2] Preliminary. *Source: Energy Information Administration, U.S. Department of Energy (EIA-DOE)*

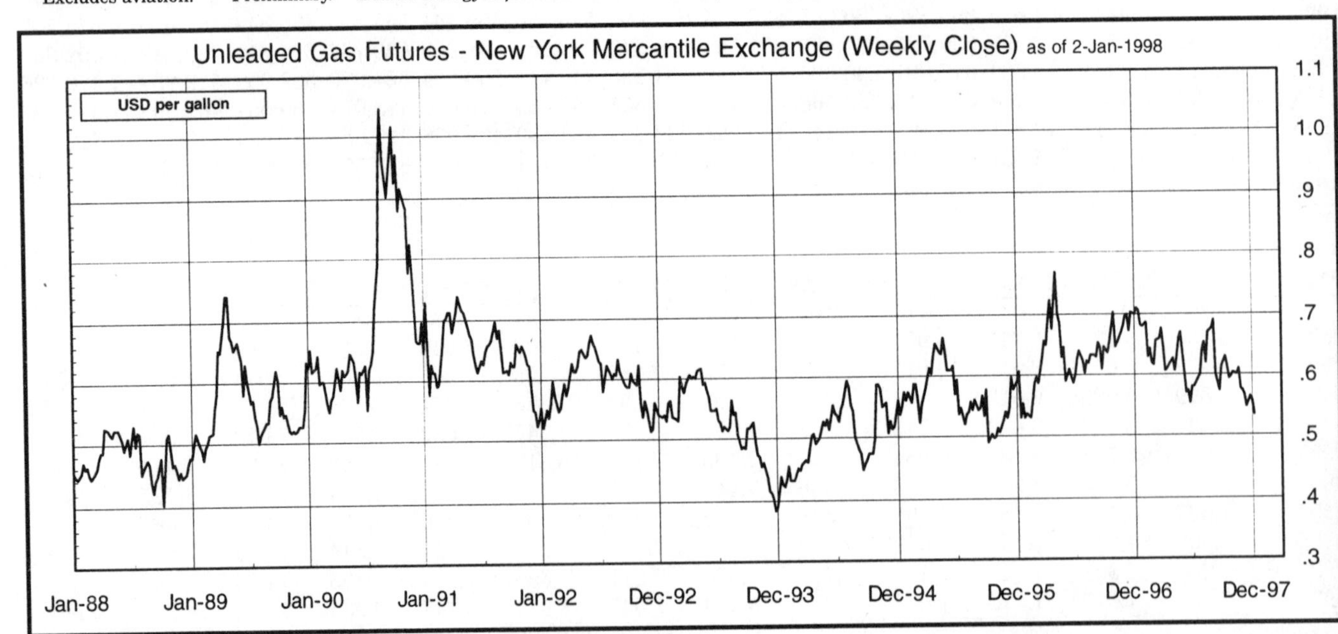

Average Retail Selling Prices of Motor Gasoline (Including Taxes) in the United States In Cents Per Gallon

Year	Jan.	Feb.	Mar.	Apr.	May	June	July	Aug.	Sept.	Oct.	Nov.	Dec.	Average
						Unleaded Premium							
1985	130.4	129.0	131.0	134.0	136.0	137.1	136.7	135.9	134.9	134.2	133.9	134.4	134.0
1986	133.6	128.2	116.0	106.1	107.5	110.0	104.5	99.9	101.0	98.7	98.0	98.4	108.5
1987	100.7	104.7	105.2	107.3	107.9	109.8	111.5	113.9	113.6	112.8	112.5	111.9	109.3
1988	109.5	108.2	107.4	108.8	110.5	111.1	112.3	113.8	113.0	111.9	111.6	110.1	110.7
1989	109.1	110.0	111.5	122.1	127.8	127.8	126.4	123.3	121.3	120.9	118.7	117.0	119.7
1990	123.0	122.7	121.8	123.3	124.8	127.1	127.2	136.9	146.7	155.4	155.9	153.7	134.9
1991	143.1	132.1	126.4	128.1	133.1	133.8	131.3	131.8	132.4	130.7	131.8	130.9	132.1
1992	126.7	124.8	125.0	126.8	131.7	135.9	136.3	134.8	134.6	134.5	135.1	133.0	131.6
1993	131.3	130.1	129.4	130.4	131.9	132.1	130.5	129.4	128.2	132.3	130.5	126.8	130.2
1994	124.0	124.5	124.3	126.0	127.4	130.0	132.7	136.7	136.4	134.5	135.4	133.7	130.5
1995	132.4	131.6	130.6	132.5	138.3	141.1	138.4	135.2	133.2	131.5	129.2	129.0	133.6
1996	131.7	131.1	134.8	143.1	150.7	148.1	145.3	142.1	141.7	140.8	142.8	143.8	141.3
1997[1]	144.1	143.4	141.5	141.3	140.9	141.1	138.8	143.3	145.8	142.6	139.7		142.0
						Unleaded Regular							
1985	114.8	113.1	115.9	120.5	123.1	124.1	124.2	122.9	121.6	120.4	120.7	120.8	120.2
1986	119.4	112.0	98.1	88.8	92.3	95.5	89.0	84.3	86.0	83.1	82.1	82.3	92.7
1987	86.2	90.5	91.2	93.4	94.1	95.8	97.1	99.5	99.0	97.6	97.6	96.1	94.8
1988	93.3	91.3	90.4	93.0	95.5	95.5	96.7	98.7	97.4	95.7	94.9	93.0	94.6
1989	91.8	92.6	94.0	106.5	111.9	111.4	109.2	105.7	102.9	102.7	99.9	98.0	102.1
1990	104.2	103.7	102.3	104.4	106.1	108.8	108.4	119.0	129.4	137.8	137.7	135.4	116.4
1991	124.7	114.3	108.2	110.4	115.6	116.0	112.7	114.0	114.3	112.2	113.4	112.3	114.0
1992	107.3	105.4	105.8	107.9	113.6	117.9	117.5	115.8	115.8	115.4	115.9	113.6	112.7
1993	111.7	110.8	109.8	111.2	112.9	113.0	110.9	109.7	108.5	112.7	111.3	107.0	110.8
1994	104.3	105.1	104.5	106.4	108.0	110.6	113.6	118.2	117.7	115.2	116.3	114.3	111.2
1995	112.9	112.0	111.5	114.0	120.0	122.6	119.5	116.4	114.8	112.7	110.1	110.1	114.7
1996	112.9	112.4	116.2	125.1	132.3	129.9	127.2	124.0	123.4	122.7	125.0	126.0	123.1
1997[1]	126.1	125.5	123.5	123.1	122.6	122.9	120.5	125.3	127.7	124.2	121.3		123.9
						All-Types[2]							
1985	114.5	112.8	115.5	119.9	122.3	123.3	123.3	122.2	120.9	119.8	120.1	120.3	119.6
1986	119.0	111.9	98.3	89.5	92.7	95.8	89.5	84.8	86.4	83.7	82.7	83.0	93.1
1987	86.8	91.1	91.8	94.0	94.8	96.6	98.0	100.4	100.0	98.8	98.7	97.5	95.7
1988	94.7	92.8	92.0	94.6	97.0	97.1	98.4	100.4	99.2	97.6	97.2	95.3	96.3
1989	94.4	95.5	97.4	109.8	115.2	115.0	113.2	109.6	107.3	107.1	104.6	103.0	106.0
1990	109.0	108.6	107.6	109.6	111.4	114.0	113.9	124.6	134.7	143.1	143.2	141.0	121.7
1991	130.4	119.8	113.8	115.9	120.9	121.4	118.5	119.6	119.9	118.0	119.3	118.2	119.6
1992	113.5	111.7	112.2	114.3	119.7	123.9	123.8	122.1	122.2	121.9	122.3	120.1	119.0
1993	118.2	117.2	116.3	117.5	119.3	119.4	117.4	116.3	115.1	119.3	117.8	113.6	117.3
1994	110.9	111.4	110.9	112.8	114.3	116.7	119.9	124.3	123.7	121.2	122.2	120.3	117.4
1995	119.0	118.1	117.3	119.7	125.6	128.1	125.2	122.2	120.6	118.5	116.1	116.0	120.5
1996	118.6	118.1	121.9	130.5	137.8	135.4	132.8	129.8	129.3	128.7	130.8	131.8	128.8
1997[1]	131.8	131.2	129.3	128.8	128.4	128.6	126.3	131.0	133.4	130.0	127.1		129.6

[1] Preliminary. [2] Also includes types of motor oil not shown separately. *Source: Energy Information Administration, U.S. Department of Energy (EIA)*

Refiner Sales Prices of Finished Aviation Gasoline to End Users[2] in the United States In Cents Per Gallon

Year	Jan.	Feb.	Mar.	Apr.	May	June	July	Aug.	Sept.	Oct.	Nov.	Dec.	Average
1985	121.7	121.1	121.4	121.2	121.9	121.7	120.2	118.9	119.5	118.9	118.3	117.0	120.1
1986	116.2	117.2	111.5	104.3	102.2	101.0	98.2	94.9	93.2	91.2	87.2	88.8	101.1
1987	87.9	89.7	90.3	89.8	90.6	91.3	91.5	92.4	91.9	91.4	91.0	90.0	90.7
1988	88.4	88.2	87.7	87.6	89.2	87.2	89.7	92.2	90.8	88.7	89.2	89.2	89.1
1989	89.2	89.7	90.6	99.1	107.0	107.1	105.5	101.9	100.7	100.4	98.6	97.3	99.5
1990	102.0	102.4	100.9	101.4	103.6	104.2	103.9	112.8	125.6	134.4	131.7	122.5	112.0
1991	112.1	106.4	101.3	101.2	105.3	105.2	103.6	105.8	105.7	104.6	104.3	102.0	104.7
1992	98.5	98.5	98.0	99.1	102.4	106.4	106.8	105.7	104.9	104.3	103.4	101.3	102.7
1993	100.3	99.9	99.4	100.7	102.2	102.5	99.7	98.8	98.2	98.0	95.7	91.2	99.0
1994	88.6	88.4	89.0	91.3	92.3	95.6	95.9	101.7	101.1	100.0	100.0	99.2	95.6
1995	99.6	99.8	99.0	101.3	105.8	106.4	101.8	99.2	101.3	96.8	95.4	96.0	100.5
1996	97.6	100.6	105.0	111.2	114.4	113.5	113.7	114.4	114.3	115.0	115.1	115.3	111.6
1997[1]	113.7	114.9	113.8	114.7	115.7	114.6	112.5	114.6	115.6	113.9			114.4

[1] Preliminary. [2] Excluding taxes. *Source: Energy Information Administration, U.S. Department of Energy (EIA-DOE)*

Gold

Gold prices collapsed to an eighteen year low during 1997. Gold began the year at $360 per ounce but finished the year at $290. Technically oriented traders favored the short side during the year with the selling accelerating when the emotionally and technically important $300 level failed to hold. The overriding rational for gold's weakness, however, was that central banks were selling--or threatening to sell--their huge gold inventories, estimated at 25 percent of the world's total gold supply; but in doing so the banks undermined a long held faith towards gold as the traditional store of value and hedge against inflation. The latter belief was already weakening during the first half of the 1990's in the wake of broadening traders access to the world's currency and interest rate markets. Moreover, inflationary pressures were dormant in most of the world. Waning speculative interest towards gold was redirected to the burgeoning world equity markets as a haven for capital. Ironically, even in the wake of the late 1997 crack in Asia's stock and currency markets, the selling pressure on gold did not lift enough to carry spot gold back over $300.

How far gold's price will slide and/or how long it might take for fresh buying enthusiasm to resurface is not discernible, but the damage seen in 1997 runs deep. Moreover, the metal's fundamentals are not encouraging. Should prices carry down to $250 an ounce a number of marginal producing mines will likely close down, but the loss of new supply would be minor should the huge above-ground supplies in the central banks become available.

A major uncertainty overhanging the gold market is the potential consolidation of the European central banks, which if realized may indeed see a liquidation of gold bullion inventory in favor of assets that yield a return, a view that was indicated in 1997 by Switzerland's central bank, whose gold holdings are estimated at 2,600 tonnes. E.U. members with large gold reserves are: Germany with 3,700 tonnes; France, 3,200 tonnes; Italy, 2,600 tonnes and the Netherlands with 1,050 tonnes. The U.S. is the world's largest holder with about 8,150 tonnes.

Annual world gold production (mined) so far in the 1990's has held around 2,250,000 kilograms. South Africa, the world's largest producer, mined 497,583 kg. in 1996, the lowest of the 1990's and compared to 523,809 kg. in 1995. The U.S., the second largest producer since 1991, produced 318,000 kg. in 1996 vs. the 1990's high of 331,000 in 1993. Australia, the third largest producer, mined 289,000 kg. in 1996 vs. 253,504 in 1995. Total world gold supplies for 1996 of 3,490 tonnes compares with 3,330 tonnes in 1995. World demand in 1996 was estimated at a record 3,290 tonnes, up one percent from 1995. Total world demand for gold in jewelry fabrication in 1996 of 2,800 tonnes was up 1.4 percent from 1995. However, jewelry fabrication demand has shown virtually no growth in the industrial nations since 1990, but has jumped as much as 40 percent in some developing nations. Identified world gold resources are estimated at 75,000 tonnes with South Africa having about one-half of the resources and the U.S. 12 percent. Of the estimated 123,000 tonnes of gold mined from historical times through 1996, about 15 percent is believed to have been lost or unaccounted for and two-thirds of the remainder is privately held in the form of coin, jewelry and bullion.

The U.S. is a net gold exporter, most of which is refined bullion shipped to Europe. Exports in 1996 of 471,000 kg. compares with 347,000 in 1995. U.S. gold imports in 1996 of 159,000 kg. compares with 126,000 in 1995.

Futures Markets

Gold futures are traded on the Bolsa de Mercadorias & Futuros (BM&F), The Hong Kong Futures Exchange Ltd. (HKFE), the Tokyo Commodity Exchange (TOCOM), the Singapore International Monetary Exchange Ltd. (SIMEX), the Chicago Board of Trade (CBOT), the Mid America Commodity Exchange, (MidAm), and the New York Mercantile Exchange, COMEX division (COMEX). Gold options are traded on the the Vancouver Stock Exchange (VSE), the European Options Exchange (EOE-Optiebeurs), the MidAm, and the COMEX. Futures and options on Krugerrands are traded on the South Africa Futures Exchange (SAFEX).

World Mine Production of Gold In Kilograms (1 Kilogram = 32.1507 Troy Ounces)

Year	Australia	Brazil	Canada	Chile	China	Ghana	Indo-nesia	Papua N.Guinea	Russia[3]	South Africa	United States	Uzeb-istan[3]	World Total
1986	75,079	67,500	102,899	17,947	66,000	8,931	3,304	35,075	275,000	638,047	116,297	------	1,606,570
1987	110,696	83,700	115,818	17,035	72,000	10,201	3,643	33,250	260,000	607,000	153,870	------	1,660,535
1988	156,950	112,159	134,813	20,614	78,000	11,601	4,738	38,129	277,600	621,000	200,914	------	1,873,803
1989	203,563	52,527	159,527	22,559	90,000	13,358	6,155	27,538	304,000	607,460	265,731	------	2,013,913
1990	244,137	101,913	169,412	27,503	100,000	16,840	11,158	31,938	302,000	605,100	294,189	------	2,180,000
1991	234,218	89,578	176,552	28,879	120,000	26,311	16,879	60,780	260,000	601,110	294,062	------	2,190,000
1992	243,400	85,862	161,402	33,774	125,000	31,032	37,983	71,190	146,000	614,071	330,212	70,000	2,290,000
1993	247,196	74,219	152,929	33,638	130,000	39,235	42,097	60,587	149,500	619,201	331,013	70,000	2,310,000
1994	256,188	70,535	146,428	38,786	132,000	44,505	42,600	58,654	146,600	580,201	327,000	70,000	2,240,000
1995[1]	253,504	62,424	150,967	39,180	140,000	52,200	62,800	51,701	132,170	523,809	317,000	70,000	2,220,000
1996[2]	289,000	62,500	164,136	39,600	145,000	50,100	65,000	51,573	120,000	497,583	318,000	72,000	2,250,000

[1] Preliminary. [2] Estimate. [3] Formerly part of the U.S.S.R.; data not reported separately until 1992. NA = not avaliable.

Source: U.S. Geological Survey (USGS)

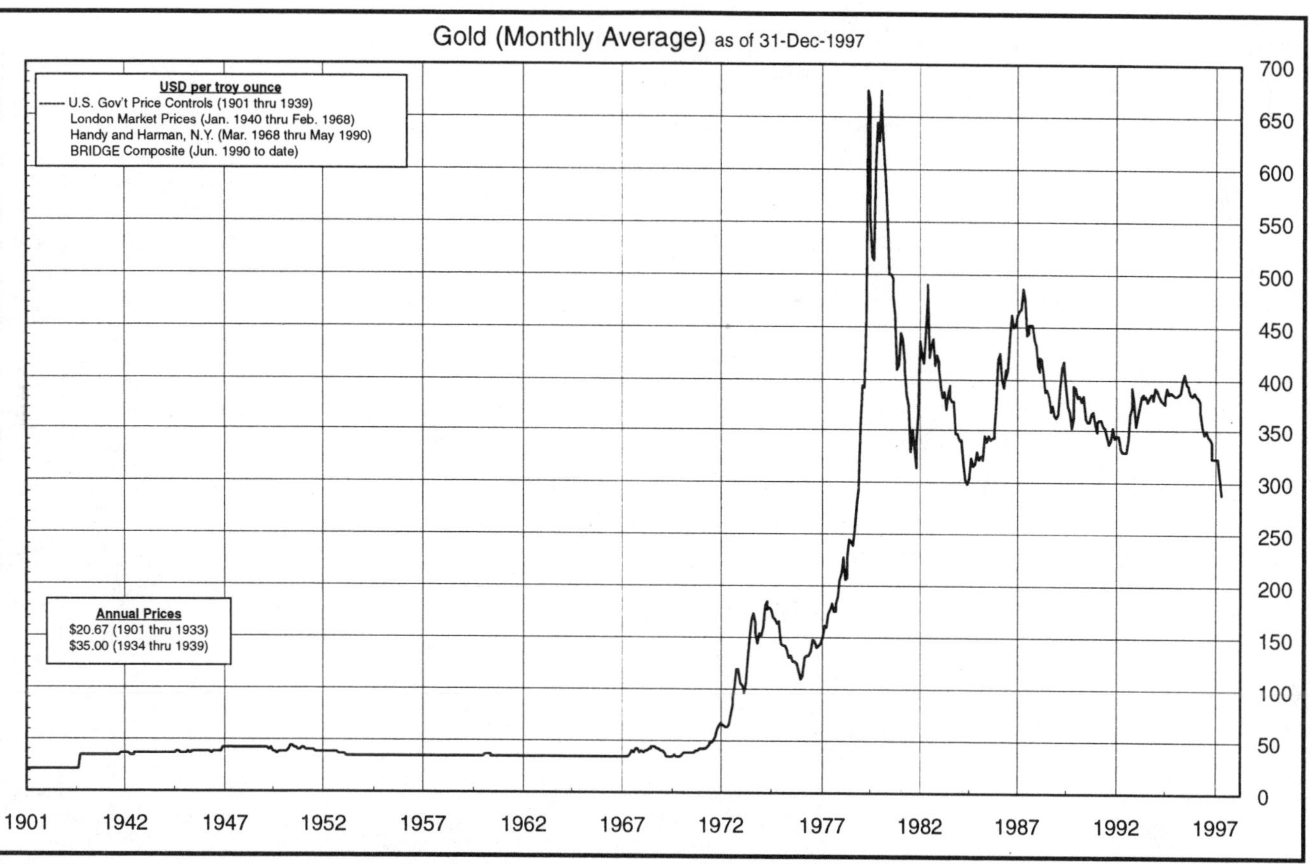

Salient Statistics of Gold in the United States In Kilograms (1 Kilogram = 32.1507 Troy Ounces)

Year	Mine Production	Value Million $	Refinery Production: Domestic & Foreign Ores	Refinery Production: Secondary (Old Scrap)	Exports (Excluding Coinage)	Imports for Consumption	Stocks, Dec. 31: Treasury Department[3]	Stocks, Dec. 31: Futures Exch.	Stocks, Dec. 31: Industry	Official World Reserves[4]	Consumption: Dental	Consumption: Industrial[5]	Consumption: Jewelry & Arts	Consumption: Total
1987	153,870	2,216.0	112,368	63,843	119,630	119,539	8,160,251	81,647	23,390	35,655	6,944	35,245	71,024	113,319
1988	200,914	2,831.3	137,829	61,391	328,237	92,457	8,145,696	44,634	38,360	35,829	7,576	37,226	67,027	111,836
1989	265,731	3,268.6	183,685	51,943	211,091	152,504	8,147,169	69,727	30,462	35,603	7,927	37,621	69,524	115,078
1990	294,189	3,640.8	225,183	43,980	296,397	97,519	8,146,432	50,881	37,065	35,572	8,700	30,996	78,514	118,216
1991	294,062	3,434.7	224,675	48,088	284,127	178,749	8,145,696	49,893	39,411	35,501	8,485	21,793	84,096	114,375
1992	330,212	3,662.4	283,951	53,396	368,851	174,341	8,145,000	46,453	36,713	35,199	6,543	20,360	83,508	110,410
1993	331,013	3,840.9	243,135	65,964	792,680	169,305	8,143,000	78,514	34,400	34,700	6,173	19,663	65,600	91,400
1994	327,000	4,050.0	240,584	74,332	471,000	114,000	8,142,000	49,100	32,700	34,800	5,430	17,013	53,700	76,100
1995[1]	317,000	3,950.0	NA	NA	347,000	126,000	8,140,000	45,400	NA	34,600	NA	NA	NA	NA
1996[2]	318,000	3,980.0	NA	NA	471,000	159,000	8,140,000	20,700	NA	34,400	NA	NA	NA	NA

[1] Preliminary. [2] Estimate. [3] Includes gold in Exchange Stabilization Fund. [4] Held by market economy country central banks and governments and international monetary organizations. [5] Including space and defense. *Source: U.S. Geological Survey (USGS)*

Monthly Average Gold Price (Handy & Harman) in New York Dollars Per Troy Ounce

Year	Jan.	Feb.	Mar.	Apr.	May	June	July	Aug.	Sept.	Oct.	Nov.	Dec.	Average
1988	476.60	441.90	443.60	451.80	450.80	451.30	437.60	431.30	412.80	406.80	420.10	418.50	436.93
1989	404.01	387.78	390.14	384.40	371.32	367.60	394.71	364.92	361.89	366.88	392.32	408.12	382.92
1990	410.10	416.80	393.10	374.30	369.20	352.30	362.50	395.00	389.50	380.70	381.70	378.20	383.61
1991	383.60	363.80	363.40	358.40	356.80	366.70	367.50	356.20	348.80	358.70	359.50	361.10	362.18
1992	354.50	353.90	344.30	338.50	337.20	340.80	353.00	343.00	345.40	344.40	335.10	334.70	343.74
1993	329.00	329.40	330.10	341.90	366.70	371.90	392.40	378.50	354.90	364.20	373.50	383.70	359.67
1994	387.02	382.01	384.13	378.20	381.21	385.64	385.44	380.43	391.80	389.77	349.43	379.60	384.14
1995	378.55	376.51	382.12	391.11	385.46	387.56	386.40	383.63	382.22	383.14	385.53	387.42	384.22
1996	399.59	404.73	396.21	392.96	391.98	385.58	383.69	387.43	382.97	381.07	378.46	369.02	387.81
1997[1]	355.10	346.71	351.67	344.47	343.75	340.75	324.08	324.03	322.74	324.87	307.10		335.02

[1] Preliminary. *Sources: U.S. Geological Survey (USGS)*

GOLD

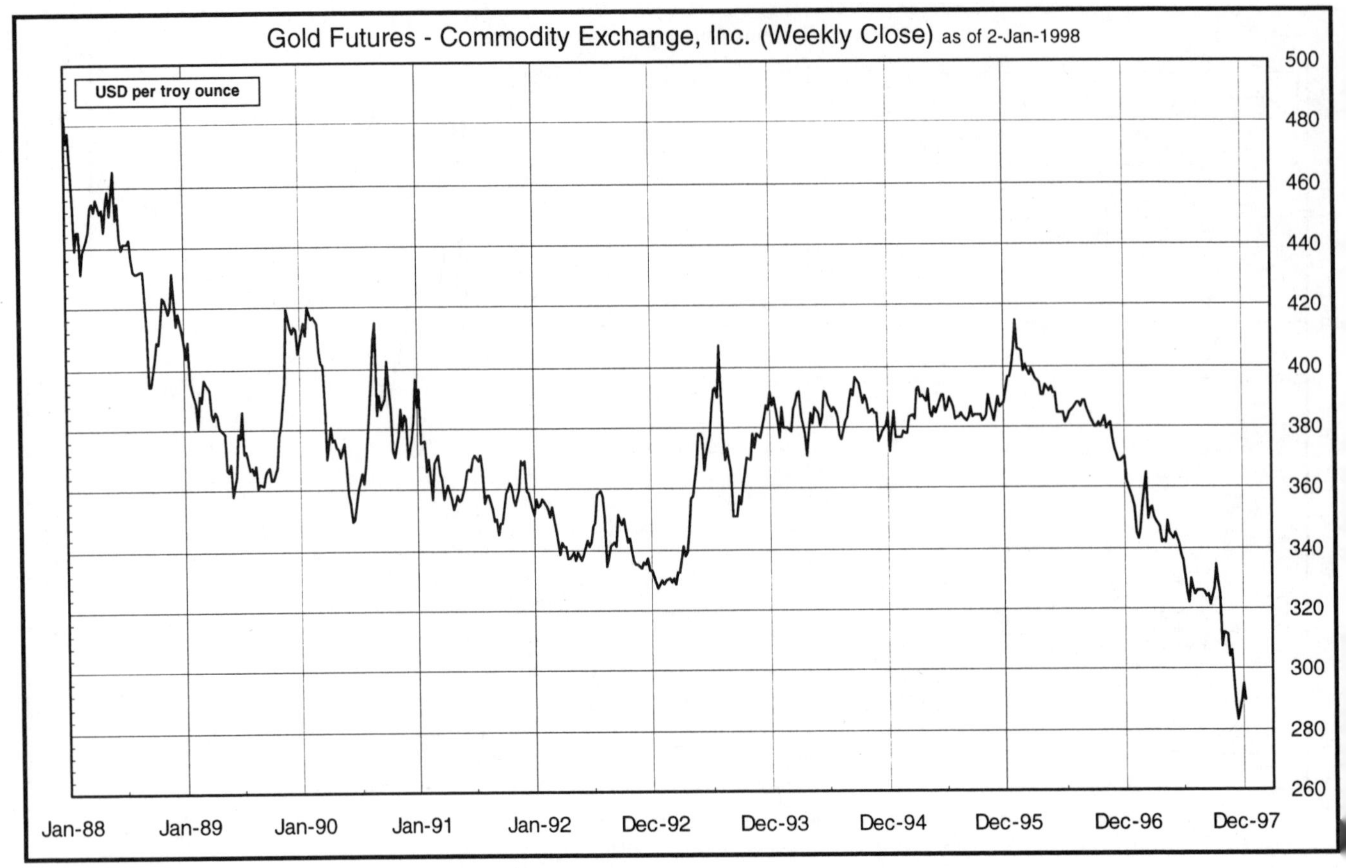

Average Open Interest of Gold Futures in New York (COMEX) In Thousands of Contracts

Year	Jan.	Feb.	Mar.	Apr.	May	June	July	Aug.	Sept.	Oct.	Nov.	Dec.
1988	147,067	152,789	158,224	154,788	153,465	145,951	147,822	140,311	153,556	160,591	153,497	144,839
1989	162,226	166,455	167,419	160,215	180,709	164,196	154,517	150,414	151,836	146,262	154,927	151,788
1990	147,884	132,400	126,890	118,750	117,707	113,958	105,496	120,579	116,331	113,873	111,638	110,343
1991	104,666	98,000	98,429	101,266	100,341	88,961	94,467	99,790	105,053	96,302	109,030	109,004
1992	106,110	103,319	109,796	106,485	109,947	98,127	111,039	102,239	102,376	102,232	109,965	100,328
1993	112,420	109,093	115,505	142,208	172,491	170,829	200,168	180,509	166,201	152,531	152,853	154,730
1994	156,045	139,354	146,269	144,386	147,738	146,255	148,915	155,641	167,981	166,041	166,536	178,998
1995	184,549	170,972	168,651	191,667	173,805	174,075	175,727	176,135	185,128	185,854	170,674	141,751
1996	210,695	226,160	203,968	201,826	203,056	192,423	185,374	159,435	185,907	192,606	187,145	185,994
1997	199,710	190,524	167,595	157,176	160,512	170,640	207,352	198,099	201,267	188,365	212,757	188,558

Source: New York Mercantile Exchange, COMEX Division

Volume of Trading of Gold Futures in New York (COMEX) In Thousands of Contracts

Year	Jan.	Feb.	Mar.	Apr.	May	June	July	Aug.	Sept.	Oct.	Nov.	Dec.	Total
1988	815.0	778.7	965.0	637.7	866.2	946.3	884.2	587.5	790.9	694.5	895.5	634.9	9,49[illegible]
1989	900.4	800.0	993.8	682.4	932.0	936.6	756.1	591.1	630.0	681.2	1,228.4	876.4	9,98[illegible]
1990	1,327.1	885.1	975.6	472.4	745.2	541.0	747.4	1,191.5	729.4	879.9	705.3	530.1	9,73[illegible]
1991	957.3	497.8	617.7	446.1	584.4	520.0	551.4	457.2	429.1	551.0	677.3	510.6	6,77[illegible]
1992	729.8	388.4	607.3	425.4	485.4	427.2	734.6	500.2	465.3	414.1	504.1	320.1	6,00[illegible]
1993	506.0	446.2	661.4	640.4	1,140.7	809.6	1,171.7	808.8	728.9	565.2	892.3	533.2	8,91[illegible]
1994	981.8	584.0	889.5	589.2	922.6	740.2	723.8	626.0	645.6	651.2	687.8	461.5	8,50[illegible]
1995	881.9	420.0	1,087.5	613.0	777.0	588.1	669.9	500.5	495.5	387.7	982.5	378.1	7,78[illegible]
1996	1,384.7	987.5	943.6	647.1	858.5	582.1	749.8	541.9	541.9	528.5	795.2	458.8	8,69[illegible]
1997	1,102.8	830.2	899.4	508.5	762.1	522.7	1,147.5	667.8	715.8	988.0	808.8	588.1	9,54[illegible]

Source: New York Mercantile Exchange, COMEX Division

Commodity Exchange, Inc. (COMEX) Depository Warehouse Stocks of Gold In Thousands of Troy Ounces

Year	Jan. 1	Feb. 1	Mar. 1	Apr. 1	May 1	June 1	July 1	Aug. 1	Sept. 1	Oct. 1	Nov. 1	Dec. 1
1988	2,624	2,605	2,586	1,596	1,566	1,675	1,834	2,099	2,189	1,949	1,629	1,267
1989	1,434	1,408	1,454	1,532	1,606	1,634	1,602	1,602	1,433	1,483	1,731	2,263
1990	2,241	2,225	2,245	2,220	2,048	1,809	1,582	1,530	1,539	1,564	1,585	1,347
1991	1,636	1,686	1,540	1,298	1,458	1,711	1,772	1,875	1,220	1,342	1,302	1,479
1992	1,605	1,362	1,435	1,411	1,591	1,618	1,605	1,733	1,688	1,947	1,766	1,524
1993	1,507	1,340	1,365	1,426	1,383	2,231	2,247	2,448	2,437	2,425	2,349	2,552
1994	2,524	2,955	2,958	2,862	2,802	2,434	2,665	2,574	2,030	1,904	1,843	1,867
1995	1,577	1,498	1,386	1,360	1,391	1,488	1,505	1,608	1,448	1,745	1,395	1,315
1996	1,460	1,869	1,412	1,429	1,335	1,711	1,263	1,273	1,402	1,283	1,060	1,104
1997	666	837	583	1,000	946	878	850	914	733	894	615	761

Source: New York Mercantile Exchange, COMEX division

Central Gold Bank Reserves In Millions of Troy Ounces

	Industrial Countries															
Year	Belgium	Canada	France	Germany	Italy	Japan	Netherlands	Switzerland	United Kingdom	United States	Industrial Total	Developing Oil	Developing Non-Oil	IMF[2]	Bank for Int'l Settlements	World Total
1987	33.6	18.5	81.9	95.2	66.7	24.2	43.9	83.3	19.0	262.4	894.3	43.6	99.1	103.4	6.1	1,146.5
1988	33.7	17.1	81.9	95.2	66.7	24.2	43.9	83.3	19.0	261.9	895.1	42.0	99.1	103.4	6.4	1,146.1
1989	30.2	16.1	81.9	95.2	66.7	24.2	43.9	83.3	19.0	261.9	891.5	42.1	103.3	103.4	6.1	1,146.4
1990	30.2	14.8	81.9	95.2	66.7	24.2	43.9	83.3	18.9	261.9	889.4	41.5	101.3	103.4	6.6	1,142.2
1991	30.2	13.0	81.9	95.2	66.7	24.2	43.9	83.3	18.9	261.9	887.3	42.0	101.6	103.4	6.6	1,141.0
1992	25.0	9.9	81.9	95.2	66.7	24.2	43.9	83.3	18.6	261.8	877.4	42.0	101.7	103.4	6.8	1,131.3
1993	25.0	6.1	81.9	95.2	66.7	24.2	35.1	83.3	18.5	261.8	860.4	42.0	100.1	103.4	8.6	1,114.6
1994	25.0	3.9	81.9	95.2	66.7	24.2	34.8	83.3	18.4	261.7	856.9	42.0	106.6	103.4	7.0	1,115.8
1995	20.5	3.4	81.9	95.2	66.7	24.2	34.8	83.3	18.4	261.7	848.8	41.4	110.4	103.4	7.3	1,111.3
1996[1]	15.3	3.1	81.9	95.2	66.7	24.2	34.8	83.3	18.4	261.7	840.2	41.4	113.2	103.4	6.7	1,104.9

[1] Preliminary. [2] International Monetary Fund. *Source: American Metal Market (AMM)*

Mine Production of Recoverable Gold in the United States, by States In Kilograms

Year	Arizona	California	Idaho	Montana	Nevada	Alaska	Colorado	South Dakota	New Mexico	Utah	Other States	Total
1988	4,549	22,442	3,218	9,175	114,322	4,210	5,126	13,981	W	W	23,891	200,914
1989	2,768	29,804	3,057	12,434	153,995	5,756	3,448	16,123	1,076	W	37,270	265,731
1990	5,000	29,607	W	13,012	179,078	3,232	2,357	17,870	888	W	43,145	294,189
1991	6,195	30,404	3,348	13,715	178,488	3,200	3,181	16,371	W	W	39,161	295,957
1992	6,656	33,335	4,037	13,994	203,393	5,003	3,763	18,681	W	W	41,350	329,124
1993	2,710	35,800	4,324	14,300	211,000	2,780	W	19,200	995	W	37,300	331,000
1994	2,540	28,880	3,610	13,300	203,000	5,740	4,420	W	W	W	50,100	306,000
1995	1,920	25,600	8,850	12,400	210,000	4,410	W	W	W	W	53,700	317,000
1996[1]	1,740	23,800	7,410	9,110	213,000	5,020	W	W	W	W	57,500	318,000
1997[2]	176	18,000	W	5,290	199,000	W	W	W	W	W	56,500	278,000

[1] Preliminary. [2] January through October. W = Withheld proprietary data, included in "Other States." *Source: U.S. Geological Survey (USGS)*

Consumption of Gold, by End-Use in the United States In Kilograms

	Jewelry and the Arts					Industrial				
Year	Gold-filled & Other	Electro-plating	Karat Gold	Total	Dental	Gold-filled & Other	Electro-plating	Karat Gold	Total	Grand Total
1987	9,256	3,133	58,635	71,024	6,944	21,010	12,343	1,892	35,245	113,319
1988	7,598	1,469	57,959	67,027	7,576	21,034	15,088	1,104	37,226	111,836
1989	7,364	1,283	60,877	69,524	7,927	15,723	20,684	1,215	37,621	115,078
1990	8,132	429	69,952	78,514	8,700	12,725	17,251	1,020	30,996	118,216
1991	3,848	373	79,875	84,096	8,485	8,102	12,624	1,068	21,793	114,375
1992	3,546	581	79,381	83,508	6,543	8,802	10,476	1,082	20,360	110,410
1993	3,532	373	61,700	65,600	6,173	9,474	9,094	1,095	19,663	91,400
1994	3,650	369	49,700	53,700	5,430	7,450	9,470	96	17,000	76,100
1995	NA	NA	NA	NA	NA	NA	NA	NA	NA	NA
1996[1]	NA	NA	NA	NA	NA	NA	NA	NA	NA	NA

[1] Preliminary. *Source: U.S. Geological Survey (USGS)*

GOLD

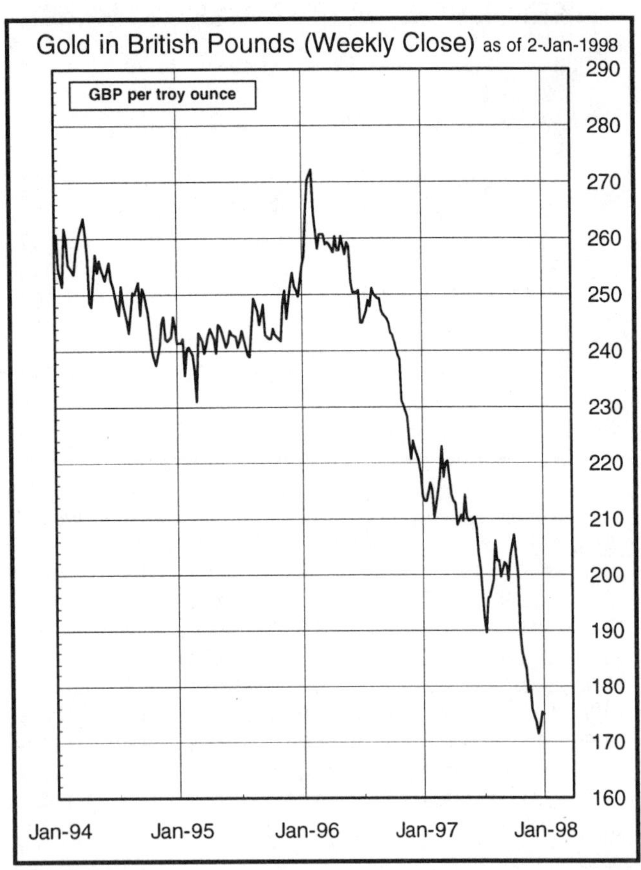

Gold in British Pounds (Weekly Close) as of 2-Jan-1998
GBP per troy ounce
290
280
270
260
250
240
230
220
210
200
190
180
170
160
Jan-94
Jan-95
Jan-96
Jan-97
Jan-98

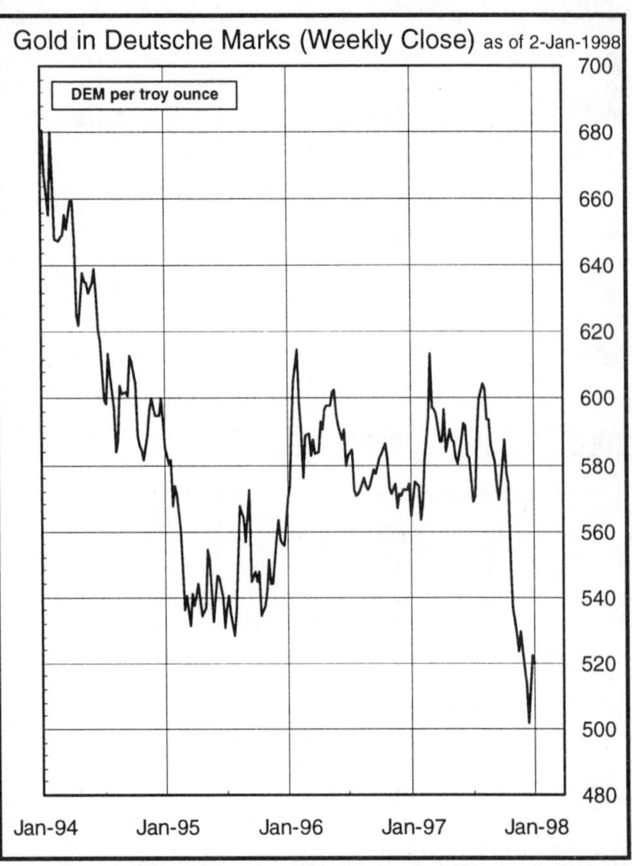

Gold in Deutsche Marks (Weekly Close) as of 2-Jan-1998
DEM per troy ounce
700
680
660
640
620
600
580
560
540
520
500
480
Jan-94
Jan-95
Jan-96
Jan-97
Jan-98

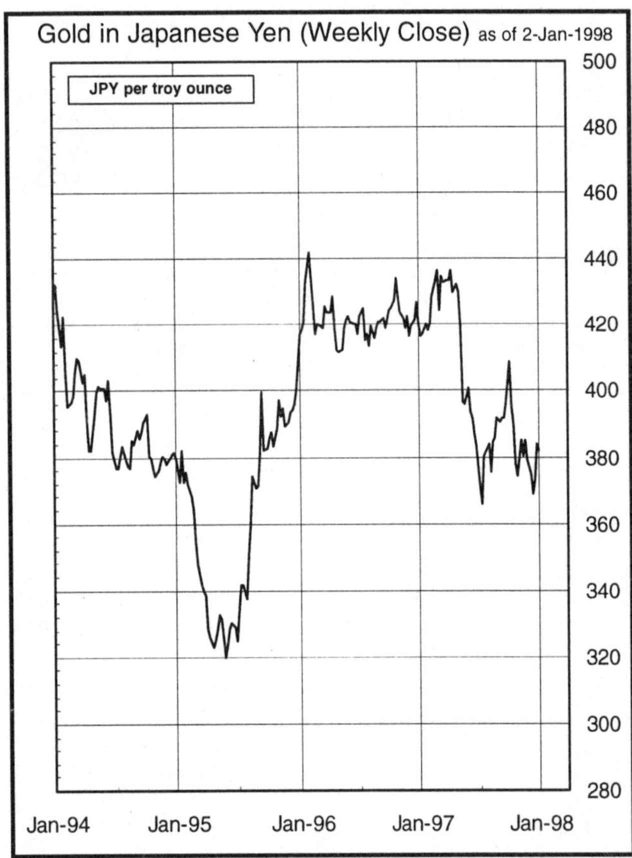

Gold in Japanese Yen (Weekly Close) as of 2-Jan-1998
JPY per troy ounce
500
480
460
440
420
400
380
360
340
320
300
280
Jan-94
Jan-95
Jan-96
Jan-97
Jan-98

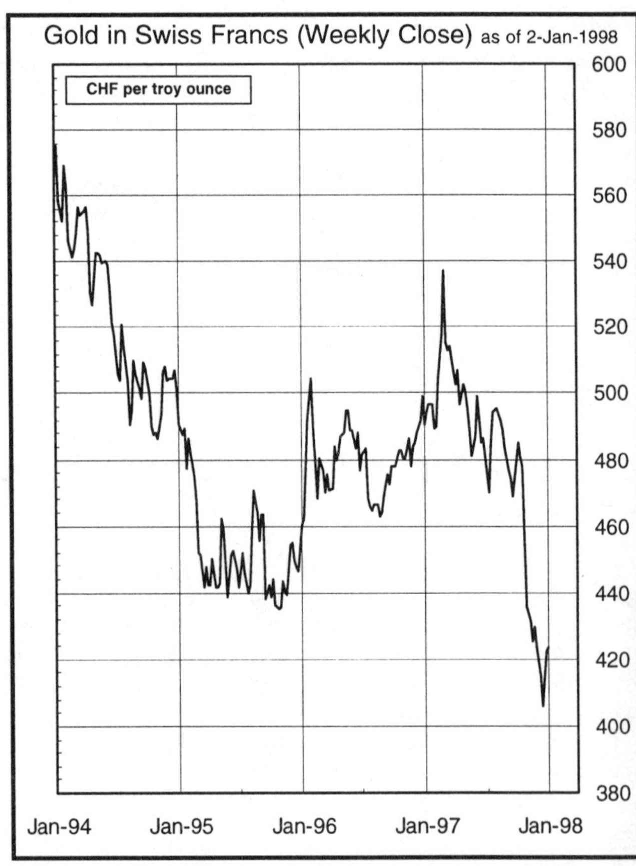

Gold in Swiss Francs (Weekly Close) as of 2-Jan-1998
CHF per troy ounce
600
580
560
540
520
500
480
460
440
420
400
380
Jan-94
Jan-95
Jan-96
Jan-97
Jan-98

Grain Sorghum

The U.S. is the world's largest producer of grain sorghum (milo) with India a distant second. World production in 1996/97 of 64.8 million metric tons compares with 54.5 million in 1995/96. The U.S. produced nearly a third of the world crop at 20.2 million tons; but in 1995/96 U.S. production of 11.7 million tons was the lowest of the 1990's and only 21 percent of world output. However, unlike most of the world's sorghum producing nations who consume their production domestically, the U.S. generally consumes two-thirds and exports the balance.

India's 1996/97 crop of 11 million tons compares with 9.7 million in 1995/96. Significantly, India sorghum acreage of 12.6 million hectares in 1996/97 accounts for nearly a third of the world's acreage of 41.7 million, but India's average yield appears to be the world's lowest; 0.87 mt/hectare vs. a world average in 1996/97 of 1.55 and a U.S. average of 4.14 mt/hectare. In contrast, China's 1996/97 average yield was one of the highest at 4.75 mt/hectare on acreage of only 1.2 million hectares yielding a crop of 4.75 million tons vs. 3.9 million in 1995/96.

World sorghum trade is small; 6.5 million tons in 1996/97 vs. 6.1 million in 1995/96 and an early 1990's average of 9 million tons. The U.S. is by far the largest exporter, mostly to Mexico and Japan, the two largest importers. Argentina is the second largest 1996/97 exporter with 500,000 tons vs. the U.S. total of 5.7 million. The world carryover totaled 9.4 million tons at the end of 1992/93, falling to 2.6 million by the end of 1995/96, but was expected to rebound to 3.7 million at the end of 1996/97, almost half of which will be in the U.S.

The U.S. sorghum crop year begins September 1. Kansas and Texas are the largest producing states with Nebraska a distant third. Production rebounded sharply in 1996/97 to 797 million bushels from 460 million in 1995/96. The Kansas crop nearly doubled to 350 million bushels from 174 million. The overall increase, however, largely reflected an increase in harvested acreage; to 12 million acres from 8.3 million and an average yield of 66.4 bushels per acre vs. 55.6 bushels, respectively.

Total U.S. supplies in 1996/97 of 815 million bushels compares with 532 million in 1995/96. No sorghum is imported into the U.S. Disappearance in 1996/97 of 754 million bushels compares with 514 million in 1995/96, of which 525 million bushels will be used in 1996/97 as a feed and 225 million exported vs. 310 million and 200 million, respectively. The projected 1996/97 carryover of 61 million bushels compares with a carryin of 18 million.

Sorghum prices received by farmers during 1996/97 were forecast to have a range of $2.55-$2.95 per bushel vs. a 1990's high of $3.19 in 1995/96 when prices were buoyed by low production.

World Supply and Demand of Grain Sorghum In Thousands of Metric Tons

	Exports				Imports				Total	Utilization				Ending Stocks		
Crop Year	Argentina	Non-U.S.	U.S.	Total	Japan	Mexico	Unaccounted	Total	Production	China	Mexico	U.S.	Total	Non-U.S.	U.S.	Total
1992-3	1,023	2,244	6,634	8,878	3,221	4,021	134	8,878	65,387	4,585	7,409	12,091	61,809	4,952	4,446	9,398
1993-4	426	1,750	5,318	7,068	2,852	3,089	548	7,068	56,680	6,205	6,307	11,687	61,997	2,873	1,208	4,081
1994-5	192	756	5,653	6,409	2,334	2,544	118	6,409	57,986	6,355	5,644	10,223	57,954	2,294	1,819	4,113
1995-6[1]	811	1,691	4,757	6,448	2,298	1,764	484	6,448	55,252	4,927	6,500	8,021	56,705	2,193	467	2,660
1996-7[2]	615	920	5,207	6,127	2,597	2,091	377	6,127	68,343	5,377	6,600	14,441	66,647	3,150	1,206	4,356
1997-8[3]	700	1,050	5,250	6,300	2,700	2,200	367	6,300	63,374	5,675	7,000	11,686	64,105	2,595	1,030	3,625

[1] Preliminary. [2] Estimate. [3] Forecast. *Source: Foreign Agricultural Service, U.S. Department of Agriculture (FAS-USDA)*

Salient Statistics of Grain Sorghum in the United States

	Acreage Planted[4] for All Purposes	For Grain						For Silage			Sorghum Grain Stocks			
		Acreage Harvested	Production 1,000	Yield Per Harvested Acre	Price in Cents Per	Value of Production	Acreage Harvested 1,000	Production 1,000	Yield Per Harvested Acre	Dec. 1		June 1	
Year	1,000 Acres	1,000 Acres	Bushels	Bushels	Bushel	Million $	Acres	Tons	Tons	On Farms (1,000 Bushels)	Off Farms	On Farms	Off Farms
1992-3	13,177	12,050	875,022	72.6	189	1,666.9	453	5,468	12.1	110,200	340,262	58,465	206,348
1993-4	9,882	8,916	534,172	59.9	231	1,234.5	351	3,914	11.2	105,950	340,198	32,075	96,035
1994-5	9,827	8,917	649,206	72.8	213	1,323.8	329	3,932	12.0	126,650	295,809	44,570	114,212
1995-6[1]	9,454	8,278	460,373	55.6	319	1,395.4	368	3,652	9.9	79,090	222,186	13,955	56,433
1996-7[2]	13,188	11,901	802,974	67.5	234	2,004.2	371	4,356	11.7	144,590	322,767	38,815	80,329
1997-8[3]	10,108	9,391	653,106	69.5	210-240	1,455.7	310	3,885	12.5	96,625	273,834		

[1] Preliminary. [2] Estimate. [3] Forecast. NA = Not available. *Source: Economic Research Service, U.S. Department of Agriculture (ERS-USDA)*

Production of All Sorghum for Grain in the United States, by States In Thousands of Bushels

Year	Arkansas	Colorado	Illinois	Kansas	Louisiana	Mississippi	Missouri	Nebraska	New Mexico	Oklahoma	South Dakota	Texas	Total
1992	31,160	6,660	26,780	244,000	15,232	10,500	62,080	143,820	12,300	17,490	14,060	279,000	875,022
1993	12,470	7,140	17,430	176,400	7,200	4,225	39,420	73,750	7,425	14,500	10,500	156,750	534,172
1994	18,375	7,140	17,820	231,000	8,364	5,250	49,500	117,600	7,410	14,000	11,375	153,400	649,206
1995	13,135	4,620	11,730	173,600	5,880	2,665	35,770	56,840	3,380	12,800	4,800	129,600	460,373
1996	16,280	13,260	18,480	354,200	11,628	5,040	52,780	97,850	7,425	28,910	7,975	182,400	802,974
1997[1]	11,100	5,600	14,105	273,000	7,546	2,475	40,920	61,500	10,340	24,500	11,360	185,850	653,106

[1] Preliminary. *Source: National Agricultural Statistics Service, U.S Department of Agriculture (NASS-USDA)*

GRAIN SORGHUM

Grain Sorghum Quarterly Supply and Disappearance in the United States   In Millions of Bushels

Crop Year Beginning Sept. 1	Supply: Beginning Stocks	Supply: Pro-duction	Supply: Imports	Supply: Total Supply	Disappearance: Domestic Use: Food, Alcohol & Industrial	Domestic Use: Seed	Domestic Use: Feed & Residual	Domestic Use: Total	Export	Total Disappearance	Ending Stocks: Gov't. Owned[3]	Ending Stocks: Privately Owned[4]	Ending Stocks: Total Stocks
1994-5	47.6	655.0	0	702.6	5.8	1.2	401.7	408.7	222.7	631.4	1.0	70.2	71.2
Sept.-Nov.	47.6	655.0	0	702.6	1.7	0	214.4	216.1	64.1	280.1	3.0	419.5	422.5
Dec.-Feb.	422.5	------	0	422.5	1.4	0	79.2	80.6	60.9	141.5	2.0	278.9	280.9
Mar.-May	280.9	------	0	280.9	1.5	.4	65.9	67.8	54.4	122.2	1.0	157.8	158.8
June-Aug.	158.8	------	0	158.8	1.2	.8	42.2	44.2	43.3	87.6	1.0	70.2	71.2
1995-6	72.0	460.0	0	532.0	5.8	1.2	312.0	322.0	198.0	514.0	1.0	40.0	18.0
Sept.-Nov.	72.0	460.0	0	532.0			176.0		54.0	231.0			301.0
Dec.-Feb.	301.0	------	0	301.0			71.0		67.0	139.0			163.0
Mar.-May	163.0	------	0	163.0			55.0		36.0	92.0			70.0
June-Aug.	70.0	------	0	70.0			7.0		41.0	52.0			18.0
1996-7[1]	18.0	803.0	0	821.0			529.0		205.0	774.0			47.0
Sept.-Nov.	18.0	803.0	0	821.0			287.0		56.0	354.0			467.0
Dec.-Feb.	467.0	------	0	467.0			124.0		59.0	193.0			274.0
Mar.-May	274.0	------	0	274.0			82.0		61.0	155.0			119.0
June-Aug.	119.0	------	0	119.0			36.0		29.0	72.0			47.0
1997-8[2]	47.0	653.0	0	701.0			425.0		200.0	660.0			41.0
Sept.-Nov.	47.0	653.0	0	701.0			276.0		45.0	330.0			370.0

[1] Preliminary. [2] Forecast. [3] Uncommitted inventory. [4] Includes quantity under loan & farmer-owned reserve. *Source: Economic Research Service, U.S. Department of Agriculture (ERS-USDA)*

Average Price of Sorghum Grain, No. 2, Yellow at Kansas City   In Dollars Per Hundred Pounds (Cwt.)

Year	Sept.	Oct.	Nov.	Dec.	Jan.	Feb.	Mar.	Apr.	May	June	July	Aug.	Average
1990-1	3.89	3.79	3.85	3.97	4.12	4.21	4.35	4.34	4.13	4.02	4.05	4.22	4.08
1991-2	4.24	4.30	4.27	4.35	4.44	4.62	4.78	4.41	4.54	4.51	4.05	3.77	4.36
1992-3	3.76	3.60	3.61	3.70	3.70	3.66	3.70	3.72	3.82	3.58	3.99	4.01	3.74
1993-4	3.89	4.03	4.60	4.91	4.93	4.81	4.64	4.33	4.38	4.43	3.79	3.73	4.37
1994-5	3.72	3.55	3.60	3.81	3.92	3.90	4.01	4.08	4.27	4.50	4.93	4.85	4.10
1995-6	5.08	5.45	5.68	6.19	6.39	6.58	6.81	7.79	8.17	7.79	7.24	6.74	6.66
1996-7[1]	5.29	4.64	4.31	4.22	4.24	4.46	4.88	4.83	4.63	4.48	4.18	4.28	4.54
1997-8[1]	4.13	4.36											4.25

[1] Preliminary. *Source: Economic Research Service, U.S. Department of Agriculture (ERS-USDA)*

Exports of Grain Sorghum, by Country of Destination from the United States   In Metric Tons

Year Beginning October	Canada	Ecuador	Ethiopia	Israel	Japan	Jordon	Mexico	South Africa	Spain	Sudan	Turkey	World Total
1990-1	1,325	33,060	0	165,906	1,853,079	20,500	3,015,944	0	181,501	91,400	114,636	5,778,792
1991-2	1,613	36,000	42,150	104,952	1,738,075	120,001	4,956,607	19,031	174,758	122,183	99,394	7,454,616
1992-3	1,795	9,501	0	217,110	1,933,012	0	3,970,069	56,186	188,893	4,287	132,182	6,651,528
1992-3	1,795	9,501	0	217,110	1,933,012	0	3,970,069	56,186	188,893	4,287	132,182	6,651,528
1993-4	1,699	0	86,697	66,264	1,681,976	0	3,118,139	0	169,454	48,042	0	5,245,524
1994-5[1]	3,713	0	0	214,073	1,987,738	0	2,543,696	0	398,339	12,304	0	5,652,585
1995-6[2]	5,734	0	0	356,868	1,616,384	0	1,633,386	332	431,578	0	0	4,757,055

[1] Preliminary. [2] Estimate. *Source: Economic Research Service, U.S. Department of Agriculture (ERS-USDA)*

Grain Sorghum Price Support Program and Market Prices in the United States

Year	Price Support Operations: Put Under Price Support: Quantity (Million Cwt.)	Put Under Price Support: % of Pro-duction	Aquired by CCC (Million Cwt.)	Owned by CCC at Year End (Million Cwt.)	Basic Loan Rate ($ Per Bushel)	Target Price ($ Per Bushel)	Findley Loan Rate ($ Per Bushel)	Effective Base[3] Mil. Acres	Partici-pation Rate[4] % of Base	No. 2 Yellow ($ Per Cwt.): Kansas City	Texas High Plains	Los Angeles	Gulf Ports
1990-1	12.1	3.8	5.0	36.4	1.86	2.61	1.49	15.4	70.2	4.08	4.48	5.52	4.65
1991-2	9.5	2.9	5.4	4.5	1.80	2.61	1.54	13.5	77.1	4.36	4.78	5.69	4.86
1992-3	27.2	5.5	0	2.2	1.91	2.61	1.63	13.6	78.6	3.74	4.06	5.11	4.27
1993-4	8.2	2.6	0	1.4	1.89	2.61	1.63	13.5	81.6	4.37	4.95	----	4.90
1994-5	25.2	6.9	0	.4	1.89	2.61	1.80	13.5	81.1	4.10	4.75	----	4.62
1995-6[1]	7.2	1.6	0	0	1.84	2.61	1.80	13.3	76.9	6.66	7.30	----	7.19
1996-7[2]	----	----	----	----	----	[5]	1.81	13.2	98.8	4.54	5.02	----	5.03

[1] Preliminary. [2] Estimate. [3] National effective crop acreage base as determined by ASCS. [4] Percentage of effective base acres enrolled in acreage reduction programs. [5] Beginning 1996-7, target prices are no longer applicable. *Source: Economic Research Service, U.S. Department of Agriculture (ERS-USDA)*

Hay

U.S. total hay production in 1996/97 (marketing year, May 1 to April 30) of 149 million tonnes was down 3 percent from 1995/96. Harvested acreage of 61 million acres compared with 59.6 million, but average yield dipped to 2.45 tonnes per acre from 2.59. California is generally the largest producing state, but South Dakota's 8.2 million tonnes was the highest output in 1996/97. Alfalfa and alfalfa mixtures account for more than half of total hay production, 79 million tonnes in 1996 vs. 85 million in 1995. Alfalfa yields are nearly twice as high as other types of hays. Hay production in 1997/98 was forecast at 152 million tonnes, slightly lower than expected, but up 2% from 1996. Significantly, all of the increase was in non-alfalfa hay as alfalfa hay acreage was reduced. Hay supplies in 1997/98 were estimated to be unchanged from 1996/97 as the larger crop was offset by a lower 1996/97 carryover.

Roughage consuming animal units (RCAU) in 1997/98 were expected to be down from 1996/97 because of fewer cattle. The supply of hay per RCAU was forecast at 2.28 tonnes vs. 2.24 tonnes a year earlier. The key to hay prices generally rests on the number of dairy cows and producer intentions to plant acreage to hay for forage. Alfalfa farm prices in 1996/97 averaged $97.20 per ton vs. $87.20 in 1995/96. In the first third of the 1997/98 season prices averaged $113 a ton vs. $96 a year earlier. The difference might have been even greater had not stable prices for non-alfalfa hay checked the strength.

Salient Statistics of All Hay in the United States

Year Crop Beginning May	Acres Harvested 1,000 Acres	Yield Per Acre Tons	Production (Millions of Tons)	Carryover May 1 (Millions of Tons)	Disappearance (Millions of Tons)	Supply Per Animal Unit (In Tons)	Disappearance Per Animal Unit (In Tons)	Animal Units Fed[3] Millions	Farm Price $ Per Ton	Farm Production Value Million $	Retail Price Paid by Farmers for Seed, April 15 (Dollars Per Cwt.): Alfalfa (Certified)	Timothy	Red Clover	Sudan-Grass
1992-3	58,903	2.49	146.9	28.2	154.1	2.32	2.04	75.3	74.3	10,436	252.00	66.30	122.00	47.10
1993-4	59,679	2.46	146.8	21.0	145.7	2.21	1.91	76.4	84.7	10,957	269.00	80.60	148.00	45.20
1994-5	58,735	2.55	150.1	22.1	151.4	2.21	1.94	77.9	86.7	11,114	266.00	76.00	148.00	47.90
1995-6	59,629	2.59	154.2	20.8	154.2	2.24	1.97	78.3	82.2	11,042	274.00	71.00	134.00	51.80
1996-7[1]	60,879	2.45	149.5	20.7	NA	2.21	NA	76.9	95.8	12,723	277.00	76.00	172.00	51.90
1997-8[2]	60,815	2.50	152.1						102.5	13,417				

[1] Preliminary. [2] Estimate. [3] Roughage-consuming animal units fed annually. *Source: Economic Research Service, U.S. Department of Agriculture (ERS)*

Production of All Hay in the United States, by States In Thousands of Tons

Year	California	Idaho	Iowa	Minnesota	Missouri	New York	North Dakota	Ohio	Oklahoma	South Dakota	Texas	Wisconsin	Total
1992	7,755	3,655	6,615	6,550	6,780	7,793	3,515	4,240	4,750	6,780	9,800	6,090	146,903
1993	7,590	4,844	4,803	5,970	7,335	7,323	5,043	3,475	4,248	8,190	7,506	6,260	146,799
1994	8,210	4,438	5,775	7,530	6,770	7,415	4,510	4,384	4,198	7,330	8,455	6,550	150,060
1995	8,341	5,080	5,665	6,943	6,818	6,975	5,095	4,035	4,174	9,050	8,136	6,820	154,166
1996	8,008	4,760	5,310	5,998	6,920	7,455	4,825	3,400	5,045	8,200	7,815	6,050	149,457
1997[1]	8,616	5,148	5,190	6,488	7,194	6,505	4,130	3,850	5,052	8,090	10,790	5,900	152,120

[1] Preliminary. *Source: Agricultural Statistics Board, U.S. Department of Agriculture (ASB-USDA)*

Hay Production and Farm Stocks in the United States In Thousands of Short Tons

Year	Production: Alfalfa & Mixtures	All Others	All Hay	Corn for Silage[1]	Sorghum Silage[1]	Farm Stocks: May 1	Dec. 1
1992	79,140	67,763	146,903	87,663	5,468	28,216	105,290
1993	80,305	66,494	146,799	81,829	3,914	21,010	100,953
1994	81,336	68,724	150,060	88,588	3,932	22,096	105,296
1995	84,515	69,651	154,166	77,867	3,652	20,775	109,438
1996	79,517	69,940	149,457	83,594	4,356	20,739	104,832
1997[2]	79,242	72,878	152,120	91,903	3,885	17,372	102,517

[1] Not included in all tame hay. [2] Preliminary. *Source: Agricultural Statistics Board, U.S. Department of Agriculture (ASB-USDA)*

Mid-Month Price Received by Farmers of All Hay (Baled) in the United States In Dollars Per Ton

Year	May	June	July	Aug.	Sept.	Oct.	Nov.	Dec.	Jan.	Feb.	Mar.	Apr.	Average[2]
1992-3	79.50	75.80	69.70	71.90	70.10	70.30	71.00	73.50	76.10	78.00	80.50	83.60	74.30
1993-4	86.60	79.60	76.90	77.50	78.80	82.30	84.20	83.50	85.70	86.90	90.80	98.20	84.70
1994-5	100.00	88.70	82.50	83.10	82.40	86.80	86.60	85.50	84.80	85.00	86.70	90.30	86.00
1995-6	90.40	83.90	80.60	81.10	80.30	83.00	81.00	80.30	81.70	81.20	83.40	90.30	82.10
1996-7	97.10	92.30	89.60	92.90	90.10	93.00	92.00	90.80	97.90	105.00	108.00	117.00	97.14
1997-8[1]	118.00	108.00	98.40	101.00	103.00	103.00	101.00	97.70	98.10				103.13

[1] Preliminary. [2] Marketing year average. *Source: Economic Research Service, U.S. Department of Agriculture (ERS-USDA)*

Heating Oil

After a sharp price increase in September-October 1997, heating oil prices declined into the end of the year. A combination of a mild winter in the Northeastern United States, large stocks of distillate, and high output of heating oil from refineries all contributed to the decline in prices. Through the end of 1997, weather in the Northeastern states had been milder than normal. Heating oil use in the U.S. is concentrated in the Northeast where it is used primarily for residential heating. The weather, combined with the fact that stocks of distillate are large and production remains strong, likely means that heating oil prices could move to still lower levels in the first part of 1998.

U.S. production of distillate fuel oil in August 1997 averaged 3.45 million barrels per day. That was almost three percent above the level in July 1997. It was five percent more than the average production in August 1996. In the January-August 1997 period, U.S. distillate fuel oil production averaged 3.33 million barrels per day. In the comparable period of 1996, production averaged 3.20 million barrels per day.

U.S. imports of distillate fuel oil in August 1997 were 213,000 barrels per day. In August 1996, imports averaged 195,000 barrels per day. In the first eight months of 1997, U.S. imports of distillate fuel oil averaged 239,000 barrels per day. That was almost three percent more than in the comparable period of 1996, and 26 percent more than in the same period of 1995. For all of 1996, imports averaged 230,000 barrels per day. Imports have shown wide variation. In 1989 imports were 309,000 barrels per day while in 1982 they averaged 93,000 barrels per day.

The U.S. also exports distillate fuel oil. In August 1997, exports averaged 190,000 barrels per day which was some 26 percent more than in the previous month. In August 1996, exports averaged 182,000 barrels per day. During January-August 1997, exports of distillate fuel oil averaged 150,000 barrels per day which was 11 percent less than in the comparable period of 1996 and nine percent less than in the same period of 1995. For all of 1996, exports averaged 190,000 barrels per day. Exports have also seen wide variation over the past few years. In 1993 they averaged 274,000 barrels per day while in 1981 they averaged 5,000 barrels per day.

Product supplied in August 1997 averaged 3.20 million barrels per day which was down two percent from the previous month but one percent more than in August 1996. During January-August 1997, product supplied averaged 3.40 million barrels per day, up almost two percent from the comparable period of 1996 and seven percent more than in the same period of 1995. For all of 1996, product supplied averaged 3.37 million barrels per day.

U.S. stocks of distillate fuel oil at the end of August 1997 were 131 million barrels, almost seven percent more than at the end of July 1997. In August 1996, stocks were 110 million barrels or 16 percent less. At the end of December 1997, stocks were 127 million barrels.

U.S. production of residual fuel oil in August 1997 was 649,000 barrels per day, up less than one percent from the previous month. In August 1996, production averaged 732,000 barrels per day. During January-August 1997, residual fuel oil production averaged 684,000 barrels per day. That was down six percent from the comparable period in 1996 and 14 percent less than the same period in 1995. For all of 1996, production of residual fuel oil averaged 726,000 barrels per day.

U.S. imports of residual fuel oil in August 1997 were 193,000 barrels per day, up almost 14 percent from the previous month. In January-August 1997, imports averaged 210,000 barrels per day. Stocks at the end of August 1997 were 36 million barrels, almost three percent above the previous month. At the end of 1996, U.S. residual fuel oil stocks were 46 million barrels. A year earlier stocks were 37 million barrels.

Futures Markets

Heating oil futures and options are traded on the New York Mercantile Exchange (NYMEX). In London, gasoil futures and options are listed on the International Petroleum Exchange (IPE).

Average Price of No. 2 Heating Oil in New York In Cents Per Gallon

Year	Jan.	Feb.	Mar.	Apr.	May	June	July	Aug.	Sept.	Oct.	Nov.	Dec.	Average
1987	52.34	47.36	49.18	48.58	51.75	52.30	54.62	52.46	52.33	56.14	55.84	53.75	52.22
1988	51.73	48.10	47.43	51.46	50.82	44.76	42.79	43.41	40.71	40.52	44.84	50.91	46.46
1989	54.35	51.47	56.86	53.98	50.76	48.51	49.35	49.75	55.78	58.80	59.20	80.91	55.81
1990	73.26	57.48	57.93	58.51	53.99	48.22	53.14	75.23	88.82	93.95	87.51	79.73	68.98
1991	74.96	70.80	61.92	56.36	55.04	53.67	57.74	60.48	61.54	66.58	64.33	53.35	61.31
1992	51.72	53.39	52.49	56.22	57.38	61.26	60.24	58.29	61.90	62.72	56.52	54.98	57.25
1993	53.14	56.02	58.13	55.49	54.53	52.62	49.74	50.70	51.96	54.00	50.30	43.47	52.51
1994	49.93	55.81	49.18	48.01	47.98	49.37	49.93	49.51	47.90	48.23	49.62	48.41	49.49
1995	47.98	47.64	45.95	49.40	50.31	47.75	46.65	49.14	50.21	48.89	51.89	57.76	49.46
1996	55.64	61.24	65.19	67.90	57.59	51.56	55.58	60.42	67.61	72.34	70.13	72.13	63.11
1997	69.90	61.15	54.83	57.74	56.31	52.32	53.11	54.02	53.19	57.24	56.23	51.09	56.43

Source: New York Mercantile Exchange (NYMEX)

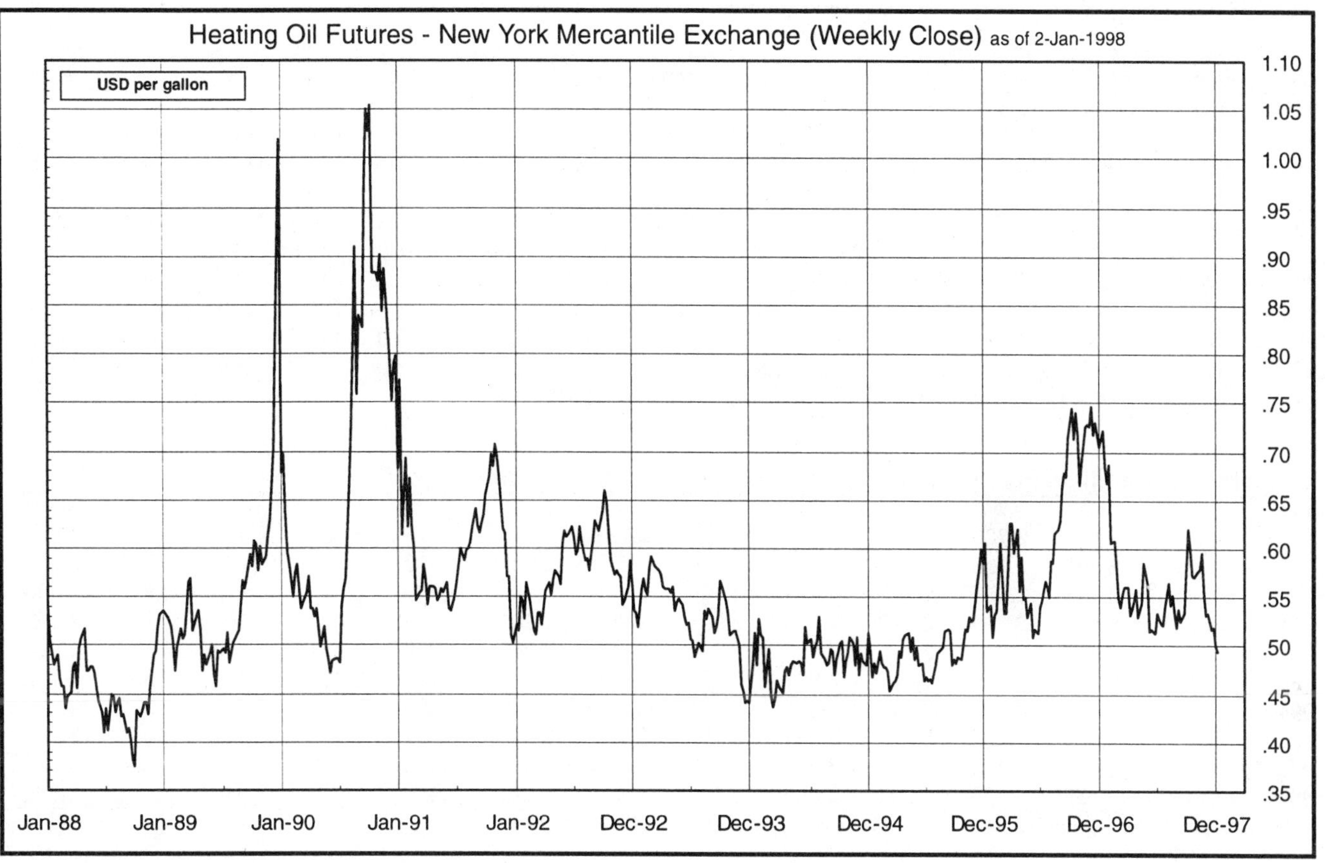

Average Open Interest of No. 2 Heating Oil Futures in New York In Contracts

Year	Jan.	Feb.	Mar.	Apr.	May	June	July	Aug.	Sept.	Oct.	Nov.	Dec.
1988	59,605	51,640	49,705	44,674	49,155	58,960	77,018	77,777	87,942	93,762	85,350	80,093
1989	75,038	63,791	60,455	57,533	49,174	49,527	59,799	69,578	88,642	97,064	99,293	105,240
1990	83,020	68,065	67,389	76,954	85,349	112,506	116,108	103,280	97,589	93,631	92,399	81,864
1991	74,216	81,742	81,103	82,419	89,482	102,887	115,896	125,463	135,804	144,026	128,330	117,182
1992	108,337	96,543	91,508	90,816	87,459	101,185	98,623	109,787	119,595	129,951	140,952	135,380
1993	130,536	125,603	130,438	107,363	102,708	113,898	131,816	142,054	166,253	172,940	175,781	199,299
1994	196,390	185,607	186,539	164,417	140,658	129,005	124,764	149,571	172,071	165,475	152,570	148,298
1995	128,664	112,508	118,700	121,974	115,501	122,163	136,722	140,214	149,934	152,244	139,232	138,596
1996	114,324	95,745	90,080	94,161	98,038	97,699	109,524	119,366	138,513	141,217	127,512	108,558
1997	100,333	105,223	122,149	139,981	135,523	141,864	151,403	149,243	151,407	141,008	126,528	145,153

Source: New York Mercantile Exchange (NYMEX)

Volume of Trading of No. 2 Heating Oil Futures In New York In Thousands of Contracts

Year	Jan.	Feb.	Mar.	Apr.	May	June	July	Aug.	Sept.	Oct.	Nov.	Dec.	Total
1988	506.2	377.4	403.2	267.2	286.4	380.6	431.2	363.3	441.9	578.6	475.7	423.4	4,935.0
1989	534.0	422.7	430.4	372.6	335.0	445.8	372.4	402.4	475.4	554.7	574.7	820.7	5,741.0
1990	754.9	415.4	462.5	451.7	517.0	463.3	519.0	723.2	505.8	612.3	522.0	429.8	6,376.9
1991	603.7	523.9	392.5	387.2	399.9	425.1	507.8	595.9	538.2	689.1	781.3	835.6	6,680.2
1992	815.2	574.0	550.1	592.1	586.7	601.1	645.0	663.7	625.7	709.5	808.2	807.1	8,005.5
1993	829.0	660.5	747.3	537.5	482.0	543.4	632.2	721.9	833.8	761.8	886.6	988.9	8,625.1
1994	1,085.7	875.7	766.8	631.7	629.3	723.7	612.3	783.2	706.8	721.4	652.3	798.1	8,986.8
1995	779.8	608.7	716.0	622.8	729.8	618.8	612.7	563.6	714.2	650.8	659.5	990.1	8,266.8
1996	977.2	768.1	666.2	586.5	530.9	402.0	530.2	624.4	766.5	1,014.2	725.0	750.7	8,341.9
1997	794.4	719.0	588.6	710.1	592.0	679.4	679.6	694.7	828.3	742.7	619.3	722.9	8,371.0

Source: New York Mercantile Exchange (NYMEX)

HEATING OIL

Stocks of Distillate and Residual Fuel in the United States, on First of Month   In Millions of Barrels

Year	Jan.	Feb.	Mar.	Apr.	May	June	July	Aug.	Sept.	Oct.	Nov.	Dec.	Residual Fuel ---- Oil Stocks ---- Jan. 1	July 1
1988	134.5	128.1	110.3	89.8	95.0	104.9	110.4	120.0	125.7	131.5	128.2	128.8	47.4	42.2
1989	123.5	120.3	107.5	96.6	98.4	99.3	99.6	115.0	116.3	123.2	121.7	119.8	44.6	44.1
1990	105.7	118.0	112.2	99.7	99.5	102.8	109.4	125.2	136.0	136.3	132.4	132.2	43.8	46.8
1991	112.1	111.7	101.6	98.2	102.9	106.9	113.7	124.7	131.4	140.1	138.3	144.5	47.6	43.7
1992	143.5	126.7	108.8	97.7	92.1	96.4	104.5	114.6	122.8	127.8	136.8	146.3	49.9	40.9
1993	140.6	130.7	110.4	97.3	99.5	102.8	110.0	120.7	128.2	131.3	145.3	149.2	42.6	45.7
1994	140.9	117.5	102.9	99.4	102.6	112.4	119.5	134.2	138.6	144.7	146.0	147.3	44.2	39.4
1995	140.2	122.1	115.4	114.6	118.3	114.7	125.0	130.9	131.7	131.4	135.4	130.2	41.9	36.0
1996	130.2	113.8	97.3	89.7	90.1	95.7	101.6	106.8	110.3	115.0	114.7	121.8	36.8	34.8
1997[1]	126.7	111.3	105.9	101.8	97.5	108.4	118.2	123.0	132.9	138.9	136.2	140.5	45.9	39.2

[1] Preliminary. *Source: Energy Information Administration, U.S. Department of Energy (EIA-DOE)*

Production of Distillate Fuel Oil in the United States   Thousand Barrels Per Day

Year	Jan.	Feb.	Mar.	Apr.	May	June	July	Aug.	Sept.	Oct.	Nov.	Dec.	Average
1988	3,010	2,667	2,706	2,867	2,936	2,893	2,784	2,848	2,778	2,827	2,909	3,068	2,859
1989	2,974	2,797	2,713	2,789	2,750	2,809	2,848	2,907	2,952	2,906	3,063	3,266	2,899
1990	3,130	2,753	2,657	2,803	2,874	2,996	3,008	3,131	2,968	2,928	2,915	2,917	2,925
1991	2,845	2,870	2,865	2,819	2,929	2,941	2,998	2,961	3,055	3,040	3,103	3,107	2,962
1992	2,818	2,661	2,749	2,930	2,933	2,995	3,067	2,865	2,983	3,251	3,240	3,179	2,974
1993	2,914	2,815	2,919	3,047	2,994	3,093	3,186	3,100	3,205	3,432	3,474	3,382	3,132
1994	3,114	3,018	3,096	3,249	3,317	3,285	3,191	3,187	3,285	3,203	3,270	3,232	3,205
1995	3,054	2,954	3,157	3,126	3,111	3,109	3,056	3,145	3,287	3,169	3,341	3,344	3,155
1996	3,110	3,145	3,110	3,305	3,258	3,291	3,139	3,295	3,403	3,626	3,665	3,558	3,325
1997[1]	3,119	3,089	3,258	3,291	3,525	3,517	3,362	3,427	3,452	3,488	3,543	3,684	3,398

[1] Preliminary. *Source: Energy Information Administration, U.S. Department of Energy (EIA-DOE)*

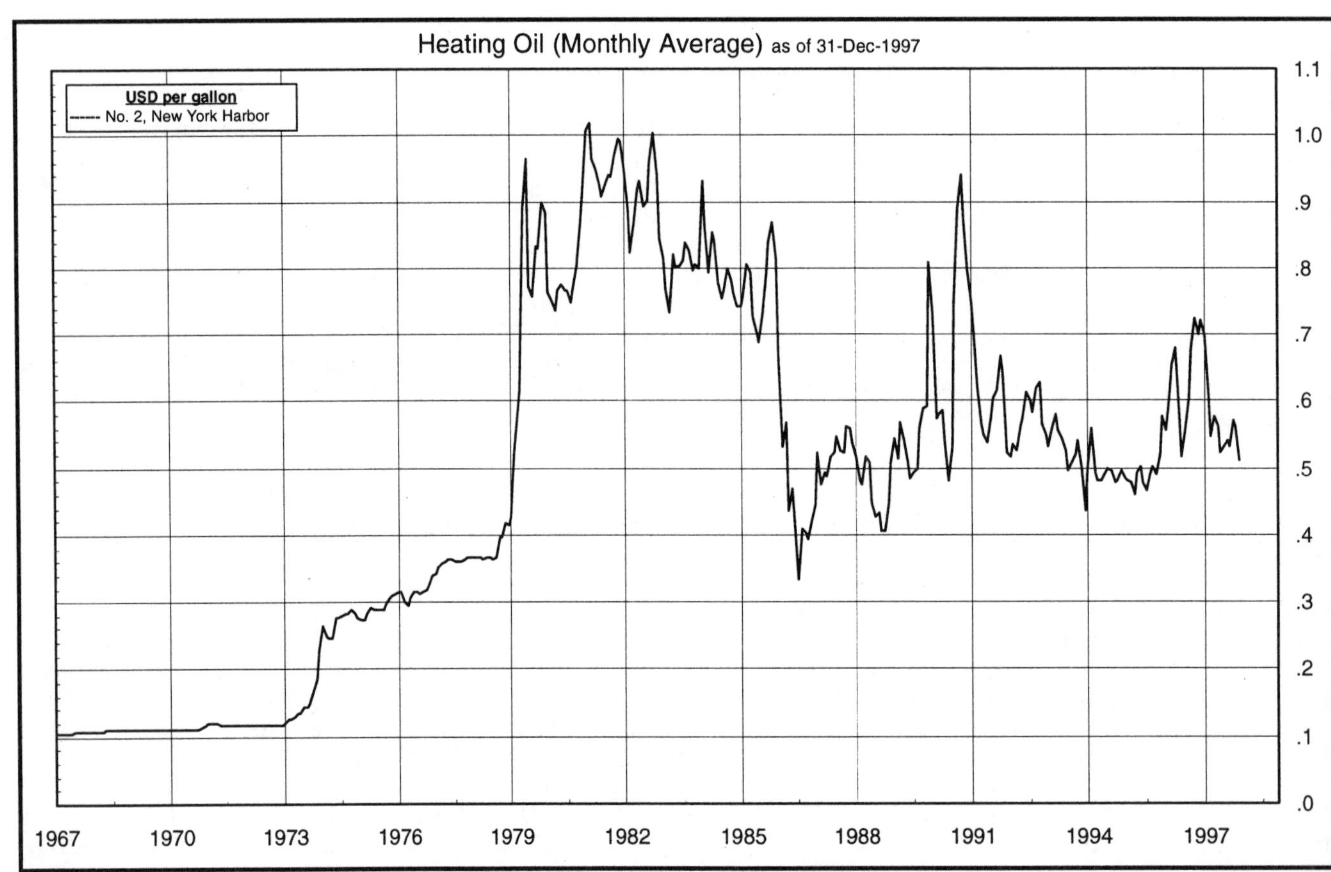

Imports of Distillate Fuel Oil in the United States Thousand Barrels Per Day

Year	Jan.	Feb.	Mar.	Apr.	May	June	July	Aug.	Sept.	Oct.	Nov.	Dec.	Average
1988	424	383	247	210	253	222	222	279	307	336	327	409	302
1989	346	331	439	301	290	233	334	254	249	261	307	324	306
1990	505	357	281	308	209	257	236	293	226	190	238	239	278
1991	192	139	206	258	186	209	155	168	237	207	249	252	205
1992	232	217	238	202	179	157	172	229	237	263	236	229	216
1993	182	224	235	209	153	168	130	159	137	242	214	160	184
1994	161	276	318	226	202	182	164	211	193	159	166	187	203
1995	313	289	188	125	109	176	157	171	142	162	262	235	193
1996	243	271	253	258	215	185	194	195	187	246	192	253	224
1997[1]	293	246	245	256	220	219	223	202	210	213	161	214	225

[1] Preliminary. *Source: Energy Information Administration, U.S. Department of Energy (EIA-DOE)*

Disposition of Distillate Fuel Oil, Total Product Supplied in the United States Thousand Barrels Per Day

Year	Jan.	Feb.	Mar.	Apr.	May	June	July	Aug.	Sept.	Oct.	Nov.	Dec.	Average
1988	3,558	3,557	3,539	2,864	2,765	2,854	2,640	2,873	2,821	3,218	3,183	3,560	3,122
1989	3,303	3,427	3,428	2,975	2,954	3,002	2,596	2,966	2,889	3,127	3,311	3,914	3,157
1990	3,185	3,260	3,277	3,043	2,900	2,923	2,726	3,218	2,864	2,960	3,094	2,816	3,021
1991	3,367	2,976	2,984	2,839	2,765	2,775	2,648	2,770	2,865	3,047	2,921	3,087	2,921
1992	3,231	3,219	3,207	3,039	2,753	2,679	2,710	2,705	2,908	3,056	2,929	3,316	2,979
1993	3,128	3,465	3,420	2,943	2,685	2,863	2,674	2,820	2,973	2,983	3,218	3,357	3,041
1994	3,698	3,581	3,307	3,116	2,912	3,062	2,663	3,063	3,133	3,066	3,180	3,203	3,162
1995	3,389	3,675	3,344	3,106	2,899	3,267	2,732	3,044	3,285	3,104	3,233	3,449	3,207
1996	3,681	3,722	3,453	3,385	3,118	3,194	3,046	3,184	3,178	3,575	3,460	3,434	3,368
1997[1]	3,780	3,422	3,515	3,523	3,240	3,235	3,279	3,124	3,302	3,659	3,411	3,632	3,428

[1] Preliminary. *Source: Energy Information Administration, U.S. Department of Energy (EIA-DOE)*

Production of Residual Fuel Oil in the United States Thousand Barrels Per Day

Year	Jan.	Feb.	Mar.	Apr.	May	June	July	Aug.	Sept.	Oct.	Nov.	Dec.	Average
1988	1,002	994	948	960	862	880	906	866	852	852	916	1,069	926
1989	949	930	937	904	934	953	862	903	856	1,001	1,075	1,140	954
1990	1,163	1,060	976	882	884	926	987	944	909	799	846	1,021	950
1991	1,001	1,050	995	916	929	933	871	925	838	814	896	1,051	934
1992	965	957	990	900	964	894	838	815	810	818	895	862	892
1993	820	840	818	896	908	795	762	752	822	841	899	869	835
1994	809	852	859	846	860	779	807	838	800	755	835	871	826
1995	903	776	778	789	748	746	797	801	811	724	705	874	788
1996	774	776	701	671	732	731	646	732	713	693	712	753	719
1997[1]	800	789	639	617	618	727	645	643	688	711	786	781	703

[1] Preliminary. *Source: Energy Information Adminstration, U.S. Department of Energy (EIA-DOE)*

Supply and Disposition of Residual Fuel Oil in the United States

	Supply		Disposition				
Year	Total Production	Imports	Stock Change	Exports	Product Supplied	Ending Stocks	Average Sales to End Users[3]
	Thousand Barrels per Day					Mil. Barrels	¢ per Gallon
1988	889	669	-8	147	1,418	47	33.4
1989	885	565	[2]	186	1,264	47	38.5
1990	950	504	13	211	1,229	49	44.4
1991	934	453	4	226	1,158	50	34.0
1992	892	375	-20	193	1,094	43	33.6
1993	835	373	4	123	1,080	44	33.7
1994	826	314	-6	125	1,021	42	35.2
1995	788	187	-13	136	852	37	39.2
1996	726	248	24	102	848	46	45.5
1997[1]	703	200	-16	119	799	40	34.0

[1] Preliminary. [2] Less than +500 barrels per day and greater than -500 barrels per day. [3] Refiner price excluding taxes.
Source: Energy Information Administration, U.S. Department of Energy (EIA-DOE)

Hides and Leather

The major producers of bovine hides and skins are the U.S., Argentina, Brazil and Russia. The U.S. is the largest producer. The U.S. inventory of cattle in 1997 is forecast to be just over 102.1 million head. That represents a decline of about two percent from 1996. Brazil's cattle inventory in 1997 was forecast to grow to 153.2 million head, an increase of one percent from the previous year. Argentina's cattle inventory was put at 51.7 million head in 1997, down four percent from 1996. Argentina's cattle inventory has been trending lower for several years while Brazil's has been trending higher. Russia's cattle inventory has been trending lower. For 1997, the forecasted cattle inventory is 57.3 million head which represents an 11 percent decline from 1996. Other large cattle producers, outside of India, include Western and Eastern Europe, Australia, Mexico, Colombia, Venezuela and Canada.

The U.S. commercial cattle slaughter in 1996 was 36.8 million head, up three percent from 1995. U.S. exports of cattle hides in 1996 were 20.3 million hides which was almost two percent more than in 1995. The U.S. also imported 1.7 million cattle hides in 1996, down three percent from 1995. Net exports of U.S. cattle hides in 1996 were 18.6 million hides.

In 1996, the major export markets for U.S. cattle hides and their market share were: South Korea, 39 percent; Taiwan, 14 percent; Japan, 12 percent; Mexico, ten percent; China, eight percent; Canada, six percent; and Italy, three percent.

Most U.S. leather is used in the shoe industry. In the first quarter of 1997, production of nonrubber footwear and slippers was 35.6 million pair. That represented a 17 percent increase from the first quarter of 1996. Of the total U.S. production, women's shoes made up 34 percent of the total with men's shoes 28 percent. Slippers were 27 percent of the total.

In the second quarter of 1997, U.S. nonrubber footwear and slipper production was 37.1 million pair. Women's shoes made up 32 percent of the total with men's shoes 25 percent and slippers 32 percent. For the first half of 1997, U.S. nonrubber footwear and slipper production was 72.7 million pair. This represents a substantial increase for the first half of 1996 when production was 59 million pair. For all of 1996, nonrubber footwear and slipper production was 115 million pair. That was down significantly from 1995 when it was 147 million pair and from 1994 when it totaled 163 million pair.

U.S. production of rubber or plastic protective footwear in the first six months of 1997 was nine million pair. That represented an increase of 2 percent from the comparable period of 1996. For all of 1996, U.S. rubber or plastic protective footwear production was 16.6 million pair while for 1995 it was 17.4 million and in 1994 20.2 million pair.

World Production of Bovine Hides and Skins In Thousands of Metric Tons

Year	Argentina	Australia	Brazil	Canada	Colombia	France	Germany	Italy	Mexico	Russia[3]	United Kingdom	United States	World Total
1989	304	137	429	84	97	170	228	88	222	1,090	91	1,086	4,623
1990	307	149	447	78	105	175	247	92	181	503	92	1,057	4,077
1991	308	153	448	75	104	182	251	95	155	502	93	1,061	4,076
1992	298	162	442	77	88	180	205	98	160	466	88	1,073	3,983
1993	303	154	565	73	79	160	175	95	161	460	77	1,078	3,969
1994	305	152	573	74	77	151	158	93	166	350	81	1,106	3,850
1995	301	145	608	75	84	154	156	93	170	310	85	1,160	3,901
1996	306	141	615	78	88	158	164	92	160	280	90	1,197	3,929
1997[1]	298	145	605	82	89	154	159	92	165	270	82	1,167	3,871
1998[2]	286	144	602	85	91	151	156	92	170	240	78	1,155	3,823

[1] Preliminary. [2] Forecast. [3] Formerly part of the U.S.S.R.; data not reported separately until 1990. *Source: Foreign Agricultural Service, U.S. Department of Agriculture (FAS-USDA)*

Salient Statistics of Hides and Leather in the United States

	New Supply of Cattle Hides – Domestic Slaughter				Wholesale Prices - ¢ Lb.		Production			Wholesale Leather Indexes – Upper		Footwear	
Year	Federally Inspected	Uninspected[4]	Total Production	Net Exports	Heavy Native Cows[2]	Heavy Native[3] Steers	All U.S. Tanning	Cattle-Hide	Value of Leather Exports	Men	Women	Production[5]	Export
	Thousands of Equivalent Hides						In 1,000 Equiv. Hides		$1,000	1982 = 100		Mil. Pairs	
1987	34,468	1,179	35,647	24,007	83.43	79.9	14,750	12,754	395,536	111.4	107.2	225,888	14,575
1988	34,048	1,031	35,079	24,527	86.50	87.3	13,300	11,475	506,483	121.3	112.5	234,852	18,394
1989	33,010	907	33,917	22,500	83.16	89.4	12,932	11,242	624,925	127.5	116.2	221,790	14,358
1990	32,391	851	33,242	20,920	92.58	92.0	14,820	13,018	750,836	135.8	120.9	184,568	15,174
1991	31,887	803	32,690	18,636	76.92	78.9	14,800	13,021	680,348	141.0	124.0	167,386	18,109
1992	32,094	780	32,874	17,810	81.71	75.9	15,900	14,474	705,038	145.0	126.4	168,451	21,401
1993	32,593	731	33,324	17,117	82.16	78.9	18,057	16,931	764,120	145.3	129.3	171,733	20,700
1994	33,483	713	34,196	16,259	94.99	87.3	18,842	18,117	811,951	144.7	127.2	163,000	22,505
1995	34,879	760	35,639	18,336	93.89	87.6	18,092	17,480	869,991	150.1	129.0	147,559	20,571
1996[1]	36,583	177	36,760	18,626	92.15	86.4	18,769	18,135	950,510	152.4	132.1	143,758	23,726

[1] Preliminary. [2] Central U.S., heifers. [3] FOB, Chicago. [4] Includes farm slaughter; diseased and condemned animals and hides taken off fallen animals. [5] Other than rubber. *Sources: Leather Industries of America; Bureau of the Census, U.S. Department of Commerce*

Production of All Footwear (Shoes, Sandals, Slippers, Athletic, Etc.) in the U.S. In Millions of Pairs

Year	First Quarter	Second Quarter	Third Quarter	Fourth Quarter	Total	Year	First Quarter	Second Quarter	Third Quarter	Fourth Quarter	Total
1988	59.1	59.2	56.7	60.1	234.8	1993	43.3	44.6	42.8	41.0	171.7
1989	56.2	52.8	50.8	50.8	221.9	1994	42.5	40.8	40.1	39.5	163.0
1990	53.5	52.3	49.6	46.2	184.6	1995	37.2	38.3	34.8	36.7	147.0
1991	48.1	37.8	41.8	41.2	169.0	1996	30.3	28.7	27.0	29.1	115.0
1992	41.1	40.8	43.6	39.3	164.8	1997[1]	35.6	37.3	31.7		139.5

[1] Preliminary. *Source: Bureau of the Census, U.S. Department of Commerce*

Average Factory Price[2] of Footwear in the United States In Dollars Per Pair

Year	First Quarter	Second Quarter	Third Quarter	Fourth Quarter	Total	Year	First Quarter	Second Quarter	Third Quarter	Fourth Quarter	Total
1988	15.08	14.73	15.84	15.63	15.32	1993	21.62	21.67	21.37	21.79	21.61
1989	15.43	16.37	16.97	17.87	16.98	1994	25.77	23.60	21.49	22.44	23.22
1990	18.04	18.65	19.91	20.72	19.37	1995	20.86	23.42	22.72	19.53	21.54
1991	22.14	20.40	19.74	18.52	20.14	1996	23.84	22.97	22.32	20.55	22.25
1992	20.19	22.21	21.15	20.46	20.96	1997[1]	20.51	19.72	20.32		20.18

[1] Preliminary. [2] Average value of factory shipments per pair. *Source: Bureau of the Census, U.S. Department of Commerce*

Imports and Exports of All Cattle Hides in the United States In Thousands of Hides

	------- Imports -------		------- U.S. Exports -- By Country of Destination -------										
Year	Total	From Canada	Total	Canada	Italy	Japan	Rep. of Korea	Mexico	Portugal	Romania	Spain	Taiwan	Thailand
1987	490	338	24,235	924	394	5,998	10,077	1,437	82	308	200	3,184	37
1988	642	481	24,687	759	319	7,140	9,986	1,865	44	624	142	2,493	35
1989	901	1,043	23,401	614	343	6,268	10,322	1,284	46	1,154	64	1,886	70
1990	661	678	21,582	674	136	6,802	9,839	1,438	29	253	175	1,476	91
1991	1,549	1,088	20,185	561	138	4,662	9,300	2,702	7	0	39	2,058	123
1992	1,536	1,457	19,347	684	107	4,647	8,589	2,729	100	4	30	1,823	160
1993	1,660	1,597	18,777	965	354	4,167	7,919	2,217	79	1	60	1,950	386
1994	1,731	-----	17,990	995	309	3,133	7,472	1,553	168	72	141	2,491	332
1995	1,759	-----	20,095	952	332	3,246	8,283	899	111	63	215	3,017	781
1996[1]	1,702	-----	20,328	1,149	522	2,372	7,956	2,123	64	171	189	2,871	455

[1] Preliminary. *Source: Leather Industries of America (LIA)*

Imports of Bovine Hides and Skins by Selected Countries In Metric Tons

Year	Brazil	Canada	Hong Kong	Italy	Japan	Mexico	Portugal	Rep. of Korea	Spain	Taiwan	Turkey	United States	World Total
1991	8	18	67	156	206	70	30	392	39	100	15	67	1,249
1992	11	17	80	131	188	71	32	385	26	91	28	65	1,266
1993	21	26	81	141	188	71	39	372	35	94	37	57	1,352
1994	16	28	95	243	139	60	56	356	29	112	17	56	1,417
1995	33	35	100	250	152	30	43	342	42	112	43	55	1,363
1996	20	33	79	263	123	71	42	341	33	124	50	56	1,360
1997[1]	30	38	75	250	120	75	40	320	41	140	60	55	1,364
1998[2]	40	35	72	250	115	75	40	300	40	140	70	54	1,350

[1] Preliminary. [2] Forecast. *Source: Foreign Agricultural Service, U.S. Department of Agriculture (FAS-USDA)*

Exports of Bovine Hides and Skins by Selected Countries In Metric Tons

Year	Australia	Brazil	Canada	Germany	Hong Kong	Italy	Nether-lands	New Zealand	Poland	Russia	United Kingdom	United States	World Total
1991	149	60	90	63	69	8	70	33	13	22	18	637	1,288
1992	144	71	74	38	75	9	66	31	17	28	19	610	1,261
1993	142	76	87	40	76	7	35	21	5	150	25	581	1,290
1994	96	84	79	24	93	10	37	22	2	216	22	602	1,343
1995	85	148	90	34	100	10	47	22	2	195	22	667	1,478
1996	93	174	97	33	72	20	47	21	3	212	24	675	1,526
1997[1]	95	180	98	25	70	23	40	21	12	210	27	665	1,520
1998[2]	94	185	100	22	68	24	40	21	15	205	27	651	1,516

[1] Preliminary. [2] Forecast. *Source: Foreign Agricultural Service, U.S. Department of Agriculture (FAS-USDA)*

HIDES AND LEATHER

Utilization of Bovine Hides and Skins by Selected Countries In Metric Tons

Year	Argentina	Brazil	Colombia	Germany	Italy	Japan	Mexico	Rep. of Korea	Spain	Taiwan	Turkey	United States	World Total
1989	304	383	94	173	422	263	262	363	115	81	70	460	3,576
1990	307	395	100	176	425	261	233	380	129	74	74	388	3,960
1991	308	396	98	143	435	253	225	400	119	101	78	491	4,009
1992	298	382	97	129	435	229	231	400	98	91	90	528	3,977
1993	302	510	94	100	435	226	232	385	98	94	95	554	3,905
1994	304	505	96	83	550	200	226	374	94	112	85	560	3,865
1995	300	493	89	79	570	191	200	355	98	112	100	548	3,767
1996	308	461	91	85	615	165	230	353	95	124	110	578	3,788
1997[1]	297	455	92	94	570	155	240	345	105	140	120	557	3,743
1998[2]	285	457	93	90	560	150	240	325	107	140	130	558	3,681

[1] Preliminary. [2] Forecast. *Source: Foreign Agricultural Service, U.S. Department of Agriculture (FAS-USDA)*

Wholesale Price of Hides (Packer Native Steer) F.O.B. Chicago In Cents Per Pound

Year	Jan.	Feb.	Mar.	Apr.	May	June	July	Aug.	Sept.	Oct.	Nov.	Dec.	Average
1988	82.90	86.25	97.46	100.00	99.21	87.55	84.15	93.70	87.29	80.52	77.10	76.71	87.74
1989	83.95	87.42	94.61	87.50	85.18	85.03	90.35	92.39	95.90	94.68	92.91	90.85	90.06
1990	92.68	92.76	95.50	99.95	99.57	97.90	96.69	91.74	87.51	84.70	82.90	84.40	82.19
1991	81.64	75.84	76.50	86.32	88.77	86.60	84.05	77.18	74.05	75.30	75.30	71.29	79.40
1992	70.55	67.84	69.68	75.95	80.05	76.77	76.50	72.76	77.62	81.18	80.05	81.00	75.83
1993	79.82	81.05	81.48	81.44	80.35	76.95	76.62	79.27	80.52	81.76	80.81	79.83	79.99
1994	75.07	75.08	79.00	84.75	87.33	88.77	90.38	89.76	93.90	93.67	93.19	91.13	86.84
1995	90.10	91.42	97.99	102.32	99.64	92.45	85.74	82.46	82.45	82.16	78.02	73.02	88.15
1996	73.67	75.11	77.96	84.58	87.56	82.51	89.45	96.06	98.91	101.51	94.60	90.65	87.71
1997	89.77	93.47	99.44	99.40	89.44	81.45	80.20	83.92	84.86	86.35	89.20	82.61	88.34

Source: The Wall Street Journal

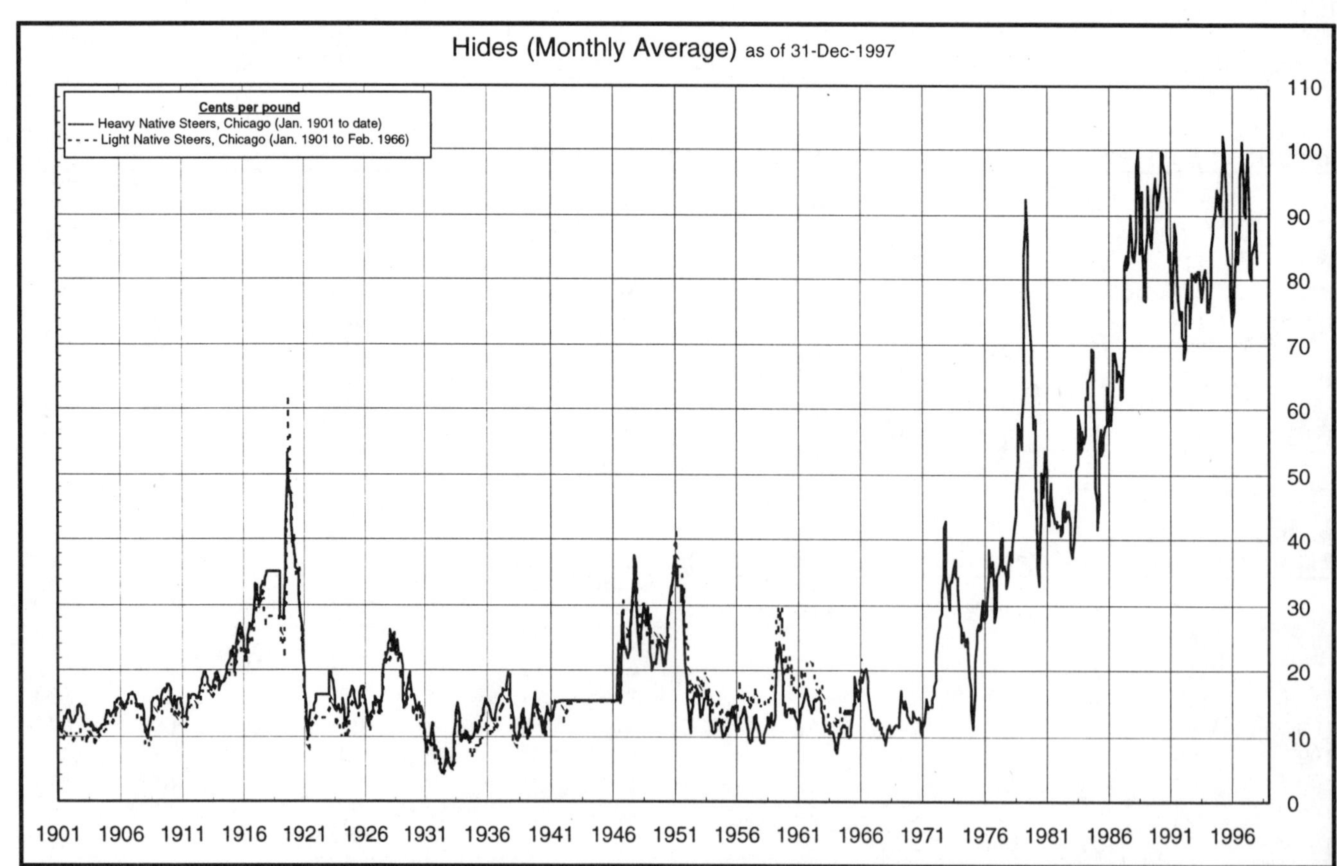

Hogs

The world's hog inventory is slowly increasing, 802 million head as of January 1, 1998, vs. 792 million a year earlier. China is the world's largest hog producer with at least half the total while the U.S. is a distant second. China's 1998 inventory of a record 475 million head compares with an annual 1990's average of 380 million. U.S. hog numbers since 1992 have shown little change, averaging around 58 million head due largely to a record 60 million head herd in early 1995; two years later the U.S. inventory totaled less than 56.5 million head. Germany's inventory dropped from over 30 million in the early 1990's to the mid-20's by 1997; but the most pronounced decline occurred in Russia and the Ukraine whose 1992 combined total of 53 million head compares with only 27 million by 1998.

The September 1, 1997 U.S. inventory of 60.3 million head compares with 58.2 million a year earlier. Almost seven million head were kept for breeding in late 1997 vs. 6.8 million a year earlier. The increase in 1997's inventory from 1996 was expected given the high mid-1997 hog prices and prospects for lower feed costs in 1998. Farrowing intentions during the fourth quarter of 1997 and into the first quarter of 1998 were seven percent above the year earlier period and a similar gain was forecast for the March-May 1998 period. If the latter is realized, it would suggest a fourth quarter 1998 slaughter of about 26.2 million head, eight percent over the like 1997 quarter. Although the U.S. hog inventory is only eight percent of the world total, U.S. slaughter runs 10-12 percent and pork production higher still compared to world totals.

More than half the inventory share of U.S. hog marketings now come from contract hog operations. In a contractual agreement, the contractor provides the hogs, feed, medication and supplies while the contractee provides the housing, utilities and labor. Most hog production still occurs in Corn Belt states with Iowa the top producing state. Southern states, led by North Carolina, have seen dramatic growth in contractual operations in recent years. Still, most U.S. producers continue to raise hogs in farrow-to-finish operations. However, as of September 1, 1997, the total number of hogs under contract, owned by operations with over 5,000 head total inventory but raised by contractees, accounted for 26 percent of the total U.S. inventory.

Commercial U.S. hog slaughter in the January-October 1997 period of 75.3 million head compared with the record setting pace of 77.2 million in the like 1996 period, with an average dressed weight of 186 pounds in both years. Pork production for the year 1997 was estimated at 17.0 billion pounds vs. 17.1 billion in 1996. Based upon the Fall 1997 hog inventory and breeding intentions, a slightly larger percentage of the pig crop will be slaughtered in 1998, but at a higher average weight, lifting pork production to about 18.5 billion pounds.

The U.S. is the world's largest pork exporter--1.06 billion pounds in 1997, up 12 percent from 1996--largely to Japan and Canada. However, shipments to Japan in 1998, while large, could be contained by macroeconomic factors affecting their economy. However, demand from Mexico and Hong Kong may increase as well as exports to the European Union. Pork exports in 1998 are expected to rise about eight percent, but much of the increase is apt to be lower-valued pork products to low income countries. The U.S. imports pork products, mostly from Canada and Denmark. Live hogs are imported from Canada. 1997's total of 2.9 million head was about 200,000 less than expected; the forecast for 1998 is 2.6 million head.

Wholesale barrow and gilt hog prices during 1997 averaged about \$51-\$54 per cwt., basis Iowa/Minnesota vs. \$53.39 in 1996, and forecast of \$46-\$49 in 1998, the decline reflecting greater hog supplies and increased competition from poultry. Composite retail pork prices are expected to decline about 2-3 percent in 1998.

Futures Markets

Lean hog futures and options are traded on the Chicago Mercantile Exchange (CME); futures settle to the CME lean hog Index (TM) which tracks the value of lean pork at select U.S. packing plants. Live hog futures are traded on the Mid-America Commodity Exchange (MidAm)and the Budapest Commodity Exchange.

Salient Statistics of Pigs and Hogs in the United States

	Pig Crop						Value of Hogs on Farms, Dec. 1		Hog Marketings	Quantity Produced	Value of Production	Hogs Slaughtered in Thousand Heads				
	Spring[3]			Fall[4]								Commercial				
Year	Sows Farrowed - 1,000s of Head -	Pig Crop - 1,000s of Head -	Pigs Per Liter	Sows Farrowed - 1,000s of Head -	Pig Crop - 1,000s of Head -	Pigs Per Liter	$ Per Head	Total Million $	Thousand Head	(Live Wt.) Mil. Lbs.	Mil. $	Federally Inspected	Other	Total	Farm	Total
1988	6,030	46,883	7.77	6,036	46,000	7.62	66.3	3,678	90,420	21,697	9,156	85,517	2,278	87,795	341	88,136
1989	6,028	47,141	7.82	5,767	44,779	7.76	79.1	4,253	92,432	21,907	9,281	86,328	2,364	88,692	315	89,007
1990	5,732	45,223	7.89	5,709	44,877	7.86	85.4	4,648	89,240	21,287	11,346	82,901	2,235	85,136	296	85,431
1991	5,988	47,413	7.92	6,071	47,902	7.89	68.8	3,966	92,220	22,727	11,067	85,952	2,217	88,169	276	88,445
1992	6,260	50,466	8.06	6,012	48,676	8.10	71.2	4,147	98,589	23,947	9,854	92,611	2,278	94,889	268	95,157
1993	6,028	49,006	8.13	5,954	48,044	8.07	74.9	4,338	98,351	23,693	10,628	90,933	2,135	93,068	229	93,296
1994	6,275	51,352	8.18	6,104	50,064	8.20	53.2	3,192	100,747	24,437	9,692	93,435	2,261	95,696	208	95,905
1995	6,056	50,224	8.29	5,791	48,292	8.34	70.7	4,120	100,309	24,121	9,750	94,203	2,123	96,325	210	96,535
1996[1]	5,712	48,200	8.44	5,475	46,756	8.54	94.0	5,284				90,534	1,905	92,439		
1997[2]	5,610	48,450	8.64	5,830	50,522	8.67						90,224	1,826	92,050		

[1] Preliminary. [2] Estimate. [3] December-May. [4] June-November. *Source: Economic Research Service, U.S. Department of Agriculture (ERS-USDA)*

HOGS

World Hog Numbers in Specified Countries as of January 1 In Thousands of Head

Year	Brazil	Canada	China	Denmark	France	Germany	Philip-pines	Poland	Russia	Spain	Ukraine	United States	World Total
1989	31,700	11,018	342,218	9,105	11,706	35,235	7,909	19,605	39,800	16,100	19,471	55,469	755,537
1990	32,120	10,650	352,810	9,120	12,275	34,178	8,124	18,685	40,000	16,910	19,947	53,788	795,188
1991	32,550	10,468	362,408	9,282	12,013	30,818	8,007	19,739	38,500	16,001	19,427	54,416	760,788
1992	33,050	10,498	369,646	9,767	12,067	26,063	8,022	20,725	35,384	17,209	17,839	57,469	728,789
1993	31,050	10,577	384,210	10,345	13,015	26,514	7,954	21,059	31,520	18,260	16,175	58,202	740,758
1994	31,200	10,851	393,000	10,870	14,791	26,075	8,227	17,422	28,600	18,234	15,298	57,904	744,211
1995	31,338	11,673	414,619	10,864	14,593	24,698	8,941	19,138	24,859	18,295	13,946	59,990	761,835
1996	32,068	12,040	441,692	10,709	14,523	23,737	9,023	20,343	22,630	18,600	13,070	58,264	785,318
1997[1]	31,369	12,101	457,130	11,081	14,968	24,283	9,750	17,697	19,500	18,479	11,175	56,171	792,126
1998[2]	31,427	12,325	475,000	11,400	15,450	24,800	10,465	18,500	17,000	18,500	10,000	60,250	802,957

[1] Preliminary. [2] Forecast. *Source: Foreign Agricultural Service, U.S. Department of Agricultures (FAS-USDA)*

Hogs and Pigs on Farms in the United States on December 1 In Thousands of Head

Year	Georgia	Illinois	Indiana	Iowa	Kansas	Minne-sota	Missouri	Nebraska	North Carolina	Ohio	South Dakota	Wis-consin	Total
1988	1,210	5,600	4,300	14,000	1,500	4,690	2,850	4,150	2,700	2,210	1,810	1,275	55,469
1989	1,200	5,700	4,350	13,500	1,450	4,450	2,700	4,200	2,570	2,080	1,720	1,150	53,821
1990	1,100	5,700	4,400	13,800	1,500	4,500	2,800	4,300	2,800	2,000	1,770	1,200	54,477
1991	1,130	5,900	4,600	15,000	1,430	4,900	2,700	4,500	3,650	1,925	1,950	1,180	57,684
1992	1,100	5,900	4,600	16,400	1,440	4,700	2,850	4,650	4,500	1,800	1,830	1,210	59,815
1993	1,000	5,450	4,300	15,000	1,350	4,750	3,000	4,300	5,400	1,630	1,750	1,170	57,904
1994	1,020	5,350	4,500	14,500	1,310	4,850	3,500	4,350	7,000	1,800	1,740	1,040	59,990
1995	900	4,800	4,000	13,400	1,230	4,950	1,100	4,050	8,200	1,800	1,450	900	58,264
1996	800	4,400	3,750	12,200	1,450	4,850	3,450	3,600	9,300	1,500	1,200	800	56,171
1997[1]	720	4,750	3,800	14,000	1,430	5,400	3,500	3,550	9,700	1,620	1,250	730	59,920

[1] Preliminary. *Source: National Agricultural Statistics Service, U.S. Department of Agriculture (NASS-USDA)*

Hog-Corn Price Ratio[1] in the United States

Year	Jan.	Feb.	Mar.	Apr.	May	June	July	Aug.	Sept.	Oct.	Nov.	Dec.	Average
1988	15.7	15.6	15.1	14.4	16.1	17.9	18.6	20.1	15.7	15.0	14.4	15.7	16.7
1989	20.5	20.8	21.6	21.4	23.4	22.9	23.2	23.3	19.0	21.0	20.1	21.2	22.1
1990	22.0	22.5	21.5	21.0	22.7	23.7	23.9	22.0	22.3	23.3	25.9	21.5	22.4
1991	22.0	22.5	21.5	21.0	22.7	23.7	23.9	22.0	19.9	18.9	16.6	16.6	20.9
1992	15.3	16.3	15.7	16.5	18.1	18.9	19.1	20.5	19.5	20.5	20.8	21.2	18.5
1993	20.3	22.0	22.1	21.0	21.9	23.0	20.6	21.0	21.6	20.6	17.3	15.2	20.6
1994	16.1	17.2	16.2	16.1	16.4	16.3	18.6	19.4	16.2	15.4	14.1	14.5	16.4
1995	16.8	17.5	16.4	15.1	15.4	16.8	17.6	18.5	18.0	16.4	13.9	14.2	16.4
1996	13.7	13.8	13.9	12.9	13.7	13.4	13.2	13.9	15.4	19.2	20.5	21.1	15.4
1997[2]	20.0	19.9	17.6	19.2	21.6	22.6	24.2	22.1	20.0	18.6	18.0	16.5	20.0

[1] Bushels of corn equal in value to 100 pounds of hog, live weight [2] Preliminary. *Source: Economic Research Service, U.S. Department of Agriculture*

Cold Storage Holdings of Frozen Pork[1] in the United States, on First of Month In Millions of Pounds

Year	Jan.	Feb.	Mar.	Apr.	May	June	July	Aug.	Sept.	Oct.	Nov.	Dec.
1988	285.4	291.5	308.2	345.8	397.3	388.6	362.8	337.2	287.0	288.0	320.8	361.3
1989	357.9	377.6	393.5	392.8	432.6	428.1	380.1	342.6	277.9	278.0	275.8	279.2
1990	255.8	272.5	303.9	294.6	320.3	320.3	292.6	256.4	224.7	225.8	231.9	221.5
1991	233.6	247.0	281.2	289.0	340.0	333.3	312.3	277.9	282.4	280.5	299.7	308.0
1992	311.1	341.2	364.0	372.2	362.6	344.9	319.0	307.0	266.7	297.3	306.8	316.7
1993	314.5	329.5	344.4	330.4	378.5	371.6	351.3	342.5	308.9	311.2	324.8	313.0
1994	299.2	348.8	356.9	393.1	429.7	437.6	410.8	393.7	364.0	352.7	385.4	383.2
1995	365.3	389.6	395.1	416.8	422.3	434.9	431.1	408.3	354.0	332.6	321.6	347.1
1996	334.8	382.2	385.5	352.9	385.5	381.3	351.8	322.7	322.9	340.3	333.3	316.4
1997[2]	313.8	342.2	386.6	404.7	440.2	410.8	398.3	387.7	371.7	347.4	354.2	334.1

[1] Excludes lard. [2] Preliminary. *Source: Economic Research Service, U.S. Department of Agriculture (ERS-USDA)*

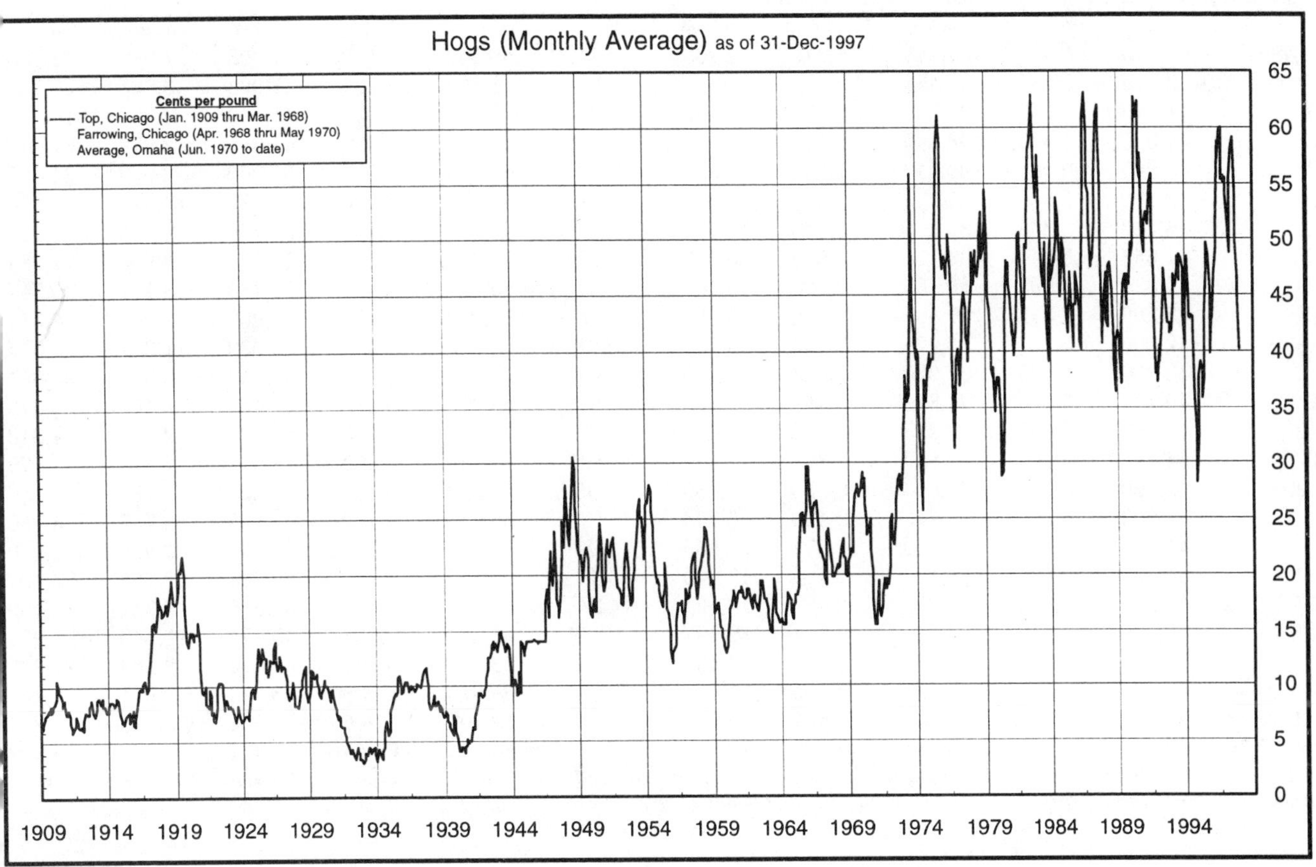

Average Wholesale Price of Hogs, Average (All Weights) in Sioux City In Dollars Per Hundred Pounds (Hwt.)

Year	Jan.	Feb.	Mar.	Apr.	May	June	July	Aug.	Sept.	Oct.	Nov.	Dec.	Average
1988	44.59	47.45	43.19	42.28	47.75	48.26	45.60	45.98	41.28	38.92	36.52	40.58	43.53
1989	41.64	41.11	39.88	37.22	42.40	46.24	47.26	47.04	44.58	47.49	47.21	49.65	44.31
1990	48.41	49.48	52.56	54.63	62.80	61.34	62.54	56.37	55.64	58.02	50.17	48.96	55.08
1991	51.32	52.31	51.92	51.42	54.83	54.79	55.74	51.11	46.76	43.51	38.29	38.93	49.24
1992	37.15	40.45	39.09	42.01	45.90	47.59	44.98	44.88	42.50	42.57	41.98	42.12	42.60
1993	41.66	44.57	46.76	45.46	47.10	48.52	46.38	48.67	48.40	47.27	42.76	40.38	45.66
1994	43.99	48.12	44.30	42.72	42.27	42.76	42.62	42.37	35.49	32.56	28.25	31.59	39.75
1995	37.82	39.09	37.94	35.88	37.35	43.03	47.18	49.46	48.67	45.42	40.02	43.80	42.14
1996	42.39	46.93	49.06	50.88	58.29	56.45	59.47	60.49	54.60	55.41	54.42	55.47	53.66
1997[1]	52.96	51.36	48.52	54.41	57.84	57.43	58.89	54.17	49.45	46.12	44.86	40.33	51.36

[1] Preliminary. *Source: Economic Research Service, U.S. Department of Agriculture (ERS-USDA)*

Average Price Received by Farmers for Hogs in the United States In Cents Per Pound

Year	Jan.	Feb.	Mar.	Apr.	May	June	July	Aug.	Sept.	Oct.	Nov.	Dec.	Average
1988	43.00	45.80	42.20	41.90	46.30	47.10	44.10	44.70	40.70	38.70	36.20	39.70	42.53
1989	40.90	40.40	39.30	36.90	41.60	45.10	45.90	45.60	43.40	46.60	45.00	48.20	43.24
1990	47.30	48.20	51.30	53.80	61.20	60.30	60.80	55.90	54.30	56.80	50.20	47.80	53.99
1991	50.00	52.20	51.50	50.90	54.10	54.70	54.20	51.20	46.40	43.60	38.00	38.60	48.78
1992	36.80	40.20	39.10	41.00	45.10	46.70	44.60	44.10	42.10	42.00	41.10	41.70	42.04
1993	41.20	44.00	46.50	45.40	46.90	48.10	45.70	47.30	47.80	46.90	42.50	40.40	45.23
1994	43.50	47.90	44.40	42.70	42.70	42.70	42.20	41.80	35.40	31.80	28.00	30.80	39.49
1995	36.90	39.10	37.80	35.70	37.20	42.30	46.30	48.60	48.40	45.70	39.90	43.50	41.78
1996	42.30	46.50	48.70	49.70	56.80	56.40	58.60	59.70	54.70	55.60	54.40	55.60	53.25
1997[1]	53.80	52.80	49.40	53.80	58.20	57.80	58.90	55.30	50.40	47.30	45.10	41.60	52.03

[1] Preliminary. *Source: Economic Research Service, U.S. Department of Agriculture (ERS-USDA)*

HOGS

Quarterly 10 -- U.S. State Hogs & Pigs Report   In Thousands of Head

Year[2]	Inventory[3]	Breeding[3]	Market[3]	Farrowings	Pig Crop	Year[2]	Inventory[3]	Breeding[3]	Market[3]	Farrowings	Pig Crop
1988	42,675	5,435	37,240	9,370	72,268	1993	58,202	7,109	51,093	11,982	97,050
I	42,675	5,435	37,485	2,123	16,489	I	58,202	7,109	51,093	3,665	29,739
II	41,345	5,555	35,825	2,578	20,175	II	47,145	5,735	41,410	2,363	19,267
III	44,065	5,630	38,435	2,358	18,000	III	58,395	7,320	51,075	2,972	24,041
IV	45,000	5,460	39,540	2,301	17,520	IV	59,030	7,130	51,900	2,982	24,003
1989	43,210	5,335	37,875	9,203	71,807	1994	57,904	7,130	50,739	12,376	101,400
I	43,210	5,335	37,875	2,109	16,439	I	57,904	7,130	50,739	2,885	23,368
II	41,655	5,440	36,215	2,580	20,309	II	57,350	7,210	50,140	3,390	27,984
III	44,020	5,565	38,455	2,324	18,167	III	60,715	7,565	53,150	3,107	25,547
IV	45,200	5,335	39,865	2,190	16,890	IV	62,320	7,415	54,905	2,997	24,517
1990	42,200	5,275	36,925	8,960	70,589	1995	59,990	7,060	52,930	11,847	98,516
I	42,200	5,275	36,925	2,013	15,748	I	59,990	7,060	52,930	2,886	23,851
II	40,190	5,245	34,945	2,458	19,576	II	58,465	6,998	51,467	3,170	26,373
III	42,630	5,405	37,225	2,236	17,684	III	59,560	7,180	52,380	2,976	24,813
IV	44,120	5,300	38,820	2,238	17,459	IV	60,540	6,898	53,642	2,815	23,479
1991	42,900	5,257	37,643	9,516	75,330	1996	58,264	6,839	51,425	11,187	94,956
I	42,900	5,257	37,643	2,129	16,700	I	58,264	6,839	51,425	2,757	23,160
II	41,990	5,450	36,540	2,577	20,555	II	56,340	6,765	49,575	2,955	25,040
III	44,520	5,700	38,820	2,413	19,260	III	57,150	6,860	50,290	2,758	23,597
IV	46,950	5,685	41,265	2,433	18,551	IV	58,150	6,765	51,385	2,717	23,159
1992	45,735	5,610	40,125	10,202	82,497	1997[1]	56,141	6,667	49,474	11,440	98,972
I	45,735	5,610	40,125	2,296	18,532	I	56,141	6,667	49,474	2,669	22,990
II	44,800	5,555	39,245	2,663	21,570	II	55,810	6,838	48,972	2,941	25,460
III	47,255	5,845	41,410	2,501	20,395	III	58,100	6,945	51,155	2,899	25,220
IV	49,175	5,840	43,335	2,398	19,351	IV	60,384	6,943	53,441	2,931	25,302

[1] Preliminary. [2] Quarters are December preceding year-February (I), March-May (II), June-August (III) and September-November (IV). [3] Beginning of period. *Source: National Agricultural Statistics Service, U.S.Department of Agriculture (NASS-USDA)*

Federally Inspected Hog Slaughter in the United States   In Thousands of Head

Year	Jan.	Feb.	Mar.	Apr.	May	June	July	Aug.	Sept.	Oct.	Nov.	Dec.	Total
1988	6,803	6,518	7,505	6,929	6,713	6,715	6,199	7,101	7,534	7,887	7,908	7,703	85,516
1989	7,116	6,619	7,569	7,199	7,277	6,881	6,131	7,392	7,493	7,823	7,815	7,012	86,328
1990	7,407	6,643	7,279	6,785	6,799	6,152	5,938	7,110	6,716	7,546	7,334	7,140	82,901
1991	7,461	6,469	7,044	7,320	6,948	6,296	6,557	7,098	7,177	8,292	7,744	7,708	85,951
1992	8,144	7,153	7,934	7,610	6,897	7,166	7,461	7,494	8,217	8,599	7,796	8,142	92,613
1993	7,649	6,921	7,958	7,840	6,988	7,338	7,010	7,473	7,763	7,857	7,952	8,184	90,993
1994	7,285	6,783	8,148	7,609	7,383	7,452	6,941	7,997	8,192	8,585	8,516	8,547	93,435
1995	7,882	7,157	8,628	7,379	8,012	7,731	6,918	8,083	7,752	8,358	8,424	7,881	94,203
1996	8,129	7,506	7,549	7,886	7,485	6,395	7,187	7,509	7,541	8,423	7,469	7,455	90,534
1997[1]	7,610	6,836	7,438	7,591	6,971	6,860	7,170	7,198	7,873	8,625	7,601	8,459	90,229

[1] Preliminary. *Source: National Agricultural Statistics Service, U.S. Department of Agriculture (NASS-USDA)*

Average Live Weight of All Hogs Slaughtered Under Federal Inspection   In Pounds Per Head

Year	Jan.	Feb.	Mar.	Apr.	May	June	July	Aug.	Sept.	Oct.	Nov.	Dec.	Average
1988	248	247	247	249	250	250	249	247	248	251	253	251	249
1989	249	247	247	251	251	251	247	247	246	248	251	250	249
1990	249	248	248	250	251	252	249	249	248	250	253	252	250
1991	251	250	250	252	254	253	251	250	251	253	256	255	252
1992	255	253	252	253	254	254	251	250	252	252	255	255	253
1993	254	253	253	254	254	256	254	252	252	254	257	258	254
1994	254	254	254	256	255	256	252	252	255	259	261	260	256
1995	258	256	257	258	258	258	256	253	252	255	259	258	257
1996	257	254	255	255	255	256	251	250	250	255	258	257	254
1997[1]	257	256	256	256	256	257	253	252	254	254	257	261	256

[1] Preliminary. *Source: Economic Research Service, U.S. Department of Agriculture (ERS-USDA)*

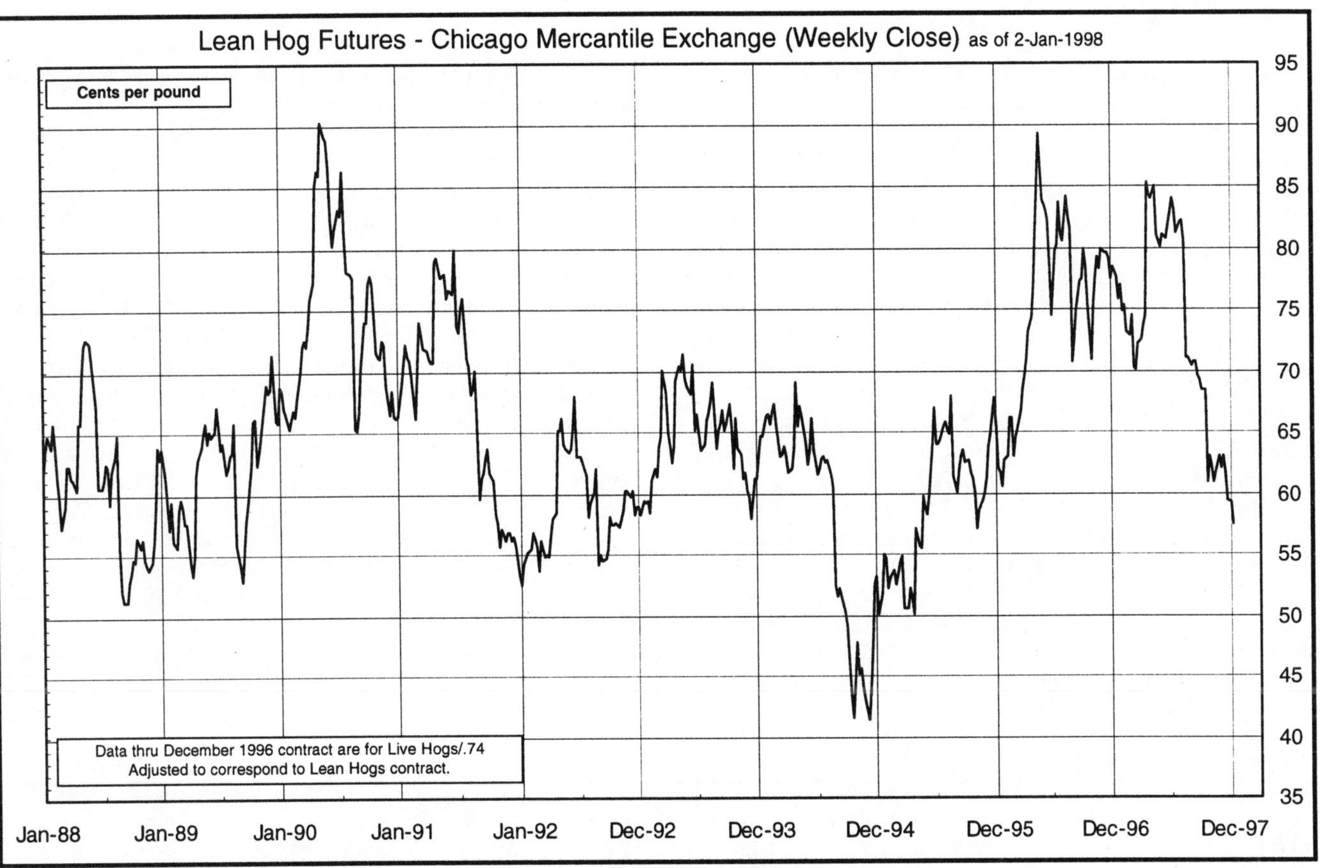

Average Open Interest of Lean Hogs Futures[1] in Chicago In Contracts

Year	Jan.	Feb.	Mar.	Apr.	May	June	July	Aug.	Sept.	Oct.	Nov.	Dec.
1988	26,681	30,532	31,329	28,156	31,801	31,221	27,466	26,476	31,507	30,092	34,251	31,458
1989	31,923	30,853	29,014	30,414	29,646	27,353	25,375	25,345	28,308	33,936	35,913	29,693
1990	30,335	31,018	37,789	39,257	47,291	43,631	32,942	29,964	26,982	25,691	27,648	25,757
1991	22,742	24,798	24,449	22,400	25,871	21,275	18,154	16,771	17,281	18,462	21,572	19,167
1992	23,854	31,545	32,441	32,430	30,947	26,362	24,935	24,535	27,535	32,555	32,738	30,468
1993	27,210	25,620	28,264	24,139	22,581	19,840	19,026	20,761	20,544	20,051	21,167	24,096
1994	31,899	32,123	31,012	31,713	30,889	27,327	26,414	25,335	28,957	32,077	36,304	33,516
1995	36,705	30,958	30,736	28,035	28,294	28,729	29,959	31,599	34,183	31,312	31,519	35,127
1996	35,253	34,823	38,730	42,900	41,916	36,620	35,616	32,541	32,591	34,329	33,148	32,163
1997	33,105	33,953	31,289	34,071	41,978	37,398	36,141	33,712	31,483	36,928	39,363	39,394

[1] Data prior to November 1995 are for Live Hogs, November 1995 thru December 1996 are Live Hogs and Lean Hogs, January 1997 to date are Lean Hogs.
Source: Chicago Mercantile Exchange (CME)

Volume of Trading of Lean Hogs Futures[1] in Chicago In Thousands of Contracts

Year	Jan.	Feb.	Mar.	Apr.	May	June	July	Aug.	Sept.	Oct.	Nov.	Dec.	Total
1988	172.9	143.0	172.4	137.6	169.6	267.0	171.4	140.3	160.7	150.3	166.8	156.7	2,008.8
1989	188.2	135.0	152.8	130.7	175.2	147.5	141.9	131.8	149.6	181.5	205.9	151.6	1,891.9
1990	181.0	119.9	189.7	188.8	278.3	277.0	212.5	170.4	147.0	160.3	186.1	130.4	2,241.3
1991	177.9	150.3	148.0	157.0	155.7	120.8	131.1	120.9	102.9	118.4	104.5	94.8	1,695.8
1992	135.2	137.0	140.4	138.2	116.7	131.2	148.8	102.2	116.6	149.5	117.0	123.3	1,556.1
1993	131.5	101.9	160.0	131.0	120.2	121.1	112.5	91.5	109.4	102.7	116.1	103.0	1,401.8
1994	144.7	97.6	146.9	93.1	127.4	144.4	116.2	122.1	110.7	129.0	150.7	172.1	1,554.0
1995	155.8	115.8	181.9	116.8	145.4	155.3	139.0	144.6	135.3	132.1	142.5	136.2	1,700.7
1996	177.3	138.0	150.1	216.5	208.7	177.4	185.9	157.5	158.1	203.8	170.6	152.1	2,095.9
1997	180.2	159.6	200.1	212.8	222.8	188.6	181.6	146.3	150.0	175.1	152.9	130.9	2,100.9

[1] Data prior to November 1995 are for Live Hogs, November 1995 thru December 1996 are Live Hogs and Lean Hogs, January 1997 to date are Lean Hogs.
Source: Chicago Mercantile Exchange (CME)

Honey

1997 honey production in the world's six major producing countries of 395,000 metric tonnes compares with 381,416 tonnes in 1996 and a 1990-95 annual average of more than 500,000 tonnes. Production in other countries is small. China is the world's largest producer followed by the U.S. and Argentina. Several factors influence annual honey production, weather being foremost; but the long-term downtrend in production also reflects a contraction in the number of beekeepers and producing bee colonies in some countries, the U.S. being one. A lingering problem is the more aggressive Africanized bees which have virtually wiped out honey production in some countries.

China's annual honey production held steady during 1992-1995 at about 177,000 tonnes, but poor weather and fewer beekeepers have since hampered production, estimated at 150,000 tonnes in 1997 vs. 147,000 tonnes in 1996. In China honey is considered a healthy food, but demand for pharmaceutical purposes has fallen. China is the world's largest honey exporter for which more stringent quality control standards are set, still China's 1997 exports of 65,000 tonnes compare with 83,462 in 1996 and 102,285 in 1994. China's major export markets are Japan, Germany, the U.S., and the U.K. China's yearend 1997 honey stocks of 10,830 tonnes compare with 5,750 a year earlier and the unusually large 15,169 tonnes two years earlier.

Argentina's 1997 honey production of 65,000 tonnes compares with 57,000 in 1996; Mexico's production of 46,000 tonnes compares with 47,997 in 1996. U.S. production in 1997 of 90,000 tonnes was marginally higher than in 1995. Five states account for more than half of U.S. production paced by California, followed by the Dakotas, Minnesota, and Florida. U.S. imports of 70,000 tonnes in 1997 compares with 68,307 tonnes in 1996. The U.S. is one of the world's largest markets for industrial honey (used in cereals, bakery and health food products) which accounts for about 45 percent of total domestic use, estimated at 153,000 tonnes in 1997 vs. 151,526 in 1996. The food service industry takes about 15 percent of domestic use. Yearend 1997 U.S. stocks of 24,007 tonnes compare with 21,307 a year earlier and over 53,000 at yearend 1993. The U.S. average honey yield per colony in 1997 of 77.2 pounds compares with 79.5 pounds in 1996; bee colonies of 2.56 million compare with 2.64 million, respectively.

U.S. prices for the 1996 honey crop averaged a record high 89.4 cents per pound vs. the previous record of 68.5 cents in 1995.

World Production of Honey In Metric Tons

Year	Argentina	Australia	Brazil	Canada	China	Germany[2]	Japan	Mexico	Russia[3]	United States	Total[4]
1986	36,000	25,077	27,000	34,041	160,000	16,000	5,553	54,000	210,000	90,900	658,571
1987	44,000	28,000	30,500	39,776	204,000	16,000	6,023	47,850	219,245	102,875	738,269
1988	46,000	27,622	30,000	37,105	156,000	18,000	4,870	46,140	243,000	97,114	705,851
1989	40,000	26,198	32,000	27,815	189,000	29,000	5,343	48,530	225,000	80,266	703,152
1990	47,000	27,561	30,000	32,115	193,000	23,000	4,854	51,000	236,219	89,717	732,466
1991	54,000	20,604	32,300	31,606	206,000	25,000	4,202	58,770	240,000	99,414	714,790
1992	61,000	18,948	18,841	30,339	178,000	24,677	3,800	48,852	47,000	100,055	531,512
1993	59,000	22,556	19,000	30,760	176,000	26,357	3,500	48,000	49,600	104,620	539,393
1994	64,000	24,000	19,000	32,920	177,000	22,233	3,500	41,500	43,900	98,500	526,553
1995	70,000	24,000	19,200	30,575	178,000	36,685	3,500	49,228	44,000	95,490	550,678
1996[1]	57,000	NA	NA	24,895	147,000	14,674	NA	47,997	NA	89,850	381,416
1997[1]	65,000	NA	NA	29,000	150,000	15,000	NA	46,000	NA	90,000	395,000

[1] Preliminary. [2] Data prior to 1989 are for West Germany. [3] Formerly part of the U.S.S.R.; data not reported separately until 1992. [4] Only for countries listed. *Source: Foreign Agricultural Service, U.S. Department of Agriculture (FAS-USDA)*

Salient Statistics of Honey in the United States In Millions of Pounds

									------- Program Activity -------					
Year	Number of Colonies (1,000)	Yield Per Colony Pounds	Stocks Jan. 1	Total U.S. Production	Imports for Consumption	Domestic Disappearance	Exports	Total Supply	Placed Under Loan	CCC Take Over	Net Gov't. Expenditure[3] Mil. $	Domestic Avg. Price All Honey ---------- ¢ Lb.	National Avg. Price Support --------	Per Capita Consumption Lbs.
1986	3,205	62.5	234.3	200.4	120.0	282.9	9.2	554.7	180.4	41.0	89.4	51.3	64.0	1.0
1987	3,190	71.1	262.6	226.8	58.3	320.9	12.4	547.7	218.0	52.7	72.6	50.3	61.0	1.1
1988	3,219	66.3	214.4	214.1	55.9	278.0	14.0	484.4	209.5	32.0	100.1	50.0	59.1	.9
1989	3,443	51.4	192.4	177.0	77.3	292.0	10.0	446.7	161.7	2.8	41.7	49.8	56.4	1.0
1990	3,210	61.6	144.7	197.8	77.0	303.4	12.4	419.5	183.5	1.1	46.7	53.7	53.8	1.0
1991	3,181	68.9	103.7	219.2	92.2	303.4	9.6	415.1	112.9	3.2	18.6	55.6	53.8	1.0
1992	3,030	72.8	109.3	220.6	114.6	330.5	10.4	444.5	122.7	4.1	16.6	55.0	53.8	1.0
1993	2,876	80.2	103.5	230.6	133.6	342.0	8.5	467.8	136.8	16.4	22.1	53.9	53.8	1.0
1994	2,770	78.4	117.3	217.2	123.2	355.2	8.3	457.7	73.4	0	-.2	52.8	50.0	1.0
1995	2,648	79.5	94.1	210.5	88.6	341.6	9.3	393.2	64.4	0	-9.3	68.5	50.0	1.0
1996[1]	2,566	77.2	42.2	198.1	150.6	334.1	9.9	390.9	NA	NA	NA	89.4	NA	NA
1997[2]	2,500	79.4	47.0	198.4	154.3	337.3	9.5	399.7	NA	NA	NA	NA	NA	NA

[1] Preliminary. [2] Forecast. [3] Fiscal year. *Source: Economic Research Service, U.S. Department of Agriculture (ERS-USDA)*

Interest Rates, U.S.

Federal Reserve policy held basically steady during 1997 although market expectations were not nearly as subdued. Prior to each of the Fed's open market committee meetings traders nerves were frayed in anticipation of some definitive action by the Fed. A case could be made for rate moves in either direction, especially during the second half of the year, but the Fed opted to hold a steady course. Short term rates, however, were lifted in March, the only official change made in 1997 with a 25 basis point increase in Fed funds to 5.50 percent. As the year progressed rates held in a narrow range, but market emphasis focused on long-term rates with the 30-year bond falling under 6.00 percent. At yearend 1997, the 30 year T-bond yield of 5.92 percent compared with 6.64 percent a year earlier; 3 month T-bills were at 5.19 percent vs. 5.04 percent; Fed funds were 5.50 percent vs. 5.25 percent, the prime rate 8.50 percent vs. 8.25 percent and the discount rate was 5.00 percent, unchanged from the previous year.

1997 was a good year for the U.S. economy, suggesting to some a need for Fed tightening to cool the economic strength. The odds seemed to be in their favor in early 1997 as the economy's cyclical expansion had persisted for five years raising fears that inflationary pressures would soon surface. The Fed's March tightening was seen as only the first of several upward moves, however, traditional economics proved to have weak legs in 1997. The U.S. economy continued strong with an ever tightening labor market but inflationary pressures proved non-existent. Moreover, the strong economy generated higher tax revenues which greatly narrowed the federal deficit, with talk surfacing of a sooner than expected surplus. And by yearend there was talk of deflation, if not in the U.S., than in other key world economies. Unlikely as that scenario may be, it gave the Fed breathing room to hold its monetary policy steady and await economic developments in 1998.

In October, the Fed chairman stated to Congress that the sizzling annualized pace of two million new jobs created in 1997 could not be sustained without inflation taking root. A clear message was sent to the marketplace; either employment growth slows or the Fed will tighten. Ironically, as the government revised its labor data towards yearend, it found that new job creation was running at nearly twice what was earlier stated as being unsustainable, and unemployment, at 4.6 percent, was at a 24-year low. Even more surprisingly, the producer price index was projecting the first yearly decline since 1986. The Fed was in a box. How could rates be raised if inflation was in check, but how could they not be raised as a pre-emptive move against anticipated higher labor costs and cost/push inflationary pressure? The answer, which put the Fed squarely on the fence, came in the fourth quarter of 1997: economic trouble in several Pacific Rim countries.

Following the late 1997 collapse in Asia, and the need for bailouts by the International Monetary Fund, The Fed could not tighten U.S. interest rates even if it wanted to, as doing so would enhance the U.S. dollar's strength and further intensify Asian financial troubles.

Futures Markets

A futures (and options) contract exists for almost every maturity on the yield curve, as well as for municipal and commercial credit risks. Major U.S. contracts include T-bills and Eurodollars on Chicago's International Monetary Market (IMM), and T-bonds and 10-year T-notes on the Chicago Board of Trade (CBOT). Futures are also traded in Chicago on 2 and 5-Year T-notes, municipal bonds, 30 day fed funds, and one month LIBOR. Smaller size contracts on some interest rate instruments are listed at the MidAmerica Commodity Exchange (MidAm).

U.S. Producer Price Index[2] (Wholesale, All Commodities) 1982 = 100

Year	Jan.	Feb.	Mar.	Apr.	May	June	July	Aug.	Sept.	Oct.	Nov.	Dec.	Average
1989	110.5	110.8	111.5	112.3	113.2	112.9	112.8	112.0	112.3	112.7	112.7	113.0	112.2
1990	114.9	114.4	114.2	114.1	114.6	114.3	114.5	116.5	118.3	120.8	120.1	118.7	116.3
1991	119.0	117.2	116.2	116.0	116.5	116.4	116.1	116.2	116.1	116.4	116.4	115.9	116.5
1992	115.6	116.0	116.1	116.3	117.2	118.0	117.9	117.7	118.0	118.1	117.8	117.6	117.2
1993	118.0	118.4	118.7	119.3	119.7	119.5	119.2	118.7	118.7	119.1	119.0	118.6	118.9
1994	119.1	119.3	119.7	119.7	119.9	120.5	120.7	121.2	120.9	120.9	121.5	121.9	120.4
1995	122.9	123.5	123.9	124.6	124.9	125.3	125.3	125.1	125.2	125.3	125.4	125.7	124.8
1996	126.3	126.2	126.4	127.4	128.1	128.0	128.0	128.3	128.2	128.0	128.2	129.1	127.7
1997[1]	129.7	128.5	127.3	127.0	127.4	127.2	126.9	127.2	127.5	127.8	127.8	126.7	127.6

[1] Preliminary. [2] Not seasonally adjusted. *Source: Bureau of Labor Statistics, U.S. Department of Commerce (BLS)*

U.S. Consumer Price Index[2] (Retail Price Index for All Items: Urban Consumers) 1982-1984 = 100

Year	Jan.	Feb.	Mar.	Apr.	May	June	July	Aug.	Sept.	Oct.	Nov.	Dec.	Average
1989	121.1	121.6	122.3	123.1	123.8	124.1	124.4	124.6	125.0	125.6	125.9	126.1	124.0
1990	127.4	128.0	128.7	128.9	129.2	129.9	130.4	131.6	132.7	133.5	133.8	133.8	130.7
1991	134.6	134.8	135.0	135.2	135.6	136.0	136.2	136.6	137.2	137.4	137.8	137.9	136.2
1992	138.1	138.6	139.3	139.5	139.7	140.2	140.5	140.9	141.3	141.8	142.0	141.9	140.3
1993	142.6	143.1	143.6	144.0	144.2	144.4	144.4	144.8	145.1	145.7	145.8	145.8	144.5
1994	146.2	146.7	147.2	147.4	147.5	148.0	148.4	149.0	149.4	149.5	149.7	149.7	148.2
1995	150.3	150.9	151.4	151.9	152.2	152.5	152.5	152.9	153.2	153.7	153.6	153.5	152.4
1996	154.4	154.9	155.7	156.3	156.6	156.7	157.0	157.3	157.8	158.3	158.6	158.6	156 9
1997[1]	159.1	159.6	160.0	160.2	160.1	160.3	160.5	160.8	161.2	161.6	161.5	161.3	160.5

[1] Preliminary. [2] Not seasonally adjusted. *Source: Bureau of Labor Statistics, U.S. Department of Commerce (BLS)*

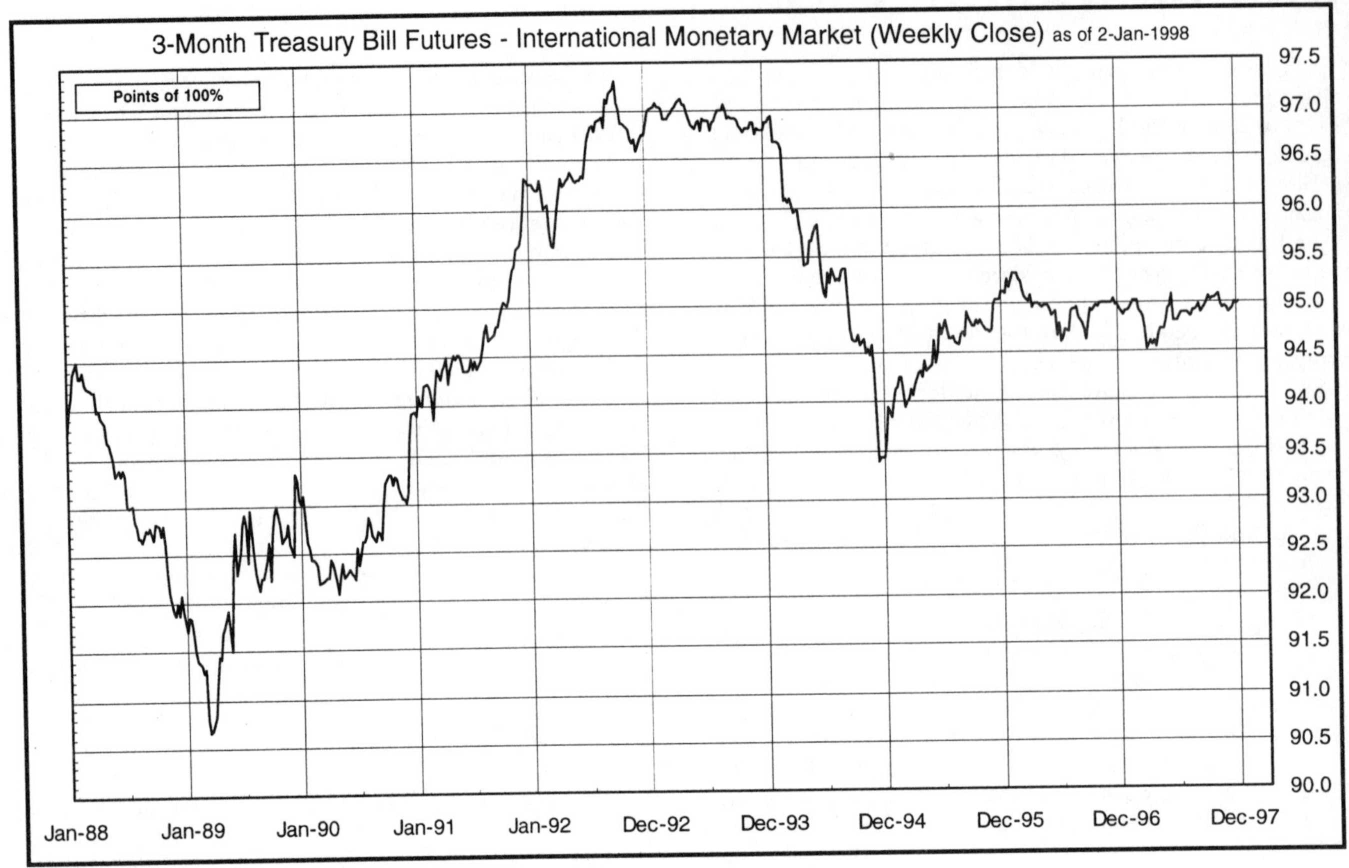

Average Open Interest of 3-Month[1] Treasury Bill Futures in Chicago   In Thousands of Contracts

Year	Jan.	Feb.	Mar.	Apr.	May	June	July	Aug.	Sept.	Oct.	Nov.	Dec.
1988	19,571	22,956	21,460	26,134	28,166	19,081	21,812	21,626	21,374	21,930	24,711	26,923
1989	29,023	26,612	25,672	20,433	21,864	19,934	20,950	22,687	25,216	29,118	34,224	33,469
1990	39,168	38,358	27,668	31,274	25,128	21,171	26,524	37,903	35,723	46,974	53,284	50,146
1991	55,371	53,484	38,259	43,538	53,941	51,178	55,514	55,999	47,509	50,865	57,680	51,750
1992	51,312	45,902	35,539	44,757	47,734	41,091	38,399	35,638	29,781	32,556	35,379	29,566
1993	32,544	35,756	32,556	39,115	40,724	34,614	30,895	34,177	28,983	30,121	33,800	30,996
1994	36,456	41,150	43,243	51,485	41,164	34,580	32,572	29,559	24,522	32,325	30,077	22,322
1995	21,065	26,289	33,420	35,873	34,608	25,930	20,534	19,195	18,929	16,781	16,384	11,279
1996	14,769	16,906	14,161	14,460	15,709	10,285	8,973	9,770	6,536	6,906	7,516	7,002
1997	8,114	9,793	9,968	10,390	10,048	8,949	8,425	9,760	7,899	9,497	11,223	10,679

[1] 90-day U.S. Treasury Bill.   *Source: International Monetary Market (IMM), division of the Chicago Mercantile Exchange (CME)*

Volume of Trading of 3-Month[1] Treasury Bill Futures in Chicago   In Thousands of Contracts

Year	Jan.	Feb.	Mar.	Apr.	May	June	July	Aug.	Sept.	Oct.	Nov.	Dec.	Total
1988	103.2	111.6	129.2	125.6	163.4	105.3	84.3	117.9	97.9	101.6	129.1	104.5	1,373.6
1989	109.6	146.5	143.2	119.2	126.3	101.4	89.3	126.9	135.9	149.1	130.1	124.9	1,502.4
1990	169.3	153.6	118.5	120.3	102.4	96.7	138.1	206.6	168.9	178.5	223.7	193.1	1,869.6
1991	252.9	197.9	166.8	164.0	188.2	173.3	141.7	223.2	111.0	110.8	140.8	141.6	1,912.2
1992	143.8	137.9	145.0	115.9	106.5	106.1	85.8	76.2	103.0	127.0	106.5	83.4	1,337.1
1993	86.1	100.4	97.0	65.6	103.2	106.0	71.7	75.7	89.3	69.1	87.4	66.0	1,071.3
1994	59.8	137.0	115.9	104.4	99.4	89.4	53.7	60.9	77.6	57.4	81.2	83.8	1,020.5
1995	72.2	80.0	90.3	37.4	58.7	49.9	28.1	41.5	44.4	36.9	46.6	34.2	620.2
1996	32.0	36.0	36.5	17.9	16.6	25.2	12.0	19.4	19.8	10.8	10.4	14.3	250.9
1997	10.6	19.4	20.6	11.6	16.6	14.9	11.5	15.4	19.0	20.4	16.8	22.1	199.1

[1] 90-day U.S. Treasury Bill.   *Source: International Monetary Market (IMM), division of the Chicago Mercantile Exchange (CME)*

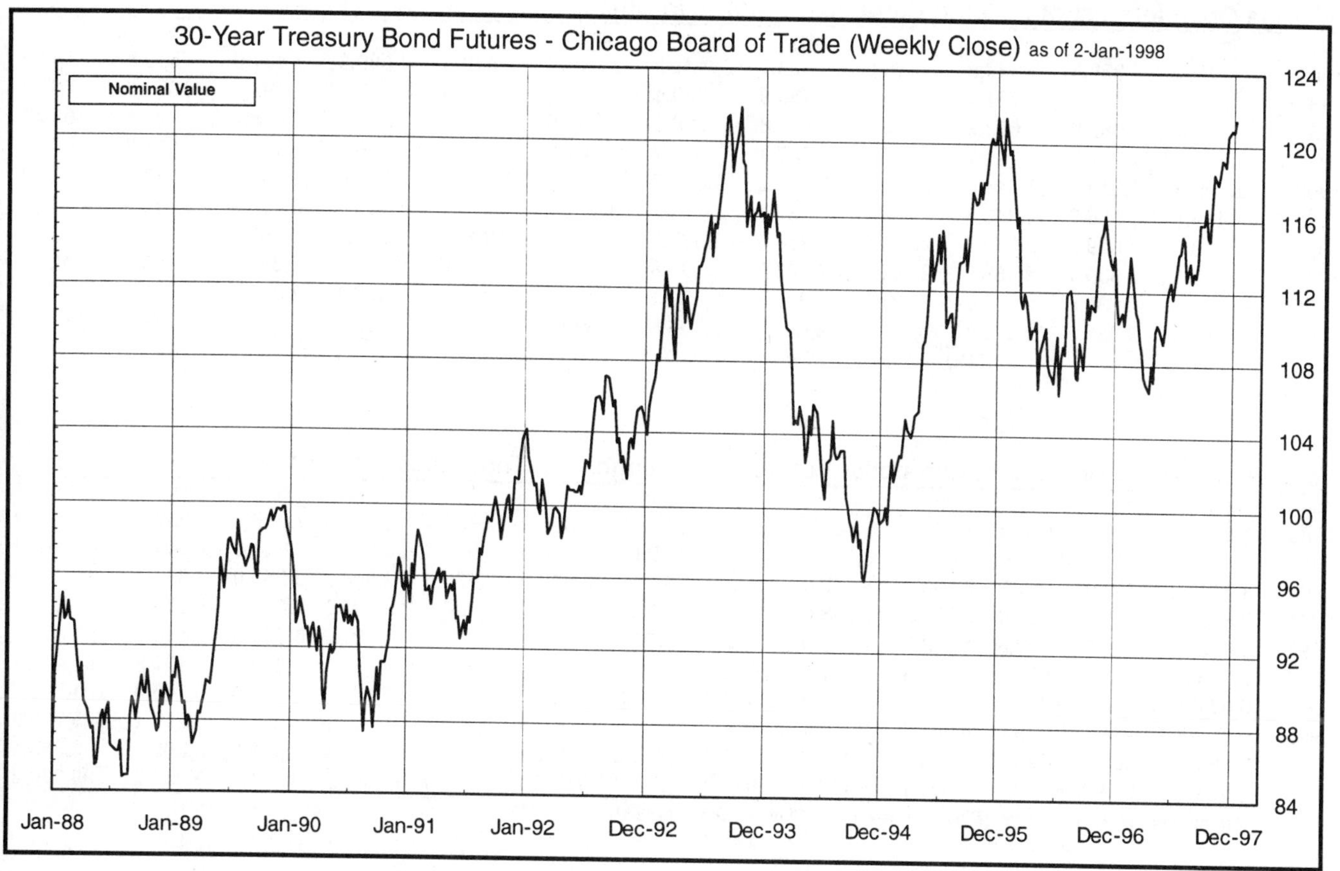

Average Open Interest of 30-Year U.S. Treasury Bond Futures in Chicago In Thousands of Contracts

Year	Jan.	Feb.	Mar.	Apr.	May	June	July	Aug.	Sept.	Oct.	Nov.	Dec.
1988	296,133	328,081	307,004	317,891	366,723	406,493	441,064	489,339	475,841	478,585	472,628	411,888
1989	395,874	366,704	303,891	308,850	330,016	312,318	325,851	321,493	283,133	301,719	355,555	314,252
1990	315,671	324,954	294,968	280,745	303,544	278,889	285,934	317,197	297,075	286,291	288,581	254,775
1991	257,229	279,378	250,028	283,473	279,443	254,983	273,774	325,303	310,110	304,198	317,445	301,604
1992	343,156	353,782	318,737	313,742	346,542	347,293	370,850	427,723	385,645	364,250	362,231	321,706
1993	336,327	375,435	361,675	362,404	370,485	349,285	361,393	396,411	388,188	360,859	359,739	337,575
1994	380,057	422,902	454,539	500,790	497,296	421,286	441,884	451,462	447,924	436,684	449,642	397,554
1995	384,356	389,908	369,989	367,964	399,500	421,234	438,267	381,237	361,394	395,346	447,409	426,384
1996	382,001	403,403	395,338	381,926	413,944	443,644	464,145	471,203	420,622	409,950	463,731	479,086
1997	497,539	545,775	509,573	493,511	554,418	480,669	530,011	608,474	624,231	723,321	719,186	737,703

Source: Chicago Board of Trade (CBT)

Volume of Trading of 30-Year U.S. Treasury Bond Futures in Chicago In Thousands of Contracts

Year	Jan.	Feb.	Mar.	Apr.	May	June	July	Aug.	Sept.	Oct.	Nov.	Dec.	Total
1988	5,550.0	5,765.0	6,088.0	4,984.0	5,570.0	7,495.0	5,133.0	6,346.0	5,641.0	6,136.0	6,431.0	5,171.0	70,307.0
1989	5,806.0	6,300.0	5,605.0	4,858.0	6,673.0	7,995.0	5,231.0	7,640.0	4,792.0	6,329.0	5,828.0	3,244.0	70,303.0
1990	7,215.0	7,438.0	7,175.0	5,653.0	6,189.0	5,279.0	4,895.0	8,855.0	4,939.0	6,659.0	6,570.0	4,691.0	75,559.0
1991	5,804.0	5,717.0	5,658.0	5,957.0	6,186.0	5,582.0	4,293.0	6,592.0	4,765.0	6,450.0	6,239.0	4,643.0	67,886.0
1992	7,523.4	6,270.1	6,793.4	4,810.1	5,417.7	4,828.8	6,081.0	6,085.5	5,953.3	6,870.7	5,287.8	4,083.0	70,004.8
1993	5,577.4	6,482.7	7,902.9	6,156.1	6,799.8	5,817.2	6,218.4	6,914.5	7,443.9	6,537.4	8,193.5	5,384.5	79,428.5
1994	7,287.8	8,430.2	10,836.7	9,557.4	9,999.0	9,804.0	6,987.0	7,910.0	7,913.0	7,004.0	8,533.0	5,699.0	99,960.0
1995	7,058.0	7,714.0	9,623.8	5,835.4	8,721.5	8,446.7	5,790.2	7,083.7	7,317.1	6,927.2	6,626.3	5,232.1	86,375.9
1996	7,528.6	8,781.4	7,199.3	6,010.6	7,932.3	6,520.6	6,422.1	6,625.8	6,926.1	6,772.4	7,297.7	6,708.4	84,725.1
1997	8,104.7	7,522.8	7,493.3	7,519.9	8,339.1	7,400.2	7,679.8	10,228.1	8,356.2	12,467.6	7,735.5	6,980.4	99,827.7

Source: Chicago Board of Trade (CBT)

INTEREST RATES

Average Open Interest of 3-Month Eurodollar Futures in Chicago   In Thousands of Contracts

Year	Jan.	Feb.	Mar.	Apr.	May	June	July	Aug.	Sept.	Oct.	Nov.	Dec.
1988	317.4	358.5	340.9	376.0	422.7	421.9	440.6	510.2	509.2	477.9	519.8	567.0
1989	574.8	672.3	731.3	749.7	756.9	720.4	690.2	714.0	637.9	591.5	663.6	661.9
1990	638.5	662.9	653.2	616.9	662.8	676.3	690.6	740.0	697.8	678.2	728.4	664.1
1991	630.9	722.7	741.1	767.6	857.4	835.2	797.9	883.1	916.7	949.5	1,054.7	1,067.2
1992	1,129.8	1,213.7	1,244.6	1,269.1	1,377.2	1,382.7	1,434.1	1,549.9	1,537.0	1,537.6	1,547.0	1,418.7
1993	1,429.4	1,586.7	1,643.3	1,653.4	1,782.8	1,739.1	1,777.7	1,918.4	1,940.7	2,026.5	2,149.0	2,150.2
1994	2,300.5	2,529.5	2,568.1	2,627.3	2,734.3	2,565.2	2,599.1	2,703.8	2,699.6	2,561.2	2,660.3	2,606.3
1995	2,443.6	2,535.4	2,463.9	2,447.4	2,503.3	2,390.8	2,279.5	2,374.6	2,347.2	2,290.3	2,405.5	2,480.5
1996	2,519.4	2,638.6	2,511.4	2,483.5	2,571.8	2,590.1	2,504.4	2,485.5	2,392.4	2,349.7	2,378.2	2,225.7
1997	2,190.8	2,333.2	2,423.1	2,523.1	2,671.3	2,706.5	2,699.2	2,788.0	2,769.3	2,815.1	2,799.5	2,661.6

Source: International Monetary Market (IMM), division of the Chicago Mercantile Exchange (CME)

Volume of Trading of 3-Month Eurodollar Futures in Chicago   In Thousands of Contracts

Year	Jan.	Feb.	Mar.	Apr.	May	June	July	Aug.	Sept.	Oct.	Nov.	Dec.	Total
1988	1,466.0	1,681.0	1,635.0	1,575.0	1,830.0	2,288.0	1,604.0	1,893.0	1,957.0	1,586.0	2,236.0	1,952.0	21,705.0
1989	2,257.0	3,107.0	3,848.0	4,471.0	3,941.0	4,116.0	3,193.0	3,980.0	2,977.0	3,971.0	2,914.0	2,043.0	40,818.0
1990	3,244.0	2,459.0	2,727.0	2,566.0	3,132.0	2,473.0	2,947.0	3,857.0	2,730.0	2,898.0	2,982.0	2,680.0	34,696.0
1991	2,859.0	2,635.0	3,445.0	3,208.0	2,458.0	2,972.0	2,629.0	4,035.0	3,000.0	3,505.0	3,301.0	3,196.0	37,243.0
1992	5,365.7	4,418.5	5,582.8	4,942.2	4,819.0	4,602.6	5,357.8	4,016.3	4,705.2	6,691.6	5,461.3	4,568.1	60,531.1
1993	5,556.8	5,003.8	6,013.8	4,059.4	5,977.8	5,672.9	5,656.7	4,494.2	6,340.6	4,888.4	6,269.8	4,477.3	64,411.4
1994	6,074.8	8,745.3	9,468.9	9,639.2	11,494.0	9,348.0	7,810.0	7,128.0	7,641.0	7,992.0	9,715.0	9,766.0	104,823.0
1995	10,341.1	10,429.3	9,549.0	6,069.2	9,897.1	10,104.7	6,669.9	7,013.5	7,171.1	6,477.9	6,055.2	5,952.1	95,730.0
1996	7,485.7	9,267.2	9,526.3	6,872.4	7,413.7	7,415.0	8,323.2	6,967.5	8,232.5	7,014.5	5,056.9	5,308.1	88,883.1
1997	7,903.4	6,918.0	8,936.4	9,351.7	8,447.4	8,049.7	7,291.6	9,295.4	7,634.7	12,569.7	6,314.1	7,058.2	99,770.2

Source: International Monetary Market (IMM), division of the Chicago Mercantile Exchange (CME)

Average Open Interest of 10-Year U.S. Treasury Note Futures in Chicago In Contracts

Year	Jan.	Feb.	Mar.	Apr.	May	June	July	Aug.	Sept.	Oct.	Nov.	Dec.
1988	76,066	75,884	73,083	75,836	78,038	84,349	84,612	101,470	96,821	91,811	89,307	74,602
1989	76,964	84,605	78,966	86,661	88,511	76,364	77,211	76,538	71,138	82,844	82,149	72,238
1990	73,155	82,211	76,939	76,030	82,174	78,498	71,413	75,644	72,900	67,309	73,744	76,697
1991	72,621	79,355	79,413	71,451	84,203	81,884	85,527	94,379	96,836	93,187	95,450	87,063
1992	119,739	114,521	106,497	102,862	112,666	126,228	143,924	158,831	179,045	191,725	199,990	195,705
1993	190,018	206,852	198,653	209,221	229,378	217,521	233,458	238,189	237,243	237,877	273,336	262,831
1994	264,848	258,643	300,080	328,821	294,091	254,612	232,373	253,233	273,564	277,313	301,000	271,992
1995	282,978	285,187	265,747	263,816	273,945	289,052	306,046	323,078	277,011	278,832	270,527	249,073
1996	260,374	297,850	285,501	319,234	331,032	293,416	302,330	326,391	291,208	284,581	313,298	303,702
1997	332,285	343,661	323,982	348,683	350,814	336,927	363,744	407,147	387,284	398,645	404,980	374,448

Source: Chicago Board of Trade (CBT)

Volume of Trading of 10-Year U.S. Treasury Note Futures in Chicago In Thousands of Contracts

Year	Jan.	Feb.	Mar.	Apr.	May	June	July	Aug.	Sept.	Oct.	Nov.	Dec.	Total
1988	335.3	462.8	420.6	298.8	467.8	469.6	327.4	566.0	455.4	383.2	537.4	476.7	5,201.0
1989	450.5	547.9	468.3	431.6	625.6	637.3	453.0	629.6	465.8	555.8	516.7	327.4	6,109.5
1990	491.3	650.5	480.9	381.1	638.7	427.4	415.0	703.0	399.3	449.6	574.3	442.6	6,053.7
1991	507.7	519.6	508.3	466.5	566.9	456.6	318.9	705.9	467.2	573.2	661.3	591.4	6,342.0
1992	929.6	866.4	824.9	531.2	758.9	683.3	859.4	1,047.7	1,138.5	1,300.2	1,225.8	1,052.1	11,218.0
1993	1,134.6	1,286.3	1,763.1	1,089.5	1,341.4	1,390.6	1,147.0	1,390.7	1,523.7	1,279.5	1,926.6	1,328.2	16,601.2
1994	1,484.3	1,935.7	2,572.4	2,213.5	2,399.4	2,250.2	1,621.8	2,028.7	1,932.9	1,635.1	2,253.6	1,750.2	24,078.0
1995	1,752.6	1,978.8	2,458.7	1,368.2	2,236.5	2,495.8	1,588.9	2,028.7	1,859.0	1,459.7	1,730.8	1,487.6	22,445.4
1996	1,649.1	2,313.1	2,075.8	1,632.1	2,211.3	1,715.6	1,556.3	1,865.7	1,810.4	1,494.7	1,904.5	1,711.2	21,939.7
1997	1,780.5	1,939.9	2,051.8	1,703.2	2,025.6	1,942.3	1,509.6	2,535.9	2,062.5	2,593.7	1,825.6	1,991.2	23,961.8

Source: Chicago Board of Trade (CBT)

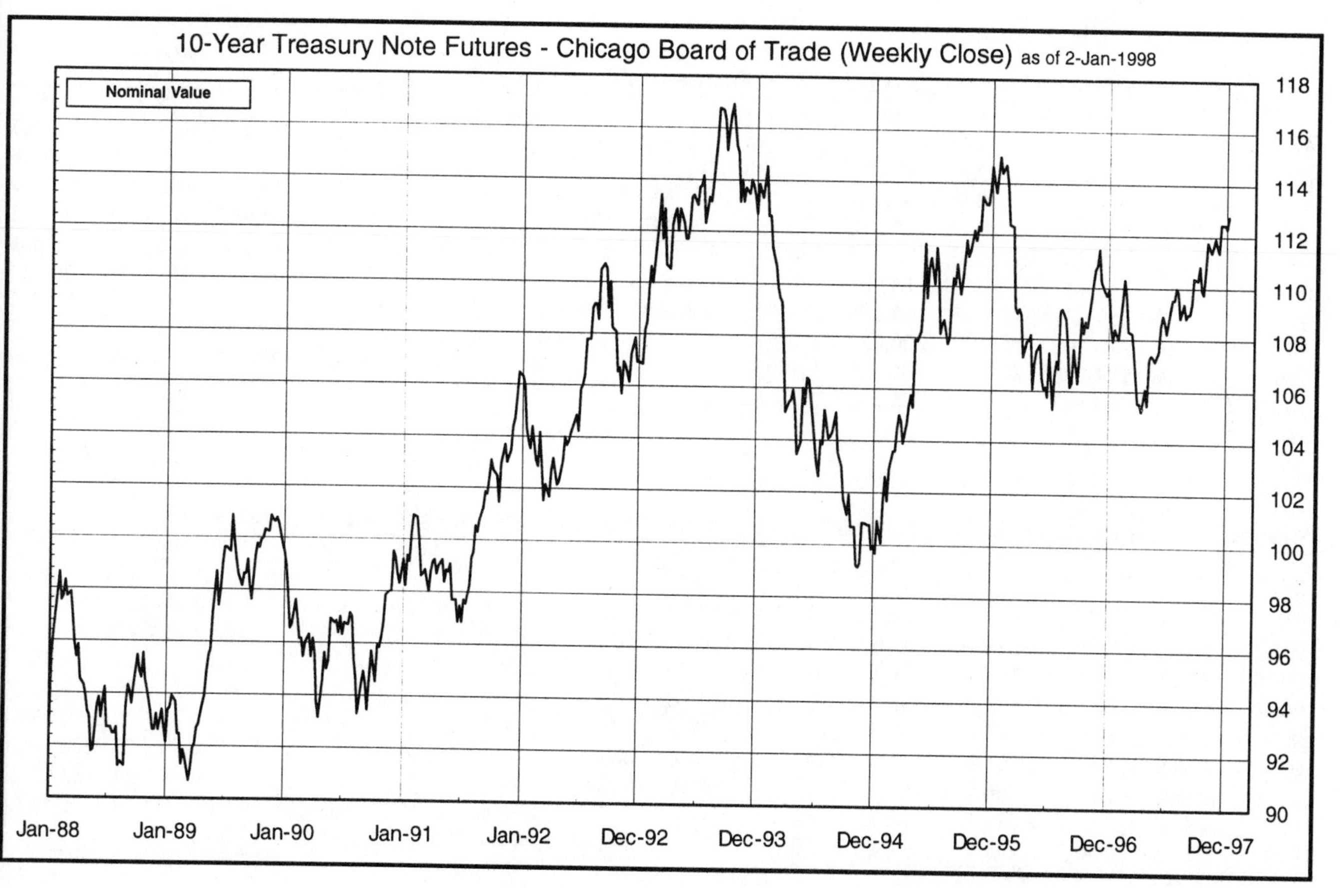

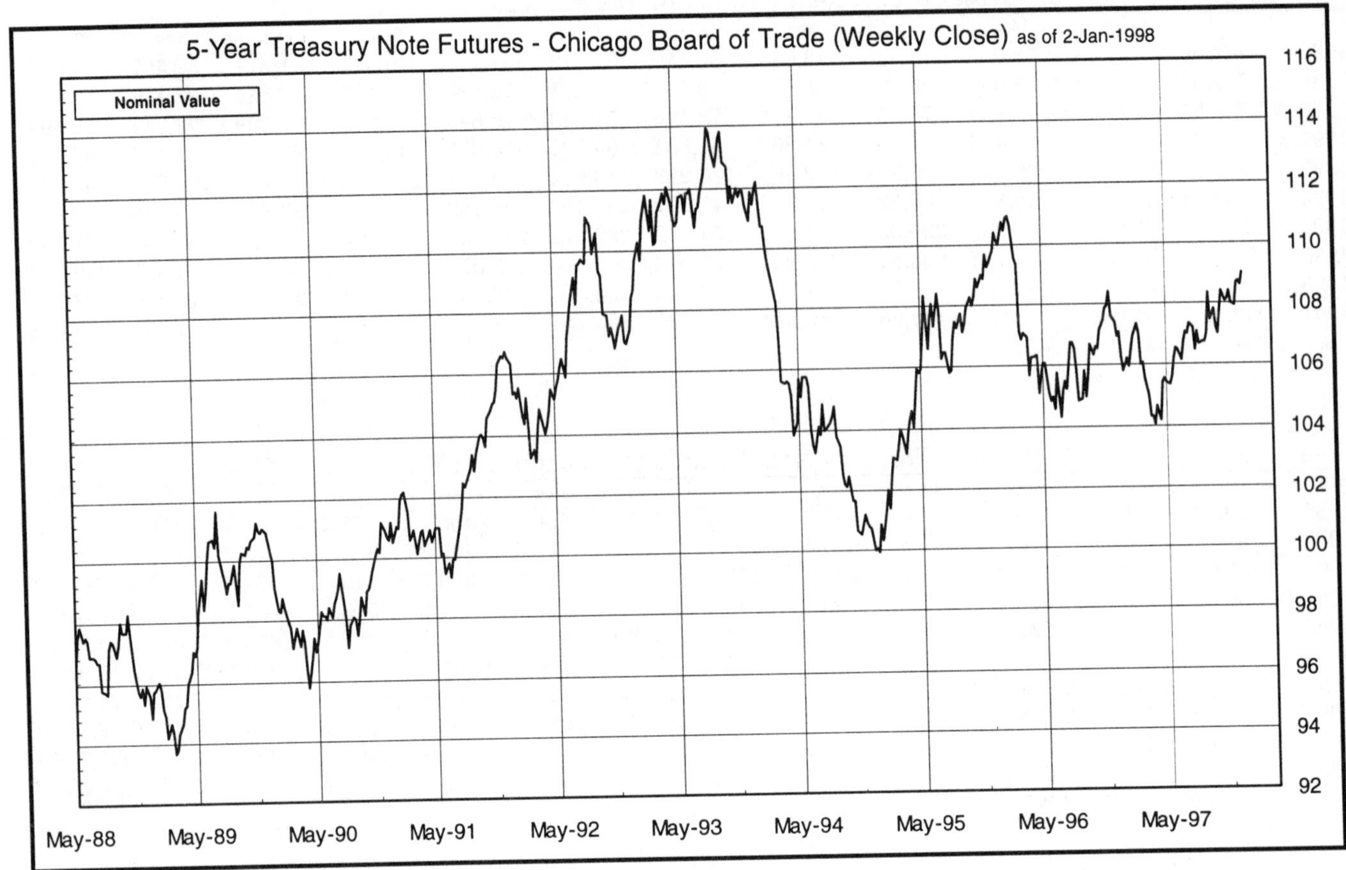

Average Open Interest of 5-Year Treasury Note Futures in Chicago In Contracts

Year	Jan.	Feb.	Mar.	Apr.	May	June	July	Aug.	Sept.	Oct.	Nov.	Dec.
1988					2,545	5,292	10,584	11,424	12,677	18,403	24,569	34,267
1989	34,728	40,203	45,320	46,371	48,195	42,496	44,985	34,675	37,474	42,669	57,901	73,798
1990	81,705	74,568	74,999	60,841	59,417	56,485	54,004	64,100	75,955	78,370	82,981	93,549
1991	80,059	82,666	83,109	74,612	75,799	65,543	72,197	86,981	85,794	91,096	102,890	99,291
1992	116,322	121,667	125,155	130,826	135,111	144,386	143,928	143,203	127,418	122,113	129,548	127,690
1993	139,207	150,443	152,711	158,607	169,234	152,262	152,403	160,258	159,754	154,501	181,492	206,914
1994	200,812	213,037	200,626	185,083	192,659	186,026	189,828	182,027	181,518	181,578	176,322	205,150
1995	206,539	210,192	199,357	200,087	213,531	189,332	176,329	173,897	163,419	162,121	177,915	171,023
1996	163,026	184,523	200,253	191,690	179,951	177,370	174,484	179,599	154,764	138,246	155,820	154,764
1997	176,691	208,928	219,540	235,543	227,882	225,691	226,306	225,792	234,309	233,480	248,377	257,886

Source: Chicago Board of Trade (CBT)

Volume of Trading of 5-Year Treasury Note Futures in Chicago In Thousands of Contracts

Year	Jan.	Feb.	Mar.	Apr.	May	June	July	Aug.	Sept.	Oct.	Nov.	Dec.	Total
1988					20.6	56.5	45.6	66.4	73.8	54.8	97.1	91.8	243.7
1989	91.1	156.8	128.1	89.2	167.3	162.0	142.3	205.2	121.2	148.3	253.4	116.9	518.6
1990	184.5	277.5	164.9	107.6	266.6	140.8	131.6	320.4	189.0	197.9	305.7	40.8	544.4
1991	220.5	318.5	252.3	181.4	307.6	232.4	179.7	385.4	243.9	291.5	419.9	353.1	1,064.5
1992	498.6	543.8	560.0	322.2	590.1	551.5	484.2	565.7	582.1	539.0	640.8	563.2	1,743.0
1993	539.5	673.1	886.0	447.6	755.9	753.8	506.4	711.3	753.8	472.6	908.0	715.8	2,096.4
1994	695.9	1,235.1	1,295.4	917.1	1,202.0	1,154.9	834.8	944.9	1,107.3	840.6	1,156.7	1,078.0	12,463.0
1995	988.5	1,296.2	1,386.9	783.4	1,291.1	1,402.9	828.6	1,100.5	1,008.7	769.6	996.0	784.7	12,637.1
1996	837.3	1,312.0	1,084.6	815.7	1,135.5	878.3	881.7	1,061.8	979.0	689.5	831.1	957.1	11,463.4
1997	927.5	1,156.7	1,271.1	984.4	1,190.6	1,143.8	761.4	1,244.6	1,243.7	1,314.1	1,068.1	1,182.8	13,488.7

Source: Chicago Board of Trade (CBT)

nited States Federal Funds Rate In Percent

ar	Jan.	Feb.	Mar.	Apr.	May	June	July	Aug.	Sept.	Oct.	Nov.	Dec.	Annual
988	6.83	6.58	6.58	6.87	7.09	7.51	7.76	8.01	8.19	8.30	8.35	8.76	7.57
989	9.12	9.36	9.85	9.84	9.81	9.53	9.24	8.99	9.02	8.84	8.55	8.45	9.22
990	8.23	8.24	8.28	8.26	8.18	8.29	8.15	8.13	8.20	8.11	7.81	7.31	8.10
991	6.91	6.25	6.12	5.91	5.78	5.90	5.82	5.66	5.45	5.21	4.81	4.43	5.69
992	4.03	4.06	3.98	3.73	3.82	3.76	3.25	3.30	3.22	3.10	3.09	2.92	3.52
993	3.02	3.03	3.07	2.96	3.00	3.04	3.06	3.03	3.09	2.99	3.02	2.96	3.02
994	3.05	3.25	3.34	3.56	4.01	4.25	4.26	4.47	4.73	4.76	5.29	5.45	4.20
995	5.53	5.92	5.98	6.05	6.01	6.00	5.85	5.74	5.80	5.76	5.80	5.60	5.84
996	5.56	5.22	5.31	5.22	5.56	5.27	5.40	5.22	5.30	5.24	5.31	5.29	5.30
997	5.25	5.19	5.39	5.51	5.50	5.56	5.52	5.54	5.54	5.50	5.52	5.50	5.46

Source: Bureau of Economic Analysis (BEA), U.S. Department of Commerce

nited States Municipal Bond Yield[1] In Percent

ear	Jan.	Feb.	Mar.	Apr.	May	June	July	Aug.	Sept.	Oct.	Nov.	Dec.	Annual
988	7.70	7.49	7.74	7.81	7.90	7.78	7.76	7.79	7.66	7.47	7.46	7.61	7.68
989	7.35	7.44	7.59	7.49	7.25	7.02	6.96	7.06	7.26	7.22	7.14	6.98	7.23
990	7.10	7.22	7.29	7.39	7.35	7.24	7.19	7.32	7.53	7.49	7.18	7.09	7.28
991	7.08	6.91	7.10	7.02	6.95	7.13	7.05	6.90	6.80	6.68	6.73	6.69	6.92
992	6.54	6.74	6.76	6.67	6.57	6.49	6.13	6.16	6.25	6.41	6.36	6.22	6.44
993	6.16	5.86	5.85	5.76	5.73	5.63	5.57	5.45	5.29	5.25	5.47	5.35	5.61
994	5.31	5.40	5.91	6.23	6.19	6.11	6.23	6.21	6.28	6.52	6.97	6.80	6.18
995	6.53	6.22	6.10	6.02	5.95	5.84	5.92	6.06	5.91	5.80	5.64	5.45	5.95
996	5.43	5.43	5.79	5.94	5.98	6.02	5.92	5.76	5.87	5.72	5.59	5.64	5.76
997	5.72	5.63	5.76	5.88	5.70	5.53	5.35	5.41	5.39	5.38	5.33	5.19	5.52

[1] 20-bond average. *Source: Bureau of Economic Analysis (BEA), U.S. Department of Commerce*

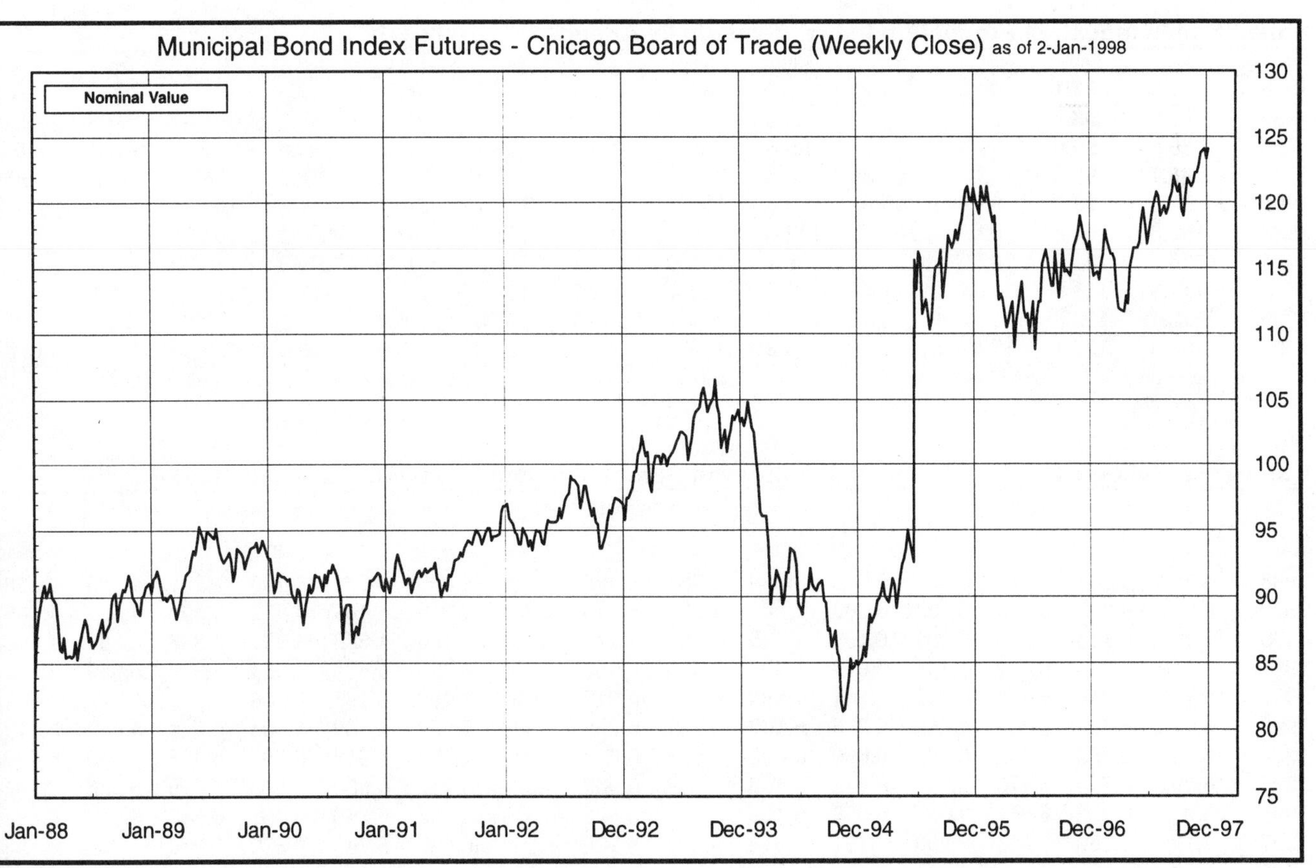

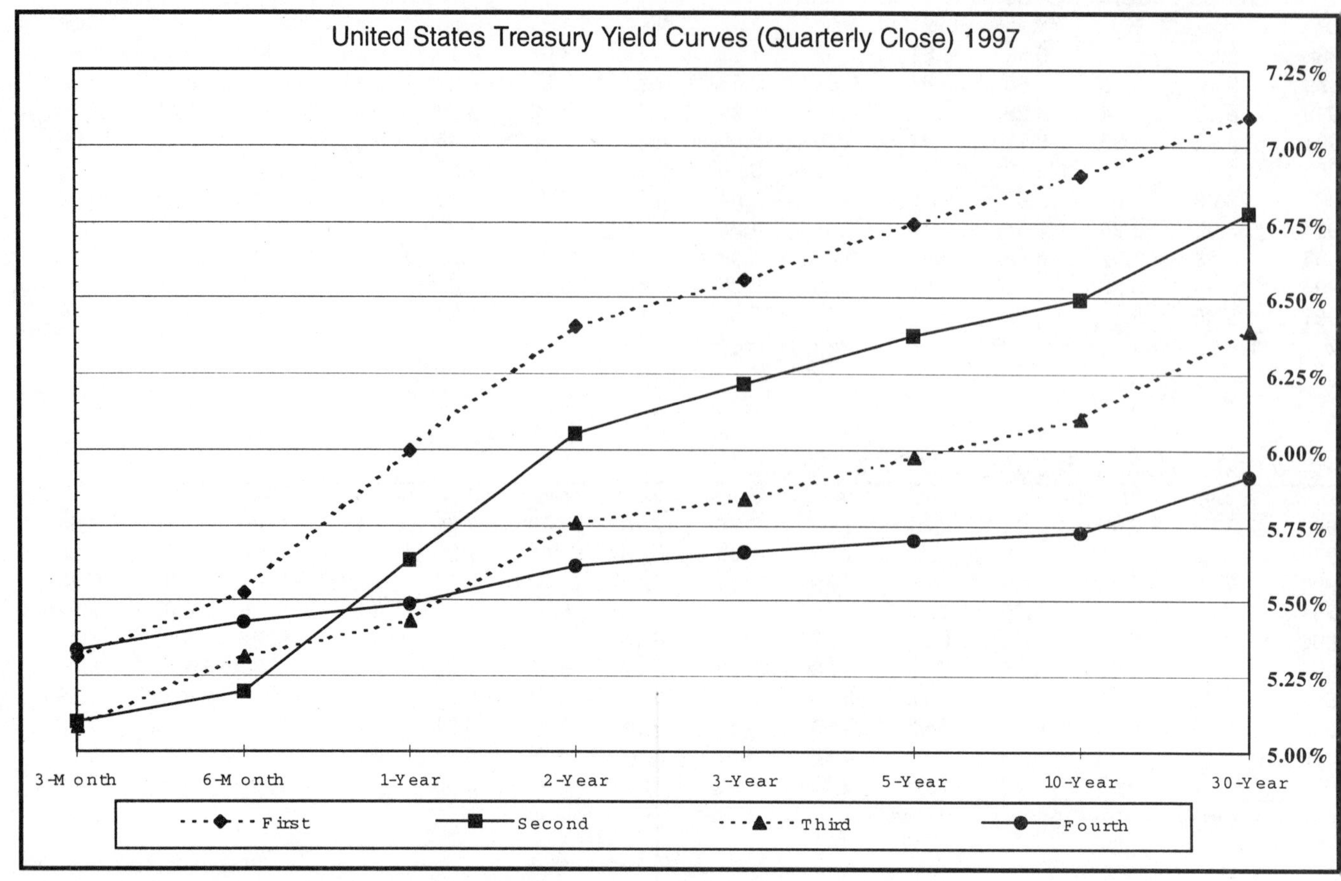

United States Industrial Production Index[1] (Seasonally Adjusted) 1992 = 100

Year	Jan.	Feb.	Mar.	Apr.	May	June	July	Aug.	Sept.	Oct.	Nov.	Dec.	Average
1988	95.8	96.1	96.2	96.7	96.8	96.8	97.4	98.0	97.6	97.9	98.6	99.1	97.3
1989	99.7	98.9	99.8	100.1	99.5	99.3	98.3	98.7	98.5	98.1	98.5	98.9	99.0
1990	98.5	99.0	99.4	98.9	99.3	99.3	99.2	99.4	99.5	99.0	97.7	97.1	98.9
1991	96.7	95.9	95.0	95.3	96.0	97.2	97.2	97.4	98.3	98.2	98.1	97.4	96.9
1992	97.5	98.1	98.9	99.6	100.0	99.7	100.4	100.1	100.5	101.3	101.9	101.9	100.0
1993	102.3	102.8	102.8	103.2	102.6	102.8	103.1	102.8	103.9	104.1	104.6	105.4	103.4
1994	105.7	106.2	107.0	107.4	108.1	108.6	109.1	109.2	109.3	109.9	110.6	111.6	108.6
1995	111.9	111.6	111.7	111.4	111.5	111.7	111.7	112.6	113.0	112.5	112.7	112.8	114.5
1996	112.4	113.8	113.2	114.3	114.8	115.5	115.5	115.8	116.0	116.2	120.6	120.9	118.5
1997[2]	121.3	122.1	122.5	123.1	123.3	123.5	124.5	125.2	125.6	126.5	127.5	128.1	124.4

[1] Total Index of the Federal Reserve Index of Quantity Output. [2] Preliminary. *Source: Bureau of Economic Analysis, U.S. Department of Commerce*

U.S. Gross National Product, National Income, and Personal Income In Billions of Current Dollars[1]

	Gross Domestic Product					National Income					Personal Income				
Year	I	II	III	IV	Annual Average	I	II	III	IV	Annual Average	I	II	III	IV	Annual Average
1988	5,783	5,842	5,877	5,951	5,863	3,889	3,966	4,028	4,128	4,003	4,064	4,135	4,207	4,285	4,173
1989	6,009	6,053	6,086	6,093	6,060	4,203	4,231	4,245	4,301	4,245	4,409	4,472	4,502	4,574	4,489
1990	6,154	6,174	6,145	6,081	6,139	4,396	4,461	4,475	4,507	4,460	4,689	4,772	4,838	4,868	4,792
1991	6,048	6,074	6,089	6,104	6,079	4,493	4,529	4,555	4,599	4,720	4,885	4,951	4,979	5,059	4,969
1992	6,175	6,214	6,261	6,327	6,244	4,889	4,941	4,912	5,103	4,990	5,161	5,236	5,233	5,429	5,277
1993	6,326	6,357	6,393	6,469	6,386	5,160	5,237	5,282	5,389	5,267	5,369	5,504	5,544	5,659	5,519
1994	6,509	6,588	6,645	6,694	6,609	5,423	5,556	5,636	5,747	5,591	5,616	5,767	5,838	5,946	5,792
1995	6,701	6,714	6,776	6,781	6,742	5,808	5,862	5,953	6,026	5,912	6,053	6,115	6,179	6,256	6,151
1996	6,814	6,892	6,944	7,017	6,928	6,109	6,229	6,303	6,377	6,255	6,359	6,461	6,542	6,618	6,495
1997[2]	7,102	7,160	7,214	7,290	7,191	6,510	6,599	6,700		6,603	6,746	6,829	6,910		6,828

[1] Seasonally adjusted at annual rates. [2] Preliminary *Source: Bureau of Economic Analysis, U.S. Department of Commerce (BEA)*

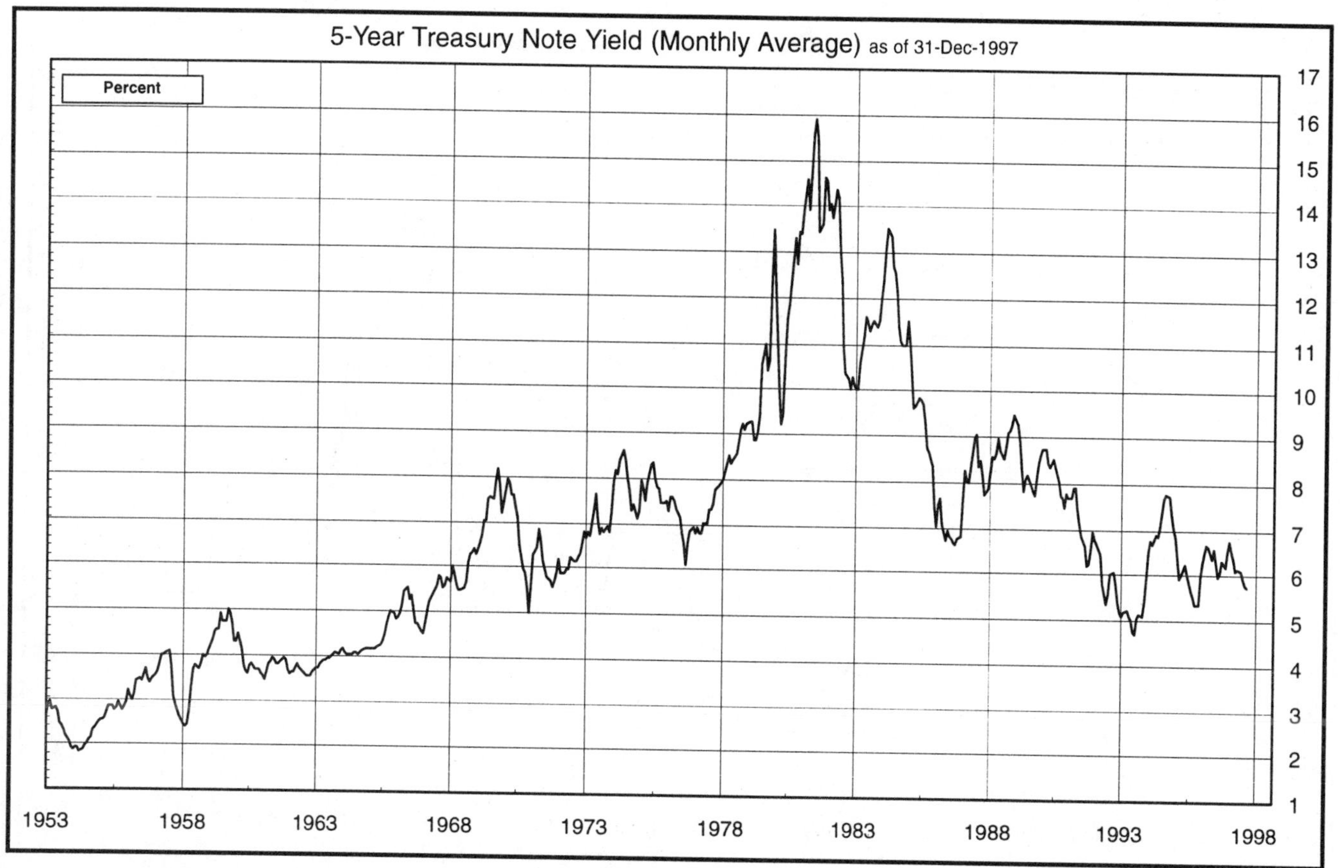

United States Money Supply M1[2] In Billions of Dollars

Year	Jan.	Feb.	Mar.	Apr.	May	June	July	Aug.	Sept.	Oct.	Nov.	Dec.	Average
1988	757.1	757.8	761.4	768.6	771.9	778.5	782.7	783.3	783.5	784.4	785.1	787.0	775.1
1989	786.0	784.2	782.9	780.1	774.9	773.4	778.7	779.3	781.6	787.0	788.1	794.2	782.5
1990	795.3	798.2	801.7	806.3	804.6	810.3	810.4	816.0	821.6	819.8	822.0	825.8	811.0
1991	826.7	832.8	839.8	842.5	849.1	858.6	861.3	867.2	870.6	877.5	888.6	897.3	859.3
1992	910.0	926.2	936.8	944.3	952.4	954.2	963.2	975.4	988.2	1,003.9	1,016.7	1,025.0	966.4
1993	1,032.0	1,034.0	1,038.4	1,047.8	1,067.5	1,075.4	1,084.7	1,094.5	1,104.2	1,114.3	1,123.6	1,129.8	1,078.9
1994	1,132.8	1,137.3	1,140.1	1,142.4	1,143.5	1,144.7	1,150.9	1,149.7	1,150.8	1,150.4	1,150.4	1,150.7	1,145.3
1995	1,150.3	1,148.4	1,147.1	1,150.4	1,145.1	1,142.7	1,145.0	1,144.0	1,141.6	1,135.7	1,133.1	1,129.0	1,142.7
1996	1,122.2	1,119.8	1,126.2	1,123.5	1,117.1	1,115.5	1,108.8	1,099.8	1,093.3	1,080.3	1,080.1	1,081.1	1,105.7
1997[1]	1,079.7	1,080.7	1,075.4	1,065.3	1,062.8	1,063.1	1,062.1	1,069.6	1,060.8	1,057.4	1,064.0	1,068.7	1,067.5

[1] Preliminary. [2] M1--This measure is currency, travelers checks, plus demand deposits at commercial banks and interest-earning checkable deposits at all depository institutions. *Source: Bureau of Economic Analysis, U.S. Department of Commerce (BEA)*

United States Money Supply M2[2] In Billions of Dollars

Year	Jan.	Feb.	Mar.	Apr.	May	June	July	Aug.	Sept.	Oct.	Nov.	Dec.	Average
1988	2,855.3	2,877.5	2,897.4	2,918.3	2,933.0	2,945.2	2,955.9	2,959.6	2,964.6	2,974.7	2,988.6	2,996.3	2,938.9
1989	2,999.8	3,000.4	3,007.2	3,014.3	3,019.1	3,034.8	3,060.2	3,081.5	3,100.8	3,122.5	3,141.1	3,160.9	3,061.9
1990	3,173.1	3,185.3	3,196.9	3,209.3	3,207.0	3,221.0	3,230.2	3,248.4	3,262.3	3,265.3	3,269.6	3,279.5	3,229.0
1991	3,293.4	3,311.1	3,329.4	3,337.9	3,348.0	3,359.1	3,361.0	3,360.5	3,360.0	3,363.9	3,372.5	3,379.6	3,348.0
1992	3,387.7	3,407.1	3,410.5	3,408.8	3,407.4	3,401.3	3,402.2	3,408.9	3,418.2	3,432.0	3,435.3	3,434.0	3,412.8
1993	3,431.3	3,424.0	3,420.4	3,423.6	3,447.6	3,452.9	3,452.7	3,456.8	3,463.6	3,469.7	3,480.2	3,486.6	3,450.8
1994	3,490.8	3,491.7	3,494.3	3,503.0	3,504.0	3,493.7	3,502.1	3,498.2	3,498.4	3,499.4	3,500.9	3,502.1	3,498.2
1995	3,506.3	3,506.1	3,506.7	3,519.1	3,534.9	3,562.9	3,583.1	3,604.4	3,620.1	3,629.8	3,639.3	3,655.0	3,572.3
1996	3,669.9	3,685.0	3,713.9	3,724.5	3,725.6	3,741.9	3,750.0	3,762.7	3,775.3	3,788.1	2,798.3	3,819.3	3,745.1
1997[1]	3,836.9	3,852.3	3,867.9	3,885.7	3,883.3	3,896.8	3,907.1	3,941.3	3,959.8	3,975.0	3,997.8	4,020.7	3,918.7

[1] Preliminary. [2] M2--This measure adds to M1 overnight repurchase agreements (RPs) issued by commercial banks and certain overnight Eurodollars (those issued by Caribbean branches of member banks) held by U.S. nonbank residents, general purpose and broker/dealer money market mutual shares (MMMF), and savings and small-denomination time deposits. *Source: Bureau of Economic Analysis, U.S. Department of Commerce (BEA)*

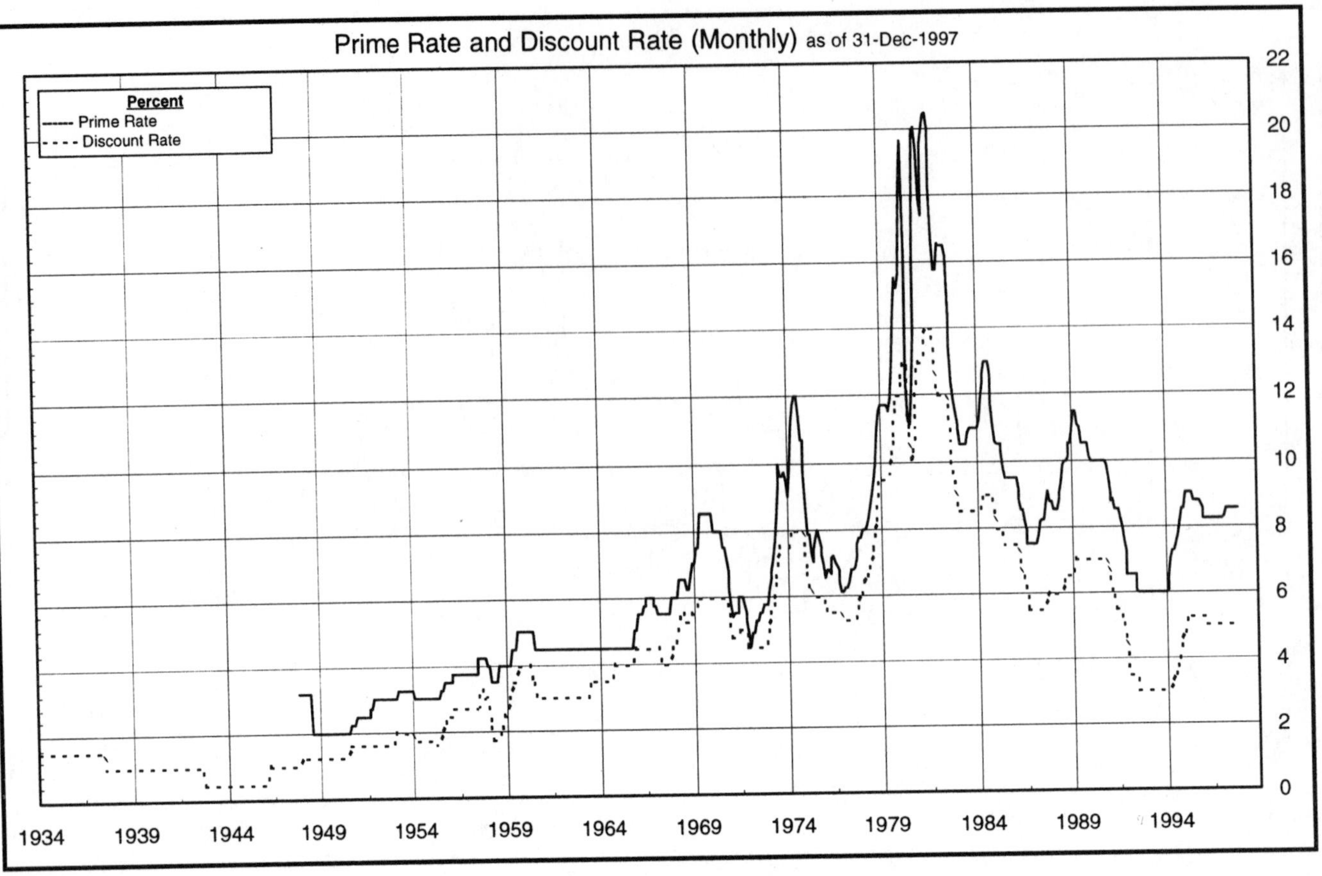

INTEREST RATES

Prime Rate and Discount Rate (Monthly) as of 31-Dec-1997

Percent
Prime Rate
Discount Rate

0 2 4 6 8 10 12 14 16 18 20 22

1934 1939 1944 1949 1954 1959 1964 1969 1974 1979 1984 1989 1994

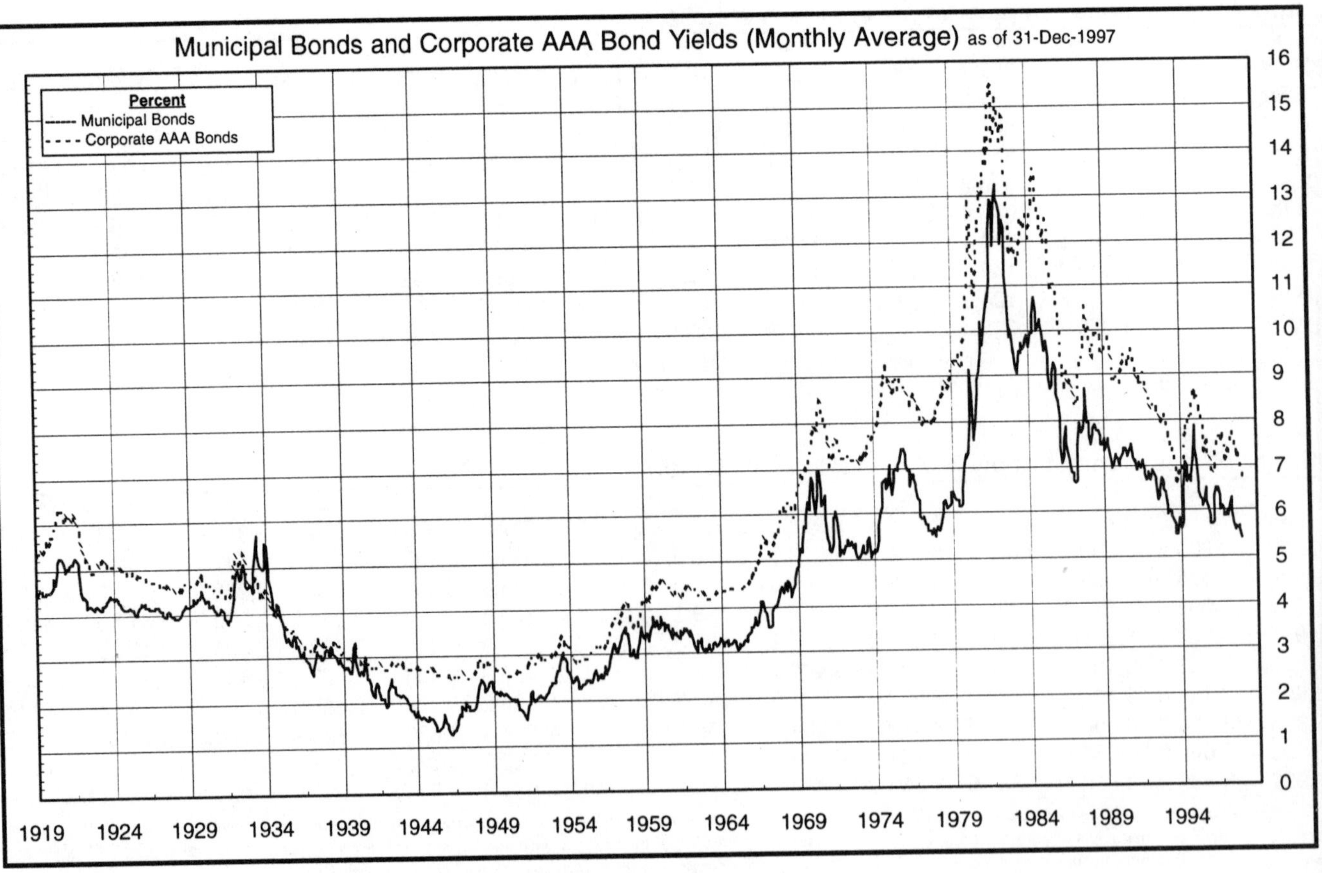

Municipal Bonds and Corporate AAA Bond Yields (Monthly Average) as of 31-Dec-1997

Percent
Municipal Bonds
Corporate AAA Bonds

0 1 2 3 4 5 6 7 8 9 10 11 12 13 14 15 16

1919 1924 1929 1934 1939 1944 1949 1954 1959 1964 1969 1974 1979 1984 1989 1994

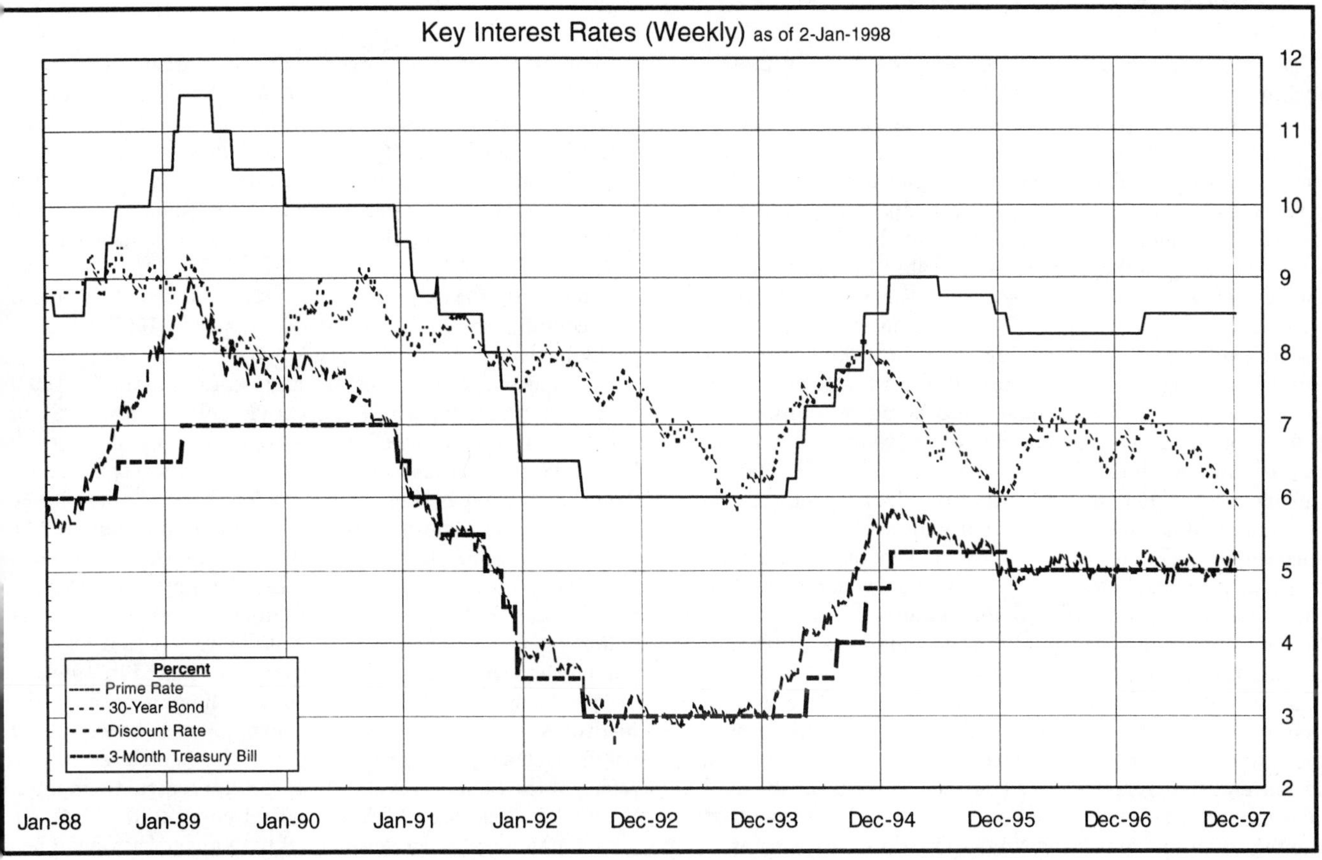

Key Interest Rates (Weekly) as of 2-Jan-1998
Percent
Prime Rate
30-Year Bond
Discount Rate
3-Month Treasury Bill
12
11
10
9
8
7
6
5
4
3
2
Jan-88
Jan-89
Jan-90
Jan-91
Jan-92
Dec-92
Dec-93
Dec-94
Dec-95
Dec-96
Dec-97

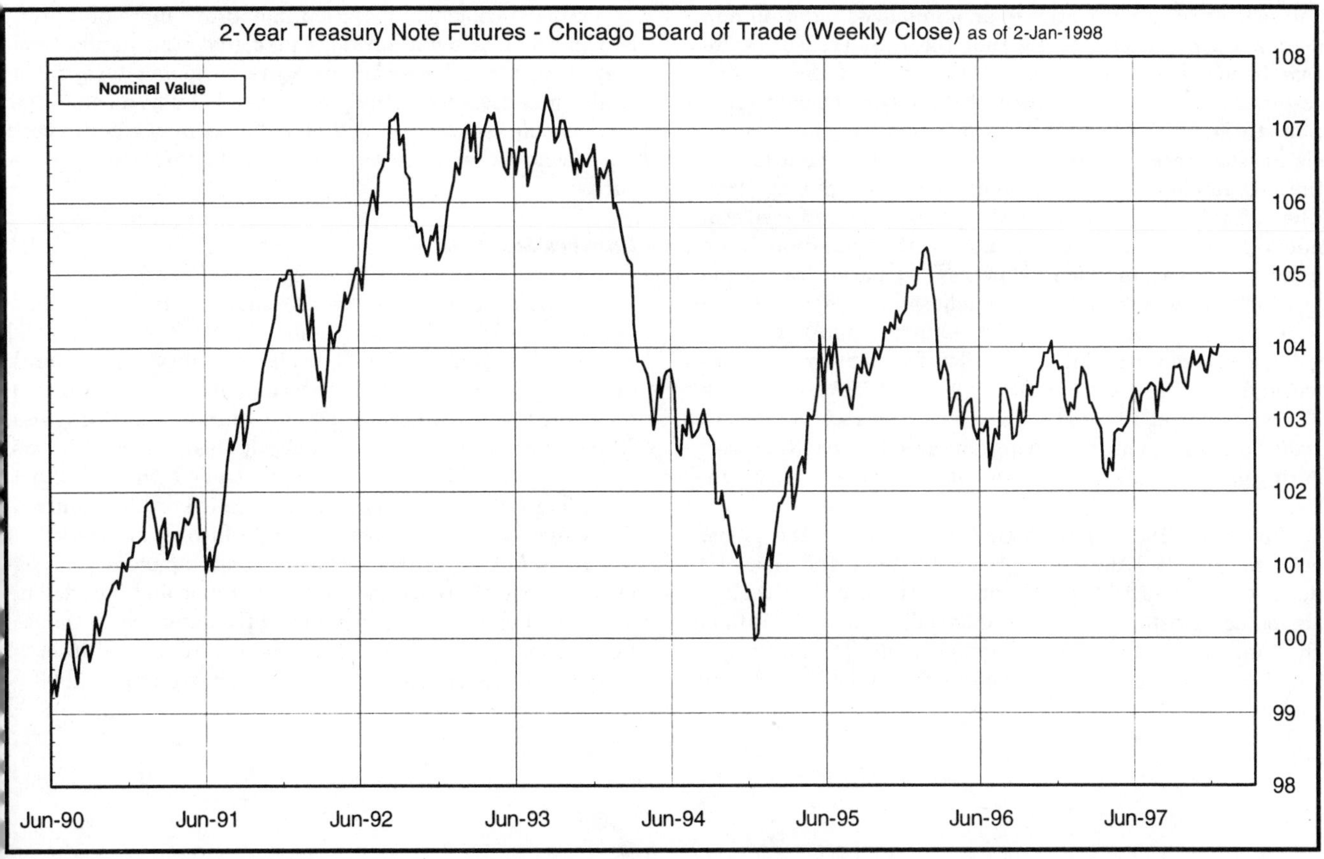

2-Year Treasury Note Futures - Chicago Board of Trade (Weekly Close) as of 2-Jan-1998
Nominal Value
108
107
106
105
104
103
102
101
100
99
98
Jun-90
Jun-91
Jun-92
Jun-93
Jun-94
Jun-95
Jun-96
Jun-97

Interest Rates, Worldwide

Central bank monetary policies were generally muted during 1997; the U.S. Federal Reserve officially changed short term rates only once during the year: a 25 basis point increase in March. In Europe, Germany's Bundesbank in a surprise move lifted the securities repurchase rate to 3.3 percent from 3.0 percent in October, an action that was viewed as symbolic rather than any real shift in policy, but it was quickly followed by small rate increases across Europe. However, in absolute terms, the yield on longer term German obligations declined in line with the downward trend in global yields. The rational for the Bundesbank tightening was more of a reminder that once the single euro-currency comes into being on January 1, 1999, as many as eleven countries will have to accept a one-size-fits-all monetary policy set by an independent European central bank based in Frankfurt. In effect, the countries will no longer be able to use interest rates to influence the performance of their national economies or implement any major independent fiscal policy changes. The Bundesbank's action, while defended as a check on inflation, was really designed to stiffen the will of the future central bank to uphold a strong euro.

At the start of 1997, a sense of optimism seemed to have taken root that the world economies were in a real growth mode and basically free of inflationary pressures. Ironically, at yearend the greater concern seemed to focus on the dangers of world deflation. What was clearly evident was that the big inflationary based swings in world interest rates in the 1970' and 1980's dissipated in the mid-1990's. Indeed, in the U.S. at yearend, long term rates under 6.0 percent were still seen as too high relative to an annualized inflation rate near 2.0 percent, suggesting that the U.S. Treasury's 30-year bond yield could slide to 5.0 percent in 1998, if one assumes that a real net return of three percent over inflation still holds true. In the U.S., inflation has fallen to levels unseen since the mid-1960's which would seem to give the Fed ample room to ease short term rates during 1998. The question is whether they will, as deflation can seed economic problems, perhaps even more so than inflation. Since interest rates cannot fall below zero, deflation raises the possibility of high real, i.e., price adjusted, interest rates.

On a world basis, the OECD estimates that the aggregate general government fiscal deficit for member countries will fall to 1.7 percent of GDP by yearend 1998, vs. a peak of 4.3 percent in 1993. The lower debt levels should lead to reduced government borrowing and freed-up capital, pressuring governments to ease fiscal, if not also monetary, policies.

Moreover, 1997 highlighted the threads of the global economy in the wake of the Asian currency and financial debacle which spread quickly around the world. Although the panic was stopped in the industrialized nations, it took the concerted damage control action of the IMF and major western banks to cool fears before they took root in the economies of the emerging nations. It's estimated that it will take at least a year or two before Asia's problems are resolved. Still, the Asian shock undermined the economic outlook for many countries who will face increased trade competition because of Asian devaluations, forcing central banks, like those of Australia and New Zealand, to lower interest rates so that their countries can remain competitive.

South America could be the next troublespot although the economic backdrop for most countries in 1997 was generally healthier than a few years ago.

Japanese interest rates are almost an enigma for 1998: long-term yields fell a full percentage point in mid-1997 in the wake of a tax induced plunge in spending, but domestic bondholders continued to buy the obligations despite a sub-2.0 percent yield as there was more fear of foreign exchange losses if higher yielding foreign bonds were purchased. The scenario puts the Bank of Japan in an almost no-win position: if Japanese rates are lifted the economy is apt to stagnate further, but any easing could further weaken the yen's value. Japan's economic growth rate in 1997 was under one percent and not much improvement is expected in 1998.

In Europe, the U.K. stands out as having perhaps the healthiest economy, whereas any expansion is barely under way in Germany and France.The U.K. is ahead of Europe in terms of the business cycle and corporate restructuring, but if the U.K. joins the EMU on the first go-around, U.K. bond yields may have to converge quickly to lower European levels, suggesting that the U.K. may opt to remain outside the EMU for the time being.

On balance, global deflation may prove more of a problem in 1998. If deflation does take root, the implications may favor more downward pressure on longer term rates, while the front-end of the yield curve is buoyed somewhat by uncertainties as to how central banks may react to curb any economic slowing associated with deflationary pressures.

Futures Markets

A number of actively traded interest rate futures markets exist worldwide. The London International Financial Futures Exchange (LIFFE) trades contracts on 3-month Sterling prices and British government bonds, called long gilts. LIFFE also offers futures on Euromarks, Euroswiss, Italian government bonds and German government bonds, called bunds. The latter is also traded in Frankfurt. Canadian Bankers Acceptances are traded on the Montreal Exchange. Notional bond and PIBOR futures are traded on the Paris MATIF. Euroyen futures and Japanese yen government bonds are traded in Tokyo. Libor and eurodollars are traded on Chicago's Mercantile Exchange, with the latter also on the Mid-America Exchange. Additional interest rate futures contracts are likely to begin trading in 1998.

Long Gilt Futures - London International Financial Futures Exchange (Weekly Close) as of 2-Jan-1998

Nominal Value

124 120 116 112 108 104 100 96 92 88 84 80 76

Jan-88 Jan-89 Jan-90 Jan-91 Jan-92 Dec-92 Dec-93 Dec-94 Dec-95 Dec-96 Dec-97

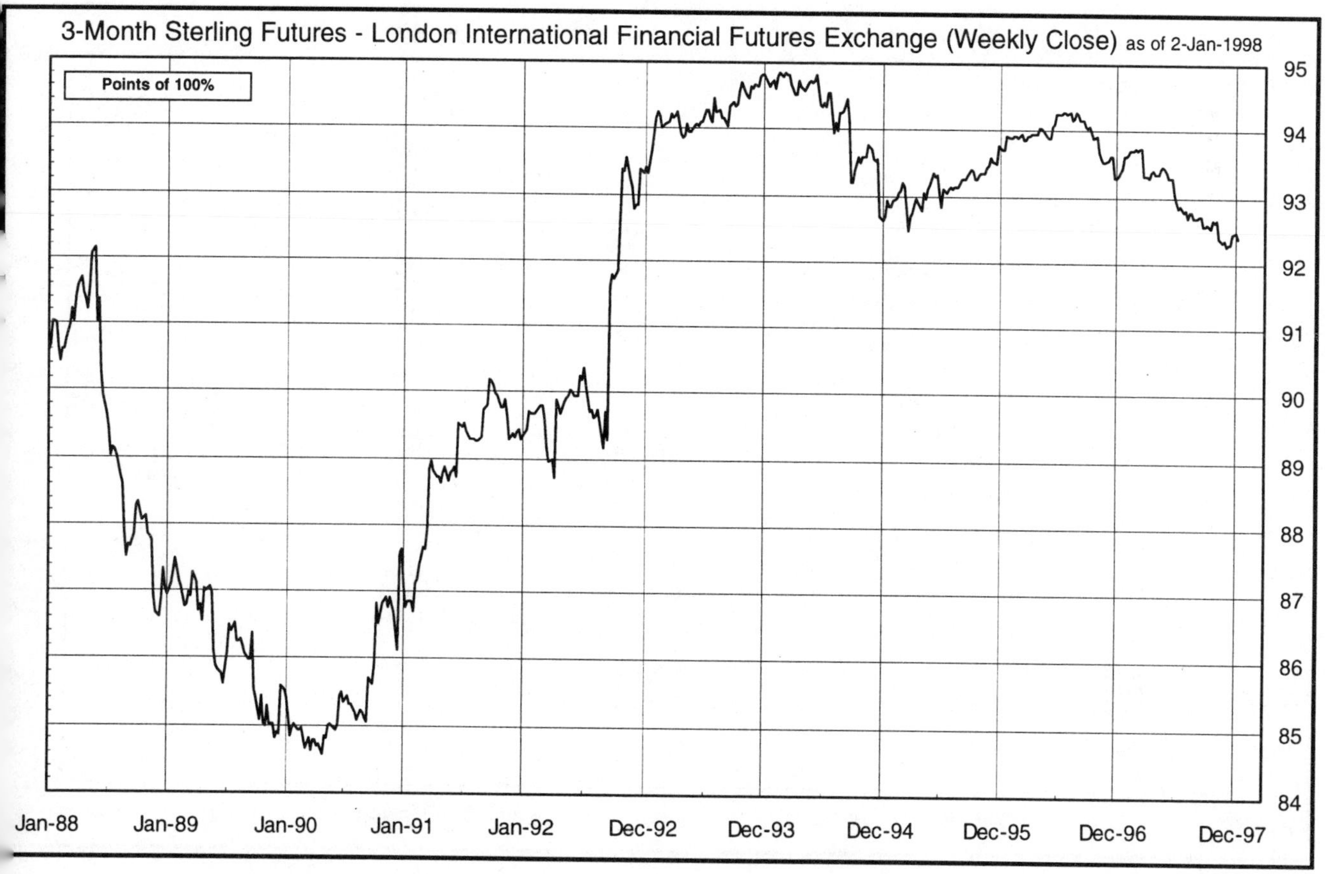

3-Month Sterling Futures - London International Financial Futures Exchange (Weekly Close) as of 2-Jan-1998

Points of 100%

95 94 93 92 91 90 89 88 87 86 85 84

Jan-88 Jan-89 Jan-90 Jan-91 Jan-92 Dec-92 Dec-93 Dec-94 Dec-95 Dec-96 Dec-97

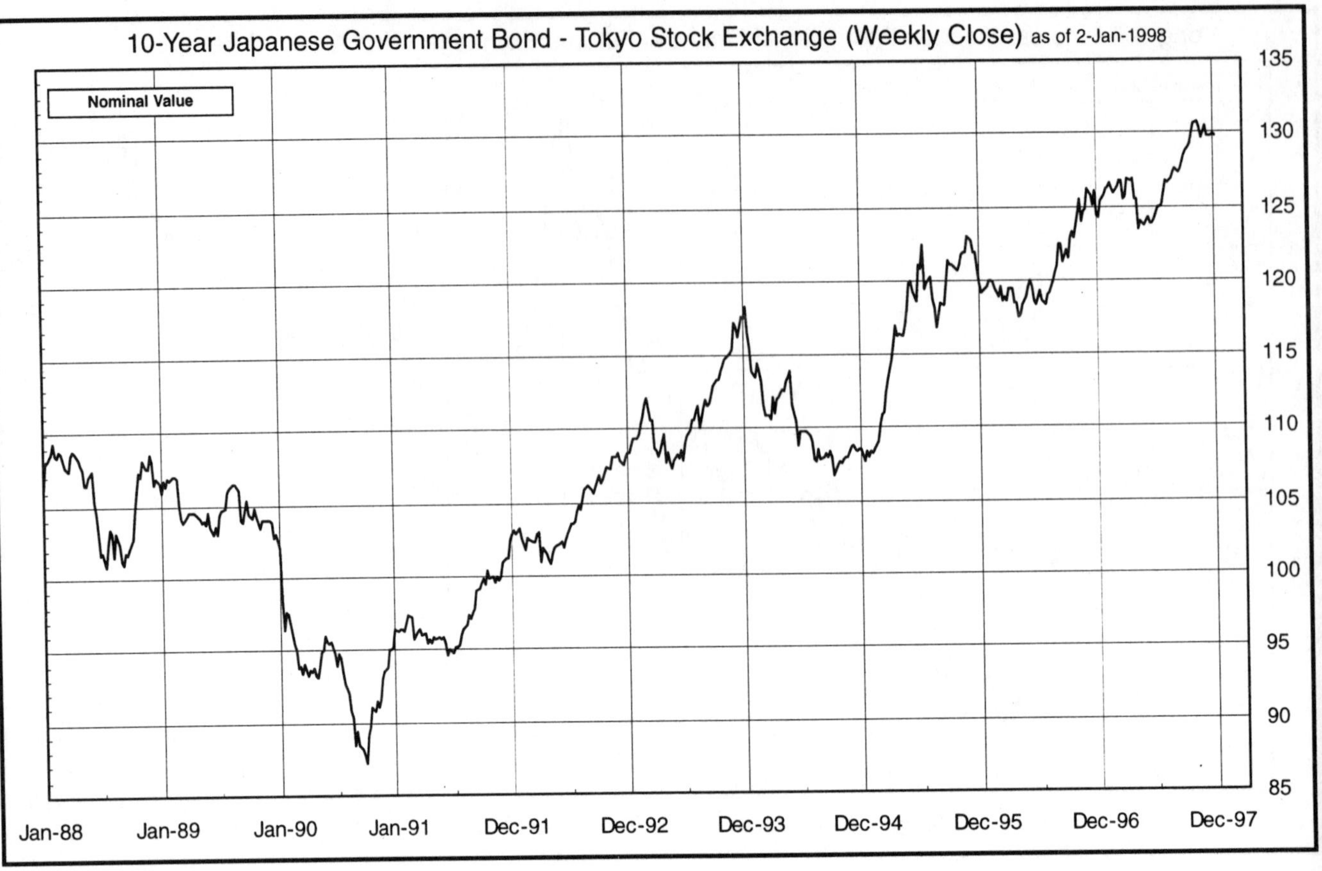

10-Year Japanese Government Bond - Tokyo Stock Exchange (Weekly Close) as of 2-Jan-1998

Nominal Value

135 130 125 120 115 110 105 100 95 90 85

Jan-88 Jan-89 Jan-90 Jan-91 Dec-91 Dec-92 Dec-93 Dec-94 Dec-95 Dec-96 Dec-97

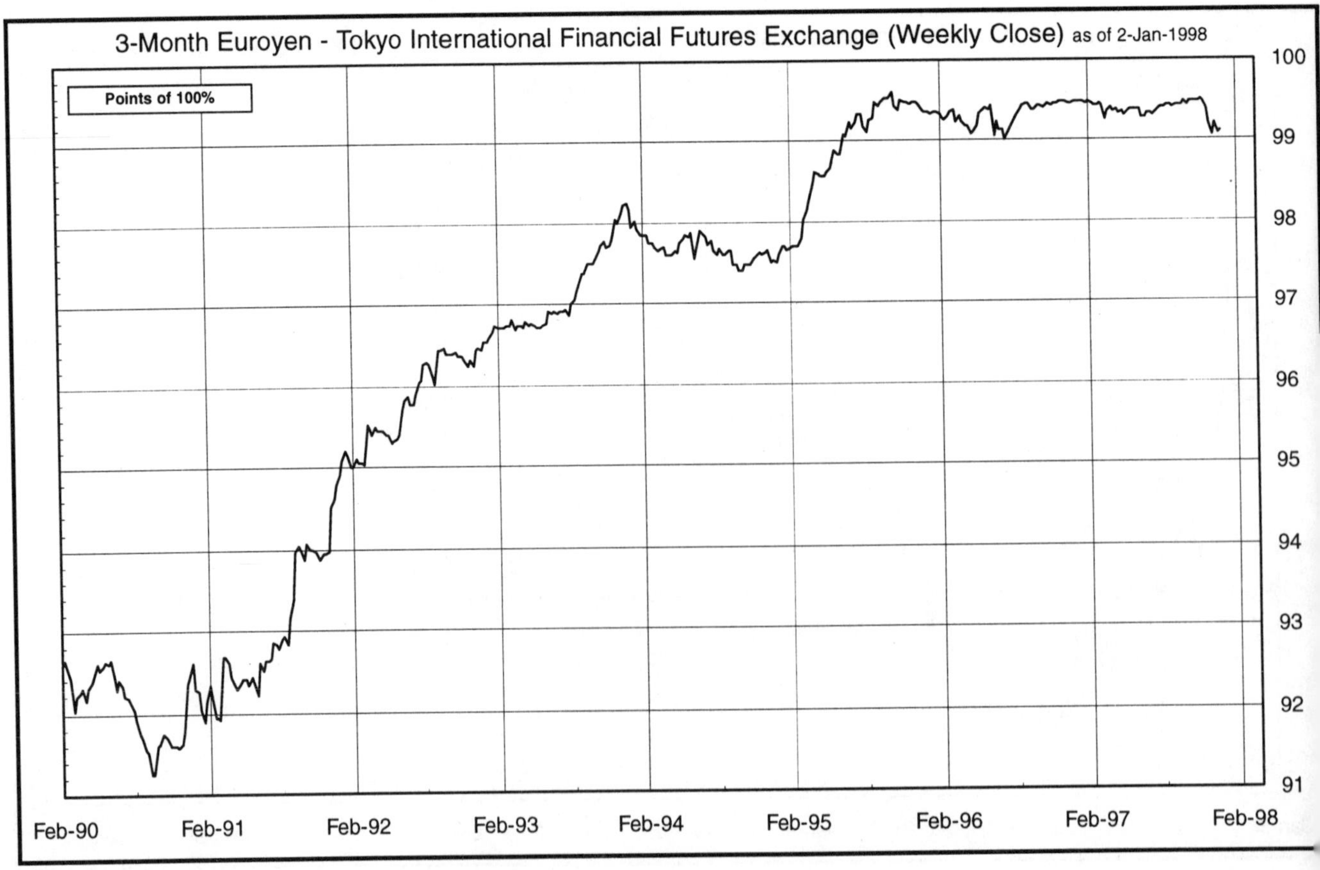

3-Month Euroyen - Tokyo International Financial Futures Exchange (Weekly Close) as of 2-Jan-1998

Points of 100%

100 99 98 97 96 95 94 93 92 91

Feb-90 Feb-91 Feb-92 Feb-93 Feb-94 Feb-95 Feb-96 Feb-97 Feb-98

3-Month Euromark - London International Financial Futures Exchange (Weekly Close) as of 2-Jan-1998

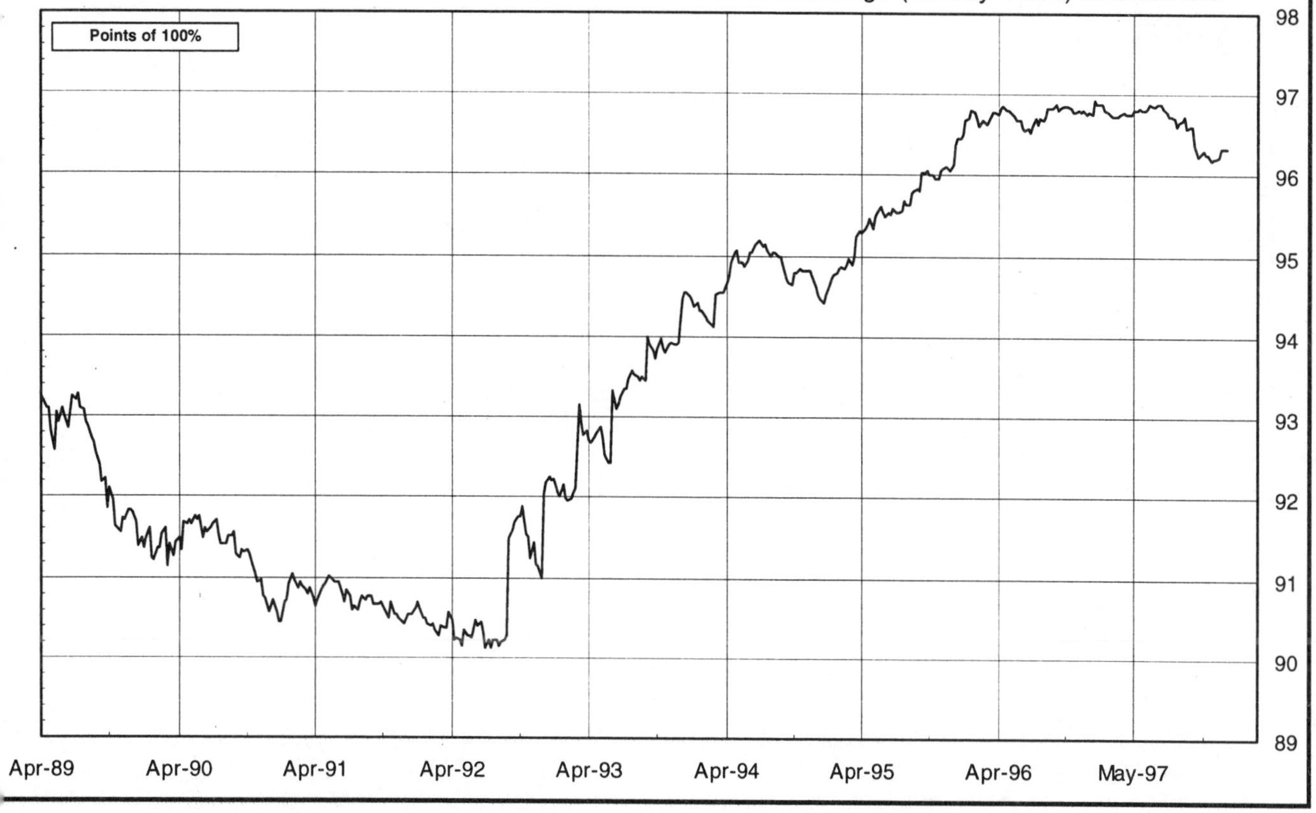

German Bond (Bund) - London International Financial Futures Exchange (Weekly Close) as of 2-Jan-1998

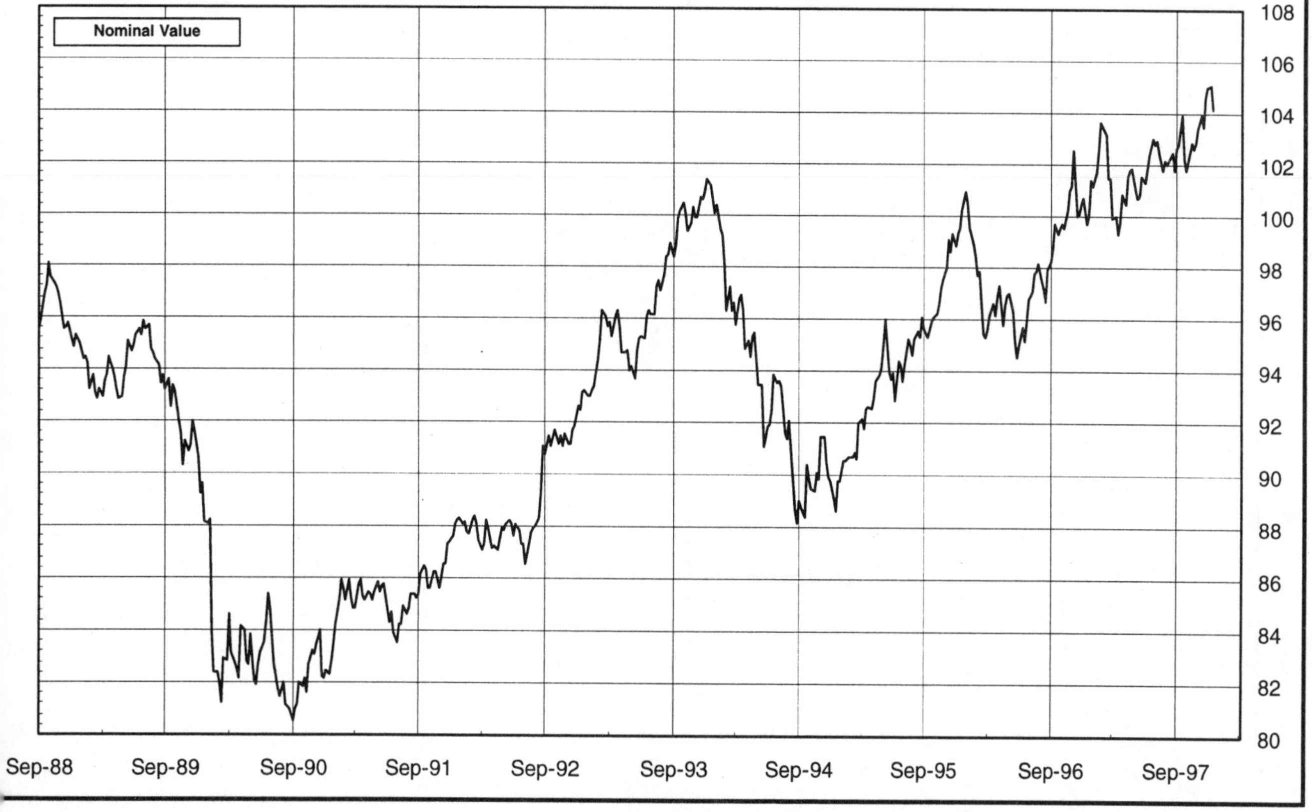

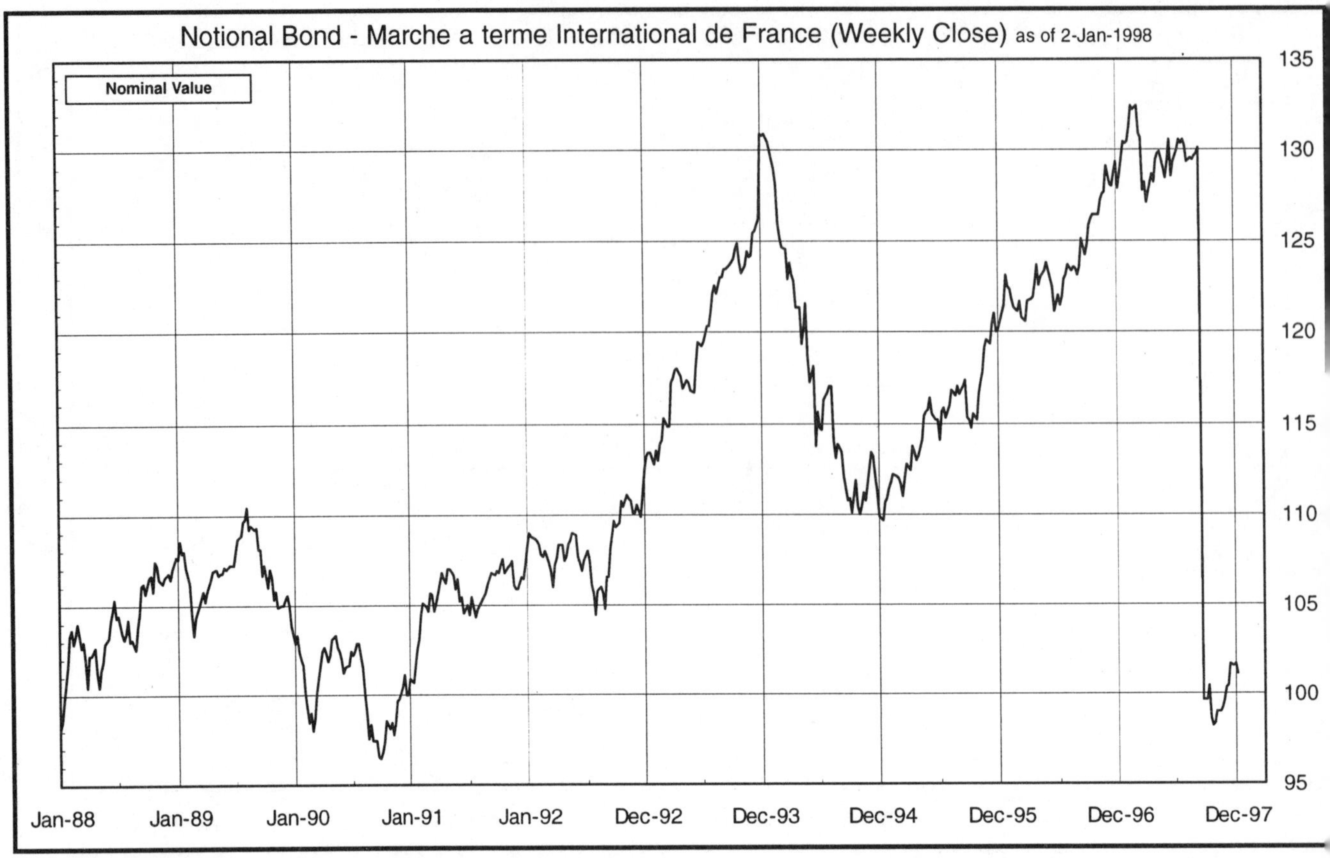

INTEREST RATES, WORLDWIDE

Notional Bond - Marche a terme International de France (Weekly Close) as of 2-Jan-1998

Nominal Value

135 130 125 120 115 110 105 100 95

Jan-88 Jan-89 Jan-90 Jan-91 Jan-92 Dec-92 Dec-93 Dec-94 Dec-95 Dec-96 Dec-97

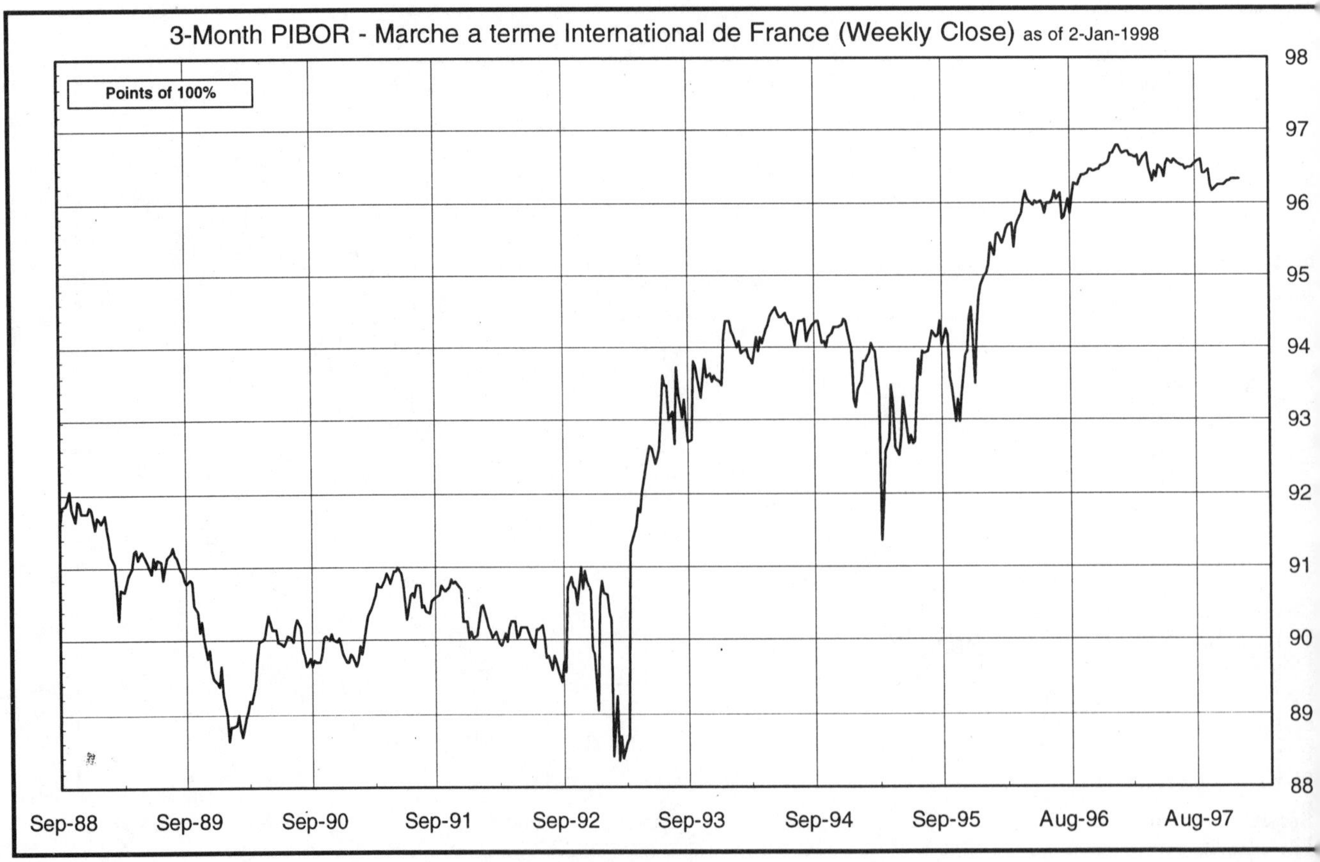

3-Month PIBOR - Marche a terme International de France (Weekly Close) as of 2-Jan-1998

Points of 100%

98 97 96 95 94 93 92 91 90 89 88

Sep-88 Sep-89 Sep-90 Sep-91 Sep-92 Sep-93 Sep-94 Sep-95 Aug-96 Aug-97

Japan--Economic Statistics Percentage Change from Previous Period

Year	Real GDP	Nominal GDP	Real Private Consumption	Real Public Consumption	Grossed Fixed Investment	Real Total Domestic Demand	Real Exports of Goods & Services	Real Imports of Goods & Services	Consumer Prices[1]	Unemployment Rate
1989	4.8	7.0	4.8	2.0	8.2	5.6	9.1	18.6	2.3	2.3
1990	5.1	7.5	4.4	1.5	8.5	5.2	6.9	7.9	3.1	2.1
1991	3.8	6.6	2.5	2.0	3.3	2.9	5.2	-3.1	3.3	2.1
1992	1.0	2.8	2.1	2.0	-1.5	.4	5.0	-.7	1.7	2.2
1993	.3	.9	1.2	2.4	-2.0	.1	1.3	-.3	1.2	2.5
1994	.6	.8	1.9	2.4	-.8	1.0	4.6	8.9	.7	2.9
1995	1.4	.8	2.0	3.5	1.1	2.2	5.4	14.3	-.1	3.1
1996	3.5	3.6	2.8	2.3	8.7	4.5	2.3	10.5	.1	3.4
1997[2]	.5	1.6	1.4	.8	-4.2	-.5	10.4	2.2	NA	3.4
1998[2]	1.7	2.5	1.7	-.2	1.5	1.5	8.2	6.8	NA	3.4

[1] National accounts implicit private consumption deflator. [2] Forecast. *Source: Organization for Economic Co-operation and Development (OECD)*

United Kingdom--Economic Statistics Percentage Change from Previous Period

Year	Real GDP	Nominal GDP	Real Private Consumption	Real Public Consumption	Grossed Fixed Investment	Real Total Domestic Demand	Real Exports of Goods & Services	Real Imports of Goods & Services	Consumer Prices[1]	Unemployment Rate
1989	2.2	9.4	3.2	1.4	6.0	2.9	4.7	7.4	7.8	6.1
1990	.4	6.8	.6	2.5	-3.5	-.6	5.0	.5	9.5	5.9
1991	-2.0	4.5	-2.2	2.6	-9.5	-3.1	-.7	-5.2	5.9	8.2
1992	-.5	4.0	-.1	-.1	-1.5	.2	4.4	6.9	3.7	10.2
1993	2.1	5.4	2.5	-.2	.6	2.0	3.5	3.0	1.6	10.3
1994	4.3	6.0	2.8	2.2	4.3	3.4	9.3	5.5	2.5	9.4
1995	2.7	5.2	1.7	1.3	1.5	1.8	7.8	4.2	3.4	8.6
1996	2.3	5.4	3.5	2.4	1.8	2.7	6.9	8.5	2.4	8.0
1997[2]	3.4	5.8	4.4	.7	4.3	3.7	6.4	7.4	NA	6.9
1998[2]	2.2	4.6	3.7	.8	5.5	3.4	3.9	7.9	NA	6.5

[1] National accounts implicit private consumption deflator. [2] Forecast. *Source: Organization for Economic Co-operation and Development (OECD)*

France--Economic Statistics Percentage Change from Previous Period

Year	Real GDP	Nominal GDP	Real Private Consumption	Real Public Consumption	Grossed Fixed Investment	Real Total Domestic Demand	Real Exports of Goods & Services	Real Imports of Goods & Services	Consumer Prices[1]	Unemployment Rate
1989	4.3	7.4	3.1	.5	7.9	3.9	10.2	8.1	3.6	9.4
1990	2.5	5.7	2.7	2.1	2.8	2.8	5.4	6.1	3.4	8.9
1991	.8	4.1	1.4	2.8	2.8	.6	4.1	3.0	3.2	9.4
1992	1.2	3.3	1.4	3.4	-2.8	.2	4.9	1.2	2.4	10.4
1993	-1.3	1.1	.2	3.4	-6.7	-2.2	-.4	-3.5	2.1	11.7
1994	2.8	4.4	1.4	1.1	1.3	3.0	6.0	6.7	1.7	12.2
1995	2.1	3.7	1.7	1.1	2.5	1.8	6.3	5.1	1.7	11.5
1996	1.5	2.8	2.1	1.4	-.5	1.0	4.7	2.8	2.0	12.3
1997[2]	2.3	3.3	.6	1.6	.6	.9	9.2	4.5	NA	12.4
1998[2]	2.9	4.3	2.2	1.0	3.2	2.3	7.5	6.0	NA	12.0

[1] National accounts implicit private consumption deflator. [2] Forecast. *Source: Organization for Economic Co-operation and Development (OECD)*

Germany[2]--Economic Statistics Percentage Change from Previous Period

Year	Real GDP	Nominal GDP	Real Private Consumption	Real Public Consumption	Grossed Fixed Investment	Real Total Domestic Demand	Real Exports of Goods & Services	Real Imports of Goods & Services	Consumer Prices[1]	Unemployment Rate
1989	3.6	6.1	2.8	-1.6	6.3	2.9	10.2	8.3	2.8	6.9
1990	5.7	9.1	5.4	2.2	8.5	5.2	11.0	10.3	2.7	6.2
1991	5.0	9.1	5.6	.5	6.0	4.8	12.3	12.8	3.6	6.7
1992	2.2	7.9	2.8	4.1	3.5	2.8	-.3	2.0	5.1	7.7
1993	-1.2	2.8	.1	-.5	-5.6	-1.4	-5.0	-5.9	4.5	8.8
1994	2.7	5.2	1.2	2.1	3.5	2.7	7.9	7.7	2.7	9.6
1995	1.8	3.9	1.9	2.2	.8	2.0	6.2	6.9	1.8	9.4
1996	1.4	2.4	1.3	1.8	-1.2	.8	4.5	2.2	1.5	10.3
1997[3]	2.4	3.3	.9	.8	.8	1.3	10.4	6.4	NA	11.4
1998[3]	3.0	4.3	1.9	1.3	3.2	2.3	9.1	6.7	NA	11.4

[1] National accounts implicit private consumption deflator. [2] Data are for Western Germany only, except for foreign trade statistics. [3] Forecast.
Source: Organization for Economic Co-operation and Development (OECD)

Iron and Steel

Iron and steel scrap are the basic raw materials for the production of new steel and cast iron products. Since scrap is readily available from manufacturing operations and from the recovery of products that have reached the end of their useful lives, both the steel and the foundry industries in the United States have been structured to recycle scrap; resulting in a high dependence on scrap.

Iron and steel slags are the coproducts of the iron and steel industry. They have a variety of uses ranging from construction to road building to waste stabilization. Slags are used in cement manufacture, concrete aggregates, fill, glass manufacturing and in agricultural applications. Slags are produced in many metallurgical operations. Iron and steel slags are produced during iron and steel manufacture. In the production of iron, slag is typically produced at a rate of 220 to 370 kilograms per ton of pig iron. Slag is also produced in the process of making steel. Steel slag is hard and dense and is particularly suitable for use in road construction.

In 1996, total slag sold or used in the U.S. was 20.5 million metric tonnes. That was down from 21 million tonnes in 1995. Total blast furnace slag sold or used in the U.S. in 1996 was 13.9 million tonnes, up from 13.8 million tonnes in 1995. Steel slag sold or used in the U.S. in 1996 totaled 6.6 million tonnes, down seven percent from 1995.

U.S. production of iron ore in July 1997 was 5.1 million tonnes. That represented a decline of 11 percent from the same month a year ago. Over the January-July 1997 period, cumulative production of iron ore was 35.3 million tonnes. For the same period of 1996, iron ore production was 34.5 million tonnes. For all of 1996, U.S. iron ore production was 62.1 million tonnes. In July 1997, U.S. stocks of iron ore were 9.1 million tonnes.

U.S. imports of iron ore in June 1997 were 1.7 million tonnes. The major supplier was Canada followed by Brazil. Over the first half of 1997, U.S. imports for consumption of iron ore were 7.8 million tonnes.

U.S. iron and steel scrap receipts from dealers and other sources in June 1997 were 3.4 million tonnes. For the first half of 1997, total scrap receipts were 20 million tonnes. Production of recirculating iron and steel scrap in June 1997 was 1.2 million tonnes while for first half 1997 it was 7.0 million tonnes.

Total U.S. consumption of iron and steel scrap in June 1997 was 4.7 million tonnes while for the first half of 1997 it was 28 million tonnes. Most scrap was consumed in electric furnaces. Iron and steel scrap stocks at the end of June 1997 were 4.6 million tonnes. Integrated steel producers held stocks of 2.0 million tonnes while electric furnace steel producers held 2.6 million tonnes.

U.S. exports of iron and steel scrap in May 1997 were 410,000 tonnes. For January-May 1997, exports of iron and steel scrap totaled 1.9 million tonnes. The major market for iron and steel scrap so far in 1997 was South Korea followed by Mexico and Canada.

World Production of Raw Steel (Ingots and Castings) In Thousands of Metric Tons

Year	Brazil	Canada	China	France	Germany	Italy	Japan	Rep. of Korea	Russia[3]	Ukraine[3]	United Kindom	United States	World Total
1987	22,231	14,737	56,280	17,693	44,491	22,859	98,513	16,782	161,887	------	17,425	80,877	734,319
1988	24,657	14,866	59,430	19,122	49,154	23,760	105,681	19,117	163,037	------	19,013	90,650	780,318
1989	25,055	15,458	61,200	19,335	48,902	25,213	107,908	21,873	160,096	------	18,813	88,852	786,712
1990	20,567	12,281	66,100	19,032	43,981	25,439	110,339	23,125	154,414	------	17,908	89,726	771,169
1991	22,616	12,987	70,600	18,434	42,169	25,046	109,649	26,001	77,093	45,002	16,474	79,738	737,000
1992	23,900	13,924	80,900	17,961	39,711	24,904	98,132	28,054	67,029	41,759	16,212	84,322	724,000
1993	25,170	14,300	89,600	17,179	37,625	25,701	99,623	33,000	58,346	32,357	16,625	88,793	730,000
1994	25,700	13,897	92,600	18,028	40,847	26,114	98,295	33,745	48,812	24,111	17,286	91,200	730,000
1995[1]	25,100	14,415	93,000	18,100	42,100	27,800	101,640	36,772	51,300	22,300	17,600	95,172	752,000
1996[2]	25,239	14,695	100,350	17,599	39,802	24,453	98,799	38,860	49,180	22,050	18,022	94,610	750,359

[1] Preliminary. [2] Estimate. [3] Formerly part of the U.S.S.R.; data not reported separately until 1992. *Source: U.S. Geological Survey (USGS)*

Average Wholesale Prices of Iron and Steel in the United States

Year	No. 1 Heavy Melting Steel Scrap: Pittsburgh ($ Per Gross Ton)	No. 1 Heavy Melting Steel Scrap: Chicago ($ Per Gross Ton)	Pittsburgh Prices: Hot Rolled Sheet[2] (Cents Per Pound)	Sheet Bars: Hot Rolled (Cents Per Pound)	Sheet Bars: Cold Finished (Cents Per Pound)	Hot Rolled Strip (Cents Per Pound)	Carbon Steel Plates (Cents Per Pound)	Cold Rolled Strip (Cents Per Pound)	Galvanized Sheets (Cents Per Pound)	Rail Road Steel Scrap[3] ($ Per Gross Ton)	Used Steel Cans[4] ($ Per Gross Ton)
1987	90.58	87.22	21.92	17.12	21.23	22.50	19.29	37.24	29.97	117.65	NA
1988	113.78	113.47	21.50	17.25	21.23	22.10	21.64	37.24	31.05	150.25	NA
1989	106.80	108.33	22.21	19.60	25.21	22.10	23.50	37.24	32.48	145.23	60.18
1990	106.61	108.62	22.25	20.43	25.37	22.10	23.75	37.24	33.55	131.59	77.16
1991	95.18	95.19	22.88	20.60	25.75	23.15	24.50	38.86	35.35	129.69	89.00
1992	88.72	88.52	19.13	17.48	24.03	23.50	24.50	39.40	30.88	117.40	88.73
1993	116.30	115.26	20.99	18.44	23.83	23.50	25.12	39.40	30.90	142.18	91.79
1994	136.76	131.91	22.93	NA	25.70	23.50	27.61	39.40	32.24	169.00	102.33
1995	142.34	143.17	25.32	NA	25.70	24.88	29.98	39.40	34.47	NA	126.32
1996[1]	137.28	136.07	23.94	NA	25.81	25.00	31.16	NA	35.90	NA	122.29

[1] Preliminary. [2] 10 gauge. [3] Specialties scrap. [4] Consumer buying prices. NA = Not available. *Source: American Metal Market (AMM)*

Salient Statistics of Steel in the United States In Thousands of Net Tons

Year	Pig Iron Production	Producer Price Index for Steel Mill Products (1982=100)	Raw Steel Production — By Type of Furnace — Basic Oxygen	Open Hearth	Electric[2]	Stainless	Carbon	Alloy	Total	Net Shipments Steel Mill Products	Total — Steel Products — Exports	Imports
1988	55,745	110.7	57,960	5,118	36,846	2,199	86,823	10,902	99,924	83,840	2,469	22,989
1989	55,873	114.5	58,348	4,442	35,154	1,926	86,230	9,786	97,943	84,100	5,098	19,699
1990	54,750	112.1	58,471	3,496	36,939	2,037	86,590	10,279	98,606	84,981	5,001	19,401
1991	48,637	109.5	52,714	1,408	33,774	1,878	77,879	8,139	87,896	78,846	7,112	17,743
1992	52,224	106.4	57,642	NA	35,308	1,993	82,458	8,498	92,949	82,241	5,016	19,033
1993	53,082	108.2	59,353	NA	38,524	1,956	86,865	9,056	97,877	89,022	4,727	21,796
1994	54,426	113.4	61,028	NA	39,551	2,022	89,535	9,022	100,579	95,084	4,852	32,705
1995	56,097	120.1	62,523	NA	42,407	2,265	92,656	10,009	104,930	97,494	7,080	24,409
1996	54,428	115.7	60,433	NA	43,923	1,943	93,026	5,562	100,531	100,531	5,031	29,164

[1] Preliminary. [2] Includes crucible sheets. NA = Not available. *Sources: American Iron & Steel Institute (AISI); U.S. Geological Survey (USGS)*

Production of Steel Ingots, Rate of Capability Utilization[1] in the United States In Percents

Year	Jan.	Feb.	Mar.	Apr.	May	June	July	Aug.	Sept.	Oct.	Nov.	Dec.	Average
1988	88.1	89.7	92.2	91.4	93.1	87.4	88.0	86.6	90.1	87.7	85.8	83.8	89.2
1989	88.2	89.8	90.9	92.2	88.1	86.2	80.8	79.2	80.0	83.0	77.4	73.3	84.5
1990	83.1	85.1	85.7	85.2	85.7	84.5	82.0	85.5	84.6	85.1	83.8	75.0	84.0
1991	74.6	73.1	71.7	72.5	70.0	71.7	74.8	75.2	78.5	78.0	78.0	74.4	74.2
1992	80.5	82.4	83.5	85.3	83.5	82.1	78.9	78.7	78.3	80.9	80.4	77.7	82.2
1993	84.8	89.0	87.0	87.4	88.3	87.5	86.9	86.2	87.7	90.2	86.3	85.9	89.1
1994	87.7	92.2	91.3	91.4	91.2	88.7	87.1	87.7	90.0	92.0	92.6	94.3	93.0
1995	93.8	95.6	96.0	92.9	91.6	90.1	86.8	88.3	93.6	90.3	92.1	90.2	91.7
1996	92.2	92.6	93.8	90.5	89.7	91.3	86.6	87.1	87.7	88.0	87.0	87.9	89.5
1997[2]	85.3	89.3	89.6	89.2	87.9	87.0	85.1	86.4	91.2	86.9	89.6	86.3	87.8

[1] Based on tonnage capability to produce raw steel for a full order book. [2] Preliminary. *Sources: American Iron and Steel Institute; U.S. Geological Survey*

Production of Steel Ingots in the United States In Thousands of Short Tons

Year	Jan.	Feb.	Mar.	Apr.	May	June	July	Aug.	Sept.	Oct.	Nov.	Dec.	Total
1988	8,380	7,984	8,763	8,398	8,832	8,031	8,313	8,181	8,237	8,332	7,883	7,954	99,924
1989	8,729	8,022	8,997	8,738	8,633	8,171	7,955	7,790	7,617	8,175	7,386	7,222	97,943
1990	8,241	7,624	8,505	8,209	8,529	8,142	8,101	8,452	8,094	8,424	8,021	7,422	98,906
1991	7,577	6,608	7,283	7,089	7,076	7,017	7,338	7,386	7,457	7,711	7,461	7,348	87,896
1992	7,754	7,432	8,043	7,875	7,968	7,584	7,542	7,526	7,249	7,742	7,449	7,438	92,949
1993	7,942	7,528	8,148	7,926	8,278	7,937	8,066	8,001	7,878	8,409	7,786	8,008	97,877
1994	8,003	7,598	8,323	8,180	8,437	7,941	7,996	8,053	7,993	8,477	8,256	8,684	100,579
1995	8,918	8,211	9,131	8,548	8,696	8,286	8,308	8,455	8,668	8,685	8,574	8,678	103,142
1996	8,981	8,438	9,136	8,588	8,798	8,661	8,585	8,627	8,407	8,702	8,276	8,689	104,356
1997[1]	8,735	8,266	9,175	8,882	9,048	8,662	8,692	8,818	9,006	9,128	9,116	9,071	107,488

[1] Preliminary. *Source: American Iron and Steel Institute (AISI)*

Shipments of Steel Products[1] by Market Classifications in the United States In Thousands of Net Tons

Year	Appliances Utensils & Cutlery	Auto-motive	Con-tainers, Packaging & Shipping Materials	Cons-truction Including Maint.	Con-tactors Products	Electrical Equip-ment	Export	Machinery, Industrial Equipment & Tools	Oil and Gas	Rail Trans-portation	Steel for Converting & Pro-cessing[2]	Steel Service Center & Dis-tributors	All Other[3]	Total Ship-ments
1988	1,638	12,555	4,421	8,607	3,495	2,459	1,233	2,798	1,477	1,146	8,792	21,037	14,182	83,840
1989	1,721	11,763	4,459	8,318	3,182	2,449	3,183	2,409	1,203	1,229	8,235	20,769	15,180	84,100
1990	1,540	11,100	4,474	9,245	2,870	2,453	2,487	2,388	1,892	1,080	9,441	21,111	14,900	84,981
1991	1,388	10,015	4,278	9,161	2,306	2,102	4,476	1,982	1,425	999	8,265	19,464	12,985	78,846
1992	1,503	11,092	3,974	9,536	2,694	2,136	2,650	1,951	1,454	1,052	9,226	21,328	13,645	82,241
1993	1,592	12,719	4,355	10,516	2,913	2,213	2,110	2,191	1,526	1,223	9,451	23,714	14,499	89,022
1994	1,736	14,753	4,495	10,935	3,348	2,299	1,710	2,427	1,703	1,248	10,502	24,153	15,775	95,084
1995	1,538	13,512	3,877	11,761	3,337	2,320	3,767	2,024	2,736	1,136	8,444	20,573	21,832	96,859
1996	1,648	14,400	3,998	12,981	-----	2,329	2,211	2,329	2,987	1,134	8,070	22,156	26,286	100,531
1997[4]	1,633	14,342	4,140	14,295	-----	2,390	2,511	1,684	3,154	1,117	9,085	21,670	29,518	105,538

[1] All grades including carbon, alloy and stainless steel. [2] Net total after deducting shipments to reporting companies for conversion or resale. [3] Includes agricultural; bolts, nuts, rivets and screws; forgings (other than automotive); shipbuilding and marine equipment; aircraft; mining, quarrying and lumbering; other domestic and commercial equipment machinery; ordinance and other direct military; seven shipments of non-reporting companies. [4] Preliminary.
Source: American Iron and Steel Institute (AISI)

IRON AND STEEL

Net Shipments of Steel Products[1] in the United States — In Thousands of Net Tons

Year	Cold Finished Bars	Rails & Acces-sories	Wire Drawn	Tin Mill Products	Plates (Cut & Coils)	Sheet & Strip Galv. (Hot Dipped)	Hot Rolled Bars	Pipe & Tubing	Structural Shapes & Steel Piling	Rein-forcing Bars	Hot Rolled Sheets	Cold Rolled Sheets	Carbon	Alloy	Stain-less
1988	1,499	118	1,073	4,069	7,328	8,115	6,460	4,443	4,860	5,091	12,969	13,871	77,702	4,552	1,586
1989	1,472	562	1,002	4,126	7,384	8,543	6,301	4,011	4,987	5,015	13,281	13,854	78,485	4,143	1,472
1990	1,486	519	918	4,031	7,945	7,878	6,655	4,652	5,670	5,305	13,388	13,199	78,818	4,647	1,516
1991	1,341	486	865	4,041	6,942	6,910	5,431	4,488	5,245	4,859	13,161	11,532	73,480	3,917	1,449
1992	1,458	562	900	3,927	7,102	8,199	5,806	4,198	5,081	4,781	13,361	12,692	76,625	4,101	1,514
1993	1,580	679	802	4,123	7,538	9,712	6,339	4,445	4,973	5,033	14,873	12,758	83,106	4,381	1,534
1994	1,786	631	788	4,137	8,556	10,943	7,088	4,965	5,506	4,929	15,654	13,016	88,505	4,859	1,720
1995	1,758	609	703	3,942	9,044	11,345	7,004	5,436	6,611	4,714	16,402	12,677	90,485	5,115	1,894
1996	1,685	721	652	4,108	8,673	11,456	6,999	5,895	6,140	5,762	17,466	14,089	93,019	5,948	1,911
1997[2]	1,796	825	619	4,058	8,855	12,369	8,045	6,548	6,011	6,142	18,136	13,317	97,032	6,449	2,057

[1] All grades, including carbon, alloy and stainless steel. [2] Preliminary. *Source: American Iron and Steel Institute (AISI)*

World Production of Pig Iron (Excludes Ferro-Alloys) — In Thousands of Metric Tons

Year	Belgium	Brazil	China	France	Ger-many	India	Italy	Japan	Russia[4]	Ukraine[4]	United Kindom	United States	World Total
1987	8,244	21,509	55,030	13,449	31,272	11,083	11,335	73,418	115,038	------	12,017	44,034	522,720
1988	9,147	23,649	57,040	14,786	34,676	11,925	11,349	79,295	116,158	------	13,056	50,861	553,395
1989	8,868	24,621	58,200	15,071	35,197	12,420	11,795	80,197	116,628	------	12,638	50,977	561,762
1990	9,416	21,360	62,380	14,415	32,058	13,395	11,883	80,229	111,763	------	12,277	50,058	549,000
1991	9,354	22,926	67,650	13,408	30,608	14,176	10,856	79,985	90,900	------	11,883	44,510	528,000
1992	8,533	23,152	75,890	12,730	28,547	15,126	10,462	73,144	45,824	34,663	11,542	47,890	523,000
1993	8,178	23,982	87,390	12,679	26,970	15,674	11,066	73,738	40,871	26,999	11,534	48,200	531,000
1994	8,974	25,177	97,409	13,293	29,923	17,808	11,157	73,776	36,116	21,200	11,943	49,400	543,000
1995[1]	9,199	25,090	105,300	13,154	29,828	18,626	11,684	74,905	39,762	20,000	12,238	50,900	564,000
1996[2]	9,000	25,100	105,300	13,000	30,000	20,000	12,000	74,597	36,061	18,143	12,225	49,400	562,000

[1] Preliminary. [2] Estimate. [4] Formerly part of the U.S.S.R.; data not reported separately until 1992. *Source: U.S. Geological Survey (USGS)*

Production of Pig Iron (Excludes Ferro-Alloys) in the United States — In Thousands of Short Tons

Year	Jan.	Feb.	Mar.	Apr.	May	June	July	Aug.	Sept.	Oct.	Nov.	Dec.	Total
1988	4,683	4,443	4,842	4,699	4,932	4,497	4,762	4,584	4,612	4,646	4,455	4,712	55,745
1989	4,964	4,654	5,112	4,990	4,917	4,707	4,604	4,172	4,403	4,692	4,322	4,202	55,873
1990	4,638	4,221	4,681	4,549	4,746	4,530	4,656	4,788	4,629	4,673	4,523	4,264	54,925
1991	4,077	3,470	4,047	3,830	3,885	3,830	4,179	4,121	4,175	4,251	4,300	4,338	48,503
1992	4,390	4,175	4,524	4,400	4,444	4,232	4,347	4,299	4,065	5,329	4,268	4,306	52,224
1993	4,503	4,503	4,454	4,328	4,555	4,351	4,522	4,504	4,367	4,652	4,218	4,514	53,103
1994	3,970	3,858	3,957	4,099	4,394	4,519	4,518	4,446	4,320	4,564	4,619	4,928	54,426
1995	4,820	4,453	4,916	4,568	4,674	4,499	4,576	4,688	4,727	4,687	4,738	4,762	56,115
1996	4,811	4,476	4,813	4,430	4,556	4,578	4,524	4,498	4,404	4,443	4,307	4,523	54,485
1997[1]	4,489	4,243	4,713	4,440	4,690	4,452	4,420	4,443	4,605	4,662	4,717	4,861	54,680

[1] Preliminary. *Source: American Iron and Steel Institute (AISI)*

Salient Statistics of Ferrous Scrap and Pig Iron in the United States — In Thousands of Metric Tons

	Consumption: Ferrous Scrap & Pig Iron Charged To												Stocks--Dec. 31 Ferrous Scrap & Pig Iron at Consumers		
	Mfg. of Pig Iron & Steel Ingots & Castings			Iron Foundries & Misc. Users			Mfg. of Steel Castings	All Uses							
Year	Scrap	Pig Iron	Total	Scrap	Pig Iron	Total	(Scrap)	Ferrous Scrap	Pig Iron	Grand Total	Imports of Scrap[2]	Exports of Scrap[3]	Scrap	Pig Iron	Total Stocks
1987	46,870	44,421	91,291	13,371	955	14,326	1,723	61,964	45,387	107,351	765	9,405	4,394	255	4,649
1988	51,054	52,163	103,217	16,513	1,393	17,906	2,126	69,692	53,567	123,259	942	9,161	4,131	188	4,319
1989	52,733	50,210	102,943	13,270	892	14,162	1,894	67,897	51,122	119,019	1,016	11,149	4,293	246	4,539
1990	54,361	49,337	103,698	13,085	835	13,920	1,850	69,296	50,193	119,489	1,324	11,580	4,292	147	4,439
1991	48,778	44,095	92,873	11,126	656	11,782	1,609	61,513	44,765	106,278	1,073	9,502	4,072	190	4,262
1992	50,144	47,263	97,407	11,444	619	12,063	1,640	63,228	47,894	111,122	1,316	9,262	3,752	181	3,933
1993	53,084	48,092	101,176	12,658	676	13,334	1,900	68,000	48,777	116,777	1,390	9,805	3,725	220	3,945
1994	53,801	50,257	104,057	14,000	1,000	15,000	2,000	70,000	51,000	121,000	1,740	8,813	4,100	400	4,500
1995	56,000	51,000	107,000	13,000	1,100	14,100	2,000	72,000	52,000	124,000	2,090	10,400	4,200	620	4,820
1996[1]	56,000	50,000	106,000	13,000	1,100	14,100	2,700	72,000	52,000	124,000	2,600	8,440	5,200	600	5,800

[1] Preliminary. [2] Includes tinplate and terneplate. [3] Excludes used rails for rerolling and other uses and ships, boats, and other vessels for scrapping.
Source: U.S. Geological Survey (USGS)

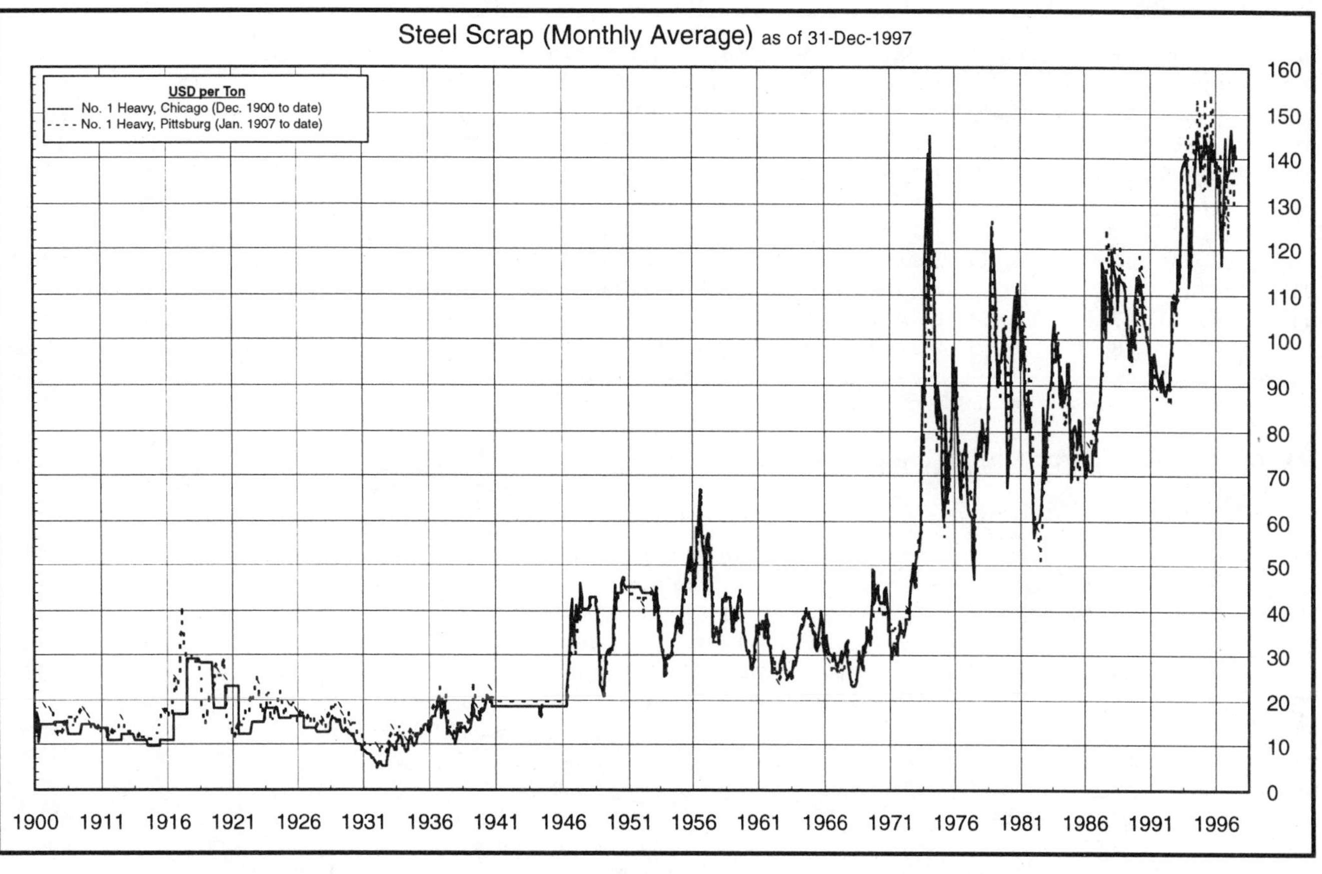

Consumption of Pig Iron in the U.S., by Type of Furnace or Equipment In Thousands of Metric Tons

Year	Open Hearth	Electric	Cupola	Basic Oxygen Process	Air & Other Furnace	Direct Casting	Total
1988	3,500	1,269	679	47,199	40	879	53,566
1989	1,582	1,051	389	49,380	30	536	52,968
1990	2,072	982	332	47,307	19	387	51,099
1991	997	574	265	42,955	13	106	44,910
1992	-----	429	215	47,194	7	49	47,894
1993	-----	519	292	47,848	34	84	48,777
1994	-----	1,700	520	49,138	4	39	51,401
1995	-----	1,700	500	50,000	W	72	52,272
1996[1]	-----	2,900	-----	45,000	-----	W	47,900
1997[2]	-----	1,500	-----	45,000	-----	W	46,500

[1] Preliminary. [2] Estimate. W = withheld. *Source: U.S. Geological Survey (USGS)*

Wholesale Price of No. 1 Heavy Melting Steel Scrap in Chicago In Dollars Per Gross Ton

Year	Jan.	Feb.	Mar.	Apr.	May	June	July	Aug.	Sept.	Oct.	Nov.	Dec.	Average
1988	100.80	119.43	119.02	117.24	111.38	108.55	120.00	119.78	115.00	115.00	109.16	106.33	113.47
1989	114.10	118.32	113.00	113.00	113.00	113.00	108.00	108.00	108.00	101.09	96.00	94.50	108.33
1990	104.00	102.29	98.00	109.43	114.55	111.67	108.50	116.00	113.76	112.50	107.73	105.00	108.62
1991	104.76	100.74	98.00	97.80	93.18	87.50	87.74	94.14	98.50	97.50	91.97	90.50	95.19
1992	90.50	90.50	90.50	90.50	89.70	87.68	87.50	87.55	88.50	85.50	85.50	88.36	88.52
1993	98.34	109.50	109.50	106.50	106.50	111.27	118.50	114.18	113.50	125.88	131.50	138.00	115.26
1994	138.00	138.00	138.00	138.00	123.64	110.50	117.20	133.63	134.50	132.50	137.50	141.50	131.91
1995	152.05	147.50	140.20	141.50	144.50	141.64	141.50	149.76	144.90	141.50	136.50	136.50	143.17
1996	143.41	144.50	139.50	139.50	142.50	139.50	134.50	136.95	140.35	130.89	120.76	120.50	136.07
1997	131.14	143.50	139.70	132.59	136.50	136.50	143.50	146.50	139.60	139.63	142.50	142.50	139.51

Source: American Metal Market (AMM)

IRON AND STEEL

World Production of Iron Ore[3] In Thousands of Metric Tons (Gross Weight)

Year	Australia	Brazil	Canada	China	India	Maur-itania	Russia[4]	South Africa	Sweden	Ukraine[4]	United States	Vene-zula	World Total
1987	101,748	134,497	37,702	113,000	51,018	9,002	250,874	22,008	19,636	------	47,648	17,782	902,737
1988	99,450	146,008	39,934	154,380	49,961	10,004	249,754	25,248	20,440	------	57,515	18,932	967,218
1989	105,810	157,900	40,509	171,850	53,418	12,110	241,348	29,958	21,763	------	59,032	18,053	1,013,383
1990	110,508	152,300	34,855	168,300	53,700	11,590	236,000	30,291	19,877	------	56,408	20,119	983,000
1991	117,134	151,500	39,307	176,070	56,880	10,246	199,000	29,075	19,328	------	56,761	21,296	955,618
1992	112,101	146,447	33,167	197,600	54,870	8,202	82,100	28,226	19,277	75,700	55,593	18,070	924,887
1993	120,534	150,000	31,830	234,660	57,375	9,360	76,100	29,385	18,728	65,000	55,661	16,841	953,099
1994	128,493	167,900	37,703	240,200	60,473	11,440	73,300	30,489	19,663	51,300	58,382	18,318	981,403
1995[1]	142,936	177,000	36,628	249,350	66,751	11,330	75,900	31,946	19,058	50,400	62,489	19,484	1,027,136
1996[2]	147,100	180,000	36,030	249,550	67,000	11,400	69,600	30,830	20,273	48,000	62,073	18,480	1,020,266

[1] Preliminary. [2] Estimate. [3] Iron ore, iron ore concentrates and iron ore agglomerates. [4] Formerly part of the U.S.S.R.; data not reported separately until 1992. *Source: U.S. Geological Survey (USGS)*

Salient Statistics of Iron Ore[3] in the United States In Thousands of Metric Tons

Year	Net Import Reliance % of Apparent Consumption	Production Total	Production Lake Superior	Production Other Regions	Ship-ments	Value Million $ (at Mine)	Average Value $ at Mine Per Ton	Stocks--Dec. 31 Mines	Stocks--Dec. 31 Con-suming Plants	Stocks--Dec. 31 Lake Erie Docks	Imports	Exports	Con-sumption	Value Million $ Imports
1987	22	47,648	46,756	892	47,983	1,503.1	31.33	2,402	16,565	2,056	16,849	5,093	67,768	408.8
1988	18	57,515	56,038	1,477	57,113	1,716.7	30.06	2,957	18,005	2,537	20,183	5,285	83,694	484.5
1989	22	59,032	56,981	2,052	58,299	1,939.9	33.27	4,575	15,730	2,171	19,596	5,365	80,447	522.3
1990	21	56,408	54,628	1,780	57,010	1,570.0	27.52	4,795	15,911	2,273	18,054	3,199	76,855	559.5
1991	14	56,761	55,636	1,124	56,775	1,900.0	33.40	4,850	17,612	2,981	13,335	4,045	66,366	436.8
1992	10	55,593	55,018	575	55,569	1,730.0	31.10	3,780	16,093	2,981	12,504	5,055	75,067	395.8
1993	14	55,661	54,814	848	56,300	1,380.0	24.50	2,500	16,500	2,290	14,100	5,060	76,800	419.0
1994	18	58,382	57,848	367	57,610	1,410.0	24.50	2,790	16,300	2,230	17,500	4,980	80,200	499.0
1995[1]	14	62,489	62,026	427	61,100	1,730.0	28.40	4,240	17,100	2,140	17,600	5,270	83,100	491.0
1996[2]	17	62,073	61,748	383	62,200	1,770.0	28.50	4,650	18,800	2,260	18,400	6,260	79,300	556.0

[1] Preliminary. [2] Estimate. [3] Usable iron ore exclusive of ore containing 5% or more manganese and includes byproduct ore. *Source: U.S. Geological Survey (USGS)*

U.S. Imports (for Consumption) of Iron Ore[2] In Thousands of Metric Tons

Year	Australia	Brazil	Canada	Chile	Maur-itania	Peru	Sweden	Vene-zuela	Total
1988	1,076	4,935	9,157	139	522	181	88	3,568	20,183
1989	394	5,169	8,538	61	594	186	57	4,232	19,596
1990	14	4,276	9,344	138	666	59	54	3,503	18,054
1991	NA	2,481	7,299	103	459	157	51	2,763	13,335
1992	163	2,442	6,834	107	280	70	64	2,540	12,504
1993	254	2,872	7,442	68	206	1	60	3,170	14,097
1994	675	3,610	10,073	134	124	2	45	2,778	17,466
1995	570	4,810	9,050	57	317	54	47	2,500	17,600
1996	511	5,170	9,800	164	275	43	48	2,140	18,400
1997[1]	475	3,498	5,860	162	-----	183	1	1,232	11,480

[1] Preliminary. [2] Including agglomerates. *Source: U.S. Geological Survey (USGS)*

Total[1] Iron Ore Stocks in the United States, at End of Month In Thousands of Metric Tons

Year	Jan.	Feb.	Mar.	Apr.	May	June	July	Aug.	Sept.	Oct.	Nov.	Dec.
1987	21,472	21,406	20,580	19,571	18,875	19,008	19,235	19,085	19,343	19,994	20,264	20,613
1988	20,997	20,925	20,041	20,119	19,789	19,341	19,835	20,801	22,210	22,140	22,485	22,755
1989	23,189	23,252	22,685	21,145	21,670	21,544	22,286	22,275	22,588	21,429	21,448	22,476
1990	22,088	21,986	20,958	20,609	20,501	21,019	21,863	22,110	22,268	22,027	22,042	22,978
1991	22,572	22,218	21,316	20,757	21,756	23,174	23,319	24,329	25,148	25,117	25,358	25,445
1992	24,527	23,162	20,922	20,550	21,501	22,492	23,046	21,721	22,735	23,190	23,433	22,856
1993	21,296	20,806	19,235	18,996	19,180	22,036	22,905	21,575	22,629	21,355	21,615	21,341
1994	19,013	17,816	15,953	14,883	15,251	16,592	17,864	18,931	20,554	20,760	21,552	21,339
1996	22,277	20,744	19,779	20,104	23,426	21,822	22,445	23,663	24,116	24,866	25,465	25,701
1997[2]	25,913	25,262	24,745	24,812	25,001	25,620	26,076	26,971	27,562	28,029		

[1] All stocks at mines, furnance yards and at U.S. docks. [2] Preliminary. *Source: U.S. Geological Survey (USGS)*

Lard

Production of lard is directly related to commercial pork production. As such, the largest producers of hogs are the largest producers of lard. China is by far the largest producer of lard followed by the U.S. Production of lard in China and the U.S. has been increasing at about the population rate.

The USDA reported that beginning stocks of lard in the U.S. in August 1997 were 23 million pounds. Lard production in August 1997 was 79.4 million pounds which was slightly higher than in July. In the October-August 1996-97 marketing year, U.S. lard production was 892 million pounds and averaged 81 million pounds a month. For all of the 1995-96 marketing year, U.S. lard production was 1.01 billion pounds.

The U.S. imports very small amounts of lard. In the October-July 1996-97 period, imports amounted to 836,000 pounds. The total supply of lard in July 1997 was 102 million pounds.

U.S. domestic use of lard in July 1997 was 71.4 million pounds. Over the October-July 1996-97 period, domestic consumption of lard was 725 million pounds. For the October-September 1995-96 marketing year, U.S. domestic consumption of lard was 922 million pounds.

U.S. exports of lard in July 1997 were 7.5 million pounds. In the October-July 1996-97 period, lard exports were 88 million pounds. For the 1995-96 marketing year, lard exports were just over 94 million pounds. For the same marketing year, total disappearance of lard was 1.02 billion pounds.

U.S. stocks of lard at the end of August 1997 were 21 million pounds, the same amount as the year before.

World Production of Lard In Thousands of Metric Tons

Year Beginning Oct. 1	Brazil	Canada	China	France	Germany	Italy	Japan	Poland	Romania	Spain	United States	Former U.S.S.R.	World Total
1988-9	147.5	79.0	1,438.3	126.5	518.7	181.0	91.0	137.7	130.4	154.8	426.2	852.1	5,382.8
1989-90	151.0	75.6	1,519.5	129.2	534.4	178.5	91.0	136.8	130.1	156.1	412.3	844.4	5,441.8
1990-1	158.6	75.6	1,605.6	137.3	476.3	187.6	87.0	288.3	129.0	169.7	415.0	762.8	5,586.2
1991-2	165.7	76.9	1,698.4	135.5	411.3	188.0	85.0	303.3	117.7	170.6	447.7	653.6	5,497.5
1992-3	175.5	77.0	1,767.6	142.9	418.2	192.1	85.8	292.9	113.7	185.8	445.0	573.8	5,523.6
1993-4	186.2	76.0	1,984.8	151.3	409.5	189.5	82.4	243.3	115.9	192.8	451.0	509.6	5,648.5
1994-5[1]	202.9	78.3	2,178.6	153.2	404.8	191.3	83.8	275.1	110.5	196.7	471.2	426.3	5,836.5
1995-6[2]	217.2	79.8	2,338.0	154.5	405.8	199.5	76.3	292.8	109.6	206.5	449.3	367.4	5,976.2
1996-7[3]	230.2	80.3	2,439.0	156.6	410.2	199.9	73.7	283.7	110.2	209.7	442.2	355.3	6,075.4

[1] Preliminary. [2] Estimate. [3] Forecast. *Source: The Oil World*

Supply and Distribution of Lard in the United States In Millions of Pounds

	Supply			Disappearance						
Year	Production	Stocks Oct. 1	Total Supply	Domestic	Baking or Frying Fats	Margarine[2]	Exports	Total Disappearance	Direct Use	Per Capita (Lbs.)
1989-90	909.0	42.0	972.0	845.0	295.0	32.0	85.0	940.0	442.0	3.3
1990-1	933.6	22.9	959.9	825.4	264.0	35.0	110.0	935.8	439.2	3.3
1991-2	1,016.3	24.1	1,042.9	884.8	274.0	43.0	131.0	1,015.7	423.7	3.3
1992-3	1,011.2	27.2	1,041.5	886.1	310.0	37.0	129.2	1,015.3	438.6	3.5
1993-4	1,014.7	26.2	1,043.6	890.4	296.0	31.0	118.8	1,009.2	573.0	3.4
1994-5	1,052.4	34.4	1,089.0	924.4	306.0	43.0	140.4	1,064.7	584.4	3.4
1995-6	1,012.6	24.3	1,038.8	921.8	266.0	33.0	94.3	1,016.1	600.5	3.5
1996-7[1]	979.1	22.7	1,002.9	879.7	254.7	15.0	103.3	983.0	602.5	3.5
1997-8[2]	1,020.0	19.9	1,040.9	935.0	NA	NA	80.0	1,015.0	NA	NA

[1] Preliminary. [2] Includes edible tallow. [3] Forecast. NA = not avaliable. *Source: Economic Research Service, U.S. Department of Agriculture (ERS)*

Consumption of Lard (Edible and Inedible) in the United States In Millions of Pounds

Year	Jan.	Feb.	Mar.	Apr.	May	June	July	Aug.	Sept.	Oct.	Nov.	Dec.	Total
1989	28.9	27.5	34.0	31.1	33.5	32.2	28.9	33.5	34.1	39.0	42.5	32.7	397.9
1990	27.0	27.3	30.9	26.3	32.1	29.2	22.8	32.0	31.3	34.6	33.8	30.6	357.9
1991	----------	97.3	----------	----------	94.7	----------	----------	95.2	----------	----------	105.9	----------	393.1
1992	33.9	31.6	39.9	40.0	38.7	39.6	42.9	41.1	47.6	46.4	41.0	37.2	479.9
1993	40.1	34.4	45.9	36.8	38.2	38.8	32.6	38.4	41.8	44.0	43.0	40.3	474.3
1994	33.5	33.9	36.2	34.6	35.9	34.4	32.4	37.5	43.4	43.8	44.7	41.7	452.0
1995	37.5	34.7	41.2	36.2	42.2	44.4	34.9	35.9	35.9	40.1	38.9	36.8	458.7
1996	30.5	35.4	36.7	46.9	36.8	31.4	32.6	33.9	30.9	34.5	34.7	33.6	417.9
1997[1]	26.5	30.5	31.0	36.5	39.9	36.2	36.1	35.0	37.4	39.0	41.5	39.4	428.8

[1] Preliminary. *Source: Bureau of the Census, U.S. Department of Commerce*

LARD

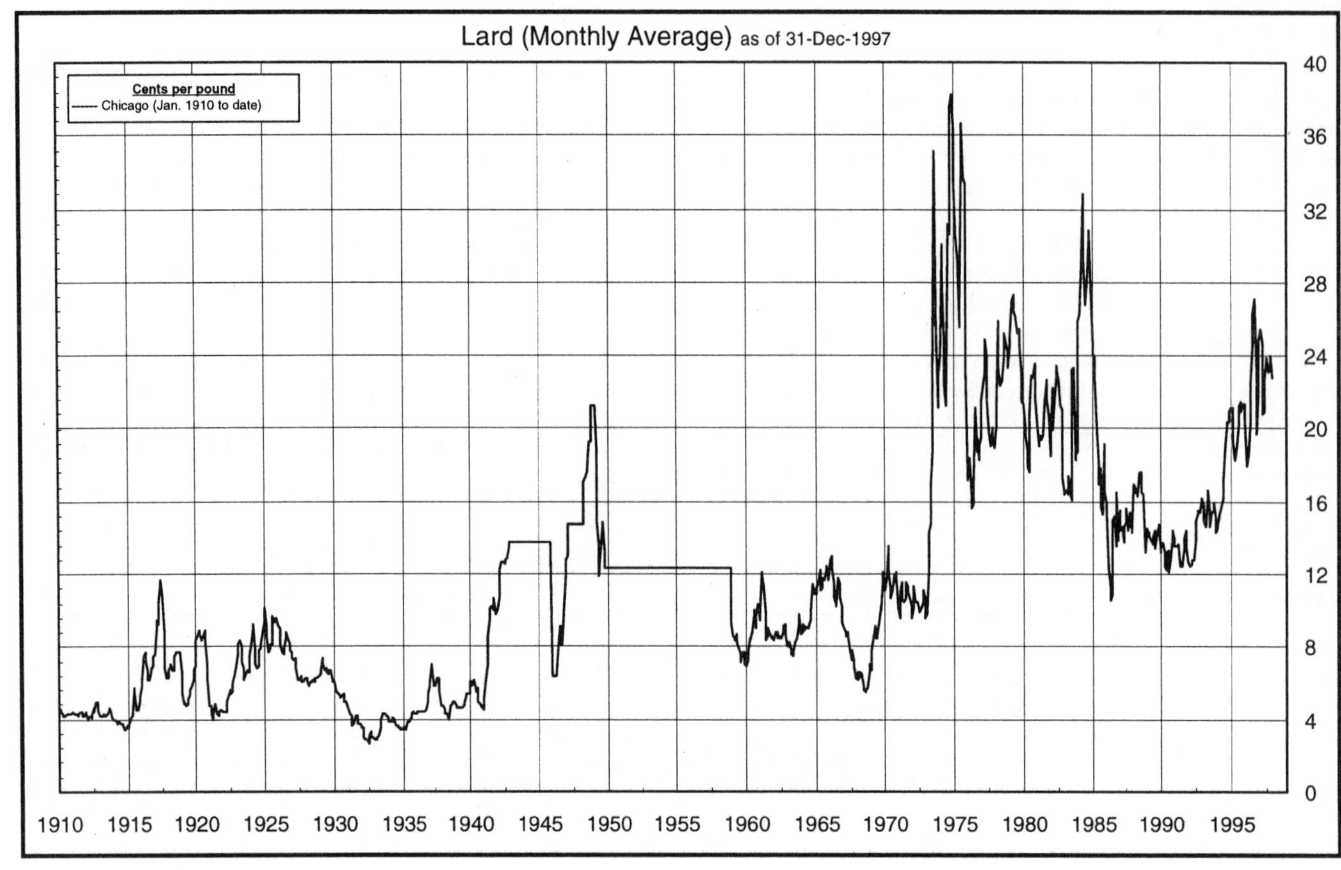

Average Wholesale Price of Lard--Loose, Tank Cars, in Chicago In Cents Per Pound

Year	Jan.	Feb.	Mar.	Apr.	May	June	July	Aug.	Sept.	Oct.	Nov.	Dec.	Average
1988	17.00	16.70	16.60	16.40	16.30	17.60	17.70	16.50	16.40	16.30	13.20	14.60	16.28
1989	14.50	14.40	14.10	13.80	13.70	14.10	14.40	13.50	14.20	14.60	14.80	13.20	14.11
1990	13.50	13.80	13.20	12.50	12.30	13.20	13.40	12.10	12.70	14.00	14.50	14.10	13.28
1991	13.50	13.50	13.50	13.70	12.50	12.50	12.40	13.40	14.00	14.40	13.60	12.20	13.27
1992	12.50	12.50	12.60	12.60	13.90	15.00	15.00	15.30	15.50	15.40	16.10	16.30	14.39
1993	15.80	15.00	14.70	16.20	16.70	15.50	14.60	15.40	15.50	15.90	15.30	14.30	15.41
1994	14.50	14.60	15.40	15.70	15.80	16.30	17.20	18.90	20.10	20.40	20.40	20.90	17.52
1995	21.21	21.13	19.25	18.34	18.25	19.02	20.25	21.30	21.48	20.90	21.38	21.35	20.32
1996	20.52	18.17	18.01	18.67	20.47	22.61	24.55	26.30	27.09	23.11	19.70	22.17	21.78
1997	24.93	25.47	24.69	20.82	20.94	22.68	23.83	23.95	23.14	23.41	23.97	22.85	23.39

Source: *The Wall Street Journal*

Cold Storage Holdings of All Lard[1] in the United States, on First of Month In Millions of Pounds

Year	Jan.	Feb.	Mar.	Apr.	May	June	July	Aug.	Sept.	Oct.	Nov.	Dec.
1988	33.0	37.2	33.8	37.1	31.2	31.9	37.8	41.1	30.1	39.0	41.7	36.7
1989	37.4	38.2	37.1	27.3	34.2	37.6	41.3	32.4	28.9	41.6	29.0	36.6
1990	32.0	33.7	37.6	28.5	31.6	27.4	25.2	25.9	22.8	22.9	22.2	30.3
1991	----------	24.4	----------	----------	28.3	----------	----------	24.0	----------	----------	24.1	----------
1992	37.4	27.2	28.9	28.3	26.7	23.2	24.8	29.2	26.9	27.2	22.2	24.8
1993	22.7	25.9	27.2	24.0	22.8	25.8	31.1	27.4	23.6	26.2	24.6	30.1
1994	37.7	38.0	31.8	28.8	25.1	27.4	27.0	25.5	29.7	34.4	34.0	35.8
1995	40.6	50.3	46.4	43.0	36.8	27.1	25.8	22.1	30.2	24.3	19.9	21.6
1996	38.4	38.6	25.8	28.8	21.5	23.2	23.7	30.5	20.7	22.7	20.1	18.8
1997[2]	18.9	16.3	18.5	19.2	18.9	18.7	23.0	23.2	21.5	19.9	21.3	19.7

[1] Stocks in factories and warehouses (except that in hands of retailers). [2] Preliminary. *Source: Bureau of the Census, U.S. Department of Commerce*

Lead

Lead is used in the production of batteries, fuel tanks, ammunition, electrical equipment, cans and containers, and as solder for pipes and plumbings. Lead and the compounds that contain lead are very toxic. There has been a concerted effort to reduce the use of lead, especially in those areas where humans are exposed to it. Some of the substitutes for lead include plastic, aluminum, tin and iron. There has been research into the use of bismuth to replace lead in solder, ammunition and in ceramic glazes. One area where there may be a significant reduction in lead use is in batteries. Current development efforts center on lithium-polymer batteries as a replacement for lead-acid batteries. One advantage is that lithium is one of the lightest of materials while lead is one of the heaviest. Despite this, lead-acid batteries continue to account for about 87 percent of lead consumption, over one million metric tonnes a year.

In other developments, the U.S. Geological Survey reported that two U.S. government agencies issued several rules and notices pertaining to lead use and lead-based paint abatement. Another government agency and industry announced a new voluntary initiative to significantly reduce worker exposure to lead. Congress passed an amendment to the Safe Drinking Water Act, thereby placing added restrictions on the use and sale of lead-containing materials in pipes and plumbing fixtures.

In 1996, lead was mined in 45 countries. For 1996, world mine production of lead was 2.92 million tonnes, some five percent more than in 1995. The largest producing country was Australia with 1996 output of 522,000 tonnes. China was the next largest producer with 500,000 tonnes followed by the United States at 436,000 tonnes. Peru was the fourth largest producer of lead at 248,787 tonnes with Canada next at 240,835 tonnes. World refinery production of lead in 1996 was 5.48 million tonnes of which 2.83 million tonnes was primary refinery production and 2.65 million tonnes was secondary production.

U.S. production of mine lead in July 1997 was 34,700 tonnes which was two percent more than in June. In the January-July 1997 period, mine production of lead was 256,000 tonnes which was almost two percent more than in the comparable period of 1996. For all of 1996, mine production was 426,000 tonnes. U.S. production of primary refinery lead in July 1997 was 259,000 tonnes, down from 28,700 tonnes in June 1997. In the January-July 1997 period, primary refinery lead production was 205,000 tonnes, up three percent from the comparable period of 1996. For all of 1996, production was 326,000 tonnes.

Secondary refinery production of lead in July 1997 was 86,700 tonnes, up one percent from the month before. In the January-July 1997 period, secondary refinery production was 616,000 tonnes. Of that total, some 600,000 tonnes was from smelter and refineries. In the comparable period of 1996, secondary refinery production was 566,000 tonnes while for all of 1996 it was 1.1 million tonnes.

U.S. stocks of lead at primary refineries at the end of July 1997 were 6,530 tonnes. That was down sharply from stocks at the end of June 1997 of 10,900 tonnes. Stocks at secondary smelters and held by consumers were 60,400 tonnes at the end of July 1997, down from 64,400 tonnes a month earlier.

World Smelter (Primary and Secondary) Production of Lead In Thousands of Metric Tons

Year	Australia[3]	Belgium[4]	Canada[3]	China[2]	France	Germany	Italy	Japan	Mexico[3]	Spain	United Kingdom[3]	United States	World Total
1989	205.0	109.4	242.8	260.0	427.6	363.9	186.2	332.4	235.0	114.5	350.5	1,288	6,077
1990	229.0	105.8	183.6	296.0	432.7	411.0	166.8	327.4	232.2	110.0	329.4	1,330	5,950
1991	239.4	110.7	212.4	330.0	438.0	362.5	208.2	332.4	161.8	169.0	311.0	1,230	5,770
1992	231.8	116.3	252.9	365.0	444.6	354.3	186.3	330.2	177.0	120.0	346.8	1,220	5,420
1993	243.0	131.1	217.0	412.0	258.7	334.2	182.8	309.5	188.0	123.0	364.0	1,230	5,250
1994	232.5	123.5	251.6	468.0	260.0	331.7	205.9	292.3	180.0	140.0	352.5	1,280	5,260
1995[1]	235.4	121.7	281.4	608.0	290.1	335.0	180.4	286.5	170.0	150.0	320.7	1,390	5,590
1996[2]	224.0	120.8	309.4	530.0	295.0	340.0	143.0	287.4	154.0	155.0	345.6	1,430	5,480

[1] Preliminary. [2] Estimate. [3] Refined & bullion. [4] Includes scrap. NA - not avaliable. *Source: U.S. Geaological Survey (USGS)*

Consumption of Lead in the United States, by Products In Metric Tons

Year	Ammunition	Bearing Metals	Pipes, Traps & Bends[2]	Cable Covering	Calking Lead	Casting Metals	Other Metal Products[3]	Total Other Oxides[4]	Sheet Lead	Solder	Storage Battery: Grids, Post, etc.	Storage Battery: Oxides	Brass and Bronze	Total Consumption
1989	57,310	2,586	9,818	22,605	1,831	16,175	6,850	57,984	20,987	17,009	552,308	459,847	9,610	1,283,234
1990	58,210	5,212	9,281	18,253	1,688	14,843	3,812	56,484	21,013	16,490	571,187	448,450	9,943	1,275,226
1991	58,458	3,669	8,975	17,472	1,074	14,141	3,254	59,617	22,334	14,750	591,884	415,233	8,997	1,246,337
1992	64,845	4,785	11,652	15,992	1,045	17,111	3,024	63,225	21,006	13,518	629,147	373,185	9,175	1,236,571
1993	65,100	4,830	5,740	17,165	961	18,500	5,360	63,600	21,200	14,400	677,000	374,000	5,750	1,290,000
1994	62,400	5,560	3,370	16,000	764	18,900	5,330	62,700	21,500	12,200	797,000	425,000	6,320	1,450,000
1995	70,900	6,490	2,210	5,640	935	18,100	5,220	61,700	27,900	16,200	711,000	618,000	5,260	1,560,000
1996[1]	52,100	4,350	1,810	W	767	18,800	3,830	56,900	21,200	9,020	655,000	681,000	5,460	1,530,000

[1] Preliminary. [2] Including building. [3] Including terne metal, type metal, and lead consumed in foil, collapsible tubes, annealing, plating, galvanizing and fishing weights. [4] Includes paints, glass and ceramic products, and other pigments and chemicals. NA = not avaliable. W = Withheld proprietary data.
Source: U.S. Geological Survey (USGS)

LEAD

Salient Statistics of Lead in the United States   In Thousands of Metric Tons

Year	Net Import Reliance as a % of Apparent Consumption	Production of Refined Lead from: Domestic Ores[3]	Foreign Ores[3]	Total Primary	Total Value of Refined Million $	Secondary Lead Recovered: As Soft Lead	In Antimonial Lead	In Other Alloys	Total	Total Value of Secondary Million $	Stocks, Dec. 31: Primary	Consumer[4]	Average Price ¢ Per Pound: New York	London[5]
1987	17	336.5	37.1	373.6	296.0	345.1	323.3	41.7	710.1	562.6	21.6	88.6	35.94	26.99
1988	13	371.3	20.7	392.1	321.0	367.1	331.3	38.0	736.4	603.0	15.4	89.9	37.14	29.73
1989	8	379.0	17.4	396.5	343.9	438.0	418.6	34.7	891.3	773.3	15.6	82.4	39.35	30.63
1990	3	385.6	18.0	403.7	409.5	461.4	425.4	35.6	922.2	935.6	25.5	86.3	46.02	37.05
1991	E	323.9	21.9	345.7	255.2	421.9	426.9	35.8	884.6	652.9	9.1	71.7	33.48	25.30
1992	4	284.0	20.8	304.8	235.9	452.9	424.5	23.1	916.3	709.1	20.5	82.3	35.10	24.50
1993	15	310.7	24.9	335.6	234.4	444.0	417.0	17.0	893.0	625.0	14.3	80.5	31.74	18.42
1994	19	328.0	23.4	351.4	288.0	527.0	371.0	16.1	931.0	763.0	9.3	68.8	37.17	24.83
1995[1]	17	374.0	W	374.0	348.0	584.0	400.0	19.2	1,020.0	951.0	14.2	79.4	42.28	28.60
1996[2]	17	326.0	W	326.0	351.0	652.0	424.0	8.0	1,100.0	1,190.0	8.2	71.7	48.83	35.10

[1] Preliminary. [2] Estimate. [3] And base bullion. [4] Also at secondary smelters. [5] LME data in dollars per metric ton beginning July 1993. W = Withheld Proprietary data. E = Net exporter. *Source: U.S. Geological Survey (USGS)*

United States Foreign Trade of Lead   In Thousands of Metric Tons

Year	Exports: Ore Concentrate	Unwrought Lead[3]	Wrought Lead[4]	Scrap	Ash & Residues[5]	Imports for Consumption: Ores, Flue Dust or Fume & Mattes	Base Bullion	Pigs & Bars	Reclaimed Scrap, Etc.	Value Million $	General Imports From: Ore, Flue Dust & Matte: Australia	Canada	Peru	Pigs & Bars: Canada	Mexico	Peru
1987	8.8	4.4	5.8	52.8	3.5	0.9	10.8	185.7	6.6	133.8	1.7	201.2	19.1	92.6	42.6	0.4
1988	20.9	7.5	6.0	81.9	15.5	20.6	4.0	148.6	7.3	124.8	1.4	221.8	11.4	104.8	30.9	-----
1989	57.0	28.5	5.4	59.9	10.0	5.1	5.8	115.7	0.7	95.7	1.9	189.9	12.9	90.5	19.2	2.3
1990	56.6	57.2	6.8	75.0	13.0	10.7	2.7	90.6	0.3	91.2	1.2	124.3	7.1	70.7	25.0	1.0
1991	88.0	94.4	7.6	72.0	11.0	12.4	0.4	116.5	0.1	82.6	1.0	226.7	3.9	83.6	11.9	0.5
1992	72.3	64.3	5.3	63.2	2.1	5.3	0.2	190.7	0.2	120.6	-----	239.9	21.2	124.7	56.1	9.8
1993	41.8	51.4	7.1	54.1	1.7	0.5	-----	195.6	0.1	99.4	-----	55.7	13.6	130.8	40.3	18.3
1994	38.7	48.2	5.3	88.1	20.6	0.5	0.6	230.8	0.1	146.6	0.5	0.2	-----	159.0	31.9	25.6
1995[1]	65.5	48.2	9.0	105.0	8.0	2.6	-----	264.0	0.1	191.7	1.5	-----	0.1	182.0	54.3	22.1
1996[2]	59.7	85.2	16.7	85.3	19.4	6.6	-----	268.0	0.2	233.1	-----	4.4	-----	192.0	56.9	17.1

[1] Preliminary. [2] Estimate. [3] And lead alloys. [4] Blocks, pigs, etc. [5] Formerly drosses and flue dust. *Source: U.S. Geological Survey (USGS)*

Annual Mine Production of Recoverable Lead in the United States   In Metric Tons

Year	Total	Idaho	Missouri	Montana	Other States	Missouri's % of Total
1987	311,381	W	W	W	W	NA
1988	384,983	W	353,194	8,266	23,523	92%
1989	410,915	W	366,931	W	43,984	89%
1990	483,704	W	380,781	W	102,923	79%
1991	465,931	W	351,995	W	113,936	76%
1992	397,923	W	300,589	W	97,334	76%
1993	353,607	W	276,569	W	77,800	78%
1994	363,443	W	290,738	9,940	63,100	80%
1995[1]	386,000	W	359,000	8,350	18,200	93%
1996[2]	426,000	W	397,000	7,970	21,200	93%

[1] Preliminary. [2] Estimate. W = Withheld. NA = Not available. *Source: U.S. Geological Survey (USGS)*

Mine Production of Recoverable Lead in the United States   In Thousands of Metric Tons

Year	Jan.	Feb.	Mar.	Apr.	May	June	July	Aug.	Sept.	Oct.	Nov.	Dec.	Total
1988	27.9	28.2	36.0	32.7	30.3	32.5	30.4	36.3	33.1	34.4	31.1	31.8	385.0
1989	33.3	31.0	34.4	33.2	33.8	36.1	33.2	38.6	34.3	35.1	32.9	30.1	410.9
1990	42.4	39.0	39.9	37.4	40.8	38.8	42.3	47.2	37.9	43.0	38.5	36.6	483.7
1991	41.5	41.1	41.6	37.8	43.5	36.4	47.5	41.1	36.1	38.9	28.0	26.1	465.9
1992	36.0	34.0	34.0	31.2	31.5	32.4	33.8	32.5	32.5	33.3	30.8	31.7	392.7
1993	33.3	30.5	34.2	30.6	28.5	29.5	25.8	27.5	28.4	27.3	29.5	28.5	355.2
1994	27.6	28.8	33.0	31.3	32.4	29.1	29.4	30.4	31.2	28.0	31.7	29.9	363.4
1995	29.6	30.3	35.2	28.9	32.7	34.8	32.5	33.5	29.9	34.1	31.6	32.1	385.0
1996	36.9	36.4	35.6	35.9	37.5	33.8	35.6	34.1	26.9	35.2	33.6	35.7	426.0
1997[1]	38.0	36.7	37.2	38.6	38.6	35.1	33.4	33.7	34.4	35.4	31.7		392.8

[1] Preliminary. *Source: U.S. Geological Survey (USGS)*

Average Price of Pig Lead, U.S. Primary Producers (Common Corroding)[1] In Cents Per Pound

Year	Jan.	Feb.	Mar.	Apr.	May	June	July	Aug.	Sept.	Oct.	Nov.	Dec.	Average
1988	38.00	34.83	34.00	34.00	34.67	36.59	37.00	37.04	38.81	39.58	40.75	42.04	37.28
1989	40.22	37.00	35.00	35.03	36.14	38.82	39.97	41.30	43.00	43.00	40.55	38.55	39.05
1990	39.73	41.74	54.45	48.10	45.00	45.14	50.62	51.00	49.08	44.52	41.33	37.03	45.65
1991	34.18	33.00	33.00	33.00	32.00	31.80	33.00	33.00	33.70	35.00	35.00	35.00	33.47
1992	35.00	35.00	35.00	35.00	35.00	35.00	36.91	40.00	40.00	36.64	32.63	32.00	35.68
1993	32.00	32.00	32.00	32.00	32.00	32.00	32.00	32.00	32.00	32.00	32.00	33.00	32.08
1994	34.00	34.00	34.00	34.00	34.00	35.73	37.70	38.00	40.00	42.00	43.70	44.00	37.59
1995	44.00	44.00	42.00	42.00	42.00	42.00	42.00	43.65	44.00	44.00	46.10	48.00	43.65
1996	48.00	49.50	50.96	52.00	52.00	52.00	50.29	49.18	50.00	50.00	50.00	50.00	50.33
1997	50.00	50.00	48.70	48.00	48.00	48.00	48.00	48.00	48.00	48.00	48.00	48.00	48.39

[1] New York Delivery. *Source: American Metal Market (AMM)*

Refiners Production[1] of Lead in the United States In Metric Tons

Year	Jan.	Feb.	Mar.	Apr.	May	June	July	Aug.	Sept.	Oct.	Nov.	Dec.	Total
1988	31,117	32,115	35,472	31,117	32,841	31,571	28,849	22,952	29,121	44,997	36,288	35,653	392,087
1989	37,195	32,659	35,381	30,845	32,841	32,206	32,387	34,474	35,653	31,480	32,024	29,303	396,455
1990	34,927	34,383	33,476	35,018	33,022	30,210	30,845	34,474	33,929	38,375	33,476	31,571	403,657
1991	30,763	30,863	33,771	30,248	27,031	22,371	27,973	28,204	29,411	29,846	26,428	28,813	345,714
1992	29,121	27,691	33,366	27,456	26,742	22,441	24,993	21,587	19,365	22,945	23,674	25,414	304,791
1993	29,627	26,693	30,197	27,578	29,814	28,253	16,734	22,817	32,725	31,220	27,953	31,312	335,014
1994	29,908	30,685	31,420	29,059	31,588	31,707	30,661	27,335	31,185	32,874	29,301	30,447	366,170
1995	32,100	29,100	32,600	32,300	32,600	28,300	31,000	29,300	30,600	34,200	30,100	31,500	374,000
1996	34,700	30,400	30,900	28,600	27,500	21,700	25,500	24,700	25,400	25,300	26,100	25,500	326,000
1997[2]	28,800	28,500	31,900	30,400	30,800	28,700	25,900	28,000	21,600	30,500	29,000		314,100

[1] Represents refined lead produced from domestic ores by primary smelters plus small amounts of secondary material passing through these smelters. Includes GSA metal purchased for remelt. [2] Preliminary. *Source: U.S. Geological Survey (USGS)*

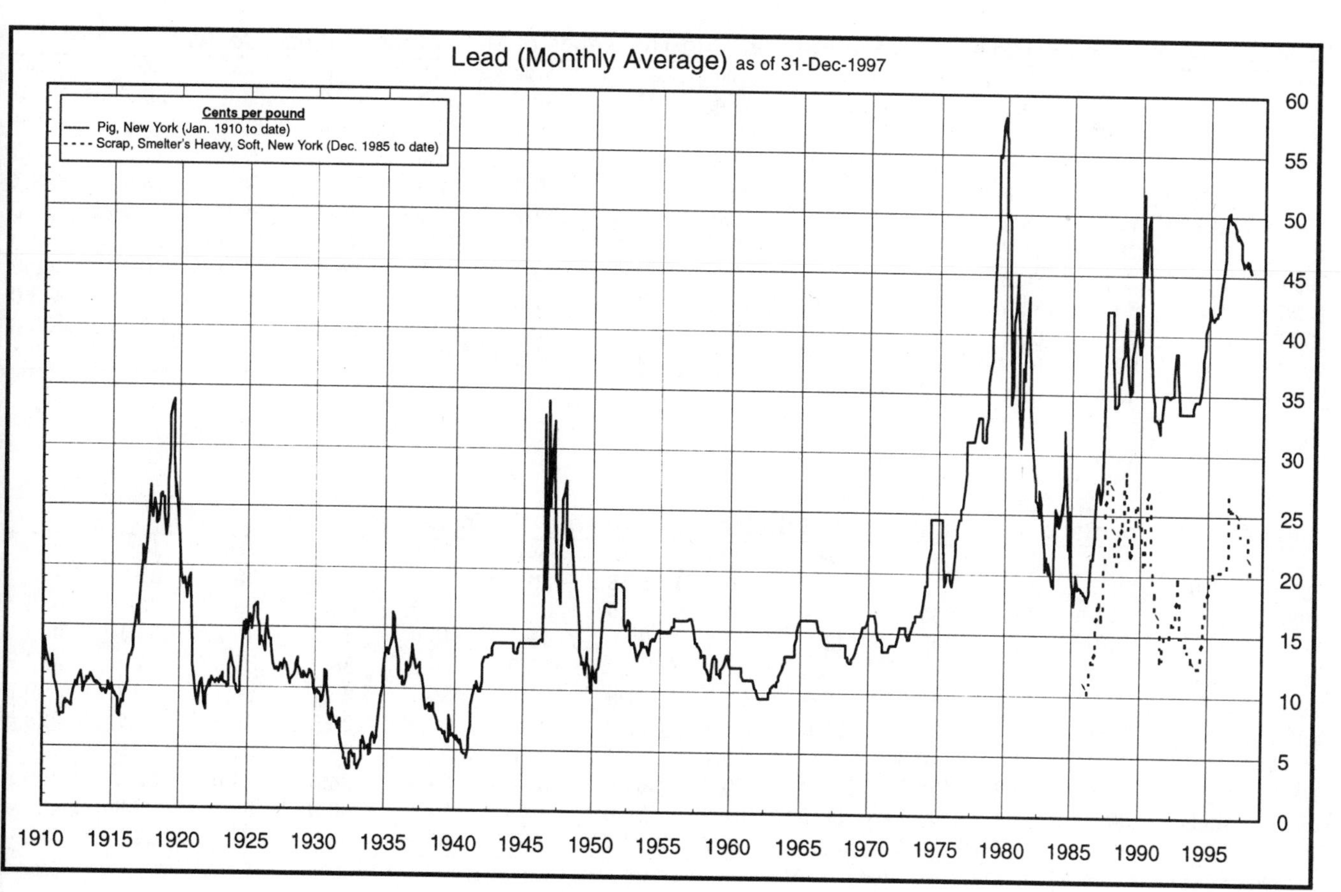

LEAD

Total Stocks of Lead[1] in the United States at Refiners, at End of Month In Metric Tons

Year	Jan.	Feb.	Mar.	Apr.	May	June	July	Aug.	Sept.	Oct.	Nov.	Dec.
1988	22,408	27,670	27,397	28,849	24,041	15,060	14,697	5,988	4,627	10,524	11,884	15,422
1989	26,037	32,931	39,191	37,558	29,665	28,940	31,389	27,942	27,488	18,779	14,606	15,604
1990	14,697	18,325	16,420	21,138	19,323	19,596	20,775	19,958	20,593	23,769	22,771	25,492
1991	24,177	24,333	26,990	21,261	17,474	16,195	15,362	9,072	6,608	4,091	4,491	9,089
1992	9,774	15,785	21,682	25,220	28,940	26,490	26,634	22,347	17,736	14,971	14,796	20,543
1993	28,069	33,338	34,058	34,306	35,775	32,162	22,753	14,797	15,086	14,408	13,456	14,289
1994	11,964	12,633	12,048	11,445	11,598	10,251	12,368	9,256	8,897	10,659	9,060	9,271
1995	8,200	9,750	11,500	14,500	16,700	16,200	21,300	14,000	12,800	9,820	9,830	14,200
1996	15,000	15,000	15,000	15,000	15,000	19,600	19,900	14,200	12,200	7,060	7,830	8,160
1997[2]	8,460	11,800	21,400	19,900	15,000	10,900	6,530	7,790	5,370	7,310	8,710	

[1] Primary refineries. [2] Preliminary. *Source: U.S. Geological Survey (USGS)*

Total[1] Lead Consumption in the United States In Thousands of Metric Tons

Year	Jan.	Feb.	Mar.	Apr.	May	June	July	Aug.	Sept.	Oct.	Nov.	Dec.	Total
1988	99.8	101.4	116.0	99.3	104.0	103.6	92.1	102.5	103.0	110.6	103.4	95.1	1,231
1989	104.7	98.3	101.2	99.2	101.3	101.6	95.2	102.7	105.9	114.0	106.2	97.3	1,283
1990	104.1	106.7	111.9	101.1	106.2	103.2	97.7	112.4	104.6	109.0	104.3	97.3	1,275
1991	101.3	105.3	101.2	101.3	98.4	92.4	90.8	101.9	102.7	106.9	102.4	92.7	1,246
1992	102.5	99.3	108.3	98.5	96.0	103.5	94.8	104.8	106.6	105.4	98.2	92.9	1,215
1993	108.9	107.5	112.3	104.6	109.2	113.8	106.8	112.6	117.1	113.2	109.3	102.2	1,357
1994	107.0	115.2	112.8	111.6	113.5	115.2	114.3	115.5	115.9	121.2	118.7	113.0	1,384
1995	119.0	119.0	119.0	109.0	110.0	113.0	115.0	105.0	115.0	116.0	118.0	116.0	1,370
1996	107.0	100.0	106.0	111.0	113.0	106.0	104.0	146.0	140.0	147.0	163.0	143.0	1,530
1997[2]	139.0	138.0	138.0	140.0	137.0	141.0	116.0	119.0	122.0	123.0	119.0		1,432

[1] Represents total consumption of primary and secondary lead as metal, in chemicals, or in alloys. [2] Preliminary. *Source: U.S. Bureau of Mines (USGS)*

Lead Recovered from Scrap in the United States In Thousands of Metric Tons (Lead Content)

Year	Jan.	Feb.	Mar.	Apr.	May	June	July	Aug.	Sept.	Oct.	Nov.	Dec.	Total
1988	52.2	57.5	60.1	55.9	52.2	59.4	55.3	56.3	60.7	61.8	61.6	59.7	737.0
1989	62.1	58.6	67.5	64.1	65.3	66.3	61.6	65.9	64.4	73.5	67.1	66.9	808.6
1990	68.7	69.6	73.0	69.4	66.9	67.9	67.0	71.8	71.0	77.5	72.3	77.3	923.0
1991	79.0	74.4	71.0	72.0	72.0	70.7	69.8	70.0	72.3	74.6	70.7	75.9	883.7
1992	76.1	71.5	66.5	71.0	73.3	72.3	71.1	77.7	77.5	79.6	76.9	74.3	888.5
1993	71.1	76.8	71.7	80.2	78.9	72.5	70.3	76.6	76.3	77.0	77.9	79.3	903.6
1994	74.0	76.0	84.2	81.7	81.1	79.0	78.9	79.8	78.4	76.4	81.0	80.4	949.0
1995	82.5	80.8	84.4	72.8	73.7	72.5	79.9	71.5	82.3	80.0	82.3	82.1	945.0
1996	75.7	76.2	84.2	83.7	84.7	80.7	81.2	89.0	92.1	98.8	97.3	93.2	1,100.0
1997[1]	88.0	89.8	91.7	86.0	88.2	85.7	86.7	94.7	97.3	96.2	95.2		1,090.4

[1] Preliminary. *Source: U.S. Geological Survey (USGS)*

Domestic Shipments[1] of Lead in the United States, by Refiners In Thousands of Short Tons

Year	Jan.	Feb.	Mar.	Apr.	May	June	July	Aug.	Sept.	Oct.	Nov.	Dec.	Total
1987	27.0	30.5	34.1	41.1	34.8	40.0	37.8	30.1	33.1	33.8	35.7	32.7	410.7
1988	33.5	29.5	39.2	33.0	41.4	44.7	32.0	34.7	33.7	43.0	38.5	35.5	438.7
1989	29.3	28.5	32.2	35.7	45.1	36.4	32.8	41.5	40.0	44.2	40.2	31.1	437.1
1990	39.3	33.9	39.1	33.5	38.4	32.9	32.6	38.9	36.6	38.9	37.9	31.7	433.7
1991	35.4	33.8	34.3	39.8	33.9	26.0	31.8	37.9	35.1	35.7	28.7	26.7	399.2
1992	31.3	23.9	30.4	26.3	25.6	27.2	27.3	28.7	26.3	28.5	26.3	21.7	323.5
1993	24.6	23.6	32.5	30.0	31.3	35.1	28.9	34.0	35.5	35.5	31.7	33.5	376.2
1994	35.9	32.8	35.2	32.7	34.7	36.7	31.6	33.4	34.8	34.3	34.0	33.3	409.3
1995	36.5	30.3	35.1	31.1	33.7	31.9	28.6	40.3	34.9	40.9	33.2	29.8	406.4
1996[2]	37.2	32.4	29.5	30.2	29.4	26.7	27.7	33.5	30.1	33.6	28.1	27.6	366.0

[1] Includes GSA metal. *Source: American Metal Market (AMM)*

Lumber & Plywood

U.S. production of softwood lumber in July 1997 increased over six percent from June 1996, and was up marginally from the total in June 1997. Total softwood production in July 1997 was 3.1 billion board feet. That compared with three billion board feet in June 1997. In July 1997, the Southern Pine region produced 1.48 billion board feet, up from 1.42 billion board feet in June 1997. West Coast region production in July 1997 was 703 million board feet, up from 688 million in June 1997. Inland region softwood production was 609 million board feet in July 1997 while California Redwood region production was 134 million board feet. Other softwoods totaled production of 168 million board feet.

U.S. shipments of softwood lumber in July 1997 were 313 billion board feet which was about the same level as in June 1997. Shipments from the Southern Pine region were 1.54 billion board feet, up slightly from the 1.5 billion board feet in June 1997. West Coast region shipments were 682 million board feet while shipments from the Inland region were 587 million board feet. Softwood lumber shipments from the California Redwood region were 142 million board feet while other softwood lumber shipments were 170 million board feet.

Orders received for softwood lumber in July 1997 were 2.85 billion board feet, down 14 percent from June 1997. Orders received from the Southern Pine region were 1.32 billion board feet, down 19 percent from June 1997. Orders received from the West Coast region were 658 million board feet while from the Inland region they were 587 million board feet. Orders received from the California Redwood region were 122 million board feet while other softwoods orders received were 155 million board feet.

At the end of July 1997, unfilled orders for softwood lumber were 1.39 billion board feet. Gross stocks of softwood lumber were 3.87 billion board feet at the end of July 1997. The disposition of the stocks was: Southern Pine region, 1.65 billion board feet; West Coast region, 775 million board feet; Inland region 902 million board feet; California Redwood region, 291 million board feet; other softwoods, 256 million board feet.

In July 1997, oak flooring shipments were 29.2 million board feet. Unfilled orders for oak flooring on July 31, 1997 were 23.7 million board feet. Gross stocks at the end of July 1997 were four million board feet. In July 1997, maple flooring production was 1.79 million square feet, down nine percent from June 1997. Shipments of maple flooring were 2.59 million square feet in July 1997, up three percent from June 1997. Orders received for maple flooring in July 1997 were 2.27 million square feet, up seven percent from June 1997.

Structural panel production in July 1997 was 2.35 billion square feet, up one percent from June 1997. Shipments of structural panels in July 1997 were 2.32 billion square feet, down four percent from June 1997. Orders received for structural panels were 2.47 billion square feet, up four percent from June 1997. Particle board shipments in July 1997 were 392 million square feet which was up six percent from June 1997.

In the January-July 1997 period, U.S. softwood lumber production was 20.6 billion square feet. That was 7.1 percent above the comparable period of 1996. Softwood lumber production in the Southern Pine region in the first seven months of 1997 was 9.57 billion square feet, up 6.5 percent from the same period of 1996. West Coast region softwood lumber production was 4.8 billion square feet, up over ten percent from the first seven months of 1996. Inland region softwood lumber production was 4.2 billion square feet, over three percent higher than in 1996. California Redwood region softwood lumber production in the first seven months of 1997 was 917 million board feet, over 17 percent above the same period in 1996. Other softwoods production in January-July 1997 was 1.12 billion board feet, over seven percent more than in 1996.

Softwood lumber shipments in January-July 1997 were 20.7 billion board feet, 6.1 percent more than in the same period of 1996. New orders for softwood lumber in the period were 20.5 billion board feet, 6.1 percent more than in the same period of 1996. New orders for softwood lumber in the period were 20.5 billion board feet, up almost three percent from 1996. Oak flooring shipments in January-July 1997 were 233.6 million square feet, up 17.3 percent from 1996.

Futures Markets

Lumber futures and options are traded on the Chicago Mercantile Exchange (CME). The CME also began trading an Oriented Strand Board contract late in 1996.

United States Housing Starts: Seasonally Adjusted Annual Rate In Thousands

Year	Jan.	Feb.	Mar.	Apr.	May	June	July	Aug.	Sept.	Oct.	Nov.	Dec.	Average
1988	1,271	1,473	1,532	1,573	1,421	1,478	1,467	1,493	1,492	1,522	1,569	1,563	1,488
1989	1,621	1,425	1,422	1,339	1,331	1,397	1,427	1,332	1,279	1,410	1,351	1,251	1,382
1990	1,551	1,437	1,289	1,248	1,212	1,177	1,171	1,115	1,110	1,014	1,145	969	1,203
1991	798	965	921	1,001	996	1,036	1,063	1,049	1,015	1,079	1,103	1,079	1,009
1992	1,176	1,250	1,297	1,099	1,214	1,145	1,139	1,226	1,186	1,244	1,214	1,227	1,201
1993	1,210	1,210	1,083	1,258	1,260	1,280	1,254	1,300	1,343	1,392	1,376	1,533	1,292
1994	1,272	1,337	1,564	1,465	1,526	1,409	1,439	1,450	1,474	1,450	1,511	1,455	1,446
1995	1,383	1,325	1,246	1,278	1,309	1,294	1,464	1,404	1,378	1,382	1,451	1,404	1,360
1996	1,444	1,520	1,429	1,522	1,476	1,488	1,492	1,515	1,470	1,407	1,486	1,353	1,467
1997[1]	1,375	1,554	1,479	1,483	1,402	1,503	1,465	1,395	1,507	1,527	1,531	1,519	1,478

[1] Preliminary. Total privately owned. *Source: Bureau of the Census, U.S. Department of Commerce*

LUMBER

World Production of Industrial Roundwood by Selected Countries In Thousands of Cubic Meters

Year	Austria	Canada	Czech[3] Republic	Finland	France	Germany	Japan	Poland	Russia[4]	Spain	Sweden	Turkey	United States
1989	13,575	170,625	16,856	42,670	34,276	41,806	31,202	18,980	305,300	15,691	51,430	5,728	416,900
1990	14,160	173,897	16,398	40,196	34,913	40,934	29,300	15,549	305,300	13,790	49,071	5,960	430,200
1991	12,535	159,039	13,770	31,616	33,754	29,823	27,938	14,334	275,300	12,988	47,600	5,502	388,310
1992	9,255	165,436	8,820	35,279	32,596	29,159	26,934	15,720	164,000	11,624	49,720	8,458	403,100
1993	9,107	173,133	9,706	37,758	29,563	29,357	25,570	15,940	136,030	11,419	50,200	9,408	401,520
1994	11,101	181,054	11,172	44,319	32,442	36,018	25,696	16,711	83,650	12,990	52,100	9,211	410,781
1995[1]	10,746	181,054	11,716	45,799	33,561	35,210	25,696	17,677	83,050	12,997	59,800	10,745	408,948
1996[2]			12,317	42,178				17,696	67,000		52,600	10,229	406,625

[1] Preliminary. [2] Estimate. [3] Formerly part of Czechoslovakia; data not reported separately until 1992. [4] Formerly part of the U.S.S.R.; data not reported separately until 1992. NA = Not available. *Source: Food and Agricultural Organization of the United Nations (FAO-UN)*

Lumber Production and Consumption in the United States In Millions of Board Feet

	Production						Domestic Consumption							
	Softwood						Softwood							
Year	California Redwood	Inland Region	Southern Pine	West Coast	Total	Total Hardwood	Inland Region	Southern Pine	West Coast	Softwood Imports	Total	U.S. Hardwood	Hardwood Imports	Total Lumber
1989	2,181	11,407	12,473	10,354	38,235	11,695	11,008	12,240	9,117	14,680	50,558	11,235	511	62,304
1990	2,214	11,395	12,676	10,029	38,130	12,170	11,180	12,108	8,096	13,806	48,513	10,636	390	59,539
1991	2,053	11,348	12,544	9,811	37,545	12,415	11,134	12,125	7,950	13,638	47,966	11,970	375	60,311
1992	1,972	10,452	12,911	8,751	35,791	12,660	10,390	12,388	7,184	12,148	45,003	11,070	255	56,328
1993	1,657	9,510	12,507	7,908	33,161	11,633	9,302	12,147	6,454	11,742	42,225	10,278	226	52,730
1994	1,474	8,097	15,010	7,902	34,107	12,311	7,856	14,618	6,833	16,380	48,104	11,127	394	59,625
1995	1,305	7,015	14,708	7,452	32,233	12,434	6,956	14,384	6,530	17,396	47,749	11,372	379	59,501
1996	1,371	7,079	15,262	7,745	33,266	NA	7,073	15,112	6,821	18,214	49,883	NA	NA	NA
I	319	1,702	3,616	1,745	7,807	NA	1,665	3,511	1,494	4,496	11,778	NA	NA	NA
II	348	1,776	4,001	1,935	8,523	NA	1,794	4,001	1,743	4,558	12,793	NA	NA	NA
III	360	1,822	3,984	2,081	8,721	NA	1,896	3,990	1,847	4,893	13,346	NA	NA	NA
IV	344	1,779	3,661	1,984	8,215	NA	1,718	3,610	1,737	4,267	11,966	NA	NA	NA
1997[1] I	373	1,749	3,875	1,983	8,438	NA	1,736	3,765	1,676	4,063	11,832	NA	NA	NA
II	410	1,838	4,228	2,113	9,083	NA	1,802	4,289	1,970	4,823	13,572	NA	NA	NA
III	385	1,833	4,120	2,048	8,868	NA	1,761	4,099	1,873	4,680	13,131	NA	NA	NA

[1] Preliminary. NA = not avaliable. *Source: American Forest & Paper Association (AF&PA)*

Stocks (Gross) of Softwood Lumber in the United States, on First of Month In Millions of Board Feet

Year	Jan.	Feb.	Mar.	Apr.	May	June	July	Aug.	Sept.	Oct.	Nov.	Dec.
1988	4,771	4,867	4,950	4,994	4,939	4,894	4,685	4,677	4,765	4,823	4,951	4,979
1989	4,999	4,896	4,818	4,837	4,810	4,740	4,746	4,748	4,797	4,762	4,908	4,934
1990	4,898	5,022	5,022	5,020	4,961	5,043	4,831	4,783	4,752	4,810	4,834	4,809
1991	4,734	4,925	4,949	4,946	4,849	4,600	4,699	4,684	4,793	4,786	4,741	4,710
1992	4,616	4,603	4,567	4,608	4,730	4,731	4,678	4,606	4,418	4,419	4,365	4,263
1993	4,669	4,217	4,166	4,239	4,490	4,618	4,599	4,526	4,418	4,445	4,282	4,298
1994	4,207	4,512	4,656	4,816	4,883	4,649	4,738	4,432	4,349	4,539	4,235	4,294
1995	4,403	4,336	4,344	4,653	4,352	4,663	4,508	4,323	4,342	4,359	4,361	4,335
1996	4,293	4,435	4,459	4,357	4,251	4,153	4,156	4,038	3,918	3,965	3,939	3,906
1997[1]	3,973	4,019	4,113	4,067	3,963	4,017	3,915	3,871	3,875	3,927	3,925	3,865

[1] Preliminary. *Source: American Forest & Paper Association (AF&PA)*

Lumber (Softwood)[2] Production in the United States In Millions of Board Feet

Year	Jan.	Feb.	Mar.	Apr.	May	June	July	Aug.	Sept.	Oct.	Nov.	Dec.	Total
1988	3,814	4,042	4,389	4,247	4,245	4,137	3,671	4,056	4,180	4,040	3,715	3,641	48,177
1989	3,849	3,311	3,758	3,773	4,025	4,273	3,683	4,023	3,787	4,172	3,811	3,615	46,080
1990	4,160	3,862	4,300	4,121	4,084	3,944	3,976	4,060	3,602	4,015	3,412	2,914	46,450
1991	3,534	3,410	3,661	3,958	3,837	3,762	3,664	3,808	3,682	3,933	3,473	3,254	43,976
1992	3,836	3,628	4,121	3,862	3,632	3,911	3,882	3,746	3,736	4,048	3,617	3,425	45,444
1993	3,545	3,596	3,954	3,809	3,555	3,787	3,685	3,930	3,824	4,103	3,883	3,576	45,247
1994	3,839	3,662	4,097	3,735	3,972	4,113	3,785	4,124	4,135	4,145	3,636	3,851	47,094
1995	4,084	3,577	3,931	3,675	3,805	3,897	3,641	3,866	3,757	4,105	3,549	3,297	45,184
1996	2,600	2,606	2,757	2,903	2,833	2,819	2,942	3,077	2,858	3,179	2,758	2,424	33,756
1997[1]	3,012	2,791	2,866	3,149	2,890	3,027	3,097	2,889	2,905	3,094	2,507		35,157

[1] Preliminary. [2] Data prior to 1996 are for Softwood and Hardwood. *Source: American Forest & Paper Association (AF&PA)*

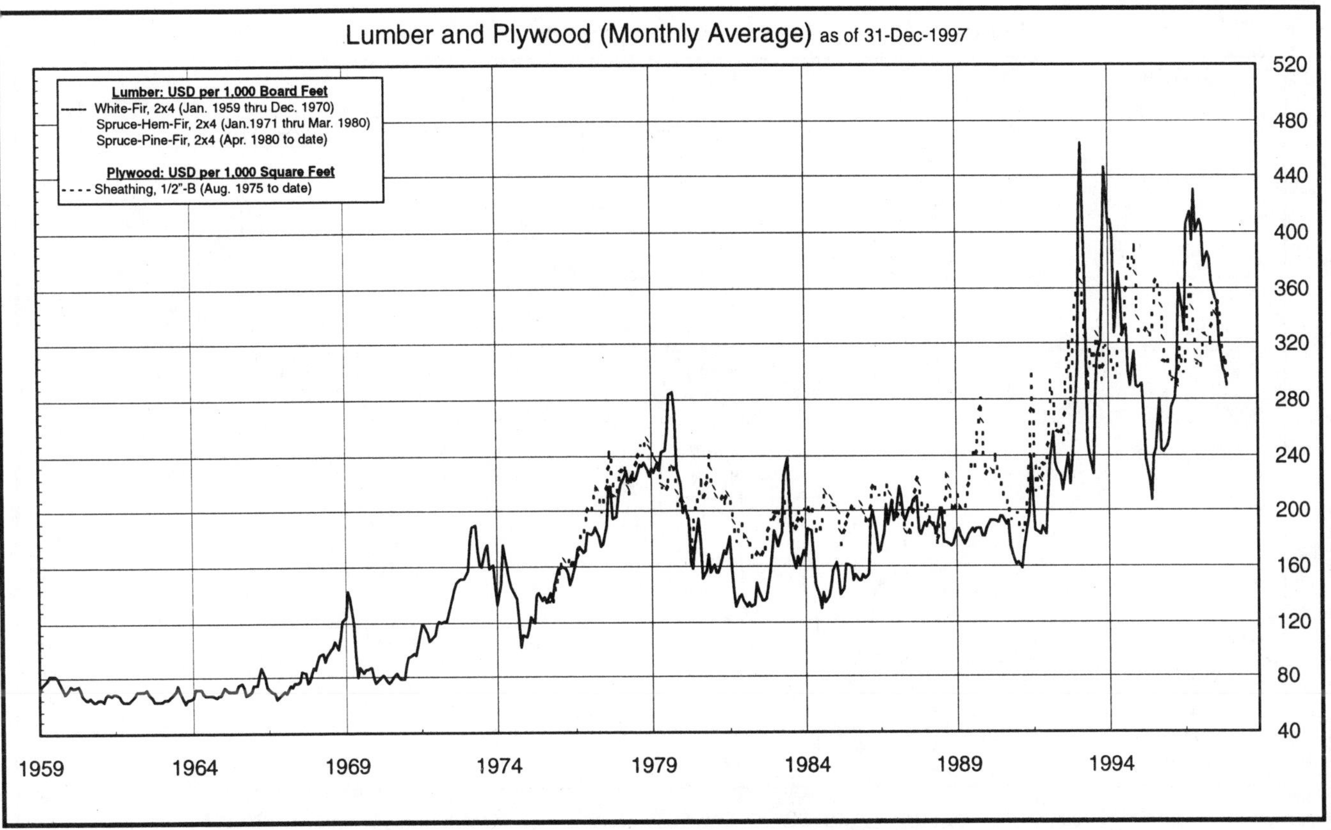

Lumber (Softwood)[2] Shipments in the United States In Millions of Board Feet

Year	Jan.	Feb.	Mar.	Apr.	May	June	July	Aug.	Sept.	Oct.	Nov.	Dec.	Total
1988	3,790	4,092	4,320	4,257	4,261	4,309	3,688	3,929	4,038	3,871	3,656	3,649	49,839
1989	3,914	3,417	3,877	3,846	4,163	4,420	3,760	3,977	3,823	4,081	3,854	3,626	50,476
1990	4,035	3,870	4,317	4,173	3,952	4,176	3,912	3,987	3,453	3,890	3,357	2,873	47,773
1991	3,240	3,301	3,617	4,037	4,028	3,764	3,412	3,926	3,676	4,012	3,477	3,370	44,559
1992	3,912	3,693	4,078	3,682	3,565	3,936	3,884	3,878	3,692	4,147	3,745	3,491	45,703
1993	3,575	3,649	3,852	3,563	3,402	3,759	3,721	3,997	3,724	4,211	3,798	3,617	44,868
1994	3,576	3,663	3,912	3,761	4,192	4,091	4,039	4,163	3,914	4,321	3,603	3,696	46,931
1995	3,971	3,584	3,855	3,831	3,765	4,026	3,826	3,870	3,760	4,055	3,478	3,367	45,388
1996	2,460	2,581	2,863	3,002	2,934	2,813	3,058	3,196	2,813	3,206	2,792	2,353	34,071
1997[1]	2,966	2,697	2,890	3,253	2,834	3,126	3,139	2,885	2,852	3,096	2,568		35,243

[1] Preliminary. [2] Data prior to 1996 are for Softwood and Hardwood. *Source: American Forest & Paper Association (AF&PA)*

Imports and Exports of Lumber in the United States, by Type In Millions of Board Feet

	Imports[2]								Exports[2]						
	Softwood								Softwood						
Year	Cedar	Douglas Fir	Hemlock	Pine	Spruce	Total	Total Hardwood	Total Lumber	Douglas Fir	Hemlock	Ponderosa/White Pine	Southern Pine	Total	Total Hardwood	Total Lumber
1988	786.8	721.4	539.7	332.3	10,284.5	13,806.0	390.1	14,225.3	888.6	714.9	233.4	492.3	3,263.9	1,232.0	4,528.0
1989	786.0	603.4	469.5	335.8	7,387.4	13,638.4	375.1	14,022.5	1,018.2	670.9	197.0	442.3	3,319.1	856.0	4,213.1
1990	652.8	375.4	362.4	87.6	3,535.7	12,148.2	255.4	12,429.4	818.5	549.4	215.2	374.7	2,970.4	877.7	3,900.0
1991	700.6	354.1	287.8	55.7	2,248.3	11,741.5	226.2	11,998.2	798.1	497.7	222.9	396.0	2,863.2	934.3	3,858.9
1992	666.4	355.3	300.0	91.4	2,410.5	13,380.5	276.4	13,681.9	735.0	396.7	308.7	440.5	2,650.7	977.2	3,687.1
1993	615.3	327.6	354.9	84.6	3,104.1	15,259.9	335.0	15,625.4	664.9	340.4	273.3	339.6	2,376.4	1,008.9	3,468.9
1994	702.6	336.2	399.2	97.2	2,948.5	16,380.3	394.4	16,787.1	591.9	283.2	157.2	356.7	2,186.6	1,040.9	3,333.4
1995	768.0	395.4	258.1	97.1	2,827.7	17,395.3	379.7	17,786.9	637.9	227.0	106.7	334.6	1,987.5	1,100.5	3,189.5
1996	726.6	264.4	257.1	133.4	1,988.8	18,213.5	396.8	18,640.6	685.4	194.9	96.6	314.5	1,935.3	1,141.0	3,173.4
1997[1] I	145.7	37.6	47.9	62.8	245.5	4,062.6	98.9	4,165.5	161.3	43.4	36.4	78.0	563.5	319.3	901.0
II	161.7	75.6	55.8	76.7	255.3	4,823.4	118.9	4,950.3	108.6	22.3	30.6	76.4	483.8	351.1	856.8
III	145.1	71.2	67.7	87.5	287.0	4,679.9	117.4	4,804.6	91.9	20.5	25.7	69.1	401.5	614.9	1,040.8

[1] Preliminary. [2] Includes sawed timber, board planks and scantings, flooring, box shook and railroad ties. *Source: American Forest & Paper Association*

Average Open Interest of Random Lumber[1] Futures in Chicago In Contracts

Year	Jan.	Feb.	Mar.	Apr.	May	June	July	Aug.	Sept.	Oct.	Nov.	Dec.
1988	6,212	6,701	5,791	6,395	5,548	5,644	5,586	6,272	5,527	5,697	5,368	5,919
1989	7,982	7,484	7,436	8,244	7,363	7,921	8,248	8,055	7,065	7,192	6,600	6,167
1990	6,078	6,061	4,991	4,957	4,538	4,359	3,570	3,028	2,881	3,105	2,632	2,001
1991	1,922	2,003	2,023	2,354	2,076	2,601	2,571	2,181	2,276	2,480	2,206	1,606
1992	1,969	2,651	2,743	2,467	1,900	1,774	1,338	1,369	1,507	1,441	1,745	2,155
1993	2,194	2,432	2,163	2,055	2,302	2,658	2,254	2,141	2,011	2,080	2,140	2,721
1994	2,571	2,814	2,638	2,563	1,936	1,838	1,705	1,854	2,102	2,169	1,702	1,967
1995	1,757	1,923	2,142	2,509	2,742	3,252	2,896	2,918	2,809	3,039	2,626	2,940
1996	3,378	4,040	3,752	4,395	5,666	4,972	3,280	5,243	4,743	4,797	4,341	3,691
1997	3,745	3,211	3,048	3,337	2,895	3,137	2,767	3,119	3,267	4,006	3,606	4,068

[1] Data July 1995 thru March 1996, Lumber and Random Lumber. *Source: Chicago Mercantile Exchange (CME)*

Volume of Trading of Random Lumber[1] Futures in Chicago In Contracts

Year	Jan.	Feb.	Mar.	Apr.	May	June	July	Aug.	Sept.	Oct.	Nov.	Dec.	Total
1988	35,451	32,410	32,886	30,386	28,100	37,508	27,550	33,454	29,743	24,632	26,131	23,238	371,489
1989	29,963	25,857	23,947	31,427	26,789	26,712	20,258	19,514	18,790	18,965	17,286	14,395	273,903
1990	27,416	21,914	20,948	18,362	19,053	16,084	16,465	13,446	8,914	11,839	15,794	11,749	201,984
1991	10,535	13,460	10,326	11,309	15,135	19,029	19,350	14,912	12,214	14,054	10,295	9,902	160,521
1992	17,073	16,778	17,557	13,713	14,059	13,807	12,177	13,043	12,127	11,261	11,514	17,425	170,534
1993	14,915	15,080	14,808	14,661	14,241	15,308	13,287	13,358	12,400	13,248	18,150	18,728	178,184
1994	16,837	15,204	17,323	17,380	14,996	14,348	11,542	13,327	14,856	13,032	10,997	13,121	172,963
1995	12,150	12,909	15,088	12,139	14,536	20,126	13,766	16,919	15,718	18,981	15,551	14,803	182,686
1996	22,954	19,960	20,956	27,094	28,271	26,100	19,302	27,792	31,982	32,042	25,236	22,525	304,214
1997	28,561	20,946	21,071	24,624	18,248	24,797	20,308	18,503	21,736	24,416	15,131	21,977	260,318

[1] Data July 1995 thru March 1996, Lumber and Random Lumber. *Source: Chicago Mercantile Exchange (CME)*

Production of Plywood by Selected Countries In Thousands of Cubic Meters

Year	Austria	Canada	Finland	France	Germany	Italy	Japan	Poland	Romania	Russia[3]	Spain	Sweden	United States
1991	140	1,927	477	470	424	450	6,588	111	51	1,548	140	67	16,508
1992	150	1,838	462	484	429	427	5.954	132	100	1,268	120	55	17,109
1993	150	1,824	621	460	416	415	5,263	133	100	1,042	200	73	17,093
1994	150	1,834	700	594	397	427	4,865	124	97	890	210	85	17,380
1995	150	1,831	778	559	498	418	4,865	115	83	939	210	108	17,140
1996[1]	150	1,814	869	537	507	402	NA	109	83	928	210	115	16,975
1997[2]	150	1,850	850	470	310	400	NA	113	95	1,020	125	120	16,000

[1] Preliminary. [2] Estimate. [3] Formerly part of the U.S.S.R.; data not reported separately until 1992. NA = Not available.
Source: Food and Agricultural Organization of the United Nations (FAO-UN)

Imports of Plywood by Selected Countries In Thousands of Cubic Meters

Year	Austria	Belgium	Canada	Denmark	France	Germany	Italy	Japan	Nether-lands	Sweden	Switzer-land	United Kingdom	United States
1991	76	385	262	161	414	664	204	3,046	619	131	121	1,271	1,338
1992	79	300	242	198	423	879	216	3,003	583	106	110	1,397	1,649
1993	77	436	288	152	263	865	241	4,105	612	98	118	1,157	1,630
1994	104	267	288	171	234	1,003	257	4,074	560	126	144	1,202	1,547
1995	116	146	353	188	260	1,177	323	4,074	552	112	136	1,127	1,769
1996[1]	110	215	422	167	256	1,549	140	NA	524	122	129	1,132	1,769
1997[2]	110	270	100	170	300	1,080	300	NA	549	125	130	1,025	1,800

[1] Preliminary. [2] Estimate. NA = Not available. *Source: Food and Agricultural Organization of the United Nations (FAO-UN)*

Exports of Plywood by Selected Countries In Thousands of Cubic Meters

Year	Austria	Baltic States[3]	Belgium	Canada	Finland	France	Germany	Italy	Nether-lands	Poland	Russia[3]	Spain	United States
1991	130	240	169	288	347	222	81	95	63	49	-------	39	1,374
1992	119	25	132	412	348	228	122	90	72	56	226	32	1,618
1993	129	90	87	416	542	194	110	104	99	41	464	60	1,562
1994	158	143	134	511	627	193	131	108	102	66	568	67	1,346
1995	130	138	88	818	668	183	149	96	72	60	670	48	1,395
1996[1]	160	151	88	872	794	214	133	15	58	50	619	77	1,106
1997[2]	160	NA	120	650	750	245	110	100	70	55	720	40	1,400

[1] Preliminary. [2] Estimate. [3] Formerly part of the U.S.S.R.; data not reported separately until 1992. NA = Not available. *Source: Food and Agricultural Organization of the United Nations (FAO-UN)*

Selected World Prices of Plywood

Year	Jan.	Feb.	Mar.	Apr.	May	June	July	Aug.	Sept.	Oct.	Nov.	Dec.	Average
Southeast Asia, Lauan, Wholesale Price, Spot Tokyo In U.S. Cents Per Sheet[1]													
1993	512.0	611.8	700.4	708.0	712.0	715.0	696.2	703.8	664.8	617.3	644.3	630.7	659.7
1994	565.0	600.3	617.1	647.1	637.2	629.6	649.7	631.0	566.5	567.9	562.7	540.0	601.2
1995	551.0	599.1	656.5	665.1	635.4	627.0	562.7	560.6	527.4	526.6	539.7	540.2	582.6
1996	529.1	548.6	529.2	521.1	535.5	523.6	521.4	538.3	528.5	525.1	526.2	518.6	528.8
1997	500.3	479.6	489.4	485.6	511.9	524.9	512.1	500.7					500.6
Canada, Export Unit Value, F.O.B. In Canadian Dollar Per Cubic Meter													
1992	426.14	409.62	373.22	396.94	387.59	395.95	354.61	373.58	385.20	395.29	410.59	353.95	388.56
1993	392.59	396.65	393.73	424.19	515.51	448.76	408.39	435.72	505.58	517.58	494.52	476.08	450.78
1994	442.04	574.74	553.92	553.81	542.95	458.48	472.29	510.01	526.42	454.20	462.90	499.71	504.29
1995	473.77	480.78											477.28
Finland, Export Unit Value, F.O.B. In Markka Per Cubic Meter													
1993	4,135	3,939	4,088	3,752	3,876	3,906	3,962	3,817	3,914	4,046	3,890	3,719	3,920
1994	3,758	3,518	3,829	3,822	3,800	4,029	3,963	3,916	4,041	3,680	3,631	3,569	3,796
1995	3,681	3,809	3,751	3,897	3,752	3,769	3,771	3,543	3,430	3,370	3,268	2,923	3,579
1996	3,084	2,548	3,129	3,296	3,075	3,225	3,070	3,003	3,245	3,036	3,264	2,900	3,060
United Kingdom, Import Unit Value, C.I.F. In Pound Sterling Per Cubic Meter													
1993	227.26	255.36	269.62	204.76	270.40	249.27	265.25	273.33	291.90	261.68	328.13	304.04	266.75
1994	256.36	252.50	263.47	299.61	291.19	209.08	275.85	272.06	294.44	276.46	213.94	247.54	262.71
1995	232.68	239.77	257.68	264.72	229.18	268.11	256.09	241.61	263.31	285.36	275.38	282.68	258.05
1996	238.86	249.65	224.40	273.23	256.16	275.38	269.36	247.83	253.37	261.66	260.77	293.42	258.67

[1] Sheet measurement = 1.2cm X 90.0cm X 1.8cm. *Source: Food and Agricultural Organization of the United Nations (FAO-UN)*

Magnesium

Magnesium has a density that is two-thirds of aluminum. Because of that property, it finds widespread use in aircraft and automobile parts, photo optical instruments, engines, luggage, water heaters and dry-cell batteries. Among the magnesium compounds, magnesium sulfate is consumed in explosives, fertilizers and paper production. Magnesium oxide is used in water treatment, household cleaners and pharmaceuticals. Demand for magnesium is expected to increase as U.S. automobile manufacturers introduce new magnesium compounds in the 1998 models.

The U.S. Geological Survey indicated that a world oversupply of magnesium in 1996 led to a sharp decline in prices throughout the year. As a result of the oversupply, production in the U.S. declined. Russia continued to be the largest source of primary magnesium. Canada is the largest source of alloy magnesium. For the first time in twenty years, the U.S. imported more magnesium than it exported. Automotive applications continued to dominate new applications for magnesium. The 1997 model year cars were estimated to contain an average of 2.9 kilograms per vehicle of magnesium alloys. New applications in the 1997 model year included instrument panel support beams in some luxury sedans and steering column support brackets. Rapidly changing magnesium costs were cited as the reason for two U.S. auto manufacturers to cancel some programs to incorporate more magnesium diecastings into domestic passenger vehicles.

U.S. domestic primary magnesium production in the second quarter of 1997 was 30,000 metric tonnes, virtually the same as production in the first quarter. Producers shipments in the second quarter of 1997 were 32,500 tonnes and inventories decreased to 13,600 tonnes.

U.S. imports for consumption of magnesium in May 1997 were 4,920 tonnes. Of that total, 1,540 tonnes were magnesium metal; 217 tonnes were waste and scrap; 3,130 tonnes (magnesium content) were alloys, and 34 tonnes (magnesium content) were sheet, tubing, ribbons, wire, powder and other materials. For the January-May 1997 period, imports of magnesium totaled 23,300 tonnes. For all of 1996, they totaled 46,600 tonnes.

U.S. exports of magnesium in May 1997 were 3,120 tonnes of which 1,270 tonnes were magnesium metal; 752 tonnes were waste and scrap; 777 tonnes were alloys (gross weight), and 314 tonnes were sheet, tubing and other magnesium materials. In 1996, the U.S. exported 40,500 tonnes of magnesium.

World Production of Magnesium (Primary and Secondary) In Metric Tons

	Primary Production								Secondary Production				
Year	Brazil	Canada	China	France	Norway	Russia[4]	United States	World Total	Japan	United Kingdom	United States	Former USSR	World Total
1987	5,488	8,800	3,000	13,601	56,907	90,000	124,396	323,930	10,124	1,000	45,165	8,000	65,665
1988	5,865	7,600	3,200	13,776	50,317	91,000	141,983	334,348	15,099	1,000	50,207	8,000	75,825
1989	6,200	7,000	3,500	14,600	49,827	91,000	152,066	344,447	20,270	1,000	51,200	8,000	81,970
1990	8,700	25,300	5,900	14,000	48,222	88,000	139,333	354,000	23,308	900	54,808	7,500	88,100
1991	7,800	35,512	8,600	14,050	44,322	80,000	131,288	342,000	17,158	800	50,543	7,000	77,100
1992	7,300	25,800	10,600	13,660	30,404	40,000	137,000	295,000	12,978	800	57,000	6,500	78,900
1993	9,700	23,000	11,800	10,982	27,300	30,000	132,000	269,000	13,215	1,000	58,900	6,000	80,700
1994	9,700	28,900	24,000	12,280	27,635	35,400	128,000	282,000	19,009	1,000	62,100	5,000	88,700
1995[1]	9,700	48,100	93,600	14,450	28,000	37,500	142,000	389,000	11,767	1,000	65,000	6,000	85,500
1996[2]	9,000	54,000	50,000	14,000	30,000	35,000	133,000	341,000	12,500	1,000	70,900	6,000	92,000

[1] Preliminary. [2] Estimate. [4] Formerly part of the U.S.S.R.; data not reported separately until 1992. *Source: U.S. Geological Survey (USGS)*

Salient Statistics of Magnesium in the United States In Metric Tons

	Production								Domestic Consumption of Primary Magnesium					
		Secondary												
						Imports		$ Price						
	Primary	New	Old			for Con-	Stocks	per	Castings	Wrought	Total	Aluminum	Other	
Year	(Ingot)	Scrap	Scrap	Total	Exports[3]	sumption	Dec. 31[4]	Pound[5]	Structural Products			Alloys	Uses[6]	Total
1987	134,396	21,712	23,452	45,164	44,182	10,851	28,000	1.53	6,285	8,300	14,585	52,172	27,863	94,620
1988	141,983	22,567	27,640	50,207	49,802	14,407	25,000	1.58-1.63	7,069	10,138	17,207	53,671	29,915	100,793
1989	152,066	23,229	27,971	51,200	56,631	12,289	26,000	1.63	7,455	9,653	17,108	53,821	34,297	88,118
1990	139,333	23,424	31,384	54,808	51,834	26,755	26,000	1.43-1.63	9,078	10,944	20,022	45,060	31,026	76,086
1991	131,288	23,059	27,484	50,543	55,160	31,863	27,000	1.43	8,857	8,802	17,659	45,809	28,404	74,213
1992	136,947	26,191	30,854	57,045	51,951	11,844	13,000	1.46-1.53	10,223	8,843	19,066	41,003	33,758	74,761
1993	132,144	28,313	30,577	58,890	38,815	37,248	26,000	1.43-1.46	12,543	9,870	22,413	46,498	32,202	78,700
1994	128,000	32,500	29,600	62,100	45,200	29,100	20,030	1.63	15,676	7,690	23,366	61,100	27,900	89,000
1995[1]	142,000	35,400	29,800	65,100	38,300	34,800	21,193	1.93-2.25	15,231	8,510	23,741	60,200	25,100	85,300
1996[2]	133,000	40,800	30,100	70,900	40,500	46,600	25,000	1.70-1.80	16,400	8,080	24,480	52,300	25,500	77,800

[1] Preliminary. [2] Estimate. [3] Metal & alloys in crude form & scrap. [4] Estimate of Industry Stocks, metal. [5] Magnesium (99.8%), F.O.B. Valasco, Texas. [6] Distributive or sacrificial purposes. *Source: U.S. Geological Survey (USGS)*

Manganese

Manganese is primarily used in the steel industry as an alloy. Virtually all steel contains some amount of manganese, which increases the metal's hardness. Manganese is essential to iron and steel production due to its sulfur-fixing, deoxidizing and alloying properties. No practical approach exists for replacing it with other materials or for obtaining the bulk of U.S. requirements from domestic sources. Manganese ore, when converted to a metallic alloy with iron, forms the compound ferromanganese. Nonmetallurgical uses for manganese include plant fertilizer and animal feeds. Manganese is the key component of some widely used aluminum alloys and is used in oxide form in dry cell batteries.

U.S. imports for consumption of manganese in June 1997 were 41,500 metric tonnes, manganese content. Of the total, some 8,090 tonnes were in the form of manganese ore and manganese dioxide. Another 33,400 tonnes were in the form of manganese ferroalloy and manganese metal. The June 1997 import total of 41,500 tonnes is well below the June 1996 total of 75,400 tonnes. In the January-June 1997 period, U.S. imports of manganese were 252,000 tonnes. Some 66,000 tonnes were manganese ore and dioxide and 186,000 tonnes were ferroalloy and manganese metal. In the comparable period of 1996, U.S. imports were 397,000 tonnes.

U.S. imports of silicomanganese in June 1997 were 17,800 tonnes, gross weight, with 11,800 tonnes manganese content. In the first half of 1997, silicomanganese imports were 117,000 tonnes, gross weight, with 78,600 tonnes manganese content. The major suppliers of silicomanganese to the U.S. in the first half of 1997 were South Africa, Australia, Mexico and India. Together they supplied over 80 percent.

U.S. imports for consumption of ferromanganese in June 1997 were 26,200 tonnes, gross weight, with 20,600 tonnes manganese content. Of the total, low carbon manganese was 1,190 tonnes, gross weight, 1,070 tonnes manganese content. Another 4,560 tonnes, gross weight, 3,550 tonnes manganese content was medium carbon manganese. High carbon ferromanganese imports in June 1997 were 20,500 tonnes, gross weight, 15,900 tonnes manganese content. In the January-June 1997 period, U.S. imports of ferromanganese were 128,000 tonnes, gross weight, 100,000 tonnes manganese content. The major suppliers of ferromanganese were South Africa, Brazil, France, Australia, Mexico and Japan.

U.S. imports of manganese ore in June 1997 were 122,000 tonnes, gross weight, with 57,500 tonnes manganese content. The major suppliers were Gabon and Mexico.

World Production of Manganese Ore   In Thousands of Metric Tons (Gross Weight)

Year	Australia[2] 37-53[4]	Brazil 30-50	China 30	Gabon 50-53	Georgia[5] 29-30	Ghana 30-50	Hungary[3] 30-33	India 10-54	Mexico 27-50	Morocco 50-53	South Africa 30-48 +	Ukraine[5] 29-30	World Total
1987	1,853	2,068	2,631	2,403	-----	275	78	1,302	386	43	3,294	9,356	23,954
1988	1,985	1,991	3,212	2,254	-----	260	81	1,333	444	30	4,023	9,108	25,013
1989	2,124	1,904	3,200	2,592	-----	297	84	1,334	394	32	4,884	9,141	26,260
1990	1,920	2,300	4,080	2,423	-----	247	60	1,385	451	49	4,402	8,500	26,108
1991	1,412	2,000	5,150	1,620	-----	320	30	1,401	254	59	3,146	7,240	22,900
1992	1,251	1,703	5,300	1,556	500	276	18	1,810	407	44	2,464	5,819	21,800
1993	2,092	1,837	5,860	1,290	300	295	59	1,655	363	43	2,507	3,800	20,800
1994	1,920	2,100	3,570	1,436	150	270	55	1,632	307	31	2,851	2,979	18,000
1995	2,177	2,105	6,900	1,934	100	176	-----	1,764	472	-----	3,199	3,200	23,000
1996[1]	2,109	2,200	6,000	2,000	97	436	-----	1,740	485	-----	3,240	3,000	22,300

[1] Preliminary. [2] Metallurgical Ore. [3] Concentrate. [4] Range of percentage of manganese. [5] Formerly part of the U.S.S.R.; data not reported separately until 1992. *Source: U.S. Geological Survey (USGS)*

Salient Statistics of Manganese in the United States   In Thousands of Metric Tons (Gross Weight)

		Manganese Ore (35% or More Manganese)				Ferromanganese				Silicomanganese	
Year	Net Import Reliance as a % of Apparent Consumption	Imports for Consumption	Exports	Consumption	Stocks, Dec. 31[3]	Imports for Consumption	Exports	Consumption	Avg. Price Mn. Metallurgical Ore $ Lg. Ton Unit[4]	Exports	Imports
1987	100	309	57	484	414	334	3	371	1.27	0.6	176.6
1988	100	464	62	503	415	482	3	425	1.75	8.3	256.0
1989	100	580	52	559	470	432	8	399	2.76	6.5	281.5
1990	100	307	70	497	379	380	7	413	3.78	1.8	224.5
1991	100	234	66	473	275	320	15	346	3.72	2.9	258.3
1992	100	247	13	438	276	304	13	339	3.25	9.2	257.2
1993	100	232	16	389	302	347	18	341	2.60	9.4	316.0
1994	100	331	15	449	269	336	11	347	2.40	6.8	273.0
1995[1]	100	394	15	486	309	310	11	348	2.40	7.8	305.0
1996[2]	100	478	32	478	319	374	10	326	2.55	5.3	323.0

[1] Preliminary. [2] Estimate. [3] Including bonded warehouses; excludes Government stocks; also excludes small tonnages of dealers' stocks. [4] 46-48% Mn, C.I.F., U.S. Ports. *Source: U.S. Geological Survey (USGS)*

MANGANESE

Imports[3] of Manganese Ore (20% or More Mn) in the United States In Metric Tons (Mn Content)

Year	Australia	Brazil	Gabon	Mexico	Morocco	South Africa	Total	Customs Value Thous. $
1987	44,223	26,919	80,208	3,368	27	-----	154,747	15,079
1988[4]	35,675	24,498	133,045	32,197	85	-----	225,499	29,074
1989	54,828	84,626	99,463	8,916	18	19,612	270,786	43,794
1990	32,544	20,662	67,828	2,732	18	9,958	148,944	40,054
1991	16,485	2,583	79,997	4,673	44	-----	117,255	40,332
1992	25,519	15,541	75,354	3,930	56	-----	120,400	29,967
1993	30,171	5,573	66,659	7,317	43	6,006	115,770	24,927
1994	23,200	4,530	112,000	13,700	56	7,780	161,000	29,800
1995[1]	31,600	7,080	104,000	23,600	37	13,100	187,000	33,300
1996[2]	48,900	5,640	140,000	16,100	9	20,800	231,000	42,400

[1] Preliminary. [2] Estimate. [3] Imports for consumption. [4] Manganese content of 35% or more prior to 1989. *Source: U.S. Geological Survey (USGS)*

Average Price of Ferromanganese[1] (High Carbon - F.O.B. Plant) In Dollars Per Gross Ton -- Carloads

Year	Jan.	Feb.	Mar.	Apr.	May	June	July	Aug.	Sept.	Oct.	Nov.	Dec.	Average
1987	NQ	NQ	NQ	NQ	326.25	331.88	339.50	345.00	355.00	358.00	363.00	373.00	348.95
1988	382.50	382.50	414.50	422.50	435.63	440.00	457.50	475.00	530.00	550.00	550.00	550.00	465.84
1989	550.00	550.50	573.75	597.50	640.00	640.00	640.00	634.00	610.00	610.00	610.00	610.00	605.48
1990	610.00	610.00	610.00	610.00	610.00	610.00	610.00	610.00	610.00	610.00	610.00	610.00	610.00
1991	610.00	610.00	610.00	610.00	610.00	610.00	610.00	610.00	610.00	610.00	610.00	610.00	610.00
1992	610.00	610.00	610.00	610.00	610.00	610.00	610.00	610.00	610.00	610.00	610.00	610.00	610.00
1993	610.00	610.00	610.00	610.00	610.00	610.00	610.00	610.00	610.00	610.00	610.00	610.00	610.00
1994	610.00	610.00	610.00	610.00	610.00	527.50	500.00	500.00	500.00	500.00	500.00	500.00	548.13
1995	500.00	500.00	500.00	500.00	500.00	500.00	500.00	518.75	525.00	525.00	542.50	560.00	514.27
1996	560.00	552.50	550.00	550.00	541.00	535.00	533.13	527.50	527.50	527.50	501.25	477.50	531.91

[1] Domestic standard. NQ = No quote. *Source: American Metal Market (AMM)*

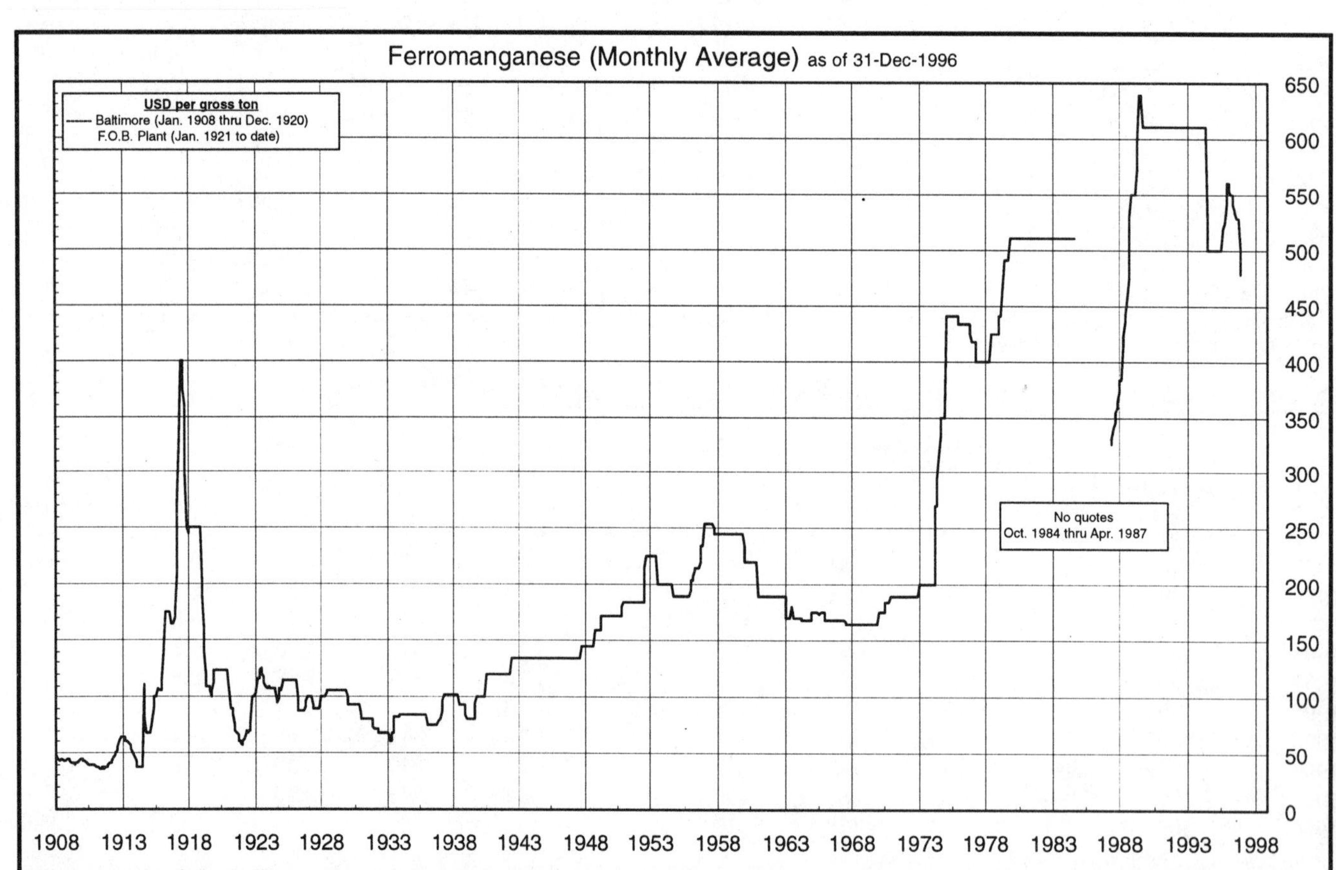

Meats

U.S. commercial red meat production, the combined total of beef, veal, lamb and pork output in 1997, failed to reach initial expectations, but a recovery is expected in 1998 that carries output to a record high. Red meat accounts for nearly 60 percent of total U.S. meat production. Poultry accounts for the balance with a combined total of 76.1 billion pounds in 1997 vs. 75.3 billion in 1996, and forecasts of 79.1 billion in 1998. Beef production in 1997 of 25.3 billion pounds compares with 25.4 billion in 1996, while pork production of 17.0 billion pounds compares with 17.1 billion, respectively. Estimates for 1998 place beef output at 24.8 billion pounds and pork at 18.5 billion. U.S. veal and lamb production are insignificant. Worldwide, China is the largest red meat producer with 43 million metric tons in 1997, about one-third of the world total with the U.S. second at slightly less than one-half of China's output. The slide in red meat production in the former USSR still shows little sign of abating, estimated at 6.0 million tons in 1997 vs. 6.4 million in 1996, and about 12 million in 1990.

U.S. per capita beef consumption (retail weight) in 1997 of 67.2 pounds compares with 67.7 in 1996 and a forecast of 65.7 pounds in 1998; pork use of 48 pounds compares with 49.1 in 1996 and 51.7 pounds in 1998. The slippage in pork usage in 1997 was surprising considering the aggressive advertising campaign by the pork industry associating pork as a white, and not a red meat. The beef industry's advertising campaign focuses on the ease (timewise) of preparing beef for dinner. For both meats, however, consumer preferences have still shifted to foods containing less fat which has benefitted poultry at red meat's expense. Per capita retail broiler and turkey consumption totaled 91.2 pounds in 1997 and is forecast at a record high 96.2 pounds in 1998.

Choice steers (basis Nebraska) averaged \$64-69/cwt. in 1997 vs. \$65.21 in 1996; forecasts for 1998 are from \$71 to \$76. Midwest barrow prices of \$51-54/cwt. in 1997 compare with \$53.39 in 1996 and estimates for 1998 of \$46-49/cwt., which if realized is the primary reason for the anticipated increase in per capita pork use.

U.S. red meat imports in 1997 of 3.1 billion pounds compares with 2.7 billion in 1996 and forecasts of 3.3 billion in 1998, with beef imports accounting for about 80 percent of the totals. U.S. red meat exports, again mostly beef, totaled 1.9 billion pounds in 1997, marginally higher than in 1996, and a 1998 estimate of 2.1 billion pounds. Japan is the world's largest red meat importer with 1.9 million tons in 1996, and Australia is the largest exporter (mostly beef) with about 1.4 million tons in 1997. The U.S. imports live cattle from Canada and Mexico while beef and veal are mostly imported from Australia and New Zealand.

World Total Meat Production[3] In Thousands of Metric Tons

Year	Argentina	Australia	Brazil	Canada	China[4]	France	Germany	Italy	Mexico	Russia[5]	United Kingdom	United States	World Total
1989	2,696	2,452	4,750	2,164	23,262	3,670	6,006	2,515	3,125	16,501	2,326	17,963	116,992
1990	2,738	2,683	4,650	2,022	25,132	3,816	6,111	2,583	2,658	8,204	2,331	17,597	120,078
1991	2,735	2,704	5,513	2,022	27,238	3,963	5,552	2,608	2,535	7,526	2,389	17,956	121,244
1992	2,602	2,810	5,620	2,107	29,406	3,997	4,994	2,648	2,626	6,748	2,297	18,589	116,309
1993	2,630	2,780	5,795	2,052	32,254	3,901	4,796	2,642	2,718	6,260	2,236	18,488	115,852
1994	2,682	2,807	5,850	2,137	36,968	3,868	5,092	2,618	2,852	5,659	2,323	19,361	123,388
1995	2,630	2,644	6,200	2,209	42,653	3,941	5,053	2,602	2,934	4,860	2,359	19,820	128,792
1996	2,636	2,552	7,750	2,238	47,721	4,059	5,163	2,668	2,832	4,497	2,088	19,449	134,673
1997[1]	2,602	2,661	7,590	2,301	50,500	4,093	4,929	2,656	2,840	3,990	2,104	19,348	135,805
1998[2]	2,526	2,653	7,640	2,343	52,700	4,068	4,993	2,656	2,850	3,575	2,060	19,793	137,849

[1] Preliminary. [2] Forecast. [3] Includes beef, veal, pork, sheep and goat meat. [4] Predominately pork production. [5] Formerly part of the U.S.S.R.; data not reported separately until 1990. *Source: Foreign Agricultural Service, U.S. Department of Agriculture (FAS-USDA)*

Production and Consumption of Red Meats in the United States (Carcass Weight)

	Beef			Veal			Lamb & Mutton			Pork (Excluding Lard)			All Meats		
	Commercial Production	Consumption		Commercial Production	Consumption		Commercial Production	Consumption		Commercial Production	Consumption		Commercial Production	Consumption	
Year	-- Million Pounds --	Total	Per Capita Lb.[4]	- Million Pounds -	Total	Per Capita Lb.[4]	- Million Pounds -	Total	Per Capita Lb.[4]	-- Million Pounds --	Total	Per Capita Lb.[4]	-- Million Pounds --	Total	Per Capita Lb.[4]
1989	22,974	24,030	98.4	355	344	1.4	341	386	1.6	15,759	16,571	67.0	39,418	41,644	168.4
1990	22,634	24,114	96.2	327	316	1.3	358	397	1.6	15,300	16,030	64.1	38,608	40,782	163.2
1991	22,800	24,261	95.4	306	296	1.2	358	397	1.6	15,948	16,399	64.9	39,402	41,214	163.1
1992	22,968	24,261	95.0	310	299	1.2	343	388	1.5	17,185	17,475	68.4	40,795	42,437	166.1
1993	22,942	24,006	93.0	267	286	1.1	329	381	1.5	17,030	17,419	67.5	40,568	42,092	163.1
1994	24,278	25,124	96.4	283	290	1.2	304	345	1.3	17,658	17,829	68.4	42,523	43,588	167.3
1995	25,115	25,534	97.0	308	319	1.2	264	338	1.1	17,085	16,826	63.3	42,772	43,017	162.6
1996[1]	25,419	25,863	97.4	367	378	1.4	264	334	1.1	17,085	16,814	63.3	43,135	43,389	163.2
1997[2]	25,137	25,706	95.9	312	323	1.2	243	324	1.1	17,119	16,460	61.4	42,811	42,813	159.6
1998[3]	24,800	25,231	93.3	260	272	1.0	227	306	1.0	18,475	17,667	65.3	43,762	43,476	160.6

[1] Preliminary. [2] Estimate. [3] Forecast. [4] Carcass Weight. *Source: Economic Research Service, U.S. Department of Agriculture (ERS-USDA)*

MEATS

Total Red Meat Imports (Carcass Weight Equivalent) of Principal Countries   In Thousands of Metric Tons

Year	Canada	France	Germany	Hong Kong	Italy	Japan	Rep. of Korea	Nether- lands	Russia[3]	Singa- pore	United Kingdom	United States	World Total
1990	198	967	1,033	311	1,025	1,153	120	143	545	971	76	1,503	6,450
1991	232	1,035	1,240	306	1,106	1,206	201	181	740	140	896	1,463	6,509
1992	237	1,027	1,338	265	1,231	1,388	187	208	292	147	885	1,424	5,733
1993	292	1,010	1,319	280	1,139	1,480	134	207	227	150	889	1,449	6,118
1994	313	1,044	1,447	298	1,103	1,628	191	238	865	28	785	1,434	6,844
1995	283	40	149	223	37	1,840	247	25	1,084	28	285	1,284	7,024
1996	276	45	137	202	62	1,904	240	31	939	41	276	1,253	6,944
1997[1]	285	51	140	207	40	1,660	331	30	1,005	36	280	1,440	7,129
1998[2]	290	51	140	206	40	1,796	468	35	1,015	33	283	1,537	7,676

[1] Preliminary. [2] Forecast. [3] Formerly part of the U.S.S.R.; data not reported separately until 1992. *Source: Foreign Agricultural Service, U.S. Department of Agriculture (FAS-USDA)*

Total Red Meat Exports (Carcass Weight Equivalent) of Principal Countries   In Thousands of Metric Tons

Year	Argentina	Australia	Brazil	Canada	China	Denmark	France	India	Ireland	Nether- lands	New Zealand	United States	World Total
1990	461	1,312	243	424	395	995	644	133	469	1,395	794	565	7,941
1991	402	1,391	290	375	494	1,097	757	151	529	1,438	845	669	8,040
1992	301	1,510	470	453	195	1,657	864	110	643	1,491	884	789	7,484
1993	283	1,469	425	494	315	1,272	917	120	672	1,470	858	779	7,290
1994	378	1,473	383	518	295	1,394	1,054	110	613	1,499	896	976	7,675
1995	463	1,329	315	520	310	1,313	999	129	372	1,425	923	1,211	7,954
1996	472	1,291	333	655	279	445	181	177	304	195	985	1,285	8,329
1997[1]	432	1,384	310	755	218	503	162	188	316	170	964	1,357	8,035
1998[2]	452	1,376	340	810	148	527	152	198	330	135	930	1,476	8,099

Preliminary. [2] Estimate. [3] Formerly part of the U.S.S.R.; data not reported separately until 1992. *Source: Foreign Agricultural Service, U.S. Department of Agriculture (FAS-USDA)*

United States Meat Imports by Type of Product   In Metric Tons

	Beaf and Veal			Lamb Mutton and Goat, Except Canned	Pork							
Year	Fresh, Chilled & Frozen	Canned, including Sausage	Other Pre- pared or Preserved		Fresh and Frozen	Canned[2]	Other Pre- pared or Preserved	Sausage, all Types	Mixed Sausage	Other Meats[3]	Variety Meats, Fresh or Frozen	Total
1989	638,999	56,302	13,842	20,917	226,172	118,598	10,328	2,656	2,620	3,509	11,102	1,105,045
1990	694,163	57,636	10,939	19,056	233,536	31,539	13,375	3,421	1,874	1,239	11,423	1,083,389
1991	709,997	60,511	12,929	19,100	215,935	82,339	16,948	2,144	1,533	3,904	18,266	1,143,606
1992	728,922	64,303	10,641	23,853	185,671	61,005	16,553	2,453	1,674	1,607	20,059	1,116,741
1993	720,079	59,786	14,560	24,468	207,653	75,440	17,689	2,695	1,368	2,274	25,298	1,151,309
1994	714,450	61,575	13,335	23,277	209,026	75,443	17,577	2,237	1,900	2,045	27,407	1,148,272
1995	641,918	52,012	13,528	29,919	194,387	61,904	15,571	2,553	1,935	2,008	27,728	1,043,463
1996[1]	640,679	63,472	14,000	33,009	183,555	70,527	11,580	2,418	1,639	4,028	31,345	1,056,252
1997[1]	621,557	50,054	3,315	32,009	156,830	51,243	8,559	1,975	1,392	5,399	2,623	934,956

[1] Preliminary. [2] Includes canned hams, shoulders and bacon. [3] Mostly mixed lucheon meats. *Source: Foreign Agricultural Service, U.S. Department of Agriculture (FAS-USDA)*

United States Meat Exports by Type of Product   In Metric Tons

	Beef and Veal			Pork			Other Pork Prepared or Preserved					
Year	Fresh, Chilled & Frozen	Prepared and Preserved	Lamb and Mutton, Fresh or Frozen	Fresh, Chilled & Frozen	Hams & Shoul- ders, Cured	Bacon	Not Canned	Canned	Sausage, Bologna & Frank- furters	Variety Meats, Fresh, Chilled & Frozen	Other Meats[2]	Total
1989	373,110	8,810	2,076	79,318	6,101	3,788	2,204	1,395	11,968	245,235	78,550	812,555
1990	339,925	7,783	2,490	66,756	5,567	4,518	4,310	1,036	14,208	226,623	70,558	743,774
1991	395,697	10,251	3,790	76,193	4,702	5,443	6,133	1,278	24,025	280,721	61,440	869,673
1992	436,455	12,064	3,278	116,496	8,181	7,396	5,812	2,352	22,796	303,295	57,154	975,279
1993	411,003	14,464	3,605	129,240	5,208	7,092	4,579	2,350	34,198	338,689	45,905	996,333
1994	517,507	13,545	3,766	149,318	8,477	12,076	4,470	2,973	46,925	373,662	34,734	1,167,453
1995	581,731	13,653	2,509	228,164	12,074	13,830	6,263	3,564	56,829	449,599	34,118	1,402,334
1996[1]	596,891	14,565	2,475	267,419	9,733	15,838	7,541	5,343	92,476	469,320	42,166	1,523,767
1997[1]	557,910	12,362	2,078	231,783	7,357	10,338	7,286	6,701	104,524	341,381	49,233	1,330,953

[1] Preliminary. [2] Includes sausage ingredients, cured (excluding canned); meat and meat products canned; and baby food, canned.
Source: Foreign Agricultural Service, U.S. Department of Agriculture (FAS-USDA)

Exports and Imports of Meats in the United States (Carcass Weight Equivalent)[3]

Year	Exports: Beef and Veal	Exports: Lamb and Mutton	Exports: Pork[4]	Exports: All Meat	Imports: Beef and Veal	Imports: Lamb and Mutton	Imports: Pork[4]	Imports: All Meat
	In Millions of Pounds							
1989	1,023	5	262	1,290	2,178	46	896	3,120
1990	1,006	6	238	1,250	2,356	41	898	3,295
1991	1,188	10	283	1,481	1,406	41	775	3,223
1992	1,324	8	407	1,739	2,440	50	645	3,135
1993	1,275	8	435	1,718	2,401	53	740	3,194
1994	1,611	9	532	2,152	2,369	49	743	3,161
1995	1,821	6	771	2,598	2,103	64	664	2,831
1996[1]	1,878	4	970	2,852	2,072	72	619	2,764
1997[2]	2,136	5	1,037	3,179	2,343	83	632	3,058

[1] Preliminary. [2] Estimate. [3] Includes meat content of minor meats and of mixed products. *Source: Economic Research Service, U.S. Department of Agriculture (ERS-USDA)*

Average Wholesale Prices of Meats in the United States In Cents Per Pound

Year	Composite Retail Price of Beef, Choice, Grade 3	Composite Retail Price of Pork[3]	Wholesale Value[4] Beef	Wholesale Value[4] Pork	Net Farm Value of Pork[5]	Cow Beef Canner & Cutter, Central US	Boxed Beef Cut-out, Choice 1-3, Central US, 550-700 lbs.	Pork Carcass Cut-out, U.S., No. 2	Lamb Carcass, Choice-Prime, East Coast, 55-65 lbs.	Pork Loins, Central US, 14-18 lbs.	Skinned Ham, Central US, 20-26 lbs.[6]	Pork Bellies, Central US, 12-14 lbs.
1989	265.70	182.90	176.80	99.20	70.40	94.43	114.78	60.62	131.35	101.11	69.25	34.14
1990	281.00	212.60	189.60	118.30	87.20	102.41	123.21	74.00	121.47	117.52	84.87	53.80
1991	288.30	211.90	182.50	108.90	78.40	99.42	118.31	67.02	117.33	108.39	75.68	47.79
1992	284.60	198.00	179.60	98.90	67.80	93.85	116.73	58.37	131.66	101.41	67.42	30.39
1993	293.40	197.60	182.50	102.90	72.50	95.43	118.74	62.19	143.97	107.47	67.85	41.62
1994	282.90	198.10	166.70	98.90	62.90	84.39	108.47	57.29	147.62	101.50	58.12	40.00
1995	284.30	194.80	163.90	98.80	66.70	68.22	106.68	59.98	163.45	107.74	58.56	43.04
1996[1]	280.20	220.90	158.10	117.20	84.60	58.18	103.09	72.39	177.58	118.49	72.41	69.97
1997[2]	279.53	231.54				64.30	103.26	70.87	178.99	108.06	62.75	71.41

[1] Preliminary. [2] Estimate. [3] Sold as retail cuts (ham, bacon, loin, etc.). [4] Quantity equivalent to 1 pound of retail cuts. [5] Portion of gross farm value minus farm by-product allowance. [6] Prior to 1995, 17-20 pounds. *Source: Economic Research Service, U.S. Department of Agriculture (ERS-USDA)*

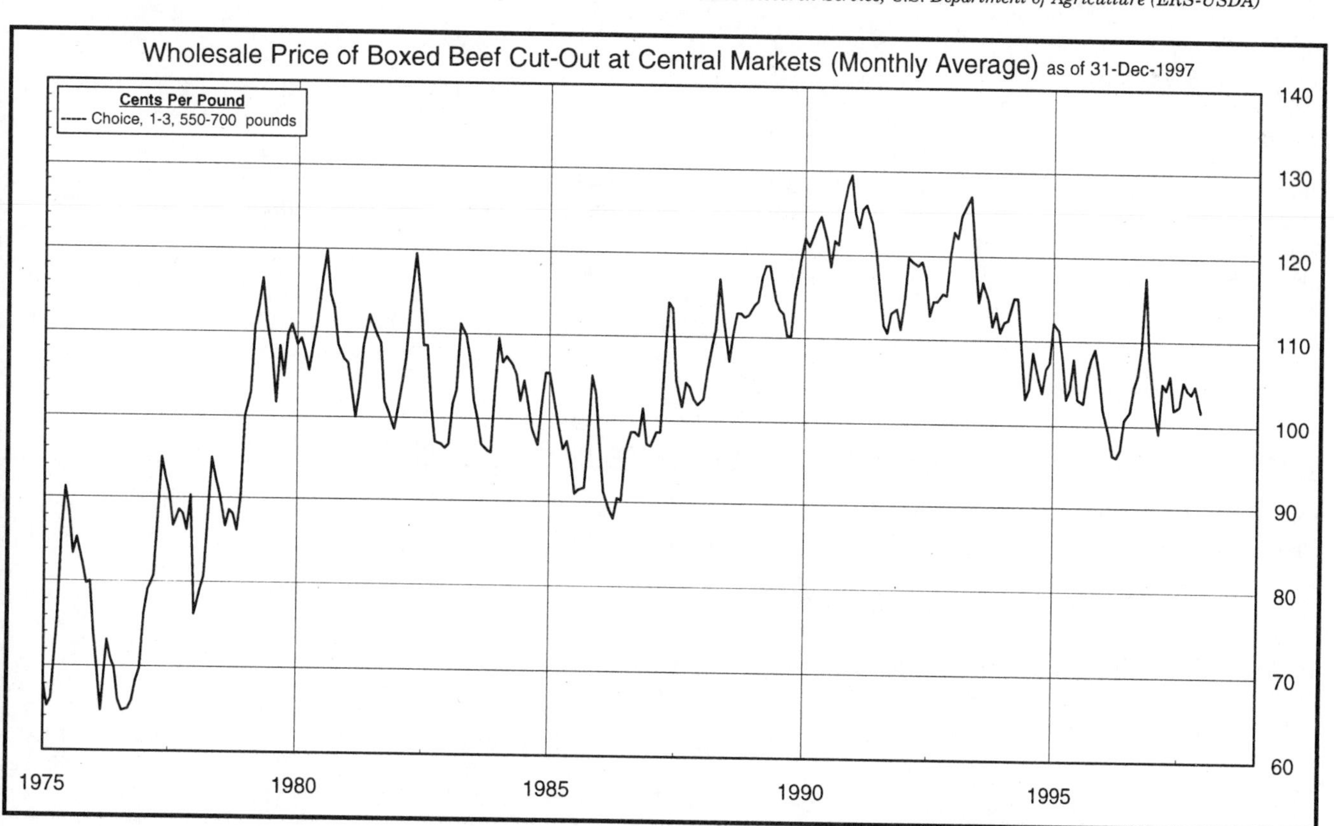

MEATS

Average Wholesale Price of Boxed Beef Cut-Out[1], Choice, at Central Markets — In Cents Per Pound

Year	Jan.	Feb.	Mar.	Apr.	May	June	July	Aug.	Sept.	Oct.	Nov.	Dec.	Average
1987	96.71	98.56	98.40	106.45	114.03	113.18	104.55	101.52	104.33	103.97	102.62	101.82	103.85
1988	102.55	105.94	108.50	110.79	116.73	111.96	107.09	110.37	112.72	112.74	112.37	112.45	110.35
1989	113.62	114.30	117.09	118.58	118.53	114.53	113.17	112.83	110.08	110.04	115.06	119.52	114.78
1990	121.75	120.97	122.10	123.62	124.56	121.53	118.54	121.52	121.18	124.96	128.32	129.48	123.21
1991	125.04	123.24	125.45	125.96	123.76	120.61	115.82	111.54	110.61	113.04	113.43	111.18	118.31
1992	114.38	119.65	119.14	118.66	119.18	117.53	112.79	114.36	114.40	115.51	115.26	119.95	116.73
1993	122.69	122.13	124.80	126.12	127.19	120.52	114.48	116.73	114.65	111.52	113.26	110.83	118.74
1994	112.11	112.23	115.03	114.98	108.85	102.92	104.19	108.38	105.49	103.63	106.66	107.22	108.47
1995	112.17	111.12	107.87	103.03	104.21	107.65	103.03	102.55	105.82	107.77	108.88	106.08	106.68
1996	101.71	98.86	96.36	96.01	96.90	100.70	101.53	104.43	105.93	109.10	117.53	108.03	103.09
1997[2]	101.90	98.98	104.87	104.17	105.97	101.83	102.38	105.14	104.06	103.72	104.63	101.50	103.26

[1] Choice 1-3, 550-700 pounds. [2] Preliminary. *Source: Economic Research Service, U.S. Department of Agriculture (ERS-USDA)*

Production (Commercial) of All Red Meats in the United States — In Millions of Pounds (Carcass Weight)

Year	Jan.	Feb.	Mar.	Apr.	May	June	July	Aug.	Sept.	Oct.	Nov.	Dec.	Total
1987	3,410	2,875	3,198	3,161	2,976	3,103	3,158	3,135	3,330	3,521	3,197	3,378	38,442
1988	3,246	3,071	3,355	3,158	3,206	3,319	3,170	3,507	3,462	3,512	3,399	3,358	39,763
1989	3,265	3,004	3,325	3,131	3,397	3,343	3,048	3,483	3,317	3,523	3,411	3,171	39,418
1990	3,354	2,972	3,259	3,049	3,320	3,175	3,100	3,431	3,096	3,499	3,273	3,080	38,608
1991	3,430	2,954	3,081	3,285	3,291	3,059	3,253	3,425	3,308	3,708	3,324	3,284	39,402
1992	3,623	3,090	3,376	3,259	3,237	3,423	3,441	3,406	3,560	3,656	3,289	3,434	40,794
1993	3,304	3,012	3,396	3,299	3,212	3,481	3,342	3,504	3,516	3,499	3,449	3,554	40,568
1994	3,366	3,126	3,591	3,382	3,431	3,615	3,361	3,756	3,720	3,795	3,666	3,714	42,523
1995	3,560	3,210	3,751	3,304	3,758	3,798	3,424	3,860	3,697	3,795	3,748	3,553	43,458
1996	3,823	3,519	3,512	3,690	3,767	3,439	3,585	3,707	3,396	3,827	3,435	3,432	43,132
1997[1]	3,715	3,257	3,418	3,570	3,549	3,471	3,637	3,600	3,644	3,983	3,433	3,692	42,969

[1] Preliminary. *Source: Economic Research Service, U.S. Department of Agriculture (ERS-USDA)*

Cold Storage Holdings of All[1] Meat in the United States, at End of Month — In Millions of Pounds

Year	Jan.	Feb.	Mar.	Apr.	May	June	July	Aug.	Sept.	Oct.	Nov.	Dec.
1987	597.6	599.0	598.2	590.8	560.2	498.7	515.6	495.9	523.0	575.6	613.8	622.9
1988	664.6	689.5	716.6	759.4	721.2	670.7	670.7	633.9	644.3	644.0	701.5	716.4
1989	745.0	758.7	474.5	747.5	763.7	683.5	652.0	576.3	557.0	538.2	554.2	536.0
1990	564.7	609.6	637.5	653.0	632.8	591.6	565.9	507.4	507.5	536.7	536.7	536.4
1991	566.2	588.6	606.2	597.7	640.1	614.1	589.7	593.2	592.8	594.7	650.2	644.9
1992	707.9	690.5	725.4	706.8	692.2	665.3	646.0	595.6	613.4	637.8	626.6	615.1
1993	649.4	654.6	652.9	692.0	671.0	660.8	664.2	650.7	671.7	702.4	720.3	726.7
1994	807.7	800.5	842.5	858.0	837.5	822.6	816.2	771.9	788.5	822.7	827.5	802.0
1995	838.7	833.8	834.0	852.7	831.2	820.8	803.6	733.4	711.3	732.3	757.0	749.7
1996	779.5	781.6	729.3	748.6	716.2	687.9	642.7	657.4	678.4	655.5	627.1	621.3
1997[2]	655.9	672.6	719.5	752.5	717.1	734.9	725.3	731.6	728.9	739.1	741.0	722.4

[1] Includes beef and veal, mutton and lamb, pork and products, rendered pork fat, and miscellaneous meats. Excludes lard. [2] Preliminary.
Source: Economic Research Service, U.S. Department of Agriculture (ERS-USDA)

Cold Storage Holdings of Frozen Beef in the United States, on First of Month — In Millions of Pounds

Year	Jan.	Feb.	Mar.	Apr.	May	June	July	Aug.	Sept.	Oct.	Nov.	Dec.
1987	310.6	320.6	306.0	311.1	312.3	280.1	252.7	278.7	269.3	286.5	307.6	304.3
1988	288.7	316.7	325.4	313.2	305.0	275.1	248.4	269.6	294.9	307.6	296.5	300.4
1989	317.5	315.1	313.4	298.9	275.4	244.1	241.8	249.2	242.4	231.8	220.7	237.6
1990	251.7	259.8	267.6	304.3	293.3	270.4	256.5	265.4	240.5	243.0	267.4	277.2
1991	300.4	298.9	271.3	276.9	265.6	234.7	247.1	273.2	259.4	276.7	298.2	306.3
1992	315.9	329.1	298.9	313.7	302.1	303.5	299.4	294.1	288.9	275.2	291.2	275.9
1993	272.8	286.4	279.9	293.9	276.7	262.1	271.7	285.3	307.5	326.8	344.4	376.3
1994	401.0	430.2	414.4	423.2	399.5	367.9	379.4	388.9	377.2	406.8	410.6	419.5
1995	411.2	420.3	407.7	385.4	392.2	359.1	352.3	359.3	344.9	347.7	381.6	381.4
1996	389.6	367.9	362.6	347.3	335.6	307.4	306.7	291.1	305.2	312.2	295.9	288.1
1997[1]	284.9	290.3	260.8	290.4	285.4	278.7	308.3	302.7	324.7	349.0	351.6	378.2

[1] Preliminary. *Source: Economic Research Service, U.S. Department of Agriculture (ERS-USDA)*

Mercury

Strict U.S. and foreign environmental policies and the advancement of new technology are increasingly affecting both primary and secondary mercury production and use. Secondary mercury, however, will become a more important factor of domestic supply, especially if the ban (imposed in 1994) on U.S. Government sales of mercury continues as seems likely.

Both U.S. primary mercury production and mercury consumption have declined since the early 1970's. The trend for the past several years has been to substitute for mercury rather than develop large-scale recycling programs. On a global basis, secondary mercury now accounts for a large part of supply as more chloralkali plants are dismantled and recycling of other products increases.

Mercury is the only common metal that is liquid at room temperatures. It is also highly toxic. In the U.S., the last producing primary mercury mine closed in 1990. Since then the only prime virgin mercury produced in the U.S. has been recovered as a by-product of gold mining operations at six mines in California, Nevada and Utah. The recovery is required to prevent environmental contamination.

World production of mercury is limited to four main countries and six marginal producers. World production in 1996 of 2,890 metric tonnes compares with 3,160 tonnes in 1995. The latter was the highest total since 1990 and reflected an increase in output from Spain, the world's largest producer whose major mine reopened following plant repairs. Spain's 1996 output of 1,500 tonnes compares with 1,497 in 1995 and total 1992-94 production of less than 500 tonnes. (One tonne equals 29+ flasks of 76 pounds each.) In Kyrgyzstan, the government has opted to privatize a 650-tonne capacity mining complex by opening ownership to foreign investors; production at which totaled 580 tonnes in 1996 vs. 380 in 1995. Algeria and China produced 300 and 240 tonnes, respectively in 1996 vs. 292 and 780 in 1995.

Mercury is a recoverable metal. U.S. secondary production totaled 446 tonnes in 1996 vs. 534 in 1995, and an annual average under 200 tonnes in the early 1990's. EPA restrictions banning landfill disposal and/or transport of mercury-containing wastes has encouraged more efficient recovery methods, especially from fluorescent lamps. The U.S. government has a mercury stockpile; tight restrictions are in place as to how much can be sold, if any, each year. Reportedly, the goal is to reduce the inventory to zero, but the timeframe is uncertain.

U.S. industrial consumption of refined mercury totaled 372 metric tonnes in 1996, down from 436 tonnes in 1995. In the mid-1980's battery production alone consumed 30,000 tonnes, now manufacturers produce alkaline and zinc-carbon batteries without mercury. Chlorine and caustic soda manufacture is the largest domestic use for mercury, 136 tonnes in 1996 vs. 154 tonnes in 1995. Substitutes for mercury include lithium and composite ceramic materials.

U.S. foreign trade in mercury is small. Imports, mostly from Canada and Russia, totaled 340 tonnes in 1996 vs. 377 tonnes in 1995 while exports fell to 45 tonnes from 179 tonnes, respectively.

Mercury is usually sold in 34.5 kilogram flasks. The U.S. average dealer price in 1996 was $262/flask (N.Y.) vs. $247 in 1995. European prices are generally lower than in the U.S. and considered more reflective of true market values.

World Mine Production of Mercury   In Metric Tons (1 tonne = 29.008216 flasks)

Year	Algeria	China	Finland	Kyrgyzstan[3]	Mexico	Spain	Tajikistan[3]	Turkey	Ukraine[3]	United States	World Total
1988	662	940	130	------	345	1,716	------	97	850	378	5,357
1989	587	1,200	159	------	651	1,224	------	197	850	414	5,464
1990	637	1,000	141	------	735	425	------	60	800	562	4,100
1991	431	760	74	------	340	100	------	25	750	58	2,540
1992	476	580	85	300	21	36	100	5	100	64	1,920
1993	459	520	101	350	12	64	80	------	80	W	1,800
1994	414	470	90	379	10	393	55	------	50	W	1,980
1995[1]	292	780	90	380	15	1,497	50	------	40	W	3,160
19962	300	240	90	580	15	1,500	45	------	30	W	2,890

[1] Preliminary. [2] Estimate. [3] Formerly part of the U.S.S.R.; data not reported separately until 1992. NA = Not available. *Source: U.S. Geological Survey*

Salient Statistics of Mercury in the United States   In Metric Tons

		Secondary Production						
Year	Producing Mines	Industrial	Government[3]	N.D.S.[4] Shipments	Consumer & Dealer Stocks, Dec. 31	Industrial Demand	Exports	Imports
1988	10	278	214	52	338	1,503	-----	329
1989	10	137	180	170	217	121	221	131
1990	9	108	193	52	197	720	311	15
1991	8	165	215	103	313	554	786	56
1992	9	176	103	267	436	621	977	92
1993	9	350	-----	543	384	558	389	40
1994	7	466	-----	86	469	483	316	129
1995[1]	8	534	-----	-----	321	436	179	377
1996[2]	6	446	-----	-----	446	372	45	340

[1] Preliminary. [2] Estimate. [3] Secondary mercury shipped from the Department of Energy. [4] National Defense Stockpile. NA = Not available.
Source: U.S. Geological Survey (USGS)

MERCURY

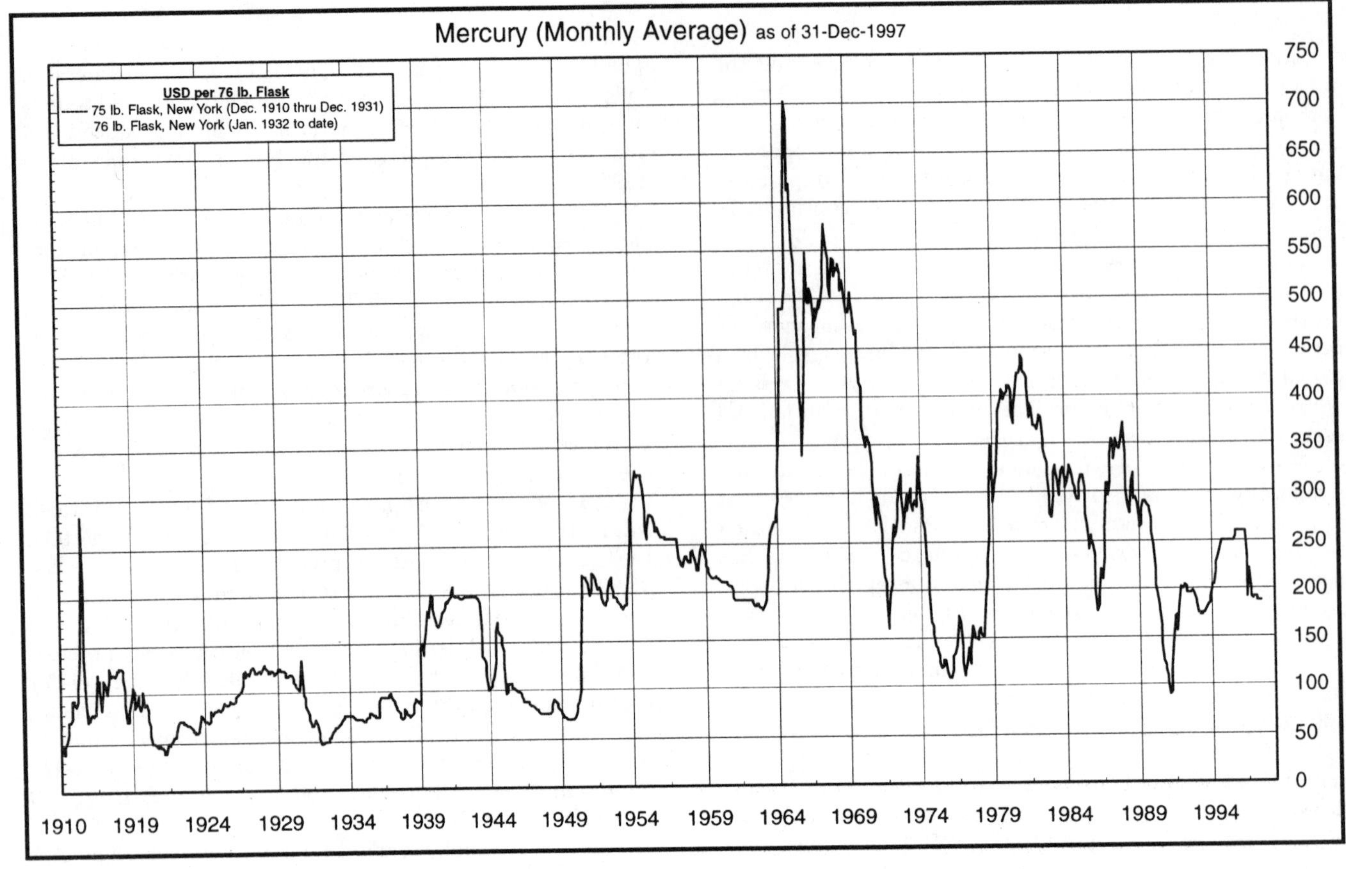

Average Price of Mercury in New York In Dollars Per Flask of 76 Pounds (34.5 Kilograms)

Year	Jan.	Feb.	Mar.	Apr.	May	June	July	Aug.	Sept.	Oct.	Nov.	Dec.	Average
1988	354.00	357.00	350.00	337.14	326.90	352.28	367.13	360.43	349.29	322.74	299.34	293.45	339.14
1989	292.50	318.42	330.00	327.50	315.68	308.86	293.03	273.80	265.13	267.61	282.50	292.50	297.29
1990	292.50	292.50	287.84	285.00	285.00	285.00	281.45	262.50	259.34	235.54	198.75	182.50	262.33
1991	181.55	169.08	150.36	140.68	129.77	119.75	110.36	102.50	98.00	94.02	127.50	150.12	131.14
1992	162.86	177.24	180.00	180.00	190.63	202.50	202.50	203.45	207.50	207.50	207.50	207.50	194.10
1993	207.50	207.50	207.50	207.50	207.50	201.30	191.00	191.00	185.00	185.00	181.00	175.00	195.57
1994	175.00	175.00	179.78	180.00	180.95	186.64	196.50	200.00	203.10	205.00	217.50	230.71	194.18
1995	235.00	240.00	241.30	250.00	250.00	250.00	250.00	250.00	250.00	250.00	250.00	250.00	247.19
1996	250.00	250.00	261.67	268.33	265.00	265.00	265.00	265.00	265.00	265.00	262.63	235.48	259.84
1997	233.98	232.76	228.88	228.64	220.00	199.05	200.00	198.10	190.83	198.83	191.47	187.00	209.13

Source: American Metal Market (AMM)

Mercury Consumed in the United States In Metric Tons

Year	Batteries	Chlorine & Caustic Soda	Catalysts, Misc.	Dental Equip.	Electrical Lighting	General Lab Use	Measuring Control Instrument	Paints	Wiring Devices & Switches	Other Uses	Grand Total
1987	533	311	59	56	45	20	59	198	131	34	1,446
1988	448	354	86	53	31	26	77	197	176	55	1,503
1989	250	379	40	39	31	18	87	192	141	32	1,212
1990	106	247	29	44	33	32	108	14	70	38	720
1991	18	184	26	41	39	30	90	6	71	49	554
1992	13	209	20	42	55	28	80	-----	82	92	621
1993	10	180	18	35	38	26	65	-----	83	103	558
1994	6	135	25	24	27	24	53	-----	79	110	483
1995[1]	-----	154	-----	32	30	-----	43	-----	84	93	436
1996[2]	-----	136	-----	31	29	-----	41	-----	49	86	372

[1] Preliminary. [2] Estimate. NA = Not available. *Source: U.S. Geological Survey (USGS)*

Milk

U.S. milk production in 1997 of 70.5 million metric tonnes was up one percent from 1996. The 1997 milk-cow inventory was smaller, but the increase in milk-per-cow production lifted output. Initial estimates for 1998 suggest a moderate increase in production over 1997, but if feed conditions are good milk output could prove much larger. Moreover, it is believed that a relatively large pool of farmers may be ready to expand milk production in 1998 while the number of producers abandoning dairying may slow. The annual average number of dairy cows in 1997 of 9.2 million head was one percent lower than in 1996, the largest decrease since 1992.

As of mid-1997, U.S. farm milk prices were down with the June Basic Formula Prices (BFP) 23 percent below a year earlier. Although the cold spring limited milk production throughout much of the northern half of the country, slow dairy product demand bolstered stocks and depressed prices. For 1997, BFP prices were estimated at $11.5-$12.3 per cwt. vs. $13.39 in 1996. The BFP average in 1998 is forecast to be unchanged from 1997. Milk's average plant market price in 1997 of $12.8-$13.6 per cwt. compares with $14.74 in 1996; 1998 is forecast to be unchanged from 1997. Retail prices generally show more variance than wholesale values largely due to differences in transportation and marketing costs.

The milk industry continues to aggressively advertise milk as a beverage in an effort to reverse the tide of fluid milk's 30-plus year consumption decline, and defend itself from competing iced teas and bottled water. This strategy of employing well known celebrities as promoters may work with children but the adult response is still questionable. It is believed that more than half of U.S. adults over age 35 have eliminated milk from their diets. U.S. consumer milk usage patterns have changed; in 1996, plain whole milk sales were 18.8 billion pounds vs. 26.4 billion ten years earlier, but over the same period plain low-fat milk sales went from 21.1 billion pounds to 24.1 billion, and skim milk sales jumped to 8.9 billion pounds from 3.2 billion. About 87 percent of U.S. milk output is produced in 22 states led by California and Wisconsin. Seasonally, milk production is highest during the Apr.-June quarter during which 40.6 billion pounds were produced in 1997 vs 39.6 billion in 1996.

The U.S. is the world's largest fluid milk producer with average annual production during 1995-97 of 70.2 million metric tonnes. Total world production of 387 million tonnes compares with 384 million in 1996. Russia and the Ukraine together produced 49 million tonnes in 1996, continuing the steady decline in the 1990's. In 1992 their production totaled 66 million tonnes. Other major producers include India, Germany and France, each in excess of 25 million tonnes during 1997. The U.S., however, is not the world's largest consumer of fluid milk, that honor goes to India with a record 32 million tonnes consumed in 1997 vs. the U.S. total of 26.9 million tonnes. On a per capita basis the U.S. total of 100 kg. is well below most European nations. Pricewise, U.S. fluid milk prices are lower than abroad, but dried milk prices tend to be higher due largely to a government support program. Generally, fluid milk prices average near $20/cwt. in Europe and are even higher in Japan.

Futures Markets

Nonfat dry milk and raw milk futures and options are traded on the Coffee, Sugar, & Cocoa Exchange Inc. (CSCE). Fluid milk futures and options are traded on the Chicago Mercantile Exchange (CME).

World Fluid Milk Production (Cow's Milk) In Thousands of Metric Tons

Year	Brazil	France	Germany	India	Italy	Netherlands	New Zealand	Poland	Russia[3]	Ukraine[3]	United Kingdom	United States	World Total
1991	14,200	25,700	28,916	28,200	11,400	11,047	8,122	14,504	51,971	22,409	14,503	66,994	385,197
1992	15,538	25,315	28,106	29,400	11,300	10,901	8,603	13,060	46,776	19,114	14,428	68,440	379,917
1993	16,250	25,049	28,080	30,600	10,400	10,953	8,735	12,650	46,300	18,377	14,645	68,303	377,633
1994	16,700	25,322	27,866	31,000	10,365	10,964	9,719	11,822	42,800	18,138	14,920	69,701	378,408
1995	18,375	25,413	28,621	32,500	10,500	11,294	9,684	11,420	39,300	17,181	14,700	70,500	380,752
1996	19,480	25,083	28,776	33,500	10,800	11,013	10,405	11,690	35,700	16,000	14,700	70,004	379,789
1997[1]	20,600	24,980	28,700	34,500	10,600	11,140	11,500	11,980	33,000	14,600	14,675	71,150	381,305
1998[2]	21,800	24,700	28,700	35,500	10,500	11,200	11,600	12,200	33,000	13,000	14,650	71,260	383,249

[1] Preliminary. [2] Estimate. [3] Formerly part of the U.S.S.R.; data not reported separately until 1989. *Source: Foreign Agricultural Service, U.S. Department of Agriculture (FAS-USDA)*

Milk-Feed Price Ratio[1] in the United States In Pounds

Year	Jan.	Feb.	Mar.	Apr.	May	June	July	Aug.	Sept.	Oct.	Nov.	Dec.	Average
1990	3.25	3.02	2.84	2.59	2.54	2.72	2.79	2.92	2.93	2.82	2.83	2.59	2.82
1991	2.57	2.52	2.42	2.34	2.41	2.54	2.73	2.82	2.94	3.14	3.25	3.19	2.74
1992	3.04	2.86	2.77	2.79	2.68	2.81	3.06	3.20	3.22	3.23	3.23	3.13	3.00
1993	2.96	2.87	2.77	2.79	2.81	2.91	2.78	2.70	2.80	2.79	2.77	2.65	2.80
1994	2.62	2.51	2.51	2.50	2.36	2.44	2.61	2.74	2.81	2.92	2.96	2.81	2.65
1995	2.73	2.75	2.73	2.60	2.53	2.46	2.39	2.50	2.55	2.60	2.69	2.55	2.59
1996	2.57	2.44	2.30	2.16	2.07	2.18	2.21	2.30	2.65	2.94	2.85	2.70	2.45
1997[2]	2.42	2.36	2.26	2.17	2.11	2.15	2.26	2.34	2.46	2.59	2.70	2.72	2.38

[1] Pounds of 16% protein mixed dairy feed equal in value to one pound of whole milk. [2] Preliminary. *Source: Economic Research Service, U.S. Department of Agriculture (ERS-USDA)*

Salient Statistics of Milk in the United States In Millions of Pounds

Year	Number of Milk Cows on Farms[3] (Thousands)	Supply: Production: Per Cow[4] (Pounds)	Supply: Production: Total[4]	Supply: Beginning Stocks[5]	Supply: Imports	Supply: Total Supply	Utilization: Exports[5]	Utilization: Domestic: Fed to Calves	Utilization: Domestic: Humans	Utilization: Domestic: Total Use	Average Farm Price Received Per Cwt.: All Milk, Wholesale	Average Farm Price Received Per Cwt.: Milk Eligible for Fluid Market	Average Farm Price Received Per Cwt.: Milk, Manufacturing Grade	Per Capita Consumption[6] (Fluid Milk in Lbs.)
1990	9,993	14,782	147,721	9,036	2,690	159,447	1,886	1,484	142,067	146,088	13.68	13.80	12.28	234
1991	9,826	15,031	147,697	13,359	2,625	163,681	2,845	1,480	142,897	147,841	12.24	12.33	11.12	233
1992	9,688	15,570	150,847	15,840	2,520	169,246	7,569	1,436	144,519	155,032	13.09	13.16	11.87	231
1993	9,589	15,704	150,582	14,214	2,806	167,602	7,894	1,408	148,178	158,032	12.84	12.88	11.80	226
1994	9,500	16,175	153,664	9,570	2,880	166,072	5,555	1,305	152,791	160,312	13.01	13.02	11.85	226
1995[1]	9,458	16,433	155,425	5,760	2,936	164,121		1,216			12.78	12.80	11.79	223
1996[2]	9,351	16,498	154,268	4,168	2,911	161,347					14.74	14.80	13.40	224

[1] Preliminary. [2] Estimate. [3] Average number on farms during year including dry cows, excluding heifers not yet fresh. [4] Excludes milk sucked by calves. [5] Government and commercial. [6] Product pounds of commercial sales and on farm consumption. *Source: Economic Research Service, U.S. Department of Agriculture (ERS-USDA)*

Utilization of Milk in the United States In Millions of Pounds (Milk Equivalent)

Year	Butter from Whey Cream	Creamery Butter[2]	Cheese[3]	Cottage Cheese (Creamed)	Canned Milk[4]	Bulk Condensed Whole Milk: Unsweetened	Bulk Condensed Whole Milk: Sweetened	Dry Whole Milk Products	Ice Cream[5]	Other Frozen Dairy Products	Other Manufactured Products[6]	Used on Farms: Farm-Churned Butter	Used on Farms: Total
1990	4,348	29,391	47,368	672	1,332	351	243	1,292	2,014	12,307	332	512	1,996
1991	4,296	30,039	46,769	644	1,194	364	236	785	2,092	12,726	356	494	1,974
1992	4,150	30,478	49,458	592	1,872	417	301	1,227	2,367	11,825	188	455	1,892
1993	4,500	29,493	49,871	557	1,178	244	324	1,130	1,995	12,063	199	428	1,836
1994	4,592	29,127	51,143	524	1,184	205	277	1,227	2,083	13,182	216	394	1,700
1995[1]	4,724	28,353	53,063	488	1,050	203	254	1,262	2,044	12,890	224	346	1,562

[1] Preliminary. [2] Excludes whey butter. [3] American and other. [4] Includes evaporated and sweetened condensed. [5] Milk equivalent of butter and condensed milk used in ice cream. [6] Whole milk equivalent of dry cream, malted milk powder, part-skim milk, dry or concentrated ice cream mix, dehydrated butterfat and other miscellaneous products using milkfat. *Source: National Agricultural Statistics Service, U.S. Department of Agriculture (NASS-USDA)*

Milk Production[1] in the United States In Millions of Pounds

Year	Jan.	Feb.	Mar.	Apr.	May	June	July	Aug.	Sept.	Oct.	Nov.	Dec.	Total
1991	12,587	11,732	13,106	12,888	13,268	12,477	12,348	12,202	11,705	12,102	11,763	12,347	148,477
1992	12,671	12,132	13,155	12,838	13,346	12,893	12,844	12,577	12,094	12,476	12,064	12,626	150,847
1993	10,728	9,908	11,060	10,927	11,410	12,957	12,894	12,492	11,978	12,272	11,872	12,427	150,582
1994	12,721	11,662	13,209	13,118	13,719	13,079	13,020	12,837	12,360	12,732	12,330	12,871	153,664
1995	13,147	12,142	13,640	13,343	13,875	13,302	13,152	12,793	12,381	12,716	12,297	12,844	155,425
1996	13,085	12,431	13,537	13,230	13,576	12,832	12,809	12,624	12,241	12,714	12,324	12,928	154,331
1997[2]	13,126	12,141	13,694	13,406	13,902	13,375	13,319	13,059	12,427	12,814	12,362	12,978	156,603

[1] Excludes milk sucked by calves. [2] Preliminary. *Source: Economic Research Service, U.S. Department of Agriculture (ERS-USDA)*

Average Price Received by U.S. Farmers for All Milk (Sold to Plants) In Dollars Per Hundred Pounds (Cwt.)

Year	Jan.	Feb.	Mar.	Apr.	May	June	July	Aug.	Sept.	Oct.	Nov.	Dec.	Average
1991	11.70	11.60	11.40	11.30	11.30	11.40	11.80	12.40	12.80	13.50	13.90	13.80	12.24
1992	13.40	12.90	12.50	12.60	12.80	13.20	13.40	13.50	13.50	13.40	13.10	12.80	13.09
1993	12.50	12.20	12.20	12.60	12.90	13.00	12.80	12.40	12.80	13.10	13.60	13.50	12.80
1994	13.60	13.40	13.50	13.40	12.80	12.60	12.20	12.40	12.80	13.00	13.10	12.80	12.97
1995	12.60	12.60	12.70	12.30	12.30	12.10	12.00	12.40	12.80	13.40	14.00	13.90	12.76
1996	14.00	13.80	13.70	13.90	14.30	14.80	15.40	15.90	16.50	16.40	15.20	14.30	14.85
1997[1]	13.40	13.50	13.50	13.40	13.00	12.40	12.20	12.70	13.20	14.00	14.60	14.60	13.38

[1] Preliminary. *Source: Economic Research Service, U.S. Department of Agriculture (ERS-USDA)*

Average Farm Price of Milk Eligible for Fluid Market In Dollars Per Hundred Pounds (Cwt.)

Year	Jan.	Feb.	Mar.	Apr.	May	June	July	Aug.	Sept.	Oct.	Nov.	Dec.	Average
1991	11.80	11.70	11.50	11.40	11.40	11.50	11.90	12.40	12.90	13.60	13.90	13.90	12.33
1992	13.50	13.00	12.50	12.60	12.90	13.30	13.40	13.50	13.60	13.50	13.20	12.90	13.16
1993	12.60	12.30	12.20	12.70	13.00	13.10	12.80	12.50	12.80	13.10	13.60	13.60	12.86
1994	13.60	13.50	13.50	13.50	12.90	12.70	12.20	12.50	12.80	13.10	13.10	12.90	13.03
1995	12.70	12.60	12.60	12.30	12.30	12.20	12.10	12.50	12.80	13.40	14.00	14.00	12.79
1996	14.00	13.90	13.70	13.90	14.30	14.90	15.50	16.00	16.60	16.40	15.30	14.40	14.91
1997[1]	13.40	13.50	13.60	13.40	13.10	12.40	12.30	12.70	13.20	14.00	14.60	14.70	13.41

[1] Preliminary. *Source: Economic Research Service, U.S. Department of Agriculture (ERS-USDA)*

Molasses

Molasses is a heavy, viscous fluid produced as a by-product of raw sugar production. About 50 gallons of molasses are produced for each ton of raw sugar refined. Molasses contains about 33 percent sucrose. U.S. supplies of molasses total about three million tonnes per year. Of this total, about a third comes from mainland sugar mills, a quarter from beet sugar refiners and smaller amounts from Hawaiian cane and cane refiners. Beet molasses is used primarily as a livestock food and as a yeast by the pharmaceutical industry.

The USDA reported that world production of sugar in the 1997-98 season was 122.4 million metric tonnes, up very slightly from the 122.3 million tonnes produced in the 1996-97 season. The European Union is the largest producer of sugar with production estimated at 17.4 million tonnes, down four percent from the previous season. Brazil is the next largest producer with 1997-98 production estimated 14.8 million tonnes, up one percent from the previous year. India's sugar production was estimated at 13.7 million tonnes, down seven percent from a year ago.

U.S. sugar production in the 1997-98 (October-September) marketing year was estimated at 7.64 million short tons, raw value, up five percent from the previous season. Beet sugar production was estimated at 4.3 million tons and cane sugar production at 3.3 million tons. U.S. consumption of sugar in 1997-98 is forecast at 9.9 million tons, up less than two percent from the previous season.

U.S. imports of molasses in calendar year 1996 were 1.37 million tonnes. The major supplier of molasses to the U.S. was Australia which in calendar year 1996 exported 284,277 tonnes of molasses to the U.S. The next largest supplier of molasses was Mexico with 254,166 tonnes.

U.S. imports of molasses in July 1997 were 97,413 tonnes, down 15 percent from July 1996. The major suppliers of molasses were Colombia, the Dominican Republic and Poland. Imports of molasses in July 1997 were 18 percent above the previous month's total of 82,592 tonnes. For the January-July 1997 period, U.S. imports of molasses were 990,364 tonnes with the major suppliers being Mexico and the Dominican Republic.

World Production of Sugarcane, by Selected Countries   In Thousands of Metric Tons

Crop Year	Australia	Brazil	China	Cuba	India	Indonesia	Mexico	Pakistan	Phillip-pines	South Africa	Thailand	United States	World Total
1990-1	25,140	75,000	57,620	67,500	135,494	28,074	36,000	22,604	18,600	18,083	40,563	24,018	707,497
1991-2	21,306	87,000	67,898	62,000	148,814	28,100	35,300	24,796	22,816	20,078	47,505	26,272	753,303
1992-3	29,400	90,000	73,011	47,150	123,985	32,000	39,700	27,276	23,850	12,955	34,711	26,264	719,671
1993-4	31,951	91,000	63,549	46,000	116,638	33,000	34,100	34,182	22,753	11,244	37,569	26,680	706,433
1994-5	34,860	110,000	60,300	39,000	159,593	30,545	40,134	34,193	18,415	15,683	50,459	25,485	783,373
1995-6	37,378	93,000	65,417	45,500	184,708	30,000	42,300	28,151	22,774	16,750	57,693	25,835	842,937
1996-7[1]	39,878	101,000	68,500	45,000	147,858	28,600	42,000	25,580	23,500	22,512	59,000	24,055	845,645
1997-8[2]	40,878	105,000	69,400	45,500	137,184	29,000		31,600			60,000		

[1] Preliminary. [2] Estimate. *Source: Economic Reseach Service, U.S. Department of Agriculture (ERS-USDA)*

World Production of Sugarbeets, by Selected Countries   In Thousands of Metric Tons

Crop Year	Belgium-Luxembrg	China	France	Germany	Italy	Poland	Russia[3]	Spain	Turkey	Ukraine[3]	United Kingdom	United States	World Total
1990-1	6,857	14,525	25,520	30,366	11,600	16,721	31,091	7,358	13,986	44,265	8,000	24,959	303,149
1991-2	6,043	16,289	24,403	25,926	11,400	11,412	24,280	6,679	15,474	36,168	7,672	25,485	277,368
1992-3	6,174	15,069	26,491	27,177	14,762	11,052	25,548	7,234	15,563	28,783	9,180	26,438	274,751
1993-4	6,120	11,938	25,514	28,606	10,510	15,621	25,468	8,622	15,463	33,717	8,988	23,813	272,746
1994-5	5,729	12,406	23,943	24,211	11,905	11,630	13,945	8,100	12,757	28,138	8,360	29,024	247,798
1995-6	6,291	13,984	25,121	26,049	12,932	13,309	19,110	7,450	10,989	28,000	8,360	25,460	257,984
1996-7[1]	6,100	13,900	24,400	27,000	11,150	17,460	16,500	7,700	14,383	25,500	8,432	24,104	254,335
1997-8[2]	6,000	14,000	24,500	26,500	12,500	14,000	17,000	6,800	15,100	25,400	8,400	26,134	256,393

[1] Preliminary. [2] Estimate. [3] Formerly part of U.S.S.R. *Source: Economic Reseach Service, U.S. Department of Agriculture (ERS-USDA)*

U.S. Annual Average Prices of Molasses, by Types (F.O.B. Tank Car or Truck)   In Dollars Per Short Ton[2]

	Blackstrap							Beet Molasses	
Year	New Orleans	South Florida	Baltimore	Upper Mississippi	Savannah	California Ports[3]	Houston	Montana/ Wyoming & Nebraska	Red River Valley[4]
1990	61.70	68.37	80.59	88.48	76.13	75.40	64.26	75.00	58.33
1991	67.02	74.58	89.15	94.78	82.52	80.00	69.52	71.92	66.16
1992	61.27	68.36	80.41	92.95	76.70	78.43	63.75	67.81	57.50
1993	55.48	62.36	76.03	89.26	70.00	74.24	57.12	72.63	64.44
1994	65.53	72.23	85.94	91.97	79.23	83.31	69.86	NA	NA
1995	72.00	79.92	86.30	99.11	87.48	90.30	76.37	NA	NA
1996	74.95	86.56	91.98	104.97	95.75	97.25	83.09	NA	NA
1997[1]	58.16	68.00	76.90	90.70	77.65	83.50	62.88	NA	NA

[1] Preliminary. [2] To convert dollars per short ton to cents per gallon divide by 171. [3] Los Angeles and Stockton. [4] North Dakota and Minnesota. NA = Not available. *Source: Agricultural Marketing Service, U.S. Department of Agriculture (AMS-USDA)*

MOLASSES

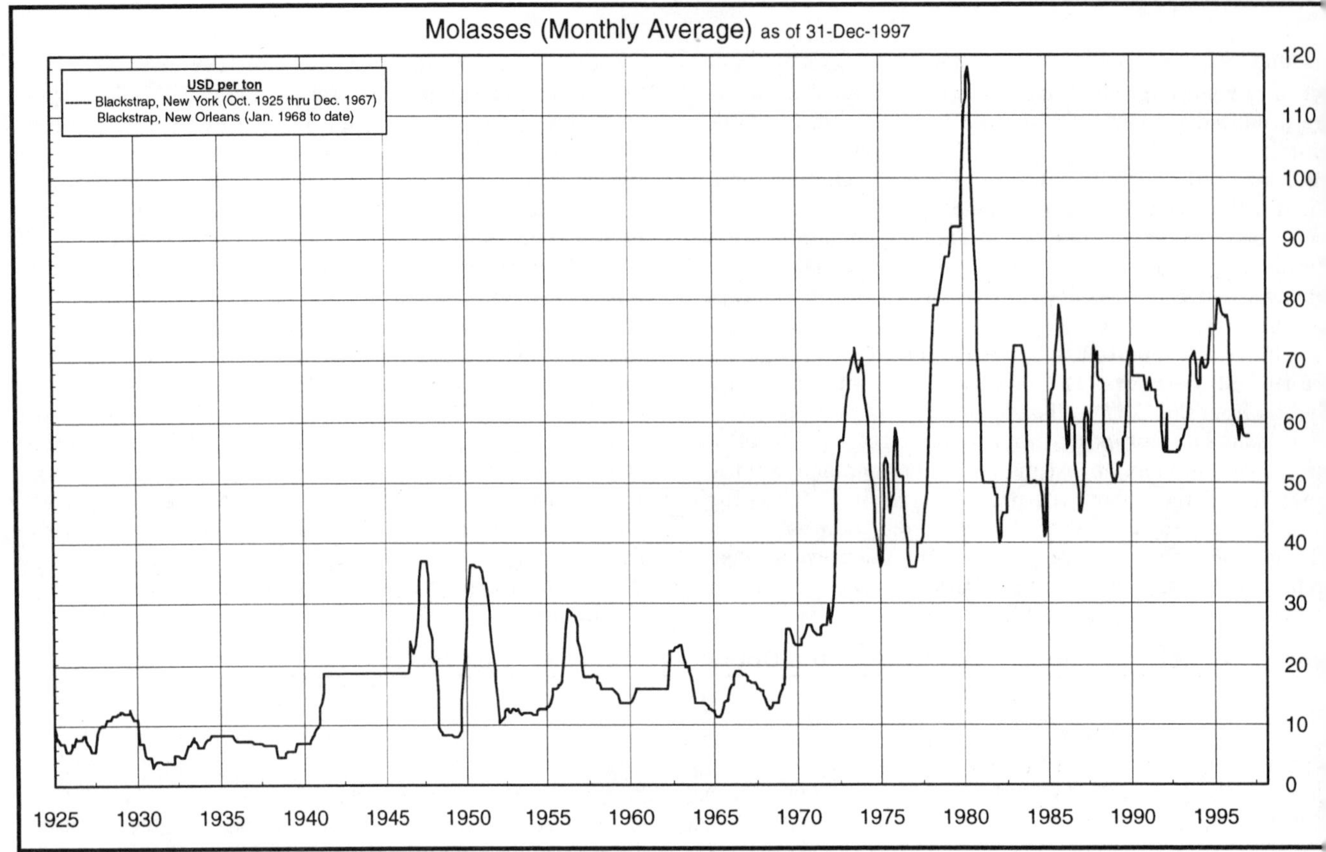

Salient Statistics of Molasses[3] in the United States In Metric Tons

	Production						Inedible Imports From						Production of Edible Molasses
		Mainland				In Shipments							
Year	Hawaii	Mainland Mills[4]	Refiners Black-strap	Beet	Puerto Rico	From Hawaii	Total Imports	Brazil	Dominican Republic	Mexico	Mainland Exports[5]	Total U.S. Supply	(1,000 Gallons)
1987	260,930	726,854	110,784	1,137,014	35,385	152,087	962,151	95,004	123,619	183,525	366,957	2,721,954	1,630
1988	252,516	775,936	101,257	1,006,353	40,694	178,476	969,870	142,897	102,792	93,605	299,217	2,749,692	1,925
1989	218,009	808,355	122,786	974,179	34,864	169,270	926,870	107,109	147,235	75,634	293,535	2,707,925	1,990
1990	228,968	741,749	105,124	948,820	24,959	214,045	1,078,924	70,986	145,543	88,401	212,263	2,876,399	1,405
1991	188,252	807,652	126,000	1,165,962	27,882	184,337	1,258,637	10,342	137,271	235,244	242,635	3,299,953	1,825
1992	182,849	782,566	123,000	950,312	25,097	183,657	1,115,863	-----	127,500	117,722	282,098	2,873,300	1,460
1993	187,915	831,661	113,000	692,465	22,802	190,371	1,040,858	-----	163,180	47,596	255,907	2,612,448	1,480
1994[1]	180,884	824,453	114,000	1,200,000	18,531	151,172	1,556,640	-----	121,320	197,753	277,098	3,459,167	1,500
1995[2]	146,000	886,826	114,000	1,040,000	16,156	146,000	1,048,726	-----	132,983	172,177	274,868	2,960,684	

[1] Preliminary. [2] Estimate. [3] Feed and industrial molasses. [4] Includes high-test molasses from frozen cane. [5] Excluding exports from Hawaii and Puerto Rico. NA = Not available. *Source: Agricultural Marketing Service, U.S. Department of Agriculture (AMS-USDA)*

Wholesale Price of Blackstrap Molasses (Cane) at New Orleans In Dollars Per Short Ton

Year	Jan.	Feb.	Mar.	Apr.	May	June	July	Aug.	Sept.	Oct.	Nov.	Dec.	Average
1988	60.30	62.00	60.60	56.90	55.50	62.50	72.50	72.50	70.00	71.50	67.50	66.90	64.89
1989	66.90	66.25	57.50	56.90	55.75	55.60	55.00	51.25	50.00	50.50	50.00	51.25	55.58
1990	52.75	53.13	52.50	54.25	57.19	57.50	62.75	68.75	70.63	72.25	71.25	67.50	61.70
1991	67.50	67.50	67.50	67.50	67.50	67.50	67.50	67.50	65.25	65.00	65.00	65.00	66.69
1992	65.00	65.00	65.00	65.00	63.75	62.50	62.50	62.50	58.75	55.31	55.00	55.00	61.28
1993	55.00	55.00	55.00	55.00	55.00	55.00	55.00	55.25	55.31	56.25	56.75	57.19	55.48
1994	57.75	57.50	59.38	62.50	68.00	70.00	70.63	71.25	69.38	67.50	66.25	66.25	65.53
1995	69.00	70.31	68.75	68.75	68.75	69.38	74.25	75.00	75.00	75.00	75.00	75.00	72.02
1996	80.00	80.00	80.00	78.00	77.50	77.50	77.50	77.50	75.00	70.00	65.63	60.75	74.95
1997[1]	60.00	60.00	59.00	56.56	56.88	60.31	57.50	57.50	57.50	57.50	57.50	57.50	58.15

[1] Preliminary. *Source: Agricultural Marketing Service, U.S. Department of Agriculture (AMS-USDA)*

Molybdenum

Molybdenum is a silver-gray metal which retains strength at high temperatures and is hard and resistant to corrosion. It is a refractory metallic element used principally as an alloying agent in steels, cast irons and superalloys to enhance strength, toughness and wear resistance. Primarily added in the form of molybdic oxide or ferromolybdenum, it is frequently used in combination with chromium, manganese nickel, tungsten or other alloy metals to achieve desired metallurgical properties. Molybdenum's versatility ensures a significant role in contemporary technology and industry. Molybdenum finds significant usage as a refractory metal in numerous chemical applications, including catalysts, lubricants and pigments. The variety of uses for molybdenum materials, few of which afford acceptable substitutions, has resulted in a demand that is expected to increase at a greater rate than most other ferrous metals.

U.S. production of molybdenum concentrate in July 1997 was 4,800 metric tonnes, contained molybdenum. Production in June 1997 was 4,390 tonnes. In the January-July 1997 period, molybdenum concentrate production was 36,100 tonnes. For all of 1996, production was 56,000 tonnes.

U.S. domestic shipments of molybdenum concentrate in July 1997 were 1,070 tonnes which was up from 943 tonnes in June 1997. For the first seven months of 1997, molybdenum concentrate domestic shipments were 7,720 tonnes. For all of 1996 they were 16,100 tonnes. U.S. exports of molybdenum concentrate in July 1997 were 1,430 tonnes which was down from 1,600 tonnes in June 1997. In the January-July 1997 period, molybdenum concentrate exports were 11,800 tonnes. For all of 1996, they were 19,700 tonnes. Exports and domestic shipments include molybdic oxides, metal powder, ammonium molybdate, sodium molybdate and other materials.

U.S. reported production of molybdenum products in July 1997 was 2,340 tonnes. In June 1997 production was 2,380 tonnes. In the January-July 1997 period, U.S. production was 26,100 tonnes. 1996 production was 46,300 tonnes.

U.S. internal consumption of molybdenum products, including molybdic oxides, metal powder, ammonium molybdate, sodium molybdate and other materials, was 1,570 tonnes in July 1997. Consumption in June 1997 was 1,620 tonnes. For January-July 1997, consumption was 13,200 tonnes. For all of 1996, consumption of molybdenum products was 23,900 tonnes.

World Mine Production of Molybdenum In Metric Tons (Contained Molybdenum)

Year	Bulgaria	Canada[3]	Chile	China	Iran	Kazakhstan[4]	Mexico	Mongolia	Peru	Russia[4]	United States	Uzbekisten[4]	World Total
1987	200	14,771	16,941	12,000	500	------	4,400	1,400	3,353	11,500	34,063	------	89,871
1988	200	13,535	15,515	14,400	700	------	4,456	1,400	2,444	17,000	43,051	------	112,860
1989	190	14,073	16,550	15,700	785	------	4,189	1,580	3,177	17,000	63,105	------	136,494
1990	150	11,994	13,830	15,700	542	------	2,000	1,578	2,510	17,000	61,611	------	127,028
1991	120	11,329	14,434	13,200	395	------	1,716	1,716	3,031	16,000	53,364	------	115,000
1992	120	9,405	14,840	19,200	1,320	700	1,458	1,610	3,220	5,000	49,725	700	108,000
1993	120	9,700	14,899	18,300	1,000	600	1,705	2,050	2,980	10,300	36,800	700	99,500
1994	100	10,250	16,028	21,400	1,000	500	2,610	2,100	2,765	7,700	46,800	700	112,000
1995[1]	400	9,113	17,889	32,000	1,200	700	3,810	1,830	3,411	8,800	60,900	500	141,000
1996[2]	400	8,845	18,000	25,000	1,200	800	3,900	2,200	3,711	8,500	54,900	500	128,000

[1] Preliminary. [2] Estimate. [3] Shipments. [4] Formerly part of the U.S.S.R.; data not reported separately until 1992. *Source: U.S. Geological Survey*

Salient Statistics of Molybdenum in the United States In Metric Tons (Contained Molybdenum)

	Concentrate							Primary Products[4]							
		Shipments						Net Production				Shipments			
Year	Production	Total (Includes Exports)	Value Mil. $	For Exports	Consumption	Imports for Consumption	Stocks, Dec. 31[3]	Grand Total	Molybdic Oxide[5]	Molybdenum Metal Powder	Price Avg. Value $ Kl.[6]	To Domestic Destinations	Oxide for Exports (Gross Weight)	Consumption	Producer Stocks, Dec. 31
1987	34,073	31,692	179.3	18,377	16,983	573	6,841	11,257	7,076	4,181	7.28	18,447	5,567	14,800	10,055
1988	43,051	45,240	266.9	23,500	35,690	514	4,777	29,782	25,404	4,378	7.61	20,535	W	17,422	7,116
1989	63,105	61,733	421.4	51,232	41,877	238	6,969	16,545	16,545	W	8.05	18,277	1,391	17,204	6,675
1990	61,611	61,580	346.3	41,380	35,455	478	7,672	15,727	15,727	W	7.39	17,983	787	18,060	5,919
1991	53,364	53,607	249.9	22,424	32,998	161	5,291	20,782	18,739	2,043	5.27	19,105	1,571	16,901	9,422
1992	49,725	45,098	189.9	33,439	15,243	831	11,905	13,880	11,916	1,964	4.85	17,305	557	17,200	7,480
1993	36,800	39,200	165.1	28,280	13,800	3,400	11,200	11,989	10,697	1,292	5.13	16,000	1,042	17,700	6,150
1994	46,800	40,000	284.0	14,568	17,200	2,280	5,510	16,000	14,900	1,070	4.60	21,400	2,240	19,100	3,940
1995[1]	60,900	61,700	651.0	18,600	25,500	5,570	5,390	22,900	20,900	1,970	17.47	24,000	2,840	19,900	4,820
1996[2]	54,900	57,900	456.0	19,700	24,500	5,480	2,470	24,100	20,400	1,970	7.50	24,100	1,790	20,300	5,780

[1] Preliminary. [2] Estimate. [3] At mines and at plants making molybdenum products. [4] Comprises ferromolybdenum, molybdic oxide, and molybdenum salts and metal. [5] Includes molybdic oxide briquets, molybdic acid, molybdenum trioxide, and all others. [6] U.S. producer price per kilogram of molybdenum contained in technical-grade molybdic oxide. W = Withheld proprietary data. *Source: U.S. Geological Survey (USGS)*

Nickel

Most commercial nickel is used in the production of stainless steel and other corrosion-resistant alloys. About one-fifth of the nickel produced in the U.S. is used in plating to give hard, tarnish-resistant, polishable surfaces. Plating techniques, like electroless coating or single-slurry coating, are employed for such applications as helicopter rotors, turbine blades, extrusion dies and rolled steel strip. Nickel finds use in coins to replace silver and is used in rechargeable batteries and electronic circuity. Nickel-base alloys are used in wire, bars, sheets and tubular forms.

U.S. production of nickel, exclusive of scrap, in March 1997 was 11,000 metric tonnes, nickel content. Total reported consumption in March 1997 was 7,540 tonnes. That compared with 7,590 tonnes in February 1997 and 9,000 tonnes in January. In the January-March 1997 quarter, U.S. nickel consumption was 24,100 tonnes, seven percent less than in the first quarter of 1996. For all of 1996, U.S. consumption of nickel was 98,700 tonnes. Of that total, 78,100 tonnes was in the form of cathodes, pellets, briquets and powder. Another 17,600 tonnes of consumption was in the form of ferronickel. Some 2,980 tonnes of use was in the form of oxide-sinter, salts, and other forms.

U.S. stocks of nickel, exclusive of scrap, at the end of March 1997, were 4,860 tonnes, nickel content. Of the total, 4,020 tonnes were in the form of cathodes, pellets, briquets and powder. There were 227 tonnes of ferronickel in stock while stocks of oxide-sinter, salts, and other forms were 617 tonnes. Stocks of nickel at the end of February were 4,390 tonnes; at the end of Dec. 1996 they were 6,610 tonnes.

U.S. consumption of secondary nickel, or nickel scrap, in March 1997 was 5,260 tonnes, nickel content. Of the total, ferrous scrap was 4,250 tonnes and nonferrous scrap was 1,010 tonnes. For all of 1996, U.S. consumption of secondary nickel was 53,500 tonnes.

U.S. stocks of secondary nickel at the end of March 1997 were 4,210 tonnes, nickel content. Of the total, 4,110 tonnes were ferrous scrap and 100 tons were nonferrous scrap. February 1997 ending stocks were 3,420 tonnes vs. 3,610 tonnes at the end of December 1996.

U.S. imports of nickel for consumption in February 1997 were 13,200 tonnes, nickel content vs. 10,800 tonnes in January. The major suppliers were Canada, Norway, Russia and Australia. For all of 1996, nickel imports were 150,000 tonnes. U.S. imports of nickel alloys in February 1997 were 926 tonnes, gross weight. The major suppliers were Germany, the United Kingdom, Sweden, and Australia. Imports of nickel alloys for all of 1006 were 10,200 tonnes.

U.S. exports of nickel in February 1997 were 3,920 tonnes vs. 46,800 tonnes for all of 1996. The major markets were Canada, Spain, Japan and South Korea.

Futures Markets

Nickel is traded on the London Metals Exchange (LME).

World Mine Production of Nickel In Metric Tons (Contained Nickel)

Year	Australia[3]	Botswana	Brazil	Canada	China	Dominican Republic	Greece	Indonesia	New Caledonia	Philippines	Russia[4]	South Africa	World Total
1987	74,554	25,900	22,092	189,086	25,000	32,521	9,202	57,764	56,850	7,819	270,000	34,300	890,539
1988	62,358	26,000	18,677	216,589	32,700	29,345	13,131	57,982	71,200	10,349	280,000	30,000	952,215
1989	67,041	23,700	18,826	200,899	34,250	31,264	16,097	62,987	96,200	15,380	280,000	28,900	984,078
1990	67,000	23,200	24,100	196,225	33,000	28,700	18,500	68,308	85,100	15,818	280,000	29,000	974,000
1991	69,000	23,500	26,400	192,259	31,000	29,062	19,300	71,681	114,492	13,658	245,000	27,700	991,000
1992	57,683	23,000	29,372	186,384	32,800	42,641	17,000	77,600	113,000	13,022	280,000	28,400	1,010,000
1993	64,717	23,000	32,154	188,080	30,700	37,423	12,940	65,757	97,092	7,663	244,000	29,868	926,000
1994	78,962	19,041	32,663	149,886	36,900	45,588	18,821	81,175	97,323	9,895	240,000	30,751	929,000
1995[1]	98,467	18,672	25,469	180,984	41,800	44,051	19,947	88,183	121,457	15,075	251,000	29,803	1,030,000
1996[2]	113,134	24,200	25,600	183,059	43,000	45,000	20,000	90,000	142,200	14,700	230,000	33,613	1,080,000

[1] Preliminary. [2] Estimate. [3] Content of nickel and sulfate and concentrates. *Source: U.S. Geological Survey (USGS)*

Salient Statistics of Nickel in the United States In Metric Tons (Contained Nickel)

Year	Net Import Reliance as a % of Apparent Consumption	Production: Plant[4]	Production: Secondary[5]	Nickel Consumed[1], By Uses: Alloy Steels	Cast Irons	Copper Base Alloys	Electroplating Anodes	Nickel Alloys	Stainless & Heat Resisting Steels	Super Alloys	Chemicals	Apparent Consumption	Stocks, Dec. 31: At Consumers' Plants	At Producer Plants	Primary & Secondary Nickel: Exports	Imports	Avg Price LME $ Lb
1987	79	-----	32,331	8,139	1,591	10,169	20,548	17,377	71,797	16,605	1,765	183,397	13,474	6,191	20,951	134,511	2.1
1988	74	-----	49,371	7,330	2,359	6,890	19,520	19,046	80,107	13,537	1,816	159,156	15,081	6,967	27,916	127,680	6.2
1989	71	347	52,131	6,094	2,318	9,928	21,604	18,757	68,866	10,956	1,164	157,103	16,562	6,326	31,460	137,017	6.0
1990	64	3,701	57,367	7,007	2,646	7,594	15,550	16,315	96,120	15,713	1,500	170,042	13,971	8,065	37,057	145,600	4.0
1991	61	7,065	53,521	5,536	1,185	6,938	15,474	16,882	84,292	13,787	1,363	156,663	15,940	11,794	36,902	138,210	3.7
1992	59	8,960	55,871	4,988	1,202	6,313	16,538	15,946	83,460	10,872	51	159,373	17,480	10,140	33,860	128,510	3.1
1993	63	4,880	54,702	4,940	805	6,078	16,611	17,004	87,300	10,783	1,170	158,000	14,430	15,700	33,180	132,710	2.4
1994	64	-----	58,590	5,930	499	7,940	15,500	20,500	88,700	11,700	2,670	164,000	11,000	10,200	41,920	133,070	2.8
1995[2]	59	8,290	64,600	9,570	491	8,510	15,600	21,800	103,000	14,100	5,210	181,000	12,300	12,700	51,550	156,930	3.7
1996[3]	63	15,100	59,200	6,240	563	7,300	16,200	19,700	94,000	12,600	5,310	183,000	12,900	11,200	46,700	150,060	3.4

[1] Exclusive of scrap. [2] Preliminary. [3] Estimate. [4] Smelter & refinery. [5] From purchased scrap (ferrous & nonferrous). [6] London Metal Exchange
W = Withheld proprietary data. *Source: U.S. Geological Survey (USGS)*

Oats

U.S. oats production has declined sharply in recent years with little sign of any viable trend reversal taking hold. Within the U.S., feed grain complex oats production is the smallest, totaling about two percent that of corn. The 1997/98 crop (June to May) of 176 million bushels compares with the 1996/97 record low 155 million bushels. Production in the early 1990's averaged near 300 million bushels. The harvested oats acreage in 1997/98 of 2.9 million acres compares with 2.7 million in 1996/97; with an average yield of 60.5 bushels per acre vs. 57.8, respectively. Wisconsin was the largest producing state in 1997 with 20.8 million bushels followed by North Dakota, Minnesota and Iowa, each with 18 million bushels. A sharp variance in average yield is evident among the North Central states: Wisconsin's average 1997 yield of 63 bushels per acre compares to North Dakota's 45 bushels and South Dakota's 55 bushels. The small oats production in recent years has helped boost imports, mostly from Canada. The 1997/98 estimate of 100 million bushels compares with 97 million in 1996/97 and an early 1990's average of about 65 million bushels.

U.S. oats 1997/98 carryin stocks on June 1, 1997 of a near record low 67 million bushels compares with 66 million a year earlier. The total supply for 1997/98 of 343 million bushels compares with 319 million in 1996/97. Disappearance was estimated at 273 million vs. 252 million, respectively. Feed and residual usage was forecast at 175 million bushels vs. 155 million in 1996/97, the increase apparently reflecting increased harvesting of oats for hay in the northern producing states. Feed/seed/industrial use in 1997/98 of 95 million bushels was unchanged from 1996/97. U.S. oats exports are insignificant. Carryover stocks on May 31, 1998 are estimated at 70 million bushels. The average farm price for 1997/98 was forecast at $1.55-$1.75/bus. vs. $1.96 in 1996/97, the latter being the highest farm price of the 1990's.

World oats production has declined about 40 percent from the mid-1980's. Production in 1997/98 of 29.9 million metric tonnes compares with 30.5 million in 1996/97. Less acreage is being allocated to oats; 1997/98 world acreage of 17.1 million hectares compares with 17.8 million in 1996/97 and 18.5 million in 1995/96. Average yield, however, in 1997/98 of 1.75 tonnes per hectare compares with 1.72 in 1996/97 and 1.56 in 1995/96. Russia is the world's largest producer, but their 1997/98 crop of 8.5 million tonnes is less than half the mid 1980's. Among the few major producers only Canada so far in the 1990's has shown any real growth in production, although due to both reduced acreage and yield the 1997/98 crop dipped to 3.5 million tonnes from the record high 4.4 million tonnes in 1996/97 and the 1980's average of about 3.0 million tonnes. Most of the world's oats production is consumed domestically and world trade is small. In 1997/98, total world exports were put at 2.2 million tonnes with Canada accounting for 1.4 million vs. 2.4 million and 1.6 million, respectively in 1996/97. EU exports of 500,000 tonnes compares with 450,000 in 1996/97 and only 124,000 in 1995/96. Importing nations are more numerous, but the U.S. is the consistent leader with 1.8 million tonnes forecast for 1997/98, followed by Japan with imports of only 90,000 tonnes.

Futures Markets

Oat futures and options are traded on the Chicago Board of trade (CBOT) and the Winnipeg Commodity Exchange (WCE). Oats futures are traded on the Mid-America Commodity Exchange (MidAm).

World Production of Oats In Thousands of Metric Tons

Crop Year	Argentina	Australia	Canada	China	France	Germany	Italy	Poland	Sweden	Turkey	United States	Former U.S.S.R.	World Total
1988-9	451	1,867	2,993	670	984	2,941	383	2,222	1,330	300	3,158	15,287	37,506
1989-90	620	1,640	3,546	622	970	2,010	296	2,186	1,455	270	5,423	14,972	39,554
1990-1	434	1,530	2,692	685	830	2,104	298	2,119	1,584	270	5,189	15,081	39,042
1991-2	400	1,690	1,794	650	740	1,867	359	1,873	1,426	280	3,534	12,342	32,785
1992-3	450	1,937	2,823	640	700	1,314	333	1,229	807	280	4,298	13,974	33,587
1993-4	440	1,652	3,550	640	710	1,730	370	1,500	1,295	280	2,994	14,422	35,162
1994-5	350	920	3,640	600	680	1,660	360	1,240	990	300	3,320	13,850	33,160
1995-6[1]	350	1,880	2,860	640	620	1,420	300	1,500	950	280	2,350	10,690	28,830
1996-7[2]	310	1,700	4,360	650	620	1,610	350	1,580	1,200	250	2,250	10,030	30,650
1997-8[3]	500	1,200	3,490	650	550	1,600	300	1,800	1,280	250	2,560	11,480	31,170

[1] Preliminary. [2] Estimate. [3] Forecast. *Source: Foreign Agricultural Service, U.S. Department of Agriculture (FAS-USDA)*

Official Oats Crop Production Reports in the United States In Thousands of Bushels

Year	July 1	Aug. 1	Sept. 1	Oct. 1	Dec.	Final	Year	July 1	Aug. 1	Sept. 1	Oct. 1	Dec.	Final
1986	-----	443,183	413,025	-----	383,553	386,356	1992	256,381	276,381	-----	-----	-----	294,229
1987	-----	392,843	-----	-----	-----	373,713	1993	262,860	249,830	249,830	208,138	-----	206,770
1988	-----	206,330	206,330	210,766	-----	217,375	1994	248,151	247,753	247,753	229,717	-----	229,008
1989	387,593	380,690	380,690	370,693	-----	373,587	1995	181,508	186,167	186,167	-----	-----	162,027
1990	374,457	365,337	365,337	358,288	-----	357,654	1996	154,968	157,663	-----	-----	-----	155,273
1991	280,016	259,666	259,666	242,526	-----	243,851	1997	182,672	187,127	-----	-----	-----	176,104

Source: National Agricultural Statistics Service, U.S. Department of Agriculture (NASS-USDA)

OATS

Oat Stocks in the United States   In Thousands of Bushels

Year	On Farms Mar. 1	On Farms June 1	On Farms Sept. 1	On Farms Dec. 1	Off Farms Mar. 1	Off Farms June 1	Off Farms Sept. 1	Off Farms Dec. 1	Total Stocks Mar. 1	Total Stocks June 1	Total Stocks Sept. 1	Total Stocks Dec. 1
1988	------	76,900	------	------	------	35,129	------	------	------	112,029	------	------
1989	------	59,930	------	------	------	38,404	------	------	------	98,334	------	------
1990	140,000	82,850	234,700	194,700	74,749	74,062	117,009	99,398	214,749	156,912	351,709	294,098
1991	138,600	92,400	173,600	148,100	90,659	78,831	110,487	96,508	229,259	171,231	284,087	244,608
1992	98,150	61,000	199,900	161,200	76,735	66,721	94,717	81,292	174,885	127,721	294,617	242,492
1993	110,250	66,130	161,000	124,200	64,875	47,063	58,004	69,517	175,125	113,193	219,004	193,717
1994	85,050	53,940	144,300	113,400	61,502	51,583	75,551	78,664	146,552	105,523	219,851	192,064
1995	78,400	46,750	107,200	87,200	70,575	53,848	72,967	65,804	148,975	100,598	180,167	153,004
1996	57,350	32,600	93,400	80,650	55,268	33,708	38,716	45,218	112,618	66,308	132,116	125,868
1997[1]	56,200	33,100	107,950	83,400	39,362	33,576	48,972	60,679	95,562	66,676	156,922	144,079

[1] Preliminary. *Source: National Agriucultural Statistics Service, U.S. Department of Agriculture (NASS-USDA)*

Oats Supply and Utilization in the United States

Crop Year Beginning June 1	Acreage Planted (1,000 Acres)	Acreage Harvested (1,000 Acres)	Yield Per Acre (Bushels)	Production	Imports	Total Supply	Feed & Residual	Food, Alcohol & Industrial	Seed	Exports	Total Use	Ending Stocks	Farm Price	Findley Loan Rate	Target Price
				In Millions of Bushels									Dollars Per Bushel		
1988-9	13,910	5,533	39.3	217.6	62.9	392.5	193.8	72.7	27.1	.6	294.2	98.3	2.61	.90	1.55
1989-90	12,085	6,882	54.3	373.6	66.4	538.3	265.6	91.6	23.4	.8	381.4	156.9	1.49	.85	1.50
1990-1	10,423	5,945	60.1	357.5	63.4	578.0	286.1	100.9	19.1	.6	406.7	171.2	1.14	.81	1.45
1991-2	8,654	4,806	50.6	243.5	74.8	489.4	235.2	107.2	17.8	1.9	362.1	127.7	1.21	.83	1.45
1992-3	7,961	4,492	65.4	294.8	55.0	476.9	233.0	107.2	17.8	5.7	363.7	113.2	1.32	.88	1.45
1993-4	7,937	3,803	54.4	206.8	106.8	426.8	193.3	110.0	15.0	3.0	321.3	105.5	1.36	.88	1.45
1994-5	6,639	4,010	57.1	229.0	93.2	427.7	201.1	79.2	12.8	1.0	327.1	100.6	1.22	.97	1.45
1995-6	6,336	2,962	54.7	162.0	80.5	343.2	155.0	80.0	11.9	2.1	276.9	66.3	1.68	.97	1.45
1996-7[1]	4,661	2,685	57.8	155.3	97.0	319.0	155.0	80.8	12.0	2.5	252.0	67.0	1.96	1.03	-----
1997-8[2]	5,169	2,911	60.5	176.1	100.0	343.0	175.0			2.0	272.0	71.0	1.55-1.65	1.11	-----

[1] Preliminary. [2] Forecast. *Source: Economic Research Service, U.S. Department of Agriculture (ERS-USDA)*

Production of Oats in the United States, by States   In Thousands of Bushels

Year	Illinois	Iowa	Michigan	Minnesota	Nebraska	New York	North Dakota	Ohio	Penn-slyvania	South Dakota	Texas	Wisconsin	Total
1988	9,180	25,000	6,000	24,750	12,160	7,540	7,200	9,000	13,000	20,000	9,000	46,860	217,375
1989	16,000	54,000	20,100	46,750	8,640	9,145	20,150	15,750	13,770	44,000	6,600	46,860	373,587
1990	11,560	40,800	13,050	48,180	13,440	8,235	16,100	2,280	15,840	53,200	9,225	47,570	357,654
1991	6,600	21,250	5,400	22,800	11,880	5,000	10,200	1,292	8,400	38,500	7,200	26,500	243,851
1992	7,930	25,125	8,400	35,000	15,400	7,700	37,400	12,070	13,735	42,900	5,720	34,410	294,229
1993	4,590	9,000	7,150	23,750	6,880	6,510	37,100	9,000	10,000	26,520	7,420	24,150	206,770
1994	5,490	26,660	6,270	24,750	7,500	7,040	33,550	6,720	8,480	31,360	5,200	25,380	229,008
1995	5,360	14,625	5,130	18,000	4,500	5,310	21,600	6,900	9,440	11,500	5,040	18,700	162,027
1996	4,620	12,920	3,600	15,120	7,455	4,275	19,000	5,130	7,560	21,600	3,400	17,400	155,273
1997[1]	5,550	17,885	5,490	17,980	4,550	7,700	18,000	7,800	9,440	17,050	5,720	20,790	176,104

[1] Preliminary. *Source: National Agricultural Statistics Service, U.S. Department of Agriculture (NASS-USDA)*

Average Cash Price of No. 2 Heavy White Oats in Toledo   In Dollars Per Bushel

Year	June	July	Aug.	Sept.	Oct.	Nov.	Dec.	Jan.	Feb.	Mar.	Apr.	May	Average
1987-8	1.56	1.24	1.55	1.62	1.62	1.77	1.83	1.83	1.87	1.77	1.73	1.73	1.68
1988-9	2.71	2.79	2.66	2.55	2.41	2.04	2.08	2.25	2.10	1.96	1.83	1.79	2.26
1989-90	1.53	1.39	1.30	1.30	1.34	1.37	1.46	1.40	1.37	1.41	1.46	1.47	1.40
1990-1	1.33	1.19	1.14	1.09	1.11	1.10	1.15	1.12	1.12	1.22	1.22	1.26	1.17
1991-2	1.14	1.24	1.29	1.28	1.31	1.30	1.34	1.41	1.58	1.61	1.48	1.50	1.37
1992-3	1.46	1.47	1.46	1.58	1.54	1.58	1.55	1.54	1.49	1.43	1.53	1.50	1.51
1993-4	1.42	1.50	1.49	1.43	1.41	1.38	1.37	1.43	1.40	1.37	1.37	1.25	1.40
1994-5	1.35	1.26	1.26	1.32	1.35	1.28	1.27	1.34	1.45	1.43	1.48	1.59	1.37
1995-6	1.65	1.76	1.83	1.90	1.76	1.91	2.21	2.14	2.06	2.17	2.32	2.05	1.98
1996-7	NQ	2.45	2.34	2.19	2.02	1.96	1.96	1.99	2.16				2.13

[1] Preliminary. NQ = No Quote. *Source: Economic Research Service, U.S. Department of Agriculture (ERS-USDA)*

Volume of Trading in Oat Futures in Chicago In Contracts

Year	Jan	Feb	Mar	Apr	May	June	July	Aug	Sept	Oct	Nov	Dec	Total
1988	18,420	24,240	29,320	32,420	32,520	53,420	32,060	24,220	21,520	21,620	36,600	28,220	354,580
1989	33,700	27,320	30,140	37,740	27,740	39,040	29,740	34,980	20,840	17,340	38,380	12,900	349,860
1990	24,660	31,740	33,880	45,140	54,000	46,360	32,040	49,600	25,200	27,800	47,380	15,560	433,360
1991	20,040	30,280	30,320	42,720	20,580	44,940	37,100	41,060	17,860	20,300	34,560	15,200	354,960
1992	31,020	84,020	42,260	47,060	42,020	54,540	22,200	40,160	25,100	16,580	35,220	19,400	459,580
1993	20,480	26,500	26,060	63,140	33,420	43,120	33,300	32,080	26,880	40,780	72,320	37,260	455,340
1994	47,980	57,060	39,800	53,820	34,300	69,760	20,760	39,340	28,840	24,900	56,940	19,680	493,180
1995	13,512	37,014	29,490	45,536	34,116	107,082	29,862	45,677	31,676	38,641	52,321	47,005	511,932
1996	61,451	52,079	34,608	77,395	47,161	34,498	38,960	33,316	30,801	37,579	37,856	16,154	501,858
1997	34,238	51,608	39,607	41,988	27,028	29,632	25,473	26,486	21,241	42,630	38,187	19,214	397,332

Source: Chicago Board of Trade (CBT) *Note: The CBT changed the Volume figures from Bushels to Contracts in January 1998.*

Average Open Interest of Oat Futures in Chicago In Contracts

Year	Jan.	Feb.	Mar.	Apr.	May	June	July	Aug.	Sept.	Oct.	Nov.	Dec.
1988	7,002	8,417	7,842	8,626	8,719	9,626	8,046	7,187	6,819	7,196	9,169	9,368
1989	10,068	10,245	10,152	10,057	9,521	9,766	9,793	9,454	9,765	11,167	11,862	11,248
1990	11,227	11,809	11,355	12,243	12,513	10,891	10,743	12,112	12,965	14,804	15,115	11,758
1991	11,890	12,832	13,895	15,620	14,223	13,091	11,117	10,894	10,368	11,560	11,257	9,355
1992	9,555	15,499	15,359	15,052	15,329	14,773	12,759	11,100	9,869	9,178	8,781	7,287
1993	7,398	7,739	7,655	11,579	13,357	12,020	10,894	11,381	11,171	14,116	20,057	20,547
1994	21,193	20,137	20,194	19,882	18,312	14,575	11,710	13,923	14,743	16,266	15,354	13,376
1995	13,133	13,231	13,000	15,426	16,054	13,611	11,019	11,348	11,012	11,970	12,542	13,003
1996	13,253	14,095	14,231	14,497	13,897	11,697	11,336	11,803	11,457	11,918	11,150	8,550
1997	8,088	9,650	12,649	11,024	9,830	9,395	8,131	8,606	8,618	10,953	11,816	10,964

Source: Chicago Board of Trade (CBT) *Note: The CBT changed the Open Interest figures from Bushels to Contracts in January 1998.*

OATS

Average Cash Price of No. 2 Heavy White Oats in Minneapolis In Dollars Per Bushel

Year	June	July	Aug	Sept	Oct	Nov	Dec	Jan	Feb	Mar	Apr	May	Average
1988-9	3.26	3.25	3.09	3.07	2.99	2.71	2.74	2.87	2.59	2.49	2.30	2.22	2.80
1989-90	1.97	1.72	1.59	1.58	1.61	1.68	1.70	1.56	1.48	1.57	1.63	1.68	1.65
1990-1	1.52	1.37	1.25	1.23	1.29	1.30	1.24	1.22	1.18	1.27	1.32	1.36	1.30
1991-2	1.25	1.33	1.38	1.35	1.41	1.42	1.49	1.50	1.68	1.66	1.57	1.59	1.47
1992-3	1.55	1.49	1.45	1.58	1.52	1.59	1.63	1.66	1.63	1.63	1.66	1.57	1.58
1993-4	1.54	1.63	1.63	1.66	1.56	1.51	1.56	1.57	1.52	1.55	1.46	1.37	1.55
1994-5	1.47	1.36	1.44	1.44	1.44	1.41	NQ	1.46	1.42	1.54	1.62	1.76	1.36
1995-6	1.73	1.92	1.96	2.04	2.11	2.63	2.50	2.40	2.31	2.47	2.56	2.68	2.28
1996-7	2.11	2.48	2.36	2.08	2.06	1.87	1.86	1.89	1.94	1.99	1.88	1.81	2.03
1997-8[1]	1.89	1.76	1.80	1.78	1.75	1.65							1.77

[1] Preliminary. NQ = No Quote. *Source: Economic Research Service, U.S. Department of Agriculture (ERS-USDA)*

Average Price Received by Farmers for Oats in the United States In Dollars Per Bushel

Year	June	July	Aug	Sept	Oct	Nov	Dec	Jan	Feb	Mar	Apr	May	Average
1988-9	2.41	2.86	2.54	2.57	2.56	2.41	2.47	2.52	2.46	2.41	2.24	2.13	2.61
1989-90	1.82	1.53	1.47	1.38	1.47	1.48	1.53	1.47	1.43	1.39	1.44	1.45	1.49
1990-1	1.33	1.15	1.06	1.09	1.14	1.16	1.17	1.13	1.13	1.16	1.16	1.16	1.14
1991-2	1.08	1.08	1.09	1.12	1.21	1.25	1.25	1.31	1.44	1.44	1.46	1.43	1.21
1992-3	1.38	1.32	1.23	1.28	1.31	1.35	1.36	1.42	1.42	1.43	1.45	1.51	1.32
1993-4	1.43	1.36	1.32	1.31	1.33	1.39	1.42	1.42	1.42	1.39	1.32	1.49	1.36
1994-5	1.31	1.20	1.16	1.18	1.21	1.18	1.18	1.22	1.22	1.33	1.36	1.41	1.22
1995-6	1.38	1.52	1.48	1.43	1.50	1.72	1.91	1.93	1.96	2.04	2.13	2.48	1.46
1996-7	2.16	2.12	2.00	1.83	1.84	1.85	1.72	1.83	1.81	1.90	1.87	1.86	1.90
1997-8[1]	1.81	1.68	1.55	1.48	1.57	1.62	1.56	1.59	1.59				1.61

[1] Preliminary. *Source: National Agricultural Statistics Service, U.S. Department of Agriculture (ERS-USDA)*

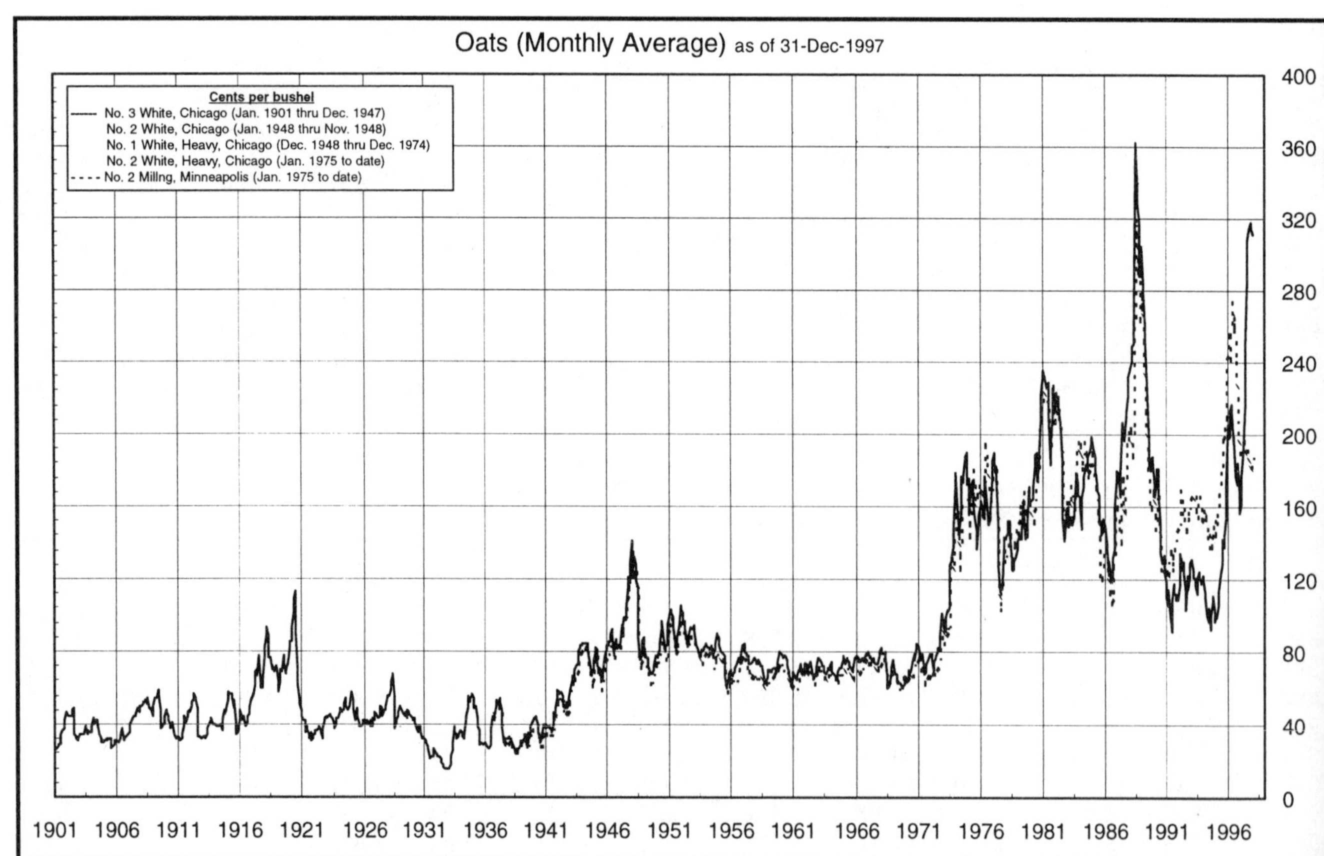

Olive Oil

Olive oil remains the cooking oil of choice for many due to its taste and widely advertised health benefits. Olive oil maintains a large price premium to other cooking oils and perhaps because of that, olive oil consumption has shown little growth in recent years. The olive harvest begins in the northern Mediterranean in mid-November and moves south, ending in March. The major producers are Italy, Spain, and Greece, with Tunisia, Turkey and Morocco accounting for smaller crops. As a tree crop, olives and olive oil production are cyclical with large crops typically followed by smaller ones in a two year cycle.

The newsletter Oil World indicated that world olive oil consumption in 1997-98 (September-October) would reach a record high 2.36 million metric tonnes, up close to four percent from the 1996-97 season. The reason for the increase was a large European crop. It was reported that high stocks of olive oil at the end of the 1997-98 season would keep prices at comparatively low levels. Olive oil price premiums over competitive oils like sunseed oil and soybean oil were expected to narrow as the prices of these other oils are increasing.

Oil world indicated that Canada could increase 1998 olive oil imports to 22,000 tonnes, Brazil to 27,000 tonnes, Japan to 28,000 tonnes and Australia to 21,000 tonnes. The U.S. is one of the largest importers of olive oil. Imports are expected to reach between 160,000 tonnes and 165,000 tonnes, up from the previous year's 148,000 tonnes.

In terms of production, Italy was expected to have a very large crop in 1997-98. Part of the reason is the inherent cyclicality in production. The 1996-97 crop was a low 380,000 tonnes which was down sharply from the previous year's 600,000 tonnes. It would follow that the small crop in 1996-97 would be followed by a large crop in 1997-98.

In the U.S., olives are grown in California. In 1996, total production of olives was 166,000 short tons. Of the total, 7,000 tonnes were crushed for oil. Planted olive acreage was 33,700 acres.

World Production of Olive Oil (Pressed Oil) In Thousands of Metric Tons

Crop Year	Algeria	Argentina	Greece	Italy	Jordan	Libya	Morocco	Portugal	Spain	Syria	Tunisia	Turkey	World Total
1987-8	10.0	9.5	322.0	742.5	3.1	6.5	41.5	38.0	792.0	36.0	101.5	63.0	2,198.0
1988-9	10.0	11.0	319.2	390.0	13.0	6.0	31.5	24.6	431.4	100.0	61.0	102.0	1,552.0
1989-90	16.0	10.5	316.3	624.2	7.5	8.0	70.0	44.3	594.9	33.0	137.0	39.0	1,938.6
1990-1	6.0	11.0	187.0	176.4	9.0	7.0	40.0	22.0	690.6	92.0	189.0	92.0	1,579.1
1991-2	37.0	9.5	423.5	727.9	5.5	10.0	55.5	72.7	640.5	47.0	264.0	70.0	2,393.5
1992-3	26.5	10.5	339.0	469.8	15.5	6.0	43.0	26.9	673.9	95.0	133.0	65.0	1,974.0
1993-4	21.0	8.5	275.0	451.5	9.5	8.0	45.5	36.1	593.2	71.0	251.0	55.0	1,875.2
1994-5[1]	14.0	10.0	389.8	464.4	15.0	6.5	50.0	36.2	547.0	101.5	106.5	181.5	1,963.6
1995-6[2]	23.0	7.9	362.0	540.0	14.5	4.0	40.0	49.9	347.8	84.0	64.5	50.5	1,632.9
1996-7[3]	46.0	8.5	368.0	507.0	15.5	9.0	70.0	51.0	755.0	128.0	239.0	202.0	2,425.2

[1] Preliminary. [2] Estimate. [3] Forecast. *Source: The Oil World*

Average Unit Value of Olive Oil Imports in the United States In Dollars Per Metric Ton

Year	Jan.	Feb.	Mar.	Apr.	May	June	July	Aug.	Sept.	Oct.	Nov.	Dec.	Average
1988	1,682	1,694	1,736	1,699	1,701	1,669	1,465	1,562	1,691	1,582	1,493	1,606	1,632
1989	1,642	1,642	1,890	1,930	2,005	1,981	1,919	1,919	1,862	1,917	1,910	2,017	1,886
1990	1,892	1,940	1,931	2,034	2,047	2,047	2,044	2,169	2,142	2,029	2,245	2,170	2,058
1991	2,195	2,213	2,355	2,188	2,283	2,274	2,281	2,282	2,401	2,250	2,417	2,523	2,305
1992	2,448	2,365	2,317	2,271	2,270	2,267	2,299	2,302	2,206	2,204	2,189	2,295	2,286
1993	2,132	2,071	1,853	1,823	1,779	1,820	1,805	1,815	1,836	1,788	1,885	1,852	1,872
1994	1,838	1,752	1,891	1,850	1,872	1,889	1,943	2,001	2,032	2,141	2,215	2,126	1,963
1995	2,245	2,316	2,470	2,629	2,795	2,857	3,032	3,112	3,110	3,253	3,256	3,322	2,866
1996	3,704	4,056	4,267	4,411	4,361	4,233	4,300	4,149	4,131	4,129	4,114	3,932	4,149
1997[1]	3,580	3,138	2,962	2,781	2,732	2,496	2,482	2,431	2,401	2,393	2,429		2,711

[1] Preliminary. *Source: Foreign Agricultural Service, U.S. Department of Agriculture (FAS-USDA)*

World Supply and Distribution of Olive Oil In Thousands of Metric Tons

Crop Year	Production	Exports	Imports	Consumption	Ending Stocks	Crop Year	Production	Exports	Imports	Consumption	Ending Stocks
1985-6	1,626	367	500	1,718	839	1991-2	2,394	346	349	1,931	836
1986-7	1,670	746	730	1,849	764	1992-3	1,974	380	373	2,068	735
1987-8	2,095	509	519	1,929	1,936	1993-4	1,875	407	413	2,041	575
1988-9	1,552	558	575	1,870	634	1994-5[1]	1,964	471	467	1,982	553
1989-90	1,939	579	573	1,861	706	1995-6[2]	1,633	321	324	1,855	334
1990-1	1,579	316	333	1,879	419	1996-7[3]	2,425	456	445	2,036	712

[1] Preliminary. [2] Estimate. [3] Forecast. *Source: The Oil World*

Onions

The USDA forecast U.S. fresh onion production in 1997 at 5.11 billion pounds, down three percent from 1996. In 1995, U.S. production set a record at 5.47 billion pounds. Imports of fresh onions in 1997 were 645 million pounds, a three percent increase from 1996. Imports of fresh onions have been trending higher for several years. Season-beginning stocks of onions were 943 million pounds. The total supply of onions in 1997 was 6.70 billion pounds.

In terms of utilization, U.S. exports of onions in 1997 were 560 million pounds, down four percent from the previous year. Exports set a high in 1994 at 802 million pounds. Shrink and loss accounted for 590 million pounds, down six percent from 1996. Domestic usage of fresh onions in 1997 was 4.67 billion pounds, down two percent from the previous year. Ending stocks of fresh onions were 875 million pounds. Per capita use of fresh onions in 1997 was 17.5 pounds. This was down slightly from the 1996 per capita usage of 17.9 pounds.

Usage of fresh onions has been trending higher for many years. In 1973, per capita use was 10.2 pounds. By 1980, per capita use had risen to 11.4 pounds. Ten years later in 1990, per capita use had increased to 15.1 pounds. Since 1973, U.S. per capita use of fresh onions is over 70 percent higher.

Salient Statistics of Onions in the United States

Crop Year	Harvested Acres	Yield Per Acre	Production 1,000 Cwt.	Price Per Cwt.	Farm Value $1,000	Jan. 1 Stocks Frozen (Millions of Pounds)	Annual Pack Frozen (Millions of Pounds)	Imports Canned (Millions of Pounds)	Exports (Fresh) (Millions of Pounds)	Imports (Fresh) (Millions of Pounds)	Per Capita[3] Utilization --Lbs., Farm Weight-- All	Per Capita[3] Utilization --Lbs., Farm Weight-- Fresh
1992	141,730	386	54,731	13.00	629,019	32.1	202.3	3.4	359.9	421.4	17.6	16.2
1993	152,580	380	57,956	16.80	831,986	34.2	213.7	4.7	437.9	510.2	18.5	16.5
1994	160,350	396	63,531	9.87	626,778	36.1	241.3	4.2	802.1	544.7	17.5	16.5
1995	164,000	391	64,182	11.10	633,692	51.2	246.8	4.0	662.1	483.7	18.9	17.6
1996[1]	159,310	385	61,369	10.60	581,571	48.8	259.5	3.6	586.3	625.2	18.7	17.9
1997[2]	154,920	404	63,883	11.50	648,437	40.8			560.0	645.0	18.6	17.5

[1] Preliminary. [2] Forecast. [3] Includes fresh and processing. *Source: Economic Research Service, U.S. Department of Agriculture (ERS-USDA)*

Production of Onions in the United States In Thousands of Hundred Pounds (Cwt.)

Year	Spring: Arizona	Spring: California	Spring: Texas	Spring: Total (All)	Summer: California	Summer: Colorado	Summer: Idaho	Summer: Michigan	Summer: Minnesota	Summer: New Mexico	Summer: New York	Summer: Oregon (Malheur)	Summer: Texas	Summer: Total (All)	Grand Total
1992	450	3,600	2,793	8,229	10,313	5,460	5,063	2,448	285	3,200	4,392	6,649	740	46,502	54,213
1993	631	3,300	2,768	8,193	13,035	5,735	4,698	2,201	22	4,074	3,720	5,940	936	49,763	57,956
1994	688	2,948	4,704	10,297	12,710	6,125	5,547	2,178	312	3,318	3,844	7,378	837	53,324	63,531
1995	672	3,300	3,763	10,110	12,658	6,141	5,481	1,856	125	4,095	4,032	7,134	870	54,072	64,182
1996	760	2,736	4,030	9,290	13,330	5,200	5,590	1,798	114	3,266	2,736	7,080	924	52,079	61,369
1997[1]	746	3,204	1,661	9,087	12,760	5,355	5,658	1,952	165		3,660	7,440		54,796	63,883

[1] Preliminary. *Source: Agricultural Statistics Board, U.S. Department of Agriculture (ASB-USDA)*

Cold Storage Stocks of Fresh Onions in the United States In Thousands of Pounds

Year	Jan.	Feb.	Mar.	Apr.	May	June	July	Aug.	Sept.	Oct.	Nov.	Dec.
1992	24,920	27,601	25,800	22,858	21,522	21,168	18,535	22,040	25,126	27,207	27,195	27,100
1993	25,634	25,246	24,648	21,336	19,061	16,384	17,571	24,457	26,828	26,219	26,145	29,205
1994	27,349	25,740	21,630	20,530	20,156	21,067	21,877	30,794	35,832	38,571	42,691	41,044
1995	37,472	36,240	35,402	33,906	30,071	30,790	31,309	32,175	32,081	33,594	36,360	34,877
1996	35,354	35,819	31,784	32,782	27,670	29,200	27,511	27,536	27,659	30,288	27,889	32,261
1997[1]	30,481	29,255	32,227	31,811	29,693	28,060	29,318	28,524	27,331	26,908	29,831	30,513

[1] Preliminary. *Source: National Agricultural Statistics Service, U.S. Department of Agriculture (NASS-USDA)*

F.O.B. Price Received by Growers for Onions in the United States In Dollars Per Hundred Pounds (Cwt.)

Year	Jan.	Feb.	Mar.	Apr.	May	June	July	Aug.	Sept.	Oct.	Nov.	Dec.	Season Average
1992	10.70	12.80	20.80	23.60	12.40	10.00	12.20	13.80	12.40	11.60	12.00	14.80	13.00
1993	16.60	14.00	17.30	31.00	23.60	10.40	12.70	14.80	13.30	12.10	18.70	24.50	16.80
1994	31.40	33.90	18.80	10.80	8.64	8.49	12.30	9.54	9.32	10.60	12.20	12.70	9.87
1995	13.50	17.50	17.90	20.00	14.60	10.50	13.70	9.67	10.00	9.89	9.52	10.00	9.87
1996	10.70	10.10	8.07	8.72	9.67	11.10	12.10	12.70	12.80	11.40	10.40	10.30	9.58
1997[1]	9.46	7.81	8.47	17.40	13.60	15.40	14.20	14.40	10.70	9.14			

[1] Preliminary. *Source: Economic Research Service, U.S. Department of Agriculture (ERS-USDA)*

Oranges and Orange Juice

U.S. production of frozen concentrated orange juice (FCOJ) continued to trend higher in the 1996-97 season as another record crop was harvested in Florida. Initial forecasts are that the 1997-98 season will see yet another record crop. There is also every indication that the next few years will see still larger crops because of several factors. One factor which is increasing production potential is that there is more bearing acreage planted to orange trees. USDA estimated that in the 1996-97 season, Florida bearing acreage was almost 625,000 acres. In 1985-86, bearing acreage was 368,000. Following freezes in the late 1980's many new trees were planted further south. The net effect of this was to reduce the potential for damage from cold weather while increasing productivity. The trees planted in the late 1980's are now reaching their most productive years. As a result, it looks like Florida orange production will continue to increase.

In December 1997, the USDA issued the second crop production report of the season. That report indicated that Florida's 1997-98 orange crop would be a record 254 million boxes, 12 percent more than the 1996-97 crop. That record crop was 226.2 million boxes. For 1997-98, the early, mid-season and navel orange crops were forecast at 146 million boxes, up almost nine percent from the previous year. The Valencia crop was estimated at 108 million boxes, up 17 percent from the previous year. The yield in 1997-98 was forecast at 1.55 gallons per box, down from 1.57 gallons in 1996-97.

U.S. orange production in the 1997-98 season was estimated at 330.55 million boxes, 11 percent higher than in 1996-97. California orange production was forecast at 74 million boxes, up nine percent from the previous season. Texas and Arizona produce smaller orange crops.

The Florida Citrus Processors reported that for the 1996-97 (December-November) season, movement of FCOJ was 265.4 million gallons, excluding deliveries on futures contracts. For the season, movement averaged 5.1 million gallons per week. Imports of FCOJ for the season were 43.19 million gallons and averaged just over 830,000 gallons per week. The net cumulative pack was 241.8 million gallons. That represented an increase of 19 million gallons from the 1995-96 season. The inventory of FCOJ at the end of the season was 68.97 million gallons. That represented a considerable amount of product to carry into a season which promised a record crop.

Brazilian fresh orange production in 1997 was estimated at a record 18.3 million metric tonnes, up eight percent from the previous year. Brazil is the world's largest producer of FCOJ.

Futures Market

Frozen concentrated orange juice futures and options are traded on the Citrus Associates of the New York Cotton Exchange (NYCE).

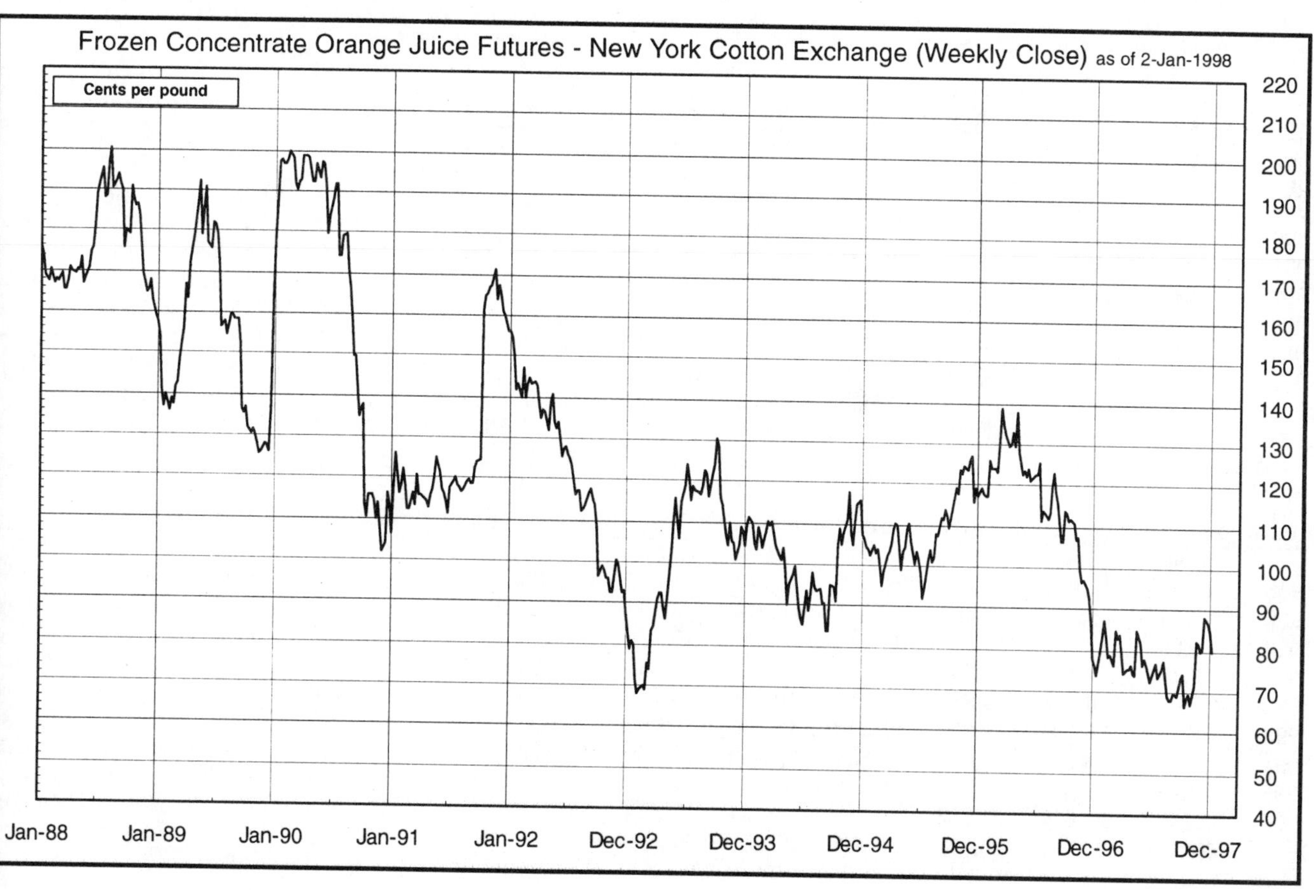

ORANGES AND ORANGE JUICE

World Production of Oranges In Thousands of Metric Tons

Season	Argentina	Australia	Brazil	Egypt	Greece	Italy	Mexico	Morocco	South Africa	Spain	Turkey	United States	World Total
1987-8	650	394	10,400	1,387	462	1,343	1,942	891	681	2,442	700	7,903	30,990
1988-9	620	544	14,150	1,199	770	2,170	2,000	994	629	2,216	740	8,272	35,835
1989-90	750	458	12,036	1,397	932	2,067	1,900	775	697	2,400	740	7,083	33,361
1990-1	600	485	12,362	1,574	819	1,760	2,300	1,103	648	2,590	735	7,222	33,938
1991-2	640	595	14,974	1,694	820	1,842	2,100	780	680	2,651	830	8,175	38,193
1992-3	660	578	14,484	1,771	1,042	2,111	2,913	874	712	2,926	820	10,074	41,582
1993-4	746	651	13,710	1,324	854	2,100	3,174	916	739	2,509	840	9,462	39,595
1994-5[1]	712	416	16,520	1,513	865	1,710	3,500	657	770	2,644	920	10,641	43,539
1995-6[2]	640	543	16,450	1,360	850	1,770	2,600	870	850	2,440	880	10,747	42,932
1996-7[3]	NA	NA	NA	1,608	850	1,515	2,800	780	NA	2,153	1,000	11,333	43,000

[1] Preliminary. [2] Estimate. [3] Forecast. NA = Not available. *Source: Foreign Agricultural Service, U.S. Department of Agriculture (FAS-USDA)*

Salient Statistics of Oranges & Orange Juice in the United States

	Production[4]					Florida Crop Processed				Frozen Concentrated Orange Juice-Florida				Brazilian U.S. Imports of Frozen Concentrated OJ		
															Exports	
Season	California	Florida	Total U.S.	Farm Price $ Per Box	Farm Value Million $	Frozen Concentrates	Chilled Products	Total Processed	Yield Per Box Gallons[5]	Carry-in	Pack	Total Supply	Total Season Movement	Pack	Total	To U.S.
	Million Boxes					Million Boxes				In Million Gallons (42° Brix)						
1987-8	59.0	138.0	200.3	8.52	1,773.7	110.2	23.3	134.4	1.6	39.8	240.9	280.7	238.5	244.8	254.5	120.5
1988-9	58.9	146.6	207.2	8.90	1,848.5	107.4	29.5	146.6	1.5	42.1	239.1	281.2	235.0	245.8	243.8	123.1
1989-90	71.4	110.2	184.5	7.96	1,465.1	70.1	33.5	110.2	1.2	46.3	184.7	231.0	191.1	362.0	330.7	132.4
1990-1	25.6	151.6	179.0	8.70	1,584.7	100.4	38.2	151.6	1.5	40.0	221.2	261.2	229.2	294.8	284.5	87.7
1991-2	67.4	139.8	209.6	7.43	1,545.2	90.6	37.0	139.8	1.6	31.8	211.7	243.5	212.6	274.1	279.3	107.8
1992-3	66.8	186.6	255.8	5.77	1,489.9	128.3	47.2	186.6	1.6	31.0	292.0	322.9	269.4	394.8	418.2	103.1
1993-4	63.6	174.4	240.5	6.37	1,541.3	111.7	51.0	174.4	1.6	53.5	261.7	315.2	256.6	388.2	387.5	102.0
1994-5[1]	56.0	205.5	263.6	6.08	1,624.1	144.7	54.8	199.8	1.5	58.6	274.2	332.8	290.4	356.9	370.7	96.5
1995-6[2]	58.0	203.3	263.9	6.85	1,822.6	132.9	64.5	197.7	1.5	42.4	284.5	326.9	285.7		360.8	65.9
1996-7[3]	68.0	226.2	296.6	6.41	1,936.4	153.8	68.8	222.8	1.6						398.3	67.5

[1] Preliminary. [2] Estimate. [3] Forecast. [4] Fruit ripened on trees, but destroyed prior to picking in not included. [5] 42° Brix equivalent.
Sources: Economic Research Service, U.S. Department of Agriculture (ERS-USDA); Florida Department of Citrus

Cold Storage Stocks of Orange Juice Concentrate in the U.S., on First of Month In Millions of Pounds

Year	Jan.	Feb.	Mar.	Apr.	May	June	July	Aug.	Sept.	Oct.	Nov.	Dec.
1988	662.4	903.8	1,072.9	1,004.1	1,019.0	1,122.1	1,171.8	998.5	827.0	693.3	638.7	589.5
1989	721.6	980.9	1,155.9	1,087.0	1,144.8	1,296.1	1,324.8	1,167.5	932.6	808.4	725.7	669.7
1990	749.6	926.6	1,046.5	1,119.2	980.9	1,148.2	1,074.8	1,008.1	901.4	797.1	802.0	871.3
1991	1,031.6	1,195.8	1,199.5	1,236.9	1,363.2	1,304.7	1,110.6	1,007.5	876.9	765.2	617.3	655.4
1992	828.4	1,130.7	1,150.0	1,102.9	1,269.3	1,294.8	1,143.8	978.0	874.9	741.9	665.5	638.0
1993	892.9	1,135.9	1,282.8	1,297.5	1,440.9	1,462.3	1,351.8	1,147.0	1,029.6	875.7	813.3	890.9
1994	955.5	1,248.9	1,429.0	1,273.8	1,499.6	1,615.2	1,521.8	1,449.1	1,257.5	1,119.6	1,026.1	1,055.9
1995	1,353.1	1,704.0	1,685.1	1,773.3	1,864.6	1,833.8	1,631.6	1,424.1	1,233.7	1,038.3	830.3	897.7
1996	1,050.6	1,295.4	1,353.0	1,322.3	1,443.9	1,596.9	1,535.0	1,423.6	1,238.6	965.6	732.7	691.0
1997[1]	1,069.4	1,522.6	1,677.6	1,759.4	1,993.9	2,176.0	1,977.7	1,761.8	1,571.8	1,293.3	1,140.9	1,214.4

[1] Preliminary. *Source: Agricultural Statistics Board, U.S. Department of Agriculture (ASB-USDA)*

Average Open Interest of Frozen Concentrated Orange Juice Futures in New York In Contracts

Year	Jan.	Feb.	Mar.	Apr.	May	June	July	Aug.	Sept.	Oct.	Nov.	Dec.
1988	11,683	14,089	16,708	14,576	11,861	11,427	11,235	11,192	9,708	6,564	9,170	8,697
1989	7,169	6,959	7,009	7,821	8,374	9,767	8,340	7,531	6,857	7,218	7,029	9,887
1990	9,667	11,067	11,877	11,952	10,528	10,229	9,413	7,485	6,867	5,939	5,802	6,983
1991	6,773	6,457	5,739	6,255	5,762	6,338	5,653	6,556	9,854	11,924	9,877	9,101
1992	9,095	10,033	9,872	11,309	10,791	9,776	10,109	12,132	11,910	14,224	16,669	17,455
1993	17,733	18,199	19,030	20,210	18,525	19,267	20,000	18,899	18,287	18,825	18,422	20,367
1994	17,544	18,137	19,073	21,607	21,450	23,530	24,829	21,874	22,739	23,385	26,859	26,413
1995	27,439	25,885	26,407	30,172	27,057	26,844	23,537	17,881	20,918	22,460	26,303	24,202
1996	22,943	21,670	25,232	23,788	21,724	20,934	20,159	19,834	18,029	18,000	22,513	26,405
1997	29,171	26,929	26,331	28,955	29,868	33,639	31,799	34,339	36,057	40,365	41,811	46,169

Source: Citrus Association of the New York Cotton Exchange (NYCE)

Volume of Trading of Frozen Concentrated Orange Juice Futures in New York In Contracts

Year	Jan.	Feb.	Mar.	Apr.	May	June	July	Aug.	Sept.	Oct.	Nov.	Dec.	Total
1988	40,976	42,153	37,295	28,937	22,931	36,877	23,752	27,118	26,228	26,922	19,399	25,451	358,039
1989	26,156	26,419	28,501	26,855	30,272	32,051	23,403	19,698	17,119	18,069	15,893	39,668	304,104
1990	53,133	32,035	31,676	28,025	23,656	45,028	21,302	24,029	13,131	21,793	16,473	30,739	342,574
1991	35,037	28,221	17,298	17,116	17,991	20,956	14,905	20,187	26,412	42,016	23,228	24,171	287,076
1992	30,508	28,177	21,371	31,725	21,253	22,473	21,877	27,208	26,912	29,604	33,133	44,979	339,230
1993	43,634	46,067	58,298	52,554	53,566	60,330	49,415	52,381	56,838	63,808	44,167	58,073	640,131
1994	46,166	51,123	43,075	55,955	48,236	60,110	37,069	55,711	52,209	73,155	54,978	76,037	653,824
1995	50,875	66,370	51,292	78,288	32,607	80,165	41,357	67,528	38,781	64,904	45,688	71,077	688,932
1996	59,666	82,057	46,272	65,752	62,247	44,827	40,884	58,346	44,239	40,680	39,291	70,676	654,937
1997	84,982	89,875	66,340	82,772	62,890	78,690	47,242	118,286	55,081	108,413	100,941	134,349	1,029,861

Source: Citrus Association of the New York Cotton Exchange (NYCE)

Retail and Nonretail Sales of Orange Juice in the United States In Millions of SSE Gallons

Crop Year	Retail Sales	% Change[2]	Nonretail Sales	% Change[2]	Apparent Con-sumption	% Change[2]	Per Capita Con-sumption	% Change[2]
1987-8	667	-4.9%	432	12.2%	1,229	-1.1%	5.0	-2.0%
1988-9	690	3.4%	401	-7.2%	1,238	.7%	5.0	0
1989-90	628	-9.0%	317	-20.9%	1,079	-12.8%	4.3	-14.0%
1990-1	701	11.6%	296	-6.6%	1,146	6.2%	4.5	4.7%
1991-2	689	-1.7%	268	-9.5%	1,112	-3.0%	4.3	-4.4%
1992-3	748	8.6%	371	38.4%	1,328	19.4%	5.1	18.6%
1993-4	740	-1.1%			1,368	3.0%	5.2	2.0%
1994-5	740	0			1,355	-1.0%	5.1	-1.9%
1995-6[1]	718	-2.9%			1,363	.6%	4.9	-3.9%
1996-7[1]	700	-2.5%			1,320	-3.1%	NA	NA

[1] Estimate. [2] Percentage change from previous period. *Source: Florida Department of Citrus*

Producer Price Index of Frozen Orange Juice Concentrate 1982 = 100

Year	Jan.	Feb.	Mar.	Apr.	May	June	July	Aug.	Sept.	Oct.	Nov.	Dec.	Average
1988	132.1	140.1	142.4	140.5	142.0	141.1	141.6	142.0	141.7	140.7	140.8	139.1	140.3
1989	136.4	127.7	126.5	126.5	131.7	139.2	140.6	140.3	134.0	131.6	123.1	121.7	131.6
1990	137.6	162.4	162.8	159.9	159.7	160.0	160.4	160.8	150.9	147.2	120.9	117.8	150.0
1991	114.4	114.4	111.7	111.7	111.0	111.0	111.0	107.2	107.4	116.0	127.3	131.5	114.6
1992	135.1	134.7	134.7	134.3	126.2	118.5	115.5	114.5	112.5	106.5	104.2	98.8	119.6
1993	91.6	88.8	88.2	89.0	89.3	97.5	104.5	104.5	104.7	104.7	107.9	107.9	98.2
1994	107.9	104.8	104.2	104.2	102.7	101.2	100.2	100.1	99.9	99.8	100.7	100.5	102.2
1995	107.4	105.4	107.6	107.6	109.1	109.1	109.1	105.3	101.0	101.6	106.1	107.3	106.4
1996	109.4	112.5	117.2	119.5	119.5	119.5	115.3	113.6	113.6	112.8	112.8	108.8	114.5
1997[1]	106.9	106.9	106.0	107.6	107.7	107.3	105.3	105.8	102.7	101.7	94.1	93.9	103.7

[1] Preliminary. *Source: Bureau of Labor Statistics, U.S. Department of Commerce (BLS)*

Average Price of Oranges (Equivalent On-Tree) Received by Growers in the U.S. In Dollar Per Box

Year	Jan.	Feb.	Mar.	Apr.	May	June	July	Aug.	Sept.	Oct.	Nov.	Dec.	Average
1988	6.43	6.59	6.87	7.76	8.79	8.78	6.47	5.44	5.56	3.39	6.15	6.76	6.58
1989	6.51	6.45	6.26	7.28	8.39	8.51	7.27	6.52	6.54	6.29	7.34	6.34	6.98
1990	5.92	5.82	6.00	6.47	6.97	6.61	5.74	4.38	4.48	5.04	5.78	5.76	5.75
1991	5.64	6.28	6.94	7.09	7.95	19.43	17.40	18.45	21.39	9.87	6.27	5.79	11.04
1992	5.90	6.02	5.81	6.14	6.16	4.26	1.85	1.02	1.05	2.43	4.10	3.67	4.03
1993	3.37	3.21	3.41	4.00	4.03	4.09	5.02	7.25	11.85	11.44	5.95	3.81	5.62
1994	3.76	3.90	4.66	4.83	5.04	4.94	4.08	4.24	3.44	2.92	3.44	3.43	4.06
1995	3.43	3.59	4.22	4.61	4.90	5.63	7.44	7.30	7.26	7.90	3.57	3.55	5.28
1996	3.97	4.39	5.20	6.11	6.63	6.72	6.97	8.15	13.70	10.94	4.30	3.91	6.75
1997[1]	3.97	3.98	3.88	4.65	4.76	4.62	5.08	6.93	6.95	3.69	2.15	2.53	4.43

[1] Preliminary. *Source: Economic Research Service, U.S. Department of Agriculture (ERS-USDA)*

Palm Oil

Palm oil is the world's second largest vegetable oil crop, but first in foreign trade. Palm oil is a tropical oil, but competes directly with other cooking oils such as soybean and sunflower oils that are grown in more temperate climates. Almost all the world's production comes from Malaysia and Indonesia.

Palm oil production in 1997/98 (October/September) reached a record 17.5 million metric tonnes vs. 17.1 million in 1996/97. More than half of the world's production is exported to meet global consumption, estimated at a record 17.6 million tonnes in 1997/98 vs 16.7 million in 1996/97, and annual usage of 11.5 million tonnes early in the 1990's. Palm oil exports go mostly to Europe, the world's largest importer of crude vegetable oils. World palm oil stocks were estimated at 1.59 million tonnes at yearend 1997/98 (September) vs. 1.71 million a year earlier.

Malaysia's 1997/98 production was forecast at 8.8 million tonnes vs. a record 8.9 million tonnes in 1996/97. However, below normal rainfall in mid-1997 in Southeast Asia could trim the area's production. Assuming the initial crop forecasts are realized, Malaysia's 1997/98 exports are forecast to be a record 7.4 million tons, marginally above 1996/97. Carryover stocks, however, are forecast to dip for the first time in four years to 825,000 tonnes vs. 900,000 a year earlier. Indonesia's crop in recent years has totaled about half that of Malaysia's. Palm kernel production is likewise concentrated, notably in Malaysia; world 1997/98 palm kernal production of 2.4 million tons compares with 2.3 million in 1996/97.

U.S. palm oil imports during the first nine months of the 1996/97 crop year (through June) totaled 113,424 tonnes vs. 88,140 in the like 1995/96 period with a value of $49.8 million vs. $46.1 million, respectively.

World palm oil prices traversed a wide range over the last 10 years averaging $391 per metric ton. For 1996/97 the average was $529, basis Malaysia FOB vs. $523 in 1995/96. Helping to support prices is the strong growth in consumption from Europe, China and India. 1997/98 consumption in China is forecast at 1.7 million tonnes vs. 1.4 million in 1996/97; India's numbers are 1.1 million tonnes vs 1 million.

Futures Markets

Crude Palm Oil and Crude Palm Kernal Oil are traded on the Kuala Lumpur Commodity Exchange (KLCE).

World Palm Oil Statistics In Thousands of Metric Tons

Crop Year	Production: Colombia	Indonesia	Ivory Coast	Malaysia	Nigeria	Thailand	World Total	Imports: China	Pakistan	World Total	Exports: Indonesia	Malaysia	World Total
1991-2	281	2,853	278	6,224	633	254	11,834	847	1,002	8,382	1,268	5,783	8,305
1992-3	303	3,453	302	7,122	640	289	13,486	1,107	1,102	9,319	1,733	6,212	9,377
1993-4	348	3,630	305	7,103	640	311	13,782	1,653	1,080	10,354	1,965	6,737	10,372
1994-5	391	4,039	282	7,771	638	346	14,945	1,786	1,215	10,643	1,904	6,728	10,624
1995-6[1]	393	4,587	277	8,264	607	369	16,062	1,178	1,156	10,472	2,082	6,896	10,598
1996-7[2]	441	4,873	276	9,000	615	386	17,212	1,851	1,033	11,574	2,419	7,794	11,839
1997-8[3]	430	5,230	286	8,610	610	375	17,183	1,815	1,100	12,078	2,620	7,700	11,900

[1] Preliminary. [2] Estimate. [3] Forecast. *Source: The Oil World*

Supply and Distribution of Palm Oil in the United States In Thousands of Metric Tons

Year Beginning Oct.	Stocks Oct. 1	Imports	Total Supply	Consumption (In Millions of Pounds): Edible Products	Inedible Products	Total End Products	Total Disappearance	Exports	Prices (U.S. $ Per Metric Ton): U.S. Import Value[4]	Malaysia, F.O.B., RBD	Palm Kernel Oil, Malaysia, C.I.F. Rotterdam
1992-3	20.1	120.6	140.7	83.5	113.5	197.0	122.5	3.3	377	379	439
1993-4	14.9	167.0	181.9	86.2	118.2	204.4	162.0	3.6	370	451	566
1994-5	16.4	98.7	115.1	38.1	113.6	151.7	101.8	5.9	538	647	680
1995-6[1]	7.4	106.9	114.3	6.7	103.9	110.6	91.0	6.4	511	545	729
1996-7[2]	14.0	140.0	154.0		91.8	91.8	135.0	9.0	432	544	734
1997-8[3]	17.0	150.0	167.0		108.3	108.3	144.0	11.0	420	595	

[1] Preliminary. [2] Estimate. [3] Forecast. [4] Market value in the foreign country, excluding import duties, ocean freight and marine insurance.
Sources: The Oil World; Economic Research Service, U.S. Department of Agriculture (ERS-USDA)

Average Wholesale Palm Oil Prices, CIF, Bulk, U.S. Ports In Cents Per Pound

Year	Jan.	Feb.	Mar.	Apr.	May	June	July	Aug.	Sept.	Oct.	Nov.	Dec.	Average
1991	19.49	19.50	19.25	19.18	19.05	19.40	20.32	19.14	18.86	20.63	21.63	18.99	19.62
1992	21.91	21.05	21.92	22.05	21.51	21.77	21.19	21.00	21.50	21.86	22.18	22.24	21.68
1993	23.18	23.09	22.99	22.26	21.95	21.01	20.31	19.84	19.43	18.83	19.74	21.90	21.21
1994	21.91	21.67	21.72	23.08	26.27	28.94	27.44	30.18	32.15	31.93	34.95	36.83	28.09
1995	34.26	33.82	36.18	35.56	32.80	33.06	33.68	32.59	30.86	31.45	31.96	30.00	33.02
1996	27.08	26.52	26.33	27.52	28.57	25.43	24.78	24.46	27.24	26.13	26.95	27.45	26.54
1997[1]	28.68	29.25	28.00	28.18	28.93	27.25	26.17	25.55	25.37				27.49

[1] Preliminary. *Source: Economic Research Service, U.S. Department of Agriculture (ERS-USDA)*

Paper

The world's largest producer of paper and paperboard is he United States. Between 1990 and 1994, U.S. paper and aperboard production averaged close to 76 million metric onnes. Another large producer is Canada which averaged .7.1 million tonnes between 1990 and 1994. Other large roducers include Japan, Germany and Sweden. Canada is he world's largest producer of newsprint. In 1996, production was estimated at 744,100 tonnes per month, down four ercent from the previous year. The U.S. is the second argest producer of newsprint. In 1996, production averaged 519,200 tonnes per month, down two percent from the previous year. Japan is the third largest producer with 1996 output of 259,000 tonnes per month.

U.S. production of newsprint in the January-February 1997 period was 1.07 million tonnes averaging 535,000 tonnes a month. For the same period, Canadian newsprint production was 1.58 million tonnes, averaging 790,000 tonnes per month. Japan reported that newsprint production in May 1997 was 276,000 tonnes. Over the first five months of 1997, Japan produced 1.32 million tonnes of newsprint. Sweden produced 207,200 tonnes of newsprint in May 1997. Over the first five months of 1997, Sweden produced 962,700 tonnes of newsprint. Germany produced 156,300 tonnes of newsprint in June 1997. In the first half of 1997, Germany produced 897,000 tonnes of newsprint.

Production of Paper and Paperboard by Selected Countries In Thousands of Metric Tons

Year	Austria	Canada	Finland	France	Germany	Italy	Japan	Netherlands	Russia[2]	Spain	Sweden	United Kingdom	United States
1991	3,090	16,559	8,776	7,190	12,904	5,795	29,056	2,862	9,590	3,579	8,349	4,951	72,724
1992	3,252	16,585	9,147	7,690	13,214	6,040	28,324	2,835	5,765	3,449	8,378	5,151	75,161
1993	3,300	17,528	9,990	7,975	13,034	6,019	27,764	2,855	4,459	3,348	8,781	5,406	77,167
1994	3,603	18,349	10,909	8,701	14,457	6,705	28,527	3,011	3,412	3,503	9,284	5,829	80,948
1995	3,599	18,713	10,942	8,619	14,827	6,810	28,527	2,967	4,073	3,684	9,159	6,093	85,526
1996[1]		18,414	10,441			6,358		2,987	3,212		9,038	6,188	85,173

[1] Preliminary. [2] Formerly part of the U.S.S.R.; data not reported separately until 1992. *Source: Food and Agricultural Organization of the United Nations (FAO-UN)*

Production of Newsprint by Selected Countries (Monthly Average) In Thousands of Metric Tons

Year	Australia	Brazil	Canada	China	Finland	France	Germany	India	Japan	Rep. of Korea	Russia[3]	Sweden	United States
1992	33.6	18.9	729.0	40.8	104.8	55.8	94.2	24.7	271.1	50.2	78.6	147.5	535.3
1993	33.1	22.2	761.0	48.3	118.7	66.7	105.8	23.5	243.1	61.9	70.4	193.8	534.3
1994	33.5	22.1	776.8	52.6	119.4	70.3	156.3	22.3	247.7	72.3	86.5	201.3	528.3
1995	37.4	23.5	768.8	64.0	117.8	56.4	146.0	24.9	258.2	79.7	-----	196.1	529.3
1996[1]	37.1	23.0	751.3	68.4	110.6	-----	142.4	26.1	261.7	99.2	-----	181.9	525.3
1997[2]	34.8	21.4	793.5	65.9	123.2	-----	149.7	24.2	265.8	115.6	-----	200.4	534.5

[1] Preliminary. [2] Estimate. [3] Formerly part of the U.S.S.R.; data not reported separately until 1992. *Source: Statistical Division, United Nations (UN)*

Salient Statistics of Newsprint in the the United States and Canada In Thousands of Metric Tons

	United States										Canada		
			Imports by Countries of Origin						-Stocks, Dec. 31-				
Year	Production	Exports	Canada	Finland	Norway	Sweden	Total	Consumption	At Mills	At Publishers	Production	Exports	Stocks at Mills
1991	6,206	570	5,623	22	29	46	6,795	11,268	98	932	8,855	9,165	565
1992	6,424	753	5,690	14	25	38	6,658	11,505	59	938	8,753	7,924	351
1993	6,412	768	5,805	14	37	54	7,061	11,535	81	956	9,130	8,003	362
1994	6,984	672	5,906	12	28	30	7,150	11,695	66	879	9,321	8,326	246
1995[1]	7,002	829	7,722						84	1,133	9,252	8,062	252
1996[1]	6,945	591	6,881						104				

[1] Preliminary. Not seasonally adjusted. *Source: Newsprint Division, American Forest & Paper Association (AF&PA)*

Index Price of Paperboard 1982 = 100

Year	Jan.	Feb.	Mar.	Apr.	May	June	July	Aug.	Sept.	Oct.	Nov.	Dec.	Average
1991	132.6	132.0	129.6	128.4	127.0	127.2	127.1	127.8	131.8	132.7	132.8	132.9	130.2
1992	133.4	133.6	133.4	134.3	134.3	134.3	134.2	134.6	135.9	135.7	133.9	133.6	134.3
1993	133.0	131.6	131.3	130.6	129.9	128.9	128.6	128.0	128.0	129.7	130.2	130.5	130.0
1994	130.2	130.1	131.1	133.4	133.1	133.5	137.8	143.5	146.9	153.6	156.0	156.7	140.5
1995	165.3	171.2	172.3	183.8	188.2	188.4	189.9	190.6	190.3	188.8	185.7	182.2	183.1
1996	175.7	172.6	166.6	161.8	154.0	150.6	148.0	145.5	145.6	146.6	146.9	147.6	155.1
1997[1]	147.1	144.2	139.7	137.2	136.8	137.5	137.8	143.8	148.4	150.5	155.8	156.0	144.7

[1] Preliminary. *Source: Bureau of Labor Statistics, U.S. Department of Commerce (BLS - 0914)*

PAPER

Index Price of Wood Pulp, Bleached Suphate Softwood 1982 = 100

Year	Jan.	Feb.	Mar.	Apr.	May	June	July	Aug.	Sept.	Oct.	Nov.	Dec.	Average
1991	152.2	150.0	143.6	142.1	136.8	132.4	126.2	124.2	123.2	120.0	120.7	114.8	132.2
1992	121.6	123.7	125.2	131.8	132.1	131.4	134.2	136.1	135.1	133.7	132.0	132.8	130.8
1993	121.6	118.1	112.7	112.3	112.7	112.7	110.7	108.9	108.6	107.1	105.5	104.0	111.2
1994	106.7	106.9	109.6	113.5	113.4	118.0	119.4	124.3	130.3	137.1	141.4	142.2	121.9
1995	150.9	153.0	187.5	193.0	202.4	215.2	217.8	223.3	218.8	223.3	217.0	212.7	201.2
1996	195.0	175.4	155.5	123.5	111.1	120.1	126.9	129.0	129.4	130.3	129.3	131.5	138.1
1997[1]	129.6	125.9	123.9	119.0	121.8	123.9	130.9	134.4	135.7	135.8	136.8	136.2	129.5

[1] Preliminary. *Source: Bureau of Labor Statistics, U.S. Department of Commerce (BLS - 0911-0211)*

Index Price of Shipping Sack Paper[2] 1982 = 100

Year	Jan.	Feb.	Mar.	Apr.	May	June	July	Aug.	Sept.	Oct.	Nov.	Dec.	Average
1991	148.9	148.9	148.9	148.9	148.9	148.9	148.9	148.9	148.9	148.9	148.9	148.9	148.9
1992	148.9	148.9	154.0	154.0	154.0	148.9	148.9	148.9	155.7	155.7	155.7	155.7	152.4
1993	155.7	155.7	155.7	155.7	151.8	151.8	151.8	151.8	151.8	151.8	152.5	152.5	153.2
1994	151.3	150.9	154.3	154.5	159.3	163.9	169.9	170.3	176.6	178.2	184.9	185.5	166.6
1995	190.4	204.5	209.5	212.0	221.5	224.2	224.2	224.2	224.0	223.4	212.8	207.3	214.8
1996	205.2	202.2	201.5	194.7	194.3	193.1	189.9	185.7	183.0	183.0	185.8	185.8	192.0
1997[1]	185.8	186.4	186.7	186.5	184.3	184.1	183.9	188.1	182.0	188.5	196.9	197.6	187.5

[1] Preliminary. [2] Unbleached kraft. NA = Not avaliable. *Source: Bureau of Labor Statistics, U.S. Department of Commerce (BLS - 0913-0307)*

Producer Price Index of Standard Newsprint 1982 = 100

Year	Jan.	Feb.	Mar.	Apr.	May	June	July	Aug.	Sept.	Oct.	Nov.	Dec.	Average
1991	126.8	127.2	127.1	121.7	121.4	120.1	119.5	118.8	118.1	117.3	116.4	115.8	120.9
1992	115.3	114.8	112.3	108.8	108.3	106.6	106.6	106.7	109.5	109.2	110.6	109.6	109.9
1993	110.4	111.2	114.1	113.9	113.0	113.1	112.7	112.6	111.3	111.2	111.0	111.0	112.1
1994	109.9	109.5	110.7	110.6	112.2	113.8	116.9	116.9	121.7	123.8	126.8	127.3	116.7
1995	135.8	134.6	140.1	147.4	152.3	164.8	166.1	166.1	174.5	186.2	186.2	186.2	161.8
1996	186.2	186.2	185.2	182.7	173.5	164.4	157.4	148.7	145.7	133.1	127.3	123.1	159.5
1997[1]	121.1	120.9	123.1	128.6	135.9	137.2	138.6	139.4	138.9	138.9	142.4	142.8	134.0

[1] Preliminary. *Source: Bureau of Labor Statistics, U.S. Department of Commerce (BLS - 0913-02)*

Index Price of Coated Printing Paper, No. 3 1982 = 100

Year	Jan.	Feb.	Mar.	Apr.	May	June	July	Aug.	Sept.	Oct.	Nov.	Dec.	Average
1991	129.3	129.4	129.4	129.1	128.7	128.1	128.1	128.1	128.1	128.7	128.7	127.8	128.6
1992	126.8	123.6	123.7	123.7	122.3	121.7	122.1	121.7	121.7	124.2	123.4	123.3	123.2
1993	123.4	123.3	123.3	123.4	123.4	123.3	123.0	123.0	123.2	122.9	122.9	122.9	123.2
1994	122.0	122.1	121.8	122.2	121.6	121.6	121.6	125.2	130.7	131.7	132.9	136.3	125.8
1995	139.5	145.8	150.2	153.1	147.7	152.0	159.3	159.3	160.4	160.3	160.3	160.3	154.0
1996	160.2	159.7	159.4	159.2	155.6	153.5	153.0	152.5	152.2	151.8	151.9	152.9	155.2
1997[1]	152.7	153.1	152.9	153.2	153.2	154.6	154.5	154.5	153.2	155.0	154.8	153.0	153.8

[1] Preliminary. *Source: Bureau of Labor Statistics, U.S. Department of Commerce (BLS - 0913-0113)*

International Paper Prices--Export Unit Value

Year	Jan.	Feb.	Mar.	Apr.	May	June	July	Aug.	Sept.	Oct.	Nov.	Dec.	Average
NEWSPRINT - Canada	In Canadian Dollars Per Metric Ton												
1993	687	676	668	690	692	690	676	674	664	666	658	642	674
1994	634	618	638	657	656	642	663	672	658	657	749	755	667
1995	781	787											784
NEWSPRINT - Finland	In Markka Per Metric Ton												
1994	2,339	2,273	2,320	2,366	2,349	2,364	2,318	2,360	2,295	2,262	2,236	2,275	2,313
1995	2,563	2,589	2,577	2,614	2,598	2,667	3,037	3,122	3,172	3,187	3,214	3,191	2,885
1996	3,320	3,412	3,438	3,463	3,442	3,362	3,265	3,110	3,010	3,709	2,899	2,841	3,207
PRINTING AND WRITING - Canada	In Canadian Dollars Per Metric Ton												
1993	885	861	860	891	902	920	923	921	924	919	927	931	905
1994	910	920	925	923	915	922	955	978	987	1,024	1,078	1,127	972
1995	1,225	1,240											1,233
PRINTING AND WRITING - Finland	In Markka Per Metric Ton												
1994	3,471	3,290	3,370	3,375	3,484	3,507	3,524	3,490	3,498	3,472	3,501	3,666	3,471
1995	3,816	3,897	3,905	4,066	4,165	4,284	4,473	4,416	4,439	4,555	4,569	4,400	4,235
1996	4,556	4,555	4,503	4,374	4,265	4,069	3,871	3,743	3,644	3,644	3,667	3,654	4,027

Source: Food and Agricultural Organization of the United Nations (FAO-UN)

Peanuts and Peanut Oil

World raw peanut (groundnut) production in 1997/98 dipped from the 1996/97 record high: 24.6 million metric tonnes vs. 26.7 million due to lower average yield, notably in China, and a marginal decline in acreage. On a shelled basis the totals would be about 25 percent lower. Among the world's major oilseed, peanut production ranks fourth, but that position is shaky as sunflowerseed production gains. Unlike most oilseeds in the 1990's whose acreage has been increased, peanut acreage has held at about 19.6 million hectares.

China and India produced about two-thirds of the world's crop in 1997/98, and the U.S. less than 10 percent. China's crop, however, dropped 20 percent, to 8.0 million tonnes from 10 million in 1996/97, as average yield fell to 2.2 tonnes per hectare from 2.8 tonnes. India's crop of 8.0 million tonnes compares with 8.2 million in 1996/97. However, India's peanut acreage is more than double China's, but India's average yield is about a third of China's yield.

Foreign trade in peanuts is small as most of the crop is consumed locally; world imports in 1997/98 of 1.6 million tonnes were marginally higher than in 1996/97. The world's peanut crush is among the smallest of the major oilseeds, 13.0 million tonnes in 1997/98 vs. 14.6 million in 1996/97. More of the world's peanut crop is allocated to meal production than oil, production of which totaled 5.3 million tonnes in 1997/98, the lowest since 1993/94, compared to 5.9 million in 1996/97 and about par with consumption in all years. Peanut oil production in 1997/98 of 3.9 million tonnes compares with 4.3 million in 1996/97. Foreign trade in both products is small.

The average world peanut oilseed prices in 1996/97 (October/September) of $922 per metric ton, basis Rotterdam, compares with $986 in 1995/96 and a 1985/86-1995/96 average of $976 per ton, during which time the season average saw a high of $1539 and a low of $818. Rotterdam meal prices in 1996/97 averaged $237 per metric ton vs. $201 in 1995/96, and the ten year average of $194. Oil prices of $947 per ton compare with $928 and $777, respectively. In the U.S., the average price for peanut meal, basis Southeast mills-FOB, during 1996/97 of $229 per ton compares with $223 in 1995/96, and a ten-average of $194 per ton. Crude peanut oil prices, basis Southeast mills-FOB-tank cars, of $980 per ton compare with $890 in 1995/96 and ten-year average of $790 per ton.

In the U.S., a record large 4.9 billion pounds (in shell) were produced in 1991/92 vs. a lower than expected 3.5 billion in 1997/98 and 3.7 billion in 1996/97. U.S. peanut production is largely concentrated in the Southeast. Peanuts are also grown in the Southern Plains states where irrigation may be needed and production costs run higher. The average yield for the 1997 crop of 2.96 tonnes per hectare was about unchanged from 1996/97, as was acreage at about 1.23 million acres. Georgia is the largest producing state with at least a third of total production followed by North Carolina and Alabama. Total supplies in 1997/98 of 4.44 billion pounds compares with 4.55 billion in 1996/97, and include an August 1, 1997 carryin of 795 million pounds vs. stocks of 758 million a year earlier. The carryin for the 1998/99 crop was forecast at 750 million pounds. Peanut imports are small, averaging about 130 million pounds in recent years, whereas exports have averaged about 700 million pounds.

Total in-shell U.S. peanut disappearance in 1997/98 of 3.7 billion pounds compares with 3.75 billion in 1996/97. The decline largely reflects a smaller crush of 650 million pounds vs. 692 million in 1996/97, and a strong 999 million in 1995/96. Peanut use as a direct foodstuff in 1997/98 of 2.1 billion pounds compares with 2.0 billion in 1996/97. However, on a per capita basis, U.S. peanut use in the 1990's has shown little growth, and at less than six pounds compares with the record high of seven pounds in 1989, reflecting little if any growth in peanut based candies as well as snack peanut consumption. Exports of peanut oil in 1997/98 of 30 million pounds compares with 21 million in 1996/97, and 108 million in 1995/96. Exports of peanut meal of only 5.0 million pounds were marginally under 1996/97.

The average peanut price received by farmers in 1997/98 was forecast at 27.5-29.5 cents per pound vs. 28.5 cents in 1996/97.

For peanut oil the 1997-98 range of $0.41-$0.44 per pound compares with $0.437 in 1996/97. Meal's estimated average price of $1.50-$1.80 per pound compares with $2.078 in 1996/97, respectively.

Futures Markets

Peanut futures are traded on the Beijing Commodity Exchange (BCE).

World Production of Peanuts (in the Shell) In Thousands of Metric Tons

Crop Year	Argentina	Burma	China	India	Indonesia	Nigeria	Senegal	South Africa	Sudan	Thailand	United States	Zaire	World Total
1988-9	243	438	5,693	9,000	843	350	163	350	450	164	1,806	380	23,279
1989-90	336	459	5,365	8,088	875	350	113	350	400	161	1,810	380	22,059
1990-1	574	440	6,368	7,514	860	250	703	112	325	162	1,634	380	22,206
1991-2	400	440	6,300	7,065	890	220	724	114	400	160	2,235	380	22,138
1992-3	225	425	5,953	8,850	890	250	580	172	390	162	1,943	380	23,050
1993-4	210	390	8,420	7,760	870	250	620	190	390	170	1,540	380	23,990
1994-5	280	445	9,682	8,255	880	250	720	105	390	165	1,927	380	26,278
1995-6	460	500	10,200	7,400	1,040	1,580	830	190	400	170	1,570	380	27,610
1996-7[1]	300	500	10,140	8,200	1,000	1,720	600	140	400	170	1,660	380	28,160
1997-8[2]	430	500	8,000	8,000	1,000	1,750	720	170	400	170	1,590	380	26,000

[1] Preliminary. [2] Estimate. *Source: Foreign Agricultural Service, U.S. Department of Agriculture (FAS-USDA)*

PEANUTS AND PEANUT OIL

Salient Statistics of Peanuts in the United States

Crop Year	Acreage Planted (1,000 Acres)	Acreage Harvested for Nuts (1,000 Acres)	Average Yield Per Acre In Lbs.	Production 1,000 Lbs.	Season Farm Price ¢ Lb.	Farm Value Million Dollars	Exports Unshelled (Thousand Pounds, Year Beg. August)	Exports Shelled	Imports Unshelled	Imports Shelled
1984-5	1,558.6	1,528.0	2,883	4,405,745	27.9	1,230.8	72,907	592,333	79	2,167
1985-6	1,490.4	1,467.4	2,810	4,122,787	24.3	1,003.4	83,747	721,690	1,493	1,942
1986-7	1,564.7	1,535.2	2,408	3,700,745	29.2	1,073.3	75,687	441,954	328	1,598
1987-8	1,567.4	1,547.4	2,337	3,619,440	28.0	1,021.9	76,345	407,557	880	1,949
1988-9	1,657.4	1,628.4	2,445	3,980,917	27.9	1,115.2	105,746	437,867	650	2,094
1989-90	1,665.2	1,644.7	2,426	3,989,995	28.0	1,116.5	126,682	577,807	55	1,477
1990-1	1,840.0	1,809.5	1,991	3,602,770	34.7	1,257.2	250,851	401,149	6,429	20,571
1991-2	2,039.2	2,015.7	2,444	4,926,570	28.3	1,392.0	997,000	630,000	5,000	27,000
1992-3	1,686.6	1,669.1	2,567	4,284,416	30.0	1,285.4	951,000	611,250	2,000	2,000
1993-4	1,733.5	1,689.8	2,008	3,392,415	30.4	1,030.9	555,000	352,500	2,000	1,420
1994-5	1,641.0	1,618.5	2,624	4,247,455	28.9	1,229.0	878,000	659,905	74,000	55,385
1995-6	1,537.5	1,517.0	2,282	3,461,475	29.3	1,013.3	824,000	564,021	153,000	108,303
1996-7[1]	1,401.5	1,380.0	2,653	3,661,205	28.5	1,043.4	666,000		127,000	
1997-8[2]	1,429.0	1,405.8	2,523	3,546,360	28.5	1,001.7	675,000		-139,000	

[1] Preliminary. [2] Estimate. *Source: Economic Research Service, U.S. Department of Agriculture (ERS-USDA)*

Supply and Disposition of Peanuts (Farmer's Stock Basis) & Support Program in the United States

Crop Year Beginning Aug. 1	Supply: Production (Million Pounds)	Imports	Stocks Aug. 1	Total	Disposition: Exports	Crushed for Oil	Seed, Loss & Residual	Food	Total Disappearance	Support Price (¢ per Lb.)	Additional (¢ per Lb.)	Amount Put Under Support: Quantity Mil. Lbs.	% of Prod.
1984-5	4,406	2	611	5,019	860	625	199	1,911	3,595	27.50	9.3	1,370	30.9
1985-6	4,123	2	1,424	5,549	1,043	812	826	2,023	4,704	27.95	7.4	1,359	33.0
1986-7	3,697	2	845	4,544	663	514	291	2,073	3,541	30.37	7.5	290	7.8
1987-8	3,616	2	1,003	4,621	618	560	539	2,071	3,788	30.41	7.5	700	19.3
1988-9	3,981	2	833	4,816	688	814	217	2,254	3,974	30.76	7.5	540	13.6
1989-90	3,990	2	843	4,835	989	624	211	2,312	4,136	30.79	7.5	401	10.0
1990-1	3,603	27	701	4,331	652	689	288	2,020	3,649	31.57	7.5	576	16.0
1991-2	4,927	5	683	5,615	997	1,103	254	2,207	4,561	32.14	7.5	1,070	21.7
1992-3	4,284	2	1,055	5,341	951	891	227	2,122	3,991	33.75	6.6	436	10.2
1993-4	3,392	2	1,350	4,744	553	670	372	2,088	3,683	33.75	6.6	324	9.6
1994-5	4,247	74	1,061	5,382	878	982	316	2,009	4,184	33.92	6.6	820	19.3
1995-6	3,461	153	1,198	4,812	824	999	238	1,993	4,054	33.92	6.6	818	24.0
1996-7[1]	3,661	127	758	4,545	666	692	363	2,029	3,751	30.50	6.6	-----	-----
1997-8[2]	3,546	139	795	4,480	675	650	308	2,065	3,698	30.50	6.6	-----	-----

[1] Preliminary. [2] Estimate. *Source: Economic Research Service, U.S. Department of Agriculture (ERS-USDA)*

Production of Peanuts (Harvested for Nuts) in the United States, by States

In Thousands of Pounds

Crop Year	Alabama	Florida	Georgia	New Mexico	North Carolina	Oklahoma	South Carolina	Texas	Virgina	Total
1984	648,550	246,400	2,160,000	32,190	449,500	189,000	39,150	371,295	269,660	4,405,745
1985	590,000	216,000	1,921,320	31,992	451,990	170,980	34,200	422,625	283,680	4,122,787
1986	494,940	233,160	1,632,575	28,700	440,440	184,500	25,530	385,000	275,900	3,700,745
1987	465,300	215,800	1,575,000	29,760	392,200	222,750	31,200	441,000	243,000	3,616,010
1988	561,680	228,600	1,801,550	30,552	419,985	225,040	32,110	417,500	263,900	3,980,917
1989	537,750	214,890	1,849,500	43,680	370,120	210,700	32,500	484,700	246,155	3,989,995
1990	386,560	233,120	1,347,500	50,000	475,600	235,320	30,105	534,650	309,915	3,602,770
1991	638,485	279,660	2,228,550	51,075	461,700	243,800	33,600	682,500	307,200	4,926,570
1992	591,180	202,510	1,820,465	58,236	406,980	236,180	32,500	680,150	256,215	4,284,416
1993	473,220	194,880	1,383,545	56,680	299,585	233,580	24,500	550,175	176,250	3,392,415
1994	446,220	207,480	1,862,630	51,660	485,465	261,000	36,250	605,570	291,180	4,247,455
1995	483,360	193,590	1,414,880	43,000	347,040	201,880	30,800	540,000	206,925	3,461,475
1996	449,805	236,160	1,433,770	37,950	367,500	195,210	32,550	689,000	219,260	3,661,205
1997[1]	364,800	230,160	1,336,440	46,710	324,000	202,800	30,450	811,200	199,800	3,546,360

[1] Preliminary. *Source: Agricultural Statistics Board, U.S. Department of Agriculture (ASB-USDA)*

Supply and Reported Uses of Shelled Peanuts and Products in the United States In Thousands of Pounds

Crop Year Beginning Aug. 1	Shelled Peanuts -- Stocks Aug.1 --- Edible	Oil Stock[2]	Shelled Peanuts ------ Production ----- Edible	Oil Stock[2]	Reported Used (Shelled Peanuts--Raw Basis) --- Edible Grades Used in --- Candy[3]	Snacks[4]	Sandwich Spread	Butter[5]	Other Products	Total	Shelled Peanuts Crushed[6]	Crude Oil Production	Cake & Meal Production
1988-9	565,779	22,647	2,095,351	406,626	326,907	381,481	28,373	831,928	35,978	1,604,667	612,200	250,498	348,662
1989-90	513,679	44,397	2,319,780	374,859	330,158	392,811	----- 897,318 -----		36,682	1,656,969	469,351	193,000	261,465
1990-1	455,586	15,194	1,836,052	330,102	305,324	355,258	----- 742,384 -----		37,888	1,440,854	517,712	213,112	299,820
1991-2	386,155	65,950	2,538,398	616,170	327,617	346,255	----- 886,367 -----		34,173	1,594,412	828,986	356,276	459,457
1992-3	871,207	57,829	2,376,782	533,641	328,324	352,775	----- 797,910 -----		24,981	1,503,990	669,942	285,904	377,301
1993-4	679,639	42,054	1,748,734	425,710	362,418	348,867	----- 727,006 -----		36,301	1,474,592	503,674	212,216	292,093
1994-5	732,272	57,188	1,741,824	511,635	349,630	301,548	----- 709,823 -----		36,854	1,397,855	738,221	314,189	415,394
1995-6	752,814	58,188	1,253,451	491,818	350,663	277,089	----- 728,076 -----		32,015	1,387,843	751,281	320,909	420,919
1996-7[1]	499,035	41,000	1,692,581	305,674	351,652	289,962	----- 727,520 -----		33,825	1,402,959	520,413	220,877	294,590

[1] Preliminary. [2] Includes straight run oil stock peanuts. [3] Includes peanut butter made by manufacturers for own use in candy. [4] Formerly titled "Salted Peanuts." [5] Includes peanut butter made by manufacturers for own use in cookies and sandwiches, but excludes peanut butter used in candy. [6] All crushings regardless of grade. *Source: National Agricultural Statistics Service, U.S. Department of Agriculture (NASS-USDA)*

Shelled Peanuts (Raw Basis) Used in Primary Products, by Type In Thousands of Pounds

Crop Year Beginning Aug. 1	Virginia Candy[2]	Virginia Snack Peanuts	Virginia Peanut Butter[3]	Virginia Total	Runner Candy[2]	Runner Snack Peanuts	Runner Peanut Butter[3]	Runner Total	Spanish Candy[2]	Spanish Snack Peanuts	Spanish Peanut Butter[3]	Spanish Total
1988-9	37,145	112,101	75,436	241,130	259,680	237,008	644,555	1,256,252	30,082	32,372	43,668	107,285
1989-90	28,701	130,000	90,622	263,014	278,062	234,661	773,985	1,306,810	23,395	28,150	32,711	87,145
1990-1	26,043	142,113	101,069	286,242	259,995	189,254	580,691	1,049,423	19,286	23,841	60,624	105,189
1991-2	51,312	142,514	89,045	297,570	244,815	180,609	759,747	1,203,233	31,490	23,132	37,575	93,609
1992-3	49,223	124,875	92,355	275,895	259,498	203,732	674,962	1,152,775	19,603	24,168	30,593	75,320
1993-4	44,889	99,381	63,270	222,641	298,325	227,286	365,047	1,179,396	19,204	22,200	28,689	72,555
1994-5	26,857	97,389	51,354	190,916	302,697	185,377	644,711	1,152,110	20,076	18,782	13,758	54,829
1995-6	25,176	93,041	71,310	203,183	304,285	169,142	634,350	1,123,719	21,202	14,906	22,416	60,941
1996-7[1]	24,162	91,911	64,262	193,187	318,972	176,663	634,388	1,149,208	8,518	21,388	28,870	60,564

[1] Preliminary. [2] Includes peanut butter made by manufacturers for own use in candy. [3] Includes peanut butter made by manufacturers for own use in cookies and sandwiches, but excludes peanut butter used in candy. *Source: National Agricultural Statistics Service, U.S. Department of Agriculture (NASS-USDA)*

Production, Consumption, Stocks and Foreign Trade of Peanut Oil in the U.S. In Millions of Pounds

Crop Year Beginning Aug. 1	Production Crude	Production Refined	Consumption In Refining	Consumption In End Products	Stocks Dec. 31 Crude	Stocks Dec. 31 Refined	Imports for Consumption	Exports
1989-90	193.0	212.5	192.4	NA	17.6	4.1	5.0	19.0
1990-1	213.1	131.7	229.1	169.0	19.3	5.8	10.0	25.0
1991-2	261.5	125.6	132.3	141.0	27.5	3.1	1.0	151.0
1992-3	285.9	181.1	188.4	182.1	46.2	5.3	0	59.0
1993-4	212.2	155.2	163.7	149.1	6.5	3.9	11.0	61.0
1994-5	319.9	120.0	126.1	118.9	5.0	2.8	5.0	21.5
1995-6	329.0	125.7	129.9	126.0	19.9	2.8	3.2	47.8
1996-7[1]	233.9	133.5	138.9	138.4	85.6	2.8	5.0	13.0
1997-8[2]	144.7	123.8	133.0	136.4	42.6	31.2	5.0	35.0

[1] Preliminary. [2] Forecast. NA = Not available. *Source: Bureau of the Census, U.S. Department of Commerce*

Production of Crude Peanut Oil in the United States In Millions of Pounds

Year	Jan.	Feb.	Mar.	Apr.	May	June	July	Aug.	Sept.	Oct.	Nov.	Dec.	Total
1988	13.8	14.9	10.1	8.3	19.5	12.5	17.0	11.4	2.8	9.7	17.0	18.4	155.4
1989	10.5	20.8	27.8	24.3	19.0	33.4	26.6	22.4	NA	7.4	11.6	9.8	213.6
1990	11.1	15.8	14.2	22.2	24.9	24.1	14.0	8.5	2.1	14.4	12.5	15.9	179.7
1991		----------- 70.8 -----------			----------- 71.1 -----------			----------- 59.5 -----------			----------- 60.1 -----------		261.5
1992	28.0	26.8	42.5	40.9	39.8	40.6	37.3	31.3	35.1	24.2	19.2	15.6	381.3
1993	16.9	17.0	24.1	28.8	23.3	29.0	25.6	22.5	3.6	8.6	16.4	14.6	230.4
1994	18.1	18.3	21.2	18.7	25.6	15.4	21.7	16.8	17.2	11.9	18.4	24.2	227.5
1995	27.9	28.6	42.7	36.9	39.2	29.2	26.9	26.3	17.4	13.2	19.5	24.3	332.0
1996	29.2	31.9	36.8	36.8	36.7	33.3	31.4	31.5	27.1	21.1	20.6	21.8	358.2
1997[1]	19.9	16.1	18.8	17.9	13.3	15.9	9.9	12.1	6.1	12.2	11.6	14.0	167.7

[1] Preliminary. NA = Not available. *Source: Bureau of the Census, U.S. Department of Commerce*

PEANUTS AND PEANUT OIL

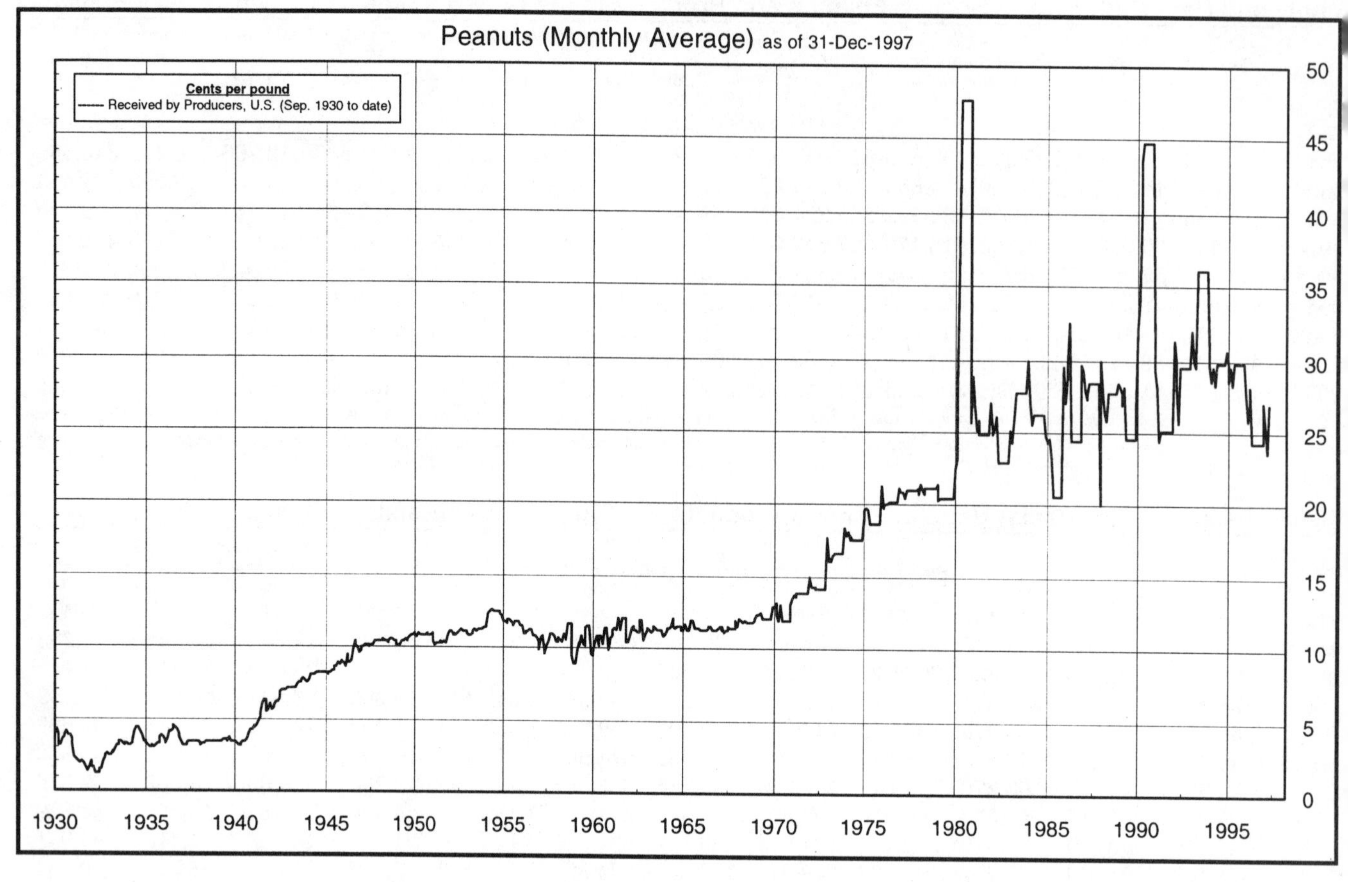

Average Price Received by Producers in United States for Peanuts in the Shell In Cents Per Pound

Crop Year	Aug.	Sept.	Oct.	Nov.	Dec.	Jan.	Feb.	Mar.	Apr.	May.	June	July	Average[1]
1988-9	20.0	29.9	28.0	26.4	25.8	27.8	NQ	NQ	NQ	NQ	NQ	NQ	26.3
1989-90	28.4	28.2	27.7	26.9	28.2	24.6	NQ	NQ	NQ	NQ	NQ	NQ	27.3
1990-1	26.5	32.2	34.0	40.1	43.6	44.8	NQ	NQ	NQ	NQ	NQ	NQ	34.7
1991-2	30.4	29.3	28.1	24.4	25.1	NQ	NQ	NQ	NQ	NQ	NQ	NQ	28.3
1992-3	NQ	31.3	29.9	28.2	25.7	29.5	NQ	NQ	NQ	NQ	NQ	NQ	30.0
1993-4	NQ	32.0	30.0	29.5	29.7	36.1	NQ	NQ	NQ	NQ	NQ	NQ	30.4
1994-5	NQ	30.6	28.6	25.9	25.8	25.7	NQ	NQ	NQ	NQ	NQ	NQ	27.9
1995-6	30.6	29.7	28.6	29.5	28.3	29.8	NQ	NQ	NQ	NQ	NQ	NQ	29.4
1996-7	NQ	27.6	25.8	27.1	28.1	24.3	NQ	NQ	NQ	NQ	NQ	NQ	26.6
1997-8[2]	NQ	27.1	25.4	23.6	26.9	24.7							25.5

[1] Weighted average by sale. [2] Preliminary. NQ = No quote. *Source: National Agricultural Statistics Service, U.S. Department of Agriculture (NASS)*

Average Price of Domestic Crude Peanut Oil (in Tanks) F.O.B. Southeast Mills In Cents Per Pound

Year	Oct.	Nov.	Dec.	Jan.	Feb.	Mar.	Apr.	May	June	July	Aug.	Sept.	Average
1988-9	42.50	36.75	34.25	26.50	25.09	29.98	32.39	36.25	39.80	NA	35.75	34.40	33.97
1989-90	39.06	41.50	41.60	43.25	46.00	43.40	41.25	45.25	46.90	46.88	49.05	51.13	44.64
1990-1	48.13	44.20	43.00	41.00	42.83	47.60	46.75	43.33	42.25	41.50	35.33	30.66	42.22
1991-2	34.33	27.67	23.50	23.50	23.63	23.17	25.00	27.88	25.60	26.19	23.88	22.00	25.53
1992-3	23.63	25.58	30.30	30.88	27.17	26.00	27.50	30.00	30.20	33.00	39.50	35.93	29.97
1993-4	40.20	43.33	43.17	46.10	46.12	44.50	43.40	44.25	43.75	44.00	45.00	43.10	43.91
1994-5	46.00	50.88	53.80	50.25	41.83	41.00	41.25	40.25	39.00	39.13	41.50	41.30	43.85
1995-6	42.50	41.63	39.20	37.25	36.00	36.60	39.25	42.80	43.00	43.00	42.60	40.80	40.39
1996-7	41.50	39.20	40.75	43.50	43.88	44.75	45.00	46.20	47.88	48.06	48.00	47.25	44.66
1997-8[1]	49.63	51.00	51.25	51.60									50.87

[1] Preliminary. *Source: Agricultural Marketing Service, U.S. Department of Agriculture (AMS-USDA)*

Pepper

Pepper prices increased rather sharply in 1997 as the production of pepper declined. The price of black pepper (Malabar-Lampong-Brazilian) in January 1997 was nearly $1.39 per pound. That was substantially higher than the price in January 1996 of $0.99 per pound. Prices increased on a fairly steady basis during 1997 reaching $2.63 per pound in October 1997. That was a near 90 percent increase in the first ten months of 1997.

The price increase was not as large for white pepper (Muntok). In January 1997, the New York spot price was $2.56 per pound, up from $1.75 per pound in January 1996. In October 1997, the price had risen to $3.42 per pound. Over the ten months of 1997, white pepper prices had risen almost 34 percent.

Part of the reason for higher pepper prices has been the decline in production of pepper in the major producing countries. The International Pepper Community (IPC) reported that IPC countries in 1996 produced 144,785 metric tonnes which was down ten percent from the previous year. World production of pepper in 1996 was estimated at 179,389 tonnes which was down eight percent from 1995.

India is the world's largest producer of pepper with 1996 production of 60,000 tonnes, or about a third of the world total. Indian production in 1996 increased from the 1995 total of 55,000 tonnes. India plants about 200,000 hectares to black pepper and exports about 70 percent of its production. The next largest producer of pepper is Indonesia with 1996 output estimated at 39,200 tonnes or some 34 percent less than in 1995. Indonesia could continue to have production problems as a severe drought occurred in 1997. In a number of countries that produce pepper, such as Indonesia, Thailand and Malaysia, there was dry to extremely dry weather due to the 1997/98 El Nino weather event.

After Indonesia, the next largest pepper producer in 1996 was Vietnam with production of 20,000 tonnes, unchanged from 1995. Vietnam's weather was not adversely influenced by El Nino. Brazil's pepper production in 1996 was 19,500 tonnes, down slightly from 1995. Malaysian pepper production in 1996 was estimated at 12,000 tonnes, down eight percent from 1995. China showed a sharp increase in pepper production. For 1996, production was estimated at 11,754 tonnes, up almost 42 percent from 1995. Thailand has seen dry weather related to El Nino. The 1996 pepper output was 9,773 tonnes which was 11 percent less than 1995.

World Exports of Pepper (Black and White) and Prices in the United States

	Exports (In Metric Tons)								New York Spot Prices (¢ Per Pound)				
									Indonesian			Indian	
Year	Brazil	India	Indonesia	Madagascar	Malaysia	Mexico	Sri Lanka	Vietnam	Lampong Black	Muntok White	Brazilian Black	Malabar Black	Tellicherry[2]
1987	26,260	32,971	29,995	1,851	14,185	2,125	2,014	4,275	237.1	267.7	235.9	236.0	262.8
1988	24,393	47,258	41,568	2,497	19,190	2,602	2,714	2,612	173.9	243.4	170.3	170.3	220.6
1989	27,717	25,120	42,138	1,417	26,260	2,388	1,576	7,551	138.2	146.2	136.2	135.9	174.8
1990	28,014	34,429	47,675	1,222	27,706	2,663	2,609	1,288	99.1	90.3	97.1	97.1	139.1
1991	47,553	18,735	49,667	1,844	25,458	1,861	2,058	16,252	71.1	70.1	67.1	67.1	117.8
1992	26,277	22,684	62,136	1,948	22,919	3,636	2,143	22,347	56.1	70.8	54.7	54.7	86.1
1993	26,254	47,677	27,684	2,001	16,737	2,430	5,032	20,138	62.5	114.6	62.3	62.3	84.0
1994	22,231	36,536	36,036	2,066	23,275	2,615	1,850	19,500	95.3	151.9	95.0	95.0	110.7
1995[1]	22,158	22,000	57,781	1,274	14,869	3,085	2,082	17,000	116.8	182.3	116.8	116.8	150.9
1996[1]									114.8	178.9	114.8	114.8	140.0

[1] Preliminary. [2] Extra bold. *Sources: Foreign Agricultural Service, U.S. Department of Agriculture; Food and Agricultural Organization of the United Nations*

United States Imports of Unground Pepper from Specified Countries In Metric Tons

	Black Pepper							White Pepper					
Year	Brazil	India	Indonesia	Malaysia	Singapore	Sri Lanka	Total	Brazil	China	Indonesia	Malaysia	Singapore	Total
1987	11,981	9,341	6,958	1,667	379	388	31,372	65	6	4,238	22	110	4,533
1988	6,033	7,481	11,131	1,400	104	344	26,939	20	2	4,169	12	26	4,326
1989	11,038	1,272	11,016	6,732	324	375	31,819	37	38	5,272	63	90	5,549
1990	8,778	6,679	8,444	6,768	457	644	32,980	17	15	5,506	24	86	5,721
1991	15,069	2,308	11,330	8,154	391	396	38,860	2	7	4,938	37	96	5,174
1992	6,601	9,892	20,768	2,073	52	310	40,590	51	2	5,089	29	261	5,544
1993	4,580	21,985	7,666	209	-----	539	35,969	322	114	4,304	137	363	5,481
1994	8,215	21,097	11,877	829	90	386	43,011	312	756	3,974	228	302	6,102
1995	3,165	10,836	19,630	268	30	327	34,465	414	280	4,037	164	211	5,266
1996[1]	4,267	18,350	17,213	1,084	101	411	41,602	519	54	4,370	150	391	5,765

[1] Preliminary. *Source: Foreign Agricultural Service, U.S. Department of Agriculture (FAS-USDA)*

PEPPER

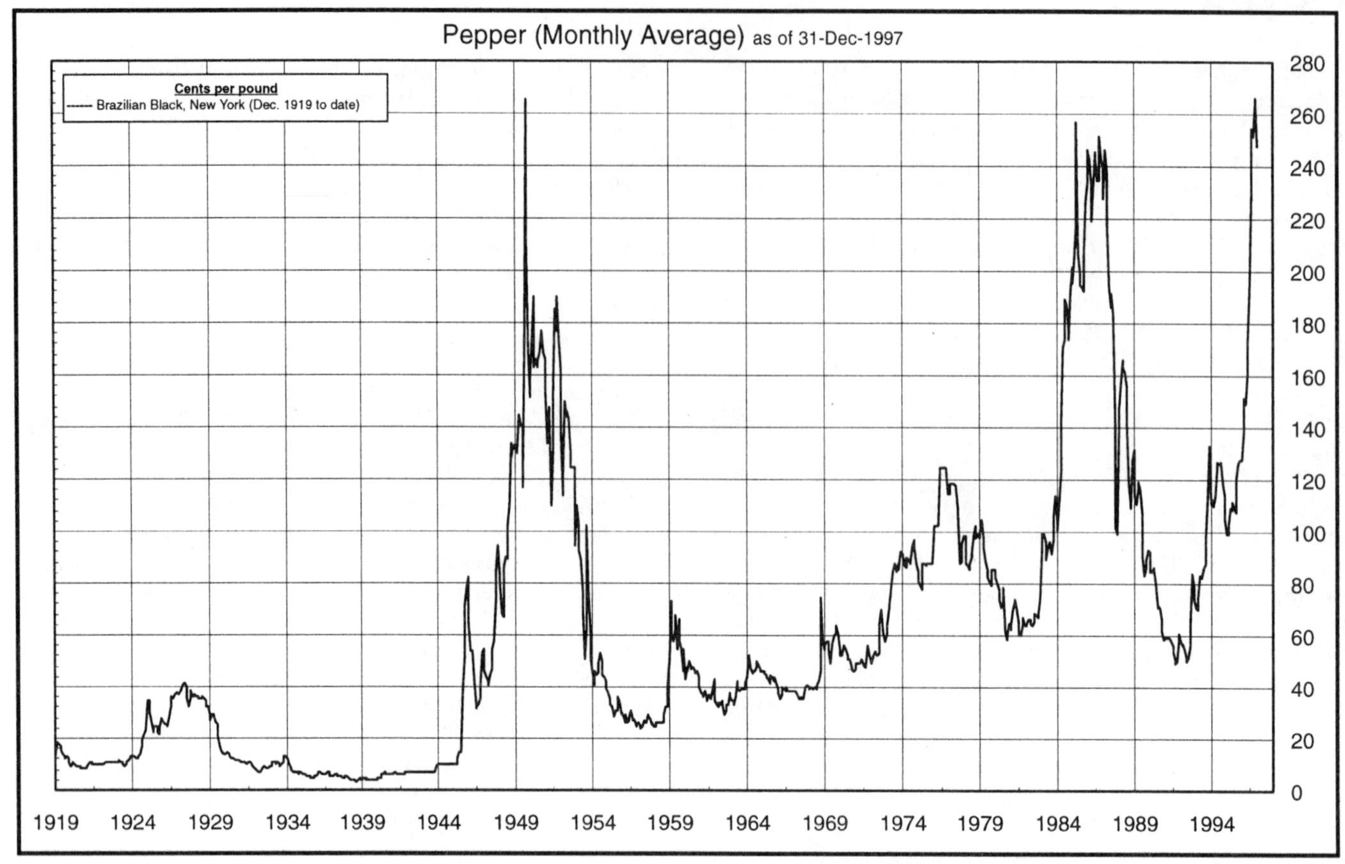

Average Black Pepper Prices in New York (Brazilian) In Cents Per Pound

Year	Jan.	Feb.	Mar.	Apr.	May	June	July	Aug.	Sept.	Oct.	Nov.	Dec.	Average
1988	233.3	228.8	210.5	190.3	184.3	190.5	182.8	141.5	100.2	99.5	138.3	143.0	170.3
1989	156.8	161.8	159.0	160.0	154.5	141.8	115.5	108.0	108.2	124.7	131.3	112.4	136.2
1990	107.0	110.8	115.4	115.0	106.0	91.0	82.3	85.8	88.5	92.3	89.6	81.8	97.1
1991	79.0	78.5	78.6	74.5	66.8	70.0	68.8	61.6	59.5	56.8	55.8	55.0	67.1
1992	55.6	54.5	56.0	55.3	54.0	54.0	50.8	49.0	50.0	57.8	61.0	58.0	54.7
1993	56.0	56.5	54.3	51.2	50.0	51.5	55.8	64.8	84.0	79.0	74.2	70.8	62.3
1994	69.3	74.3	82.0	82.8	82.0	86.5	87.8	97.8	112.2	131.5	123.5	110.4	95.0
1995	111.0	110.0	114.2	124.8	127.3	126.0	127.0	126.3	118.2	113.5	104.8	99.0	116.8
1996	99.3	103.3	109.2	108.3	111.2	109.5	108.0	119.8	126.5	127.5	127.6	128.0	114.8
1997	138.6	151.8	149.0	161.8	173.4	193.8	229.5	255.0	251.3	264.8	266.3	247.5	206.9

Source: Foreign Agricultural Service, U.S. Department of Agriculture (FAS-USDA)

Average White Pepper Prices in New York (Indonesian)[1] In Cents Per Pound

Year	Jan.	Feb.	Mar.	Apr.	May	June	July	Aug.	Sept.	Oct.	Nov.	Dec.	Average
1988	273.3	275.0	277.5	285.0	291.3	296.3	262.0	235.0	204.0	172.5	177.8	171.2	243.4
1989	176.3	178.8	179.8	169.2	156.3	147.6	141.5	135.0	125.6	121.2	116.0	107.6	146.2
1990	102.3	100.5	99.2	95.5	93.8	82.8	80.0	88.2	91.5	88.0	83.2	78.0	90.3
1991	77.0	72.5	71.4	70.0	67.4	66.0	66.3	63.2	67.0	70.8	78.6	71.5	70.1
1992	70.0	70.0	70.0	70.0	68.0	65.0	64.2	65.0	72.7	79.2	78.5	77.4	70.8
1993	79.0	89.0	85.3	84.0	81.3	87.3	97.0	121.5	181.3	172.6	154.7	142.4	114.6
1994	144.5	139.5	141.3	140.8	137.0	143.3	143.4	156.3	159.2	167.5	176.5	173.0	151.9
1995	179.5	175.8	168.0	181.3	195.0	184.2	187.5	190.8	191.0	182.0	178.5	174.2	182.3
1996	174.5	177.5	181.6	179.5	172.6	164.8	154.0	169.6	181.5	193.5	191.8	205.8	178.9
1997	256.0	264.5	255.0	250.0	241.0	248.8	280.3	324.0	332.5	362.0	433.8	415.0	305.2

[1] Muntok white. *Source: Foreign Agricultural Service, U.S. Department of Agriculture (FAS-USDA)*

Petroleum

U.S. domestic field production of crude oil, natural gas, plant liquids and other liquids in August 1997 was 8.45 million barrels per day. That represented a decline of one percent from the previous month and a one percent decline from August 1996. In the January-August 1997 period, total domestic field production of crude oil and petroleum products averaged 8.59 million barrels per day. In the comparable period of 1996, the average production was 8.56 million barrels, while in the same period of 1995 it was 8.67 million barrels. For all of 1996, total domestic production averaged 8.61 million barrels per day.

In August 1997, natural gas plant liquids production averaged 1.83 million barrels per day, down one percent from the previous month and one percent less than a year ago. During the January-August 1997 period, natural gas plant liquids production averaged 1.85 million barrels per day. That was three percent more than in the comparable period in 1995. For all of 1996, production averaged 1.83 million barrels per day.

U.S. production of crude oil in August 1997 averaged 6.29 million barrels per day, down very slightly from the July production average of 6.32. Production in August 1997 was down one percent from a year ago in the same month. During January-August 1997, domestic crude oil production averaged 6.40 million barrels per day, down one percent from the comparable period in 1996, and some three percent less than the same period in 1995. For all of 1996, crude oil production averaged 6.47 million barrels per day. U.S. production of crude oil has been declining for several years. In 1985, crude oil production averaged 8.97 million barrels per day.

Production of crude oil in Alaska in August 1997 averaged 1.17 million barrels per day, down five percent from the previous month and down 12 percent from the same month a year before. During the January-August 1997 period, Alaskan crude oil production averaged 1.30 million barrels per day, down seven percent from the same period in 1996, and 14 percent less than in 1995. For all of 1996, production averaged 1.39 million barrels per day. Alaskan oil production peaked in 1988 when it averaged 2.02 million barrels per day.

U.S. imports of crude oil in August 1997 averaged 8.46 million barrels per day, almost seven percent more than in the month before and five percent more than in August 1996. During January-August 1997, imports of crude oil averaged 7.92 million barrels per day, up almost five percent from the comparable period in 1996, and 10 percent above 1995. For all of 1996, U.S. imports of crude oil averaged 7.51 million barrels per day. U.S. crude oil imports have been increasing for a number of years. In 1985 they were 3.20 million barrels per day.

Refinery inputs in August 1997 averaged 15.2 million barrels per day, almost two percent above the previous month and five percent more than a year ago. In the first eight months of 1996, refinery inputs averaged 14.5 million barrels per day. That was two percent more than in the comparable period of 1996 and almost four percent above 1995. For all of 1996, refinery inputs averaged 14.2 million barrels per day.

U.S. exports of crude oil in August 1997 averaged 102,000 barrels per day, much above the 70,000 barrel daily average in July 1997. In the first eight months of 1997, exports averaged 105,000 barrels per day. In the same period of 1996, exports averaged 96,000 barrels per day.

U.S. stocks of crude oil at the end of August 1997 were 868 million barrels, down one percent from the previous month and three percent less than a year before. Crude oil stocks at the end of 1996 were 850 million barrels. The Strategic Petroleum Reserve held 563 million barrels of oil at the end of August 1997.

Futures Markets

Futures and options contracts on light sweet crude oil, heating oil and unleaded gasoline are traded on the New York Mercantile Exchange (NYMEX). Propane and natural gas futures also are traded there. London's International Petroleum Exchange (IPE) trades Brent crude oil futures and options on those futures. The IPE also trades heating oil futures and options (termed gas oil) and unleaded gasoline futures. High-sulfur fuel oil futures are traded on the SIMEX in Singapore.

World Production of Crude Petroleum In Thousands of Barrels Per Day

Year	Canada	China	Indo-nesia	Iran	Kuwait	Mexico	Nigeria	Russia[3]	Saudi Arabia	United Kingdom	United States	Vene-zuela	Total World
1988	1,616	2,730	1,342	2,240	1,492	2,512	1,450	12,053	5,086	2,232	8,140	1,903	58,737
1989	1,560	2,757	1,409	2,810	1,783	2,520	1,716	11,715	5,064	1,802	7,613	1,907	59,863
1990	1,553	2,774	1,462	3,088	1,175	2,553	1,810	10,975	6,410	1,820	7,355	2,137	60,566
1991	1,548	2,835	1,592	3,312	190	2,680	1,892	9,992	8,115	1,797	7,417	2,375	60,207
1992	1,605	2,845	1,504	3,429	1,058	2,669	1,943	7,632	8,332	1,825	7,171	2,371	60,216
1993	1,679	2,890	1,511	3,540	1,852	2,673	1,960	6,730	8,198	1,915	6,847	2,450	60,246
1994	1,746	2,939	1,510	3,618	2,025	2,685	1,931	6,135	8,120	2,375	6,662	2,588	61,003
1995	1,805	2,990	1,503	3,643	2,057	2,618	1,993	5,995	8,231	2,489	6,560	2,750	62,446
1996[1]	1,823	3,131	1,547	3,686	2,062	2,855	2,188	5,774	8,218	2,568	6,465	3,053	63,972
1997[2]	1,884	3,214	1,546	3,662	2,074	3,020	2,320	5,884	8,547	2,500	6,401	3,299	66,221

Includes lease condensate. [1] Preliminary. [2] Estimate. [3] Formerly part of the U.S.S.R.; data not reported separately until 1992.
Source: Energy Information Administration, U.S. Department of Energy (EIA-DOE)

Refiner Sales Prices of Petroleum Products for Resale (Excluding Taxes) In Cents Per Gallon

Year	Jan.	Feb.	Mar.	Apr.	May	June	July	Aug.	Sept.	Oct.	Nov.	Dec.	Average
						Residual Fuel Oil (Sulfur 1% or less)							
1991	52.1	36.5	36.0	33.6	36.6	32.1	32.6	33.4	33.7	34.1	36.6	34.8	36.4
1992	30.3	32.7	30.8	31.6	33.1	35.9	38.0	37.7	37.9	41.4	39.2	35.9	35.1
1993	36.8	35.5	39.1	38.4	34.8	33.7	32.7	31.6	31.9	32.1	30.7	27.5	33.7
1994	33.8	39.3	30.0	29.4	31.7	35.8	37.8	37.1	32.6	32.6	35.7	36.9	34.5
1995	39.1	37.1	38.3	36.8	40.4	39.9	36.8	35.5	36.4	35.3	36.6	44.7	38.3
1996	49.9	42.8	47.1	48.3	45.0	40.4	41.4	42.0	42.8	47.9	49.1	51.4	45.7
1997[1]	46.2	43.7	39.6	37.6	36.6	39.4	38.5	39.4	40.1	44.6	46.5		41.1
						No. 2 Fuel Oil							
1991	76.6	67.9	59.6	57.2	56.0	54.0	56.7	60.6	62.1	66.3	66.6	55.9	62.2
1992	51.9	54.0	53.7	56.5	58.8	61.7	61.3	60.1	62.7	64.6	58.8	55.7	57.9
1993	54.4	56.9	59.0	57.5	56.9	55.0	51.0	51.0	54.8	58.1	53.1	45.1	54.4
1994	50.7	54.2	49.7	48.9	49.0	49.8	50.9	51.4	50.1	50.8	51.0	49.5	50.6
1995	49.4	49.1	48.1	50.4	52.4	49.3	48.1	51.0	52.0	50.5	53.4	57.3	51.1
1996	56.8	58.9	62.8	67.5	61.1	53.7	57.1	62.1	68.7	72.7	71.4	71.2	63.9
1997[1]	69.8	64.5	57.7	58.6	58.8	54.5	53.8	55.3	54.3	59.0	58.4		58.6
						No. 2 Diesel Fuel							
1991	75.5	67.4	57.7	57.4	57.2	54.5	57.1	61.9	62.9	65.6	66.5	55.6	61.5
1992	51.4	54.1	54.0	57.0	60.1	62.7	61.8	60.4	63.3	65.5	60.4	56.4	59.1
1993	54.9	57.4	60.0	59.8	59.6	57.2	53.2	53.2	58.9	65.8	58.9	46.8	57.0
1994	49.1	52.8	52.9	52.3	51.7	52.2	53.7	54.1	54.2	55.2	55.1	50.8	52.9
1995	50.1	50.6	51.2	54.8	55.9	52.6	51.4	54.2	55.7	54.6	56.3	57.6	53.8
1996	56.2	57.9	61.9	70.1	67.0	59.1	60.0	64.9	71.7	75.4	73.2	71.0	65.9
1997[1]	69.9	67.8	62.5	61.7	60.7	56.5	55.8	58.9	57.8	61.7	61.5		61.3
						Kerosine-Type Jet Fuel							
1991	82.0	74.0	62.4	58.9	60.8	58.8	59.4	63.3	65.9	67.1	68.2	60.1	65.0
1992	53.9	55.2	54.6	56.9	60.8	63.3	64.8	63.9	64.3	66.0	61.5	58.9	60.5
1993	57.7	60.4	60.3	59.8	60.1	58.5	55.1	55.1	56.6	60.5	58.7	51.0	57.7
1994	52.6	56.0	52.4	50.8	50.6	51.5	53.8	54.4	54.0	54.4	56.3	53.1	53.4
1995	52.3	52.1	50.1	52.6	54.7	53.1	51.3	53.1	55.2	54.1	56.3	58.6	53.9
1996	60.3	57.2	59.6	65.3	62.2	57.5	59.6	64.5	71.6	73.6	72.2	73.0	64.6
1997[1]	73.5	71.4	61.8	60.5	59.4	58.1	56.8	59.4	58.8	61.3	61.3		62.0
						Propane (Consumer Grade)							
1991	42.2	31.6	31.3	31.8	31.9	29.3	27.6	29.6	34.9	40.2	43.0	37.7	34.9
1992	30.9	30.2	29.5	29.0	29.4	31.6	31.5	32.9	35.4	36.6	36.2	36.3	32.8
1993	40.2	36.7	38.2	36.2	34.0	33.8	33.3	33.3	34.1	34.7	33.6	30.9	35.1
1994	32.3	34.0	31.8	30.5	30.4	29.9	29.8	31.0	31.7	33.5	35.0	35.8	32.5
1995	35.6	34.5	34.3	33.0	33.2	32.6	32.1	33.2	33.8	34.4	34.7	37.9	34.4
1996	41.6	44.1	41.1	37.8	36.2	36.2	36.9	38.9	45.3	51.1	58.0	67.7	46.1
1997[1]	59.9	44.7	41.3	37.7	36.9	36.4	35.9	37.5	39.5	41.1	39.6		41.0

[1] Preliminary. *Source: Energy Information Administration, U.S. Department of Energy (EIA-DOE)*

Supply and Disposition of Crude Oil in the United States

Yearly Average	Supply: Field Production: Total Domestic	Supply: Field Production: Alaskan	Supply: Imports: Total	Supply: Imports: SPR[2]	Supply: Imports: Other	Supply: Unaccounted for Crude Oil	Stock Withdrawal[3]: SPR[2]	Stock Withdrawal[3]: Other	Disposition: Refinery Inputs	Disposition: Exports	Ending Stocks: Total	Ending Stocks: SPR[2]	Ending Stocks: Other Primary
	Thousands of Barrels Per Day										Million of Barrels		
1988	8,140	2,017	5,107	51	5,055	196	52	-51	13,246	155	890	560	330
1989	7,613	1,874	5,843	56	5,787	200	56	30	13,401	142	921	580	341
1990	7,355	1,773	5,894	27	5,867	258	16	-51	13,409	109	908	586	323
1991	7,417	1,798	5,782	0	5,782	195	-47	5	13,301	116	893	569	325
1992	7,171	1,714	6,083	10	6,073	258	17	-18	13,411	89	893	575	318
1993	6,847	1,582	6,787	15	6,772	168	34	47	13,613	98	922	587	335
1994	6,662	1,559	7,063	12	7,051	266	13	5	13,866	99	929	592	337
1995	6,560	1,484	7,230	0	7,230	193	0	-93	13,973	95	895	592	303
1996	6,465	1,393	7,508	0	7,508	215	-71	-53	14,195	110	850	566	284
1997[1]	6,411	1,296	7,996	0	7,996	377	-7	55	14,626	108	868	563	305

[1] Preliminary. [2] Strategic Petroleum Reserve. [3] A negative number indicates a decrease in stocks and a positive number indicates an increase. Note: Crude oil includes lease condensate. Stocks of Alaskan crude oil in transit were included beginning in January 1981. *Source: Energy Information Administration, U.S. Department of Energy (EIA-DOE)*

Crude Petroleum Refinery Operations Ratio[1] in the United States In Percent of Capacity

Year	Jan.	Feb.	Mar.	Apr.	May	June	July	Aug.	Sept.	Oct.	Nov.	Dec.	Average
1988	83.0	81.0	83.0	84.0	86.0	86.0	86.0	87.0	84.0	83.0	84.0	85.0	84.3
1989	86.0	83.0	84.0	84.0	86.0	90.0	89.0	89.0	88.0	86.0	86.0	84.0	86.3
1990	88.0	88.0	84.0	85.0	87.0	89.0	93.0	91.0	91.0	84.0	84.0	83.0	87.3
1991	83.0	84.0	83.0	85.0	87.0	90.0	89.0	89.0	88.0	83.0	84.0	87.0	86.0
1992	83.0	81.0	85.0	86.0	89.0	92.0	92.0	89.0	91.0	89.0	90.0	88.0	87.9
1993	87.0	87.0	89.0	91.0	93.0	95.0	95.0	93.0	93.0	92.0	92.0	91.0	91.5
1994	89.8	88.7	87.6	92.4	95.4	95.8	95.5	96.4	94.4	89.8	92.7	92.6	92.6
1995	89.6	87.9	86.7	90.5	94.0	95.6	94.0	94.0	95.6	90.5	92.1	93.3	92.0
1996	90.6	89.1	90.6	93.7	94.4	95.4	93.9	95.0	95.5	94.6	94.7	94.3	93.5
1997[2]	89.3	87.3	90.7	92.6	97.3	97.7	97.1	98.6	99.7	96.7	95.6		94.8

[1] Based on the ration of the daily average crude runs to stills to the rated capacity of refineries per day. [2] Preliminary.
Source: Energy Information Administration, U.S. Department of Energy (EIA-DOE)

Crude Oil Refinery Inputs in the United States In Thousands of Barrels Per Day

Year	Jan.	Feb.	Mar.	Apr.	May	June	July	Aug.	Sept.	Oct.	Nov.	Dec.	Average
1988	12,920	12,644	13,016	13,135	13,425	13,487	13,617	13,752	13,261	13,126	13,156	13,381	13,246
1989	13,330	12,765	12,963	12,956	13,405	13,905	13,848	13,861	13,791	13,360	13,420	13,165	13,401
1990	13,491	13,487	12,876	13,051	13,386	13,689	14,212	14,142	14,104	12,825	12,953	12,708	13,409
1991	12,735	13,046	12,839	13,042	13,539	13,918	13,703	13,800	13,694	12,896	12,929	13,465	13,301
1992	12,923	12,486	13,083	13,260	13,679	14,059	13,953	13,426	13,714	13,584	13,547	13,194	13,411
1993	12,938	12,865	13,200	13,538	13,829	14,129	14,136	13,844	13,841	13,729	13,686	13,571	13,613
1994	13,286	13,130	12,985	13,809	14,272	14,351	14,344	14,491	14,234	13,529	13,968	13,951	13,866
1995	13,604	13,365	13,480	13,817	14,303	14,553	14,403	14,276	14,402	13,598	13,833	14,011	13,973
1996	13,708	13,529	13,755	14,263	14,401	14,535	14,319	14,423	14,483	14,276	14,276	14,194	14,181
1997[1]	13,632	13,425	14,047	14,283	15,083	15,139	14,958	15,217	15,297	14,790	14,654	14,898	14,626

[1] Preliminary. *Source: Energy Information Administration, U.S. Department of Energy (EIA-DOE)*

Production of Major Refined Petroleum Products in the Continental United States In Millions of Barrels

Year	Asphalt	Aviation Gasoline	Fuel Oil: Distillate	Fuel Oil: Residual	Gasoline	Jet Fuel	Kerosene	Natural Gas Plant Liquids	Lubricants	Liquefied Gases: Total	Liquefied Gases: at L.P.G.[2]	Liquefied Gases: at L.P.G.[3]
1987	158.4	9.1	996.6	323.2	2,506	490.1	28.7	605.6	60.9	638.2	474.5	163.7
1988	162.1	9.3	1,046.3	338.7	2,555	501.3	28.8	614.2	62.3	665.2	482.6	182.6
1989	154.9	9.2	1,152.2	500.1	2,684	543.6	30.8	586.1	58.1	653.5	451.3	202.2
1990	164.0	8.5	1,067.5	346.6	2,650	555.6	15.5	598.3	59.7	638.4	456.2	182.2
1991	156.8	8.0	1,081.0	341.1	2,554	525.0	14.0	639.2	57.0	683.1	487.5	195.6
1992	153.0	7.9	1,088.4	326.1	2,591	512.0	14.8	668.0	57.5	721.9	499.7	222.2
1993	165.6	7.9	1,139.7	303.9	2,644	518.8	17.5	631.2	58.4	849.4	633.5	215.9
1994	164.8	7.9	1,169.7	301.4	2,621	528.4	21.1	630.2	62.1	734.2	511.1	223.2
1995	170.4	7.8	1,151.7	287.6	2,722	516.8	19.2	643.2	63.7	759.9	521.1	238.8
1996[1]	167.8	7.3	1,213.6	265.5	2,769	554.5	22.8	669.8	63.3	789.1	546.7	242.5

[1] Preliminary. *Source: Energy Information Administration, U.S. Department of Energy (EIA-DOE)*

Stocks of Petroleum and Products in the United States on January 1 In Millions of Barrels

Year	Crude Petroleum	Strategic Reserve	Refined Products: Total	Asphalt	Aviation Gasoline	Fuel Oil: Distillate	Fuel Oil: Residual	Finished Gasoline	Jet Fuel	Kerosene	Liquefied Gases[2]	Lubricants	Motor Gasoline: Total	Motor Gasoline: Finished[3]
1988	889.6	540.6	579.5	18.8	2.3	134.5	47.4	191.1	49.9	8.4	97.1	13.3	226	189
1989	889.9	559.5	561.6	20.8	2.1	123.5	44.6	192.0	43.8	7.3	97.3	13.3	228	190
1990	921.1	579.9	508.3	20.6	2.1	105.7	43.8	179.1	40.9	5.1	80.2	13.8	213	177
1991	908.4	585.7	566.8	18.7	1.7	132.2	48.6	182.4	52.1	5.6	97.9	12.4	220	181
1992	893.1	568.5	576.7	22.3	1.6	143.5	49.9	183.3	48.8	5.8	92.3	12.3	219	182
1993	892.9	574.7	549.1	17.7	1.6	140.6	42.6	179.1	43.1	5.7	88.7	13.3	216	178
1994	922.5	587.1	465.8	19.1	1.8	140.9	44.2	185.7	40.4	4.1	106.6	11.8	226	187
1995	928.9	591.7	468.0	18.6	2.3	145.2	41.9	175.9	46.8	8.0	108.0	11.5	215	176
1996	895.0	591.6	401.2	26.3	2.2	106.3	34.8	162.8	38.4	4.0	99.2	11.7	206	161
1997[1]	849.7	565.8	425.9	20.5	2.3	126.7	45.9	157.0	39.9	7.0	92.6	12.7	203	157

1 Preliminary. [2] Includes ethane and ethylene at plants and refineries. [3] Includes oxygenated. *Source: Energy Information Administration, U.S. Department of Energy (EIA-DOE)*

PETROLEUM

Stocks of Crude Petroleum in the United States, on First of Month In Millions of Barrels

Year	Jan.	Feb.	Mar.	Apr.	May	June	July	Aug.	Sept.	Oct.	Nov.	Dec.
1988	889.6	888.3	892.2	898.9	904.6	907.6	908.9	900.8	885.7	883.2	895.6	895.7
1989	889.9	894.8	896.6	892.5	907.4	915.7	903.0	907.6	916.3	912.0	914.3	930.5
1990	921.1	932.9	924.0	955.9	953.1	968.7	970.9	966.2	959.2	932.7	935.7	924.7
1991	908.4	905.3	912.8	905.3	907.2	924.3	915.3	910.6	913.8	909.1	910.7	912.0
1992	893.1	909.7	914.8	907.1	916.5	912.0	894.6	902.2	898.3	893.5	906.2	899.4
1993	892.9	902.0	908.1	914.7	930.4	935.0	935.1	935.2	919.6	906.4	916.5	924.1
1994	922.5	925.3	922.6	932.6	930.6	922.7	919.6	924.2	920.2	927.0	934.9	938.0
1995	922.2	920.8	931.0	929.4	924.1	919.6	907.3	899.5	897.5	902.8	910.6	894.9
1996	894.9	894.7	892.9	888.8	889.7	889.7	898.9	891.3	890.8	875.8	881.5	869.1
1997[1]	849.7	865.9	862.1	877.6	883.9	890.5	885.3	873.0	864.2	866.6	879.3	886.9

[1] Preliminary. *Source: Energy Information Administration, U.S. Department of Agriculture (EIA-DOE)*

Production of Crude Petroleum in the United States In Thousands of Barrels Per Day

Year	Jan.	Feb.	Mar.	Apr.	May	June	July	Aug.	Sept.	Oct.	Nov.	Dec.	Average
1988	8,250	8,374	8,374	8,288	8,229	8,170	8,040	8,079	7,895	8,023	8,023	7,942	8,140
1989	7,937	7,788	7,575	7,772	7,816	7,624	7,444	7,544	7,548	7,453	7,536	7,337	7,613
1990	7,546	7,497	7,433	7,407	7,328	7,106	7,173	7,287	7,224	7,542	7,387	7,338	7,355
1991	7,500	7,637	7,546	7,509	7,409	7,320	7,347	7,316	7,368	7,437	7,328	7,299	7,417
1992	7,361	7,389	7,348	7,293	7,169	7,167	7,131	6,922	7,030	7,126	7,024	7,103	7,171
1993	6,961	6,943	6,974	6,881	6,847	6,795	6,688	6,758	6,712	6,839	6,912	6,858	6,847
1994	6,817	6,770	6,746	6,612	6,688	6,611	6,501	6,544	6,609	6,658	6,628	6,760	6,662
1995	6,682	6,794	6,600	6,604	6,629	6,579	6,449	6,447	6,416	6,421	6,585	6,530	6,560
1996	6,495	6,577	6,571	6,444	6,394	6,458	6,338	6,360	6,482	6,481	6,476	6,506	6,465
1997[1]	6,387	6,514	6,470	6,483	6,401	6,341	6,316	6,282	6,388	6,435	6,450	6,475	6,411

[1] Preliminary. *Source: Energy Information Administration, U.S. Department of Energy (EIA-DOE)*

U.S. Foreign Trade of Petroleum and Products In Thousands of Barrels Per Day

	Exports		Imports						Exports		Imports				
Year	Total[2]	Petroleum Products	Crude	Petroleum Products	Distillate Fuel Oil	Residual Fuel Oil	Net Imports[3]	Year	Total[2]	Petroleum Products	Crude	Petroleum Products	Distillate Fuel Oil	Residual Fuel Oil	Net Imports[3]
1978	362	204	6,356	2,008	173	1,355	8,002	1988	815	661	5,107	2,295	302	644	6,587
1979	471	236	6,519	1,937	193	1,151	7,985	1989	859	717	5,843	2,217	306	629	7,202
1980	544	258	5,263	1,646	142	939	6,365	1990	857	748	5,894	2,123	278	504	7,161
1981	595	367	4,396	1,599	173	800	5,401	1991	1,001	885	5,782	1,844	205	453	6,626
1982	815	579	3,488	1,325	93	776	4,298	1992	950	861	6,083	1,805	216	375	6,938
1983	739	575	3,329	1,722	174	699	4,312	1993	1,003	904	6,787	1,833	184	373	7,618
1984	722	541	3,426	2,011	272	681	4,715	1994	942	843	7,063	1,933	203	314	8,054
1985	781	577	3,201	1,866	200	510	4,286	1995	949	855	7,230	1,605	193	187	7,886
1986	785	631	4,178	2,045	247	669	5,439	1996	981	871	7,508	1,971	230	248	8,498
1987	764	613	4,674	2,004	255	565	5,914	1997[1]	1,003	896	7,996	1,912	227	196	8,904

[1] Preliminary. [2] Includes crude oil. [3] Equals imports minus exports. *Source: Energy Information Administration, U.S. Department of Energy (EIA)*

Domestic First Purchase Price of Crude Petroleum at Wells[1] In Dollars Per Barrel

Year	Jan.	Feb.	Mar.	Apr.	May	June	July	Aug.	Sept.	Oct.	Nov.	Dec.	Average
1988	13.64	13.43	12.96	13.92	14.12	13.59	12.38	12.22	11.63	10.62	10.31	11.99	12.58
1989	13.80	14.24	15.65	17.04	16.76	16.42	16.32	15.01	15.58	16.25	16.30	17.01	15.86
1990	18.49	18.16	16.57	14.52	13.82	12.79	14.03	21.87	28.46	30.86	27.53	22.63	20.03
1991	19.60	16.28	15.13	16.16	16.44	15.58	16.36	16.60	16.71	17.72	17.12	14.68	16.54
1992	13.99	14.04	14.12	15.36	16.38	17.96	17.80	17.07	17.20	17.16	16.00	14.94	15.99
1993	14.70	15.53	15.94	16.15	16.03	15.06	13.83	13.75	13.39	13.72	12.45	10.38	14.25
1994	10.49	10.71	10.94	12.31	14.02	14.93	15.34	14.50	13.62	13.84	14.14	13.43	13.19
1995	14.00	14.69	14.68	15.84	15.85	15.02	14.01	14.13	14.49	13.68	14.03	15.02	14.62
1996	15.43	15.54	17.63	19.58	17.94	16.94	17.63	18.29	19.93	21.09	20.20	21.34	18.46
1997[2]	21.76	19.38	17.85	16.64	17.24	15.90	15.91	16.21	16.44	17.68	16.84		17.44

[1] Buyers posted prices. [2] Preliminary. *Source: Energy Information Adiministration, U.S. Department of Energy (EIA-DOE)*

Volume of Trading of Crude Oil Futures in New York   In Thousands of Contracts

Year	Jan.	Feb.	Mar.	Apr.	May	June	July	Aug.	Sept.	Oct.	Nov.	Dec.	Total
1988	1,626.0	1,336.0	1,809.0	1,352.0	1,205.0	1,507.0	1,754.0	1,219.0	1,956.0	2,040.0	1,609.0	1,450.0	18,859.0
1989	1,919.0	1,524.0	2,053.0	2,070.0	1,911.0	2,082.0	1,663.0	1,343.0	1,541.0	1,521.0	1,425.0	1,483.0	20,535.0
1990	2,164.0	1,790.0	1,794.0	1,813.0	1,945.0	1,839.0	2,046.0	2,716.0	2,073.0	2,437.0	1,769.0	1,302.0	23,687.0
1991	1,997.0	1,478.0	1,605.0	1,885.0	1,741.0	1,411.0	1,675.0	1,598.0	1,543.0	2,064.0	2,051.0	1,960.0	21,008.0
1992	2,097.0	1,630.0	1,620.0	1,889.0	1,885.0	2,006.0	1,796.0	1,531.0	1,541.0	1,797.0	1,542.0	1,778.0	21,110.0
1993	2,139.0	1,886.0	1,895.0	1,459.0	1,641.0	2,018.0	2,616.0	2,200.0	2,679.0	1,945.0	2,378.0	2,122.0	24,869.0
1994	2,296.0	1,933.0	2,228.0	2,382.0	2,602.0	2,576.0	2,186.0	2,544.0	1,897.0	2,195.0	2,195.9	1,778.2	16,812.0
1995	2,133.5	1,657.3	2,289.8	2,220.1	2,408.9	2,172.4	1,749.3	1,793.8	1,968.0	1,834.6	1,739.1	1,647.2	23,614.0
1996	2,260.1	1,928.3	2,399.3	2,489.9	2,161.3	1,601.7	1,732.1	1,657.0	1,912.6	2,098.0	1,643.1	1,604.3	23,487.8
1997	1,949.9	1,973.7	2,086.6	2,033.7	2,134.9	2,098.6	2,221.4	2,053.7	2,027.5	2,574.0	1,770.2	1,847.2	24,771.4

Source: New York Mercantile Exchange (NYMEX)

Average Open Interest of Crude Oil Futures in New York   In Contracts

Year	Jan.	Feb.	Mar.	Apr.	May	June	July	Aug.	Sept.	Oct.	Nov.	Dec.
1988	202,830	200,813	210,878	192,074	177,155	180,019	177,978	177,879	220,973	221,628	196,454	196,109
1989	204,066	210,299	224,322	248,032	231,390	222,748	221,389	209,702	230,990	235,716	242,677	257,974
1990	273,193	300,069	287,013	287,538	278,600	285,384	275,771	262,746	266,313	269,167	242,500	232,405
1991	249,759	272,396	285,417	303,942	286,159	277,587	278,704	267,186	264,223	298,434	292,889	284,453
1992	310,763	331,050	316,544	340,315	335,545	364,155	331,972	316,066	314,446	301,381	308,467	330,134
1993	352,316	369,180	385,768	381,954	384,309	396,832	423,041	428,418	404,172	397,121	404,046	427,756
1994	427,705	438,929	424,462	410,974	427,071	414,257	409,251	396,657	395,194	413,206	388,932	391,151
1995	373,798	379,329	353,805	364,929	350,826	346,051	357,718	343,636	342,360	334,170	329,786	348,954
1996	389,935	400,236	427,306	460,841	424,994	376,164	367,405	364,458	395,358	410,387	385,415	368,331
1997	365,522	384,737	408,751	409,719	401,663	397,245	411,292	424,529	405,389	419,821	404,597	424,333

Source: New York Mercantile Exchange (NYMEX)

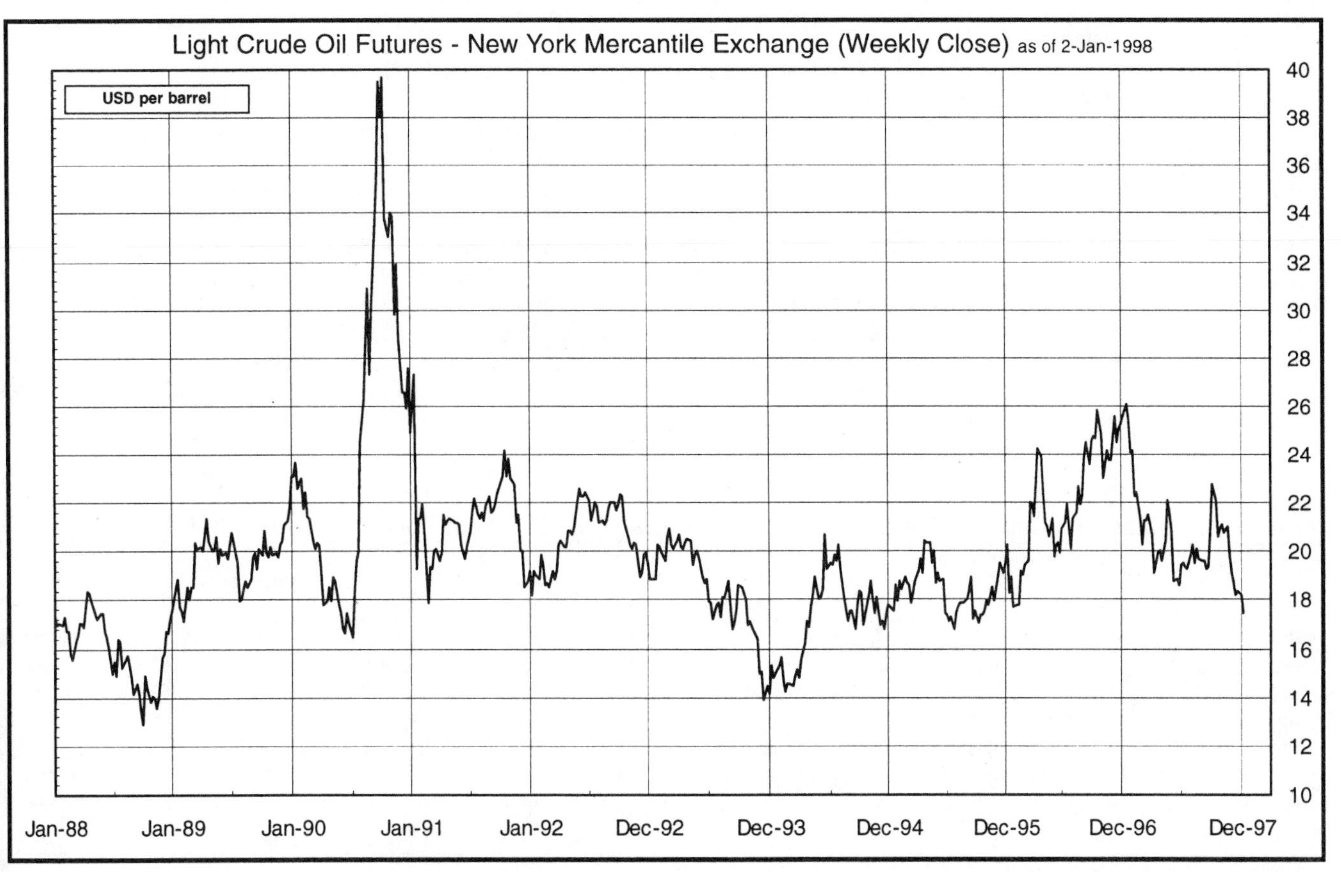

Plastics

Plastics, on a volume basis, are one of the most used materials in the U.S. for industrial and commercial purposes. The plastics industry in the U.S. is now in its second century but the most important developments in the industry have occurred since 1910. The period of 1930-1940 saw the initial commercial development of today's major thermoplastics: polyvinyl chloride, low density polyethylene, polystyrene and polymethyl methacrylate. In 1939, World War II brought plastics in great demand mostly as substitutes for material that was in short supply, such as natural rubber. In the U.S., the production of synthetic rubbers led to the development of more plastic materials. The demand for plastics has increased steadily and plastics are now accepted as basic materials along with more traditional materials.

Plastics find a wide use in a variety of products ranging from packaging materials to replacement material for wood, metals, glass and paper. The environmental impact of the disposal of plastic materials has led to the development of a recycling industry. One area where plastic is making an important contribution is in the automobile industry. Part of this is due to the need by automakers to keep the prices of cars down while at the same time making materials lighter to improve gasoline efficiency. Plastic material is finding use in bumpers, gas tanks, hoods, fenders and body panels.

U.S. plastic resin sales in 1996 were 78.7 billion pounds, dry weight basis, up 11 percent from 1995. Sales of plastic resin continue to increase. Of the total, plastic resin sales for the packaging industry in 1996 were 21.3 billion pounds or 27 percent of the total. The building and construction industry took 16.2 billion pounds or 21 percent of the total sales. Other major users of plastic resins were consumer and institutional markets, transportation, furniture and furnishings, electrical and adhesives, inks and coatings.

Of the total plastic resin sales in 1996 of 78.7 billion pounds, thermoplastics were 70.6 billion pounds. In terms of major markets, the packaging industry took 30 percent of the thermoplastics, consumer and institutional products took almost 14 percent, building and construction 15 percent, transportation took almost 5 percent, furniture and furnishings 4 percent and electrical and electronic products 4 percent.

The remaining 8.1 billion pounds of plastic resins are in the form of thermosets. Of this total, the major markets were building and construction, 66 percent; transportation, 8 percent; furniture and furnishings, 6 percent; adhesives, inks and coatings, 4 percent; consumer and institutional products, 4 percent; electrical and electronic products, 3 percent; industrial and machinery products, almost 3 percent; and other products, almost 3 percent. While packaging took 30 percent of thermoplastics, packaging was less than 1 percent of total thermoset use. Of all the plastic resin sales, 11 percent was exported.

Plastics Production by Resin in the United States In Millions of Pounds

	Thermosets				Thermoplastics										
Year	Polyester Unsaturated	Phenolic	Epoxy	Total Thermosets	Thermoplastic Polyester	Polyvinyl Chloride	Polystyrene	Polypropylene	Nylon	Low Density Polyethylene[1]	High Density Polyethylene	Total Thermoplastics	Total Selected Plastics	Other Plastics	Total Plastics
1987	1,367	2,869	433	6,263	1,394	7,971	4,780	6,647	507	9,599	7,995	40,194	46,457	9,294	55,751
1988	1,404	3,066	486	6,588	1,652	8,350	5,187	7,274	566	10,397	8,400	43,251	49,839	9,923	59,762
1989	1,319	2,879	510	6,407	1,630	8,478	5,104	7,238	569	9,695	8,102	42,189	48,596	9,933	58,529
1990	1,221	2,946	499	6,364	1,879	9,096	5,021	8,310	558	11,148	8,337	45,646	52,010	9,950	61,960
1991	1,075	2,658	497	5,909	2,115	9,164	4,954	8,330	576	11,582	9,213	47,146	53,055	9,731	62,786
1992	1,175	2,923	457	6,335	2,413	9,989	5,096	8,421	668	11,917	9,808	49,751	56,086	10,285	66,371
1993	1,264	3,078	512	6,868	2,549	10,257	5,382	8,628	768	12,067	9,941	51,159	58,027	10,777	68,854
1994	1,468	3,229	601	7,513	3,196	11,712	5,848	9,539	943	12,600	11,117	56,794	64,307	11,664	75,971
1995	1,577	3,204	632	7,519	3,785	12,295	5,656	10,890	1,020	12,886	11,211	59,331	66,850	11,834	78,684
1996	1,557	3,476	662	8,129	4,031	13,220	6,065	11,991	1,103	14,145	12,373	64,526	72,655	11,640	84,295

[1] Includes LDPE and LLDPE. *Source: The Society of the Plastics Industry, Inc. (SPI)*

Total Resin Sales and Captive Use by Important Markets In Millions of Pounds (Dry Weight Basis)

Year	Adhesive, Inks & Coatings	Building & Construction	Consumer & Industrial	Electrical & Electronics	Exports	Furniture & Furnishings	Industrial & Machinery	Packaging	Transportation	Other	Total
1989	1,211	11,096	6,217	3,145	[1]	2,285	475	14,711	2,547	10,911	52,598
1990	1,373	11,803	5,861	3,165	[1]	2,190	636	16,568	2,504	11,811	55,910
1991	1,391	10,650	5,689	2,896	7,418	2,255	587	16,723	2,328	6,616	56,553
1992	1,723	11,876	6,093	2,766	6,950	2,559	617	18,284	2,817	6,877	60,562
1993	1,572	12,885	6,015	2,981	6,632	2,759	768	19,569	3,221	7,234	63,636
1994	1,789	14,715	9,266	3,325	6,889	3,118	836	19,551	3,795	7,515	70,799
1995	1,795	14,321	9,054	2,966	7,742	3,198	818	19,334	3,916	8,050	71,194
1996	1,833	16,199	9,804	3,137	8,722	3,477	980	21,271	3,964	9,361	78,748

[1] Included in other. *Source: The Society of the Plastics Industry, Inc. (SPI)*

Average Producer Price Index of Plastic Materials in the United States 1982 = 100

Year	Jan.	Feb.	Mar.	Apr.	May	June	July	Aug.	Sept.	Oct.	Nov.	Dec.	Average
					Plastic Resins and Materials (066)								
1989	140.3	141.1	140.6	140.7	139.8	138.0	135.3	127.7	126.1	124.7	123.7	123.3	133.4
1990	122.2	121.6	122.2	123.0	123.5	123.0	122.1	122.3	123.6	125.1	128.6	131.2	124.0
1991	131.1	128.7	125.4	122.9	120.6	117.0	115.0	114.9	114.9	116.4	116.7	116.0	120.0
1992	115.4	115.6	114.2	114.2	114.7	115.2	115.9	117.7	117.5	118.2	118.1	118.1	116.2
1993	118.3	118.0	117.6	117.1	116.3	116.9	116.9	117.6	117.4	116.9	116.2	116.2	117.1
1994	115.0	114.7	114.5	116.5	117.7	119.1	119.6	121.5	126.3	131.9	134.1	138.1	122.4
1995	142.5	144.1	145.9	148.5	149.0	148.9	147.0	144.8	142.7	139.2	135.8	132.2	143.4
1996	129.9	128.4	128.4	127.7	130.6	132.1	133.2	135.2	137.9	138.0	138.0	137.7	133.1
1997[1]	137.0	137.5	138.7	138.9	139.1	139.6	139.3	137.4	136.0	136.7	134.3	133.2	137.3
					Thermoplastic Resins (0662)								
1989	114.5	145.2	144.4	143.9	143.2	141.1	137.7	128.5	126.7	125.1	124.0	124.0	133.2
1990	122.9	121.9	122.5	123.5	124.1	123.4	122.4	122.5	124.1	125.8	130.5	134.0	124.8
1991	132.1	129.4	125.5	122.9	120.2	116.2	113.8	113.7	114.6	115.5	116.0	115.3	119.6
1992	114.7	114.7	113.0	112.9	113.4	114.1	114.8	117.1	116.8	117.6	117.6	117.5	115.4
1993	117.5	117.1	116.3	115.8	114.8	115.4	115.5	116.4	116.4	116.4	115.5	114.6	116.0
1994	113.0	112.7	112.5	115.0	116.2	117.9	118.4	120.1	125.4	131.6	133.9	138.4	121.3
1995	143.1	145.0	147.1	150.3	151.0	151.2	148.7	146.2	143.7	139.6	135.5	131.1	144.4
1996	128.4	126.7	126.8	125.9	129.4	131.1	132.5	134.8	137.8	137.9	137.9	137.6	132.2
1997[1]	136.7	137.3	138.6	138.8	139.0	139.7	139.3	137.0	135.5	136.3	133.4	132.2	137.0
					PE Resin, Low, Film & Sheeting (0662-0301)								
1989	202.0	206.6	206.0	204.0	200.8	195.3	191.9	151.5	150.3	150.9	152.3	153.0	180.4
1990	151.9	145.3	146.1	145.9	152.5	151.7	144.9	141.9	152.3	145.6	149.8	157.4	148.8
1991	158.1	150.7	142.6	135.8	130.1	121.9	117.8	114.8	113.9	123.2	131.3	124.6	130.4
1992	126.5	130.9	126.7	121.3	123.5	122.4	132.9	138.9	145.2	149.3	148.6	150.6	134.7
1993	NA	151.4	145.6	141.8	135.5	137.1	132.2	136.6	129.2	128.4	127.6	127.4	135.7
1994	121.6	119.4	119.3	120.8	127.6	134.5	136.3	140.8	146.6	155.4	172.8	182.2	139.8
1995	188.5	196.0	202.0	210.6	215.4	211.1	205.7	194.4	185.0	173.4	167.5	157.4	192.3
1996	146.4	139.9	137.6	139.5	147.6	158.8	166.0	165.3	190.1	195.2	195.9	196.6	164.9
1997[1]	191.8	189.0	189.7	193.8	196.8	199.4	197.9	201.0	190.2	185.1	182.5	177.2	191.2
					Styrene Plastics Materials (0662-06)								
1989	135.3	136.3	134.4	135.8	135.1	133.1	124.6	119.5	119.0	116.8	114.2	114.4	126.5
1990	113.1	114.7	117.2	116.8	116.8	115.2	113.7	113.7	116.8	123.4	127.8	124.2	117.8
1991	123.3	122.7	115.4	115.5	112.4	121.9	109.2	107.7	108.3	113.0	113.0	111.5	114.5
1992	109.5	109.6	109.1	109.1	110.3	109.4	110.4	112.6	111.2	112.5	111.7	111.5	110.6
1993	110.7	110.5	110.0	110.4	111.0	111.3	111.2	111.1	110.6	109.1	106.5	106.4	109.9
1994	105.8	104.1	104.1	108.1	108.3	109.2	110.4	110.6	116.0	123.3	125.3	126.2	112.6
1995	129.0	127.0	132.5	134.7	135.9	137.5	135.1	133.2	132.1	130.1	127.9	126.1	131.8
1996	125.7	123.5	125.0	118.3	120.1	122.7	123.4	123.3	123.6	122.8	122.0	120.9	122.6
1997[1]	120.6	123.1	123.0	121.6	121.6	121.6	122.7	117.7	118.0	117.0	112.8	113.7	119.4
					Thermosetting Resins (0663)								
1989	122.4	124.0	124.9	127.9	126.6	126.5	126.8	127.5	126.9	126.6	125.9	123.8	125.8
1990	122.8	124.0	124.1	124.4	124.3	124.7	124.7	124.8	125.0	125.6	124.0	126.6	124.6
1991	130.1	129.1	128.9	127.1	126.3	125.2	124.9	124.9	123.9	124.5	123.8	123.1	126.0
1992	123.1	124.1	123.9	124.3	124.4	124.4	124.7	125.0	125.0	125.3	125.1	125.2	124.5
1993	126.1	126.5	127.4	127.5	127.8	128.0	127.7	127.7	127.9	127.8	127.8	128.3	127.5
1994	128.2	128.1	128.1	127.8	128.7	129.1	129.7	132.1	134.9	137.7	140.1	141.5	132.2
1995	144.3	145.1	145.4	145.2	144.7	143.5	144.0	143.5	142.9	142.3	142.4	142.1	143.8
1996	141.8	141.9	141.2	141.3	141.4	141.2	140.6	141.5	141.7	142.0	142.0	142.2	141.6
1997[1]	142.1	142.3	142.7	143.1	143.2	143.0	142.8	142.9	143.0	143.0	143.0	143.0	142.8
					Phenolic & Tar Acid Resins (0663-02)								
1989	156.7	158.9	162.6	166.8	164.2	164.4	166.2	159.5	158.6	158.0	156.9	152.3	160.4
1990	148.2	149.4	149.1	148.7	148.5	147.3	143.9	142.5	141.5	139.0	138.2	143.7	145.0
1991	146.4	147.3	142.4	140.7	138.3	132.8	131.6	131.5	128.3	129.7	126.5	125.5	135.1
1992	125.4	126.4	125.1	124.7	125.6	125.6	127.7	127.6	127.9	129.7	128.8	128.5	126.9
1993	128.5	130.3	130.5	131.4	133.7	134.1	133.9	132.8	133.1	132.1	132.0	132.9	132.1
1994	133.0	130.9	129.7	131.3	134.1	135.9	139.2	143.7	147.2	154.7	161.0	161.5	141.9
1995	164.6	166.4	165.1	162.5	158.6	153.5	152.0	148.5	147.7	146.2	143.2	142.6	154.2
1996	142.7	142.6	141.9	142.2	143.1	143.4	143.2	147.2	148.7	149.1	149.8	150.5	145.4
1997[1]	150.5	151.2	150.9	152.7	152.9	152.6	151.9	152.7	153.1	152.6	151.9	151.8	152.0

[1] Preliminary. NA = Not available. *Source: Bureau of Labor Statistics, U.S. Department of Commerce (BLS)*

Platinum-Group Metals

Given the strong world goal for a cleaner environment and focusing on the use of catalytic converters to stringently control emissions from gasoline-powered vehicles, the demand for platinum group metals (PGM) is expected to grow moderately during the next few years. Both platinum and palladium are used in converters, but over the short term, platinum is expected to remain the dominant metal, primarily due to the need to use up to three times as much palladium to obtain the same desired emissions reduction. Despite the apparent positive attitude towards platinum, the marketplace during 1997 viewed palladium more positively, at least based on the NYMEX futures action. In 1996, unfabricated platinum's average price of $398.17 per ounce compared with palladium's $130.41, a spread of $267.76. During the second half of 1997, platinum futures, basis nearest contract, hit a summer high of $454.00 and towards yearend were trading near $370.00. During the same timeframe, palladium futures went from about $160.00 per ounce up to $210.00, dipping back towards $203.00 at yearend, a differential of only $167.00. Clearly, the impetus favored palladium, apparently reflecting the view that the metal's demand has outdistanced supply, perhaps by as much as 20 percent.

Platinum tends to be viewed as a precious metal and its price, justified or not, has mirrored gold and silver's price action, and most of the time, palladium follows platinum. In 1997, speculative interest in the precious metals complex, notably gold, dropped due (1) to the buoyancy in the equity markets that siphoned capital away from the metals; (2) the absence of inflation fears which weighed notably on gold and in turn platinum even though the latter lacks the inflation hedge psychology; (3) the absence of any serious problems in South Africa that may have hindered mine production and/or shipments of the metals. Generally the short term variables on platinum's price are more supply sensitive. PGM prices pushed higher during September/October on fears that Russia, the world's second largest producer, would either be unable or unwilling to export the metals. As the fears dissipated, platinum, but not palladium prices, dropped quickly and later accelerated downward on fresh fears of a fall in demand from Asia, but the slide was braked by renewed concerns about Russian supplies.

Six metals make up the platinum group (PGM); statistical data is limited to platinum and palladium; for iridium, osmium, rhodium (the most expensive) and ruthenium (the least expensive) the data is spotty at best. Minable deposits of the PGM's are rare, production occurs as a byproduct of some other metal, usually nickel or copper. World production in 1996 of 284,000 kilograms compares with 287,000 in 1995. However, a shift has developed in the production breakdown, until 1991 more palladium was produced than platinum, generally by about 10,000 kg.; in 1996 about 146,000 kg. of platinum were produced and 111,000 kg. of palladium. Other 1996 PGM metals production of 26,800 kg. compares with 27,200 kg. in 1995. Identified world PGM resources at yearend 1966 totaled 100 million kilograms. The reserve base was estimated at 66 million kg. of which South Africa had nearly 90 percent of each and Russia 9 percent and 11 percent, respectively.

South Africa is the largest producer with 117,000 kg. of platinum in 1996 vs. 118,000 in 1995; palladium production at a near record high 48,900 kg. compares with 49,400 in 1995. Russia is believed to have produced 18,000 kg. of platinum in 1996 and 48,000 kg. of palladium, both unchanged from 1995, but well under production in the first half of the 1990's. U.S. production trails demand, leaving the U.S. dependent on imports. The Stillwater Mine in Montana accounts for nearly all domestic PGM production. Stillwater smelts the ore locally, but the resulting PGM-bearing matte is shipped to Belgium for refining. Stillwater was expected to nearly double ore production, to more than 660,000 metric tonnes by mid-1997, from 336,000 tonnes annually in the first half of the 1990's. Reportedly there are large deposits of PGM in the Montana region, but high extracting costs is a restraining factor. The U.S. produced 1840 kg. of platinum in 1996 and 6100 kg. of palladium vs. 1590 kg. and 5260 kg., respectively, in 1995.

In the U.S. the automotive industry is the largest consumer of PGM. The metal(s) have no competitive substitutes when used as an emission control catalyst, but the percentage of each metal used in the catalysts can be varied. On a world basis, demand for "platinum" in 1996 is forecast at 152 tonnes, about unchanged from 1995, with 40 percent used by the automotive industry, 35 percent for jewelry, 20 percent for industrial and the balance for investment.

The U.S. imports half of the world's PGM production. U.S. imports of platinum during 1992-96 totaled about 318,000 kg. with South Africa supplying about 60 percent; and during the period the U.S. imported about 500,000 kg. of palladium with Russia supplying about 42 percent and South Africa 22 percent. The U.S. exports PGM's, most of which is refined palladium, 26,700 kg. in 1996, with Japan, Belgium, Mexico and the Netherlands taking 16,360 kg.

Producers maintain an artificial price for the platinum group metals, but dealer or market prices are generally much lower. Generally platinum has a premium to gold; at yearend 1997 the metal was about $80 an ounce over gold vs. a year earlier differential near $5/oz.

Futures Markets

Platinum and palladium futures and options are traded on the New York Mercantile Exchange (NYMEX). In Japan platinum and palladium futures are listed on the Tokyo Commodity Exchange (TOCOM).

World Mine Production of Platinum In Kilograms

Year	Australia	Canada	Colombia[3]	Finland	Japan	Russia[4]	Serbia/ Montenegro[5]	South Africa	United States	Zimbabwe	World Total
1988	106	5,393	815	54	647	32,000	23	80,322	1,240	28	120,629
1989	100	4,467	973	60	1,031	32,000	23	82,884	1,430	25	122,994
1990	100	5,040	1,320	60	1,430	31,000	21	87,800	1,810	21	129,000
1991	100	4,680	1,600	60	988	30,000	22	88,900	1,500	19	128,000
1992	100	4,800	1,956	60	629	28,000	19	94,900	1,650	9	132,000
1993	100	5,000	1,722	60	661	20,000	10	109,000	2,050	4	139,000
1994	100	6,000	1,084	60	691	15,000	10	114,000	1,960	7	139,000
1995[1]	100	9,320	673	60	730	18,000	10	118,000	1,590	10	149,000
1996[2]	100	8,260	669	60	850	18,000	10	117,000	1,840	10	146,000

[1] Preliminary. [2] Estimate. [3] Placer platinum. [4] Formerly part of the U.S.S.R.; data not reported separately until 1992 [5] Formerly part of Yugoslavia.; data not reported separately until 1992 *Source: U.S. Geological Survey (USGS)*

World Mine Production of Palladium and Other Group Metals In Kilograms

Year	Palladium										Other Group Metals		
	Australia	Canada	Finland	Japan	Russia[3]	Serbia[4] Montenegro	South Africa	United States	Zimbabwe	World Total	Russia[3]	South Africa	World Total
1988	411	5,643	106	1,170	85,000	142	34,400	3,730	46	130,648	10,500	17,000	29,005
1989	400	4,676	100	821	85,000	199	35,800	4,850	43	131,889	10,500	15,000	26,746
1990	400	5,270	100	1,050	84,000	130	38,300	5,930	31	135,000	10,000	15,800	27,200
1991	400	6,440	100	1,050	82,000	155	38,000	5,200	30	133,000	9,500	16,000	26,100
1992	400	5,800	100	986	70,000	130	41,000	5,440	19	124,000	6,000	17,000	24,300
1993	400	6,000	100	1,183	50,000	72	48,000	6,780	11	113,000	4,000	19,000	24,400
1994	400	7,000	100	1,277	40,000	50	47,800	6,440	17	103,000	3,000	22,100	27,100
1995[1]	400	5,950	100	2,174	48,000	50	49,400	5,260	20	111,000	3,600	22,800	27,200
1996[2]	400	5,270	100	2,300	48,000	50	48,900	6,100	20	111,000	3,600	22,500	26,800

[1] Preliminary. [2] Estimate. [3] Formerly part of the U.S.S.R.; data not reported separately until 1992 [4] Formerly part of Yugoslavia.; data not reported separately until 1992 *Source: U.S. Geological Survey (USGS)*

Platinum–Group Metals Sold to Consuming Industries in the United States In Kilograms

Year	Automotive		Chemical		Electrical		Dental & Medical		Jewelry & Decorative		Petroleum		All Platinum–Group Metals			
	Platinum	Other[3]	Platinum	Other[3]	Platinum	Other[3]	Platinum	Other[3]	Platinum	Other[3]	Platinum	Other[3]	Platinum	Palladium	Other[3]	Total
1986	19,438	7,234	2,416	2,346	3,219	11,082	645	8,363	352	304	951	1,896	30,509	27,677	6,511	64,698
1987	18,816	6,935	1,919	1,283	1,821	10,879	479	10,526	177	478	543	1,286	25,469	30,953	3,851	60,273
1988	19,346	7,186	3,184	4,499	3,494	14,429	581	6,650	385	407	1,027	1,560	31,125	34,241	5,632	70,998
1989	18,774	6,869	2,424	2,233	3,894	19,514	632	8,601	418	396	2,859	2,570	33,698	39,273	5,512	78,483
1990	20,967	5,990	2,080	2,574	3,907	19,791	687	6,287	431	387	3,274	1,488	36,055	35,116	6,316	77,487
1991	18,643	5,338	861	1,749	3,910	14,428	598	4,918	626	500	3,163	181	31,112	25,747	5,738	62,597
1992	20,290	5,789	1,716	2,297	2,922	15,738	640	5,386	881	1,417	1,036	790	31,095	28,935	6,816	66,846
1993[1]	19,444	10,123	2,364	3,121	2,125	12,699	687	5,562	1,024	1,422	1,204	709	29,879	26,840	8,544	65,063
1994[2]	21,754	11,412	3,104	1,889	2,790	7,961	902	5,092	1,345	824	1,581	422	34,044	21,509	7,387	62,940

[1] Preliminary. [2] Estimate. [3] Includes palladium, iridium, osmium, rhodium, and ruthenium. *Source: U.S. Geological Survey (USGS)*

Salient Statistics of Platinum and Allied Metals[3] in the United States In Kilograms

Year	Net Import Reliance as a % of Apparent Consumption	Mine Production		Refinery Production (Secondary)	Total Refined	Refiner, Importer & Dealer Stocks as of Dec. 31				Imports for Consumption		Exports		Apparent Consumption
		Platinum	Palladium			Platinum	Palladium	Other[4]	Total	Refined	Total	Refined	Total	
1988	91	1,240	3,730	51,190	51,488	18,438	14,837	2,239	35,514	110,947	124,324	20,301	28,787	103,302
1989	90	1,430	4,850	50,186	50,525	14,791	15,182	2,570	32,543	111,107	113,278	23,082	38,301	101,209
1990	88	1,810	5,930	71,248	71,312	13,421	14,425	2,478	30,324	120,631	125,354	20,148	55,044	117,043
1991	90	1,730	6,050	72,349	72,564	10,349	12,263	1,701	24,313	121,741	125,661	27,401	39,624	111,798
1992	87	1,840	6,470	64,309	64,309	14,187	10,641	2,118	26,946	129,419	132,006	31,060	57,830	109,469
1993	89	2,050	6,780	65,792	65,792	10,263	8,324	176	18,763	148,790	153,165	43,798	78,486	123,273
1994	91	1,960	6,440	63,000	63,000	10,304	9,345	123	19,772	167,681	170,907	46,259	88,561	127,000
1995[1]	NA	1,590	5,260	NA	NA	NA	NA	NA	NA	214,143	220,613	41,825	50,575	NA
1996[2]	NA	1,840	6,100	NA	NA	NA	NA	NA	NA	248,860	255,880	39,709	48,836	NA

[1] Preliminary. [2] Estimate. [3] Includes platinum, palladium, iridium, osmium, rhodium, and ruthenium. [4] Includes iridium, osmium, rhodium, and ruthenium. NA = Not available. *Source: U.S. Geological Survey (USGS)*

PLATINUM-GROUP METALS

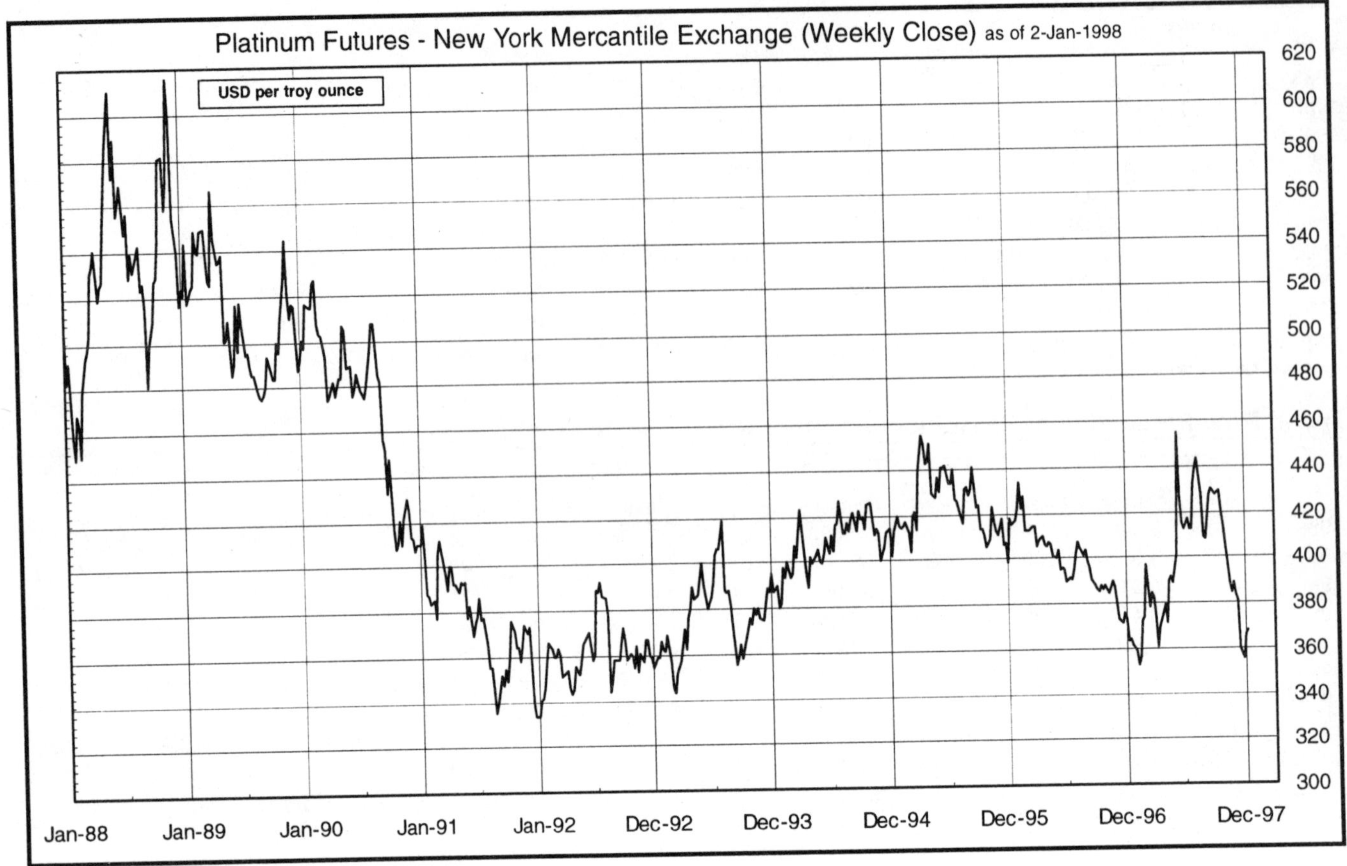

Average Open Interest of Platinum Futures in New York In Contracts

Year	Jan.	Feb.	Mar.	Apr.	May	June	July	Aug.	Sept.	Oct.	Nov.	Dec.
1988	17,133	18,080	16,737	16,718	18,643	22,735	19,668	17,671	19,936	19,097	22,022	24,384
1989	19,334	18,648	19,736	19,895	19,661	20,597	17,310	19,121	19,165	16,981	19,934	20,392
1990	19,510	17,970	15,888	15,915	16,688	15,652	15,496	17,254	18,494	17,472	16,313	16,994
1991	15,497	16,043	16,083	14,334	15,779	18,273	17,503	19,214	18,611	15,933	13,579	14,533
1992	15,464	14,231	14,272	14,130	15,353	19,070	20,402	18,444	17,574	14,079	13,532	14,282
1993	11,889	14,315	12,990	15,490	19,641	17,919	20,931	18,892	16,883	15,690	16,658	19,633
1994	18,779	19,655	21,673	22,834	21,880	22,835	24,804	25,049	24,245	24,159	26,287	26,661
1995	23,285	23,058	23,470	23,657	20,984	21,533	20,801	25,288	23,489	24,498	22,137	21,534
1996	23,130	21,535	23,156	25,081	26,343	27,720	25,861	25,455	28,511	28,305	27,423	29,143
1997	25,890	26,092	22,364	16,568	18,933	18,440	13,280	14,180	13,639	13,466	12,396	13,501

Source: New York Mercantile Exchange (NYMEX)

Volume of Trading of Platinum Futures in New York In Thousands of Contracts

Year	Jan.	Feb.	Mar.	Apr.	May	June	July	Aug.	Sept.	Oct.	Nov.	Dec.	Total
1988	82.8	77.6	119.2	74.3	123.3	182.2	111.5	105.8	125.1	114.6	164.8	179.2	1,460.5
1989	113.6	96.6	148.5	107.3	111.6	126.9	69.8	86.8	85.1	56.4	99.8	88.1	1,190.5
1990	85.6	80.9	81.3	55.3	65.2	70.1	52.7	73.8	77.2	68.0	50.1	56.8	817.1
1991	50.8	42.3	72.7	43.0	51.1	55.7	40.6	45.7	55.8	42.9	41.9	60.3	598.6
1992	47.9	38.3	54.1	29.3	37.7	82.0	61.0	50.6	51.8	28.5	42.3	53.8	577.3
1993	29.4	55.6	61.4	50.6	65.8	72.5	59.8	56.4	58.6	37.0	44.0	60.3	651.2
1994	48.3	65.3	94.4	62.6	65.1	88.3	84.2	75.4	92.4	60.9	77.3	81.6	895.8
1995	61.4	38.6	131.3	69.9	60.4	75.4	53.4	62.5	98.8	55.9	56.3	82.8	846.7
1996	80.5	70.3	86.3	54.2	47.9	88.8	53.3	53.7	90.1	47.1	42.0	88.3	802.5
1997	60.5	83.3	86.2	57.7	67.0	72.5	38.7	36.4	62.5	46.2	28.9	58.6	698.6

Source: New York Mercantile Exchange (NYMEX)

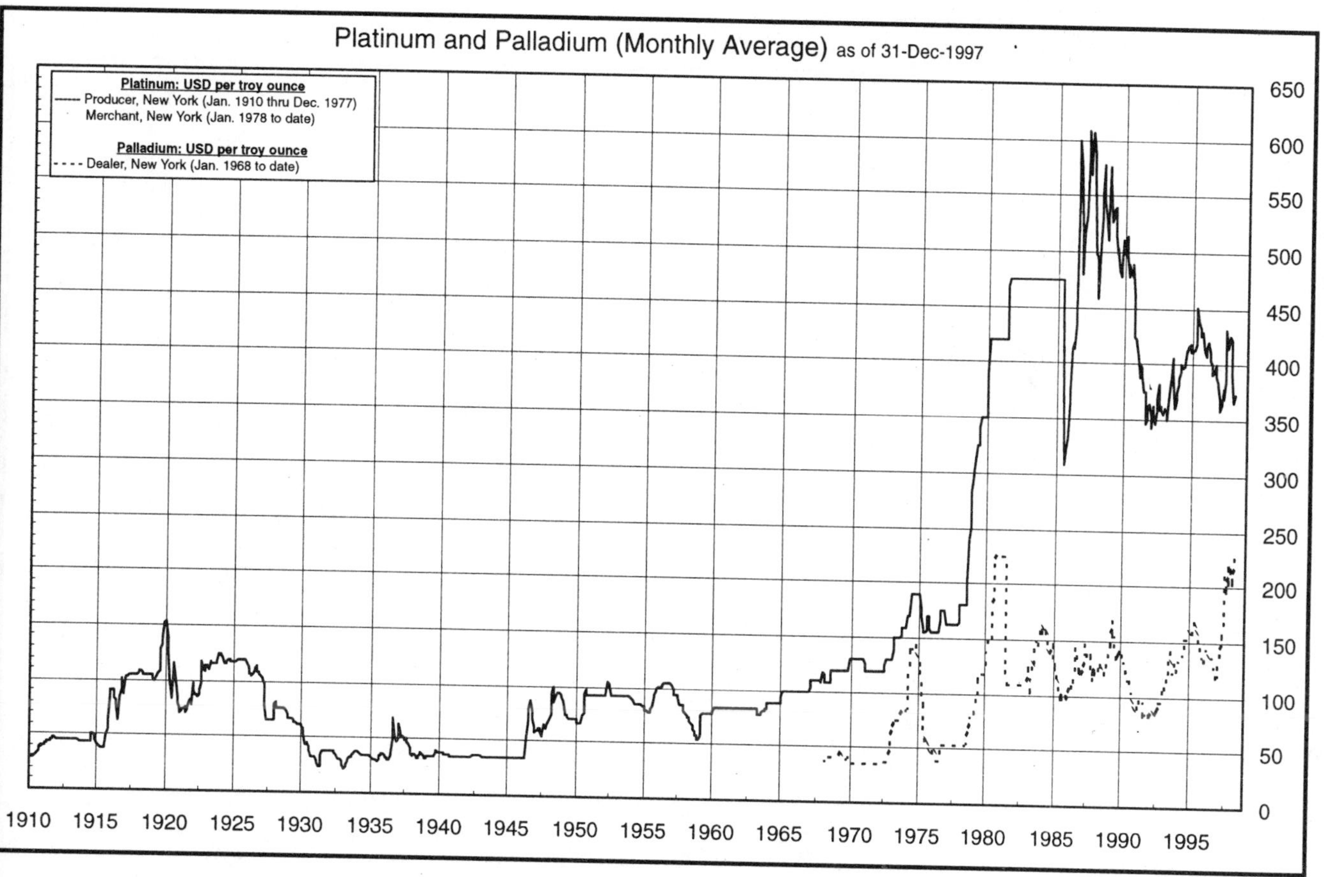

Average Merchant's Price of Platinum in the United States In Dollars Per Troy Ounce

Year	Jan	Feb	Mar	Apr	May	Jun	Jul	Aug	Sep	Oct	Nov	Dec	Average
1988	494.14	458.64	496.49	527.73	548.91	581.32	548.51	532.80	513.16	527.35	577.74	567.36	531.18
1989	528.69	532.66	538.26	539.96	517.20	498.81	503.16	485.20	479.29	485.48	508.73	507.24	510.39
1990	949.93	517.34	500.32	478.33	485.89	486.60	476.93	492.02	463.87	423.78	424.12	446.94	474.26
1991	408.92	385.53	403.12	398.16	373.06	374.25	375.38	351.68	348.01	362.52	364.01	356.65	375.11
1992	341.88	362.97	356.84	347.73	354.75	368.17	378.89	360.20	361.60	359.75	355.81	361.98	359.21
1993	359.99	361.53	349.31	365.98	385.50	384.54	401.10	394.69	365.29	369.19	376.98	383.85	374.75
1994	390.30	393.95	398.29	400.38	395.41	401.42	408.25	411.91	415.93	421.11	415.73	408.83	405.13
1995	414.27	415.22	415.37	446.24	439.02	436.58	435.21	425.61	430.31	414.49	413.55	410.17	424.67
1996	416.13	420.02	411.19	404.28	401.60	392.64	393.86	400.03	389.86	384.24	382.36	370.60	397.23
1997[1]	359.66	364.99	379.18	370.39	387.14	430.79	415.23	424.55	425.48	423.20	392.83	365.76	394.93

[1] Preliminary. *Source: American Metal Market (AMM)*

Average Dealer[1] Price of Palladium in the United States In Dollars Per Troy Ounce

Year	Jan.	Feb.	Mar.	Apr.	May	June	July	Aug.	Sept.	Oct.	Nov.	Dec.	Average
1988	125.26	120.40	122.67	123.62	124.06	128.77	126.25	123.84	121.04	122.59	126.80	133.30	124.89
1989	135.74	141.79	152.84	165.46	155.17	152.92	151.36	135.97	137.85	137.84	139.35	139.75	145.50
1990	135.80	136.63	131.25	128.18	120.08	117.40	116.60	116.17	106.62	96.12	94.84	90.93	115.89
1991	86.61	85.11	86.44	95.25	96.61	97.39	95.57	84.55	82.49	81.87	85.96	82.72	88.38
1992	82.96	86.04	84.50	83.71	82.90	80.98	86.49	86.04	90.67	95.07	95.01	104.88	88.27
1993	110.39	112.57	106.22	113.79	119.94	125.36	139.74	137.37	121.95	130.04	123.62	125.60	122.22
1994	124.40	130.92	132.43	133.22	135.76	137.03	145.28	151.83	152.99	154.90	158.10	153.80	142.56
1995	156.67	157.53	161.18	170.91	160.87	158.59	156.27	138.81	143.76	137.36	135.57	132.37	150.83
1996	131.59	142.10	140.67	138.05	134.36	132.95	134.55	128.82	123.10	119.39	119.30	119.90	130.40
1997[2]	124.73	141.26	139.55	143.73	173.38	209.47	195.73	221.57	200.38	214.21	217.05	202.64	181.98

[1] Based on wholesale quantities, prompt delivery. [2] Preliminary. *Sources: American Metal Market (AMM); U.S. Geological Survey (USGS)*

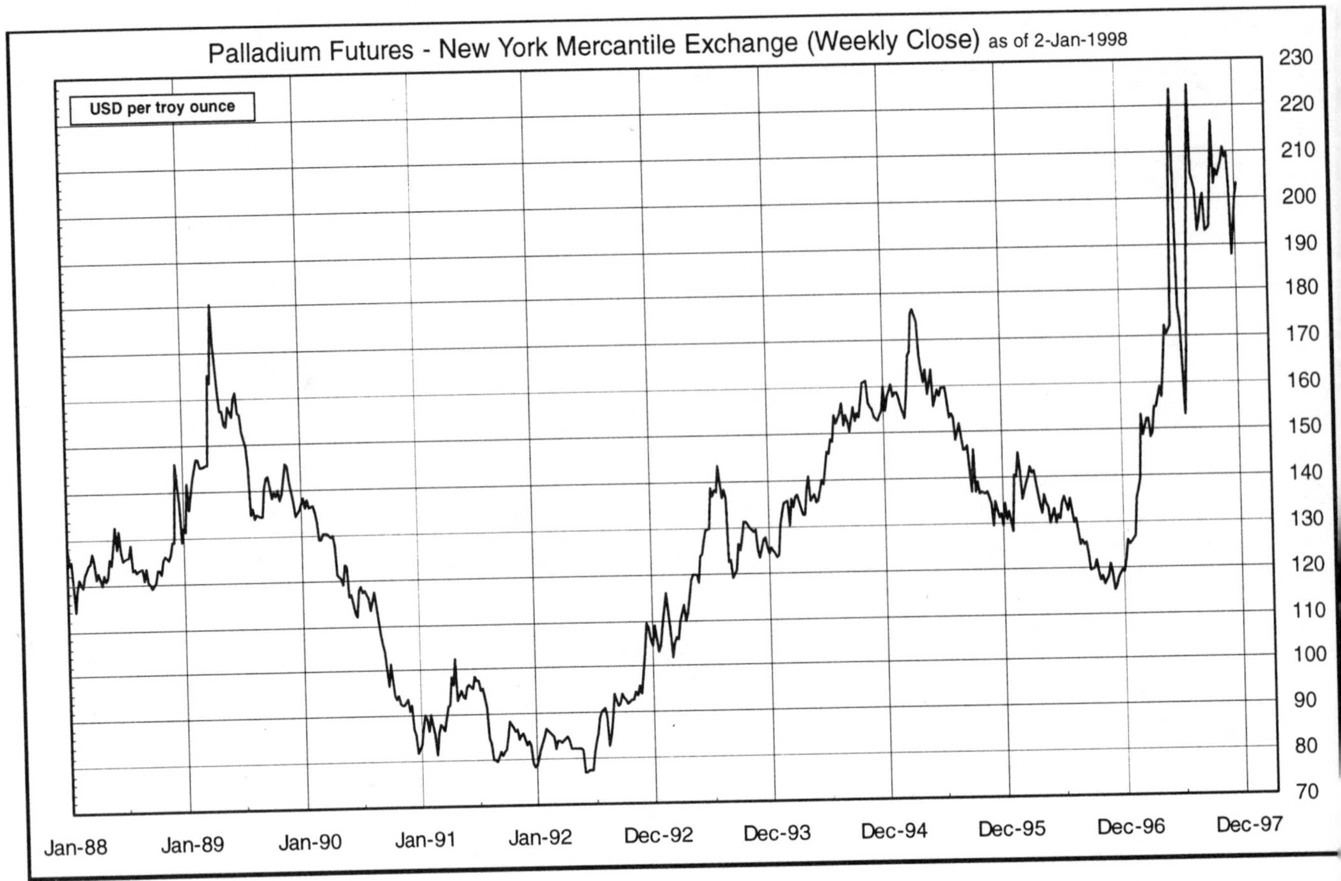

Volume of Trading of Palladium Futures in New York In Contracts

Year	Jan.	Feb.	Mar.	Apr.	May	June	July	Aug.	Sept.	Oct.	Nov.	Dec.	Total
1988	12,348	16,065	8,673	11,970	15,435	15,456	15,393	11,781	6,363	7,077	14,973	11,739	147,273
1989	12,852	16,296	12,978	48,699	28,266	13,062	15,477	15,351	11,235	8,862	17,745	10,836	211,659
1990	4,893	19,026	6,930	5,355	13,104	5,670	4,452	11,130	5,407	7,150	9,592	3,178	95,887
1991	5,017	10,542	5,380	7,245	10,521	4,447	5,230	10,114	2,914	5,668	8,150	2,971	78,199
1992	7,217	7,323	3,429	2,833	8,011	2,881	4,965	6,752	5,066	5,359	6,461	7,912	68,209
1993	7,708	14,461	8,057	10,034	12,190	7,368	7,043	13,356	6,977	9,220	12,477	4,790	113,681
1994	8,250	14,953	6,067	6,676	15,481	6,514	9,024	21,741	15,690	9,603	21,384	8,390	143,773
1995	10,684	17,092	21,001	12,775	17,413	9,615	11,816	18,948	9,754	9,320	16,662	11,633	166,713
1996	13,725	33,519	11,931	16,416	27,467	8,989	9,896	23,740	10,721	8,149	28,870	12,187	205,610
1997	13,908	43,160	22,796	21,604	36,422	17,647	18,097	18,751	8,331	13,094	13,143	11,763	238,716

Source: New York Mercantile Exchange (NYMEX)

Average Open Interest of Palladium Futures in New York In Contracts

Year	Jan.	Feb.	Mar.	Apr.	May	June	July	Aug.	Sept.	Oct.	Nov.	Dec.
1988	6,094	6,434	6,194	6,269	6,419	7,038	7,330	7,160	6,360	6,263	6,188	6,289
1989	6,460	6,758	6,636	9,082	9,173	9,116	8,307	7,616	7,105	6,847	7,123	6,660
1990	6,296	6,350	5,276	5,359	5,476	5,361	5,493	5,717	5,165	5,100	5,316	4,565
1991	4,658	4,559	4,319	4,686	4,559	4,302	4,454	4,429	4,429	4,384	4,337	4,042
1992	3,984	4,071	4,101	4,206	4,137	3,852	3,762	3,362	3,041	2,982	2,901	3,246
1993	3,718	4,213	4,365	4,897	5,312	4,513	4,655	5,080	4,360	4,495	4,472	4,484
1994	4,626	4,995	4,672	4,303	5,116	4,530	5,807	6,851	6,625	6,511	7,726	6,917
1995	7,484	7,579	7,102	7,231	6,519	6,413	6,739	6,852	5,950	6,120	6,486	6,090
1996	6,365	7,539	6,682	7,099	8,713	8,143	7,977	8,805	8,129	7,971	8,227	7,727
1997	8,291	10,946	10,528	9,759	9,947	7,072	5,538	4,973	3,822	4,282	4,291	4,030

Source: New York Mercantile Exchange (NYMEX)

Pork Bellies

Wholesale pork belly prices, basis Chicago futures, piv- ted around 75 cents per pound in the first quarter of 1997, oved about 10 cents higher in the second quarter, and fell 60 cents in mid-summer, a near two-year low, reflecting a rojected hefty increase in hog production in 1998. lthough the futures market now lacks much of the specu- tive following it formerly attracted, it remains a viable ricing hedging media for producers and users.

Pork bellies, more commonly known as bacon, are btained from the underside of a hog. A hog has two bellies, enerally weighing about 8-18 pounds, depending on the og's commercial slaughter weight. Slaughter weights now verage about 255 pounds per head, equal to a dressed eight of about 190 pounds. Bellies account for about 12% f a hog's live weight, but represent a somewhat larger per- entage of the total cutout value of the realized pork prod- cts. Bellies deliverable against futures generally weigh etween 12-14 pounds.

There are definitive seasonal trends for pork bellies. ellies are storable and the movement into cold storage uilds early in the calendar year and peaks about mid-year. et withdrawals from storage then carry stocks to a low round October. The cycle then begins anew. Retail bacon emand also follows a time tested pattern; peaking in the ummer when consumer preference shifts to lighter foods nd tapering off to a low during the winter months. While emand patterns would suggest the highest prices in the ummer and the lowest in the winter, the opposite is not nusual. Such contra-seasonal price moves can be partially ttributed to supply logistics; notably, the availability of torage stocks deliverable against futures at exchange approved warehouses. When it happens, underlying demand factors for bacon are on the backburner as a market making variable. The fact that no contract months are traded between August and the following February adds to the price distortion as evidenced by the late 1997 price weakness in anticipation of large supplies in 1998.

Belly prices (cash and futures) are sensitive to the inventory in cold storage during the year and to the weekly net movement in and out of storage. Storage movements can afford a clue to demand although a better measure is the weekly quantity of bellies being sliced into bacon. Higher prices tend to (1) encourage placing more supply into storage and (2) discourage retail bacon demand. Bacon is not a consumer necessity but demand can be buoyed by favorable consumer disposable income as was the case during 1997. Consumer dietary standards have changed dramatically in recent years, but the earlier negative effects on bacon consumption may have run their course by now. Retail bacon prices in the first half of 1997 averaged about $2.65 a pound, up 20 cents from a year earlier. By late summer retail prices around $2.75 were five cents lower compared to 1996.

U.S. foreign trade in bacon as a processed product is small. Imports are largely from Denmark and exports go to Eastern Europe.

Futures Markets

Pork belly futures and options are traded on the Chicago Mercantile Exchange (CME).

verage Bureau of Labor Statistics Retail Price of Bacon, Sliced In Dollars Per Pound

ear	Jan.	Feb.	Mar.	Apr.	May	June	July	Aug.	Sept.	Oct.	Nov.	Dec.	Average
988	1.95	1.94	1.92	1.91	1.90	1.90	1.91	1.88	1.84	1.86	1.80	1.79	1.88
989	1.80	1.80	1.79	1.75	1.68	1.69	1.71	1.72	1.72	1.77	1.82	1.96	1.77
990	1.97	2.01	1.99	1.98	2.04	2.15	2.21	2.24	2.18	2.21	2.24	2.28	2.13
991	2.26	2.30	2.32	2.27	2.31	2.31	2.31	2.22	2.16	2.12	2.07	1.99	2.22
992	1.96	1.95	1.92	1.92	1.90	1.93	1.95	1.94	1.93	1.89	1.85	1.86	1.92
993	1.87	1.84	1.80	1.89	1.91	1.95	2.00	1.95	1.98	1.99	2.01	2.02	1.93
994	2.04	2.02	2.02	2.06	1.99	1.99	2.00	1.99	1.97	1.97	1.92	1.89	1.99
995	1.93	1.93	1.91	1.89	1.92	1.90	1.91	1.97	2.04	2.12	2.16	2.17	1.99
996	2.14	2.20	2.20	2.24	2.35	2.49	2.54	2.68	2.81	2.72	2.66	2.64	2.47
997[1]	2.66	2.65	2.66	2.66	2.63	2.69	2.72	2.76	2.75	2.73	2.67	2.61	2.68

[1] Preliminary. *Source: Economic Research Service, U.S. Department of Agriculture (ERS-USDA)*

rozen Pork Belly Storage Stocks in the United States, on First of Month In Thousands of Pounds

ear	Jan.	Feb.	Mar.	Apr.	May	June	July	Aug.	Sept.	Oct.	Nov.	Dec.
988	62,089	62,996	67,035	90,347	102,543	111,484	103,401	73,747	42,623	31,054	49,550	93,254
989	113,137	116,191	121,556	127,617	143,751	142,340	126,676	94,107	49,083	32,031	39,358	67,489
990	85,026	77,255	85,789	96,945	102,899	105,482	87,983	55,859	23,352	4,785	5,506	24,044
991	46,998	48,750	54,529	68,094	80,382	79,936	72,032	45,915	29,832	15,944	25,558	48,311
992	71,318	76,894	75,925	85,095	96,653	92,677	78,646	54,544	26,854	21,973	26,044	49,970
993	70,576	65,280	65,919	66,064	79,430	77,903	70,251	46,630	20,811	10,964	14,345	33,563
994	53,168	55,999	54,921	63,099	72,230	79,018	73,583	57,747	30,636	18,260	22,656	40,725
995	61,073	62,776	64,228	78,975	78,539	77,919	67,607	47,055	17,435	6,255	13,478	37,092
996	47,587	46,498	46,381	47,655	57,174	63,522	56,767	28,533	18,996	12,702	16,206	30,943
997[1]	37,930	38,030	44,277	54,767	54,015	55,274	52,274	33,657	18,346	11,154	14,408	25,365

[1] Preliminary. *Source: National Agricultural Statistics Service, U.S. Department of Agriculture (NASS-USDA)*

PORK BELLIES

Weekly Pork Belly Storage Movement

1996 Week Ending		Stocks[1] in Thousands of Pounds In	Out	On Hand	Net Movement	1997 Week Ending		Stocks[1] in Thousands of Pounds In	Out	On Hand	Net Movement
Jan.	6	1,119	83	33,884	1,036	Jan.	4	2,868	6	30,680	2,862
	13	749	439	34,194	310		11	1,094	165	31,609	929
	20	995	827	34,362	168		18	429	270	31,768	159
	27	546	1,320	33,588	-774		25	402	685	31,485	-283
Feb.	3	844	1,842	32,590	-998	Feb.	1	837	813	31,345	24
	10	69	692	31,967	-623		8	880	720	31,659	160
	17	61	1,390	30,638	-1,329		15	2,035	380	33,314	1,655
	24	315	485	30,468	-170		22	1,459	586	34,187	873
Mar.	2	1,599	552	31,515	1,047	Mar.	1	1,220	489	34,918	731
	9	488	1,151	30,852	-663		8	1,902	57	36,763	1,845
	16	815	594	31,073	221		15	2,536	9	39,290	2,527
	23	1,014	305	31,782	709		22	968	6	40,252	962
	30	499	399	31,882	100		29	277	41	40,488	236
Apr.	6	1,407	682	32,607	725	Apr.	5	798	541	40,745	257
	13	2,951	488	35,070	2,463		12	1,030	677	41,098	353
	20	2,093	293	36,870	1,800		19	161	570	40,715	-383
	27	999	735	37,134	264		26	189	1,394	39,510	-1,205
May	4	739	397	37,476	342	May	3	415	1,369	38,556	-954
	11	1,289	381	38,384	908		10	1,530	337	39,749	1,193
	18	3,101	291	41,194	2,810		17	1,415	469	40,695	946
	25	1,992	286	42,900	1,706		24	531	813	40,413	-282
June	1	2,026	1,824	43,102	202		31	213	350	40,276	-137
	8	2,058	1,630	43,530	428	June	7	262	368	40,170	-106
	15	564	366	43,728	198		14	1,545	392	41,323	1,153
	22	182	1,210	42,700	-1,028		21	457	252	41,258	205
	29	227	1,385	41,542	-1,158		28	16	1,195	40,349	-1,179
July	6	4	1,854	39,692	-1,850	July	5	92	1,633	38,808	-1,54
	13	0	3,414	36,278	-3,414		12	75	2,284	36,599	-2,20
	20	12	4,364	31,926	-4,352		19	239	3,164	33,674	-2,92
	27	0	3,577	28,349	-3,577		26	97	3,687	30,084	-3,59
Aug.	3	162	3,721	24,790	-3,559	Aug.	2	79	3,503	26,660	-3,42
	10	0	3,723	21,067	-3,723		9	6	3,603	23,063	-3,59
	17	0	1,802	19,265	-1,802		16	41	2,600	20,504	-2,55
	24	235	486	19,014	-251		23	66	2,779	17,791	-2,71
	31	490	1,638	17,866	-1,148		30	NA	NA	15,757	-2,03
Sept.	7	664	1,746	16,784	-1,082	Sept.	6	38	1,722	14,073	-1,68
	14	1,268	1,526	16,526	-258		13	44	2,259	11,858	-2,21
	21	906	2,857	14,575	-1,951		20	57	2,945	8,970	-2,88
	28	122	3,069	11,628	-2,947		27	9	1,378	7,601	-1,36
Oct.	5	43	2,549	9,122	-2,506	Oct.	4	222	1,143	6,680	-92
	12	981	970	9,133	11		11	181	1,382	5,479	-1,20
	19	1,765	893	10,005	872		18	876	774	5,581	10
	26	1,932	946	11,091	1,086		25	1,065	994	5,652	7
Nov.	2	2,165	697	12,559	1,468	Nov.	1	232	1,042	4,842	-81
	9	3,108	278	15,389	2,830		8	NA	NA	NA	N
	16	2,409	167	17,631	2,242		15	1,836	42	8,062	1,79
	23	1,134	296	18,469	838		22	622	0	8,684	62
	30	3,626	313	21,782	3,313		29	2,058	90	10,652	1,96
Dec.	7	2,244	465	23,561	1,779	Dec.	6	2,241	66	12,827	2,17
	14	2,154	410	25,305	1,744		13	1,693	85	14,435	1,60
	21	1,323	138	26,490	1,185		20	1,505	96	15,844	1,40
	28	1,328	0	27,818	1,328		27	4,735	216	20,363	4,51

[1] 57 Chicago and Outside Combined Chicago Mercantile Exchange approved warehouses. *Source: Chicago Mercantile Exchange (CME)*

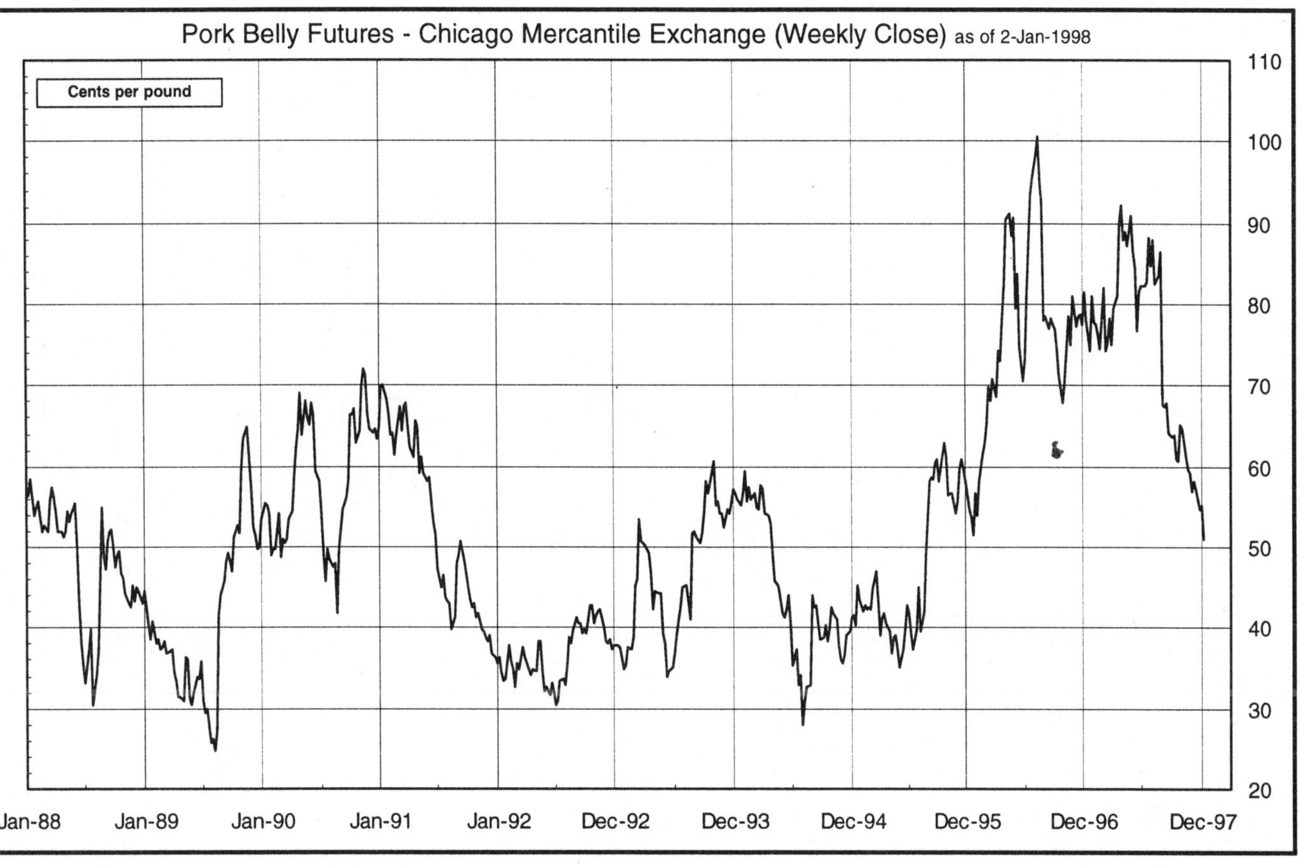

Average Open Interest of Pork Belly Futures in Chicago In Contracts

Year	Jan.	Feb.	Mar.	Apr.	May	June	July	Aug.	Sept.	Oct.	Nov.	Dec.
1988	11,250	10,942	13,421	16,229	17,887	18,428	15,782	11,874	14,678	15,860	19,292	19,723
1989	20,453	20,444	21,897	22,117	24,931	25,898	20,053	12,724	11,916	12,501	14,802	13,844
1990	12,885	12,114	13,017	15,338	14,513	13,038	11,146	6,104	6,059	7,851	11,419	12,589
1991	11,777	10,187	9,776	11,509	10,436	10,111	7,356	6,176	7,532	10,813	13,173	12,844
1992	12,521	12,195	11,901	12,345	12,497	13,598	12,623	7,149	6,540	7,033	9,251	10,953
1993	10,623	9,244	8,283	8,626	10,096	11,092	9,031	5,427	4,644	7,241	8,701	9,121
1994	11,053	10,426	9,375	9,894	8,092	8,248	7,836	7,841	8,398	10,072	10,141	10,216
1995	10,294	9,080	7,809	7,367	8,017	7,036	5,666	4,271	6,246	7,007	7,103	7,282
1996	7,094	8,028	10,521	10,753	10,018	8,136	6,432	6,296	6,056	6,395	6,050	6,480
1997	7,504	7,930	7,260	7,165	8,950	7,203	5,905	4,791	5,242	7,520	8,302	9,009

Source: Chicago Mercantile Exchange (CME)

Volume of Trading of Pork Belly Futures in Chicago In Contracts

Year	Jan.	Feb.	Mar.	Apr.	May	June	July	Aug.	Sept.	Oct.	Nov.	Dec.	Total
1988	70,150	76,741	85,947	99,754	116,780	179,505	112,356	90,371	79,667	94,646	84,236	96,446	1,186,599
1989	107,577	89,922	84,768	90,353	145,975	152,207	119,733	91,200	75,155	106,389	141,983	105,714	1,310,976
1990	109,036	100,813	129,476	133,946	165,880	143,663	122,187	74,653	53,428	76,549	112,752	80,746	1,303,129
1991	106,078	89,975	88,056	111,195	119,773	96,273	74,255	59,176	65,604	80,707	63,331	50,773	1,005,196
1992	80,697	79,700	67,470	57,565	73,137	73,081	78,588	54,663	39,839	64,248	60,724	54,440	784,152
1993	77,380	62,871	63,988	62,403	62,400	70,124	65,496	42,613	37,992	47,780	60,163	49,099	698,799
1994	60,316	67,250	58,183	53,839	56,575	58,424	50,450	47,626	38,375	45,525	49,280	47,803	633,646
1995	62,994	54,330	59,324	43,501	49,453	53,571	45,869	36,623	31,112	35,444	47,061	42,631	561,913
1996	48,563	56,623	61,669	61,703	61,868	55,337	55,121	45,399	39,182	48,973	42,709	35,502	612,649
1997	60,761	53,604	56,750	76,072	62,190	54,043	55,043	36,153	31,154	44,277	31,663	33,609	595,319

Source: Chicago Mercantile Exchange (CME)

PORK BELLIES

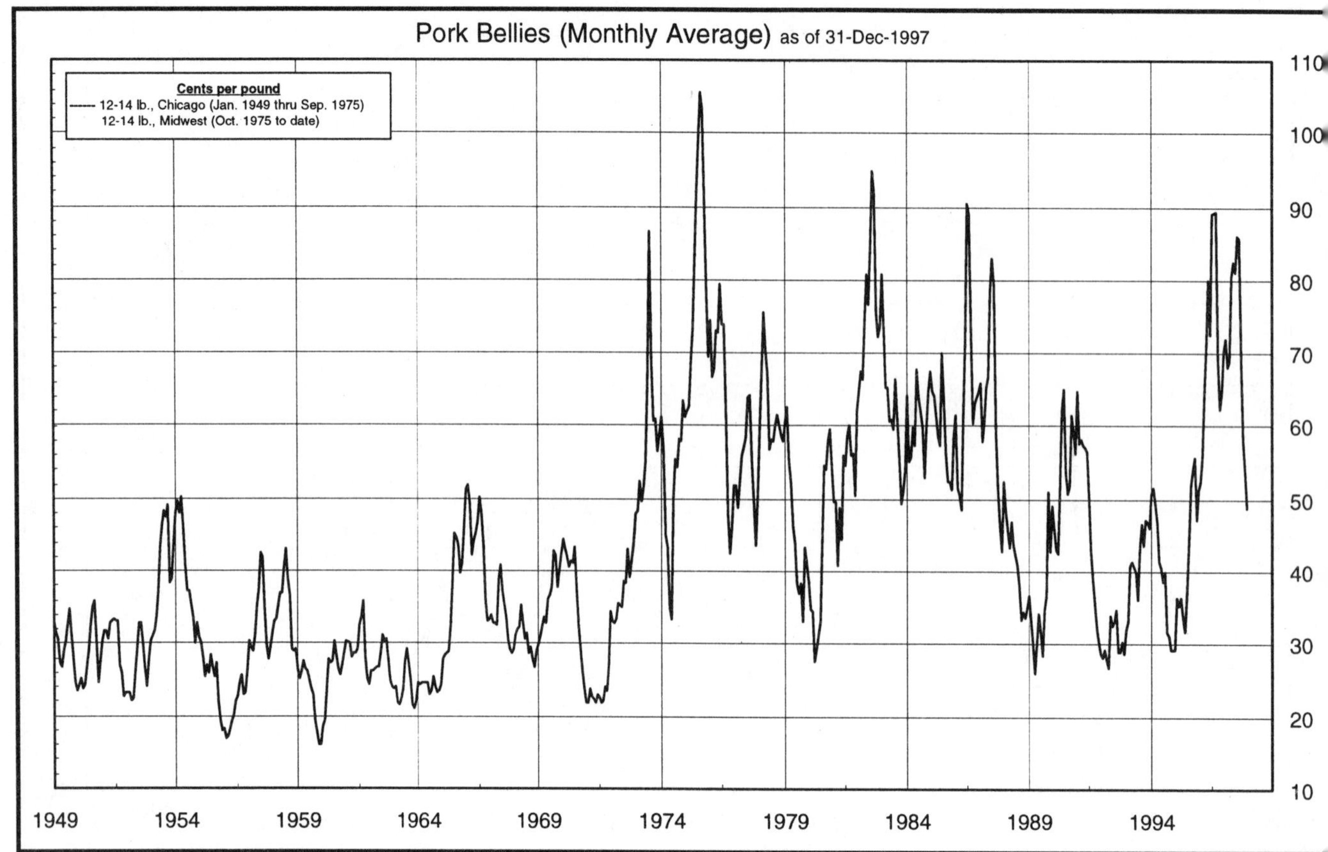

Average Price of Pork Bellies (12-14 lbs.) Midwest In Cents Per Pound

Year	Jan.	Feb.	Mar.	Apr.	May	June	July	Aug.	Sept.	Oct.	Nov.	Dec.	Average
1988	51.82	48.40	45.32	43.13	46.09	45.51	40.84	37.46	33.05	34.97	33.64	34.82	41.25
1989	36.91	31.41	30.19	25.49	29.11	32.90	31.52	28.82	34.23	36.88	49.96	42.23	34.14
1990	48.65	42.53	42.60	52.60	61.48	65.15	53.18	51.08	51.31	59.83	60.57	56.58	53.80
1991	64.11	57.20	58.52	57.25	57.50	56.48	50.40	42.01	38.97	32.26	30.04	28.79	47.79
1992	28.05	29.44	28.01	26.93	34.09	32.78	32.77	35.13	29.09	29.13	30.48	28.80	30.39
1993	31.97	33.22	41.28	41.19	39.86	36.24	44.51	46.68	43.82	47.25	47.21	46.21	41.62
1994	50.63	51.66	49.68	46.84	41.40	40.39	38.64	39.60	31.50	31.33	29.09	29.29	40.00
1995	36.03	35.80	36.30	33.83	31.70	37.94	43.10	52.42	54.43	56.20	47.28	51.45	43.04
1996	52.33	56.33	64.50	69.86	79.50	72.64	89.49	88.40	68.12	63.07	65.27	70.07	69.97
1997[1]	72.04	68.42	59.05	80.54	82.58	80.68	86.70	85.43	72.25	57.97	53.77	47.52	70.58

[1] Preliminary. *Source: Economic Research Service, U.S. Department of Agriculture (ERS-USDA)*

Average Price of Pork Loins (14-18 lbs.) Central, U.S. In Cents Per Pound

Year	Jan.	Feb.	Mar.	Apr.	May	June	July	Aug.	Sept.	Oct.	Nov.	Dec.	Average
1988	102.43	94.93	87.82	94.03	112.74	111.31	104.96	106.88	97.92	85.33	77.87	93.61	97.49
1989	89.35	90.97	91.77	91.59	99.95	108.28	115.10	110.03	105.25	111.98	91.75	107.28	101.11
1990	101.36	107.75	117.26	120.68	136.06	125.62	144.14	119.56	121.64	113.71	98.94	103.50	117.52
1991	107.67	109.13	110.33	104.81	120.48	123.49	121.73	117.54	105.85	100.87	88.63	90.19	108.39
1992	96.89	99.13	94.10	98.65	108.94	113.94	108.22	111.18	102.98	96.98	89.64	96.22	101.41
1993	98.22	100.05	100.61	107.61	111.16	122.28	113.40	116.73	116.74	111.85	98.68	92.33	107.47
1994	103.90	110.75	100.45	101.89	103.99	103.84	109.79	112.86	105.34	95.65	80.00	89.50	101.50
1995	96.94	102.20	95.30	93.33	103.50	118.81	124.65	127.98	117.63	108.23	93.94	110.39	107.74
1996	110.00	116.43	120.49	119.70	131.61	115.73	126.16	118.18	112.28	115.40	115.39	120.45	118.49
1997[1]	112.50	109.50	106.58	117.16	125.68	116.28	122.53	119.28	112.07	99.68	85.99	79.44	108.89

[1] Preliminary. *Source: Economic Research Service, U.S. Department of Agriculture (ERS-USDA)*

Potatoes

Potatoes are the largest vegetable crop grown in the U.S. 1996 production reached a record 499 million cwt., up 12 percent from 1995 and seven percent over the previous record of 467 million cwt. in 1994. The two primary reasons for the large 1996 crop were an average yield at a record high 350 cwt. per acre and a four percent increase in harvested acreage over 1995.

Total consumption also rose to a record in 1996, suggesting that the 1995 contraction in demand was only a temporary pause in a steady annualized growth in demand. Total foodstock usage rose to 283.4 million cwt. in 1996 vs. 255.8 million in 1995, of which frozen french fries accounted for a record high 145.5 million cwt., up 16 million cwt. from the previous year. For a time, in the mid-1990's, there was concern that the U.S. consumer affinity for deep-fried processed potatoes may have peaked, 1996's demand proved otherwise. Tablestock use (fresh potatoes) in 1996 of 131 million cwt. compares with 123 million in 1995.

Potatoes are grown in all fifty states, but the crop is divided into four seasonal groups based on harvest time. The fall crop, consisting of about two dozen states, accounts for 85-90 percent of total production and is usually harvested from September through November. The winter crop is the smallest and harvested only in Florida and California from January into March. Spring and summer crop production tends to be fairly close in size. The seasonal disparities reflect major differences in planted acreage and realized yield which is consistently higher in the fall producing states. The marketing season follows the harvest, but the movement of the fall crop can extend into the following July with supplies drawn from storage. The inventoried fall crop can serve as a supply buffer in the event the spring and summer crops are short. Large fall stocks can be a depressant on prices should earlier crops prove large. Generally about one third of farm marketings occur during September and October.

Harvested acreage in 1996 of 1.43 million acres compares with 1.37 million in 1995, of which fall acreage accounted for 1.25 million acres and 1.21 million, respectively. Idaho is the nation's largest producer with a 1996 fall crop of 143 million cwt. vs. 133 million in 1994. Washington's crop, at a distant second, of 95 million cwt. compares with 81 million in 1995. As usual, Washington's average yield was the nation's highest, 590 cwt. per acre in 1996 compared to Idaho's 346 cwt. per acre. Maine, once the largest fall producing state, realized a crop of only 22 million cwt. vs. 17 million in 1995. Maine's decline in ranking largely reflects the wide variety of potatoes grown in the state, about 80, whereas in Idaho production is focused on one type of potato, the Russet Burbank, enhancing marketing consistency and consumer preference.

The value of the 1996 crop was estimated at $2.4 billion, down 19 percent from the 1995 record high and in fact the lowest dollar value since 1992. The average price received by farmers in 1996 of $4.93 per cwt., the lowest since 1987, compares with $6.77 in 1995. On the retail level, the price of processed potatoes is usually about three times higher than tablestock.

Some 60 percent of U.S. production is processed, either into frozen products or as a direct consumer food, such as potato chips. Frozen french fries account for most of all frozen use. Chips and shoestrings account for about 20 percent of total processing use. In 1996 there were 122 chip producing plants in the U.S. vs. 130 in 1995, most of which are located in the eastern half of the U.S. Foreign trade in U.S. potatoes is small. Japan imports processed potatoes, mostly french fries, while Canada exports fresh potatoes which are used mostly for seed.

Futures Markets

Potato futures and options are traded on the New York Cotton Exchange (NYCE) and the London Commodity Exchange (LCE). Potato futures are traded on the Marche a Terme International de France (MATIF).

Salient Statistics of Potatoes in the United States

Crop Year	Acreage: Planted (1,000 Acres)	Acreage: Harvested (1,000 Acres)	Yield Per Harvested Acre Cwt.	Total Production (In Thousands of Cwt.)	Farm Disposition – Used Where Grown: Seed & Feed (In Thousands of Cwt.)	Farm Disposition – Used Where Grown: Shrinkage & Loss (In Thousands of Cwt.)	Farm Disposition: Sold[2] (In Thousands of Cwt.)	Farm Price $ Cwt.	Value of Production[3] (Million $)	Value of Sales (Million $)	Stocks on Jan. 1 1,000 Cwt	Foreign Trade[5] (Fresh): Domestic Exports (Millions of Lbs.)	Foreign Trade[5] (Fresh): Imports (Millions of Lbs.)	Consumption[5] Per Capita in Pounds: Fresh	Consumption[5] Per Capita in Pounds: Total
1988	1,285	1,259	283	356,438	5,810	25,067	325,561	6.02	2,144	1,958	177,750	421,985	388,394	49.6	122.4
1989	1,305	1,282	289	370,444	5,722	24,974	339,748	7.36	2,717	2,501	173,550	467,836	509,347	50.0	127.1
1990	1,400	1,371	293	402,110	5,949	28,329	367,832	6.08	2,409	2,240	194,460	327,333	482,903	45.8	127.7
1991	1,408	1,374	304	417,622	5,995	32,429	379,198	4.96	2,043	1,880	211,005	341,682	437,349	46.4	130.4
1992	1,339	1,315	323	425,367	5,925	33,807	385,637	5.52	2,336	2,129	215,990	537,939	273,515	48.9	132.4
1993	1,385	1,317	326	428,693	5,931	30,152	392,610	6.17	2,637	2,424	217,800	539,345	541,382	49.7	136.9
1994	1,416	1,380	339	467,054	5,878	37,166	424,010	5.58	2,590	2,367	237,960	655,026	405,899	48.6	140.2
1995	1,398	1,372	323	443,606	5,745	29,530	408,331	6.77	2,992	2,762	223,150	583,938	458,926	50.7	137.9
1996[1]	1,456	1,426	350	498,633	6,231	41,234	451,168	4.93	2,431	2,225	262,120	564,010	690,768	48.8	142.8
1997[1]	1,362	1,326	347	459,912							240,850			50.8	142.4

[1] Preliminary. [2] For all purposes, including food, seed processing & livestock feed. [3] Farm weight basis, excluding canned and frozen potatoes.

Source: Economic Research Service, U.S. Department of Agriculture (ERS-USDA)

POTATOES

Cold Storage Stocks of All Frozen Potatoes in the United States, on First of Month   In Millions of Pounds

Year	Jan.	Feb.	Mar.	Apr.	May	June	July	Aug.	Sept.	Oct.	Nov.	Dec.
1988	882.6	899.0	977.7	965.1	950.7	963.9	1,000.8	882.5	835.0	917.9	1,047.5	1,044.4
1989	988.7	927.4	944.3	947.3	968.7	986.7	961.5	739.9	611.3	734.2	878.7	938.0
1990	917.3	932.7	995.6	1,041.2	1,059.0	1,061.3	977.6	769.3	688.1	852.5	995.6	999.5
1991	975.8	993.3	988.9	1,041.5	1,052.3	1,167.2	1,216.5	935.5	880.1	985.5	1,148.0	1,037.2
1992	980.8	996.5	1,036.3	1,082.7	1,077.6	1,137.3	1,131.4	966.4	948.7	949.1	1,067.1	1,038.7
1993	963.2	971.2	1,028.2	1,046.6	912.7	979.5	989.8	932.8	902.8	1,019.5	1,184.7	1,130.7
1994	1,006.4	1,019.9	1,057.1	1,054.4	1,050.5	1,118.9	1,099.9	979.8	1,028.2	1,108.7	1,189.0	1,163.5
1995	1,096.6	1,156.0	1,179.9	1,169.0	1,138.0	1,125.4	1,116.5	992.4	992.6	1,145.3	1,225.6	1,174.5
1996	1,123.7	1,147.2	1,172.5	1,164.6	1,112.1	1,076.4	1,059.7	907.1	957.8	1,124.9	1,225.2	1,146.3
1997[1]	1,098.4	1,111.5	1,180.1	1,177.1	1,195.8	1,213.3	1,271.3	1,214.2	1,130.8	1,269.0	1,354.8	1,314.0

[1] Preliminary. *Source: Agricultural Statistics Board, U.S. Department of Agriculture (ASB-USDA)*

Potato Crop Production Estimates, Stocks and Disappearance in the United States   In Millions of Cwt.

	Crop Production Estimates					Total Storage Stocks[2]						Fall Crop				
	Total Crop			Fall Crop		Following Year						1,000 Cwt.				
Year	Oct. 1	Nov. 1	Dec. 1	Oct. 1	Nov. 1	Dec. 1	Jan. 1	Feb. 1	Mar. 1	Apr. 1	May 1	Production	Disappearance (Sold)	Dec. 1 Stocks	Average Price $/Cwt.	Value of Sales $1,000
1988	------	352.1	------	------	322.7	206.4	177.8	151.1	124.5	92.6	59.4	305,623	284,205	206,420	5.82	1,652,864
1989	------	367.3	------	------	342.5	202.1	173.6	144.3	116.6	84.3	50.7	316,097	295,605	202,050	6.76	1,999,104
1990	------	393.2	------	------	371.7	225.5	194.5	162.9	134.5	101.2	63.0	344,200	320,033	225,500	5.42	1,734,476
1991	------	417.6	------	------	379.5	242.1	211.0	178.5	145.8	108.9	69.1	363,541	334,893	242,070	4.16	1,393,749
1992	------	425.4	------	------	372.4	246.8	216.0	184.6	152.8	115.8	75.0	368,516	341,209	246,820	5.17	1,762,984
1993	------	428.7	------	------	372.4	249.7	217.8	186.1	154.1	116.0	73.9	375,004	351,161	249,710	5.65	1,981,017
1994	------	467.9	------	------	412.4	272.3	238.0	201.9	168.1	128.4	87.4	408,139	378,333	272,290	5.06	1,914,311
1995	------	444.8	------	------	402.4	256.3	223.2	189.0	155.7	116.3	76.2	392,942	368,946	256,310	6.43	2,590,294
1996	------	491.5	------	------	447.9	291.3	256.5	220.5	184.6	143.2	100.8	441,083	407,326	295,100	4.35	1,964,766
1997[1]	------	459.4	------	------	417.5	274.3	240.9	205.9				406,964		274,250		

[1] Preliminary. [2] Held by growers and local dealers in the fall producing areas. *Source: Agricultural Statistics Board, U.S. Department of Agriculture*

Production of Potatoes by Seasonal Groups in the United States   In Thousands of Cwt.

		Spring			Summer			Fall								
Year	Winter	California	Florida	Total	New Mexico	Virgina	Total	Colorado	Idaho	Maine	Minnesota	North Dakota	Oregon	Washington	Wisconsin	Total
1988	2,616	7,546	6,753	20,110	3,060	2,048	20,154	19,040	102,610	22,000	13,860	15,525	20,735	63,250	20,000	313,55
1989	2,764	7,875	6,860	20,852	4,025	1,440	22,155	20,603	102,475	22,000	13,860	15,070	23,308	64,310	23,120	324,67
1990	2,343	8,438	8,714	24,163	3,400	1,980	23,097	22,750	119,070	20,520	14,280	16,675	23,450	67,980	23,075	352,50
1991	2,609	8,284	6,600	20,636	3,450	1,485	22,647	23,800	122,175	18,170	17,160	30,030	22,170	75,435	23,275	371,73
1992	2,998	7,238	7,750	21,535	952	1,980	21,309	22,110	127,050	24,300	16,080	27,690	21,075	69,300	25,160	379,52
1993	2,552	7,508	6,068	19,654	1,290	1,760	14,922	25,270	126,192	19,890	14,780	21,090	23,103	88,500	22,588	391,56
1994	2,372	7,790	8,588	22,646	1,088	1,425	17,381	25,795	138,801	18,375	20,035	28,200	27,514	88,920	25,740	424,65
1995	2,473	6,230	7,830	20,193	1,344	2,040	17,931	23,808	132,657	17,160	20,790	25,410	24,788	80,850	26,000	403,00
1996	3,273	7,538	7,765	22,417	1,404	1,688	19,507	29,175	142,800	21,175	24,600	28,820	30,124	94,990	31,590	453,43
1997[1]	3,124	8,280	6,641	21,749	1,376	1,463	17,951	25,377	135,430	19,170	20,440	21,525	27,161	88,060	27,923	417,08

[1] Preliminary. *Source: Agricultural Statistics Board, U.S. Department of Agriculture (ASB-USDA)*

Utilization of Potatoes in the United States   In Thousands of Cwt.

	Sales											Non-sales			
		For Processing							Other Sales						
Crop Year	Table Stock	Chips, Shoe-strings	For Dehyd-ration	Frozen French Fries	Other Frozen Products	Canned Potatoes	Other Canned Products[2]	Starch & Flour	Livestock Feed	Seed	Total Sale	Used on Farms Where Grown	Shrink-age & Loss	Total Non-sales	Total
1987	129,097	40,593	30,823	101,377	18,305	2,958	1,597	2,184	3,808	21,023	351,765	4,521	31,901	37,555	389,32
1988	108,348	44,539	28,786	95,466	17,558	2,941	2,031	1,416	3,330	21,146	325,561	4,827	25,067	30,877	356,43
1989	113,932	43,071	32,187	100,459	19,115	3,138	1,858	898	2,800	22,290	339,748	4,735	24,974	30,696	370,44
1990	119,545	44,489	38,838	108,455	23,915	2,526	2,075	1,699	3,264	23,026	367,832	5,035	28,329	34,278	402,11
1991	126,953	45,850	40,395	111,128	23,097	2,465	1,886	1,739	3,652	22,033	379,198	4,988	32,429	38,424	417,62
1992	127,215	48,455	38,078	112,496	23,016	2,710	2,557	1,610	3,928	23,529	385,637	4,746	33,807	39,730	425,36
1993	123,802	48,987	40,795	121,087	25,190	1,879	2,458	1,691	2,498	24,223	392,610	4,808	30,152	36,083	428,69
1994	133,989	49,299	41,381	136,531	26,362	2,503	3,006	2,176	4,147	24,616	424,010	4,732	37,166	43,044	467,05
1995	123,462	47,284	45,065	129,029	27,073	3,342	2,385	1,668	3,224	25,799	408,331	4,783	29,530	35,275	443,60
1996[1]	131,402	47,969	54,261	145,489	28,728	2,828	2,211	1,956	12,073	24,251	451,168	4,690	41,234	47,465	498,63

[1] Preliminary. [2] Hash, stews and soups. *Source: Agricultural Statistics Board, U.S. Department of Agriculture (ASB-USDA)*

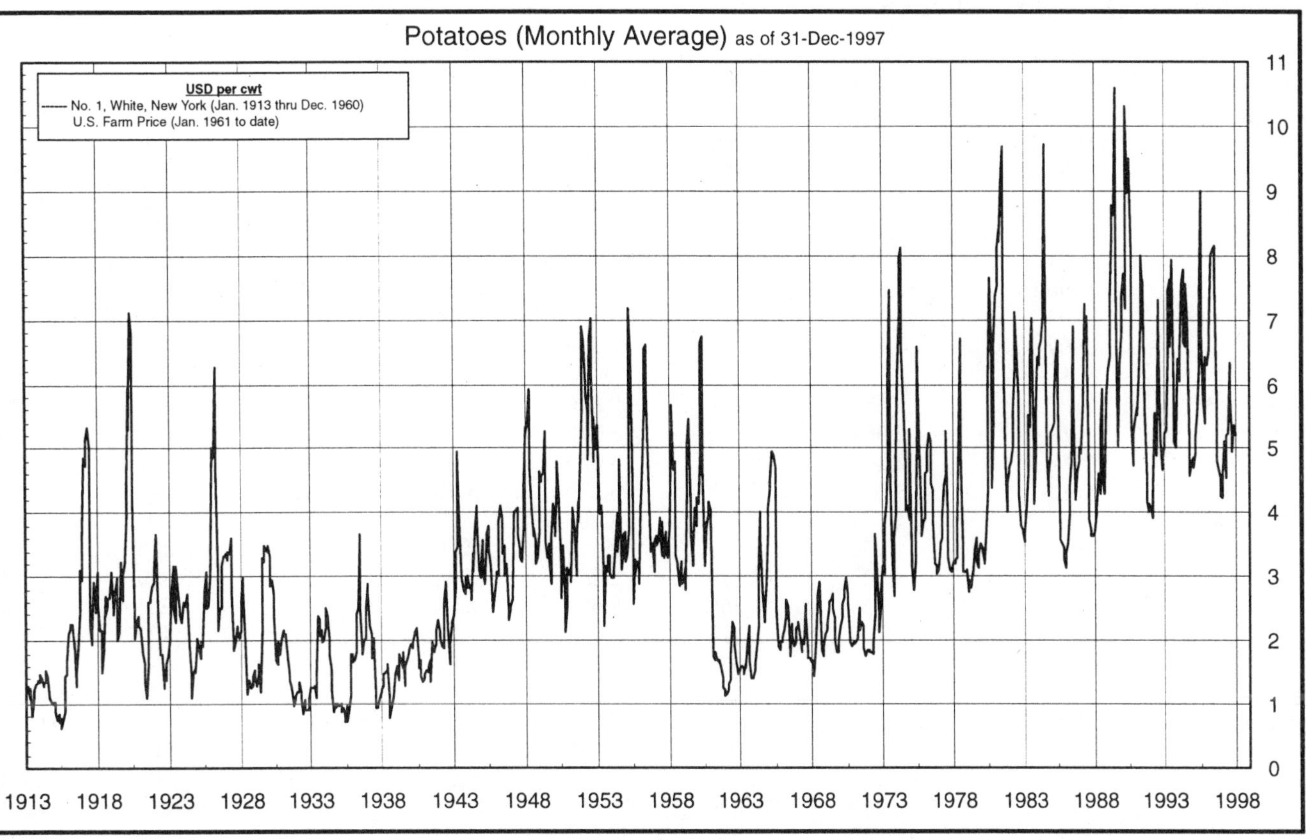

Per Capita Utilization of Potatoes in the United States in Pounds (Farm Weight)

			Processing				
Year	Total	Fresh	Freezing	Chips & Shoe-string	Dehy-drating	Canning	Total
1989	127.1	50.0	46.8	17.5	10.8	2.0	77.1
1990	127.7	45.8	50.2	17.0	12.8	1.9	81.9
1991	130.4	46.4	51.3	17.3	13.7	1.7	84.0
1992	132.4	48.9	51.0	17.5	13.2	1.8	83.5
1993	136.9	49.7	54.5	17.6	13.4	1.7	87.2
1994	140.2	48.6	59.3	17.1	13.5	1.7	91.6
1995	137.9	50.7	55.3	16.9	13.0	2.0	87.2
1996	142.8	48.8	59.8	17.0	15.1	2.1	94.0
1997[1]	142.4	50.8	57.7	16.9	14.9	2.1	91.6
1998[2]	140.2	49.0	57.0	17.0	15.2	2.0	91.2

[1] Preliminary. [2] Forecast. *Source: Agricultural Statistics Board, U.S. Department of Agriculture (ASB-USDA)*

Average Price Received by Farmers for Potatoes in the United States In Dollars Per Cwt.

Year	Jan.	Feb.	Mar.	Apr.	May	June	July	Aug.	Sept.	Oct.	Nov.	Dec.	Season Average
1988	3.70	3.74	4.02	4.11	4.62	4.30	5.28	5.91	4.55	4.30	5.72	5.79	6.02
1989	6.24	6.43	7.34	8.33	8.78	8.61	10.60	7.58	5.06	5.03	6.32	6.81	7.36
1990	7.36	7.71	9.17	10.30	9.32	8.96	9.50	8.09	5.36	4.73	5.24	5.46	6.08
1991	5.66	5.53	6.15	7.03	7.98	7.51	7.95	5.39	4.51	4.06	3.99	4.29	4.96
1992	4.07	4.08	4.64	5.16	4.43	4.71	7.00	6.64	4.89	4.55	4.90	5.06	5.52
1993	5.15	5.29	6.06	7.19	7.18	6.45	7.61	6.05	5.12	4.96	6.40	6.12	6.17
1994	6.02	6.43	7.67	6.69	6.59	6.67	7.49	6.99	5.03	4.57	4.80	4.86	5.58
1995	4.88	4.90	5.39	5.54	5.77	6.98	8.60	6.81	5.76	5.38	6.42	6.29	6.77
1996	6.65	6.92	7.51	7.83	8.09	8.14	8.09	5.79	4.83	4.76	4.43	4.32	5.11
1997[1]	4.23	4.50	5.12	4.55	5.19	5.23	6.34	6.33	5.16	4.96	5.36	5.40	

[1] Preliminary. *Source: Agricultural Statistics Board, U.S. Department of Agriculture (ASB-USDA)*

POTATOES

Potatoes Processed[1] in the United States, Eight States In Thousands of Cwt.

States	Storage Season	to Dec. 1	to Jan. 1	to Feb. 1	to Mar. 1	to Apr. 1	to May 1	Entire Season
Idaho and Oregon-Malheur Co	1988-9	18,740	24,270	29,420	34,720	41,360	48,080	64,425
	1989-90	22,200	28,140	34,240	40,270	46,330	51,810	66,010
	1990-1	24,780	31,100	37,550	44,220	51,030	58,660	78,500
	1991-2	22,980	28,910	35,700	42,840	50,260	57,290	78,690
	1992-3	22,180	29,080	35,710	42,800	50,090	57,090	80,570
	1993-4	24,090	30,540	37,150	44,720	53,070	61,440	85,780
	1994-5	26,620	34,230	42,330	49,890	57,990	66,680	90,300
	1995-6	27,310	35,040	43,260	51,530	59,060	66,690	89,250
	1996-7	31,060	38,210	45,420	54,640	62,570	70,720	96,970
	1997-8	26,880	33,950	41,050				
Maine[2]	1988-9	1,685	2,190	2,830	3,455	4,230	4,915	6,915
	1989-90	2,055	2,660	3,510	4,000	4,620	5,210	6,900
	1990-1	2,105	2,690	3,420	3,900	4,460	5,120	6,750
	1991-2	2,015	2,450	3,050	3,350	3,900	4,445	5,210
	1992-3	1,195	1,630	2,205	2,720	3,390	4,020	5,055
	1993-4	1,350	1,720	2,210	2,505	2,890	3,275	4,555
	1994-5	1,505	1,840	2,265	2,540	2,985	3,330	4,770
	1995-6	1,455	1,850	2,430	2,850	3,435	3,965	5,725
	1996-7	1,790	2,115	2,820	3,280	3,820	4,420	6,495
	1997-8	1,245	1,655	2,285				
Washington and Oregon-Other	1988-9	19,200	23,455	27,280	31,960	37,575	41,795	51,555
	1989-90	23,635	28,015	33,170	38,610	44,510	49,595	57,695
	1990-1	24,780	29,830	35,170	39,950	45,600	50,780	61,450
	1991-2	26,345	30,570	35,320	41,320	47,120	52,605	65,210
	1992-3	26,840	31,550	35,950	41,670	46,530	51,630	63,510
	1993-4	28,260	33,350	39,010	45,020	51,290	57,180	70,690
	1994-5	28,670	33,480	39,120	46,070	52,940	59,540	76,780
	1995-6	30,000	35,170	39,460	45,280	51,730	57,360	70,250
	1996-7	31,670	36,660	41,700	48,740	55,570	62,320	80,970
	1997-8	28,580	33,990	38,690				
Other States[3]	1988-9	5,805	7,450	9,040	10,645	12,340	14,075	18,385
	1989-90	6,340	8,010	9,860	11,535	13,240	15,100	20,610
	1990-1	6,585	8,605	10,405	12,425	14,635	17,010	24,005
	1991-2	7,515	9,350	11,580	13,585	15,685	17,935	24,990
	1992-3	7,140	9,220	11,265	13,305	15,550	17,555	25,070
	1993-4	7,605	9,515	11,605	13,720	16,080	18,705	25,690
	1994-5	9,725	13,110	15,630	18,260	21,115	24,060	32,260
	1995-6	12,650	15,630	18,815	21,985	25,510	28,610	33,580
	1996-7	13,660	16,570	20,140	23,510	26,990	29,890	40,275
	1997-8	11,335	13,550	16,615				
Total	1988-9	45,430	57,365	68,570	80,780	95,505	108,865	144,280
	1989-90	54,230	66,825	80,780	94,415	108,700	121,715	151,215
	1990-1	58,250	72,225	86,545	100,495	115,725	131,570	170,705
	1991-2	58,855	71,280	85,650	101,095	116,965	132,275	174,100
	1992-3	57,355	71,480	85,130	100,495	115,560	130,295	174,205
	1993-4	61,305	75,125	89,975	105,965	123,330	140,600	186,715
	1994-5	66,520	82,660	99,345	116,760	135,030	153,610	204,110
	1995-6	71,415	87,690	103,965	121,645	139,735	156,625	198,805
	1996-7	78,180	93,555	110,080	130,170	148,950	167,350	224,710
	1997-8	68,040	83,145	98,640				

[1] Total quantity received and used for processing regardless of the state in which the potatoes were produced. Excluding quantities used for potato chips in Maine, Michigan, Minnesota, North Dakota or Wisconsin. [2] Includes Maine grown potatoes only. [3] Michigan, Minnesota, North Dakota and Wisconsin.
Source: National Agricultural Statistics Service, U.S. Department of Agriculture (NASS-USDA)

Rayon and Other Synthetic Fibers

World Cellulosic Fiber Production In Thousands of Metric Tons

Year	Austria	Brazil	China	Czech Republic	Finland	Germany	India	Japan	Taiwan	United Kingdom	United States	Former U.S.S.R.	Total
1988	132.0	51.5	184.4	58.3	60.4	277.1	174.1	290.6	125.8	64.0	278.3	601.0	2,896
1989	136.0	55.0	204.0	56.9	64.8	278.4	198.7	272.9	147.6	55.0	263.3	584.0	2,943
1990	135.0	54.5	214.3	55.0	63.8	199.1	216.7	275.8	147.9	71.0	229.2	544.0	2,757
1991	120.0	53.0	242.0	33.5	47.4	118.0	215.4	266.4	149.1	63.0	220.7	401.7	2,433
1992	128.3	54.2	249.0	39.3	56.0	139.9	219.9	254.4	139.3	65.0	224.5	292.3	2,327
1993	131.2	56.7	276.2	41.0	56.5	127.1	238.9	244.4	130.8	67.2	228.9	258.3	2,286
1994	134.3	62.8	336.1	41.7	58.5	136.2	239.7	218.9	149.3	67.4	226.0	176.0	2,340
1995	139.4	53.1	435.0	35.0	57.5	143.5	262.1	212.7	139.6	67.1	226.0	188.4	2,247
1996[1]	145.0	50.1	432.0	31.5	49.8	143.6	251.9	160.5	144.7	62.3	215.9	127.3	2,066
1997[2]	145.0	61.9	540.0	51.2	62.0	155.0	304.1	282.9	163.9	70.0	283.1	401.2	2,937

[1] Preliminary. [2] Producing capacity. *Source: Fiber Economics Bureau, Inc. (FEB)*

World Noncellulosic Fiber Production (Except Olefin) In Thousands of Metric Tons

Year	Brazil	China	Germany	India	Italy/ Malta	Japan	Rep. of Korea	Mexico	Spain	Taiwan	United States	Former U.S.S.R.	Total
1988	239.7	1,074.5	926.3	321.6	568.2	1,351.9	1,115.0	340.3	302.3	1,430.2	3,146.9	601.0	14,418
1989	245.8	1,223.2	952.3	366.7	547.7	1,380.9	1,189.9	352.8	252.3	1,523.1	3,119.4	874.0	14,747
1990	207.8	1,342.8	777.0	436.6	578.3	1,425.0	1,269.7	366.8	255.0	1,621.5	2,886.0	893.5	14,894
1991	219.1	1,488.9	797.0	439.6	564.6	1,429.8	1,365.2	395.3	241.1	1,841.4	2,902.9	804.8	15,273
1992	218.2	1,586.7	817.3	538.0	589.9	1,448.8	1,451.4	426.6	257.0	2,042.6	2,980.6	656.8	15,911
1993	233.3	1,871.9	758.8	608.9	551.6	1,365.1	1,581.3	406.5	240.3	2,122.8	3,016.1	669.8	16,653
1994	239.1	2,299.2	807.6	681.0	599.9	1,374.0	1,673.5	418.4	273.6	2,295.9	3,193.3	658.1	17,908
1995	227.4	2,282.0	771.3	738.0	551.3	1,400.0	1,859.2	516.5	252.3	2,410.5	3,225.2	636.1	18,482
1996[1]	236.3	2,627.0	-----	897.6	-----	1,395.0	2,025.6	552.9	-----	2,561.0	3,254.0	1,359.8	19,667
1997[2]	336.1	3,499.0	-----	1,622.5	-----	1,812.8	2,633.4	632.0	-----	3,017.7	3,844.5	-----	25,659

[1] Preliminary. [2] Producing capacity. *Source: Fiber Economics Bureau, Inc. (FEB)*

World Production of Synthetic Fibers In Thousands of Metric Tons

	Noncellulosic Fiber Production (Except Olefin)							Glass Fiber Production							
	By Fibers				World Total										
Year	Acrylic & Mod-acrylic	Nylon & Aramid	Polyester	Other Fibers[3]	Yarn & Monofil-aments	Staple & Tow & Fiberfill	Total	Europe	Japan	Other Americas	United States	Total	China	Former U.S.S.R.	Cigarette Tow Pro-duction
1988	2,452	3,725	8,102	138	6,572	7,845	14,417	465	340	65	730	1,655	65	125	412
1989	2,341	3,795	8,459	152	6,847	7,900	14,747	470	345	65	735	1,680	70	133	443
1990	2,320	3,738	8,678	158	7,035	7,859	14,894	445	371	60	675	1,631	75	120	464
1991	2,385	3,605	9,116	167	7,241	8,032	15,273	441	293	75	650	1,561	65	133	480
1992	2,363	3,662	9,729	157	7,673	8,238	15,911	442	307	83	700	1,652	75	130	475
1993	2,297	3,707	10,512	136	8,478	8,174	16,652	508	312	86	794	1,865	77	69	482
1994	2,472	3,770	11,500	162	9,107	8,797	17,904	545	313	87	959	2,076	78	64	536
1995	2,436	3,816	12,003	227	9,863	8,619	18,483	567	318	96	981	2,141	85	55	550
1996[1]	2,577	3,921	12,941	227	10,318	9,348	19,666	585	316	94	996	2,175	98	54	584
1997[2]	3,048	5,212	17,048	352	13,572	12,087	25,659	757	324	105	1,180	2,581	130	83	-----

[1] Preliminary. [2] Producing capacity. [3] Alginate, azion, spandex, saran, etc. *Source: Fiber Economics Bureau, Inc. (FEB)*

Artificial (Cellulosic) Fiber Distribution in the United States In Millions of Pounds

	Yarn & Monofilament					Staple & Tow					
	Producers' Shipments					Producers' Shipments					
Year	Domestic	Exports	Total	Imports	Domestic Con-sumption	Domestic	Exports	Total	Imports	Domestic Con-sumption	Glass Fiber Ship-ments
1988	182.6	34.1	216.7	17.6	200.2	386.0	20.5	406.5	20.4	406.4	1,587.6
1989	187.3	31.7	219.0	26.3	213.6	338.2	16.2	354.4	54.0	392.2	1,530.1
1990	172.7	34.0	206.7	24.2	196.9	291.7	12.5	304.2	111.6	403.3	1,519.1
1991	179.9	32.3	212.2	30.8	210.7	255.5	8.1	263.6	92.0	347.5	1,488.5
1992	182.9	35.1	218.0	32.1	215.0	260.7	6.9	267.6	85.6	346.3	1,629.7
1993	196.5	31.5	228.0	40.4	236.9	273.6	10.3	283.9	89.5	363.1	1,780.6
1994	190.3	32.9	223.2	32.9	223.2	252.3	30.7	283.0	65.7	318.0	2,016.0
1995	169.3	41.5	210.8	34.0	203.3	259.8	28.7	288.5	40.8	300.6	2,089.0
1996[1]	168.9	49.7	218.6	39.3	208.2	225.4	20.0	245.4	35.3	260.7	2,326.0

[1] Preliminary. *Source: Fiber Economics Bureau, Inc. (FEB)*

RAYON AND OTHER SYNTHETIC FIBERS

Man-Made Fiber Production in the United States In Millions of Pounds

	Artificial (Cellulosic) Fibers - Rayon & Acetate			Synthetic (Noncellulosic) Fibers											
				Yarn & Monofilament				Staple & Tow							
Year	Filament Yarn & Monofil-ament	Staple & Tow	Total Cellu-lostic	Nylon	Polyester	Olefin	Total Yarn	Nylon	Polyester	Acrylic & Mod-acrylic	Olefin	Total Staple	Total Noncel-lulosic	Total Manu-factured Fibers	Total Glass Fiber
1988	214	400	614	1,728	1,228	1,224	4,180	942	2,452	588	364	4,346	8,526	9,140	1,609
1989	217	363	580	1,759	1,209	1,257	4,225	981	2,385	543	382	4,291	8,516	9,096	1,620
1990	206	299	505	1,671	1,107	1,417	4,194	990	2,090	505	406	3,991	8,185	8,690	1,488
1991	213	273	486	1,667	1,208	1,408	4,282	869	2,202	454	459	3,984	8,266	8,752	1,433
1992	220	275	495	1,651	1,270	1,528	4,449	904	2,308	439	474	4,125	8,573	9,068	1,543
1993	227	278	505	1,700	1,284	1,659	4,643	959	2,274	433	483	4,149	8,791	9,296	1,751
1994	225	273	498	1,805	1,492	1,870	5,167	935	2,366	442	549	4,292	9,459	9,957	2,114
1995	208	290	498	1,829	1,597	1,907	5,333	874	2,290	432	521	4,117	9,450	9,948	2,282
1996[1]	219	245	464	1,920	1,560	1,957	5,437	875	2,259	478	465	4,078	9,515	9,979	2,326
1997[2]	187	266	453	2,005	1,642	2,058	5,704	793	2,424	440	468	4,126	9,830	10,282	2,408

[1] Preliminary. [2] Estimate. *Source: Fiber Economics Bureau, Inc. (FEB)*

Domestic Distribution of Synthetic (Noncellulosic) Fibers in the United States In Millions of Pounds

	Yarn & Monofilament								Staple & Tow								
	Producers' Shipments								Producers' Shipments								
	Domestic								Domestic								
Year	Nylon	Pol-yester	Olefin	Total	Exports	Total	Imports	Dome-stic Con-sumption	Nylon	Pol-yester	Acrylic & Mod-acrylic	Olefin	Total	Exports	Total	Imports	Dome-stic Con-sumption
1988	1,572.4	1,157.4	1,199.8	3,929.6	260.5	4,190.1	116.3	4,045.9	944.9	2,311.8	421.1	344.2	4,022.0	344.8	4,366.8	196.2	4,218.2
1989	1,575.3	1,110.7	1,226.0	3,912.0	237.9	4,149.9	182.2	4,094.2	955.3	2,261.3	414.8	363.4	3,994.8	253.3	4,248.1	192.4	4,187.2
1990	1,537.5	1,046.2	1,404.9	3,988.6	265.1	4,253.7	154.7	4,143.3	950.2	2,015.4	352.2	387.9	3,705.7	278.9	3,984.6	209.8	3,915.5
1991	1,493.9	1,114.0	1,380.6	3,988.5	246.9	4,235.4	174.8	4,163.3	835.0	2,127.9	319.2	437.5	3,719.6	277.8	3,997.4	263.1	3,982.7
1992	1,570.1	1,229.6	1,496.1	4,295.8	194.8	4,490.6	209.3	4,505.1	891.7	2,202.1	322.3	441.0	3,857.1	267.2	4,124.3	397.7	4,255.0
1993	1,612.7	1,228.4	1,631.5	4,472.6	174.6	4,647.2	295.8	4,768.4	907.9	2,157.8	333.0	468.2	3,866.9	297.1	4,164.0	509.0	4,375.9
1994	1,700.0	1,402.8	1,838.2	4,941.0	204.9	5,145.9	377.7	5,318.7	911.7	2,221.3	319.6	489.0	3,941.6	390.9	4,332.5	622.9	4,564.5
1995	1,741.1	1,439.8	1,870.3	5,051.2	259.0	5,310.2	393.6	5,445.1	828.5	2,100.2	266.1	458.0	3,653.0	398.7	4,051.7	624.9	4,277.9
1996[1]	1,801.0	1,427.9	1,933.8	5,162.7	275.2	5,437.9	482.0	5,644.7	843.4	2,015.2	283.4	439.2	3,581.2	492.2	4,073.4	607.7	4,188.9

[1] Preliminary. *Source: Fiber Economics Bureau, Inc. (FEB)*

Mill Consumption of Fiber & Products and Per Capita Consumption in the U.S. In Millions of Pounds

	Cellulosic Fibers				Noncellulosic Fibers								Per Capita[4] Mill Consumption (Pounds)				
Year	Yarn & Monofi-lament	Staple & Tow	Net Waste	Total Cellu-lostic	Noncellu-lostic	Net Waste	Total Noncellu-lostic	Total Manu-factured Fibers[2]	Cotton	Wool	Other Fibers[3]	Grand Total	Man-made Fibers[2]	Cotton	Wool	Other Fibers[3]	Total All Fibers
1988	200.2	406.4	5.8	612.4	8,264.1	140.9	8,405.0	9,017.4	3,470.1	156.1	83.8	12,727.4	40.9	21.4	1.5	2.1	65.9
1989	213.6	392.2	-5.0	600.8	8,281.4	127.4	8,408.8	9,009.6	3,985.9	139.6	77.9	13,213.0	40.6	23.4	1.1	2.0	67.1
1990	196.9	403.3	-1.3	598.9	8,058.8	179.3	8,238.1	8,837.0	4,036.5	135.4	75.7	13,084.6	39.3	23.2	1.1	2.2	65.8
1991	210.7	347.5	-1.7	556.5	8,135.9	168.8	8,304.7	8,861.2	4,347.5	159.0	78.6	13,446.3	39.1	24.6	1.2	2.0	66.9
1992	215.0	346.3	-3.6	557.7	8,760.1	181.1	8,941.2	9,498.9	4,714.7	159.1	76.3	14,449.0	41.5	27.6	1.2	1.9	72.2
1993	236.9	363.1	-5.6	594.4	9,144.3	189.8	9,334.1	9,928.5	4,921.9	166.6	73.8	15,090.8	43.2	29.2	1.3	1.8	75.5
1994	223.2	318.0	-21.4	519.8	9,883.2	102.4	9,985.6	10,505.4	5,191.6	168.1	54.8	15,919.9	45.4	30.2	1.4	2.7	79.7
1995	203.3	300.6	-22.7	481.2	9,722.7	76.3	9,799.0	10,280.2	5,199.9	161.5	65.6	15,707.5	43.7	30.2	1.5	2.5	77.8
1996[1]	208.2	260.7	-12.8	456.1	9,833.5	99.8	9,933.3	10,389.4	5,145.0	143.3	45.8	15,723.6	43.7	29.3	1.3	1.8	76.0

[1] Preliminary. [2] Excludes Glass Fiber. [3] Includes silk, linen, jute and sisel & others. [4] Mill consumption plus imports less exports of semimanufactured and unmanufactured products. *Source: Fiber Economics Bureau, Inc. (FEB)*

Producer Price Index of Grey Synthetic Broadwovens 1982 = 100

Year	Jan.	Feb.	Mar.	Apr.	May	June	July	Aug.	Sept.	Oct.	Nov.	Dec.	Average
1988	110.0	111.1	111.6	111.8	112.2	113.0	113.4	113.8	113.0	113.5	113.9	114.6	112.7
1989	114.3	112.0	112.2	112.2	112.1	113.1	114.7	115.0	115.0	115.8	115.9	115.3	114.0
1990	115.6	115.7	115.6	115.7	115.5	115.6	115.7	115.2	115.3	115.6	115.8	116.1	115.7
1991	115.7	114.7	114.4	114.1	114.3	113.9	114.8	116.4	116.5	116.5	116.8	118.2	115.5
1992	119.0	119.9	120.3	120.9	121.8	122.0	122.6	122.0	121.7	120.8	119.4	119.9	120.9
1993	119.6	119.1	119.1	119.2	117.1	118.4	118.0	118.0	116.9	117.3	115.2	114.5	117.7
1994	113.5	112.8	112.9	113.2	113.2	113.3	113.1	113.3	114.1	111.8	112.9	113.8	113.2
1995	114.8	116.8	116.7	116.3	116.6	117.1	115.4	114.8	116.9	116.4	114.7	116.2	116.1
1996	114.3	114.1	116.9	117.9	116.8	115.7	116.1	117.1	116.9	117.2	116.6	117.0	116.4
1997[1]	117.9	118.3	118.3	117.9	118.4	119.0	118.8	118.5	119.4	119.3	117.5	118.6	118.5

[1] Preliminary. *Source: Bureau of Labor Statistics, U.S. Department of Commerce (BLS)*

Rice

International trading in rice, the world's second most opular foodstock after wheat, is light as most rice is conumed where it is produced. Global rice trade during 1997 f 17.9 million metric tonnes (milled basis) compares with 9.5 million tonnes in 1996 and the record 21 million in 995; initial forecasts for 1998 center on 19 million tonnes.

Asia accounts for most of the world's exports with Thailand the largest exporting nation at 4.8 million tonnes n 1997 vs. 5.3 million in 1996. The U.S. ranks among the op exporters with 2.5 million tonnes in 1997 vs. 2.6 million n 1996. The Western hemisphere is the primary destination or U.S. rice and is generally higher priced than Asian rice. mporting nations are numerous, but in 1996 and 1997 only wo nations imported at least one million tonnes although ive nations may do so in 1998. Indonesia is generally the argest importer but their needs have dropped since 1995. On a regional basis, the Middle East tends to be the largest mporter, paced by Iran's annual need of more than one milion tonnes. Low quality rice, an extremely price sensitive sector and dominated by Asian sellers, constitutes a major portion of total world rice imports International prices, notably Asian, fell in mid-1997 when Thailand allowed its currency to float, the impact of which contracted export activity.

The long term trend for world stocks has been down, reflecting higher exports and consumption, but the slippage may have bottomed. Carryover 1996/97 stocks of 53.9 million metric tonnes compares with 50.1 million a year earlier and are forecast at 53.3 million for the end of 1997/98. China holds half the total and India 20 percent. World rice production in 1997/98 of a record 380.9 million metric tonnes (milled) compares with the previous year's high of 380 million. World consumption of a record 381.5 million tonnes in 1997/98 compares with 376.2 million in 1996/97.

China is the world's largest producer and consumer with about a third of each; production in 1997/98 of 136 million tonnes (milled) was unchanged from 1996/97. China's recent annual rice acreage has been holding near 31 million hectares. China's consumption in 1997/98 of 135 million tonnes compares with 132 million in 1996/97. India, the second largest producer and consumer, produced 82 million tonnes in 1997/98, up one million from 1996/97.

1997/98 U.S. rough rice production (August/July) of 179.4 million cwt. (rough) compares with 171.3 million in 1996/97 and the record 197.8 million cwt. in 1994/95. Domestic rice usage of 99 million cwt. in 1997/98 compares with 98 million in 1996/97, most of which is consumed directly as a foodstuff. U.S. ending 1997/98 stocks of 22 million cwt. (rough) compares with 24 million a year earlier.

The U.S. average farm price in 1997/98 was forecast to range between $9 to $10 per cwt. vs $9.90 in 1996/97.

Futures Market

Rough rice futures and options are traded on the Chicago Board of Trade (CBOT).

World Rice Supply and Distribution[4] In Thousands of Metric Tons

	Exports			Imports					Utilization			Ending Stocks		
Year	U.S.	Non-U.S.	Total	Brazil	Iran	Saudi Arabia	Unaccounted	Total	China	India	Total	China	India	Total
1993-4	2,794	13,671	16,465	1,098	645	698	1,591	16,465	128,000	76,045	358,968	25,173	14,230	51,622
1994-5	3,073	17,924	20,997	987	1,633	615	817	20,997	129,000	77,307	367,078	21,256	14,083	49,019
1995-6[1]	2,624	16,836	19,460	786	1,294	786	1,166	19,460	130,035	78,000	370,036	21,456	12,203	50,175
1996-7[2]	2,300	16,520	18,820	1,000	1,000	750	2,309	18,820	132,070	79,250	375,310	25,556	11,743	53,294
1997-8[3]	2,700	17,411	20,111	1,000	1,250	700	1,060	20,111	135,000	80,250	379,327	28,306	11,243	55,773

[1] Preliminary. [2] Estimate. [3] Forecast. [4] Production is on a rough basis; all other data are reported on a milled basis. *Source: Foreign Agricultural Service, U.S. Department of Agriculture (FAS-USDA)*

World Production of Rough Rice In Thousands of Metric Tons

Year	Bangladesh	Brazil	Burma	China	India	Indonesia	Japan	Rep. of Korea	Pakistan	Philippines	Thailand	Vietnam	World Total
1993-4	27,064	10,515	15,086	177,700	120,462	46,638	9,793	6,404	5,993	9,923	19,200	24,317	527,156
1994-5	25,252	10,885	16,000	175,930	121,752	49,743	14,977	6,882	5,171	10,475	21,400	24,615	540,134
1995-6[1]	26,533	10,050	17,000	185,214	119,442	51,100	13,435	6,386	5,905	11,174	21,800	26,792	550,939
1996-7[2]	27,633	9,747	15,517	195,100	120,822	48,500	12,930	7,189	6,461	11,177	20,758	27,273	560,567
1997-8[3]	27,753	9,559	16,552	197,857	122,262	47,692	12,363	7,365	6,451	10,769	21,667	27,273	565,708

[1] Preliminary. [2] Estimate. [3] Forecast. *Source: Foreign Agricultural Service, U.S. Department of Agriculture (FAS-USDA)*

World Exports of Rice (Milled Basis) In Thousands of Metric Tons

Year	Argentina	Australia	Burma	China	European Union	Guyana	India	Pakistan	Thailand	Uruguay	Vietnam	United States	World Total
1993	276	540	223	1,374	153	122	625	937	4,798	451	1,765	2,644	14,915
1994	215	570	619	1,519	185	183	600	1,399	4,738	396	2,222	2,794	16,465
1995	342	519	645	32	323	203	4,201	1,592	5,931	470	2,308	3,073	20,997
1996[1]	367	475	265	265	301	233	3,556	1,663	5,280	596	3,040	2,624	19,460
1997[2]	525	700	15	900	350	225	1,750	1,650	5,275	650	3,500	2,300	18,820
1998[3]	600	650	100	1,500	350	200	1,750	1,700	5,800	675	3,500	2,700	20,111

[1] Preliminary. [2] Estimate. [3] Forecast. *Source: Foreign Agricultural Service, U.S. Department of Agriculture (FAS-USDA)*

RICE

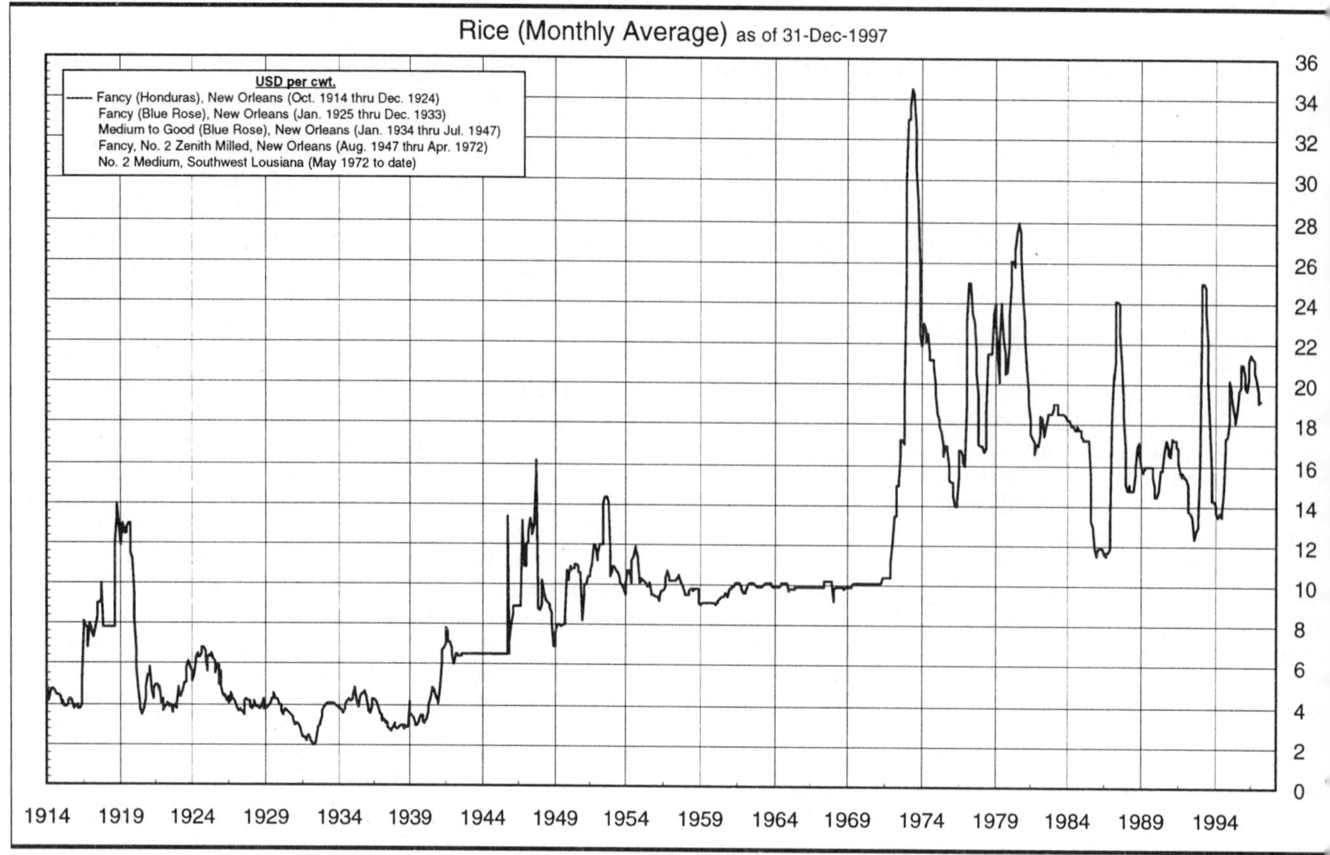

Average Wholesale Price of Rice No. 2 (Medium)[1] Southwest Louisiana In Dollars Per Cwt. Bagged

Year	Aug.	Sept.	Oct.	Nov.	Dec.	Jan.	Feb.	Mar.	Apr.	May	June	July	Average
1987-8	11.10	11.95	16.60	17.25	16.75	18.50	19.80	20.15	20.00	18.00	17.40	16.70	17.00
1988-9	16.40	16.20	14.50	14.50	14.00	13.90	13.75	13.50	13.50	14.60	14.65	15.75	14.60
1989-90	15.55	15.30	14.80	14.30	14.04	14.80	15.13	15.13	15.50	15.75	15.65	15.30	15.10
1990-1	14.75	13.90	13.50	13.50	13.50	14.90	14.90	15.05	16.05	16.15	16.50	16.35	14.90
1991-2	15.85	16.00	16.00	16.00	16.00	16.00	15.90	15.50	15.50	15.15	14.50	14.50	15.60
1992-3	14.50	14.00	14.50	14.15	13.40	13.40	13.00	12.80	12.40	11.94	12.00	12.00	13.15
1993-4	12.25	12.45	15.65	21.95	24.00	24.00	23.88	23.80	24.00	23.70	22.00	20.00	20.65
1994-5	18.30	15.88	15.00	15.00	14.00	13.80	14.16	14.38	14.38	14.70	14.75	14.55	14.91
1995-6	15.44	17.50	20.25	20.13	20.00	20.00	19.88	19.25	19.13	19.38	19.40	19.50	19.15
1996-7[2]	19.50	19.50	19.25	19.25	19.00	18.81	19.19	19.25	19.25	19.25	18.40	19.00	19.14

[1] U.S. No. 2--broken not to exceed 4%. [2] Preliminary. *Source: Economic Research Service, U.S. Department of Agriculture (ERS-USDA)*

Average Price Received by Farmers for Rice (Rough) in the U.S. In Dollars Per Hundred Pounds (Cwt.)

Year	Aug.	Sept.	Oct.	Nov.	Dec.	Jan.	Feb.	Mar.	Apr.	May	June	July	Average[2]
1988-9	7.49	6.97	6.85	6.81	6.68	6.58	6.67	6.60	6.74	6.78	7.05	7.45	6.83
1989-90	7.41	7.59	7.41	7.03	7.05	7.44	7.57	7.55	7.41	7.28	7.18	7.05	7.35
1990-1	6.66	6.21	6.02	6.29	6.13	6.39	6.75	7.07	7.43	7.44	7.43	7.21	6.68
1991-2	7.16	7.67	7.65	7.84	7.98	7.84	7.97	7.78	7.46	7.18	6.97	6.99	7.58
1992-3	6.60	6.41	6.40	6.42	6.39	6.36	6.06	5.64	5.52	5.24	5.02	4.92	5.89
1993-4	5.19	5.21	6.10	8.06	8.91	8.98	10.10	10.20	9.93	10.00	8.88	7.80	7.98
1994-5	6.87	6.89	6.47	6.53	6.56	6.78	6.71	6.64	6.70	6.75	7.03	7.17	6.78
1995-6	7.64	7.95	8.77	9.12	9.36	9.33	9.10	9.31	9.34	9.69	9.74	9.68	9.15
1996-7	9.99	9.95	9.75	9.36	9.63	9.87	10.10	10.20	10.20	10.10	9.88	10.00	9.90
1997-8[1]	9.94	9.85	10.10	9.71	10.10								9.94

[1] Preliminary. [2] Weighted average by sales. *Source: Economic Research Service, U.S. Department of Agriculture*

alient Statistics of Rice, Rough & Milled (Rough Equivalent) in the United States In Millions of Cwt.

op ear eginning gust	Supply				Disappearance								Government Support Program				
					Domestic									Loan Rate ($ Per Cwt.)			
														Rough[3]			
	Stocks August 1	Pro-duction	Imports	Total Supply	Food	Brewers	Seed	Total	Resi-dual	Exports	Total Disap-pearance	CCC Stocks July 31	Put Under Price Support	Long	Medium	All Classes	Milled Long
992-3	27.4	179.7	6.1	213.2	69.0	15.1	3.8	87.9	8.8	77.0	173.7	.1	125.8	6.66	6.13	6.50	10.74
993-4	39.4	156.1	6.9	202.5	71.2	14.3	4.3	89.8	11.6	75.3	176.7	0	30.9	6.67	6.11	6.50	10.75
994-5	25.8	197.8	7.0	230.9	74.0	14.5	4.1	92.5	8.2	98.9	199.6	.1	131.2	6:64	6.13	6.50	10.72
995-6	31.3	173.9	7.4	212.6	77.0	15.6	3.7	96.3	8.3	83.0	187.6	0	100.9	6.68	6.12	6.50	10.69
996-7[1]	25.0	171.3	10.0	206.3	80.0	15.4	4.0	99.4	3.4	76.4	179.2	0	68.9	6.68	6.17	6.50	10.77
997-8[2]	27.1	180.0	10.0	217.1	83.0	15.4	4.0	102.4	5.5	83.0	190.9	0	66.5	6.67	6.14	6.50	10.69

[1] Preliminary. [2] Estimate. [3] Loan rate for each class of rice is the sum of the whole kernels' loan rate weighted by its milling yield (average 56%) and the roken kernels' loan rate weighted by its milling yield (average 12%). *Source: Economic Research Service, U.S. Department of Agriculture (ERS-USDA)*

creage, Yield, Production and Prices of Rice in the United States

rop ear	Acreage Harvested (1,000 Acres)			Yield Per Harvested Acre (In Lbs.)		Production 1,000 Cwt.			Value of Production $1,000	Wholesale Prices ($ Per Cwt.)		Milled Rice, Average C.I.F. at Rotterdam		
	Southern States	California	United States	California	United States	Southern States	California	United States		Arkan-sas[2]	Hous-ton[3]	U.S. No. 2[4]	Thai "A"[5]	Thai "B"[5]
												$ Per Metric Ton		
992-3	2,738	394	3,132	8,500	5,736	146,168	33,490	179,658	1,057,272	14.30	15.25	287	385	290
993-4	2,396	437	2,833	8,300	5,510	119,839	36,271	156,110	1,246,875	21.15	20.75	413	413	335
994-5	2,831	485	3,316	8,500	5,964	156,555	41,224	197,779	1,336,570	14.47	14.70	325	412	331
995-6	2,628	465	3,093	7,600	5,621	138,519	35,352	173,871	1,587,236	19.10	19.15	404	NA	407
996-7	2,299	500	2,799	7,490	6,121	133,862	37,459	171,321	1,687,407	19.02	20.95	428	NA	380
997-8[1]	2,524	510	3,034	8,300	5,896	136,555	42,341	178,896	1,728,687	18.35	20.16	418	NA	320

[1] Preliminary. [2] F.O.B. mills, Arkansas, medium. [3] Houston, Texas (long grain). [4] Milled, 4%, container, FAS. 5 SWR, 100%, bulk. NA = Not available. *Source: Economic Research Service, U.S. Department of Agriculture (ERS-USDA)*

J.S. Exports of Milled Rice, by Country of Destination In Thousands of Metric Tons

ear Beginning October	Canada	Germany	Haiti	Iran	Ivory Coast	Jamaica	Mexico	Nether-lands	Peru	Russia[2]	Saudi Arabia	Senegal	South Africa	Switzer-land	United Kingdom	Total
1990-1	127.4	49.9	124.8	0	69.4	75.5	96.5	91.6	61.5	0	189.1	63.2	115.9	108.6	38.8	2,395.1
1991-2	143.7	44.9	116.9	11.6	73.4	46.3	157.0	67.7	43.6	55.6	179.6	61.7	136.6	94.2	59.8	2,279.0
1992-3	146.0	67.6	152.9	184.3	107.3	39.4	241.5	120.9	61.6	74.8	223.5	91.5	122.1	71.2	72.2	2,709.9
1993-4	141.3	41.7	57.2	60.4	34.2	53.8	234.0	92.8	47.0	6.4	180.5	90.1	110.9	64.8	82.4	2,432.5
1994-5	160.0	43.1	210.2	240.6	92.0	88.5	309.6	170.3	81.8	0	176.1	28.1	106.1	91.2	58.7	3,763.1
1995-6[1]	172.1	42.7	149.6	24.5	61.3	63.1	359.1	113.9	97.7	0	141.5	0	169.9	80.3	85.4	2,825.9

[1] Preliminary. [2] Formerly part of the U.S.S.R.; data not reported separately until 1992. *Source: Economic Research Service, U.S. Department of Agriculture*

J.S. Exports of Rice, by Export Program In Thousands of Metric Tons

Fiscal Year	PL 480	Section 416	CCC Credit Pro-grams[2]	CCC African Relief Exports	EEP[3]	Export Pro-grams[4]	Exports Outside Specified Export Programs	Total U.S. Rice Exports	% Export Programs as a Share of Total Exports
1992	229	0	220	0	358	823	1,456	2,279	36
1993	199	0	235	0	278	850	1,860	2,710	31
1994	222	0	155	0	46	433	2,001	2,433	18
1995	196	0	321	0	113	644	3,119	3,763	17
1996	182	0	215	0	23	420	2,406	2,826	15
1997[1]	116	0	89	0	0	205	2,355	2,560	8

[1] Preliminary. [2] May not completely reflect exports made under these programs. [3] Sales not shipments. [4] Adjusted for estimated overlap between CCC export credit and EEP shipments. *Source: Economic Research Service, U.S. Department of Agriculture*

Production of Rice (Rough) in the United States, by Type and Variety In Thousands of Cwt.

Year	Long Grain	Medium Grain	Short Grain	Total	Year	Long Grain	Medium Grain	Short Grain	Total
1988	119,364	36,891	3,642	159,897	1993	103,064	51,873	1,173	156,110
1989	109,161	41,441	3,885	154,487	1994	133,445	63,390	944	197,779
1990	107,806	47,328	954	156,088	1995	121,730	51,241	900	173,871
1991	109,137	47,567	753	157,457	1996	113,351	56,901	1,069	171,321
1992	128,015	50,633	1,010	179,658	1997[1]	121,647	55,833	1,416	178,896

[1] Preliminary. *Source: National Agricultural Statistics Service, U.S. Department of Agriculture (NASS-USDA)*

Rubber

According to the International Rubber Study Group, world production of natural rubber in 1996 was 6.34 million metric tonnes. That represented an increase of almost five percent from 1995. Estate production of natural rubber in 1996 was 1.67 million tonnes, up two percent from 1995. Small holding production of natural rubber was 4.67 million tonnes, a six percent increase from 1995. Over the first five months of 1997, world production of natural rubber was 2.56 million tonnes. Estate production was 700,000 tonnes while smallholdings production was 1.86 million tonnes.

World consumption of natural rubber in 1996 was 6.13 million tonnes, an increase of two percent from 1995. Over the January-May 1997 period, consumption of natural rubber was 904,000 tonnes. Producer stocks of natural rubber at the end of May 1997 were 470,000 tonnes. At the end of December 1996, producer stocks were also 470,000 tonnes. Consumer's reported stocks of rubber at the end of May 1997 were 337,000 tonnes while at the end of December 1996 they were 419,000 tonnes. Consumer's total stocks in May 1997 were 800,000 tonnes while at the end of December 1996 they were 880,000 tonnes. Stocks afloat in May 1997 were 410,000 tonnes while at the end of 1996 they were 510,000 tonnes. World stocks of natural rubber in May 1997 were 1.68 million tonnes. That was ten percent less than stocks at the end of 1996 which were 1.86 million tonnes.

World production of synthetic rubber in 1996 was 9.76 million tonnes. That was almost three percent above 1995. Production of synthetic rubber in the January-May 1997 period was 422,000 tonnes. Global consumption of synthetic rubber in 1996 was 9.59 million tonnes, up over three percent from 1995. In the first five months of 1997, world consumption of synthetic rubber was 423,000 tonnes.

Reported world stocks of synthetic rubber at the end of May 1997 were 1.07 million metric tonnes. At the end of 1996 they were 1.05 million tonnes. Russian Federation stocks of synthetic rubber in May 1997 were 230,000 tonnes while China's stocks in May 1997 were 130,000 tonnes. Stocks elsewhere were 640,000 tonnes while stocks afloat were 250,000 tonnes. World stocks of synthetic rubber in May 1997 were 2.32 million tonnes. down very slightly from the December 1996 stocks of 2.33 million tonnes.

U.S. consumption of synthetic and natural rubber in 1996 was 3.19 million tonnes, nearly the same as in 1995. In the January-May 1997, U.S. consumption of natural and synthetic rubber was 1.43 million tonnes. Japan's consumption of rubber in 1996 was 1.84 million tonnes, a three percent increase from 1995. China's consumption of rubber in 1996 was 1.68 million tonnes, an increase of nine percent from 1995. Other major users of rubber were South Korea, India, France and Germany.

U.S. reported stocks of natural rubber held by consumers in May 1997 were 62.2 million pounds, down from 79.3 million pounds at the end of 1996. U.S. stocks of synthetic rubber in May 1997 were 408.2 million pounds, up two percent from stocks at the end of 1996.

The major producers of natural rubber are Thailand, Indonesia and Malaysia. In 1996, Thailand's production of natural rubber was 1.98 million tonnes. That was almost ten percent more than in 1995. In 1996, Indonesian production of natural rubber was 1.54 million tonnes, a five percent increase from 1995. Indonesian estates produced 337,000 tonnes in 1996 while small holdings produced 1.21 million tonnes. Malaysian production of natural rubber in 1996 was 1.08 million tonnes. Other producers of natural rubber include Sri Lanka, Vietnam, China, India and Nigeria.

The major exporters of natural rubber are also the largest producers. In 1996, Thailand exported 1.76 million tonnes of natural rubber, up almost eight percent from 1995. Indonesia's exports in 1996 were 1.43 million tonnes, up eight percent from 1995. Malaysian natural rubber exports in 1996 were almost 710,000 tonnes, a decline of nine percent from 1996.

Futures Markets

Rubber futures are traded on the Kobe Rubber Exchange (KRE), the Tokyo Commodity Exchange, (TOCOM), the Kuala Lumpur Commodity Exchange (KLCE), and the Singapore Commodity Exchange Ltd.

U.S. Imports of Natural Rubber (Includes Latex & Guayule) In Thousands of Metric Tons

Year	Jan.	Feb.	Mar.	Apr.	May	June	July	Aug.	Sept.	Oct.	Nov.	Dec.	Total
1988	83.2	69.6	87.0	68.6	67.2	64.9	49.5	83.3	59.1	69.3	77.4	74.7	791.8
1989	99.3	52.2	99.1	74.6	87.5	63.8	77.9	65.6	69.1	69.5	78.9	69.1	880.9
1990	72.3	58.6	81.9	63.1	89.5	77.7	60.4	61.0	83.0	55.7	81.7	75.7	820.1
1991	59.9	54.1	69.5	90.9	59.6	56.7	53.4	52.4	65.5	74.4	71.3	68.9	776.2
1992	77.5	75.2	84.7	64.7	79.0	73.8	80.5	77.2	73.9	81.3	68.1	77.5	913.4
1993	95.3	79.9	93.9	86.3	74.1	81.2	83.6	77.8	69.2	73.4	86.0	86.9	987.6
1994	87.5	74.7	102.6	78.9	88.3	77.8	66.7	85.0	78.8	89.3	70.0	76.0	975.6
1995	81.7	86.9	102.3	90.2	94.1	93.4	78.0	81.0	81.5	89.2	79.1	68.7	1,026.1
1996	105.4	86.1	82.2	90.6	65.1	70.4	79.0	81.0	82.1	113.6	73.5	85.0	1,014.0
1997[1]	94.2	92.0	93.9	88.2	93.0	65.1	76.8	90.1	87.5				1,041.1

[1] Preliminary. *Source: International Rubber Study Group (IRSG)*

World Production[1] of Rubber In Thousands of Metric Tons

	Natural								Synthetic				
Year	China	India	Indo-nesia	Malaysia	Sri Lanka	Thailand	Vietnam	World Total	Ger-many	Japan	United States	Russia[3]	World Total
1987	237.6	227.4	1,203.3	1,578.7	121.8	925.6	55.0	4,840	468.4	1,191.9	2,182.1	2,366	9,450
1988	239.8	254.8	1,235.0	1,661.6	122.4	978.9	60.0	5,020	499.6	1,298.8	2,334.7	2,435	10,160
1989	242.8	288.6	1,256.0	1,415.6	110.7	1,178.9	85.0	5,150	507.6	1,352.7	2,261.4	2,358	10,150
1990	264.2	323.5	1,262.0	1,291.0	113.1	1,275.3	103.0	5,120	524.5	1,425.8	2,114.5	2,277	9,910
1991	296.4	360.2	1,284.0	1,255.7	103.9	1,341.2	87.0	5,170	504.4	1,377.3	2,050.0	2,105	9,270
1992	309.3	383.0	1,387.0	1,173.2	106.1	1,531.0	114.0	5,440	544.7	1,389.9	2,300.0	1,611	9,300
1993	326.1	428.1	1,301.3	1,074.3	104.2	1,553.4	97.0	5,290	569.7	1,309.8	2,180.0	1,103	8,600
1994	374.0	464.0	1,360.8	1,100.6	105.3	1,717.9	121.0	5,710	621.6	1,349.0	2,390.0	632	8,880
1995	424.0	499.6	1,466.8	1,089.3	105.7	1,804.8	123.0	6,040	480.0	1,497.6	2,530.0	837	9,480
1996[2]	430.0	540.2	1,543.0	1,082.5	112.5	1,978.0	132.0	6,340	485.0	1,519.9	2,486.0	775	9,740

[1] Including rubber in the form of latex. [2] Preliminary. *Source: International Rubber Study Group (IRSG)*

World Consumption of Natural and Synthetic Rubber In Thousands of Metric Tons

	Natural							Synthetic					
Year	Brazil	France	Ger-many	Japan	United Kingdom	United States	World Total	France	Ger-many	Japan	United Kingdom	United States	World Total
1987	115.4	170.0	198.5	568.0	134.0	789.0	4,800	316.4	453.4	946.0	216.0	2,017.3	9,650
1988	125.3	181.0	203.6	623.0	140.0	858.3	5,100	315.0	471.0	1,042.0	226.5	2,016.8	9,940
1989	124.3	184.0	221.1	657.0	132.5	866.9	5,190	358.0	476.0	1,103.0	240.0	2,051.0	10,070
1990	121.3	179.0	208.7	677.0	136.0	807.5	5,200	351.0	511.0	1,133.0	223.0	1,820.8	9,710
1991	125.0	183.0	210.7	689.5	119.0	755.8	5,100	342.0	502.0	1,118.5	201.0	1,768.1	9,310
1992	123.4	179.0	212.8	685.4	124.5	910.2	5,320	365.4	506.0	1,080.6	231.0	1,959.6	9,380
1993	131.7	168.5	174.9	631.0	119.0	966.7	5,440	314.7	488.0	1,022.0	212.0	2,001.0	8,640
1994	144.7	179.8	186.4	639.8	135.0	1,001.7	5,680	400.1	512.2	1,026.2	217.0	2,117.6	8,820
1995	155.2	176.0	211.7	692.0	118.0	1,003.9	6,000	430.2	426.4	1,085.0	233.0	2,172.0	9,290
1996[1]	145.0	182.2	193.0	714.5	111.0	1,001.7	6,130	436.1	416.0	1,124.5	277.0	2,186.6	9,550

[1] Preliminary. *Source: International Rubber Study Group (IRSG)*

World Stocks of Natural & Synthetic Rubber (by Countries) on January 1 In Thousands of Metric Tons

		In Producing Countries							In Consuming Countries (Reported Stocks)				
Year	Total Synthetic	Africa	Indo-nesia	Malaysia	Sri Lanka	Thailand	Vietnam	Total Natural	Brazil	India	Japan	United States	Total
1988	1,520	19.1	100	208.5	20.0	37.8	6.0	510	13.5	58.2	70.7	95.2	224
1989	1,800	23.2	100	286.5	23.2	53.0	6.0	540	20.5	80.9	97.2	61.7	260
1990	988	26.9	110	248.3	27.0	53.7	8.0	510	16.0	78.4	105.6	92.0	292
1991	1,011	21.7	114	190.3	29.8	83.7	11.0	490	12.0	92.9	91.6	94.3	291
1992	973	24.4	68	196.1	17.3	89.3	9.0	460	9.0	106.0	92.7	109.4	317
1993	982	19.6	110	187.2	16.0	89.0	12.0	540	17.0	90.9	82.9	108.0	442
1994	924	21.6	80	159.2	17.2	115.4	9.0	520	25.0	96.4	85.4	71.3	410
1995	888	16.9	80	187.0	16.5	96.1	11.0	430	17.0	94.1	72.9	45.2	363
1996	977	21.2	90	175.6	17.0	112.2	12.0	450	13.0	127.4	77.1	67.1	414
1997[1]	1,046	20.5	60	190.3	17.6	153.5	13.0	470	5.0	123.4	86.8	79.3	419

[1] Preliminary. *Source: International Rubber Study Group (IRSG)*

Net Exports of Natural Rubber from Producing Areas In Thousands of Metric Tons

Year	Cambodia	Guat-emala	Indonesia	Liberia	Malaysia	Nigeria	Sri Lanka	Thailand	Vietnam	Other Africa[2]	Other Asia[3]	World Total
1987	20.0	10.4	1,092.8	91.1	1,578.5	43.7	106.0	873.2	35.0	94.0	28.1	3,950
1988	21.0	9.8	1,132.0	105.6	1,563.6	65.8	99.3	906.4	37.9	107.0	36.8	4,070
1989	32.0	11.0	1,151.8	106.0	1,364.8	101.3	86.0	1,100.6	57.7	115.0	38.2	4,170
1990	28.0	13.4	1,077.3	19.0	1,185.6	121.0	86.7	1,150.8	75.9	118.0	37.6	3,990
1991	21.0	14.3	1,220.0	32.0	1,041.2	63.0	76.4	1,231.9	62.9	126.0	44.0	3,950
1992	20.0	15.7	1,268.1	30.0	939.1	70.4	78.6	1,412.9	80.9	135.0	44.6	4,060
1993	21.0	16.9	1,214.3	45.0	769.8	79.7	69.6	1,396.8	65.0	134.0	52.8	3,840
1994	32.0	22.3	1,244.8	31.0	782.1	49.6	69.1	1,605.0	80.0	143.0	63.9	4,200
1995	34.0	23.2	1,323.8	13.0	777.5	99.2	68.2	1,635.5	82.0	142.0	60.5	4,250
1996[1]	33.0	29.2	1,434.3	13.5	709.8	69.0	72.1	1,763.0	88.0	164.0	69.9	4,450

[1] Preliminary. [2] Includes Cameroon, Cote d'Ivoire, Gabon, Ghana and Zaire. [3] Includes Myanmar, Papua New Guinea and the Philippines.
Source: International Rubber Study Group (IRSG)

RUBBER

Average Spot Crude Rubber Prices (Smoked Sheets[1]) in New York In Cents Per Pound

Year	Jan.	Feb.	Mar.	Apr.	May	June	July	Aug.	Sept.	Oct.	Nov.	Dec.	Average
1988	54.59	53.75	54.92	55.68	58.62	70.69	66.05	63.84	60.08	55.17	52.98	54.10	58.37
1989	55.95	59.34	56.69	55.23	52.07	49.50	49.20	47.21	46.13	46.09	45.63	44.84	50.66
1990	44.72	45.75	45.92	45.64	45.80	46.00	45.80	47.46	48.43	46.50	46.23	47.03	46.27
1991	47.47	48.92	48.09	45.92	45.17	45.26	44.59	44.45	44.25	44.52	44.75	44.16	45.63
1992	43.11	43.95	44.50	45.86	46.41	46.57	46.78	47.05	46.86	47.83	48.00	48.03	46.25
1993	48.51	48.30	46.41	44.15	43.78	43.78	43.30	43.85	44.54	44.23	44.90	44.70	45.04
1994	44.92	46.11	49.62	50.83	51.43	55.13	62.49	66.35	67.15	73.51	71.76	77.35	59.72
1995	85.68	92.61	94.15	93.43	89.50	80.57	72.13	68.54	70.70	73.59	83.19	83.39	82.29
1996	80.25	79.90	79.76	75.08	76.99	75.10	71.03	69.13	68.75	66.32	66.32	66.14	72.90
1997	65.06	64.76	63.53	59.97	57.71	57.30	51.96	52.45	51.89	51.36	47.99	40.53	55.38

[1] No. 1 ribbed, plantation rubber. *Source: Wall Street Journal*

Natural Rubber Prices in London In British Pounds Per Metric Ton

Year	Jan.	Feb.	Mar.	Apr.	May	June	July	Aug.	Sept.	Oct.	Nov.	Dec.	Average
Buyers' Price RSS 1 (CIF)													
1994	612.6	639.5	686.0	698.9	712.6	771.7	878.5	886.8	884.7	911.8	875.8	1,004.5	797.0
1995	1,141.9	1,170.8	1,209.6	1,189.2	1,174.9	1,004.9	894.9	886.0	921.4	946.7	1,082.6	1,099.7	1,060.2
1996	1,063.1	1,066.1	1,057.3	990.8	1,025.1	999.6	912.0	881.2	880.5	829.8	803.3	800.3	942.4
1997	777.6	783.6	800.9	731.3	715.1	699.6	605.9	604.1	592.5	573.9			688.5
Buyers' Prices RSS 3 (CIF)													
1994	586.2	629.2	671.0	688.2	706.0	766.0	872.6	880.8	875.0	901.8	866.8	975.2	784.9
1995	1,122.9	1,157.0	1,188.2	1,174.2	1,161.0	988.2	882.7	859.2	911.3	941.4	1,074.2	1,093.6	1,046.2
1996	1,057.3	1,058.6	1,049.9	981.4	1,015.5	984.6	895.2	863.0	862.0	814.7	790.7	782.1	929.6
1997	762.2	769.4	788.7	721.3	708.9	696.9	588.7	592.1	575.8	553.0			675.7
Sellers' Prices SMR 20 (CIF)													
1994	619.4	658.8	718.5	757.5	713.8	719.8	780.6	821.0	823.1	877.5	897.5	1,088.1	789.6
1995	1,227.5	1,228.8	1,151.5	1,116.9	1,053.0	926.3	796.9	839.1	871.2	887.5	1,066.5	1,065.0	1,019.2
1996	1,059.5	1,019.4	1,006.3	915.0	894.0	838.1	821.0	830.6	844.4	814.5	778.8	777.5	883.3
1997	767.5	769.4	765.0	697.5	663.1	653.8	597.0	600.0	580.6	567.5			666.1

Source: International Rubber Study Group (IRSG)

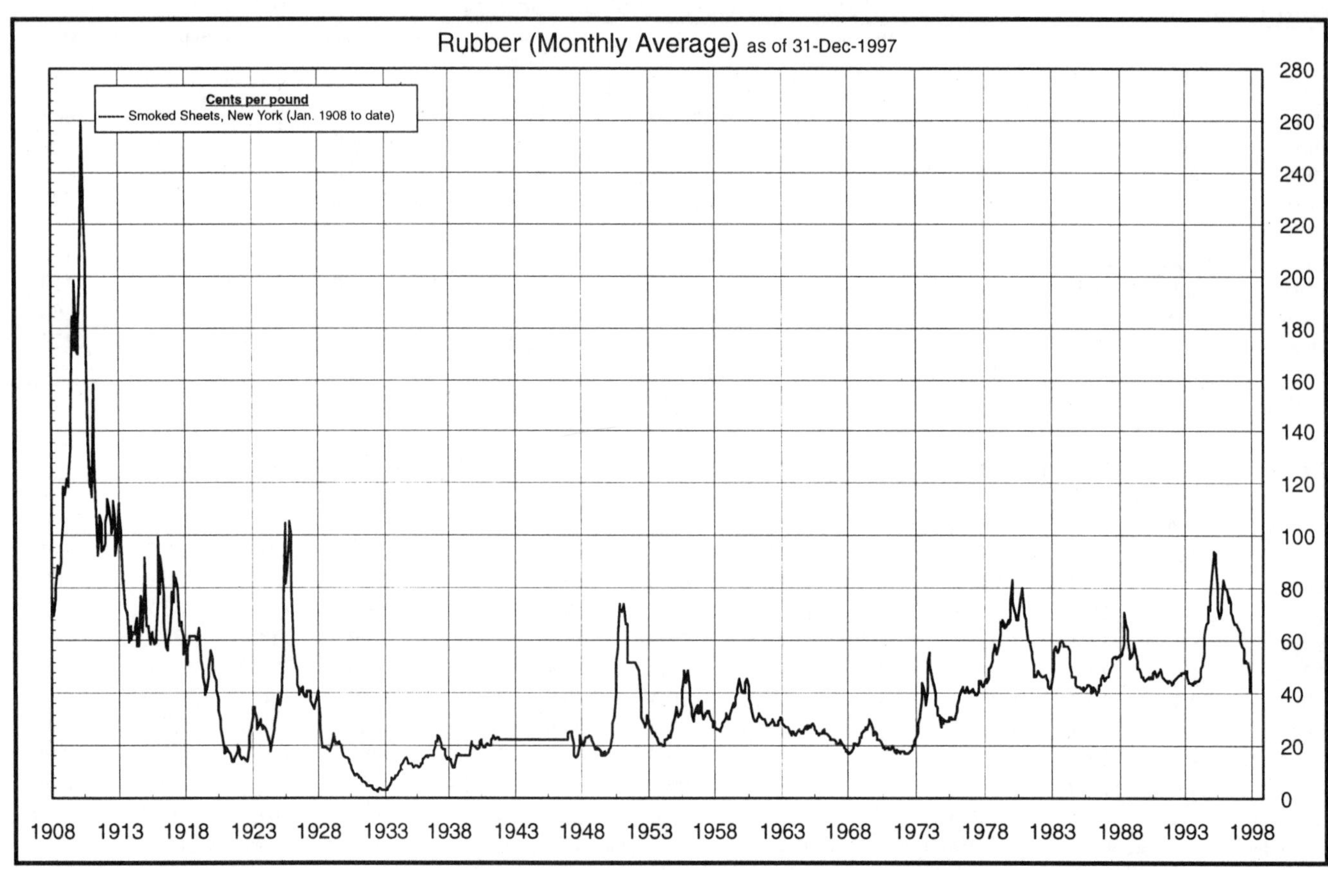

Consumption of Natural Rubber in the United States In Thousands of Metric Tons

Year	Jan.	Feb.	Mar.	Apr.	May	June	July	Aug.	Sept.	Oct.	Nov.	Dec.	Total
1988	80.9	66.3	91.6	60.8	68.7	66.2	53.5	80.6	64.6	74.5	75.4	75.2	858.3
1989	89.9	51.1	96.6	68.4	87.9	65.1	82.7	70.8	72.0	62.1	84.6	50.9	866.9
1990	62.6	57.3	79.0	65.2	87.4	73.9	57.4	74.1	78.8	59.8	75.6	69.8	807.5
1991	60.0	60.0	65.0	65.0	65.0	60.0	55.0	55.0	65.0	70.0	65.0	66.0	755.8
1992	83.4	63.3	85.9	66.9	80.6	78.6	82.6	79.5	70.2	84.6	64.4	70.2	910.2
1993	96.3	76.0	93.4	93.4	67.9	76.8	77.3	84.9	72.0	73.6	82.9	72.2	966.7
1994	92.8	84.9	93.1	82.7	89.6	84.6	76.2	87.8	74.8	90.1	66.4	78.7	1,001.7
1995	70.5	75.8	98.4	90.3	92.2	93.3	85.0	82.7	83.1	89.9	81.4	61.3	1,003.9
1996	102.5	85.8	81.2	87.9	65.6	76.7	81.9	88.1	83.3	108.4	72.1	68.2	1,001.7
1997[1]	99.2	92.0	91.2	87.6	108.4	72.0	78.4	91.5	88.5				1,078.4

[1] Preliminary. *Source: International Rubber Study Group (IRSG)*

Stocks of Natural Rubber in the United States, on First of Month In Thousands of Metric Tons

Year	Jan.	Feb.	Mar.	Apr.	May	June	July	Aug.	Sept.	Oct.	Nov.	Dec.
1988	72.5	74.9	75.3	70.7	74.6	72.9	71.6	68.7	71.2	63.9	57.9	58.4
1989	61.7	71.1	67.5	77.4	82.2	86.7	86.2	86.2	88.1	83.3	87.7	83.9
1990	92.0	100.2	100.2	101.6	97.1	97.3	99.8	101.6	87.2	90.3	84.7	89.6
1991	94.3	94.0	88.0	93.0	119.0	113.0	110.0	108.0	106.0	106.0	110.0	117.0
1992	109.4	103.6	112.7	110.4	107.5	105.9	101.1	99.0	96.7	100.3	97.0	100.7
1993	108.0	49.4	53.3	53.7	46.7	52.9	57.3	63.6	56.5	53.7	53.4	56.5
1994	71.3	65.9	55.7	65.2	61.4	60.0	53.2	43.8	41.0	45.0	44.2	47.8
1995	45.2	56.4	67.5	71.4	71.2	72.6	73.0	66.0	64.4	62.8	62.1	59.8
1996	67.1	70.0	70.3	71.2	73.9	73.4	67.1	64.2	57.2	56.0	61.1	62.4
1997[1]	79.3	74.2	74.2	76.9	77.5	62.2	55.2	53.6	52.1	51.2		

[1] Preliminary. *Source: International Rubber Study Group (IRSG)*

Stocks of Synthetic Rubber in the United States, on First of Month In Thousands of Metric Tons

Year	Jan.	Feb.	Mar.	Apr.	May	June	July	Aug.	Sept.	Oct.	Nov.	Dec.
1988	229.0	237.8	235.1	229.6	237.5	246.2	249.6	261.0	259.9	258.6	259.0	258.2
1989	276.3	288.9	287.7	294.4	289.6	300.4	303.7	308.7	314.1	323.4	329.6	414.8
1990	404.0	393.5	392.5	385.8	406.8	397.5	395.0	414.9	420.8	419.6	405.0	393.9
1991	403.7	406.0	403.0	404.0	402.0	388.0	394.0	385.0	356.0	334.0	330.0	325.0
1992	403.7	386.0	381.2	383.9	393.2	389.2	372.8	382.7	382.1	375.1	378.6	401.1
1993	406.9	345.9	345.7	346.0	340.5	351.8	342.1	341.6	333.6	326.4	319.9	321.4
1994	331.1	313.3	313.3	307.9	306.0	314.2	302.5	323.2	318.5	304.6	299.4	299.5
1995	305.4	307.4	302.8	293.5	319.4	315.6	325.9	349.2	355.7	354.6	347.0	351.5
1996	366.2	355.3	342.0	354.8	365.4	360.0	367.0	377.3	366.0	362.8	354.1	370.6
1997[1]	400.0	402.5	402.6	410.7	415.0	412.0	406.1	397.1	382.6	386.8		

[1] Preliminary. *Source: International Rubber Study Group (IRSG)*

Production of Synthetic Rubber in the United States In Thousands of Metric Tons

Year	Jan.	Feb.	Mar.	Apr.	May	June	July	Aug.	Sept.	Oct.	Nov.	Dec.	Total
1988	166.5	156.7	189.1	178.6	167.8	164.9	155.3	170.5	178.6	186.7	145.6	174.7	2,335
1989	206.3	177.5	193.6	174.1	179.7	175.0	186.2	164.2	176.0	191.0	182.9	194.8	2,261
1990	173.5	180.1	182.5	187.8	174.6	172.0	171.9	180.9	180.4	190.3	167.4	153.1	2,115
1991	168.0	163.0	184.0	174.0	173.0	159.0	154.0	133.0	159.0	159.0	173.0	164.0	2,050
1992	180.0	190.0	200.0	210.0	200.0	190.0	190.0	200.0	210.0	200.0	195.0	175.0	2,300
1993	120.0	160.0	220.0	190.0	200.0	180.0	190.0	180.0	180.0	180.0	190.0	180.0	2,180
1994	180.0	180.0	210.0	200.0	210.0	200.0	200.0	210.0	190.0	210.0	200.0	200.0	2,390
1995	220.0	200.0	210.0	210.0	240.0	220.0	210.0	230.0	210.0	200.0	200.0	190.0	2,540
1996	200.0	190.0	220.0	210.0	200.0	210.0	200.0	210.0	200.0	210.0	220.0	216.0	2,486
1997[1]	220.0	200.0	220.0	230.0	220.0	200.0	220.0	220.0	230.0				2,613

[1] Preliminary. *Source: International Rubber Study Group (IRSG)*

RUBBER

Consumption of Synthetic Rubber in the United States   In Thousands of Metric Tons

Year	Jan.	Feb.	Mar.	Apr.	May	June	July	Aug.	Sept.	Oct.	Nov.	Dec.	Total
1988	162.8	166.1	182.8	160.6	163.1	157.8	161.9	163.6	172.2	185.1	167.6	174.1	2,017
1989	158.5	166.8	186.8	163.1	172.1	166.3	160.9	171.1	162.5	170.6	180.5	150.5	2,051
1990	159.6	158.7	161.6	144.1	161.5	151.6	137.1	149.5	155.6	175.3	147.1	119.1	1,821
1991	145.0	140.0	160.0	150.0	160.0	135.0	140.0	140.0	160.0	140.0	150.0	149.0	1,768
1992	167.8	159.5	174.7	158.9	162.6	184.2	154.5	177.7	180.2	171.5	155.1	148.2	1,960
1993	161.3	154.4	189.4	172.8	164.5	173.6	166.0	173.9	162.0	169.4	162.3	151.4	2,001
1994	177.7	160.8	191.8	173.0	173.5	187.5	164.9	187.1	176.0	178.8	175.7	170.8	2,118
1995	188.6	182.2	194.3	179.1	212.7	188.7	160.0	190.7	182.4	178.1	169.7	145.5	2,172
1996	188.0	173.7	186.9	176.8	184.9	178.5	177.0	197.3	182.9	201.0	177.8	165.5	2,190
1997[1]	192.4	181.6	190.6	188.5	194.8	183.8	204.7	206.4	201.9				2,326

[1] Preliminary. *Source: International Rubber Study Group (IRSG)*

Exports of Synthetic Rubber in the United States   In Thousands of Metric Tons

Year	Jan.	Feb.	Mar.	Apr.	May	June	July	Aug.	Sept.	Oct.	Nov.	Dec.	Total
1988	39.7	37.4	41.8	41.7	40.4	41.1	29.8	44.0	38.6	37.2	36.3	32.1	514.0
1989	42.4	45.7	55.0	41.3	54.4	51.3	43.7	48.2	54.5	54.6	43.6	44.4	450.6
1990	45.6	39.0	50.2	42.6	42.7	41.0	37.4	43.1	42.0	50.8	50.3	39.0	523.7
1991	43.8	46.1	44.0	45.2	47.9	40.4	42.8	43.2	43.1	46.3	47.3	42.2	532.3
1992	52.3	55.1	51.3	59.1	58.2	51.6	46.5	52.8	58.0	51.4	48.1	39.7	624.1
1993	47.1	34.1	57.7	47.4	52.4	46.9	46.9	43.8	48.8	46.6	49.0	41.9	562.6
1994	48.8	46.4	55.4	57.0	52.4	49.6	50.2	62.8	60.7	59.9	56.9	55.0	655.1
1995	54.9	51.6	62.7	55.6	58.6	58.6	50.0	54.9	53.0	60.4	53.9	52.6	666.8
1996	61.1	57.7	64.0	68.0	48.2	66.8	62.3	57.1	63.9	65.2	58.6	58.6	731.5
1997[1]	63.1	58.2	57.5	74.2	66.9	61.6	64.1	70.0	65.6				774.9

[1] Preliminary. *Source: International Rubber Study Group (IRSG)*

Production of Tyres (Car and Truck) in the United States   In Thousands of Units

Year	First Quarter	Second Quarter	Third Quarter	Fourth Quarter	Total	Year	First Quarter	Second Quarter	Third Quarter	Fourth Quarter	Total
1979	61,751	52,756	47,800	44,595	206,687	1988	54,677	52,986	51,195	52,493	211,351
1980	45,329	35,764	36,174	41,997	159,263	1989	56,716	56,626	50,086	49,444	212,870
1981	47,853	46,042	45,658	42,209	181,762	1990	55,915	53,856	51,163	49,729	210,663
1982	47,304	45,602	42,656	42,938	178,500	1991	51,296	52,796	49,183	51,115	202,391
1983	45,859	47,451	45,370	47,353	186,923	1992	57,890	57,319	57,554	57,487	230,250
1984	53,369	53,588	50,957	51,463	209,375	1993	61,809	60,752	57,702	57,184	237,447
1985	54,460	49,385	46,468	46,610	196,923	1994	63,586	63,331	57,018	59,442	243,377
1986	49,240	45,687	46,855	48,507	190,289	1995	63,800	63,800	63,800	63,754	255,154
1987	51,205	50,210	49,723	51,839	202,978	1996[1]	64,000	64,000	64,000	63,700	255,700

[1] Preliminary. [2] Estimate. *Source: International Rubber Study Group (IRSG)*

Foreign Trade of Tyres (Car and Truck) in the United States   In Thousands of Units

	Imports					Exports				
Year	First Quarter	Second Quarter	Third Quarter	Fourth Quarter	Total	First Quarter	Second Quarter	Third Quarter	Fourth Quarter	Total
1987	11,584	12,820	11,722	11,341	47,467	2,095	2,327	2,389	3,371	10,182
1988	11,383	12,059	12,383	12,783	48,608	4,203	4,120	3,712	4,034	16,069
1989	12,802	14,518	12,609	12,749	52,678	4,104	4,254	5,267	4,704	18,329
1990	13,713	13,564	11,951	11,633	50,861	5,453	5,532	6,031	6,730	23,746
1991	12,011	13,008	11,320	10,158	46,497	6,407	6,388	6,623	6,342	25,760
1992	10,760	12,496	11,850	12,285	47,391	6,243	6,475	7,125	6,646	26,489
1993	11,519	13,045	12,688	13,036	50,288	7,266	6,930	7,163	7,133	28,492
1995	14,883	14,977	13,762	12,718	56,340	8,438	8,502	8,478	9,174	34,592
1996[1]	13,163	13,864	-----	-----	54,054	8,244	10,013	-----	-----	36,514
1997[2]	13,359	14,487	-----	-----	55,692	9,466	11,386	-----	-----	41,704

[1] Preliminary. [2] Estimate. *Source: International Rubber Study Group (IRSG)*

Rye

The slippage in U.S. rye production shows little sign of abating. During the 1980's annual production averaged more than 20 million bushels and has since been more than halved. Rye is now a minor U.S. crop, leaving the U.S. as a net importer of rye, importing almost half of domestic production. The major producing states are Georgia and South Dakota, the two accounting for about a third of 1997/98 (June/May) total production of a record low 8.9 million bushels (226,380 metric tons) vs 9 million in 1996/97. Although average yield has held steady near 1.64 metric tons/hectare (26.1 bu./acre), the area planted and harvested continues to set new lows with only 138,000 hectares harvested for the 1997/98 crop.

In the U.S. rye is used as an animal feed and as an ingredient in bread and some whiskeys, with about a third of the total supply used as a feedstuff, a third as a foodstuff and the balance as seed and for whisky. U.S. rye exports are minimal. Carryover stocks are also small of late at under one million bushels. Current carryover stocks stand in sharp contrast to the late 1980's when carryover averaged near 18 million bushels. The contraction in U.S. supply/demand statistics reflects the lack of interest towards the grain by producers and users alike; a trend that has yet to show any sign of bottoming.

On a world basis the slippage is not as intense. Indeed, production in the mid-1990's appears to have stabilized in the 20 to 25 million metric ton range although those totals pale against the mid-1980's average of more than 30 million tons. World production in 1997/98 of 23 million metric tons compares with the previous two crop years of 22.2 and 21.9 million tons, respectively, reflecting steady planted acreage totals and average yield. Eastern Europe is the major producing area with more than half of the world's crop; 12.5 million tons in 1997/98 with Poland accounting for 5.5 million tons. Russia is the largest single producing country; 6 million tons in 1997/98 vs. 5.9 millon in 1996/97. Germany is third with 4.55 million tons in 1997/98. Canada, whose output is not much larger than the U.S., exports most of its crop to the U.S. The estimated world carryover as of June 1, 1998, of 19,000 tons, is unchanged from a year earlier, the lowest so far in the 1990's.

World trade in 1997/98 (October/September) of slightly less than 1.7 million metric tons compares with 1.75 million in 1996/97, and a recent high of 2.66 million in 1994/95. Importing nations show a wide year-to-year variance. China's 1997/98 imports of 50,000 tons compares with a high of 696,000 in 1994/95 and nothing in 1993/94; South Korea imported 952,000 tons in 1995/96 but only 300,000 in 1997/98. U.S. imports are fairly consistent at 100,000 tons as are Japan's needs of 400,000 tons. The largest exporter is the European Union with 1.3 million tons in 1997/98 vs. 1.2 million in 1996/97, but in 1994/95 the EU exported almost 2 million tons vs. only 715,000 the previous year.

World Production of Rye In Thousands of Metric Tons

Crop Year	Austria	Canada	Czech Republic[5]	Denmark	France	Germany	Poland	Russia[4]	Spain	Turkey	Ukraine[4]	United States	World Total
1988-9	356	267	530	366	260	3,419	7,232	-----	357	360	18,517	373	32,989
1989-90	381	873	708	487	270	3,867	6,216	-----	336	320	18,288	347	33,412
1990-1	396	599	736	545	240	3,988	6,044	-----	267	240	21,193	258	36,861
1991-2	350	339	484	395	210	3,324	5,899	-----	242	240	14,061	248	27,359
1992-3	278	265	255	308	205	2,422	3,981	13,890	230	240	1,160	304	28,656
1993-4	290	320	300	323	190	2,984	5,000	9,150	300	230	1,180	263	26,090
1994-5	320	400	280	380	180	3,450	5,300	6,000	220	250	940	290	21,890
1995-6[1]	310	310	260	500	200	4,520	6,290	4,100	170	260	1,210	260	21,890
1996-7[2]	150	310	200	340	230	4,210	5,650	5,900	300	250	1,100	230	22,220
1997-8[3]	200	300	270	480	200	4,550	5,320	7,500	230	250	1,350	230	24,310

[1] Preliminary. [2] Estimate. [3] Forecast. [4] Formerly part of the U.S.S.R.; data not reported separately until 1992. [5] Formerly part of Czechoslovakia; data not reported separately until 1992. *Source: Foreign Agricultural Service, U.S. Department of Agriculture (FAS-USDA)*

Production of Rye in the United States, by States In Thousands of Bushels

Year	Georgia	Kansas	Michigan	Minnesota	Nebraska	North Dakota	Oklahoma	Penns-ylvania	South Carolina	South Dakota	Texas	Wisconsin	Total
1988	1,890	130	650	920	1,375	1,350	720	684	720	2,250	150	120	14,689
1989	1,610	80	825	1,088	600	1,064	532	576	644	3,240	126	360	13,647
1990	1,320	130	580	868	750	780	420	496	594	1,870	140	465	10,176
1991	1,300	115	360	648	1,000	992	665	297	630	1,152	228	435	9,761
1992	1,560	130	496	720	1,040	1,496	798	720	675	1,666	280	330	11,952
1993	1,380	693	420	667	500	1,050	660	340	380	1,600	363	260	10,340
1994	1,890	325	442	810	546	700	945	320	600	1,485	435	875	11,341
1995	1,155	400	544	609	480	726	810	330	440	1,650	380	480	10,064
1996	1,820	150	351	480	418	528	900	216	520	1,476	190	384	9,016
1997[1]	1,430	300	416	546	340	667	1,265	400	435	735	330	432	8,912

[1] Preliminary. *Source: Agricultural Statistics Board, U.S. Department of Agriculture (ASB-USDA)*

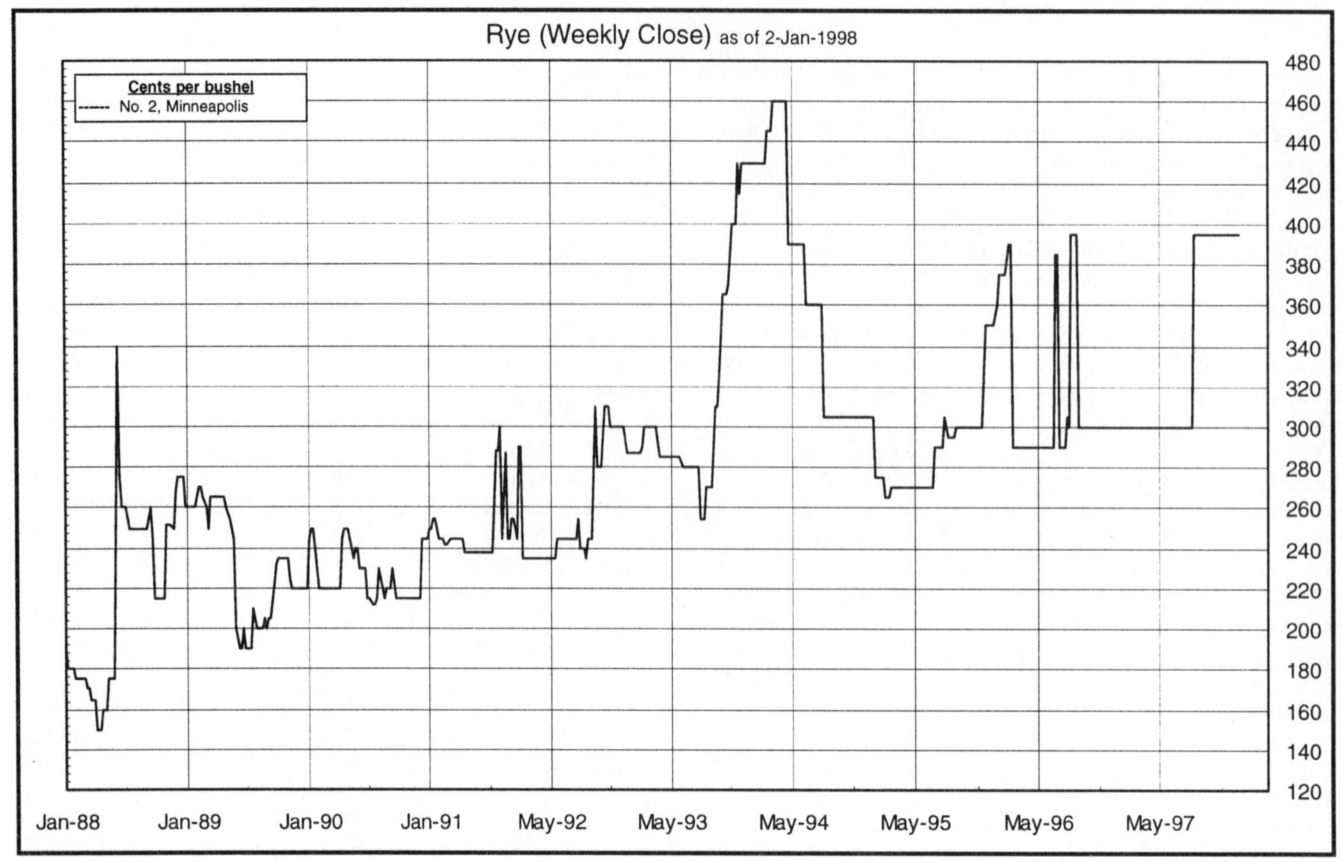

Salient Statistics of Rye in the United States In Thousands of Bushels

Crop Year Beginning June 1	Supply: Stocks June 1	Supply: Production	Supply: Imports	Supply: Total Supply	Disappearance: Domestic Use: Food	Domestic Use: Industry	Domestic Use: Seed	Domestic Use: Feed & Residual	Domestic Use: Total	Exports	Total Disappearance	Acreage: Planted (1,000 Acres)	Acreage: Harvested for Grain (1,000 Acres)	Yield Per Harvested Acre Bushels
1988-9	18,912	14,689	200	33,801	3,500	2,000	3,200	11,401	20,101	3,400	23,501	2,374	595	24.7
1989-90	10,300	13,647	30	23,977	3,500	2,000	3,000	9,035	17,535	800	18,335	2,014	484	28.2
1990-1	5,642	10,176	3,895	19,713	3,500	2,000	3,000	7,670	16,173	213	16,383	1,625	375	27.1
1991-2	3,327	9,761	4,542	17,630	3,500	2,000	3,000	7,528	16,028	53	16,081	1,671	396	24.6
1992-3	1,523	11,952	3,099	16,100	3,500	2,000	3,000	5,984	14,484	14	14,498	1,582	406	29.4
1993-4	1,555	10,340	4,607	16,502	3,600	2,000	3,000	6,915	15,515	16	15,531	1,493	381	27.1
1994-5	971	11,341	4,386	16,698	3,600	2,000	3,000	6,612	15,212	35	15,247	1,613	407	27.9
1995-6[1]	1,451	10,064	3,760	15,275	3,200	2,000	3,000	6,136	14,336	41	14,377	1,602	385	26.1
1996-7[2]	898	9,016	4,000	13,914	3,200	2,000	3,000	4,700	12,900	100	12,900	1,467	347	26.0
1997-8[3]		8,912										1,433	341	26.1

[1] Preliminary. [2] Estimate. [3] Forecast. *Source: Economic Research Service, U.S. Department of Agriculture (ERS-USDA)*

United States Rye Crop Production Reports and CCC Operations In Thousands of Bushels

Crop Year Beginning June 1	Official Crop Reports: July 1	Official Crop Reports: Aug. 1	Official Crop Reports: Dec. 1	Official Crop Reports: Final	National Average Support Rate: $ Per Bushel	National Average Support Rate: % of Parity	Placed Under Loan Total	Percentage of Production	Acquired by CCC
1989-90	------	13,610	------	13,647	1.40	32	600	4.4	0
1990-1	------	10,098	------	10,176	1.33	31	200	2.0	0
1991-2	------	9,761	------	9,761	1.38	32	100	1.0	0
1992-3	------	11,952	------	11,952	1.46	34	200	1.7	0
1993-4	------	10,340	------	10,340	1.46	35	100	1.0	0
1994-5	------	11,138	------	11,341	1.61	38	100	0.9	0
1995-6[1]	------	9,928	------	10,064	1.61	42	100	1.0	0
1996-7[2]	------	------	------	9,016	[4]	------	------	------	------
1997-8[3]	------	------	------	8,912	[4]	------	------	------	------

[1] Preliminary. [2] Estimate. [3] Forecast. [4] The Federal Agriculture Improvement and Reform Act of 1996 did not extend authority for price support for rye beyond the 1995-6 marketing year. *Source: National Agricultural Statistics Service, U.S. Department of Agriculture (NASS-USDA)*

Average Price of Cash Rye No. 2 in Minneapolis In Cents Per Bushel

Year	July	Aug.	Sept.	Oct.	Nov.	Dec.	Jan.	Feb.	Mar.	Apr.	May	June	Average
1988-9	266	264	264	247	269	280	268	268	264	270	257	201	260
1989-90	206	203	214	235	229	225	245	220	222	241	242	232	226
1990-1	215	222	220	220	190	245	252	243	242	242	245	245	232
1991-2	216	238	195	288	288	279	251	263	235	235	235	245	247
1992-3	245	241	267	295	303	298	288	290	300	289	285	282	282
1993-4	280	270	280	354	387	427	430	430	452	460	400	383	372
1994-5	360	336	305	305	305	305	285	267	270	270	270	270	296
1995-6	287	298	299	300	300	350	368	346	290	290	290	304	310
1996-7	325	364	314	300	300	300	300	300	300	300	300	300	309
1997-8[1]	300	327	395	395	395	395	396						372

[1] Preliminary. *Source: Agricultural Marketing Service, U.S. Department of Agriculture (AMS-USDA)*

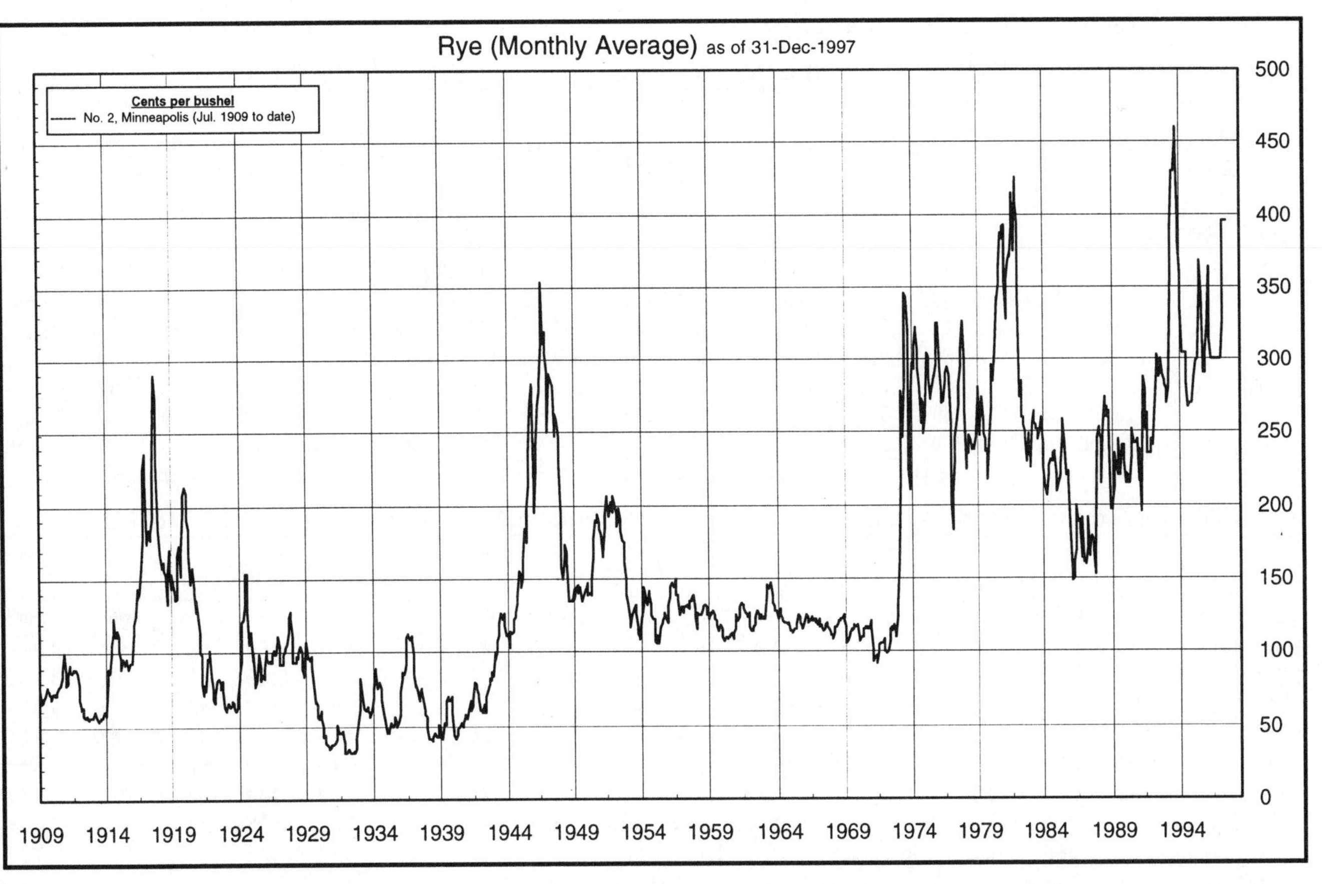

Salt

Salt, or sodium chloride, is a basic commodity with many uses. Salt is added to food to enhance flavor and to remove ice in the winter. Salt is used in the manufacture of caustic soda and as a feedstock for chlorine. Salt is produced in the U.S. by a number of companies using a number of methods. Salt is produced by solar evaporation, by vacuum pan, rock salt and brine. In 1996, the five leading states in terms of total salt sold or used were Louisiana 33 percent, Texas 24 percent, New York 11 percent, Kansas 7 percent and Utah 4 percent. Louisiana, New York and Ohio were the major rock salt producing states. U.S. salt production comprises about 22 percent of total world production. World salt production has remained steady. The world chloralkali industry is the largest single consumer of salt.

The U.S. Geological Survey reported that U.S. production of salt in 1996 was 42.2 million metric tonnes, up from 42.1 million tonnes in 1995. Brine salt production was 21.5 million tonnes, up four percent from 1995. Rock salt production in 1996 was 13.5 million tonnes, down four percent from the previous year. Solar salt production was 3.27 million tonnes, down eight percent from 1995. Vacuum pan and open pan salt production was 3.92 million tonnes, down one percent from the previous year.

U.S. exports of salt in 1996 were 869,000 tonnes, up 30 percent from the previous year. U.S. imports for consumption of salt in 1996 were 10.6 million tonnes, some 50 percent more than in 1995. U.S. apparent consumption of salt in 1996 was 50.6 million tonnes, up seven percent from 1995. U.S. reported consumption of salt in 1996 was 52.8 million tonnes, up 14 percent from the previous year. World salt production in 1996 was 192 million tonnes, unchanged from the previous year.

World Production of All Salt — In Thousands of Metric Tons

Year	Australia	Canada	China	France	Germany	India	Italy	Mexico	Poland	Spain	United Kingdom	United States	World Total
1989	7,069	11,021	28,000	8,267	17,129	9,603	4,186	6,703	4,670	3,090	6,720	35,251	191,660
1990	7,227	11,261	20,000	6,605	15,719	9,503	4,432	7,135	4,055	3,377	6,434	36,918	183,000
1991	7,791	11,993	24,100	6,500	14,870	9,503	3,954	7,533	3,840	4,070	6,828	36,400	191,000
1992	7,693	11,171	28,100	6,116	12,708	9,503	3,821	7,395	3,887	3,610	6,101	36,100	184,000
1993	7,737	10,900	29,500	6,980	12,688	9,503	3,730	7,490	3,817	3,410	6,790	39,300	187,000
1994	7,685	11,700	29,700	7,536	10,532	9,503	3,953	7,458	4,074	4,932	7,000	39,800	191,000
1995[1]	8,148	10,957	29,800	7,539	10,800	9,503	3,552	7,670	4,214	4,776	6,650	42,200	192,000
1996[2]	7,905	12,289	28,900	7,660	10,800	9,503	3,600	8,508	4,163	4,000	6,700	42,300	192,000

[1] Preliminary. [2] Estimate. *Source: U.S. Geological Survey (USGS)*

Salient Statistics of the Salt Industry in the United States — In Thousands of Metric Tons

Year	Net Import Reliance as a % of Apparent Consumption	Average Value FOB Mine Vacuum & Open Pan $ Ton	Production: Total	Production: Open & Vacuum Pan	Production: Solar	Production: Rock	Production: Brine	Sold or Used by Producers: Open & Vacuum Pan	Sold or Used by Producers: Rock Salt	Sold or Used by Producers: Brine	Sold or Used by Producers: Total Salt	Value[3] Million $	Imports for Consumption	Exports: Total	Exports: To Canada	Apparent Consumption
1989	10	102.22	35,632	3,606	2,849	12,682	16,496	3,599	15,364	16,509	35,250	776.8	5,519	1,422	1,240	39,347
1990	9	110.58	36,794	3,662	2,985	12,772	17,374	3,655	13,056	17,724	36,916	826.7	5,969	2,266	2,087	40,619
1991	11	114.75	36,316	3,654	2,813	11,188	18,660	3,623	11,064	18,640	35,902	801.5	6,188	1,777	1,288	40,313
1992	11	113.20	36,016	3,811	3,221	11,411	17,574	3,763	10,910	34,784	34,784	802.6	5,394	992	718	39,186
1993	12	111.97	39,200	3,864	2,960	14,253	18,100	3,850	13,401	18,100	38,200	904.0	5,868	688	499	43,400
1994	18	115.35	40,100	3,960	3,020	15,100	18,000	3,930	14,900	18,000	39,700	990.0	9,630	742	573	48,600
1995[1]	14	118.63	42,100	3,950	3,540	14,000	20,600	3,920	13,000	20,500	40,800	1,000.0	7,090	670	558	47,200
1996[2]	18	120.54	40,100	3,920	3,270	13,500	21,500	3,900	14,500	21,500	42,900	1,060.0	10,600	869	710	50,600

[1] Preliminary. [2] Estimate. [3] Values are fob mine or refinery and do not include cost of cooperage or containers. *Source: U.S. Geological Survey (USGS)*

Salt Sold or Used by Producers in the U.S. by Classes & Consumers or Uses — In Thousands of Metric Tons

Year	Chemical[2]	Tanning Leather	Textile & Dyeing	Meat Packers	Canning	Baking	Agricultural Distribution	Feed Dealers	Feed Manufacturers	Rubber	Oil	Paper & Pulp	Metal Processing	Water Treatment	Grocery Stores	Water Conditioning Distrib.	Ice Control and/or Stabilization
1989	18,105	105	211	394	263	152	530	810	363	31	653	338	363	469	880	880	10,397
1990	19,258	99	206	543	288	155	562	999	495	41	719	257	314	449	811	1,019	10,253
1991	20,014	76	232	370	255	142	546	1,097	335	138	554	237	293	432	897	889	9,360
1992	18,538	67	271	389	252	161	553	1,020	392	34	1,208	230	217	435	849	899	7,814
1993	19,273	67	313	418	322	152	808	1,120	476	37	1,220	110	216	419	823	527	13,600
1994	18,400	82	304	410	342	157	842	1,070	478	33	1,290	150	239	440	934	505	16,400
1995	21,100	74	290	410	332	155	726	1,040	407	67	2,420	152	236	413	847	563	12,900
1996[1]	22,400	83	288	407	336	169	661	1,150	403	71	2,430	122	199	534	855	719	17,700

[1] Preliminary. [2] Chloralkali producers and other chemical. *Source: U.S. Geological Survey (USGS)*

Sheep & Lambs

The contraction in the U.S. sheep inventory shows little sign of abating; the mid-1997 total of all sheep and lambs of 9.9 million head compares with 10.3 million a year earlier. Of the total, the breeding inventory was down to 5.8 million head vs. 6.2 million in mid-1996. The 1997 lamb crop dipped below 5.0 million head, six percent under mid-1996.

Commercial lamb production in 1997 of 250 million pounds compares with 264 million in 1996 and annual totals in excess of 300 million pounds in the early 1990's. Production in 1998 is forecast at a record low 227 million pounds. The U.S. is a net importer of lamb, mostly from New Zealand and Australia, totaling 42.4 million pounds through the first eight months of 1997 vs. 34.9 million in the like 1996 period. However, the U.S. imports live sheep from Canada. Per capita retail weight disappearance of lamb in the U.S. is small, only 1.1 pounds in 1997.

Choice slaughter lamb prices in mid-1997 were higher than a year earlier, peaking at $89.50/cwt. in August vs. $83.75 a year earlier, basis San Angelo.

Although the demand for sheep meat is low in the U.S., foreign demand is higher, especially in those countries with large sheep herds utilized for wool production from which there is a derived demand for meat. Thus, the price of wool is a key factor in determining the availability of sheep meat. World sheep numbers declined steadily during the first half of the 1990's, but have since recovered largely due to increases in China and India, which have more than offset declines in Australia and New Zealand inventories.

World Sheep and Goat Numbers in Specified Countries on January 1 In Thousands of Head

Year	Argentina	Australia	China	India	Kazak-hstan[3]	New Zealand	Romania	Russia[3]	South Africa	Spain	Turkey	United Kingdom	World Total
1990	28,571	177,841	211,642	157,706	36,223	60,569	15,442	61,300	38,349	22,730	45,300	29,521	975,553
1991	27,552	173,982	210,021	160,207	35,700	57,852	14,062	58,200	37,585	24,037	45,000	30,147	962,853
1992	25,706	161,073	206,210	161,084	34,556	55,162	13,879	55,255	36,076	24,625	44,700	28,932	931,903
1993	24,500	140,542	207,329	162,155	34,420	52,568	12,079	51,368	35,770	24,615	44,600	29,493	900,400
1994	23,500	132,569	217,314	163,156	34,208	50,298	12,276	43,700	33,800	23,872	44,000	29,333	886,483
1995	21,626	123,210	240,528	164,242	25,132	50,135	12,119	34,500	33,385	23,058	43,000	29,484	876,169
1996	17,956	126,320	276,857	165,384	19,600	48,816	11,086	28,336	35,145	21,322	42,400	28,797	895,370
1997[1]	17,295	126,800	304,150	166,209	14,896	47,394	10,317	23,519	35,830	21,727	41,300	27,896	908,562
1998[2]	16,775	127,300	335,000	167,330	11,915	46,970	9,400	20,697	36,980	21,827	40,100	27,861	932,011

[1] Preliminary. [2] Forecast. [3] Formerly part of the U.S.S.R.; data not reported separately until 1986. *Source: Foreign Agricultural Service, U.S. Department of Agriculture (FAS-USDA)*

Salient Statistics of Sheep & Lambs in the United States In Thousands of Head

	--Inventory, Jan. 1 --				--- Marketings[3]---		---------- Slaughter ----------					Production	Farm Value, ------ Jan. 1 ------	
Year	Without New Crop Lambs	With New Crop Lambs	Lamb Crop	Total Supply	Sheep	Lambs	Farm	Commercial	Total[4]	Net Exports	Total Disappearance	(Live Weight) Mil. Lbs.	All Million $	$ Per Head
1989	10,853	11,674	7,721	19,395	1,129	7,201	97	5,466	5,563	188	12,412	811.3	894.4	82.4
1990	11,358	12,132	7,685	19,817	1,628	6,823	96	5,654	5,750	448	12,290	780.8	901.1	79.3
1991	11,174	11,930	7,651	19,581	1,719	7,187	91	5,722	5,813	787	11,763	796.1	732.6	65.6
1992	10,797	11,507	7,225	18,732	1,923	7,007	88	5,497	5,585	770	11,173	746.0	660.7	61.2
1993	10,201	10,906	6,379	17,285	1,952	6,752	84	5,184	5,268	750	10,159	688.6	714.2	70.6
1994	9,079	9,714	5,897	15,611	1,527	6,358	69	4,939	5,008	760	8,899	625.9	681.4	69.9
1995	8,886	8,886	5,648	14,534	990	6,228	69	4,560	4,628	680	5,807	599.4	663.4	74.7
1996[1]	8,461	8,461	5,328	13,789	1,019	5,923	65	4,184	4,249	264	5,488	560.2	732.2	86.5
1997[2]	7,937	7,937	5,295	13,232	-----	-----	-----	3,911	3,861	-----	5,946	-----	761.7	96.0

[1] Preliminary. [2] Estimate. [3] Excludes interfarm sales. [4] Includes all commercial and farm. *Source: Economic Research Service, U.S. Department of Agriculture (ERS-USDA)*

Sheep and Lambs[3] on Farms in the United States on January 1 In Thousands of Head

Year	California	Colorado	Idaho	Iowa	Minnesota	Montana	New Mexico	Ohio	South Dakota	Texas	Utah	Wyoming	Total
1990	1,000	840	286	490	285	663	495	270	590	2,090	509	805	11,363
1991	1,015	710	272	465	300	683	462	305	640	2,000	508	830	11,200
1992	995	710	273	345	293	658	445	215	602	2,140	488	870	10,749
1993	995	685	250	320	245	554	405	190	591	2,000	490	885	10,500
1994	1,120	647	266	267	231	534	340	198	550	1,895	442	813	9,742
1995	1,060	545	270	294	190	490	315	162	530	1,700	445	790	8,886
1996	1,000	535	273	345	185	465	265	153	500	1,650	395	680	8,461
1997[1]	960	575	285	285	180	432	235	130	450	1,400	375	720	7,937
1998[2]	870	575	285	235	170	410	240	117	400	1,500	350	680	7,616

[1] Preliminary. [2] Estimate. [3] Includes sheep & lambs on feed for market and stock sheep & lambs. *Source: Economic Research Service, U.S. Department of Agriculture (ERS-USDA)*

SHEEP AND LAMBS

Average Wholesale Price of Slaughter Lambs (Choice) at San Angelo, Texas — In Dollars Per 100 Pounds

Year	Jan.	Feb.	Mar.	Apr.	May	June	July	Aug.	Sept.	Oct.	Nov.	Dec.	Average
1989	68.13	68.83	70.90	78.17	73.56	72.63	67.79	67.28	63.81	59.63	56.06	60.83	67.30
1990	54.80	60.38	63.69	63.13	62.25	53.56	53.25	51.20	51.75	52.50	50.42	48.08	55.42
1991	47.63	45.81	54.88	55.50	57.70	55.75	55.50	54.31	53.25	51.20	52.08	54.92	53.21
1992	58.56	57.69	66.55	74.63	68.88	64.50	58.17	52.38	53.61	52.81	56.93	67.25	61.00
1993	69.88	73.38	75.50	71.25	62.50	57.75	57.00	58.97	66.08	63.75	65.69	68.44	65.85
1994	56.67	62.31	61.19	51.25	60.94	66.92	75.33	79.50	76.08	69.96	73.60	67.50	66.77
1995	65.38	75.08	73.75	68.58	77.20	81.63	83.70	87.00	80.00	75.50	72.00	70.50	75.86
1996	74.44	85.63	84.07	83.10	86.17	97.50	92.67	83.75	84.40	82.58	80.00	88.88	85.27
1997[1]	94.63	100.81	97.50	95.50	83.17	83.25	79.69	89.50	85.45	82.75	80.33	83.52	88.01

[1] Preliminary. *Source: Economic Research Service, U.S. Department of Agriculture (ERS-USDA)*

Federally Inspected Slaughter of Sheep & Lambs in the United States — In Thousands of Head

Year	Jan.	Feb.	Mar.	Apr.	May.	June	July	Aug.	Sept.	Oct.	Nov.	Dec.	Total
1989	418	415	505	393	435	423	398	476	440	468	467	457	5,295
1990	479	431	481	466	465	426	430	463	422	490	465	449	5,467
1991	495	449	546	436	442	388	431	438	456	501	449	471	5,502
1992	468	422	481	503	374	419	427	400	470	452	413	460	5,289
1993	380	384	476	461	396	462	394	413	410	391	403	430	5,000
1994	383	409	515	402	418	377	302	382	384	381	393	411	4,756
1995	373	363	456	420	355	347	296	355	344	356	364	358	4,388
1996	352	353	403	374	313	271	313	315	313	365	324	336	4,032
1997[1]	294	317	386	321	308	293	295	288	310	324	299	337	3,771

[1] Preliminary. *Source: Economic Research Service, U.S. Department of Agriculture (ERS-USDA)*

Cold Storage Holdings of Lamb and Mutton in the U.S., on First of Month — In Thousands of Pounds

Year	Jan.	Feb.	Mar.	Apr.	May	June	July	Aug.	Sept.	Oct.	Nov.	Dec.
1989	6,115	7,267	6,487	6,947	6,135	6,827	8,003	7,841	7,731	7,057	7,707	7,990
1990	7,625	7,844	8,468	7,905	8,390	8,052	9,685	10,107	9,144	8,929	8,458	8,099
1991	8,414	9,438	9,829	8,070	7,277	8,436	8,002	6,917	6,130	5,287	5,739	6,659
1992	6,296	7,255	6,670	8,455	8,580	9,870	10,968	11,711	9,314	8,751	8,520	8,406
1993	7,864	6,343	6,620	6,661	11,064	11,181	13,152	13,495	12,241	12,615	11,843	10,161
1994	8,372	9,198	9,507	11,194	11,505	11,368	12,124	12,026	11,016	9,261	8,946	8,796
1995	10,913	11,621	10,825	12,679	14,934	13,992	12,306	10,679	10,240	7,412	7,503	7,846
1996	7,606	9,794	13,017	12,247	13,649	12,187	13,726	13,164	14,645	11,249	10,494	9,788
1997[1]	8,899	9,473	9,861	11,163	13,027	15,220	16,594	18,535	19,383	16,116	16,894	16,534

[1] Preliminary. *Source: Economic Research Service, U.S. Department of Agriculture (ERS-USDA)*

Average Price Received by Farmers for Sheep in the U.S. — In Dollars Per Hundred Pounds (Cwt.)

Year	Jan.	Feb.	Mar.	Apr.	May	June	July	Aug.	Sept.	Oct.	Nov.	Dec.	Average
1989	34.20	35.70	30.30	25.40	21.60	22.20	24.60	23.40	23.10	22.70	29.50	31.10	26.98
1990	32.20	30.90	30.00	23.50	19.70	19.60	24.70	24.30	18.90	19.20	20.40	22.40	23.82
1991	23.50	19.90	21.50	21.30	18.30	21.00	20.30	19.20	18.90	18.20	19.80	22.60	20.38
1992	28.10	29.80	31.60	28.30	23.10	22.60	24.00	25.80	25.00	25.30	25.50	33.20	26.86
1993	33.10	35.20	36.10	27.30	29.10	28.90	29.00	28.50	25.80	24.60	25.70	30.30	29.47
1994	35.10	37.00	34.30	29.60	29.30	33.60	30.10	29.40	27.90	27.30	30.50	34.70	31.57
1995	32.80	37.50	31.90	29.50	27.90	28.30	28.60	27.00	26.00	24.50	23.80	26.00	28.65
1996	34.40	33.80	34.00	27.30	25.30	26.60	30.50	29.10	30.20	28.80	29.80	34.20	30.33
1997[1]	41.80	41.30	42.70	37.60	33.40	36.20	40.20	38.60	33.80	35.90	39.20	37.80	38.21

[1] Preliminary. *Source: Economic Research Service, U.S. Department of Agriculture (ERS-USDA)*

Average Price Received by Farmers for Lambs in the U.S. — In Dollars Per Hundred Pounds (Cwt.)

Year	Jan.	Feb.	Mar.	Apr.	May	June	July	Aug.	Sept.	Oct.	Nov.	Dec.	Average
1989	67.40	68.40	72.50	75.20	73.10	70.60	68.60	66.60	65.90	62.00	58.70	59.00	67.33
1990	56.40	59.80	66.00	62.90	59.80	55.40	54.40	54.00	52.80	51.90	50.10	48.60	56.01
1991	48.00	45.80	51.10	54.80	57.60	55.30	57.70	53.40	51.80	51.70	50.70	52.00	52.49
1992	53.50	55.20	63.40	69.30	68.80	65.60	62.20	55.90	56.70	55.40	58.20	65.20	60.78
1993	67.30	72.70	76.00	68.10	61.50	55.70	53.90	59.20	64.50	64.50	65.80	66.00	64.60
1994	60.60	59.40	58.60	54.50	54.50	63.00	72.80	75.50	71.20	68.00	70.60	69.10	64.82
1995	67.50	70.40	74.80	74.60	80.40	85.70	85.70	85.60	82.70	77.60	77.10	76.50	78.22
1996	76.10	84.30	86.60	85.90	90.30	100.70	98.30	89.10	88.50	87.00	84.60	88.20	88.30
1997[1]	94.60	99.80	99.60	96.60	90.90	86.60	81.30	92.70	90.60	87.40	83.50	84.10	90.64

[1] Preliminary. *Source: Economic Research Service, U.S. Department of Agriculture (ERS-USDA)*

Silk

Silk is the cloth and thread made from silkworms. The fiber used in commercial silk production is produced primarily by the mulberry silkworm. Silk is produced in a number of countries depending mostly on a favorable climate and adequate labor. A primary requirement of silk production is an ample supply of mulberry trees. The mulberry leaf-feeding silkworm thrives on mulberry leaves. The silkworm spins a cocoon made of silk fiber which is then collected for a process called reeling. Reeling is the bringing together of two or more cocoons to form them into one continuous strand of raw silk.

World production of silk between 1990 and 1994 averaged just over 102,000 metric tonnes. China is by far the world's largest producer of silk, producing about three-quarters of the world total. Silk production in China has been trending higher on a steady basis. In 1996, China's silk production was estimated at 80,000 tonnes, the same total as in 1995. 1994 production was 84,000 tonnes. Between 1989-91, Chinese silk production averaged 55,000 tonnes.

World exports of silk average about 30 percent of total production. China is the world's largest exporter of silk with a market share of about 50 percent.

India is the next largest producer of silk. In 1996 production was estimated at 16,000 tonnes, up from 15,000 tonnes in 1995 and 15,000 tonnes in 1994. In the 1989-91 period, Indian silk production averaged 12,000 tonnes. North Korea is the world's third largest producer of silk with production in 1996 estimated at 5,000 tonnes. Japan's silk production has been trending lower for several years. In 1996 production was estimated at 3,000 tonnes, the same amount as in 1995. In 1994 production was 4,000 tonnes while in the 1989-91 period it averaged 6,000 tonnes. In the 1986-88 period, Japanese silk production averaged over 9,000 tonnes per year. Japan, along with Italy and India, are the major importers of silk.

Futures Markets

Raw silk is traded in Japan on the Kobe Raw Silk Exchange (KSE). Dry Cocoons are traded on the Manila International Futures Exchange Inc., (MIFE).

World Production of Raw Silk — In Metric Tons

Year	Brazil	China	India	Iran	Japan	North Korea	South Korea	Kyrgyzstan[3]	Thailand	Turkmenistan[3]	Uzbekistan[3]	Viet Nam	World Total
1985	1,200	38,956	7,029	280	9,591	3,500	1,436	-----	1,300	-----	3,908	330	68,090
1986	1,200	39,098	9,300	280	8,336	3,600	1,342	-----	1,400	-----	3,710	350	69,178
1987	1,800	40,940	9,498	900	7,864	3,700	1,413	-----	1,200	-----	4,200	360	72,597
1988	1,900	42,041	10,255	900	6,862	3,800	1,355	-----	1,250	-----	4,300	420	73,866
1989	1,697	50,244	10,500	537	6,078	4,000	1,400	-----	1,250	-----	3,900	400	80,745
1990	1,693	55,003	11,000	537	6,000	4,200	971	-----	1,250	-----	4,094	500	85,987
1991	2,077	60,002	14,000	537	5,527	4,400	837	-----	1,300	-----	4,100	500	93,880
1992	2,296	70,302	15,000	537	5,085	4,500	870	1,200	1,300	600	2,200	500	105,220
1993	2,450	76,801	14,168	480	4,254	4,600	683	1,000	1,500	500	2,000	550	109,790
1994	2,450	84,001	14,500	600	2,400	4,700	700	1,000	1,600	500	2,000	600	115,796
1995[1]	2,450	80,001	15,000	600	2,400	4,700	700	1,000	1,600	500	2,000	650	112,350
1996[2]	2,000	80,000	16,000	1,000	3,000	5,000	-----	1,000	2,000	1,000	2,000	1,000	113,000

[1] Preliminary. [2] Estimate. [3] Formerly part of the U.S.S.R.; data not reported separately until 1992. *Source: Food and Agricultural Organization of the United Nations (FAO-UN)*

World Trade of Silk by Selected Countries — In Metric Tons

	Imports							Exports					
Year	France	Hong Kong	India	Italy	Japan	South Korea	World Total	Brazil	China	Hong Kong	Japan	North Korea	World Total
1985	919	3,233	2,000	6,463	7,928	2,567	27,929	581	15,939	3,911	897	850	27,855
1986	572	3,179	2,100	7,133	8,943	3,747	29,835	692	16,349	4,115	586	1,060	27,931
1987	770	6,652	2,100	7,339	8,342	5,582	35,864	648	18,368	7,778	794	1,200	34,886
1988	771	7,489	1,411	8,094	10,259	4,851	39,216	670	20,168	8,553	442	1,200	37,276
1989	1,012	6,362	1,400	7,740	8,512	3,763	35,968	534	19,314	6,748	417	1,100	39,064
1990	796	3,928	1,647	4,775	7,111	3,204	27,322	1,064	13,066	4,102	380	1,200	27,977
1991	579	4,347	2,100	5,297	6,933	3,519	29,623	2,052	15,178	4,186	405	900	29,188
1992	693	4,400	2,843	4,337	5,137	3,627	28,239	1,552	13,474	4,358	701	800	26,433
1993	1,001	5,475	4,977	5,634	5,982	4,494	36,086	1,495	15,652	7,204	904	1,200	35,634
1994	1,047	6,165	5,750	9,235	5,772	4,128	44,124	1,739	21,004	6,149	1,265	1,400	41,996
1995[1]	663	4,775	4,200	5,612	4,331	3,513	37,096	966	16,788	5,176	925	1,000	36,052

[1] Preliminary. *Source: Food and Agricultural Organization of the United Nations (FAO-UN)*

Silver

Silver prices witnessed an occasional hefty swing during 1997, but a bearish bias prevailed until the fourth quarter. However, the action did not mirror 1996 when prices were under constant downward pressure. Prices during the first quarter of 1997 rallied almost 80 cents an ounce from the late 1996 value of $4.75. By mid-1997, March '98 COMEX futures were trading near $4.40/oz., the metal's lowest value since early 1995. Towards yearend 1997, prices rallied towards $6.50/oz., basis March, a nine-year high with the buying, in a perverse way, partly reflecting the weakness in gold. However, the late 1997 bullish enthusiasm did not appear to run deep if one uses as a clue daily futures trading volume and changes in open interest, both of which were generally routine. By yearend, March '98 silver was again under $6.00/oz. Contributing to the curtailed 1997 trading interest were (1) the strong equity markets which siphoned risk capital away from silver and (2) the persistent assurance from the Federal Reserve and world credit markets of little, if any, inflationary pressures.

Many variables impact on silver's price, but which are more important at any given time is not easily discernible. The fundamental approach focuses on tangible supply and demand data which can then be rationalized to support price swings in either direction, which are then exaggerated, as likely occurred in late 1997, by chart and computer generated buy or sell signals. Further clouding the market's outlook is that silver's price is quoted in different markets and perhaps at the same time, different prices. The primary price references are: (l) the London spot which is fixed daily at 12:15 P.M., (2) the COMEX spot settlement and (3) the Handy & Harmon price which is the cash quotation accepted by most commercial users.

Silver prices are also influenced by inflation fears, real and perceived, coupled with a long standing belief that a direct tandem price correlation exists between gold and silver. This relationship is currently under heavy doubt, although silver is likely to retain its nickname as the poor man's gold. If nothing else, the late 1997 price action of the two metals seemed to underscore an underlying speculative demand for silver and very little such demand for gold. The drawdown on COMEX approved vault silver stocks to a twelve year low (about 122 million ounces) during 1997 helped reawaken fundamentalist buying interest. However, declining COMEX silver inventories do not necessarily mean increased consumption, but perhaps a reallocation of inventory placement, either in U.S. vaults and/or exported for inventory placement abroad.

World mine production of silver in 1996 of 493 million ounces compares with 449 million in 1995, which was the lowest since 1986. Only 17 percent of 1996's silver came from primary mines, most was obtained as a by-product of copper, lead, zinc and gold mining. Forecasts for the next few years put mine production around 500 million ounces with production more a function of the price of the host metals associated with silver. Mexico is the world's largest producer with 81 million ounces in 1996 vs. 75 million in 1995, followed by Peru at 63 million (vs. 61 million). U.S. primary production in 1996 of 50.3 million ounces compares with 49.8 million in 1995.

The worldwide recovery of silver from secondary supplies such as scrap and old coinage totaled 151 million ounces in 1996 vs. 149 million in 1995. U.S. recycling of old silver scrap of 42 million ounces in 1996, vs. 40.5 million in 1995, was the world's largest recovery. Next came Japan with 27 million ounces, and Germany at 15 million, both about unchanged from 1995.

World silver fabrication demand in 1996 of 803 million ounces was the highest so far of the 1990's and compares with 769 million in 1995. U.S. demand of 150.7 million ounces compares with 147.7 million in 1995. Japanese demand of 112.1 million in 1996 compares to 112.7 million in 1995. Collectively, European demand was the largest at 221 million ounces vs. 223 million in 1995, with Italy and Germany accounting for almost 100 million ounces in each year. Fabrication demand includes (1) industrial and decorative, (2) photography, (3) jewelry/silverware and (4) coinage; of the four only world coinage use fell in 1996, to 20.7 million ounces, the lowest total since 1989.

Futures Markets

Silver futures are traded on the Tokyo Commodity Exchange (TOCOM), the Chicago Board of Trade (CBOT), the Mid America Commodity Exchange (MidAm), and the New York Mercantile Exchange, COMEX division (COMEX). Options are traded on the European Options Exchange (EOE-Optiebeurs), the CBOT, and the COMEX.

World Mine Production of Silver In Thousands of Kilograms (Metric Tons)

Year	Australia	Bolivia	Canada[3]	Chile	China	Kazakhstan[4]	Rep. of Korea	Mexico	Peru	Poland	Sweden	United States	World Total[2]
1987	1,119	142	1,375	500	100	1,510	209	2,415	2,054	831	254	1,241	14,019
1988	1,118	232	1,443	507	110	2,500	227	2,359	1,552	1,063	208	1,661	15,484
1989	1,075	267	1,371	545	125	2,500	239	2,400	1,840	1,003	228	2,008	16,425
1990	1,173	311	1,501	655	130	2,500	238	2,425	1,930	832	243	2,121	16,600
1991	1,180	376	1,339	678	150	2,200	265	2,295	1,927	899	239	1,860	15,600
1992	1,218	282	1,220	1,029	170	900	333	2,098	1,614	798	210	1,800	14,600
1993	1,092	333	896	970	840	500	215	2,420	1,631	767	255	1,640	14,400
1994	1,045	352	740	983	810	500	257	2,330	1,742	1,064	276	1,490	14,200
1995[1]	939	425	1,245	1,032	910	489	299	2,496	1,909	1,001	268	1,560	15,100
1996[2]	1,020	380	1,228	1,035	930	480	254	2,500	1,968	1,100	270	1,570	15,200

[1] Preliminary. [2] Estimate. [3] Shipments. [4] Formerly part of the U.S.S.R.; data not reported separately until 1992

Source: U.S. Geological Survey (USGS)

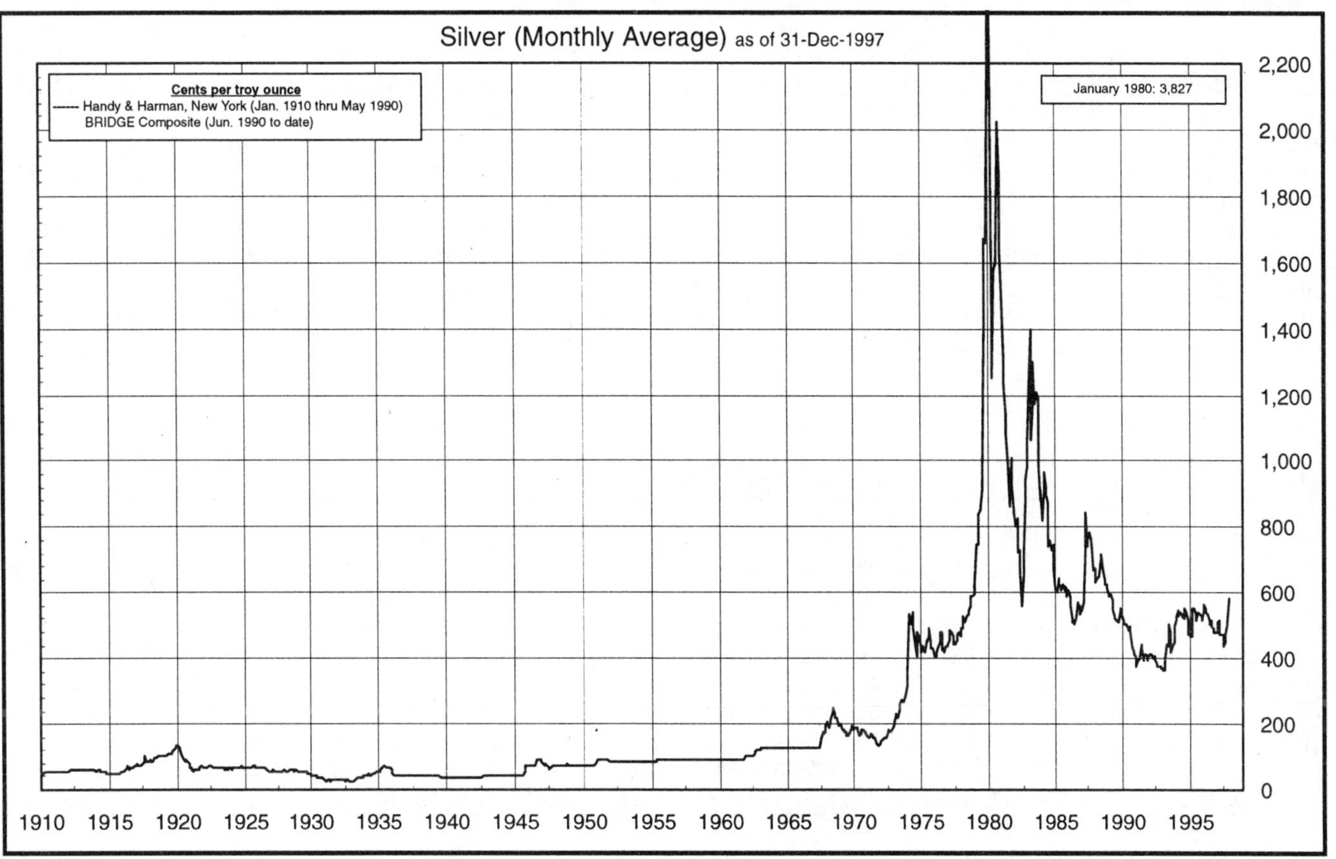

Average Price of Silver in New York (Handy & Harman) In Cents Per Troy Ounce (.999 Fine)

Year	Jan.	Feb.	Mar.	Apr.	May	June	July	Aug.	Sept.	Oct.	Nov.	Dec.	Average
1988	673.25	632.48	641.28	647.83	654.26	703.68	714.65	670.80	636.48	628.45	627.53	610.83	653.46
1989	597.17	589.08	592.98	579.08	544.70	528.02	523.65	517.93	513.30	513.30	546.53	554.28	550.00
1990	524.30	527.84	505.82	504.58	507.39	490.60	485.90	498.15	479.03	436.59	416.90	406.84	482.00
1991	402.82	372.34	396.90	397.07	404.07	438.85	430.38	393.80	403.60	410.22	406.05	390.90	403.92
1992	412.08	413.71	410.36	403.00	406.83	405.64	394.89	379.67	376.33	373.66	376.32	370.98	393.62
1993	367.93	364.39	364.80	396.36	445.02	437.50	503.74	480.61	417.19	433.45	450.25	496.83	429.84
1994	513.14	527.24	545.11	530.87	543.64	539.34	528.65	519.54	552.88	544.10	519.60	476.88	528.42
1995	476.36	469.53	464.83	552.42	555.25	535.27	517.58	539.59	540.78	534.48	529.30	514.75	519.18
1996	547.03	562.75	551.38	540.14	536.02	513.58	502.95	500.98	510.50	492.76	482.76	479.23	518.34
1997	476.39	508.76	519.88	476.41	475.80	474.60	435.96	451.36	472.69	501.15	506.00	571.53	489.21

Source: American Metal Market (AMM)

Average Price of Silver London (Spot Fix) In Pence Per Troy Ounce (.999 Fine)

Year	Jan.	Feb.	Mar.	Apr.	May	June	July	Aug.	Sept.	Oct.	Nov.	Dec.	Average
1987	366.59	359.00	355.64	457.59	507.47	455.07	474.70	493.26	462.20	457.53	378.40	391.31	429.90
1988	373.09	361.12	350.19	343.97	349.76	393.77	416.27	392.67	378.37	361.99	348.15	334.87	367.02
1989	337.32	335.09	346.81	341.28	333.69	340.21	322.29	324.61	326.77	323.99	348.64	348.92	335.80
1990	317.67	311.77	312.45	309.08	302.29	287.85	269.56	263.50	255.45	225.76	212.45	210.97	273.23
1991	209.50	190.10	216.00	227.61	234.43	266.86	263.97	235.06	234.22	238.90	229.09	228.03	231.15
1992	227.68	233.21	238.36	230.72	225.02	219.32	206.74	197.03	203.89	226.06	246.94	240.01	224.58
1993	240.39	254.41	249.55	256.16	287.61	289.42	335.27	324.64	276.85	285.48	306.07	332.78	286.55
1994	344.48	354.77	364.74	358.95	360.86	353.28	341.86	336.67	353.15	339.73	326.64	306.49	345.14
1995	302.80	300.36	290.35	341.95	248.74	336.31	323.80	343.72	348.99	340.29	339.90	336.05	329.44
1996	359.20	367.64	362.03	392.85	354.25	334.68	325.81	330.93	322.98	310.78	290.51	289.77	336.79

Source: American Metal Market (AMM)

SILVER

Average Open Interest of Silver Futures in New York In Contracts

Year	Jan.	Feb.	Mar.	Apr.	May	June	July	Aug.	Sept.	Oct.	Nov.	Dec.
1988	76,788	79,031	68,994	66,187	69,137	83,428	84,517	82,793	82,369	85,261	92,026	90,081
1989	93,582	95,876	93,953	99,598	90,996	86,804	83,466	88,886	85,248	88,406	91,459	93,606
1990	94,397	93,713	96,182	96,701	95,784	103,575	99,098	99,668	92,436	91,093	84,181	80,364
1991	91,685	101,352	99,564	99,791	94,921	105,646	97,554	95,536	87,079	90,791	89,765	91,390
1992	97,179	93,352	88,445	96,427	87,355	84,002	80,879	81,695	74,265	72,090	77,633	72,296
1993	80,155	86,241	87,127	100,985	105,931	102,539	107,537	109,427	93,891	93,316	101,576	110,029
1994	112,584	116,652	112,745	119,314	121,296	126,255	122,138	118,081	113,261	117,224	126,666	134,099
1995	132,158	139,806	132,317	129,063	112,723	108,941	101,842	111,251	95,433	101,763	105,453	95,551
1996	99,316	107,667	92,186	101,011	99,529	110,247	105,627	103,618	93,448	95,809	93,238	83,879
1997	91,385	94,539	90,531	97,434	87,510	90,145	96,777	89,250	79,344	100,464	96,695	93,761

Source: New York Mercantile Exchange, COMEX Division

Volume of Trading of Silver Futures in New York In Thousands of Contracts

Year	Jan.	Feb.	Mar.	Apr.	May	June	July	Aug.	Sept.	Oct.	Nov.	Dec.	Total
1988	274,098	301,119	348,905	313,927	341,145	726,860	638,934	411,665	299,858	268,383	475,374	264,387	4,664,655
1989	317,152	408,485	447,323	354,235	278,496	484,711	272,254	360,381	244,926	261,102	622,123	345,423	4,376,611
1990	343,175	413,287	210,193	364,055	328,804	433,848	242,288	524,815	201,273	308,449	323,664	219,758	3,913,609
1991	309,841	420,092	446,491	395,957	255,548	547,495	344,683	320,639	268,660	252,983	349,698	242,617	4,154,704
1992	408,179	320,226	229,010	322,364	184,825	295,358	197,946	266,347	173,165	125,537	355,728	127,654	3,016,339
1993	167,201	315,916	242,974	476,554	433,460	523,961	503,935	531,772	428,366	338,189	520,591	373,005	4,855,924
1994	489,055	555,136	484,134	585,058	516,396	729,414	339,298	535,722	377,540	455,049	589,220	348,323	5,994,345
1995	390,453	501,454	541,807	592,620	500,522	476,481	280,651	655,854	344,182	272,362	447,095	179,755	5,183,236
1996	415,801	583,767	368,175	547,629	334,973	549,631	296,905	460,686	316,366	321,781	415,441	259,653	4,870,808
1997	401,995	530,514	360,871	493,999	280,536	472,306	340,245	425,471	335,400	430,397	488,024	333,762	4,893,520

Source: New York Mercantile Exchange, COMEX Division

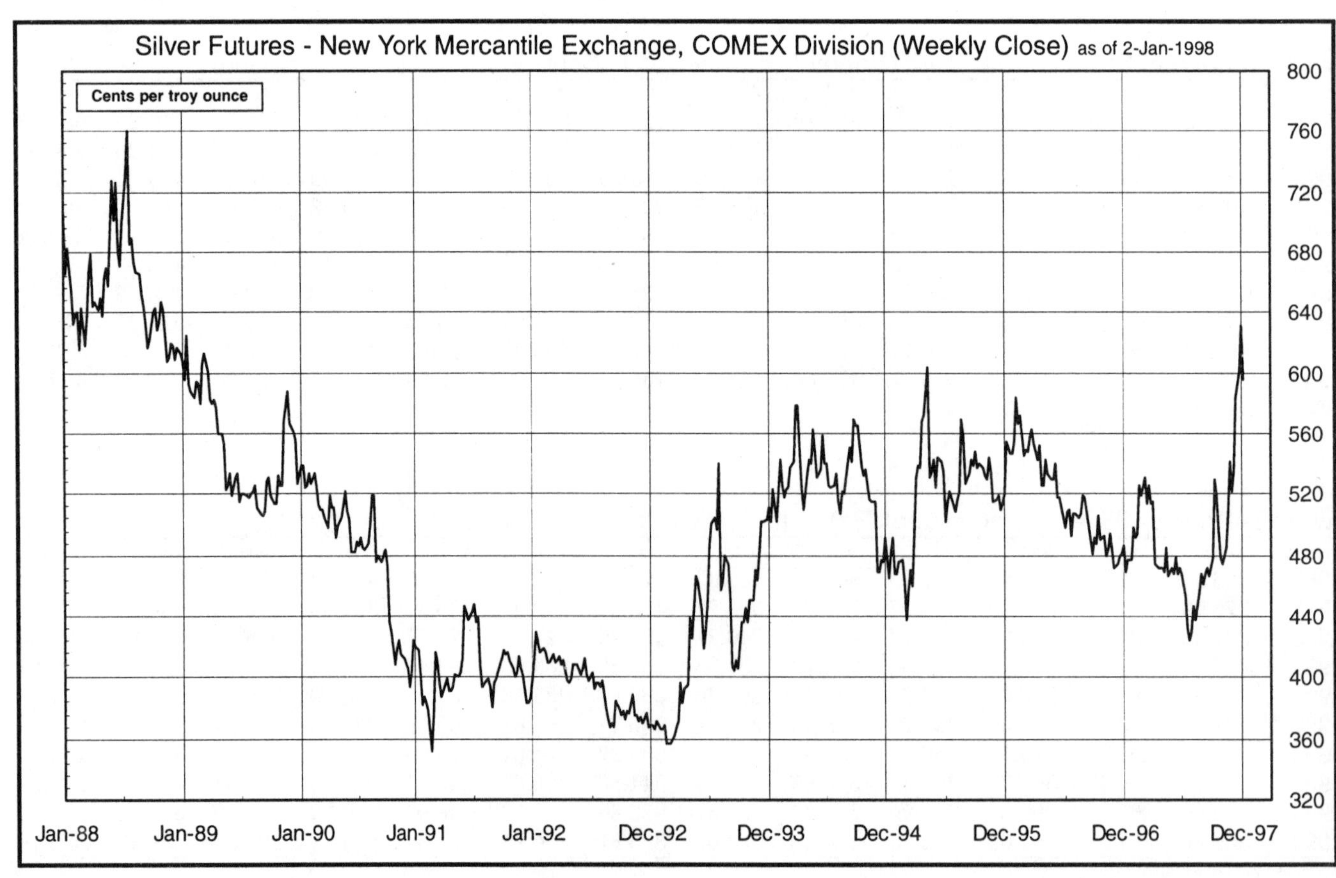

Mine Production of Recoverable Silver in the United States, by State In Metric Tons

Year	Arizona	Idaho	Montana	Nevada	Total	Year	Arizona	Idaho	Montana	Nevada	Total
1985	152	586	125	154	1,227	1991	148	337	222	578	1,848
1986	140	349	148	199	1,074	1992	153	255	195	586	1,740
1987	114	NA	185	379	1,241	1993	157	190	125	713	1,610
1988	152	340	192	608	1,661	1994	183	158	71	602	1,390
1989	171	439	194	625	2,007	1995	220	182	76	766	1,640
1990	173	442	220	646	2,125	1996[1]	188	229	11	605	1,570

[1] Preliminary. [2] Estimate. NA = Not available. *Source: U.S. Geological Survey (USGS)*

Consumption of Silver in the United States, by End Use In Millions of Troy Ounces

Year	Brazing Alloys & Solders	Catalysts	Batteries[2]	Mirrors	Electrical Contacts - Conductors	Photo-graphic Materials[3]	Silver-plate	Jewelry[4]	Sterling Ware	Total Net Industrial Con-sumption	Coinage	Total Con-sumption
1987	5.6	2.4	2.4	1.0	22.7	60.2	2.5	4.2	3.8	115.1	12.2	127.3
1988	NA	2.6	2.5	1.1	23.0	62.5	2.6	2.9	3.5	117.5	7.9	125.4
1989	NA	2.8	2.8	1.1	23.5	65.2	2.7	2.4	3.4	126.0	6.8	132.8
1990	2.8	3.0	3.0	1.2	23.3	67.0	2.8	2.0	3.5	118.2	9.4	131.0
1991	5.6	3.3	3.1	1.1	21.2	65.0	2.8	2.0	3.5	112.3	10.8	128.2
1992	6.5	3.8	3.1	1.2	23.1	63.5	2.9	3.0	3.9	114.5	8.4	128.6
1993	7.2	4.0	3.3	1.3	24.7	64.0	3.0	3.3	4.0	117.4	8.2	131.7
1994	7.7	--------	16.9	--------	28.2	------ 67.8	------	----- 12.0	------	132.6	8.7	141.3
1995	8.0	--------	17.9	--------	31.0	------ 70.3	------	----- 12.5	------	139.7	8.1	147.7
1996[1]	8.2	--------	18.2	--------	31.3	------ 74.4	------	----- 12.4	------	144.6	6.1	150.7

[1] Preliminary. [2] Beginning 1994; includes batteries, catalysts, and mirrors. [3] Beginning 1994; includes photographic materials and silverplate [4] Beginning 1994; includes jewelry and sterlingware. *Source: The Silver Institute*

Commodity Exchange, Inc. (COMEX) Warehouse of Stocks of Silver In Thousands of Troy Ounces

Year	Jan. 1	Feb. 1	Mar. 1	Apr. 1	May 1	June 1	July 1	Aug. 1	Sept. 1	Oct. 1	Nov. 1	Dec. 1
1988	155,429	157,592	155,755	161,276	164,348	168,198	169,743	176,309	178,773	175,282	178,457	174,359
1989	182,657	190,243	194,802	200,995	203,207	206,049	210,385	207,286	212,283	226,570	237,946	238,773
1990	240,796	243,421	252,104	253,773	255,421	251,626	253,326	255,814	260,184	258,614	257,685	265,339
1991	266,206	263,832	257,851	263,563	263,686	266,087	276,961	270,804	269,661	265,874	262,835	270,734
1992	271,692	278,990	270,449	262,239	267,003	267,818	271,259	273,743	278,575	278,526	280,712	275,156
1993	272,824	273,629	271,856	265,580	270,800	273,947	277,228	278,745	276,819	275,370	277,666	263,138
1994	251,685	250,730	239,374	240,187	233,950	236,459	246,291	249,417	255,198	259,634	265,710	258,618
1995	260,708	264,045	235,114	211,028	189,668	184,570	181,269	175,764	156,544	156,529	156,110	156,932
1996	159,695	143,426	151,336	139,059	141,789	150,141	168,079	155,441	151,283	141,673	129,911	148,451
1997	204,051	195,450	193,381	191,676	189,498	201,682	184,691	169,079	164,296	138,775	133,470	128,252

Source: New York Mercantile Exchange, COMEX Division

Production[1] of Refined Silver in the United States, from All Sources In Metric Tons

Year	Jan.	Feb.	Mar.	Apr.	May	June	July	Aug.	Sept.	Oct.	Nov.	Dec.	Total
1988	244	226	294	247	245	294	329	308	229	251	297	303	3,268
1989	312	295	307	300	373	279	240	290	248	246	314	280	3,485
1990	278	244	221	271	267	274	256	241	237	249	303	252	3,093
1991	273	209	229	228	285	236	220	254	263	259	250	268	2,973
1992	414	388	396	375	408	295	366	350	323	393	331	364	4,403
1993	359	406	374	357	315	266	293	275	292	293	261	303	3,794
1994	278	327	319	307	209	371	239	288	273	254	297	281	3,443
1995	279	273	340	281	381	355	331	404	364	340	384	351	4,083
1996	373	299	332	321	327	316	354	314	333	344	304	403	4,020
1997[1]	343	262	296	331	247	326	290	342	329	278			3,653

[1] Preliminary. [2] Through 1991; output of commercial bars .999 fine, including U.S. Mint purchases of crude. Production is from both foreign and domestic silver.Beginning 1992; U.S. mine production of recoverable silver plus imports of refined silver. [2] Preliminary. *Source: U.S. Geological Survey (USGS)*

SILVER

U.S. Exports of Refined Silver to Selected Countries In Thousands of Troy Ounces

Year	Canada	France	Germany	Hong Kong	Japan	Singapore	South Korea	Switzer-land	United Arab Emirates	United Kingdom	Uruguay	Other Countries	Total
1987	2,086	134	261	[2]	5,426	[2]	[2]	[2]	[2]	2,568	[2]	157	11,241
1988	1,073	157	480	[2]	6,030	[2]	166	70	[2]	4,894	[2]	82	14,270
1989	2,597	61	519	[2]	5,997	[2]	588	88	[2]	3,722	[2]	55	13,828
1990	2,586	64	749	[2]	16,568	1,005	298	74	[2]	2,060	152	93	23,664
1991	736	22	350	755	6,519	1,593	2,823	8	3,462	8,628	259	73	25,318
1992	2,177	44	140	497	4,554	2,126	[2]	70	6,922	10,856	671	47	29,274
1993	4,910	[2]	34	1,002	3,414	2,500	1,492	38	4,403	3,673	530	44	22,673
1994	4,289	[2]	8	456	9,275	16	3,084	[2]	3,627	4,896	1,353	193	27,902
1995	1,667	431	[3]	[2]	2,737	2,209	2,929	1,170	10,285	63,882	937	41	86,644
1996[1]	[2]	[2]	[3]	265	18,100	[2]	[2]	[2]	52,800	67	[2]	[2]	71,232

[1] Preliminary. [2] Included in "other countries", if any. *Source: American Bureau of Metal Statistics (ABMS)*

U.S. Imports of Silver from Selected Countries In Thousands of Troy Ounces

	Ores and Concentrates				Refined Bullion						
Year	Canada	Mexico	Other Countries	Total	Canada	Chile	Mexico	Peru	Uruguay	Other Countries	Total
1987	650	1,561	59	2,681	16,665	113	40,779	243	[2]	71	67,959
1988	288	1,511	31	6,151	31,361	211	37,471	11	[2]	139	72,663
1989	56	129	28	225	37,203	724	53,262	2,761	1,958	0	98,429
1990	12	189	2	203	33,518	1,671	40,204	8,141	2,265	165	86,741
1991	42	277	29	348	25,389	6,640	34,448	13,748	[2]	17	81,198
1992	646	126	11	814	24,937	2,002	40,230	16,841	400	2	85,572
1993	299	836	12	1,147	28,622	1,058	27,241	12,709	[2]	28	70,189
1994	369	3,805	97	4,271	28,678	1,923	22,135	12,663	[2]	32	66,141
1995	312	6,269	-----	6,825	27,640	4,694	29,200	13,732	[2]	78	84,446
1996[1]	189	3,890	-----	4,079	30,640	2,424	46,940	9,002	[2]	28	89,034

[1] Preliminary. [2] Included in "other countries", if any. *Source: American Bureau of Metal Statistics (ABMS)*

World Silver Consumption[1] In Millions of Troy Ounces

	Industrial Uses										Coinage							
Year	Canada	France	Ger-many	India	Italy	Japan	Mexico	United Kingdom	United States	World Total	Austria	Canada	France	Ger-many	Mexico	United States	World Total	World Total
1987	10.4	17.6	39.1	20.1	38.6	90.9	6.9	21.1	115.1	538.7	.6	1.2	2.2	3.2	2.3	12.2	30.4	569.1
1988	11.0	21.3	44.0	22.4	37.9	100.4	7.1	22.8	112.0	568.6	.6	1.1	2.2	3.2	2.0	7.9	25.3	593.9
1989	12.0	22.1	46.7	25.6	43.1	100.8	7.2	24.6	120.0	599.2	.4	3.3	2.2	3.2	1.7	6.8	26.3	625.5
1990	4.0	22.4	51.7	42.3	45.7	106.9	14.1	24.7	118.9	651.8	.5	1.9	2.2	2.4	1.2	9.1	31.6	683.4
1991	3.8	26.9	52.2	44.9	57.4	109.3	14.3	24.7	112.3	672.3	.6	.9	2.0	5.5	1.6	10.5	28.4	700.7
1992	1.6	29.7	49.3	58.1	61.1	105.4	15.6	26.3	114.5	687.7	.5	.8	2.1	5.4	8.7	8.1	32.8	720.5
1993	1.6	27.6	45.6	109.9	57.5	105.5	15.6	27.9	123.5	736.1	.5	1.2	2.1	2.6	17.1	8.2	40.5	776.6
1994	1.6	26.5	45.8	91.8	53.2	108.4	15.3	31.4	132.6	716.9	.5	1.5	1.0	7.0	13.0	8.7	42.9	759.9
1995	2.0	29.2	43.6	98.7	51.2	112.7	17.7	32.5	139.7	743.7	.6	.7	1.2	2.3	.6	8.1	25.1	768.8
1996[2]	2.0	24.8	40.8	129.6	52.7	112.1	21.0	34.8	144.6	782.5	.4	.7	.3	3.9	.5	6.1	20.8	803.3

[1] Non-communist areas only. [2] Preliminary. NA = Not available. *Source: The Silver Institute*

Soybean Meal

Soybean meal, a high-protein feed used in formulating livestock and poultry rations, is obtained from the processing (crush) of soybeans and is the world's top protein meal with about 60 percent of total production. Cottonseed and rapeseed meal account for a combined total of about 20 percent, and sunflowerseed meal about 7 percent. The U.S. is the largest producer of soybean meal with Brazil a distant second.

World soybean meal production has increased steadily during the 1990's, from about 70 million metric tonnes in 1990, to a record large 96 million tonnes in 1997/98. U.S. meal production in 1997/98 of 32 million tonnes compares with Brazil's 16 million, Argentina's 9.45 million, and China's 7.8 million, all of which were higher than in 1996/97.

The growth in meal production reflects both increasing global livestock numbers and a directly derived expanding need for high-protein feed, and strong worldwide demand for vegetable oils. Percentagewise, much of the recent gain in foreign trade has come from developing nations in Latin America and Asia, but the European Union is the largest importing region, paced by France who imports about ten percent of the the world total.

World meal consumption in 1997/98 of a record 96.2 million tonnes compares with 92.1 million in 1996/97. The U.S. is the largest single consumer using just under 26 million tonnes. Asia's use in 1997/98, of a record 25.4 million tonnes, has nearly doubled during the past decade. As recently as 1993/94, Asia's meal usage was only 17 million tonnes vs. the EU's 22.7 million. Total European Union consumption ranked third globally in 1997/98 at 22.7 million tonnes. Contributing to the gain in both E.U. and Asian usage (and imports) is the strong growth in poultry production (notably in China), the primary user of soybean meal.

World carryover at the end of the 1997/98 season is forecast at 4.0 million tonnes vs. a year earlier carryin of 4.1 million, with Argentina and Brazil accounting for a combined total of at least 1.2 million tonnes.

U.S. soymeal production (October/September) in 1997/98 of a record 35.5 million short tons compares with 34.2 million in 1996/97. A decade earlier, production totaled 28 million tons. Total 1997/98 supplies of 35.9 million tons compares with 34.5 in 1996/97, and includes a carryin of about .25 million tons as of October 1, 1997 and imports of .12 million tonnes. Domestic usage has climbed steadily during the 1990's and for 1997/98 is forecast at a record high 28.2 million tons vs. 27.2 million in 1996/97, the steady gain largely due to increases in poultry production. As has been the case in recent years, it's likely that poultry demand will continue to be the controlling factor influencing the size of the U.S. crush, and not the demand for soybean oil. Cattle accounts for little soybean meal use, hogs a little more.

U.S. soybean meal exports of 7.4 million short tons in 1997/98 compares with 7.1 million in 1996/97, and the 1979/80 record of 7.9 million tonnes. Major foreign buyers of U.S. soybean meal include Canada, China, Japan, Saudi Arabia and the Netherlands. China, as recently as 1994/95, was a net exporter of soybean meal, but their intensive domestic demand growth has recently made them dependent on U.S. meal imports. If the 1997/98 supply/demand forecasts are realized, ending carryover on September 30, 1998 of 250,000 tonnes will be unchanged from a year earlier.

U.S. soybean meal prices were expected to average between $195-$225 per ton in 1997/98 vs. $270.90 in 1996/97, basis 48 percent protein, Decatur, Illinois. Generally, U.S. soybean meal prices are higher than those abroad.

Futures Markets

Soybean meal futures and options are traded on the Chicago Board of Trade. A smaller futures contract is traded on the Mid-America Commodity Exchange.

World Supply and Demand of Soybean Meal In Thousands of Metric Tons

Year Beginning Oct. 1	Production					Exports			Imports		Consumption			Ending Stocks		
	Brazil	China	EC-12	United States	Total	Brazil	United States	Total	France	Total	EC-12	United States	Total	Brazil	United States	Total
1988-9	11,360	3,570	9,100	22,630	64,230	8,680	4,940	24,980	2,910	26,310	17,810	17,680	66,050	790	160	3,220
1989-90	12,350	3,020	10,580	25,150	70,089	9,430	4,830	26,010	3,480	25,730	19,900	20,220	68,950	1,114	290	4,070
1990-1	11,160	3,280	9,950	25,700	69,500	8,200	4,960	26,890	3,430	27,200	20,190	20,810	70,130	860	260	3,660
1991-2	11,740	2,750	10,530	27,060	73,200	8,780	6,300	28,620	3,550	28,250	21,170	20,870	73,360	520	210	3,140
1992-3	12,170	3,630	10,980	27,550	76,380	8,170	5,650	27,550	3,500	27,870	22,240	22,000	76,050	600	190	3,800
1993-4	14,500	6,160	9,850	27,680	81,200	10,310	4,860	29,950	3,800	29,260	22,680	22,940	80,600	610	140	3,710
1994-5	15,870	6,550	11,490	30,180	87,170	10,450	6,090	30,920	3,790	31,270	24,420	24,080	87,100	980	200	4,370
1995-6	17,040	5,830	10,910	29,510	88,830	11,940	5,450	33,770	3,340	32,700	22,600	24,140	87,750	970	190	4,400
1996-7[1]	15,880	6,480	11,960	31,030	92,150	10,660	6,350	33,910	3,300	34,210	22,780	24,790	92,820	990	190	4,040
1997-8[2]	16,390	7,490	12,270	32,520	98,080	10,900	6,760	35,910	3,410	35,720	23,520	25,850	97,790	990	200	4,140

[1] Preliminary. [2] Forecast. *Source: Foreign Agricultural Service, U.S. Department of Agriculture (FAS-USDA)*

SOYBEAN MEAL

Average Open Interest of Soybean Futures in Chicago In Contracts

Year	Jan.	Feb.	Mar.	Apr.	May	June	July	Aug.	Sept.	Oct.	Nov.	Dec.
1988	65,643	63,960	61,100	66,950	73,264	80,444	71,643	76,295	80,753	75,439	77,466	71,44
1989	71,792	71,599	67,542	58,923	58,794	64,212	59,547	60,925	59,271	60,038	63,552	57,21
1990	60,010	71,773	74,762	76,897	77,307	69,658	63,824	62,033	58,915	68,888	76,899	70,90
1991	62,172	60,017	56,179	59,107	49,973	57,068	55,629	54,342	67,765	68,627	68,263	71,90
1992	67,575	56,453	55,370	59,528	57,204	60,519	66,315	66,861	66,648	72,403	73,255	72,88
1993	63,178	70,384	64,550	66,121	78,386	74,191	91,435	73,770	75,267	77,065	83,802	85,03
1994	87,612	91,142	82,193	89,453	85,553	81,721	84,461	82,691	85,508	94,483	101,030	98,71
1995	97,661	101,253	101,846	99,898	90,237	86,090	83,712	74,233	79,450	85,290	103,824	110,19
1996	95,903	90,010	87,468	101,204	91,453	88,641	77,961	80,727	93,373	88,969	90,007	84,39
1997	86,204	97,618	107,763	111,413	113,848	110,780	114,372	108,923	111,447	118,409	125,201	116,76

Source: Chicago Board of Trade (CBT)

Volume of Trading of Soybean Meal Futures in Chicago In Thousands of Contracts

Year	Jan.	Feb.	Mar.	Apr.	May	June	July	Aug.	Sept.	Oct.	Nov.	Dec.	Tota
1988	393.7	371.5	350.4	396.3	497.3	584.3	482.0	427.7	449.6	446.3	533.1	424.0	5,35
1989	408.1	320.7	382.4	388.8	406.7	403.8	410.7	393.1	382.8	364.8	330.1	294.8	4,48
1990	308.6	276.4	400.2	428.4	421.0	398.3	460.2	435.3	401.6	476.3	448.7	448.5	4,90
1991	323.4	281.8	310.3	429.3	296.8	412.5	484.3	463.6	394.7	410.8	351.6	339.6	4,49
1992	368.7	290.5	312.6	312.2	388.1	381.0	426.0	333.6	327.6	320.2	327.9	357.1	4,14
1993	295.5	288.1	346.6	307.9	356.7	518.2	575.5	460.5	402.4	315.6	469.3	380.6	4,71
1994	405.6	339.8	330.7	380.7	467.2	456.3	384.5	354.4	366.3	317.4	370.4	420.5	4,59
1995	283.6	307.5	404.4	410.9	532.7	479.6	610.8	491.8	481.9	449.0	523.4	625.6	5,60
1996	496.4	442.9	435.8	656.0	439.2	442.4	507.2	490.3	425.9	581.1	491.9	452.1	5,86
1997	479.0	481.8	509.5	576.6	581.9	569.8	579.7	452.2	531.3	589.5	561.1	512.5	6,42

Source: Chicago Board of Trade (CBT)

Supply and Distribution of Soybean Meal in the United States — In Thousands of Short Tons

Year Beginning Oct. 1	Supply: For Stocks Oct. 1	Supply: Production	Supply: Total Supply	Distribution: Domestic	Distribution: Exports	Distribution: Total	$ Ton Decatur 48% Protein Solvent	$ Tonne: Decatur 44% Solvent	$ Tonne: Brazil FOB 45-46% Protein	$ Tonne: Rotterdam CIF
1988-9	153	24,943	25,113	19,496	5,444	24,940	252.40	257	241	259
1989-90	173	27,719	27,928	22,291	5,319	27,610	186.48	192	181	204
1990-1	318	28,325	28,688	22,934	5,469	28,403	181.40	187	178	198
1991-2	285	29,831	30,183	23,008	6,945	29,953	189.20	194	184	203
1992-3	230	30,364	30,687	24,251	6,232	30,483	193.75	201	185	207
1993-4	204	30,514	30,788	25,282	5,356	30,638	192.86	199	182	202
1994-5	150	33,269	33,483	26,542	6,717	33,260	162.55	167	172	184
1995-6[1]	223	32,527	32,826	26,611	6,002	32,613	236.00	248	256	256
1996-7[2]	212	34,209	34,522	27,322	6,994	34,316	270.90	286	289	278
1997-8[3]	207	35,843	36,175	28,500	7,450	35,950	195-210	236	256	258

[1] Preliminary. [2] Estimate. [3] Forecast. *Source: Economic Research Service, U.S. Department of Agriculture (ERS-USDA)*

U.S. Exports of Soybean Cake & Meal, by Country of Destination — In Thousands of Metric Tons

Year	Algeria	Australia	Canada	Dominican Republic	Italy	Japan	Mexico	Netherlands	Philippines	Russia[2]	Spain	Venezuela	Total
1987	131.5	29.4	753.0	79.6	726.8	21.1	50.6	764.0	87.5	270.9	98.3	695.5	5,929
1988	411.4	35.5	718.1	92.7	543.6	33.0	332.3	553.9	110.6	1,122.0	71.2	851.3	6,348
1989	389.1	7.7	569.2	66.2	188.6	10.8	269.5	269.0	59.1	1,417.9	44.2	283.8	4,712
1990	373.5	28.2	555.5	130.5	146.4	20.8	253.0	229.7	200.7	1,568.4	19.6	332.2	4,826
1991	323.5	99.4	651.2	142.6	33.5	24.1	303.6	339.8	150.4	2,271.0	5.5	405.9	5,536
1992	237.8	75.9	582.5	146.7	93.4	167.2	454.4	420.0	434.8	765.1	92.3	473.8	6,236
1993	266.1	90.6	646.7	200.8	91.5	208.7	187.8	580.8	295.7	697.1	203.8	425.0	5,536
1994	248.3	247.0	706.3	209.2	27.1	76.9	367.5	465.6	257.9	159.5	92.6	258.9	4,825
1995	216.7	190.2	798.7	219.2	70.2	246.7	340.0	751.6	593.4	11.1	127.7	181.4	5,890
1996[1]	203.4	157.2	687.3	260.7	85.9	225.5	292.2	452.6	423.2	5.1	51.8	274.9	5,860

[1] Preliminary. [2] Formerly part of the U.S.S.R.; data not reported separately until 1992. *Source: The Oil World*

Production of Soybean Cake & Meal[2] in the United States — In Thousands of Short Tons

Crop Year	Oct.	Nov.	Dec.	Jan.	Feb.	Mar.	Apr.	May	June	July	Aug.	Sept.	Total	Yield of Meal from Soybeans in lbs.
1988-9	2,235.5	2,399.4	2,390.0	2,359.8	2,036.3	2,218.8	2,126.6	2,061.2	1,802.9	1,749.2	1,804.4	1,758.6	24,943	47.43
1989-90	2,246.2	2,492.5	2,519.6	2,548.6	2,187.2	2,432.3	2,263.7	2,224.2	2,183.4	2,196.6	2,237.1	2,187.3	27,718	47.63
1990-1	2,508.8	2,513.2	2,431.5	----------	7,082.0	----------	----------	6,640.8	----------	----------	7,148.9	----------	28,325	47.47
1991-2	----------	7,920.4	----------	2,665.5	2,393.8	2,544.4	2,411.3	2,262.5	2,372.4	2,434.2	2,429.0	2,397.3	29,831	47.51
1992-3	2,698.1	2,697.3	2,763.4	2,781.2	2,430.4	2,691.3	2,519.1	2,536.3	2,373.0	2,324.1	2,188.3	2,361.8	30,364	47.54
1993-4	2,707.1	2,714.8	2,696.7	2,632.3	2,458.1	2,696.3	2,510.0	2,446.4	2,330.7	2,398.0	2,406.6	2,517.1	30,514	47.62
1994-5	2,812.5	2,903.5	3,027.8	3,007.5	2,755.0	3,048.5	2,829.8	2,697.9	2,492.1	2,565.4	2,589.8	2,535.8	33,269	47.33
1995-6	2,893.2	2,948.9	2,972.3	2,945.2	2,652.1	2,757.5	2,683.1	2,534.6	2,566.2	2,656.3	2,513.4	2,404.1	32,527	47.69
1996-7	2,992.8	3,151.8	3,263.8	3,251.7	2,966.8	3,089.1	2,709.1	2,618.1	2,573.2	2,517.4	2,465.2	2,609.6	34,209	47.37
1997-8[1]	3,320.0	3,390.6	3,624.4										41,340	

[1] Preliminary. [2] At oil mills; including millfeed and lecithin. *Source: Economic Research Service, U.S. Department of Agriculture (ERS-USDA)*

Stocks (at Oil Mills)[2] of Soybean Cake & Meal in the U.S., on First of Month — In Thousands of Short Tons

Year	Oct.	Nov.	Dec.	Jan.	Feb.	Mar.	Apr.	May	June	July	Aug.	Sept.
1988-9	153.5	267.8	295.6	353.6	442.3	395.7	237.9	296.8	260.4	218.0	264.9	152.0
1989-90	172.9	220.5	194.3	328.2	254.0	262.0	311.8	307.9	252.6	262.5	267.7	232.0
1990-1	318.3	290.9	313.6	----------	455.8	----------	----------	527.8	----------	----------	425.0	----------
1991-2	----------	285.0	----------	281.0	258.3	291.3	315.6	310.4	310.2	274.7	260.5	209.9
1992-3	230.0	307.9	411.3	360.8	440.0	420.5	336.9	268.5	328.4	257.3	386.1	353.8
1993-4	204.4	375.1	282.3	290.1	230.0	283.1	277.3	333.0	325.2	254.3	267.5	144.9
1994-5	149.6	240.9	231.6	241.1	197.7	227.1	173.1	382.7	337.6	222.6	252.0	203.8
1995-6	223.4	196.9	241.3	394.8	302.2	229.9	369.3	382.1	306.8	406.2	298.8	218.3
1996-7	212.4	200.2	291.8	254.4	263.0	198.5	322.6	280.1	256.5	317.3	303.2	257.4
1997-8[1]	206.6	218.2	412.2									

[1] Preliminary. [2] Including millfeed and lecithin. *Source: Economic Research Service, U.S. Department of Agriculture (ERS-USDA)*

SOYBEAN MEAL

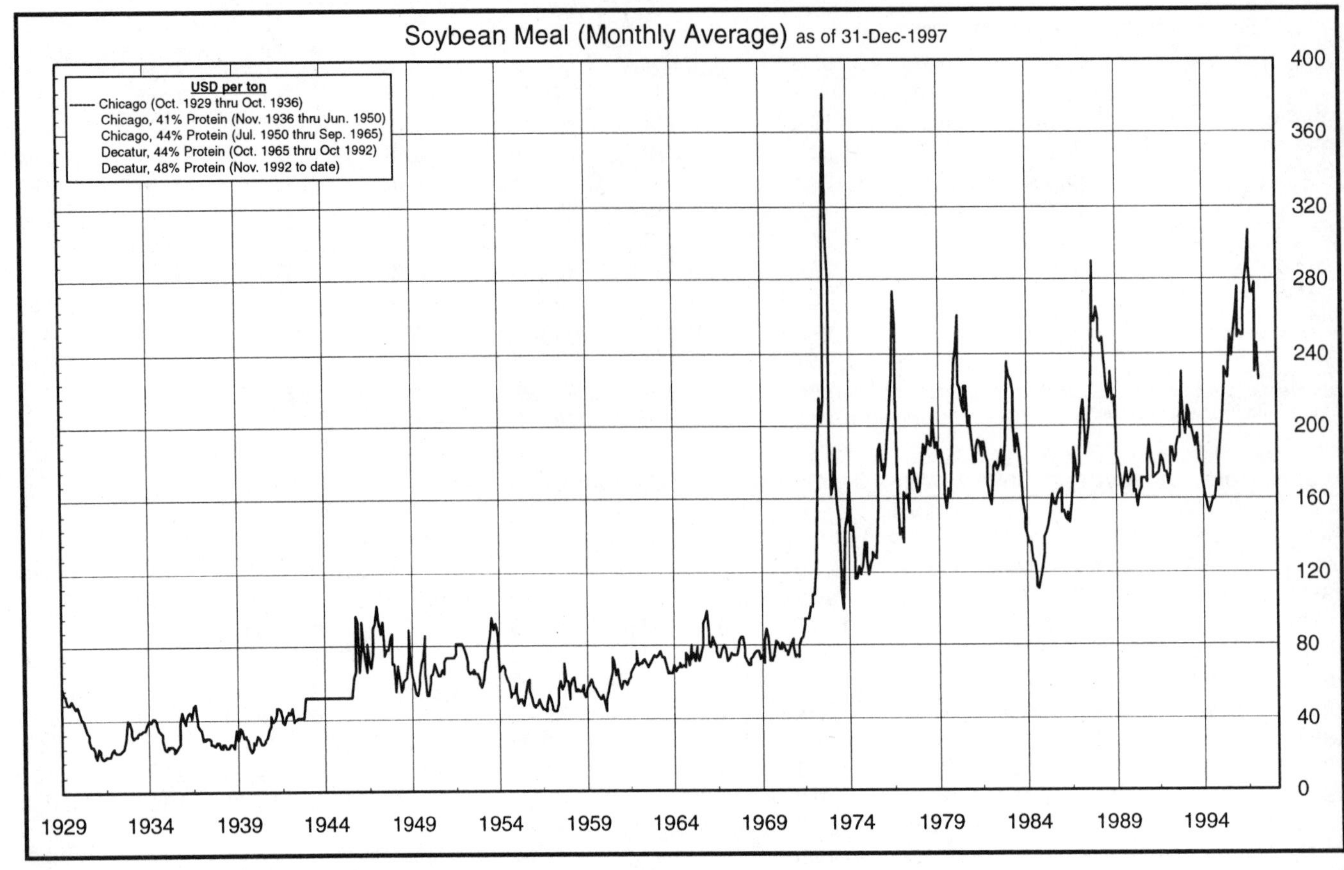

Average Price of Soybean Meal (44% Solvent) at Decatur In Dollars Per Short Ton--Bulk

Year	Oct.	Nov.	Dec.	Jan.	Feb.	Mar.	Apr.	May	June	July	Aug.	Sept.	Average
1987-8	185.50	206.60	214.80	193.75	183.00	191.80	200.40	223.50	287.80	255.60	255.10	264.90	221.90
1988-9	259.75	248.20	246.00	249.30	234.10	237.10	220.75	214.70	227.50	231.50	215.50	227.50	234.33
1989-90	191.60	183.40	179.40	172.30	161.90	165.10	165.40	176.20	169.10	171.30	172.40	176.90	173.75
1990-1	172.50	163.80	164.80	153.70	163.50	165.75	171.50	171.00	171.10	169.70	177.60	191.90	169.74
1991-2	183.00	178.00	170.70	172.70	174.30	174.20	174.80	182.75	181.70	173.90	174.40	175.10	176.30
1992-3	168.60	170.90	176.40	175.60	167.50	172.40	175.60	181.70	181.30	217.60	206.90	186.50	181.75
1993-4	180.60	195.70	192.50	185.90	184.40	182.00	176.40	191.10	183.00	168.10	165.60	162.50	180.65
1994-5	156.40	150.90	145.40	145.10	149.40	145.70	151.00	148.10	149.10	160.10	157.50	171.75	152.54
1995-6	183.40	194.10	213.60	220.50	216.70	215.70	237.90	232.30	227.90	242.30	251.10	265.50	225.08
1996-7	238.00	242.70	240.90	240.70	253.60	270.40	277.70	296.00	275.90	261.49	261.60	265.70	260.39

Source: Economic Research Service, U.S. Department of Agriculture (ERS-USDA)

Average Price of Soybean Meal (48% Solvent) at Decatur In Dollars Per Short Ton--Bulk

Year	Oct.	Nov.	Dec.	Jan.	Feb.	Mar.	Apr.	May	June	July	Aug.	Sept.	Averag
1988-9	280.10	268.90	266.90	270.10	252.10	254.00	238.00	232.30	246.25	251.00	234.30	234.90	252.4
1989-90	208.10	194.90	191.60	183.80	172.90	176.40	178.00	189.40	182.00	183.92	186.75	190.00	186.4
1990-1	185.40	174.25	175.90	167.00	174.50	177.60	182.50	182.10	183.25	181.00	188.75	204.25	181.4
1991-2	196.30	190.25	183.10	184.00	185.40	185.90	187.20	195.25	203.90	186.25	186.00	187.00	189.2
1992-3	180.60	181.90	187.60	188.75	179.90	183.60	187.40	193.25	193.10	229.90	219.10	199.90	193.7
1993-4	194.50	209.40	206.00	198.30	198.40	195.40	188.90	193.75	195.50	181.10	178.60	174.50	192.8
1994-5	168.50	161.00	156.90	156.40	151.30	156.90	161.90	159.10	160.40	170.45	166.70	180.99	162.5
1995-6	193.90	204.10	223.60	232.00	228.30	226.57	249.30	244.30	238.80	252.50	261.20	276.40	235.9
1996-7	248.50	251.50	250.60	249.20	262.40	280.50	288.60	306.40	287.90	273.60	273.30	278.30	270.9
1997-8	229.30	245.30	222.50										232.3

Source: Economic Research Service, U.S. Department of Agriculture (ERS-USDA)

Soybean Oil

During each crop year of the 1990's, world soybean oil production and consumption set new records; 1997/98 output of 21.7 million metric tonnes compares with 20.6 million in 1996/97, and 15.9 million in 1990/91. The U.S., the world's largest soyoil producer, generally accounts for about a third of total production and produces twice that of Brazil, the second largest producer. Of the important edible vegetable oils, soyoil is the world's largest--about 29 percent in 1997/98--followed by palm oil (23 percent) and rapeseed oil (14 percent). World soyoil use in 1997/98 was forecast at a record 21.8 million tonnes vs. 20.6 million in 1996/97. The U.S. is the largest consumer with 6.49 million tonnes in 1997/98, and China is now second at 3.0 million tonnes with their intake more than doubling since the early 1980's. World carryover stocks at the end of 1997/98 were estimated at 2.4 million tonnes, a shade higher than a year earlier.

World soybean oil exports in 1997/98 of a record 6.0 million tonnes compares to 5.8 million in 1996/97. Argentina is the largest exporter with Brazil second. U.S. exports in 1997/98 of one million tonnes compare with 910,000 in 1996/97. China is the world largest importer with 1.6 million tonnes in 1997/98, followed by Iran with 410,000 tonnes. Total world imports in 1997/98 of a record 6.1 million tonnes compares with 5.7 million in 1996/97. U.S. bean oil imports are insignificant.

U.S. soyoil production in 1997/98 (October/September) of a record high 16.7 billion pounds compares with the previous high of 15.7 billion in 1996/97. Carryin stocks on October 1, 1997 of 1.55 billion pounds compares with 2.0 billion a year earlier. The U.S. bean oil supply in 1997/98 of a record 18.3 billion pounds compares with 17.8 billion in 1996/97. 1997/98 disappearance of a record 16.7 billion pounds compares to 16.3 billion in 1996/97.

There is a mild seasonality to domestic soybean oil usage, generally peaking during October and setting a low in the following calendar year's first quarter. Domestic use in 1997/98 of a record high 14.3 billion pounds compares with 14.2 billion in 1996/97. Exports of 2.4 billion pounds compares with 2.1 billion, respectively, the increase partially reflecting the comparative price advantage of U.S. oil relative to other key oilseeds, notably palm oil, in the wake of the Southeast Asian drought that has tightened palm oil supplies.

Crude soybean oil prices (basis Decatur) in 1997/98 were expected to range from 23.0¢ to 26.0¢ per pound vs. a 22.50¢ per pound average in 1996/97, and the high so far in the 1990's of 27.6 cents, made during 1994/95.

Futures Markets

Soybean oil futures and options are traded on the Chicago Board of Trade (CBT).

World Supply and Demand of Soybean Oil — In Thousands of Metric Tons

Year Beginning Oct. 1	Production				Exports			Imports		Consumption					Stocks[3]	
	Brazil	EC-12	United States	Total	Brazil	United States	Total	India	Total	Brazil	EC-12	India	United States	Total	United States	Total
1988-9	2,740	2,010	5,320	14,630	700	750	3,710	30	3,490	2,140	1,590	410	4,800	14,870	780	1,660
1989-90	2,980	2,350	5,900	16,000	870	610	3,940	30	3,970	2,000	1,610	340	5,480	15,950	590	1,740
1990-1	2,679	2,243	6,082	15,909	686	356	3,635	20	3,587	2,136	1,661	370	5,515	15,886	810	1,988
1991-2	2,815	2,337	6,507	16,851	658	748	3,558	100	3,487	2,167	1,703	442	5,554	16,366	1,016	2,470
1992-3	2,910	2,540	6,250	17,200	690	640	4,210	40	3,900	2,280	2,000	560	5,920	17,220	710	2,050
1993-4	3,470	2,240	6,330	18,250	1,350	690	4,850	40	4,730	2,320	1,850	710	5,870	18,410	500	1,770
1994-5	3,800	2,580	7,080	19,710	1,550	1,220	6,080	60	6,100	2,470	1,920	560	5,860	19,440	520	2,050
1995-6	4,030	2,470	6,910	20,140	1,600	450	5,280	60	5,160	2,530	1,950	770	6,110	19,640	910	2,520
1996-7[1]	3,760	2,710	7,140	20,710	1,330	930	5,910	90	5,930	2,600	1,990	740	6,460	20,860	690	2,380
1997-8[2]	3,880	2,770	7,700	22,200	1,350	1,130	6,350	100	6,360	2,700	2,110	950	6,580	22,260	700	2,330

[1] Preliminary. [2] Forecast. [3] End of season. *Source: Foreign Agricultural Service, U.S. Department of Agriculture (FAS-USDA)*

Supply and Distribution of Soybean Oil in the United States — In Millions of Pounds

Year Beginning Oct. 1	Production	Imports	Stocks Oct. 1	Exports	Domestic Disappearance: Total Domestic	Food: Shortening	Food: Margarine	Food: Cooking & Salad Oils	Food: Other Edible	Food: Total Food	Non-Food: Paint & Varnish	Non-Food: Resins & Plastics	Non-Food: Total Non-Food	Total Disappearance
1988-9	11,737	137	2,092	1,661	10,591	3,419	1,537	4,497	137	9,636	35	124	282	12,252
1989-90	13,004	22	1,715	1,353	12,083	3,934	1,754	4,726	124	10,537	38	112	272	13,436
1990-1	13,408	17	1,305	780	12,164	4,090	1,811	4,693	130	10,722	49	106	295	12,944
1991-2	14,345	1	1,786	1,648	12,245	4,091	1,911	4,961	148	11,112	46	98	301	13,893
1992-3	13,778	10	2,239	1,419	14,473	4,465	1,970	4,717	254	11,505	38	95	296	14,473
1993-4	13,951	68	1,555	1,529	14,471	4,773	1,840	4,999	221	11,832	46	115	304	14,471
1994-5	15,613	17	1,103	2,680	15,597	4,714	1,693	5,546	222	12,175	49	124	287	15,597
1995-6	15,240	95	1,137	992	13,465	4,702	1,699	5,317	159	11,877	48	119	297	14,457
1996-7[1]	15,743	53	2,015	2,050	14,242	4,578	1,667	6,116	60	12,421	51	132	333	16,291
1997-8[2]	16,725	60	1,520	2,400	14,350						45	123	412	16,750

[1] Preliminary. [2] Forecast. *Source: Economic Research Service, U.S. Department of Agriculture (ERS-USDA)*

SOYBEAN OIL

Stocks of Soybean Oil (Crude & Refined) in the United States, at End of Month In Millions of Pounds

Crop Year Beginning Oct.		Oct.	Nov.	Dec.	Jan.	Feb.	Mar.	Apr.	May	June	July	Aug.	Sept.
1991-2	Crude	----------	----------	1,955.9	1,915.8	2,156.8	2,175.8	2,211.3	2,213.9	2,216.8	2,205.0	2,126.8	2,026.2
	Refined	----------	----------	259.8	243.7	245.7	224.3	211.2	219.6	209.7	215.9	236.0	213.2
1992-3	Crude	1,856.1	1,885.0	2,041.5	2,177.8	2,110.4	2,029.0	2,068.9	2,006.4	1,967.0	1,848.8	1,518.6	1,352.9
	Refined	220.2	220.2	238.6	232.3	226.4	217.1	229.0	234.3	207.0	211.8	201.2	201.9
1993-4	Crude	1,239.6	1,209.9	1,189.3	1,184.2	1,184.0	1,192.3	1,329.8	1,346.2	1,330.0	1,352.6	1,124.0	904.7
	Refined	213.1	189.7	217.5	230.4	216.9	209.8	223.5	220.6	223.8	218.2	215.4	198.4
1994-5	Crude	850.8	811.4	826.6	880.6	876.7	838.3	860.5	893.9	885.9	906.3	895.3	905.7
	Refined	204.7	215.5	231.7	236.2	252.1	221.3	229.1	236.5	225.8	235.7	204.7	231.0
1995-6	Crude	990.4	908.9	1,154.3	1,237.4	1,264.2	1,366.6	1,490.1	1,531.7	1,672.4	1,951.4	1,874.3	1,799.3
	Refined	990.4	908.9	1,154.3	1,237.4	1,264.2	1,366.6	1,490.1	1,531.7	1,672.4	1,951.4	1,874.3	1,799.3
1996-7	Crude	1,796.5	1,711.6	1,805.1	1,928.5	1,982.6	1,938.2	1,929.9	1,919.4	1,917.8	1,760.3	1,492.8	1,321.1
	Refined	196.4	186.8	222.0	243.8	220.6	233.1	233.9	223.9	220.1	217.8	207.1	199.0
1997-8[1]	Crude	1,307.0	1,303.6	1,439.8	1,518.2								
	Refined	218.6	221.9	239.8	269.2								

[1] Preliminary. *Source: Bureau of the Census, U.S. Department of Commerce*

U.S. Exports of Soybean Oil[1], by Country of Destination In Metric Tons

Year Beginning Oct. 1	Canada	Ecuador	Ethiopia	Haiti	India	Mexico	Morocco	Pakistan	Panama	Peru	Turkey	Vene-zuela	Grand Total
1986-7	6,940	18,814	561	6,940	47,098	21,883	59,547	146,663	2,975	1,292	0	18,652	538,466
1987-8	7,344	19,050	17,605	3,411	151,600	11,537	35,821	396,737	3,736	1,144	17,098	4,866	850,015
1988-9	5,364	30,930	8,960	2,846	28,127	17,730	80,023	453,067	6,695	5,778	0	29,055	753,576
1989-90	5,443	26,314	22,858	1,688	16,391	4,435	77,985	309,502	3,174	5,206	0	8,198	613,902
1990-1	3,790	20,832	14,948	4,946	13,544	11,087	73,255	66,209	8,123	6,566	16,460	0	353,959
1991-2	11,153	528	19,619	4,737	67,577	23,383	127,602	250	11,143	32,696	81,976	13	747,465
1992-3	28,585	17	8,272	6,753	49,452	44,194	57,995	0	641	36,340	58,436	0	643,796
1993-4	4,401	0	24,509	1,747	46,846	18,499	31,563	72,204	248	24,081	34,920	26	693,697
1994-5	24,886	12,698	8,391	49,793	28,949	58,623	29,053	25,500	13,342	8,692	5,750	2,016	1,215,804
1995-6[2]	43,910	1,155	4,546	15,040	20,841	46,645	0	0	9,512	35,999	1,960	1,876	449,869

[1] Crude & refined oil combined as such. [2] Preliminary. *Source: Foreign Agricultural Service, U.S. Department of Agriculture (FAS-USDA)*

Production of Crude Soybean Oil[2] in the United States In Millions of Pounds

Year	Oct.	Nov.	Dec.	Jan.	Feb.	Mar.	Apr.	May	June	July	Aug.	Sept.	Total
1988-9	1,047	1,109	1,110	1,106	952	1,041	1,010	977	856	836	855	843	11,737
1989-90	1,057	1,146	1,161	1,187	1,022	1,142	1,067	1,050	1,036	1,038	1,059	1,038	13,004
1990-1	1,188	1,168	1,138	------------	3,331	------------	------------	3,171	------------	------------	3,412	------------	13,408
1991-2	------------	3,772	------------	1,270	1,147	1,228	1,167	1,096	1,152	1,177	1,179	1,158	14,345
1992-3	1,238	1,200	1,239	1,247	1,102	1,216	1,148	1,152	1,083	1,070	1,006	1,078	13,778
1993-4	1,241	1,228	1,218	1,192	1,122	1,231	1,155	1,123	1,070	1,099	1,104	1,168	13,951
1994-5	1,328	1,342	1,403	1,400	1,289	1,419	1,333	1,275	1,183	1,205	1,228	1,208	15,61
1995-6	1,354	1,360	1,382	1,360	1,236	1,292	1,259	1,197	1,221	1,263	1,171	1,139	15,234
1996-7	1,401	1,430	1,473	1,474	1,348	1,413	1,254	1,216	1,196	1,176	1,141	1,222	15,74
1997-8[1]	1,584	1,572											18,93

[1] Preliminary. [2] Not seasonally adjusted. *Source: Economic Research Service, U.S. Department of Agriculture (ERS-USDA)*

Production of Refined Soybean Oil in the United States In Millions of Pounds

Year	Oct.	Nov.	Dec.	Jan.	Feb.	Mar.	Apr.	May	June	July	Aug.	Sept.	Total
1988-9	867.1	826.9	800.8	776.7	709.6	830.1	800.6	867.4	801.4	791.4	866.6	866.6	9,80
1989-90	936.8	912.0	873.9	887.8	800.6	800.6	812.7	952.8	915.1	903.7	931.1	935.7	10,74
1990-1	1,028.0	980.6	934.7	------------	2,717.1	------------	------------	2,865.5	------------	------------	2,952.8	------------	11,47
1991-2	------------	2,918.1	------------	933.8	876.7	1,041.3	973.1	993.3	977.9	979.2	997.6	1,040.7	11,73
1992-3	1,095.6	999.4	951.0	960.1	935.4	1,054.9	1,039.7	950.6	1,042.8	978.2	1,066.7	1,109.7	12,18
1993-4	1,094.3	1,053.5	1,030.8	960.1	945.5	1,056.6	1,018.5	1,012.0	1,017.3	968.0	1,107.2	1,044.6	12,30
1994-5	1,123.0	1,079.2	1,060.6	1,002.5	968.2	1,063.6	1,010.4	1,077.0	993.5	940.9	1,076.8	1,039.8	12,43
1995-6	1,119.2	1,088.8	1,018.5	979.9	934.3	1,042.6	997.3	1,009.3	962.8	971.9	1,115.8	1,058.7	12,29
1996-7	1,111.7	1,064.1	1,025.7	969.8	931.5	1,057.1	1,023.7	1,026.2	984.8	1,019.1	1,094.3	1,072.5	12,38
1997-8[1]	1,173.9	1,156.3	1,110.1	1,093.6									13,60

[1] Preliminary. *Source: Bureau of the Census, U.S. Department of Commerce*

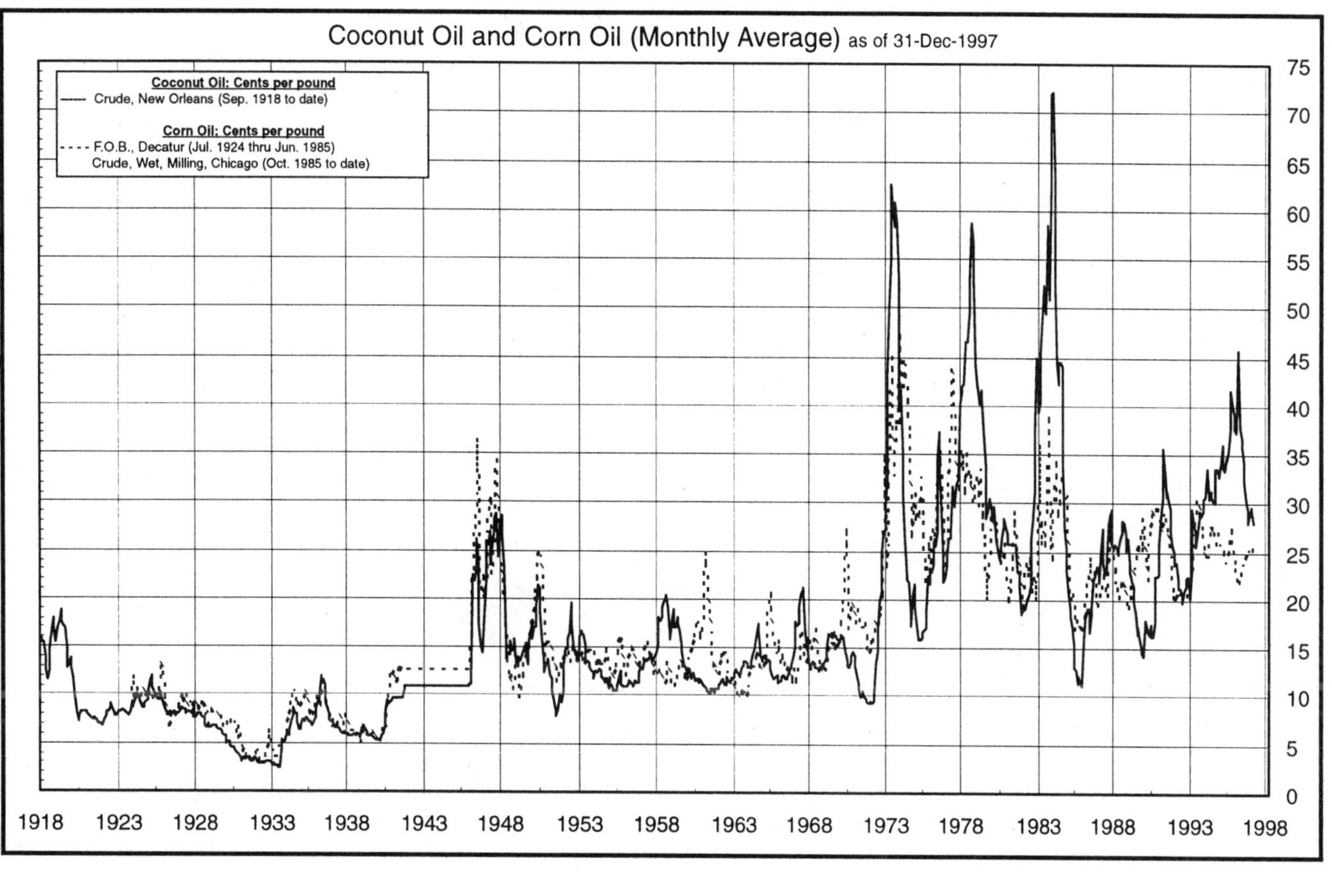

Consumption of Soybean Oil in End Products in the United States In Millions of Pounds

Year	Jan.	Feb.	Mar.	Apr.	May	June	July	Aug.	Sept.	Oct.	Nov.	Dec.	Total
1988	913.9	820.5	930.0	839.9	870.5	937.9	936.5	907.3	829.1	862.2	829.1	846.6	10,524
1989	780.8	729.5	834.7	800.8	851.9	854.2	774.7	876.9	876.2	923.2	889.7	887.0	10,080
1990	901.3	815.7	952.0	893.6	950.9	927.8	866.0	905.4	895.7	984.1	912.9	878.0	10,883
1991	--------	2,690.3	------------	--------	2,831.8	------------	--------	2,837.7	------------	--------	2,907.8	------------	11,268
1992	880.4	867.0	1,010.1	947.9	956.7	962.1	935.5	932.4	1,019.8	1,061.7	951.8	946.1	11,472
1993	934.5	942.2	1,092.6	1,044.6	981.2	1,036.0	1,019.3	1,097.3	1,103.3	1,123.6	1,092.1	1,029.2	12,496
1994	924.5	939.1	1,084.7	1,040.6	1,001.4	1,023.8	974.9	1,119.2	1,075.4	1,123.3	1,103.4	1,063.8	12,474
1995	991.1	950.0	1,093.8	1,006.2	1,077.3	1,020.8	948.7	1,046.1	1,042.3	1,092.0	1,067.7	1,002.6	12,339
1996	964.9	927.4	1,026.4	999.8	1,020.6	946.2	959.9	1,123.3	1,042.8	1,137.1	1,080.9	1,093.1	12,322
1997[1]	1,086.0	979.7	1,104.9	1,060.4	1,034.1	995.2	991.4	1,126.1	1,067.8	1,128.5	1,100.0	1,087.8	12,762

[1] Preliminary. *Source: Bureau of the Censue, U.S. Department of Commerce*

U.S. Exports of Soybean Oil (Crude and Refined) In Millions of Pounds

Year	Jan.	Feb.	Mar.	Apr.	May	June	July	Aug.	Sept.	Oct.	Nov.	Dec.	Total
1988	25.7	281.0	279.4	87.7	138.6	269.0	157.2	78.1	183.2	200.1	110.6	119.9	1,931
1989	104.5	65.8	112.4	105.5	161.4	72.1	159.3	181.1	265.6	116.2	82.5	113.4	1,540
1990	95.4	136.2	164.4	33.0	112.0	161.9	122.6	82.8	132.9	85.4	43.9	12.1	1,183
1991	--------	71.8	------------	--------	132.3	------------	--------	434.8	------------	--------	336.1	------------	975
1992	140.0	171.9	134.6	155.4	69.1	129.1	163.7	205.2	142.5	169.5	113.2	91.6	1,686
1993	146.8	188.0	143.3	61.1	154.8	75.4	59.9	116.0	99.7	190.4	88.6	200.2	1,524
1994	120.4	144.6	94.4	46.1	111.6	36.1	57.7	184.6	254.0	154.8	303.2	305.9	1,813
1995	217.4	367.6	564.2	236.2	90.8	160.4	91.0	109.4	79.4	69.3	205.4	95.9	2,287
1996	189.1	97.0	68.0	75.3	63.9	16.1	27.1	28.0	56.7	121.0	303.8	213.3	1,259
1997[1]	190.7	239.2	301.1	84.9	28.9	44.9	144.1	212.9	152.1	217.2			1,939

[1] Preliminary. *Source: Economic Research Service, U.S. Department of Agriculture (ERS-USDA)*

SOYBEAN OIL

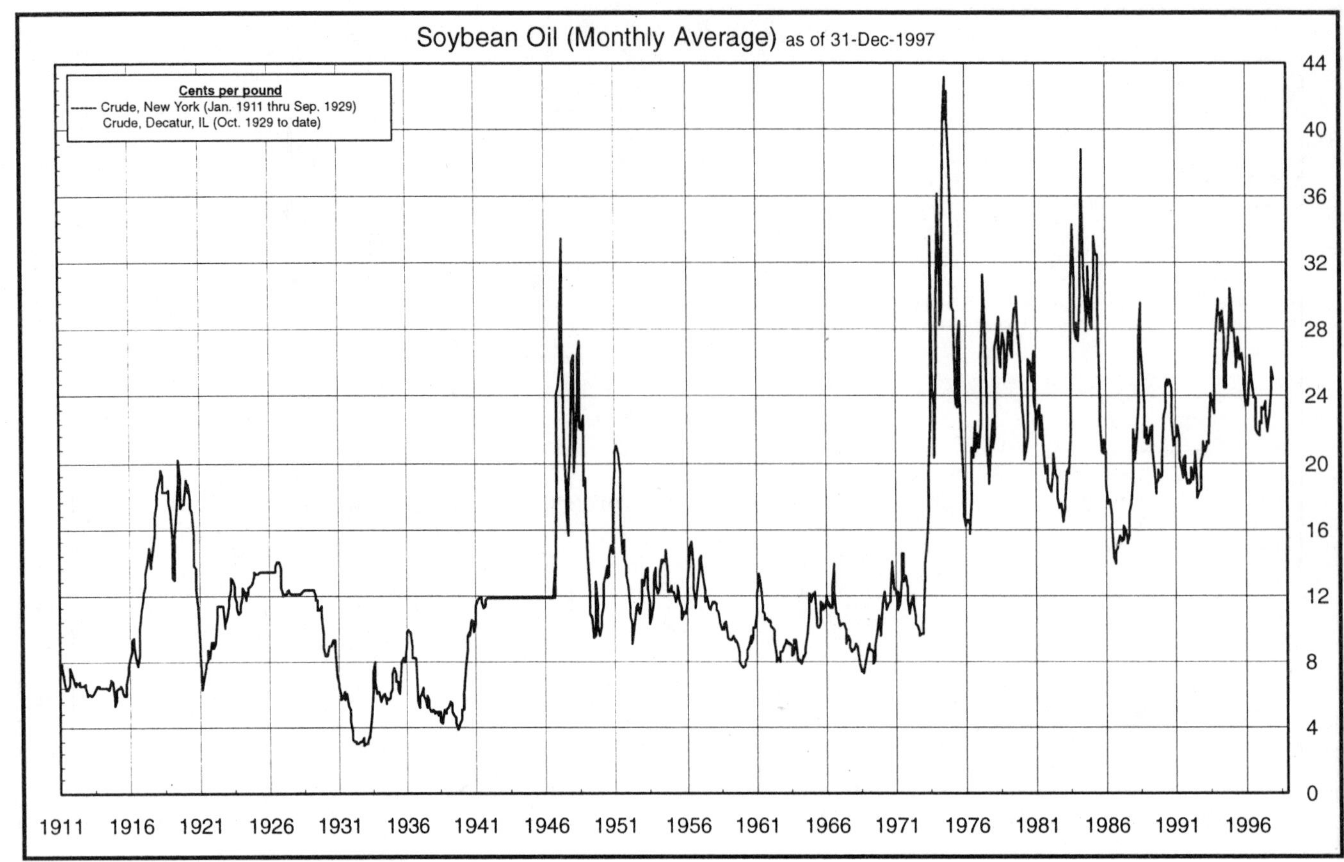

Stocks of Soybean Oil (Crude and Refined) at Factories and Warehouses in the U.S. In Millions of Pounds

Year	Oct. 1	Nov. 1	Dec. 1	Jan. 1	Feb. 1	Mar. 1	Apr. 1	May 1	June 1	July 1	Aug. 1	Sept. 1
1988-9	2,092	2,046	2,303	2,540	2,703	2,902	2,893	2,759	2,743	2,683	2,427	2,070
1989-90	1,715	1,515	1,532	1,605	1,718	1,703	1,695	1,716	1,551	1,422	1,433	1,380
1990-1	1,305	1,216	1,320	--------	1,464	------------	--------	1,875	------------	--------	1,853	------------
1991-2	--------	1,786	------------	2,217	2,159	2,402	2,400	2,423	2,433	2,427	2,421	2,363
1992-3	2,239	2,076	2,111	2,280	2,410	2,337	2,246	2,298	2,241	2,174	2,061	1,720
1993-4	1,555	1,453	1,400	1,407	1,415	1,401	1,402	1,553	1,567	1,554	1,571	1,339
1994-5	1,103	1,056	1,027	1,055	1,117	1,129	1,060	1,090	1,130	1,112	1,142	1,100
1995-6	1,137	1,196	1,132	1,409	1,513	1,521	1,654	1,747	1,759	1,888	2,156	2,091
1996-7	2,015	1,993	1,898	2,027	2,172	2,203	2,171	2,164	2,143	2,138	1,978	1,700
1997-8[1]	1,520	1,526										

[1] Preliminary. *Source: Economic Research Service, U.S. Department of Agriculture (ERS-USDA)*

Average Price of Crude Domestic Soybean Oil (in Tank Cars) F.O.B. Decatur In Cents Per Pound

Year	Oct.	Nov.	Dec.	Jan.	Feb.	Mar.	Apr.	May	June	July	Aug.	Sept.	Average
1988-9	23.42	21.55	22.16	21.13	21.21	22.11	21.97	22.23	20.75	19.66	18.08	18.77	21.09
1989-90	19.02	19.57	19.11	19.28	20.27	22.80	23.35	24.72	25.03	24.69	25.05	24.45	22.28
1990-1	22.59	21.05	21.55	21.56	21.66	22.21	21.50	20.23	19.65	19.05	20.23	20.46	21.00
1991-2	19.57	18.78	18.99	18.77	18.88	19.74	19.00	20.15	20.71	18.82	17.87	18.28	19.10
1992-3	18.36	20.10	20.52	21.23	20.72	21.00	21.24	21.15	21.30	24.13	23.47	23.61	21.40
1993-4	22.98	25.37	28.09	29.91	28.84	29.03	27.94	29.10	27.60	24.53	24.51	26.11	27.00
1994-5	27.06	29.84	30.61	29.01	28.15	28.33	27.16	26.00	26.78	27.60	26.56	26.26	27.71
1995-6	26.56	25.41	24.76	23.69	23.65	23.60	25.82	26.50	24.95	24.10	23.99	23.92	24.70
1996-7	21.95	21.80	21.60	22.45	22.41	23.29	23.17	23.68	22.97	21.89	22.06	22.88	22.51
1997-8[1]	24.31	25.73	25.08										25.04

[1] Preliminary. *Source: Economic Research Service, U.S. Department of Agriculture (ERS-USDA)*

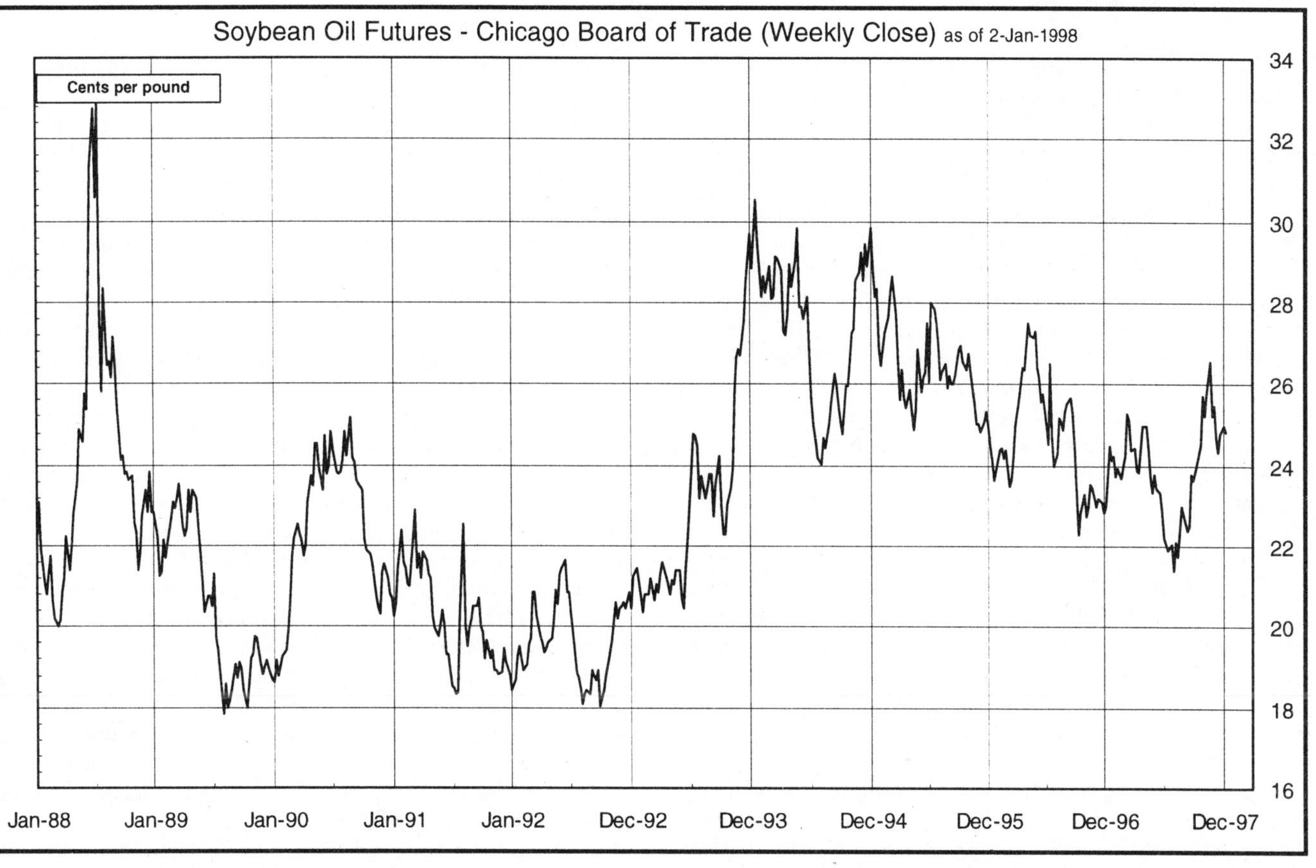

Average Open Interest of Soybean Oil Futures in Chicago In Contracts

Year	Jan.	Feb.	Mar.	Apr.	May	June	July	Aug.	Sept.	Oct.	Nov.	Dec.
1988	85,953	88,260	86,472	85,712	87,253	94,791	95,931	87,566	86,994	82,541	82,477	75,688
1989	77,741	81,676	78,235	77,249	73,623	76,572	70,644	68,652	63,751	63,911	69,248	68,166
1990	73,368	80,842	87,615	92,845	103,116	103,747	88,763	81,310	73,841	78,548	86,786	75,995
1991	72,987	71,607	76,800	70,361	70,954	73,870	73,864	70,058	66,128	61,227	69,657	63,901
1992	68,619	73,919	75,508	68,749	65,084	71,507	64,450	72,569	70,228	65,243	76,168	76,908
1993	73,683	68,887	66,803	68,598	65,814	73,892	83,730	72,746	64,927	62,348	80,136	94,990
1994	97,198	99,640	100,334	98,659	97,595	83,165	93,994	88,196	81,735	86,901	108,327	114,928
1995	101,171	103,856	97,715	87,300	76,175	75,171	81,650	77,064	70,410	71,652	85,241	84,138
1996	87,214	85,611	87,859	95,954	95,422	86,366	81,440	80,090	83,211	98,514	97,496	86,119
1997	89,112	89,348	102,388	101,191	101,544	104,433	105,346	95,282	94,521	107,471	119,877	106,406

Source: Chicago Board of Trade (CBT)

Volume of Trading of Soybean Oil Futures in Chicago In Thousands of Contracts

Year	Jan.	Feb.	Mar.	Apr.	May	June	July	Aug.	Sept.	Oct.	Nov.	Dec.	Total
1988	437.0	390.7	346.8	442.7	399.2	580.2	461.4	403.6	390.0	303.1	377.3	364.2	4,896.2
1989	317.8	347.7	368.1	384.7	426.4	386.3	414.5	348.8	320.8	341.0	344.2	298.6	4,298.9
1990	294.1	397.1	413.9	447.7	488.8	441.5	462.3	405.6	319.2	344.1	370.2	266.3	4,650.8
1991	330.2	259.4	355.0	342.1	364.6	322.9	433.8	399.8	303.2	340.6	297.9	369.3	4,118.8
1992	344.2	293.1	400.0	255.8	381.8	352.3	413.1	298.0	425.9	346.8	365.8	405.5	4,282.3
1993	341.4	281.1	378.4	291.5	261.6	434.7	513.3	444.6	449.3	302.1	465.2	448.6	4,611.8
1994	442.0	401.6	366.0	391.2	442.4	378.2	397.5	357.9	415.4	476.9	516.7	477.4	5,063.2
1995	424.4	363.7	464.4	355.9	457.7	418.2	377.4	330.5	303.9	317.2	431.7	366.4	4,611.3
1996	354.6	355.2	375.2	443.4	376.7	423.1	512.6	449.0	425.9	414.0	396.2	454.3	4,980.3
1997	473.3	381.9	504.0	445.8	389.7	439.6	442.8	375.1	418.0	413.7	489.5	511.4	5,285.0

Source: Chicago Board of Trade (CBT)

Soybeans

The U.S. record high soybean crop in 1997/98 (September/August) of a better than expected 2.74 billion bushels compares with the previous year's record of 2.38 billion; the increase due largely to favorable weather that advanced the crop's maturity followed by a swift harvest pace. The U.S. produced more than half (51 percent) of the world's soybeans in 1997/98, and Brazil, the second largest producer, about 19 percent. World production in 1997/98 of a record large 147.5 million metric tonnes proved marginally larger than expected and compares with 131.6 million tonnes in 1996/97. The previous record of 137.6 million tonnes was realized in 1994/95. World soybean production in the late-1980's averaged under 100 million tonnes; in the first half of the 1990's the average neared 120 million tonnes, suggesting that if the trend is maintained world production will average more than 150 million tonnes in the second half of the 1990's.

The expected large world crop weighed on prices during the second half of calendar 1997 which more than erased a rally during the first half that carried to $9.00 per bushel, basis nearby Chicago futures. The bearish pressure carried into early fall with futures at $6.25, the lowest prices since late 1995. Although a subsequent moderate recovery took hold, at yearend 1997 nearby futures were reasonably close to year earlier values.

World soybean production is expanding is a number of countries, but the U.S. ranking is well entrenched as is Brazil's runner-up slot. China's year-to-year production growth, however, has apparently slowed, especially when measured against expectations. China in recent years was the third largest producer; however, production in 1997/98 of about 13.5 million tonnes was unchanged from 1996/97, while Argentina's bumper crop of 14.2 million tonnes compares with 11.5 million, respectively. China's slippage in 1997/98 may prove an aberration and reflective of reduced average yield; China's longer term setting would seem to favor greater bean production in line with their expanding poultry flocks and the derived need for high protein soybean meal. However, the acreage planted to soybeans in China has been held near 8 million hectares for some time due to prospective bean acreage being allocated to other crops, notably corn and cotton. Brazil's soybean crop is sown about the time the U.S. crop has been harvested and was forecast at a record high 28 million tonnes in 1997/98 vs. 26.6 million in 1996/97. Unlike Brazil, Argentine soybean farmers have significantly lower production costs and have a better transportation structure. Brazil's soybean acreage is generally about twice that of Argentina's, 12.6 million hectares vs. 6.5 million in 1997/98, respectively, but yield per acre is not much different, 2.22 tonnes per hectare vs. 2.18 tonnes. Brazil's crop year encompasses February to January; Argentina's is April to March.

World soybean trade in 1997/98 of a record 38.3 million tonnes compares with 36.2 million in 1996/97. The U.S. accounted for about two-thirds (26 million tonnes) of each year's total and Brazil nearly 20 percent. Importing nations are numerous, the biggest in 1997/98 were Japan (4.8 million tonnes), Germany (3.4 million) and the Netherlands (4.5 million). The primary recipients of U.S. soybean exports in 1996/97 were Japan, the Netherlands and Mexico. The ending 1997/98 world soybean carryover of 18.5 million tonnes compares with the year earlier 12.7 million, most of which is in the U.S., Brazil and Argentina.

U.S. farmers harvested a record 28.3 million hectares in 1997/98, up from 25.7 million in 1996/97, with an average yield of 2.64 metric tonnes per hectare vs. 2.53 tonnes, respectively. Total U.S. disappearance in 1997/98 of a record 2.6 billion bushels compares with 2.4 billion in 1997/98, of which 1.5 billion will be crushed, 1.0 billion exported and about 133 million allocated to seed and residual. Carryover as of August 31, 1998 is forecast at a lower than expected 255 million bushels vs. 132 million a year earlier. Whether disappearance during 1997/98 reaches expectations will depend largely on the crush (and export demand) during December-February which tends to be the seasonal high. Historically, when a more positive soybean usage outlook shows signs of materializing it's apt to show in early calendar year prices. Demand bull years in soybeans generally show counterseasonal strength in January and February, however, if total usage holds neutral then prices, manifested chiefly in futures, tend to witness what is referred to as the "February break." If the latter develops it's not unusual for prices to penetrate the harvest lows of the previous October-December quarter.

The USDA's average price received by farmers in 1997/98 was forecast at $5.75 to $6.85 per bushel vs. $7.38 in 1996/97. The highest farm price during the past decade was $7.42 in 1988/89 and the low was $4.78 in 1986/87. On the world market, U.S. prices tend to run higher than South American prices.

Futures Markets

Soybean futures are traded on the Bolsa de Mercadorias & Futuros (BM&F), the Kansai Agricultural Commodities Exchange (KANEX), the Tokyo Grain Exchange (TGE), the Manila International Futures Exchange Inc. (MIFE), the Chicago Board of Trade (CBOT), and the Mid America Commodity Exchange (MidAm). Options are traded on the TGE, the CBOT, and the MidAm.

World Production of Soybeans In Thousands of Metric Tons

Crop Year[4]	Argentina	Bolivia	Brazil	Canada	China	India	Indonesia	Mexico	Paraguay	Thailand	United States	Former USSR	World Total
1988-9	6,500	294	23,600	1,100	11,650	1,400	1,285	300	1,620	517	42,153	880	95,650
1989-90	10,750	173	20,340	1,219	10,227	1,806	1,315	984	1,575	672	52,354	956	107,367
1990-1	11,500	352	15,750	1,262	11,000	2,602	1,400	575	1,300	530	52,416	880	104,155
1991-2	11,315	384	19,456	1,460	9,713	2,492	1,555	725	1,315	436	54,065	830	108,050
1992-3	11,240	278	22,710	1,455	10,304	3,106	1,870	573	1,794	435	59,546	620	117,508
1993-4	12,200	491	24,963	1,851	14,600	3,700	1,709	497	1,890	480	50,919	660	117,058
1994-5	12,500	710	26,068	2,251	15,200	3,150	1,565	523	2,100	528	68,494	496	136,941
1995-6[1]	12,430	887	24,150	2,293	13,500	4,350	1,680	190	2,400	386	59,240	370	124,940
1996-7[2]	11,200	886	27,000	2,170	13,220	3,800	1,510	65	2,600	352	64,840	410	131,790
1997-8[3]	16,000		30,000		13,800				2,900		74,220		152,300

[1] Preliminary. [2] Estimate. [3] Forecast. [4] Split year includes Northern Hemisphere crops harvested in the late months of the first year shown combined

Supply and Distribution of Soybeans in the United States In Millions of Bushels

Crop Year Beginning Sept. 1	Supply: Stocks, Sept. 1: Farms	Mills, Elevators[3]	Total	Production	Total Supply	Distribution: Crushings	Exports	Seed, Feed & Residual	Total Distribution
1988-9	105.1	197.4	302.5	1,548.8	1,854.9	1,057.7	526.5	88.7	1,672.9
1989-90	87.3	94.7	182.0	1,923.7	2,108.2	1,146.4	622.9	99.7	1,869.1
1990-1	86.0	153.1	239.1	1,925.9	2,168.6	1,187.3	557.3	94.9	1,839.5
1991-2	118.4	210.6	329.0	1,986.5	2,319.0	1,253.5	683.9	103.1	2,040.6
1992-3	105.0	173.4	278.4	2,190.4	2,470.8	1,279.0	769.6	130.0	2,178.6
1993-4	125.0	167.3	292.3	1,871.0	2,169.7	1,275.6	589.1	95.8	1,960.5
1994-5	59.1	150.0	209.1	2,516.7	2,731.3	1,405.2	838.1	153.2	2,396.5
1995-6	105.1	229.7	334.8	2,176.8	2,516.1	1,369.5	851.2	111.9	2,332.6
1996-7[1]	59.5	123.9	183.5	2,382.0	2,574.7	1,435.9	881.8	125.6	2,443.3
1997-8[2]	43.6	87.8	131.4	2,727.0	2,859.3	1,520.0	960.0	139.0	2,619.0

[1] Preliminary. [2] Estimate. [3] Also warehouses. *Source: Economic Research Service, U.S. Department of Agriculture*

U.S. Soybean Price Support Program & Official Crop Production Reports In Millions of Bushels

Crop Year Beginning Sept.	Quantity Put Under Support	% of Production	Stocks Sept. 1	National Average Support: % of Parity	$ Per Bu.	Crop Production Reports In Thousands of Bushels: Aug. 1	Sept. 1	Oct. 1	Nov. 1	Dec. 1	Final
1988-9	120.1	7.8	302.5	40	4.77	1,473,986	1,472,376	1,501,381	1,511,876	----------	1,548,841
1989-90	208.9	10.9	182.0	37	4.53	1,905,300	1,889,265	1,926,385	1,936,545	----------	1,926,806
1990-1	241.4	12.5	239.1	36	4.50	1,836,017	1,834,602	1,823,462	1,903,832	----------	1,925,947
1991-2	158.8	8.0	329.0	40	5.02	1,868,825	1,816,825	1,933,570	1,961,840	----------	1,986,539
1992-3	182.1	8.3	278.4	41	5.02	2,079,487	NA	NA	NA	----------	2,190,354
1993-4	87.1	4.8	292.3	40	5.02	1,902,023	1,909,188	1,890,808	1,833,788	----------	1,870,958
1994-5	375.0	14.9	209.1	40	4.92	2,282,367	2,316,077	2,458,087	2,522,527	----------	2,516,694
1995-6	181.8	8.4	334.8	39	4.92	2,245,901	2,284,551	2,190,661	2,182,991	----------	2,176,814
1996-7	195.9	-----	183.5	-----	4.97	2,299,675	2,269,505	2,346,220	2,402,610	----------	2,382,364
1997-8[1]	253.6	-----	131.4	-----	5.26	2,744,451	2,745,891	2,721,843	2,736,115	----------	2,727,254

[1] Preliminary. NA = Not available. *Source: National Agricultural Statistics Service, U.S. Department of Agriculture*

Soybean Stocks in the United States In Thousands of Bushels

Year	On Farms: Mar. 1	Jun. 1	Sept. 1	Dec. 1	Off Farms[1]: Mar. 1	Jun. 1	Sept. 1	Dec. 1	Total Stocks: Mar. 1	Jun. 1	Sept. 1	Dec. 1
1988	553,100	304,900	105,050	650,000	594,620	351,382	197,426	716,812	1,147,720	656,282	302,476	1,366,812
1989	415,000	229,200	87,320	793,400	475,246	235,311	94,709	816,583	890,246	464,511	182,029	1,609,983
1990	535,800	255,300	86,000	754,000	519,705	340,614	153,139	929,963	1,055,505	595,914	239,139	1,683,963
1991	555,500	336,500	118,400	810,000	634,619	387,022	210,642	968,957	1,190,119	723,522	329,042	1,778,957
1992	505,000	279,000	105,000	876,100	672,343	416,671	173,437	959,885	1,177,343	695,671	278,437	1,835,985
1993	576,900	319,800	124,970	697,400	638,667	363,613	167,314	876,220	1,215,567	683,413	292,284	1,573,620
1994	425,700	195,000	59,080	985,800	595,917	360,260	150,037	1,116,156	1,021,617	555,260	209,117	2,101,956
1995	635,300	348,800	105,130	861,500	734,898	443,072	229,684	971,929	1,370,198	791,872	334,814	1,833,429
1996	512,000	234,100	59,523	935,100	678,356	388,701	123,935	889,984	1,190,356	622,801	183,458	1,825,084
1997	514,000	216,000	43,600	1,050,000	541,912	283,890	87,786	944,968	1,055,912	499,890	131,386	1,994,968

[1] Includes stocks at mills, elevators, warehouses, terminals and processors. NA = Not available. *Source: National Agricultural Statistics Service, U.S. Department of Agriculture*

SOYBEANS

Commercial Stocks of Soybeans in the United States, on First of Month In Millions of Bushels

Year	Jan.	Feb.	Mar.	Apr.	May	June	July	Aug.	Sept.	Oct.	Nov.	Dec.
1988	63.0	66.9	63.6	61.2	54.6	51.7	53.2	54.5	46.0	41.6	74.7	80.9
1989	81.3	75.6	63.8	53.4	35.8	31.2	21.1	18.6	14.1	11.4	62.1	71.3
1990	65.8	62.1	57.8	53.2	56.2	54.4	48.1	41.4	26.1	24.1	89.7	90.7
1991	90.2	78.1	70.5	56.2	43.5	35.5	33.3	25.5	25.3	29.7	80.6	84.0
1992	76.0	75.9	67.1	67.8	58.5	57.2	51.7	32.1	18.6	59.0	75.1	79.9
1993	71.5	63.5	54.5	48.5	44.0	32.1	26.6	24.4	15.8	9.6	52.3	60.2
1994	62.6	65.3	54.4	46.3	40.7	34.7	29.9	24.3	19.8	11.5	68.1	83.4
1996	57.2	57.2	59.2	54.7	56.2	44.9	36.9	32.7	12.0	5.3	55.2	50.6
1997	32.6	28.8	22.9	26.0	29.2	24.7	14.3	12.8	6.3	4.5	50.2	49.4
1998	35.3	31.2	22.9									

Source: Livestock Division, U.S. Department of Agriculture (LD-USDA)

Salient Statistics of Soybeans in the United States

Crop Year	Planted (--- 1,000 Acres ---)	Acreage Harvested (--- 1,000 Acres ---)	Yield Per Acre (Bu.)	Farm Price ($ Bu.)	Farm Value (Million Dollars)	Pounds Per Bushel Crushed: Yield of Oil	Pounds Per Bushel Crushed: Yield of Meal	-U.S. Exports of Soybeans Crop Year (Oct-Sept) in Thous of Metric Tons-: Grand Total	Germany	Japan	Netherlands	Spain	Taiwan	former USSR
1988-9	58,840	57,373	27.0	7.42	11,488	11.16	47.43	14,356	601	3,251	2,531	1,152	1,439	240
1989-90	60,820	59,538	32.3	5.69	10,916	11.17	47.63	16,933	818	3,480	2,721	1,565	2,016	342
1990-1	57,795	56,512	34.1	5.74	11,042	11.23	47.47	15,161	760	3,584	2,085	1,027	1,087	354
1991-2	59,180	58,011	34.2	5.58	11,092	11.42	47.51	19,277	814	3,891	3,167	1,459	2,034	543
1992-3	59,180	58,233	37.6	5.56	12,168	10.84	47.54	20,400	893	3,984	3,362	1,424	2,369	46
1993-4	60,135	57,347	32.6	6.40	11,950	10.87	47.62	16,364	807	3,527	2,661	921	1,700	0
1994-5	61,670	60,859	41.4	5.48	13,756	11.08	47.33	23,584	1,228	4,061	4,130	1,714	2,586	0
1995-6	62,575	61,624	35.3	6.72	14,737	11.15	47.69	22,372	1,286	3,730	3,706	1,218	2,631	16,578
1996-7[1]	64,205	63,409	37.6	7.35	17,582	10.91	47.37							
1997-8[2]	70,850	69,884	39.0	6.69	17,154	11.13	47.24							

[1] Preliminary. [2] Forecast. NA = Not available. *Source: Economic Research Service, U.S. Department of Agriculture (ERS-USDA)*

Production of Soybeans for Beans in the United States, by State In Millions of Bushels

Year	Arkansas	Illinois	Indiana	Iowa	Kentucky	Michigan	Minnesota	Mississippi	Missouri	Nebraska	Ohio	Tennessee	Total
1988	83.2	234.9	115.5	251.1	24.1	35.1	124.8	49.5	112.1	70.8	99.9	32.0	1,548.8
1989	75.2	354.0	166.1	322.9	36.9	38.9	185.0	40.0	121.8	81.9	125.4	29.8	1,923.7
1990	90.5	354.9	171.4	327.9	39.0	43.3	179.4	39.9	124.5	81.4	135.7	33.8	1,925.9
1991	89.6	341.3	171.6	349.5	36.7	52.8	195.3	46.8	135.1	82.4	135.7	31.5	1,986.5
1992	104.3	405.5	194.4	359.5	42.2	47.5	172.8	59.5	161.5	103.3	147.2	33.3	2,190.4
1993	92.3	387.0	223.1	257.3	38.0	54.7	115.0	42.9	118.8	90.0	156.2	32.2	1,871.0
1994	115.6	429.1	215.3	442.9	42.4	57.0	224.0	57.0	173.3	134.4	173.6	38.3	2,516.7
1995	88.4	378.3	196.7	407.4	41.4	59.6	234.9	37.8	132.8	101.0	153.1	34.6	2,176.8
1996	112.0	398.9	203.7	415.8	44.8	46.7	224.2	54.3	149.9	135.5	157.2	40.3	2,382.0
1997[1]	108.3	427.9	237.6	483.6	44.2	72.8	261.3	64.2	177.0	141.5	197.6	43.5	2,727.0

[1] Preliminary. *Source: Agricultural Statistics Board, U.S. Department of Agriculture (ASB-USDA)*

Stocks of Soybeans at Mills in the United States, on First of Month In Millions of Bushels

Crop Year	Sept.	Oct.	Nov.	Dec.	Jan.	Feb.	Mar.	Apr.	May	June	July	Aug.
1988-9	59.7	61.4	136.6	147.4	138.6	131.9	112.0	99.2	72.8	52.5	46.1	31.0
1989-90	23.8	24.5	96.3	108.5	89.7	93.6	91.4	83.5	73.0	67.5	58.8	46.9
1990-1	45.2	34.5	130.1	130.7	------	106.5	------------	------	78.5	------------	------	61.2
1991-2	------	------	67.0	------------	126.9	121.4	109.6	94.7	79.8	73.5	65.7	56.2
1992-3	43.8	46.3	132.3	137.4	119.1	111.2	97.2	90.1	83.6	67.7	67.1	55.3
1993-4	42.0	28.0	108.6	114.9	120.9	126.1	118.5	119.7	98.7	97.8	90.0	63.5
1994-5	47.9	46.8	114.1	124.3	108.0	114.7	114.3	112.6	94.1	81.2	69.1	55.1
1995-6	52.8	54.2	125.6	129.1	120.0	123.3	121.9	110.6	104.2	92.5	70.4	57.4
1996-7	40.7	23.4	101.1	117.4	106.0	112.6	122.2	104.9	89.2	78.2	64.0	43.6
1997-8[1]	27.7	36.8										

[1] Preliminary. *Source: Economic Research Service, U.S. Department of Agriculture (ERS-USDA)*

U.S. Exports of Soybeans In Millions of Bushels

Year	Sept.	Oct.	Nov.	Dec.	Jan.	Feb.	Mar.	Apr.	May	June	July	Aug.	Total
1988-9	26.7	50.2	61.3	69.3	66.3	56.1	66.8	40.8	23.2	31.2	16.4	18.3	526.5
1989-90	17.9	74.0	76.6	65.7	76.3	74.9	87.3	43.6	22.8	35.2	20.8	28.3	623.4
1990-1	27.9	29.8	62.8	55.8	------	190.1	-----------	------	117.7	-----------	------	73.9	557.9
1991-2	26.8	------	235.6	-----------	73.8	90.6	63.3	56.6	28.3	27.3	42.6	39.2	683.9
1992-3	50.1	98.0	84.2	73.6	89.1	104.7	79.7	48.7	34.6	39.4	42.7	24.6	769.5
1993-4	30.1	73.6	72.4	73.9	71.0	67.8	53.6	34.8	27.5	26.7	17.1	40.7	589.1
1994-5	42.3	99.9	78.5	104.2	89.3	91.4	83.1	80.7	45.2	35.5	41.2	46.7	838.1
1995-6	70.7	77.4	65.5	89.6	106.2	82.9	93.5	52.9	42.1	51.8	46.0	52.6	851.2
1996-7	41.6	95.7	152.4	121.7	106.0	105.4	66.9	58.2	40.8	32.3	23.2	37.5	881.8
1997-8[1]	42.6												511.0

[1] Preliminary. *Source: Economic Research Service, U.S. Department of Agriculture (ERS-USDA)*

Spread Between Value of Products and Soybean Price in the United States In Cents Per Bushel

Year	Sept.	Oct.	Nov.	Dec.	Jan.	Feb.	Mar.	Apr.	May	June	July	Aug.	Average
1988-9	111	131	109	95	90	73	70	72	61	93	107	155	97
1989-90	171	141	113	87	78	58	70	85	109	103	97	99	101
1990-1	99	77	58	64	63	73	79	75	72	74	91	99	77
1991-2	118	120	94	82	74	74	75	78	87	104	80	83	89
1992-3	98	93	87	93	94	77	77	79	82	84	120	97	90
1993-4	95	108	105	92	93	99	88	85	89	88	94	118	96
1994-5	146	167	143	137	130	109	114	109	86	102	87	90	118
1995-6	88	107	82	88	82	77	79	94	73	76	77	71	82
1996-7	109	117	126	115	94	95	86	80	107	96	123	151	108
1997-8	212	128	137										159

Source: Economic Research Service, U.S. Department of Agriculture (ERS-USDA)

Soybean Crushed (Factory Consumption) in the U.S. In Millions of Bushels--One Bushel=60 Pounds

Year	Sept.	Oct.	Nov.	Dec.	Jan.	Feb.	Mar.	Apr.	May	June	July	Aug.	Total
1988-9	79.9	94.4	101.0	100.7	99.8	85.8	93.5	89.6	87.0	76.0	74.0	75.9	1,058
1989-90	74.1	94.8	104.1	105.4	107.2	91.8	102.1	95.1	93.4	92.0	92.2	94.2	1,146
1990-1	92.1	106.1	106.0	102.7	--------	297.9	-----------	--------	280.1	-----------	--------	202.5	1,187
1991-2	98.9	--------	333.3	-----------	112.0	100.8	107.2	101.6	95.2	100.0	102.3	102.3	1,254
1992-3	101.2	113.9	113.1	116.2	116.8	102.2	113.0	105.9	106.5	99.9	98.0	92.2	1,279
1993-4	98.4	113.7	114.4	114.1	110.7	103.3	113.3	105.6	103.0	97.2	101.0	101.0	1,276
1994-5	105.9	119.3	122.5	128.5	127.3	116.5	128.1	119.4	114.2	105.6	108.4	109.5	1,405
1995-6	107.4	120.6	123.4	125.1	122.8	111.2	115.5	112.1	106.3	107.5	111.9	105.7	1,370
1996-7	100.9	127.0	133.1	138.1	137.3	125.1	130.1	114.8	110.7	108.9	106.1	103.7	1,436
1997-8[1]	110.0	140.4											1,503

[1] Preliminary. *Source: Economic Research Service, U.S. Department of Agriculture (ERS-USDA)*

SOYBEANS

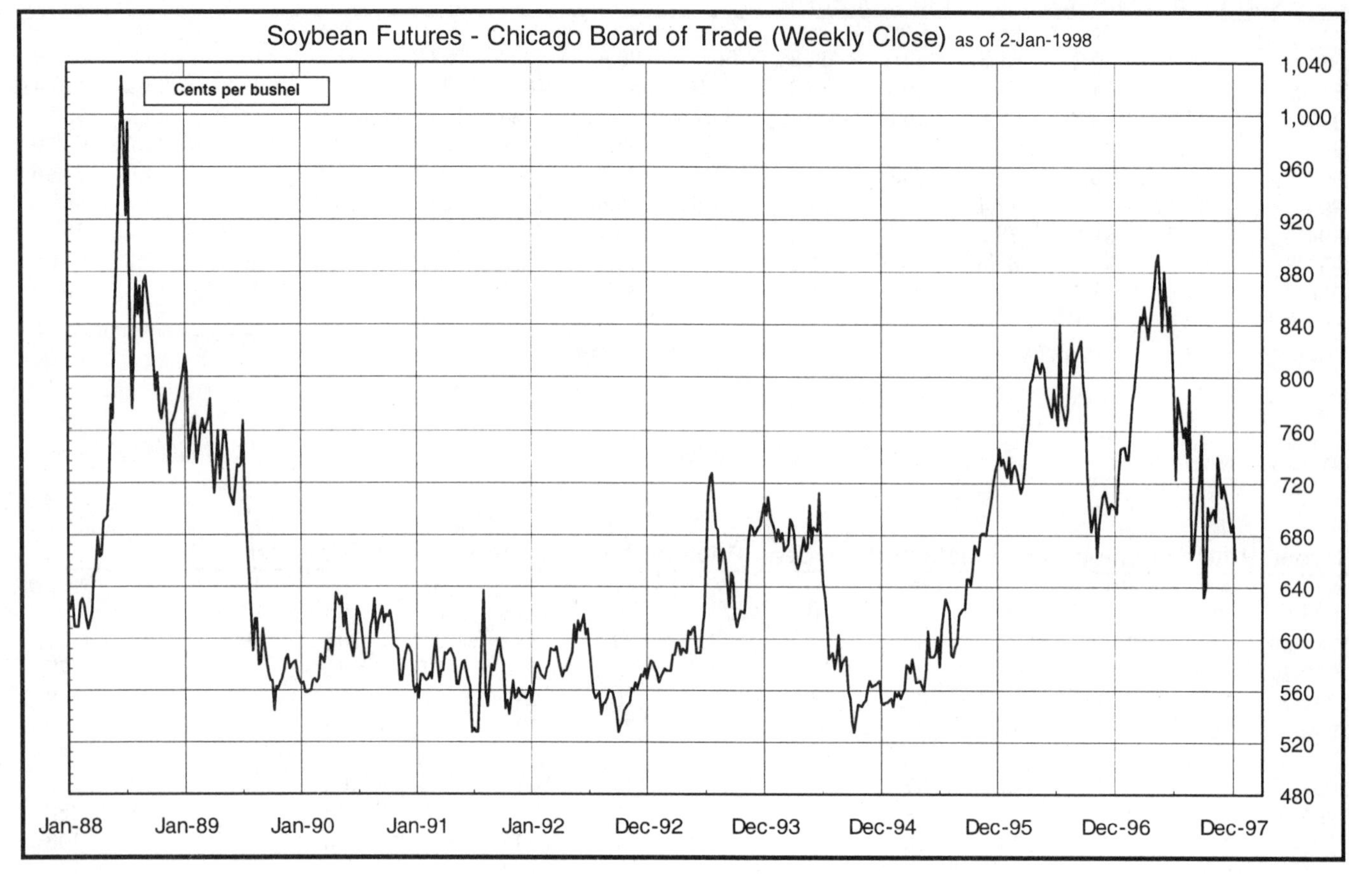

Average Open Interest of Soybean Futures in Chicago In Millions of Bushels

Year	Jan.	Feb.	Mar.	Apr.	May	June	July	Aug.	Sept.	Oct.	Nov.	Dec.
1988	118,512	123,586	121,862	138,515	152,695	169,954	128,962	114,830	119,790	121,481	111,722	120,710
1989	119,700	114,468	115,992	102,736	96,802	94,453	83,407	75,926	80,966	100,793	96,432	98,672
1990	95,718	99,367	111,395	123,005	131,173	118,009	96,789	91,706	97,929	119,841	125,136	123,552
1991	109,311	110,421	110,318	106,995	102,369	103,362	91,449	86,132	98,050	114,206	112,407	112,782
1992	114,871	118,317	132,639	121,171	121,398	137,896	116,208	106,830	104,115	125,734	118,877	114,261
1993	121,726	126,682	126,681	138,155	137,821	142,721	199,681	183,422	163,647	159,641	161,170	168,694
1994	177,648	167,217	156,059	147,569	145,798	150,203	132,010	121,126	126,947	147,198	137,187	136,351
1995	138,345	138,794	137,843	138,624	133,533	143,119	143,671	135,584	144,409	167,200	174,775	194,021
1996	198,731	199,150	192,927	207,284	191,989	179,548	180,817	182,324	196,361	178,872	155,937	152,966
1997	157,728	176,242	189,352	188,617	186,792	159,720	141,658	133,732	150,606	172,098	148,760	150,201

Source: Chicago Board of Trade (CBT) *Note: The CBT changed the open interest figures from Bushels to Contracts in January 1998.*

Volume of Trading of Soybean Futures in Chicago In Thousands of Contracts

Year	Jan.	Feb.	Mar.	Apr.	May	June	July	Aug.	Sept.	Oct.	Nov.	Dec.	Total
1988	887.2	850.4	856.8	964.4	1,267.8	1,595.0	1,114.8	1,042.8	903.2	1,047.0	1,000.2	955.4	12,497
1989	1,044.4	853.0	952.0	944.0	917.4	893.2	795.4	634.4	570.8	802.2	649.4	578.6	9,635
1990	655.6	534.6	826.6	884.4	1,126.0	1,041.8	1,037.6	905.6	642.8	1,132.0	859.8	655.0	13,577
1991	745.0	620.8	715.4	808.0	684.4	776.2	992.4	943.2	662.4	876.2	571.2	619.0	8,974
1992	804.4	738.4	688.0	558.8	873.8	1,054.6	933.2	630.8	572.2	867.4	613.2	665.4	9,000
1993	683.4	624.6	675.8	761.2	778.0	1,287.0	1,643.2	1,180.0	925.0	962.2	1,188.0	941.4	11,649
1994	1,134.6	898.5	922.0	919.3	1,158.4	1,197.0	892.4	688.4	622.6	857.0	825.8	633.2	10,749
1995	614.0	572.0	799.6	698.3	949.4	1,050.8	1,196.7	817.0	800.2	1,127.8	840.4	1,145.4	10,612
1996	1,302.6	1,122.9	1,009.4	1,683.2	1,149.3	989.5	1,295.9	989.8	1,050.2	1,002.7	1,695.6	940.1	14,231
1997	1,119.8	1,254.2	1,405.9	1,585.5	1,391.1	1,355.6	1,217.4	835.0	852.3	1,505.8	1,010.7	1,006.6	14,540

Source: Chicago Board of Trade (CBT) *Note: The CBT changed the volume figures from Bushels to Contracts in January 1998.*

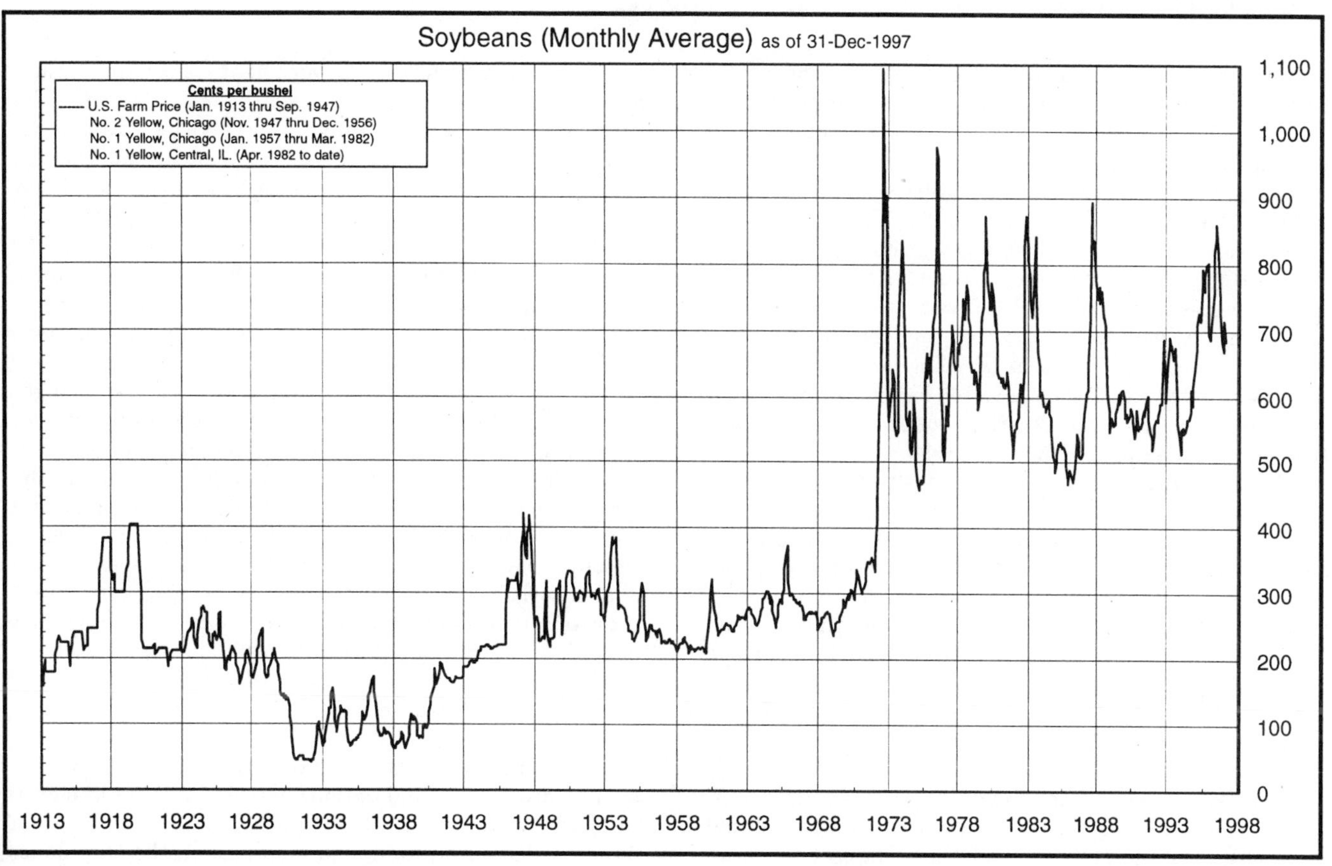

Average Cash Price of No. 1 Yellow Soybeans at Illinois Processor In Cents Per Bushel

Year	Sept.	Oct.	Nov.	Dec.	Jan.	Feb.	Mar.	Apr.	May	June	July	Aug.	Average
1988-9	852	792	767	783	783	760	778	739	740	725	708	606	753
1989-90	600	564	570	582	572	585	600	600	620	609	619	626	596
1990-1	628	614	587	591	576	585	592	601	589	583	554	578	590
1991-2	598	568	571	568	577	581	593	585	609	619	580	564	584
1992-3	554	535	560	572	582	575	587	597	607	606	689	679	595
1993-4	643	606	664	694	701	686	692	670	689	685	603	576	659
1994-5	557	531	566	567	558	560	574	578	580	577	623	602	573
1995-6	632	656	686	717	737	730	726	791	808	778	795	816	739
1996-7	820	711	704	708	737	769	833	854	878	837	769	741	780
1997-8[1]	703	684	727										705

[1] Preliminary. *Source: Economic Research Service, U.S. Department of Agriculture (ERS-USDA)*

Average Price Received by Farmers for Soybeans in the United States In Cents Per Bushel

Year	Sept.	Oct.	Nov.	Dec.	Jan.	Feb.	Mar.	Apr.	May	June	July	Aug.	Average
1988-9	793	753	743	753	769	741	751	729	720	705	683	607	742
1989-90	570	555	566	564	565	556	565	582	597	588	597	600	569
1990-1	599	588	578	572	571	565	576	577	567	556	536	566	574
1991-2	564	548	548	545	554	559	567	566	587	594	559	540	558
1992-3	536	526	536	546	558	556	565	573	581	590	656	656	556
1993-4	621	601	632	664	672	671	673	657	677	672	592	558	640
1994-5	547	530	536	541	547	540	551	555	556	568	590	583	548
1995-6	598	615	640	676	677	701	700	743	769	741	762	782	672
1996-7	779	695	690	691	713	738	797	823	840	816	752	725	755
1997-8[1]	672	650	685	671	669	663							668

[1] Preliminary. *Source: Economic Research Service, U.S. Department of Agriculture (ERS-USDA)*

Stock Index Futures, U.S.

1997 proved to be record year for U.S. Stock Markets by almost every measure. All the major stock indices showed strong advances, adding about $2.6 trillion of value. It was also the first time the bellwether Dow-Jones Industrials ever gained 20 percent or more for three consecutive years; the Dow closing 1997 at 7,908.25 up 22.6 percent and only four percent shy of its mid-summer record high 8,259.31. The S&P 500 index gained 31 percent; the Wilshire 5000 rose 29 percent; the Russell 2000 was up 21 percent; the Value Line "A" gained 28.5 percent; and the Nasdaq composite index rose 21.6 percent. Trading volume soared on the New York Stock Exchange to 134 billion shares vs. 105 billion in 1996, while the Nasdaq's volume reached nearly 164 billion shares vs. 138 billion in 1996.

However, 1997 witnessed some nasty declines in the equity markets and a sharp increase in volatility. In late October, the Dow fell 873 points in three days with a 554 point drop on October 27, the biggest one-day point loss in the Dow's 101-year history as the market reacted to currency devaluations and equity market meltdowns in Southeast Asia. The panic selling proved shortlived as the Dow jumped a record 337 points on October 28. The Asian uncertainties weighed on U.S. equities during the closing weeks of 1997 with the Dow lapsing into a trading range between 7500 and 8000.

Wall street analysts and many economists viewed 1997 as the "goldilocks economy"--not too hot, not too cold, but just right; the best of all possible worlds. The economy grew robustly with the gross domestic product up 3.2 percent. Unemployment fell to just 4.6 percent, corporate earnings grew nearly 12 percent, and the consumer price index gained just 1.8 percent for the year. The producer price index at times actually showed deflation.

Moreover, the Federal Government's shrinking deficit meant the Treasury issued fewer bonds to finance the Government's needs, resulting in lower yields and making equities even more attractive. Indeed, mainstream America viewed equities as the best of all possible investments and poured more than $100 billion into stocks during 1997, with much of the capital allocated to retirement programs. In mid-1997, mutual fund assets in stocks, bonds and money market funds topped $4 trillion for the first time with more than half the total in stock funds, ownership of which was in the hands of nearly 40 million American households.

At yearend 1997, consumer confidence reached its highest level in 30 years. However, there were reasons for caution with the financial crisis in Asia clouding the 1998 U.S. economic outlook. Corporate profits may not repeat the strong growth of 1997 and real gross domestic product will likely dip below three percent. On the other hand, deflationary fears may prove a greater concern, especially abroad, which could force the Fed to ease short-term interest rates, maintaining the opportunity cost's attractiveness of equities vs. capital inflows into bank deposits.

Futures Markets

The Chicago Mercantile Exchange's (CME) IOM division trades futures and options on the S&P 500, the S&P MidCap 400, and the NASDAQ 100. The Chicago Board of Trade (CBOT) lists futures and options on the Dow Jones Industrial Average. The New York Futures Exchange (NYFE) trades futures and options on the New York Stock Exchange Composite Index. The Kansas City Board of Trade (KCBT) lists futures and options on the Value Line Index.

Dow Jones Industrial Average (30 Stocks)

Year	Jan.	Feb.	Mar.	Apr.	May	June	July	Aug.	Sept.	Oct.	Nov.	Dec.	Average
1988	1,947.4	1,981.4	2,044.3	2,036.1	1,988.9	2,104.9	2,104.2	2,051.3	2,080.1	2,144.3	2,099.0	2,148.6	2,060.9
1989	2,234.7	2,304.3	2,283.1	2,348.9	2,439.5	2,494.9	2,554.0	2,691.1	2,693.4	2,692.0	2,642.5	2,728.5	2,508.9
1990	2,679.2	2,614.2	2,700.1	2,708.4	2,793.8	2,894.8	2,934.2	2,681.9	2,550.7	2,460.5	2,518.6	2,610.9	2,679.0
1991	2,587.6	2,863.0	2,920.1	2,925.5	2,928.4	2,968.1	2,978.2	3,006.1	3,010.4	3,019.7	2,986.1	2,958.6	2,929.3
1992	3,227.1	3,257.3	3,247.4	3,294.1	3,376.8	3,337.8	3,329.4	3,307.4	3,293.9	3,198.7	3,238.5	3,303.1	3,284.3
1993	3,277.7	3,367.3	3,440.7	3,423.6	3,478.2	3,513.8	3,529.4	3,597.0	3,592.3	3,625.8	3,674.7	3,744.1	3,522.1
1994	3,868.4	3,905.6	3,817.0	3,661.5	3,708.0	3,737.6	3,718.3	3,797.5	3,880.6	3,868.1	3,792.5	3,770.3	3,793.8
1995	3,872.5	3,953.7	4,062.8	4,230.7	4,391.6	4,510.8	4,684.8	4,639.3	4,746.8	4,760.5	4,935.8	5,136.1	4,493.8
1996	5,179.4	5,518.7	5,612.2	5,579.9	5,616.7	5,671.5	5,496.3	5,685.5	5,804.0	5,995.1	6,318.4	6,435.9	5,742.8
1997	6,707.0	6,917.5	6,901.1	6,657.5	7,242.4	7,599.6	7,990.7	7,948.4	7,866.6	7,875.8	7,677.4	7,909.8	7,441.1

Monthly average. *Source: The Wall Street Journal*

Dow Jones Transportation Average (20 Stocks)

Year	Jan.	Feb.	Mar.	Apr.	May	June	July	Aug.	Sept.	Oct.	Nov.	Dec.	Average
1988	756.0	790.2	860.5	853.9	820.2	873.1	881.2	856.1	879.4	923.1	916.2	955.4	863.8
1989	1,009.3	1,073.0	1,046.3	1,098.0	1,139.8	1,159.3	1,223.1	1,407.1	1,462.7	1,342.0	1,188.1	1,183.0	1,194.3
1990	1,139.8	1,083.4	1,160.3	1,164.8	1,163.1	1,181.9	1,150.0	951.1	881.3	850.8	848.1	908.5	1,040.3
1991	962.2	1,110.4	1,113.5	1,138.8	1,167.6	1,205.2	1,204.7	1,204.7	1,182.3	1,241.5	1,237.1	1,233.3	1,166.8
1992	1,378.7	1,412.2	1,409.0	1,356.9	1,380.4	1,333.3	1,303.1	1,254.6	1,275.2	1,286.1	1,375.9	1,430.2	1,349.6
1993	1,488.1	1,533.2	1,541.6	1,619.7	1,583.4	1,533.9	1,553.7	1,631.6	1,623.9	1,660.5	1,732.6	1,763.2	1,605.5
1994	1,812.1	1,810.4	1,719.9	1,614.7	1,602.2	1,619.2	1,596.2	1,602.8	1,553.7	1,485.8	1,473.7	1,415.3	1,608.8
1995	1,515.8	1,547.2	1,584.6	1,648.9	1,646.2	1,699.3	1,852.1	1,883.9	1,961.4	1,922.9	2,008.3	2,029.5	1,775.0
1996	1,932.7	2,030.0	2,136.0	2,180.0	2,229.1	2,213.4	2,053.1	2,060.4	2,050.8	2,100.1	2,224.3	2,273.9	2,123.7
1997	2,295.0	2,341.4	2,427.8	2,464.0	2,635.1	2,711.4	2,858.0	2,925.8	3,086.0	3,239.9	3,155.7	3,233.5	2,781.1

Monthly average. *Source: The Wall Street Journal*

Dow Jones Public Utilities (15 Stocks)

Year	Jan.	Feb.	Mar.	Apr.	May	June	July	Aug.	Sept.	Oct.	Nov.	Dec.	Average
1988	182.2	185.0	177.7	171.4	169.3	180.0	178.7	178.6	179.8	185.0	184.1	185.2	179.8
1989	188.9	186.6	182.8	188.0	196.3	206.7	215.5	218.1	216.0	215.7	221.0	232.1	205.6
1990	223.2	221.2	217.0	210.7	212.4	211.2	205.0	201.2	199.8	207.2	210.3	210.6	210.8
1991	205.3	213.7	213.2	214.4	211.2	204.6	199.6	204.4	208.0	213.6	216.7	219.3	210.3
1992	215.7	206.8	204.4	206.1	213.2	212.5	219.1	220.2	220.0	217.2	217.7	220.2	214.4
1993	222.0	234.2	240.0	242.1	237.8	241.5	246.5	252.0	253.0	243.1	227.1	227.1	238.9
1994	222.3	215.6	207.0	196.5	185.5	182.9	181.8	188.9	179.6	179.9	177.7	181.0	191.6
1995	186.9	194.0	187.9	192.7	197.6	204.5	202.5	202.8	207.2	216.4	215.3	221.4	202.4
1996	228.4	228.6	216.3	209.5	211.2	210.0	212.8	214.8	217.2	222.3	234.0	232.1	219.8
1997	235.8	230.5	223.7	213.8	222.1	223.5	232.0	231.9	238.9	242.9	249.2	263.9	234.0

Source: The Wall Street Journal

Standard & Poor's 500 Composite Price Index

Year	Jan.	Feb.	Mar.	Apr.	May	June	July	Aug.	Sept.	Oct.	Nov.	Dec.	Average
1988	250.5	258.2	265.7	262.7	256.1	270.7	269.1	263.7	268.0	277.4	271.0	276.5	265.8
1989	285.4	294.0	292.7	302.3	313.9	323.7	331.9	346.6	347.3	347.4	340.2	348.6	322.8
1990	340.0	330.5	338.5	338.2	350.3	360.4	360.0	330.8	315.4	307.1	315.3	328.8	334.6
1991	325.5	362.3	372.3	379.7	378.0	378.3	380.2	389.4	387.2	386.9	385.9	388.5	376.2
1992	416.1	412.6	407.4	407.4	414.8	408.3	415.1	417.9	418.5	412.5	422.8	435.6	415.7
1993	435.2	441.7	450.2	443.1	445.3	448.1	447.3	454.1	459.2	463.9	462.9	466.0	451.4
1994	473.0	471.6	463.8	447.2	451.0	454.8	451.4	464.2	467.0	463.8	461.0	455.2	460.3
1995	465.3	481.9	493.2	507.9	523.8	539.4	557.4	559.1	578.8	582.9	595.5	614.6	541.6
1996	614.4	649.5	647.1	547.2	661.2	668.5	644.1	662.7	674.9	701.5	735.7	743.3	662.5
1997	766.1	798.4	792.2	763.9	833.1	876.3	925.3	927.7	937.0	951.2	938.9	962.4	872.7

Source: The Wall Street Journal

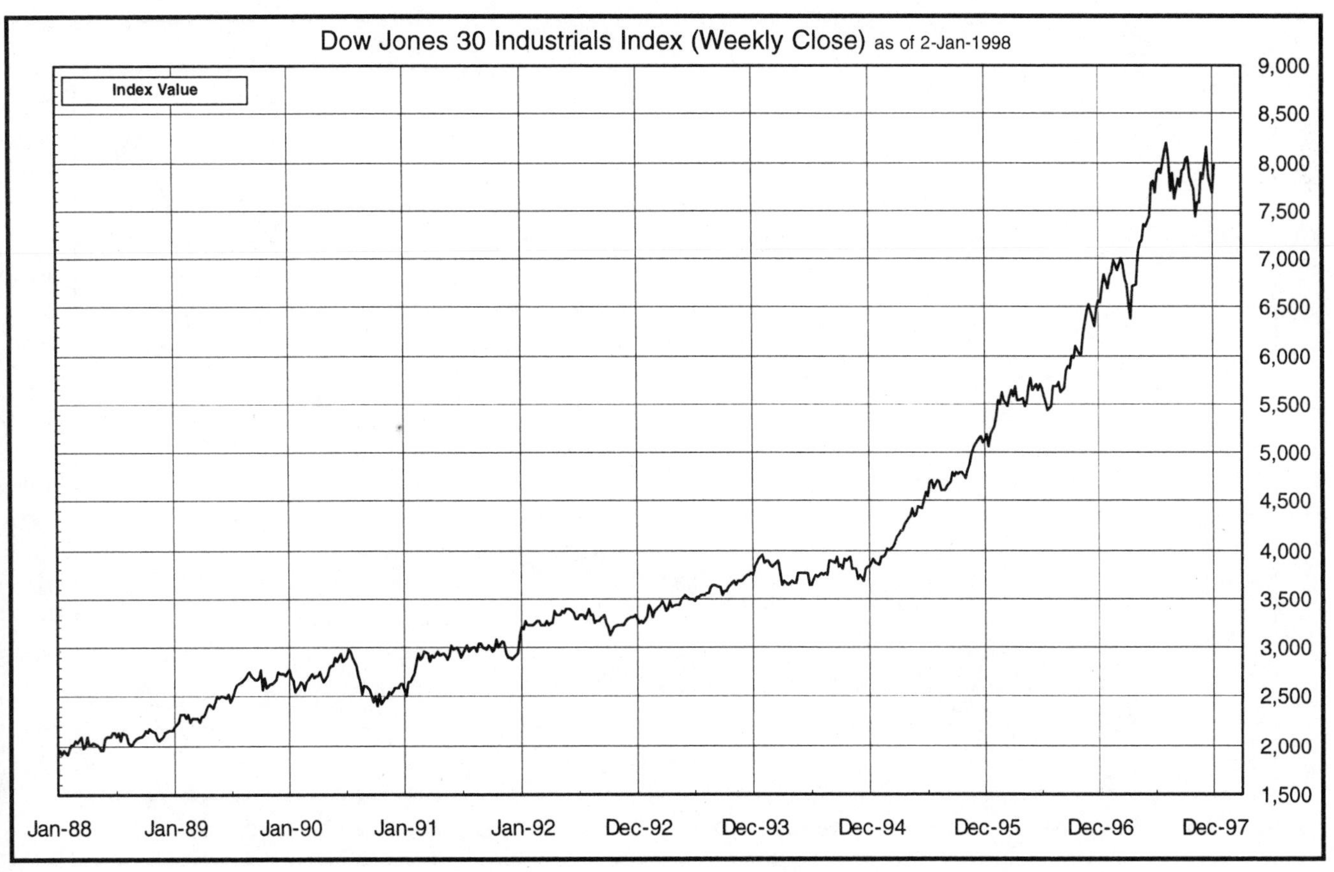

STOCK INDEX FUTURES, U.S.

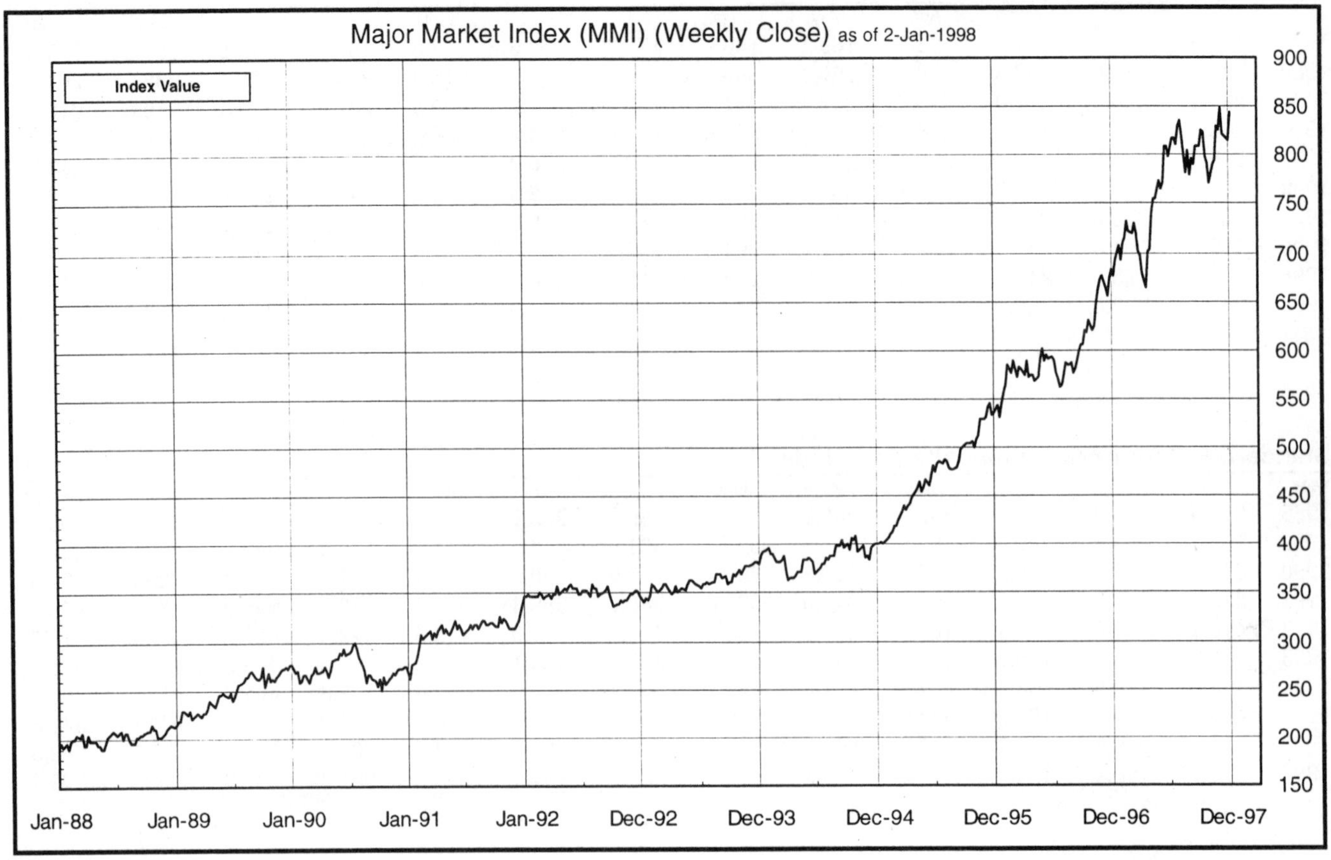
Major Market Index (MMI) (Weekly Close) as of 2-Jan-1998
Index Value
900
850
800
750
700
650
600
550
500
450
400
350
300
250
200
150
Jan-88
Jan-89
Jan-90
Jan-91
Jan-92
Dec-92
Dec-93
Dec-94
Dec-95
Dec-96
Dec-97

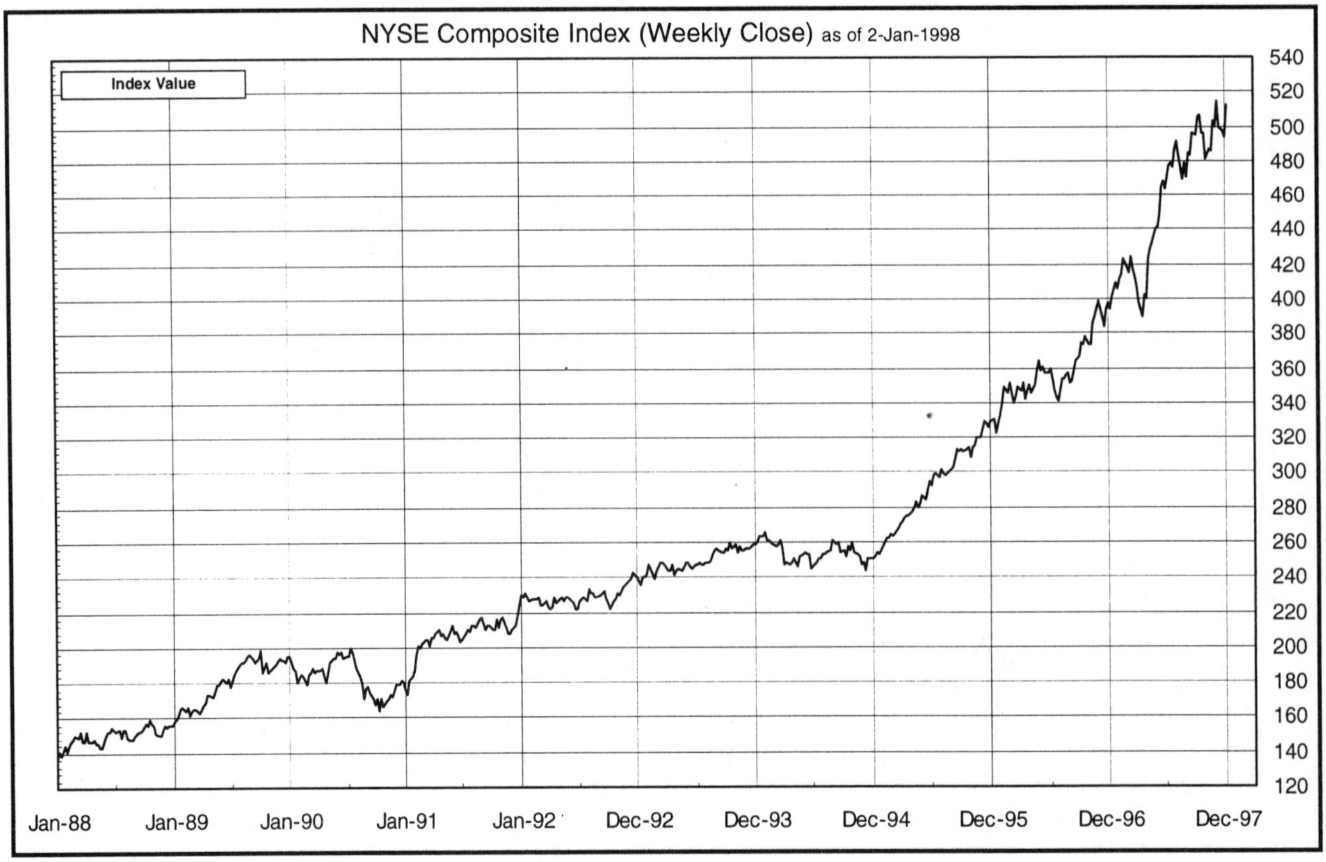
NYSE Composite Index (Weekly Close) as of 2-Jan-1998
Index Value
540
520
500
480
460
440
420
400
380
360
340
320
300
280
260
240
220
200
180
160
140
120
Jan-88
Jan-89
Jan-90
Jan-91
Jan-92
Dec-92
Dec-93
Dec-94
Dec-95
Dec-96
Dec-97

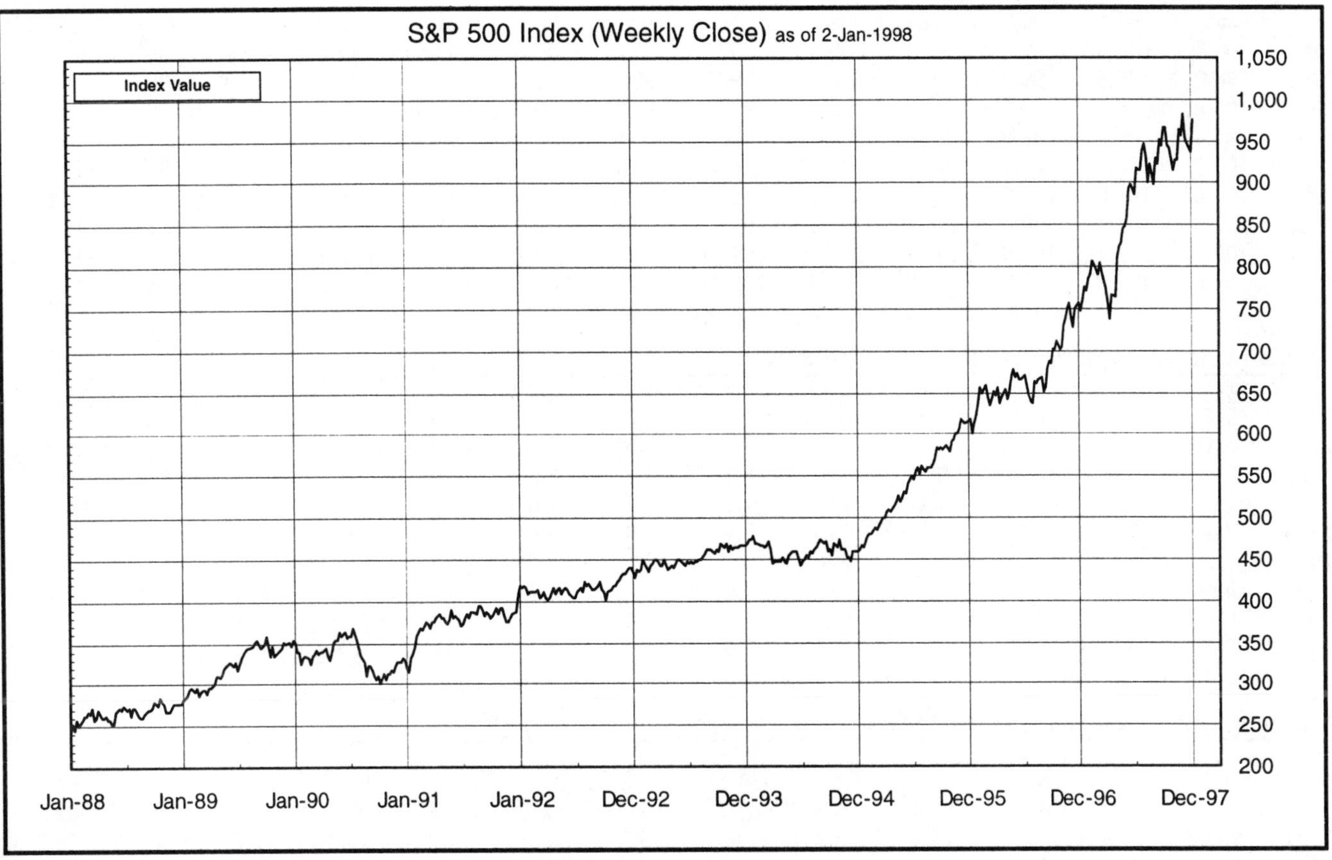

S&P 500 Index (Weekly Close) as of 2-Jan-1998

Index Value

1,050
1,000
950
900
850
800
750
700
650
600
550
500
450
400
350
300
250
200

Jan-88 Jan-89 Jan-90 Jan-91 Jan-92 Dec-92 Dec-93 Dec-94 Dec-95 Dec-96 Dec-97

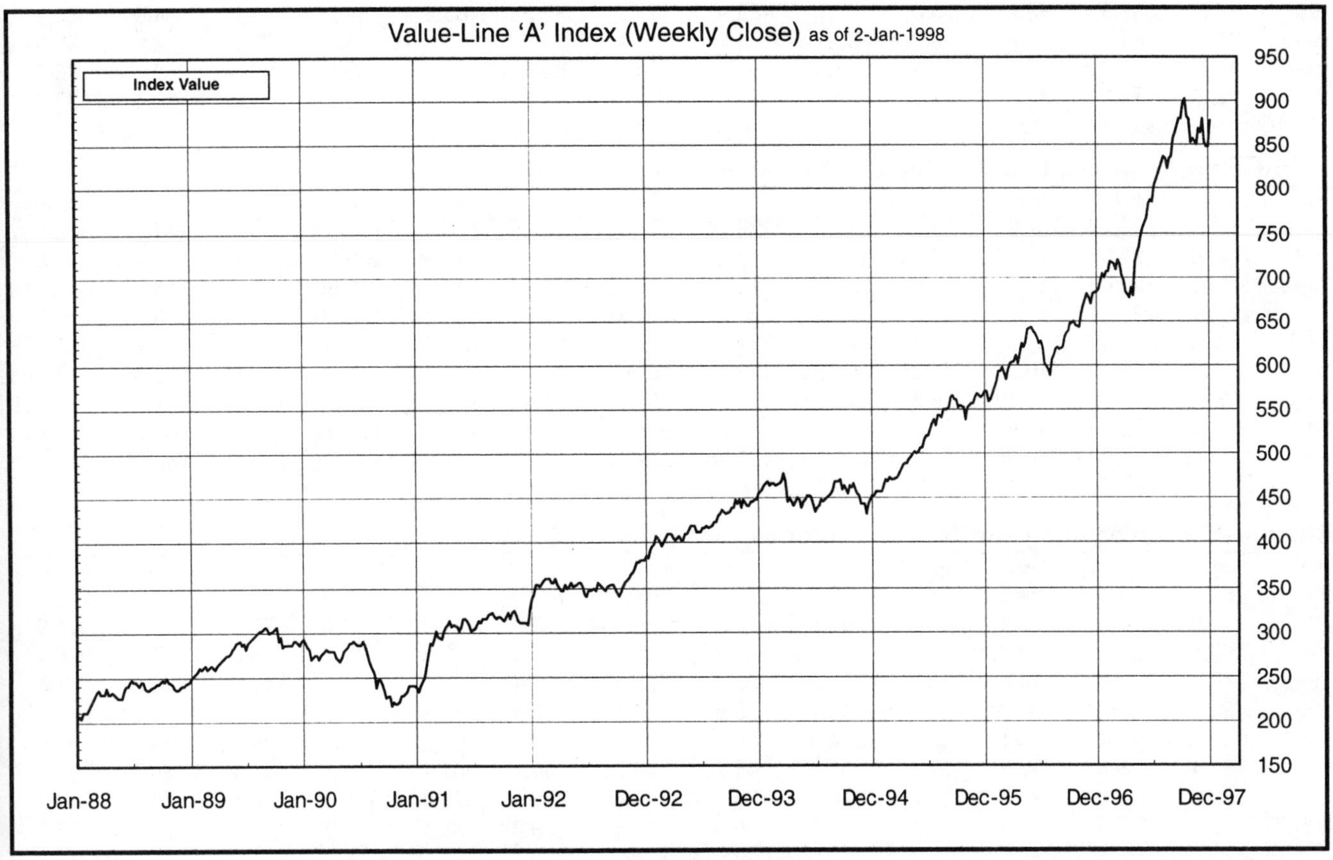

Value-Line 'A' Index (Weekly Close) as of 2-Jan-1998

Index Value

950
900
850
800
750
700
650
600
550
500
450
400
350
300
250
200
150

Jan-88 Jan-89 Jan-90 Jan-91 Jan-92 Dec-92 Dec-93 Dec-94 Dec-95 Dec-96 Dec-97

STOCK INDEX FUTURES, U.S.

Composite Index of Leading Indicators 1987 = 100

Year	Jan.	Feb.	Mar.	Apr.	May	June	July	Aug.	Sept.	Oct.	Nov.	Dec.	Average
1989	100.3	100.0	99.6	99.9	99.4	99.3	99.3	99.5	99.6	99.4	99.6	99.7	99.6
1990	100.0	99.6	99.9	99.7	99.7	99.7	99.6	99.1	98.8	98.2	97.9	98.0	99.2
1991	97.8	98.1	98.5	98.8	99.1	99.3	99.8	99.5	99.5	99.5	99.4	99.1	99.0
1992	99.4	99.7	99.9	99.9	100.0	99.9	99.9	99.9	99.9	100.1	100.4	101.0	100.0
1993	100.7	100.7	100.1	100.4	100.2	100.3	100.1	100.3	100.4	100.5	100.8	101.2	100.5
1994	101.2	101.0	101.5	101.4	101.4	101.4	101.2	101.5	101.4	101.5	101.6	101.6	101.4
1995	101.5	101.1	100.7	100.6	100.4	100.5	100.7	101.0	101.1	100.9	100.9	101.2	100.9
1996	100.5	101.4	101.6	101.8	102.1	102.3	102.3	102.4	102.5	102.5	102.5	102.6	102.0
1997[1]	102.8	103.3	103.4	103.3	103.6	103.6	103.9	104.1	104.3	104.4	104.5	104.5	103.8

[1] Preliminary. *Source: Bureau of Economic Analysis, U.S. Department of Commerce (BEA)*

Civilian Unemployment Rate in the United States

Year	Jan.	Feb.	Mar.	Apr.	May	June	July	Aug.	Sept.	Oct.	Nov.	Dec.	Average
1989	5.4	5.2	5.0	5.2	5.2	5.3	5.2	5.2	5.3	5.3	5.4	5.4	5.3
1990	5.4	5.3	5.2	5.4	5.4	5.2	5.5	5.7	5.9	5.9	6.2	6.3	5.6
1991	6.4	6.6	6.8	6.7	6.9	6.9	6.8	6.9	6.9	7.0	7.0	7.3	6.9
1992	7.3	7.4	7.4	7.4	7.6	7.8	7.7	7.6	7.6	7.3	7.4	7.4	7.5
1993	7.3	7.1	7.0	7.1	7.1	7.0	6.9	6.8	6.7	6.8	6.6	6.5	6.9
1994	6.7	6.6	6.5	6.4	6.0	6.1	6.1	6.1	5.9	5.8	5.6	5.4	6.1
1995	5.6	5.5	5.4	5.7	5.6	5.6	5.7	5.7	5.7	5.5	5.6	5.6	5.6
1996	5.7	5.5	5.5	5.5	5.5	5.3	5.4	5.2	5.2	5.2	5.3	5.3	5.4
1997[1]	5.4	5.3	5.2	4.9	4.8	5.0	4.9	4.9	4.9	4.8	4.6	4.7	5.0

[1] Preliminary. *Source: Bureau of Economic Analysis, U.S. Department of Commerce (BEA)*

Capacity Utilization Rates (Total Industry) Percent

Year	Jan.	Feb.	Mar.	Apr.	May	June	July	Aug.	Sept.	Oct.	Nov.	Dec.	Average
1989	85.3	84.5	85.1	85.2	84.6	84.3	83.3	83.5	83.2	82.7	82.9	83.2	84.0
1990	82.6	82.9	83.2	82.6	82.8	82.7	82.5	82.5	82.5	81.9	80.7	80.1	82.3
1991	79.6	78.9	78.1	78.2	78.7	79.5	79.5	79.5	80.1	79.9	79.7	79.1	79.2
1992	79.0	79.4	79.9	80.4	80.6	80.2	80.6	80.2	80.5	81.0	81.3	81.2	80.4
1993	81.4	81.7	81.6	81.7	81.2	81.2	81.3	81.0	81.7	81.8	82.1	82.5	81.6
1994	82.6	82.8	83.2	83.3	83.7	83.9	84.1	83.9	83.8	84.1	84.4	84.9	83.9
1995	84.9	84.5	84.3	83.9	83.7	83.6	83.4	83.8	83.9	83.3	83.2	83.0	83.4
1996	82.4	83.2	82.6	83.1	83.2	83.5	83.2	83.2	83.1	83.0	82.5	82.5	82.4
1997[1]	82.4	82.6	82.5	82.6	82.4	82.3	82.6	82.8	82.7	83.0	83.3	83.4	82.7

[1] Preliminary. *Source: Bureau of Economic Analysis, U.S. Department of Commerce (BEA)*

Manufacturers New Orders, Durable Goods In Billions of Constant Dollars

Year	Jan.	Feb.	Mar.	Apr.	May	June	July	Aug.	Sept.	Oct.	Nov.	Dec.	Average
1989	137.70	133.27	132.31	133.42	126.53	129.50	127.01	125.49	128.47	123.84	131.25	134.44	130.27
1990	124.02	127.57	135.14	127.83	131.90	129.10	131.58	127.67	128.36	130.67	117.87	123.12	127.90
1991	119.26	120.00	112.54	117.55	120.64	116.85	132.82	125.62	122.36	123.66	124.96	116.97	121.10
1992	122.15	122.14	124.63	127.60	125.65	128.77	125.51	123.79	125.86	128.69	125.49	135.19	126.29
1993	129.56	133.47	128.50	130.20	126.93	131.29	128.27	128.99	130.31	133.01	135.60	136.82	131.08
1994	142.23	138.88	140.91	141.21	142.61	146.15	142.60	145.92	146.93	145.72	149.89	152.88	144.66
1995	153.42	151.82	151.72	146.32	149.74	148.21	147.45	152.12	156.78	154.37	154.09	158.89	154.10
1996	158.86	155.10	157.67	156.01	162.59	162.67	168.25	162.76	170.45	170.59	169.34	166.02	165.14
1997[1]	171.73	174.80	170.02	173.13	177.05	177.78	178.17	182.82	182.98	182.93	192.42	180.92	178.73

[1] Preliminary. *Source: Bureau of Economic Analysis, U.S. Department of Commerce (BEA)*

Change in Manufacturing and Trade Inventories In Billions of Dollars

Year	Jan.	Feb.	Mar.	Apr.	May	June	July	Aug.	Sept.	Oct.	Nov.	Dec.	Average
1989	84.5	71.6	54.7	77.5	82.9	76.1	54.3	22.3	-11.5	37.0	47.6	-17.7	48.3
1990	19.9	7.6	22.2	39.8	64.5	-15.2	64.0	55.9	41.3	24.2	25.3	-50.3	24.9
1991	60.8	-24.8	-99.2	-25.7	-50.0	-32.7	-10.5	-1.1	37.2	16.2	8.8	47.3	-6.1
1992	-60.6	-0.3	13.8	28.3	-22.3	53.6	28.4	21.4	-8.4	4.6	11.8	23.9	7.9
1993	34.9	31.8	66.7	43.7	12.9	25.6	7.3	39.0	34.8	27.2	63.2	1.6	32.4
1994	15.3	45.1	-8.1	42.1	114.2	56.3	60.8	98.6	60.3	71.8	65.3	64.5	57.2
1995	127.4	78.5	100.6	97.6	54.4	48.1	42.9	50.6	51.4	61.8	24.1	-39.7	58.5
1996	66.2	14.2	-27.7	61.5	-8.4	80.3	123.6	-272.1	90.6	143.4	86.1	72.0	58.5
1997[1]	46.6	27.7	20.6	-6.0	22.5	86.8	18.4	29.5	83.1	37.1	48.2		37.7

[1] Preliminary. *Source: Bureau of Economic Analysis, U.S. Department of Commerce (BEA)*

Comparison of International Stock Price Indexes 1990 = 100

Year	Jan.	Feb.	Mar.	Apr.	May	June	July	Aug.	Sept.	Oct.	Nov.	Dec.	Average
United States													
1992	122.9	124.1	121.3	124.7	124.9	122.7	127.5	124.5	125.6	125.9	129.7	131.0	125.4
1993	131.9	133.3	135.8	132.3	135.3	135.4	134.7	139.3	137.9	140.6	138.8	140.2	136.3
1994	144.8	140.4	134.0	135.5	137.2	133.5	137.7	142.9	139.1	142.0	136.4	138.1	138.5
1995	141.4	146.5	150.5	154.7	160.3	163.7	168.9	168.9	175.7	174.8	182.0	185.1	164.4
1996	191.2	192.5	194.0	196.6	201.1	201.6	192.4	196.0	206.6	212.0	227.6	222.7	202.9
1997[1]	236.3	237.7	227.6	240.9	255.0	266.1	286.8	270.4	284.7	274.9	287.2	291.7	263.3
Canada													
1992	105.1	104.7	99.7	98.1	99.0	99.0	100.7	99.5	96.4	97.5	96.0	97.9	99.5
1993	96.6	100.9	105.3	110.8	113.5	115.9	116.0	120.9	116.6	124.4	122.2	126.3	114.1
1994	133.1	129.3	126.6	124.7	126.5	117.7	122.2	127.1	127.3	125.4	119.7	123.2	125.2
1995	117.4	120.6	126.1	125.1	130.0	132.3	134.9	132.0	132.4	130.3	136.2	137.8	129.6
1996	145.2	144.2	145.3	150.4	153.4	147.4	144.1	150.3	154.7	163.7	175.9	173.2	154.0
1997[1]	178.6	180.0	171.0	174.7	186.6	188.2	201.0	193.3	205.8	200.0	190.4	195.8	188.8
France													
1992	103.2	109.1	106.9	111.8	111.9	104.6	96.5	92.7	95.6	95.9	97.5	102.2	102.3
1993	97.5	109.1	111.8	106.7	103.9	108.5	114.8	122.0	116.4	120.1	116.1	124.8	112.6
1994	128.4	123.1	114.6	119.2	111.7	104.1	114.2	113.8	103.4	104.9	108.7	103.5	112.5
1995	98.9	97.8	102.3	105.6	107.2	102.3	105.6	103.6	98.4	99.8	100.6	103.0	102.1
1996	111.2	109.5	112.5	118.1	116.1	116.9	109.8	108.4	117.4	117.8	127.4	127.4	116.0
1997[1]	138.5	143.5	146.2	145.2	142.2	157.3	169.2	152.4	165.5	150.7	157.3	165.0	152.8
Germany[2]													
1992	93.5	97.2	95.4	95.4	98.4	94.8	86.9	82.6	79.6	80.7	82.9	82.4	89.2
1993	84.3	90.2	91.2	88.1	88.0	90.6	96.6	102.8	101.4	110.0	109.3	117.5	97.5
1994	115.1	110.7	112.3	117.8	109.7	106.4	111.5	114.5	105.2	107.7	105.9	108.3	110.4
1995	103.8	108.2	98.6	103.5	106.6	106.6	112.8	113.7	111.4	109.3	111.9	114.0	108.4
1996	123.7	123.2	123.3	123.0	124.4	126.3	122.1	125.6	130.4	130.6	139.0	139.7	127.6
1997[1]	147.0	157.8	167.8	167.1	172.2	183.8	209.6	184.1	195.3	177.8	186.0	196.3	178.7
Italy													
1992	84.3	83.4	78.2	78.3	77.3	70.7	62.5	60.9	56.6	68.3	68.2	69.5	71.5
1993	75.8	79.9	73.9	81.9	83.9	83.5	87.7	98.4	92.8	90.8	85.4	96.4	85.9
1994	103.1	102.5	112.6	124.5	113.8	107.4	110.5	107.5	105.8	98.9	97.4	98.5	106.9
1995	102.8	97.5	93.3	99.8	98.8	94.9	98.8	99.0	96.1	90.5	86.1	91.8	95.8
1996	96.5	94.5	90.4	102.4	104.1	102.4	93.4	93.2	99.0	94.0	102.4	103.7	98.0
1997[1]	119.8	115.4	115.3	119.5	117.9	130.0	144.5	136.6	155.0	144.6	149.4	164.0	134.3
Japan													
1992	76.4	74.0	67.1	60.3	63.6	55.3	55.2	62.7	60.4	58.2	61.3	58.7	62.8
1993	59.1	58.8	64.5	72.6	71.3	68.0	70.7	72.9	69.7	68.4	56.9	60.4	66.1
1994	70.2	69.4	66.3	68.4	72.8	71.6	70.9	71.6	67.9	69.3	66.2	68.4	69.4
1995	64.7	59.2	56.0	58.3	53.6	50.4	57.9	62.9	62.1	61.2	65.0	68.9	60.0
1996	72.2	69.8	74.3	76.5	76.2	78.2	71.8	70.0	74.8	71.0	72.9	67.2	72.9
1997[1]	63.6	64.4	62.5	66.4	69.6	71.5	70.5	63.2	62.1	57.1	57.7	52.9	63.5
United Kingdom													
1992	113.4	113.6	108.2	118.5	121.2	112.4	105.6	101.3	111.4	116.1	121.3	126.0	114.1
1993	126.0	129.0	130.1	128.3	129.6	132.3	133.8	142.0	139.2	144.6	143.8	155.4	136.2
1994	161.3	154.8	144.3	146.0	138.7	135.2	142.8	150.3	139.6	141.9	141.2	140.5	144.7
1995	136.8	137.4	142.1	145.8	150.8	150.0	157.3	158.8	160.2	160.2	165.2	166.6	152.6
1996	170.2	170.0	170.3	176.9	174.2	171.5	169.6	177.0	179.7	180.8	183.4	186.0	175.8
1997[1]	192.8	194.7	194.0	197.3	203.3	201.8	212.0	210.3	226.8	211.9	211.4	222.7	206.6

[1] Preliminary. [2] Federal Republic of Germany. Not seasonally adjusted. *Source: Economic and Statistics Administration, U.S. Department of Census*

Corporate Profits After Tax--Quarterly In Billions of Dollars

Year	I	II	III	IV	Average	Year	I	II	III	IV	Average
1986	112.5	113.1	115.7	123.0	116.1	1992	267.2	275.2	240.4	270.6	263.4
1987	144.4	167.3	173.8	180.6	166.5	1993	282.5	296.1	298.4	324.0	300.3
1988	201.0	217.1	220.3	231.0	217.4	1994	312.1	342.5	361.6	377.7	348.5
1989	219.3	206.7	196.9	204.4	206.8	1995	401.0	405.9	411.8	418.8	409.4
1990	221.7	232.2	233.9	237.1	231.2	1996	438.7	450.0	447.5	454.0	447.6
1991	240.7	236.4	238.6	247.6	240.8	1997[1]	467.2	475.3	495.2		479.2

[1] Preliminary. *Source: Bureau of Economic Analysis, U.S. Department of Commerce (BEA)*

STOCK INDEX FUTURES, U.S.

Productivity: Index of Output Per Hour, All Persons, Nonfarm Business--Quarterly 1992 = 100

Year	I	II	III	IV	Average	Year	I	II	III	IV	Average
1986	94.7	95.1	95.0	94.7	94.9	1992	99.3	99.9	99.7	101.1	100.0
1987	94.1	94.7	94.5	95.2	94.6	1993	100.1	99.7	100.1	100.8	100.2
1988	94.9	95.0	95.4	95.9	95.3	1994	100.2	100.5	101.0	101.2	100.7
1989	95.5	95.7	96.0	96.1	95.8	1995	100.5	100.9	101.3	101.1	100.7
1990	96.4	96.7	96.4	95.5	96.3	1996	101.5	101.7	102.0	102.4	102.1
1991	96.1	96.8	97.4	97.6	97.0	1997[1]	102.8	103.4	104.4		103.5

[1] Preliminary. *Source: Bureau of Economic Analysis, U.S. Department of Commerce (BEA)*

Consumer Confidence, The Conference Board 1985 = 100

Year	Jan.	Feb.	Mar.	Apr.	May	June	July	Aug.	Sept.	Oct.	Nov.	Dec.	Average
1989	115.8	120.7	117.4	116.6	116.7	117.2	120.4	115.4	116.3	117.0	115.1	113.0	116.8
1990	106.5	106.7	110.6	107.3	107.3	102.4	101.7	84.7	85.6	62.6	61.7	61.3	91.5
1991	55.1	59.4	81.1	79.4	76.4	78.0	77.7	76.1	72.9	60.1	52.7	52.5	68.5
1992	50.2	47.3	56.5	65.1	71.9	72.6	61.2	59.0	57.3	54.6	65.6	78.1	61.6
1993	76.7	68.5	63.2	67.6	61.9	58.6	59.2	59.3	63.8	60.5	71.9	79.8	65.9
1994	82.6	79.9	86.7	92.1	88.9	92.5	91.3	90.4	89.5	89.1	100.4	103.4	90.6
1995	101.4	99.4	100.2	104.6	102.0	94.6	101.4	102.4	97.3	96.3	101.6	99.2	100.0
1996	88.4	98.0	98.4	104.8	103.5	100.1	107.0	112.0	111.8	107.3	109.5	114.2	104.6
1997[1]	118.7	118.9	118.5	118.5	127.9	129.9	126.3	127.6	130.2	123.4	127.9	129.9	124.8

[1] Preliminary. *Source: The Conference Board (Copyrighted)*

Average Open Interest of NYSE Composite Stock Index Futures in New York In Contracts

Year	Jan.	Feb.	Mar.	Apr.	May	June	July	Aug.	Sept.	Oct.	Nov.	Dec.
1989	6,460	7,211	7,860	7,605	8,001	6,771	6,386	6,247	6,449	7,045	6,491	6,084
1990	6,350	6,098	5,443	4,925	5,129	5,160	4,732	6,079	6,003	5,272	4,983	4,554
1991	4,736	5,720	5,264	5,488	6,190	6,010	5,056	5,997	5,869	5,512	6,438	6,195
1992	5,216	5,290	5,469	4,575	4,867	5,858	6,491	7,049	6,647	6,034	6,430	5,890
1993	5,033	5,083	4,113	3,613	4,222	4,340	3,714	4,178	3,997	4,315	4,721	4,539
1994	4,653	4,471	4,823	3,720	3,839	3,969	3,903	3,982	4,142	4,494	4,244	4,617
1995	3,695	4,159	4,113	3,476	3,396	3,254	3,205	3,029	2,966	2,683	3,125	3,403
1996	3,644	4,139	3,245	2,822	2,839	2,547	2,492	2,526	2,759	2,798	2,649	3,050
1997	3,126	3,232	3,194	2,801	3,154	2,744	2,316	2,823	2,780	2,384	3,005	4,354

Source: New York Futures Exchange (NYFE)

Average Open Interest of Value Line Stock Index Futures in Kansas City In Contracts

Year	Jan.	Feb.	Mar.	Apr.	May	June	July	Aug.	Sept.	Oct.	Nov.	Dec.
1989	1,394	1,189	1,288	1,262	1,421	1,513	1,615	1,710	1,522	1,250	1,200	1,182
1990	1,245	1,355	1,463	1,514	1,544	1,404	1,311	1,297	1,250	1,210	1,325	1,381
1991	1,534	2,211	2,107	2,326	2,384	2,138	1,860	1,884	1,764	1,509	1,857	2,100
1992	2,127	2,208	1,657	1,169	1,117	1,049	833	867	1,029	962	1,101	1,632
1993	1,999	1,822	1,356	934	1,188	1,118	1,100	1,181	1,039	1,057	1,302	1,461
1994	1,921	1,649	1,289	768	839	823	812	850	898	915	1,011	1,478
1995	1,600	1,365	1,077	802	759	648	580	565	568	489	627	1,025
1996	1,163	783	571	530	418	435	347	411	403	318	370	503
1997	548	447	352	218	321	361	324	342	313	255	202	211

Source: Kansas City Board of Trade (KCBT)

Average Open Interest of Maxi Major Market Stock Index Futures in Chicago In Contracts

Year	Jan.	Feb.	Mar.	Apr.	May	June	July	Aug.	Sept.	Oct.	Nov.	Dec.
1989	7,060	6,421	5,554	6,335	6,280	4,130	6,213	5,235	4,043	7,169	4,835	5,552
1990	5,274	4,273	5,261	5,847	7,686	8,773	8,398	6,480	7,837	8,106	7,873	9,891
1991	9,705	9,856	7,894	7,739	7,715	7,130	5,519	5,501	5,042	4,296	3,877	5,118
1992	5,326	5,568	4,627	4,776	5,495	5,518	4,505	4,336	4,681	4,409	4,236	5,771
1993	5,880	5,122	3,730	3,137	3,116	2,913	2,033	1,903	1,849	2,040	2,867	3,699
1994	3,467	3,722	4,048	4,280	4,516	5,015	4,517	3,690	2,937	3,842	3,511	1,899
1995	2,009	3,457	2,397	1,263	1,297	1,048	1,015	746	705	334	313	344
1996	333	302	208	165	116	86	81	99	92	46	6	21
1997	48	62	58	34	17	18	21	64	76	22	20	22

Source: Index and Option Market (IOM), division of the Chicago Mercantile Exchange (CME)

Average Open Interest of S & P 500 Index Futures in Chicago In Contracts

Year	Jan.	Feb.	Mar.	Apr.	May	June	July	Aug.	Sept.	Oct.	Nov.	Dec.
1988	230,012	241,818	229,584	228,538	258,268	233,048	209,288	236,016	241,314	243,940	275,430	262,268
1989	258,906	272,570	274,136	273,328	281,254	257,156	233,870	259,978	259,898	252,078	252,888	235,750
1990	224,392	248,558	248,920	236,700	255,436	237,730	226,100	265,136	319,214	303,980	314,880	320,520
1991	296,224	337,606	317,988	296,212	314,206	309,696	285,330	304,134	303,218	288,558	307,796	290,648
1992	294,868	286,026	283,884	273,982	283,514	299,924	306,070	327,226	336,526	340,130	356,684	359,884
1993	329,228	347,382	357,878	348,554	365,792	380,106	364,378	382,622	416,780	390,218	402,748	392,350
1994	376,450	391,648	420,130	401,636	438,218	599,134	434,056	455,742	475,868	461,188	487,162	502,740
1995	427,004	442,628	445,584	420,104	443,296	453,364	420,024	422,608	417,812	402,794	441,780	447,528
1996	406,400	428,058	419,688	368,620	399,070	407,914	369,248	382,266	413,944	374,726	416,102	448,382
1997	393,086	396,528	417,542	377,100	392,034	417,006	372,274	392,812	423,449	391,922	402,044	417,717

Source: International Monetary Market (IMM); division of the Chicago Mercantile Exchange (CME)

Average Open Interest of S & P 400 Midcap Index Futures in Chicago In Contracts

Year	Jan.	Feb.	Mar.	Apr.	May	June	July	Aug.	Sept.	Oct.	Nov.	Dec.
1992		2,776	3,060	3,017	3,712	4,476	4,073	4,350	4,762	4,355	5,778	6,883
1993	7,197	9,048	9,095	8,759	8,640	9,336	8,731	10,183	10,728	12,955	13,343	13,261
1994	13,183	11,999	12,748	10,801	10,829	11,902	11,970	12,369	15,002	13,702	13,896	14,494
1995	13,787	13,355	11,130	9,275	9,329	9,929	11,198	11,708	13,107	11,702	12,341	12,863
1996	11,088	10,474	11,375	8,700	9,254	10,403	9,763	10,867	11,168	9,641	10,596	11,107
1997	11,215	11,825	11,258	9,721	10,807	10,877	11,292	12,346	13,505	11,595	11,874	13,329

Source: International Monetary Market (IMM); division of the Chicago Mercantile Exchange (CME)

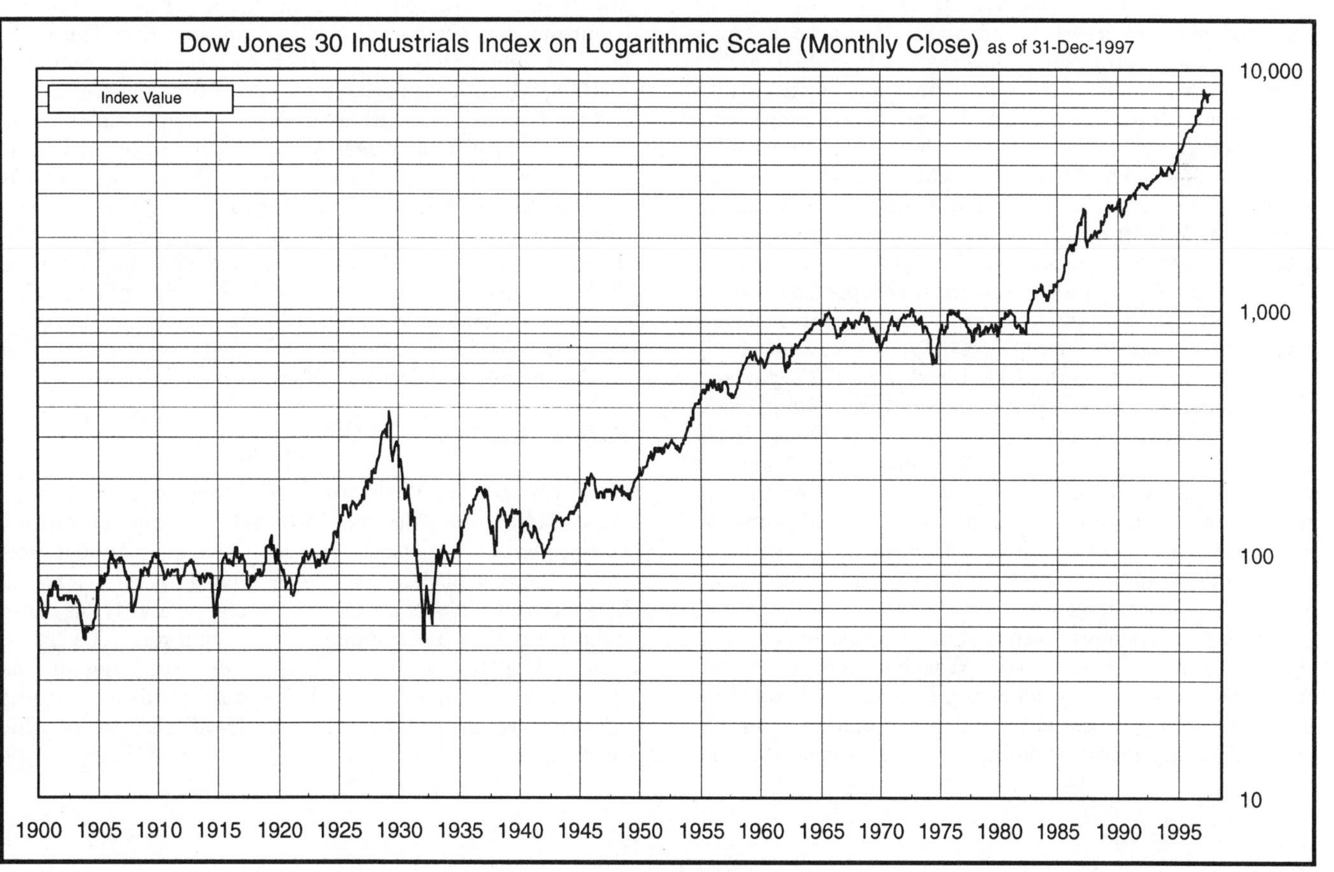

Stock Index Futures, Worldwide

The world's equity markets generally began 1997 on a firm footing and the strength persisted through the first half of the year. The second half, notably the fourth quarter, proved unnerving. Russia's equity market led the pack upward with a near 200 percent gain, statistically, however, it's an unfair comparison to the world's major equity markets whose gains were considerably less. The losers were all Asian markets. For the year, in U.S. dollars, Australia's stock market lost 11 percent; the U.K. gained 16 percent; Canada and France both gained 9 percent; Germany gained 19 percent; Switzerland gained 40 percent; Brazil gained 20 percent; Mexico gained 41 percent; Hong Kong lost 32 percent; Indonesia was down 70 percent; Japan lost 28 percent; Singapore lost 46 percent; and Thailand's market lost almost 81 percent. In the U.S., the Dow Jones Industrial Average advanced 22.6 percent in 1997, but closed the year four percent below its mid-summer record high. The S & P 500 composite gained 31 percent; the Nasdaq composite 21.6 percent, and the Wilshire 5000, which measures almost all U.S. stocks, gained 29 percent.

In almost all markets price volatility seemed the rule rather than the exception, reflecting burgeoning public participation throughout the first half of the year. Price corrections, when they occurred, generally proved short-lived and were viewed as buying opportunities. However, a surprise was in the offing and the impact moved quickly through the world's equity markets during 1997's fourth quarter.

It started with Thailand's currency debacle in late October. Traders began to perceive that Thailand's seemingly booming economy had very weak legs with an over extended national treasury and highly leveraged banking system. Panic selling in Southeast Asia rolled across Malaysian and Indonesian equity markets, spilling into Hong Kong, Japan and South Korea, into Europe, and across the Atlantic. The more developed economies were able to absorb much of the selling, but not so in the world's emerging economies, including Latin America, where fears mounted that their economies were vulnerable to the same pressures that were evident in Asia. During the closing ten weeks of 1997, Thailand's equity market dropped 57 percent in U.S. dollar terms, Indonesia was off 54 percent, Malaysia was down 45 percent, South Korea 67 percent, Hong Kong 31 percent, and Japan's Nikkei lost about 21 percent. Canada's index lost 6.6 percent, Mexico was off 4.4 percent, Germany 1.0 percent, but the U.K's Financial Times Index gained 0.4 percent while the U.S. managed a 2.0 percent gain. Clearly, the so-called global economy seemed to have two halves; the question for 1998 is which would prove the more dominant. On balance, an underlying optimism seemed to prevail by the start of 1998 that the Asian shakeout had been contained.

Stock markets have taken root in a number of countries that only a few years ago perceived such symbols of capitalism as decadent; worldwide, nearly one hundred countries now have equity markets. Russia's stock market strength, percentile gain notwithstanding, reflected a view that the government would accelerate state asset sales, reduce the budget deficit, and achieve a two percent economic growth rate in 1998, which if realized, would be Russia's first expansion since the USSR's collapse in 1991. However, among Eastern Europe's stock markets, attention seems to have focused on Hungary as a hot spot in 1998, notwithstanding a 45 percent gain in 1997.

In the U.S., stocks once again reacted positively to a robust low inflation economy. Cyclically, the economy's expansionary phase has persisted for an unprecedented 80 months and appears likely to carry into 1998 although at a somewhat slower growth rate. The Federal Reserve did tighten monetary policy 25 basis points in March, 1997, but it failed to slow the flow of capital into equities, estimated at nearly $2 billion per week on average, much of it emanating from retirement programs. While the U.S. equity markets would seem ripe for the long awaited pause, and a case could be made that yearend 1997 prices were high relative to seemingly normal price/earning ratios, the underlying bias was still solidly positive.

The economic outlooks are less sanguine in other key industrialized nations, but their equity markets were less overvalued relative to the U.S. In Europe, the coming monetary union and single currency early in 1999 clouds the outlook. Moreover, the growing competitiveness in the global economy will likely trigger a restructuring in many corporations to cut costs and enhance profit margins, the impact of which will likely show huge variances across countries. Germany, for example, is making good strides in the direction of increased efficiency, but in France corporate profit margins are more likely to drop than rise. The U.K., however, seems to be in good position for a decent economy in 1998, which if realized, should favor further strength in their F-T index. The outlook in Japan remains almost dire. Corporate profitability seems almost out of reach in their near deflationary economy since unit costs can never be cut enough to compensate for declining revenues. This suggests continued pressure on the Nikkei index during 1998. The index closed 1997 at 15,258 vs. a mid-1997 high of over 20,000. Along the Asian rim, Hong Hong's Hang Seng index could lead a mid-1998 recovery in the region's equity markets, assuming no further economic meltdowns in other rim nations during the first half of the year.

Futures Markets

During the 1990's, futures and options on stock indices have taken their place alongside debt instrument futures and options as the most successful exchange traded contracts. Because of this, nearly every global futures exchange lists a variety of stock index contracts, primarily on those indices based on their domestic stock markets. The list of stock indices traded worldwide has grown too large for this space, but a listing is available in the worldwide futures exchange volume tables in the front section of this Yearbook.

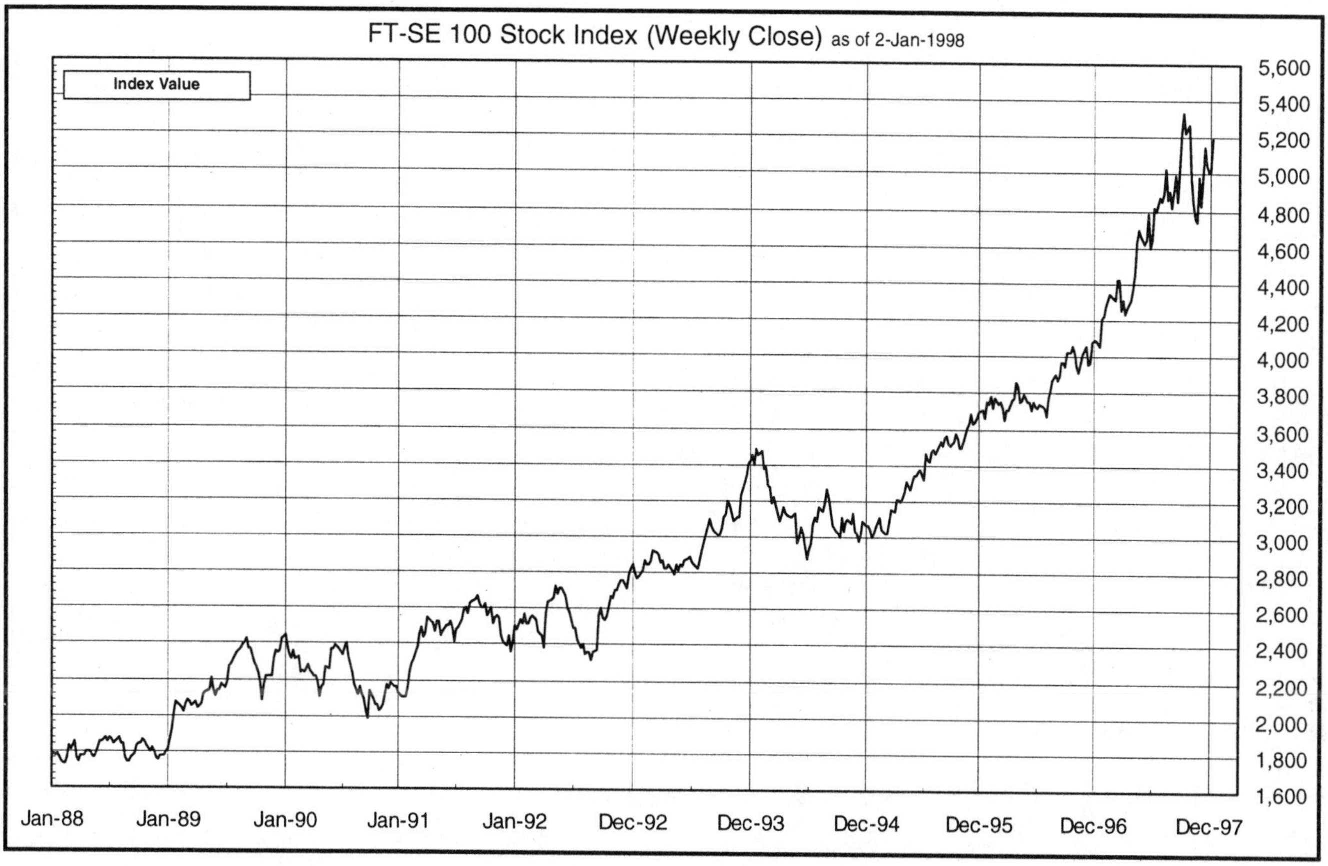

FT-SE 100 Stock Index (Weekly Close) as of 2-Jan-1998

Index Value

5,600
5,400
5,200
5,000
4,800
4,600
4,400
4,200
4,000
3,800
3,600
3,400
3,200
3,000
2,800
2,600
2,400
2,200
2,000
1,800
1,600

Jan-88 Jan-89 Jan-90 Jan-91 Jan-92 Dec-92 Dec-93 Dec-94 Dec-95 Dec-96 Dec-97

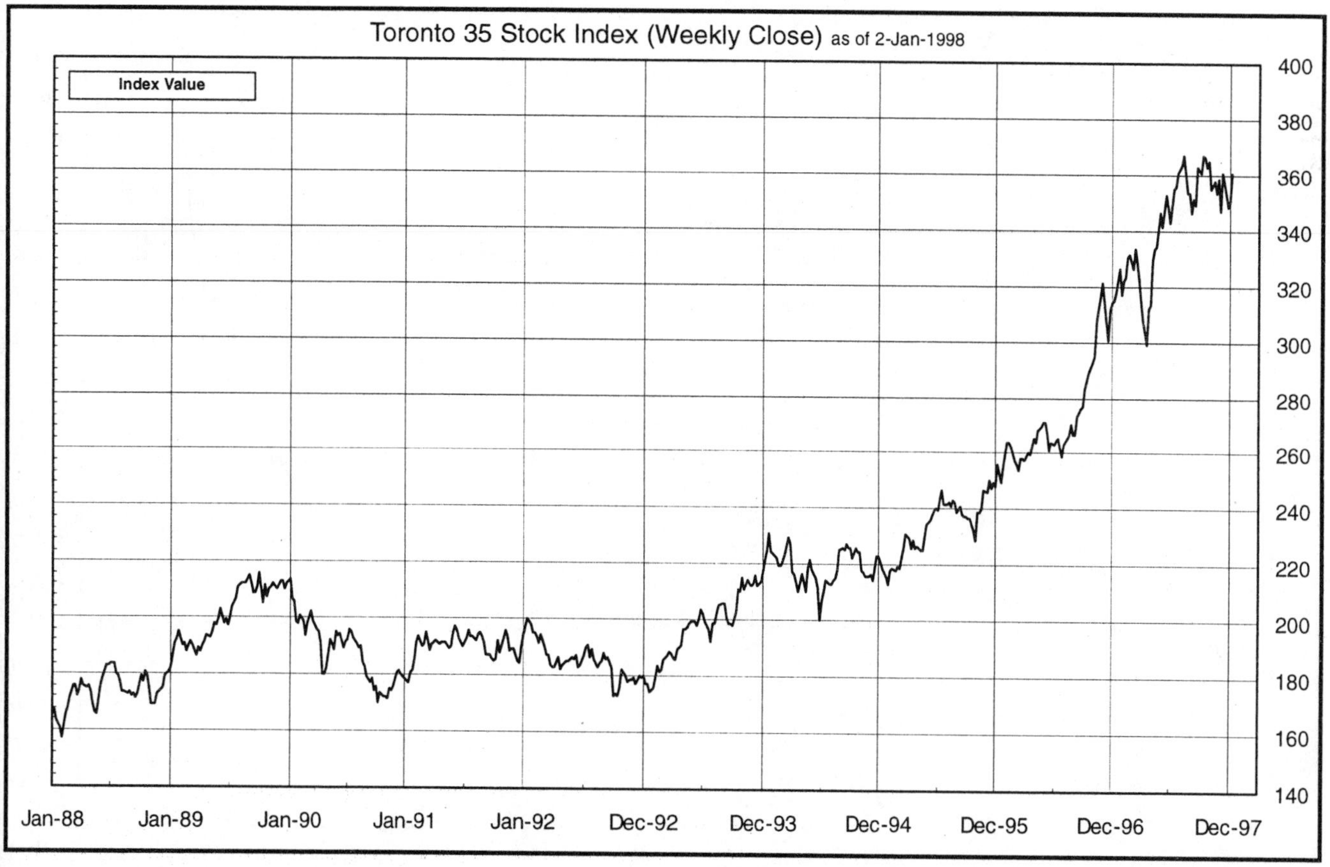

Toronto 35 Stock Index (Weekly Close) as of 2-Jan-1998

Index Value

400
380
360
340
320
300
280
260
240
220
200
180
160
140

Jan-88 Jan-89 Jan-90 Jan-91 Jan-92 Dec-92 Dec-93 Dec-94 Dec-95 Dec-96 Dec-97

STOCK INDEX FUTURES, WORLDWIDE

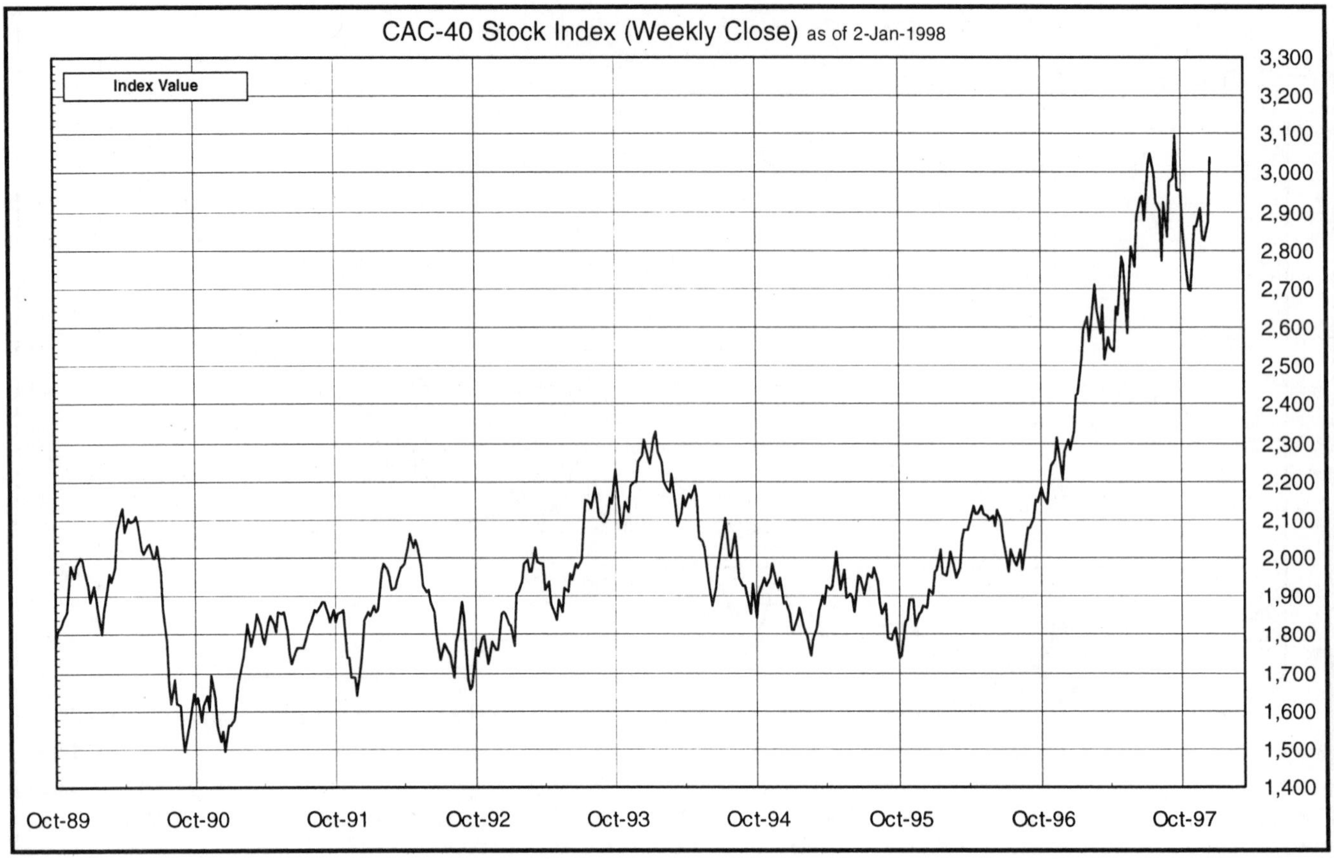

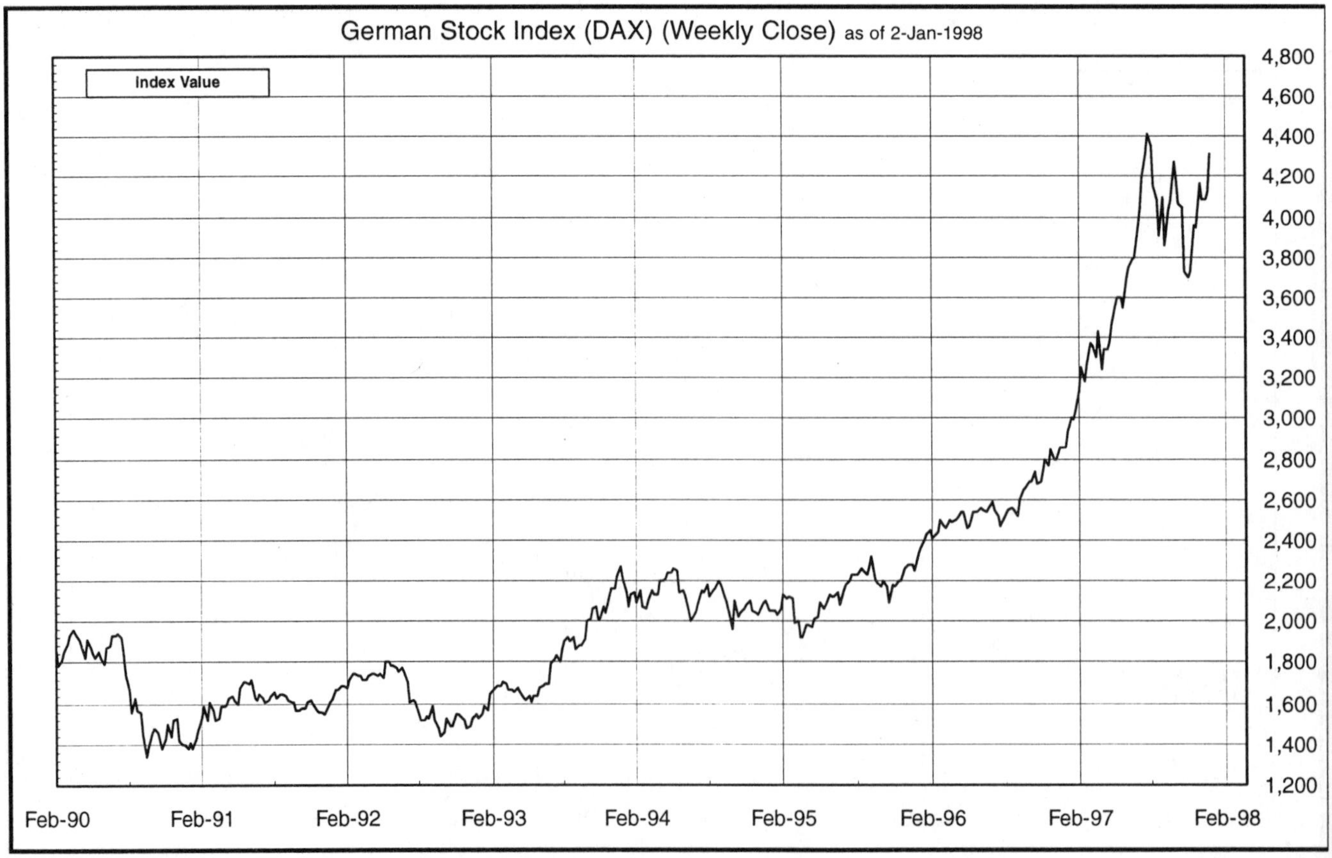

CAC-40 Stock Index (Weekly Close) as of 2-Jan-1998

German Stock Index (DAX) (Weekly Close) as of 2-Jan-1998

Hang Seng Stock Index (Weekly Close) as of 2-Jan-1998
Index Value
17,000
16,000
15,000
14,000
13,000
12,000
11,000
10,000
9,000
8,000
7,000
6,000
5,000
4,000
3,000
2,000
1,000
Jan-88
Jan-89
Jan-90
Jan-91
Jan-92
Dec-92
Dec-93
Dec-94
Dec-95
Dec-96
Dec-97

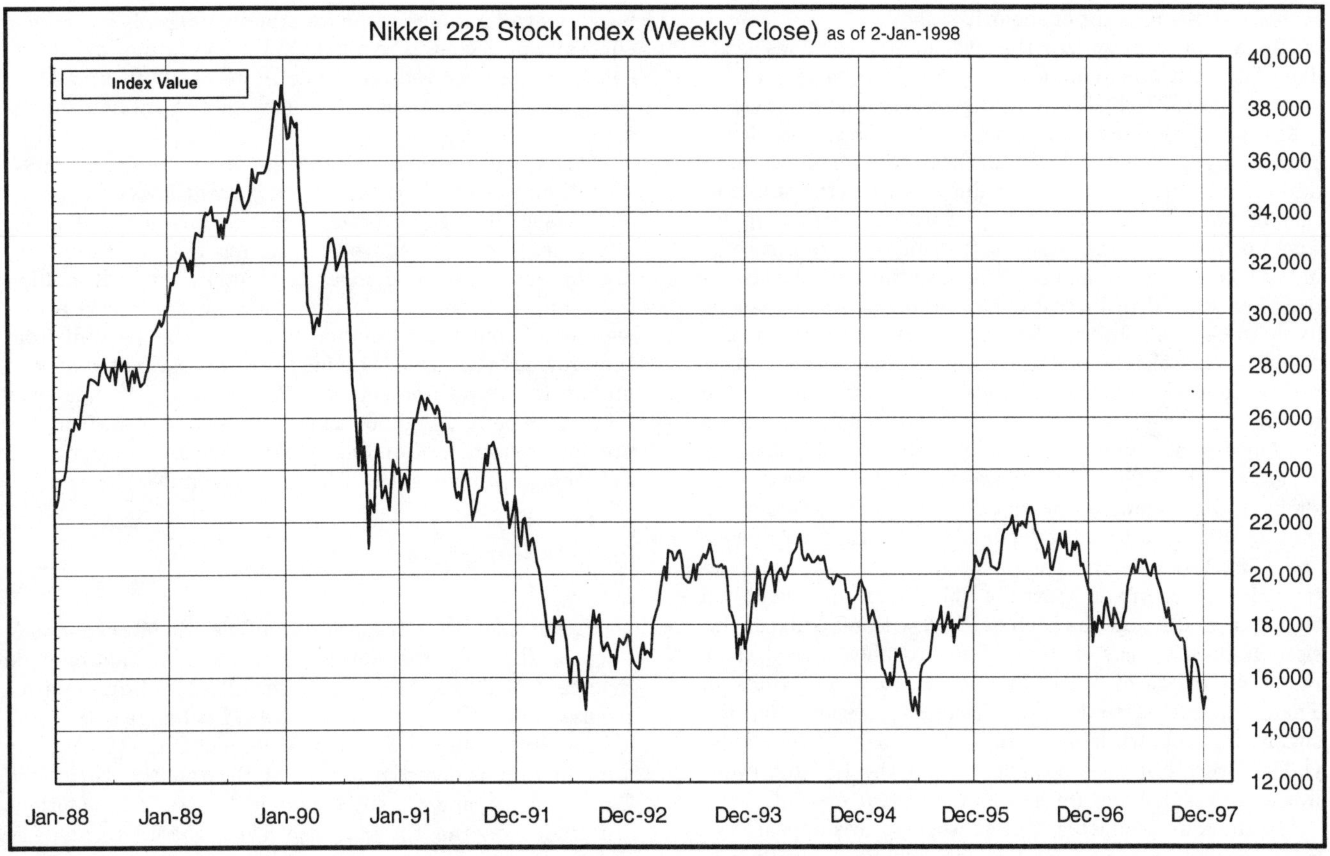

Nikkei 225 Stock Index (Weekly Close) as of 2-Jan-1998
Index Value
40,000
38,000
36,000
34,000
32,000
30,000
28,000
26,000
24,000
22,000
20,000
18,000
16,000
14,000
12,000
Jan-88
Jan-89
Jan-90
Jan-91
Dec-91
Dec-92
Dec-93
Dec-94
Dec-95
Dec-96
Dec-97

Sugar

Sugar prices trended higher in 1997 though the gains were not substantial. The major fundamental support for the market appeared to be the expectation that the 1997-98 season (September-August) world stocks of sugar would decline. Sugar prices have been stagnant for some time as world stocks of sugar have been increasing. They were higher at the end of the 1995-96 season and in 1996-97 they increased again. The 1997-98 season should see a decline in stocks due mostly to a reduction in Indian sugar production. Still, world stocks of sugar remain fairly large and prices are likely to hold near current levels until stocks are reduced.

World consumption of sugar in 1997-98 is expected to be about 124 million metric tonnes. That would represent an increase of about one percent from the previous season. World sugar consumption is trending higher for several reason. Among them are increasing rates of use in countries that produce sugar, like Brazil. Other areas, like Eastern Europe, are also showing signs of increased sugar consumption. While the industrialized countries of North America and Western Europe are showing little increase in sugar use, due in part to the use of artificial sweeteners and corn sweeteners, countries in Asia, South America and Africa are showing increased rates of use. Consumption in 1998 could in part be affected by the financial turmoil in Asia which could act to slow use. A country like India has shown a very high rate of sugar consumption, while in Japan sugar consumption is slowing. China remains a mixed picture in terms of sugar use. Per capita consumption of sugar in the rural areas of China is very low relative to the urban areas. With a very large rural population, China would appear set to increase the amount of sugar it uses.

Sugar consumption in the developing countries looks like it will continue to increase by perhaps three percent per year. In the 1997-98 season, that number could be adversely affected by the financial turmoil in Asia. In the developed countries, sugar consumption has been trending lower for a number of years. This has been due in part to the substitution of sweeteners such as high fructose corn syrup for sugar in processed foods and soft drinks. There are some indications now that the use of sugar in the developed countries has started to increase again, though the increase is likely to be small. In the countries of Eastern Europe, particularly Russia, the Ukraine and Poland, use of sugar remains high. Part of that is due to availability and part due to consumer preference for sugar over artificial sweeteners.

World production of sugar in the 1997-98 season is expected to be 122 million tonnes. That would represent a slight decline from the previous season. Production areas that are expected to show declines include Eastern Europe and Asia. Western Europe is expected to increase production. How much of an impact the El Nino weather event had on sugar production has been debated with no firm conclusion. It does appear that El Nino probably caused some reduction in world sugar production. Dry conditions in Thailand, related to El Nino, reduced prospects for the sugar cane crop, while in Brazil heavy rains worked against yields. Overall, it does not appear that the El Nino event was or will be a major influence in the sugar market.

In the fourth quarter of 1997, sugar prices appeared to be supported by persistent Russian buying of mostly raw sugar. The Russian sugar beet harvest was disrupted by poor weather and part of the crop was lost. As a result, Russian raw sugar production in the 1997-98 season is estimated at 1.4 million tonnes, over 20 percent less than the previous season. With domestic consumption of five million tonnes, Russia will import four million tonnes of sugar. Further complicating the situation is the fact that traditionally Russia obtained sugar from the Ukraine and Cuba who are both projected to have smaller crops in 1997-98.

The Ukraine is a major producer and exporter of white sugar. This season poor weather damaged the sugar beet crop with the result that sugar production was projected to fall to 2.1 million tonnes. That would represent a decline of over 20 percent from the previous season. Russia and the Ukraine reached an agreement where the Ukraine would be allowed to export to Russia 600,000 tonnes of white sugar under a duty free quota. Given the extent of the decline in Ukrainian production, it is likely that the Ukraine will have to import sugar just to meet the quota.

Cuba is also projected to produce less sugar in 1997-98. After reaching a multiyear production low in 1994-95 of just over three million tonnes, Cuban sugar production began to increase again. Now it is declining. Raw sugar production in 1997-98 was projected to fall to about 3.8 million tonnes, down 10 percent from the previous season. Brazil continues to be the dominant Southern Hemisphere sugar producer. The 1997-98 crop was about 14 million tonnes, down four percent from 1996-97. Poor weather late in the season had some effect on the crop.

After producing very large crops in 1994-95 and 1995-96, India will produce a smaller crop in 1997-98. The crop is currently projected to be about 13 million tonnes or 10 percent less than last season. While India has built up a large stockpile of sugar, imports of close to one million tonnes could be needed.

The USDA forecast U.S. raw sugar production in 1997-98 at 7.86 million short tons, nine percent above the previous season. Beet sugar production was forecast at 4.4 million tons, 10 percent above the year ago output of four million tonnes, while cane sugar production was 3.46 million tons, up eight percent. U.S. imports of sugar in 1997-98 were estimated at 2.33 million tons, down 16 percent from the previous year. Domestic food use was estimated at 9.84 million tons, up three percent. U.S. total use of sugar was forecast to be 10.15 million tonnes, up two percent from the previous season. U.S. ending stocks of sugar were projected to increase two percent to 1.52 million tonnes.

Futures Markets

Sugar futures are traded on the Bolsa de Mercadorias & Futuros (BM&F), the Marche a Terme International de France (MATIF), Kansai Agricultural Commodities Exchange (KANEX), the Tokyo Grain Exchange (TGE), the Manila International Futures Exchange Inc. (MIFE), the London Commodity Exchange (LCE), and the New York Coffee, Sugar, and Cocoa Exchange Inc. (CSCE). Options are traded on the KANEX, the TGE, the LCE, and the CSCE.

World Production, Supply & Stocks/Consumption Ratio of Sugar   In Thousands of Metric Tons (Raw Value)

Marketing Year	Beginning Stocks	Production	Imports	Total Supply	Exports	Domestic Consumption	Ending Stocks	Stocks/ Consumption Percentage
1988-9	20,349	105,562	28,671	154,582	28,671	106,516	19,395	18.2
1989-90	19,395	108,772	33,179	161,346	33,179	108,709	19,458	17.9
1990-1	19,458	113,458	32,538	165,391	32,538	111,926	20,927	18.8
1991-2	20,967	116,512	30,802	168,281	30,802	113,929	23,550	20.7
1992-3	23,550	112,089	29,022	164,661	29,022	114,102	21,537	18.9
1993-4	21,537	109,787	29,753	161,077	29,753	112,801	18,523	16.4
1994-5	18,574	115,842	30,532	164,948	30,532	113,622	20,794	18.3
1994-5	19,238	116,161	30,601	166,000	30,601	112,886	22,513	19.9
1995-6	22,513	122,324	34,732	179,569	34,732	118,272	26,565	22.5
1996-7[1]	26,565	122,776	35,813	185,154	35,813	123,225	26,116	21.2

[1] Preliminary. [2] Forecast. *Source: Foreign Agricultural Service, U.S. Department of Agriculture (FAS-USDA)*

World Production of Sugar (Centrifugal Sugar-Raw Value)   In Thousands of Metric Tons

Year	Australia	Brazil	China	Cuba	France	Germany	India	Indonesia	Mexico	Thailand	United States	Ukraine[3]	World Total
1988-9	3,680	8,582	5,312	8,100	4,372	3,003	10,150	1,889	3,678	4,055	6,089	8,900	105,562
1989-90	3,797	7,793	5,618	8,000	4,204	4,087	12,575	2,080	3,100	3,502	6,070	5,627	108,772
1990-1	3,637	7,900	6,765	7,620	4,736	4,675	13,707	2,120	3,900	3,954	6,330	5,369	113,484
1991-2	3,192	9,200	8,492	7,030	4,413	4,250	15,249	2,250	3,500	5,062	6,627	4,178	116,512
1992-3	4,367	9,800	8,300	4,280	4,723	4,401	12,456	2,300	4,330	3,750	7,111	3,965	112,088
1993-4	4,412	9,930	6,505	4,000	4,725	4,736	11,660	2,480	3,780	3,975	6,945	4,188	109,787
1994-5	5,196	12,500	5,900	3,300	4,363	3,991	16,410	2,450	4,556	5,448	7,191	3,600	115,842
1995-6	5,049	13,700	6,686	4,450	4,601	4,150	18,225	2,090	4,660	6,223	6,686	3,800	122,324
1996-7[1]	5,659	14,650	7,267	4,200	4,400	4,550	14,610	2,094	4,835	6,013	6,557	2,900	122,776
1997-8[2]	5,866	15,200	7,500	3,900			13,370	2,050	5,000	4,600	7,017	2,200	122,229

[1] Preliminary. [2] Forecast. [3] Formerly part of the U.S.S.R.; data not reported separately until 1989. *Source: Foreign Agricultural Service, U.S. Department of Agriculture (FAS-USDA)*

World Stocks of Centrifugal Sugar at Beginning of Marketing Year   In Thousands of Metric Tons (Raw Value)

Year	Australia	Brazil	China	Cuba	France	Germany	India	Iran	Mexico	Philippines	United Kingdom	United States	World Total
1988-9	236	771	2,575	460	710	432	2,700	246	577	160	338	1,194	20,349
1989-90	256	1,382	2,674	340	642	409	1,315	246	605	275	343	1,128	19,395
1990-1	256	1,164	1,350	475	434	330	2,376	220	750	308	300	1,111	19,458
1991-2	220	757	1,350	500	689	428	3,563	275	1,505	242	228	1,371	21,016
1992-3	194	950	2,002	500	589	340	5,245	300	910	515	281	1,340	23,602
1993-4	156	880	905	130	701	358	3,501	400	1,040	679	416	1,546	21,063
1994-5	125	455	573	170	784	511	2,731	400	575	412	450	1,213	18,574
1995-6	152	710	3,215	400	437	271	5,990	270	601	100	453	1,126	22,513
1996-7[1]	101	510	2,648	400	684	331	8,455	300	714	634	457	1,354	26,565
1997-8[2]	542	860	2,530	300			6,696	280	699	550		1,368	26,116

[1] Preliminary. [2] Forecast. *Source: Foreign Agricultural Service, U.S. Department of Agriculture (FAS-USDA)*

Average Wholesale Price of Refined Beet Sugar[1]--Midwest Market   In Cents Per Pound

Year	Jan.	Feb.	Mar.	Apr.	May	June	July	Aug.	Sept.	Oct.	Nov.	Dec.	Average
1988	23.25	22.75	22.75	23.45	24.19	25.25	27.10	27.75	27.50	27.25	26.75	27.80	25.44
1989	28.75	29.00	29.50	29.50	29.50	29.50	29.38	29.25	29.06	28.20	29.50	31.38	29.06
1990	30.50	30.50	30.50	30.50	30.50	30.50	30.50	30.50	30.50	29.13	28.60	27.38	29.97
1991	26.88	26.50	26.50	26.13	26.00	25.75	25.50	25.50	25.00	24.94	24.60	24.50	25.65
1992	25.40	26.50	26.50	26.50	26.40	26.00	25.00	25.00	25.00	24.90	24.13	23.90	25.44
1993	23.25	23.00	23.00	23.50	23.50	23.50	25.50	27.75	27.50	27.50	27.25	26.50	25.15
1994	25.75	25.50	25.50	24.50	24.75	25.25	25.00	25.00	24.70	25.00	25.38	26.50	25.15
1995	25.50	25.50	25.50	25.50	25.13	25.10	24.75	24.75	25.50	25.75	28.13	28.85	25.83
1996	28.69	29.00	29.50	29.50	29.70	29.50	29.50	29.00	29.00	29.00	29.00	29.00	29.20
1997[2]	29.00	29.00	28.13	28.00	28.00	27.50	27.00	26.65	26.38	24.90	25.00		27.23

[1] These are f.o.b. basis prices in bulk, not delivered prices. [2] Preliminary. *Source: Economic Research Service, U.S. Department of Agriculture (ERS)*

SUGAR

Average Price of World Raw Sugar[1] In Cents Per Pound

Year	Jan.	Feb.	Mar.	Apr.	May	June	July	Aug.	Sept.	Oct.	Nov.	Dec.	Average
1988	9.64	8.40	8.48	8.49	8.85	10.52	14.04	11.09	10.18	10.29	10.82	11.28	10.17
1989	6.69	10.49	11.54	12.14	11.93	12.63	14.01	13.96	14.13	14.42	15.02	13.52	12.79
1990	14.38	14.63	15.39	15.24	14.62	12.99	11.92	10.92	11.00	9.77	10.00	9.72	12.55
1991	8.88	8.57	9.22	8.55	7.88	9.37	10.26	9.45	9.39	9.10	8.79	9.03	9.04
1992	8.43	8.06	8.22	9.53	9.62	10.52	10.30	9.78	9.28	8.66	8.54	8.15	9.09
1993	8.27	8.61	10.75	11.30	11.87	10.35	9.60	9.30	9.52	10.27	10.10	10.47	10.03
1994	10.29	10.80	11.71	11.10	11.79	12.04	11.73	12.05	12.62	12.75	13.88	14.76	12.13
1995	14.87	14.43	14.58	13.63	13.49	13.99	13.46	13.75	12.72	11.94	11.96	12.40	13.44
1996	12.57	12.97	13.07	12.43	11.94	12.54	12.83	12.33	11.87	11.65	11.29	11.38	12.24
1997[2]	11.13	11.06	11.17	11.50	11.54	12.02	12.13	12.54	12.65	12.86	13.19	12.90	12.58

[1] Contract No. 11 fob stowed Caribbean port, including Brazil, bulk spot price. [2] Preliminary. *Source: Economic Research Service, U.S. Department of Agriculture (ERS-USDA)*

Average Price of Raw Sugar New York (C.I.F., Duty/Free Paid, Contract #12 & #14) In Cents Per Pound

Year	Jan.	Feb.	Mar.	Apr.	May	June	July	Aug.	Sept.	Oct.	Nov.	Dec.	Average
1988	21.83	22.11	22.16	22.16	22.13	22.54	23.43	21.90	21.77	21.74	21.70	21.99	22.12
1989	21.88	22.07	22.12	22.30	22.45	22.99	23.56	23.57	23.50	23.14	23.24	22.84	22.81
1990	23.11	22.93	23.58	23.81	23.58	23.33	23.42	23.27	23.23	23.29	23.15	22.47	23.26
1991	21.86	21.42	21.46	21.23	21.29	21.42	21.25	21.83	22.06	21.76	21.75	21.50	21.57
1992	21.38	21.56	21.36	21.38	21.04	20.92	21.10	21.34	21.55	21.61	21.39	21.11	21.31
1993	20.76	21.16	21.56	21.76	21.36	21.42	21.89	21.85	21.97	21.80	21.87	22.00	21.62
1994	22.00	21.95	21.95	22.08	22.18	22.44	22.72	21.84	21.78	21.58	21.57	22.35	22.04
1995	22.65	22.69	22.46	22.76	23.10	23.09	24.47	23.18	23.21	22.67	22.60	22.63	22.96
1996	22.39	22.68	22.57	22.71	22.62	22.48	21.80	22.51	22.38	22.37	22.12	22.14	22.40
1997[1]	21.88	22.07	21.81	21.79	21.70	21.62	22.04	22.21	22.30	22.27	21.90	21.93	21.96

[1] Preliminary. *Source: Economic Research Service, U.S. Department of Agriculture (ERS-USDA)*

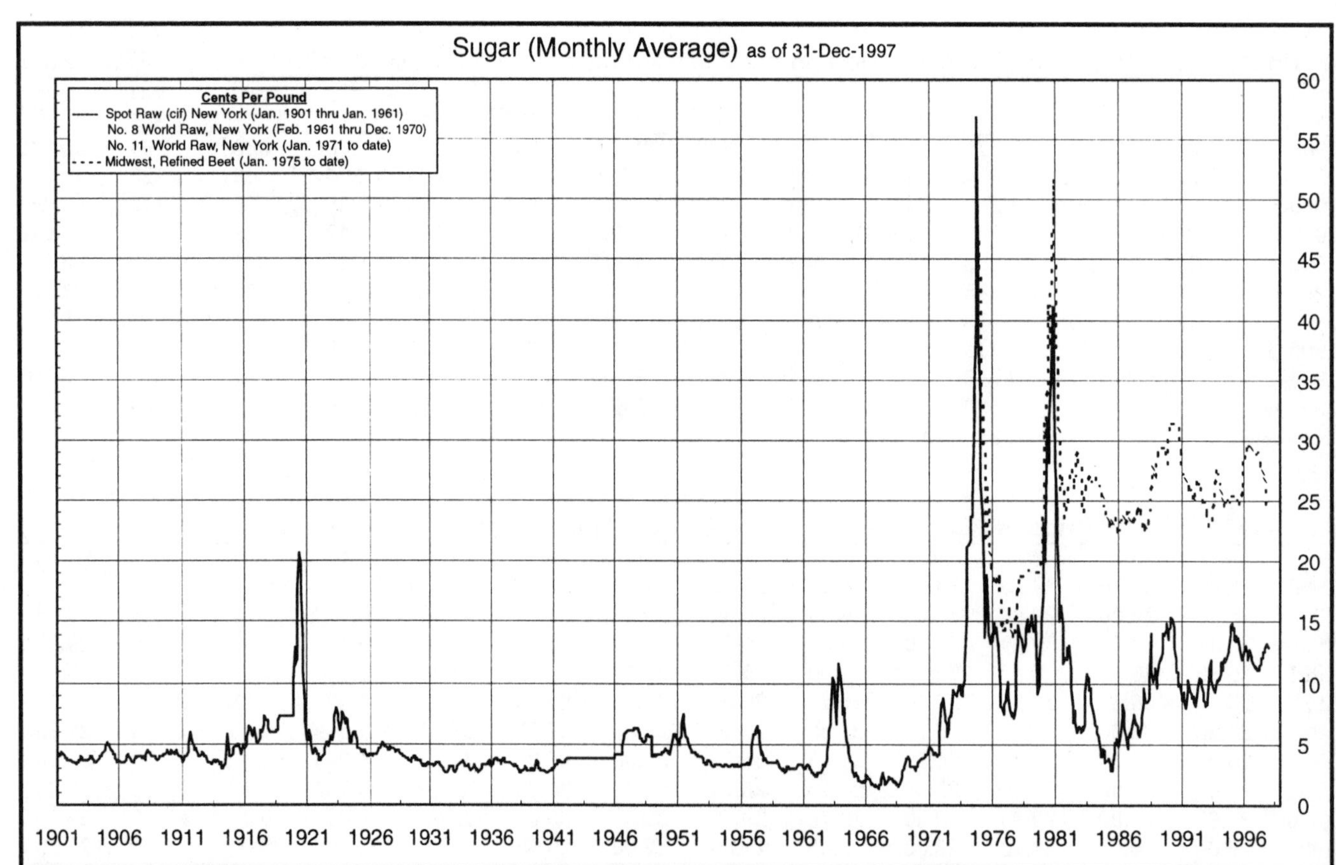

Centrifugal Sugar (Raw Value) Imported into Selected Countries In Thousands of Metric Tons

Year	Algeria	Canada	China	France	Iran	Rep. of Korea	Malaysia	Morocco	Nigeria	Russia[4]	United Kingdom	United States	World Total
1989-90	840	824	1,132	357	774	1,110	841	276	396	4,550	1,350	2,351	33,179
1990-1	990	1,109	1,055	343	875	1,233	900	350	480	3,580	1,143	2,619	32,558
1991-2	980	961	1,230	398	825	1,258	921	380	560	3,850	1,442	2,071	30,822
1992-3	980	1,095	506	487	780	1,233	900	408	430	3,500	1,352	1,827	29,605
1993-4	990	1,219	874	156	950	1,258	958	417	510	3,150	1,363	1,604	29,753
1994-5	990	1,020	4,110	361	800	1,345	1,030	455	460	2,700	1,261	1,664	30,601
1995-6[1]	1,000	1,192	2,075	523	940	1,411	1,120	477	447	3,200	1,361	2,536	34,732
1996-7[2]	1,000	1,099	1,514	553	1,150	1,500	1,195	471	470	3,300	1,260	2,508	35,813
1997-8[3]	1,010	1,129	2,100		1,150	1,550	1,340	470	530	3,300		2,111	35,900

[1] Preliminary. [2] Estimate. [3] Forecast. [4] Formerly part of the U.S.S.R.; data not reported separately until 1989-90. *Source: Foreign Agricultural Service, U.S. Department of Agriculture (FAS-USDA)*

Centrifugal Sugar (Raw Value) Exported from Selected Countries In Thousands of Metric Tons

Year	Australia	Brazil	Cuba	Dominican Republic	France	Germany	Mauritius	Mexico	South Africa	Swaziland	Thailand	United Kingdom	World Total
1989-90	2,927	1,500	7,065	393	2,748	1,539	589	17	927	449	2,611	385	33,179
1990-1	2,819	1,300	6,800	328	2,751	1,857	621	285	757	469	2,741	255	32,558
1991-2	2,345	1,607	6,100	344	2,682	1,557	590	50	969	474	3,657	368	30,822
1992-3	3,476	2,425	3,800	327	2,822	1,607	621	0	123	409	2,332	300	29,605
1993-4	3,663	2,861	3,300	346	2,636	1,785	590	0	27	395	2,718	410	29,753
1994-5	4,321	4,300	2,600	295	3,004	1,417	508	235	369	296	3,809	263	30,601
1995-6[1]	4,242	5,800	3,800	325	2,735	1,180	560	587	399	307	4,537	327	34,732
1996-7[2]	4,310	5,800	3,600	351	2,730	1,430	575	750	1,059	293	4,200	388	35,813
1997-8[3]	4,539	6,400	3,200	300			580	750	1,150	272	3,700		35,900

[1] Preliminary. [2] Estimate. [3] Forecast. *Source: Foreign Agricultural Service, U.S. Department of Agriculture (FAS-USDA)*

Supply and Utilization of Sugar (Cane & Beet) in the United States In Thousands of Short Tons (Raw Value)

	Supply								Utilization						
	Production			Offshore Receipts									Domestic Disappearance		
Year	Cane	Beet	Total	Foreign	Territories	Total	Beginning Stocks	Total Supply	Total Use	Exports	Net Changes in Invisible Stocks	Refining Loss Adjustment	In Polyhydric Alcohol[4]	Total	Per Capita
1989-90	3,157	3,466	6,623	2,568	0	2,568	1,244	10,503	9,279	561	53	7	10	7,933	63.7
1990-1	3,124	3,854	6,978	2,825	0	2,825	1,224	11,027	9,503	627	-86	61	8	9,503	64.6
1991-2	3,641	3,845	7,486	2,194	0	2,194	1,524	11,024	9,547	554	-13	0	11	9,547	64.4
1992-3	3,446	4,392	7,838	2,039	0	2,039	1,477	11,354	9,650	405	48	0	15	8,916	64.6
1993-4	3,565	4,090	7,655	1,772	0	1,772	1,704	11,131	9,794	454	7	0	15	9,794	66.1
1994-5	3,434	4,494	7,927	1,853	0	1,853	1,337	11,117	9,876	502	37	0	10	9,876	65.5
1995-6[1]	3,454	3,916	7,370	2,772	0	2,772	1,241	11,383	9,891	385	-48	0	13	9,891	66.5
1996-7[2]	3,203	4,050	7,253	2,784	0	2,784	1,492	11,529	9,975	225	0	0	16	9,975	67.2
1997-8[3]	3,335	4,300	7,635	2,372	0	2,372	1,554	11,561	10,100	200	0	0	10	10,100	67.7

[1] Preliminary. [2] Estimate. [3] Forecast. [4] Includes feed use. *Source: Economic Research Service, U.S. Department of Agriculture (ERS-USDA)*

Sugar Cane for Sugar & Seed and Production of Cane Sugar and Molasses in the United States

			Production					Farm Value		Sugar Production				
										Raw Value			Molasses Made	
Year	Acreage Harvested 1,000 Acres	Yield of Cane Per Havested Acre Net Tons	for Sugar (1,000 Tons)	for Seed (1,000 Tons)	Total (1,000 Tons)	Sugar Yield Per Acre Short Tons	Farm Price $ Per Ton	of Cane Used for Sugar (1,000 Dollars)	of Cane Used for Sugar & Seed (1,000 Dollars)	Total 1,000 Tons	Per Ton of Cane Lbs.	Refined Basis 1,000 Tons	Edible (1,000 Gallons)	Total[3] (1,000 Gallons)
1989	852.0	34.5	28,069	1,357	29,426	3.83	29.2	819,057	857,678	3,244	226	2,967	1,990	197,732
1990	794.0	35.4	26,475	1,661	28,136	4.20	30.8	815,630	863,497	3,226	238	2,945	1,405	186,487
1991	897.0	33.7	28,960	1,292	30,252	3.95	29.0	840,194	876,479	3,497	237	3,206	1,825	193,117
1992	925.0	32.8	28,873	1,490	30,363	3.79	28.1	811,350	852,235	3,437	234	3,193	1,460	184,974
1993	924.0	32.8	29,652	1,449	31,101	3.82	28.5	846,132	886,285	3,532	235	3,351	1,480	198,167
1994	936.8	33.0	29,405	1,524	30,929	3.96	29.2	857,438	900,827	3,595	NA	3,308	NA	193,628
1995	932.3	33.0	29,155	1,641	30,796	3.90	29.5	859,604	906,956	3,489	NA	NA	NA	195,429
1996[1]	888.9	33.1	27,686	1,776	29,462		28.3	780,745	833,245		NA	NA	NA	
1997[2]	915.5	34.5	29,913	1,650	31,563									

[1] Preliminary. [2] Estimate. [3] Excludes edible molasses. *Source: Economic Research Service, U.S. Department of Agriculture (ERS-USDA)*

SUGAR

U.S. Sugar Beets, Beet Sugar, Pulp & Molasses Produced from Sugar Beets and Raw Sugar Spot Prices

Year of Harvest	Acreage (1,000 Acres) Planted	Acreage (1,000 Acres) Harvested	Yield Per Harvested Acre Tons	Production 1,000 Tons	Sugar Yield Per Acre Sh. Tons	Price[3] Dollars	Farm Value $1,000	Sugar Production (1,000 Short Tons) Equivalent Raw Value[4]	Sugar Production (1,000 Short Tons) Refined Basis	Raw Sugar Prices (Cents Per Pound) World[5] Refined #5	Raw Sugar Prices (Cents Per Pound) Cof., Sugar Exch. #11 World	Raw Sugar Prices (Cents Per Pound) Cof., Sugar Exch. N.Y. Duty Paid	Wholesale List Price HFCS (42%) Midwest
1988	1,327	1,301	19.1	24,810	2.70	41.20	1,022,284	3,507	3,278	12.01	10.17	22.12	16.47
1989	1,324	1,295	19.4	25,131	2.66	42.10	1,058,298	3,442	3,217	17.15	12.79	22.81	19.24
1990	1,400	1,377	20.0	27,513	2.79	43.00	1,182,221	3,842	3,591	17.32	12.55	23.26	19.69
1991	1,427	1,412	20.3	28,203	2.68	38.50	1,085,728	3,729	3,485	13.41	9.04	21.57	20.93
1992	1,437	1,412	20.6	29,143	3.10	41.40	1,206,480	4,386	4,099	12.39	9.09	21.31	20.70
1993	1,438	1,409	18.6	26,249	2.87	38.50	1,023,687	4,047	3,792	12.79	10.03	21.62	18.83
1994	1,476	1,443	22.1	31,853	3.17	38.80	1,234,470	4,578	4,090	15.66	12.13	22.04	20.17
1995	1,445	1,417	19.8	28,065	2.78	38.10	1,070,663	3,944	NA	17.99	13.44	22.96	15.63
1996[1]	1,368	1,323	20.2	26,680	3.06	45.40	1,211,001	3,900	NA	16.64	12.24	22.40	14.46
1997[2]	1,459	1,428	20.9	29,874	3.00						12.06	21.96	

[1] Preliminary. [2] Estimate. [3] Includes support payments, but excludes Government sugar beet payments. [4] Refined sugar multiplies by the factor of 1.07. [5] F.O.B. Europe. *Source: Economic Research Service, U.S. Department of Agriculture (ERS-USDA)*

Sugar Deliveries and Stocks in the United States In Thousands of Short Tons (Raw Value)

Year	Quota Allocation	Actual Imports	Deliveries by Primary Distributors: Cane Sugar Refineries	Beet Sugar Factories	Importers of Direct Consumption Sugar	Mainland Cane Sugar Mills[3]	Total Deliveries	Total Domestic Consumption	Stocks (January 1): Cane Sugar Refineries[4]	Beet Sugar Factories	Commodity Credit Corp.	Refiners' Raw	Mainland Cane Mills	Total
1988	1,056.7	1,024.8	4,290	3,832	20	5	8,147	8,557	184	1,546	0	401	996	3,128
1989	3,093.1	2,995.8	4,764	3,449	76	6	8,295	8,952	187	1,372	0	487	1,008	3,053
1990	2,314.9	2,242.8	4,998	3,570	39	8	8,615	9,309	155	1,412	0	381	899	2,947
1991	1,526.7	1,477.0	4,786	3,713	30	11	8,540	9,470	168	1,327	0	371	812	2,729
1992	2,500.0	2,275.4	4,808	3,966	52	7	8,936	8,772	194	1,336	0	619	890	3,039
1993	[5]	[5]	4,781	4,087	52	10	9,064	9,577	183	1,640	0	507	895	3,225
1994	[5]	[5]	4,929	4,170	78	NA	9,321	9,813	218	1,696	0	438	1,160	3,512
1995	2,413.2	2,308.0	5,397	4,645	43	15	10,100	9,971	185	1,594	6	448	906	3,139
1996[1]	2,339.1								195	1,383	0	334	996	2,908
1997[2]									196	1,520	0	323	1,156	3,195

[1] Preliminary. [2] Estimate. [3] Sugar for direct consumption only. [4] Refined. [5] Combined with 1992. *Source: Economic Research Service, U.S. Department of Agriculture (ERS-USDA)*

Sugar, Refined--Deliveries to End Users in the United States In Thousands of Short Tons

Year	Bakery & Cereal Products	Beverages	Confectionery[2]	Hotels, Restaurant & Institutions	Ice Cream & Dairy Products	Canned, Bottled & Frozen Foods	All Other Food Uses	Retail Grocers[3]	Wholesale Grocers[4]	Non-food Uses	Non-Industrial Uses	Industrial Uses	Total Deliveries
1988	1,541	237	1,107	89	394	354	529	940	2,200	121	3,316	4,283	7,614
1989	1,532	215	1,187	106	426	342	637	1,026	2,051	126	3,259	4,465	7,730
1990	1,608	228	1,279	108	462	332	642	1,077	2,130	109	3,391	4,660	8,051
1991	1,632	204	1,277	100	439	331	623	1,182	2,079	88	3,469	4,594	8,063
1992	1,719	164	1,246	101	429	315	649	1,230	2,104	69	3,668	4,591	8,259
1993	1,785	158	1,292	108	424	336	725	1,235	2,075	85	3,589	4,805	8,394
1994	1,952	156	1,313	93	453	322	704	1,269	2,039	77	3,598	4,977	8,575
1995	1,905	169	1,372	103	452	279	863	1,236	2,173	64	3,701	5,103	8,804
1996[1]	1,993	196	1,335	80	445	318	849	1,263	2,241	66	3,759	5,202	8,962

[1] Preliminary. [2] And related products. [3] Chain stores, supermarkets. [4] Jobbers, sugar dealers. *Source: Economic Research Service, U.S. Department of Agriculture (ERS-USDA)*

U.S. Deliveries[1] of All Sugar by Primary Distributors, by Quarters In Thousands of Short Tons (Raw Value)

Year	First Quarter	Second Quarter	Third Quarter	Fourth Quarter	Total	Year	First Quarter	Second Quarter	Third Quarter	Fourth Quarter	Total
1986	1,819	1,907	2,069	1,991	7,786	1992	1,985	2,178	2,390	2,273	8,826
1987	1,908	2,001	2,146	2,112	8,167	1993	2,039	2,172	2,432	2,277	8,920
1988	1,951	1,983	2,147	2,107	8,188	1994	2,121	2,265	2,532	2,260	9,177
1989	1,923	2,051	2,181	2,185	8,340	1995	2,105	2,311	2,542	2,379	9,337
1990	1,837	1,911	2,154	2,149	8,051	1996	2,191	2,355	2,519	2,445	9,511
1991	1,878	1,955	2,173	2,057	8,063	1997[2]	2,143	2,408	2,593		9,525

[1] Includes for domestic consumption and for export. [2] Preliminary. *Source: Economic Research Service, U.S. Department of Agriculture (ERS-USDA)*

Average Open Interest of World Sugar No. 11 Futures in New York In Contracts

Year	Jan.	Feb.	Mar.	Apr.	May	June	July	Aug.	Sept.	Oct.	Nov.	Dec.
1988	147,508	147,629	132,539	133,524	137,472	167,829	159,071	137,351	135,121	115,138	119,873	144,931
1989	123,554	126,504	146,798	157,254	146,878	162,097	186,211	179,077	168,840	152,276	171,354	164,757
1990	164,235	160,509	163,155	168,962	170,351	161,320	133,208	121,665	112,065	109,986	110,047	108,939
1991	124,637	129,361	114,432	115,704	110,142	105,607	106,406	107,852	102,546	91,649	90,976	93,827
1992	96,255	105,166	93,774	109,137	95,101	106,310	96,038	87,089	77,740	69,023	74,292	93,039
1993	91,426	105,147	123,023	115,400	112,085	101,843	94,296	94,932	91,312	92,832	96,246	99,592
1994	108,936	123,148	137,582	115,060	117,030	126,843	106,749	118,057	141,361	140,011	171,843	191,801
1995	186,893	167,451	149,027	152,600	127,978	121,877	114,027	119,787	114,069	119,561	140,008	157,779
1996	156,047	159,563	150,093	142,773	137,897	148,447	144,527	153,845	153,202	144,830	150,866	150,573
1997	155,156	147,198	143,623	166,143	150,480	175,139	165,884	197,331	187,477	158,065	200,486	201,922

Source: Coffee, Sugar & Cocoa Exchange, Inc. (CSCE)

Volume of Trading of World Sugar No. 11 Futures in New York In Contracts

Year	Jan.	Feb.	Mar.	Apr.	May	June	July	Aug.	Sept.	Oct.	Nov.	Dec.	Total
1988	603,565	605,773	348,510	391,971	474,693	705,498	807,381	422,101	450,116	276,010	332,463	381,040	5,819,121
1989	499,199	520,018	575,486	600,852	557,386	660,521	624,969	517,295	526,834	328,469	456,485	375,927	6,243,361
1990	519,886	523,591	588,021	505,492	598,320	532,937	384,116	441,608	448,195	372,925	303,065	206,645	5,424,801
1991	313,915	510,163	388,672	477,954	286,120	534,639	309,836	352,351	366,007	240,812	253,201	234,876	4,268,546
1992	376,704	395,793	255,501	583,535	246,360	454,854	264,528	275,677	334,962	163,263	168,470	147,844	3,667,481
1993	330,474	481,506	507,370	518,292	415,283	390,261	255,581	307,181	368,194	222,082	272,579	217,142	4,285,945
1994	289,593	486,222	360,787	472,388	407,343	443,002	252,012	349,079	471,899	316,330	484,943	387,620	4,719,218
1995	591,861	489,274	472,519	478,757	352,000	485,131	298,756	402,358	360,086	246,584	278,906	254,850	4,711,082
1996	550,780	544,514	341,940	526,255	384,302	496,745	279,707	290,732	562,082	264,290	203,921	306,584	4,751,852
1997	436,935	493,199	268,343	618,176	308,563	575,264	400,150	427,082	580,551	440,208	323,286	413,214	5,284,971

Source: Coffee, Sugar & Cocoa Exchange, Inc. (CSCE)

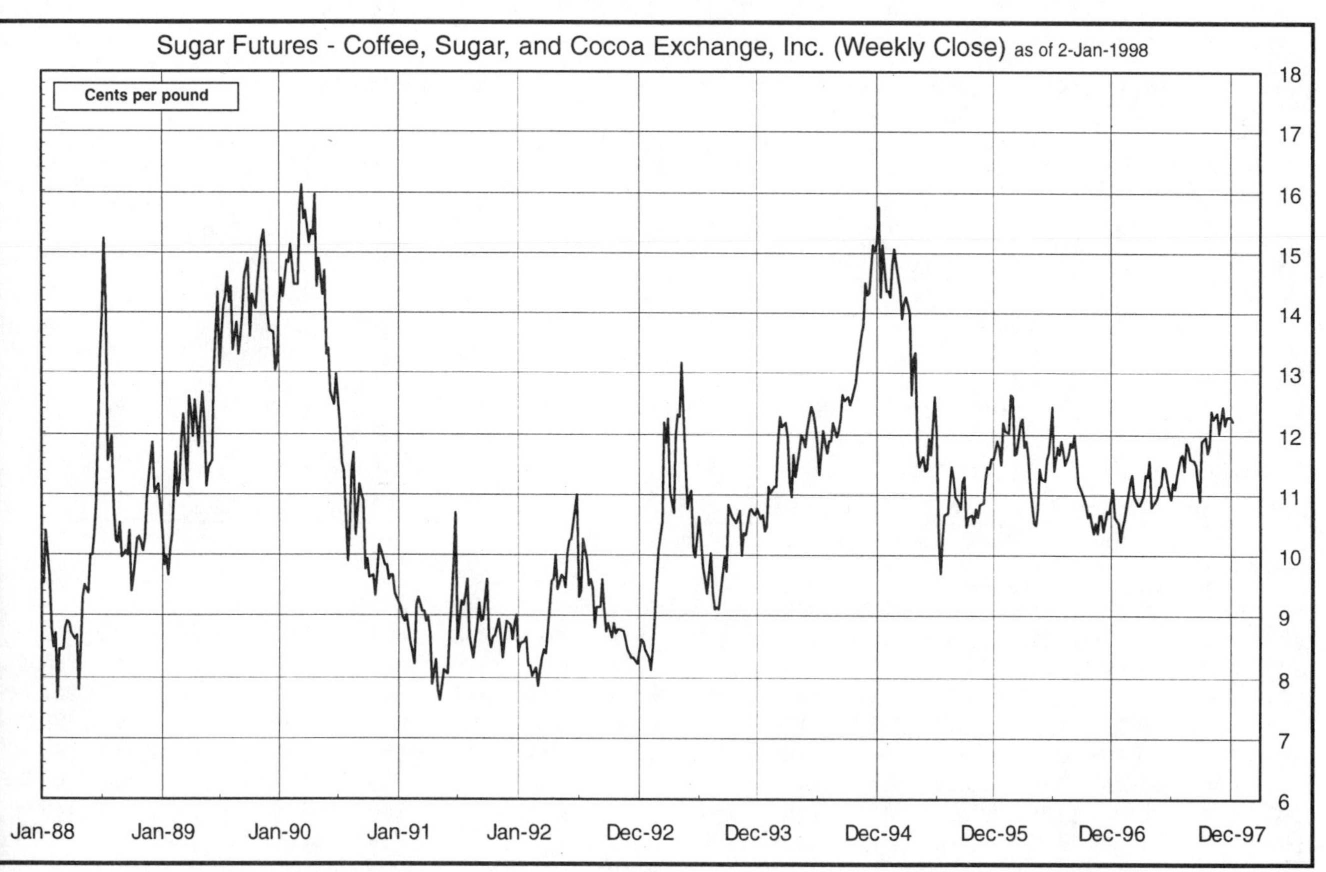

Sulfur

Elemental sulfur is used in the synthesis of sulfur compounds. It finds use in construction where it is added to concrete to aide corrosion resistance. It is also added to asphalt for highway construction.

According to the U.S. Geological Survey, U.S. production of sulfur in July 1997 was 885,000 metric tonnes. That was about four percent above the June production total of 851,000 tonnes. In July 1997, production of sulfur from petroleum, including coking operations, was 480,000 tonnes. Production from natural gas, including Frasch producers, was 405,000 tonnes. For the January-July 1997 period, production of sulfur was 6.2 million tonnes. Production from petroleum operations was 3.22 million tonnes, while production from natural gas operations was 2.98 million tonnes. In the comparable period of 1996, sulfur production was 6.0 million tonnes. For all of 1996, U.S. sulfur production was 10.4 million tonnes. Of the total, 5.37 million tonnes came from petroleum operations and 4.99 million tonnes was from natural gas operations.

U.S. imports of sulfur in June 1997 were 126,000 tonnes. That was up from 108,000 tonnes in May 1997. The major suppliers are Canada and Mexico. In the first half of 1997, U.S. imports of sulfur were 754,000 tonnes, down 16 percent from the comparable period of 1996. For all of 1996, imports of sulfur were 1.73 million tonnes.

U.S. imports of sulfuric acid in June 1997 were 138,000 tonnes, with sulfur content of 45,000 tonnes. Almost all of this supply originated in Canada. For the first half of 1997, imports of sulfuric acid were 921,000 tonnes, with sulfur content of 300,000 tonnes. In the comparable period of 1996, imports were 1.07 million tonnes with sulfur content of 349,000 tonnes. For all of 1996, U.S. imports of sulfuric acid were 2.08 million tonnes with sulfur content of 682,000 tonnes.

World Production of Sulfur (All Forms) In Thousands of Metric Tons

Year	Canada	China	France	Germany	Iraq	Japan	Mexico	Poland	Russia[3]	Saudi Arabia	Spain	United States	World Total
1989	6,600	5,170	1,036	1,701	1,330	2,559	2,372	5,137	9,900	1,423	1,211	11,592	58,924
1990	6,790	5,370	1,049	1,550	1,180	2,630	2,413	4,902	9,025	1,435	1,147	11,560	57,800
1991	7,130	5,910	1,200	1,282	300	2,626	2,094	4,104	8,100	2,000	905	10,820	54,600
1992	7,487	5,900	1,150	1,164	350	2,745	2,300	3,087	3,500	2,370	860	10,663	50,700
1993	8,430	6,360	1,260	1,171	450	2,922	1,640	2,119	3,600	2,400	687	10,959	51,300
1994	8,850	6,900	1,180	1,010	475	2,820	2,890	2,398	3,510	2,300	788	11,500	53,700
1995[1]	9,010	5,430	1,170	1,110	475	2,810	2,880	2,660	4,000	2,200	756	11,800	53,200
1996[2]	9,014	5,470	1,200	1,110	475	2,800	2,890	1,769	4,020	2,000	752	11,800	52,200

[1] Preliminary. [2] Estimate. [3] Formerly part of the U.S.S.R.; data not reported separately until 1992. *Source: U.S. Geological Survey (USGS)*

Salient Statistics of Sulfur in the United States In Thousands of Metric Tons (Sulfur Content)

	Production of											Sales Value of Shipments F.O.B. Mine/Plant		
	Elemental Sulfur											$ Per Tonne		
	Native - Sulfur[3] -	Recovered												
Year	Frasch	Petroleum & Coke	Natural Gas	Total	By-product Sulfuric Acid[4]	Other Sulf. Acid Compounds	Production (All Forms)	Imports Sulfuric Acid[4]	Exports Sulfuric Acid[4]	Producer Stocks, Dec. 31[5]	Apparent Consumption (All Forms)	Frasch	Recovered	Average
1989	3,888	3,971	2,539	6,510	1,190	4	11,592	2,260	146	1,301	12,685	100.18	78.70	86.62
1990	3,726	4,199	2,337	6,536	1,294	4	11,560	2,571	162	1,423	13,056	91.17	73.89	80.14
1991	2,869	4,243	2,402	6,645	1,302	4	10,820	3,020	149	1,194	12,932	87.05	64.17	71.45
1992	2,320	4,524	2,524	7,048	1,292	3	10,663	2,725	139	809	12,747	58.15	44.47	48.14
1993	1,904	4,820	2,905	7,725	1,430	3	11,100	2,440	145	1,382	12,600	51.60	25.06	31.86
1994	2,960	4,930	2,240	7,160	1,380	0	11,500	2,130	140	1,160	13,100	W	W	28.60
1995[1]	3,150	5,040	2,210	7,250	1,400	0	11,800	1,920	170	583	14,300	W	W	43.74
1996[2]	2,900	5,370	2,090	7,470	1,430	0	11,800	2,070	117	639	13,200	W	W	38.00

[1] Preliminary. [2] Estimate. [3] Or sulfur ore. [4] Basis 100% H_2SO_4, sulfur equivalent. [5] Frasch & recovered. W = Withheld. *Source: U.S. Geological Survey*

Sulfur Consumption & Foreign Trade of the United States In Thousands of Metric Tons (Sulfur Content)

	Consumption			Sulfuric Acid Sold or Used, by End Use[2]					Foreign Trade					
									Exports			Imports		
Year	Native Sulfur (Frasch)	Recovered Sulfur	Total Elemental Form	Total Sulfuric Acid	Pulpmills & Paper Products	Inorganic Chemicals[3]	Synthetic Rubber & Plastic	Phosphatic Fertilizers	Petroleum Refining[4]	Frasch	Recovered	Value Thous. $	Frasch	Recovered	Value Thous. $
1989	4,536	6,955	11,491	12,563	320	423	383	8,642	683	330	694	107,126	1,086	1,174	209,465
1990	4,457	7,301	11,758	12,600	290	653	273	8,664	400	348	624	109,327	1,129	1,442	206,450
1991	3,931	7,694	11,625	12,842	279	901	272	8,311	383	448	748	119,713	1,259	1,760	241,749
1992	3,083	8,368	11,451	12,340	296	617	278	8,300	385	362	604	69,662	845	1,877	129,894
1993	1,331	9,046	10,377	11,886	304	549	259	7,906	388	246	656	39,726	100	2,070	49,800
1994	W	11,100	11,100	11,300	295	448	256	8,040	236	-----	899	48,400	-----	1,650	62,000
1995	W	12,300	12,300	11,500	319	170	245	8,200	479	-----	906	66,200	-----	2,510	143,000
1996[1]	W	11,200	11,200	11,000	343	152	270	7,380	525	-----	855	51,700	-----	1,620	60,500

[1] Preliminary. [2] Sulfur equivalent. [3] Including inorganic pigments, paints & allied products, and other inorganic chemicals & products. [4] Including other pertroleum and coal products. NA = Not available. W = Withheld. *Source: U.S. Geological Survey (USGS)*

Sunflowerseed, Meal, and Oil

1997/98 world sunflowerseed production ranked fourth among the world's major oilseed crops, although still less ıan 20 percent of soybeans. However, unlike soybeans for 'hich most of the crop is crushed for meal, sunflowerseed as nearly equal amounts of meal and oil produced. The J.S. produces six percent of world sunflowerseed produc- .on, but has a larger role in world trade.

World production in 1997/98 of a near record 25 million ıetric tonnes was higher than expected and compares with 3.7 million in 1996/97. Argentina is the largest producer 'ith 5.6 million tonnes in 1996/97 down from the previous ear's record 5.9 million tonnes. The Russian Federation FSU-12) remains the largest producing area--6.1 million onnes in 1997/98 vs. 5.2 million in 1996/97; production in he E.U. in 1997/98 of 3.5 million tonnes compares with 3.9 nillion, respectively. Sunflowerseed is the third largest ilseed in foreign trade, 1997/98 exports of 3.7 million onnes compares with 2.7 million in 1996/97. World stocks enerally average about one million tonnes. Sunflower meal roduction in 1997/98 of 10 million tonnes compares with .9 million in 1996/97; sunflower oil of 8.8 million tonnes ompares with 8.6 million, respectively; but more oil moves n foreign trade than meal.

The acreage planted to sunflowerseed production in the J.S. shows an irregular pattern, as does average yield. In he 1990's the highest acreage planted was 3.6 million acres 1994/95), for 1997/98 about 2.9 million were planted vs. 2.6 million in 1996/97. Production (September/August) in 1997/98 of 1.7 million metric tonnes compares with 1.6 million in 1996/97, and the 1990's high of 2.2 million (1994/95). The Dakotas, notably North, are the largest producing states, with about two-thirds of total production.

U.S. sunflower meal production in 1997/98 (October/September) of 417,000 metric tonnes was unchanged from a year earlier. Disappearance in 1997/98 of 422,000 tonnes was also unchanged from 1996/97, with about five percent exported. Sunflower oil production in 1997/98 of 362,000 tonnes compares with 365,000 in 1996/97. However, unlike meal, most U.S. sunflower oil production is exported; 283,000 tonnes in 1997/98 vs. 325,000 in 1996/97, with Mexico the largest buyer. Domestic oil use has recently hovered around 75,000 tonnes. The U.S. also exports sunflower seed, much of it going to the European Union. Seed exports of 177,000 tonnes in 1997/98 compare with 147,000 in 1996/97.

The 1997/98 sunflower oil price was forecast at $507-$573 per metric tonne vs. $497 in 1996/97, basis average crude Minneapolis. The sunflower meal price was forecast to range from $90-$123 per metric tonne vs. $136 in 1996/97, basis 28 percent protein.

Abroad, the 1996/97 average sunflowerseed oil price of $545 per metric tonne, basis Rotterdam, compares with $617 the year before; for protein meal the average of $139 compares with $151, respectively.

Vorld Production of Sunflowerseed In Thousands of Metric Tons

rop ear	Argen-tina	Bulgaria	China	France	Hungary	India	Romania	South Africa	Spain	Turkey	United States	Former U.S.S.R.	World Total
993-4	4,010	442	1,340	1,643	702	1,400	696	362	1,309	815	1,167	5,230	21,390
994-5	5,900	596	1,367	2,053	664	1,204	764	352	979	740	2,194	4,612	24,020
995-6	5,556	655	1,269	1,993	785	1,324	931	546	588	800	1,819	7,296	25,970
996-7[1]	5,350	530	1,420	1,996	905	1,270	1,096	755	1,138	660	1,627	5,470	24,849
997-8[2]	6,100	475	1,350	2,105	700	1,200	800	450	1,359	730	1,699	5,200	24,680

[1] Preliminary. [2] Forecast. *Source: The Oil World*

Sunflowerseed Statistics in the United States In Thousands of Metric Tons

rop ear eginning eptember	Harvested Acres 1,000	Harvested Yield Per Cwt.	Farm Price $ Per Metric Ton	Value of Production Mil. $	Supply: Stocks, Sept. 1	Supply: Production	Supply: Imports	Supply: Total	Disappearance: Crush	Disappearance: Exports	Disappearance: Non-Oil Use & Seed	Disappearance: Total
993-4	2,486	10.35	284	332.0	69	1,167	25	1,261	661	99	429	1,189
994-5	3,430	14.10	236	512.8	71	2,194	42	2,306	1,313	287	604	2,203
995-6	3,368	11.90	254	457.6	103	1,819	21	1,943	915	224	598	1,737
996-7[1]	2,499	14.35	260	417.9	205	1,627	18	1,850	844	149	661	1,654
997-8[2]	2,852	13.20	230-260	426.6	196	1,707	25	1,928	1,055	154	676	1,884

[1] Preliminary. [2] Forecast. *Source: Economic Research Service, U.S. Department of Agriculture (ERS-USDA)*

Sunflower Oil and Meal Statistics in the United States In Thousands of Metric Tons

rop ear eginning ctober	Sunflower Oil: Supply: Stocks, Oct. 1	Supply: Production	Supply: Total[3]	Disappearance: Exports	Disappearance: Domestic	Disappearance: Total	Price $ Per Metric Ton[4]	Sunflower Meal: Supply: Stocks, Oct. 1	Supply: Production	Supply: Total[3]	Disappearance: Exports	Disappearance: Domestic	Disappearance: Total	Price $ Per Metric Ton 28% Protein
993-4	25	263	292	204	59	262	683	2	327	331	37	291	328	104
994-5	29	528	558	444	78	521	622	5	653	660	89	566	655	72
995-6	37	390	428	285	76	361	560	5	458	463	25	433	458	136
996-7[1]	67	385	462	322	98	420	497	5	440	445	21	419	440	122
997-8[2]	42	454	504	386	86	472	552-607	5	522	527	23	499	522	87-101

[1] Preliminary. [2] Forecast. [3] Includes imports. [4] Crude at Minneapolis. *Source: Economic Research Service, U.S. Department of Agriculture (ERS)*

Tall Oil

Tall oil is the major by-product of the kraft or sulfate processing of pinewood. After the lumber is pulped, the resulting liquor concentrate is skimmed. These skimmings are then acidified to produce crude tall oil.

Crude tall oil contains 40-50 percent fatty acids; 5-10 percent sterols, alcohols and other neutral components. When distilled, these resins and fatty acids are consumed in alkyd and synthetic resins, lubricants, adhesives, soaps and detergents, linoleum, flotation agents and waterproofing agents.

The U.S. Department of Commerce, Bureau of Census, reported that U.S. tall oil production in January 1997 was 124.1 million pounds, eight percent higher than production in December 1996 and seven percent higher than in January 1996. In the fourth quarter of 1996, U.S. production of tall oil was 347.6 million pounds, eight percent higher than in the fourth quarter of 1995. In the 1995-96 (October-September) marketing year, U.S. production of tall oil was 1.28 billion pounds.

U.S. tall oil consumption in December 1996 was reported to be 98.8 million pounds, down three percent from November 1996. Production in December 1996 was up 11 percent from the same month a year earlier. In calendar year 1996, U.S. consumption of tall oil was 1.18 billion pounds, up almost four percent from 1995.

U.S. stocks of tall oil on February 1, 1997 were 179.4 million pounds, up 46 percent from February 1, 1996. Stocks of crude tall oil on February 1, 1997 were 173 million pounds, while stocks of refined tall oil were 6.4 million pounds. On January 1, 1997, U.S. tall oil stocks were 191.3 million pounds. Crude tall oil stocks were 182.4 million pounds while refined tall oil stocks were 8.9 million pounds.

Consumption of Tall Oil in Inedible Products in The United States In Millions of Pounds

Year	Jan.	Feb.	Mar.	Apr.	May	June	July	Aug.	Sept.	Oct.	Nov.	Dec.	Total
1991	-------	249.1	-------	-------	237.3	-------	-------	223.1	-------	-------	230.5	-------	940
1992	77.8	7.5	73.2	67.6	77.8	74.8	71.5	78.4	77.1	78.9	63.8	69.2	884
1993	68.6	64.8	73.1	68.1	76.3	68.8	79.0	78.1	78.0	75.4	78.4	83.2	892
1994	117.4	98.8	124.0	118.4	115.0	118.8	106.8	114.9	119.8	113.7	101.9	113.0	1,363
1995	99.8	93.6	96.9	95.8	87.3	96.5	93.1	102.3	89.4	91.6	100.5	88.9	1,136
1996	93.1	103.4	89.2	104.1	100.5	96.6	85.4	100.7	94.9	111.5	101.4	98.8	1,180
1997[1]	111.5	89.0	91.0	99.5	97.0	105.8	103.7	94.4	84.7	87.2	87.3	88.4	1,139

[1] Preliminary. *Source: Bureau of the Census, U.S. Department of Commerce*

Tall Oil Production in the United States In Millions of Pounds

Crop Year		Oct.	Nov.	Dec.	Jan.	Feb.	Mar.	Apr.	May	June	July	Aug.	Sept.	Total
1991-2	Crude	-------	342.7	-------	131.4	121.5	131.2	133.2	121.9	129.8	130.6	129.9	119.7	1,372.[illegible]
	Refined	-------	15.7	-------	5.4	5.6	6.2	W	W	W	W	W	W	W
1992-3	Crude	120.2	114.7	122.7	119.4	128.4	142.1	131.8	120.0	126.6	117.0	104.3	117.3	1,347.[illegible]
1993-4	Crude	107.5	120.7	124.6	127.0	115.4	148.1	131.0	119.1	109.1	108.7	110.8	117.4	1,322.[illegible]
1994-5	Crude	111.1	114.5	115.1	108.3	108.1	123.0	111.1	116.5	118.2	116.4	119.2	102.9	1,261.[illegible]
1995-6	Crude	109.8	105.2	105.2	115.5	123.3	126.9	108.9	120.3	120.3	120.5	124.9	112.9	1,281.[illegible]
1996-7	Crude	119.2	113.9	114.5	119.9	125.1	125.1	118.5	116.6	116.4	135.0	132.9	130.8	1,337.[illegible]
1997-8[1]	Crude	122.7	115.4	135.4	133.7									1,522.[illegible]

[1] Preliminary. W = Withheld proprietary data. *Source: Bureau of Census, U.S. Department of Commerce*

Stocks of Tall Oil in the United States, on First of Month In Millions of Pounds

Crop Year		Oct.	Nov.	Dec.	Jan.	Feb.	Mar.	Apr.	May	June	July	Aug.	Sept.
1991-2	Crude	-------	139.1	-------	188.9	153.9	163.1	163.2	156.9	158.4	161.0	190.7	186.[illegible]
	Refined	-------	36.0	-------	35.0	35.0	35.7	36.2	13.5	16.1	15.2	15.9	28.[illegible]
1992-3	Crude	173.3	167.5	143.7	137.8	162.5	170.8	184.7	187.3	165.3	179.2	173.1	149.[illegible]
	Refined	17.4	18.1	13.8	14.1	14.0	12.6	13.7	9.4	7.7	7.3	7.5	7.[illegible]
1993-4	Crude	132.8	124.0	113.0	103.7	109.5	109.7	118.2	124.4	112.6	105.3	101.1	97.[illegible]
	Refined	7.0	7.5	8.5	10.7	13.7	13.5	13.5	12.0	10.2	9.7	11.6	10.[illegible]
1994-5	Crude	86.3	82.7	94.1	104.1	107.6	117.2	123.4	132.1	118.1	132.3	134.7	135.[illegible]
	Refined	12.0	14.4	16.3	13.5	15.4	14.1	11.7	10.8	10.2	10.0	9.9	8.[illegible]
1995-6	Crude	120.9	117.5	112.9	100.7	105.7	120.3	146.0	131.8	127.0	130.5	138.7	147.[illegible]
	Refined	10.1	11.6	7.9	6.0	7.9	9.7	8.5	10.4	8.5	6.0	6.1	7.[illegible]
1996-7	Crude	172.3	192.1	167.4	182.4	173.0	196.0	200.8	220.6	187.3	237.5	248.5	242.[illegible]
	Refined	8.3	7.0	7.5	8.9	6.5	26.5	17.4	31.7	20.9	32.0	13.2	16.[illegible]
1997-8[1]	Crude	208.6	187.9	209.7	202.1	203.6							
	Refined	32.3	25.6	34.9	21.4	29.8							

[1] Preliminary. *Source: Bureau of the Census, U.S. Department of Commerce*

Tallow and Greases

Production of tallow and greases is related to the number of cattle produced. Tallow finds widespread use in baking and cooking. The USDA reported that U.S. edible tallow stocks on August 1, 1997 were 55 million pounds. This was up almost eight percent from stocks in July 1997. Edible tallow stocks in August 1997 were also some 38 percent higher than stocks in August 1996. The marketing year for tallow extends from October to September. On October 1, 1996, edible tallow stocks were 34 million pounds.

In August 1997, U.S. production of edible tallow was 118 million pounds, down two percent from the July total of 120 million pounds. Over the October-August 1996-97 period, edible tallow production was 1.29 billion pounds and was averaging about 117 million pounds a month. For all of the 1995-96 marketing year, tallow production was 1.56 billion pounds, averaging almost 130 million pounds a month.

The U.S. imports minor amounts of tallow. In the October-July 1996-97 period, imports were only four million pounds or some 400,000 pounds per month. For the 1996-97 marketing season, U.S. tallow imports were eight million pounds. The year prior to that they were 18 million pounds. The U.S. supply of edible tallow in the October-August 1996-97 period was 1.33 billion pounds. For the 1995-96 marketing year the total supply of tallow was 1.62 billion pounds. The previous high supply level before that was in the 1991-92 season when tallow supplies were 1.94 billion pounds.

In terms of usage, the USDA estimated domestic use of tallow in the October-July 1996-97 period at just over a billion pounds, averaging 100 million pounds a month. For the 1995-96 marketing year domestic use of tallow was 1.36 billion pounds. That represented an average of 113 million pounds per month.

The U.S. exports smaller amounts of tallow. In July 1997, the last month of available data, tallow exports were 17 million pounds. For the October-July 1996-97 period, U.S. exports of edible tallow were 150 million pounds, averaging 15 million pounds per month. For the 1995-96 marketing year exports were 229 million pounds, averaging 19 million pounds a month. The previous high in exports was in the 1991-92 season when they totaled 333 million pounds.

Total disappearance of edible tallow in the October-August 1996-97 period was 1.28 billion pounds. In August 1997, disappearance of tallow was 122 million pounds. For the 1995-96 marketing year, total disappearance of tallow in the U.S. was 1.59 billion pounds, averaging 132 million pounds a month. Direct use of tallow in the October-July 1996-97 period was 740 million pounds, averaging 74 million pounds a month. For the October-September 1995-96 marketing year, direct use of tallow was 974 million pounds.

U.S. ending stocks of tallow in August 1997 were 51 million pounds. A year earlier they were 35 million pounds.

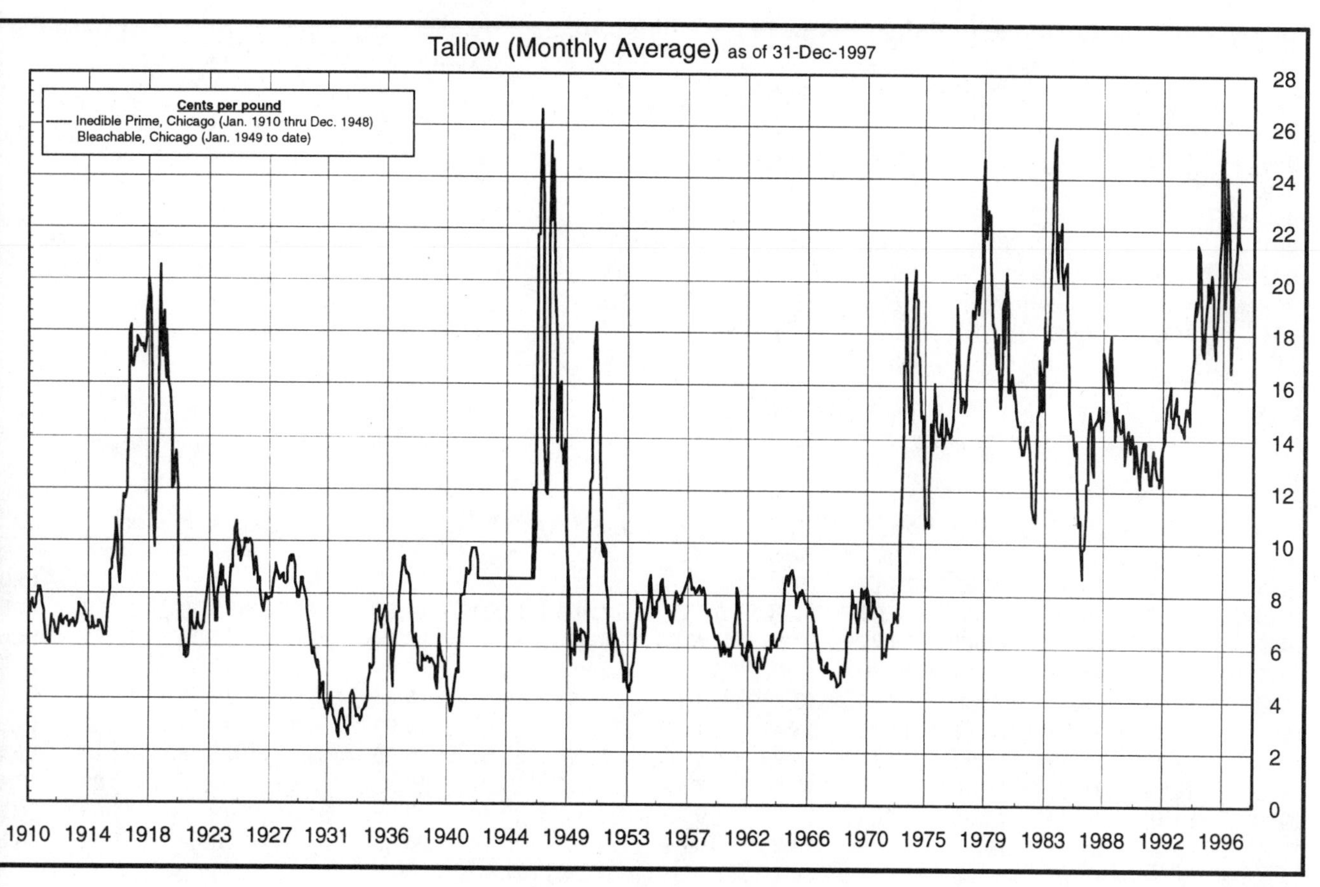

TALLOW AND GREASES

World Production of Tallow and Greases (Edible and Inedible) In Thousands of Metric Tons

Year	Agrentina	Australia	Brazil	Canada	France	Germany	Rep. of Korea	Netherlands	New Zealand	Russia[4]	United Kingdom	United States	World Total
1988	279	456	190	200	186	278	53	125	146	370	200	3,382	6,726
1989	278	489	272	203	179	280	60	125	133	400	207	3,212	6,614
1990	285	530	340	193	185	270	85	150	132	108	230	3,180	6,538
1991	268	472	336	212	275	197	121	150	134	106	225	3,309	6,677
1992	260	526	345	209	240	178	115	163	145	115	212	3,487	7,511
1993	250	446	350	213	206	167	120	159	135	90	215	3,851	7,716
1994	248	423	462	217	220	166	118	158	147	377	230	3,756	8,253
1995	240	407	467	245	220	168	198	161	151	348	165	3,500	8,000
1996[1]	235	427	460	260	220	167	182	180	155	295	145	3,490	8,037
1997[2]	230	387	458	265	220	168	175	168	155	270	140	3,426	7,937

[1] Preliminary. [2] Estimate. [3] Forecast. [4] Formerly part of the U.S.S.R.; data not reported separately until 1990. *Source: Foreign Agricultural Service, U.S. Department of Agriculture (FAS-USDA)*

Salient Statistics of Tallow and Greases (Inedible) in the United States In Millions of Pounds

	Supply				Consumption			Wholesale Prices, ¢ Per Lb.	
Year	Production	Stocks Jan. 1	Total	Exports	Soap	Feed	Total	Edible, (Loose) Chicago	Inedible, Chicago No. 1
1988	6,158	407	6,565	2,807	461	1,864	3,147	17.9	16.6
1989	5,848	399	6,247	2,679	368	1,919	3,194	15.8	14.4
1990	5,217	374	6,097	2,267	402	2,000	3,061	14.6	13.7
1991	5,759	357	6,116	1,936	392	1,748	2,949	14.3	13.3
1992	5,768	349	6,117	2,276	334	1,954	3,050	15.5	14.4
1993	6,621	309	6,930	2,117	300	1,995	3,018	16.2	14.9
1994	6,364	320	6,684	3,039	301	2,183	3,246	18.4	17.4
1995	6,481	350	6,831	2,486	264	2,071	2,334	21.4	19.2
1996[1]	6,242	373	6,615	1,807	245	2,389	2,634	22.0	20.1
1997[2]	6,249	266	6,515		245	2,401	2,646	23.4	20.8

[1] Preliminary. [2] Estimate. *Sources: Economic Research Service, U.S. Department of Agriculture; Bureau of the Census, U.S. Department of Commerce*

Supply and Disappearance of Edible Tallow in the United States In Millions of Pounds, Rendered Basis

	Supply			Disappearance					
Year	Stocks Jan. 1	Production	Total	Domestic	Exports	Total	Direct Use	Baking or Frying Fats	Per Capita (Lbs.)
1988	40	1,296	1,336	1,149	139	1,288	197	840	4.7
1989	48	1,167	1,215	975	202	1,177	223	752	3.9
1990	34	1,202	1,247	955	251	1,206	342	637	3.8
1991	41	1,515	1,944	1,197	333	1,530	604	460	3.9
1992	33	1,414	1,456	1,109	306	1,415	537	427	4.7
1993	41	1,499	1,556	1,204	316	1,519	700	404	4.4
1994	33	1,510	1,559	1,228	295	1,523	731	405	4.7
1995	36	1,536	1,591	1,268	279	1,548	711	374	4.8
1996[1]	43	1,520	1,568	1,317	218	1,535	997	311	5.0
1997[2]	33	1,416	1,450	1,190	203	1,393		312	

[1] Preliminary. [2] Forecast. *Sources: Economic Research Service, U.S. Department of Agriculture; Bureau of the Census, U.S. Department of Commerce*

Average Wholesale Price of Tallow, Inedible, No. 1 Packers (Prime), Delivered, Chicago In Cents Per Lb.

Year	Jan.	Feb.	Mar.	Apr.	May	June	July	Aug.	Sept.	Oct.	Nov.	Dec.	Average
1988	18.00	17.08	17.25	16.17	15.93	17.18	18.81	17.44	16.00	15.02	14.18	16.33	16.62
1989	14.90	16.00	14.86	14.60	14.70	15.10	14.48	13.52	14.13	15.25	15.50	15.50	14.88
1990	14.87	14.50	14.47	13.77	13.66	NA	13.50	10.12	12.00	13.42	14.09	14.75	13.56
1991	13.88	14.28	14.43	14.80	13.02	12.36	12.96	14.00	13.50	13.68	13.08	12.50	13.54
1992	12.25	12.63	12.68	13.25	13.75	13.98	14.75	15.42	15.25	15.94	16.75	16.13	14.40
1993	15.36	14.70	15.24	16.15	15.41	14.51	14.36	14.53	14.66	14.62	14.69	14.63	14.91
1994	15.00	15.00	15.22	15.19	15.25	15.63	16.67	18.64	19.50	19.78	20.38	22.48	17.40
1995	21.75	18.86	18.00	17.75	17.50	17.89	19.61	19.81	19.53	19.46	19.75	20.08	19.17
1996	19.45	17.00	17.03	17.54	19.37	19.50	20.98	22.40	25.98	21.05	19.65	21.63	20.13
1997[1]	23.40	22.88	19.35	17.39	18.09	19.64	19.65	20.10	20.88	23.73	21.68	21.44	20.69

[1] Preliminary. *Source: Economic Research Service, U.S. Department of Agriculture (ERS-USDA)*

Tea

Tea is produced in a number of countries around the world. It is usually grown on plantations. The tea plant is an evergreen shrub which can grow 15-30 feet tall in its natural state, though on a plantation it is kept to a height of about five feet. It thrives in tropical climates with plenty of rain. It does well at higher altitudes though it can be grown at sea level. Most commercial production of tea takes place near the equator.

Tea is usually classified into three classes. The first is black tea or fermented tea; second is also green tea or unfermented tea; and third oolong tea or semifermented. All of these teas are differentiated in processing, the tea leaves used are all the same. Black tea is made by taking tea leaves and fermenting them under damp cloths, then drying the leaves until they are black. The fermentation reduces astringency and changes flavor. Green tea is steamed in a boiler with fermentation and the leaves are dried. Oolong teas are partially fermented. After drying, teas are graded with orange pekoe being the highest quality.

The world's largest producer of tea is India with 1995 production estimated at 715,000 metric tonnes. India produces mostly black tea and has recently been putting more emphasis on producing higher quality tea. Tea is grown principally in the Assam valley and in the south in Kerala.

China is the second largest producer of tea with production in 1995 of 590,000 tonnes. China also has been looking to improve the quality of its tea. Green tea is produced for local use while black tea is exported.

Sri Lanka is the world's third largest producer of mostly black tea. Production in 1995 was estimated at 240,000 tonnes. The Sri Lanka Tea Board indicated that in August 1997, tea production was 22,510 tonnes, an increase of 6 percent from August 1996. Over the January-August 1997 period, Sri Lanka produced 178,850 tonnes of tea, up five percent from the comparable period of 1996. At the current rate of production, it appears that Sri Lanka will increase production in 1997 by five percent to about 260,000 tonnes.

The U.S. is a major importer of tea. The USDA reported that imports of tea in 1995 were 87,556 tonnes, down eight percent from the previous year. Of the total, 92 percent was in the form of black tea. The major supplier was Argentina with 25,191 tonnes, followed by China with 20,634 tonnes. Other major suppliers include Sri Lanka, Indonesia and Brazil. The U.S. also exports a small amount of tea. The U.S. Commerce Department reported that in October 1997, tea exports were 358 tonnes, up from 266 tonnes in September 1997. Tea re-exports in October 1997 were 107 tonnes compared to 263 tonnes in September 1997. U.S. per capita consumption of tea in 1996 was estimated at just over nine gallons. In contrast, per capita consumption of coffee is about 22 gallons.

World Tea Production, in Major Producing Countries In Thousands of Metric Tons

Year	Argentina	Bangladesh	China	India	Indonesia	Iran	Japan	Kenya	Malawi	Sri Lanka	Turkey	Former USSR[2]	Wprld Total
1987	43.0	40.6	508.0	665.3	126.1	45.6	96.3	155.8	31.9	214.6	140.7	120.0	2,356
1988	44.0	43.6	545.0	700.0	133.8	55.6	89.8	164.0	40.2	228.2	166.4	118.0	2,490
1989	48.0	39.1	535.0	688.1	141.4	46.0	90.5	180.6	39.5	208.0	141.6	119.2	2,444
1990	50.0	45.9	540.0	720.3	145.2	44.0	89.9	197.0	39.1	234.1	126.7	123.2	2,528
1991	40.0	45.2	542.0	741.7	133.4	45.0	87.9	203.6	40.5	241.6	135.3	110.0	2,541
1992	43.0	46.0	580.0	704.0	163.0	55.0	92.0	188.0	28.0	179.0	144.0	57.0	2,439
1993	55.0	49.0	600.0	757.0	169.0	57.0	92.0	211.0	39.0	232.0	117.0	81.0	2,645
1994	50.0	51.0	613.0	744.0	136.0	56.0	86.0	209.0	35.0	242.0	134.0	66.0	2,615
1995	50.0	52.0	609.0	715.0	155.0	54.0	90.0	245.0	34.0	246.0	103.0	43.0	2,581
1996[1]	42.0	48.0	609.0	715.0	169.0	56.0	90.0	255.0	37.0	246.0	124.0	38.0	2,622

[1] Preliminary. [2] Mostly Georgia and Azerbaijan. *Sources: Food and Agriculture Organization of the United Nations (FAO-UN)*

World Tea Exports from Producing Countries In Metric Tons

Year	Argentina	Bangladesh	Brazil	China	India	Indonesia	Kenya	Malawi	P. New Guinea	Sri Lanka	Vietnam	Zimbabwe	World Total
1986	36,279	27,675	10,851	172,028	203,149	78,957	116,456	40,189	5,213	207,567	12,500	11,819	997,534
1987	33,647	21,606	8,073	174,274	201,891	90,422	134,779	33,404	5,491	200,774	13,000	10,105	978,368
1988	34,258	26,187	9,686	198,289	200,956	92,687	138,201	36,961	5,834	219,710	14,800	14,190	1,039,313
1989	43,335	23,426	9,400	204,584	211,622	114,709	163,188	39,891	5,439	203,763	15,016	12,768	1,121,251
1990	45,966	26,970	7,976	195,471	209,085	110,964	169,586	43,039	5,375	215,251	24,698	11,507	1,141,026
1991	36,029	26,860	7,347	190,188	215,144	110,207	175,625	41,185	3,747	212,017	7,953	11,304	1,206,282
1992	36,530	24,990	8,211	180,834	166,359	121,243	172,053	37,056	5,638	181,259	12,967	6,088	1,130,355
1993	44,258	29,620	8,335	206,659	153,159	123,925	199,379	35,264	6,441	134,742	21,200	8,065	1,193,144
1994[1]	43,355	27,415	8,377	184,071	150,874	84,916	174,926	38,670	3,400	115,097	17,300	9,688	1,052,117
1995[2]	41,175	26,445	7,252	169,744	157,500	79,227	217,937	32,600	4,200	178,005	15,000	9,156	1,118,029

[1] Preliminary. [2] Estimate. *Source: Food and Agriculture Organization of the United Nations (FAO-UN)*

Tin

Tin is used in the manufacture of coatings for steel containers used to preserve foods and beverages. It also finds use in solder alloys, electroplating, ceramics and in plastic. Tin is mined in 23 countries with the five largest producers accounting for over 80 percent of world output. China is the world's largest producer of tin with 1996 production of 60,000 metric tonnes. That represented almost a third of the total world output of 196,000 tonnes. The second largest producer was Indonesia with 1996 output of 38,500 tonnes. The third largest producer of tin in 1996 was Peru with output of 27,004 tonnes. Brazil followed with 19,500 tonnes with Bolivia at 15,200 tonnes. Other large tin producers are Australia, Russia and Malaysia. World production of tin has been on the increase. In 1996, world output was 196,000 tonnes which was up from 195,000 tonnes in 1995. In 1994, world production was 182,000 tonnes.

World tin reserves are estimated by the U.S. Geological Survey at seven million tonnes. They are considered adequate to meet the world's future tin requirements. Using the assumption that world primary tin consumption will be 200,000 tonnes a year, current reserves will last 35 years. The bulk of the world's tin reserves are in Asia and South America. In the U.S., there was no domestic tin production in 1996. This marks the third consecutive year in which there was no domestic tin mine production in the U.S. For many years there were one or two small mines operating.

The U.S. is believed to be the world's largest producer of secondary tin. Tin metal recovered from new tinplate scrap and used in tin cans was the only type of secondary tin available in the marketplace as free tin; most secondary tin was produced from the various scrapped alloys of tin and recycled in those same alloy industries. Secondary tin from recycled fabricated parts was used in many kinds of products and was a major source of material, particularly for the solder and bronze and brass industries.

World smelter production of tin in 1996 was 207,000 tonnes which was down from 220,000 tonnes in 1995. The world's largest producer of smelter tin was China with 1996 output of 55,800 tonnes. The next largest producer was Indonesia with 39,000 tonnes, followed by Malaysia with 38,051 tonnes. Other large producers of smelter tin include Brazil with 19,800 tonnes in 1996 and Bolivia at 16,000 tonnes.

U.S. production of secondary tin recovered from alloys and tinplate in June 1997 was 900 metric tonnes, the same amount that was produced in May 1997. In the January-June 1997 period, U.S. production of secondary tin was 5,400 tonnes. For all of 1996, production of secondary tin was 10,800 tonnes.

U.S. consumption of primary tin in June 1997 was 3,190 tonnes which was up slightly from 3,110 tonnes in May 1997. In the first six months of 1997, consumption of primary tin was 19,000 tonnes while for all of 1996 it was 37,700 tonnes. U.S. consumption of secondary tin in June 1997 was 889 tonnes, which was down slightly from 899 tonnes in May 1997. For the first half of 1997, consumption of secondary tin was 5,370 tonnes while for all of 1996 it was 11,100 tonnes.

U.S. imports for consumption of tin metal in May 1997 were 2,670 tonnes. In the January-May 1997 period, U.S. imports of unwrought tin metal were 15,900 tonnes. During that period, the major supplier was Brazil with 3,780 tonnes, followed by Peru with 3,090 tonnes and Indonesia with 3,050 tonnes. Other major suppliers were Bolivia, China and India. U. S. imports of other tin materials in May 1997 were 614 tonnes, gross weight. That was down from 733 tonnes in May 1997. In the January-June 1997 period, U.S. imports of other tin materials were 4,770 tonnes. Of the total, tin alloys were 2,930 tonnes and waste and scrap 952 tonnes. For all of 1996, imports of other tin materials were 21,300 tonnes. U.S. exports of tin metal in May 1997 were 400 tonnes, while for all of 1996 they were 4,780 tonnes.

U.S. stocks of tin at the end of June 1997 were 5,080 tonnes. That was down four percent from stocks at the end of May 1997. At the end of 1996, U.S. tin stocks were 4,670 tonnes. The U.S. Defense Logistics Agency has a program to dispose of tin stocks. Disposals in June 1997 were 60 tonnes. In the first half of 1997 they were 850 tonnes while for all of 1996 disposals were 6,670 tonnes.

Futures Markets

Tin futures are traded on the London Metals Exchange (LME) and on the Kuala Lumpur Commodity Exchange (KLCE). Options are traded on the LME.

World Mine Production of Tin (Contained) In Metric Tons

Year	Australia	Bolivia	Brazil	China	Indonesia	Malaysia	Nigeria	Peru	Portugal	Russia[3]	Thailand	United Kingdom	World Total
1987	7,691	8,128	30,405	20,000	26,093	30,388	844	5,263	64	16,000	14,852	4,003	179,902
1988	7,009	10,504	44,102	29,500	29,590	28,866	300	4,181	81	16,000	14,225	3,454	204,654
1989	7,709	15,849	50,232	40,000	31,263	32,034	217	5,082	63	16,000	14,922	3,846	232,857
1990	7,377	17,249	39,149	42,000	30,200	28,468	192	5,134	4,780	15,000	14,635	3,400	221,000
1991	5,708	16,830	29,253	42,100	30,061	20,710	217	6,558	8,333	13,500	14,937	2,326	201,000
1992	6,609	16,516	27,000	43,800	29,400	14,339	415	10,044	6,560	15,160	11,484	2,044	191,000
1993	8,057	18,634	26,900	49,100	29,000	10,384	400	14,310	5,334	13,100	6,363	2,232	191,000
1994	7,100	16,169	20,400	54,100	30,610	6,458	185	20,275	4,332	10,460	3,926	1,922	182,000
1995[1]	8,656	14,419	19,500	61,900	38,378	6,402	185	22,331	4,627	9,000	2,201	1,973	195,000
1996[2]	8,828	15,200	19,500	60,000	38,500	5,174	150	27,004	4,800	8,000	1,450	2,103	196,000

[1] Preliminary. [2] Estimate. [3] Formerly part of the U.S.S.R.; data not reported separately until 1992. *Source: U.S. Geological Survey (USGS)*

World Smelter Production of Primary Tin In Metric Tons

Year	Australia	Bolivia	Brazil	China	Indo-nesia	Japan	Malaysia	Mexico	Russia[2]	South Africa	Spain	Thailand	World Total
1987	563	2,667	29,446	20,000	24,200	895	44,363	1,734	18,500	1,508	1,671	15,438	188,156
1988	439	5,373	41,857	29,500	28,365	846	49,945	1,812	18,500	1,377	806	14,675	215,163
1989	424	9,448	44,240	29,500	29,916	808	50,874	4,752	18,000	1,306	1,767	14,571	221,569
1990	312	12,567	37,580	35,000	30,389	816	49,067	5,004	16,000	1,140	600	15,512	246,000
1991	340	14,663	25,776	36,400	30,415	716	42,722	2,262	13,000	1,042	600	11,255	205,000
1992	240	14,393	27,000	39,600	31,915	821	45,598	2,590	15,200	592	600	10,679	194,000
1993	222	14,541	26,900	52,000	30,415	804	40,079	1,640	13,400	452	500	8,099	193,000
1994	315	15,285	20,400	67,800	31,100	706	37,990	768	11,500	43	500	7,759	198,000
1995	570	17,709	19,500	62,100	38,628	630	39,433	770	9,500	-----	500	8,243	201,000
1996[1]	460	16,000	19,500	55,800	39,000	524	38,051	770	9,000	-----	150	8,000	191,000

[8] Preliminary. [2] Formerly part of the U.S.S.R.; data not reported separately until 1992. *Source: U.S. Geological Survey (USGS)*

United States Foreign Trade of Tin In Metric Tons

		Imports (For Consumption)											
		Concentrates[2] (Ore)			Unwrought Tin Metal								
Year	Exports (Metal)	Total All Ore	Bolivia	Peru	Total All Metal	Bolivia	Brazil	China	Indo-nesia	Malaysia	Singa-pore	Thailand	United Kingdom
1987	1,318	2,953	732	2,165	41,150	3,476	13,089	8,044	4,001	4,959	743	1,460	467
1988	1,209	2,837	923	1,914	43,493	3,926	16,213	6,223	5,334	5,317	1,342	670	1,354
1989	904	216	-----	149	33,988	4,795	10,572	4,793	5,162	2,392	456	180	391
1990	658	-----	-----	-----	33,810	8,472	6,535	4,339	4,695	3,873	40	60	227
1991	970	1	1	-----	29,102	8,912	4,489	5,281	4,425	1,751	100	-----	344
1992	1,888	-----	-----	-----	27,314	4,623	8,167	5,389	3,854	2,799	320	427	-----
1993	2,598	-----	-----	-----	33,682	8,027	11,366	4,202	5,678	846	220	-----	6
1994	2,560	-----	-----	-----	32,400	7,260	9,990	3,230	6,620	1,390	142	-----	666
1995	2,790	-----	-----	-----	33,200	6,630	8,070	5,610	7,230	3,810	40	-----	97
1996[1]	3,670	-----	-----	-----	30,200	6,290	9,460	2,760	7,550	965	120	-----	243

[1] Preliminary. [2] Tin content. *Source: U.S. Geological Survey (USGS)*

Consumption (Total) of Tin (Pig) in the United States In Metric Tons

Year	Jan.	Feb.	Mar.	Apr.	May	June	July	Aug.	Sept.	Oct.	Nov.	Dec.	Total
1988	4,600	4,700	4,800	4,700	5,300	5,600	5,300	5,300	5,500	5,600	4,900	4,900	45,073
1989	4,800	4,700	4,300	4,500	4,500	4,100	4,000	4,200	4,100	4,300	4,000	3,300	46,371
1990	4,000	4,000	4,200	4,100	4,200	4,100	4,100	4,300	4,100	4,100	4,200	3,900	44,363
1991	4,100	3,900	4,100	4,300	4,100	4,200	3,900	4,100	4,000	4,300	4,100	4,000	49,000
1992	3,800	3,800	3,800	3,800	3,700	3,800	3,800	3,500	3,600	3,600	3,400	3,300	45,090
1993	3,400	3,500	3,600	3,600	3,500	3,600	3,500	3,600	3,500	3,500	3,500	3,400	47,107
1994	3,500	3,700	3,700	3,600	3,600	3,700	3,500	3,400	2,500	3,600	3,600	3,400	42,700
1995	3,500	3,600	3,680	3,726	3,877	3,833	3,544	3,895	3,825	3,823	3,735	3,770	44,808
1996	3,862	3,938	3,940	3,878	3,894	3,976	3,926	3,996	3,687	3,779	3,908	3,730	48,800
1997[1]	4,953	4,025	4,023	4,067	3,999	4,079	3,936	3,912	4,050	4,098	3,954		49,196

[1] Preliminary. *Source: U.S Geological Survey (USGS)*

Tin Stocks (Pig -- Industrial) in the United States, on First of Month In Metric Tons

Year	Jan.	Feb.	Mar.	Apr.	May	June	July	Aug.	Sept.	Oct.	Nov.	Dec.
1988	4,428	4,490	5,989	5,631	5,868	6,128	6,456	5,665	4,350	4,171	4,371	4,781
1989	4,943	4,242	3,894	4,320	3,717	4,945	4,912	5,597	5,872	6,241	5,313	5,530
1990	6,072	5,975	5,824	6,401	4,959	3,298	3,792	3,592	3,836	4,762	4,819	4,829
1991	6,337	6,677	6,688	6,177	5,993	5,991	6,348	6,739	6,544	8,544	6,616	6,347
1992	3,024	3,022	3,369	2,844	2,877	2,901	2,651	3,111	3,321	3,454	3,654	3,178
1993	3,221	3,572	4,450	4,483	3,898	3,609	4,648	4,652	4,561	3,709	3,262	3,535
1994	3,651	4,635	3,775	3,967	3,471	3,470	3,825	3,027	2,891	2,980	2,844	2,908
1995	2,741	3,931	3,850	2,780	3,000	3,080	3,210	3,910	3,800	3,880	4,380	4,290
1996	4,580	6,000	5,200	4,390	4,880	5,590	5,760	5,640	4,790	4,580	4,810	6,810
1997[1]	4,670	5,100	5,610	5,600	5,070	5,270	5,180	5,650	5,590	5,420	5,290	5,290

[1] Preliminary. *Source: U.S. Geological Survey (USGS)*

TIN

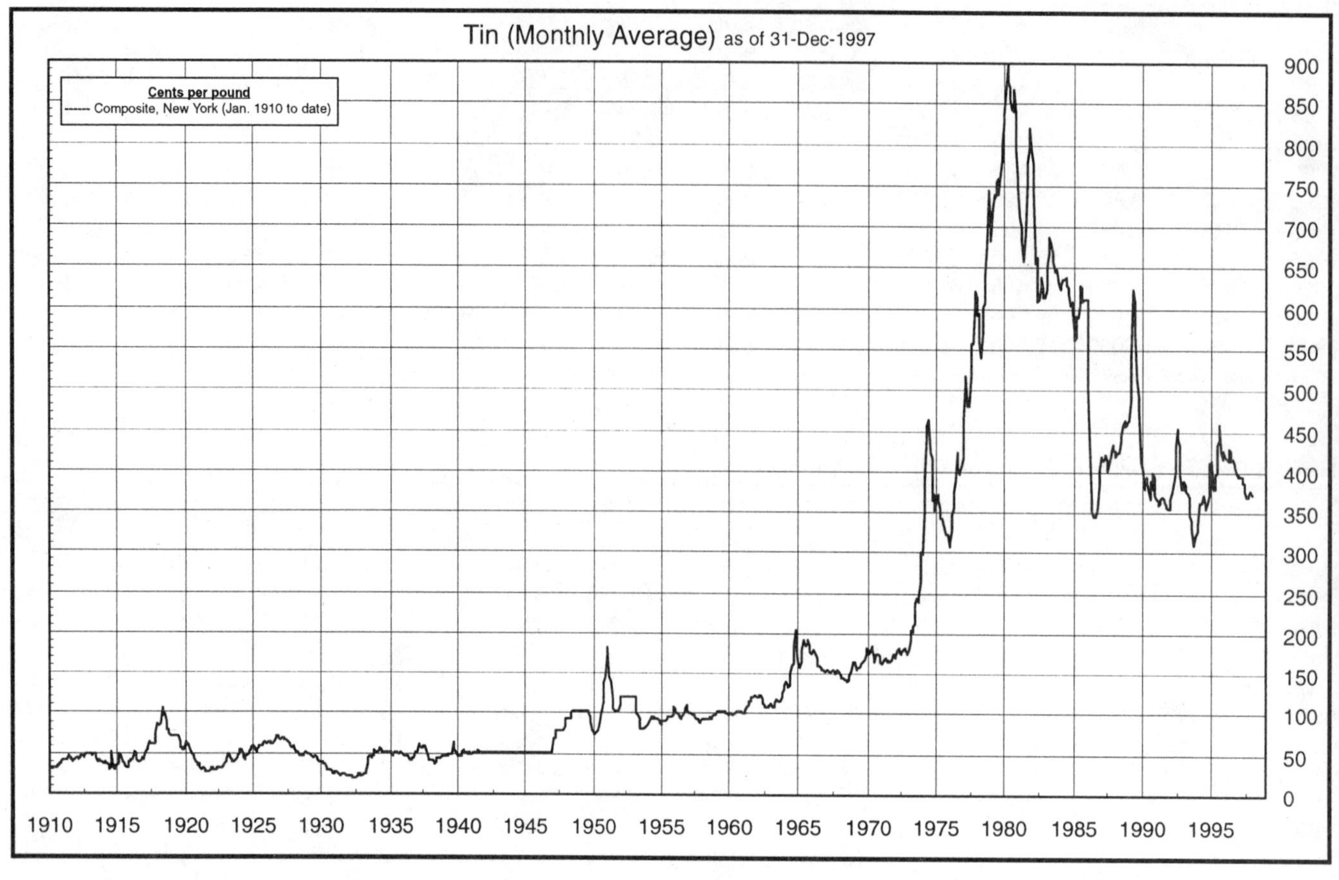

Average Price of Ex-Dock Tin in New York In Cents Per Pound

Year	Jan.	Feb.	Mar.	Apr.	May	June	July	Aug.	Sept.	Oct.	Nov.	Dec.	Average
1988	326.68	321.12	324.79	323.85	325.28	337.37	342.18	351.14	355.20	347.84	351.10	352.42	338.25
1989	355.80	377.77	419.64	486.72	484.42	474.15	458.64	415.80	395.99	379.67	329.10	324.79	408.54
1990	317.89	296.28	302.41	308.97	307.02	295.86	288.09	287.48	279.20	296.11	292.27	261.82	295.41
1991	269.97	268.00	264.51	265.78	271.78	272.30	270.55	269.02	265.86	264.50	262.26	262.05	267.21
1992	261.30	267.79	267.52	277.20	290.05	313.07	331.10	322.19	315.66	291.60	268.54	271.76	289.81
1993	280.40	280.91	277.43	275.67	269.62	255.35	252.31	230.17	213.22	220.02	224.88	236.90	251.41
1994	249.55	267.55	261.20	258.49	277.79	282.43	276.11	265.35	279.39	292.17	325.83	346.21	281.84
1995	374.77	260.25	266.45	288.00	283.62	314.33	316.06	331.64	304.12	297.77	304.47	300.28	303.48
1996	299.55	297.45	296.68	308.49	306.71	296.20	298.47	291.30	292.13	285.11	285.87	280.61	294.88
1997	281.91	281.34	281.51	274.36	274.19	267.31	261.03	259.85	262.56	266.77	268.39	262.61	270.15

Source: American Metal Market (AMM)

Average Price of Tin (Straights) in New York In Cents Per Pound

Year	Jan.	Feb.	Mar.	Apr.	May	June	July	Aug.	Sept.	Oct.	Nov.	Dec.	Average
1988	426.59	419.49	424.07	422.90	424.93	439.47	446.63	457.66	462.63	455.42	457.58	460.10	441.46
1989	464.49	488.17	542.72	622.13	624.62	607.96	568.59	515.89	493.12	477.14	419.57	413.34	519.81
1990	403.31	380.61	387.60	394.20	389.34	376.17	367.19	390.25	380.34	399.32	394.50	372.81	386.30
1991	368.22	364.86	360.89	362.04	368.33	368.95	367.07	365.06	361.19	358.63	355.35	354.27	362.91
1992	367.89	375.70	375.25	386.88	402.70	431.63	453.05	441.89	434.02	398.27	380.41	380.89	402.38
1993	390.01	384.48	378.36	374.06	369.82	347.55	339.79	330.63	310.94	322.67	322.26	326.72	349.77
1994	334.38	362.81	361.86	363.65	371.63	372.59	360.45	353.85	362.48	371.82	411.63	401.31	369.04
1995	415.05	379.08	378.61	395.99	399.17	433.75	438.04	458.66	423.71	417.23	425.41	419.75	415.37
1996	418.68	415.65	414.71	429.34	427.24	413.65	416.63	409.12	407.79	400.25	400.65	394.46	412.35
1997	396.18	395.50	395.64	386.52	386.58	377.83	369.97	369.01	372.45	377.39	378.00	371.35	381.37

Source: Wall Street Journal (WSJ)

Tin Plate Production & Tin Recovered in the United States In Metric Tons

Year	Tinplate Waste (Gross Weight)	Tin Content of Tinplate Produced – Tinplate (All Forms) – Gross Weight	Tin Content (Tonne)	Tin per Tonne of Plate (Kilograms)	Tin Recovered from Scrap by Form of Recovery – Tin Metal	Bronze & Brass	Solder	Type Metal	Babbitt	Anti-monial Lead	Chemical Com-pounds	Misc.[2]	Grand Total
1983	166,186	2,586,810	9,328	3.6	1,180	8,517	3,072	172	185	803	182	94	14,205
1984	151,540	2,409,399	8,659	3.6	1,107	9,146	3,653	142	123	894	301	51	15,417
1985	146,041	2,215,042	9,321	4.2	1,302	8,045	3,565	122	88	791	186	10	14,109
1986	120,186	2,068,246	8,660	4.2	1,134	7,996	3,676	197	66	891	W	17	13,977
1987	141,842	2,302,173	10,357	4.5	1,353	10,245	3,765	66	77	623	W	30	16,159
1988	149,054	2,375,809	11,582	4.9	578	9,939	3,619	70	112	902	W	29	15,249
1989	153,542	2,263,769	11,764	5.2	569	10,305	3,225	46	116	952	W	W	15,213
1990	156,419	2,467,205	11,750	4.8	186	13,312	2,876	46	28	739	W	4	17,187
1991	166,647	2,468,769	11,482	4.7	234	11,719	W	44	24	928	W	2,705	12,949
1992	195,760	1,620,007	9,821	6.1	137	12,761	W	47	78	704	W	181	13,727
1993	196,874	1,625,132	9,945	6.0	112	10,670	W	43	51	796	W	W	11,672
1994	188,921	1,528,303	9,396	6.1	NA	NA	NA	NA	NA	NA	NA	NA	NA
1995	205,000	1,660,000	9,600	5.8	W	11,200	W	39	W	335	W	W	11,600
1996[1]	181,100	1,551,000	9,617	6.2	W	10,800	W	37	34	171	W	W	11,000

[1] Preliminary. [2] Includes foil, terne metal, cable lead, and items indicated by symbol "W". W = Withheld proprietary data.
Source: U.S. Geological Survey (USGS)

Consumption of Primary and Secondary Tin in the United States In Metric Tons

Year	Net Import Reliance as a % of Apparent Consumption	Industry Stocks Jan. 1[2]	Net Receipts – Primary	Secondary	Scrap	Total	Available Supply	Stocks Dec. 31 (Total Available Less Total Processed)	Total Processed	Consumed in Manu-facturing Products
1983	73	7,549	36,494	5,412	7,435	49,341	56,890	11,098	45,792	45,547
1984	74	8,063	38,813	6,110	6,791	51,714	59,777	11,145	48,632	48,315
1985	72	8,430	38,006	8,904	7,471	54,381	62,811	13,928	48,883	48,669
1986	74	9,336	35,475	11,636	6,346	53,457	62,793	18,915	43,878	43,524
1987	74	9,876	38,401	11,707	6,635	56,743	66,619	21,887	44,731	44,219
1988	78	10,217	39,421	12,472	6,707	58,600	68,817	23,586	46,232	45,602
1989	77	9,242	37,760	10,901	8,168	56,829	66,071	19,184	46,887	46,463
1990	71	13,551	38,473	9,501	6,534	54,508	68,059	22,578	45,481	45,165
1991	74	12,502	36,126	1,622	8,370	46,118	58,620	13,540	45,080	44,805
1992	80	12,038	34,327	2,279	8,412	45,018	57,056	11,669	45,387	45,120
1993	84	8,556	37,700	3,280	8,768	49,700	58,300	11,566	46,700	46,600
1994	83	9,540	35,400	4,210	4,940	44,500	54,100	11,600	42,500	42,200
1995	84	8,480	39,400	5,020	6,240	50,600	59,100	13,000	46,100	46,000
1996[1]	83	9,180	39,200	2,730	6,340	48,300	57,400	12,600	44,800	44,700

[1] Preliminary. [2] Includes tin in transit to the U.S. *Source: U.S. Geological Survey (USGS)*

Consumption of Tin in the United States, by Finished Products In Metric Tons (Contained Tin)

Year	Tinplate[2]	Solder	Babbitt	Bronze & Brass	Tinning	Chemicals[3]	Tin Powder	Bar Tin & Anodes	White Metal	Other	Total	Total – Primary	Secondary
1983	9,462	14,120	2,881	4,583	1,759	W	793	654	937	10,358	45,547	34,301	11,246
1984	8,825	17,249	2,684	4,998	1,748	W	1,057	526	958	11,396	48,315	37,201	11,114
1985	9,321	18,621	1,488	4,330	1,511	W	976	466	937	12,100	48,669	36,524	12,145
1986	8,660	15,810	1,324	3,502	1,437	W	1,002	449	1,134	10,204	43,522	33,324	10,198
1987	10,357	15,240	1,060	3,559	1,398	W	W	703	1,175	10,704	44,219	35,620	8,599
1988	11,582	15,288	926	3,934	1,406	W	W	557	1,131	10,777	45,601	37,529	8,072
1989	11,764	16,370	794	3,693	1,505	W	711	619	1,074	9,926	46,456	36,603	9,853
1990	11,750	16,443	763	3,166	1,707	6,275	563	603	1,045	2,850	45,165	36,770	8,395
1991	11,482	16,296	941	2,896	1,465	6,564	539	436	868	3,318	44,805	35,138	9,667
1992	9,821	18,461	916	2,916	1,275	6,301	573	919	974	2,964	45,090	34,983	10,137
1993	9,650	19,000	823	3,093	1,249	6,446	608	946	789	3,927	46,600	34,600	11,900
1994	9,480	15,100	831	3,080	1,230	5,740	625	1,190	992	3,990	42,200	33,700	8,530
1995	9,670	17,700	871	2,830	1,110	7,060	W	1,200	965	4,550	46,000	35,200	10,800
1996[1]	9,350	15,600	851	2,760	2,030	7,520	573	1,150	1,340	3,230	44,700	36,500	8,180

[1] Preliminary. [2] Includes small quantity of secondary pig tin and tin acquired in chemicals. [3] Including tin oxide. W = Withheld proprietary data.
Source: U.S. Geological Survey (USGS)

Titanium

Titanium's unique properties of being one-half the density of steel, excellent strength, and immunity to corrosion, make it an ideal construction material for engines and air frames. Pure titanium metal is called "sponge" because of its porous cellular form. Titanium sponge is processed to form an ingot and the ingot is processed by mills to make plate sheet tubing. There are titanium sponge plants in the U.S., Japan, Great Britain, China and Russia. Because of its unique combination of high strength and light weight, titanium is finding a growing number of uses. One of the more publicized is in golf clubs. There continue to be new applications in the automotive industry as well as in heavy military vehicles. There is even work being done on using titanium substrate in computer disk drives. Other uses of titanium mill products are in pollution control devices, desalination plants, chemical processing, and in tubing for power plants and oil refineries. Titanium dioxide finds use as a white pigment for exterior paints, paper production, and pigment for ink and porcelain enamels.

In one development in the market, E.I. du Pont de Neumours and Company, a major producer of titanium dioxide, announced that it will indefinitely delay the development of a titanium deposit near the eastern edge of the Okefenokee National Wildlife Refuge. DuPont indicated that it planned to hold discussions with interested parties regarding the environmental impact of developing the 38,000 acres.

U.S. production of titanium ingot in the first quarter of 1997 was 13,800 metric tonnes. That was some 12 percent above the first quarter of 1996. For all of 1996, ingot production was 51,400 tonnes. U.S. data on production of titanium sponge was withheld by the U.S. Geological Survey to avoid disclosing company proprietary data. U.S. production of titanium mill products in the first quarter of 1997 was 8,330 tonnes, which was up almost 17 percent from the first quarter of 1996. For all of 1996, titanium mill product production was 30,700 tonnes.

U.S. exports of titanium in the January-February 1997 period were 2,190 tonnes. Exports of titanium sponge were 160 tonnes; titanium scrap, 160 tonnes; titanium ingot, slab, sheet, and bar, 635 tonnes; other unwrought titanium, 66 tonnes; titanium bars, rods, profiles and wire, 177 tonnes; other wrought titanium products, 599 tonnes. For all of 1996, U.S. exports of titanium products were 12,100 tonnes. U.S. imports of titanium products in the first two months of 1997 were 6,450 tonnes. For all of 1996, imports were 35,800 tonnes.

Average Prices of Titanium in the United States

Year	Ilmenite F.O.B. Australian Ports $ Tonne	Slag, 85% TiO_2 F.O.B. Richards Bay, South Africa $ Tonne	Rutile Large Lots Bulk, F.O.B. U.S. East Coast $ Tonne	Rutile Bagged F.O.B. Australian Ports $ Tonne	Avg. Price of Grade A Titanium Sponge, F.O.B. Shipping Point	Titanium Metal Sponge	Titanium Dioxide Pigments, F.O.B. U.S. Plants: Anatase	Titanium Dioxide Pigments, F.O.B. U.S. Plants: Rutile
					Dollars Per Pound			
1988	64-77	250-275	NA	547-572	4.21	4.25-4.75	.92-.95	.95-.97
1989	67-75	275-300	540-550	553-632	5.11	4.80-5.30	1.01-1.02	1.04-1.05
1990	69-77	285-310	550-580	693-770	5.31	4.75	.99	1.01
1991	68-76	295-325	606-650	515-545	5.25	4.75	.99	.99
1992	58-62	310	510-520	380-414	3.96	3.50-4.00	.99	.92-.95
1993	61-64	330	NA	370-400	3.75	3.50-4.00	.99	.92-.95
1994	74-80	334	410-430	450-480	3.96	3.75-4.25	.94-.96	.92-.94
1995	81-85	349	550-650	650-800	4.06	4.25-4.50	.92-.96	.99-1.03
1996[1]	82-92	353	525-600	700-800	NA	4.25-4.50	1.06-1.08	1.08-1.10
1997[2]	76-87	390	650-750	640-700	NA	4.25-4.50	.90-.94	.92-.94

[1] Preliminary. [2] Estimate. NA = Not available. *Source: U.S. Geological Survey (USGS)*

Salient Statistics of Titanium in the United States In Metric Tons

Year	Titanium Dioxide Pigment: Production	Titanium Dioxide Pigment: Imports[3]	Titanium Dioxide Pigment: Apparent Consumption	Ilmenite: Imports[3]	Ilmenite: Consumption	Titanium Slag: Imports[3]	Titanium Slag: Consumption	Rutile[4]: Imports[3]	Rutile[4]: Consumption	Exports of Titanium Products: Ores & Concentrates	Exports: Scrap	Exports: Dioxide & Pigments	Exports: Ingots, Billets, Etc.
1987	878,558	174,219	966,169	307,515	744,266	408,785	251,423	197,937	320,505	4,023	5,083	108,889	2,467
1988	926,746	185,468	991,536	394,170	679,008	434,641	300,013	231,124	352,356	9,368	5,939	118,422	2,083
1989	1,006,581	166,346	947,259	411,751	659,584	386,146	414,830	264,895	366,143	19,832	5,474	212,197	2,702
1990	978,659	147,592	925,447	345,907	688,948	373,623	390,537	274,605	369,454	18,765	5,487	202,288	2,371
1991	991,976	166,094	935,829	213,886	738,089	408,302	341,379	240,120	368,643	26,912	4,568	211,854	1,700
1992	1,137,038	169,260	999,930	294,585	684,882	537,118	539,323	317,399	460,969	34,665	2,770	270,422	1,455
1993	1,161,561	171,939	1,028,311	301,000	693,940	476,000	545,809	371,481	464,825	15,202	3,893	261,000	1,511
1994	1,250,000	176,000	1,090,000	808,000	W	472,000	583,000	332,000	510,000	19,000	4,120	313,000	1,559
1995[1]	1,250,000	183,000	1,080,000	861,000	1,410,000	388,000	582,000	318,000	480,000	32,300	3,420	306,000	2,560
1996[2]	1,230,000	167,000	1,070,000	939,000	1,400,000	421,000	NA	324,000	398,000	15,500	3,410	292,000	3,130

[1] Preliminary. [2] Estimate. [3] For consumption. [4] Natural and synthetic. W = Withheld proprietary data. *Source: U.S. Geological Survey (USGS)*

World Production of Titanium Ilmenite Concentrates In Thousands of Metric Tons

Year	Australia[2]	Brazil	China	India	Malaysia	Norway	Sierra Leone	Sri Lanka	Thailand	Ukraine[3]	World Total	-- Titaniferous Slag[4] -- Canada	South Africa
1983	910	30.5	139.7	134.4	222.7	555.9	-----	81.7	-----	435	3,727	635	417
1984	1,525	40.9	139.7	140.0	268.5	651.8	-----	102.1	-----	440	4,619	726	417
1985	1,433	76.4	140.0	143.0	314.7	735.8	-----	114.9	1.00	445	4,737	845	435
1986	1,252	75.5	140.0	140.0	414.9	803.6	-----	129.9	13.50	450	4,705	850	435
1987	1,509	169.3	140.0	140.0	509.2	852.3	5.6	128.5	27.10	455	3,937	925	650
1988	1,622	142.2	150.0	229.7	486.3	898.0	42.1	74.3	18.30	460	4,033	1,025	400
1989	1,714	144.2	150.0	240.7	533.7	929.8	62.3	101.4	16.99	460	4,353	1,040	725
1990	1,621	114.1	150.0	280.0	530.2	814.5	54.6	66.4	10.67	430	4,072	1,046	840
1991	1,381	69.1	150.0	311.5	336.3	625.0	60.4	60.9	17.08	400	3,360	701	808
1992	1,806	76.6	150.0	300.0	337.7	708.0	60.3	33.3	2.97	450	3,920	753	884
1993	1,825	90.6	155.0	320.0	289.0	713.0	62.9	76.9	20.82	450	4,000	653	892
1994	1,817	97.4	155.0	300.0	115.9	826.0	47.4	60.4	1.68	530	3,950	764	744
1995	2,011	102.1	160.0	300.0	151.7	833.0	-----	49.7	.03	359	3,970	815	990
1996[1]	2,058	105.0	165.0	300.0	244.6	750.0	-----	62.8	-----	300	3,990	950	990

[1] Preliminary. [2] Includes leucoxene. [3] Formerly part of the U.S.S.R.; data not reported separately until 1992. [4] Approximately 10% of total production is ilmenite. Beginning in 1988, 25% of Norway's ilmenite production was used to produce slag containing 75% TiO_2. NA = Not available.
Source: U.S. Geological Survey (USGS)

World Production of Titanium Rutile Concentrates In Metric Tons

Year	Australia	Brazil	India	Sierre Leone	South Africa	Sri Lanka	Thailand	Ukraine[2]	World Total
1983	163,377	463	5,534	71,801	56,246	8,093		9,979	315,493
1984	170,427	412	5,988	91,302	56,246	6,467		9,979	340,821
1985	211,615	713	6,800	80,611	55,000	8,558	110	10,000	373,407
1986	215,774	495	7,000	97,100	55,000	8,443	48	10,000	393,860
1987	246,263	324	7,000	113,300	55,000	7,200	92	10,000	439,179
1988	230,637	1,514	5,000	126,358	55,000	5,255	128	10,000	433,892
1989	243,000	2,613	9,931	128,198	60,000	5,589	150	10,000	459,331
1990	245,000	1,814	11,000	144,284	64,056	5,460	NA	9,500	481,114
1991	201,000	1,094	13,635	154,800	77,000	3,085	76	9,000	460,000
1992	183,000	1,798	10,000	148,990	84,000	2,741	281	60,000	491,000
1993	186,000	1,744	13,900	152,000	85,000	2,643	87	60,000	501,000
1994	233,000	1,911	14,000	137,000	78,000	2,410	49	80,000	546,000
1995	195,000	1,985	14,000		90,000	2,697		112,000	416,000
1996[1]	180,000	2,000	14,000		115,000	3,532		100,000	415,000

[1] Preliminary. [2] Formerly part of the U.S.S.R.; data not reported separately until 1992. NA = Not available. *Source: U.S. Geological Survey (USGS)*

World Production of Titanium Sponge Metal & U.S. Consumption of Titanium Concentrates

	Production of Titanium (In Metric Tons)						------ U.S. Consumption of Titanium Concentrates, by Products (In Metric Tons) ------						
	---- Sponge Metal[2] ----						------- Ilmenite (TiO_2 Content) ------			---- Rutile (TiO_2 Content) ----			
Year	China	Japan	Russia[3]	United Kingdom	United States	Total	Pigments	Misc.	Total	Welding Rod Coatings	Pigments	Misc.	Total
1983	1,814	10,524	40,824	1,814	12,670	67,133	424,823	5,449	430,272	3,310	191,373	32,496	227,179
1984	1,814	15,366	41,731	2,268	22,069	83,462	446,939	5,733	452,672	3,548	210,296	57,081	270,925
1985	1,814	15,366	42,638	1,361	21,099	82,555	430,522	5,751	436,273	4,428	217,631	37,843	259,902
1986	1,814	16,330	43,546	1,361	15,876	78,926	463,643	1,501	465,144	6,956	221,518	52,199	280,673
1987	1,814	10,074	44,453	1,361	17,849	75,298	420,099	1,648	421,747	3,781	246,448	51,309	301,538
1988	2,000	16,500	46,000	1,500	24,000	88,000	429,736	590	430,326	3,737	262,998	64,641	331,376
1989	2,000	21,000	46,000	1,500	25,225	95,725	419,329	414	419,743	3,603	271,208	71,178	345,989
1990	2,000	25,630	47,000	1,500	24,679	101,000	445,502	726	446,228	4,047	271,637	71,373	347,057
1991	2,000	18,945	20,000	2,000	13,366	56,000	476,145	495	476,640	6,931	286,741	42,200	335,872
1992	2,000	14,554	20,000	2,000	W	38,554	425,876	647	426,523	W	405,875	32,553	438,428
1993	2,000	14,400	20,000	1,000	27,938	37,000	434,097	451	434,548	W	405,784	30,223	436,007
1994	2,000	14,400	12,000	-----	29,510	33,000	W	637	W	W	460,000	18,500	478,500
1995	2,000	16,000	12,000	-----	W	35,000	1,010,000	[4]	1,010,000	W	417,000	22,300	439,300
1996[1]	2,000	21,100	18,000	-----	W	51,000	1,010,000	[4]	1,010,000	W	341,000	24,200	365,200

[1] Preliminary. [2] Unconsolidated metal in various forms. [3] Formerly part of the U.S.S.R.; data not reported separately until 1993. [4] Included in Pigments. NA = Not available. W = Withheld proprietary data. *Source: U.S. Geological Survey (USGS)*

Tobacco

The major development in the tobacco market in 1997 was the Global Settlement between the State Attorney Generals and the cigarette manufacturers. The settlement was signed on June 20, 1997. While the settlement will still be reviewed by the Congress, in essence it will result in an increase in the retail price of cigarettes. The agreement will require the cigarette manufacturers to pay a substantial amount of money to settle lawsuits and to reimburse states for smoking-related medicaid expenses. The settlement also covers areas such as advertising, which will be limited, and teenage smoking which is expected to decline. One major aim of the agreement is to sharply limit teenage smoking. The final details of the agreement have not been worked out.

The USDA indicated that U.S. cigarette consumption in 1997 was expected to decline about two percent to 475 billion pieces. U.S. consumption of cigarettes has been trending lower for some time. As recently as 1988, consumption was 563 billion pieces. Production of cigarettes in 1997 was 733 billion pieces, down three percent from 1996. In contrast to U.S. consumption of cigarettes, production has been increasing. In 1988, U.S. output of cigarettes was almost 695 billion pieces. The difference is in exports which have been trending sharply higher.

Cigarette prices in 1997 were increased twice, in March they were raised $2.50 per 1000 pieces, and in September they were increased $3.50 per 1000 pieces. A number of factors have been cited for the decline in U.S. cigarette consumption. These include the higher prices, an increasing number of prohibitions on where smoking is allowed, and continuing publicity about the health hazards of smoking.

A number of states increased their taxes on cigarettes. On July 1, New Hampshire's excise tax rose 12 cents per pack to 37 cents, while Rhode Island's increased 10 cents per pack to 71 cents. On September 1, Hawaii's excise tax rose 20 cents per pack to 80 cents and that tax will rise another 20 cents on July 1, 1998. On October 1, Alaska's cigarette excise tax rose from 29 cents per pack to $1.00, the highest in the nation. On August 5, 1997, the President signed legislation increasing the federal cigarette tax from 24 cents per pack to 34 cents per pack, starting January 1, 2000. Taxes on other tobacco products will also increase. On January 1, 2005, the Federal cigarette tax will increase another 5 cents to 39 cents per pack and other tobacco product taxes will also increase.

Per capita cigarette consumption in 1997 is forecast to be 2,399 cigarettes. That is almost 120 packs of 20 cigarettes. Consumption is down from 2,482 cigarettes in 1996, and 3,103 cigarettes in 1988. 120 packs of cigarettes is equivalent to four pounds of tobacco. Per capita consumption of snuff in 1997 was .31 pounds which was unchanged from 1996. Per capita consumption of all tobacco products in 1997 was 4.6 pounds, down from 4.7 pounds in 1996 and 6.1 pounds in 1988.

Per capita male consumption (18 years and over) of large cigars and cigarillos in 1997 was 33.6, up from 32.7 in 1996. After a period of decline, cigar consumption has increased for four consecutive years. U.S. large cigar and cigarillo output will increase by 600 million to an estimated 3.1 billion in 1997. Cigar consumption, including imports, could reach 3.3 billion cigars. Output of small cigars (which weigh three pounds or less per 1,000 cigars) increased five percent in 1996 to 1.5 billion. Small cigar output reached a high of 4.4 billion in 1973 and fell to under one billion in 1986. Per capita consumption of smoking tobacco in 1997 was .12 pounds, unchanged from 1996 while per capita consumption of chewing tobacco was .64 pounds, unchanged from 1996.

U.S. exports of cigarettes in the July-June 1996-97 period were 232.8 billion pieces. That was down three percent from 1996. U.S. exports of tobacco have been trending higher. In the comparable period ending June 30, 1998, exports were 112.1 billion pieces. In ten years, exports have risen over 100 percent. In the current period, the major export destinations were Japan with 66.8 billion pieces, Belgium-Luxembourg with 53.1 billion pieces, Cyprus with 11.7 billion pieces and Lebanon with 11.5 billion.

U.S. tobacco production on September 1, 1997 was forecast at 1.61 billion pounds. The 1997 tobacco crop is six percent larger than in 1996 due to increased acreage. Estimated U.S.-grown leaf use increased about 12 percent in 1996-97 to 1.65 billion pounds from 1.47 billion in the previous year. The increase in leaf use was a result of larger cigarette production. U.S. leaf tobacco exports in 1996-97 (July-June) increased nine percent to 534 million pounds, declared weight.

World Production of Leaf Tobacco In Metric Tons

Year	Brazil	Canada	China	Greece	India	Indonesia	Italy	Japan	Pakistan	Turkey	United States	Zimbabwe	World Total
1988	419,000	69,776	2,731,251	184,355	367,400	137,775	184,355	85,790	69,530	218,774	621,205	123,671	6,835,351
1989	462,000	75,573	2,830,353	197,316	492,800	146,914	197,316	74,397	71,089	269,517	620,152	135,205	7,110,889
1990	435,000	63,057	2,627,500	134,368	564,400	158,865	214,846	80,542	68,040	295,599	737,710	139,803	7,106,502
1991	422,000	78,704	3,030,700	165,650	555,900	164,850	193,296	69,897	80,806	239,405	754,949	178,107	7,563,836
1992	577,000	71,775	3,499,000	196,500	584,400	145,420	150,784	79,366	107,980	331,786	780,944	211,394	8,293,001
1993	608,000	86,094	3,451,000	148,000	580,600	152,800	135,698	67,430	105,966	338,068	731,914	235,286	8,300,069
1994	442,000	71,500	2,238,000	135,400	528,000	160,000	131,010	79,503	100,351	187,733	717,955	177,816	6,391,942
1995	398,000	79,287	2,317,700	131,875	587,100	171,400	124,492	78,212	80,917	204,900	575,380	209,042	6,354,987
1996[1]	452,000	79,287	2,900,000	131,500	562,750	177,000	136,000	66,031	80,760	229,400	688,222	207,767	7,175,429
1997[2]	545,000	79,287	2,900,000	132,000	604,500	184,300	136,000	75,600	78,320	235,400	781,949	210,580	7,513,370

[1] Preliminary. [2] Estimate. *Source: Foreign Agricultural Service, U.S. Department of Agriculture (FAS-USDA)*

Production and Consumption of Tobacco Products in the United States

Year	Cigarettes -Billions-	Cigars[3] -Millions-	Chewing Tobacco: Plug	Chewing Tobacco: Twist	Chewing Tobacco: Loose-leaf	Chewing Tobacco: Total	Smoking Tobacco	Snuff[4]	Consumption[5] of Per Capita[6]: Cigarettes (Number)	Cigars[3] (Number)	Cigarettes (Pounds)	Cigars[3] (Pounds)	Smoking Tobacco (Pounds)	Chewing Tobacco (Pounds)	Total Products (Pounds)
			Million Pounds												
1988	694.5	1,980	8.9	1.4	65.6	75.9	17.8	48.6	3,096	29.1	5.40	.47	.25	.86	6.11
1989	677.2	2,010	8.3	1.3	64.9	74.5	17.0	49.7	2,926	27.9	4.90	.46	.22	.82	5.67
1990	709.7	1,896	7.4	1.3	64.3	72.9	16.4	53.1	2,817	26.2	4.80	.43	.20	.79	5.48
1991	694.5	1,740	6.7	1.2	64.3	72.2	15.7	54.3	2,713	24.9	4.70	.41	.19	.79	5.41
1992	718.5	1,741	5.9	1.2	61.6	69.7	14.9	57.5	2,640	24.1	4.70	.40	.17	.74	5.38
1993	661.0	1,795	5.3	1.1	58.0	64.4	13.7	59.1	2,539	23.9	4.50	.39	.17	.70	5.12
1994	725.5	1,942	4.6	1.1	56.8	62.5	13.4	59.5	2,527	25.3	4.23	.41	.16	.67	4.90
1995	746.5	2,040	4.1	1.1	57.4	62.6	12.2	60.2	2,505	27.5	4.22	.45	.13	.67	4.70
1996[1]	755.4	2,430	3.9	1.1	56.0	61.1	12.0	61.5	2,482	32.7	4.20	.54	.12	.64	4.70
1997[2]	724.6	2,900	3.5	1.0	51.4	55.8	11.5	64.3	2,399	33.6	4.00	.54	.12	.64	4.70

[1] Preliminary. [2] Estimate. [3] Large cigars and cigarillos. [4] Includes loose-leaf. [5] Consumption of tax-paid tobacco products. Unstemmed processing weight. [6] 18 years and older. *Source: Economic Research Service, U.S. Department of Agriculture (ERS-USDA)*

Production of Tobacco in the United States, by States In Thousands of Pounds

Year	Florida	Georgia	Indiana	Kentucky	Maryland	North Carolina	Ohio	Pennsylvania	South Carolina	Tennessee	Virginia	Wisconsin	Total
1988	17,152	85,880	10,945	355,024	11,970	552,627	14,497	18,175	100,125	93,142	92,177	6,906	1,369,500
1989	17,755	87,200	13,237	366,551	8,103	541,056	15,925	17,925	103,680	79,820	93,814	11,248	1,367,188
1990	19,044	103,845	15,050	442,253	9,656	639,639	18,915	19,780	109,905	112,218	110,269	13,346	1,626,380
1991	15,312	80,600	18,920	479,794	12,900	634,655	22,776	20,765	111,180	121,524	116,849	15,191	1,664,372
1992	19,575	100,980	18,900	524,378	11,931	609,873	21,840	20,840	112,320	146,556	111,459	13,100	1,721,671
1993	18,673	96,320	17,415	455,080	12,255	608,415	18,900	18,260	110,760	139,423	99,544	6,643	1,613,319
1994	16,575	80,660	15,265	453,687	12,750	599,853	18,360	18,360	108,100	132,289	106,092	5,866	1,582,896
1995	17,676	84,000	13,601	328,581	11,475	484,599	15,015	15,685	105,000	92,907	81,269	6,220	1,268,538
1996	20,100	113,620	14,972	395,542	10,000	585,542	12,640	15,464	117,810	109,888	103,543	5,145	1,517,351
1997[1]	19,635	89,320	18,690	427,715	12,000	714,120	18,620	15,360	126,360	104,488	111,112	5,453	1,678,821

[1] Preliminary. *Source: Agricultural Statistics Board, U.S. Department of Agriculture (ASB-USDA)*

Salient Statistics of Tobacco in the United States

Year	Acres Harvested 1,000 Acres	Yield Per Acre Pounds	Production Million Pounds	Farm Price ¢ Lb.	Farm Value Million $	Tobacco (July-June) Exports[2]	Tobacco (July-June) Imports[3]	U.S. Exports of Cigarettes	U.S. Exports of Cigars & Cheroots	U.S. Exports of All Tobacco	U.S. Exports of Smoking Tobacco[4]	Stocks of Tobacco[5] All Tobacco	Various Types: Fire Cured[6]	Various Types: Cigar Filler[7]	Various Types: Maryland
						-- Million Pounds --		------- Millions -------				Million Pounds			
1988	634.0	2,160	1,370	164.6	2,254	476.7	394.6	118,499	87	555	43.9	2,909	79.2	35.1	37.6
1989	678.4	2,016	1,367	170.8	2,335	485.9	365.0	141,782	78	582	46.6	2,714	75.9	31.8	27.0
1990	732.3	2,218	1,625	173.8	2,827	487.4	415.0	164,301	72	631	58.0	2,401	70.2	26.9	19.3
1991	763.4	2,179	1,664	177.3	2,951	511.0	502.2	179,200	70	499	63.2	2,232	66.7	25.6	12.1
1992	784.4	2,195	1,722	177.7	3,059	528.8	881.0	205,600	76	574	59.1	2,280	61.6	26.7	9.4
1993	746.4	2,161	1,613	175.3	2,830	529.7	707.8	195,476	67	458	62.5	2,412	64.0	26.7	7.5
1994	671.1	2,359	1,583	177.4	2,779	442.1	537.5	220,200	75	434	77.0	2,588	69.7	24.1	8.4
1995	663.1	1,913	1,269	182.0	2,305	432.6	623.3	231,100	94	462	91.8	2,541	80.5	20.5	11.7
1996	732.7	2,071	1,517	188.2	2,852	539.9	717.2	243,900	105	490	110.4	2,225	80.2	17.9	15.0
1997[1]	797.3	2,106	1,679	181.3	3,039	350.7	653.8	230,000	90	507	114.6	2,055	83.3	13.2	18.5

[1] Preliminary. [2] Domestic. [3] For consumption. [4] In bulk. [5] Flue-cured and cigar wrapper, year beginning July1; for all other types, October 1. [6] Kentucky-Tennessee types 22-23. [7] Types 41-46. *Source: Economic Research Service, U.S. Department of Agriculture (ERS-USDA)*

Tobacco Production in the United States, by Types In Thousands of Pounds (Farm-Sale Weight)

Types	11-14	21	22	23	31	32	35-36	37	41	41-61	51	54	55	61
1988	813,212	2,920	19,804	8,020	477,208	18,445	7,415	127	11,700	22,372	1,630	5,016	1,890	2,108
1989	808,350	2,480	18,463	7,980	482,568	17,825	6,430	104	10,725	25,512	1,256	7,648	3,600	2,283
1990	939,234	2,762	22,931	9,285	597,927	16,316	7,491	102	13,120	30,278	1,160	9,328	4,018	2,652
1991	911,887	3,563	20,620	8,704	658,181	19,920	8,776	156	13,735	32,587	1,433	9,799	5,392	2,228
1992	906,025	2,567	23,736	10,486	719,552	18,771	10,332	124	14,000	30,098	1,484	8,460	4,640	1,514
1993	886,908	1,872	26,985	12,060	633,838	18,335	11,123	104	12,180	22,094	1,694	4,690	1,953	1,577
1994	869,920	2,403	31,723	14,205	612,398	19,770	11,797	124	11,340	20,680	1,808	4,180	1,686	1,666
1995	746,616	1,540	26,609	11,041	436,343	17,935	8,488	79	9,225	19,887	2,441	4,513	1,707	2,001
1996	908,345	1,738	29,461	13,029	520,483	16,080	8,550	112	9,384	19,553	2,901	3,610	1,552	2,106
1997[1]	1,024,785	1,800	27,075	12,875	565,260	17,700	8,653	112	9,660	20,561	3,383	4,140	1,313	2,065

[1] Preliminary. *Source: Agricultural Statistics Board, U.S. Department of Agriculture (ASB-USDA)*

TOBACCO

U.S. Exports of Unmanufactured Tobacco In Millions of Pounds (Declared Weight)

Year	Australia	Belgium-Luxem.	Denmark	France	Germany	Italy	Japan	Nether-lands	Sweden	Switzer-land	Thailand	United Kingdom	Total U.S. Exports
1988	9.0	9.7	16.4	5.7	87.2	32.4	70.4	41.0	12.0	15.5	13.5	19.6	481.8
1989	6.2	12.3	13.8	4.8	75.4	17.1	105.3	43.2	8.3	10.4	15.7	18.4	485.9
1990	8.3	12.4	15.1	5.7	75.9	19.3	106.5	45.3	9.5	13.3	22.2	20.5	492.5
1991	7.7	11.0	14.8	6.5	82.8	19.9	83.1	42.8	8.3	14.8	19.5	18.9	499.3
1992	6.9	21.4	15.6	4.2	93.3	19.0	131.0	49.9	8.8	7.5	16.9	24.3	574.4
1993	5.7	12.8	15.5	4.3	52.1	7.3	124.7	38.1	8.1	6.1	17.8	20.8	458.0
1994	6.4	12.3	14.9	3.1	54.1	11.3	126.2	30.9	7.3	6.0	19.0	14.7	433.9
1995	4.8	17.9	14.6	3.9	70.7	14.8	106.9	39.2	3.0	14.4	19.0	14.2	461.8
1996	5.6	39.7	15.1	3.2	60.1	17.3	88.7	40.4	3.7	14.9	15.9	34.4	485.5
1997[1]	5.6	40.6	16.1	6.4	74.7	17.2	76.1	28.3	5.2	12.4	18.2	19.7	484.8

[1] Preliminary. *Source: Economic Research Service, U.S. Department of Agriculture (ERS-USDA)*

Salient Statistics for Flue-Cured Tobacco (Types 11-14) in the United States In Millions of Pounds

Crop Year	Acres Harvested 1,000	Yield Per Acre Pounds	Mar-ketings	Stocks July 1	Total Supply	Exports	Domestic Disap-pearance	Total Disap-pearance	Farm Price ¢ Lb.	Placed Under Gov't Loan Mil. Lb.	Price Support Level ¢ Lb.	Loan Stocks Nov. 30	Loan Stocks Uncom-mitted
1988-9	366.4	2,219	796	1,513	2,309	363	522	885	161.3	15.2	144.2	421.9	328.4
1989-90	390.7	2,069	838	1,424	2,262	387	567	954	167.4	28.4	146.8	314.5	218.2
1990-1	416.9	2,253	920	1,308	2,228	403	609	1,012	167.3	74.4	148.8	226.4	223.8
1991-2	402.6	2,265	882	1,216	2,098	403	472	875	172.3	49.9	152.8	153.7	174.5
1992-3	401.5	2,257	901	1,223	2,124	420	509	929	172.6	81.8	156.0	223.6	129.0
1993-4	400.1	2,217	892	1,195	2,087	359	433	792	168.1	204.9	157.7	330.5	317.5
1994-5	359.5	2,420	807	1,295	2,102	346	569	915	169.8	97.7	158.3	298.5	396.5
1995-6	386.2	1,933	854	1,187	2,041	345	531	875	179.4	12.0	159.7	157.6	62.3
1996-7[1]	422.2	2,151	897	1,166	2,063	391	555	947	183.7	1.8	160.1	181.0	.0
1997-8[2]	455.7	2,249	1,014	1,117	2,131	380	525	905	172.4	195.5	162.1		.0

[1] Preliminary. [2] Estimate. *Source: Economic Research Service, U.S. Department of Agriculture (ERS-USDA)*

Salient Statistics for Burley Tobacco (Type 31) in the United States In Millions of Pounds

Crop Year	Acres Harvested 1,000	Yield Per Acre Pounds	Mar-ketings	Stocks Oct. 1	Total Supply	Exports	Domestic Disap-pearance	Total Disap-pearance	Farm Price ¢ Lb.	Gross Sales[3]	Price Support Level ¢ Lb.	Loan Stocks Nov. 30	Loan Stocks Uncom-mitted
1988-9	226.4	2,109	468	1,073	1,541	164	414	578	161.0	351.5	150.0	243.4	117.7
1989-90	244.4	1,975	498	963	1,461	169	446	614	167.2	398.1	153.2	314.5	91.6
1990-1	270.6	2,204	592	847	1,439	199	475	674	175.3	467.8	155.8	226.4	52.0
1991-2	312.0	2,110	657	765	1,422	209	407	616	178.8	501.5	158.4	62.3	32.8
1992-3	332.7	2,163	700	807	1,507	183	385	568	181.5	502.4	164.9	131.2	71.7
1993-4	299.7	2,115	627	939	1,566	152	400	552	181.6	492.4	168.3	178.8	141.9
1994-5	266.3	2,300	568	1,014	1,582	159	464	623	184.1	455.7	171.4	345.2	380.8
1995-6	234.2	1,863	483	959	1,441	165	386	551	185.5	321.1	172.5	212.5	50.8
1996-7[1]	268.3	1,940	516	890	1,407	209	422	631	192.2	403.4	173.7	216.8	27.1
1997-8[2]	299.3	1,889	563	776	1,339	180	390	570	191.0	337.9	176.0		24.1

[1] Preliminary. [2] Estimate. [3] Before Christmas holidays. *Source: Economic Research Service, U.S. Department of Agriculture (ERS-USDA)*

Exports of Tobacco from the United States (Quantity and Value) In Metric Tons

Year	Unmanufactured: Flue-Cured	Value $1,000	Burley	Value $1,000	Total	Value $1,000	Manufactured	Value $1,000
1988	121,444	758,504	46,655	307,584	218,542	1,252,771	NA	2,900,864
1989	120,344	782,337	47,498	327,988	220,408	1,301,173	NA	3,662,176
1990	131,155	883,155	50,262	349,561	223,413	1,441,116	NA	5,038,830
1991	115,481	776,654	61,852	441,223	226,463	1,427,630	NA	4,574,086
1992	146,100	983,478	64,481	483,743	260,526	1,650,559	58,115	4,509,395
1993	111,636	752,646	51,892	389,964	207,747	1,306,067	49,669	4,253,286
1994	107,411	749,305	49,859	380,993	196,792	1,302,744	63,837	5,367,220
1995	123,040	866,208	47,129	365,206	209,481	1,399,863	77,135	5,221,487
1996	112,797	786,473	52,202	380,012	222,316	1,390,311	83,383	5,238,340
1997[1]	116,457	832,381	56,803	454,849	221,510	1,553,314	85,734	4,956,392

[1] Preliminary. [2] Forecast. NA = Not available. *Source: Foreign Agricultural Service, U.S. Department of Agriculture (FAS-USDA)*

Tung Oil

Tung oil is derived from the seeds of the tung tree and is used as an industrial lubricant and drying agent. The tung tree is found mainly in China which produces about 75 percent of world output. China is also the world's largest exporter of tung oil. Other producers include Argentina and Paraguay.

Among the major importers of tung oil are Japan, Taiwan, South Korea and the United States. World import demand for tung oil averages about 40,000 metric tonnes per year. U.S. consumption of tung oil in inedible products in 1996 was 21.6 million pounds, up five percent from the previous year. U.S. consumption has shown wide variability over the last several years. In 1989 consumption was 33.7 million pounds, while in 1990 that fell to 10.2 million pounds.

The USDA reported that in June 1997, U.S. imports of tung oil were 311 metric tonnes. That was well above the June 1996 total of 15 metric tonnes. In the October-June 1996-97 period, U.S. imports of tung oil were 3,478 tonnes. That was eight percent more than the import total of 3,216 tonnes in the comparable period on 1995-96. The USDA reported that the value of tung oil imports in June 1997 were $516,000. That was up from $16,000 in June 1996. In October-June 1996-97, the value of tung oil imports was $4.99 million compared to $2.97 million in the comparable period of 1995-96.

World Tung Oil Trade In Metric Tons

	Imports								Exports				
Year	Germany	Hong Kong	Japan	Netherlands	South Korea	Taiwan	United States	World Total	Argentina	China	Hong Kong	Paraguay	World Total
1990	1,078	4,176	12,424	1,095	3,249	3,152	4,046	36,590	8,557	16,069	4,454	8,347	38,500
1991	1,138	6,476	11,890	543	3,035	4,957	5,646	39,766	8,522	14,485	7,182	9,039	40,600
1992	1,036	8,509	13,326	782	3,722	6,676	4,996	44,146	5,808	20,867	8,174	4,221	40,269
1993	720	5,222	6,549	1,351	3,490	3,595	4,270	29,793	2,497	16,990	6,004	2,295	29,200
1994	912	7,843	8,628	1,663	4,294	7,454	5,401	43,082	2,415	30,582	6,476	4,603	45,182
1995[1]	825	3,671	8,429	2,174	7,200	5,777	4,427	38,306	4,319	25,620	3,838	3,400	38,629
1996[2]	653	1,247	3,619	1,253	6,577	4,244	3,944	36,424	2,427	16,850	1,266	3,450	26,021

[1] Preliminary. [2] Estimate. *Source: The Oil World*

Consumption of Tung Oil in Inedible Products in the United States In Thousands of Pounds

Year	Jan.	Feb.	Mar.	Apr.	May	June	July	Aug.	Sept.	Oct.	Nov.	Dec.	Total
1991	----------	1,953	----------	----------	1,555	----------	----------	1,334	----------	----------	1,100	----------	5,942
1992	435	459	574	498	502	694	572	705	674	873	530	790	7,306
1993	958	966	693	1,041	833	1,022	867	1,427	1,354	860	585	593	11,199
1994	608	592	635	1,408	1,558	840	861	910	480	392	660	382	9,326
1995	427	503	976	1,389	1,437	1,387	1,886	2,830	2,549	2,645	2,455	2,126	20,610
1996	1,724	1,427	1,730	1,750	1,498	1,813	2,214	2,024	1,431	2,045	1,908	2,081	21,645
1997[1]	934	1,922	2,720	2,170	1,335	2,034	2,618	1,262	1,267	1,099	857	1,157	19,375

[1] Preliminary. *Source: Bureau of the Census, U.S. Department of Commerce*

Stocks of Tung Oil at Factories & Warehouses in the U.S., on First of Month In Thousands of Pounds

Year	Jan.	Feb.	Mar.	Apr.	May	June	July	Aug.	Sept.	Oct.	Nov.	Dec.
1991	1,829	----------	----------	2,997	----------	----------	1,379	----------	----------	963	----------	----------
1992	1,608	2,421	2,439	1,605	1,323	1,540	847	1,348	2,162	1,724	2,560	3,545
1993	3,122	2,038	2,390	2,120	2,966	1,773	866	815	1,596	1,217	1,635	1,752
1994	1,551	2,053	1,507	2,049	2,091	2,591	2,148	1,562	820	2,455	1,712	1,909
1995	1,764	1,490	1,055	3,193	2,554	2,551	2,369	2,116	2,038	2,361	2,210	2,048
1996	2,013	1,635	2,232	3,018	2,386	2,532	2,641	2,381	2,670	2,525	2,459	2,834
1997[1]	2,373	2,754	3,417	2,808	2,134	2,230	2,230	1,561	2,525	2,535	2,311	2,326

[1] Preliminary. *Source: Bureau of the Census, U.S. Department of Commerce*

Average Price of Tung Oil (Imported, Drums) F.O.B. in New York In Cents Per Pound

Year	Jan.	Feb.	Mar.	Apr.	May	June	July	Aug.	Sept.	Oct.	Nov.	Dec.	Average
1991	70.00	63.00	61.50	63.00	63.00	61.50	61.00	61.00	61.00	61.00	61.00	70.00	63.08
1992	70.00	70.00	70.00	76.00	82.00	130.00	130.00	130.00	132.00	131.50	132.00	130.00	106.96
1993	130.00	130.00	130.00	130.00	117.00	130.00	130.00	130.00	107.50	100.00	94.75	93.00	118.52
1994	93.00	79.25	78.00	78.00	78.00	78.00	78.00	78.00	78.00	74.40	60.00	60.00	76.05
1995	60.00	60.00	60.00	60.00	60.00	60.00	60.00	60.00	60.00	60.00	60.00	60.00	60.00
1996	60.00	60.00	64.00	64.00	64.00	64.00	64.00	64.00	64.00	64.00	64.00	64.00	63.33
1997[1]	74.00	92.00	92.00	103.00	103.00	103.00	103.00	108.00	110.00				98.67

[1] Preliminary. *Source: Economic Research Service, U.S. Department of Agriculture (ERS-USDA)*

Tungsten

Tungsten has unique high-temperature properties that can be used in the production of numerous items. It has a high melting point, high density, good corrosion resistance, and good thermal and electrical conductivity properties. It has excellent wear-resistance and cutting properties. Almost 60 percent of tungsten is used to produce tungsten carbide. Tungsten carbide is used for cutting tools, mining and drilling equipment, dies, bearings and armor-piercing military projectiles. Nearly 25 percent of tungsten use is in unalloyed tungsten, which is formed into wire and manufactured into filaments for incandescent and fluorescent lamps. Tungsten is also used in fireproofing materials.

U.S. reported consumption of concentrate tungsten in June 1997 was 674 metric tonnes, tungsten content. That was up 26 percent from May 1997. In the January-June 1997 period, U.S. reported consumption of tungsten was 3,450 tonnes. For calendar 1996, reported consumption was 5,420 tonnes. U.S. imports for consumption of concentrate tungsten in May 1997 were 753 tonnes, up sharply from 202 tonnes in April 1997. For the January-May 1997 period, U.S. imports for consumption were 1,971 tonnes. For calendar 1997, tungsten concentrate imports were 4,190 tonnes. Consumption of tungsten scrap in June 1997 was 228 tonnes, up from 173 tonnes in May 1997. For January-June 1997, reported tungsten scrap consumption was 1,270 tonnes. For 1996, scrap consumption was 2,450 tonnes. U.S. tungsten concentrate stocks at the end of June 1997 were 596 tonnes, up from 542 tonnes at the end of May 1997.

U.S. production of ammonium paratungstate in the first half of 1997 was 1,950 tonnes, tungsten content. Consumption in the same period was 3,570 tonnes.

World Concentrate Production of Tungsten In Metric Tons (Contained Tungsten[3])

Year	Australia	Austria	Bolivia	Brazil	Burma	China	Kazakhstan[4]	Mongolia	Peru	Portugal	Rep. of Korea	Russia[4]	World Total
1988	1,261	1,235	900	738	307	30,000	------	1,000	432	1,382	2,029	9,200	50,869
1989	1,371	1,517	1,118	679	233	30,200	------	600	970	1,376	1,701	9,300	51,038
1990	1,086	1,378	1,014	316	443	32,000	------	500	1,536	1,410	1,361	8,800	51,900
1991	237	1,314	1,065	223	356	31,800	------	300	1,232	971	780	8,000	48,200
1992	159	1,490	851	205	531	25,000	200	260	802	1,870	247	6,500	40,400
1993	23	104	287	245	524	21,600	150	250	398	1,280	200	8,000	35,100
1994	11	------	462	155	548	27,000	200	150	259	100	------	4,000	34,300
1995[1]	------	188	655	98	531	27,400	225	200	728	1,511	------	5,400	38,500
1996[2]	------	360	582	100	328	24,000	220	200	331	1,343	------	3,000	31,900

[1] Preliminary. [2] Estimate. [3] Conversion factors: WO_3 to W, multiply by 0.7931; 60% WO_3 to W, multiply by 0.4758. [4] Formerly part of the U.S.S.R.; data not reported separately until 1992. *Source: U.S. Geological Survey (USGS)*

Salient Statistics of Tungsten in the United States In Metric Tons (Contained Tungsten)

			Consumption of Tungsten Products by End Uses										Stocks at End of Year	
			Steel										Concentrates	
Year	Net Import Reliance as a % Apparent Consumption	Total Consumption	Tool	Stainless & Heat Assisting	Alloy Steel[3]	Superalloys	Cutting & Wear Resistant Materials	Products Made from Metal Powder	Miscellaneous	Chemical and Ceramic	Exports	Imports for Consumption	Consumers	Producers
1989	84	7,725	258	62	W	258	5,018	1,828	476	52	203	7,896	1,261	10
1990	81	5,878	342	64	74	325	4,985	2,181	464	50	139	6,420	1,077	16
1991	91	5,309	243	44	W	287	4,801	1,941	614	44	21	7,837	1,778	26
1992	86	4,313	407	52	66	25	4,211	1,309	828	W	38	2,477	702	44
1993	82	2,866	388	43	40	282	5,064	1,434	2	37	63	1,721	592	44
1994	81	3,630	529	20	19	300	5,920	1,200	W	108	44	2,960	756	44
1995[1]	84	6,320	265	W	18	215	6,590	1,200	3,600	W	20	4,660	631	44
1996[2]	82	5,420	434	2	33	W	W	551	6,420	90	72	4,190	569	44

[1] Preliminary. [2] Estimate. [3] Other than tool. W = Withheld proprietary data. *Source: U.S. Geological Survey (USGS)*

Average Prices of Tungsten In U.S. Dollars

Year	Jan.	Feb.	Mar.	Apr.	May	June	July	Aug.	Sept.	Oct.	Nov.	Dec.	Average
					European Market (London), 65% WO_3 Basis, C.I.F.[1] -- $ Per Metric Ton								
1993	45.00	42.63	37.50	36.38	33.94	33.00	32.44	27.75	27.89	32.13	33.00	33.00	34.56
1994	29.94	29.94	37.71	35.38	35.38	37.09	38.10	38.10	42.03	45.36	47.63	49.56	38.85
1995	56.00	60.00	64.00	64.00	65.00	66.00	67.00	66.00	66.00	66.00	66.00	62.50	64.04
1996	56.00	54.00	56.00	57.00	57.00	57.00	53.50	50.00	50.00	47.50	45.00	48.00	52.58
					U.S. Spot Quotations, 65% WO_3, Basis C.I.F., U.S. Ports (Including Duty) -- $ Per Short Ton								
1993	43.50	43.50	42.00	40.50	40.50	40.50	40.50	35.63	34.00	34.00	34.00	34.00	38.55
1994	37.48	40.79	44.10	44.10	44.10	44.53	47.95	48.50	48.50	48.50	48.50	48.50	45.46
1995	44.00	44.00	44.00	44.00	55.00	65.00	65.00	62.50	60.00	60.00	60.00	60.00	55.29
1996	60.00	60.00	60.00	60.00	60.00	60.00	60.00	60.00	60.00	60.00	60.00	60.00	60.00

[1] Combined wolframite and scheelite quoations. *Source: U.S. Geological Survey (USGS)*

Turkeys

U.S. turkey production rose steadily during the first half of the 1990's, from 4.50 billion pounds in 1990, to 5.42 billion in 1996. To help iron out the pronounced yearend holiday seasonality for whole birds, the industry has shifted a larger proportion of retail sales to prepackaged turkey parts. The additional processing required to cut up and package turkey cuts, such as breasts and legs, has increased the supply of edible trimmings which processors sell in several forms, including mechanically deboned turkey (MDT). A promising market for MDT is the export market; also, as a relatively low-cost meat protein MDT can easily be incorporated into sausage and other meat products.

U.S. per capita ready-to-cook retail weight turkey consumption reached a record high 18.5 pounds in 1996 vs. 17.9 pounds in 1995. An increase to 18.8 pounds is forecast for 1997. In the mid 1980's, per capita use averaged about 12 pounds. The October-December quarter accounts for more than a third of total use followed by a sharp tapering off in the January-March period. Traditionally, November is the highest slaughter month with a recent average of about 25 million birds. Prices follow a similar pattern, peaking generally in the fourth quarter and trending lower during the first quarter, basis 8-16 pound hens in New York. Turkeys of 14-22 pound weight are classified as toms. However, changes in consumer food tastes that favor poultry could be altering turkey's traditional marketing and price seasonality.

Federally inspected turkey production in 1996 was estimated at a record high 5.4 billion pounds vs. 5.1 billion in 1995. Net returns to producers during 1996 were not as favorable as in 1995 due to higher feed costs and smaller increases in competing meat prices. With little improvement expected in net returns, at least early in 1997, producers are apt to hold production to about 5.5 billion pounds, still a new record high if realized.

U.S. turkey exports rose to a record high 383 million pounds in 1996 vs. 348 million pounds in 1995. Estimates for 1997 focus on a rise to 405 million pounds. In the first quarter of 1996, exports climbed 60 percent over the like 1995 period on the strength of large purchases by Russia and Poland. The Eastern European pace tapered off in the rest of 1996, but some of the slack was offset by larger shipments to Mexico, traditionally the largest export market. The bulk of low priced turkey shipments to Russia are defined as "other prepared or preserved meat, meat offal, or blood of turkey."

Wholesale turkey prices edged towards 68 cents per pound in late 1996, but the average for the year of 65 cents was about unchanged from 1995. Prices for 1997 were forecast to average in the mid 60 cent per pound range.

Production and Consumption of Turkey Meat, by Selected Countries In Thous. of Metric Tons (RTC)

	Production							Consumption						
	Canada	France	Germany	Italy	United Kingdom	United States	World Total	Canada	France	Germany	Italy	United Kingdom	United States	World Total
1989	120	387	118	257	230	1,876	3,300	119	301	172	256	210	1,863	3,284
1990	129	432	145	279	223	2,048	3,600	125	315	208	272	211	1,992	3,486
1991	131	487	149	273	242	2,088	3,722	126	342	240	265	236	2,060	3,630
1992	132	558	159	269	246	2,167	3,892	129	354	272	268	228	2,072	3,732
1993	128	532	169	266	252	2,176	3,902	126	321	280	256	249	2,075	3,759
1994	133	568	183	269	253	2,239	4,040	128	330	295	245	258	2,110	3,756
1995	141	650	206	294	289	2,299	4,295	126	353	196	262	287	2,133	3,921
1996	146	671	211	315	293	2,450	4,530	123	352	217	277	298	2,225	4,170
1997[1]	142	725	217	316	295	2,448	4,618	133	372	224	277	299	2,207	4,214
1998[2]	145	730	224	316	300	2,565	4,766	134	359	234	277	304	2,309	4,345

[1] Preliminary. [2] Estimate. [3] Forecast. *Source: Foreign Agricultural Service, U.S. Department of Agriculture (FAS-USDA)*

Salient Statistics of Turkeys in the United States

Year	Poults Placed[3] (In Thousands)	Number Raised[4] (In Thousands)	Liveweight Produced Mil. Lbs.	Liveweight Price ¢ Per Lb.	Value of Production Million $	Ready-to-Cook-Basis Production (Million Pounds)	Beginning Stocks (Million Pounds)	Exports (Million Pounds)	Consumption Total (Million Pounds)	Consumption Per Capita Lbs.	Production Costs Feed (Liveweight Basis)	Production Costs Total (Liveweight Basis)	Wholesale Ready-to-Cook Production Costs	Wholesale 3-Region Weighted Average Price[5]
1987	264,228	240,438	4,894.9	34.8	1,703.1	3,745	178	33	3,580	14.7	19.40	33.10	57.60	57.21
1988	261,406	242,421	5,059.1	38.6	1,957.3	3,930	266	51	3,844	15.7	24.60	38.30	64.20	60.69
1989	290,678	261,280	5,465.5	40.9	2,234.4	4,181	250	41	4,109	16.6	26.70	40.40	66.80	65.75
1990	304,863	282,450	6,029.6	39.4	2,378.6	4,567	236	54	4,390	17.6	23.40	37.10	62.60	62.35
1991	308,083	285,110	6,110.7	38.4	2,344.7	4,658	306	103	4,541	18.0	22.72	36.42	61.83	60.79
1992	307,823	288,980	6,333.8	37.7	2,387.7	4,835	264	171	4,599	18.0	23.06	36.76	62.25	60.48
1993	308,871	287,650	6,432.6	39.0	2,509.1	4,798	272	244	4,577	17.7	22.20	35.86	61.12	62.83
1994	317,468	289,025	6,332.4	40.4	2,643.8	4,937	249	280	4,652	17.8	24.00	37.70	63.40	65.90
1995[1]	320,882	292,856	6,506.1	41.0	2,776.4	5,069	254	348	4,705	17.9	21.90	35.60	60.80	66.20
1996[2]	325,375	301,378	6,925.5	43.3	3,102.1	5,400	271	461	4,910	18.5	35.00	48.70	77.10	67.40

[1] Preliminary. [2] Estimate. [3] Poults placed for slaughter by hatcheries. [4] Turkeys placed August1-July 31. [5] Regions include central, eastern and western. Central region receives twice the weight of the other regions in calculating the average. *Source: Economic Research Service, U.S. Department of Agriculture*

TURKEYS

Turkey-Feed Price Ratio[1] in the United States In Pounds

Year	Jan.	Feb.	Mar.	Apr.	May	June	July	Aug.	Sept.	Oct.	Nov.	Dec.	Average
1988	6.2	5.5	5.2	5.0	4.9	4.5	5.3	5.6	6.2	6.7	6.7	5.3	5.6
1989	4.8	5.3	5.5	5.9	6.1	6.3	6.1	6.6	6.0	6.4	6.8	6.5	6.0
1990	5.9	5.7	6.1	5.9	6.0	6.2	6.4	6.7	7.0	7.6	7.7	6.7	6.5
1991	6.0	6.3	6.4	6.5	6.7	6.9	7.2	7.1	7.0	6.5	6.4	6.5	6.6
1992	6.0	5.8	6.0	6.0	6.0	6.1	6.5	6.8	6.7	7.1	7.2	7.1	6.4
1993	6.3	6.4	6.6	6.5	6.6	6.7	6.4	6.4	6.9	7.2	6.7	6.1	6.5
1994	5.4	5.4	5.5	5.8	5.9	6.0	7.0	7.4	7.4	7.9	8.0	7.3	6.6
1995	6.7	6.4	6.5	6.4	6.3	6.3	6.0	6.3	6.4	6.3	6.5	5.7	6.3
1996	5.3	5.2	5.1	4.7	4.6	4.9	4.9	4.8	5.3	6.1	6.4	6.2	5.3
1997[2]	5.4	5.0	5.0	5.0	5.3	5.6	6.0	5.9	6.1	6.1	6.3	5.8	5.6

[1] Pounds of feed equal in value to one pound of turkey, liveweight. [2] Preliminary. *Source: Economic Research Service, U.S. Department of Agriculture*

Average Price Received by Farmers for Turkeys in the United States (Liveweight) In Cents Per Pounds

Year	Jan.	Feb.	Mar.	Apr.	May	June	July	Aug.	Sept.	Oct.	Nov.	Dec.	Average
1988	32.3	29.7	28.4	28.4	29.8	32.1	40.4	42.0	45.4	48.4	47.9	38.3	36.9
1989	35.5	38.4	40.3	42.0	43.6	43.8	41.2	40.8	36.4	38.2	40.7	39.3	40.0
1990	35.4	33.7	36.4	36.6	38.3	38.7	39.1	40.2	40.3	42.5	42.3	36.9	38.4
1991	33.6	35.1	37.0	37.6	38.3	38.7	39.1	40.1	40.2	37.0	37.0	38.1	37.7
1992	36.3	35.5	37.0	37.0	37.7	37.7	37.9	37.8	37.5	38.5	39.4	39.3	37.6
1993	35.6	35.7	37.6	37.6	37.7	37.6	38.7	39.6	41.1	43.2	42.7	40.8	39.0
1994	37.0	37.3	38.4	39.2	39.9	40.3	40.6	42.1	43.1	44.5	44.3	42.2	40.7
1995	39.3	37.2	38.3	38.3	38.4	39.3	39.6	41.9	43.6	45.2	47.3	44.0	41.0
1996	40.9	42.4	41.8	42.2	43.2	44.4	45.0	44.3	44.2	45.1	45.5	43.2	43.5
1997[1]	38.6	36.4	37.8	39.5	41.2	41.5	41.1	40.7	41.1	40.3	42.3	38.6	39.9

[1] Preliminary. *Source: Economic Research Service, U.S. Department of Agriculture (ERS-USDA)*

Average Wholesale Price of Turkeys[1] (Hens, 8-16 Lbs.) in New York In Cents Per Pound

Year	Jan.	Feb.	Mar.	Apr.	May	June	July	Aug.	Sept.	Oct.	Nov.	Dec.	Average
1988	52.79	47.09	47.01	46.90	49.29	57.14	70.82	70.46	76.02	79.64	75.97	61.59	61.23
1989	59.03	62.17	65.71	68.33	72.08	72.98	66.40	62.61	57.88	67.61	72.45	72.70	66.66
1990	55.55	55.16	58.86	59.62	61.27	62.88	63.37	66.57	68.99	76.15	73.70	56.05	63.18
1991	53.49	55.76	59.10	60.32	62.32	62.68	63.41	64.66	64.38	60.52	63.07	65.18	61.24
1992	58.74	55.00	58.77	60.00	60.03	59.46	57.02	57.80	61.02	63.92	65.57	65.14	60.21
1993	58.05	56.83	58.41	58.98	58.81	58.35	59.76	63.43	66.73	71.28	71.76	68.20	62.55
1994	60.09	59.32	60.98	61.58	63.14	64.61	65.26	66.39	68.98	73.13	74.01	70.35	65.65
1995	60.71	58.54	60.04	60.05	60.57	62.76	64.78	68.52	72.92	76.73	80.31	70.35	66.36
1996	64.60	64.65	65.07	64.82	65.39	65.85	65.66	64.94	64.16	69.09	73.58	70.05	66.49
1997[2]	59.71	57.84	59.30	62.93	66.60	68.60	68.59	68.14	67.89	67.33	70.07	62.18	64.93

[1] Ready-to-cook. [2] Preliminary. *Source: Economic Research Service, U.S. Department of Agriculture (ERS-USDA)*

Certified Federally Inspected Turkey Slaughter in the U.S. (Ready-to-Cook Weights) In Millions of Pounds

Year	Jan.	Feb.	Mar.	Apr.	May	June	July	Aug.	Sept.	Oct.	Nov.	Dec.	Total
1988	255.7	266.9	314.0	276.6	331.3	373.2	322.4	377.3	365.8	395.7	371.7	272.8	3,923
1989	254.1	248.1	301.3	268.8	356.9	388.6	360.4	430.3	385.7	422.6	423.1	334.9	4,175
1990	334.0	298.3	351.1	328.4	384.1	389.2	395.7	444.0	382.9	478.4	446.2	328.6	4,561
1991	365.6	322.0	329.7	375.8	398.2	380.7	402.2	421.8	404.8	482.0	419.2	349.9	4,652
1992	362.9	331.7	361.3	385.2	374.2	435.0	451.8	411.9	431.3	467.6	423.0	393.1	4,829
1993	354.1	322.7	382.9	391.9	378.7	446.7	419.3	426.9	436.0	451.4	461.8	375.3	4,848
1994	347.8	342.0	400.9	380.6	415.6	457.9	405.6	483.6	447.7	453.6	453.9	397.5	4,992
1995	386.3	368.9	433.1	369.6	441.4	478.4	409.1	447.3	419.5	480.2	463.0	394.4	5,091
1996	412.4	426.5	422.3	430.9	483.0	454.7	484.8	476.6	440.9	518.1	465.9	406.1	5,422
1997[1]	439.7	389.5	399.3	446.6	459.9	480.1	487.4	452.7	457.0	508.3	453.8	453.6	5,428

[1] Preliminary. *Source: Economic Research Service, U.S. Department of Agriculture (ERS-USDA)*

Per Capita Consumption of Turkeys in the United States In Pounds

Year	First Quarter	Second Quarter	Third Quarter	Fourth Quarter	Total	Year	First Quarter	Second Quarter	Third Quarter	Fourth Quarter	Total
1987	2.5	2.8	3.5	5.8	14.7	1993	3.5	3.7	3.9	6.5	17.7
1988	3.1	3.4	3.8	5.4	15.7	1994	3.6	3.9	4.4	6.2	17.8
1989	3.2	3.2	4.2	6.0	16.6	1995	3.6	3.9	4.2	6.2	17.9
1990	3.5	3.6	4.2	6.2	17.6	1996	3.7	3.9	4.6	6.2	18.5
1991	3.7	4.0	4.1	6.4	18.0	1997[1]	3.5	4.0	4.2	6.0	17.8
1992	3.4	3.8	4.2	6.5	18.0	1998[2]	3.5	4.0	4.3	5.9	18.0

[1] Preliminary. [2] Estimate. *Source: Economic Research Service, U.S. Department of Agriculture (ERS-USDA)*

Storage Stocks of Turkeys (Frozen) in the United States, on First of Month In Millions of Pounds

Year	Jan.	Feb.	Mar.	Apr.	May	June	July	Aug.	Sept.	Oct.	Nov.	Dec.
1988	282.4	281.8	321.5	339.0	370.7	410.1	456.8	496.2	551.9	572.8	583.3	303.5
1989	249.7	262.5	263.1	269.2	298.7	355.6	454.6	496.9	574.3	569.3	571.8	258.6
1990	235.9	268.4	276.3	317.9	354.9	405.6	481.3	541.7	593.1	623.6	625.1	338.4
1991	306.4	302.5	342.2	370.0	408.5	453.4	503.1	571.3	625.8	667.2	653.0	305.5
1992	264.1	325.5	354.1	392.3	430.2	486.8	580.1	662.1	684.2	734.4	714.7	320.5
1993	271.7	314.7	359.8	359.2	424.4	474.0	556.1	624.2	678.6	713.8	683.6	290.6
1994	249.1	279.8	304.8	346.5	399.1	461.4	539.2	288.1	623.4	648.6	636.2	280.7
1995	254.4	312.9	359.5	432.1	466.2	536.3	598.8	651.1	678.2	686.0	644.2	270.1
1996	271.3	339.2	423.1	445.4	514.5	587.4	679.7	718.2	723.2	721.0	658.3	347.8
1997[1]	328.0	401.0	446.4	496.5	543.3	611.8	667.7	713.8	742.0	771.5	736.6	438.6

[1] Preliminary. *Source: Economic Research Service, U.S. Department of Agriculture (ERS-USDA)*

Average Retail Price[2] of Turkeys (Whole frozen) in the United States In Cents Per Pound

Year	Jan.	Feb.	Mar.	Apr.	May	June	July	Aug.	Sept.	Oct.	Nov.	Dec.	Average
1988	63.30	58.00	57.60	56.40	57.80	68.30	72.30	78.50	83.30	87.50	84.50	70.40	69.83
1989	67.60	66.90	71.90	75.10	79.40	80.60	74.40	71.80	67.80	73.28	79.80	79.60	74.02
1990	65.20	64.60	67.30	69.40	70.10	70.10	68.70	73.60	76.60	81.90	82.30	66.40	71.35
1991	62.30	63.06	66.61	66.78	69.70	70.00	70.30	72.20	72.80	69.10	70.80	73.90	68.96
1992	67.90	65.80	68.10	68.70	69.24	69.04	65.70	68.10	69.60	72.30	74.00	74.90	69.45
1993	67.85	67.22	67.94	68.80	68.40	68.19	67.08	72.07	74.91	78.37	80.08	75.03	71.33
1994	70.30	69.40	70.60	70.90	72.00	72.58	72.77	74.75	77.32	79.89	83.33	77.34	74.27
1995	69.54	67.08	68.47	68.62	70.05	72.49	74.18	77.77	81.60	84.89	86.50	77.50	74.89
1996	103.50	104.70	106.90	101.40	104.30	104.10	104.40	108.60	106.50	107.40	98.10	102.00	104.33
1997[1]	106.30	106.70	104.70	103.20	104.50	107.80	107.40	109.20	108.90	106.20	97.60	98.20	105.06

[1] Preliminary. [2] Data prior to 1996 are prices to selected retailers. *Source: Economic Research Service, U.S. Department of Agriculture (ERS-USDA)*

Turkey (Whole) Retail-to-Consumer Price Spread in the U.S. In Cents Per Pound

Year	Jan.	Feb.	Mar.	Apr.	May	June	July	Aug.	Sept.	Oct.	Nov.	Dec.	Average
1988	29.8	34.9	33.4	33.0	35.1	24.6	23.7	21.0	17.3	16.5	14.7	26.7	25.9
1989	29.8	29.9	25.7	23.2	20.7	20.7	30.2	32.3	34.2	28.9	13.4	15.4	25.4
1990	33.7	33.7	32.1	27.7	29.8	29.7	32.1	27.8	26.7	23.7	8.8	29.6	27.9
1991	37.1	38.1	31.2	33.7	30.9	32.0	32.6	31.2	30.3	34.9	20.8	17.5	30.9
1992	28.2	29.2	27.0	29.4	29.6	29.5	33.3	32.5	31.4	27.2	15.4	18.1	27.5
1993	30.0	31.7	32.6	31.9	32.3	34.5	35.8	29.7	27.7	25.0	13.6	20.4	28.8
1994	27.5	29.7	28.1	25.1	27.1	28.8	28.7	27.6	27.1	25.5	13.9	20.3	25.8
1995	28.5	32.0	33.7	32.1	32.7	32.8	30.8	28.2	27.0	20.1	10.6	21.2	27.5
1996	30.4	30.7	33.6	28.0	29.3	28.0	27.9	32.1	30.3	28.9	18.0	26.6	28.7
1997[1]	38.3	40.7	37.5	32.0	29.6	32.0	32.0	34.5	34.3	31.9	20.0	26.9	32.5

[1] Preliminary. *Source: Economic Research Service, U.S. Department of Agriculture (ERS-USDA)*

Uranium

There were a number of developments in the uranium market in 1997. In one important development, Russia and the U.S. agreed to stop production of weapons-grade plutonium by the year 2000. The agreement also called for the final three Russian nuclear reactors that produce plutonium to be converted to civilian use. The U.S. will pay most of the cost of the conversion. The U.S. unilaterally stopped weapons-grade plutonium production in 1989. Russia had 13 reactors that produced plutonium and has shut all but three of them. Plutonium is used in the production of nuclear weapons. The U.S. and Russia agreed to stop plutonium production in 1994 but Russia had to use the three reactors for civilian electricity production.

In another development, Russia indicated it will sell $1.5 billion of natural uranium to the U.S. Under a pact made by the U.S. and Russia in 1994 to deal with nuclear material obtained from the scrapping of Russian nuclear warheads, Russia will be allowed to sell uranium in the U.S.

Jordan announced that uranium deposits had been discovered in that country in amounts large enough to encourage commercial exploitation. Initial reports indicate that about 8,000 tonnes of uranium dioxide were found in central Jordan. The deposits were located near the surface indicating that mining the deposit would be low cost.

U.S. net generation of electricity from nuclear power in July 1997 was 57.4 billion kilowatthours. That was up from 52.1 billion kilowatthours in June 1997. In June 1996, nuclear power generated 61 billion kilowatthours of electricity. In the January-July 1997 period, some 361.8 billion kilowatthours of electricity were generated by nuclear power. That was down over nine percent from the comparable period in 1996. For all of 1996, electric power generation from nuclear power was 674.7 billion kilowatthours, while for 1995 it was 673.4 billion kilowatthours. In the January-July 1997 period, electric power generation in the U.S. by all sources was 1.8 trillion kilowatthours. Nuclear power generated 20 percent of all U.S. electric utility generated electric power.

In the January-July 1997 period, most nuclear-powered net generation of electricity was in the South Atlantic states with 98.6 billion kilowatthours. South Carolina produced 25.8 billion kilowatthours. The Middle Atlantic states produced 65.3 billion kilowatthours with Pennsylvania producing 39.7 billion kilowatthours. In the East North Central census division, 53.9 billion kilowatthours of electricity were produced by nuclear power with Illinois producing 29.8 billion kilowatthours.

Electric power generation by nuclear-powered facilities continues to increase. The future of uranium dioxide use in the U.S. remains questionable due to continued public resistance to the development of new nuclear power facilities.

World Production of Uranium Oxide (U_3O_8) Concentrate In Short Tons (Uranium Content)

Year	Australia	Canada	China	Czech Rep. & Slovakia	France	Gabon	Germany	Namibia	Niger	South Africa	United States	Former U.S.S.R.	World Total
1987	4,902	16,127	-----	-----	4,377	1,030	26	4,590	3,848	5,219	6,500	-----	47,745
1988	4,580	15,646	-----	-----	4,377	1,194	58	4,551	3,845	5,039	6,500	-----	46,846
1989	4,752	14,855	1,039	2,989	4,183	1,157	4,961	4,000	3,874	3,810	6,919	18,849	75,264
1990	4,589	11,400	1,039	2,600	3,661	922	3,864	4,030	3,682	3,169	4,443	18,199	64,642
1991	4,909	10,609	1,039	2,340	3,204	882	1,569	3,185	3,853	2,248	3,975	13,650	53,458
1992	3,032	12,087	1,039	2,040	2,755	702	325	2,199	3,855	2,449	2,822	11,205	46,124
1993	2,949	11,990	1,300	911	2,220	769	195	2,168	3,786	2,261	2,587	10,491	43,027
1994	3,050	11,950	NA	NA	1,700	750	NA	2,500	3,800	2,250	1,950	NA	41,750
1995[1]	4,900	13,600	NA	NA	1,250	800	NA	2,600	3,750	1,850	3,050	NA	42,650
1996[2]	6,450	15,250	NA	NA	1,200	750	NA	3,150	4,300	2,200	3,150	NA	47,600

[1] Preliminary. [2] Estimate. NA = Not available. *Source: American Bureau of Metal Statistics, Inc. (AMBS)*

Month-End Uranium (U_3O_8) Transaction Values[1] In Dollars Per Pound

Year	Jan.	Feb.	Mar.	Apr.	May	June	July	Aug.	Sept.	Oct.	Nov.	Dec.	Average
1987	17.35	16.90	16.95	17.00	17.20	17.10	17.30	17.55	18.20	18.05	17.80	17.20	17.38
1988	16.85	16.65	16.55	16.45	16.10	15.80	15.45	15.00	14.50	14.40	13.30	12.50	15.30
1989	12.25	12.00	11.25	11.00	10.75	10.45	9.95	9.80	9.80	9.65	9.55	9.40	10.49
1990	9.25	9.05	8.75	8.65	8.55	8.80	9.75	10.80	11.40	10.10	9.30	9.15	9.46
1991	9.40	9.45	9.35	9.30	9.30	9.20	9.15	8.95	8.70	8.35	7.45	7.50	8.84
1992	7.55	7.80	7.95	7.90	7.85	7.80	7.75	7.85	7.95	8.40	8.55	8.75	8.01
1993[2]	8.80	8.60	8.80	9.20	8.70	8.90	8.20	8.80	9.05	8.45	8.60	8.71	8.74
1994	8.58	8.45	8.25	8.25	8.23	8.25	8.23	8.15	8.13	8.10	8.13	8.25	8.25
1995	8.30	8.45	8.65	8.78	9.18	9.48	9.50	9.83	9.83	9.83	9.95	10.05	9.32
1996	10.20	10.48	10.93	11.70	13.03	13.25	14.93	15.18	15.40	15.53	15.48	15.38	13.45

[1] Transaction value is a weighted average price of recent natural uranium sales transactions, based on prices paid on transactions closed within the previous 3 month period for which delivery is scheduled within one year of the transaction date; at least 10 transactions involving a sum total of at least 2 million pounds of U_3O_8 equivalent. 2 Data beginning December 1993 represents average of Unrestricted and Restricted. *Source: American Metal Market (AMM)*

Reported Average Price Settlements for Purchases by U.S. Utilities and Domestic Suppliers In $ Per Lb.[2]

Year of Delivery	Contract Price	Market Price[1]	Price & Cost Floor	Total	Contract & Market	Year of Delivery	Contract Price	Market Price[1]	Price & Cost Floor	Total	Contract & Market
	Averages of Reported Prices						Averages of Reported Prices				
1987	29.16	17.53	34.34	22.85	27.37	1992	13.16	8.65	18.35	13.89	13.45
1988	28.20	16.12	33.52	21.59	26.15	1993	14.96	9.57	14.87	11.03	13.14
1989	20.87	11.48	22.50	15.42	19.56	1994	10.68	9.76	20.03	10.57	10.63
1990	17.94	9.18	19.40	11.65	15.70	1995	10.58	10.19	17.86	12.05	10.79
1991	13.94	9.04	21.84	12.62	13.66	1996	13.40	13.66	16.13	14.91	13.72

[1] No floor. [2] U_3O_8 equivalent. Note: Price excludes uranium delivered under litigation settlements. Price is given in year-of-delivery dollars.
Source: Energy Information Adminstration, U.S. Department of Energy (EIA-DOE)

Uranium Industry Statistics in the United States In Millions of Pounds U_3O_8

Year	Production: Mine	Production: Concentrate	Concentrate Shipments	Employment – Person Years: Exploration	Mining	Milling	Processing	Total	Deliveries to U.S. Utilities[1]	Avg. Price Delivered Uranium $/lb. U_3O_8	Imports	Avg. Price Delivered Uranium Imports $/lb. U_3O_8	Exports
1987	6.0	12.991	11.558	183	819	432	568	2,002	20.8	27.37	15.9	19.14	1.0
1988	9.5	13.130	12.791	144	849	572	576	2,141	17.6	26.15	17.0	19.03	4.3
1989	9.7	13.837	14.808	86	659	367	471	1,583	18.4	19.56	13.7	16.75	2.5
1990	5.9	8.885	12.957	73	664	304	293	1,335	20.5	15.70	26.6	12.55	2.4
1991	5.2	7.952	8.437	52	411	191	361	1,016	26.8	13.66	23.1	15.55	3.5
1992	1.0	5.645	6.853	51	219	129	283	682	23.4	13.45	45.4	11.34	20.9
1993	2.0	3.063	3.374	36	133	65	145	380	15.5	13.14	41.9	10.53	21.3
1994	2.5	3.352	6.319	41	157	105	149	980	38.3	10.40	36.6	8.95	17.7
1995	3.5	6.000	5.500	27	226	121	161	1,107	43.4	11.25	41.3	10.20	9.8
1996	4.7	6.300	6.000	27	333	155	175	1,118	47.3	14.12	45.4	13.15	11.5

[1] From suppliers under domestic purchases. *Source: Energy Information Administration, U.S. Department of Energy (EIA-DOE)*

Commercial and U.S. Government Stocks of Uranium, End of Year In Millions of Pounds U_3O_8 Equivalent

Year	Utility: Natural Uranium	Utility: Enriched Uranium[1]	Domestic Supplier: Natural Uranium	Domestic Supplier: Enriched Uranium[1]	Total Commercial Stocks	DOE-Owned & USEC-Held: Natural Uranium	DOE-Owned & USEC-Held: Enriched Uranium
1989	67.3	48.5	21.2	1.0	138.1	77.5	24.7
1990	61.5	41.2	22.0	4.4	129.1	59.8	32.8
1991	70.9	27.1	18.7	2.0	118.7	46.8	36.7
1992	66.5	25.5	19.1	6.1	117.3	45.8	23.1
1993	57.9	23.3	19.1	5.4	105.7	52.4	26.9
1994	42.4	23.0	17.4	4.1	86.9	57.2	28.0
1995	41.2	17.5	13.2	.5	72.5	82.0	28.8
1996	42.2	25.3	13.0	.7	81.2	82.4	25.3

[1] Includes amount reported as UF_6 at enrichment suppliers. DOE = Department of Energy USEC = U.S. Energy Commission.
Source: Energy Information Administration, U.S. Department of Energy (EIA-DOE)

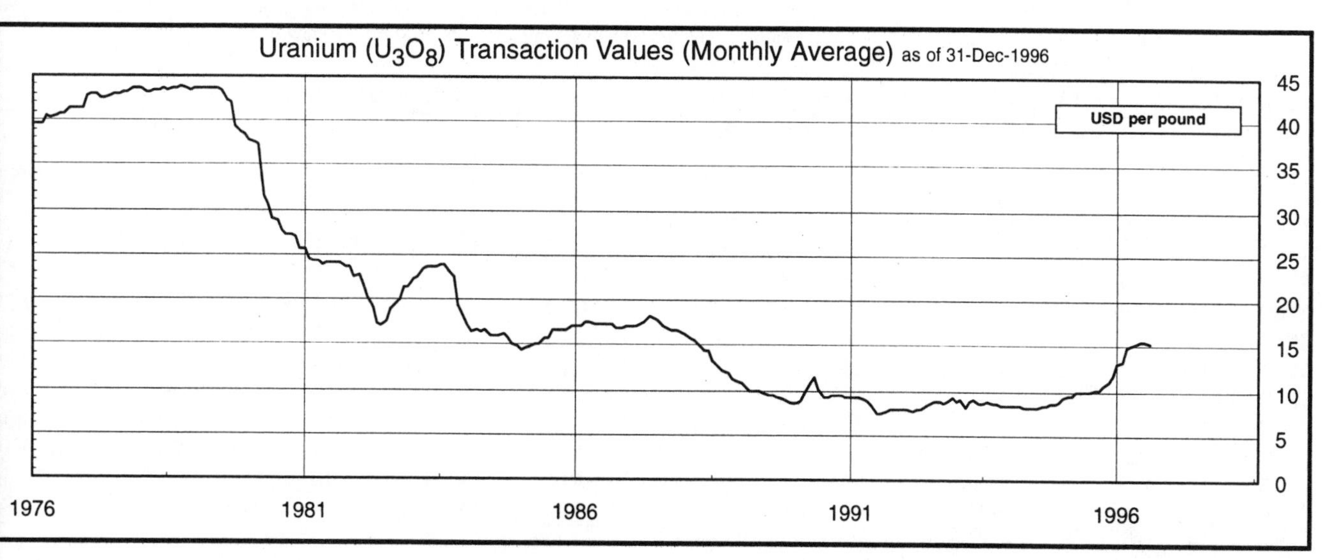

Vanadium

Vanadium is used in the production of carbon and alloy plates and steels, pipe steels, and structural bars. It has commercial importance as an oxidation catalyst. Vanadium is used in tool production to provide strength and toughness. Ferrovanadium is an iron alloy used in steel. Vanadium is used in ceramics production as a coloring agent. Vanadium pentoxide is used in dyeing and printing applications. Vanadium is important in the production of aerospace titanium alloys and as a catalyst in the production of maleic anhydride and sulfuric acid. The major producers of vanadium are presently South Africa, China and Russia.

Consumption of vanadium within the United States in July 1997 was 374,000 kilograms, contained vanadium. Of the total, ferrovanadium consumption was 330,000 kilograms. That included vanadium-iron-carbon alloys as well as vanadium oxides added directly to steel. Vanadium oxide consumption in July 1997 was 1,120 kilograms. Other vanadium material consumption totaled 42,600 kilograms. Consumption of vanadium in June 1997 was 337,000 kilograms. For all of 1996, vanadium consumption was 4.5 million kilograms.

U.S. stocks of vanadium at the end of July 1997 were 290,000 kilograms, vanadium content. Ferrovanadium stocks were 268,000 kilograms, while stocks of vanadium oxides were 6,780 kilograms. Vanadium-aluminum alloy stocks at the end of July 1997 were 10,700 kilograms. Other vanadium material stocks were 4,520 kilograms. That included vanadium alloys, vanadium metal and vanadium chemicals. At the end of 1996, U.S. stocks of vanadium were 334,000 kilograms.

U.S. exports of aluminum-vanadium master alloy in June 1997 were 52,300 kilograms, vanadium content. The major destinations were Mexico, the United Kingdom, Germany and Israel. For the first half of 1997, U.S. exports of aluminum-vanadium master alloy were 371,000 kilograms. Ferrovanadium exports in June 1997 were 17,800 kilograms, all of which went to Canada. For the January-June 1997 period, ferrovanadium exports were 218,000 kilograms. U.S. exports of vanadium pentoxide (anhydride) in June 1997 were 40,400 kilograms. The major destinations were the Czech Republic, Germany, Belgium and France. In the January-June 1997 period, exports were 415,000 kilograms.

World Production of Vanadium — In Metric Tons (Contained Vanadium)

	From Ores, Concentrates and Slag						From Petroleum Residues, Ash, Spent Catalysts			
			Republic of South Africa							
Year	China[3]	Russia[4]	Content of Pentoxide & Vanadate Products	Content of Vanadiferous Slag Product	Total	Total[5]	Japan[6]	United States[7]	Total	World Grand Total
1987	4,500	9,600	5,842	10,100	15,942	30,042	728	2,275	3,003	33,045
1988	4,500	9,600	6,330	11,300	17,631	31,731	728	2,950	3,678	35,409
1989	4,500	9,600	7,270	11,300	18,567	32,967	868	2,389	3,257	36,224
1990	4,500	9,000	7,100	10,000	17,106	33,900	700	2,308	3,008	36,900
1991	4,500	8,500	6,500	8,460	14,962	31,700	404	2,250	2,650	34,300
1992	4,700	11,000	6,300	7,730	14,033	29,900	245	1,347	1,590	31,500
1993	5,000	10,000	6,650	8,400	15,051	31,500	252	2,867	3,120	34,600
1994	5,400	10,000	6,050	9,600	15,229	31,700	252	2,740	2,990	34,700
1995[1]	7,000	11,000	6,500	9,000	16,297	35,400	245	1,990	2,240	37,700
1996[2]	7,000	11,000	NA	NA	16,000	35,100	245	3,730	3,980	39,100

[1] Preliminary. [2] Estimate. [3] In vanadiferous slag product. [4] Formerly part of the U.S.S.R.; data not reported separately until 1992. [5] Excludes U.S. production. [6] In vanadium pentoxide products. [7] In vandium pentoxide and ferrovandium products. *Source: U.S. Geological Survey (USGS)*

Salient Statistics of Vanadium in the United States — In Metric Tons (Contained Vanadium)

		Vanadium Consumption by Uses in U.S.									Exports			Imports			
Year	Consumer & Producer Stocks, Dec. 31	Tool Steel	Cast Irons	Hign Strength, Low Alloy	Stainless & Heat Resisting	Superalloys	Carbon	Full Alloy	Total	Average $ Per Lb. V_2O_5	Vanadium Pentoxide, Anhydride	Oxides & Hydroxides	Ferro-Vanadium	Ores, Slag, Residues	Vanadium Pentoxide, Anhydride	Oxides & Hydroxides	Ferro-Vanadium
1987	2,057	422	23	1,212	59	9	1,086	740	4,221	3.50	742	-----	311	2,054	207	-----	310
1988	1,266	481	20	1,339	41	9	1,259	887	4,834	3.40	620	-----	462	2,025	219	-----	108
1989	1,736	420	18	1,225	96	38	1,103	898	4,646	6.17	1,171	1,080	399	4,210	133	106	527
1990	1,082	421	18	1,122	38	42	994	814	4,081	4.21	819	976	271	3,826	83	217	244
1991	935	242	15	919	37	14	919	739	3,293	2.85	700	1,110	94	882	133	110	420
1992	1,084	453	17	989	28	13	1,262	828	4,079	2.28	26	1,113	213	838	206	103	592
1993	900	373	21	981	33	13	1,413	789	3,973	1.45	126	895	219	1,454	70	19	1,630
1994	1,110	424	31	979	26	16	1,680	777	4,290	1.55	335	1,050	374	1,900	294	3	1,910
1995[1]	1,100	443	40	1,070	32	20	1,870	833	4,640	4.63	229	1,010	340	2,530	547	36	1,950
1996[2]	980	433	W	890	22	16	1,820	1,030	4,200	3.11	241	2,670	479	2,270	485	11	1,880

[1] Preliminary. [2] Estimate. W = Withheld proprietary data. *Source: U.S. Geological Survey (USGS)*

Vegetables

U.S. production of fresh tomatoes in 1997 was estimated by the USDA to be 3.1 billion pounds. That was up four percent from 1996 but well below the production levels of previous years. U.S. imports of fresh tomatoes in 1997 were 1.77 billion pounds, up from 1.63 billion pounds in 1996. The total supply of U.S. fresh tomatoes in 1997 was 4.87 billion pounds. In terms of use, exports of fresh tomatoes were 305 million pounds, up three percent from 1996. Domestic use of fresh tomatoes was 4.57 billion pounds, up three percent from 1996. U.S. per capita use of fresh tomatoes in 1997 was 17 pounds.

U.S. production of fresh head lettuce in 1997 was 6.57 billion pounds, about the same as in 1996. Imports of lettuce were 31 million pounds with the total supply of lettuce in 1997 being 6.60 billion pounds. In terms of usage, U.S. lettuce exports in 1997 were 435 million pounds, up four percent from 1996. Domestic utilization of fresh lettuce was 6.16 billion pounds, down one percent from 1996. U.S. per capita use of lettuce was 23 pounds in 1997.

U.S. production of fresh sweet corn in 1997 was 2.25 billion pounds, slightly less than in 1996. U.S. imports of sweet corn in 1997 were 25 million pounds. The total supply of sweet corn in 1997 was 2.28 billion pounds. In terms of use, exports of sweet corn in 1997 were 95 million pounds. Domestic utilization of sweet corn was 2.18 billion pounds, down one percent from 1996. Per capita use of fresh sweet corn in 1997 was 8.1 pounds.

Production of potatoes for freezing in 1997 was 16.4 billion pounds, down one percent from 1996. Imports in 1997 were 1.05 billion pounds with a total supply of 19.6 billion pounds. Exports of potatoes were 1.89 billion pounds with domestic use of 15.5 billion pounds. Per capita utilization in 1997 was 57.7 pounds.

Commercial and Fresh Vegetables: Indices of Prices Received by Growers in the United States

Year	Jan.	Feb.	Mar.	Apr.	May	June	July	Aug.	Sept.	Oct.	Nov.	Dec.	Annual
					Commercial[1] 1990-92 = 100								
1991	95	84	114	107	131	109	91	88	90	88	109	88	100
1992	97	118	144	106	93	94	102	113	115	125	109	121	111
1993	119	125	108	164	126	100	105	109	112	95	102	124	116
1994	114	111	92	87	97	104	97	94	104	117	123	163	109
1995	120	115	147	172	155	122	98	101	117	98	98	101	120
1996	93	108	140	118	100	115	97	114	100	107	119	123	111
1997[2]	110	105	117	113	109	116	111	125	117	139			116
					Fresh[3] 1982 = 100								
1991	89.3	87.3	88.4	112.8	157.0	138.0	102.0	82.6	81.8	73.5	113.1	76.1	100.2
1992	117.5	154.7	147.9	99.7	89.9	81.3	85.5	114.8	115.1	149.4	108.2	133.4	116.5
1993	128.8	125.8	117.4	178.5	163.5	80.7	98.4	110.5	117.0	89.5	141.1	167.0	126.5
1994	146.3	99.3	96.1	91.4	91.2	94.9	104.8	95.7	107.1	113.8	128.1	244.7	117.8
1995	163.5	149.2	159.2	199.1	167.2	127.2	107.3	94.8	152.9	116.0	115.8	125.5	139.8
1996	133.9	119.4	202.5	155.6	108.2	96.6	108.8	97.2	91.3	106.0	131.5	99.3	120.9
1997[2]	105.2	126.2	150.4	109.6	103.2	112.2	115.7	125.2	121.8	143.1	124.7	118.5	121.3

Not seasonally adjusted. [1] Includes fresh and processing vegetable. [2] Preliminary. [3] Producer Price Index (0113-02). *Source: National Agricultural Statistics Service, U.S. Department of Agriculture (NASS-USDA)*

Processed Vegetables in the United States: Producer Price Indices 1982 = 100

Year	Jan.	Feb.	Mar.	Apr.	May	June	July	Aug.	Sept.	Oct.	Nov.	Dec.	Annual
						Canned[1] (0244)							
1991	114.8	114.8	115.1	113.8	114.0	113.3	114.0	112.2	110.9	111.2	110.1	109.8	112.8
1992	110.3	109.7	109.3	108.9	109.8	109.4	109.5	109.6	109.2	109.1	109.5	109.8	109.5
1993	110.1	109.8	109.7	109.1	108.8	109.9	111.1	109.6	110.4	111.5	112.3	112.6	110.4
1994	113.1	115.1	116.8	116.5	117.9	118.0	118.9	118.1	116.0	116.0	114.0	112.4	116.1
1995	112.6	114.3	114.7	112.9	115.6	117.5	118.2	117.5	117.6	117.8	118.4	119.6	116.4
1996	120.4	119.8	120.4	120.4	120.8	121.0	122.6	122.1	121.9	121.8	121.9	121.8	121.2
1997[2]	121.5	121.1	120.5	120.1	119.8	119.9	119.1	119.3	119.3	120.2	120.3	120.4	120.2
						Frozen (0245)							
1991	118.4	118.5	118.3	117.9	118.1	117.5	117.8	117.2	117.4	116.6	116.5	116.8	117.6
1992	116.8	116.1	116.2	116.6	116.3	115.5	115.3	115.4	116.8	116.3	117.5	118.2	116.4
1993	118.0	118.0	117.9	118.7	119.9	121.1	121.3	122.1	122.6	123.2	123.7	124.7	120.9
1994	125.5	126.1	126.1	126.4	126.9	127.0	126.4	126.4	125.2	124.9	124.7	125.0	126.0
1995	125.1	124.7	124.9	125.1	124.3	123.6	123.2	123.6	124.4	124.6	123.7	124.0	124.3
1996	125.1	124.8	124.6	124.9	125.0	125.4	125.5	125.8	126.0	125.7	125.8	126.0	125.4
1997[2]	125.9	125.7	125.6	125.6	125.7	125.7	126.9	125.6	125.7	126.6	125.8	125.0	125.8

Not seasonally adjusted. [1] Includes canned vegetables and juices, including hominy and mushrooms. [2] Preliminary. *Source: Bureau of Labor Statistics, U.S. Department of Labor (BLS)*

VEGETABLES

Per Capita Use of Selected Commercially Produced Fresh and Processing Vegetables in the United States

Pounds, Farm Weight Basis

Crop	1987	1988	1989	1990	1991	1992	1993	1994	1995	1996[9]	1997[10]
Asparagus, all	1.0	1.0	1.0	1.0	1.0	1.0	1.0	.9	1.0	.9	.9
Fresh	.6	.6	.6	.6	.6	.6	.6	.6	.6	.6	.6
Canning	.3	.3	.3	.3	.3	.3	.3	.2	.3	.2	.2
Freezing	.1	.1	.1	.1	.1	.1	.1	.1	.1	.1	.1
Snap Beans, all	6.7	6.7	7.1	6.7	7.0	7.2	7.3	7.4	6.9	7.1	7.1
Fresh	1.2	1.2	1.2	1.1	1.1	1.5	1.5	1.6	1.7	1.4	1.5
Canning	3.8	3.8	3.9	3.7	4.1	4.0	4.0	3.8	3.5	3.8	3.7
Freezing	1.7	1.7	2.0	1.9	1.8	1.7	1.8	2.0	1.7	1.9	1.9
Broccoli, all[1]	5.3	6.2	6.0	5.6	5.4	5.8	5.2	6.2	6.6	6.7	6.7
Fresh	3.1	3.8	3.8	3.4	3.1	3.4	2.9	3.9	4.0	4.1	4.1
Freezing	2.2	2.4	2.2	2.2	2.3	2.4	2.3	2.3	2.6	2.6	2.6
Carrots, all[2]	11.3	10.4	11.5	11.9	11.2	12.3	12.0	12.8	13.2	14.6	14.4
Fresh	8.3	7.1	8.1	8.3	7.7	8.3	8.2	8.7	9.0	10.2	10.2
Canning	.9	1.0	.9	1.3	1.1	1.7	1.0	1.3	1.7	1.6	1.6
Freezing	2.1	2.3	2.5	2.3	2.4	2.3	2.8	2.8	2.5	2.8	2.6
Cauliflower, all[1]	3.0	3.1	3.1	3.0	2.6	2.5	2.4	2.2	2.0	1.9	2.1
Fresh	2.1	2.2	2.3	2.2	2.0	1.8	1.7	1.6	1.4	1.4	1.5
Freezing	.9	.9	.8	.8	.6	.7	.7	.6	.6	.5	.6
Celery, fresh	6.6	7.2	7.5	7.2	6.8	7.4	7.1	6.8	6.4	6.3	6.3
Sweet Corn, all[3]	24.7	24.9	24.4	26.3	26.4	27.8	28.0	27.6	28.8	29.3	28.6
Fresh	6.3	5.8	6.5	6.7	5.9	6.9	7.0	8.2	7.8	8.3	8.1
Canning	10.6	10.4	9.5	11.0	11.1	11.9	11.2	10.2	10.5	10.5	10.0
Freezing	7.8	8.7	8.4	8.6	9.4	9.0	9.8	9.2	10.5	10.5	10.5
Cucumbers, all	10.6	10.1	10.0	9.7	9.7	9.6	9.7	10.2	10.9	10.2	10.6
Fresh	5.1	4.8	4.8	4.7	4.6	5.0	5.3	5.5	5.7	6.0	6.0
Pickles	5.5	5.3	5.2	5.0	5.1	4.6	4.4	4.7	5.2	4.2	4.6
Melons	24.3	23.8	26.5	24.6	23.4	25.4	25.0	25.8	26.8	30.3	29.7
Watermelon	13.0	13.5	13.6	13.3	12.8	14.8	14.6	15.4	15.7	17.4	17.0
Cantaloupe	9.1	7.9	10.4	9.2	8.7	8.5	8.7	8.6	9.2	10.6	10.4
Honeydew	2.2	2.4	2.5	2.1	1.9	2.1	1.7	1.8	1.9	2.3	2.3
Lettuce, Head	25.7	27.0	28.8	27.8	26.1	25.9	24.6	24.3	22.5	23.3	23.0
Onions, all	14.9	16.2	16.4	17.1	17.3	17.6	18.5	17.5	18.9	18.7	18.6
Fresh	13.4	14.5	14.8	15.1	15.7	16.2	16.5	16.5	17.6	17.9	17.5
Green peas, all[4]	3.7	3.7	3.7	4.2	4.2	4.1	3.5	3.7	3.7	3.4	3.5
Canning	2.0	1.8	1.7	2.0	1.9	2.1	1.6	1.5	1.6	1.5	1.5
Freezing	1.7	1.9	2.0	2.2	2.3	2.0	1.9	2.2	2.1	1.9	2.0
Tomatoes, all	81.0	78.1	86.2	90.9	92.8	89.2	92.4	90.1	92.8	90.8	92.5
Fresh	15.8	16.8	16.8	15.5	15.4	15.5	16.0	16.5	17.2	16.6	17.0
Canning	65.2	61.3	69.4	75.4	77.4	73.7	76.4	73.6	75.6	74.2	75.5
Subtotal, all[8]	248.7	249.5	263.7	268.1	267.2	271.7	274.6	273.2	276.7	283.2	283.2
Fresh	132.4	135.5	142.6	138.5	134.3	141.6	141.7	146.1	145.9	153.5	153.1
Canning	95.5	91.2	98.7	107.3	109.8	108.1	108.7	104.0	106.6	105.4	106.4
Freezing	19.3	21.1	20.8	20.3	21.5	20.6	22.2	22.1	22.9	23.5	23.3
Potatoes, all	126.0	122.4	127.1	127.6	130.4	132.4	136.9	140.7	137.9	142.8	142.4
Fresh	47.9	49.6	50.0	45.7	46.4	48.9	49.7	49.1	50.7	48.8	50.8
Processing	78.1	72.8	77.1	81.9	84.0	83.5	87.2	91.6	87.2	94.0	91.6
Sweetpotatoes, all	4.4	4.1	4.1	4.6	4.0	4.3	3.9	4.7	4.5	4.6	4.6
Total, all items	387.1	386.9	406.7	411.1	413.1	420.3	426.9	430.5	431.5	442.6	443.2

[1] All production for processing broccoli and cauliflower is for freezing. [2] Industry allocation suggests that 27% of processing carrot production is for canning and 73% is for freezing. [3] On-cob basis. [4] In-shell basis. [5] Includes artichokes, brussel sprouts, eggplant, endive/excarole, garlic, radishes and spinach. [6] Includes beets, chile peppers and spinach. [7] Includes green lima beans, spinach and miscellaneous freezing vegetables. [8] Fresch, canning and freezing data do not add to the total because onions are for dehydrating are included in total. [9] Preliminary. [10] Forecast. *Source: Economic Research Service, U.S. Department of Agriculture (ERS-USDA)*

Fresh Vegetables: Average Prices Received by Growers in the United States   Dollars Per Cwt.

Year	Jan.	Feb.	Mar.	Apr.	May	June	July	Aug.	Sept.	Oct.	Nov.	Dec.	Season Average
						Broccoli							
1995	24.70	34.30	54.40	34.00	26.50	27.30	19.50	31.30	27.70	23.60	20.80	26.90	29.30
1996	34.60	22.00	30.90	25.20	28.20	30.60	24.10	24.10	23.90	24.30	37.90	40.00	28.50
1997[1]	39.90	28.90	26.20	24.20	23.10	30.30	27.50	23.30	31.20	45.30			29.99
						Carrots							
1995	19.20	16.90	18.70	19.40	19.20	15.20	15.00	16.10	16.10	15.30	15.50	13.00	16.80
1996	12.60	13.80	15.90	15.70	12.00	11.00	10.50	14.50	12.60	12.00	13.60	14.20	12.80
1997[1]	14.50	14.30	13.40	12.70	12.60	12.60	12.50	13.90	12.30	11.80			13.06
						Cauliflower							
1995	31.40	31.50	53.90	68.40	47.70	37.60	26.70	34.20	25.40	21.10	22.60	33.20	34.70
1996	35.20	36.10	52.80	37.00	37.70	35.70	24.30	27.20	23.80	29.20	36.20	38.00	33.90
1997[1]	30.50	34.80	32.80	28.20	20.70	31.20	38.90	22.90	34.50	60.80			33.53
						Celery							
1995	24.30	26.00	20.60	33.30	24.50	14.40	11.50	10.50	16.50	13.20	12.90	11.40	16.30
1996	7.90	8.50	12.20	11.60	8.90	11.50	11.50	10.20	11.50	9.79	12.80	13.00	10.50
1997[1]	16.20	16.20	12.30	10.50	15.40	9.89	19.40	17.10	14.40	12.10			14.35
						Corn, Sweet							
1995	25.00	44.70	27.80	16.70	24.80	18.90	17.70	15.50	16.30	17.90	24.00	24.80	18.20
1996	37.10	24.10	29.40	21.10	15.60	13.80	19.40	17.40	16.70	18.40	16.60	18.70	16.60
1997[1]	26.80	36.60	27.40	16.20	19.60	18.00	18.20	18.80	17.30	16.60			21.55
						Lettuce, Head							
1995	13.40	9.33	27.20	48.20	47.00	15.60	12.60	15.20	25.60	13.30	11.50	16.20	23.50
1996	11.20	14.90	16.50	13.20	13.30	15.20	12.70	23.50	13.70	15.40	23.40	24.90	14.80
1997[1]	14.90	9.66	13.50	15.70	10.50	14.70	17.00	22.80	22.30	31.60			17.27
						Tomatoes							
1995	41.60	27.00	37.10	20.50	16.70	34.20	20.60	15.60	18.70	22.10	32.80	24.90	25.80
1996	18.40	40.00	81.70	50.50	23.60	25.90	27.00	22.00	23.20	29.30	31.50	28.00	28.50
1997[1]	31.40	45.70	58.00	27.60	33.80	32.70	26.80	26.10	23.30	23.60			32.90

[1] Preliminary. *Source: National Agricultural Statistics Service, U.S. Department of Agriculture (NASS-USDA)*

Frozen Vegetables: January 1 and July 1 Cold Storage Holdings in the U.S.   In Thousands of Pounds

	1993	1994		1995		1996		1997		1998[1]
Crop	July 1	Jan. 1	July 1	Jan. 1	July 1	Jan. 1	July 1	Jan. 1	July 1	Jan. 1
Asparagus	22,307	14,782	19,175	9,808	15,493	9,689	14,001	8,353	12,276	6,908
Lima Beans	26,164	49,594	24,093	59,440	29,783	60,208	33,350	60,696	28,015	72,221
Snap Beans	73,907	184,418	71,457	244,681	87,436	224,297	80,224	202,648	95,868	230,661
Broccoli	194,061	134,774	152,312	109,076	110,075	136,850	150,883	120,972	108,411	112,311
Brussels sprouts	12,029	34,338	20,166	30,191	18,181	18,883	9,533	16,314	7,975	19,926
Carrots	176,830	260,993	165,748	271,244	176,054	307,645	177,248	283,770	162,153	300,870
Cauliflower	32,461	60,683	40,077	77,243	49,561	65,008	38,355	54,376	32,785	58,512
Corn, Sweet[2]	239,379	371,151	119,206	485,361	199,148	498,626	215,553	494,308	203,740	532,645
Mixed vegetables	42,013	44,916	51,737	58,272	59,414	60,492	67,031	54,208	50,755	45,744
Okra	18,387	16,341	31,799	62,491	43,367	39,954	23,902	28,576	18,711	52,230
Onions	24,787	36,101	31,296	51,244	42,810	48,761	38,342	40,790	37,817	42,218
Black-eyed peas	4,636	9,605	3,159	13,157	3,145	9,994	3,529	9,795	2,952	9,344
Green peas	177,245	261,338	218,032	260,487	219,669	281,349	163,293	224,134	137,615	219,533
Peas and carrots	7,506	15,363	14,063	9,329	9,034	10,401	8,340	6,731	6,840	5,760
Spinach	79,337	47,159	120,542	70,010	100,274	68,940	86,281	46,890	104,073	67,092
Squash	40,941	61,679	53,763	64,533	39,494	57,785	44,785	58,749	48,184	75,397
Southern greens	22,251	31,786	29,194	29,993	30,079	21,659	32,363	26,936	16,681	20,771
Other vegetables	211,523	258,611	238,554	241,252	189,124	319,519	235,880	314,640	253,158	285,670
Total	1,405,764	2,015,892	1,404,373	2,288,336	1,422,141	2,390,428	1,422,893	2,185,704	1,317,049	2,303,007
Potatoes	989,818	1,006,416	1,099,850	1,083,747	1,116,454	1,123,744	1,057,470	1,131,642	1,271,316	1,163,547
Grand total	2,395,582	3,022,308	2,504,223	3,372,083	2,538,595	3,514,172	2,480,363	3,317,346	2,588,365	3,466,554

[1] Preliminary. [2] Cut-basis with cob corn converted to cut-basis using a factor of 0.4706. *Source: National Agricultural Statistics Service, U.S. Department of Agriculture (NASS-USDA)*

Wheat

World wheat production in 1997/98 topped 600 million metric tonnes for the first time, up from 583 million in 1996/97, and the previous record high of 588 million in 1990/91. The large crop, for the second year in a row, exceeds estimated world usage and allows a further rebuilding of carryover from the severely depleted reserves of the mid-1990's. World consumption was forecast at a record high 582 million tonnes vs. 580 million in 1996/97. The projected 1997/98 carryover of 128 million tonnes compares with 109 million a year earlier, and 105 million two years ago. Although world stock levels have rebounded, the supplies required to maintain the current high rate of consumption remains largely dependent upon continued high production.

Since the late 1980's, China has been the world's largest wheat producer with about 20 percent of total production. A a record large crop of 121 million tonnes in 1997/98, if realized, will for the first time exceed China's consumption. Production in 1996/97 totaled 111 million tonnes. Both China's wheat acreage (30 million hectares in 1997/98) and average yield (4.03 tonnes per hectare) continue to trend higher. China's year-to-year wheat consumption has been edging higher and for 1997/98 is expected to reach a record large 114 million tonnes vs. 113 million in 1996/97. Despite China's large 1997/98 crop, some imports may be apparently needed, estimated at 2.0 million tonnes vs. 2.8 million in 1996/97, and 13 million in 1995/96. However, China's import needs have little consistency as their wheat inventory is uncertain as is the government's willingness to utilize carryover supplies. What remains apparent on the world market is that China's import needs are very price sensitive and world prices quickly strengthen on talk, real or rumored, of Chinese buying, which in turn brakes both their interest and market strength.

The persistent decline during the first half of the 1990's in the former USSR's wheat production may be finally over. Production in 1997/98 in the key republics was forecast at: Russia, 42 million tonnes vs. 35 million in 1996/97; Kazakstan, 9 million vs. 7.7 million; and the Ukraine, 19 million vs. 13.5 million. Russia's 1997/98 imports are forecast at only one million tonnes, with the Ukraine at perhaps 50,000 tonnes. Russia's lack of foreign exchange and credit still accounts for some of the drop in imports, but higher production is also a factor. The drop in consumption among the Russian republics also appears to have been braked with Russia's domestic use estimated at 37.4 million tonnes in 1997/98 vs. 37.8 million in 1996/97 and more than 50 million on average early in the 1990's; the Ukraine's usage of 16.7 million tonnes is about unchanged from 1996/97.

The 1997/98 world wheat trade is forecast at 96 million tonnes vs. 96.9 million in 1996/97. Four nations account for the bulk of 1997/98 world wheat exports: Argentina, 9.2 million tonnes; Australia, 13.5 million; Canada, 19 million; and the U.S., the world's largest exporter, at 29 million tonnes. Collectively, the European Union is forecast to export 15.5 million tonnes. Among the exporting nations, only Australia was expected to have much of a difference from 1996/97's totals when 18 million tonnes were exported. Importing nations are scattered. Among those forecast to take at least five million tonnes in 1997/98 are Brazil, Iran, Egypt, and Japan.

The 1997 U.S. (June/May) wheat crop of 2.53 billion bushels compares with 2.28 billion in 1996/97. The increase reflected a higher average yield of 39.7 bushels per acre vs. 36.3, and harvested acreage of 63.6 million acres vs. 62.9 million, respectively. Winter wheat accounts for most of U.S. production, 1.9 billion bushels in 1997/98 vs. 1.5 billion in 1996/97. The increase reflected a jump in average yield to 45.0 bushels per acre from 37.2 in 1996/97. Kansas is the largest winter wheat producing state with 506 million bushels in 1997/98. North Dakota is the largest spring wheat (210 million bushels) and durum (57 million bushels) producing state. The 1997/98 durum wheat crop of 86 million bushels compares with 116 million in 1996/97; other spring wheat production was put at 558 million bushels vs. 692 million. Generally durum wheat has the lowest yield per acre, but the 1997/98 average yield in the spring producing states was at least five bushels per acre under 1996/97.

The U.S. imports some wheat, mostly from Canada. Carryin stocks on June 1, 1997, of 444 million bushels compares with 376 million a year earlier. The U.S. wheat supply for 1997/98 of 3.1 billion bushels compares with 2.75 billion in 1996/97. Total usage in 1997/98 of 2.4 billion bushels compares with 2.3 billion in 1996/97. Exports account for almost half of total disappearance. Food use takes about two-thirds of domestic usage; feed about 20 percent and seed the balance. If the 1997/98 supply/demand estimates are realized, ending stocks on May 31, 1998 would rise to 665 million bushels.

The 1997/98 average price received by farmers was forecast to range from \$3.30 to \$3.70 a bushel vs. \$4.30 in 1996/97.

Futures Markets

Wheat futures and options are traded on the London Commodity Exchange (LCE), the Chicago Board of Trade (CBOT), the Kansas City Board of Trade (KCBT), the Minneapolis Grain Exchange (MGE), and the Mid America Commodity Exchange (MidAm). Feed wheat futures and options are traded on the Winnipeg Commodity Exchange (WCE).

World Production of Wheat In Thousands of Metric Tons

Crop Year	Argentina	Australia	Canada	China	France	Germany	India	Pakistan	Russia[4]	Turkey	United Kingdom	United States	World Total
1988-9	8,400	14,060	15,995	85,432	29,660	11,922	46,169	12,675	84,445	16,000	11,750	49,320	500,300
1989-90	10,150	14,214	24,796	90,807	32,100	14,482	54,110	14,419	87,151	12,500	14,030	55,428	533,001
1990-1	10,900	15,066	32,098	98,229	33,600	15,242	49,850	14,429	49,596	16,000	14,000	74,292	587,995
1991-2	9,880	10,557	31,946	96,000	34,594	16,610	55,134	14,565	38,900	16,500	14,400	53,891	542,132
1992-3	9,800	16,184	29,871	101,590	32,777	15,542	55,690	15,684	46,170	15,500	14,000	67,135	561,807
1993-4	9,700	16,479	27,232	106,390	29,630	15,767	57,210	16,157	43,500	16,500	12,900	65,220	559,216
1994-5	11,300	8,903	23,122	99,300	30,550	16,480	59,840	15,212	32,100	14,700	13,314	63,167	524,602
1995-6[1]	8,600	16,504	25,037	102,215	30,860	17,760	65,470	17,002	30,100	15,500	14,310	59,400	537,532
1996-7[2]	15,900	23,586	29,801	110,570	35,940	18,920	62,620	16,907	34,900	16,000	16,100	62,191	582,552
1997-8[3]	13,900	19,000	24,300	124,000	34,000	19,900	68,700	17,000	44,200	16,000	15,000	68,761	609,351

[1] Preliminary. [2] Estimate. [3] Forecast. [4] Formerly part of the U.S.S.R.; data not reported separately until 1990-91. *Source: Foreign Agricultural Service, U.S. Department of Agriculture (FAS-USDA)*

World Supply and Demand of Wheat In Millions of Metric Tons/Hectares

Crop Year	Area Harvested	Yield	Production	World Trade	Utilization Total	Ending Stocks	Stocks as % of Utilization
1988-9	217.4	2.28	495.0	104.3	524.3	118.4	22.6
1989-90	225.8	2.36	533.2	103.9	532.7	118.9	22.3
1990-1	231.4	2.54	588.0	101.0	561.5	145.4	25.9
1991-2	222.5	2.44	542.1	110.8	554.7	132.8	23.9
1992-3	223.1	2.52	561.8	112.7	549.9	144.8	26.3
1993-4	222.3	2.52	559.2	100.2	561.9	142.1	25.3
1994-5	215.2	2.44	524.6	98.2	547.7	118.4	21.6
1995-6[1]	219.5	2.45	537.5	95.5	550.5	105.4	19.2
1996-7[2]	230.7	2.52	582.6	97.7	578.2	109.8	19.0
1997-8[3]	229.2	2.66	609.4	98.2	585.7	133.4	22.8

[1] Preliminary. [2] Estimate. [3] Forecast. *Source: Foreign Agricultural Service, U.S. Department of Agriculture (FAS-USDA)*

Salient Statistics of Wheat in the United States

Crop Year	Planting Intentions	Acreage Harvested: Winter	Acreage Harvested: Spring	Acreage Harvested: All	Average - All Yield Per Acre	Value of Production	Foreign Trade[5]: Domestic Exports[2]	Foreign Trade[5]: Imports[3]	Per Capita[4] Consumption: Flour	Per Capita[4] Consumption: Cereal
	1,000 Acres	1,000 Acres	1,000 Acres	1,000 Acres	in Bushels	$1,000	Millions of Bushels	Millions of Bushels	In Pounds	In Pounds
1988-9	65,529	39,800	13,389	53,189	34.1	6,683,999	1,414.9	22.7	130.0	3.8
1989-90	76,615	41,509	20,680	62,189	32.7	7,542,464	1,232.0	22.5	129.6	4.0
1990-1	77,041	49,721	19,382	69,103	39.5	7,184,427	1,069.5	36.4	135.8	4.3
1991-2	69,881	39,506	18,297	57,803	34.3	5,956,642	1,282.3	40.7	136.5	4.5
1992-3	72,219	42,123	20,638	62,761	39.3	7,978,911	1,353.6	70.0	138.3	4.7
1993-4	72,168	43,811	18,901	62,712	38.2	7,647,527	1,227.8	108.9	143.0	5.0
1994-5	70,349	41,335	20,415	61,770	37.6	7,968,237	1,188.3	91.9	144.0	5.1
1995-6	69,132	40,972	19,973	60,945	35.8	9,787,213	1,241.1	67.9	142.0	5.4
1996-7	75,639	39,679	23,248	62,927	36.3	9,814,961	1,001.0	92.3	149.0	
1997-8[1]	70,767	41,813	21,764	63,577	39.7	8,611,684	1,075.0	90.0	148.0	

[1] Preliminary. [2] Includes flour milled from imported wheat. [3] Total wheat, flour & other products. [4] Civilian only. [5] Year beginning June. *Source: Economic Research Service, U.S. Department of Agriculture (ERS-USDA)*

Supply and Distribution of Wheat in the United States In Millions of Bushels

Crop Year Beginning June	Supply: Stocks, June 1: On Farms	Supply: Stocks, June 1: Mills, Elevators[3]	Supply: Stocks, June 1: Total Stocks	Supply: Production	Supply: Imports[4]	Supply: Total Supply	Domestic Disappearance: Food	Domestic Disappearance: Seed	Domestic Disappearance: Feed & Residual[5]	Domestic Disappearance: Total	Exports[4]	Total Disappearance
1988-9	525.0	735.8	1,260.8	1,812.2	22.7	3,096.0	725.8	103.0	150.5	979.2	1,414.9	2,394.0
1989-90	289.0	412.6	701.6	2,036.6	22.5	2,761.0	748.9	104.3	139.1	992.3	1,232.0	2,224.0
1990-1	212.5	324.0	536.5	2,729.8	36.4	3,303.0	789.8	92.9	482.1	1,365.1	1,069.5	2,435.0
1991-2	341.2	524.7	868.1	1,980.1	40.7	2,889.0	789.5	97.7	244.5	1,131.6	1,282.3	2,414.0
1992-3	144.6	327.2	475.0	2,466.8	70.0	3,011.8	834.8	99.1	193.6	1,127.5	1,353.6	2,481.2
1993-4	183.8	345.3	530.7	2,396.4	108.8	3,035.9	871.7	96.3	271.7	1,239.7	1,227.8	2,467.4
1994-5	175.3	393.2	568.5	2,321.0	91.9	2,981.4	852.9	89.2	344.4	1,286.5	1,188.3	2,474.8
1995-6	163.4	343.2	506.6	2,182.6	67.9	2,757.1	883.0	104.1	151.9	1,139.0	1,241.1	2,381.1
1996-7[1]	74.6	301.4	376.0	2,281.8	92.0	2,749.8	892.0	103.0	313.8	1,308.8	1,001.0	2,309.9
1997-8[2]	154.6	289.7	443.6	2,526.6	90.0	3,060.2	910.0	96.0	300.0	1,306.0	1,075.0	2,381.0

[1] Preliminary. [2] Estimate. [3] Also warehouses and all off-farm storage not otherwise disignated, including flour mills. [4] Imports & exports are for wheat, including flour & other products in terms of wheat. [5] Mostly feed use. *Source: Economic Research Service, U.S. Department of Agriculture (ERS-USDA)*

WHEAT

Stocks, Production and Exports of Wheat in the United States, by Class In Millions of Bushels

Year Beginning June	Hard Spring June 1 Stocks	Hard Spring Production	Hard Spring Exports[3]	Durum[2] June 1 Stocks	Durum[2] Production	Durum[2] Exports[3]	Hard Winter June 1 Stocks	Hard Winter Production	Hard Winter Exports[3]	Soft Red Winter June 1 Stocks	Soft Red Winter Production	Soft Red Winter Exports[3]	White June 1 Stocks	White Production	White Exports[3]
1988-9	402	181	194	83	45	20	567	882	639	75	473	315	135	232	247
1989-90	219	433	280	60	92	55	302	711	359	39	549	345	81	251	193
1990-1	155	555	201	50	122	53	215	1,196	369	32	344	230	85	313	216
1991-2	279	431	380	62	104	45	360	901	559	80	325	105	87	219	193
1992-3	131	707	438	55	100	47	194	967	464	41	427	210	54	266	195
1993-4	171	512	266	49	70	54	204	1,066	486	43	401	173	64	347	249
1994-5	201	515	292	28	97	40	227	971	422	45	434	212	67	304	222
1995-6	193	475	330	26	102	39	194	825	384	37	456	250	57	325	238
1996-7	106	631	300	26	116	38	154	762	286	35	422	140	55	355	237
1997-8[1]	166	501	230	31	86	40	143	1,121	385	45	484	195	59	335	225

[1] Preliminary. [2] Includes "Red Durum." [3] Includes flour made from U.S. wheat & shipments to territories. [4] Estimate. *Source: Economic Research Service, U.S. Department of Agriculture (ERS-USDA)*

Seeded Acreage, Yield and Production of Wheat in the United States

Year	Seeded Acreage--1,000 Acres Winter	Other Spring	Durum	All	Yield Per Harvested Acre (Bushels) Winter	Other Spring	Durum	All	Production (1,000,000 Bushels) Winter	Other Spring	Durum	All
1988	48,800	13,393	3,336	65,529	39.2	19.5	15.7	34.1	1,561.9	205.5	44.8	1,812.2
1989	55,091	17,733	3,791	76,615	35.0	28.8	25.1	32.7	1,454.6	489.7	92.2	2,036.6
1990	56,748	16,723	3,570	77,041	40.7	36.7	34.9	39.5	2,024.2	583.1	122.4	2,729.8
1991	51,024	15,604	3,253	69,881	34.7	33.4	32.5	34.3	1,371.6	504.6	104.0	1,980.1
1992	50,922	18,750	2,547	72,219	38.2	41.8	39.7	39.3	1,609.3	757.6	99.9	2,466.8
1993	51,587	18,340	2,241	72,168	40.2	33.7	33.6	38.2	1,760.1	565.8	70.5	2,396.4
1994	49,197	18,329	2,823	70,349	40.2	31.8	35.6	37.6	1,661.9	562.3	96.7	2,321.0
1995	48,726	17,015	3,436	69,177	39.4	30.2	30.5	35.8	1,547.3	535.9	102.3	2,185.5
1996	51,958	20,033	3,630	75,621	37.2	35.1	32.6	36.3	1,477.1	692.0	116.1	2,285.1
1997[1]	48,342	19,397	3,250	70,989	45.0	29.9	27.7	39.7	1,882.6	557.8	86.2	2,526.6

[1] Preliminary. *Source: Economic Research Service, U.S. Department of Agriculture (ERS-USDA)*

Production of Winter Wheat in the United States, by State In Thousands of Bushels

Year	Colorado	Idaho	Illinois	Kansas	Missouri	Montana	Nebraska	Ohio	Oklahoma	Oregon	Texas	Washington	Total
1988	75,900	50,820	67,500	323,000	75,950	39,900	72,000	46,000	172,800	46,860	89,600	108,500	1,561,910
1989	57,200	56,700	105,020	213,600	86,950	54,000	55,350	62,730	153,900	48,900	60,000	68,900	1,454,642
1990	84,150	69,000	91,200	472,000	76,000	87,500	85,500	79,650	201,600	54,600	130,200	138,600	2,024,224
1991	71,300	49,000	44,800	363,000	48,000	76,000	67,200	52,920	135,000	41,600	84,000	40,600	1,371,617
1992	70,500	55,250	62,100	363,800	64,800	65,250	55,500	59,095	168,150	42,900	129,200	102,000	1,609,284
1993	94,350	67,150	68,200	388,500	53,200	102,900	73,500	52,520	156,600	61,060	118,400	162,500	1,760,143
1994	76,500	56,880	50,400	433,200	50,400	64,750	71,400	68,440	143,100	55,680	75,400	124,200	1,661,943
1995	102,600	58,520	68,110	286,000	47,970	54,800	86,100	73,810	109,200	57,750	75,600	133,300	1,544,653
1996	70,400	68,800	41,800	255,200	48,750	63,360	73,500	51,870	93,100	61,200	75,400	164,500	1,477,058
1997[1]	91,200	69,600	70,150	506,000	57,200	56,550	70,300	68,670	178,200	56,280	118,900	144,050	1,882,609

[1] Preliminary. *Source: Crop Reporting Board, U.S. Department of Agriculture (CRB-USDA)*

Official Winter Wheat Crop Production Reports in the United States In Thousands of Bushels

Crop Year	May 1	June 1	July 1	August 1	September 1	Current December	Final
1988-9	1,620,257	1,570,417	1,568,052	1,554,812	1,560,970	1,561,145	1,561,910
1989-90	1,430,148	1,407,898	1,461,924	1,466,049	1,451,746	1,453,842	1,454,642
1990-1	2,091,614	2,089,234	2,035,087	2,054,287	2,036,059	----------	2,030,874
1991-2	1,495,943	1,449,418	1,361,316	1,371,946	1,372,182	----------	1,372,617
1992-3	1,618,017	1,618,017	1,573,901	1,600,931	----------	----------	1,609,284
1993-4	1,807,657	1,824,062	1,821,345	1,788,005	1,788,005	----------	1,760,143
1994-5	1,657,938	1,674,563	1,658,426	1,670,436	1,670,436	----------	1,661,043
1995-6	1,638,211	1,608,396	1,529,950	1,552,230	1,552,230	----------	1,544,653
1996-7	1,363,851	1,369,861	1,484,836	1,494,716	----------	----------	1,477,058
1997-8[1]	1,561,470	1,603,580	1,780,554	1,855,474	----------	----------	1,882,609

[1] Preliminary. *Source: Crop Reporting Board, U.S. Department of Agriculture (CRB-USDA)*

Production of All Spring Wheat in the United States In Thousands of Bushels

	Durum Wheat						Other Spring Wheat							
Year	Arizona	California	Montana	North Dakota	South Dakota	Total Durum	Idaho	Minnesota	Montana	North Dakota	Oregon	South Dakota	Washington	Total Other
1988	4,300	5,605	2,070	31,200	816	44,831	24,700	49,450	18,000	70,500	4,940	15,600	16,120	205,460
1989	7,560	8,715	6,030	66,000	2,880	92,229	34,720	96,900	85,000	174,000	4,935	45,100	41,710	489,747
1990	4,136	5,346	4,465	103,700	3,204	122,171	30,600	134,750	53,900	277,200	3,016	67,200	11,480	583,124
1991	3,705	3,360	5,907	88,350	1,675	103,957	32,660	64,170	81,600	212,350	2,300	49,000	58,000	504,565
1992	3,740	5,115	4,851	81,700	990	99,906	44,840	137,500	79,050	382,200	4,900	85,000	17,640	757,608
1993	4,500	3,800	3,534	57,970	432	70,476	43,200	69,750	99,900	274,350	3,900	54,540	15,080	565,821
1994	8,554	5,605	5,340	76,375	598	96,747	43,400	70,000	100,500	278,775	2,900	51,480	9,800	562,291
1995	8,514	6,800	7,950	77,760	896	102,280	44,800	70,400	133,000	221,400	5,928	33,600	20,470	535,658
1996	14,760	13,800	6,750	79,380	720	115,840	50,400	100,800	106,600	313,500	6,405	83,250	18,170	687,875
1997[1]	8,277	12,350	7,750	60,950	648	90,155	40,880	77,550	121,800	212,500	7,750	69,600	23,585	561,540

[1] Preliminary. *Source: Crop Reporting Board, U.S. Department of Agriculture (CRB-USDA)*

Grindings of Wheat by Mills in the United States In Millions of Bushels (60 Pounds Each)

Year	July	Aug.	Sept.	Oct.	Nov.	Dec.	Jan.	Feb.	Mar.	Apr.	May	June	Total
1988-9	63.6	70.0	66.0	70.0	69.7	63.8	65.0	60.8	60.4	60.7	64.7	59.6	773.3
1989-90	58.5	70.6	63.6	67.4	65.1	58.7	63.4	64.0	66.7	61.6	63.6	60.6	763.8
1990-1	62.3	73.2	65.7	74.9	73.9	64.3	66.7	65.2	63.2	67.6	69.9	60.9	807.8
1991-2	65.3	71.2	67.7	72.2	73.5	65.6	65.7	66.0	65.6	67.3	67.0	67.2	814.3
1992-3	70.0	77.3	71.9	77.9	71.9	65.5	68.1	70.0	76.2	72.0	69.6	67.9	858.2
1993-4	69.2	75.2	74.1	75.8	77.0	76.3	70.0	68.3	81.1	73.0	73.0	70.6	883.8
1994-5	68.9	78.7	76.3	77.9	75.9	71.1	69.0	65.2	76.9	66.6	74.7	71.9	873.1
1995-6	69.8	77.8	74.2	78.4	74.8	70.0	70.1	72.4	72.1	69.4	72.6	67.7	869.1
1996-7	73.6	77.4	75.1	82.7	73.7	71.3	69.6	66.9	70.3	73.2	72.5	72.2	878.6
1997-8[1]	76.4	75.8	78.4	82.7	75.3	74.8							926.9

[1] Preliminary. *Source: Bureau of the Census, U.S. Department of Commerce*

Wheat Stocks in the United States In Millions of Bushels

	On Farms				Off Farms				Total Stocks			
Year	Mar. 1	June 1	Sept. 1	Dec. 1	Mar. 1	June 1	Sept. 1	Dec. 1	Mar. 1	June 1	Sept. 1	Dec. 1
1988	748.0	525.0	798.0	620.0	1,175.5	735.8	1,455.6	1,095.9	1,923.5	1,260.8	2,253.6	1,715.9
1989	463.0	289.0	832.0	592.0	764.7	412.6	1,086.0	830.5	1,227.7	701.6	1,918.0	1,422.5
1990	376.0	212.5	1,000.0	763.2	567.1	324.0	1,409.5	1,144.8	943.1	536.5	2,409.5	1,909.5
1991	532.9	341.2	828.0	564.8	863.3	524.7	1,212.7	877.3	1,396.3	865.9	2,040.7	1,442.1
1992	275.6	144.6	979.4	672.0	611.7	327.2	1,128.2	918.5	887.2	471.9	2,107.6	1,590.5
1993	378.0	183.8	987.0	653.1	670.3	346.8	1,145.6	932.6	1,048.3	530.7	2,132.6	1,585.7
1994	363.2	175.3	859.8	575.6	664.8	393.2	1,209.7	920.6	1,028.0	568.5	2,069.5	1,491.1
1995	335.3	163.4	743.6	477.0	633.8	343.2	1,137.5	861.3	969.1	506.6	1,881.1	1,338.3
1996	220.6	74.6	824.5	584.2	602.9	301.4	899.7	634.7	823.5	376.0	1,724.2	1,218.8
1997[1]	320.8	154.6	794.4	604.0	501.1	289.0	1,282.0	1,010.9	821.8	443.6	2,076.3	1,614.9

[1] Preliminary. *Source: Crop Reporting Board, U.S. Department of Agriculture (CRB-USDA)*

Wheat Supply and Distribution in Canada, Australia and Argentina In Millions of Metric Tons

	Canada (Year Beginning Aug. 1)					Australia (Year Beginning Oct. 1)					Argentina (Year Beginning Dec. 1)				
	Supply			Disappearance		Supply			Disappearance		Supply			Disappearance	
Crop Year	Stocks Aug. 1	New Crop	Total Supply	Domestic	Exports[3]	Stocks Oct. 1	New Crop	Total Supply	Domestic	Exports[3]	Stocks Dec. 1	New Crop	Total Supply	Domestic	Exports[3]
1988-9	7.3	15.9	23.2	5.8	12.4	2.8	14.1	16.8	2.9	11.3	.8	8.4	9.2	4.7	4.0
1989-90	5.0	24.8	29.8	6.5	16.9	2.6	14.2	16.8	3.0	10.8	.5	10.2	10.7	4.5	6.1
1990-1	6.4	32.1	38.5	6.5	20.5	3.0	15.1	18.1	3.5	11.7	0	10.9	10.9	4.5	4.8
1991-2	10.3	31.9	42.3	7.8	24.5	2.8	10.6	13.4	3.4	7.1	.8	9.9	10.7	4.6	5.8
1992-3	10.1	29.9	40.1	8.1	19.7	2.9	16.2	19.1	4.2	9.9	.3	9.8	10.1	4.3	5.9
1993-4	12.2	27.2	39.4	9.3	19.1	5.0	16.5	21.5	4.1	13.7	0	9.7	9.7	4.3	5.0
1994-5	11.1	23.1	34.2	7.8	20.9	3.7	8.9	12.7	3.9	6.3	.4	11.3	11.7	4.3	7.3
1995-6	5.7	25.0	30.7	7.8	16.3	2.4	16.5	18.9	3.7	13.3	.2	8.6	8.8	4.2	4.5
1996-7[1]	6.7	29.8	36.5	8.2	19.5	2.0	23.6	25.6	4.8	18.7	.2	15.9	16.1	4.8	10.5
1997-8[2]	9.1	24.3	33.4	8.5	19.0	2.1	19.0	21.1	4.9	14.0	.8	13.9	14.7	4.8	9.4

[1] Preliminary. [2] Forecast. [3] Including flour. *Source: Foreign Agricultural Service, U.S. Department of Agriculture (FAS-USDA)*

WHEAT

Quarterly Supply and Disappearance of Wheat in the United States In Millions of Bushels

Crop Year Beginning June 1	Supply				Disappearance: Domestic Use						Ending Stocks		
	Beginning Stocks	Production	Imports[3]	Total Supply	Food	Seed	Feed & Residual[7]	Total	Exports[3]	Total Disappearance	Gov't Owned[4]	Privately Owned[5]	Total Stocks
1987-8	1,821.0	2,107.7	16.1	3,944.7	720.7	85.0	290.2	1,095.9	1,587.9	2,683.8	283.0	977.8	1,260.8
June-Aug.	1,821.0	2,107.7	2.7	3,931.3	181.0	1.0	363.8	545.8	409.0	954.8	798.8	2,189.7	2,976.5
Sept.-Nov.	2,977.0	--------	4.5	2,981.0	193.0	58.0	-79.1	171.9	308.5	480.4	755.4	1,750.5	2,500.6
Dec.-Feb.	2,501.0	--------	3.7	2,504.3	172.1	3.0	-7.3	167.8	413.0	580.8	450.1	1,473.4	1,923.5
Mar.-May	1,924.0	--------	5.1	1,928.7	174.6	23.0	12.8	210.4	547.4	757.8	283.0	977.8	1,260.8
1988-9	1,261.0	1,812.2	22.6	3,095.7	725.8	103.0	150.5	979.3	1,414.9	2,394.2	190.5	511.1	701.6
June-Aug.	1,261.0	1,812.2	8.6	3,081.6	183.3	1.0	282.2	466.5	361.6	828.1	250.0	2,003.6	2,253.6
Sept.-Nov.	2,254.0	--------	6.3	2,259.8	197.3	67.0	-49.4	214.9	329.0	543.9	213.0	1,502.9	1,715.9
Dec.-Feb.	1,716.0	--------	3.7	1,719.6	173.4	3.0	-44.5	131.9	360.0	491.9	203.2	1,024.5	1,227.7
Mar.-May	1,228.0	--------	4.1	1,231.9	171.8	32.0	-37.8	166.0	364.2	530.2	190.5	511.1	701.6
1989-90	701.6	2,036.6	23.4	2,760.7	748.9	104.3	139.1	992.3	1,232.0	2,224.3	116.6	419.9	536.5
June-Aug.	701.6	2,036.6	5.9	2,744.1	190.7	1.7	264.9	457.3	368.7	826.0	167.9	1,750.1	1,918.0
Sept.-Nov.	1,918.0	--------	7.1	1,925.1	191.7	70.3	-87.8	174.2	328.6	502.8	154.5	1,268.0	1,422.5
Dec.-Feb.	1,423.0	--------	4.7	1,427.1	184.3	2.7	37.4	224.4	259.6	484.0	136.5	806.6	943.1
Mar.-May	943.1	--------	5.8	947.9	182.2	29.6	-75.4	136.4	275.1	411.5	116.6	419.9	536.5
1990-1	536.5	2,729.8	36.4	3,302.6	789.8	92.9	482.4	1,365.1	1,069.5	2,434.6	162.7	705.4	868.1
June-Aug.	536.5	2,729.8	8.0	3,274.2	194.1	1.7	399.7	595.5	267.7	863.2	104.6	2,306.5	2,411.1
Sept.-Nov.	2,409.5	--------	13.4	2,424.5	210.6	62.9	-38.3	235.2	279.4	514.6	129.9	1,780.0	1,909.9
Dec.-Feb.	1,908.0	--------	7.8	1,917.7	191.0	2.1	101.5	294.6	225.5	520.1	152.5	1,245.2	1,397.7
Mar.-May	1,396.0	--------	7.2	1,404.9	194.1	26.3	19.5	239.9	296.9	536.8	162.7	705.4	868.1
1991-2	868.1	1,980.1	40.7	2,889.0	789.5	97.2	244.5	1,131.2	1,282.3	2,413.5	152.0	323.0	475.0
June-Aug.	868.1	1,980.1	7.8	2,856.1	189.4	1.2	359.1	549.7	251.7	801.4	162.8	1,891.9	2,054.7
Sept.-Nov.	2,054.7	--------	7.3	2,062.0	213.0	62.2	-26.9	248.3	365.9	614.2	160.7	1,287.1	1,447.8
Dec.-Feb.	1,447.8	--------	10.7	1,458.5	192.9	2.4	-.5	194.8	371.7	566.5	156.9	735.1	892.0
Mar.-May	892.0	--------	14.9	906.9	194.2	31.9	-87.3	138.8	293.0	431.8	152.0	323.0	475.0
1992-3	475.0	2,466.8	70.0	3,011.8	834.3	99.1	194.2	1,127.6	1,353.6	2,481.2	150.0	380.7	530.7
June-Aug.	475.0	2,466.8	20.1	2,962.0	212.1	1.4	345.3	558.8	282.6	841.4	151.6	1,969.0	2,120.6
Sept.-Nov.	2,120.6	--------	16.4	2,137.0	218.8	63.4	-81.9	200.3	345.0	545.3	151.1	1,440.6	1,591.7
Dec.-Feb.	1,591.7	--------	17.4	1,609.1	196.7	2.6	5.2	204.5	356.3	560.8	150.4	897.9	1,048.3
Mar.-May	1,048.3	--------	16.1	1,064.4	206.7	31.7	-74.4	164.0	369.7	533.7	150.0	380.7	530.7
1993-4	530.7	2,396.4	108.8	3,035.9	871.7	96.3	271.7	1,239.7	1,227.8	2,467.4	150.3	418.2	568.5
June-Aug.	530.7	2,396.4	14.6	2,941.7	211.3	1.3	295.8	508.4	300.7	809.1	149.9	1,982.7	2,132.6
Sept.-Nov.	2,132.6	--------	30.1	2,162.7	225.3	60.9	-38.5	247.7	329.2	577.0	150.3	1,435.4	1,585.7
Dec.-Feb.	1,585.7	--------	26.9	1,612.6	211.0	2.3	39.0	252.3	332.3	584.6	150.4	877.6	1,028.0
Mar.-May	1,028.0	--------	37.2	1,065.2	224.1	31.8	-24.7	231.2	265.5	496.7	150.3	418.2	568.5
1994-5	568.5	2,321.0	92.0	2,981.4	852.5	89.2	344.9	1,286.6	1,188.3	2,474.9	142.1	364.5	506.6
June-Aug.	568.5	2,321.0	30.7	2,920.2	213.2	1.6	376.3	591.1	259.6	850.7	146.4	1,923.1	2,069.5
Sept.-Nov.	2,069.5	--------	21.4	2,090.9	229.3	61.1	-28.8	261.6	338.2	599.8	142.8	1,348.3	1,491.1
Dec.-Feb.	1,491.1	--------	17.7	1,508.8	201.5	2.2	25.6	229.3	310.4	539.7	142.3	826.8	969.1
Mar.-May	969.1	--------	22.2	991.2	208.5	24.3	-28.2	204.6	280.1	484.7	142.1	364.5	506.6
1995-6	506.6	2,182.6	67.9	2,757.1	882.9	104.1	153.0	1,139.9	1,241.1	2,381.1	118.2	257.8	376.0
June-Aug.	506.6	2,182.6	22.7	2,711.9	215.3	8.0	305.0	528.3	302.5	830.8	141.5	1,739.6	1,881.1
Sept.-Nov.	1,881.1	--------	16.3	1,897.4	232.2	64.9	-98.7	198.3	360.8	559.1	141.2	1,197.1	1,338.3
Dec.-Feb.	1,338.3	--------	11.8	1,350.0	215.8	3.0	13.3	232.1	294.5	526.6	137.5	686.0	823.5
Mar.-May	823.5	--------	17.2	840.7	219.6	28.2	-66.5	181.3	283.4	464.6	118.2	257.8	376.0
1996-7[1]	376.0	2,285.1	92.4	2,753.5	891.4	103.1	314.0	1,308.5	1,001.4	2,309.9	93.0	350.6	443.6
June-Aug.	376.0	2,285.1	14.9	2,676.0	223.7	8.8	385.3	617.8	334.1	951.9	109.5	1,614.7	1,724.2
Sept.-Nov.	1,724.2	--------	20.7	1,744.9	233.8	60.4	-76.4	217.8	308.3	526.1	96.1	1,122.7	1,218.8
Dec.-Feb.	1,218.8	--------	27.1	1,245.9	213.1	1.8	29.9	244.8	179.3	424.1	95.3	726.5	821.8
Mar.-May	821.8	--------	29.7	851.6	220.8	32.1	-24.8	228.1	179.8	407.9	93.0	350.6	443.6
1997-8[2]	443.6	2,526.6	91.0	3,060.2	936.6	123.0	573.8	1,633.4	1,075.0	2,708.4	93.0	581.2	674.2
June-Aug.	443.6	2,526.6	22.7	2,992.9	228.8	3.1	396.6	628.5	288.1	916.6	93.2	1,983.1	2,076.3
Sept.-Nov.	2,076.3	--------	22.8	2,099.1	239.5	58.4	-109.7	188.2	296.0	484.2	93.1	1,521.8	1,614.9

[1] Preliminary. [2] Forecast. [3] Imports & exports include flour and other products expressed in wheat equivalent. [4] Uncommitted, Government only. [5] Includes total loans. [6] Includes alcoholic beverages. *Source: Economic Research Service, U.S. Department of Agriculture (ERS-USDA)*

Wheat Government Loan Program Data in the United States Loan Rates (Cents Per Bushel)

Crop Year Beginning June	National Average[3]	Target Rate	Farm Loan Prices: Corn Belt (Soft Red Winter)	Central & Southern Plains (Hard Winter)	Northern Plains (Spring & Durum)	Pacific Northwest (White)	Placed Under Loan	% of Production	Acquired by CCC Under Program	Total Stocks	Total CCC Stocks	Stocks Ending May 31 — Outstanding: CCC Loans	Farmer-Owned Reserve	"Free"
							Millions of Bushels							
1989-90	206	410	214	204	206	217	113	5.6	62	536	117	30	144	245
1990-1	195	400	200	194	195	206	405	14.8	90	868	163	217	14	474
1991-2	204	400	209	200	204	214	143	7.2	1	475	152	20	50	273
1992-3	221	400	232	220	221	237	240	9.8	.1	531	150	47	28	353
1993-4	245	400	251	243	245	269	258	14.7	.3	569	150	67	6	413
1994-5	258	400	253	257	258	271	231	10.0	0	507	142	64	0	365
1995-6	258	400	254	258	258	276	114	5.2	0	376	118	13	0	258
1996-7[1]	258	NA	253	257	258	271	194	8.1	0	444	93	72	0	351
1997-8[2]	258	NA					248		0	674	93	50	0	578

[1] Preliminary. [2] Estimate. [3] The national average loan rate at the farm as a percentage of the parity-priced wheat at the beginning of the marketing year. NA = Not avaliable. *Source: Agricultural Marketing Service, U.S. Department of Agriculture (AMS-USDA)*

Exports of Wheat (Only)[2] from the United States In Thousands of Bushels

Year	June	July	Aug.	Sept.	Oct.	Nov.	Dec.	Jan.	Feb.	Mar.	Apr.	May	Total
1989-90	90,490	137,933	131,176	150,697	89,336	68,664	81,813	78,343	87,647	104,903	84,576	71,572	1,177,152
1990-1	88,235	80,831	93,617	107,786	84,488	76,800	56,444	66,473	91,313	112,809	88,526	81,760	1,029,072
1991-2	59,167	79,319	97,794	94,991	124,155	136,385	112,771	132,413	115,126	103,024	116,850	59,764	1,231,759
1992-3	75,045	96,382	99,290	92,723	132,232	108,235	111,389	111,584	118,607	118,782	126,845	104,540	1,295,653
1993-4	85,874	103,836	100,516	104,732	100,618	112,667	121,900	109,389	87,250	96,873	71,575	82,838	1,178,068
1994-5	73,364	66,314	103,941	117,555	101,450	107,549	104,139	93,735	97,478	98,876	85,251	75,006	1,124,658
1995-6	78,355	88,649	119,797	131,424	117,679	105,535	99,175	96,085	91,876	108,800	90,373	78,303	1,206,051
1996-7	73,715	108,437	145,840	125,910	98,302	75,245	50,979	63,431	59,039	55,936	69,821	47,640	974,295
1997-8[1]	65,654	92,465	123,141	119,029	89,331								1,175,088

[1] Preliminary.. [2] Grains. *Source: Economic Research Service, U.S. Department of Agriculture (ERS-USDA)*

United States Wheat and Flour Imports and Exports In Thousands of Bushels

Crop Year Beginning June	Imports — Wheat: Suitable for Milling	Unfit for Human Con-sumption	Grain	Flour & Products[2]	Total	Exports: P.L. 480	Foreign Donations Sec. 416	Aid[3]	Total con-cessional	CCC Export Credit	Export Enhance-ment Program	Total U.S. Wheat Exports
			Wheat Equivalent			In Thousands of Metric Tons						
1988-9	15,870	NA	15,870	6,798	22,668	3,020	137	806	3,963	8,897	17,906	37,660
1989-90	13,548	NA	12,583	9,884	22,467	2,985	0	28	3,065	7,759	12,806	28,064
1990-1	25,540	NA	25,574	10,832	36,407	2,975	0	0	3,159	8,339	15,150	26,792
1991-2	30,924	NA	31,019	9,675	40,694	2,286	0	0	2,416	13,334	21,111	34,322
1992-3	56,859	NA	56,859	13,142	70,001	2,043	890	0	4,001	8,538	21,806	36,081
1993-4	91,287	NA	91,288	11,086	108,860	2,801	0	0	3,527	5,874	18,157	31,145
1994-5	70,561	NA	70,562	21,386	91,946	1,491	0	NA	1,948	4,202	18,073	32,088
1995-6[1]	47,753	NA	47,754	20,179	67,933	1,530	0	NA	1,530	5,581	570	33,708

[1] Preliminary. [2] Includes macaroni, semolina & similar products. [3] Shipments mostly under the Commodity Import Program, financed with foreign aid funds. NA = Not available. *Source: Economic Research Service, U.S. Department of Agriculture (ERS-USDA)*

Comparative Average Cash Wheat Prices In Dollars Per Bushel

Crop Year Beginning June	Received by U.S. Farmers	No. 2 Soft Red Winter Chicago	No. 1 Hard Red Ordinary Protein Kansas City	No. 2 Soft Red Winter St. Louis	Minneapolis: No. 1 Dark Northern Spring 14%	No. 1 Hard Amber Durum	No. 1 Soft White Portland Oregon	No. 2 Western White Pacific N.W.	No. 2 Soft White Toledo	Export Prices[2] (U.S. $ per Metric Ton): Austr-ralian Standard Wheat	Canada Vancouver No. 1 CWRS 13 1/2 %	Argentina F.O.B. B.A.	U.S. Gulf No. 2 H.W.	Rotter-dam C.I.F. U.S. No. 2 Hard Winter
1989-90	3.72	3.92	4.22	3.94	4.16	4.25	4.28	3.88	3.80	176	202	151	171	190
1990-1	2.61	2.74	2.94	2.81	3.06	3.48	3.16	2.75	2.59	144	158	107	137	164
1991-2	3.00	3.49	3.77	3.32	3.82	3.61	4.11	3.66	3.41	137	141	99	129	154
1992-3	3.24	3.49	3.67	3.54	3.91	3.88	4.11	3.69	3.18	165	177	122	152	173
1993-4	3.26	3.20	3.60	3.23	5.02	5.76	3.53	3.12	3.16	154	192	131	141	200
1994-5	3.45	3.62	3.97	3.62	4.26	5.98	4.16	3.75	3.37	162	199	NA	150	210
1995-6	4.55	4.78	5.49	4.82	5.72	7.03	5.27	4.74	4.41	198	204	178	177	221
1996-7	4.30	NQ	4.88	4.10	4.97	5.59	4.54	4.26	3.71	237	230	218	207	235
1997-8[1]	3.45	NQ	3.83	3.53	4.38	6.26	3.99			NA	181	157	160	166

[1] Preliminary. [2] Calendar year. NA = Not available. *Source: Economic Research Service, U.S. Department of Agriculture (ERS-USDA)*

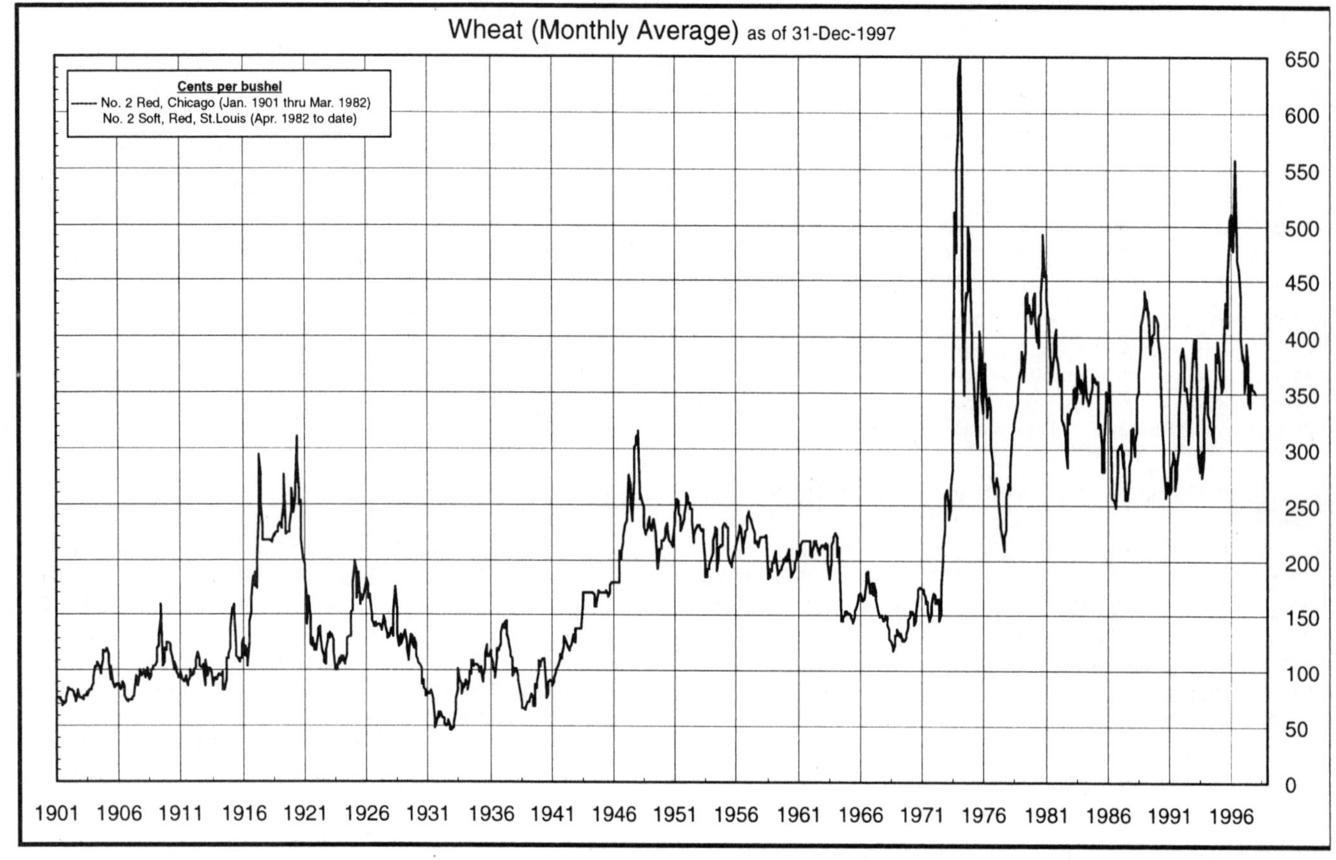

Average Price of No. 2 Soft Red Winter (30 Days) Wheat at Chicago In Dollars Per Bushel

Year	June	July	Aug.	Sept.	Oct.	Nov.	Dec.	Jan.	Feb.	Mar.	Apr.	May	Average
1988-9	3.56	3.52	3.61	3.84	4.07	4.09	4.25	4.39	4.30	4.31	4.04	4.07	4.00
1989-90	3.87	3.92	3.94	3.93	4.07	4.07	4.13	4.03	3.92	3.61	3.83	3.71	3.92
1990-1	3.26	3.04	2.83	2.62	2.62	2.41	2.52	2.50	2.53	2.76	2.80	2.83	2.73
1991-2	2.86	2.79	2.97	3.24	3.50	3.57	3.79	4.12	4.15	3.71	3.53	3.68	3.49
1992-3	3.60	3.39	3.09	3.24	3.39	3.60	3.59	3.77	3.67	3.58	3.72	3.19	3.49
1993-4	2.82	3.03	3.12	2.99	3.02	3.29	3.53	3.67	3.48	3.20	3.15	3.15	3.20
1994-5	3.21	3.14	3.34	3.63	3.97	3.85	3.99	3.88	3.74	3.49	3.51	3.64	3.62
1995-6	3.94	NQ	4.26	4.55	NQ	4.97	5.13	5.02	NQ	NQ	NQ	5.59	4.78
1996-7	4.91	4.64	4.71	4.61	NQ	NQ	NQ	NQ	NQ	NQ	NQ	NQ	4.72
1997-8[1]	NQ	NQ	NQ	NQ	NQ	NQ	NQ	NQ					

NQ = Not quoted. *Source: Economic Research Service, U.S. Department of Agriculture (ERS-USDA)*

Average Price[1] Received by Farmers for Wheat in the United States In Cents Per Bushel

Year	June	July	Aug.	Sept.	Oct.	Nov.	Dec.	Jan.	Feb.	Mar.	Apr.	May	Average[2]
1988-9	3.37	3.50	3.61	3.74	3.84	3.88	3.94	4.02	4.03	4.07	4.03	4.01	3.72
1989-90	3.85	3.78	3.74	3.72	3.75	3.72	3.79	3.71	3.56	3.48	3.49	3.40	3.72
1990-1	3.08	2.79	2.58	2.46	2.43	2.39	2.40	2.42	2.42	2.53	2.60	2.65	2.61
1991-2	2.55	2.50	2.63	2.80	3.07	3.25	3.44	3.54	3.78	3.72	3.65	3.64	3.00
1992-3	3.43	3.15	3.01	3.20	3.21	3.29	3.31	3.37	3.33	3.30	3.26	3.11	3.24
1993-4	2.84	2.85	2.96	3.10	3.25	3.47	3.63	3.58	3.60	3.70	3.56	3.43	3.26
1994-5	3.21	3.04	3.25	3.57	3.76	3.75	3.74	3.69	3.61	3.52	3.48	3.66	3.45
1995-6	3.84	4.10	4.26	4.53	4.72	4.81	4.88	4.83	4.98	5.07	5.32	5.73	4.55
1996-7	5.25	4.73	4.58	4.37	4.18	4.14	4.06	4.03	3.88	3.93	4.11	4.09	4.28
1997-8[2]	3.52	3.23	3.56	3.67	3.55	3.50	3.40						3.49

[1] Weighted average by sales. [2] Includes an allownace for unredeemed loans at average loan value. *Source: Economic Research Service, U.S. Department of Agriculture (ERS-USDA)*

Average Price of No. 1 Hard Red Winter (Ordinary Protein) Wheat in Kansas City In Dollars Per Bushel

Year	June	July	Aug.	Sept.	Oct.	Nov.	Dec.	Jan.	Feb.	Mar.	Apr.	May	Average
1988-9	3.79	3.77	3.78	4.03	4.13	4.18	4.25	4.40	4.37	4.32	4.46	4.55	4.17
1989-90	4.44	4.28	4.24	4.18	4.28	4.36	4.39	4.30	4.13	4.04	4.13	3.91	4.22
1990-1	3.60	3.11	2.89	2.82	2.81	2.78	2.78	2.71	2.77	2.94	2.98	3.04	2.94
1991-2	2.99	2.91	3.10	3.31	3.64	3.76	4.06	4.66	4.51	4.33	4.02	3.90	3.77
1992-3	3.91	3.52	3.27	3.56	3.60	3.78	3.81	3.97	3.75	3.74	3.59	3.51	3.67
1993-4	3.33	3.38	3.34	3.37	3.52	3.39	4.15	4.00	3.80	3.64	3.63	3.65	3.60
1994-5	3.60	3.48	3.70	4.05	4.31	4.24	4.27	4.06	3.98	3.87	3.86	4.22	3.97
1995-6	4.72	4.98	4.76	5.00	5.28	5.34	5.51	5.40	5.67	5.63	6.60	7.02	5.49
1996-7	6.12	5.34	5.01	4.70	4.76	4.78	4.70	4.61	4.52	4.58	4.78	4.61	4.88
1997-8[1]	4.08	3.57	3.84	3.86	3.88	3.87	3.72						3.83

Source: Economic Research Service, U.S. Department of Agriculture (ERS-USDA)

Average Price of No. 1 Dark Northern Spring (14% Protein) Wheat in Minneapolis In Dollars Per Bushel

Year	June	July	Aug.	Sept.	Oct.	Nov.	Dec.	Jan.	Feb.	Mar.	Apr.	May	Average
1988-9	4.32	4.23	4.24	4.32	4.33	4.22	4.26	4.44	4.40	4.56	4.47	4.55	4.36
1989-90	4.41	4.36	4.18	4.08	4.14	4.12	4.23	4.21	4.06	3.96	4.08	4.09	4.16
1990-1	3.96	3.56	3.05	2.84	2.85	2.80	2.82	2.83	2.85	3.00	3.07	3.10	3.06
1991-2	3.04	2.94	3.10	3.21	3.68	3.78	4.11	4.36	4.56	4.36	4.28	4.44	3.82
1992-3	4.42	4.04	3.65	3.79	3.85	3.94	3.88	4.05	3.87	3.87	3.80	3.71	3.91
1993-4	3.96	4.80	4.88	4.90	5.17	5.50	5.45	5.32	5.29	4.94	4.99	5.05	5.02
1994-5	4.20	4.14	4.00	4.27	4.40	4.41	4.37	4.21	4.09	4.11	4.30	4.61	4.26
1995-6	4.89	5.52	5.06	5.27	5.52	5.63	5.80	5.62	5.82	5.81	6.53	7.14	5.72
1996-7	6.73	6.04	5.29	4.63	4.69	4.64	4.51	4.62	4.45	4.62	4.78	4.58	4.97
1997-8[1]	4.44	4.36	4.49	4.36	4.35	4.42	4.27						4.38

Source: Economic Research Service, U.S. Department of Agriculture (ERS-USDA)

Average Wheat Farm Prices for Leading Classes in the United States In Dollars Per Bushel

Year	June	July	Aug.	Sept.	Oct.	Nov.	Dec.	Jan.	Feb.	Mar.	Apr.	May	Average
						Winter Wheat							
1989-90	3.84	3.80	3.74	3.74	3.77	3.79	3.84	3.82	3.58	3.50	3.55	3.31	3.69
1990-1	3.02	2.75	2.53	2.45	2.40	2.34	2.37	2.36	2.37	2.52	2.56	2.62	2.52
1991-2[2]	2.58	2.54	2.69	2.87	3.16	3.29	3.49	3.63	3.93	3.84	3.67	3.47	3.26
1992-3	3.36	3.13	2.99	3.24	3.30	3.31	3.41	3.47	3.39	3.32	3.20	3.03	3.26
1993-4	2.72	2.76	2.83	2.88	3.00	3.21	3.43	3.41	3.36	3.26	3.24	3.17	3.11
1994-5	3.09	2.99	3.23	3.57	3.79	3.76	3.75	3.67	3.61	3.47	3.45	3.65	3.50
1995-6	3.77	4.05	4.22	4.47	4.70	4.78	4.88	4.80	5.01	5.06	5.39	5.81	4.75
1996-7	5.14	4.67	4.52	4.28	4.07	4.05	4.04	4.02	3.90	3.98	4.14	4.14	4.25
1997-8[1]	3.42	3.16	3.39	3.47	3.42	3.31	3.25						3.35
						Durum Wheat							
1989-90	3.83	3.65	3.48	3.25	3.31	3.27	3.36	3.33	3.31	3.34	3.44	3.50	3.46
1990-1	3.36	3.11	2.53	2.39	2.44	2.44	2.47	2.61	2.55	2.62	2.61	2.61	2.63
1991-2	2.55	2.44	2.24	2.36	2.62	2.68	2.75	2.98	3.34	3.24	3.33	3.40	2.82
1992-3	3.31	3.03	2.75	2.96	2.92	3.04	3.00	3.00	3.08	3.09	3.10	3.26	3.05
1993-4	3.18	3.26	3.43	3.92	4.23	4.91	4.92	4.97	5.36	5.71	5.70	4.93	4.54
1994-5	4.59	4.32	4.30	4.51	4.89	4.88	4.67	4.61	4.68	4.61	4.48	4.82	4.61
1995-6	5.20	5.29	5.33	5.87	5.80	5.78	5.75	5.66	5.72	5.73	5.63	5.62	5.62
1996-7	5.58	5.13	5.03	4.69	4.78	4.56	4.59	4.47	4.31	4.32	4.40	4.50	4.70
1997-8[1]	4.21	4.61	5.23	5.35	5.09	5.25	5.00						4.96
						Other Spring Wheat							
1989-90	3.89	3.81	3.68	3.59	3.59	3.58	3.60	3.58	3.51	3.47	3.49	3.49	3.61
1990-1	3.33	2.96	2.58	2.46	2.44	2.40	2.43	2.45	2.44	2.52	2.60	2.65	2.61
1991-2	2.57	2.49	2.56	2.76	3.03	3.26	3.44	3.56	3.83	3.79	3.82	3.86	3.25
1992-3	3.87	3.63	3.12	3.19	3.18	3.28	3.24	3.33	3.34	3.32	3.34	3.19	3.34
1993-4	3.21	3.50	3.51	3.37	3.50	3.67	3.75	3.69	3.68	3.64	3.68	3.63	3.57
1994-5	3.51	3.28	3.19	3.38	3.52	3.51	3.56	3.50	3.40	3.38	3.34	3.53	3.43
1995-6	3.78	4.26	4.19	4.27	4.45	4.61	4.72	4.66	4.81	4.88	5.21	5.67	4.63
1996-7	5.48	5.30	4.63	4.41	4.23	4.11	4.01	3.95	3.80	3.83	4.04	3.94	4.31
1997-8[1]	3.74	3.66	3.75	3.64	3.49	3.55	3.45						3.61

[1] Preliminary. [2] Data thru 1991-2 are for Central and So. Plains (hard red winter). *Source: Agricultural Statistics Board, U.S. Department of Agriculture (ASB-USDA)*

WHEAT

Average Open Interest of Wheat Futures in Chicago In Contracts

Year	Jan.	Feb.	Mar.	Apr.	May	June	July	Aug.	Sept.	Oct.	Nov.	Dec.
1988	38,565	41,864	41,307	43,402	41,909	56,624	56,742	56,024	68,415	74,535	69,791	62,696
1989	66,904	63,154	64,669	61,729	60,391	69,898	67,118	65,463	61,511	52,246	52,023	54,117
1990	54,225	56,395	56,984	51,548	56,624	63,819	64,576	59,792	57,237	58,231	55,850	47,061
1991	48,597	51,520	55,922	53,668	53,030	58,997	54,946	52,283	55,220	61,257	57,679	51,845
1992	61,484	70,152	58,957	53,706	50,978	50,340	60,116	62,071	50,093	54,564	57,693	49,263
1993	50,329	47,858	44,885	48,354	51,353	55,829	58,705	64,335	58,603	61,496	62,877	50,523
1994	53,912	48,013	45,110	47,430	44,552	54,622	57,151	65,388	73,200	78,419	70,815	67,150
1995	66,715	67,768	55,973	55,612	67,875	90,208	101,351	90,800	91,505	103,987	102,475	99,422
1996	102,718	104,807	91,378	98,260	93,378	81,211	69,222	66,128	65,561	65,639	60,810	58,533
1997	63,388	71,304	76,747	85,516	84,721	83,675	92,815	105,320	104,587	108,480	101,089	90,386

Source: Chicago Board of Trade (CBT) *Note: The CBT changed the open interest figures from Bushels to Contract in January 1998.*

Volume of Trading of Wheat Futures in Chicago In Contracts

Year	Jan.	Feb.	Mar.	Apr.	May	June	July	Aug.	Sept.	Oct.	Nov.	Dec.	Total
1988	186,874	222,409	193,294	218,822	283,097	459,291	353,707	286,262	308,171	328,275	300,859	236,677	3,377,738
1989	283,879	255,584	326,201	244,321	281,159	347,012	333,646	287,543	233,465	243,185	209,931	191,783	3,237,709
1990	211,769	197,397	209,873	251,823	346,922	296,337	297,182	298,383	197,304	201,589	231,845	135,846	2,876,270
1991	198,340	182,158	291,762	268,560	234,880	391,134	286,097	271,625	187,232	300,628	271,927	262,501	3,146,844
1992	366,736	460,354	318,810	236,063	290,148	303,044	304,217	283,379	250,003	220,502	257,017	188,541	3,498,814
1993	246,125	237,936	277,632	217,898	173,607	268,206	366,414	266,893	202,308	256,329	310,464	195,817	3,019,629
1994	288,321	211,703	187,617	244,544	300,324	370,135	272,492	330,758	343,548	398,041	354,975	318,173	3,620,631
1995	353,603	302,950	316,330	279,099	345,455	598,762	507,876	527,716	436,145	472,794	454,352	359,985	4,955,067
1996	628,340	510,138	455,981	660,722	531,979	512,883	452,690	345,626	305,448	362,047	359,005	261,108	5,385,967
1997	312,680	373,411	368,547	567,099	422,935	469,158	470,992	493,225	401,277	405,978	432,621	340,722	5,058,645

Source: Chicago Board of Trade (CBT) *Note: The CBT changed the volume figures from Bushels to Contract in January 1998.*

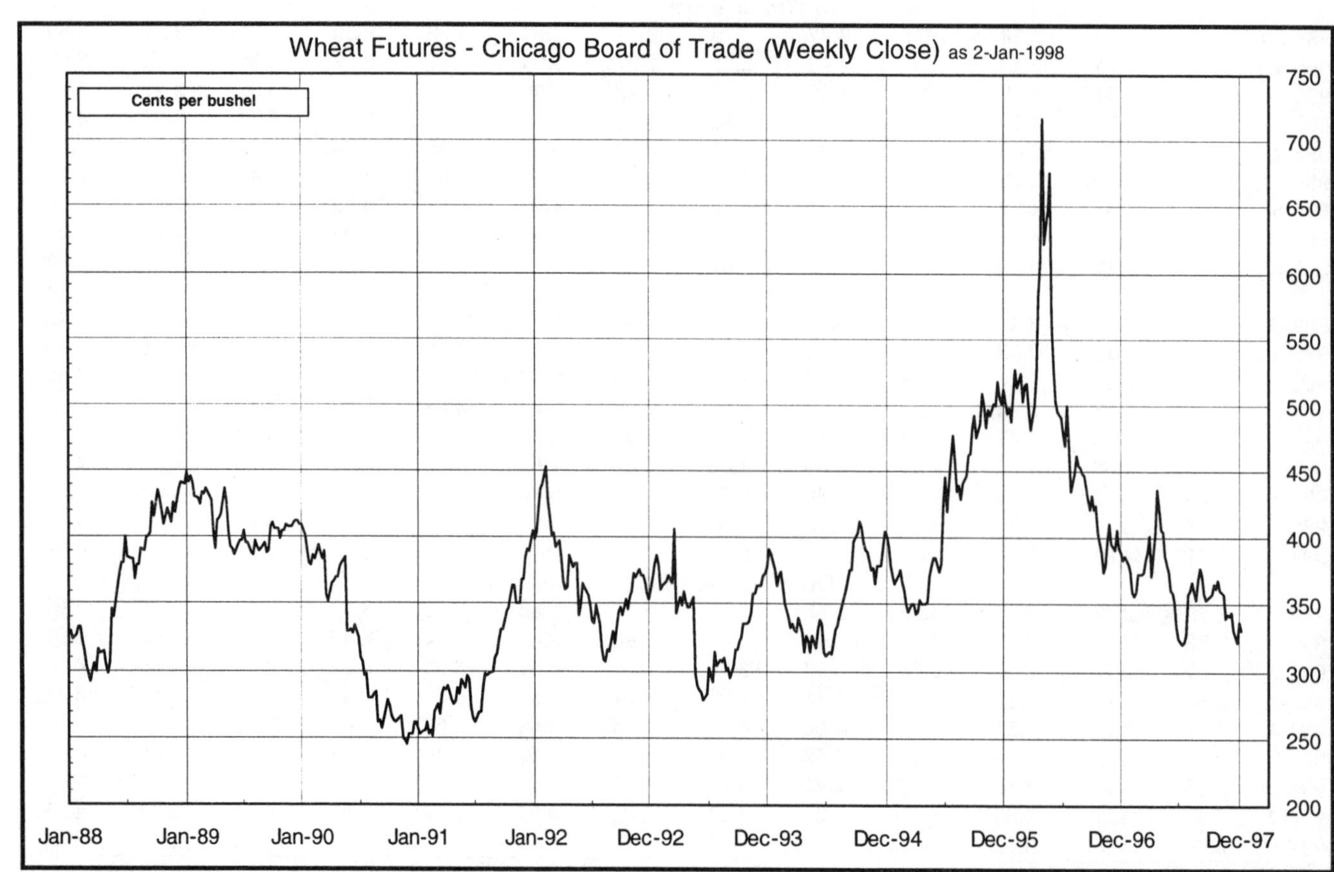

Commercial Stocks of Domestic Wheat[1] in the United States, on First of Month In Millions of Bushels

Year	July	Aug.	Sept.	Oct.	Nov.	Dec.	Jan.	Feb.	Mar.	Apr.	May	June
1988-9	291.6	334.2	342.4	340.8	331.1	297.2	293.7	266.5	213.3	181.1	150.1	114.4
1989-90	130.5	171.6	211.7	211.8	196.0	180.2	164.2	150.4	127.9	109.7	87.2	77.8
1990-1	121.8	212.7	289.7	290.2	284.6	264.8	243.7	237.7	------	------	174.5	174.5
1991-2	244.8	275.5	296.9	308.2	271.0	264.8	249.8	227.0	205.2	180.7	170.9	209.1
1992-3	269.6	290.5	202.5	228.2	231.9	202.7	185.5	169.5	153.3	132.6	112.9	87.0
1993-4	102.9	145.1	171.8	194.9	199.3	174.9	169.5	168.3	162.2	143.8	127.3	111.3
1994-5	145.7	203.9	243.0	269.7	268.6	238.2	199.5	181.0	162.5	150.2	108.7	91.8
1995-6	92.3	161.7	201.1	234.3	228.3	200.2	178.7	170.8	156.6	137.7	107.6	87.2
1996-7	86.3	112.9	128.0	145.3	117.2	94.9	89.0	80.4	77.0	75.6	68.1	64.6
1997-8	80.1	186.3	235.2	268.1	258.1	231.4	196.8	178.1	170.6			

[1] Domestic wheat in storage in public and private elevators in 39 markets and wheat afloat in vessels or barges at lake and seaboard ports, the first Saturday of the month. *Source: Livestock Division, U.S. Department of Agriculture (LD-USDA)*

Stocks of Wheat Flour Held by Mills in the United States In Thousands of Sacks (100 Pounds Each)

Year	Jan. 1	April 1	July 1	Oct. 1	Year	Jan. 1	April 1	July 1	Oct. 1
1986	4,847	4,740	5,141	5,101	1992	5,660	5,210	5,841	5,864
1987	5,228	4,900	5,581	5,258	1993	5,487	4,863	6,197	5,882
1988	5,858	4,508	4,822	5,303	1994	5,611	5,904	5,834	6,020
1989	4,800	4,423	5,116	5,489	1995	7,060	6,496	6,312	6,582
1990	5,207	5,072	5,818	7,980	1996	6,869	6,927	6,400	6,350
1991	8,051	5,474	8,115	6,336	1997[1]	6,671	6,442	6,303	6,822

[1] Preliminary. *Source: Bureau of the Census, U.S. Department of Commerce*

Average Producer Price Index of Wheat Flour (Spring[1]) June 1983 = 100

Year	Jan.	Feb.	Mar.	Apr.	May	June	July	Aug.	Sept.	Oct.	Nov.	Dec.	Average
1988	91.2	94.4	90.6	93.5	93.9	107.0	107.0	107.7	110.0	110.5	109.0	109.1	102.0
1989	110.7	110.0	112.4	109.5	112.0	112.7	112.1	110.7	109.5	108.5	108.7	109.6	110.5
1990	109.4	109.0	106.9	108.8	107.9	106.0	99.7	93.4	92.0	91.2	89.4	89.8	100.3
1991	88.7	90.2	92.0	93.0	94.0	93.7	91.3	94.1	96.3	100.1	97.5	102.7	94.5
1992	109.7	116.4	111.5	110.3	109.2	111.0	104.9	99.6	104.1	104.4	104.7	103.5	107.4
1993	107.5	108.1	107.2	108.4	105.2	104.7	103.7	107.2	102.1	107.3	108.4	112.5	106.9
1994	111.8	110.5	108.9	107.9	109.4	106.4	100.8	101.2	109.1	112.0	110.9	111.4	108.4
1995	110.7	108.5	107.9	109.8	113.5	118.6	127.4	126.7	129.5	132.6	132.3	133.5	120.9
1996	130.4	138.0	136.6	137.6	160.1	146.8	138.0	127.0	121.5	125.7	121.7	121.4	133.7
1997[2]	119.4	119.3	116.6	121.8	120.8	117.4	112.1	113.5	115.1	112.6	112.0	110.6	115.9

[1] Standard patent. [2] Preliminary. *Source: Bureau of Labor Statistics, U.S. Department of Commerce (0212-0301)*

World Wheat Flour Production (Monthly Average) In Thousands of Metric Tons

Year	Australia	France	Germany	Hungary	India	Japan	Kazakhstan	Rep. of Korea	Mexico	Poland	Russia	Turkey	United Kingdom
1988	105.5	433.6	282.0	98.0	363.3	372.1	159.1	141.0	198.6	236.3	NA	111.2	333.0
1989	109.0	435.6	280.0	102.2	391.3	381.8	164.0	134.5	207.0	241.1	NA	136.4	333.0
1990	114.9	442.7	218.1	102.4	394.3	387.7	163.5	134.7	209.4	150.6	NA	112.9	323.0
1991	112.7	464.8	341.1	97.7	398.0	389.8	167.8	130.4	207.3	128.6	NA	111.1	320.0
1992	113.9	465.2	327.0	106.9	400.0	389.0	161.0	129.4	223.3	167.1	449.5	112.2	320.0
1993	116.3	480.6	336.4	75.0	399.4	399.3	155.3	129.5	214.0	113.4	449.5	122.1	331.0
1994	116.9	470.8	378.8	62.9	400.0	387.2	157.0	132.6	219.8	150.5	348.0	104.9	337.0
1995	112.6	473.1	382.3	84.0	400.0	389.3	131.0	139.9	210.7	156.9	274.6	119.7	341.0
1996[1]	123.8	-----	394.2	75.1	400.0	389.6	105.5	141.2	215.9	108.5	309.7	119.3	353.5
1997[2]	-----	-----	398.6	77.0	403.8	382.5	98.5	142.6	211.2	115.9	339.8	160.2	351.5

[1] Preliminary. [2] Estimate. NA = Not available. *Source: United Nations*

Production of Wheat Flour in the United States In Millions of Sacks (100 Pounds Each)

Year	July	Aug.	Sept.	Oct.	Nov.	Dec.	Jan.	Feb.	Mar.	Apr.	May	June	Total
1989-90	26.6	32.3	29.8	31.8	30.0	27.8	27.9	28.0	29.2	27.0	27.6	26.7	354.3
1990-1	27.7	33.7	29.9	32.2	32.7	29.1	29.4	29.5	29.5	29.4	29.2	29.1	362.3
1991-2	29.2	31.8	30.1	32.2	32.7	29.2	29.3	29.3	29.4	30.0	29.8	29.8	363.0
1992-3	31.1	34.2	31.9	34.6	32.2	29.2	30.6	31.3	34.1	32.0	31.0	30.3	382.4
1993-4	30.7	33.3	32.9	33.5	34.0	33.8	30.9	30.2	35.9	32.3	32.2	31.1	390.8
1994-5	30.5	34.9	34.2	35.0	33.7	31.7	30.9	29.4	34.5	29.9	33.5	32.3	390.4
1995-6	31.0	34.5	33.0	35.1	33.4	31.2	31.6	32.3	32.2	31.2	33.2	30.6	389.3
1996-7	33.9	35.6	34.6	37.5	33.1	32.0	31.3	30.0	31.8	33.1	32.6	32.5	397.9
1997-8[1]	34.0	34.3	35.1	37.2	33.8	33.5							207.9

[1] Preliminary. *Source: Bureau of the Census, U.S. Department of Commerce*

United States Wheat Flour Exports (Grain Equivalent[2]) In Thousands of Bushels

Year	June	July	Aug.	Sept.	Oct.	Nov.	Dec.	Jan.	Feb.	Mar.	Apr.	May	Total
1989-90	907	1,897	5,775	8,917	3,579	6,817	3,606	4,943	3,124	4,466	6,132	3,287	53,450
1990-1	1,035	2,207	2,785	1,464	3,303	3,407	4,480	2,698	3,809	6,301	3,719	3,525	38,733
1991-2	5,582	5,362	4,207	3,743	1,179	2,222	3,140	2,549	5,549	4,630	3,771	4,579	46,513
1992-3	3,257	5,284	2,856	2,325	3,840	4,641	3,903	2,325	7,744	5,832	7,499	5,285	54,791
1993-4	4,408	3,793	1,811	3,642	3,840	3,416	3,170	5,838	4,390	6,099	4,198	3,368	47,973
1994-5	2,922	6,824	5,636	3,407	3,105	4,721	4,734	2,805	7,085	7,617	6,945	6,005	61,806
1995-6	2,822	5,018	7,520	2,249	2,080	1,221	3,458	808	2,537	1,230	2,415	1,830	33,188
1996-7	2,005	2,008	1,669	3,133	2,496	2,748	2,240	1,344	1,897	2,490	1,253	2,086	25,369
1997-8[1]	1,731	2,849	1,621	3,101	2,518								28,368

[1] Preliminary. [2] Includes meal, groats and durum. *Source: Economic Research Service, U.S. Department of Agriculture (ERS-USDA)*

Supply and Distribution of Wheat Flour in the United States

Year	Wheat Ground 1,000 Bu.	Milfeed Production 1,000 Tons	Flour Production[3]	Flour & Product Imports[2]	Total Supply	Exports: Flour	Exports: Products[2]	Domestic Disappearance	Total Population July 1 Millions	Per Capita Disappearance Pounds
			1,000 Cwt.							
1989	761,021	6,072	342,762	3,337	346,099	25,265	180	320,654	247.3	130
1990	788,186	6,109	354,348	3,623	357,971	18,872	273	338,826	249.9	136
1991	808,966	6,436	362,311	4,070	366,381	20,044	440	345,897	252.6	137
1992	833,339	6,707	370,829	5,037	375,866	20,711	619	354,536	255.4	139
1993	871,408	6,963	387,419	6,233	393,652	23,241	548	369,863	258.1	143
1994	884,707	7,186	392,519	9,048	401,567	24,234	733	376,599	260.7	144
1995	869,296	7,144	388,689	9,306	397,995	24,343	716	372,936	263.0	142
1996	878,070	7,042	397,776	8,847	406,623	11,003	714	394,906	265.6	149
1997[1]	888,257	7,143	399,198	9,190	408,388	11,229	1,095	396,064	267.8	148

[1] Preliminary. [2] Import and exports of macaroni and noodle products (flour equivalent), reporting methods changed in 1990. [3] Commercial production of wheat flour, whole wheat, industrial and durum flour and farina reported by Bureau of the Census. *Source: Economic Research Service, U.S. Department of Agriculture (ERS-USDA)*

Wheat and Flour -- Price Relationship at Milling Centers in the United States In Dollars

Crop Year (June-May)	At Kansas City: Cost of Wheat to Produce 100 lb. Flour[1]	Wholesale Price of: Bakery Flour 100 lb. Flour[2]	Wholesale Price of: By-Products Obtained 100 lb. Flour[3]	Total Products: Actual	Total Products: Over Cost of Wheat	At Minneapolis: Cost of Wheat to Produce 100 lb. Flour[1]	Wholesale Price of: Bakery Flour 100 lb. Flour[2]	Wholesale Price of: By-Products Obtained 100 lb. Flour[3]	Total Products: Actual	Total Products: Over Cost of Wheat
1989-90	9.58	10.41	1.45	11.86	2.28	9.48	10.00	1.36	11.36	1.89
1990-1	6.86	7.78	1.29	9.07	2.21	6.98	7.73	1.21	8.94	1.96
1991-2	8.58	9.53	1.26	10.79	2.21	8.71	9.39	1.16	10.55	1.84
1992-3	8.53	9.65	1.28	10.93	2.40	8.91	10.12	1.15	11.27	2.37
1993-4	10.03	10.34	1.46	11.79	1.77	11.45	12.50	1.28	13.77	2.33
1994-5	9.25	10.50	1.21	11.71	2.46	9.71	11.01	1.04	12.05	2.34
1995-6	12.97	13.35	1.93	15.28	2.31	13.04	13.03	1.68	14.71	1.67
1996-7	11.22	11.89	1.92	13.81	2.60	11.32	11.68	1.87	13.54	2.22
1997-8 I	9.20	10.42	1.20	11.62	2.42	10.10	10.98	1.28	12.27	2.17
II	9.31	10.00	1.66	11.66	2.35	9.98	10.50	1.50	12.00	2.02
Dec.[4]	9.14	9.70	1.69	11.39	2.24	9.74	10.30	1.52	11.82	2.09
Jan.[4]	8.66	9.50	1.75	11.25	2.59	9.39	10.15	1.47	11.62	2.22

[1] Based on 73% extraction rate, cost of 2.28 bushels: at Kansas City, No. 1 hard winter, 13 % protein; and at Minneapolis, No. 1 dark northern spring, 14% protein. [2] Quoted as mid-month bakers' standard patent at Kansas City and spring standard patent at Minneapolis, bulk basis. [3] Assumed 50-50 millfeed distribution between bran and shorts or middlings, bulk basis. *Source: Agricultural Marketing Service, U.S. Department of Agriculture (AMS-USDA)*

Wool

The ten-year contraction in world wool production continued in 1997/98 with output of 5.4 billion pounds (greasy) vs. 5.5 billion in 1996/97, the equivalent of 3.18 billion pounds of clean wool vs. 3.27 billion. World consumption in 1996/1997 of 3.1 billion pounds (clean) compares with 3.26 billion in 1995/96. The decline largely reflected a steady contraction in world sheep numbers, to about one billion head in 1996/97 from an average of over 1.1 billion head in the early 1990's. However, the contraction has slowed during the past few years due largely to China whose sheep flock was the world's largest at 140 million head in 1996/97 vs. 127 million in 1995/96. This lifted China's 1997/98 production to 351 million pounds (clean) from 337 million in 1996/97. In Australia, still the world largest wool producer, sheep numbers totaled 123 million head in 1996/97, down from 163 million in 1990/91, at which time production (clean) totaled 1,541 million pounds vs. only 942 million in 1997/98. New Zealand is the world's second largest producer at 439 million pounds in 1997/98 vs. 448 million in 1996/97. The former Soviet Union has seen a steady slide in both production and inventory; 1997/98 production of 183 million pounds compares with 220 million in 1996/97 and 540 million in 1990/91. The sheep inventory fell to 64 million head in 1996/97 from 135 million in 1990/91.

Wool production in the U.S. totaled a record low 52.4 million pounds (greasy) in 1997 vs. 56.7 million in 1996. The U.S. sheep inventory on January 1, 1997, of a record low 5.9 million head, compares with 6.2 million a year ago.

World wool exports in 1996/97 (greasy) of 2.6 billion pounds were unchanged from 1995/96. As usual, Australia exported about half the total, 1.3 billion pounds, and New Zealand about 0.4 billion pounds. Importing nations are numerous; China has been number one since 1993/94, followed by Japan, the U.K., Italy and France. U.S. imports fell to a record low 75 million pounds in 1996/97 from 89 million in 1995/96. Australian wool accounts for most U.S. imports.

Global wool prices are a function of origin and grade; South African wool prices were almost four times higher than Australian prices in 1996/97, while the latter were moderately higher than New Zealand's prices.

The total 1997 U.S. clean wool supply of 151 million pounds compares with 172 million in 1996. 1997 mill use and exports of 115 million pounds compares with 129 million in 1996. Yearend 1997 stocks of 35.6 million pounds compare with 42.6 million. The 1996 U.S. farm price for shorn wool, greasy, of $.70 per pound compares with $1.04 in 1995. The 1996 U.S. average price for Australian grade 64 wool of $2.34 per pound compares with $2.81 in 1995.

Futures Markets

Wool futures are traded on the Sydney Futures Exchange (SFE), the Nagoya Textile Exchange, the Osaka Textile Exchange, the Tokyo Commodity Exchange (TOCOM), and the New Zealand Futures & Options Exchange Ltd. (NZFOE).

World Production of Wool In Metric Tons-Degreased

Year	Argentina	Australia	China	Kazak-hstan[3]	New Zealand	Pakistan	Romania	Russia[3]	South Africa	United Kingdom	United States	Uruguay	World Total
1989	87,600	622,000	120,111	-----	302,800	34,800	20,900	284,400	46,500	52,765	21,665	60,000	2,011,693
1990	85,800	724,000	122,400	64,750	233,000	28,200	26,500	136,050	49,500	53,358	21,140	58,100	2,029,209
1991	75,400	699,000	123,000	62,640	227,000	28,900	19,196	122,700	51,000	51,055	20,830	56,500	1,953,339
1992	74,200	574,000	121,500	63,000	221,000	29,600	16,800	107,400	48,500	50,876	19,980	50,700	1,780,613
1993	58,000	557,000	122,000	56,800	193,000	30,300	15,600	95,000	45,000	48,329	18,520	49,410	1,688,806
1994	48,000	570,000	130,000	55,000	214,000	31,000	17,000	73,000	40,000	47,000	16,000	50,000	1,693,000
1995[1]	44,000	540,000	141,000	54,000	213,000	32,000	16,000	56,000	35,000	47,000	15,000	48,000	1,641,000
1996[2]	39,000	540,000	141,000	54,000	196,000	32,000	16,000	56,000	35,000	47,000	14,000	44,000	1,614,000

[1] Preliminary. [2] Estimate. [3] Formerly part of the U.S.S.R.; data not reported separately until 1990. *Source: Food and Agriculture Organization of the*

Production of Wool Goods[1] in the United States In Millions of Yards

Year	First Quarter	Second Quarter	Third Quarter	Fourth Quarter	Total Year	Year	First Quarter	Second Quarter	Third Quarter	Fourth Quarter	Total Year
1988	50.6	53.0	43.0	43.9	190.5	1993	48.4	48.9	43.9	42.8	184.0
1989	48.3	50.9	40.1	37.0	176.3	1994	49.1	51.1	39.4	39.0	178.6
1990	38.0	38.7	32.6	31.4	140.7	1995	46.8	45.9	35.2	34.3	162.2
1991	38.0	48.7	41.4	41.5	169.6	1996	44.8	43.6	30.8	32.8	152.0
1992	45.7	47.2	43.9	39.5	176.3	1997[2]	42.7	49.6	42.3	40.3	174.9

[1] Woolen and worsted woven goods, except woven felts. [2] Preliminary. *Source: Bureau of the Census, U.S. Department of Commerce*

Consumption of Apparel Wool in the United States In Millions of Pounds--Clean Basis

Year	First Quarter	Second Quarter	Third Quarter	Fourth Quarter	Total Year	Year	First Quarter	Second Quarter	Third Quarter	Fourth Quarter	Total Year
1988	30.9	30.1	27.4	28.7	117.1	1993	35.5	35.9	35.5	34.4	141.4
1989	35.4	31.0	29.8	26.3	120.5	1994	36.3	35.6	32.7	34.0	138.6
1990	31.5	31.7	26.9	30.5	120.6	1995	36.3	35.5	29.4	28.1	129.3
1991	31.6	37.1	34.6	33.9	137.2	1996	33.6	30.8	23.5	23.1	111.0
1992	36.4	35.1	33.6	31.1	136.1	1997[2]	27.5	28.2	25.5	27.2	108.4

[1] Preliminary. *Source: Bureau of the Census, U.S. Department of Commerce*

WOOL

Salient Statistics of Wool in the United States

Year	Sheep & Lambs Shorn[4] 1,000	Weight per Fleece Lbs.	Shorn Wool Production 1,000 Lbs	Price per Lb.	Value of Production 1,000 $	--- Shorn Wool --- Support	Payment Rate	Total Wool Production	Raw Wool (Clean Content): Domestic Production	Exports Domestic Wool	Dutiable Imports for Consump.[3] 48s&Finer	Total New Supply[2]	Duty Free Imports (Not Finer than 46's)	-- Mill Consumption -- Apparel	Carpet
						----- ¢ Per Lb. -----		---------- Thousands of Pounds ----------							
1988	11,531	7.76	89,482	138.0	124,993	178	40.0	89,482	47,246	1,247	72,324	142,740	24,417	117,069	15,633
1989	11,314	7.89	89,220	124.0	110,537	177	53.0	89,220	47,108	1,188	77,003	152,860	29,889	120,534	14,122
1990	11,222	7.84	88,033	80.0	69,534	182	102.0	88,033	46,481	2,736	50,328	115,461	21,355	120,622	12,124
1991	11,009	7.97	87,740	55.0	47,178	188	133.0	87,740	46,327	3,867	68,242	128,916	18,166	137,187	14,352
1992	10,521	7.88	82,943	74.0	60,162	197	123.0	82,819	43,728	3,413	65,457	129,599	23,802	136,143	14,695
1993	9,976	7.77	77,535	51.0	39,077	204	153.0	77,319	40,824	2,529	76,001	138,606	21,876	141,380	15,431
1994	8,882	7.73	68,643	78.0	52,419	209	131.0	68,577	36,500	2,900	64,889	122,880	24,645	138,563	14,739
1995	8,108	7.81	63,303	104.0	64,124	212	108.0	63,303	33,424	6,042	63,781	128,286	25,039	129,299	12,667
1996[1]	7,300	7.80	56,700	70.0					30,000	5,700	54,063		20,971	110,986	12,311

[1] Preliminary. [2] Production minus exports plus imports; stocks not taken into consideration. [3] Appearal wool includes all dutiable wool; carpet wool includes all duty-free wool. [4] Includes sheep shorn at commercial feeding yards. *Source: Economic Research Service, U.S. Department of Agriculture (ERS-USDA)*

Shorn Wool Prices

Year	U.S. Farm Price Shorn Wool Greasy Basis[1] ¢ per Lb.	Australian Offering Price, Clean[2]: Grade 70's Type 61	Grade 64's Type 63	Grade 64/70's Type 62	Grade 60/62's Type 64A	Grade 58's-56's 433-34	Market Indicator[3] Cents/Kg.	Graded Territory Shorn Wool, Clean Basis[4]: 64's Staple 2 3/4" & up	60's Staple 3" & up	58's Staple 3 1/4" & up	56's Staple 3 1/4" & up	54's Staple 3 1/2" & up
		---- Dollars per Pound ----						---- Dollars per Pound ----				
1988	138.0	7.43	4.77	4.16	3.62	3.08	1,003	3.47	2.78	2.39	2.08	1.90
1989	124.0	5.82	4.21	3.86	3.44	2.81	990	3.14	2.61	2.06	2.04	1.91
1990	80.0	4.76	3.60	3.26	2.87	2.46	870	2.06	1.66	1.45	1.30	1.18
1991	55.0	3.56	2.32	2.02	1.87	1.68	627	1.58	1.31	1.14	1.03	.93
1992	74.0	2.58	2.32	2.17	2.10	1.94	557	1.81	1.61	1.47	1.35	1.23
1993	51.0	2.08	1.70	1.84	1.49	1.44	488	1.37	1.13	1.05	.99	.94
1994	78.0	3.72	2.43	3.01	1.96	1.86	547	2.12	1.50	1.26	1.27	1.21
1995	104.0	3.22	2.81	3.01	2.49	2.33	888	2.49	1.93	1.77	1.63	1.53
1996	70.0	2.81	2.34	2.54	1.96	1.84	619	1.93	1.54	1.43	1.31	1.22

[1] Annual weighted average. [2] F.O.B. Australian Wool Corporation South Carolina warehouse in bond. [3] Index of prices of all wool sold in Australia for the crop year July-June. [4] Wool principally produced in Texas and Rocky Mountain States. *Source: Economic Research Service, U.S. Department of Agriculture*

Average Wool Prices[1]--Australian--64's, Type 62, Duty Paid--U.S. Mills In Cents Per Pound

Year	Jan.	Feb.	Mar.	Apr.	May	June	July	Aug.	Sept.	Oct.	Nov.	Dec.	Average
1988	391	468	496	564	564	513	489	467	461	488	472	475	487
1989	511	484	454	429	414	403	405	410	414	417	417	420	431
1990	417	404	403	414	406	342	338	352	355	343	332	332	370
1991	334	335	209	221	271	286	NA	248	229	215	274	270	242
1992	259	270	277	264	268	246	NA	224	210	192	195	193	236
1993	186	176	170	158	179	169	167	154	153	171	175	176	170
1994	204	216	205	223	249	258	243	248	259	256	273	297	244
1995	281	297	302	302	307	308	292	284	266	236	242	237	280
1996	240	237	238	234	242	245	236	234	228	220	225	232	234
1997	234	261	254	261	279	287	NA	270	262	250	245	240	258

[1] Raw, clean basis. NA = Not available. *Source: Economic Research Service, U.S. Department of Agriculture (ERS-USDA)*

Average Wool Prices--Domestic[1]--Graded Territory, 64's, Staple 2 3/4 & Up--U.S. Mills In Cents Per Pound

Year	Jan.	Feb.	Mar.	Apr.	May	June	July	Aug.	Sept.	Oct.	Nov.	Dec.	Average
1988	315	397	435	453	463	460	450	450	450	463	475	450	438
1989	450	438	410	375	375	365	350	350	350	350	333	300	370
1990	294	287	287	284	275	257	242	235	235	235	225	220	256
1991	217	210	163	167	203	230	230	167	156	148	148	155	158
1992	163	203	195	196	199	218	210	188	210	193	168	168	193
1993	158	148	132	127	135	140	138	140	130	129	133	133	124
1994	140	150	170	201	226	230	230	235	250	238	238	252	213
1995	245	252	265	288	295	285	261	250	235	185	208	192	247
1996	188	192	197	197	195	192	192	192	192	192	190	190	192
1997	190	190	208	228	248	255	255	255	255	255	260	260	238

[1] Raw, shorn, clean basis. *Source: Economic Research Service, U.S. Department of Agriculture (ERS-USDA)*

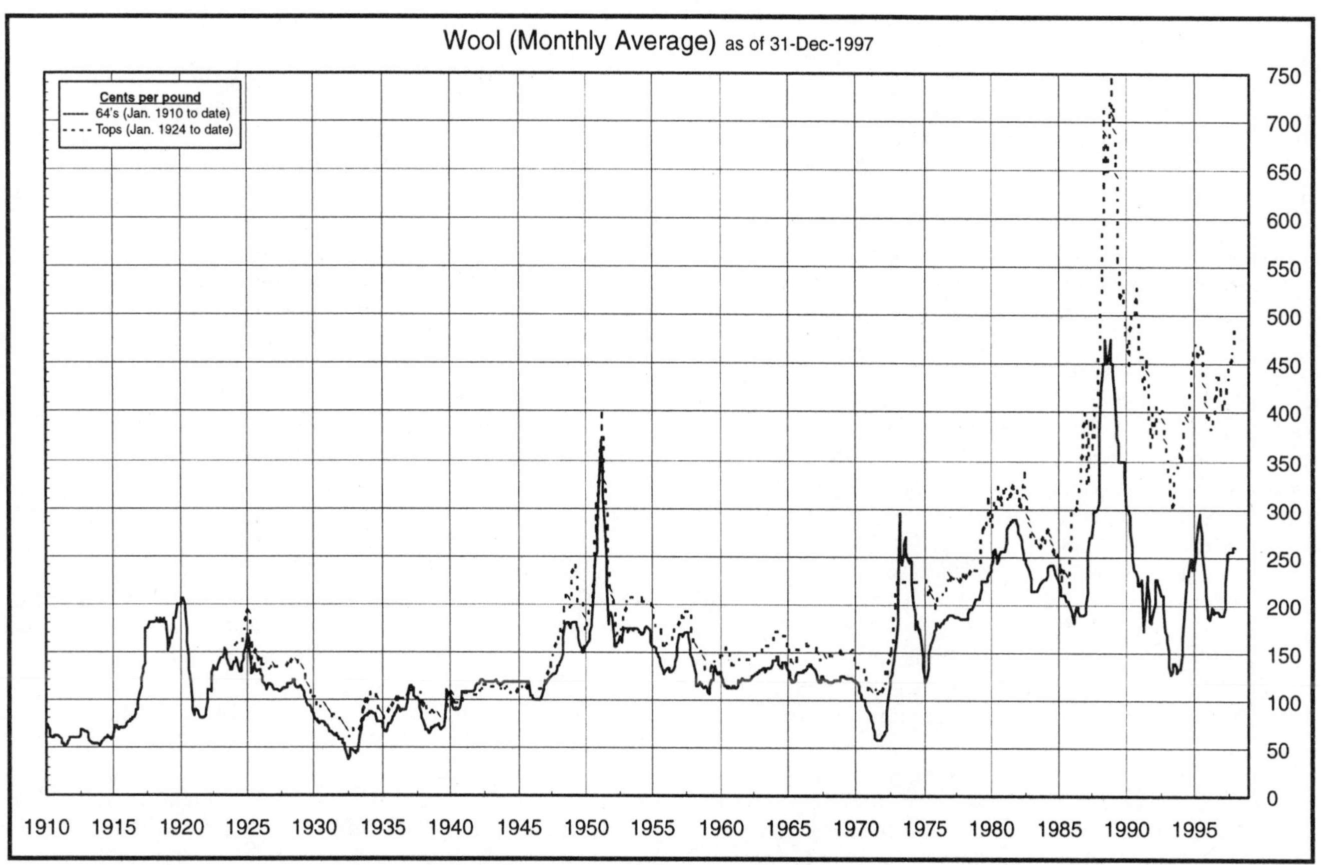

Wool: Mill Consumption, by Grades in the United States, Scoured Basis In Thousands of Pounds

	Apparel Wool[1]							
	Woolen System			Worsted System				
Year	60's & Finer	Coarser Than 60's	Total	60's & Finer	Coarser Than 60's	Total	All Total	Carpet Wool[2]
1987	32,401	28,613	61,014	53,814	14,849	68,663	129,677	13,092
1988	23,769	20,876	44,645	54,553	17,871	72,424	117,069	15,633
1989	24,123	21,803	45,935	56,065	18,534	74,599	120,534	14,122
1990	26,173	24,941	51,114	50,630	18,878	69,508	120,622	12,124
1991	31,961	26,599	58,560	56,521	22,106	78,627	137,187	14,352
1992	33,878	25,600	59,478	58,495	18,170	76,665	136,143	14,695
1993	40,895	26,624	67,519	58,834	15,027	73,861	141,380	15,431
1994	35,960	26,038	61,998	59,599	16,966	76,565	138,563	14,739
1995[3]	30,211	27,089	57,300	54,980	17,019	71,999	129,299	12,667
1996[4]	29,163	22,014	51,177	46,057	13,752	59,809	110,986	12,311

[1] Domestic & duty-paid foreign. [2] Duty-free foreign. [3] Preliminary. [4] Estimate. *Source: Economic Research Service, U.S. Department of Agriculture*

United States Imports[1] of Unmanufactured Wool (Clean Yield) In Millions of Pounds

Year	Jan.	Feb.	Mar.	Apr.	May	June	July	Aug.	Sept.	Oct.	Nov.	Dec.	Total
1988	12.0	12.7	8.8	9.1	8.6	7.4	7.7	5.0	3.3	6.7	8.6	6.7	96.7
1989	8.7	11.3	9.0	13.1	10.3	8.3	10.0	6.9	3.9	10.4	5.1	9.8	106.9
1990	7.3	9.2	4.7	8.2	5.0	4.8	3.4	5.5	5.0	6.9	7.5	4.2	71.7
1991	10.7	6.9	5.4	5.5	7.3	8.1	9.2	7.0	4.4	7.8	5.1	9.0	86.5
1992	10.2	8.1	7.3	10.6	8.8	6.2	6.9	5.0	3.9	5.5	9.1	7.8	89.3
1993	7.8	8.7	8.5	9.3	11.0	9.6	9.7	8.7	5.7	7.7	7.2	8.4	100.3
1994	10.0	7.7	7.7	12.7	7.5	7.7	6.9	6.5	4.1	5.7	8.1	7.0	91.7
1995	10.4	7.7	10.8	6.0	11.5	5.2	7.3	7.3	4.9	7.9	7.7	4.1	90.6
1996	9.6	9.1	8.8	5.6	7.0	5.9	5.3	6.6	3.1	4.6	4.6	5.1	75.3
1997[2]	5.1	5.8	6.1	6.6	5.8	4.2	4.9	4.2	4.8	8.5	7.3	8.6	71.9

[1] Data are imports for consumption. [2] Preliminary. *Source: Economic Research Service, U.S. Department of Agriculture (ERS-USDA)*

Zinc

Zinc is utilized as a protective coating for other metals, such as iron and steel, in a process known as galvanizing. Zinc also finds use as an alloy with copper to make brass and as an alloying compound with aluminum and magnesium.

The U.S. Geological Survey reported that despite numerous mine closings, world mine production of zinc increased in 1996 to an estimated 7.44 million metric tonnes, up almost 3 percent from the 1995 total of 7.24 million tonnes. In 1994, world mine production of zinc was 7.0 million tonnes. In 1996, the largest producer of zinc was Canada with 1.24 million tonnes. The next largest producer was Australia with 1996 zinc production of 1.07 million tonnes. After Australia, the next largest producer was China with 1.01 million tonnes. Other major producers include Peru with 1996 output of 760,563 tonnes; the United States with 628,000 tonnes; Mexico with 377,599 tonnes, and Kazakstan with 225,000 tonnes.

World smelter production of zinc in 1996 was 7.53 million tonnes, down less than one percent from 1995. Of the 1996 total, primary smelter production was 4.11 million tonnes or 55 percent, with secondary smelter production of 349,000 tonnes or 5 percent, and undifferentiated smelter production of 3.08 million tonnes or 40 percent.

The largest producer of zinc by smelter in 1996 was China with 1.12 million tonnes. Next was Canada with 715,553 tonnes and Japan at 642,200 tonnes. Australian smelter production of zinc in 1996 was 331,000 tonnes.

U.S. mine production of zinc content of concentrate in July 1997 was 47,200 tonnes. In the January-July 1997 period, U.S. mine production was 340,000 tonnes, down seven percent from the comparable period of 1996. For all of 1996, mine production of zinc was 628,000 tonnes.

U.S. mine production of zinc, recoverable zinc, in July 1997 was 45,100 tonnes. That was up from 44,600 tonnes in June 1997 but well below the July 1996 total of 53,800 tonnes. In the January-July 1997 period, zinc production was 325,000 tonnes, down from 351,000 tonnes in the comparable period of 1996. For all of 1996, U.S. mine production of zinc, recoverable zinc, was 600,000 tonnes.

U.S. smelter production of zinc in July 1997 was 32,500 tonnes, refined zinc. That compared with 31,600 tonnes in June 1997, and 30,800 tonnes in July 1996. In the January-July 1997 period, U.S. smelter production of zinc was 223,000 tonnes compared to 213,000 tonnes in the same period of 1996.

U.S. production of zinc oxide in July 1997 was 14,500 tonnes, gross weight, the same total as in June 1997. In July 1997, zinc oxide production was 11,500 tonnes. In the January-July 1997 period, U.S. zinc oxide production was 95,300 tonnes, up from 91,000 tonnes in the comparable period of 1996. For all of 1996, zinc oxide production was 156,000 tonnes.

U.S. reported consumption of refined zinc in July 1997 was 44,500 tonnes, down from 46,100 tonnes in June 1997, and 10 percent less than the total for July 1996. In the January-July 1997 period, consumption of refined zinc was 326,000 tonnes which was 16 percent less than in the comparable period of 1996. For all of 1996, consumption was 788,000 tonnes. U.S. consumption of zinc ores in July 1997 was 150 tonnes, zinc content, while for January-July 1997, ore consumption was 1,050 tonnes. U.S. consumption of zinc-based scrap in July 1997 was 8,300 tonnes, zinc content. That was the same amount as in the previous month and a year ago. In the January-July 1997 period, zinc-based scrap consumption was 58,100 tonnes, while for all of 1996 it was 100,000 tonnes.

U.S. apparent consumption of zinc metal in July 1997 was 108,000 tonnes, up from 106,000 tonnes in June 1997, and almost 24 percent above the total in July 1996. For the January-July 1997 period, zinc metal consumption was 781,000 tonnes, while for all of 1996 it was 1.21 million tonnes.

U.S. stocks of refined zinc at the end of July 1997 were 70,400 tonnes, down from 71,900 tonnes at the end of June 1997. A year earlier, stocks were 74,800 tonnes. U.S. imports for consumption of refined zinc in January-July 1997 were 448,000 tonnes. For all of 1996, imports for consumption of refined zinc were 827,000 tonnes.

Futures Markets

Zinc futures and options are traded on the London Metal Exchange (LME).

Salient Statistics of Zinc in the United States In Metric Tons

Year	Slab Zinc Production: Primary	Slab Zinc Production: Secondary	Mine Production (Recovered)	Imports for Consumption: Slab Zinc	Imports for Consumption: Ore (Zinc Content)	Exports: Slab Zinc	Exports: Ore (Zinc Content)	Consumption: Slab Zinc[3]	Consumption: Consumed as Ore	Consumption: All Classes[4]	Net Import as a % of Consumption	High-Grade, Price ¢ Per Lb.
1987	261,345	82,589	216,327	705,985	46,464	1,082	16,921	1,052,000	2,536	1,324,000	69	41.92
1988	241,294	88,492	244,314	748,130	62,966	482	33,590	1,089,000	2,412	1,340,000	70	60.20
1989	260,305	97,904	275,883	711,554	40,974	5,532	78,877	1,060,000	2,107	1,311,000	61	82.02
1990	262,704	95,708	515,355	631,742	46,684	1,238	220,446	992,000	2,178	1,240,000	41	74.59
1991	253,276	124,078	517,804	549,137	45,419	1,253	381,416	933,000	2,098	1,165,000	24	52.77
1992	272,000	128,000	523,430	644,482	44,523	565	307,114	1,050,000	2,400	1,290,000	30	58.38
1993	240,000	141,000	488,374	723,563	33,093	1,410	311,278	1,120,000	2,200	1,340,000	45	46.15
1994	216,600	139,000	570,000	793,000	27,374	6,310	389,000	1,180,000	2,400	1,400,000	35	49.26
1995[1]	232,000	131,000	614,000	856,000	10,300	3,080	424,000	1,230,000	2,400	1,460,000	35	55.83
1996[2]	226,000	140,000	600,000	827,000	15,100	1,970	425,000	1,210,000	1,400	1,450,000	33	51.11

[1] Preliminary. [2] Estimate. [3] Data through 1981 are reported consumption of slab zinc; 1982 forward, data are apparent consumption of slab zinc.
[4] Based on apparent consumption of slab zinc plus zinc content of ores and concentrates and secondary materials used to make zinc dust and chemicals.
Source: U.S. Geological Survey (USGS)

World Smelter Production of Zinc[3] In Thousands of Metric Tons

Year	Australia	Belgium	Canada	France	Germany	Italy	Japan	Kazakhstan[4]	Mexico	Poland	Spain	United States	World Total
1987	312.1	284.5	609.9	249.3	401.2	247.0	665.6	1,000.0	184.8	177.0	249.0	343.9	7,022
1988	307.0	298.1	703.2	274.1	376.3	242.1	678.2	963.0	192.5	174.0	256.0	329.8	7,163
1989	296.5	306.0	669.7	265.8	372.0	259.5	714.7	977.0	193.3	163.7	246.4	358.2	7,245
1990	308.5	356.5	591.8	263.1	350.3	264.4	731.6	890.0	199.3	132.2	252.7	358.4	7,178
1991	326.5	384.2	660.6	299.6	345.7	263.8	778.7	800.0	189.1	126.0	262.2	376.0	7,310
1992	333.0	310.6	671.7	318.7	383.1	252.6	780.6	260.0	151.6	134.6	351.9	399.0	7,260
1993	321.0	299.6	659.9	309.8	380.9	254.0	744.5	260.0	209.9	149.0	341.6	382.0	7,460
1994	328.0	306.2	691.0	308.6	359.9	255.9	713.3	190.0	209.2	156.0	294.7	356.0	7,450
1995[1]	324.5	301.1	720.3	290.0	322.5	267.6	716.9	168.3	222.7	166.0	358.0	363.0	7,550
1996[2]	331.0	297.4	715.6	320.0	327.0	260.0	642.2	168.5	221.7	165.0	350.0	366.0	7,530

[1] Preliminary. [2] Estimate. [3] Secondary metal included. [4] Formerly part of the U.S.S.R.; data not reported separately until 1992.
Source: U.S. Geological Survey (USGS)

Consumption (Reported) of Slab Zinc in the United States, by Industries and Grades In Metric Tons

Year	Total	By Industries: Galvanizers	Brass Products	Zinc-Base Alloy[3]	Zinc Oxide	Other	By Grades: Special High Grade	High Grade	Remelt and Other	Prime Western
1987	788,728	405,054	84,360	178,682	61,428	23,777	415,315	100,046	101,661	171,706
1988	832,425	406,541	89,995	205,566	61,367	68,956	412,417	104,235	93,852	221,921
1989	887,203	444,603	95,798	189,690	70,417	84,147	458,020	120,433	94,340	214,410
1990	801,969	388,421	104,276	171,771	67,532	69,969	445,427	92,424	78,265	210,373
1991	764,038	364,629	97,952	169,883	64,035	67,539	421,316	91,468	57,786	189,930
1992	814,228	396,480	112,990	165,598	71,224	67,936	414,661	119,660	56,185	223,723
1993	1,035,000	532,400	139,500	222,000	63,448	141,100	403,696	116,500	71,202	182,309
1994	859,000	395,000	107,000	196,000	68,300	92,400	486,000	112,000	68,400	192,000
1995[1]	1,240,000	390,000	91,500	194,000	70,900	90,800	135,000	98,200	54,400	251,000
1996[2]	788,000	398,000	87,400	142,000	[4]	161,000	385,000	111,000	54,000	238,000

[1] Preliminary. [2] Estimate. [3] Die casters. [4] Included in Other. *Source: U.S. Geological Survey (USGS)*

United States Foreign Trade of Zinc In Metric Tons

Year	Imported for Consumption: Ores[1]	Blocks, Pigs, Slabs	Sheets, Plates, Other	Waste & Scrap	Dross, Ashes, Fume	Dust, Powder & Flakes	Total Value $1,000	Zinc Ore & Manufactures Exported: Blocks, Pigs, Anodes, etc.: Unwrought	Unwrought Alloys	Wrought & Alloys: Sheets, Plates & Strips	Angles, Bars, Rods, etc.	Waste & Scrap	Dust (Blue Powder)	Zinc Ore & Concentrates
1987	46,464	705,985	960	4,025	6,727	7,001	608,256	1,082	5,825	1,732	1,271	90,204	1,927	16,921
1988	62,699	749,133	4,100	5,727	6,346	7,652	884,524	482	5,748	3,814	2,016	103,732	2,221	33,590
1989	40,974	711,554	3,066	9,367	9,031	7,253	1,241,659	5,532	2,423	16,515	2,653	108,086	8,137	78,877
1990	46,684	631,742	929	31,720	6,411	8,834	1,049,940	1,238	4,566	11,881	3,731	109,316	8,701	220,446
1991	45,419	549,137	539	31,596	6,483	15,424	687,879	1,253	4,224	10,385	6,151	96,314	5,737	381,416
1992	44,523	644,482	171	31,176	11,813	17,051	910,289	5,886	-----	-----	-----	82,088	5,889	307,114
1993	33,093	723,563	136	38,079	11,862	16,218	799,999	8,765	-----	-----	-----	46,385	6,727	311,278
1994	27,374	793,482	475	51,676	12,152	11,954	878,100	13,220	-----	-----	-----	58,297	6,603	389,488
1995[2]	10,300	856,000	332	42,300	10,900	11,700	1,018,620	-----	-----	-----	-----	55,900	8,840	424,000
1996[3]	15,100	827,000	16,900	31,900	14,500	10,300	1,001,800	-----	-----	-----	-----	45,500	11,100	425,000

[1] Zinc content. [2] Preliminary. [3] Estimate. *Source: U.S. Geological Survey (USGS)*

Mine Production of Recoverable Zinc in the United States In Thousands of Metric Tons

Year	Jan.	Feb.	Mar.	Apr.	May	June	July	Aug.	Sept.	Oct.	Nov.	Dec.	Total
1988	16.8	18.2	22.3	21.9	22.0	22.4	18.8	21.5	19.9	19.9	19.9	19.3	244.3
1989	22.2	20.8	22.9	22.4	23.4	24.3	20.8	25.3	23.1	25.1	22.8	20.9	275.9
1990	26.9	24.8	26.4	26.2	27.9	45.6	50.7	57.1	44.7	42.7	40.4	43.6	515.4
1991	45.5	41.9	43.8	45.5	49.4	36.9	43.0	47.4	49.5	39.0	33.4	38.0	517.8
1992	41.5	48.8	47.7	40.3	40.7	40.4	46.2	49.1	47.6	36.2	40.4	42.2	520.1
1993	48.0	42.5	46.4	39.5	43.0	40.7	33.5	32.1	35.9	41.8	41.4	43.4	488.3
1994	43.2	40.2	48.4	44.0	47.9	47.1	52.5	47.1	50.1	41.6	46.0	48.0	557.0
1995	49.8	48.1	52.8	45.6	54.5	50.0	50.2	55.0	48.1	52.0	47.8	48.1	601.0
1996	52.4	48.9	49.7	45.5	50.7	49.9	53.7	48.1	46.8	43.4	43.1	42.6	600.0
1997[1]	46.2	45.7	45.8	47.9	49.7	45.3	45.9	49.8	53.0	47.6	44.2	47.9	573.0

[1] Preliminary. *Source: U.S. Geological Survey (USGS)*

ZINC

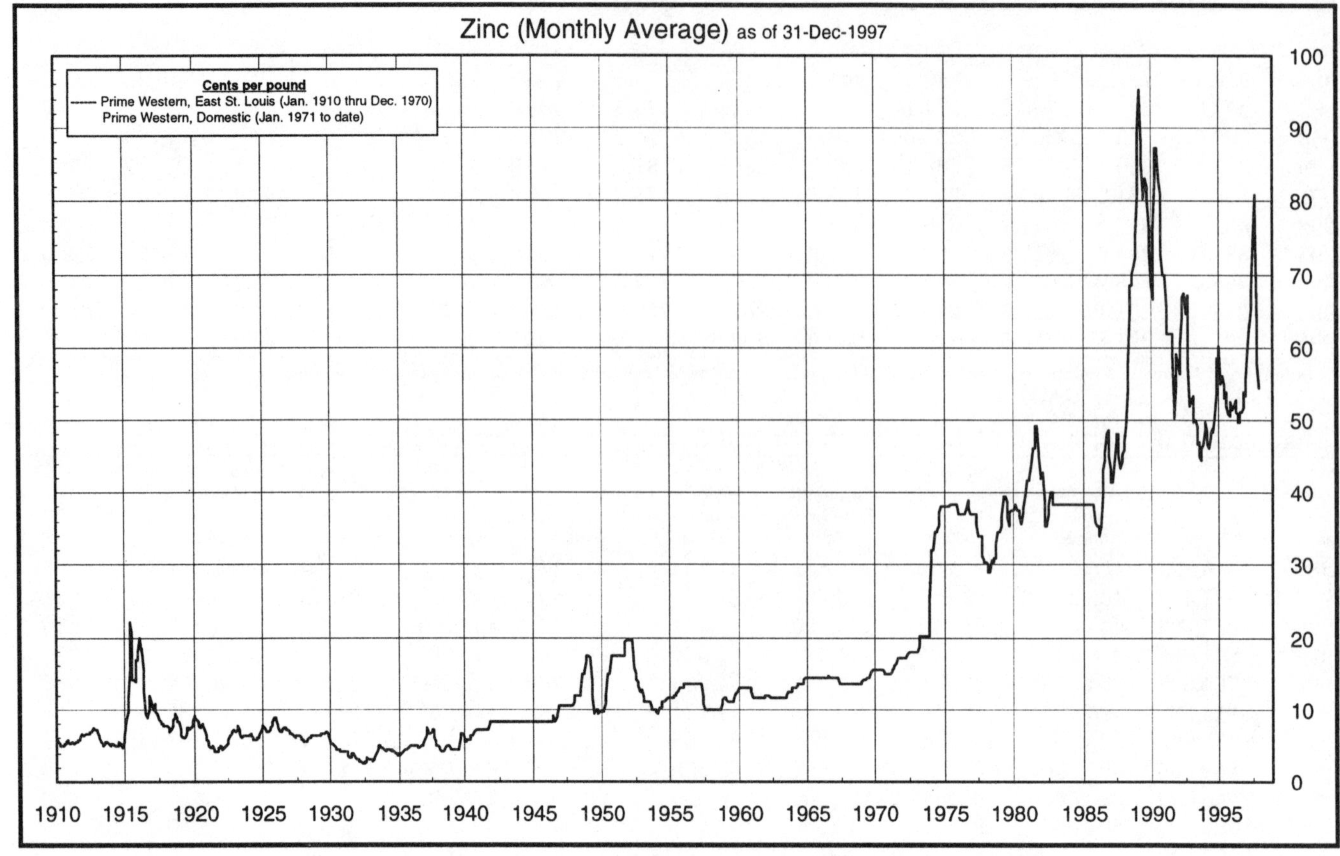

Average Price of Zinc, Prime Western Slab (Delivered U.S. Basis) In Cents Per Pound

Year	Jan.	Feb.	Mar.	Apr.	May	June	July	Aug.	Sept.	Oct.	Nov.	Dec.	Average
1988	45.90	46.93	49.36	54.14	57.74	65.08	68.38	68.38	69.88	71.07	72.54	75.37	62.06
1989	81.58	89.01	95.38	87.76	85.38	81.06	80.38	83.26	81.88	80.31	76.57	73.38	83.00
1990	71.33	66.47	77.37	83.12	87.38	87.38	86.54	82.45	81.00	72.30	70.00	70.00	77.95
1991	70.00	64.53	62.00	62.00	62.00	62.00	62.00	N.Q.	N.Q.	50.44	54.85	59.22	60.90
1992	57.62	56.40	60.19	64.12	66.83	67.29	64.57	66.47	67.12	57.84	52.16	52.71	61.11
1993	52.70	53.18	49.72	50.07	49.27	46.75	46.90	45.08	44.54	46.21	46.54	48.69	48.30
1994	49.64	48.29	46.70	46.16	47.66	48.42	48.81	48.26	50.55	53.81	58.64	57.41	50.36
1995	60.11	55.44	54.84	56.08	54.61	53.08	53.75	52.00	50.77	50.42	52.52	51.60	53.77
1996	51.35	51.86	52.66	51.03	50.76	49.75	49.86	51.22	51.11	51.76	53.81	53.78	51.58
1997	55.64	59.82	63.28	62.62	65.65	67.78	75.29	80.89	78.96	62.55	57.83	54.45	65.40

NQ = No quote. *Source: American Metal Market (AMM)*

Consumption of Slab Zinc by Fabricators in the United States In Thousands of Metric Tons

Year	Jan.	Feb.	Mar.	Apr.	May	June	July	Aug.	Sept.	Oct.	Nov.	Dec.	Total
1988	79.5	76.4	110.3	97.9	110.7	84.6	73.9	111.8	100.0	97.5	87.2	88.1	1,089.0
1989	90.0	81.4	96.0	81.6	97.0	82.1	76.1	101.2	81.2	92.0	92.7	78.0	1,060.0
1990	82.4	79.2	88.0	74.0	79.4	91.0	102.8	100.0	73.0	86.0	73.0	67.1	826.5
1991	80.0	69.0	65.9	67.8	68.3	68.8	73.6	78.0	79.3	85.9	84.2	82.0	764.0
1992	93.8	77.2	85.0	89.9	76.0	76.9	47.2	53.8	52.2	53.5	50.3	47.6	814.2
1993	50.9	49.2	55.8	59.2	60.8	55.7	44.6	49.1	47.0	52.7	50.9	51.0	774.0
1994	50.8	53.7	55.7	58.5	58.7	52.7	48.0	53.2	53.6	53.9	52.5	45.0	623.0
1995	51.3	57.8	56.3	57.9	53.4	58.0	44.0	44.0	58.8	57.0	56.0	54.5	838.0
1996	56.3	55.6	59.3	55.7	56.3	55.9	48.9	48.1	54.4	56.4	54.2	53.1	788.0
1997[1]	45.7	43.1	48.6	50.1	48.1	45.3	45.1	45.5	50.9	49.6	46.0	48.0	569.0

[1] Preliminary. *Source: U.S. Geological Survey (USGS)*